**WITHDRAWN**

PIERRE S. DU PONT AND THE MAKING
OF THE MODERN CORPORATION

Books by the authors

BY ALFRED D. CHANDLER, JR.

*The Railroads: The Nation's First Big Business*

*Giant Enterprise: Ford, General Motors, and the Automobile Industry*

*Strategy and Structure: Chapters in the History of Industrial Enterprise*

*Henry Varnum Poor: Business Editor, Analyst and Reformer*

BY STEPHEN SALSBURY

*The State, the Investor, and the Railroad: The Boston and Albany 1825–1867*

*This study has been prepared under the auspices
of The Center for the Study of Recent American History
at The Johns Hopkins University*

PIERRE SAMUEL DU PONT (ca. 1915)

# PIERRE S. DU PONT
# AND THE MAKING OF THE
# MODERN CORPORATION

By Alfred D. Chandler, Jr. and Stephen Salsbury

*With the Assistance of Adeline Cook Strange*

HARPER & ROW, PUBLISHERS

NEW YORK, EVANSTON, SAN FRANCISCO, LONDON

1817

*To the Ramsays and the Connors*

# Contents

*Acknowledgments*                                                          *xvii*

*Introduction*                                                              *xix*

## I. THE YEARS OF PREPARATION

1. The Family and the Firm                                                    3
2. The Apprenticeship                                                        23
3. The New Company                                                           47
4. The Big Company                                                           77

## II. MANAGING THE POWDER COMPANY

5. The Treasurer                                                            123
6. Formulating Financial Policy                                            149
7. Investment Overseas?                                                    169
8. Maintaining Financial Control                                           201
9. Toward Vertical Integration                                             227

## III. THE NEW CHALLENGES

10. The Powder Company Assailed                                            259
11. The Problem of Succession                                             301

12. The Cousins Split                                             322
13. Supplying the Allies                                         359
14. The American War Effort: Negotiations Begun                  390
15. The American War Effort: Negotiations Completed              410

IV. THE GENERAL MOTORS STORY

16. Initial Involvement, 1915–1917                               433
17. Du Pont "Control" at General Motors, 1918–1920               457
18. The Crisis, 1920                                             475
19. Reorganization and Regeneration, 1921                        492
20. Product Policy and Technological Innovation, 1921–1923       511
21. General Motors Rebuilt, 1923–1924                            537
22. Last Years at General Motors and Du Pont                     560
23. The Family and the Enterprise                                592

    *Appendix*                                                   605

    *Sources of Information*                                     615

    *Notes*                                                      617

    *Index*                                                      709

# Tables and Charts

TEXT TABLES

Table 3–1. Data Concerning Inventories E. I. du Pont de Nemours &
Company                                                                    55

Table 3–2. Laflin & Rand Treasurer's Statement—June 30th, 1902             67

Table 4–1. Total Sale of *Black Blasting Powder* in the United States,
1905–1907                                                                 105

Table 4–2. Total Sale of *Saltpeter Blasting Powder* in the United
States, 1905–1907                                                         106

Table 4–3. Total Sale of *Dynamite and Substitutes Therefor* in the
United States, 1905–1907                                                  107

Table 4–4. Total Sale of *Black Sporting Powder* in the United States,
1905–1907                                                                 108

Table 4–5. Total Sale of *Smokeless Sporting Powder* in the United
States, 1905–1907                                                         109


APPENDIX TABLES

Table 1. Assets and Capital, E. I. du Pont de Nemours Powder Company and Successors 1904–1919                                             607

Table 2. Du Pont Powder Company and E. I. du Pont de Nemours &
Co. Annual Common Stock Dividends 1904–1919                               608

Table 3. E. I. du Pont de Nemours Powder Co. (and its successors)
1904–1919, Income Account                                                 609

Table 4. Du Pont Company Output of Selected Products 1904–1917    610
Table 5. Du Pont Company Profits on Sales of Selected Products
1904–1917    611
Table 6. General Motors Corporation    612
Table 7. Comparison of Number and Proportion of Passenger Motor
Vehicles Sold by the Principal Manufacturers During Alter-
nate Years from 1911 to 1929    614


CHARTS                                                          *Follows page*

Chart I.    Major Explosives Companies in California    52
Chart II.   Du Pont Structure Prior to the 1911 Reorganization    306
Chart III.  Du Pont Company Structure after the Reorganization of
1911    306
Chart IV.   Du Pont Company Committee System after the Reorgan-
ization of 1911    316
Chart V.    Du Pont Company Structure after the Reorganization of
September 1914    342
Chart VI.   Organization Chart, General Motors Corporation, May
1921    500
Chart VII.  General Motors Corporation Organization, 1924    564
An Abridged Du Pont Family Genealogy    626

# Illustrations

*Frontispiece*

Pierre Samuel du Pont (ca. 1915)

*Following page 234*

Lammot du Pont
Mary (Belin) du Pont
Alexis I. du Pont and Pierre S. du Pont (ca. 1887)
Pierre S. du Pont and William H. Fenn (1890)

Family picture—St. Amour (ca. 1896)

Senior Partners in 1900

       Colonel Henry Algernon du Pont
       Francis Gurney du Pont
       Eugene du Pont
       Alexis Irénée du Pont

The Three Cousins (ca. 1903), members of the Executive Committee prior to the 1911 reorganization

       Pierre S. du Pont
       T. Coleman du Pont
       Alfred I. du Pont

Other members of the first Executive Committee, 1903

    Hamilton Barksdale
    J. Amory Haskell
    Arthur J. Moxham
    Francis Irénée du Pont

Close associates of Pierre S. du Pont

    John J. Raskob
    William du Pont
    Henry Belin, Jr.
    Tom L. Johnson

Senior executives at the Powder Company

    Russell H. Dunham
    Colonel E. G. Buckner
    Major William Ramsay
    Elias Ahuja and Walter S. Carpenter

Pierre S. du Pont and the War Executive Committee

The Family Fight—a cartoon from the Cleveland *Plain Dealer* (ca. February 1916)

Pierre S. du Pont and Alice B. du Pont on their wedding trip

Brothers-in-law of Pierre S. du Pont

    Charles Copeland
    H. Rodney Sharp
    W. W. Laird
    R. R. M. Carpenter

The conservatory at Longwood

Senior executives at General Motors

    W. C. Durant
    Alfred P. Sloan, Jr.
    Donaldson Brown

Pierre and the copper-cooled engine—a cartoon from the New York *Globe* (ca. January 1923)

General Motors Corporation guests at the Muncie Chamber of Commerce Annual Spring Dinner, May 15, 1928

Pierre S. du Pont and John J. Raskob at Longwood (ca. 1950)

# Acknowledgments

Many persons contributed to this study. The efforts of Henry B. du Pont and Lammot du Pont Copeland launched the project. They made arrangements with The Johns Hopkins University and the Eleutherian Mills Historical Library to provide the authors with the time and working space necessary for the research and writing. Of even more importance they, with members of their family, through the Eleutherian Mills-Hagley Foundation, collected and made available for study the papers of Pierre S. du Pont and T. Coleman du Pont, and the vast correspondence of many other individuals related to or associated with them. Also, at our request, these two busy men reviewed our typescript. They were most helpful in checking and adding to our factual information. They did not, however, comment on our analysis or interpretations of the information, for they did not consider it proper to do so. Hopefully, their keen appreciation of the value of scholarly history and the need to protect the integrity of the historian will provide an example for other American industrial families to follow.

We were helped daily in the research and writing of the book by the staff of the Eleutherian Mills Historical Library, and men and women at the Wilmington headquarters of the E. I. du Pont de Nemours & Company. Among the former we particularly want to thank Walter Heacock, Director of the Eleutherian Mills-Hagley Foundation, Richmond D. Williams, Director of the Eleutherian Mills Historical Library, John B. Riggs, Curator of Manuscripts, Ruthanna Hindes, Manuscripts Department, and Marie E. Windell, Research and Reference Librarian. At the Du Pont Company, D. Irving Cashell, Alice J. Blackwell, Juanita Craig, Henry Ford, Henry Bush, and particularly Ila Lee Clark and James Hart, aided us in our search for documents more than half a century old. Bettina Sargeant of the Public Relations Department at Du Pont and Elizabeth Erickson in the same department at Hercules, Inc., were able to provide us with much information on men and events associated with these two companies. Other Delawareans who assisted in our search for facts included Donald F. Carpenter, George P. Edmonds, William J. Storey, and E. Murton Carpenter. To all we owe many thanks.

We are as indebted to those who gave us assistance after the research and initial drafts were completed. Constance P. Weber typed and retyped with great accuracy and care several drafts of the chapters. Mary Day also helped with the typing. Louis Galambos provided us with an admirable critique of the typescript, and the final version of the book greatly benefited from his suggestions. Jacqueline Hinsley then carefully edited the manuscript, improving on nearly every page the style and clarity of the prose.

We are extremely grateful to William J. Reader for allowing us to read the proofs of the first volume of his *Imperial Chemical Industries—A History*.

Our greatest debt is to Adeline Cook Strange. She worked with enthusiasm, intelligence, and imagination on all phases of the study—in the search for and the compilation and duplication of documents, in reviewing the finished chapters and redrafting parts of them, and finally in carrying out that most onerous of scholarly tasks, the checking of notes. This book is as much hers as it is ours. Yet, as its authors, the responsibility for the facts and their interpretation is wholly ours. In this work we divided this responsibility, with Stephen Salsbury writing Chapters 1–2, 8–15, and Alfred Chandler, the Introduction and Chapters 3–7, 16–23.

ALFRED D. CHANDLER, JR.
STEPHEN SALSBURY

# Introduction

This study is as much history as biography. While it is the story of a man rather than of a firm, it has the same purposes as business history. It provides a way to get inside an enterprise to see how its business was carried on and how and why basic decisions affecting its destiny were made. A study of a businessman rather than a business firm has the advantage of permitting a sharp focus. It makes possible an exploration and an analysis of complex business activities, processes, and decisions in a shorter space than would be required if all the varied activities of a large enterprise were recorded.

More important, this approach permits a careful review of the relationship of the individual to the enterprise. Such an analysis has become particularly significant in the history of the modern corporation where, as was rarely true before in the history of business, the individual must work closely with many other men in the management of a single enterprise. Such a focus, for example, makes possible a detailed analysis of the inevitable conflict between personal goals and ambitions and the impersonal demands of large-scale business organization. It can also make clearer than most business histories the responses of individuals, in their corporate setting, to the larger economy and particularly to the needs and opportunities created by rapidly changing markets and increasingly complex technologies. Nevertheless, few men in American industry have had a strong enough influence within a major business enterprise to provide such a focus.

One of these is certainly Pierre Samuel du Pont. As he was the single most influential executive in not one but two of the nation's largest and most powerful business corporations during the most critical periods of their existence, his career provides an admirable subject for this type of business history. Under Pierre's guidance, the E. I. du Pont de Nemours & Company became the largest explosives and then chemical enterprise in the United States, and the General Motors Corporation became the largest maker of automobiles and, indeed, the largest manufacturing company in the world.

Pierre du Pont's career is particularly significant because the building and management of the modern Du Pont Company and of General Motors offered such different sets of business problems and challenges. The production processes at Du Pont were chemical; those at General Motors, mechanical. Du Pont sold producers goods, that is, those used by other businessmen in their industrial, mining, and transportation activities. General Motors became the greatest of the mass producers of consumer durables. Du Pont was an old firm. It celebrated its 100th birthday the year Pierre with two cousins began its modernization. General Motors was an untried speculative venture in a brand new industry. It was only seven years old when Pierre du Pont became chairman of its board of directors. For decades the Du Pont Company had been financed from within the firm and family; from the start General Motors relied on outside capital.

The varied and diverse business problems that Pierre had to face and solve were central to the development of large-scale business enterprise in the United States during the first third of the twentieth century. At Du Pont, Pierre was first involved in the transformation of a cartel of small family firms into a modern consolidated, centrally administered industrial company and in the simultaneous change of a family enterprise into a large impersonal corporation. He had to build the administrative tools and techniques necessary to manage such a big business.

As the new Du Pont Company's treasurer, acting president, and president, Pierre became responsible for the formulation of financial policies. More than any other executive in the company he determined the direction of its growth. It was he who decided, after long negotiations with the international cartels of European explosives makers, not to extend the Du Pont Company's manufacturing activities overseas but to concentrate instead on the growing domestic market. He also had the most to say in how the company carried out this expansion, particularly through a policy of vertical integration to assure itself of a steady supply of raw and semifinished materials. Most important of all, he came to be the man who selected and organized the company's top management.

At Du Pont, Pierre also had to meet challenges that were not strictly involved in the production and distribution of goods. These challenges forced him to think about defining his company's relationships with the public and the government. He had to handle its defense in one of the most important early antitrust suits and then had to work out with the government the dissolution of the Du Pont Company into three separate enterprises. Shortly afterwards he guided the massive expansion of the Du Pont Company in meeting the sudden and totally unexpected demands of the Allied Powers for ammunition. Then, when the United States entered World War I, the Du Pont Company's president had to negotiate the largest contract the United States government had ever made with an industrial corporation.

At General Motors Pierre du Pont's tasks differed from those at Du Pont not only because of the nature of the business but also because Pierre did not have the close personal relationships that he had with the men in the Powder Company. His primary aim was to bring system and order into that sprawling, young industrial giant. This goal he achieved only after the corporation had undergone a shattering crisis. While reorganizing the enterprise he turned, more than he had at Du Pont, to technological innovation; for he wanted a product to compete with Henry Ford's Model T. At General Motors, as at Du Pont, he was responsible for bringing together a managerial group, and this team became one of the most successful in American industrial history.

Pierre's story is significant for another reason. During the period of his leadership at Du Pont and General Motors, the two enterprises transmitted and developed basic financial, managerial, and operational techniques of big business in two new basic American industries—chemicals and automobiles. The methods of financing and administering large-scale economic enterprise in the United States were first devised on the railroads during the 1850s and 1860s. From the railroads they were carried by Andrew Carnegie and others during the 1870s and 1880s into the iron and steel industry. In the 1880s and 1890s more special methods for handling high-volume production were initiated in the metal-working industries, culminating in the techniques of Frederick W. Taylor's brand of "scientific management." Pierre, his cousin Coleman, and their associates brought the ways of both Carnegie and Taylor to the Du Pont Company, modifying them to meet the special needs of the explosives industry. Then, as the Du Pont Company moved into chemicals, these big business techniques were carried into that industry. At the same time Pierre and his younger colleagues took many of these methods to General Motors and the automobile industry. Thus, Pierre not only was the builder of two of the nation's leading industrial enterprises, but played a pivotal role in spreading the techniques of modern corporate enterprise within the American economy.

Much has been written in a general way on corporate administration, organizational structure, and finance, as well as vertical integration, antitrust, wartime expansion, and other matters with which Pierre was so intimately concerned. Yet rarely have these matters been seen from the inside —from the view of those who actually made the critical decisions and devised and formulated so many of the practices of modern big business.

In order to provide such an inside view, our study presents these business problems and challenges as Pierre du Pont saw them. The story is told within the subject's own frame of reference. An evaluation of this business career based on criteria outside such a frame of reference is left to the reader himself.

Because its purposes are that of an inside business history, this study is incomplete biography. Pierre's nonbusiness activities are mentioned only when they directly affect his business career. When he becomes no longer directly involved in the affairs of the Du Pont Company and General Motors, we conclude our book. Nor do we attempt to explain Pierre's personality. We say more about it than we do about his outside interests and activities, but what we say is description not analysis. We give Pierre's own comments about his early years to help the reader come to his own conclusions about why Pierre du Pont's personality evolved as it did. We also suggest his relationship with his strong-minded colleagues at Du Pont and General Motors and with the members of the larger family. An authoritative analysis, however, must wait for scholars better trained in psychoanalytic techniques than we are. Indeed, we sincerely hope that this study of his business activities will encourage the writing of a complete, well-rounded biography of Pierre S. du Pont.

PART I

THE YEARS OF PREPARATION

# The Family and the Firm

P IERRE S. DU PONT WAS almost thirty-five years old before he began to devote himself fully to the management of a large industrial enterprise. In those years he had been well prepared for this task. As a boy he had been imbued with the traditions and values of one of the nation's oldest industrial families; he had become familiar with the critical interrelationships between firm and family. His formal education provided him with chemical and engineering competence and a professional outlook.

Events conspired to give Pierre a continuing business education that few members of the larger du Pont clan ever obtained. Because of the untimely death of his father and then of his uncle, Pierre became guardian, while still a very young man, of his nine brothers and sisters. The resulting responsibilities not only gave him training in finance but soon involved him in ventures in the steel and traction businesses, two of the most technologically advanced industries of the day. The opportunities of these new businesses and the restraining hand of conservatism in the Du Pont firm caused Pierre to leave the company in 1889. He received further invaluable training in finance and business management before he came back to Wilmington in 1902 to take over the family firm with his two cousins, Alfred I. and T. Coleman du Pont.

For two years after he returned in 1902, he worked closely with Coleman in creating the modern Du Pont Company and at the same time completely transforming the structure of the American explosives industry. Once the transformation was complete, Pierre's years of preparation were over. As treasurer of the new consolidated Powder Company, he soon became its most influential executive. He did so largely because his early years had equipped him to handle the management of a huge industrial enterprise better than any other du Pont, even better than his talented cousin T. Coleman, who became president when the three young cousins assumed the leadership.

## The Brandywine

Of all the early influences on the business career of Pierre S. du Pont, none were more significant than the family and its firm. Pierre's father, Lammot, was the grandson of Eleuthère Irénée du Pont, the founder of the firm, and the great-grandson of Pierre Samuel du Pont de Nemours, the noted Physiocrat who fled the turmoil of revolutionary France in 1799 to begin a new life in America. The young Pierre, the second of the name, never forgot that he was a third-generation direct descendant of the Du Pont Company's founder; that his grandfather Alfred Victor had been its head; and that his father Lammot du Pont was the trusted partner and associate of Henry du Pont, the uncle who had succeeded Pierre's grandfather as the head of the firm.

When Pierre was born on January 15, 1870, his father was almost thirty-nine years old. In later years Pierre remembered him as six feet tall in his stocking feet and with "thin, fine straight hair. At fifty-three when he died, he was not noticeably bald or gray. . . . His eyes were gray, but as he always wore spectacles of the type with almost rectangular steel rimmed lenses, his eyes without them seemed somewhat expressionless. His nose was straight . . . and he wore a moustache and side and chin whiskers but the beard was thin and little more than slightly gray when he died. His teeth were set apart, he showed them very little, almost not at all." His hands were "large well-proportioned with large straight fingers and large nails, all characteristics of strength. . ."[1]*

Lammot had been sent to the best local school, The Reverend Samuel Maxwell Galey's Wilmington Classical Institute, from which he graduated at the age of fourteen. From there, in February 1846, he had gone to the University of Pennsylvania. Although he took many of the standard courses such as rhetoric, Greek, and Latin, his main interests and best grades were in chemistry, natural philosophy (physics), and mathematics.

Lammot graduated in July 1849 when all America had gold fever. He may have considered going to California with two of his half-uncles, but any such activity was curtailed by the ill health of his father, Alfred Victor, president of the Du Pont Company and partner of the firm. Lammot was encouraged to stay home and enter into the service of the family, which he

*Notes begin on page 617.

did in April 1850, eight months prior to his father's retirement.

During the years of Lammot's employment, the Du Pont Company was run with an iron hand by his father's brother Henry, known as "Boss Henry" or "The General."[2] Its mills extended almost three miles along the swift-flowing Brandywine Creek, approximately five miles distant from the city of Wilmington, Delaware. They were grouped in three main complexes. Farthest upstream and located on the west bank were the original Eleutherian Mills built in 1802. By Lammot's time these were called the Upper Yard. Downstream on the same side, but separated by a broad buffer zone designed to prevent an explosion in one complex from blowing up powder in another, was a "double set of works" called the Hagley Yard. Still closer to Wilmington, on the opposite or east bank and separated from Hagley by another safety zone, was the Lower Yard. These, the newest mills, were built in 1836.[3]

The Brandywine Creek supplied power for all the millsites. Above each of the three main complexes the company had built stone dams to form shallow, still pools from which water was diverted into the canals running along the banks of the Brandywine to the power equipment. Despite industrial activity the scene was one of intense natural beauty. Throughout the factory area the Brandywine coursed between steep embankments of native hardwood forests growing down to the river's edge. Here and there the ravine widened to include natural meadows. Beaches of sand and pebbles in the coves above the dams invited swimming in the summer and good skating in the winter months.

The mills themselves were constructed in such a way that, should an explosion occur, the main force would be directed harmlessly into the forest on the creek's eastern slope. On the high ground to the west, but within quick walking distance of the mills, the du Ponts built many of their own houses. They were both close to their work and vulnerable to its dangers.

Lammot lived on this western bank in a house called Nemours. It was built by his father and owned by the firm. On all sides he could see the spacious grounds and comfortable homes of his uncles and cousins and a few unrelated, company-connected families. In the valley and on the shoreline were clusters of houses constructed of Brandywine stone—two, four, and six houses in a row—for the millworkers and their families. The du Ponts donated the land and their stone masons to build St. Joseph's Roman Catholic Church for their employees, who were mostly Irish. Later Christ Episcopal Church was built for the large du Pont family and Protestant neighbors. There were several stores, a doctor's residence, blacksmiths', coopers' and carpenters' shops, a tavern and a weekly school. Except for special occasions most of the families in the valley worked, played, married, and were buried within the geographical confines of the Du Pont Company property. The company was not simply a place to work; it was a way of life.[4]

There had developed a tradition of what might be called "family communism." The firm owned most of the land and the houses in which the du Ponts lived, and accommodations were assigned by Boss Henry, the company president. The firm maintained and improved the properties and charged no rent. Pierre wrote that his father probably did not have a bank account of his own as long as he lived on the Brandywine. All transportation was in the hands of the firm. Pierre remembered that "a 'Dearborn,' as the four-wheeled, three-passenger carriages were known, made three trips daily to Wilmington carrying mail, passengers of the du Pont family and their servants, and executing commissions especially those at the meat market or at shops that sold articles unobtainable at the country store."[5]

When Lammot started work, black powder for use as gunpowder and for blasting constituted the company's main product. As in 1802, its three ingredients were charcoal made from Brandywine Valley willow trees, sulphur from Sicily, and saltpeter from India. Lammot's first task was the "stirring of the melting kettle," a process designed to purify saltpeter prior to its use in the manufacturing process. From the first, Boss Henry referred to Lammot as "our Chemist." When the Crimean War (1853-1856) made the importation of saltpeter difficult, Lammot set to work to devise a method to substitute nitrates from Chile for the scarce product. Out of his research came "B" Blasting Powder. It proved to be very important. Offering a two-to-one price advantage over the product made with saltpeter and a 20% greater oxygen content per pound, it became the leading explosive for blasting. The patent was issued to Lammot in May 1857. The new product was particularly effective for mining anthracite coal. Consequently, in 1858 the Du Pont Company bought a powder mill on Wapwallopen Creek in Luzerne County, Pennsylvania. This became the nucleus of the subsidiary Du Pont Company of Pennsylvania with its headquarters in Scranton. Lammot du Pont was sent to Wapwallopen to supervise the installation of the machinery for the new process and to organize the operation of an efficient powder mill that would meet the needs of the coal-mining district. Charles Augustus Belin was left in charge of the operation after Lammot returned to the Brandywine.

The Belins were "powder people" also. Their many years with the Du Pont Company had been primarily in the accounting office. Like the du Ponts, they lived in a company house on company property, down the hill from Christ Church, across the fields from Nemours. Lammot worked closely with the Belin brothers, Charles Augustus and Henry Hedrick, and had known their families all his life. But it was not until he was thirty-four years old that he discovered the compelling charm of Henry's daughter Mary. She was unprepared for his attention and proposal and the ladies of the Brandywine were caught by surprise when their engagement was announced. Lammot's mother wrote to Bidermann du Pont in Kentucky: "My dear son, Lammot is engaged to be married. Now guess and guess again. No one had the least idea, not a single individual and the lady, I think, was as much surprised as anyone. . . . Mary Belin? I have no objection but health. She is very delicate and certainly will go into consumption."[6]

Perhaps the little community had relegated Mary at the age of twenty-six to the ranks of spinsterhood. She had certainly settled into a busy routine within the confines of the valley. Very musical, she had become organist and choir director for Christ Church. She taught at the weekly school with several of the du Pont girls. She had attended her dying sister who had tuberculosis and then had been desperately ill herself. She was undoubtedly a community favorite. She had large brown eyes with well-shaped brows and a generous well-proportioned mouth. Her maternal great-grandfather was Moses Homberg, a Jewish merchant from Philadelphia. Her grandfather was Henry Victor d'Andelot, a French sea captain who married the merchant's daughter.

Lammot's brilliant contribution to the explosives industry was rewarded by Boss Henry's acceptance and dependence upon his nephew. The partners and Lammot's mother agreed that the time had come to make way for a new mistress at Nemours. While the Belins made preparations for Mary's wedding, Mrs. Alfred Victor du Pont packed her possessions and left the home she had known for forty-one years to move three miles farther from the mills, into a company-owned farmhouse called Goodstay.

On October the third, almost the entire community as well as many friends from Wilmington and Philadelphia arrived at Christ Church for the occasion. The wedding party consisted of ten attendants, all but one of whom were brothers or cousins of the young couple. The affair was long remembered for its exciting sendoff at the end of the reception when not only the bride and groom, but the entire wedding party, stepped aboard the train to enjoy the honeymoon trip to Niagara Falls![7]

In the next eleven years the Lammot du Ponts would fill the quiet empty rooms at Nemours with a large and active family. Eleven children would be born to this "delicate" woman and she would raise ten of them to adulthood, an amazing record in a day of high infant mortality. In 1870 Lammot's mother recorded the arrival of her daughter-in-law's first-born son: "Mary calls her son Pierre Samuel after its great-great-grandfather. She was confined the fifteenth and in such a hurry that she had neither doctor or nurse."

Pierre had vivid memories of his early years on the Brandywine. He never knew his first sister, who died as an infant, but Louisa, two years older than he, was his first companion and closest confidante for many years. Sophie, although only a year younger than Pierre, turned to younger brothers and sisters for companionship. However, it did not take long for the younger brothers, Henry Belin, William K., and Irénée, to outgrow the nursery supervision and learn to share Pierre's interests. Mineral collecting, the use of the laboratory on the property, athletic contests with their cousins, expeditions around the wooded property surrounding the mill—these filled their busy days. In the evening, as Lammot worked at home the children gathered in the parlor for endless games of cards and parchesi. Their mother played the piano and sang and the girls joined in with their voices and instruments. By 1880 sisters Mary and Isabella and then the fifth son, Lammot, had joined the tribe. But by this time Pierre had found playmates his own age among his du Pont cousins.

In the 1870s Eugene du Pont, Pierre's cousin, had charge of the Upper Yards, just below the Nemours house. Eugene's son Alexis (Lex) Irénée du Pont 2nd became Pierre's "most intimate chum." Pierre remembered him as "five months older than I and much more of a boy. He could throw a stone accurately and made his own 'sling shot' with which he brought down a goodly number of specimens. . . ." They also spent much time in search of "dusties." These small zinc balls used for mixing powder were scattered along the east bank of the Brandywine opposite an old mill that had blown up years before. The two prized the balls as ammunition for the sling shot, but Pierre remembered even with dusties he never "overcame [his] . . . inaptitude for accurate marksmanship." When they were not looking for dusties or practicing with the slingshot, Lex and Pierre often went fishing. Many times Lex's younger brother Eugene joined them.[8]

Two of Pierre's uncles, Alfred Victor (Uncle Fred) and Bidermann du Pont, migrated to Louisville. Both played an important part in Pierre's career. Alfred Victor remained a crusty old bachelor throughout his life. He dressed in a casual and unstylish manner that raised eyebrows even on the Brandywine, which was not noted for its fashion consciousness. He lived in an austere room in Louisville's Galt Hotel. A shrewd businessman, Alfred Victor made a fortune. He built up a paper company and was the owner of Louisville's street railway system, then a horsecar line. Bidermann served as president of both enterprises.

Bidermann had a son Thomas Coleman, who was born in 1863, seven years before Pierre. Young Coleman was always big for his age. Athletic and ruggedly handsome, he also had a penchant for mischief. Alfred Victor and Bidermann often came visiting to Delaware and they brought Coleman with them. Pierre remembered an early meeting. It was at a party held at what was jokingly called Snapper Beach, a pebbly-bottomed section of Brandywine Creek not far from Nemours. Pierre was just six and a half years old and the occasion also served as his first swimming lesson. At first, Coleman seemed very old to Pierre, but as they grew up the two became firm friends.

Pierre's swimming lessons "continued under the auspices of Eugene du Pont in the raceway directly beside the old 'Eagle Glazing Mill' in the Upper Yard." Unlike Coleman or Lex, Pierre was not athletically inclined and it "required two or three years of trials with the assistance of a board before . . . [his] timidity was fully overcome and . . . [he] succeeded in swimming without artificial aid to buoyancy." Pierre remembered that

> it was at this swimming place that four presidents (or future presidents) of E. I. du Pont de Nemours and Company met for the first and only time. General Henry du Pont, then president, clad in long blue coat and linen trousers with a tall silk hat was making his daily visit to inspect the dumping of the Eagle Powder; Eugene du Pont then in charge of the Upper Powder Yard was seated on the bank of the race; Coleman du Pont, then a visitor from Louisville, Kentucky, an expert swimmer and my very inexpert self vainly struggling with a piece of board cut [in a triangular shape] which would never "swim straight"[9]

More of Pierre's close friends on the Brandywine came from the family of the third of his father's brothers, Eleuthère Irénée. Uncle Irénée had five children, and the family occupied a house on Breck's Lane, about a mile downstream from Nemours. The name the family gave to their residence, Swamp Hall, spoofed the du Pont tradition of naming houses as had been the custom in France. Swamp Hall stood on a steep slope near the swift-flowing Brandywine. There was not a marsh or bog within miles.[10] Of the Swamp Hall group Louis Cazenove du Pont was the youngest, just two years older than Pierre, and they became firm friends, At Swamp Hall, Pierre saw much of Louis's older brothers, Maurice and Alfred Irénée. The latter, who with Coleman and Pierre would take over the Du Pont Company in 1902, was just about a year younger than Coleman and six years older than Pierre. Although not as big as Coleman, Alfred was very athletic, liked to box and wrestle, and had many friends both among the du Ponts and the powder workers' sons who lived nearby. While Pierre lived on the Brandywine, the age difference between him and Alfred was great enough that the two were not close companions. Only after Pierre moved to Philadelphia and came back to Delaware to visit did they develop a strong friendship.

Several short trips away from the Brandywine made a lasting impression on young Pierre. At the age of six he visited The Great Centennial Exposition in Philadelphia. Three years later, in 1879, his father took him to New York to consult a doctor about severe "growing pains" in his left leg. The New York doctor found a short main tendon in Pierre's left foot caused the trouble and proposed an operation, but Lammot rejected this advice. Doctors in Philadelphia recommended massage treatment to stretch the tendon. Lammot agreed, but for this Pierre had to go to Philadelphia, where he stayed with a distant cousin, Mrs. Elizabeth Graff ("Aunt Betty"), who lived in a well-appointed townhouse at 1337 Arch Street. The daily massage took a relatively short period each morning, leaving many hours to be filled. Part of the time Pierre spent walking through the great and fascinating metropolis. Often he wandered over to the Reading Railroad station (then at Broad and Callowhill), where he "thrilled with the excitement" of watching the many steam locomotives arrive and depart.

Another walk took Pierre to the old Matthias W. Baldwin mansion at 1118 Chestnut Street. From "Uncle" Fred Graff, Pierre learned that "the founder of the Baldwin locomotive works was a self made man who ... [was] a lover of flowers in his boyhood and who resented . . . that many private collections [of flowers in greenhouses] were withheld from public view. When he built the greenhouse adjoining his home . . . he placed it with one long side directly on the street line where it could be observed at all times." After hearing that story and seeing Baldwin's greenhouse, Pierre "made an inward resolve that if ever . . . [he] built a greenhouse it would be kept open to the public view within as well as from without." By the start of summer 1879, Pierre was able to return to Delaware. His leg was still imperfect, but he had the assurance that the treatment may have prevented a worse condition from developing.[11]

Pierre's childhood household environment left a lifelong impact on his thinking. He described his home as one of "a kind that belonged to what then [the 1870s] might have been classed as 'respectable gentility' not rich but comfortable without financial embarrassment." His mother had servants including "one untrained Irish girl, who could neither read nor write, to help with the children," a cook, a waitress, and chambermaid. And as the family grew, a woman " 'came in' to help with the laundry work."[12]

Though the family was well-to-do, its substance was not squandered either on material things or personal habits. "There was little spending of money on the house and its appointments," Pierre recalled. "New things made a great impression upon the children. I do not remember a repapering, inside repainting, new window hanging or new carpeting during the years 6–12 of my likely recollection excepting that the carpet of the nursery and the small 'middle room' adjacent thereto was 'turned' and a new 'Brussels' carpet laid in the small room over my father's 'office' which later became my bedroom. The oil cloth in the entrance hall was renewed but I . . . remember the old oil cloth part of which though thoroughly worn was thought sufficient for the side hall and remained there some six years longer." Though Pierre wrote that in 1935, he felt that his memory did not suffer from "forgetfulness or lack of youthful observation as I can now distinctly recall the color and pattern of the carpets and wall papers of the old house."[13]

Food appeared on the Nemours tables in ample quantities, but the fare was not luxurious. Ice cream, cake, and candy were real treats. Pierre remembered the vivid contrast between meals at his house and those at the home of his cousins who resided in Philadelphia. Life at "Aunt Betty's" "was a marvel of opulent living." In her well-furnished dining room, wrote Pierre, "one really breakfasted, dined and supped. . . . Luxury abounded, all dishes were delicious and were 'passed a second time.' Several kinds of pie were on the table at a single meal but this did not mean a choice of one only but an invitation to sample all. Ice cream might appear any day, not only by call of the ice cream man on Thursday in summer, which was our custom at home."[14]

At about age seven Pierre received the same allowance that was being given to his older sister Louisa, twenty-five cents per month. They both learned to be careful spenders. Soon afterward his cousin "Anne du Pont . . . revealed the fact that by joining the missionary society of her aunt, Miss Mary V. du Pont, free ice cream would be served at the monthly meetings. My sister and I attended once only, the ice cream and cake were offered and all seemed well until on leaving we were each presented with a small envelope and asked to return it at the next meeting with 25 cents placed therein for the regeneration of the Heathen of China. Twenty-five cents per plate seemed a high price for ice cream especially when one's entire allowance was consumed thereby. As far as I am concerned," wrote Pierre years later, "the 'Heathen Chinee' has remained in his natural state for the above was my first and last experience in foreign missionary work."[15]

Pierre's mother early taught him that good things were seldom free. She frequently went shopping at the nearby country store, and Pierre and his sister Louisa often went along. One day the two hit upon a scheme for conserving their meager allowance. Wrote Pierre, "I and my sister had observed that the remark 'charge it on the book' seemed to avoid the payment of money. There appeared no reason why this same 'charge' should not cover candy as well. The experiment was tried seemingly with success until at the end of the first month the fatal balance of 'the book' occurred and our flight in high finance came to an abrupt end with some wise remarks of my Mother that removed the something for nothing idea from my head permanently."[16]

Pierre had one dominant personality trait in childhood, shyness, which continued throughout his life. This trait made him a particularly sensitive listener. In later years as the leader of a large enterprise, his lifelong habit of listening to opposing sides made him an ideal bridge between conflicting personalities. But Pierre did not regard this characteristic as a virtue. He wrote: "Somewhere in the remote generations of the du Pont family the spirit of what has recently been called inferiority complex crept in. Formerly it was known as shyness, a word that does not altogether express the exact nature of the fault, for fault it is." Pierre considered that it was an inherited characteristic affecting many of the descendants of his great-grandfather Irénée du Pont. But it should be noted the trait did not manifest itself in Alfred I. du Pont, Coleman du Pont, or most of the other du Ponts with whom Pierre worked in his business life. He wrote: "I myself have been aware of my shyness since earliest childhood. To be conspicuous, in success or failure, has been equally distasteful. At school I never succeeded in reciting before a class even a short poem that I could have readily written down at leisure. . . . In my graduating year at [preparatory] school (I was then 16½ years old) the class asked me to be chairman of the class meeting. This request was totally unexpected and resulted in such confusion of mind that I hardly answered and refused to take part in the proceedings, a discourtesy which my associates kindly forgave." After graduation, when he attended a meeting of the Du Pont Company stockholders, Pierre recalled: "Unexpectedly, the chairman of the meeting, whom I knew well, asked me if I would present a very brief and formal resolution of no great importance at an appropriate time in the meeting which he would signify. As I awaited the fateful moment I pondered whether it was possible for me to read the few words which I was not obliged to memorize and the accomplishment of the task was a relief beyond description." Not until World War I, when Pierre had to speak often for the Red Cross, did he overcome his real dread of public appearances. Even then he never enjoyed public speaking.

Pierre's timidity was much more than reluctance to be the center of attention. It dominated his relationship with his father, producing almost extreme behavior. For example, Pierre liked music, particularly the piano. His parents had a piano at Nemours, and when his mother played he stood beside it and watched the keys being struck. Pierre often thought of trying his "ability as a musician, but the piano was always closed and," he wrote,

> I dared not risk opening it. Finally one day to my great delight I discovered the cover open and the keys in view. Cautiously I pressed the keys and produced what I thought was a fair repetition of . . . ["The Little Brown Jug"] in extreme pianissimo. This feat of daring and adventure was never repeated until after we moved to Philadelphia when I ventured to try the Piano again at age of 12.
>
> Why this secrecy? My father actually disliked music. To him it was so much noise and neither rhythm nor tone seemed to touch him. He had frequently said in my presence that no man could amount to anything if he smoked cigarettes, wore eye-glasses (pince-nez) or played on the piano. The two former were merely signs of effeminacy or degeneration I believe, as my father was a great smoker of cigars and always wore his spectacles. Piano-playing in itself was damning and I felt that having touched the keys was sufficient to draw down parental disapproval.[17]

Pierre was sensitive to his father's wishes, yet beneath this outward desire to please was a strong will of his own. Lammot had been an athlete in his younger days and he tried to encourage his son to become one, too, but "did not succeed." Wrote Pierre: "I always felt that my lack of ability in that line was a disappointment to him. He made two direct attempts to interest me [in athletics] after we moved to Philadelphia in the winter of 1881–1882. First he bought a ticket for lessons in a gymnasium which institution I disliked keenly as I was absolutely useless for anything pertaining to that establishment. I was clumsy and the instructor had as little interest in me as I had in the work. Two or three trials finished me," Pierre remembered.

Next his father tried to make Pierre into a horseback rider. His sisters Louisa and Sophie were already enjoying lessons. But commented Pierre: "I disliked everything about a horse and still do. Naturally I never acquired any control and should have been happy to have fallen off and submitted to any consequent injury if the horse could have been eliminated from my life forever. After a very few lessons I bribed my sister Sophie to use my card for riding lessons which was to be returned to me with punch marks to indicate completion of the courses." Lammot learned of Pierre's quitting the gymnasium and refusing to finish his riding lessons. Wisely the father did not say anything to Pierre about either affair.[18]

Among close friends and associates, Pierre's natural reticence did not prevent him from asserting himself. Nothing better illustrates this than an episode that occurred when he was eleven years old. The story also gives evidence of his early business interest. Pierre discovered a big stack of old paper and he asked his mother whether he and his two brothers Belin and Bill could sell it to Rockland Paper Mill. "Permission was granted," remembered Pierre, "and we dragged our express wagon filled with paper over the stony path through the woods to Rockland. . . . I received ten cents for the cargo and we returned well satisfied. My mother used to say that I gave one cent of the ten to the two brothers but I claim that they each received a cent. However, as entrepreneur and owner of the wagon, and, probably, as furnishing more than one half the horse-power for the trip, I am probably entitled to all I received."[19]

The first significant change in Pierre's life came when his family moved from the Brandywine to a house at Powelton Avenue and 35th Street in West Philadelphia. The change resulted from Lammot's dissatisfaction with the way General Henry du Pont was running the company. Lammot, from the time he joined the company, was constantly formulating and patenting new processes for making blasting powder. His interest in new developments never lagged. He eagerly followed Alfred Nobel's experiments in Europe with the new explosive nitroglycerin, and finally the development of dynamite in the late 1860s.

It did not take long for Nobel's dynamite to become accepted in America. In 1867 the Giant Powder Company was organized in San Francisco to manufacture the product for use in the California gold mining industry. In 1868, two years before Pierre's birth, production started.[20] Dynamite did not captivate General Henry du Pont. As late as March 14, 1871, he wrote: "It is only a matter of time *how soon* a man will lose his life who uses

Hercules, Giant, Dualin, Dynamite, Nitroglycerine, Guncotton, Averhard's Patent or any explosive of that nature. They are vastly more dangerous than gunpowder, and no man's life is safe who uses them."[21] In the following years nothing that Lammot du Pont could say changed the general's opinion. But Lammot became convinced that dynamite and other nitroglycerin-based powders had a more assured future than black powder and that the firm that neglected them was doomed.

The controversy led to a significant break in the traditions of the family and the firm. Since its beginning in 1802 the firm had been intimately tied to the family. "The head of the firm was *ex officio* head of the family," one of the du Ponts has written of their nineteenth-century ways.[22] Moreover, "the business was entirely managed by the senior partner." He might consult others about their specific responsibilities, "but he was in no way bound to accept their advice, and tradition made them hesitant to offer it or to ask questions." Lammot's insistence on developing dynamite against the wishes of the general thus not only caused him to leave the firm but also to move his family away from the Brandywine.

While Henry du Pont was not enthusiastic, neither was he unpleasant about the change. After much discussion he agreed to let Lammot form the Repauno Chemical Company and to take with him his own son William as its secretary and treasurer. Lammot, however, had to sell out his interest in the Du Pont partnership and with those funds subscribe to one-third of the stock in the new dynamite firm. The Du Pont Company would take another third.[23] So would the Laflin & Rand Powder Company, Du Pont's important friendly rival. Laflin & Rand's president, Solomon Turck, worked closely with the general to control competition in the black powder industry through the Gunpowder Trade Association and was very sympathetic to Lammot's views about the future of dynamite.

After the Du Pont partnership was re-formed on December 31, 1880, Lammot sought a site for the dynamite works. He viewed locations along the Wilmington and Northern Railroad running north to Reading, Pennsylvania, but never seriously considered them on the grounds that they were too close to populated areas. He finally selected a plot of land on the Delaware River in New Jersey opposite Chester, Pennsylvania. It could easily be reached by train from Philadelphia and then ferry from Chester, but it was outside commuting range from the Brandywine. This choice of a location meant that the family must be moved. It also meant that Lammot would have an autonomy in his business and industrial activities that would have been difficult to maintain if he and his family had continued to live on the banks of the Brandywine. In the spring of 1881 Pierre's mother told him and his older sister as they sat on the lawn at Nemours that the family would soon be leaving. "No order of banishment could have been more sorrowfully received," remembered Pierre.[24]

*School and College*

Philadelphia expanded Pierre's outlook beyond the horizons of his Wilmington cousins. He was one of the few Delaware du Ponts of his generation to spend so many of his formative years away from the Brandywine. He knew from his stay with "Aunt Betty" and "Uncle Fred" that Philadelphia could be as interesting in its own way as life at Nemours. The major change was in Pierre's education. In Delaware Lammot did not send his children to the "Yellow School" attended by the sons of the powdermen, but hired a procession of governesses to teach his ever-growing family. This tended to reinforce Pierre's shyness and to restrict his circle of friends.

Pierre was enrolled in the fall of 1881 at the William Penn Charter School, a private institution affiliated with the Society of Friends, and located in the center of Philadelphia near the intersection of 12th and Market Streets. Pierre entered the "class called quinta, being the fifth from the top in the Upper School." The course of study prepared him for college and included "spelling, writing, arithmetic, algebra, Latin, French, German, English Composition."

Pierre spent five years at Penn Charter and graduated at the age of sixteen. The school was small; his class contained about thirty boys at the beginning and about half that number at commencement. Pierre got along well with his fellow students, but made few intimate friends. His bent for scholarship and his quiet manner kept him apart from the more rough-and-tumble activities. So serious was he in attitude that Headmaster Richard M. Jones nicknamed him "Graveyard . . . much to the amusement of [Pierre's] . . . companions."

But even in scholarship, shyness influenced Pierre. His father "had some doubts about book learning. . . . Continued high standing indicated to him the possibility of parrot learning. This had a good effect on me," Pierre recalled, "as it prevented bragging on my part when I stood high in the class, which as a boy I frequently was guilty of doing. I have heard him say in my presence but not addressed to me—'I have observed that those who stand at the head of the class in school and college rarely amount to much in their after life.' " Thus, reluctance to assert himself discouraged Pierre from seeking the very top standing. A perfect example of this was spelling. "Usually I excelled in spelling generally standing near the top in the contests," wrote Pierre. "My diffidence as to the conspicuous position of winner and the obvious disappointment of the head boy of the class when defeated together with my father's remarks about the after success of those who stood very well at school caused me to feel quite satisfied to be second, third or fourth from the top."[25]

Pierre had especially good relations with his teachers, particularly the headmaster. "Mr. Jones was the terror of most of the boys but I always liked him." Indeed Pierre developed a lifelong friendship with Richard Jones and his wife, who also taught at the school.

It was during Pierre's years at Penn Charter that he formed his religious views. In these he was greatly influenced by his father. Pierre recalled that Lammot "was not a religious man in that he never took part in the spectacular forms of sectarian worship, and from some of his remarks, I believe he did not give much credence to biblical stories though he approved and practiced their teachings of moral conduct."[26] Pierre's exposure to the Quaker way at Penn Charter did not impress him. For his five years at school he attended a compulsory Quaker meeting every Wednesday morning. Recalled Pierre: "The boys attending the school rarely said anything about it [the meeting] and never in derogation or disrespect. Whether those of the Society of Friends received spiritual benefit I do not know but I must admit that to me it was an hour of wandering thoughts some of them far afield."[27] When he was twelve or thirteen Pierre read Robert G. Ingersoll's *Some Mistakes of Moses* in which it was claimed "that much of the Old Testament was traditional, not necessarily the word of God or even correct historically." Pierre admitted that the "noted infidel's" book "made a profound impression upon me," but he concluded that "Ingersoll's work was not satisfying in that it offered no substitute for that which he tried to destroy."[28] Out of the diversity of religious teachings and the readings that Pierre experienced came a profound respect for the ethical values of orthodox Protestant Christianity. For the mystical part of the theological issues, Pierre had little feeling. But he had respect for those whose religious views differed from his own.

Suddenly, on March 29, 1884, Pierre's life and education took a new turn. There was a violent explosion at Repauno's nitroglycerin manufacturing house. Perhaps Mary du Pont's far-reaching background in the powder business prepared her for the tragic news. The message came. Lammot was dead, killed instantly with five others at the plant. It would be six weeks before Lammot's last child, Margaretta Lammot du Pont, would be born. Mary du Pont would need great courage and support and she would find it within her own young family.

Pierre's uncle Alfred Victor du Pont, who had become the guardian of Alfred I. du Pont and his siblings upon Eleuthère Irénée and Charlotte du Pont's untimely deaths in 1877, became the guardian for Lammot's family too. Lammot's death thrust responsibility onto Pierre and at the same time removed his father's heavy restraining influence. At the time of the explosion Pierre was only fourteen years old. He was the eldest son. Of the ten children only his sister Louisa was older. Pierre quickly became the acknowledged leader of the family, and all of the children including Louisa called him Dad. His mother was grateful for his family concern. As years passed she consulted him in the many decisions involving the education and finances of his brothers and sisters. The fact that guardian Alfred Victor du Pont lived hundreds of miles away in Kentucky increased Pierre's responsibility. And, equally important, Alfred Victor had great trust in the quiet, serious, and studious Pierre and was determined to see that he got a good start in the world.

Lammot left his family well situated financially. His estate amounted to about $750,000, which included a one-third share in the Repauno Chemical Company. Since he left no will, under the laws of Pennsylvania the widow received one-third and the children the rest, equally divided. Each offspring's share, which amounted to approximately $50,000, was held in trust until he or she turned twenty-one. Meanwhile the Orphan's Court authorized allowances to provide for their education and other necessary expenses.[29]

At Penn Charter's graduation in the spring of 1886 Headmaster Jones, much to Pierre's embarrassment, announced that young du Pont had been admitted to Massachusetts Institute of Technology for the fall term. Pierre's choice of a technical college resulted partly from the influence of his father who had triggered and then encouraged his son's interest in chemistry. But the choice of M.I.T. also reflected the views of Alfred Victor du Pont. Pierre's guardian, at that moment on the threshold of converting his horse-car lines to electricity and of entering the steel rail business, looked with favor upon a scientific education. Under Alfred Victor's influence his brother Bidermann had sent his son Thomas Coleman to M.I.T. in 1881. In the fall of the next year Alfred I. du Pont of Swamp Hall went, too, and became T.C.'s roommate. But neither Coly nor Alfred finished. Coleman, gregarious and well supplied with money by an indulgent father, enjoyed Boston as much for its night life as its educational opportunities. He quit after his sophomore year to go to work for the coal mining company owned by his father. Alfred too left after two years; he never took a regular course but merely subjects that interested him, mainly chemistry. A.I. also liked the extracurricular life, frequenting boxing matches at the Old Howard theatre, where he met and became friendly with Boston's strong boy, prizefighter John L. Sullivan.[30]

Pierre's experience at M.I.T. followed a more prescribed pattern. He came to take a regular course and he stayed the full four years, receiving his degree in 1890. Indeed, M.I.T. was an enormous step forward in the enlargement of his personality; he overcame the more extreme effects of his shyness. For the first time he spent significant periods outside the family circle. But even in Boston there were many familiar faces. His childhood Brandywine chum Lex du Pont, son of Eugene du Pont, studied at Harvard. Another Brandywine cousin, Maurice, was already enrolled at M.I.T. upon Pierre's arrival. And for the last part of Pierre's stay his brothers Belin and Irénée attended preparatory school at nearby Phillips Andover.

From the day Pierre left for college the change in his mode of living impressed him. He enjoyed the all-night train ride to Boston. On his many trips he normally left Philadelphia in early evening. At 9:30 his train arrived at Jersey City, where it was put on a ferry boat, taken around lower Manhattan, and up the East River to the Bronx, where it started off again for Boston. "We passed under the Brooklyn Bridge," wrote Pierre to his sister Louisa; "it seems very very long at night and very high above the water but it looks so frail that you would think the least wind would blow it away."[31]

Tech, in Pierre's day, had yet to move to its present location in Cambridge; the school occupied buildings in the middle of Boston on Boylston Street not far from the Public Garden. The college provided no dormitories; students took rooms in private houses, most of them located in the Back Bay off Columbus Avenue. Pierre lived in four different rooming houses, one for each of his years at the school. For the last three years he had the same roommate, William H. Fenn of Jersey City. By tradition several Tech students would band together in informal eating clubs, making the best bargain they could with a local "hash house." Judging from Pierre's letters home none of the eating arrangements were very satisfactory, since they offered such gastronomic delights as "vulcanized cake." In the middle of Pierre's freshman year his eating club came up with the idea of renting a kitchen and dining room and hiring a cook and waiter. "We are not going to take a cook that knows how to make hash or fish-balls," he told his sister, "and the mere mention of baked beans on her part will cause the cook to be immediately put to death."[32]

Unlike Alfred and Coleman, Pierre spent much of his time studying. Chemistry dominated his courses, but he took solid geometry, mechanical drawing, algebra, and English composition in his freshman year as well. In his later years he had analytic geometry, carpentry, and physics. He spent much of his time in laboratories, even on weekends, and when Lex told him that class preparation at Harvard amounted to about twelve hours a week, Pierre concluded that the school across the Charles River was a country club.

Pierre did find time for recreation. On weekends he often played poker with Lex, Maurice, and his roommate, Fenn. And he joined a fraternity. Initially Pierre's choice of fraternity caused him much anguish because he did not want to offend anyone. On January 9, 1887, he wrote to his sister: "I am having the worst time imaginable about that fraternity business. Every time Maurice sees me he attacks me about it and I have given every excuse that I can think of excepting the right one but none of them seem to satisfy him. I don't know what will happen when I join one for if I choose Maurice's, Charlie [Lennig] and Ab [Smith] will be furious; if I choose theirs, Maurice will be furious; . . . and I can't join both. So you see it is just out of the frying pan into the fire whatever I do."[33] A few weeks later

Pierre screwed up his courage and acted. He told Louisa, "Today Maurice came in and I broke the news of my proposed joining of the Phi Kappa Sigma to him. I broke it very suddenly so that if the shock killed him his death would not be lingering."[34] Off-campus activities included frequent attendance at the theatre. He went as often as his budget and time allowed. And on many Sunday mornings he attended Boston's famous churches. Nearby Trinity, presided over by Phillips Brooks, impressed him the most favorably and often he could be found in its pews or seated on the chancel steps because of overflow crowds.

Pierre engaged in some of the normal college horseplay, and this undoubtedly helped draw him out of his shell. Beginning M.I.T. freshmen classes normally numbered about 300, and rivalry with the sophomores was intense. Pierre quickly developed strong class and school loyalty. When his sister humorously cheered the sophomores, Pierre wrote back: "HURRAH FOR '90!!! How can you be 'so mean,! so low!!, so base!!! so despicable!!!!' (that is from Shakespeare, I guess) as to hurrah for '89 instead of for '90. A great crime like this, my child, might bring your poor brother to an untimely end if it were repeated. I hope that by future good deeds that you may be able to atone for this terrible sin."[35]

The next year Pierre entered into the spirit of being a sophomore. "A few days ago one of the fellows made a large baby's bottle of wood and tied the freshman colors to it. Four of us went out that night to suspend this appropriate gift to the freshmen on an electric light wire in front of the Tech. There was a lecture going on in one of the buildings so Waite and I and the bottle did not find it very hard work to gain the roof. Just as we had the bottle poised on the wire ready to push out the janitor appeared on the scene and forced us to retire without accomplishing our design."[36] When in the fall of 1887 rumors swept Boston that Tech and Harvard might be merged, Pierre was horrified. "Is not that too absolutely outrageously appalling? I hope that the report is not true!" he wrote Louisa.[37]

Early in Pierre's senior year his thoughts turned toward employment. He had only one real desire—to return to the Brandywine and to enter the service of the company his ancestors had founded. The previous summer, on August 8, 1889, General Henry du Pont had died. Eugene du Pont, who had stood on the banks of the raceway at the old Eagle Mill while Pierre learned to swim, became the new president. When Pierre inquired about a job, Eugene quickly agreed. This pleased Pierre's mother, who made immediate plans to leave Philadelphia and build a new house near the Brandywine that would serve as a home for Pierre and also reunite her with her family and friends.

In the spring of 1890 Pierre learned of big changes on the Brandywine. The first news came from his sister Louisa who had visited Wilmington in search of a site for the family's new house. In conversations with Eugene,

Louisa had discovered that there had been a serious fight between General Henry's two sons, Colonel Henry and William.

William, who had kept his active interest in the Du Pont firm after joining with Lammot to form Repauno, had become the dynamite company's president in 1886 (two years after Pierre's father's death). Henry, the elder son, was a West Point graduate who had been first in his class, and during the Civil War had won the Congressional Medal of Honor. He had given up a promising military career when, in 1875, at the urging of his father he had joined the Du Pont firm. He handled the transportation of the company's products and had represented it in the Gunpowder Trade Association, but had never taken an active part in the operation of the mills themselves.

Apparently the controversy between the two brothers arose over the sensitive question of succession after their father's death in August 1889. Henry looked on himself as his father's successor as the head of the family and so the head of the firm. William, who had far more practical business experience as president of the progressive dynamite concern, thought of himself as a more logical candidate to head the family business.

At this time there were only four partners, these two sons of Henry and two of Alexis I.—Eugene and Francis G. The conflict between the first pair had led to the selection of Eugene. They then invited a third son of Alexis I., who carried the same name, to take the general's share in the partnership. They did not, however, consider asking the sons of Alfred I. to join, as both Alfred Victor and Bidermann were fully involved in their own business activities in Louisville.[38] However, all that Pierre learned from his sister Louisa in April 1890 about this succession crisis was that William was resigning his partnership in the Du Pont firm but would continue to manage Repauno.[39]

This news startled Pierre. He tried to pump Eugene's son Lex, and then wrote his sister: "Do you know if the Cousin Willie affair is known by Lex? I tried to find out but only succeeded in learning that Willie and the Col. do not speak and that the latter always visits the office by special appointment with Cousin Eugene lest he might meet his beloved brother. I supposed that Lex has, like me, been forbidden to mention the change in the firm."[40]

The change could not be kept secret, for it had important ramifications, particularly for young Alfred I. du Pont. After leaving M.I.T. Alfred had returned to Delaware to work for the company, and by 1890 he had risen to the position of assistant superintendent of the Hagley and the Lower Yards. But this did not satisfy Alfred, who wanted a partnership. William's 'retirement' made this possible; Alfred was offered one half of William's share, a 10% interest in the company, for the sum of $225,000. Alfred raised the money, using $125,000 that he had inherited and a $100,000 loan (at

7% interest), which his guardian Alfred Victor supplied.[41] The remaining half share went to Charles I., a member of one of the more distant branches of the family.[42]

The turmoil at the top levels in the company little affected Pierre at the time, for he was to start at the very bottom. But in the long run the fight between Willie and Colonel Henry would pose difficult problems. And Alfred's ownership of 10% of the firm also had long-range importance. In the meantime Pierre was thrilled to learn that Cousin Eugene wanted him to start work in the fall of 1890. This would give him a well-earned vacation after four hard, but rewarding, years at school. For Pierre, leaving Tech was a sad moment indeed. He told his sister on May 18, 1890:

> Friday afternoon which was supposed to be the last that the fourth year men would work in the lab found me still with "something left undone." Saturday morning I went back and worked until twelve. Everyone else was gone, that is of our class, and all the other men were clearing up and everything was upside down. I do not think that I have ever passed a bluer morning at Tech and when I washed up my apparatus and locked the desk for the last time I fully realized that a four year's acquaintance is pretty hard to drop without regret.[43]

Pierre's first twenty years shaped his total life. From the very first, kinfolk dominated his small world. Born on the Brandywine in relative isolation, he spent ten years surrounded by immediate family and clansmen. The larger family gave him psychological security. Pierre came to rely upon the family in almost everything he did. From it he would choose his friends and in time his wife. In business the family became an essential source of funds and of talent.

But the clan had another side. It produced not only strong loyalty but severe tensions between various branches and even between brothers. The enmity between the sons of Boss Henry (Colonel Henry and William) was symbolic of the depth of passion that could tear men apart. Because Pierre relied upon the clan it was inevitable that he would be drawn into its fights. Moreover, the clan limited Pierre's horizons. It reinforced his tendency toward shyness, and it limited his understanding of the outside world. Throughout his entire career Pierre seldom felt at ease out of the environment that he came to know as a child. In this sense Pierre was quite different from his cousin Thomas Coleman. Pierre was a Brandywine du Pont. Coleman came from Kentucky. He never felt the same deep attachment to the clan or to Wilmington as did Pierre. Coleman moved readily from place to place and from venture to venture. He could easily think of transferring the center of his interests from Delaware to New York City.

Pierre's second ten years in Philadelphia and Boston never diminished his source of identity with and loyalty to the clan. His education did accomplish important changes. He had a natural bent for scholarship and he attended schools that were academically excellent; he became the best trained of the younger du Ponts in the ways of modern science and technology. Neither Coleman nor Alfred was scholarly. Of his generation of du Ponts only Francis I., who graduated from Yale in 1893, had a similar academic background. Pierre made the most of his opportunities at Massachusetts Institute of Technology. From it he emerged with a strong sense of professional dedication, something which would have pleased his father but mystified old "Boss Henry" as it did Eugene du Pont and his lieutenant Francis G. du Pont—and as it later did cousins Alfred and William. Loyalty to family and dedication to professional ideals were to become the hallmark of Pierre's career.

# The Apprenticeship

On MONDAY, THE FIRST of September, 1890, Pierre reported for work at the Upper Powder Yard on the Brandywine. "This is where my father, grandfather and great-grandfather had entered the Company's employ," he wrote, and it fulfilled a childhood ambition. Cousin Charles I. du Pont, one of the two new partners and Pierre's immediate boss, greeted him. Together they inspected the "saltpetre refinery, nitrate of soda grinding, charcoal burning and sporting powder manufacture." Pierre recalled that "this was no novelty to me as the powder yard had been my youthful playground and I had visited all of the buildings many times."[1]

But everything looked different now that Pierre had assumed some responsibility for the firm's destiny. His assigned duties were light; they consisted of drying samples of powder, making specific gravity determinations, and preparing suggestions for future chemical work. Fresh from college, he was shocked by the firm's primitive scientific equipment. Pierre recounted that

> the laboratory, so called, was in deplorable condition. . . . The building was a one story addition to the Saltpetre Refinery, heavy stone walls and not too adequate windows. Equipment was almost nothing. A common kitchen range and one small spirit lamp were the only means of heating for chemical work. No gas or electrical facilities, and a common kitchen sink and one ordinary ¾ inch tap the water supply. Distilled water came from a supply prepared for use in the refinery; the workmen called it "still-water" which referred more to its escape from ill-treatment more or less in original condition than to any attained purity. Any unusual impurity was accounted for by the words "she must have boiled

over." The laboratory contained no chemical reagents for making ordinary tests and the chemical apparatus was equally deficient in quantity or selection. The chemical balance did not deign to respond to the added weight of a few milligrams, but as it was customary to select the weights by hand without use of forceps the rough operation of weighing powder samples for drying was sufficiently well accomplished.[2]

As Pierre became more familiar with the company's workings, he discovered that the backward conditions in the laboratory typified almost every aspect of the firm. Cousin Eugene made few significant changes from General Henry's day. The company worked with other small family partnerships through the Gunpowder Trade Association to control black powder prices and production as it had since 1872. Despite the fact that, upon Lammot's death, the Du Pont firm had purchased two-thirds of his interest in the Repauno Chemical Company (thus obtaining 5/9 of the Repauno stock outstanding), neither Boss Henry nor Eugene had attempted to integrate the growing and ever more vital high explosives industry into their planning or operations.[3] Cousin Eugene had made no systematic analysis of the firm to determine which of its plants were most efficient, which locations were best for manufacturing, or which products held the most promise for future capital expenditure. Nor did he plan any such studies. In fact, partnership records and accounting that lumped together personal and company spending made such analyses impossible.

In 1890, at age twenty, Pierre only sensed some of these faults and, as a new and inexperienced employee who was not a partner, he did not expect to initiate immediate changes. His first goals were to learn the business and to gain the confidence of the management. Then, after a period of years he could demand, as his cousin Alfred I. du Pont had done, a partnership and a real voice in building the company anew.

### Pierre's Financial Responsibilities

Meanwhile, events in faraway Louisville changed Pierre's life. On May 16, 1893, his guardian, Alfred Victor du Pont (Uncle Fred), died in a bordello. Uncle Fred's brother Bidermann and nephew Coleman, in league with Louisville's highest authorities, made every attempt to suppress the scandal, which did not emerge until after the funeral, when it was exposed in lurid detail by the Cincinnati *Enquirer*.[4] Pierre had the greatest respect and admiration for Uncle Fred, and in later years he wrote much about him. But never did he discuss the details of his demise. He merely referred to it as "sudden" or "unexpected."

Alfred Victor's death had immediate significance for Pierre. Without warning he assumed the guardianship of his seven minor brothers and sisters, Louisa and Sophie being now over twenty-one. This meant the management of estates amounting to more than $70,000 each, a task he undertook without the aid of a trust company, but with the legal advice of family lawyer Willard Saulsbury. Up to that moment Pierre's sole experience in the investment of money had been the handling of his share of his father's estate which he had received about two years earlier, just after he had come of age. Even more important was Pierre's inheritance from Uncle Fred's estate, representing a much larger sum.

Alfred Victor du Pont was a rich man. His property was appraised at $2.0 million, one-half of which was invested in the Johnson Company, a Johnstown steel rail-producing firm. Although Uncle Fred had asserted that all men should leave a will, he did not do so. Thus, under the laws of Kentucky one-half of the estate went to his mother; the rest was divided in five equal shares, which went to his living sister Paulina du Pont and brother Bidermann du Pont and to the heirs of his deceased sister and two deceased brothers, Irénée du Pont (Alfred I. du Pont's father) and Lammot du Pont (Pierre's father). Had Pierre received just this share, which amounted to $20,000, the inheritance would probably have been of little consequence. But Pierre got a large additional sum.[5]

Associated with Pierre's Uncle Fred were three men: his brother Bidermann, Tom Johnson, and Arthur Moxham. Tom Johnson was a most unusual man. In 1869, about a year before Pierre was born, Alfred Victor had hired young Johnson, who was then only fifteen years old, as a bookkeeper and cashier for the Louisville horsecar line. Johnson was quick-witted and hardworking. Before long he became the superintendent of the Louisville railways. From there, with the aid of Alfred Victor, who came to regard him as a son, Johnson began to buy and manage horsecars and, after 1888, electric trolleys in such major cities as Indianapolis, St. Louis, Cleveland, Johnstown, and Brooklyn. Among other things, Johnson had a strong bent toward invention. As a manager of trolley roads, he observed that conventional railroad tracks were unsatisfactory. Consequently he invented a girder rail especially designed for streetcars. This brought him in contact with Arthur J. Moxham, who developed a method for rolling the rails. The two patented both the design of the rails and the manufacturing process and then set about having a steel company manufacture the track.

Johnson was a born promoter. The trolley business was booming and created a vast market for rails. Between 1890 and 1902 all street railroads (horse, cable, and electric) increased in mileage from 8,100 to 22,600. But that did not tell the entire story, since during the same period electric car mileage increased from 1,200 to 22,000. Because electric trolleys required heavier rails than horsecars, virtually the entire 22,000 miles of electric road opened needed new track.[6] Tom Johnson saw the great potential for his invention and asked Uncle Fred, as he too came to call Alfred Victor du Pont, to join with him and Moxham in a company to manufacture the new rails. The resulting enterprise began in 1889 at Johnstown, Pennsylvania. Appropriately enough it was called the Johnson Company.[7]

The Johnson Company was the brainchild of Tom Johnson. He also supplied much of the original capital, which came from the sale of his interests in the Indianapolis railways. Uncle Fred and a few smaller investors supplied the rest. Arthur Moxham managed the new steel company and became its president. He not only built and managed its plant but set up a national sales force with nine regional offices throughout the country. In the early nineties Johnson and Moxham also began to manufacture their own electric traction motors. They feared that the formation of General Electric in 1892 would make them dependent on only two suppliers (General Electric and Westinghouse) for their streetcar companies. To assure their independence they formed the Steel Motors Company, with its plant in Johnstown. Although Johnson kept in close touch with these factories and sales activities, he was too busy promoting other trolley roads and becoming involved in politics to take an active part in the firm's day-to-day management.

Johnson's public life was active and interesting. Almost simultaneously with the founding of the company he launched his political career. Years before, he had become a devoted follower of Henry George and a believer in the single tax. In 1888 the Democrats nominated Johnson for Congress in Ohio's twenty-first district, which included Cleveland. He lost that vote, but the following election in 1890 he ran again and won. Altogether Johnson served four years in the House of Representatives before the Republicans retired him. This, however, did not end his public life, for in 1901 the Democrats elected him as a reform mayor in Cleveland. Considering Johnson's background, his political career was unusual. In office he attacked monopoly, especially steam railroad and trolley car corporations. He favored government ownership of such ventures, and he attempted to start a municipal electric railway in Cleveland to compete with lines he had founded but no longer owned. Out of office Johnson promoted streetcar lines and many other enterprises. And he took advantage of every loophole to advance his interests. He saw nothing inconsistent in this. He argued that as long as the system remained as it was he had to operate within it; and he emphasized that his public utilities experience made him as a public officer uniquely qualified to deal with such corporations.

Tom Johnson was indirectly responsible for the additional inheritance Pierre received from Alfred Victor's estate. Uncle Fred, sometime before his death, talked to his mother, Margaretta Lammot du Pont (Pierre's grandmother), saying that he wanted to leave something substantial in a will to Coleman du Pont (Bidermann's son), Alfred I. du Pont, and Pierre S. du Pont. Uncle Fred had been impressed by Coleman's ability as the manager of Bidermann's two Kentucky mining firms, the Central Coal & Iron Company and the Jellico Coal Company. Alfred, too, had pleased his uncle by the way he had taken hold on the Brandywine after dropping out of M.I.T. Although Pierre was as yet too young to have accomplished much in the business world, this quiet, studious eldest son of Lammot's had made a fine record at M.I.T. and showed promise of success. When Pierre's grandmother received her half of the estate it included Johnson Company stock worth $500,000. As she was financially secure without this investment, she decided to make a distribution of the stock that would honor her son's wishes. Accordingly she called upon Tom Johnson to advise her. He recommended that Bidermann du Pont, his son Coleman, Alfred I., and Pierre each be given 1,000 shares of Johnson Company stock. Margaretta agreed and thus Bidermann du Pont and the three young cousins, each the son of a different one of Uncle Fred's brothers, became major shareholders in Tom Johnson's steel and rail-making firm.

Pierre's share of the stock was valued at $100,000, and in 1893 it paid an annual dividend of $10,000. Together with his other inheritance from Uncle Fred and that from his father, Pierre's total fortune exceeded $170,-000. In addition he had the responsibility of managing a total of nearly $500,000 held in trust for Lammot's seven minor children. "I was totally unprepared for this sudden acquisition of what seemed very great wealth . . . ten thousand dollars per annum appeared an amount that could not possibly be needed nor even expended by a young man in my position. I then had few expenses, lived with my mother to whom I paid board about $1,200 per annum," Pierre recollected.[8]

Pierre later wrote that when he assumed this burden he "hardly knew the difference between a ledger book and leger-de-main; at least they were both equally incomprehensible to me."[9] Fortunately Pierre had Tom Johnson's guidance. Before 1893 the two had often met, usually in company with Uncle Fred. Johnson had early decided that Pierre was a good potential street railway or steel executive. Indeed the hope that new talent could be recruited for the Johnson Company undoubtedly added to his enthusiasm for Margaretta's distribution of the company's stock. In fact Coleman was recruited. He moved to Johnstown to become the firm's general manager. But Pierre and Alfred stayed on the Brandywine.

Pierre immediately sought advice on the investment of his own money and that for which he was the trustee. Johnson, serving his second term in Congress, often stopped by Wilmington to see Pierre, and the two frequently corresponded. As might be expected, Johnson's advice was a bit unorthodox. Uncle Fred in his role as guardian had invested nearly all the trust funds in low-paying Philadelphia mortgages favored by the Orphan's Court. Johnson preferred more speculative, high-yielding bonds. He told Pierre that 6% obligations of new and expanding traction systems such as those in Johnstown, Allentown, Cleveland, and Brooklyn could be bought below par and, as the lines were completed and began full operation, such investments would almost certainly rise in value. In short, according to Johnson, street railway bonds entailed little risk and had a high potential for appreciation. Pierre followed this advice, and his investment portfolio between 1893 and 1901 showed Johnson's influence in almost every selection.

But Pierre's decisions seemed daring and imprudent to the family lawyer, Willard Saulsbury, who informed the young trustee that the court would hold him responsible for any loss on street railroad securities. Moaned Pierre: "This practically means all of the bonds that I have so far invested in. It seems to me a pity to give up these bonds and to go back to the mortgages again. What would you advise me to do under the circumstances?" he asked Coleman.[10] T.C. wrote back approval for Pierre's actions. Thus encouraged, Pierre decided to "let remain all the investments in bonds that . . . [he had] made so far and to add to them from time to time," but he cautiously opted to keep a "large part of the estate invested in mortgages as prescribed by law."[11]

Pierre's response to this first controversial decision of his business career proved to be a forerunner of things to come. Before acting, Pierre always tried to obtain the best possible information. He bought trolley road bonds because of his enormous respect for Tom Johnson's judgment and experience in the industry and knowledge of the lines involved. Pierre liked to take prudent risks based on sound information, but he rarely ventured all on a single course of action. Cousin Coleman, on the other hand, enjoyed big risks and seldom worried about the consequences of failure. As for gambling on the stock market, which was so fashionable in the period between 1893 and 1919, Pierre had only mild curiosity. Not so his old M.I.T. roommate, William Fenn. "By the way," Pierre wrote his brother Belin after a visit to New York in December 1899, "Fenn gave me a pointer on Sugar. It is good for 140. Just keep your eye on it and see what happens. This child is not going in."[12]

*Financing the Johnson Company*

Despite the fact that during the years between 1890 and 1899 Pierre worked full time for the Du Pont Company and managed a substantial investment portfolio, the Johnson Company provided his major business experience. Almost immediately after receiving his inheritance from Uncle Fred, Pierre tightened his relationship with the company by finding a position there for his brother Bill, who detested formal education and wanted to try his hand in the business world.[13] Bill's job began on March 1, 1894, with the enthusiastic approval of Arthur Moxham, who promised personally to supervise young du Pont's progress.[14]

For the Johnson Company, 1893 proved a pivotal year. Financially it was the firm's most successful. But there were storm clouds on the horizon. Nobody realized this more than Arthur Moxham, who drew up a program to meet the challenge. Moxham put the finishing touches to his scheme in December of 1893. Early in January 1894 the Johnson Company president wrote Pierre a long letter urging him to attend a stockholders' meeting to vote upon a major increase in the company's debt for the purpose of financing an expansion program.

Pierre's stake in the Johnson Company's plan was major. He was an important stockholder, and Tom Johnson had asked him to consider still further investments in the company. Pierre responded to Moxham's letter by a trip to Johnstown to discuss the matter. This was Pierre's first exposure to the inside of corporate finance. Heretofore he had always seen Moxham as a kindly friend of Uncle Fred or of Tom Johnson. Now Pierre saw Moxham in a new light, as an industrial planner and business strategist. As Moxham explained the Johnson Company's problems, the difference between Johnstown and the Brandywine struck Pierre. He later wrote: "Moxham . . . was a master of cost sheets and orderly management. He visited his plant frequently and was interested in details but he was always accompanied by the line man in charge through whom every question or recommendation passed. His cost sheets were fascinating to me and I became hopeful that the business of [the] Du Pont Company could be presented in such a clear manner."[15]

Moxham's explanations of the Johnson Company's problems and his recommendations for changes seemed logical. The corporation's first years from 1890 to 1893 had been prosperous; the annual net earnings on an investment of $2,750,000 had averaged $528,000. The company had ridden the crest of the street railway boom and had benefited by a prosperity that permeated the entire steel industry. But 1893 marked the start of a severe depression and overcapacity in steel. For the first time in the Johnson Company's brief life such major rail producers as the Pennsylvania Steel Company had whole plants idle, with no prospect of orders from steam lines. This augured stiff competition for the trolley road business.

Moxham's statistics indicated that the Johnson Company had profited during its lush period largely by sales from its switch works which fashioned those special orders—that is, switches, curved track, and crossovers—so common on the street railroads. The profit per ton from the rail-rolling mill, however, had been comparatively small. This was because the company purchased its ingots instead of making them. This practice caused losses, Moxham asserted. The company did not often get the shapes it wanted; it had to pay the extra cost of working cold steel, "with its great waste in fuel account and relatively smaller product," and the company also "paid to others the profit on pig metal and converting."[16] Moxham recommended that the company should integrate vertically back into the production of pig iron. But he did not stop there. He analyzed the cost of steel-making to find the optimum geographic location for a new plant. He discovered that Johnstown was not well placed, and that by building on Lake Erie near Cleveland the cost of transportation for iron ore and coke would be reduced.

Therefore, Moxham proposed that the Johnson Company abandon its Johnstown rail mills and that upon an entirely new site at Lorain, Ohio, a completely integrated plant be built to combine all the "economies known to the present state of the art, not only in saving of by-products from coke ovens and blast furnaces, but in the use of the direct process, never permitting the metal to get cold from start to finish."[17] But the plan included more. Although Moxham, like Johnson, was a single tax advocate, he suggested that the company purchase 3,700 acres (nearly six square miles) of farmland surrounding the new mill. On this the firm would develop a new town with its own business district and homes for the workers. Thus the company would profit from the rise in land values caused by its industrial activities.

Moxham estimated that his program would require $4.0 million of new capital, half of which would be raised by bond sales and the rest through an issue of new stock. Encouraged by past success the stockholders overwhelmingly voted to proceed. Pierre was among those who enthusiastically endorsed the program. So did his cousin Coleman.[18]

The company immediately purchased the Lorain, Ohio, site and Coleman as general manager began to supervise the construction of the new plant. But soon it was clear that all was not well. The Johnson Company was, in fact, marginal and ill prepared to survive a prolonged period of economic distress. Johnson, Moxham, and Coleman assumed that the economic stringency of 1894 would quickly pass, but their optimism proved unfounded. Things grew steadily worse. Economic recession hurt the company in many ways. It dried up capital and made it impossible to obtain the funds to complete the Lorain complex. Although a rolling mill started production, plans for the blast furnaces and coke ovens languished. Thus the crucial part of Moxham's scheme to reduce production costs through vertical integration could not be achieved. Furthermore, overcapacity in the steel industry drove down rail prices and eliminated profits. The company suspended dividend payments. It was a vicious circle. Johnson and Moxham had counted upon stockholders to provide much of the capital for expansion by reinvesting their dividends. The end of dividends, therefore, almost insured the failure of the plans for vertical integration.

The Johnson Company faced still other problems. Its sole market was the electric street railroad industry. In most cases this meant selling to firms that were in the process of constructing their lines from nothing. Many trolley roads were speculative, and few had substantial revenues during their construction period. Because electric railways had little cash, they offered their securities, usually bonds, in payment for rails, motors, and other equipment. The Johnson Company had to either take bonds or lose business. In the firm's lush period this worked well because the securities could be taken at a discount, held until they appreciated and the lines became operational, and then sold at a substantial profit. But in the financially turbulent period between 1894 and 1899, the company found it increasingly harder to hold such bonds. The firm's Lorain expansion drained away cash in large amounts, and the company needed additional money for working capital to pay the labor force and to purchase raw materials. To obtain cash the Johnson Company had two choices. First, it could discount the bonds at a sacrifice. This meant foregoing the almost certain appreciation after the streetcars started running. Or secondly, Moxham's firm could borrow money for current expenses. This had the disadvantage of creating a large floating debt, but it promised long-term profit.

Pierre had an insider's view of every aspect of the Johnson Company's troubles. Initially he shared Johnson and Moxham's enthusiasm. He subscribed for at least 44 of the new Johnson Company bonds[19] and 173 shares of the new stock[20] for his personal account and for certain of his brothers and sisters.[21] Pierre and his cousin Alfred made several joint trips to Lorain to view progress on the new venture and to discuss prospects with their cousin Coleman and Arthur Moxham. After one trip in April 1895, in a letter to Tom Johnson, Pierre wrote, "It is needless to say that I was very much pleased and surprised to see all that has been done in the nine months work on the plant."[22] He concluded that it would not be long before Moxham's plans came true.

January of 1896 dashed all of Pierre's optimism. That month Arthur Moxham estimated that the company needed an immediate infusion of $750,000 just to meet its current obligations. Much of the cash could be raised by short-term loans in the Midwest and through Tom Johnson's Wall Street connections. Coleman, who broke the news to Pierre, asked his cousin if he could raise some money, say, $100,000, in Wilmington.

Pierre immediately went to work. He contacted two Wilmington institutions at which the Du Pont Company did its business, and where he was well known, the Union Bank and the Bank of Delaware. Acting according to Coleman's instructions Pierre sought $50,000 from each. The loans were to be in the form of personal notes, backed by collateral furnished by the Johnson Company. This was largely the bonds of various trolley roads. The signatories were to be Tom Johnson, Arthur Moxham, Coleman, Antoine Bidermann du Pont, Jr. (Coleman's brother), and Pierre. Each was to sign for a specific sum. Pierre's share was to be $20,000.

Pierre's first fling at corporate high finance proved successful. He wrote his cousin that he had secured the money at 6% interest for a period of three months with the option to renew. Coleman breathed a sign of relief. He wrote his cousin, "In both Mr. Moxham's and Mr. Johnson's letters they ask me to say to you that they appreciate very much your efforts in behalf of the Johnson Company, and it is needless to add that the writer's appreciation is equal to either of theirs. . . ."[23] In April 1896, after an initial three months, Pierre easily renewed the loans.

At mid-year Moxham wrote an optimistic letter. He told Pierre that while he would still require a renewal of the Wilmington loans, he had "completed arrangements within the last few days that will put matters with the Johnson Company on a comfortable footing so far as I can now see for many months to come." Moxham concluded that while orders were not plentiful, "they have materialized a little better so far than I figured when you were with me, and on the whole I am inclined to feel quite encouraged."[24] But the third quarter of 1896 made Moxham a bad prophet. The company's cash position was more critical than ever. And to make matters worse, Dun's Reports, a forerunner of Dun and Bradstreet credit rating service, gave the company a bad rating, asserting that the company admitted "inability to take care of their maturing obligations." "Their liability," said Dun, "is a large and pressing one, and various accounts are accruing daily with practically no resources on hand for their liquidation."[25]

Dun's report exaggerated the company's financial troubles, but not by very much. And Pierre found that it complicated his relationship with the Wilmington banks. Fortunately he had renewed the $50,000 in notes from the Union Bank before the Dun announcement, but the Bank of Delaware was pressing for payment. The company could ill afford not to have an extension on the loan. Moxham's letter on October 7, 1896, to Pierre gives a sense of the urgency: "As per my telephone message, the situation is this: The checks which Coleman will bring with him to take care of the Wilmington paper temporarily cleans out completely our bank account. If, therefore, it will be a possible thing to do anything with the Wilmington account it will be of invaluable assistance to the company."[26] Together Coleman and Pierre managed to win an extension and the crisis temporarily receded.

The year 1897 proved no more fortunate than 1896. Pierre continued his role as unofficial Wilmington financial agent for the company, providing between $150,000 and $100,000 of short-term cash. As 1898 brought continued slack orders at low prices, and the vertical integration program remained stalled, it became evident that the Johnson Company could not continue as usual. Efforts to reduce costs and improve efficiency had not yet affected the profit balance even though Coleman, as general manager, had brought Frederick W. Taylor as a consulting engineer into the Johnson Company to apply his methods of scientific management in the making of electric motors. Therefore, Moxham went to England in a vain attempt either to raise more capital or to sell the company.[27]

In 1898 hard times plagued many marginal steel producers as well as some industry giants such as the Illinois Steel, which was backed by J. P. Morgan. In an attempt to end competition and rationalize the industry, the house of Morgan began putting together a vast new combination called Federal Steel. The Johnson Company was invited to participate. Johnson and Moxham both agreed that the Morgan overtures should be accepted, but both had continued optimism that the firm's Lorain real estate venture and a wholly owned electric interurban railroad between Lorain and Elyria would appreciate in value and should be liquidated at a later date. Therefore, the agreement reached with Federal Steel sold only that part of the business that made steel rails, electric motors, and other equipment for street railways. For each share of common stock with a par value of $100, Johnson Company stockholders received Federal Steel preferred and common shares worth at market value about $28. Although Pierre did not know it at the time, this would be the only return of capital he would receive for his Johnson Company shares. Thus economic forces reduced the value of the $120,000 worth of Johnson Company stock that came to him from Uncle Fred's estate to about one-quarter of that amount.[28]

Pierre learned many important lessons from his experiences with the Johnson Company between 1893 and 1898. First, he came away profoundly impressed by analytical management. Moxham's balance sheets told at a glance which segments of the company's activities made money and compared the profitability of one part of the firm's investment with another. In this manner it was possible to have a rational basis for investment decisions. Pierre did not blame the Johnson Company's failure on Moxham's plans for expansion at Lorain. He realized that the real trouble lay in the firm's weak financial position. Because Pierre worked closely with Johnson, Moxham, and his cousin Coleman to stave off the company's financial disaster, he learned much. He gained experience in negotiating loans from banks. He discovered the importance of collateral and of business reputation. But, most important, he saw the danger of an inadequate cash reserve. The lack of working capital led to the accumulation of a substantial floating debt. This was the first step toward the loss of control of the enterprise. Pierre saw that any company with a large floating debt was prey to the least turmoil in the economy as a whole or to a minor reverse within the company itself. At that point the company's creditors, not its owners, called the tune. This was a lesson Pierre never forgot.

### Pierre Leaves the Brandywine

During the years when Pierre was learning business techniques from financial transactions with the Johnson Company, things had not gone well for him on the Brandywine. He found his labors at the Upper Yard frustrating. Charles I. du Pont gave him little authority. Pierre could make no

significant changes, not even in the backward chemical laboratory. After
eighteen months Francis G. du Pont asked Pierre if he would like to transfer
to the newly opened Smokeless Powder factory at Carney's Point, located
just across the Delaware River from Wilmington. Pierre jumped at the
chance.

Smokeless powder, or guncotton, a high explosive made by treating raw
cotton with nitric acid, was new to the United States. In 1890 the navy
began important experiments to see if guncotton, then considered highly
dangerous, could be adapted for use in the large caliber guns aboard ships.
In 1891 Du Pont had established its factory at Carney's Point.[29] The purpose of the new plant was experimental. Francis G. du Pont ran Carney's
Point. He was the brother of Eugene du Pont, the head of the firm, and was
a chemist and inventor of some note. Francis hoped to develop a powder
suitable for army and navy use, and the firm received government encouragement in the form of a small contract. Another goal was a smokeless
powder that could be used in shotgun shells. For the Du Pont Company
Carney's Point was at the frontier of research and development, and it
thrilled Pierre to go to a position where he might put the knowledge he had
gained at M.I.T. to practical use.

At first things went well. Cousin Frank assigned him the task of developing the shotgun powder. Pierre visited the Navy Torpedo Station at Newport, Rhode Island, where Professor Charles E. Munroe was conducting
advanced research on the adaptation of smokeless powder for naval guns.
At Newport Pierre familiarized himself with the navy's method of guncotton manufacture. He also learned that the Munroe process was not suitable
for commercial use in shotguns and rifles. Years later Pierre described his
early experience at Carney's Point. Returning from Newport he brought
back with him

> a quantity of wet guncotton pulp made at the Torpedo Station. Nitro benzol was
> to me an old friend of college days and . . . its preparation in laboratory apparatus
> had been one of my assignments. . . . Without any very definite plan in mind
> I transferred some of my guncotton to a pint or quart bottle about half filled with
> water, shook it well and added some nitro benzol while continuing the shaking.
> To my surprise the mixture separated into a mass of quite even spherical grains
> which remained apart—did not return to a single mass or adhere together. This
> was the discovery of Du Pont smokeless powder for shotguns.[30]

Pierre's invention needed much work before it became a commerical
product. Cousin Frank immediately started to work with him on the project.
Together they ironed out the many problems. "The inventive genius of
Francis G. du Pont brought about the ultimate success of the chance discovery, therefore, it is proper to say that he was the real *inventor,* I the chance
*discoverer.* The patent was issued in our joint names, which to me was quite

sufficient recognition," wrote Pierre. Young du Pont assessed his main contribution as dogged determination. "At one time I felt that without my insistence the project might have been abandoned."[31]

Despite initial success things turned sour. For one thing, Cousin Frank assigned his son Francis I. du Pont, who was three years Pierre's junior, to work on smokeless powder. Francis "proved much more to . . . [his] father's liking," and Pierre soon began to feel crowded out.[32]

But competition from Francis was only a minor irritant. Pierre soon found himself in fundamental disapproval of the way the Du Pont Company was managed. Partly the trouble stemmed from the wide gulf that separated the four senior partners—Eugene du Pont, his two brothers Francis G. and Alexis I. du Pont, and Colonel Henry du Pont—from the two junior partners, Charles I. du Pont and Alfred I. du Pont, and the younger du Ponts who like Pierre were just starting in the company and aspiring toward partnership. In 1895, when his brother Belin graduated from M.I.T., Pierre talked Cousin Eugene into putting him to work in the Upper Yard.[33] At home at St. Amour, where the family had lived since 1892, the two brothers spent many an evening discussing the refusal of the older generation to listen to new ideas. Fresh from college, Belin had many thoughts about increasing the efficiency of the saltpeter refinery where he worked. In exasperation he once wrote Pierre that "even if the Refinery should burn down, they would probably build it up just as it is now or if any changes were made I am sure I would not be consulted."[34]

Pierre considered things to be just as bad at Carney's Point. While he admired Francis G.'s inventive genius, he had little patience with the disorganized way he ran the works. Cousin Frank made no proper estimates of the capital improvements needed to carry out a prolonged program of experimentation with smokeless powder. Nor did he prepare adequately for manufacturing the powder required by the government contracts. As in the case of the development of the shotgun powder, Francis G. tended to be erratic and to give up easily when things did not go well. One year a cold snap hit, and conditions at Carney's Point came close to chaos. Pierre told Belin:

> The prospect is not very encouraging as there is almost nothing for me to do over there [Carney's Point] the plant being practically shut down owing principally to F.G.'s methods of doing things. The gun-cotton dripping rooms are hardly heated at all and it is impossible for the men to do anything as they can not wrap up much and must wear rubber gloves. The ice is about one or two inches thick all over the floors as all the splash and drip of water freezes immediately. Our powder presses are also in a very bad way. We are using only one but we have to keep the others running . . . all night in order to prevent freezing. It is all the same old trouble of not looking ahead and making provision for things that are bound to occur sooner or later.[35]

Pierre kept comparing the methods Moxham used in the internal management of the Johnson Company plants to F.G.'s way at Carney's Point. The comparison did not flatter Francis G.

In 1898 the Spanish-American War broke out. As usual the Du Pont Company played a vital role in supplying the armed forces with powder. The main brunt, however, fell not at Carney's Point, because smokeless powder was still considered too experimental to be used in active combat, but across the Delaware River on the Brandywine. Pierre could not help but note the uncertainty of war business and its effect upon the firm. One minute the mills under Alfred I. du Pont's capable direction turned full speed ahead producing for war. The next moment an unexpectedly quick peace left the company with mountains of surplus powder, much of which was unsuited for commerical use.

The year 1899 brought Pierre's career with the Du Pont Company to a crisis. When the Johnson Company sold its steel plants to Federal Steel, Arthur Moxham retired from the presidency to head a Nova Scotia steel firm. But the Johnson Company still needed a chief executive to direct the long-term liquidation of its other assets, the landholdings and interurban railway at Lorain. In early January 1899, with the advice of Moxham and Coleman, Tom Johnson offered the position of presidency of the Johnson Company to Pierre at a salary of $10,000 a year.

Tom Johnson's offer was attractive. The salary alone amounted to an increase of $6,000 per year over what Pierre received at the Du Pont Company. Of more importance, it would give Pierre a chance to make something out of his holdings in the company. Furthermore, Pierre would have opportunities to gain friends in the business world that would prove useful when, after the Johnson Company had been liquidated, he would strike out on his own. Pierre decided that he could afford to refuse Johnson's offer on only one condition, that he be promoted to an executive position in the Du Pont Company. This meant a place where he could have a voice in reshaping the firm along modern lines.

At the time of Johnson's offer Pierre's brother Belin was in Asheville, North Carolina, recuperating from a siege of tuberculosis. The two brothers corresponded frequently, and the letters reveal much of Pierre's frustration. On January 20, 1899, Pierre informed Eugene du Pont of Johnson's offer. Pierre asked that his future with the company be determined. On January 23, Eugene answered with vague statements. He did not promise to promote Pierre from Carney's Point to the firm's top management but did ask Pierre to meet with the partners for a formal interview.[36] About the same time, Pierre wrote his thoughts to Belin, "I do not see how they can offer an inducement that will be financially better than the Johnson Company one. It does seem like a very foolish move to think of turning down the latter when we have such large interests in it and the allied companies."[37] Belin's response precisely fitted Pierre's own views. "The Presidency of the Johnson Company not only gives you a large salary but gives you the advantage of meeting and associating with business men and thereby getting opportunities of making even more money than you do by your salary. There will be only one way of your doing as well with E. I. and that is: eventually becoming the head of the business and changing their entire business methods, so that the business will have a chance of making money as it should."[38] Belin suggested that Pierre ask for an immediate partnership in the firm and an executive position, and advised that if these goals were not met he should leave.

On January 27 Pierre wrote his brother, "I am going to leave the Brandywine and go to Lorain." He described his encounter of the previous day with the Du Pont partners:

> I went hardly hoping that they would have any definite offer. I was not disappointed for Cousin Eugene simply said that when things were organized there would be several good places to be filled and thought that I could fill any of them. No special place was mentioned and no salary offered or any mention of giving or selling me an interest in the Company. I remarked that I hoped for something more definite and Alfred, for the whole partnership was lined up against the wall, spoke up and said he thought as I had made a definite proposition that I was entitled to a definite answer. Nothing more was forthcoming so I got up with the remark that I thought that I understood the position and cleared out.[39]

Of the six partners only the two junior ones, Alfred and Charles I., made a determined effort to keep Pierre on the Brandywine. Almost as soon as Pierre arrived home at St. Amour he heard a knock on the door. It was his two young cousins, and they gave Pierre all sorts of reasons why he should stay. Both sympathized with Pierre's ideas for more businesslike management and they were full of reforms. They indicated that if Pierre stayed, he would probably become head of the business in the end. However, Pierre "told them that there had been reforms promised ever since last September and that I could not very well turn down a good offer for vague promises."[40]

Pierre left the firm with considerable bitterness. His experience at Carney's Point had been particularly distasteful, and his relations with Francis G. du Pont had been strained to the breaking point. Pierre wrote Belin: "Today at Carney's Point I told 'F.G.' of my decision. It is needless to say that he did not burst into tears or anything of the kind. I thought before that he was not anxious to have me stay and I am sure of it now."[41] Later that year Belin, who seemingly much better had returned to the Upper Yard, reported to Pierre in Lorain that Carney's Point had lost $75,000 for the year 1898.[42] A few months later Pierre read that $500,000 of Du Pont smokeless powder for army seacoast fortifications had deteriorated and become useless. Pierre could not resist gloating. "It is not always agreeable to say 'I told you so' especially for those who are told, but I think the phrase would apply very well to some of our friends." He wrote Belin, "I am still deeply interested," and asked his brother to ferret out the full details.[43]

Pierre may have left Wilmington with bitterness toward Francis G. du Pont, but his main reason was an inner frustration born of a realization that as long as the old partnership dominated the company there was no possibility that his voice would be heard. Nearly ten years on the Brandywine had sapped his youthful dreams of remaking the company. Beneath Pierre's quiet exterior there was determination to succeed. The association with men like Coleman, Moxham, and Tom Johnson only increased his drive. Pierre left with no illusions. He thought his break with Delaware permanent and that his future lay in the West. Both his brother Belin and his mother understood this and they approved, even though they would miss him at St. Amour. At the same time Coleman du Pont, who would be responsible for getting Pierre back to Wilmington, left the Johnson Company after the sale of its steel business and came east to the family town. Although he had never lived in Wilmington, he now hoped to use it as a base from which to manage his investments which were, like Tom Johnson's, mainly in street-car lines. His wife, Elsie, a sister of Charles I. du Pont, had encouraged the move east.

### New Ventures

Pierre arrived in Lorain shortly before the first of March 1899. He stayed in the large house Arthur Moxham had built for himself while he managed the steelworks. For Pierre the Johnson Company was a transitional position. His job was to liquidate its assets, a process that could take several years. Of the two main Johnson Company properties, the Lorain Street Railway was profitable, and it seemed to have potential for further growth. Although Pierre spent considerable time with the railway, working to increase its profits, the other main property, the Sheffield Land Company, absorbed most of his energy.

The Sheffield Land Company, with its more than 3,000 acres surrounding Federal Steel's Lorain plant, represented well over 80% of the Johnson Company's potential assets. But these could be realized only in the distant future. Furthermore, there was a need of substantial capital in order to develop the land. Streets had to be laid out and constructed, sewers put in, water extended, and sample homes built.

Pierre's job was largely town building. During his tenure in Lorain he started new industries on the property, some of which the Johnson Company financed. These included a brick works, a cold storage plant, and a shovel factory. He helped to found a bank. He also built houses and sold lots.

But liquidating the Johnson Company proved to be much like treading water. He got nowhere. The major problem at the outset had been the large floating debt the company had contracted in its desperate attempt to survive as a steel-making concern. This amounted to slightly more than $600,000. The difficulty was that both the Sheffield Land Company and the street railway soaked up all the revenue they generated. In the long run there was hope that the capital improvements would be completed and the profits from land sales and street railway operations could be applied toward the reduction of the firm's debt and finally toward paying off the stock-holders. But as of June 1900, more than a year after Pierre took control, there was no measurable progress toward liquidation. A lack of orders at the Lorain Steel Company kept the labor force low and reduced poten-tial town growth and land sales. Pierre could only hope things would change.[44]

In August 1900 Pierre hired John J. Raskob as a bookkeeper. Raskob previously had worked for a short time with Arthur Moxham as a stenogra-pher, going with the former Johnson Company president to his new position with the Dominion Iron & Steel Company in Sydney, Nova Scotia. Raskob, a native of upstate New York, soon tired of Canada and desired to return to the United States. Pierre hired the young bookkeeper on Moxham's recommendation.[45]

Although John Raskob was nine years younger than Pierre and came from a very different background and traditions, they soon became fast friends. Raskob was one of a large family. His father was a cigar maker of Alsatian descent, and his mother was Irish. Like his mother and father the son remained a devout Catholic throughout life. Raskob had helped support himself during the school years as a newspaper carrier and office clerk. He had a sharp, quick, ingenious mind that was especially good at the manipula-tion of figures. He began at once to help Pierre work out his financial schemes and arrangements. The two quickly developed a great mutual respect for each other. Throughout his entire business career, no other person ever was as close to Pierre du Pont as John Raskob.

Even though Pierre spent most of his time in the Middle West, he remained very much the head of his father's family. Through Pierre's influ-ence his former roommate, William H. Fenn, who had started a construc-tion company in Newark, New Jersey, hired Irénée, who had graduated from M.I.T. in 1897 and received his master's degree the following year. Pierre felt grave concern for his brother Belin, who had been forced to leave the Brandywine again for the more healthful climate of Colorado in a second attempt to win his fight with tuberculosis. In the fall of 1900 Pierre visited Belin in Colorado and then accompanied him to a new home near Phoenix, Arizona.[46]

Pierre also continued to invest the inheritances of his brothers and sisters. Under his leadership they formed a syndicate, and Pierre used the money to invest in stocks recommended mostly by Tom Johnson. In 1900 the newly formed Federal Steel was the favorite, and soon he was calling his investment group the Federal Steel Syndicate. This was the one period when Pierre came closest to gambling on the market. When Johnson and other insiders recommended purchases Pierre made them. When the stock rose he sold, buying it back again when it fell.

Toward the end of 1900 managing the Johnson Company became routine. It was merely a matter of selling lots and hoping that income from that source and from the Lorain Street Railway would provide the cash to pay the floating debt and gradually accumulate enough money to return capital to the stockholders. Pierre's plans to refinance the company were rejected by the company's stockholders mainly because the proposals called for the infusion of new capital. All hesitated to throw good money after bad.[47] The firm's floating debt remained long after Pierre submitted his resignation as president in 1904. The creditors were not repaid until after World War I, and the stockholders lost everything.[48]

In late 1900 Pierre, with the full approval of Tom Johnson, who would soon become mayor of Cleveland, began to search for a new business opportunity. Still heavily under Johnson's influence he chose trolley systems. This was the time when most street railways had just shifted or were changing from horse to electric power. It was also a time of rapid urban expansion, and almost every town of 10,000 population or more was planning to install streetcars.

By the end of 1900 Pierre was experienced in corporate finance, and he had grappled with the problems of the Lorain Street Railway. He had specific ideas about how he would make money. His formula was to find a run-down street railway property in a middle-sized, growing city. He hoped to pay for the line using little or no cash. He planned to achieve initial control by making a minimum down payment. The seed capital for this he would raise from his own resources, including the trust funds he administered, from his adult brothers and sisters, and from Coleman. Much of this money he would transfer from the Federal Steel Syndicate. Pierre, remembering the Johnson Company's experiences, was determined not to be saddled by a large floating debt. After making his down payment Pierre hoped to finance his venture with a bond issue. He would use the proceeds from bond sales to pay the former owners and to provide for needed improvements. For Pierre's plans to work he had to find a system where the current revenues would be sufficient to meet the interest on the bonds issued to pay for his purchase and for the improvements on the property. Pierre felt that savings from more efficient operations and increased business resulting from the natural growth of the city would provide enough revenue over and above that needed to service the debt to allow a 5% or 6% dividend on the common stock. This would make such securities for which he would have paid nothing become valuable.

Pierre perfected his plan with Johnson and Coleman. It seemed foolproof, provided the right opportunity could be found. Through George T. Bishop, a Cleveland financier and an acquaintance of Johnson's, Pierre's attention was directed toward a scheme that proposed to unify all electric railroads in Fort Worth and Dallas and then build an interurban between the two Texas cities. This proposal failed, but Pierre discovered that Dallas alone seemed to meet all of his requirements. In early March 1901 Pierre wrote Coleman, "I have spent several days in Dallas, Texas, looking at street railway properties. There seems to be a chance for a good deal there. The railways (three companies) owning 43.45 miles of track can be purchased for $1,300,000." Pierre felt that the price could be negotiated downward. Dallas's earnings particularly impressed him, the net being about $114,000 for 1900 and the trend rapidly upward. This would allow the servicing of $1.3 million of 5% bonds and still leave in excess of $45,000 to allow expansion of the debt for new improvements or to pay dividends on the stock.

Dallas's run-down condition met Pierre's fondest hopes. He told Coleman: "The whole street railway outfit is strictly 'bum'. . . . All but five miles or so of track is laid with 30–35 lb. Tee Rail and the alignment and special work is of the Brandywine Powder Yard order and poor of its type. There are thirty-two good motor equipments, however, and fifty-six good cars, but all of these need painting. The overhead [wire] is reported fair and may be kept up out of earnings. . . . The road is operated very badly, cars are dirty and run with little system. The track is so rough that riding is very uncomfortable, in fact, everybody keeps a horse and buggy and the streets are crowded with vehicles in the evening. . . . With the extremely poor accommodations there can be but little pleasure riding, though there should be excellent business from this as the climate is warm. . . ." He concluded, "From the earnings of the Electric Railway during the past year and the bad condition of the property, it seems to be an excellent field for investment."[49] Pierre noted that Dallas's population including suburbs was about 56,000 and rapidly growing.

Upon Pierre's return to Lorain he began to line up commitments for the initial investment. His list of backers included Coleman and his Aunt Emma Paulina du Pont, Colonel Henry, the Federal Steel Syndicate, and additional individual contributions by his sister Louisa and his brothers Belin, Irénée, and William K.

Prolonged negotiations, in which Pierre was assisted by John Raskob, were carried on with the owners of the two most important Dallas systems, The Dallas Consolidated Electric Street Railway and North Dallas Circuit Railway Company, and produced an agreement that went into effect June

11, 1901. For all the stock in the two companies (the old owners agreeing to pay off all debts from the proceeds), Pierre agreed to pay the sum of $1,075,000 in funds and $50,000 out of an issue of par value of $1,500,000 of common stock in his new company. Only $225,000 of the $1,075,000 was cash that Pierre raised through his family syndicate. In order to consummate the deal Pierre gave the old owners his notes for the remaining $850,-000. For collateral he used the stock in the old firms that he had just purchased! To retire these notes Pierre planned to have his new company issue $1,150,000 of bonds, which he would sell through eastern investment banking houses. This would be sufficient not only to pay the old owners, but with an issue of $65,000 of preferred stock at 90 would provide $168,000 for needed improvements such as laying heavier rails on improved roadbeds.

Pierre's sophistication in financial schemes shows how well and quickly he was becoming an expert financier. He wrote the members of the family syndicate that backed him:

> We have furnished two hundred twenty-five thousand dollars in cash for which we receive one million four hundred fifty thousand dollars common stock [out of $1,500,000] as soon as the bonds [which we will issue] are ready to substitute as collateral on notes. To meet the eight hundred fifty thousand dollars in outstanding notes, we will purchase one million fifty thousand dollars of the company's bonds at eighty-one; pay off the notes and use the balance of the bonds to return to us a portion of the cash put up in the first payment. The remaining one hundred thousand [dollars of] bonds will be sold for making improvements.[50]

What Pierre was telling his backers was that proceeds from the bond sales would not only pay off his notes, but return to the syndicate most of their capital. In short they would acquire their stock for nearly nothing.

All Pierre's plans contained an element of risk. He had to sell the bonds of his new company or he would lose the $225,000 his syndicate had invested. And in order to keep control he had to be able to pay the interest upon the bonded debt he was creating. Furthermore, to make his stock valuable he had to increase earnings. This was Pierre's first big financial transaction and he saw the risk clearly and was a bit nervous about it. To his brother Belin, who was desperately ill in Phoenix, Pierre wrote: "The only difficulty in the way is raising sufficient money. I hesitate to advise everyone to go into this deal as it might be financially embarrassing if we should not be able to sell the bonds."[51] At first Pierre cautiously did not want to go ahead until he had already found a market for the bonds. Significantly the more ebullient Coleman argued against this, feeling that it would be no problem to find buyers for the bonds after Pierre bought the railway. Coleman's ideas prevailed, and thus selling bonds was Pierre's first major task for the Dallas Railway.

Pierre entered the street railway business in Dallas with enthusiasm. He planned to move to Texas from Lorain as soon as he cleared up his work for the Johnson Company. He also planned to create positions for his family. He made his brother Bill (William K. du Pont) vice-president, and John J. Raskob treasurer. Pierre kept on Edward T. Moore, the Dallas company's secretary and general superintendent, as his general manager. Pierre made immediate plans to improve the company by laying new and heavier rail on the principal lines. The construction contracts for this went to William Fenn, the M.I.T. classmate for whom Irénée now worked.

Immediately after Pierre bought the Dallas Consolidated Electric Street Railway he tried to place his bond offering. Difficulties developed. Pierre had no commitment whatsoever from any financial house or bond broker when he purchased the Dallas lines. Furthermore, he was as yet little known in the money markets outside of Cleveland, Wilmington, and Philadelphia. He hoped to offer 5% gold bonds at a price of 92½. He was prepared, if a potential buyer showed interest, to offer a bonus of 5% of the value of the bonds in common stock. Either a buyer would receive this or a broker could keep it as a commission.[52]

Pierre soon discovered that there was no great demand for his wares. He went to Boston to see Stone & Webster, a financial house specializing in street railway securities, and found that they were "endeavoring to do the same kind of work that we have planned, namely, to sell bonds and to take up stock themselves."[53] From George P. Bissell, who was associated with the Philadelphia bond broker William T. Tiers, Pierre learned that Dallas had a bad reputation in the Quaker City because of the failure of the original Dallas Railway, in which Philadelphians had invested heavily.[54] Bissell held out some hope that the securities might be sold if the price were lowered. From most New York houses Pierre received polite, but firm, letters of disinterest. One exception was the Wall Street broker Alven Beveridge, who made a real effort to sell the bonds. For a while it looked as if he had found a customer in Harris & Company, but negotiations dragged on into late fall. Harris & Company wanted Pierre to limit future bond sales, establish a sinking fund to retire the bonds, and lower his price to about 90. Finally Pierre in exasperation called a halt to the negotiations. In November 1901 he wrote Beveridge: "I thank you for . . . enclosing letter of Messrs. Harris & Company. I can appreciate very much that they would be glad to have a sinking fund as I would also like it if I were in their position. One million [in] bonds at ninety-two and one-half with part redeemable at 105 each year, fifteen years, would make a very attractive investment; for instance those called the first year would bring to the lucky owner fifteen and one-half percent. This," he concluded, "is a rather high rate of interest to pay even in Texas."[55]

A continued climb in net earnings by the Dallas streetcars and the willingness of the firm's old owners not to press for payment of Pierre's notes relieved the young financier from being forced to make a deal with Harris & Company. Pierre now began to rethink the problem. The increased earnings of his railway bolstered his confidence. He had no doubt that the system could pay off all the debt he proposed to create and that there would be enough to pay dividends on the stock as well. That being the case, why deal with bankers at all? Why not keep the profit of selling the bonds for himself and his investors? Pierre began to think of cutting the bond offering up into five blocks of $200,000 each and selling them to members of the family such as Colonel Henry du Pont, Henry Belin, Jr. (Pierre's uncle), and Alexis I. du Pont (Eugene's brother), all of whom had substantial money to invest. And possibly he could dispose of a block or two to the old owners as well.

On January 28, 1902, before Pierre could put together a definite plan, Cousin Eugene died, leaving the Du Pont Company leaderless. This story is told in the next chapter, but it must be noted here that, by the end of February 1902, the three cousins—Pierre, Coleman, and Alfred—had purchased the Du Pont Company, and Pierre had returned from Lorain to Wilmington to assume the position of treasurer. Pierre did not immediately decide to sell his Dallas holdings, but instead placed much of the operational detail in the hands of his brother Bill.

In Wilmington Pierre discussed Dallas with key family members. He needed $400,000 in immediate cash so that the old owners could pay off a debt that was about to come due. In April he took advantage of his new position by having the Du Pont Company, which had some extra cash and which could use the bonds as collateral should it want to borrow money, take $400,000 worth of bonds. In addition Pierre, as guardian, took $20,000, and Colonel Henry took $25,000 worth of bonds. Other members of the family seemed interested in purchasing these securities, though probably in small lots.[56]

By mid-1902 Pierre, realizing that sharing in the management of the Du Pont Company would require his full time, decided to try to sell his Dallas property. But he could not let it be known that he wanted to sell because this would tend to force the price he might receive downward. Meanwhile, conditions in Dallas complicated any move Pierre might wish to make. When he bought Dallas Consolidated in 1901, an important factor in his estimates for the cost of operation was a favorable power contract with a local Dallas electric utility company. Pierre did not know two key facts. The two major electric companies in the city—Dallas Electric and Standard Light and Power—were controlled by the General Electric Company, and both firms were having trouble meeting operating expenses and were in need of fresh capital to improve their plants. Soon after Pierre took control, Standard Light and Power, through A. K. Bonta, manager of the Dallas Electric Company, indicated that it wanted to "revise" the railway's power contract, which still had several years to run. Since the change would increase power costs, Pierre refused.

In January 1902 Standard Light and Power broke its contract. While it continued to provide power on a day-to-day basis to the streetcars, the action threatened Pierre's carefully worked-out plans. Furthermore, Standard's arbitrary manner angered the young Wilmingtonian. He decided to fight. He promised C. H. Alexander, who owned a small power plant to service an ice factory, that, if he would start a full-fledged new power company, he would receive the contract to supply power for the trolleys. Pierre even agreed to supply some capital for the venture. Pierre's bold move triggered a sharp reaction from the Standard interests. The old company felt that it could not afford to lose the street railway business, since trolleys consumed approximately one-third of all power used in the city.[57] Consequently Bonta went to the city council and won a franchise to build a new street railway that would parallel many of Pierre's routes and in the center of the city even operate on some of the same streets as did Pierre's Dallas Consolidated Electric Street Railway.

Pierre and his general manager, Moore, spent much of their time fighting the rival line. They brought lawsuits to try to block construction of tracks on streets already occupied by Consolidated. They hired detectives to trace the movements of the Bonta group and various members of the city council whom they suspected of receiving graft for the passing of the rival franchise. But despite everything the new railway started construction. On July 7, 1902, Moore reported to Bill du Pont the details of a near battle that occurred over Bonta's attempt to build his line through a Consolidated switch on Peak Street between Live Oak and Bryan. Moore wrote:

> Last night about 12 o'clock the Bonta people, with about 200 men and a great many wagons and teams, began their work building their tracks through our switch. . . . My first thought was to allow them to begin the work and then stop them with an injunction, and after they had begun work about 12 o'clock I run [sic] two cars in on the switch and stopped them for a short time, but before I could get other cars there they piled rails and ties on the track so that it was impossible to get other cars on the switch, especially with the force of men they had to pile them on as fast as our men took them off and we finally abandoned the effort to prevent them from working.[58]

Before this skirmish took place, representatives of the General Electric Company had contacted Pierre. They informed him that they wanted to purchase Dallas Consolidated, and admitted that they controlled both Standard Light & Power and Dallas Electric.[59] By this time Pierre had decided to sell his railway, but the price offered by General Electric was too low, so he feigned lack of interest.

While Pierre fought to maintain his position in Dallas, from June 1902 onward he actively tried to sell the railways. Actually two groups wanted to buy, Stone & Webster as well as General Electric. After Pierre's initial rebuff General Electric approached him through a third party, William D'H. Washington, a New York street railway promoter. Stone & Webster operated through third parties right from the start. On July 29, 1902, Pierre wrote his brother William: "We will be willing to sell the Dallas Road upon the following basis:

| | | |
|---|---|---|
| $1,050,000 | bonds at 97½ and interest to August 1st | $1,050,000 |
| $210,000 | preferred stock at 90 | 189,000 |
| $1,500,000 | common stock at 20 | 300,000 |
| | Total | $1,539,000 |

This would have made Pierre and the holders of the common stock a profit of an even $300,000.[60]

After prolonged negotiations Pierre finally in the last week of August closed the deal. He wrote his cousin Alexis the terms of the sale. The bonds would be 97½. The common stock would be sold at 15, but prior to its sale the present holders would be paid a dividend of $4 a share. Thus Pierre came within $1 a share of getting his price.[61] The young Du Pont Company treasurer's brief fifteen-month fling with streetcars in Dallas was a financial success.

Pierre learned much from his Dallas venture. He had planned to make his money by enhancing the value of the company's stock. The present income of the traction company would cover the interest on the bonds issued to pay for it. By improving its roadbed, equipment, and management and by counting on the increase in its customers, he hoped to provide the funds for the payment of dividends on the stock he issued. But he did not have time to test his ideas fully.

He did, however, get the experience of putting together a complex financial scheme and of trying to raise money on Wall Street. He learned how difficult it was to finance such ventures and also that profits could be made through internal financing using family resources. Equally important, he learned that estimates for company profits could be upset if the prices of raw materials, in this case electric power, changed unexpectedly. He learned that even long-term contracts could not guarantee prices. The Standard Light and Power Company was able to break its contract by what Pierre believed was contrived receivership. The Dallas experience taught him the value of better research and planning for protection against unforeseeable changes in the cost of raw materials. All these lessons Pierre would use to advantage in his new Wilmington career.

# The New Company

THE RETURN TO Wilmington ended Pierre's apprenticeship. He suddenly found himself in a position of responsibility and authority where he could put to use his recent financial lessons as well as the administrative ones he had been taught by Moxham and Tom Johnson. He now had the opportunity to carry out old schemes for modernizing the Du Pont Company. By reorganizing its finances and by reshaping its business and management methods he could perhaps make as lasting a contribution to the firm as had his father, grandfather, and great-grandfather, and he could add as much as they had to the fortunes of the larger family, of which he felt so much a part.

The opportunity, when it came, was completely unanticipated. As 1902 opened, Pierre was wholly engrossed in the affairs of the Dallas street railways and the Johnson Company. He spent the first two weeks of January in Dallas preparing to give battle to the electric power company there.[1] On his return to Lorain, where he caught up on Johnson Company business, he heard the pleasant rumor that the new industrial giant, the United States Steel Corporation, was planning to enlarge the Lorain works. If this were true, the Johnson Company might still produce an adequate return for its stockholders. By the end of the month Pierre was in New York trying to market bonds of the Dallas company. On January 27 his sister Louisa wrote that Cousin Eugene was in bed with a bad cold. The old man looked so weak and haggard when she last saw him that she was afraid the illness might bring his end. The next day Raskob forwarded him this letter and sent a telegram saying that the Du Pont Company's president had died of pneumonia on the afternoon of January 28.[2]

## The Succession

Pierre's thoughts must have turned immediately to the oldest problem of family dynasties—that of succession. Who would take over the company and so, in the order of things, become head of the family? Here was a chance to bring in younger men and modernize the firm. On the other hand, succession also raised the threat of controversy. Pierre, like most of the larger family, realized that the last succession crisis had irrevocably driven apart the brothers William and Henry. The logical choice for the presidency in terms of experience and seniority was Francis G. du Pont. And Cousin Frank, Pierre knew so well, had little sympathy for young blood and new ideas. Nor were his administrative talents such as to revive confidence in the future of the family firm. Even if Francis G. turned it down, who then might take the job? Pierre was certain that Cousin Frank would not permit the company to be headed by a man without experience in the powder industry.

The answer came in less than three weeks. Over the long distance telephone Coleman's booming voice broke the news. He and Alfred were planning to buy the company, but they needed Pierre's help particularly to handle finances. Would Pierre join them? Pierre always remembered his response. "Would I do it? This was the most important far-reaching decision of my life; no position, salary or interest in the business was offered but the three minute allowance of a telephone conversation was quite long enough for me to receive the account of the proposition placed before me, and to make up my mind and give my reply in one word, *yes.*"[3]

The call, however, was not quite as unexpected nor the decision made quite as suddenly as Pierre later remembered. Pierre certainly consulted with his cousins about the possibilities of bringing in a younger management when he was in Wilmington for Eugene's funeral. A week before the phone call Coleman and Pierre had met briefly in New York City.[4] Although the meeting was scheduled to last less than an hour, Coleman must have brought Pierre up to date on the developments in Wilmington, for Coleman had surely kept in touch with Alfred and Charles I., the two junior partners, one of whom, Charles, was Coleman's brother-in-law. These younger men were clearly deeply concerned about the future of the company. On February 11, five days after meeting Coleman in New York, Pierre received a telegram from his cousin mentioning an important meeting in Wilmington the following evening. He added that he would wire him the news, which he thought would be "yes."[5] Instead of the telegram came the telephone call.

When he reached Wilmington a few days later, Pierre learned many of the details of the events that led to Coleman's phone call.[6] Shortly after Eugene's funeral the partners met to decide who would be the next presi-

dent. Because Eugene had incorporated the firm three years before, the
partners had become stockholders of the E. I. du Pont de Nemours &
Company. The senior partners, each of whom held 20% of the stock, had
included, in addition to Eugene, his two brothers, Francis G. and Alexis I.,
and Colonel Henry A. du Pont, the eldest son of old "Boss Henry." The two
junior partners, Charles I. and Alfred I., each held 10% of the stock. Of the
stockholders Alfred was the one who was most lax in attending their irregular meetings. He did not even show up for the important one on succession,
probably because he assumed that the older men had already decided and
that the meeting would be a *pro forma* ratification of their decision.

The others, who all attended the meeting, were most surprised when
Francis G. opened the discussion by saying that he "emphatically refused"
to take the presidency.[7] Although he gave no reason, the family soon were
to know that he had developed an illness that he felt would quickly force
him to retire.[8] In fact, he and his brother Alexis were to die within a few
days of each other two and a half years later, and Charles, who was also
sickly, had less than a year to live. Cousin Frank's refusal turned all eyes
on Colonel Henry. Although the old soldier had, next to Francis, the longest
service in the company, he had never played an important part in the
management of the firm. He was becoming involved in politics and hoped
before long to represent his state either as a congressman or a senator.

As Alexis was old and had had little practical experience in the business
and as Charles was in ill health, Colonel Henry's refusal left Alfred as the
only partner and stockholder available for the presidency. But neither the
colonel nor his cousins favored Alfred's candidacy. As Colonel Henry later
reported, Cousin Frank "had formed an exceedingly low estimate of Alfred
Irénée's good judgment and business ability, which he did not hesitate to
express."[9] Alexis concurred with his brother. While Henry was, in his own
words, "disposed to be more lenient," he fully agreed that Alfred I. should
not be permitted to take over the family business.

Who then could? Worried, tired, and discouraged, the four agreed that
the simplest and most direct course would be to sell the company to its
ancient competitors and closest ally, the Laflin & Rand Powder Company.
Together the two firms had dominated the black powder business for a
generation, and together they had created much of the dynamite production
in this country. The four all knew and respected Laflin & Rand's president,
J. Amory Haskell, who at one time had been the president of the Repauno
Chemical Company, the dynamite firm that Pierre's father had started. If
Laflin & Rand refused to buy or offered too low a price, the stockholders
decided to turn the presidency of their company over to Hamilton M.
Barksdale. That competent young executive, who had married another of
Charles I. du Pont's sisters, had succeeded Haskell as president of the
Repauno Company in 1895 and had with Haskell made that company one

of the most progressive in the explosives industry. The final action of the meeting was, therefore, a motion to ask Barksdale to take the presidency in order to arrange the sale of the Du Pont Company to Laflin & Rand. If he failed to obtain a satisfactory price, then he would continue to manage the firm.

Barksdale gave the proposal a few days' thought, talking it over with his brothers-in-law, Charles I. and T. Coleman du Pont. He then reported back to Alexis that he felt that a man with the family name should be given the position. Until the stockholders had, he told Alexis, "exhausted all efforts to secure such a man to take the helm, I would not accept it."[10] To Colonel Henry this meant that Barksdale was proposing Coleman.[11] But Henry realized that Francis G. would vehemently resist turning the company over to a man, even if his name was du Pont, if that man had had no experience in the powder trade.

On Thursday, February 13, after receiving Barksdale's reply, the stockholders again met and again did so without Alfred.[12] Francis and Alexis then agreed that the company should be sold to Laflin & Rand for a price of $12.0 million and that Barksdale be appointed the agent for the sale. Charles and Colonel Henry said little. They now favored Coleman's candidacy, but were uncertain how to broach the possibility without unsettling Cousin Frank and forcing him to take a position from which he could not later be moved.[13] Since these two were clearly not enthusiastic about the sale and since the fifth stockholder, Alfred, was not present, Francis G. decided to postpone further discussion until the following afternoon, when Alfred could be there.

Alfred came to that meeting from the yards dressed in his work clothes, his hands and face grimy with powder.[14] He listened with apparent inattention as Cousin Frank first reviewed the discussion and actions of the previous meeting and next offered a formal resolution to sell the company to Laflin & Rand. Alfred then proposed an amendment to the resolution that provided that the business should be sold to the highest bidder. It was accepted and the meeting seemed over.

Then Alfred rose quietly and said that he would buy the company. There was a stunned silence. Even Charles and Colonel Henry were taken by surprise. A shocked Cousin Frank told Alfred that he simply could not have the business. "Why not?" Alfred demanded. In an increasingly shrill voice he made his plea. As he later testified:

> I pointed out to him the fact that the business was mine by all rights of heritage, that it was my birthright; I told him that I would pay as much as anybody else, and further more, I proposed to have it. I told him that I would require a week to perfect the necessary arrangements looking towards the purchase of the business, and asked for that length of time.[15]

No one spoke. As Alfred moved toward the door, Colonel Henry rose. "Gentlemen, I think I understand Alfred's sentiment in desiring to purchase the business, and I wish to say that it has my hearty approval, and I shall insist that he be given the first opportunity to acquire the property."[16]

Colonel Henry then followed Alfred out of the room. Catching his younger cousin by the arm, he asked, "I assume, of course, although you said nothing about it, that Thomas Coleman and Pierre are, or will be, associated with you in the proposed purchase?" As Henry later remembered the conversation, Alfred replied, "Yes, although as a matter of fact I have not heard from Pierre as yet, to whom I have written, (or am about to write)." The colonel was satisfied. "With the understanding that Coleman and Pierre are associated with you in the proposition I assent to it most cordially and will do everything in my power to bring it about."[17]

While the colonel worked hard to convince Alexis and through him Francis G. to permit the sale of the company to the younger men, Alfred moved quickly to complete his arrangements. Immediately following the meeting of February 14 he drove to Coleman's house on Delaware Avenue to report all that had occurred.[18] Coleman had already discussed with his wife the possibility of taking over the company with Alfred. He hesitated, for he was almost as skeptical as Cousin Frank and Colonel Henry about Alfred's business abilities and his temperamental stability. Furthermore, Elsie had reminded him of the difficulties of doing business with relatives. So Coleman presented Alfred with two conditions. First, he must have a free hand in organizing and managing the new company. To assure this he, Coleman, must have the largest block of stock in that firm. Second, Pierre must join them to handle the finances. Pierre's performance as guardian and trustee for his family and his skill in financing the Lorain and Dallas ventures clearly impressed the experienced and hardheaded Coleman. Alfred readily agreed to both conditions, and Coleman then put in the long distance call to Pierre.

After receiving the call Pierre hurriedly made his plans to return permanently to Delaware. He telephoned Tom Johnson about the sudden turn of events. Johnson graciously urged him to make the most of his new opportunity. Pierre then spent some time going over the details of the Johnson Company with William A. Donaldson who, he and Johnson agreed, could take over much of Pierre's work there.[19] Then on either Saturday or Sunday night he took the train from Lorain, bringing Raskob with him.

Throughout Sunday and much of Monday a heavy snow fell. The worst blizzard of the season swept up the coast. As soon as the roads were passable Pierre and Coleman went to Swamp Hall.[20] There, sitting in Alfred's billiard room, Pierre listened to his two cousins review the events of the past two weeks. The three then discussed the mechanics of the proposed purchase. Although they had no information to go on, they agreed that the price of

$12.0 million was undoubtedly fair. The company's earnings in the past few years had been about 4% of this amount. Coleman was sure that the property was undervalued. Moreover, the conservative policies of the older generation indicated large reserves from undistributed earnings. Finally Coleman and Pierre were convinced that by introducing modern financial and management methods to the old company they could increase its profitability. Indeed from the start Pierre and Coleman looked on the purchase of the family firm in much the same way as Pierre had viewed the Dallas street railway venture. They would pay for the company in bonds and they would make their stock valuable by improving the company's technical capabilities and reorganizing its management.

Nevertheless, $12.0 million was a large sum for three young men to raise. The older stockholders would not insist on cash, but neither would they agree to finance their successors.[21] They wanted an assured 4% return on their present investment. So Pierre and Coleman proposed a plan to buy out the company. They would form a new corporation, E. I. du Pont de Nemours Company, which would issue $12.0 million worth of 4%, thirty-year bonds. These bonds would be exchanged for the stock of the old company, the E. I. du Pont de Nemours & Company, and would represent a first lien on the property. The new company was also authorized to issue capital stock up to a par value of $20.0 million. This stock was to be divided among the three cousins. In this way the older stockholders would be assured of a continuing income at the present rate of return, and the new owners would have full control. They would receive any earnings above the current 4%.

This proposal met with the full approval of the sellers. Then Coleman had some second thoughts about securing the bonds with a first lien on the property, for this would eliminate the possibility of later loans if an emergency should arise. So he asked Colonel Henry "if the sellers would be willing to waive that part of the purchase agreement and accept in lieu thereof 25% of the stock of the new company."[22] The notes would then be supported by the credit of the company alone, but the former stockholders would have a share in any increased profit. The colonel again had to work through Alexis to get the approval of crusty and conservative Cousin Frank. He was successful, for on Wednesday evening, February 10, Colonel Henry, Francis G., Charles I., and young Eugene as the representative of his father's estate met to review the younger cousins' offer. (Alexis was too ill to come.) Those present at once accepted the offer in principle.[23] All agreed that only a few days would be needed to iron out the details and put the matter into proper legal form.

The next morning Pierre jubilantly broke the news to his two brothers and William Fenn, whose company had been rebuilding the Dallas street railway company's track. "The wheel of fortune has been revolving at pretty

|          |                           |
|----------|---------------------------|
| Chemical | 1<br>Peyton Chemical      |
|          | ↑                         |
| Powder   | C.P.W.<br>(black, dynamite,<br>& smokeless)<br>(44% of stock<br>held by Du Pont Co.) |
|          | ↓                         |
| Fuse     | California Fuse Co.        |
|          |                           |
|          | ↓                         |
| Shell    | Shell-making<br>auxiliary |

|          |                           |
|----------|---------------------------|
| Chemical | Peyton Chemical           |
| Powder   | C.P.W.<br>(wholly owned<br>subsidiary of<br>Du Pont Powder Co. |
| Fuse     | Coast Manufacturing<br>& Supply Co.<br>(purchased later by<br>Ensign, Bickford) |
| Shell    | by C.P.W.                 |

high speed on the Brandy Wine during the last week or two," he wrote his brother Bill, "with the result that Coleman and Alfred and I have made E. I. du Pont & Co. an offer to buy out their property and I today received verbal acceptance of the proposition." To both he gave a brief description of the developments. To Irénée he added: "I think there is to be some tall hustling to get everything reorganized. We have not the slightest idea of what we are buying, but in that we are probably not at a disadvantage as I think the old company has a very slim idea of the property they possess."

To both brothers Pierre outlined his plans for dropping his existing commitments in order to take on the new tasks. His primary concern was the Dallas venture. He told Bill that he had checked with Tom Johnson and they both had agreed that Donaldson could do most of the work that Pierre had done in Lorain, although Pierre doubted whether he could "cut loose from there altogether." Therefore he hoped that Bill could now devote most of his time to the Dallas business. Pierre requested his brothers and Fenn not to mention these developments to anyone outside of the immediate family until they heard from him, "as the du Ponts are cranky and may not like to have news announced until they do it themselves."

By early the next week both sides had pretty well agreed on the final form of the sale. The stockholders of the old and new companies met on Wednesday, February 26, to complete and authorize the sale and transfer of property.[24] The final agreement signed shortly afterwards was dated March 1. By this agreement the old company, E. I. du Pont de Nemours & Company, would sell the entire business, good will, property, and assets to the new company, E. I. du Pont de Nemours Company, which would be capitalized at $24.0 million, $12.0 million in notes and $12.0 million in stock. The $12.0 million worth of thirty-year notes would go to the five stockholders of the company and to the estate of Eugene du Pont, with Francis, Alexis, and Henry receiving 20% each, Eugene's heirs another 20%, and Charles and Alfred getting 10% apiece. In addition, the five stockholders and Eugene's heirs would receive 28%, rather than 25%, of the stock, or 33,600 shares to be divided in the same proportion. The rest was allocated among the three purchasers, with Coleman, as part of the agreement with Alfred to have a free hand, getting half this block, or 36% of this total, which equaled 43,200 shares, while Alfred and Pierre each took 18%, or 21,600 shares. Since Alfred held 10% of the old company stock, he then had a total of 24,433 shares. In addition he received $1.2 million worth of purchase notes.

On Friday, with the agreement signed, Coleman left for the West, to begin closing out his many interests in Kentucky, Ohio, and elsewhere. Alfred returned to the yards, as the supervision of production could not wait on changes in management. Pierre, assisted by Raskob, started to inventory and appraise the property. The next day, March 1, Pierre came to the small office that had been set aside for him. Unexpectedly Cousin Frank entered, bringing in the morning mail and some items requiring immediate attention. Then to Pierre's surprise he announced that he was now turning over the company to the three cousins, since the sale had been made and the agreement signed. He shook hands, took his hat and coat and walked out of the door.[25] Significantly, this symbolic transfer of authority and control from one generation of du Ponts to another was bestowed on Pierre rather than Coleman or Alfred. The older man, who had refused the honor and responsibility as head of the family and the firm, in this way expressed his confidence in the youngest of the company's new owners.

*The New Strategy*

The three cousins now fully controlled the family birthright. For their properties they had paid almost nothing in cash. Organizing costs of about $700 had been split among the three.[26] But if they were to make a profit from their properties, they certainly had to do some "tall hustling." The company's present income would pay the interest on the purchase notes and permit amortizing of the debt; it might even cover the salaries of the three cousins and their managerial assistants. However, the 120,000 shares of stock issued by the new company would remain worth little more than the paper on which they were printed until improvements were made in the methods of manufacturing and distributing explosives and, above all, in the over-all organization of the properties.

The new owners had no trouble in the allocation of their work. Alfred, the one with the longest experience in the making of explosives, would administer production as vice-president and general manager. Pierre, with his talent and experience in finance, would be treasurer, while Coleman, as president, would supervise marketing and plan over-all strategy.[27] The cousins took up their tasks immediately. Alfred began to inspect the mills for which he had become responsible. Besides the largest black powder plant in the world, which Francis G. had built in 1888 at Mooar, Iowa, there were the black powder mills on the Brandywine, Wapwallopen near Scranton, and the small Sycamore plant at Nashville. In addition to black powder, there was the smokeless powder works at Carney's Point, New Jersey.[28] Coleman began to reshape the company's marketing, purchasing, and transportation methods, while Pierre continued to inventory the company's property and other assets.

Pierre's inventory began with the first approaches of the soft Delaware spring. He would not finish before the hot, muggy summer had descended. But almost immediately after he started, he and Coleman worked out their initial plans for reorganizing the company and with it the explosives industry in the United States. Pierre had been delighted as his practiced eye first reviewed the columns of cash balances, accounts receivable, materials on hand, valuations of the five works operated directly by the company and of its storage magazines and offices, as well as the investments in companies outside the powder business and the extensive holdings in other explosives firms. The rough, initial estimate that Pierre had drawn up with Raskob's help valued the assets at $12,214,332.42. It was drawn so that the total would be close to the sale price set by Cousin Frank. (See Table 3–1.)[29]

Table 3–1   DATA CONCERNING INVENTORIES
E. I. DU PONT DE NEMOURS & COMPANY

|  |  | Inventoried at | Oscar E. Morton Valuation |
|---|---|---|---|
| Cash |  | 1,193,533.81 | 1,141,528.67 |
| Bonds |  | 914,549.75 | 913,768.00 |
| Stocks, Powder Co. | $4,536,265.00 |  |  |
| "   Investment | 160,163.50 | 4,696,428.50 | 5,831,337.78 |
| Bills Receivable |  | 200,056.09 | 139,061.16 |
| Accounts Receivable |  |  |  |
| General | 800,397.98 |  |  |
| Misc. Assets | 239,108.18 | 1,039,506.16 | 1,039,931.56 |
| Bonds, Brown Bros. | 28,000.00 | 28,000.00 | 50,000.00 |
| Gunpowder & Supplies |  |  |  |
| Finished Prod. | 273,369.32 |  |  |
| Supplies | 402,681.59 | 676,050.91 | 894,032.92 |
| Farm |  | 15,725.50 | 15,725.50 |
| Delaware Real Estate |  | 429,814.35 | 430,562.90 |
| Magazine Lots: |  |  |  |
| To be kept | 218,802.18 |  |  |
| To be sold | 229,196.56 | 447,998.74 | 486,069.65 |
| Houses |  | 300,000.00 | 667,350.00 |
| Plants |  | 2,001,865.17 | 2,338,368.98 |
| Delaware River Real Estate |  | 270,803.44 | 400,794.68 |
| Magazines |  |  | 40,000.00 |
| Chicago Farm Property, Inventory |  |  | 1,889.25 |
| Chicago Farm Account |  |  | 1,041.70 |
| Freight on Smokeless Powder |  |  | 461.61 |
| Furniture at Agencies |  |  | 6,000.00 |
|  |  | $12,214,332.42 | $14,397,924.26 |
| Liabilities |  | 214,292.42 | 229,951.34 |
|  |  | $12,000,000.00 | $14,167,972.92 |

In making this review Pierre realized at once that he and Coleman had been correct. Over a million dollars of this total was in cash, representing undivided profits. Clearly the property's potential was undervalued. The certified public accountant hired to check Pierre's figures, Oscar E. Morton, who had done much work in the explosives industry, gave a somewhat larger figure of $14,397,924.26 for the company's assets. The primary difference between his and Pierre's figures came in the evaluation of the stocks of other companies that the Du Pont Company held. Morton listed these at $5,831,337.78 and Pierre at $4,696,428.50.

Pierre and Coleman realized immediately that the potential for profit lay in combining the separately operated properties, which these securities represented, into a single, integrated, centrally administered corporation that would do much of its own purchasing and marketing and would sell large quantities of all three of the industry's products—black powder, smokeless powder, and dynamite. To achieve this goal the two cousins decided on a fourfold strategy: first, the modernization of the existing Du Pont Company's administrative organization by setting up clear-cut functional departments for sales, purchasing, traffic, and engineering as well as for manufacturing; secondly, an immediate merger of the works and sales offices of a wholly owned subsidiary—the Hazard Powder Company—into this administrative structure; third, and most urgent, absorption of the other subsidiaries, particularly those making dynamite, into the new centrally managed organization; fourth, and finally, the expansion of smokeless powder output by purchasing a competitor in that field.

In formulating these plans Pierre realized at once the importance of Laflin & Rand for their goals. If they were to carry out the planned reorganization, they must first obtain control of their old and friendly rival. For Pierre's review of the books had made clear what he, Coleman, and Alfred only suspected. The two companies owned blocks of stocks in many explosives firms. But if these blocks were combined, their owners would control these firms and therefore a major share of the industry. Individually Du Pont and Laflin & Rand held a majority of the stock in very few of these firms. If the Du Pont Company came to control Laflin & Rand, it would then hold over 50% of the shares of stock in 17 and a substantial minority in 12 more important black powder companies and so have control of, or a voice in, approximately two-thirds of the black powder production in the United States east of the Rockies. Without Laflin & Rand, however, it controlled only two besides Hazard.[30] In the dynamite business the situation was even more critical. In March 1902 the Du Pont Company did not directly operate a single dynamite works. Even the Repauno and the Hercules Powder companies, which Pierre's father had started, were at this time controlled by the Eastern Dynamite Company in which Du Pont (and Hazard) owned 6,985 out of a total of 20,000 shares and in which Pierre and Coleman were certain that Laflin & Rand held at least 5,000 shares. So, if Du Pont could purchase Laflin & Rand, it would have control of the Eastern Dynamite

Company, which in turn controlled close to 70% of the dynamite produced in the United States east of the Rockies.

Although much needed to be done on all fronts, Pierre did not want to delay long before moving on Laflin & Rand. On March 6, less then a week after Cousin Frank had turned the office over to him and three weeks after the older stockholders had suggested selling the Du Pont Company to Laflin & Rand, Pierre wrote his uncle Henry Belin in Scranton about the possibility of buying "L & R." "Consolidation might be better than direct purchase though personally I am inclined toward the latter. . . . As soon as the preliminary skirmish is over we should meet and arrange a plan."[31]

In order to understand why Laflin & Rand and the Du Pont Company came to control jointly so many firms in the explosives industry; to appreciate the complex financial arrangements Pierre had to untangle before he could work out a plan for obtaining control of Laflin & Rand; and, indeed, to comprehend the larger industrial and competitive environment in which the Du Pont Company operated, it is essential to do just what Pierre and Coleman did after Pierre's initial check of the company's books. We must briefly review the historical development of the explosives industry during the generation before the young du Ponts took over their birthright in 1902.

The complex patterns of cross-ownership in the explosives business resulted from two separate but interrelated historical causes. The first was the attempt of the black powder manufacturers to control price and production in their industry, and the second was the methods used to finance the production and then to control the price and output of the new more technologically advanced product, dynamite. In their attempts to control price and production, the actions of the explosives manufacturers were quite similar to those in other industries during the latter part of the nineteenth century. The swift expansion of the railroad network after 1850 had stimulated demand for both consumer and producer goods. Increased construction, particularly in cities but also by the railroads themselves, new demands for coal and the other outputs of mines, all enlarged the demands for explosives after 1850. Increased demand brought an expansion of output. As production capacity caught up with demand after 1870, prices began to drop. The explosives industry's response to falling prices was precisely the same as that in the petroleum, whiskey, fertilizer, iron and steel, and other trades during this same period. The manufacturers joined together to form a federation, or association, to control price and production. Such associations were then quite legal and would remain so until the passage of the Sherman Antitrust Act of 1890. Of all the associations formed in the early 1870s, the Gunpowder Trade Association was certainly one of the longest-lived, most stable, and effective.

The leading powder makers met in New York City in April 1872 to form their association.[32] They set prices for black powder in different markets east of the Rockies. In the determination of prices and other policies each member company of the association was given a number of votes according to its size. Du Pont, Laflin & Rand, and Hazard each held ten votes. Oriental of Maine had six and Austin of Ohio had four, as did both the American and Miami companies in which the Fay family had a controlling interest. By the initial agreement members of the association held regular meetings four times a year to determine or adjust general policies. They also created a permanent board or council to meet weekly to listen and act on requests for price changes or adjustments as well as to arbitrate differences about price and competition. As was true of all such industrial alliances in the United States, the association's biggest problem was the enforcement of its rulings. A first step was taken in 1876 by imposing a fine of one dollar a keg for any sale discovered to be below the price listed by the association. In the 1880s more rigorous methods of enforcement had to be found.

The association also had to deal with competition outside the region in which its members normally sold. Because of the difficulties of transporting explosives, the California powder companies had relatively little competition from the eastern firms. Nor did the western companies find it profitable to sell their powder in the East, although one company that pioneered in the production of dynamite did set up a plant at Kenvil, New Jersey. Both eastern and western firms, however, competed for the valuable mining and construction markets in the Rocky Mountain area. To control competition in this "neutral ground," the association and the California Powder Works, the largest of the West Coast companies, signed an agreement in March 1875 that stated that the price in the area would be set by agents of the association after consultation with those of the California company.

After 1880 the most important changes in the association came in methods developed to enforce prices and output schedules. Increasingly stronger measures had to be adopted. In 1886, for example, the association gave its members carefully defined yearly quotas for production. If sales of any of the nine smaller firms (five new firms had joined since 1872) exceeded their quotas, the larger firms were to supply the amounts needed.[33] If the large firms should sell over their quotas, those of the smaller firms would be proportionally increased. In 1889 the association decided to try to strengthen and simplify its control by setting up a money pool. All income from "over sales"—the amount over the quota—would be turned over to the association, which would then use these funds to reimburse those members who sold less than their quotas. In the 1880s the association also increased its control over marketing as well as production and pricing by having principals, rather than their sales agents, sign contracts with customers.[34] Agents were admonished to seek out and report any violation of the prices set by the association.

Nevertheless, these arrangements as to quotas, pooling, and agents were not in themselves enough to assure the continuing stability, effectiveness, and even existence, of the Gunpowder Trade Association. One important reason for its success was that the industry was not one of the country's largest. According to the United States Bureau of the Census the industry had 54 establishments in 1880, 69 in 1890, 97 in 1900, and 124 in 1905.[35] Its "capital" was listed at $6.6 million in 1880, $13.5 million in 1890, $19.5 million in 1900, and $42.3 million in 1905. The average number of employees rose from approximately 1,350 in 1880 to 2,500 in 1890, to 5,350 in 1900, and 6,030 in 1905. In 1905 the value of its product was $29.6 million. This was much smaller than some other chemically oriented industries, including petroleum refining with a product value of $175.0 million or illuminating and heating gas at $125.1 million, or of the cotton seed, general chemical, patent medicine, paints, soap, and fertilizer industries, whose product value ran between $50 and $100 million. Its product value was about the same size as druggist preparations ($31.8 million) and cement ($29.9 million); and larger than the value of the output of the baking powder, starch, varnish, dye, turpentine, grease and tallow, linseed oil, and cosmetics and perfumes industries. Because the manufacturing of explosives was a middle-sized industry, a relatively few associated firms were able to make decisions about the price and output of at least two-thirds of the industry's productive capacity.

The most significant reason, however, for the association's stability was the policy of the leaders in the industry of buying into competing companies, particularly new ones. It was this strategy that provided the glue that held the association together. The depression of the 1870s gave Henry du Pont his initial opportunity to purchase control in other companies. In 1876 he bought the Sycamore Mills in Tennessee, the Hazard Powder Company with its main works in Hazardville, Connecticut, as well as a block of stock in the California Powder Works. The Hazard purchase gave the du Ponts ten more votes in the association's councils, and that of Sycamore still four more.[36] Yet these purchases severely stretched even General du Pont's ample resources. After obtaining a sizable block of the Austin Company's stock, the general decided that the members of the association, particularly Laflin & Rand, should pay a share of the cost of controlling competition. Solomon Turck, the president of Laflin & Rand, who also had been buying into new companies like Schaghticoke, Ashland, and others that were not yet members of the association, had come to the same conclusion. So the two quickly agreed on a new strategy.

From the mid-seventies on, the general left most of the problems of competition up to his nephew Lammot (Pierre's father), who had been elected first president of the association. Until the time of his death in the explosion at Repauno in 1884, he had played a major role in the federation's affairs. From 1876 on, he and Solomon Turck worked hand in hand in carrying out the policy of buying into new competition.[37] Austin, American, Miami, and other members of the association were usually invited to take a portion of the stock, but in nearly every case Du Pont and Laflin & Rand were the two firms that supplied most of the funds and received most of the shares. In late 1876 the associated companies purchased some small mills in the Pennsylvania anthracite region. Far more significant was the acquisition in the same year by Du Pont and Laflin & Rand of majority control in the Lake Superior Powder Company, a large producer formed in 1868 in the copper and iron mining region of upper Michigan that had recently enlarged its operations. Then in 1880 Lammot and Turck, working through William Barklay Parsons, purchased control of the Oriental Powder Mills with its works in Maine. That firm had gone bankrupt in 1872 and, though reorganized, remained relatively unsuccessful until the more prosperous times at the end of the decade.

Returning prosperity encouraged the founding of new, relatively large companies. The Kings' Great Western Powder Company was formed in 1878; the Ohio Powder Company and the Marcellus Powder Company were both organized in 1881. These soon came into the association and in 1886 Du Pont, Hazard, and Laflin & Rand were able to buy control of Marcellus and 38% of the stock of Ohio, with Oriental taking a share of the Ohio stock.[38] An arrangement with the King company did not come until later.

The pattern was repeated with the formation of new companies after the depression of the mid-1880s. Phoenix, founded in 1889; Chattanooga in 1890; Equitable in 1893; and Southern in 1894 became members of the association.[39] For even after the passage of the Sherman Antitrust Act in 1890, the association carried on. The legal status of such cartels remained uncertain, and the government did not aggressively enforce the act. In time Laflin & Rand and the Du Pont Company purchased 55% of Chattanooga, 49% of Equitable, and control of the Southern Powder Company. About the same time the two leading firms plus American and Austin purchased control of Phoenix and placed at its head Franklin W. Olin, an able powder maker who had helped establish the Equitable Powder Company. As the country revived from the depression of the mid-nineties, the cycle started again. Between 1898 and 1902 four new large powder makers, Birmingham, Indiana, Northwestern, and Fairmont, and a number of smaller firms were formed.[40] By 1902 Laflin & Rand and Du Pont had bought into Birmingham and Northwestern, and Du Pont by itself into Indiana.

The purpose of this strategy of buying into competition so consistently adhered to for nearly thirty years was clear enough. First, as stockholders the members of the association, and particularly Du Pont and Laflin & Rand, would have a say in the policies of the new companies. But, more important, they would have the right to look at the books of those firms to see how rigorously they were abiding by their agreements with the association. Of course not all of those competitors intended to join the association when they built their plants. Often Du Pont and Laflin & Rand and the others subjected them to strong pressure to bring them into line. Friends and agents of the old firms secretly became directors and provided funds in the new companies. The du Ponts and others formed dummy corporations to undersell the new concerns by providing powder with other brand names or to market in areas where the miners and other customers favored or helped to organize the new independents.

While Lammot du Pont and Solomon Turck were working closely together in the Gunpowder Trade Association to stabilize the black powder trade, they were also cooperating in the development of dynamite.[41] Turck had helped to finance Lammot's initial venture, the Repauno Chemical Company. After Lammot was killed in 1884 Turck became its president, staying on for two years, when he turned it over to General Henry's son William. In 1882 Lammot and Turck had formed the Hercules Powder Company with a dynamite-producing plant in Cleveland (in 1893 it moved to Ashburn, Missouri) and purchased stock in the Atlantic Giant Company, with a large factory in Kenvil, New Jersey, which had been built by the Giant Powder Company of California. Du Pont and Laflin & Rand purchased the stocks of two more small dynamite companies before Turck's retirement in 1895. At that time Turck, J. Amory Haskell, the new president of Repauno, and Eugene du Pont formed the Eastern Dynamite Company. The stocks of this holding company were exchanged for those of Repauno, Hercules, and other jointly owned firms.

The purpose of the holding company was to control price and output. Not only did it set prices at home but it also negotiated for distant markets. Like the Gunpowder Trade Association it completed an agreement with the California companies for marketing in the "neutral belt," an agreement it soon discovered was usually honored in the breach. In 1897 Eastern Dynamite, the California companies, and a few small dynamite producers signed a broad agreement with the leading French, English, and German firms allocating markets throughout the world.[42]

Like the Gunpowder Trade Association, the Eastern Dynamite Company began to buy out competitors, particularly new ones. But, unlike the black powder group, it purchased stocks in its own name because it was a holding company rather than an association. By 1902 Eastern Dynamite controlled the Forcite Powder Company and two other firms that had been formed in 1897, the New York Powder, and the Enterprise High Explosives companies. Hamilton Barksdale, as president of Eastern Dynamite, kept his eye on the Oliver Dynamite and Climax Powder companies and in 1902 was negotiating for their purchase.[43]

The importance of Eastern Dynamite to the plans of Pierre and Coleman went beyond merely obtaining control of a major share of that part of the industry. By the end of the century dynamite was rapidly replacing both types of black powder—"A" and Soda "B"—as a standard blasting explosive. Moreover, the most progressive plants and executives were in the dynamite rather than the black powder business, possibly because the plants had been built more recently, and dynamite manufacturing and selling was more complex. At Repauno, Barksdale and Amory Haskell's younger brother Harry had built a modern administrative organization, while the Du Pont Company continued to be run in the old-fashioned way.[44] The manufacturing works at Repauno were carefully designed to assure the most efficient use of personnel. In marketing, their sales manager, Charles L. Patterson, replaced the agency system with a large salaried force by having branch offices in nearly every major American city. Patterson also pioneered in training his salesmen to show the customers how to make best use of their explosives. The Repauno engineering staff, headed by Major William G. Ramsay and his assistant Harry Pierce, had few equals in the construction, maintenance, and repair of explosives plant and equipment. The systematic management at Repauno extended, however, only to the Ashburn plant, for the other works controlled by Eastern Dynamite continued to be operated quite independently.

After making their brief review of the history of the American explosives, Pierre and Coleman fully agreed that it was absolutely essential to obtain Laflin & Rand in order to produce a full line of products in large enough quantities to dominate the industry and to make use of the ablest executives available. They apparently did not confer with Alfred about this decision or tell him that they had asked Pierre's uncle Henry Belin, who had long known Turck and his associates, to make the first move.[45] Both Pierre and Coleman were delighted when Belin reported that a formal approach would not be difficult.[46] Like other firms in the industry, Laflin & Rand, with its several works and its headquarters in New York City, was still a family enterprise. As in the case of Du Pont, the older generation had long been in charge. Five men had controlled the company for years. After Solomon Turck retired in 1895, the others, except for J. Amory Haskell, were ready to follow him. Henry M. Boies, whose mother was a Laflin and whose father was a partner in the firm, had come to Scranton in 1865 to manage the company's mills in the anthracite area. The most important of these had a separate corporate identity as the Moosic Powder Company. John L. Riker had served Laflin & Rand's interests in various capacities since 1864, including that of vice-president and director. The third man, Schuyler Parsons, had followed his father, William Barklay Parsons, one of the company's original trustees, on the board in 1888. Schuyler Parsons had never played an important role in the company's management, but had acted for many years as the purchaser of nearly all the nitrates of soda used by Laflin & Rand and the Du Pont Company. The only young man in the group, Riker's son-in-law, J. Amory Haskell, had become president of Laflin & Rand in 1895 when Turck put down the reins and had since then made nearly all its important business decisions.[47]

Henry Belin was the obvious man in the Du Pont group to approach these men, as he had worked closely with them, particularly Boies, in the anthracite district. Belin had long been treasurer of one of Laflin & Rand's subsidiaries in the area, the Laflin Powder Manufacturing Company.[48] On May 13 Belin wrote his nephew Pierre: "Parsons reports having had a talk with Riker and states that everything looks favorable. Will do nothing however, until Boies' return about July 1."[49] When Belin talked with Boies in July, he found him, too, in a receptive mood. As a result, on July 22 Parsons, speaking for himself and the other three, made Belin a formal proposal.[50] The price was substantial. The four would sell the controlling block of Laflin & Rand stock, approximately 5,400 shares out of 10,000, for "$700 per share and with the same about 1,100 shares of Moosic Powder at $700 per share," the total price coming to $4.55 million. As a condition of sale Haskell and Boies were to continue work with a guaranteed salary for a ten-year period, with Haskell getting $25,000 a year and Boies $15,-000. E. P. Kingsbury and other "valued employees" were to be "retained at their present positions and salaries."

The price was indeed high. Solomon Turck had disposed of holdings less than two years before at $300 a share.[51] When the stock occasionally came on the market it sold for about $350 a share. Pierre and Henry Belin balked. But Coleman soon convinced them that the stock was worth the price.[52] Without Laflin & Rand, he reminded them, they simply could not carry out their plans to rationalize the production and distribution of the properties they had purchased from the older generation. Moreover, Coleman hoped that, as in the case of Du Pont, the transaction could be effected with little actual money, even though the Laflin & Rand group had said they wanted cash.

On August 8 Pierre, aided by Raskob, began to draw up plans for the purchase of 5,400 shares of Laflin & Rand stock and 1,100 shares of Moosic. By using the Du Pont Company's credit, they would exchange $4.55 million worth of bonds for the two sets of stock by setting up a holding company to make the exchange and hold the stock.[53] Before completing these plans, Pierre and Raskob realized they needed more information on the return they could expect from the Laflin & Rand and the Moosic stock. Also, they wanted to find out how, exactly, the sellers expected to be paid.

Coleman and Pierre decided to send Colonel Henry to get this information. Henry du Pont, like Belin, had a long acquaintance with the four men. And, while Coleman was a man of great persuasion, he, quite shrewdly, preferred to rely in these negotiations on the men who best knew the other side. On Tuesday, August 12, the colonel reported on his meeting to Coleman, who was then in New York completing arrangements to move the Hazard office to Wilmington. "The net result of Coz. Henry's talk with S.P. [Schuyler Parsons]," Coleman scribbled in a penciled note to Pierre, "was they have earned on L & R and E. DYN. STOCK for 4 years 8%. On M. [Moosic] for 3 years 7%."[54] They wanted, he continued, "⅓ cash bal in 4 years equal payments 4½% int. payable semi-annually. They want us to make prop in writing and submit it to S.P. next Tuesday at 10:30 a.m. I have arranged for you and I to meet Coz Henry at Waldorf Monday evening and talk matters over and to then make them the Proposition." As an after-thought Coleman added that they had better see Colonel Henry on Saturday if possible.

Pierre, still assisted by Raskob, was outlining a tentative plan that would allow them flexibility in negotiating.[55] They agreed that if it was absolutely necessary, they could raise the $1.5 million in cash by selling $1.0 million of the securities held by Du Pont & Company and borrowing the other half million from the banks. The rest of the payment could then be made in the securities of a holding company created to hold the Laflin & Rand and Moosic stock. The bonds of that holding company, secured by the very stock the company would hold, could then cover the remaining two-thirds of the price. Pierre hoped, however, that the sellers might be talked into taking more holding company bonds and less cash in return for a bonus in the stock in the new holding company.

Armed with this plan Pierre and Coleman met with Parsons and Haskell on Tuesday, August 19, at the Laflin & Rand offices at 99 Cedar Street in New York. Clearly much negotiating lay ahead. The sellers disliked payment in long-term bonds, but would accept them if the bonds were secured by more than just the stock that they themselves were selling. They showed some interest in taking a bonus in stock in place of cash. One particularly difficult problem to work out was to arrange the transaction so that the high price of $700 a share which the buyers were willing to pay for the stock that bought control would not inflate the price of the remaining stock too far above the going market figure of somewhat above $350 a share. Finally, arrangements had to be made for continuing the salaries of Haskell, Boies, Riker, and others.

After a long, hard bargaining session Pierre returned to his rooms at the Earlington Hotel, where he sat down with Raskob to put into writing a proposal that he thought, on the basis of the day's discussion, might be acceptable.[56] He began with a plan that involved no cash payments but instead a stock bonus in addition to bonds. In order to permit buying at market prices the remainder of the Laflin & Rand stock [the 46% not involved in this sale], the plan called for setting up two holding companies instead of the one in the original proposal. Delaware Securities Company would purchase and hold the Laflin & Rand stock, and a second company, Delaware Investment Company, would purchase and hold the Moosic stock. The sellers of control of Laflin & Rand were to receive for one share of Laflin & Rand $400 worth of Delaware Securities bonds—an exchange rate that could then be offered to the holders of the remaining Laflin & Rand stock. But in addition, the four holders of the controlling shares were to get $300 worth of Delaware Investment bonds for each Laflin & Rand share, and the holders of Moosic would get $700 worth of Delaware Investment bonds for each share of Moosic they exchanged. The holders of the stocks of both explosives companies would receive stock bonuses from both holding companies. To accomplish these ends the two holding companies would issue a total of $6.5 million worth of stock and $6.5 million worth of 5% twenty-year bonds (Delaware Securities to issue $4.0 million in stock and $4.0 million in bonds, and Delaware Investment $2.5 million in stock and $2.5 million in bonds). These securities were to be allocated in such a way that the sellers received the asking price of $4.52 million in bonds and a bonus of a little more than $1.0 million in stock.[57] The remainder of the stock stayed in the hands of the Du Pont & Company to assure its control of the two holding companies. After completing this plan, Pierre drew up alternative ones that involved more cash and smaller stock bonuses.

After outlining the procedures of the sale, Pierre wrote down the conditions that had to be met before the transaction could be carried out. First, from the buyer's position, the whole deal depended on Pierre and Coleman being satisfied that "verbal statements are correct as to earnings of L & R and Moosic and of the stocks owned by L & R and Moosic in other companies."[58] Secondly, as a seller's condition, the bonds of the holding companies were to be guaranteed by the du Ponts and this would be done by putting up a sizable amount of Du Pont & Company stock as collateral. In addition, Haskell was to continue to serve in any of the companies controlled by Du Pont, at no less than his present salary, as well as to receive an extra stock bonus of $200,000. Also, the sellers were to "use their influence and best endeavors to get in the remaining 46% of the L & R stock and will agree not to go into the explosives business either directly or indirectly in the future." The details of paying back the bonds were then outlined. A final condition, which did not appear in this proposition, but which was outlined by the sellers in their original letter, was later accepted. The sellers were to have the opportunity to buy, with the du Ponts, the remaining Laflin & Rand stock, which would then be exchanged for the securities of Delaware Securities Company.[59]

Pierre and Coleman returned the next morning to 99 Cedar Street with two documents—a "Proposition" outlining these terms, and a form for an agreement that would put them into effect. The sellers substantially accepted the proposition by which they sold their control for bonds and a stock bonus instead of cash. A few minor changes were made and the wording of the proposition was tightened up. Haskell was to receive $25,000 a year as president of either Laflin & Rand or Eastern Dynamite Company, and his $200,000 bonus in Delaware Securities Company was eliminated.

The general arrangement agreed upon, Coleman, Pierre, and Raskob returned on Wednesday to Wilmington, tired but satisfied. Parsons then sought out his associates. The meeting must have been a trying one for Parsons. He wrote the next day urging Pierre and Coleman to "accept without any changes of *any kind,* as from what passed at the meeting, I am of the opinion that any kind of proposal from you will only lead to other and not as favorable proposition being made to you; and, as I believe it to be a good thing for you, I am loath to have you run any chance of its falling through."[60]

On Friday Pierre was back in New York to check the verbal statements Parsons had first made to Colonel Henry as to the return on both blocks of stock. As he pored over Laflin & Rand's very private ledger, he became increasingly wide-eyed. Indeed, the first entry listing stocks held by Laflin & Rand in other companies brought him up short.[61] (See Table 3–2.[62]) It showed 5,807 shares of Eastern Dynamite valued at $180,869.34, or approximately $31 a share. The old Du Pont Company held only 1,805 shares and they had been conservatively estimated at $252,700, or $140 a share (the rest of the holdings were owned through Hazard). The other listings showed that Laflin & Rand held more stock in other companies than Pierre and Coleman realized and, of more importance, that they were valued far below the figures given in the Du Pont books. Possibly, these values reflected the result of doing business over the long period of declining prices between 1873 and 1897. Since these stocks were not listed on the exchanges and were rarely sold, there had been little reason to re-evaluate many of them.

A short inspection was enough. Pierre hurried out of the Cedar Street building, caught the first train to Wilmington and went right to Coleman's office. He urged his cousin to close the deal immediately, "lest our inspection might lead the owners to resurvey their property and retire from the commitment."[63] Coleman moved quickly, going to New York the next day, Saturday, August 24, to draw up the final agreements with Haskell and Parsons.[64] On Monday at one o'clock the formal contracts were signed. These final documents involved the specifications of actual payment, for the precise number of shares the four sellers were able to deliver was 5,524 of Laflin & Rand and 950 of Moosic.

In this complex way the most significant negotiation in the history of the

| ASSETS | | | EVALUATION | RE-EVALUATION |
|---|---|---|---:|---:|
| Passaic Mill Plant | | | 25,000.00 | 250,000.00 |
| Pompton Mill Plant | | | 25,000.00 | 400,000.00 |
| New Platteville Mill Plant | | | 25,000.00 | 200,000.00 |
| Cherokee Mill Plant | | | 25,000.00 | 175,000.00 |
| Empire Mill Plant | | | 5,000.00 | 75,000.00 |
| Orange Mill Plant | | | 5,000.00 | 75,000.00 |
| Old Platteville Mills Plant | | | 1,000.00 | |
| Schaghticoke Real Estate | | | 100.00 | |
| | | | $111,100.00 | 1,175,000.00 |
| Eastern Dynamite Stock | 5761 | Shs. | 180,869.34 | 806,540.00 |
| The Moosic Powder Co. | 1410 | " | 98,930.00 | 465,300.00 |
| Equitable Powder Mfg. Co. | 192 | " | 41,491.35 | 57,600.00 |
| Oriental Powder Mills | 1223 | " | 50,000.00 | 134,530.00 |
| Lake Superior Powder Co. | 826 | " | 20,532.50 | 61,950.00 |
| Schaghticoke Powder Co. | 779 | " | 19,475.00 | 77,900.00 |
| Laflin Powder Mfg. Co. | 2091 | " | 27,950.00 | 31,365.00 |
| Chattanooga Powder Co. | 544 | " | 21,760.00 | 48,960.00 |
| Ohio Powder Co. | 224 | " | 11,200.00 | 47,040.00 |
| Mahoning Powder Co. | 500 | " | 12,500.00 | 50,000.00 |
| Birmingham Powder Co. | 149 | " | 5,600.00 | 14,900.00 |
| The Hecla Powder Co. | 157 | " | 1,000.00 | 1,000.00 |
| Anthracite Powder Co. | 125 | " | 1,000.00 | 1,000.00 |
| Marcellus Powder Co. | 179 | " | 179.00 | 8,950.00 |
| King Mercantile Co. | 121 | " | 100.00 | 12,100.00 |
| Eastern Fibre Ware Co.  Subscribed $10,000.00 | | | 100.00 | 100.00 |
| Laflin & Rand Powder Co. | 200 | " | 1,000.00 | 20,000.00 |
| The Utah Powder Co. | 1569 | $5.00 shs. | 10.00 | 00 |
| Driggs, Seabury Gun & Am. Co. | 250 | Pfd. | | 00 |
| | 125 | Com. | 10.00 | 00 |
| Standard Cartridge Co. | 243 | shs. | 10.00 | 00 |
| Phoenix Powder Mfg. Co. | 2099 | " | 2,099.00 | 00 |
| Globe Powder Co. | 1 | " | 10.00 | 00 |
| Indiana Powder Co. | 476 | " | 98,297.82 | 98,297.82 |
| Northwestern Powder Co. | 143 | " | 28,672.65 | 28,672.65 |
| Shenandoah Powder Co.  Purchase | | | 7,500.00 | 7,500.00 |
| Southern Indiana Powder Co.  " | | | 3,084.89 | 00 |
| | | | 633,381.55 | 1,973,705.47 |

INVESTMENT, INSURANCE & ACCIDENT FUND

| | EVALUATION | RE-EVALUATION |
|---|---:|---:|
| Cincin. Ind. St. L. & Chi. 4% Bonds | | |
| 5 Bonds $5000. ea. 94.93 taken at par | 25,000.00 | 25,625.00 |
| Western Penna. R. R. Co. 4% Gold Bonds | | |
| 25 bonds $1000. ea. cost 99.75 at par | 25,000.00 | 20,000.00 |
| | 50,000.00 | 50,625.00 |

OTHER INVESTMENTS

| | EVALUATION | RE-EVALUATION |
|---|---:|---:|
| Pittsburgh, McKeesport & Youghioghenny R.R. Stock | | |
| 1000 shs. $50. ea. cost $58.25 taken at 57.47 | 57,470.00 | 57,470.00 |
| Morris & Essex E. E. Extension Stock | | |
| 100 shs. $100. ea. cost $102.50 taken at par | 10,000.00 | 10,250.00 |
| Jackson, Lansing & Saginaw R.R. Stock | | |
| 300 shs. $100.oo ea. cost $72.50 at cost | 21,750.00 | 21,750.00 |
| Calumet & Hecla Mining Co. Stock | | |
| 100 shs. $25. ea. cost $256.377 at cost | 25,637.70 | 55,000.00 |
| | | 144,470.00 |

American explosives industry was completed. The new company could now begin to integrate its powder and dynamite holdings into a single mass-producing, mass-marketing, centrally administered enterprise. Although Coleman probably did most of the persuading, Pierre could take the credit for working out the financial arrangements that made possible the purchase without laying out a cent of cash and without going to the nation's money markets to borrow funds. As in the case of the purchase of the Du Pont Company itself, the interest on the bonds could easily be paid out of the earnings of the purchased companies, based on their past performance. The sellers were willing to take a stock bonus instead of cash, for Pierre and Coleman had convinced them that, after a reorganization of the properties, such stock would be worth a great deal more than the cash that they had originally wanted, as it indeed became. But even if the reorganization did not work out in the way that Coleman and Pierre expected, the sellers still were assured of obtaining the same return they had been getting before they agreed to the sale.

Much still had to be done before Coleman and Pierre could reorganize these new properties into the Du Pont Company's operating structure. Contracts with Haskell, Boies, and also Riker had to be signed.[65] The first two received salaries agreed to in the basic proposal. A special arrangement was signed by Riker, in which he took an additional $500,000 in Delaware Securities Company stocks and bonds in exchange for the remaining Laflin & Rand stock he held. In return he was not to engage in the powder business for twenty-five years.

Coleman and Pierre still had to inform their own stockholders. Although Colonel Henry and Belin had been involved, no one else knew about these negotiations. Even Alfred, apparently, had not been informed until the deal was completed.[66] The purchase was such a coup that no one of the stockholders expressed disapproval, at least not in writing, even though they would all have to provide the Du Pont & Company stock as collateral (that is, security) for the bonds of the two holding companies as agreed in the final negotiations. Finally, the two holding companies had to be incorporated, and the mechanics of the exchange of stocks and bonds worked out. As Coleman had to go west in September to continue negotiations for disposing of his interests in the Kentucky coal fields, he left these arrangements to Pierre.[67]

The transactions went smoothly. Pierre arranged for the incorporation of the two holding companies and provided the necessary collateral.[68] On October 8 the actual exchange took place. After the transfer the only remaining business in connection with the purchase of Laflin & Rand was the buying of the shares still outstanding. Pierre and Coleman, aided by Haskell, wrote or talked personally with the holders of those shares to urge them to exchange their stocks for Delaware Securities bonds at $400 a share.[69] They also made occasional purchases in the open market.[70]

While Pierre and Coleman were carrying out their negotiations with Laflin & Rand, they were at the same time completing an easier part of their original plan—the merger of Hazard Powder into Du Pont. For ten years after its purchase in 1876 the Du Pont ownership of Hazard had for competitive reasons been kept secret. Even after Du Pont control became widely known, Hazard continued to operate as a completely autonomous unit. In addition to its large powder-making plant at Hazardville, near Hartford, Connecticut, it had its sales and executive offices in New York. It did its own purchasing and had its own sales agents.[71] The Gunpowder Trade Association set prices for its products as it did for Du Pont and Laflin & Rand and its other members. The only effort before 1902 to coordinate Du Pont and Hazard activities was in combining the sales offices in a number of major towns.

Coleman and Pierre had little difficulty in carrying out the merger of this wholly owned subsidiary. In July Coleman began to work out the arrangements with the company's president, William S. Colvin.[72] The New York offices were to be closed and the personnel who so desired were to move to Wilmington by mid-September. The sales offices were to come under the new Sales Department that Coleman was organizing at Du Pont, and manufacturing facilities would be under Alfred's office. By August 14 Coleman was able to write Pierre: "I have settled with Mr. Weightman [the treasurer] and he will go on the pension roll the first of September. I have practically arranged with Mr. Colvin likewise. I am arranging to leave Mr. Lequin and Mr. Lentilhon in charge of the New York office simply as a sales office for Hazard Powder putting them on a cost-sheet basis and holding them absolutely responsible for the results."[73]

The retirements were easy to arrange, since Weightman and Colvin had had long service with the company.[74] The latter began work in 1858, became treasurer after the du Ponts obtained control of Hazard, and took its presidency in 1892. Weightman had served for more than forty years, and during most of that time had heartily disliked his closest associate Colvin. Thus, as in the case of Laflin & Rand and the Du Pont Company, the end of one generation made it easier for a younger generation to make major organizational changes within the industry. The sales office in New York was short lived. Before the end of the year the cost sheets were showing that maintenance of a separate Hazard sales force was too expensive in relation to the sales it made. So they closed down Hazard's New York office, with Lentilhon moving to Wilmington while Lequin, who wanted to stay in New York, left the company.[75]

The merger with Hazard, like the purchase of Laflin & Rand, had gone well. Pierre was therefore surprised, but not too concerned, when they failed in negotiations to expand their smokeless powder capacity. In April they opened negotiations for the purchase of the E. C. Schultze Company.[76] This British-financed firm, headed by Captain Albert W. Money, was the first in this country to manufacture smokeless powder for commercial shotgun and rifle shells. Its plant at Oakland, New Jersey, had been in operation since 1890, and its powder had been sold through Von Lengerke & Detmold, agents of the British company that had financed Money.[77] Cautious negotiations between Money and the two cousins continued throughout the summer. Although Coleman appears to have given this purchase as high a priority as he did the merger of Hazard and the buying of Laflin & Rand, neither he nor Pierre could arrange a satisfactory agreement.[78] Yet, even without the Schultze Company, the new Du Pont Company with the Laflin & Rand works at Pompton, New Jersey, was producing 30% and 40% of the smokeless powder made in this country.

After the purchase of Laflin & Rand on October 8, 1902, the Du Pont Company was, for the first time, directly involved in dynamite production, fully controlling four large and four small dynamite plants.[79] It now also owned eight black powder mills formerly belonging to Laflin & Rand (at three, operations had been suspended) and the two Moosic mills. In addition the stocks that came with the Laflin & Rand purchase gave the company a majority of shares and, therefore, operating control of seven more powder mills. The Du Pont manufacturing establishment thus came to total 8 dynamite mills, 21 black powder works, and a large smokeless powder works at Pompton Lakes, New Jersey, as well as the one at Carney's Point. The company also controlled the sales offices and magazines of Laflin & Rand and Eastern Dynamite.

## A New Structure

With the purchase of Laflin & Rand the Du Pont Company had become a full line firm, by far the largest in the business. The success of Pierre and Coleman's strategy intensified the need to fashion an organizational structure to operate the combined properties of Du Pont, Hazard, Eastern Dynamite, and Laflin & Rand. As part of their initial plans the three cousins had agreed to create a modern administrative structure for the company they had purchased from the older du Ponts, and from the start they wanted to incorporate Eastern Dynamite and Laflin & Rand as well as Hazard into this organization. The creation of a large centrally administered enterprise dominating the entire industry had always been the basic strategy of Pierre and Coleman. At the end of 1902, however, neither Pierre nor Coleman had plans for incorporating the other companies they had acquired through the purchase of Laflin & Rand into this modern, large operating corporation.

Coleman's first step in the spring of 1902 in the building of this new type of administrative structure was to find space to house new administrative offices. The building on the Brandywine was far too small. He proposed the adding of two new floors to Wilmington's largest office structure, the Equitable Trust Company Building at Ninth and Market Streets.[80] The offices of the progressive Eastern Dynamite Company were already on the fifth and sixth floors and, since Coleman wanted to combine the Du Pont explosives interests into a single organization, he wanted to house them in a single building on adjoining floors. In April and May he arranged with William Fenn's Manufacturers' Contracting Company to carry out the construction of an additional two floors.[81] Much of this work came to be handled by Pierre's younger brother Irénée du Pont. Construction moved quickly enough to permit the Du Pont Company to move into its new offices by the end of the year.

Next came a search for subordinate managers. One of Coleman and Pierre's first appointments was naming Russell H. Dunham auditor. Dunham had worked with Coleman at the Lorain Steel Company where, as comptroller, he had taken part in the sale of that firm to Federal Steel.[82] He then went to a similar post with the Bethlehem Steel Company. By July Dunham was hard at work under the watchful eye of Pierre and Raskob, adapting cost sheets and other accounting devices developed in the steel industry to the explosives business. These new accounting forms were soon to be used in the purchasing and selling end of the business as well as in its manufacturing plants.

Coleman himself concentrated on improving marketing and purchasing methods and on assuring a better flow of raw materials into and finished goods out of the manufacturing plants. After appointing John Barron Niles, a New Yorker with accounting, purchasing, and financial experience, as purchasing agent and head of the new Purchasing Department, Coleman asked Robert S. Waddell, an able and aggressive sales agent who had long represented Du Pont in Cincinnati, to become the general sales agent for the Du Pont Company as a whole.[83] He and Waddell then began searching for a man to handle the movement of raw materials and finished goods and so create a Traffic Department. They also supported Dunham's request that the offices of the different sales agents send back more detailed information regularly to Wilmington.

The sales agents responded quickly and most unfavorably to the coming of centralized control. These changes challenged the existing ways of doing business. The Du Pont Company had originally sold its products through commissioned agents, as had nearly all American manufacturing companies earlier in the century. In the years after the Civil War the company increasingly used agents who alone handled all their products in one region. They may have handled those of other members of the association in selling their products to contractors, mining, and transportation companies and, in the case of sporting powder and some explosives, to wholesale jobbers, and occasionally to retailers. By the end of the century the agents, who were paid a salary as well as a commission, sold only the products of the company or its direct subsidiaries. Again they were following the normal pattern of American industry. Within the Du Pont Company, however, the agent remained far more autonomous and free-wheeling than did sales managers in branch and district offices of other American industrial firms. including even those of the Repauno Company.[84] The Du Pont agents used their own names, canvassed customers in their own way, had complete control of advertising, and arranged for shipments from the factory to their own storage magazines and then to the customer. Only in the setting of prices were agents controlled from the outside. Even here the control did not come from Wilmington, but from the Advisory Committee of the Gunpowder Trade Association, which for many years set or approved of any change in prices for much of the American powder industry.

No one was more unhappy about the introduction of new methods than Elliott S. Rice, who had been the Du Pont agent in Chicago since 1882. Rice was incensed. At the end of May he wrote Coleman a series of letters telling the president so.[85] Why should he, who had worked so long and so effectively for the interests of the company, be called on by a Mr. Dunham, whom he had never heard of, to account for all the small details of expenditure? To make matters worse, what right had Waddell, the agent for Cincinnati, who had the nerve to sign himself "General Agent of E. I. du Pont de Nemours & Co.," to ask him, Rice, the company's most trusted agent, to recommend someone as traffic manager to take over the movement of freight?[86] In this case the request was an invasion of his rights and responsibilities, for he had long handled more traffic than any of the other agents. Rice then reviewed his work in obtaining railroad rates from the Mooar plant as well as the Chicago area.

> It is to the "home town" it is to the "front yard" if you please, of him who planned and accomplished this work—that R. S. Waddell came with an application to a Traffic Manager, seeking help, for which he apparently knew not where else to look.
>
> His application is made without reference to your Chicago office, and in tone, completely usurps the rights, and disregards the feelings of that office. By this invasion he raises a question in the minds of my friends and my business associates as to my position with my employers.

Coleman tried to calm Rice. He assured him that both Dunham and Waddell had written with Coleman's knowledge, and indeed at his request. He stressed the need for a man to handle all the company's freight problems. "You have no idea how badly a freight man is needed to handle this end of the line, not only for shipments of powder but also raw materials to plants other than Mooar." He assured Rice that all requests for detailed accounts were merely normal business procedures, and he insisted that all items should be reported to the home office: "An auditor's business is to know why every cent is expended and he should have written authority for the expenditure of every penny that goes through the books."[87] However, Coleman pointed out that these accounts would be reviewed only by Dunham and Pierre du Pont and so would be kept confidential.

Rice was temporarily mollified.[88] Other agents also chafed under the new regime, but being less close to the old company and family than Rice, kept their protests out of the front office.[89] And many were unable to adjust to the new ways of the centralized organization. So, one by one, the older agents, including Rice, dropped out of active business life, usually going on the pension list.[90] Even Waddell found operating within the new structure more and more confining. At the end of 1902 he resigned from the Du Pont Company in order to set up his own Buckeye Powder Company to produce black powder for miners in the Illinois coal mining region, part of Rice's territory.

The problems arising out of the initial reorganization of the Du Pont Company's operating structure and the realization that these would grow when Laflin & Rand and Eastern Dynamite were brought into the fold had convinced Pierre and Coleman they needed help in managing the new company. Alfred, temperamental and little experienced in the ways of modern management, seemed quite content to continue to run the works of the original company. Indeed, he seemed to have little interest in supervising more than the mills on the Brandywine. Pierre and Coleman naturally thought of inviting their own mentors, Tom Johnson and Arthur Moxham, to join them. Johnson had just begun his long reign as the reform mayor of Cleveland and so was unavailable. Moxham, an even more ardent advocate of rational systematic management than Johnson, was interested. The prospect of reorganizing the American explosives industry was clearly both challenging and profitable.

Moxham arrived in Wilmington in September, 1902.[91] After helping Pierre complete the arrangements for the final exchange of Laflin & Rand stock through the two Du Pont-controlled holding companies, he made an extended tour of the properties the du Ponts had acquired by the exchange.[92] On his return he began drawing up a specific scheme for assuring the effective centralized administration of the consolidated properties. The plan, which essentially expanded the one Coleman and Pierre had already instituted, called for the formation of functional departments whose heads would form an Executive Committee to manage the company as a whole, a practice used in steel and other more progressive American industries.

After Pierre and Coleman had carefully reviewed Moxham's suggestions, Coleman sent a letter on February 4, 1903, to formalize these proposals. In this letter he authorized a single Executive Committee to have "charge of matters of all kinds pertaining to the powder and high explosives business of all the companies in which Laflin & Rand, Eastern Dynamite, or Du Pont & Co., are importantly interested."[93] The committee consisted of the president and department heads. As Moxham had written: "Each member of the Committee will take charge of and be responsible for the department of which he has charge with the power to appoint committees, himself being chairman, for such purposes as he deems advisable." There were soon to be three "operative" or product departments for the manufacture of the company's three major products, and separate sales, development, and financial departments.

The men who had played a major role in forming the enlarged company now became the department heads and members of the Executive Committee. Only Coleman, as president, was relieved of departmental responsibilities. Alfred would be in charge of all black powder operations, while young Francis I. du Pont, Cousin Frank's son, headed the much smaller Smokeless Powder Department with its plants at Pompton, New Jersey, and Carney's Point. Hamilton Barksdale, as the former chief of Repauno and Eastern Dynamite, was the logical choice to head the dynamite or High Explosives Department. Barksdale had already begun in the autumn of 1902 to bring the activities of the old Eastern Dynamite under a single centralized control. J. Amory Haskell, one of the ablest executives in the industry and the only one in the top group of the new company whose experience embraced dynamite as well as smokeless and black powder, took charge of the Sales Department. As Haskell decided to keep his residence in New York, he turned most of the department's daily work over to his assistant manager or director, Charles L. Patterson. Patterson indeed played a basic role in fashioning the new department, a creative task for which his training at Repauno had well prepared him. Waddell's resignation from the Du Pont Company in December undoubtedly made it easier for Haskell and Patterson to take full control of the new department.

The Treasurer's Department also centralized in Wilmington the administration of a single function for many plants and offices. Pierre, as treasurer, turned much of his day-to-day work over to the auditor, Dunham, who quickly began to introduce and extend uniform accounting methods and other financial controls over men and offices handling the production and sale of dynamite and smokeless and black powder, much as he had done in the preceding spring for the black powder plants and sales office of the older Du Pont Company. John Raskob, as assistant to the treasurer, also aided Pierre with much of the more routine work and assisted Dunham in devising and checking accounting techniques. Raskob's more important task, however, continued to be assisting Pierre and Coleman in working out and implementing plans for financing the company's strategic expansion.

Finally Moxham had suggested that he, as a member of the Executive

Committee, head what was a new type of office, one that existed in almost no other large American company outside of the electrical industry. As senior executive of the Development Department, Moxham was officially "in charge of competition of all kinds. In charge of developments and of experimental work."[94] He was to be responsible for the new company's strategy as well as its structure. He remained charged with defining its over-all organization and was to analyze, interpret, and plan ways to meet competition. This included the relationships with existing concerns, new concerns, those firms with whom the company had agreements, and those in which it held a stock interest. Moxham's office was also to concentrate on "improving our strategic position in the matter of raw material, e.g., charcoal, sulphur, nitrate of soda, etc., and a proper consideration of receiving points for such material as may be distributed to all the combined interests."[95] Finally, he was to investigate and develop "any new inventions or innovations" that came from within or without the company, bringing the project, as Coleman explained, "to a point where you would either yourself drop it or take up with the Executive Committee, the advisability of adopting it."[96] The mission of Moxham's office was then essentially that of a general staff, to review constantly the company's over-all situation and then to suggest plans to the Executive Committee for meeting new needs and opportunities.

The adoption of the new operating structure in February 1903 completed the plans outlined by Pierre and Coleman at the time they had purchased the old company. The potential of their purchase could now be realized. Costs of production and distribution could now be cut by reducing the number of administrative and sales offices and by concentrating production in large plants advantageously located in relation to markets and raw materials. Moreover, Pierre and Coleman had achieved this fundamental transformation in much of the explosives industry without laying out any real cash and without resorting to the banks or Wall Street. Their formula was the extremely simple one that they had learned in the traction business. They paid for their purchases in bonds, with the interest on the bonds equal to the current income from the purchased properties. In addition, to get the sellers to accept bonds rather than the cash they had first insisted upon, the buyers offered them a stock bonus in the new corporation or in a holding company controlled by the new corporation. In these years many other American industries were undergoing similar transformations. In steel, electrical manufacturing, agricultural implements and other machinery, matches, rubber, biscuits, and a host of others, small family firms were being combined into impersonal integrated industrial enterprises. By 1900 investment bankers and brokers from Wall Street were playing a critical role in the change of these industries, and they charged a high price for their services. The du Ponts and the explosives industry avoided this cost.

Although by February 1903 the first essential steps had been taken, much still needed to be done. The organizational structure was still only a plan. Much time and effort were needed before the Executive Committee and department heads would bring the activities of the company's plants and offices under their direct control; before production would be rationalized and systematized; before the overlapping sales agencies could be converted fully into branch offices and the autonomous sales agents fully replaced by salaried men; and before uniform methods of accounting, collections, and payments would be completely introduced. Time, too, was needed to define departmental boundaries and to work out methods of interdepartmental coordination. Yet during 1903 Pierre, Coleman, and their associates on the Executive Committee were unable to concentrate on building their internal organization. They had to pay close and constant attention to their external strategy. In working out this strategy, Pierre du Pont continued to play a critical role in the reorganization of the American explosives industry.

# The Big Company

THE TWELVE MONTHS following Pierre's return to Wilmington had been the most eventful and productive he had yet known. The next twelve were to be equally challenging and creative. During 1902 Pierre had effectively used the financial skills and experience that he had acquired at Lorain and Dallas. At the same time he gained new training in the ways of business planning and negotiation. The purchase of Laflin & Rand—that "monument to the diplomacy of T. C. du Pont" as he characterized it some months later—made a lasting impression. In 1903 he continued to acquire new knowledge and experience in the building and management of a large modern corporation. In these months Moxham came to overshadow even Coleman as a teacher.

The first half of 1903 was particularly significant to the career of Pierre du Pont and the Du Pont Company itself, for from January to August sickness and a trip to California kept Coleman out of the office. During that period Pierre, who had just passed his thirty-third birthday, was the chairman of the new Executive Committee and so became the company's acting president. He had to put the newly formed administrative structure through its first critical tests. Even more important, Pierre and Moxham conceived and began to carry out plans during these same months to enlarge their enterprise still further by consolidating nearly all the firms in the explosives industry into a single "Big Company." When Coleman did return from California in August, he firmly took over the administrative reins and the negotiations involved in completing the big company. Only then could Pierre begin to devote attention to his more specialized responsibilities as treasurer.

During their first year in office Coleman and Pierre had consolidated the largest makers of powder—Du Pont, Hazard, and Laflin & Rand—and the holding company that controlled the leading producers of dynamite into a single, centrally managed, modern corporation. They had done so because they believed that this was the most certain way to assure the profitableness of the properties they had purchased from their elders in February 1902. Then, early in 1903 they turned their attention to the relationship of their new company with the rest of the industry, and particularly with those firms whose stock they held. While most of the enterprises in which the Du Pont Company and Laflin & Rand had earlier purchased stock were black powder producers, some, like the Lake Superior Powder Company and the California Powder Works, also had large dynamite plants.

## Consolidation Proposed

On March 16, 1903, at the third meeting of the new Executive Committee, Pierre and Moxham proposed to bring all the companies in which the Du Pont Company held stock into a single corporation. Moxham opened that session of the Executive Committee by pointing to "the advisability of consolidating all the various interests, into one Holding Company on such a basis that outside stockholders of the various companies in which E. I. du Pont de Nemours & Co. have holdings would be invited to exchange their stock into the securities of the Holding Company upon equitable basis."[1] As Moxham and Pierre's arguments impressed the committee, Coleman appointed its two advocates as a subcommittee "to formulate in detail a plan embodying the points discussed and to report to the Executive Committee as quickly as possible."

Their initial proposal was to form only a holding company. In March they did not suggest that the firms joining the holding company might become consolidated into the operating structure that they had created for the properties purchased the previous year. They merely wanted to tighten legal, but not administrative, control over these firms. The proposal reflected Pierre and Moxham's brief experience with competitive practices in the explosives industry.

During the summer and fall of 1902, both seemed as willing as Coleman to give the existing ways a try. They agreed to have the new company work within the Gunpowder Trade Association and to continue to apply the time-tested policy of buying into competition. In addition, they hoped to get control of the explosives companies owned by two leading cartridge makers and also to obtain the California Powder Works. The control of the first two might discourage other ammunition makers, good customers of the Du Pont Company, from following their example by moving into powder making. Dominance in the California company appeared essential if price stability was ever to be reached in the Mountain and Pacific Coast states. In all these firms, the Du Pont Company held stock—49% of the Illinois-based Equitable Powder Company, 34.5% of the Austin Powder Company in Cleveland, and 44% of the California Powder Works.[2] And in all three cases, Coleman planned to purchase control, as he had done at Laflin & Rand, by setting up individual holding companies similar to Delaware Securities and Delaware Investment.

Coleman du Pont opened negotiations with Almon Lent, the president of Austin, early in December 1902 and with Frank W. Olin, president of Equitable, later that month. Both these men were major stockholders in cartridge companies as well as their powder-making enterprises. By January 5 Lent and Coleman had agreed on a value for the Austin Company's assets as a basis for an exchange of blocks of stock in a holding company that Du Pont would control.[3] Pierre then went to Cleveland to look over the Austin Company's books. On January 24 he completed his work and wrote Coleman that as far as he could see "the reports of Mr. Lent are correct, except for the earnings from Sporting Powder which I do not seem to reconcile with existing conditions." In response to Pierre's letter Coleman, on January 26, notified William S. Hilles, a leading Wilmington lawyer, to form the Columbian Investment Company "similar to the Delaware Investment Company" to buy the stock of Austin. By the end of the month the only question to be settled was the amount of the Du Pont Company's securities to be required as collateral for the bonds of the investment company.

At this critical moment illness prevented Coleman from being available to complete the final negotiations. He had been sick for two weeks in January with the flu. Then on a trip to Johnstown early in February he was struck down by a still more serious attack and for a month was unable to leave his bed.[4] During this hiatus Pierre unexpectedly received a letter from Lent notifying him that the deal was off and saying only, in explanation, that his stockholders were dissatisfied with the collateral offered. "It was the matter of the purchaser's securities entirely that prevented the consummation of a deal," wrote Lent.[5]

The negotiations with Frank Olin of Equitable followed somewhat the same course. Coleman began talking with him in New York just before Christmas. Again the Du Pont president proposed to set up a company whose bonds would be exchanged for stock on the basis of assets plus a stock bonus.[6] The situation as to a cartridge company that Olin operated became a major problem. Coleman did not get as far with Olin as he did with Lent before the sickness struck.

Clearly, despite their specific arguments, neither of these two ammunition makers was eager to sell out. Unlike the owner-managers at the old Du Pont Company and Laflin & Rand, these men were still young and vigorous. Each felt that he had a promising career in the business that he knew best.

Moreover, Coleman and Pierre only wanted to obtain control of their powder business. They expected them to continue as cartridge manufacturers. Neither of the cousins wanted the Du Pont Company to integrate forward into that type of production. "If we go into the shell business, it would license the ammunition people to go into the powder business," Coleman pointed out later during a follow-up of these negotiations.[7] In addition, such a move into cartridge manufacturing on any scale would mean purchasing costly plant and equipment and meeting new marketing and management requirements. At the same time such an increase in existing capacity would only intensify competition. On the other hand, if Olin and Lent were to stay in the cartridge business, they did not want to be dependent on the Du Pont Company for their powder supplies. Despite Coleman's promises to provide them with their basic raw material at a fair price, the two cartridge manufacturers preferred, when pressed to make a decision, to keep control of their powder mills. Pierre and Coleman continued to negotiate with them throughout 1903, but to no avail.

The move to obtain the California Powder Works raised even more problems than the attempts to acquire the companies of Olin and Lent, but it was in the end more successful. After the cousins took over the Du Pont Company, they sent Hamilton Barksdale and then Pierre's uncle Henry Belin, Jr., to the West Coast to provide firsthand reports on the situation there. Belin particularly stressed how much more competitive and chaotic the powder business was in the West than in the East.[8] The inability to control competition had encouraged the companies in the West to carry out policies of integration to a much greater degree than had those east of the Rockies. When the powder companies began to move into the making of chemicals, fuses, and other supplies, the chemical and fuse companies in turn began to move into explosives.

As to the California Powder Works itself, Belin reported that it was split into two factions: one headed by the president, Captain John Bermingham, and the other by the chairman of the Executive Committee, E. S. Pillsbury.[9] The latter and his committee knew little about operations, while Bermingham, who had long managed the firm, was not a member of the Executive Committee. But as Pillsbury's family and friends held much of the stock, he was the man the du Ponts must win over if they were to obtain full control of that company.[10] Given all these complications, Coleman decided that he must go to California himself. He was about to leave for the West Coast when he again became ill in Johnstown. As soon as the doctors would allow him, Coleman planned to depart for San Francisco.[11]

While Coleman was confined to his bed, Pierre and Moxham began to work on plans for creating a still larger consolidated enterprise. One reason was simply to provide easier financial and legal arrangements for obtaining control of Equitable, Austin, and the California Powder Works. The formation of separate holding companies for each purchase on the pattern of the Laflin & Rand deal was, they agreed, cumbersome and possibly more costly than necessary. A single holding company to permit obtaining control through exchange of stock of different companies seemed to make more sense. By this time, however, Moxham and Pierre wanted to use such a holding company for more than just the purchase of the three companies. They were ready to employ it to buy out the minority stockholders in companies in which Du Pont & Company had control and even to buy out those in which they had only a little stock. They wanted to consolidate a large part of the American explosives industry into a single legal entity. This was the plan that Pierre and Moxham proposed at the Executive Committee meeting on March 16 and on which they made a formal report at the meeting of April 6 just before Coleman was able to leave for the West Coast.[12]

The Executive Committee approved the general outline for the legal consolidation and gave Moxham and Pierre the authority to work it out. As the two studied the company's needs and opportunities, they shifted their goals. They decided that their position in the industry would in the long run be more profitable and more stable if they moved from legal combination to administrative consolidation, and if they took all the leading powder firms into the new consolidation instead of just those in which they owned stock. This meant that the proposed holding company would become an operating one and that the centralized management structure created for Du Pont, Hazard, Laflin & Rand, and Eastern Dynamite would be extended to cover nearly all of the American explosives industry. Moxham reported these basic changes in strategy to Coleman on May 2.

Pierre outlined the concepts that lay behind the formation of the "Big Company" in a report that he drafted in April 1904 as its formation was being completed.[13] Consolidation and rationalization of the lion's share of the powder industry's production and distribution facilities should lead, he pointed out, to lowered unit costs and more assured profits. The purpose was, Pierre wrote, "the avoiding of expenses incident to maintaining under separate management numerous corporations [and] the bringing [together] of the several interests in such a way as to make it possible to handle the manufacturing, shipping and selling of the business in the most economical manner." Secondly, the holding company route should assist in getting companies to join the consolidation by making easier "the bringing together of numerous minority stockholders of which each group forms an obstructive unit against changes, which though favorable to the whole business was inimical to one particular group." Particularly important here was "the absorption of the main explosives interests on the West coast none of which were controlled by the eastern companies but which were still too large and important to be acquired by direct purchase on the open market."

The new and different form of legal control would in turn allow "the adoption of a single management which could at all times command the field with sufficient power to dominate rivals and at the same time make fair returns to its stockholders without imposing burdens on the purchasing public." And it would achieve this end "by the avoidance of trade agreements contrary to law."

The decision to provide for administrative as well as legal control of nearly all the major companies in the industry reflected Moxham and Pierre's dissatisfaction with the traditional ways of doing business in the powder industry. These, they now agreed, were inefficient, costly, demoralizing, and illegal. This was particularly true of black powder, for which the Gunpowder Trade Association still set the industry's price and production schedules. But it was also true of the dynamite side of the business, where the policy of buying into new competition was still generally practiced. In addition, the reports from California continued to make it clear that until some new kinds of controls were formed neither the association nor the du Ponts themselves could make satisfactory arrangements with the West Coast companies for maintaining price stability in the rich market of the "neutral belt" in the Mountain states.

During the summer and fall of 1902 the new men at Du Pont had been willing enough to go along with the old policies of controlling price and production both through the association and the purchase of small competitors, because they realized that the purchase of Laflin & Rand would assure them complete dominance of the Gunpowder Trade Association. Coleman and, to a lesser extent, Pierre began to take part in the affairs of the association. In the summer of 1902 Coleman became a member of its Advisory Committee while Colonel Henry continued as its chairman. Its other members included Haskell, Colvin (until his retirement in September as Hazard's president), Olin, and Lent. Edward Greene, its permanent secretary, had long been active in Laflin & Rand.[14] John B. Coleman of Oriental, William Beecher of the Ohio Powder Company, and Addison G. Fay of American and Miami often met with the regular members of the committee, as did Pierre and, after September, Moxham.

These sessions differed little from those held in the 1880s. The only major formal change in the structure of the association after 1889 was the formation of a Special Committee, consisting of a few members of the Advisory Committee, which met between the regular monthly meetings of the latter group to authorize changes in price and handle other matters.[15] The Advisory Committee spent most of its time reviewing requests to adjust prices in different marketing areas, either by approving those already passed by the Special Committee or reviewing those sent in by companies or their agents. It also looked over the monthly reports on sales and made certain that those firms who oversold made their proper payments to the association and those who had undersold received their proper reimbursement from the association. The committee further checked all contracts with customers to be certain that they adhered to the regulations on car prices (which could be lower than smaller or "composite" lots), brand names, grades of powder, credit, and discounts. Discounts were permitted only at "distribution points," which were major cities where, according to the ruling passed in 1897, all storage magazines had to be placed.[16] Finally, the committee reviewed complaints about violations of the association's rules and levied fines on those found guilty.

Besides attending meetings of the Advisory Committee, Coleman, Pierre, and Moxham took part in the association's annual meeting held in October 1902.[17] In fact, at this meeting Moxham proposed a way to improve the enforcement of the association's rulings. He suggested the use of an outside auditor to act as a judge or arbitrator in determining violations of price and other agreements in order to permit more objective and impartial rulings. He then outlined the procedure that would cause the least possible "embarrassment" to all parties by having the auditor, the "complainant," and the defendant work out the matter quietly.[18] The only strong opposition to this proposal came from the companies owned by the Fay family.[19] They quite naturally were against Moxham's proposal of having an auditor "call for any book or other record he may desire." They insisted that "we and we alone, should be the judge of what books we shall show any person outside of the Company." Olin too was skeptical about parts of the plan.[20] Nevertheless, as the du Ponts had the votes, the association accepted the proposal.

The reason for the Du Pont Company's interest in improving enforcement procedures quickly became clear. Early in 1903 Moxham brought a complaint against Fay's American and Miami companies for selling at below listed prices in Iowa and Colorado.[21] However, Oscar Morton, who had become the association's auditor (he was the accountant who had worked with Pierre and Raskob on the evaluation of the Du Pont property in March 1902), found the defendant guilty on only one of four counts.

Pierre and Coleman were also troubled by indications that Lent of Austin had been returning false reports on his sales. After a careful study of the Austin books early the next summer, Pierre found that the rumors were indeed true.[22] The company had not reported and had not made payment to the association for sizable oversales above their quotas. While the Du Pont Company, as a stockholder in Austin, gained from these false reports, it lost through the interest in other associated companies. Pierre computed the gain at $40,000 and the losses at $60,000. Because of "the great difficulty in making a fair adjustment" and also because he was, by this time, anxious to get Lent to join the big company, Pierre decided that the Du Pont Company "would for the present not take action in this matter."

During his first months with the Du Pont Company Pierre received comparable lessons in the difficulty involved in the policy of buying into competition. One of Coleman and Pierre's first tasks was to complete the negotiations for the purchase of the Fairmont Mills in West Virginia, which Eugene du Pont had begun just before his death. In the following summer Coleman continued the old policy by starting to negotiate for control of Ferndale, Cambria, Shenandoah, and other small mills in Pennsylvania, and the Jellico Company in Tennessee. A little later he began discussions with Arthur Kirk & Sons for the purchase of the Climax Powder Company. The transaction, by which the Du Pont Company paid $700,000 to Kirk, was completed just before Coleman left for California in April 1903.[23]

While the Kirk purchase was straightforward, those for the small Pennsylvania mills and the Jellico Company were indirect, underhanded, and expensive. Both were carried out by agents who did not let the buyers know that the du Ponts were involved. In Pennsylvania much scheming led only to the signing of tentative agreements with two mills, the Cambria and Ferndale companies.[24] The others were willing enough to sell, but only at a price that Coleman considered too high. Even the two that were purchased were no bargains. Alfred, who investigated the Ferndale works, was hardly enthusiastic about its prospects. To reproduce it would cost, as the sellers claimed, $100,000, but the mill had, Alfred insisted, "no operative value, as the buildings were all within flash distance and liable to be destroyed at any time. The plant looks as though it were built for selling, and evidently has not been in operation very long, as everything looks freshly painted and very clean."[25] The Cambria plant was not much more promising.

Coleman expressed an interest in the Jellico Company even before that firm began construction of a small black powder works to supply nearby coal mines. He contacted an old associate, Hywel Davis, whom Coleman had known when he had managed coal mines in that area, and arranged for Davis to buy into the Jellico Company with funds provided by the Du Pont Company.[26] At the same time Coleman wrote Haskell (the serious negotiations with Laflin & Rand were only just about to begin) about the new proposed mill. "It is, of course, my intention that any or all associates [i.e., members of the association] shall be permitted to take their pro rata share of whatever is necessary to control the situation."[27] Haskell agreed to join Du Pont in taking a sizable block of the initial issue of $10,000 worth of stock made by the Jellico Company. Just before Coleman left for California, he sent Davis $5,000 more, which assured Du Pont control of 127 of the 250 shares.[28] Davis made certain that none of the other stockholders were aware of the Du Pont connection. The company thus had assured its control of another new firm, but in so doing was essentially financing the building of new and, from its point of view, unnecessary capacity.

Both Pierre and Moxham became distressed at the cost of this uncontrolled construction. This is why Moxham stressed to Coleman and the Executive Committee in March 1903 the necessity to avoid "the continual multiplication of corporations and companies that seems to be a positive mania among powder men."[29] Such a policy meant that the Du Pont Company was paying for the expansion of the industry's plant capacity in a way that Pierre and Moxham believed had little connection with the most efficient use of the industry's plant and equipment. Since the low cost of building a small works made entry into the industry easy, new competitors would continue to be attracted, as in the past, by the prices that the association was able to maintain. In some cases, like that at Ferndale, plants were actually built just to sell out to the "trust."

Moxham further insisted that the use of secret and underhanded methods demoralized the Du Pont executives and employees. It encouraged disloyalty and the use of corrupt methods against the company as well as competitors. To make his point Moxham sent Coleman and the Executive Committee a muckraking article from *McClure's* magazine on Standard Oil's methods of competition: "Illustrating as it does the detective methods of looking after competitors, I believe it will be useful to all of us." Such methods, Moxham implied, would bring outside protest as well as inside demoralization. With these views Pierre now fully concurred and in March and April 1903 he enthusiastically joined Moxham in advocating and planning the formation of the big company.

## Organizing the Powder Company

Pierre quickly took command of organizing the consolidation. He had an energy, an enthusiasm and, above all, a rationality and levelheadedness that Moxham could only admire. As the older man wrote Coleman early in June: "I have been so much impressed by the systematic and logical way that Pierre has developed each step in the consolidation, that I cannot speak too highly of him. He is worth more than the rest of the field together when he has once mastered a given line of action."[30] To this Coleman simply replied, "I am sincerely glad that Pierre is showing up so well. I always knew that he would."[31]

When Pierre and Moxham outlined their first detailed plan to form the holding company, they set down several basic conditions to be met. These Pierre outlined in a report he made on the consolidation as it was coming to completion in the spring of 1904. The first and most essential of these conditions was to assure "control of the consolidated company by E. I. du Pont de Nemours & Company or by its stockholders."[32] The second was "the bringing together of at least a majority interest in the several existing companies without the expenditure of too much money." At the same time the plan should permit "the minority interests to come into the consolidation on practically the same basis as the majority." Just as important, the arrangement had to be such that it was "a matter of indifference whether or not the minority came in." The consolidation should meet all legal requirements and needs that the present Gunpowder Trade Association did not. Finally, its financing should avoid the costs of payments for interests and sinking funds involved in the issuing of bonds and still provide a "moderate, but as far as possible fixed income to the prospective stockholders, which investment and income might be retained or sold apart from the speculative investment and income which might belong to the future of the business."

To meet these conditions Pierre and Moxham proposed the formation of a holding company to exchange shares of stock with twenty-seven firms in which the Du Pont Company held stock.[33] These included Hazard, Eastern Dynamite, and Laflin & Rand, which had already been incorporated into the Du Pont structure, as well as those firms in which they held stock but did not manage. To do this a new corporation, the E. I. du Pont de Nemours Powder Company, would issue $23,715,367 worth of preferred shares and $22.0 million worth of common. The exchange was to be based on assets, and assets were to be determined by two criteria. The first was the cost of reproducing "tangible property," that is, the physical plant and facilities including securities and cash on hand; the second was to be earning power. For the first—the agreed-upon valuation of its tangible assets—a company joining the consolidation would receive *preferred* stock at par. Later the Executive Committee decided to have the preferred stock pay 5% and gave it full voting powers. For the second—its agreed-upon earning power—the company received an amount of *common* stock of the new Powder Company, the income from which, added to the 5% return to be paid on the preferred, would provide shareholders making the exchange a return equivalent to what they had received before their company joined the consolidation and before they made the exchange. Pierre estimated that the cost of reproducing the physical assets of the twenty-eight companies (including Du Pont Company itself) came to $23,715,367. The earnings of the same companies for 1902, if capitalized on a 15% basis (less 5% paid on preferred), would come to about $20.0 million.

In addition, Moxham and Pierre proposed that the Du Pont Company receive a 5% commission in stock for organizing and underwriting the new company. As this bonus would add $2.0 million of common stock, the total capitalization of the new company would be tentatively set at $45,715,376. Should companies other than the twenty-eight listed enter the consolidation, the capital stock would be increased according to their specific assets and earning power. Of these potential joiners (in which the Du Pont Company had no stock) the most important included almost all the West Coast companies, the explosives companies owned by the Fay family, and two smokeless powder firms.

Although Pierre's criteria for the exchange of stock had been used in financing United States Steel and other combinations, it was a new idea to most powdermen. He spelled out his argument for using both physical assets and earning power as a basis for capitalization. There were, Pierre pointed out, four types of assets: first, "tangible property in permanent investment such as plant, magazines and real estate"; secondly, property "in the form of working capital such as materials, supplies, finished product on hand, commercial accounts, stocks and bonds held and cash";[34] third, intangible property including patents, trademarks, and good will; and fourth, earning power "to be represented by the income of the several investments." The first and second categories could be appraised in a uniform manner, but the third would certainly be difficult to estimate. Fortunately very few important patents existed in the explosives industry, except in the new smokeless powder business; nor had any "large sum been paid for patents or other tangible property in recent years." Hence, this item could be easily disregarded in the determination of assets which could then be based on the combination of the first, second, and fourth categories. One further advantage of basing the stock exchange on tangible property (i.e., permanent investment plus working capital and securities in hand) and earning power was that it lessened the possible "contention as to the appraisal of property, since the capitalization for Common Stock was made after subtracting the dividend on Preferred Shares." Thus, while overvaluation of tangible property would increase the preferred stock obtained, it would also reduce the amount of common stock received, "so that the measure of tangible values became more a question of what kind of a stock to be issued than of how much."

Pierre believed that the final amount of capitalization was conservative. It would permit "a moderate dividend of 3% on Common Stock if only one-half the earnings of the company were distributed. The earnings on total capitalization would then be a little over 8% [i.e., 5% on preferred and 3% on common] and on actual investment 16% which seemed a fair average for an industrial enterprise."

Finally Pierre argued that the 5% commission allotted to the Du Pont Company for handling and underwriting the consolidation was reasonable. It was less than outside financiers were charging for similar services in other industries, and he believed it would not bring criticism from the minority holders. The 5%, he admitted, would water the total issue, but the 5% water would only mean an average of 8.2% on earnings instead of 8.75% if a commission had not been taken. The smallness of the percentage involved was then a standard argument used by financiers in carrying out similar large consolidations, for they could make large profits in actual figures based on such small percentages. Still the price was low, and the increased profits resulting from probable lower costs should assure the stockholders a return well above the 5% charged. Of the more than thirty companies that were finally asked to join the consolidation, executives in only two of them openly questioned payment of the 5% commission.

Next, Pierre had to make arrangements for removing current liens or claims on the securities of E. I. du Pont de Nemours & Company that might interfere with its transfer to the new Powder Company. For the stock of the company that had been used as collateral to secure the bonds of the two holding companies in the Laflin & Rand purchase, he proposed to substitute preferred stock of the new Powder Company.[35] The Powder Company would also agree to guarantee the principal and bonds of both Delaware Securities and Delaware Investment. The other claim on Du Pont & Company was the purchase notes held by the sellers of the old company. Here Pierre thought the best answer was to replace that unfunded debt with a funded one. E. I. du Pont de Nemours & Company would issue $10.0 million worth of 5%, thirty-year, sinking fund, gold bonds.[36] These bonds, to be backed by $14.0 million worth of preferred stock of the new Powder Company, would be issued at 105 and then exchanged for purchase notes. To pay off this bond issue two sinking funds would be set up providing a total of $400,000, at least half of which was to come from dividends paid by E. I. du Pont de Nemours & Company (which in turn would come from the Powder Company).[37] Du Pont & Company, but not the Powder Company, would also guarantee not to issue any bonds having a prior lien on the new $10.0 million issue.

Once these arrangements had been accepted and approved, the assets and operating business of E. I. du Pont de Nemours & Company were to be turned over to the E. I. du Pont de Nemours Powder Company in return for the preferred and common stock on the appraised value of its physical assets and earning power. The old legal entity, E. I. du Pont de Nemours & Company, would then become solely a holding company. Since the assets and earning power of Du Pont & Company totaled close to 3/5 of the proposed consolidations, it would, after the exchange of stock, control the new Powder Company. In this way Pierre achieved the first of the objectives he outlined in planning the consolidation. And since the three cousins held the largest blocks of stock in Du Pont & Company, they would legally control nearly all of the explosives industry.

There was to be one exception to this general exchange. This was the formation of E. I. du Pont de Nemours & Company of Pennsylvania, which would operate the company's mills at Wapwallopen in the anthracite coal region along with other holdings in that Pennsylvania area, including those of Moosic, Enterprise, and the Laflin Powder Manufacturing Company, which came in with the Laflin & Rand exchange of stock, as well as the recently acquired Oliver Powder Company and the long-established Consumer Powder Company.[38] The reason for this separate regional enterprise was operational as well as legal, for these several mills produced only for nearby anthracite coal mines. The legal reason was that Pennsylvania levied high fees on "foreign" corporations. The stock of the Pennsylvania company was, like that of the Powder Company, to be held by E. I. du Pont de Nemours & Company.

As Pierre and Moxham worked out their proposals, they consulted with a well-recommended New York legal firm, Townsend and Avery, specialists in corporation law. James A. Townsend, the senior partner, approved and then strongly urged incorporating the new company in New Jersey. In his report on the formation of the consolidation Pierre summarized the lawyer's reasons that had convinced him and Moxham to incorporate the new company in that state. The New Jersey incorporation laws were not only "very liberal" but also "of long standing and have been fully interpreted by the courts."[39] The "facilities" for incorporation and continued legal operation were better than in other states. Finally, there were "so many large corporations under the New Jersey laws that adverse legislation would bring together a great body of powerful interests in strong opposition."

After working out the terms of the consolidation, Pierre's first major hurdle was to get the approval of the older du Ponts who were stockholders and directors in E. I. du Pont de Nemours & Company. Alfred had been convinced by the arguments made before the Executive Committee. Alexis, and particularly Cousin Frank, continued to be suspicious of the younger men's innovating and empire-building tendencies. Recalling the experience of the previous year, Pierre decided to work through his cousin Colonel Henry. When he reached the colonel he found that the two older cousins had already raised objections. The colonel reported, as Pierre wrote Coleman: "They started out with the remark that they did not at all approve of the consolidation plan, but after talking awhile with Cousin Henry, they left him with a better idea of the whole scheme."[40] However, even Colonel Henry was not completely satisfied. He wanted a larger share of, if not all, the dividends of Du Pont & Company to go into the sinking fund to pay off the bonds. In the resulting discussion Pierre was able not only to convince Colonel Henry of the rightness of his current proposals but also to get an explicit statement that the Powder Company (but not Du Pont & Company, the holding firm) could make short-term, unsecured bond issues, which Moxham and Pierre had decided they might find necessary in carrying on its business.

After the older du Ponts and the principal holders of Delaware Securities and Delaware Investment companies approved the plan, Pierre arranged for the incorporation of the E. I. du Pont de Nemours Powder

Company on May 19. The capitalization of the new company was finally set at $50.0 million divided equally between preferred and common stock. Pierre decided that the new enterprise should have fifteen directors. These would include the present Executive Committee of the E. I. du Pont de Nemours & Company (himself, Coleman, Alfred, Moxham, Haskell, Barksdale, and Francis I. du Pont), three members of the older generation (Cousins Henry, Alexis, and Frank), making "ten in all from our side of the house." The minority holders should have five directors, one apiece from California, Austin, Equitable—and, hopefully, if they could be induced to join—one from each of two Fay companies, leaving one to spare. The officers of the Powder Company would be the same as those of the present Du Pont Company.[41]

A few weeks later the consolidation of Du Pont's interests in the Pennsylvania anthracite district was also consummated.[42] The change in the relation to Delaware Securities and Delaware Investment went off without a hitch.[43] Moreover, Parsons and Boies seemed agreeable to exchange later the stocks and bonds of these two holding companies for preferred stock of the Powder Company. Then on July 1 the directors of Du Pont & Company authorized the transfer, as of August 1, of all properties, assets, and business to the new Du Pont Company in return for $16.5 million worth of preferred and $13.5 million worth of common stock of the Powder Company.[44] At the same time, the holders of purchase notes exchanged their notes for the bonds of Du Pont & Company. The transfer of stock went off just as smoothly with the companies in which Du Pont held all or nearly all of the control, including such large firms as Lake Superior, Marcellus, and Phoenix.

The negotiations with those companies in which the minority interests were large but Du Pont had control and with those in which Du Pont did not have control took a great deal more time and energy. The first group, in which Du Pont controlled but outsiders held large blocks of stock, included the Birmingham Powder Company, the H. A. Weldy Powder Company, Frank Connable's Chattanooga Powder Company, and John B. Coleman's Oriental Powder Mills. The second group, in which the Du Pont Company held only a minority interest, included Olin's Equitable; Lent's Austin; the California Powder Works; and the Ohio Powder Company, run by Edmund L. Brown and Walter A. Beecher. Pierre also hoped to bring in the three companies the Fay family owned and in which the du Ponts held no stock at all.

The strategy they decided upon, Moxham wrote Coleman on May 2, was first to complete the consolidation of their own interests and then "to tackle the Lent crowd, and Olin, leaving the Fay interests to the last."[45] Moxham then reviewed the continuing "conscientious" study of consolidation matters.

The plan agreed upon is to first form a Holding Company, using this as a machine to round up everything that can be rounded up. This done, the present feeling is as quickly as possible to round out the outstanding interests which do not first come into the Holding Company and at the tail end perhaps by purchase, if nothing else can be done, to even things up. When this is effected the intent is to turn it into an Operative Company pure and simple.

Of the important outside interests, Pierre, Moxham, and Coleman agreed that Olin's was the most significant and also would probably be the the most difficult to obtain.[46] Olin was at that moment disturbing the competitive situation by making machinery for the new dynamite plant being built by Norman P. Rood and his father, George L., in Missouri and also by indicating his general dissatisfaction with the association. The negotiations with the Illinois powder maker got off to a bad start, as the Executive Committee appointed a committee of three—Pierre, Alfred, and Hamilton Barksdale—to do the job. "A committee of one would have been best but we do not seem to do anything but with a crowd in the powder business," Moxham wrote Coleman.[47] In the end Pierre saw Olin alone. The difficulty remained with the cartridge company. Olin seemed willing enough to come in, Pierre reported, but his associate in the Western Cartridge Company, C. F. McMurray, strongly opposed the merger.[48] When Coleman returned from California, Olin still had not made up his mind.

By the time Coleman reached Wilmington in early August, Pierre had consulted all but the Fay interests. John B. Coleman of Oriental was the first to accept, making his agreement before the end of May. He was quickly followed by Henry A. Weldy.[49] Pierre saw Connable late in June and Beecher of Ohio shortly thereafter.[50] Both were agreeable, but Connable had to wait until his mother, who was a large stockholder, returned from Europe before making the final decision, and Beecher until his partner, Brown, returned to Youngstown from his summer vacation in Massachusetts. Pierre postponed negotiations with Lent of Austin until a decision had been reached on the false reporting to the association he had recently discovered.[51]

In addition to the black powder and dynamite makers Pierre and Moxham listed in their original proposal, they decided to bring in the two most important smokeless powder manufacturers, the Schultze Company and the International Smokeless Powder and Chemical Company. On April 14 the Executive Committee appointed Moxham and Haskell to try once again to purchase the E. C. & Schultze Company.[52] As the Schultze offices were near New York, Haskell took over most of these negotiations.[53] He was soon in correspondence with the British parent company, which by the end of July had agreed to lease the factory at Oakland, New Jersey, for an annual rental of £3,750, with an option to buy, on the condition that no powder made by the American company be sold in Great Britain. Secondly, it wanted the transfer of property to be made on January 1, 1904, rather than September 1, 1903, as originally contemplated. The shareholders believed that they would give away practically a whole year's work in return for a small rent.[54] After the Executive Committee adopted Haskell's suggestion to start payment of rent as of May 1, the British signed a contract.

Negotiations with International Smokeless Powder proved much more complicated. Late in May, after the formation of the Du Pont Powder Company, Pierre sounded out one of the senior executives, W.W. Gibbs. By mid-June Moxham reported to Coleman that Gibbs was interested in coming into the consolidation and that Pierre had worked out a proposal that Gibbs and his colleagues approved.[55] The basic plan was to form a separate company to bring in under a single corporate entity the facilities of the four producers of military powder—Du Pont, Laflin & Rand, the California Powder Works and International. Once the company was completed, it could be brought into the big company *"on its own merits."*

Pierre wrote Coleman in more detail.[56] According to the agreement that he and Gibbs initialed, the preferred stock of the new company would represent net working capital plus the cost of reproducing the plant. The common stock would represent their respective outputs. But neither Pierre nor Gibbs could agree on the period on which to determine output. Gibbs naturally wanted the last five months in which International had made its best showing; Pierre argued for a more extended period. They finally agreed that International would receive not less than 32% and not more than 39% of the common stock.

But neither Coleman nor his Executive Committee was enthusiastic about the agreement. Nor, in fact, was Pierre. Coleman wrote, "Just why I can't say."[57] Gibbs, he felt, was not telling the whole story. He simply did not "like the style of the man but I may be, and perhaps am prejudiced, 'though the feeling is more intuition than logic.'" So Pierre dropped the matter until Coleman's return.

By that time Pierre had completed most of the spade work in the creation of the consolidation. All the Du Pont interests and the negotiations with minority holders were pretty well settled, although the independents —Olin, Lent, and Gibbs—had not yet signed. Appraisals had begun to determine assets and earnings to be used as a basis for exchange of stock.[58] By that time, also, Pierre and Moxham had altered substantially the over-all objective of the consolidation from what it had been when Coleman had left Wilmington in April. The two men not only had decided to transform the holding company into an operating company, but had now come to believe that it was no longer necessary to bring in all outside interests, even such important firms as those of the Fay family or Olin or Lent.

By early summer Moxham was certain that the new company would probably make a higher return on investment without such outsiders. "I believe our greatest profit will be in giving up the attempt to buy everything in sight, and devote our investments towards greater economy in manufacturing."[59] To persuade the others he and Pierre began to use realistic and sophisticated arguments about the nature of profit-making in a high-volume business with the normal fluctuating markets. Both fully appreciated how their new industrial form would take advantage of its size. With a high volume of output produced and distributed by the new centralized management, the company should be able to lower its costs well below that of its smaller competitors. Only the efficient small firm or one with specialized local markets could stay in the business. Now Moxham moved one step further in his analysis. He decided that the continuance of small competitors could be a positive advantage to a policy of maintaining steady volume and keeping down unit costs. He wrote Coleman:

> I have been urging upon our people the following arguments. If we could by any measure buy out all competition and have an absolute monopoly in the field, it would not pay us. The essence of manufacture is steady and full product. The demand for the country for powder is variable. If we owned all therefore when slack times came we would have to curtail product to the extent of diminished demands. If on the other hand we control only 60% of it all and made that 60% cheaper than others, when slack times came we could still keep *our* capital employed to *the full* and our product to this maximum by taking from the other 40% what was needed for this purpose. In other words you could count upon always running full if you make cheaply and control only 60%, whereas, if you own it all, when slack times came you could only run a curtailed product.

Coleman was unconvinced. On his return he decided to continue the negotiations with Olin and Lent, although he did decide not to approach the Fays.

Once he was back in Wilmington, Coleman began to have a great deal more to say about the form and objectives of the big company; but by then its shape had already been defined. Although Coleman and others often made modifications that affected the final definition of the big company, there is no question that Pierre du Pont and Arthur Moxham had fashioned between April and August 1903 the legal, financial, and economic underpinnings of the modern Du Pont Company.

## Coleman in California

One reason that Coleman hesitated about taking Moxham's advice to rely wholly on economic power of the consolidated enterprise was that his experiences in California had dramatically pointed out the dangers of uncontrolled competition. There, with patience, tact, and diplomatic skill, he had brought stability to the industry for the first time in many years. Not only was Coleman able to get all but one of the major explosives firms on the West Coast to come into the new Powder Company (Chart I), but he was also able to persuade chemical and fuse companies and other suppliers to move out of the explosives business. It was an experience, however, that he did not want to repeat again. During the trip he kept in close touch with Pierre and Moxham and adjusted his plans as they brought the new Powder Company into being. From Coleman's letters Pierre received still more of an insight into the competitive world of late nineteenth-century business.

Although Coleman had been thoroughly briefed on the intricacies of the West Coast explosives industry by Belin and Barksdale and had talked personally with California powdermen when they came east, he was still quite unprepared for what he found. Writing Pierre on April 20 he reported:

> I have been here two days now, and at this time the various explosive, acid companies, match factories, chemical works, etc. are pictured on my brain like a pinwheeel at a pyrotechnic exhibition, with every fellow I have met so far turning in a different direction, and I find it is going to take more time than I think to be able to size the whole situation up. I will not say that the task is hopeless but hope to write very soon that I know in which direction some of the wheels are turning.[60]

A week later he had become a little more optimistic about the situation: "I have done a good deal of preliminary work—a good deal of talking, and a good deal of thinking and a good deal of figuring, but I have not, as yet been able to report a single concern that I have closed with."[61] To Moxham he added: "I think my trip from an educational view will be a success as far as I am personally concerned, but I am afraid to make any prediction as to which way the cats will jump, or how many cats will jump."[62]

Coleman was getting a dramatic reminder of the effective role that the Gunpowder Trade Association and the policy of buying into competition had played in providing stability to the powder business in the East. The West Coast companies all had agreements as to price and production, but these were rarely maintained. "I thought we had a good deal of internal competition in the East which is, of course, now much better," Coleman wrote Pierre, "but tell Mr. Moxham as compared with the Pacific Coast there is no internal competition in the East."[63] The Du Pont Company's president found an infinite variety of secret rebating, special discounts, and rigged accounts. As Coleman said to Moxham, "Don't worry that I have nothing to do here and no one to do it with." Every day was instructive for him as a newcomer to the powder industry, because all the men he saw "had been brought up in the Waddell or Colvin school."[64] Some practices were blatantly open. Coleman was astonished to find that the California Powder Works, in which his firm had 44% of the stock, was loading shotgun shells with its own powder and then falsely labeling them and selling them as Du

Pont products.[65] As this lesson taught him, even ownership of stock had little effect on maintaining agreements. "Each day here," Coleman pointed out, "develops a new way of cutting prices and I think the California Powder Works is entitled to a blue ribbon for their ability along these lines."[66]

In this highly competitive situation, companies involved in the different processes of manufacturing explosives had begun to obtain their own sources of supplies or their own outlets for their products. For this reason, Coleman wrote Pierre, he had to work with sixteen companies—five explosives, four fuse, four acid, two shell, and one cap—if he was to bring some kind of order to the West Coast explosives industry. Of these sixteen the explosives firms were the most important, and of the five explosives companies the oldest and the largest was the California Powder Works, in which the 44% of the stock held by the Du Pont Company amounted to 6,500 shares. The C.P.W., as it was usually called, was a full line firm that had begun to buy into chemical and fuse companies.[67] Because of its aggressiveness, its major competitor, the Giant Powder Company, had not been faring well.[68] With profits down, the value of its stock had fluctuated widely and these shares now had the reputation of being highly speculative.[69] The smaller Vigorite and Judson firms, which concentrated largely on the production of dynamite, were also involved in the integrating process.[70] The Judson Company had been founded by Egbert Judson, a pioneer dynamite producer who had first been a chemical manufacturer. He had started his own explosive company near San Francisco in 1890 when the Giant Powder Company had built its own acid works. Later, his company promoted a fuse concern.[71] In much the same way the Stauffer Chemical Company had purchased a large block of stock in the Vigorite Powder Company when the C.P.W. decided to produce its own acids.[72] In 1900, partly to protect itself from the C.P.W.'s continuing tendency for "breaking the price of acid," Stauffer's managers had Vigorite construct a dynamite plant with a capacity of over 300,000 pounds a month. Finally, early in 1902 the Metropolitan Match & Fuse Company had set up a fifth explosives works to assure itself of a supply of black powder.[73]

By early May Coleman had decided on his strategy. His argument would be a simple one. Peace was preferable to war, and the surest way to peace was for each company to concentrate on its own basic business. If each could be assured of outlets and supplies, it should be willing to give up those companies it had purchased or plants it had built for these purposes. Thus if the Stauffer Chemical Company was assured of a continuing outlet for its acid, it should be willing to sell Vigorite, and if Metropolitan was assured of getting black powder at a reasonable price, it should agree to sell the black powder plant it was constructing. If the Du Pont Company could obtain control of the powder companies in California, Coleman felt he could guarantee this stability to their suppliers and customers and at the same time make arrangements so that the explosives manufacturers (who would become Du Pont subsidiaries) would have the necessary supplies and sales. The Du Pont Company's president felt that he had a workable plan and a good slogan. Even so, he knew that success depended on using all the charm and persuasion he could muster.

The explosives companies were, then, the place to begin. Because the controversy within the California Powder Works between the president, Bermingham, and the chairman of the Executive Committee, Pillsbury, intensified the problem of getting control of that enterprise directly, Coleman decided to move first on the Judson Company. That company, now headed by Edward G. Lukens, still had close ties with the chemical company Judson had founded, but after Judson's death in 1893 the two firms became legally quite separate. Coleman hoped that by obtaining Judson he could convince the Pillsbury group of his serious intention to bring peace to the California industry and so get those stockholders to sell him the shares that would give Du Pont control of the C.P.W. That control in turn would make easier the purchase of the Giant Powder Company. Of more importance it should make it possible to persuade Stauffer Chemical and the fuse and cartridge companies to move out of the explosives industry. In first outlining his campaign Coleman did not consider the use of the consolidated company, as it was still in its embryonic stage. Instead he planned to continue the use of separate small holding companies to purchase the control of the stock he desired.

On May 19 Coleman reported to Moxham and Pierre on the progress of his campaign along its many fronts. He and Lukens, the president of Judson, had "practically agreed" on the terms of the purchase of that company.[74] But until that agreement was signed, he could not push the California Powder Works to a settlement. Coleman also had come to a tentative agreement with the president of Stauffer Chemical, Christian de Guigné, for the purchase of Vigorite, although, as he wrote Moxham, "I must say I don't feel sanguine that he will carry it out." Apparently de Guigné was at least initially impressed by Coleman's promise to get C.P.W. out of the acid business and to end Judson's alliance with its former parent. Finally, as to Giant, he was unable to find anyone "in a position to talk trade." So, he thought it best "to leave them alone until we have rounded up the other three companies when I think they will be eager for a proposition." All the above, Coleman warned, "is subject to change without notice but it is the best report I can make up to date."

Two events did materially change the process of these negotiations, and both came from the Du Pont side. The first was the completion of the plans for the big company and the second was the recurrence of Coleman's Johnstown illness, which put him to bed and then sent him to the hospital in California. The availability of the Powder Company, chartered on May

19, Coleman immediately realized, would make his proposed purchases neater and cheaper.[75] They would no longer require collateral for the several different holding companies, and all the firms could be asked to accept the same set of comparable terms. Since the agreement with Judson had already been reached, Coleman decided to let stand an arrangement that called for the formation of a California Investment Company to function much as Delaware Securities and Delaware Investment had in the buying of Laflin & Rand. He and Moxham agreed that once the deal was consummated the California Investment Company, and with it Judson, could be brought quickly into the Powder Company and then dissolved. Control of the other firms—Giant, Metropolitan Match & Fuse's subsidiary, Vigorite, and the C.P.W.—would be obtained through exchange of stock with the new Powder Company.[76]

With the control of Judson assured, the critical step became that of bringing the C.P.W. into the consolidation. As the key man, Pillsbury, was to be in the East, Coleman urged Moxham to go to New York with Haskell and Barksdale and present to Pillsbury in person the proposition to join the big company.[77] Haskell and Moxham both agreed with Coleman that Pillsbury must be treated carefully, as "his position is one of great strength in that he is really the determining element between Du Pont and the field."[78] But the older men, already impressed by Pierre's negotiating abilities, decided that he should be the one to meet with Pillsbury and that he should meet with him alone. Moxham would be ready to take "the next train" to New York if Pierre felt he needed help.

The younger man had no trouble handling the assignment by himself. Since he and Pillsbury were both members of New York's Metropolitan Club, Pierre arranged to spend a weekend there. As he reported to Coleman:

> I am taking the rest cure over Sunday at the Club, (the woods of Maine are gay by comparison) and incidentally working with Pillsbury. The work has not been difficult so far as he has favored the proposition from the start, says it is the best thing and that he will be much relieved to have powder matters settled as he had had a great deal of trouble to keep the Captain [Bermingham] and his men on "the straight and narrow path." [79]

Pillsbury seemed satisfied with the terms of the consolidation. He was quite willing to accept appraisal procedures that might be worked out in the East. He even pointed out that the reported earnings of the C.P.W. were undoubtedly inaccurate. His only concern was with the 5% commission the du Ponts were taking for underwriting the consolidation. Possibly, Pierre suggested to Coleman, "it might be well to give him back his share in return for his services in bringing in the others," but Pierre did not make the offer. After two evenings of discussion, the Californian agreed to write Coleman of his approval and on his return to San Francisco "to take up the matter of consolidation" with the two major interests he represented: the Parrot estate and the de Laveaga family. Pillsbury, Pierre further reported, was skeptical about the advisability of paying the price quoted for Giant stock, but he did feel that Judson was a good purchase and he, as a stockholder of that company as well as C.P.W., would support its sale. Pierre closed the correspondence by urging his cousin to concentrate on getting well—"make that the main issue, all the powder companies in California can go to ---- if you are all right."

Coleman's illness did slow him down.[80] By the end of July he was writing Pierre that he was up and about again and hoped to wind up his work quickly. On the other hand: "With the fuse fight, the loaded shell fight and the amount of personal feelings between the various concerns anything in the way of bringing them together is like trying to get an automobile up a steep hill and in fact the companies here are a good deal like automobiles, you can never tell just what is the matter with them except they won't do and they won't stay doing after they start to do."[81]

The negotiations did go off well. Control of Judson was acquired along the lines arranged in May.[82] On July 29 Coleman signed an agreement with the Stauffer Chemical Company to purchase Vigorite through an exchange of stock with the new Powder Company on much the same terms as the exchange made with the eastern companies. The amount of preferred stock exchanged was to be based on tangible property and common stock based on earnings on a somewhat lower scale (12½% rather than 15%).[83] On the same day, Pillsbury wrote Coleman that the California Powder Works would come in on the same terms.[84] With Giant, Coleman was less successful. He and its president could not agree on a price that Coleman thought reflected the company's assets and earnings.[85] So Giant continued as an active competitor on the West Coast. Finally Coleman convinced the Metropolitan Match & Fuse Company to sell to the Powder Company, through an exchange of stock, its nearly completed black powder subsidiary.[86]

The last deal was part of his moves to settle the fuse fight. There his most important step was to get the four companies in California that were producing fuses to form a single fuse-making enterprise, the West Coast Manufacturing Company, each taking stock in that corporation according to the value of the assets and earnings of their properties.[87] The four included the Metropolitan subsidiary, the C.P.W., the Judson subsidiary, and the Ensign, Bickford Company of Simsbury, Connecticut, the largest fuse makers in the country. Through its California and Judson purchases the new Powder Company came to control over 50% of the stock in the new fuse company. In a short time, in line with Coleman's promises, it sold its holdings in the West Coast Manufacturing Company to Ensign, Bickford.[88]

Coleman ended the acid and shell fights by completing his plans for what might be called dis-integration. Following his agreement with de Guigné, he refused to permit the C.P.W.'s acid-making subsidiary, the Peyton Chemical Company, to be brought into the Powder Company, and at the same time he ended Judson's alliance with its former parent company.[89] In the second controversy—the shell fight—Coleman finally convinced a number of leading West Coast hardware dealers to stop loading their own shotgun and rifle shells.[90] He did so by guaranteeing that the California Powder Works would load all brands they offered at a price that was satisfactory.

By the end of July Coleman's exhausting task was completed. He was still skeptical. "How many will fly the track at the last moment I cannot say," he wrote Barksdale, "but on one point I am very clear,—if there is ever another job which includes as many different phases of as many different businesses and as many different characters as this one and anybody wants it, they need not consider me as a rival."[91] The Executive Committee in Wilmington was of course highly pleased by Coleman's success. So too were the men on the West Coast. "It has been good for all, my dear sir," wrote one executive, "that you came here, and I assure [you] we greatly appreciate what you have done—no other man could have accomplished the same result as you have."[92] When the dividends from the new Powder Company reached the Coast, the enthusiasm was even greater. As one former president wrote: "For myself and stockholders I want to thank you for the promptness in paying us a div. on pref. Stock. Our friends pronounced you 'All Right' and were really astonished. The distribution of the div. was the most pleasing job I've had for a long time & I shall 'ever pray' that you may continue in your good work."[93]

On his return to Wilmington Coleman was as busy as he had been in California. The trip back across the continent provided some rest, but he plunged immediately into the mass of work waiting on his desk at the Market Street office. Pierre reviewed with him the many operative and administrative decisions made during the president's absence. Coleman also had innumerable loose ends to tie up concerning the legal aspects of the California negotiations. Plans for appraising the physical properties and auditing the accounts of the companies joining the consolidation had to be approved. In fact, it was more than two weeks before Pierre had a chance to discuss in detail with his cousin the uncompleted negotiations, particularly those with Equitable, Austin, and International.[94]

Pierre, Coleman, and Moxham, after consulting the other members of the Executive Committee, quickly agreed upon the procedures for appraising and auditing the properties and for the exchange of stock for all the firms, East and West, coming into the big company. The earnings of the eastern companies could be readily determined from the records already in Wilmington or from Gunpowder Trade Association's books. A much more searching audit would be required in the West, for those firms were not members of the association nor had any connection with Eastern Dynamite. As to appraisals, the original plan was to have them done throughout the country by the same committee.[95] But the time involved and the different requirements made this difficult. So Irénée du Pont was placed in charge of all appraisals, with assistants for making them in the East and in the West. Pierre was unquestionably responsible for his younger brother's appointment to this task. Certainly there could be no better way for the younger man, who, since leaving M.I.T., had been with Fenn's Manufacturers' Contracting Company, to get financial training and a clear picture of the industrial empire his family was acquiring. In the East Irénée's assistants for the appraising of black powder were George Patterson, who had just come to Wilmington from Laflin & Rand to be general manager of Alfred's black powder operating department, and Frank L. Connable, president of the Chattanooga Powder Company. For the appraisal of dynamite plants he had Oscar R. Jackson, who had recently retired after seventeen years as works manager at Repauno, and William G. Ramsay, who headed the Repauno engineering staff. In the West Irénée was to work with Jackson and Russell Dunham, the comptroller whom Pierre had already sent to the West Coast to audit the books of the companies coming into the consolidation and to set up procedures for the transfer of securities.

Pierre took the over-all responsibility of organizing and carrying out this industry-wide appraisal. This was no mean task. Coleman originally planned to send Pierre west to carry out the job personally, but, as the president reported to Pillsbury on September 4, "Mr. Pierre is snowed under just at this moment with the new organization but I think he will be out of deep water shortly."[96] Dunham was soon writing back from San Francisco that his task was proving much more difficult than anticipated. Except for the California Powder Works, he found that little or no attempt had been made by the western companies to develop accurate cost accounting.[97] Moreover, they recorded their stocks on hand, accounts receivable, and accident fund in a wide variety of ways. Even the California Powder Works had only begun to make a start toward using modern methods. Pierre had to reply to Dunham that he could release only one man from the Wilmington office, given the pressure he was under there. So Pierre arranged to have the closing date of the appraisal moved up a month from September 1.[98]

In the East, too, accounting difficulties, particularly in obtaining accurate, up-to-date inventories, delayed the completion of the appraisals.[99] By the end of January 1904 the appraisal committee had made its final report, and the Executive Committee had accepted it. On the basis of these estimates, Pierre and his assistants then computed the values on which stock was to be exchanged. Before the end of the year the treasurer had drafted a form letter, to be sent to all stockholders of the companies coming into the consolidation, indicating the procedures involved in the exchange and the ratio by which each shareholder would receive Powder Company stock for the shares of the stock of his company that he turned in.[100]

The companies going into the consolidation accepted the appraisals and exchange values determined by Pierre's department with little question, even though the treasurer's office had to adjust some of its accounting procedures in order to ensure uniformity. Thus, for example, after conferring with the Executive Committee and the different companies involved, Pierre set a uniform price for the several grades of powder listed in stocks on hand.[101] Since nearly every company differed in its method of accounting for explosives accidents and worthless accounts, he finally decided to "restore to earnings any amounts charged off for these funds and to then make an arbitrary and uniform percentage charge against the earnings of each company."[102] This proposal caused some concern, but there was no concerted protest. On evaluations, the only protest in all the mass of correspondence existing about the appraisal and transfer of stock was over the value of land owned by the Vigorite Powder Company on San Francisco Bay.[103] Its officers thought the land was worth $45,000, and the appraisers had set it at a good bit less. The issue was quickly settled by arbitrators, as had been provided for in the agreements to merge into the big company.

While Pierre was keeping an eye on the process of consolidation, he was also working with Coleman on the negotiations with those firms that had still not joined. By then, however, neither the cartridge makers, Olin and Lent, nor the powder makers were enthusiastic about merging. Pierre and Moxham and, to a lesser extent, Coleman, no longer considered the latter as necessary to the success of the Powder Company; while both Olin and Lent continued to resist giving up their own sources of powder for their cartridge and shell works. In addition, Lent had a more personal and easily understandable consideration. Pierre wrote Coleman that he would not join "unless we assure him of the presidency of Austin and the power to run that corporation as a separate concern."[104] Lent clearly preferred, Pierre thought, "the prestige he now holds as President of the Austin Powder Company" to becoming a plant manager for Du Pont.

The inability to get these two cartridge makers to bring their powder firms into the big company undoubtedly discouraged Pierre and Coleman from pressing the King Powder Company to join the consolidation. The King family—three brothers and a brother-in-law, Gershon M. Peters—operated an old family black powder firm and a newer Peters Cartridge Company.[105] In January 1901, a year before the cousins took charge in Wilmington, the Du Pont Company and Laflin & Rand had signed a contract with the King Company by which they agreed to take all King's output that did not go to the Peters Cartridge Company. Du Pont and Laflin & Rand, in turn, had set up the King Mercantile Company to market the powder produced by the Kings. This device gave the Kings an assured supply of sporting powder and had permitted Eugene du Pont to control the price of their output of explosives. Pierre and Coleman would have liked to terminate the agreement and bring the King Powder Company into the new Powder Company on the same terms as the others. But the Kings and Peters had no intention of selling out to the consolidation; nor did they see any advantage to themselves in terminating the earlier contract.[106]

Coleman was more successful in winning over the International Smokeless Powder and Chemical Company than he was with Olin, Lent, or the Kings. The difficulties raised by the International negotiations did, however, lead to a lengthy discussion in the Executive Committee early in September on the advisability of continuing talks with Gibbs and his associates.[107] Pierre tended to agree with those on the committee who emphasized the risks involved in investing in a business that was technologically in a state of flux and to a great extent dependent on government orders. There was, as Pierre noted, a real danger of reduction of profits and even possible losses "either through being forced to reduce prices to the Government or through lack of orders."[108] Then too there were always possible "complications with the United States Government because of creating a monopoly in the smokeless powder business." After the California Powder Works had come into the consolidation, International remained the last of the large independent producers of military smokeless powder in the country.

On the other hand, there were obvious advantages in obtaining International. It would remove a primary competitor for government business and also a potential competitor in the commercial trade. The latter was a real threat if the government demand fell off, since the capacity of existing plants already exceeded probable demand, and since a shift from military to commercial smokeless powder was technologically easy enough. In addition, International "undoubtedly has considerable valuable influence in the United States Government." Finally its control would mean "the removal from the outside field of a corporation that might make an alliance with European Manufacturers greatly to our disadvantage at the expiration of the European Agreement in 1907." Given the persuasive arguments on either side, the Executive Committee could not come to a decision. As its members were "about equally divided," they decided to refer the question to the board of directors, who finally agreed to move ahead on the purchase.[109]

As Coleman reopened negotiations with International, he learned that his earlier intuitions had been correct. Gibbs had not told all. That company's promoters had heavy debts resulting from the fact that International had been formed originally to produce smokeless powder from a process using cellulose made from cornpith.[110] W. W. Gibbs and Colonel Edmund G. Buckner were large stockholders in the Marsden Company, a Philadelphia firm producing corn products including cornpith. They had helped to finance International Smokeless Powder in 1899. Then, after building a large plant in Parlin, New Jersey, to produce smokeless powder from a corn-based cellulose, they found that the process did not work and were forced to change to one making cellulose from cotton linters. Under Harry Fletcher Brown, a Harvard-trained chemist from the Naval Torpedo Station at Newport, Rhode Island, the Parlin plant became a profitable operation by 1903, when it was already manufacturing about 35% of the powder used in large caliber army and navy guns.[111] The Marsden Company, however, remained saddled with heavy debts and had failed to make a substantial income from its other corn products. So a merger with International meant the settlement of the Marsden Company's debts.

After a series of meetings and much correspondence, Gibbs, Coleman, and Pierre decided to give up the idea of bringing International into the big company at that time.[112] In addition to the complications of the Marsden finances, both sides continued to disagree on a proper period to determine earnings on which the common stock was to be exchanged. Therefore, the cousins decided it was simpler to set up a separate company to buy out International, as they had done before they had hit upon the idea of one all-embracing holding company. Then, as had been planned for the California Investment Company and Judson, it could be brought into the consolidation at a later date. Coleman's proposal was to form the Du Pont International Powder Company to "operate in harmony with the general powder interests until such a time as their earning capacity for a year, two, three or more has been established, when they can be brought into the general Du Pont Company upon a determination of values on earning capacity at that time."[113] Gibbs and Buckner were agreeable if an arrangement could be made to pay off Marsden's debts.[114] When such an arrangement was worked out, an agreement was signed on December 21 which gave the du Ponts control of the International Smokeless Powder and Chemical Company by having the E. I. du Pont de Nemours & Company (now the family holding company) rather than the Powder Company hold the stock of the new Du Pont International Powder Company.

Pierre had always been lukewarm about the purchase of International. In February 1904, when Coleman asked him to work out the exchange values in which the common stock of Du Pont International could be turned over to the Powder Company, he made a careful survey of the books. On the basis of earning power and assets, almost any exchange seemed unfavorable. A careful computation of the profits showed that they were much less than Buckner and Gibbs had claimed. Pierre found that the old International Smokeless Powder and Chemical Company had no works accident or plant depreciation fund, and "if these were set aside I think the profit in the latter case would be practically wiped out. . . . To sum up, I think the situation an extremely difficult one and one in which the present showing does not promise much reward to the stockholders of E. I. du Pont de Nemours & Company excepting the very substantial gain made in the interest of the E. I. du Pont de Nemours Powder Company through making a definite settlement with the International Company."[115] When Coleman proposed later an exchange rate of one share of Powder Company common for three of International, Pierre protested that the rate was too high and one for which they "might be seriously criticised," even though International's profit performance was certainly improving.[116] Because Pierre, Coleman, and the stockholders of the old International company could not come to an agreement as to an exchange rate, its final merger with the Powder Company kept being put off.

By the end of 1903 the basic transactions involved in creating the "Big Company" were complete. Its final form was now clear. It was to be a large horizontal consolidation producing a full line of explosives, but not controlling manufacturers who used its products and not yet owning sources of its raw materials. It would not include those powder companies controlled by three major ammunition makers—Olin, Lent, and King. However, as stockholders in the Olin and Lent companies, and by the contract with the King company, the du Ponts still had a voice in the pricing of the powder-producing firms controlled by these three families. Nor would the big company include Giant, whose price was too high, nor the three companies owned by the Fay family and the two belonging to George L. Rood and his son, Norman P., which had not been asked to join. (See Tables 4–1 to 4–5.) International would remain a separate financial and legal entity, although its plants would be administered and its products sold through the Powder Company's new centralized administrative organization. By the middle of 1904, when the transactions involved in the consolidation were completed, the new Powder Company controlled the manufacturing of just over 70% of the dynamite sold in the United States; a little over 60% of most-used black powders; 65% of all soda blasting powder "B" sold in the United States; close to 80% of the older saltpeter blasting powder; 75% of the black sporting powder; and 70% of the military (smokeless) powder.[117] By obtaining control of International it had achieved a complete monopoly of military smokeless powder, except for a small amount made by government-owned and -operated works.

### The Powder Company Takes Final Form

As the final form of the big company took shape, arguments grew within the Executive Committee as to its precise relationship to the rest of the industry. The differences reflected the development of Pierre and Moxham's views about the economic role that a large consolidated enterprise could play in the industry it dominated. The views of these two men with

## Table 4-1

Table Showing the Total Sale (as Reported Under Oath by Themselves) of *Black Blasting Powder*[1] in the United States During the Calendar Years 1905 to 1907, Both Inclusive, by All Manufacturers of Same, Except E. I. du Pont de Nemours Powder Company and Companies of Which E. I. du Pont de Nemours Powder Company Owns or Controls All or a Majority of the Capital Stock.

| NAME | ADDRESS | 1905 | 1906 | 1907 | |
|---|---|---|---|---|---|
| Aetna Powder Company | Chicago, Ill. | 78,836 | 148,515 | 98,151 | (Fay) |
| The American Powder Mills | Boston, Mass. | 188,025 | 238,379 | 222,165 | (Fay) |
| Austin Powder Company of Cleveland | Cleveland, Ohio | 420,039 | 402,974 | 502,031 | (Lent) |
| Black Diamond Powder Company | Mahony City, Pa. | 443 | 18,069 | 32,422 | |
| Buckeye Powder Company | Peoria, Ill. | 153,543 | 73,293 | 85,309 | |
| Burton Powder Company | Pittsburgh, Pa. | 172,281 | 208,912 | 169,640 | (formed 1907) |
| Connell Powder Company | Scranton, Pa. | 32,685 | 23,835 | 58,776 | |
| Cressona Powder Company | Pottsville, Pa. | 63,568 | 48,762 | 55,345 | |
| Egyptian Powder Company | Chicago, Ill. | 144,291 | 137,652 | 257,013 | (Olin)[2] |
| Equitable Powder Manufacturing Company | East Alton, Ill. | 304,402 | 536,011 | 642,535 | (Olin) |
| Excelsior Powder Company | Kansas City, Mo. | 44,034 | 121,281 | 194,159 | (formed 1907) |
| Giant Powder Company, Consolidated | San Francisco, Cal. | 68,590 | 84,395 | 53,893 | |
| Jefferson Powder Company | Birmingham, Ala. | None | 5,089 | 40,169 | |
| King Powder Company | Cincinnati, Ohio | 259,766 | 284,979 | 224,059 | (King) |
| *Lakeside Powder Company | Shenandoah, Pa. | 69,000 | 55,344 | 27,025 | |
| Locust Mountain Powder and Dynamite Company | Mahanoy City, Pa. | 24,120 | 20,830 | 18,340 | |
| Lofty Powder Company | Hazleton, Pa. | 21,600 | 23,100 | 18,300 | |
| Miami Powder Company | Xenia, Ohio. | 433,271 | 581,235 | 584,716 | (Fay) |
| J. S. Miller Powder Company | White Haven, Pa. | 18,686 | 6,550 | 16,860 | |
| Nuremberg Powder Company | Nuremberg, Pa. | 28,773 | 23,059 | 22,207 | |
| Pennsylvania Powder, Dynamite and Fuse Company | Brandonville, Pa. | 51,863 | 40,371 | 55,931 | |
| D. C. Rand Powder Company | Pittsford, N. Y. | 23,276 | 9,659 | 11,163 | |
| *Rand Powder Company | Fairchance, Pa. | 138,000 | None | None | |
| Rand Powder Company of Tennessee | Knoxville, Tenn. | 34,368 | 135,935 | 148,765 | (formed 1905) |
| *Roberts Powder Company | Shenandoah, Pa. | *57,500 | *51,175 | 66,846 | |
| Rockdale Powder Company | York, Pa. | 39,417 | 10,294 | 4,805 | |
| Senior Powder Company | Cincinnati, Ohio | 150,000 | 193,400 | 209,100 | (formed 1907) |
| Shamokin Powder Company | Shamokin, Pa. | 86,579 | 68,507 | 76,280 | |
| Standard Powder Company | Pittsburgh, Pa. | 136,337 | 119,243 | 2,045 | |
| *Tennessee Powder Company | Jellico, Tenn. | None | None | 48,875 | |
| United States Powder Company | Terre Haute, Ind. | 160,644 | 195,635 | 265,181 | (Rood) |

SOURCE: Adapted from Government's Exhibit No. 393 (March 17, 1909), Vol. V, pp. 2748–2749. *In the Circuit Court of the United States, For the District of Delaware No. 280 in Equity. The United States of America, Petitioner v. E. I. du Pont de Nemours and Company et al., Defendants.*

1 The figures in this table are given in kegs of 25 lbs. each.   2 Formed by Peabody Coal Company in 1903 and sold to Olin in 1907.   * Du Pont estimate plus 15%.

Table 4–2

Table Showing the Total Sale (as Reported Under Oath by Themselves) of *Salpeter Blasting Powder*[1] in the United States During the Calendar Years 1905 to 1907, Both Inclusive, by All Manufacturers of Same, Except E. I. du Pont de Nemours Powder Company and Companies of Which E. I. du Pont de Nemours Powder Company Owns or Controls All or a Majority of the Capital Stock.

| NAME | ADDRESS | 1905 | 1906 | 1907 |
|---|---|---|---|---|
| The American Powder Mills | Boston, Mass. | 20,462 | 31,218 | 17,344 (Fay) |
| Cressona Powder Company | Pottsville, Pa. | None | 3,969 | 4,891 |
| Giant Powder Company, Consolidated | San Francisco, Cal. | 380 | 446 | 200 |
| King Powder Company | Cincinnati, Ohio | 491 | 280 | 66 |
| Locust Mountain Powder and Dynamite Company | Mahanoy City, Pa. | None | None | 400 |
| Miami Powder Company | Xenia, Ohio | 2 | None | 46 |
| Pennsylvania Powder Dynamite and Fuse Company | Brandonville, Pa. | 1,691 | 1,100 | 1,538 |
| Rockdale Powder Company | York, Pa. | None | None | 70 |
| Black Diamond Powder Company | Mahanoy City, Pa. | None | 400 | None |

SOURCE: Adapted from Government's Exhibit No. 394 (March 17, 1909), Vol. V, p. 2750. *In the Circuit Court of the United States, For the District of Delaware No. 280 in Equity. The United States of America, Petitioner v. E. I. du Pont de Nemours and Company et al., Defendants* (1909).

[1] The figures in this table are given in kegs of 25 lbs. each.

# Table 4-3

Table Showing the Total Sale (as Reported Under Oath by Themselves) of *Dynamite and Substitutes Therefor*[1] in the United States During the Calendar Years 1905 to 1907, Both Inclusive, by All Manufacturers of Same, Except E. I. du Pont de Nemours Powder Company and Companies of Which E. I. du Pont de Nemours Powder Company Owns or Controls All or a Majority of the Capital Stock.

| NAME | ADDRESS | 1905 | 1906 | 1907 | |
|---|---|---|---|---|---|
| Aetna Powder Company | Chicago, Ill. | 9,039,114 | 12,838,922 | 12,008,776 | (Fay) |
| Ajax Dynamite Works | Bay City, Mich. | 360,000 | 410,000 | 425,000 | |
| Allentown Non-Freezing Powder Company | Allentown, Pa. | 55,500 | 670,275 | 569,527 | |
| American High Explosives Company | Pittsburgh, Pa. | None | None | 1,247,192 | (formed 1907) |
| The American Powder Mills | Boston, Mass. | 328,950 | 296,500 | 366,875 | (Fay) |
| *Anthony Powder Company, Limited | Ishpeming, Mich. | *943,000 | None | None | |
| Burton Powder Company | Pittsburgh, Pa. | 1,580,417 | 2,282,888 | 3,766,134 | (formed 1904) |
| Cerberite Powder Manufacturing Company | Kansas City, Mo. | 472,920 | 326,405 | None | |
| Connell Powder Company | Scranton, Pa. | None | 35,250 | 140,100 | |
| Eldred Powder Company | Olean, N. Y. | 112,700 | 80,900 | 65,600 | |
| Emporium Powder Manufacturing Company | Emporium, Pa. | 4,795,613 | 5,412,125 | 6,416,653 | (formed 1904) |
| *Explosives Manufacturing Company | Elmira, N. Y. | *92,000 | None | None[2] | |
| *The New Jersey Explosives Manufacturing Company | Bonhamton, N. J. | *172,500 | 69,000 | None | |
| Equitable Powder Manufacturing Company | East Alton, Ill. | 87,700 | 157,750 | 224,330 | (Olin) |
| Excelsior Powder Company | Kansas City, Mo. | 123,550 | 224,790 | 230,823 | |
| *General Explosives Company | Wharton, N. J. | 86,250 | 1,385,750 | 1,150,000 | |
| Giant Powder Company Consolidated | San Francisco, Cal. | 10,488,826 | 14,078,970 | 13,102,525 | |
| Great Western Powder Company | Toledo, Ohio. | 50,000 | 30,000 | None | |
| Hancock Chemical Company | Dollar Bay, Mich. | 1,961,000 | 1,803,450 | 1,838,300 | |
| Illinois Powder Manufacturing Company | St. Louis, Mo. | None | None | 32,425 | |
| Independent Powder Company of Missouri | Joplin, Mo. | 3,121,150 | 3,970,850 | 6,130,250 | (Rood) |
| Jefferson Powder Company | Birmingham, Ala. | None | 533,300 | 975,050 | |
| Keystone Powder Manufacturing Company | Emporium, Pa. | 6,632,250 | 6,976,875 | 8,254,500 | (Jones & Palmer, 1900) |
| King Powder Company | Cincinnati, Ohio | None | None | 5,500 | |
| G. R. McAbee Powder and Oil Company | Pittsburgh, Pa. | 3,090,900 | 1,195,750 | None | |
| Masurite Explosives Company | Sharon, Pa. | 581,275 | 650,540 | 834,835 | |
| Maury Powder Company | Seattle, Wash. | 2,000 | 60,800 | 2,750 | |
| Miami Powder Company | Xenia, Ohio | 68,375 | 61,725 | 148,300 | |
| J. S. Miller Powder Company | White Haven, Pa. | 18,686 | 26,800 | 15,600 | |
| Nitro Powder Company | Kingston, N. Y. | 1,127,195 | 435,840 | 624,032 | |
| Pacific High Explosives Company | Oakland, Cal | None | None | 35,350 | |
| Potts Powder Company | Reynolds, Pa. | None | None | 935,300 | |
| Rockdale Powder Company | York, Pa. | 999,475 | 827,650 | 631,575 | |
| Sinnamahoning Powder Manufacturing Company | Emporium, Pa. | None | 1,255,200 | 3,288,150 | (formed 1905) |
| *Texas Dynamite Company | Beaumont, Texas | None | 34,500 | 235,750 | |
| Trojan Powder Company | Pueblo, Colo. | None | None | 37,600 | |
| West Penn Dynamite Company | Pittsburgh, Pa. | None | None | 1,706,200 | (formed 1907) |

SOURCE: Adapted from Government's Exhibit No. 395 (March 17, 1909), Vol. V, pp. 2751–2752. *In the Circuit Court of the United States, For the District of Delaware No. 280 in Equity. The United States of America, Petitioner v. E. I. du Pont de Nemours and Company et al., Defendants.* [1] The figures in this table are given in **pounds**. [2] Removed to Bonhampton, N. J. 5/15/05. * Du Pont estimate plus 15%

Table 4–4

Table Showing the Total Sale (as Reported Under Oath by Themselves) of *Black Sporting Powder*[1] in the United States During the Calendar Years 1905 to 1907, Both Inclusive, by All Manufacturers of Same, Except E. I. du Pont de Nemours Powder Company and Companies of Which E. I. du Pont de Nemours Powder Company Owns or Controls All or a Majority of the Capital Stock.

| NAME | ADDRESS | 1905 | 1906 | 1907 | |
|---|---|---|---|---|---|
| Aetna Powder Company | Chicago, Ill. | | | | |
| The American Powder Mills | Boston, Mass. | 1,800,700 | 2,000,550 | 1,784,325 | (Fay) |
| Burton Powder Company | Pittsburgh, Pa. | 4,830 | 20,235 | 29,370 | |
| Equitable Powder Manufacturing Company | East Alton, Ill. | 236,137 | 330,475 | 263,000 | (Olin) |
| Giant Powder Company, Consolidated | San Francisco, Cal. | | | 19,424½ | |
| King Powder Company | Cincinnati, Ohio. | 539,100 | 459,075 | 382,025 | (King) |
| Miami Powder Company | Xenia, Ohio. | 108,670¼ | 80,166 | 69,164¾ | (Fay) |

SOURCE: Adapted from Government's Exhibit No. 396 (March 17, 1909), Vol. V, p. 2753. *In the Circuit Court of the United States, For the District of Delaware No. 280 in Equity. The United States of America, Petitioner v. E. I. du Pont de Nemours and Company et al., Defendants.*

[1] The figures in this table are given in pounds.
[2] Included in figures on table showing sale of smokeless sporting powder.
[3] Records showing sale during 1905 and 1906 destroyed by fire.

Table 4–5

Table Showing the Total Sale (as Reported Under Oath by Themselves) of *Smokeless Sporting Powder*[1] in the United States During the Calendar Years 1905 to 1907, Both Inclusive, by All Manufacturers of Same, Except E. I. du Pont de Nemours Powder Company and Companies of Which E. I. du Pont de Nemours Powder Company Owns or Controls All or a Majority of the Capital Stock.

| NAME | ADDRESS | 1905 | 1906 | 1907 | |
|---|---|---|---|---|---|
| Aetna Powder Company | Chicago, Ill. | 20,468¾ | 44,231¼ | 51,306¼ | (Fay) |
| The American Powder Mills | Boston, Mass. | None | 131,844 | 65,863 | (Fay) |
| Giant Powder Company, Consolidated | San Francisco, Cal. | | | 150[2] | |
| King Powder Company | Cincinnati, Ohio | 493,300 | 622,237½ | 580,087½ | |
| Miami Powder Company | Xenia, Ohio | 127 | 75¼ | 3,205 | (Fay) |

SOURCE: Adapted from Government's Exhibit No. 397 (March 17, 1909), Vol. V, p. 2754. *In the Circuit Court of the United States, For the District of Delaware No. 280 in Equity. The United States of America, Petitioner v. E. I. du Pont de Nemours and Company et al., Defendants.*

[1] The figures in this table are given in pounds.
[2] Records covering sale during 1905 and 1906 destroyed by fire.

relatively little experience in the powder business increasingly ran counter to those of the veteran explosives makers Haskell and Barksdale. The controversy smoldered until Coleman's return from California. Then the issue that triggered the debate concerned the continuance of existing trade agreements, and secretly and openly held subsidiaries and other arrangements used to maintain prices, to increase sales, or to meet local legal and tax needs. The question was whether, once the big company was completed, these arrangements should be completely abrogated or a few be permitted to continue.

From the start, Moxham, supported by Pierre, wanted to get rid of the many small companies and concentrate all the Powder Company's activities in a single legal and administrative entity. After conferences with the legal counsel, James M. Townsend, about the incorporation of the Powder Company in April 1903, both men became even more convinced of the value of operating through a single company and of eliminating subordinate firms and trade agreements. This was why Moxham wrote Coleman early in May that he and Pierre hoped, once the legal and financial consolidation was completed, "to turn it into an Operative Company pure and simple."[118] This was why, too, Moxham urged Coleman to let the Powder Company rely solely on the advantages of size in meeting competition.

The new Powder Company should have just two aims, Moxham had insisted in a letter to Coleman on June 18: "First: Stop buying outside concerns and completely organize those we control. Second: Concentrate our thought upon reduced cost of manufacture."[119] Clearly Coleman was not convinced, for in his last letter to the president in San Francisco, Moxham again stressed his point:

> As quickly as possible I want to urge upon everybody that we follow the policy of wiping out the enormous number of measly, little, one-horse companies, following upon the plan agreed upon, viz: consolidating everything . . . and turning the holding Company into an *operative* company. At all events, until you see me, do not discourage this line of thought for I think I can give you arguments that will almost force you to acquiesce in it.[120]

Coleman read these comments with interest, but gave little positive backing to Moxham's views.[121]

On his return the company's president heard arguments on both sides of the question; for, although Haskell and Barksdale had listened to Moxham and Pierre and the lawyers about the need for the elimination of the old legal agreements as well as complete legal and administrative consolidation, they remained unconvinced.[122] They accepted the general policy of simplification of the legal and financial organization, but they still saw no reason to drop the old ways completely. During the summer Haskell, as vice-president in charge of sales, had become increasingly concerned by the rash of new companies formed, like the Jellico Company, to compete for local mining business. He was particularly troubled by the efforts of Robert S. Waddell, the Du Pont sales manager who had left the previous winter to found the Buckeye Powder Company to sell in the Illinois coal fields (see Chapter 3, p. 73). In his monthly report to the Executive Committee, dated September 3, 1903, Haskell stressed "the absolute necessity of not ignoring" new competition.[123]

Growing competition increased Haskell's skepticism about the policies proposed by Moxham and strongly supported by Pierre. He was probably not too happy about Moxham's pronouncement in August 1903 that the company must not use subterfuge and underhanded methods in meeting competition. "No man in our employ will be asked to do for the company anything which, as a straightforward man, he would not do for himself individually," was the way Moxham defined the new policy.[124]

Nor was the head of the Sales Department convinced by Moxham's claim that the company had little to worry about competition from Waddell's new company. Nor did he accept the head of the Development Department's position that, once the consolidation was legally and administratively completed, the company need not trouble itself with small competitors. Many of these new companies, including Waddell's, were formed, Moxham maintained, because "the trade has been educated to the belief that there is no better investment than to 'sell to the Trust.' "[125] Moxham remained unconcerned by their potential effectiveness as economic competitors, but he was afraid that Waddell and others might exploit the inevitable "coming reaction" against the consolidation. One way to protect the company against this reaction, Moxham argued, was to end the old ways of competition.

After listening to the two points of view, Coleman called a special meeting of the Executive Committee on September 24 to consider what precisely should be done about existing trade agreements and the legal status of subordinate companies. After reviewing once again the different points of view, the president appointed a subcommittee made up of advocates of both positions—Moxham, Pierre, Haskell, and Barksdale. After the four had met and conferred with the lawyers, they decided, on October 20, that each member should submit his views in writing to James Townsend. The legal counsel would read the statements, report on the problems and proposals raised, and give his recommendations for action. The subcommittee also decided, undoubtedly at Haskell's suggestion, to have the views of still another lawyer, and so they asked an expert on corporation law, Edward Walker, of Winston, Payne and Strown of Chicago, to give a second report.

Townsend completed his report on December 1 and Walker's followed on the fourth. As Townsend stressed, there was more agreement than disagreement in the four statements.[126] All favored simplification of the legal structure of the Du Pont holdings. They further unanimously agreed to accomplish this by dissolving the subordinate companies as quickly as practicable. All realized that because of financial and legal complexities, this process would have to be effected with deliberation and care. The primary point of disagreement, Townsend pointed out, was essentially over the totality of the legal transformation, since "one member of the committee advises adopting an absolute policy, setting a fixed goal toward which every effort of simplification should be directed, while another says that we cannot fix a goal but must simplify and in the process find our goal."[127]

Haskell and Barksdale pointed to the many advantages to be gained by retaining a number of separate subordinate companies. Such advantages could, occasionally, be of more value than the simplification of legal structure. The most important benefit was in the competitive arena. There were still gains to be had from selling through companies using other names and other brands besides those of Du Pont. Moreover, the use of separate companies often avoided taxes placed on out-of-state, or "foreign," corporations. They could keep down the cost of liabilities for losses, which the constant threat of explosions made an important factor in the powder industry. Haskell further maintained that the use of separate companies might prevent the spread of labor unions, because in one big company a contract signed in one plant might have to be adopted in all. Finally, Haskell and Barksdale continued to resist giving up all existing trade agreements, if for no other reason than that these had "great money value," and that "it would be too great a financial effort to abrogate them."

In their reports Moxham and Pierre readily conceded these advantages, but insisted that the legal and moral dangers of continued use of separate companies and trade agreements far outweighed their benefits. Both Townsend and Walker emphatically supported their position. Both lawyers insisted that the existing arrangements had become "absolutely illegal," and that legal safety lay in abandoning the old ways and concentrating on building one big company. Walker particularly stressed that the Supreme Court, in its interpretations of the Sherman Antitrust Act, had opposed practices restricting production. On the other hand, Walker continued, "the restrictions placed by common law and by the laws of the federal and state governments on large aggregations of capital are not intended to prevent legitimate expansion of business, however large." The Chicago lawyer pointed to the E. C. Knight case of 1895 in which the Court found the American Sugar Company not guilty, even though it controlled 90% of the sugar production in the United States, because it had "no intermediate selling company or corporation and no exclusive sales contracts." Then in the Addyston Pipe and Steel case of 1899 the Court dissolved the contract among six companies that set up exclusive marketing areas for each of the six firms.[128] Moreover, Walker was certain that in the Northern Securities case then pending before the Supreme Court, the use of a holding company to restrain production or control competition would be declared illegal. "I would avoid," he concluded, "all 'entangling alliances' or contracts, but stand simply on the legality of your incorporation and the management and conduct of its corporate business."

The advice Walker and Townsend gave must have been fairly representative of that which corporation lawyers were serving to their clients. If so, the Supreme Court's interpretation of the Sherman Antitrust Act must certainly have encouraged the shift from the old cartel to the new consolidated, centrally managed enterprises in industries other than explosives. Obviously, if the alternative offered by antitrust legislation was either to split up a cartel into its constituent parts or to consolidate them into a single centrally administered unit, most American businessmen would have preferred the second choice. But without the passage of the Sherman Act the choice would not have been forced. Many industrialists might have been content to continue on with their cartels and associations, as was certainly the case in the European nations, where no legislation similar to the Sherman Act existed.

Townsend answered, in more detail than Walker, the arguments favoring the retention of separate companies. State taxes on "foreign" corporations were relatively low as compared to the size of business of the big company, and they were usually only on the corporation's real property in that state (as would be the case for any local corporation), or on the capital stock invested in the state. Should new taxes be imposed or old ones increased, he believed that they "might be successfully resisted."[129] There was, in fact, a positive advantage to being a foreign corporation, for if suits arose, the cases would be tried in a federal rather than in a state court, where local interests and bias might prejudice the company's position.

The attorneys saw little value in having separate companies either as protection from liability for accidents and explosions or as competitive weapons. Once a "unity of interest" had been established between the parent and the subsidiary—and this was relatively easy to prove—all legal units concerned would be liable for the actions of others. "The courts," Townsend stressed, "show a very real tendency to go beyond these formal organizations and to look for real parties and interests." For example, Barksdale had asked Townsend if Company A was solely a holding company controlling Company B and C; if Company B was an operating company "selling its wares but having no trade agreements"; and if Company C carried on no business of any kind and merely held trade agreements, would the officers of Company B be liable for the activities of Company C?[130] In Townsend's opinion the courts would indeed hold that they were.

"From a lawyer's point of view," Townsend wrote in much the same vein as Walker had written in his supplementary statement,

> I cannot too strongly emphasize my opinion that the day is past when evasion will be found useful through stockholders' evading liabilities by doing business through other agencies, pretending actual competition by artificial competition, suppressing competition by quota contracts; and all other evasions are perfectly susceptible to exposure and I believe that the aggregation of capital which is found to be pursuing those methods will fare much more harshly at the hands of the court than the corporation openly avowing its purpose to extend business by legitimate means.[131]

The lawyer then added: "I could wish these properties had been openly and gradually acquired by one old and established interest."

Possibly anticipating a potential line of defense should these acquisitions be questioned, Townsend continued: "But the explanation lies in the fact that these properties were acquired in legitimate expansion of the business and that you had hitherto chosen to hold them through stock ownership." In fact, Moxham had succinctly put the basic legal line of defense for the new consolidation six months before Townsend and Walker presented their reports. "First," Moxham wrote, "that we have nothing to offer the public [i.e., no public issue of securities]; secondly, that the control has been consolidated *de facto* long before the earliest antitrust laws; and third, because of the other two, the sole object of consolidation was economy of operation."[132] Both lawyers repeatedly stressed that the company had one "great strategic advantage . . . you are an old and honorable business interest with a century of intrinsically legitimate expansion behind you. This would on general principles appeal to and be fostered by the courts, and such interests they will endeavor to protect."[133]

Moxham presented arguments other than legal ones for eliminating the separate sales companies and the trade agreements. He repeated to the subcommittee and to the Executive Committee what he had said earlier to Coleman. These practices were immoral as well as illegal. Even worse, they were bad business. For, he maintained, it was as hard in the long run to deceive the customers as it was the courts. "The advocates of selling companies for the purposes of competition must admit that the arguments in its favor are based on deluding the customer."[134] The existing evidence "at least throws grave doubts upon the extent to which the customer *has been fooled.*" Even if he was, the cost of such deception was prohibitively high. If discovered, it damaged, wrote Moxham, "what is known as good will," which businessmen "recognized as an asset worth sometimes as much as the whole investment capital in the old and well established concerns."

Still more serious, deception demoralized the employees. "To successfully fool the customers somebody has got to do the fooling. . . . Therefore, for this plan to be successful we must have a whole staff of salesmen educated on unhealthy lines. . . . Trickiness must be placed at a premium." So the company "educates a class of men whose loyalty we cannot count on, for trickiness and deceit are as universal in their application as honesty and frankness." Thus, the company is forced to rate its men on their "demerits" rather than on their merits. Moreover, such practices place the company "under obligation" to their employees, and so it loses "that absolute control over the situation without which we cannot expect to handle our men to the best advantage, nor obtain the most economical results." Finally, the Development Department's chief argued that the possible gain from all these dubious methods was minimal. At best the business acquired was 5% of the lowest priced, least profitable part of the trade, barely totaling $100,000 a year. The action of a disloyal employee could easily cost the company more than that sum of money.[135]

Nor in Moxham's opinion were separate manufacturing companies any more valuable than separate selling ones. He disagreed with Haskell that "unionism in one plant would necessitate unionism in the others." In the steel industry, he noted, many companies had both unionized and nonunionized plants. Even in a single works, often one department had its union and another an open shop. Moreover, wages in that industry depended on regional differences just as they did in the powder business.

After their reports had been reviewed, the subcommittee debated the issues on December 23, again on Christmas Eve, and still again on the thirtieth. In these debates Pierre listened again to the arguments of Moxham and Haskell and added new ones of his own. As treasurer he had strong practical reasons for achieving a swift and complete legal and financial simplification. During most of the fall he had been "snowed under" by the accounting work required in taking over the many new companies. As he wrote in his October report to the Executive Committee, the Accounting Department had to make up and consolidate thirty separate balance sheets for just the dynamite companies coming into the consolidation. "This statement alone should be sufficient to warrant rapid and thorough reorganization. At present we are expending a great deal of valuable energy and time on mechanical work of accounting. This work is so complex that it is necessary to take the time of our best men in order to get approximate accuracy."[136]

When, after all this debate, Haskell and Barksdale would not fully come over to Pierre and Moxham's position, Pierre decided to break the deadlock by agreeing to sign a report with Haskell and Barksdale in which all the debated issues were to be presented to the Executive Committee, "asking its careful consideration of the same."[137] Moxham was then to write a minority report spelling out his position and Pierre's. Actually Haskell and Barksdale had come a long way. They agreed that the general policy was to turn the big company into a single legal, financial, and administrative unit as soon as practical and to eliminate all existing agreements "as soon as consistent with good faith." The difference remained only over the possibility of making a few special exceptions to the general rule. Moxham wanted none; Haskell wanted to be able to make them if really necessary. Interestingly enough all seem to have agreed that the European Agreement on foreign markets should stand as a valid exception to the general policy. Neither Moxham nor Pierre appeared to question its value or legality.

At the Executive Committee meeting held on January 13, 1904, to act on the subcommittee's report, Pierre stood solidly with Moxham. The top committee had no trouble in quickly approving the basic agreement that the final report recommended. Subsidiary companies were to be ended as soon as practical, but such terminations were "to be undertaken on conservative lines and carefully worked out." All members agreed that the parent company should carry on manufacturing and sales and that all agreements be terminated as soon as possible. But, on permitting exceptions to the general rule, the Executive Committee, like the subcommittee, split right down the middle.[138] Francis I. supported Moxham and Pierre, while Coleman threw his critical vote the other way. Since Alfred was absent, the other six members agreed to hold off decision until he returned. At the meeting of January 21, Alfred voted with Haskell, Barksdale, and unquestionably Coleman.[139] Although the final vote permitted exceptions, Moxham and Pierre secured a statement that they would be allowed only after a full and careful discussion on each individual case by the Executive Committee. For practical purposes Pierre and Moxham thought they had achieved their goal.

The completion of the consolidation followed closely the policies set in January 1904. By April Pierre was able to present a detailed and analytical report to the board of directors describing the nearly completed transaction.[140] There were some hitches and delays. The final acceptance of appraisals and ratios of stock often had to await the approval of an important stockholder or the ratification at an annual or special meeting of shareholders. For a time Pierre and Coleman were worried that Pillsbury might block the exchange of C.P.W. stock; but at its annual meeting in April the terms of the exchange were accepted without dissent.[141] However, certain legal requirements forced the Executive Committee to agree to delay its final dissolution. The wind-up of the Vigorite Company was also delayed when one stockholder threatened legal action because he thought he had been promised a place on the Powder Company's board. Then, as value of preferred dropped in 1905, a few stockholders who had not completed the exchange refused to do so, asking to receive bonds rather than preferred stock.[142] An even more serious delay occurred in connection with the exchange of securities of the holding companies that had been used in the purchase of the Laflin & Rand Powder Company.[143] Stockholders of Laflin

& Rand who had received securities of Delaware Securities and Delaware Investment unexpectedly refused to exchange the bonds of those two holding companies for preferred stock of the Powder Company. The deadlock was not broken until early in 1906 when Pierre and Moxham devised a plan by which the Powder Company would issue bonds that could be used for the exchange. Given the legal obstacles inherent in the dissolution of many and often long-lived corporations, there were surprisingly few cases in which the completion of the exchange was not followed by the legal ending of the merged company.[144]

In these same months the Powder Company dropped nearly all its agreements. On March 30, 1904, Haskell formally notified Greene, the secretary of the Gunpowder Trade Association, of the withdrawal of Du Pont, Hazard, Laflin & Rand, Oriental, Marcellus, Lake Superior, Phoenix, and Birmingham from the association.[145] By July, Ohio, Chattanooga, and others who had joined the consolidation also withdrew. With these departures the association became, for all practical purposes, defunct. Its Advisory and Special committees no longer met to decide prices or to enforce these decisions. In the same month Haskell and Barksdale, on a visit to San Francisco, canceled the trade agreements on the Pacific Coast and the Neutral Belt. Only the existing "Mexican Agreement," which was a part of the larger treaty with the European companies, remained intact.[146]

By summer the Powder Company had dropped its sales companies and placed their offices under its new enlarged Sales Department. Haskell did, however, permit the continuance of the Explosives Supply Company, Anthony Powder Company, and Enterprise High Explosives Company.[147] But only Enterprise was continued for any length of time. Its owner, Elmer Brode, had sold the small company in Pennsylvania to Eastern Dynamite in 1897 on the condition that he would "preserve secrecy of ownership" and represent Enterprise as an independent firm.[148] Brode now insisted that if the truth came out, his reputation would suffer and his marketing agency would lose business. As Haskell was anxious to avoid a fight at this time, he apparently agreed informally to permit Brode to continue as he had been operating in the past.

Thus the wind-up of the subsidiary companies was not as complete as Pierre, Moxham, and the lawyers would have liked. The holders of Delaware Securities and Delaware Investment who refused to exchange their bonds from preferred stock of the Powder Company also opposed the final closing out of Laflin & Rand. This resistance to total merger among the Laflin & Rand stockholders delayed the dissolving of the Eastern Dynamite Company. Gibbs and the other stockholders of International Smokeless Powder and Chemical Company were also able to keep postponing the merger of that firm into the Powder Company. Nor would the King brothers and Peters let the Powder Company break the 1901 contract to take their blasting powder, although the du Ponts did dissolve the King selling company. And, of course, the European and Mexican Agreements with foreign companies remained.

Although more than sixty companies had been dissolved, and although these exceptions were wholly legal vestiges with no effect on the administrative reorganization of the properties under their control, their continuing existence did give significance to Coleman's decision to support Haskell and Barksdale in the debate over permitting exceptions to the rule of eliminating subordinate companies and trade agreements. If Pierre and Moxham had had their way, the Du Pont Company might have been less vulnerable in the antitrust suit that was brought against it by the Justice Department at the instigation of Robert S. Waddell in July 1907. The defense in that case depended largely on proving that the Du Pont Company had in actual fact given up the old methods of competition. If the Executive Committee had supported Moxham and Pierre, its minutes could have been used as evidence of an explicit shift in policy that permitted no exceptions. It might then have been more convincing to point out that the delay in winding up Laflin & Rand, Eastern Dynamite, and the California companies resulted in the normal problems involved in meeting complex legal requirements and the wishes of a few minority stockholders. If the Executive Committee had passed such a resolution, it might also have encouraged its members to push harder on the reluctant stockholders in the California companies and International; to come to terms sooner with the old Laflin & Rand stockholders to exchange bonds for Powder Company preferred stock; and to terminate the King contract and the arrangement with Brode. For the existence of these vestiges of the old ways was to prove embarrassing to the new Powder Company when, as Moxham had anticipated, the reaction to the consolidation appeared.

In the two years following March 1902, Pierre and his mentors, Coleman du Pont and Arthur Moxham, had transformed the American explosives industry. In 1902 they had consolidated the industry's two largest operating companies (both primarily makers of black powder) and its largest holding company (Eastern Dynamite, which controlled well over half of the dynamite production in the United States) into a modern, centrally administered corporation with its own operating, sales, and auxiliary departments. Then, beginning in March 1903, they used the new company as a base for completing the reorganization of the industry. At first, they and their associates on the new Executive Committee considered the all-embracing "Big Company" as a device to assure tighter legal control over the industry's prices and output. But almost immediately Pierre and Moxham decided that administrative control should follow legal control. They would make what was still a cartel into a single consolidated corporation.

By early summer they modified these objectives. They agreed that they did not need to bring all the major powder makers into the consolidation, but could achieve their goals by controlling 60% to 70% of the output. Through careful reorganization and rationalization of their properties, they expected to lower the unit costs of production and distribution of explosives. Such reduced costs meant that they could undersell small competitors, old or new, who could not get the same advantage of volume production and distribution. In fact, as Moxham had stressed, such small competitors, who could provide the marginal output the national market required, were a positive advantage.[149]

It is difficult to evaluate the effect of existing antitrust legislation on their plans. The written record does not indicate for certain whether Pierre and Moxham consulted the New York lawyers before or after they had decided to transform the holding company into an operating one. In any case, advice they did receive confirmed the value of what they had done in the consolidation of Du Pont, Laflin & Rand, and Eastern Dynamite, and the legal advantages of applying this same scheme to the industry as a whole. Undeniably, in this case, and surely in many others, the existence of the antitrust laws encouraged the transformation of an association of small family firms into a great national, centrally managed economic enterprise.

In engineering these sweeping changes, Pierre, Moxham, and Coleman were able to fulfill the conditions they had set when they began the undertaking. The "Big Company" was created at very little cash cost; minority stockholders were not able to delay its completion (although they delayed the legal "winding up" of the constituent companies); and, above all, the E. I. du Pont de Nemours & Company controlled the new Powder Company. So the transformation from a cartel of many family firms into a single giant corporation had also resulted in the dominance of a single family in the industry. In very few of the comparable combinations and consolidations that were being carried on in American industries in these same years did one family emerge with such solid control as the du Pont family did in the explosives business. A great many of the consolidations of the period were carried out by investment bankers. Once completed, the investment house, such as J. P. Morgan or Kuhn, Loeb, had as much to say on the boards of the new enterprises as did any one family group. In these companies, as in the large railroads even earlier, executives holding little stock soon came to run the enterprise. At Du Pont, on the other hand, three stockholders controlled the holding company that controlled the operating company that operated more than two-thirds of the industry. There the three owners continued to manage, and three senior managers continued to own.

As Pierre, Coleman, Alfred, and their associates on the new Executive Committee were putting together the "Big Company," they fully realized that the long-run success of their creation depended on building an effective organization for its management and on paying constant attention to its administration. In carrying out these tasks Pierre was to play an even more important role than he had had in carrying out the consolidation. In managing the Powder Company, Pierre came full into his own. During its formation he had continued to look on Coleman and Moxham as his teachers. But as he built and managed his own department and became increasingly involved in running the company itself, Pierre relied much less on his mentors. The completion of the "Big Company" marked the completion of Pierre's years of preparation.

PART II

MANAGING THE POWDER COMPANY

# The Treasurer

I N 1904 PIERRE DU PONT turned from the challenge of creating to that of governing a modern industrial empire. For the next fifteen years he, more than Coleman or any other executive, would be the person most responsible for determining the current health and continuing growth of the new Powder Company. Not only did Pierre play a decisive role in building one of the largest explosives, and what was to become the largest chemical, company in the United States, but it was on the experience of these years that he drew when in 1920 he was called on to reorganize the General Motors Corporation. Because of his experiences at Du Pont he was able to transform that financially shaky, poorly administered enterprise into the largest and one of the most profitable manufacturing companies in the world.

Pierre's career at the Du Pont Company provides a study in the formulation and execution of corporate policy. It also reveals his changing relationships with the men with whom he worked most closely in the defining and carrying out of business policy. As a senior executive of the new consolidated enterprise his duties were twofold. First, as treasurer, he was responsible for organizing and setting policies for his own department. Here he had to create for the first time in the explosives industry many of the techniques of modern management. From the start Pierre looked upon his office as the one to provide the information necessary to evaluate, appraise, and plan the company's business. Accurate data on all aspects of costs and income had to be developed. At the same time he had to be certain that his subordinates were handling properly, efficiently, and honestly the myriad complex financial transactions carried on by the company in all parts of the country and, in fact, throughout the world.

Even more significant was the part Pierre played in determining the basic policies needed to maintain and expand the Powder Company as a profit-making institution. His powerful influence in the formulation of many of these policies grew directly from his functions as treasurer. He was the executive who had to give the most attention to obtaining and allocating funds. So it was he who worked out plans to assure a continuing flow of working capital to pay for the supplies and labor needed to transform raw and semifinished materials into finished products. He also had to make sure that the company met its obligations and paid off its short-term notes as well as the interest on any bonds, and its dividends on the preferred stock. These concerns meant, in turn, that he had to take a key part in determining one of the most critical of business policies: that of deciding how much should be paid in dividends and how much should be put back into the business. Finally, as treasurer of the company, Pierre had to decide how best to raise new capital if plowed-back earnings were not enough to expand the business.

Even though Pierre usually initiated plans about financial policies, he shared their final formulation with his colleagues on the Executive Committee. In their decisions the committee members had to consider the wide variety of events and information that affected action, including the short- and long-term changes in demand for the company's different products, shifts in uses for explosives, developments in the technology of production, and the opening of new sources of supply. The continuing discussion over the formulation of financial policies vitally affected Pierre's personal relationships with Coleman, Alfred, Haskell, Barksdale, John Raskob, Russell Dunham, and other colleagues as well as with members of the larger du Pont family who were not directly involved with the management of the company.

Of these personal relationships the most important was the one with Coleman. When he and Coleman took the lead in putting together the new company and the still larger Powder Company, Pierre always considered himself the junior man. Not yet confident of his own ability he deferred to his older cousin. But, although he admired Coleman, Pierre never imitated him. After a somewhat nervous and uncertain start, Pierre, as treasurer, developed an increasingly firm grasp on the management of the Powder Company. At the same time Coleman's attention began to turn to the possibilities of more novel and exciting projects. Within five years after the completion of the consolidation Pierre, rather than Coleman, was the Powder Company's acknowledged chief.

In managing the Powder Company Pierre faced the inevitable problems involved in the transformation of a small family partnership into a large national business enterprise. This was indeed the beginning of the metamorphosis of a cartel or association into a giant corporation. The change meant more than just introducing new methods and business techniques. It meant defining and developing a new attitude toward the relations of family to firm. In bringing in new methods Pierre and his colleagues could draw on the experience of the steel and traction industries and to some extent on that of the Repauno Chemical Company. The definition of the relationship between the family and firm was in some ways more difficult.

Pierre never doubted that if the company was to be a successful profit-making enterprise, the impersonal test of return on investment must be the criterion of performance. Family loyalties and idiosyncrasies must give way to efficiency and system. A man must be placed and promoted first because of business and technical competence. He had to prove himself to be a capable professional manager. Only after ability had been demonstrated should family connections play a part. Then they could be important. For Pierre the firm no longer had the obligation to provide the family with jobs. Instead it should assure them of larger dividends. Of course, as the firm expanded, potential employment for younger relatives would be realized.

The family was not to be forgotten but rather to play a different role. To Pierre, continuing family control of the company was as important as competent professional management. Its members remained the major stockholders. Of even more importance, the du Pont group was the most certain source of capital if the market should grow and the company should need money for expansion; or if it should decline and the company should require funds to carry it through an emergency. Because of the family backing, Pierre, Coleman, and Alfred had been able to create a modern corporation without sacrificing personal control. The surest way of continuing this control was to keep the family behind the firm.

Family loyalties and traditions were as meaningful to Pierre as monetary and managerial considerations. As he became the real head of the firm, he came to act more as the head of the family. He was always more sensitive to the feelings and prejudices of the many different members of the family than was either Coleman or Alfred. He tried, more than they ever did, to keep the branches of the clan that were not in the actual management of the company involved with or at least fully informed of its affairs. He worked harder than any du Pont of his generation to keep the clan together and to soften the inevitable family frictions and disputes. For more than a decade his efforts were successful. But ultimately even Pierre was unable to prevent a disastrous family split—a split that was basically caused by the new relationship between the family and the firm.

## The Executive Committee

From early 1903 on, Pierre carried the dual responsibilities involved in the management of the new enterprise in two different formal capacities. According to the plan of management adopted in February 1903, each senior executive, except for the president, was a department head responsible for the organization and operation of a single functional activity. As a member of the Executive Committee, each department head was also expected to take part in defining the plans and policies of the total company. In the first months of the Powder Company's existence Pierre learned more about this second of the two roles, since he was, during Coleman's absence, the committee's first chairman. Later in the year he finally had a chance to concentrate his attention on creating his own treasurer's office. Only after his department was manned and working efficiently did Pierre find time to initiate basic financial policies for the company as a whole.

Under Pierre's guidance the Executive Committee quickly took hold. As Moxham reported to Coleman in distant California, when forwarding him copies of the committee's minutes: "I think you will find that they speak well for the earnest effort to introduce system and a general plan into what we are doing, particularly a proper control of finances."[1] The greatest difficulty was, as Moxham pointed out, to keep the committee's attention on broad over-all policy. "We have to learn to leave details to Heads of Departments instead of trying to make them subjects of executive action, and leave to the Executive Committee only the big questions," Moxham commented early in May.[2] "I think we are improving upon this at each meeting." Three weeks later he reported continued progress. Haskell tended to be overconcerned with details but was working hard and loyally, as was Barksdale. "Even Alfred, finding that no one objects to safety valves going off, seems to be feeling better as to the general situation all the time and looking at it from a broader point of view."[3]

Six weeks later, however, Moxham was less optimistic. Old ways were proving hard to change. "In the main Haskell has been perhaps the greatest disturbing element," he told Coleman, "his past method having been to attend to very minute matters to such an extent that practically no one under him was a free agent. He professes not to believe this, but nevertheless it is true."[4] Barksdale, Haskell's "First Lieutenant," was much the same. "To the extent that this is now done on the part of both of them, it is not with intent but from force of old habit, and it will be some time before the two of them get straightened out." On the other hand, Francis I. du Pont was increasing his grasp of administrative matters, although he was reluctant to carry his duties to other plants besides that at Carney's Point. "It is going to pay to push Francis on."[5] "Alfred," Moxham continued, "as far as organization is concerned is in no way a disturbing element, but in every way an aid." As for Pierre, Moxham had only the highest praise for his work on the committee as well as for his work on the consolidation. "Pierre has been 'the man behind the gun' doing his own work and making good, wherever possible, the deficiencies of the others."[6]

When Coleman returned in August, the committee was already working fairly harmoniously along the same lines it would follow for many years. The president took over the reins of management from his younger cousin as quickly and surely as he had engaged himself in completing the consolidation. Pierre turned over the chair at the Executive Committee meetings with relief. He was sure his cousin could handle the job more effectively than he; and in the late summer and fall of 1903 the younger man had more than he could do in completing the financial details of the consolidation and in fashioning a treasurer's office to carry on the financial activities of the new Powder Company. Even so he remained, second only to Coleman, the most influential man on the Executive Committee and, therefore, in the over-all administration of the company.

Strong and dynamic as he was, Coleman never usurped or bypassed that instrument of group management—the Executive Committee. That group, rather than the Finance Committee or the board of directors, made the decisions that counted. However, Pierre, more than Coleman, saw the value of using the other two formal governing bodies as places to tie the family to the company. Pierre proposed the formation of a Finance Committee to include himself, Coleman, and Alfred as a way of assuring Alfred of his place at the top.[7] Once Alfred seemed satisfied with the way the affairs of the big company were going, Pierre saw to it that the Finance Committee became formally a subcommittee of the Executive Committee.[8] Because Coleman and Pierre did not bring Olin, Lent, and the Fays into the Powder Company, they did not need the board to give these outside interests representation as Pierre originally had planned. The only representative of such interests to become a director was Frank Connable, who had been president of the Chattanooga Company, and he did so only after becoming an active member of the Powder Company's management.[9]

Pierre and Coleman, therefore, consciously decided to use the board as a way to bring into the company the members of the family who were not directly involved in its day-to-day management. In addition to the former partners who had sold out in 1902—Colonel Henry, Cousins Frank and Alexis—Pierre and Coleman arranged to have Eugene's oldest son and one of Pierre's favorite relatives, young Alexis I. (Lex), become a director. Victor, the brother of Charles I. (who had died in 1902), also took a directorship shortly after Charles's death. To bring these representatives of different branches of the family still closer to the company, Pierre and Coleman gave each nominal jobs, Lex as the company's secretary and assistant treasurer and Victor as the head of the Real Estate Department. In these tasks both worked directly under Pierre. On the death of two of the elder generation, Francis G. and his brother Alexis I., in 1904, Henry F. du Pont, Colonel Henry's only son, and Pierre's brother Irénée took their places on the Powder Company's board. The next year Eugene E., old Alexis I.'s son, became a member.[10]

On the other hand, Pierre had to use his most tactful and diplomatic persuasion to convince William du Pont, Colonel Henry's brother, first to go along with the consolidation and then not to ask for a seat on the board.[11] William had left Wilmington in 1892 to take up the life of a Virginia country gentleman after divorcing his first cousin, May du Pont (one of Charles and Victor's sisters), and marrying Annie Rogers Zinn, a lively divorcée from nearby New Castle. William and his brother Henry, who still considered himself as the head of the family, had not spoken to each other since the succession crisis of 1889. With the divorce, other du Ponts followed Henry's example. Pierre, however, remained on good terms with William and was careful to keep him informed of the important activities and developments in the Powder Company. His regular letters to William became, in fact, one of the most valuable sources for the company's history.

The members of the Powder Company board who were not on the Executive Committee considered themselves as the spokesmen for the several branches of the family rather than as policy makers. They were willing to be little more than ratifiers of the committee's actions. Sometimes, if the Executive Committee was unable to agree, and particularly if the disagreement came over large sums of money, it took the matter to the board. Yet such occasions were rare. No one connected with the Powder Company ever doubted for a minute that the Executive Committee ran the show. Its seven members considered themselves, and were considered by others, as the company's top management.

During the first years of its existence the committee remained relatively unchanged. Alfred and Barksdale continued to represent the Black Powder and High Explosives Operating Departments; Haskell, Sales; Pierre, the Treasurer's Department; and Moxham, Development. Francis I. stayed on the committee until the end of 1904, but took only a passive part in its deliberations after he became head of the new Experimental Station in December 1903. Coleman then put a brother-in-law, Henry F. Baldwin, in Francis's place as the head of the Smokeless Powder Operating Department.[12] Baldwin, an experienced professional railroad executive, had enjoyed a successful career, first on small New England roads and then as chief engineer of the Chicago & Alton and finally of the Erie Railroad.

All the members of the Executive Committee were young, but nevertheless experienced industrialists. All but Alfred had worked in businesses other than explosives. In fact, three of the seven members, Coleman, Moxham, and Baldwin, had had no previous experience in the powder industry. Coleman had been engaged in coal mining before he joined Moxham in steel and traction; Haskell, like Coleman, had mining experience; Haskell, Barksdale, and Baldwin had all been railroad executives; while Pierre, despite his young age, combined a detailed technical knowledge of explosives with a broad business training acquired from his brief acquaintance with two of the most progressive industries of the day, steel and traction. Because of this outside experience, the practices and procedures the Du Pont Executive Committee devised for the administration of its new enterprise probably owed more to the experience of railroads, steel, and traction businesses than to that of the explosives industry.

Broad training in similar areas undoubtedly helped the members of the committee to work together. Perhaps a similarity in age and education further aided a common approach and outlook. So too did family ties and loyalty. The managing board of the new enterprise included, besides the three du Ponts who had formed the new company, two du Pont in-laws. Only Moxham and Haskell had no connection with the family. Except for the older Moxham and the younger Pierre, the others on the Executive Committee were, in 1904, all between forty and forty-three years of age. Pierre was only thirty-four while Moxham, in many ways the wisest of them all in the ways of corporate management, was fifty. (The older man, incidentally, was the only one on the Executive Committee to whom Pierre used the title Mr. rather than a first name.) All but two of the committee members had formal engineering training. Baldwin, as well as the three du Ponts, had attended the Massachusetts Institute of Technology. Barksdale had taken the civil engineering course at the University of Virginia. Only Moxham and Haskell were not college men. And Moxham was a self-trained engineer who had helped to invent and develop a new type of steel rail. Rigorous engineering training in college as well as the engineering experience involved in their early business careers undoubtedly help account for the rational systematic approach that the members of the Executive Committee took toward the management of their enterprise.

Pierre and his associates on the committee differed more in looks and temperament than they did in business outlook and training. His two cousins were as tall as he. All three were over six feet. All three had the prominent du Pont nose and high forehead and all were beginning to show signs of baldness. The three made quite a contrast to the small, dapper, urbane Barksdale, the expansive, jovial, graying Haskell, and the short, stocky Moxham, whose crick in his neck and slight facial twitch gave him a bulldog appearance.

The personalities of the members of the Executive Committee were in even greater contrast. Coleman exuded energy, ability, optimism, and confidence. Armed with a fund of amusing, often ribald, stories, he used his quick wit and ready mind to dominate any activity, social or business, in which he entered. Yet, as his first year in the company indicated, there were physical weaknesses behind this rugged exterior. From 1903 on, Coleman du Pont became increasingly subjected to sharp, severe, and often prolonged and exceedingly painful illnesses. In the summer and fall of 1905 he was, for example, closed up in a dark room with his eyesight impaired, unable to read and able to see people only occasionally. Precisely what the trouble was the doctors of that day could not decide. As it appears to have been largely intestinal involving pancreatitis or ulcers as well as gallstones, it probably had psychological as well as physiological causes.

Temperamental and high-strung, Alfred wore his strong feelings on his sleeve. He reacted quickly and often incautiously in both business and social situations. Having more than his usual share of the du Pont stubbornness, he found it difficult to move back from a position once taken. Although he was devoted to the family business, that business continued to mean for him the production of black powder in the Brandywine Mills. He cared little for the complexities of financial and legal arrangements or for the niceties of business diplomacy. He had not been involved in the negotiations for the purchase of Laflin & Rand and he had little to do with the formation of the consolidated company. Moxham's letters to Coleman in the spring of 1904, in fact, suggest that Alfred was skeptical about these moves. He seems to have shared the distrust of his older cousins for the broad and sweeping plans to reorganize the family firm and the explosives industry. Nor was Alfred happy spending his time reviewing detailed reports and statistics— a task that took so much of the energy of the men on the Executive Committee. So even before Alfred lost an eye in a hunting accident in November 1904, he had the poorest attendance of any at the meetings of the Executive Committee.

Moxham, who had had less formal education than any one else on the committee, was certainly the most analytical and innovative thinker and the most literate writer of the group. Much more of a reader than his colleagues, he was the only member to show an awareness of the broader social, political, and economic changes that the nation was then undergoing. He had a passion for accurate data, careful analysis, system and order. He had imagination, too, seeking new methods and ways to meet old problems and new challenges. Yet he was more a man of ideas than action. Pierre remembered him half a century later as a man who "could prepare the most wonderful recommendations but would never carry them out."[13] Nevertheless, Moxham, more than any other single individual, was responsible for applying modern business practices and procedures to the Du Pont Company and to the American explosives industry.

In the first year or so, Pierre often found himself standing with Moxham against Haskell and Barksdale. Haskell's attitude and opinions and even personality were closest to the stereotype of the men of large business interests at the turn of the century. He kept in close contact with his subordinates, nearly all of whom respected and admired him. He enjoyed the rough-and-tumble of the old-time competition in the powder industry and was more concerned, or at least said more, than the others about the dangers of organized labor and the threat of government intervention. His close companion, Barksdale, was, however, much more of a spokesman for the new ways. Even more than Pierre and Moxham, Barksdale worshiped system and order. More than any other Du Pont executive, he preached and practiced modern "scientific" plant management.[14] Yet he seems to have lacked Pierre's and even Haskell's sensitivity to other people's concerns. For Barksdale, system came first. People could be easily fitted into organizational slots. For Pierre, who learned from Coleman and Moxham, the slots should be adjusted to meet individual temperaments and talents.

The correspondence and reports of these years reveal much less about the personality of the seventh member of the committee, Henry F. Baldwin, than they do about the others. Baldwin took full responsibility for smokeless powder operations and appears to have been a competent enough head of that department from January 1904 until the spring of 1907. The success may have depended in part on the talents of Harry Fletcher Brown, who came into the company with International Smokeless Powder and Chemical Company. In 1907 Brown became the *de facto* head of the department after Baldwin resigned to become chief engineer of the new Portland Tacoma Railroad, the Pacific coast outlet for the Harriman system. Brown, however, did not become a vice-president and a member of the Executive Committee until 1914. Instead, Haskell became the vice-president in charge of that department. As a result of the shift in Smokeless Powder, Patterson took Haskell's place as head of the Sales Department with William Coyne, an executive with long experience in the iron and steel industry, moving into Patterson's office as Director of Sales.

From the start Pierre was the catalyst that kept this group of seven men functioning smoothly. He had the authority that came from being a member of the larger family and one of the three cousins who had created the present company. Far more than Alfred, and even more than Coleman, he enjoyed meeting and solving complex legal and financial problems and reading and writing business reports. This commitment, and the fact that his duties took him out of town less than his colleagues, meant that of all the members his attendance record at committee meetings was the best. So he kept in closer touch with the issues and programs as they developed from meeting to meeting and understood better the nuances of the arguments of the different members of the committee on these matters. Moreover, his position as treasurer gave him a fuller, more precise picture of all the company's activities and its over-all situation than had anyone, except possibly Coleman, the president.

Pierre's influence on the Executive Committee differed from Coleman's. He relied less on personal charm and persuasion and more on detailed knowledge. His clear, penetrating, and occasionally even imaginative mind, his retiring and instinctively cautious temperament, and his engineering training—all helped to give Pierre a firm belief in the value of facts and systematic analysis in the making of decisions and in order and system in executing them. Moreover, his sensitivity continued to make him far more aware of the feelings of others than either Alfred or Coleman.

It was Pierre's good fortune to be at the right place at the right time. A man with his personality would have been far less effective in the Du Pont Company of an earlier generation when one man made nearly all the decisions. Nor could his contributions have been so significant in a later generation when the new patterns had become set, and the ladder to the top was much longer and more routinized. The coming of the large centrally administered corporation demanded group management for the first time in American business. No longer could an individual or even two or three partners make all the necessary decisions and carry out all the activities of a business. Authority had to be delegated and functions allocated to a number of top managers. These strong-minded men, trained in the old tradition, inevitably had difficulty in working as a team. The ability to keep such a group working harmoniously was one of the most valuable attributes a corporate leader could have during the first two decades of the twentieth century.

The fashioning of group management required not only a sensitivity to others but an ability to understand reports and figures. The activities of the large corporation were so complex and involved in a multitude of business transactions that not even a group of top managers could keep in personal touch with all aspects of the business. A constant flow of information on production, purchases, sales, and finances had to move into the central offices. The managers had to become sophisticated in their analyses and understanding of such data. The rise of the modern corporation thus demanded the development of the basic business techniques of control through statistics. Pierre and the Executive Committee were forced to do this for the explosives trade at a time when these methods of modern management were little known outside the railroad, steel, and electrical industries.

The Executive Committee's patterns of action worked out in 1903 and 1904, though modified in later years, remained basically those used by the Du Pont Company's Executive Committee for the next sixty years. During the first three and a half years, the regular meetings came to be held on the last Wednesday of each month. At the start they were held earlier in the month, but were pushed up on the calendars to allow the departments enough time to compile their monthly reports and for the members of the committee to read and digest them.[15] By the spring of 1904 the committee had agreed on the order of business at these regular monthly meetings and the special ones called almost weekly to handle specific problems or issues.[16] After the minutes of the previous meeting had been approved, the departmental reports were discussed in detail. Then came the reports of special committees; these in turn brought a review of old business before the committee moved on to consider new business.

The monthly reports quickly became detailed and did, indeed, require a couple of days for intelligent study. Each report included statistical information appraising the current work of a department, described problems or issues, and made suggestions for proposals or actions. Some of the statistical data were so detailed—as, for example, the consolidated sales report—that the members urged that the information be presented in the form of graphs.[17] But this suggestion proved unsatisfactory, as the graphs appeared to oversimplify the reality the statistics tried to indicate.

Often the departmental reports raised questions or issues requiring action by the Executive Committee. At other times, discussion resulting from these reports brought suggestions for changes in the existing programs and plans. If the recommendations presented were relatively routine or met with no opposition, the committee would usually act on them at that same meeting. Far more often, members would raise questions about the information presented and the courses proposed. Then Coleman would appoint a special committee of the two or three department heads most concerned to make a detailed report to the Executive Committee. As a result, executive action was rarely taken except on the basis of special, often quite thorough, studies.

Even though the committee tried to follow Moxham's admonitions to avoid detail, its members found their meetings getting longer and longer. By 1905, as the company and its activities expanded, regular meetings began to last two and even three days. By the spring of 1905 reforms in scheduling were clearly essential. Coleman then asked Pierre to work out, with the assistance of Moxham and Barksdale, a plan to assure more effective allocation and use of the committee's time.

Pierre's resulting proposal, which the Executive Committee approved, had two parts. First, there were to be two regular meetings rather than a single monthly meeting, and one of these was to be devoted solely to reviewing appropriations for plant, machinery, and other large-scale capital expenditures.[18] The members were to classify business proposed in their reports as "important," "general," or "formal" (i.e., routine). The chairman (Coleman, unless he was out of town or ill) was to make a formal agenda before the meetings, listing the matters to be considered according to their significance. The members were urged to "purge their reports of all unnecessary detail and, while not sacrificing important matters, to avoid introduction of any business not properly belonging to the Executive Committee consideration." And in the meetings a member was to be ruled out of order if he introduced anything "not germane to the particular subject of the discussion."

The second part of Pierre's plan was the formation of an Operative

Committee to meet fortnightly. It was to include the directors, that is, the second in command, of all major departments whose heads sat on the top committee, as well as the heads of smaller departments, like Purchasing and Traffic. (By Moxham's basic plan of organization, each department was to have a director who, in addition to supervising routine activities, was to be responsible for carrying out the plans and policies set by the vice-president in charge of the department and by the Executive Committee.) The new Operative Committee would handle, Pierre proposed, day-to-day operational matters and make studies of its own or at the request of the Executive Committee. On the basis of such studies, these representatives of middle management were to recommend action to the company's top management. After the Executive Committee accepted Pierre's suggestions, Coleman asked his younger cousin to work out with its members the more precise duties of the Operative Committee.[19] The Executive Committee also approved of Pierre's proposal to have his younger brother Irénée, who had moved from the Black Powder Department to the Treasurer's Office early in 1905, become the Operative Committee's chairman.

From the start the Executive Committee considered its most important functions to be three: the coordination of departmental activity, the setting of general policies affecting the personnel and work of all the departments and, most vital of all, the allocation of the company's financial resources. In the first years of the new company, the coordination of departmental activities particularly involved defining departmental boundaries.[20] Where, for example, did an operating department's responsibility for accounting in plants or branch sales offices end and that of the Treasurer's Department begin? How far should the new Purchasing Department go in buying small items locally and how many of such purchases could be shifted to plant and office managers? Should there be a single Engineering Department or should each of the three manufacturing units have its own? Did the Sales or did the Development Department have the responsibility for analyzing competition and recommending action? At what point did the manufacturing departments hand over control of product to the Sales Department?

Coordination also involved decisions about the correlation of current market demand with existing output and about the cooperation of the several departments to assure a smooth and uninterrupted flow of materials from the purchasing of nitrates and other raw materials through the manufacturing departments and then the sales offices to the ultimate consumer. Policies to assure the quality of the products through better interdepartmental coordination were also called for. If an explosive failed to do what was expected of it, then the Development Department as well as the manufacturing department involved studied the ingredients and process of its manufacture. Both departments worked closely with the sales office to produce the product the customer wanted.

    In the first year of the new organization the formulation of general
policies largely involved personnel and finances. Discussions and decisions
about both reflected the process of transformation from the old family firm
into the large, more impersonal corporation. In dealing with personnel the
Executive Committee left nearly all the decisions as to hiring, firing, and
promotion of supervisory personnel and the labor force to department heads
or even plant executives and managers. In July 1904 Pierre chaired an *ad
hoc* committee including Haskell and Alfred to study the possibility of
standardizing salaries, a course which the three quickly decided was "impractical."[21] From almost the beginning, however, the Executive Committee required the president or the Finance Committee, which Pierre chaired,
to approve salaries over $100 a month.[22] Not until the period of retrench-
ment following the nationwide financial panic of 1907 did the Executive
Committee consider making a general review of salaries and salary scales.
Nor did the committee involve itself in labor disputes. Questions involving
organization of plants by unions or meeting workers' demands the committee invariably turned back to the department involved for decision.
    The Executive Committee, however, did concentrate its attention on the
two areas where the change from family firm to modern corporation made
a clear difference. One, the development of stock buying and bonus plans,
was to give new executives somewhat the same personal and psychological
involvement in the company as had members of the family in the past. The
other, the pension plan, was to provide formally for retirement benefits that
the old company had informally granted the employees. Pierre played a
major part in the formulation of both bonus and pension arrangements. He
outlined the initial pension plan; helped to write the first bonus plan; and
proposed a supplementary bonus scheme that rewarded loyalty and hard
work.
    The initiative for these plans did, however, come from Coleman. As
early as December 1902, Coleman asked William S. Hilles, who had become
the company's local lawyer, to draw up plans "to permit important employees" to purchase stock in the new company.[23] Stock sales to employees
was a novel suggestion. The oldest of American big businesses, the railroads,
had not developed such plans, nor had well-known established industrial
companies like Standard Oil. Moreover, until Coleman made the proposal,
no one in the Du Pont Company had ever considered letting outsiders own
stock. Coleman later recalled that he had always been impressed by Andrew
Carnegie's scheme of providing his senior executives a share in the business.[24] In any case, Coleman was certain that the best way to attract and
keep able managers was to have them own stock in the company. His
arguments completely convinced Pierre who, for the rest of his business
career, believed that the success of a modern large corporation depended
on making its executives "partners" in the business by permitting them

to consider themselves owners as well as managers.

In late 1903 and early 1904, Coleman, Pierre, and the Executive Committee reviewed three different plans involving stock distribution and stock bonuses. One, which Coleman proposed on the basis of the recommendations from Hilles and which the Executive Committee had approved, permitted selected employees to buy shares "paying therefor a price approved by us."[25] The employee would make a down payment of 20% on the stock, which the company would continue to hold for him while he used the resulting dividends to pay for the unpaid portion. The second was a bonus plan in which salaries would be tied to profits. The third called for giving stock as a reward for exceptional performance. At a special meeting on December 31, 1903, to review these plans, the committee agreed that "a bonus system" based on profits was "preferable to a fixed salary system in that it permitted an advance based upon equity, if profits increased, and a reduction without question on the part of the employee" if they decreased.[26] Even so, the committee agreed that "it was inferior to the method of making the employees de facto partners in the business by the method of making stock donations."

At the meeting Coleman, Pierre, and the others decided on a combination of the three ideas. The bonus would be made in blocks of stock. Employees would not however, receive title to their stock until after future accrued dividends amounted to the value of the shares at the time they were distributed. In this manner the bonus would help to keep the employee with the company and provide an incentive to increase profits and dividends so that the stock could be paid for more quickly. The amount of stock available, they decided, would depend on the profits made that year. In the following May, the committee agreed to set aside $150,000 in common stock to be awarded at the discretion of the department heads.[27]

At the end of the year the bonus system was more fully worked out. Then the Executive Committee decided that the purpose of the bonus was to recognize "merit alone" and not to be "used for purposes of readjusting or making up inconsistencies in salaries."[28] It should be large enough "to make it worth working for," and would be paid in common stock at par with its cost being charged as an operating cost to the department employing the man receiving the bonus. The committee was to decide the total amount of the bonus, and the department heads how much each recipient would get. No member of the Executive Committee was to be entitled to a bonus.

Pierre, sensitive to the importance of personal attributes which were the strengths of a family firm, felt that these too should be rewarded. He favored the giving of bonuses for "special merit, ability, loyalty and good and faithful work," as well as for "exceptional merit."[29] In June 1906 the committee approved of a second, or class B, type of bonus, which Pierre urged successfully over the strong opposition of both Moxham and Coleman. In the next few years a sizable number of salaried managers, between fifty and a hundred, acquired stock bonuses usually running from $1,000 to $10,000 a year. These programs set up in 1904 and 1906 remained basically unchanged even after the critical review of personnel policies that followed the international financial crisis of 1907.

Pierre and his colleagues were able to decide more quickly on a pension plan. In May 1904 the Executive Committee readily agreed on the basic policy that Pierre had first outlined four months earlier.[30] All employees who had worked five years or more with the company were to retire on reaching seventy (although those with salaries over $5,000 a year had the option of continuing to work). Also, those who had worked twenty-five years and had become incapacitated would receive comparable pensions. The pension was to be computed according to length of service. To administer the new plan, the committee set up a small Pension Department which operated under Pierre's supervision. A committee consisting of the president and the department heads decided general pension policies. This plan remained little changed even during the rethinking of most of the financial commitments after the panic of 1907.[31] By these programs, then, the new Powder Company provided incentive for its executive personnel and security for all members of the company in a systematic and extensive way that no firm in the explosives industry could have done before the reorganizations of 1902 and 1903.

More important for the current health and further growth of the company than its personnel plans were its financial policies. The fundamental decisions of how precisely to determine profit and loss, to obtain and use working capital, and to determine what amount of earnings to devote to the further expansion of plant, offices, and equipment were the most complex and most important that the Executive Committee had to face. Before such policies could be rationally determined, Pierre, as treasurer, had to obtain precise information on costs and income as well as on the availability of money for working capital and fixed investments. So, also, the several departments needed to know more about their operating requirements and the demand for their products. The Executive Committee could do little about rational long-term planning and policy making until its members had their own departments in good working order.

## Department Building

As the department heads were getting the Executive Committee functioning and making the initial definition of broad policies, they were also devoting much time to building their own departments. In private discussions, at luncheons, and even in the meetings of the Executive Committee itself, the different members talked over and reviewed with Pierre the problems and challenges involved in getting their offices manned and under way. He often compared their difficulties with those he had experienced in forming the Treasurer's Office. His tasks, he thought, were even more harassing than theirs because in 1904 his was the only department still involved in wrapping up the loose ends involved in forming the "Big Company."

Pierre was particularly interested in the creation of the three manufacturing departments. They had the common problems of first setting up a new operating structure and then reshaping their productive capacity by combining, enlarging, and modernizing old plants and building new ones in order to meet more effectively a nationwide demand for their product. Yet, because of the differing and changing demands for black powder, dynamite, and smokeless powder, the specific problems in the building of each of these operating departments varied. Alfred's task was probably the most difficult because black powder, the oldest of the three products, was being replaced for many uses by the other two, particularly dynamite. Of the new Powder Company's sales and income, black powder accounted for only about 30% as compared to dynamite's 50%. The even newer smokeless powder came to 15% of the total. The remaining 5% came from special blasting supplies. Alfred's mills were small, often built for local markets in the typical pattern of the mid-nineteenth century. Barksdale's plants were larger in size, fewer in number, and equipped with more modern machinery. The Smokeless Powder Department's five plants were still larger and more modern than those making dynamite. As a result, even after the reorganization of facilities, the more than two dozen black powder plants continuing in operation hired a total of 1,600 men, while half that number of dynamite works employed over 2,500, and the five smokeless powder plants, over 1,000.[32]

Given its many mills, Alfred's was the only manufacturing department to structure itself along geographical lines with an Eastern, Southern, and Central Division. In addition the department had its engineering and accounting divisions. The chiefs of all five of these divisions reported to Frank Connable, the former president of the Chattanooga Powder Company, who became director of the Black Powder Department.[33] Two of Pierre's brothers became division heads under Connable.[34] For both, these were their first jobs with the company. Lammot, who graduated from the Massachusetts Institute of Technology in 1901, became head of the Eastern Division. Irénée briefly took charge of the department's engineering division before moving into Pierre's Treasurer's Department in January 1905.

In setting up the High Explosives Department, Barksdale's major task was to spread the system of administrative control which he and Haskell had developed at Repauno to all the dynamite plants the new Powder Company controlled. He kept his organization on functional rather than geographical lines and had his own engineering, research, and accounting divisions. In this work he relied heavily on his director, Harry G. Haskell

(J. Amory's younger brother), who was as committed to order, system, and rationality in manufacturing as was his chief. In building the Smokeless Powder Department, Baldwin and Fletcher Brown followed Barksdale's example and used the Repauno organization as their model.

In reorganizing plants and facilities to obtain greater economies of scale and to assure better integration with market demand, the three manufacturing departments first made a detailed review and classification of their existing units. Then they listed those plants which should be improved, those which should be shut down or maintained on a stand-by basis, and finally they decided where and when new plants might be constructed. These reports, which Pierre carefully reviewed in his capacity as both treasurer and Executive Committee member, listed each plant and its equipment, the volume of its output, its operating costs (including a comparison of its cost sheets over different periods of time to those of similar plants in the department), and the availability and costs of transportation, particularly the existing freight rate structure (transportation costs for each plant were compared on the same basis as operating costs).

After such a review, Alfred and Connable recommended closing down five of their thirty-two mills and keeping three on a stand-by basis, and proposed that three new ones be built.[35] Even though the Executive Committee was disturbed by the costs of maintaining the Brandywine works and those at Mooar, Iowa, Alfred insisted on keeping these familiar family mills in operation. As there was less pressure for the High Explosives Department to reorganize, Barksdale was slower in sending in his recommendations on reorganizing the fourteen dynamite plants and two others producing wood pulp and electrical fuses and batteries. As a result of preliminary analysis, one of the smaller units, the Oliver Mills, was shut down and the two specialty operations were consolidated into a single plant. More important was the proposal to expand the large works recently started near Ashland, Wisconsin, to replace the older ones at Marquette as suppliers for local iron and copper mines, and to build new plants in Colorado and the Indian Territory to meet growing demands of mining companies in the Mountain States. In October 1904 the Executive Committee had to ask Barksdale again to "make a complete study of the extent to which the High Explosives Department could be improved by relocation and improved equipment of plant."[36] The resulting investigation led Barksdale to ask for a large increase in plant capacity to meet a rapidly growing demand for dynamite. His request became, in turn, one of the major requirements that Pierre and the Executive Committee had to consider as they attempted to formulate the company's long-range financial policies in late 1904 and early 1905.

The Smokeless Powder Department required less attention, as its output was already concentrated in five works—the Du Pont Company's plant at Carney's Point, the former Laflin & Rand plant at Haskell, New Jersey, the

Schultze works at Oakland, New Jersey, the California Powder Works near San Francisco, and International's plant at Parlin, New Jersey. These five were operated by one department; but the fact that the United States government was by far the largest buyer and that International remained a separate legal entity meant that there was less need to centralize control.[37] So the plants were operated more autonomously than in other manufacturing departments.

The building of the new Sales Department involved fewer changes or additions in physical assets but more shifts in personnel than did the formation of the manufacturing departments. For Pierre and his office, the new statistical and accounting methods needed in the Sales Department were as complex as those required by the production units. J. Amory Haskell relied, as did Barksdale, on his Repauno experiences and on those of the best one of the Repauno salesmen, Charles L. Patterson, who became his director. Together they moved fast. Coleman pointed out in the fall of 1903 that, given "Mr. Haskell's talents in this direction," the Sales Department was making "more progress and is in better hands than our other departments."[38]

In March 1904 Haskell sent the Executive Committee an account of the organization of his department, a report which Pierre read with great interest.[39] The enlarged department included two (soon it would be three) geographical districts and four bureaus. Former Du Pont agencies and those of the other companies that had joined the consolidation were converted to branch offices with salesmen and office staffs being paid by salary rather than commission. Normally, several agencies in one city were combined into a single office, with each office controlling land, storage, warehouses, and transportation facilities as well as handling all the activities involved in the sale and distribution of the company's products. The heads of each branch office reported to the executive in charge of either the Eastern or Central District. After the California companies' activities became integrated into the larger structure, a third, the Far Western District, was created. (For a short period after the consolidation Coleman had placed production and distribution on the West Coast under a single manager, Russell S. Penniman.)[40] In addition, the Company had branch offices in London, Paris, and, in time, other foreign cities manned by salaried employees who reported directly to Haskell.

Two of the four smaller bureaus handled nonmilitary smokeless powder —one sold rifle and the other shotgun powder. The other two bureaus carried on key functions. The Advertising Bureau supervised nationwide promotion of the Du Pont products and checked on the method and content of advertising by local branch offices. The Information Bureau prepared the reports on sales made by the Du Pont Company and its competitors and also carried out more general studies on the nature and activity of the market and of the competition. Haskell and Patterson met regularly with their district and bureau chiefs as the Sales Board which reviewed systematically the department's activities and set sales and other policies including pricing.

Although Haskell and Patterson were able to build their new department with speed, the task was by no means easy. As Coleman had discovered in 1902, the transformation of semi-independent sales agents into salaried executives created tension and frustration. Good salesmen often proved to be poor office managers. The consolidation of several offices in a single city aggravated the situation.[41] Some men with long service found themselves working under former, sometimes younger, associates. Others had to be let go. From the start there was trouble between men in the same office and continuing protests against central control. In St. Louis the branch manager, John G. Miller, suddenly resigned. In Cincinnati, where John B. Coleman, the former president of the Oriental Powder Mills, was the new branch manager, and Frederick W. Waddell, former agent in that town, was his first assistant, there was continual friction between the two men and between that office and Wilmington.[42] In Chicago Elliott S. Rice again raised complaints about the control in Wilmington over accounts and freight rates which had so annoyed him in 1902. By the fall of 1905 Frederick Waddell had quit, as his brother Robert had already done, and Rice was retired on a pension. Due to Coleman du Pont's intervention, Frederick Waddell had actually stayed on for a year and a half after he first threatened to resign. Coleman sympathized with the position of the older salesman, pointing out to Haskell that Waddell was "probably not much on system but I believe an extremely good salesman and mixer and I would urge your very careful consideration [before] letting him go."[43]

While many older salesmen found they could not take the new system, others preferred the new methods to the old. The new ways had much in common with those adopted by Barksdale in the High Explosives Department. Haskell, Patterson, and the Wilmington headquarters paid careful attention to analyzing and compiling statistical data and gave increasing thought to cost analysis in the marketing and distribution of their products. They held, as Barksdale did for men of his department, regular meetings and conventions where Du Pont salesmen from all parts of the country gathered to compare notes, to consider departmental policies and procedures, and to enjoy themselves.[44]

In the same years in which the basic line departments of manufacturing and sales were being formed, the smaller staff departments were also taking their modern form as they expanded to meet the enlarged needs of the consolidated company. John B. Niles continued as head of the Purchasing Department, while in 1905 Frank G. Tallman, who was trained in the steel and machinery industry, took over the Traffic Department from L. Faithorne, whom Coleman had hired in 1902.[45] In addition, the Executive

Committee decided in March 1904 to create an Essential Materials Department, to be headed also by Tallman, to handle the procurement of materials purchased in bulk including nitrates, glycerin, pyrites, sheet steel, and fusel oil.[46] Niles' Purchasing Department did all the rest of the buying for the company except for small items "covered by the ordinary expense funds at the various mills."[47]

Although Pierre and Coleman strongly favored the formation of a single engineering department, all of the manufacturing departments insisted on having engineering divisions of their own.[48] For several years they had their way. The Legal Department received its autonomy much sooner. It initially came into being to meet the full-time work involved in completing the consolidation and in closing out the separate constituent companies.[49] It remained under the supervision of the Development Department until 1905, when it became an "independent department" under John P. Laffey.[50] Laffey, in making his plea for independence, indicated clearly the functions of the smaller staff departments in the new Powder Company. His, like those, had "no general department or other unit having superior claims on its services, and act[ed] in a sense as auxiliaries or helpers to all departments and agencies of the business."

The most important of the smaller departments, and one whose function was so critical that the Executive Committee considered it more of a line than a staff unit, was Moxham's Development Department. Coleman, Pierre, and Moxham all looked on it, as they had from the start, as the strategy-planning office.[51] It continued to keep a constant check on the company's competitors; to assure the manufacturing departments of a steady and reasonably priced supply of raw and semifinished materials; to carry on a constant search to improve the company's products and the processes involved in producing them; and to keep watch on organizational matters.[52] To carry out the department's three main duties, Moxham quickly formed three divisions with the titles of Competitive, Raw Materials, and Experimental.

Of these, the last was the largest and, in the long run, the most significant, for it marked the beginning of the institutionalizing of technical research and development for the Du Pont Company as a whole and therefore for two-thirds of the American explosives industry. As soon as the consolidation was completed, the Executive Committee, at the insistent urging of Pierre as well as of Moxham and Francis I. du Pont, the head of the Smokeless Powder Department, authorized the construction of an Experimental Station near the old Hagley Yards by the Brandywine.[53] Moxham and Pierre then recommended that the new unit be headed by Francis I. du Pont, whose scientific talents they both admired and whose administrative ability they were coming to appreciate. By the end of 1904 Francis I. had a staff of over one hundred technicians including several college-trained scientists.[54]

Moxham and Francis I. had expected to have all experimental work done at the Station, but Barksdale was able to persuade the Executive Committee to allow the Eastern Laboratory, which he had set up at Repauno the year before, to continue experimental and research work as well as to carry on routine control and testing of high explosives.[55] In these laboratories a large number of trained men spent all their working time on projects to improve the company's products and its manufacturing process. In time their skills and resources would greatly facilitate the company's expansion into new chemical products other than explosives. To Pierre, who always remembered his distress when he first saw the company's technical equipment after graduating from M.I.T., these large, elegantly equipped new laboratories must have symbolized, as much as anything else in and about Wilmington, the coming of a new era in a company's history.

Although Pierre listened with interest and patience as the other Executive Committee members talked about the problems of setting up their departments, he was, of course, far more concerned about those involved in building the Treasurer's Office. Several reasons had prevented him from giving any concentrated attention to the problem until the fall of 1903: the negotiations required in the formation of the big company; the efforts to get the Executive Committee functioning; a delay in moving of Laflin & Rand accounts to Wilmington; and Coleman's absence. All had forced him to put off outlining plans for the formation of the Financial and Accounting Department that became more informally known as the Treasurer's Office.[56] When he did turn attention to drawing up his plans to organize the department, Pierre kept in mind the present needs as well as those which would come from the expansion of activities after the consolidation was completed. In the fall of 1903 his department included a large accounting section with separate offices for black powder and dynamite (and in early 1904 another was added for smokeless powder) and three smaller units, Auditing, Salary, and Treasurer's Offices.

Pierre selected experienced men to head these bureaus. Dunham, whom he and Coleman had brought from Bethlehem Steel in 1902, when their company still handled only black powder, continued to take care of black powder accounting in the new organization. William J. McMannis, who had long been comptroller at Repauno and then at Eastern Dynamite, was the obvious candidate to be responsible for the accounts of the dynamite business. Edward N. Wead, who since 1900 had acted as treasurer at Laflin & Rand, took charge of the Auditing Department, a brand new unit. As Pierre reported to the Executive Committee, all bills passed upon by the Accounting Department were then sent to Wead's office "for final audit. This will permit a much closer scrutiny than we have been able to give heretofore and place with each branch of the Accounting Department the means of closely checking the systems established by them."[57] Wead, however, did not handle the basic books, such as Profit and Loss, Investment and Surplus, which were filed in the Treasurer's Office directly under the supervision of Pierre and John Raskob. Pierre placed Charles Copeland, his sister Louisa's husband, at the head of the small Salary Department, when he decided to form it as a separate office for the purpose of "reducing the number that must be acquainted with the amounts of salaries, and making it possible to properly distribute the salary roll."

As the "Big Company" came into being, Pierre's department moved swiftly to meet the new demands, expanding from a salaried force of about twenty-five in the summer of 1903 to one of over two hundred by the next summer.[58] Dunham, who impressed Pierre by his work in appraising the California plants, soon took charge of the whole Accounting Department.[59] Traveling auditors were added to Wead's office for the purpose of checking accounts in the branch offices outside of Wilmington. The work of the auditing staff was, in turn, reviewed by outside professional auditors, whose employment Pierre recommended to the Executive Committee in June 1904.[60] At this time, such use of certified public accountants by industrial companies for independent audits was, except for railroads and some steel companies, still quite rare in this country. Early in 1904 the committee authorized the formation of a Real Estate Department to be placed, like the new Pension Department, directly under Pierre.[61]

In creating and running his department, Pierre counted as heavily on John Raskob as the other Executive Committee members relied on their directors, even though Raskob only had the title of assistant to the treasurer. For the purpose of tying the family closer to the company, Pierre had brought into his office Eugene's son Lex, and had given him the title of assistant treasurer. While Pierre often talked with Lex about the company's financial affairs, and as often conferred with Dunham, Wead, and others on his staff about the more technical accounting procedures and problems on important matters, within or without the department, he always consulted Raskob first, before anyone else except Coleman. On major financial matters, the two alone made significant decisions or proposals. Sure of Raskob's complete loyalty and respectful of his ingenuity and judgment, Pierre talked over his problems and ideas with Raskob in a way that he did not, or probably could not, with his subordinates in the department or his colleagues on the Executive Committee, even Coleman and Moxham. At the same time Raskob became an increasingly useful foil to Pierre. He grew bolder and more inventive in financial matters as Pierre was becoming more cautious and conservative. Together they worked out successful complex schemes and programs—at Du Pont and, in later years, at General Motors —which either might not have done alone.[62]

At the new Powder Company, the major task Pierre and Raskob faced, once the department's structure had been outlined and personnel selected, was to bring all its activities under a single consolidated accounting system.

Balances and capital appropriations accounts had to be made for all the subsidiary companies at least until their stock had been completely exchanged for Powder Company shares and until they were legally dissolved. The making of separate balances was an arduous task; but it was little more than an accounting game, as the operations of the many subsidiaries were becoming, in actual fact, completely merged with those of the parent company.[63]

More serious than the time involved in drawing up these balances were the legal barriers to the pooling of the merged companies' capital, particularly the cash and securities they held. Pierre suddenly realized this problem when, late in 1903, an officer of one recently merged company refused to turn over to the treasurer securities that the Executive Committee had ordered to be sold, while another would not make the expenditure for capital equipment that the committee had authorized.[64] Then, in January 1904 Pierre suddenly found that the company was without funds. The resulting crisis, the first Pierre had to face as treasurer, had a profound effect on the formulation of the company's financial policies and will be discussed in detail in the next chapter.[65] One result, however, was to hasten the wind-up of the companies that had come into the big company and thus make easier Pierre's task of developing a single set of consolidated accounts.

Even before the January difficulties, Pierre had been able to consolidate in twelve banks the cash balances of many of the subsidiaries which had been scattered in 139 banks.[66] Such a combination of accounts not only simplified bookkeeping, but also enhanced the company's credit rating at the deposit banks if it needed short-term loans. Then, as legal barriers were removed in the spring of 1904, the treasurer placed all these balances in "one set of books" known as the "Alexis I. du Pont—Ass't Treasurer's Account" to be kept in the Wilmington office. The actual funds remained in the twelve banks where they were all listed as Powder Company accounts.[67]

By the summer of 1904, the treasurer could report significant progress in both the consolidation of accounts and accounting. This consolidation reflected the centralizing of managerial control in the different functional activities, including purchasing and sales. As Pierre told the Executive Committee on July 21, 1904:

> Looking back over the past year of development in the Accounting Department, I am pleased to report that there is great promise of perfecting a satisfactory plan during the next few months. The greatest difficulty to overcome has been the presentation of consolidated reports, at the same time overcoming objections in handling the several companies as a unit. Starting with interchange of accommodations between companies we have developed first, the consolidation of all cash balances, second, the consolidation of purchases of nitrate of soda, then the consolidation of Sales Accounting into practically one company; and on July 1

the consolidation of all purchases into one company. We have now reached the point where our operations will be practically accounted for in one set of records, though we still deem it necessary to carry elaborate accounts to divide the profits on our several classes of goods. We hope that at an early date we will push our consolidation plans one step further and consolidate Operating profits, returning to each company a percentage of the whole profit as may be determined from time to time.[68]

The unifying and centralizing of accounting records and procedures continued the way Pierre anticipated. Not only did the new consolidated accounts give a far more accurate picture of the company's current financial situation, but they also were drawn up much more quickly than earlier ones.[69] In November 1904, Pierre promised the Executive Committee that his consolidated balance sheets for one month would be ready within five weeks after its end; that is, the January report of December's business would be ready the first week in February, and preliminary ones even sooner.

The consolidated balance sheets, which Pierre, Raskob, Dunham, and Wead first worked out in the spring and summer of 1904, remained the company's basic set of accounts and one of its most important administrative tools for several years to come. Occasionally the Executive Committee suggested new data to add. It proposed, for example, including the cost of accounting in the statement of administrative costs given in the regular monthly treasurer's reports. At other times Pierre made an addition on his own initiative, such as putting in summaries of monthly salary rolls.

After the summer of 1904 Pierre's office prepared for each monthly meeting of the Executive Committee a consolidated profit and loss statement that showed for the preceding four months the following items: First, *income from sales* for each of the thirteen different products the company sold; then, *other income received* including that from interest on bank deposits and securities and that from bills receivable, commercial papers, rents, farms, and miscellaneous items;[70] next, the *charges against income* including interest on bonds and on bills payable, interests and discounts allowed, and miscellaneous interest. The difference between income and charges gave "net operating income" to which was added nonoperative income including losses and gains in the sale of securities, real estate, and other sales. Operative plus nonoperative income indicated net receipts from which the dividends declared were subtracted and the final figure showed profit and loss. To it was added any surplus profit carried over from earlier accounting periods.

In addition to the profit and loss sheet, the treasurer's monthly report included the basic assets and liabilities account, but the largest portion of these reports was concerned with appropriations approved and obligations outstanding. The staff provided detailed statements of how much was expended and still unexpended for each item on each appropriation in each plant and office. Pierre further gave a financial forecast of available cash with probable expenditures. The treasurer added statistics on payrolls and the cost of raw materials used in making the different products.

Pierre also made a detailed statement showing the relation between the capital expenditure for the production of each product and the earnings made by that product. This was Pierre's initial attempt to get a "return on investment" figure on the monies expended for the production of each type of goods produced. He, Raskob, and their assistants would continue to refine this analysis until the return on investment data became the company's single most important analytical tool.

The department's annual reports were essentially a compilation of the monthly reports.[71] In time, the Treasurer's Office could provide more comparative yearly figures for each item. In addition, the annual statements immediately following the consolidation included a report on the situation of the subsidiaries remaining in the consolidation and listed those that had been dissolved during the year. These reports also listed securities held, bought, and sold during the year, plant investments and capacities, details on pensions paid, taxes, worthless accounts, accidents, and number of employees. The 1905 report, the first full year in which the consolidated accounting system existed, ran to eighty-one pages, and those that followed stayed about the same size.

By the end of 1904 Pierre and his colleagues had their departmental structures worked out and their different functional activities moving along relatively smoothly. During the year Moxham, in his role of supervisor of organization, kept reminding the Executive Committee to avoid details in their deliberations. He further urged them not to bypass the channels of authority and communication which they had so recently defined, insisting that subordinates should communicate with subordinates in another department only through the departmental heads.[72] In this way a revolution in industrial control had been accomplished with astonishing swiftness. In less than two years Coleman and Pierre, Alfred, Moxham, Haskell, and Barksdale had introduced modern methods of production, distribution, cost accounting, scientific plant management, and over-all administration to two-thirds of an industry where, except for a few dynamite concerns, most of these practices had hardly been known at all.

This revolution in administrative control was capped by the construction of an office building to house the many new executives, managers, and their staffs. By 1905, as Pierre wrote William du Pont, departmental headquarters and central offices were "in temporary offices scattered through out the city."[73] The company purchased land for the building on the corner of 10th and Market Streets in 1904. In the following year, after Pierre returned from a trip to France and South America, he took over the plans for building as well as financing the structure.[74] Pierre thoroughly enjoyed planning all the details of the new headquarters and had an obvious satisfaction in watching the twelve-story edifice rise. The building, expanded in later generations, would always remain Wilmington's predominant landmark.[75]

Only when it came to naming the building did Alfred appear to show much interest in the structure. The differing responses of the three cousins to the naming of the building was quite characteristic. Coleman did not really care. Pierre saw it as a way to boost the bank which he, Coleman, and other members of the family had recently founded. Alfred looked on the building as a symbol of the family's past achievements rather than of its present enterprise. Shortly before the new building was to be opened, Alfred wrote Coleman from Miami, where he was wintering at the Royal Palm Hotel. He was disturbed by Pierre's proposal to call it the Wilmington Trust Building, merely because Pierre thought "the Trust Company needed advertising."[76] The building, Alfred insisted in a voluble two-and-a-half-page letter, should certainly be entitled "du Pont de Nemours." "There can be no question in my mind that this building should stand as a monument to our ancestors, as it is their industry and frugality which is directly responsible for its construction, and it should be so indicated to impress upon the present and future generations of the du Pont family the fact that what they now possess is due much more to the valued characteristics of their ancestors than to any personal efforts on their part."

Pierre responded in a short, single-page letter that he would be perfectly agreeable to Alfred's suggestions. He did feel, however, that "the greatest commercial value to our interest can be had by calling our new office building 'Wilmington Trust.' "[77] The new bank was not yet well known even in Wilmington, in sharp contrast to the Du Pont Company. Surely neither the new company nor the old family needed advertising. He told Alfred that he "always felt that the indiscriminate use of 'du Pont' in advertising savors more of Dr. Munyon and Lydia E. Pinkham." Coleman, in a usual terse four-sentence note, also agreed, saying merely: "The shorter any name is the better. No matter what label you put on the door I think it will be called the 'du Pont Building.' " And indeed it was.[78]

# Formulating Financial Policy

AFTER THE POWDER COMPANY'S financial offices were fully organized and running smoothly, the internal activities of his department were no longer of primary importance to Pierre. He was quite willing to leave the day-to-day operations and the solving of specialized, technical problems in the hands of competent subordinates—the ingenious Raskob, the experienced and methodical Dunham, the capable and discreet Copeland, and the hardworking Wead. He felt even more assured after his brother Irénée moved into the Treasurer's Office in the first days of 1905. Irénée began to specialize in handling appropriations. He also represented Pierre on the Executive Committee when the elder brother spent several months in 1905 in Europe and South America.

As treasurer, Pierre's interest focused increasingly on the formulation of financial policies for the Powder Company as a whole, policies which he hoped would assure him and the Executive Committee a firmer grasp on the management of their new $50.0 million business. Immediately after consolidation, Pierre gave costing and pricing policies highest priority. The first meant the development and acceptance of uniform accounting practices and procedures for the departments and other units of the company. Pricing involved setting a margin of profit above costs that would assure adequate return on investment and still not so high as to encourage increased competition by attracting new firms into the industry or causing old ones to expand production.

Another and even more important set of financial policies involved the allocation of the company's financial resources, that is, funds available from its own profits and surpluses and those it could raise from banks and the money markets. The allocation of these funds called for decisions as to how much working capital was needed and how best to obtain it, how much of the profits would be put back into offices, plant equipment, and other fixed assets, and how much into dividends, and finally, what was the best way to raise capital if surplus and dividends proved inadequate. The costs of reorganizing productive facilities, the day-to-day expenses of running the business, the need to have assured sources of supply, the opportunities created by increasing demand in the United States for explosives, and the possibility of investment in overseas productive capacity for overseas markets, all called for large sums of capital that had to be provided from the company's profits or its credit. While basic costing and pricing policies could be more or less definitely settled, the allocation of financial resources had to be constantly adjusted to meet shifts in demand for explosives, changes in supplies of raw materials, and new investment opportunities. All three of these conditions were in turn constantly affected by national and international business conditions.

In the debates over the formulation of financial policy, the different members of the Executive Committee usually reflected the interests of their departments. As treasurer, Pierre was naturally skeptical about any excessive commitment of financial resources. In private conversations and in the more formal meetings, he resisted suggestions that might even remotely threaten the company's solvency. His own instinctive cautiousness reinforced this conservative position. So too did a nervousness, an uncertainty as to his ability to meet these new complex responsibilities. Financial liquidity and soundness, he therefore insisted, must come before purchases of property or increase in capacity at home or abroad. The ability of the company to meet its financial obligations was of more significance to Pierre than the expenditure of funds for what others considered absolutely essential investment in plant, equipment, and personnel.

Still, the young treasurer was rarely dogmatic. He was willing to analyze proposals he thoroughly distrusted. While making his position clear in the meetings of the Executive Committee, he always listened to, although he refused to be intimidated by, other men's arguments. In the give and take of Executive Committee discussion he would often adjust or modify his original views. As long as the information was accurate and everyone understood the risk, Pierre was willing enough to accept the committee's decision and work for a policy he had at first opposed.

In the beginning the older and more experienced members of the Executive Committee considered their young associate too cautious. But as he learned the details of the several branches of the business from the many reports and statistics sent to the central office and from the discussions in the Executive Committee meetings, his proposals and positions became harder to debate. So their respect for him increased. In 1905 they agreed that he was the one to send abroad for delicate negotiations in France and in Chile. In the months following his return, the committee increasingly came to accept his views on both domestic and foreign expansion and on the ways to finance such growth. By early 1907 his ideas and actions had become as influential in deciding the company's policies as those of Coleman. Pierre's impressive performance in guiding the firm through the economic storms set off by the panic of 1907 further strengthened his own confidence in his abilities to manage a giant enterprise and increased the regard that his colleagues held for him. Thus, well before Pierre became acting president in 1909, he had replaced Coleman as the actual head of the Powder Company and as the most influential single individual in the American explosives industry.

## *Setting Costing and Pricing Policies*

Once the Treasurer's Department had succeeded in consolidating the accounts of the Powder Company, its next major task was to see to it that uniform accounting procedures were practiced throughout the company. All the senior executives agreed in theory on the value of having the same sets of accounts.[1] In practice, however, uniform accounting proved difficult to achieve. Pierre found Barksdale's department the hardest to bring into line. As the largest and most profitable of the operating departments, High Explosives was able to maintain a special autonomy. Despite the wishes of Pierre, Coleman, and Moxham, Barksdale had kept his own research and engineering divisions. He further wanted to have his department continue to keep its records in its own way.

For example, in March 1904 the Executive Committee approved Pierre's request to place "all employees handling records" under the control of the Accounting Department, "so far as records are concerned."[2] Barksdale, however, protested. So the committee, with Pierre and Moxham voting in the negative, agreed that the High Explosives Department would be exempted from the ruling if Barksdale promised to provide, promptly and regularly, the information needed. Even so, the cost sheets and other data remained different enough to make comparison between the works of different departments inaccurate. Therefore, in the following October Pierre proposed, and the Executive Committee agreed, that each of the manufacturing departments should "select a competent man to co-operate with the representatives of the Accounting Department who would visit the different mills and look into all inconsistencies and report upon the means of rectifying them."[3] Pierre, who took charge of this study, continued for many months to devise methods to assure that cost of materials, labor, and general overhead were allocated in each mill in the same way.[4]

In working out these uniform cost sheets, the charges for material and labor used in the manufacturing of each of the company's products were easy enough to define. The only matter here that became an issue was how to charge for materials purchased by one department or plant from another one within the company. The question was temporarily significant during 1902 and 1903 before the subsidiaries, like Laflin & Rand and the Chattanooga Powder Company, were fully amalgamated into the larger enterprise. After the completion of the consolidation, there were far fewer intracompany transactions, and those that occurred were largely between departments. Whether the transfer was between subsidiaries or departments, Pierre believed the principle on how to charge was the same. He advocated that transfers be made at cost with "a portion of Works Administration expenses [to] be added."[5] If Carney's Point was to manufacture guncotton for the Forcite Powder Company at 18¢ per pound, Pierre recommended that the Forcite Company be billed 20¢ a pound, "the additional amount covering salaries and expenses at the works."

From the accounting point of view, Pierre clearly saw the company—the new, large multifunctional enterprise—as an expanded plant or factory. In fact, he and Dunham later stressed that their whole accounting system had been worked out on this premise. The billing between the new functional departments in the company could be handled in just the same way as the billing of materials from one department to another in one of its plants or mills; that is, goods were transferred at cost.[6] The basic consolidated accounts for the company as a whole were to include the departmental costs involved in production and sales for each of the company's products, just as the cost sheet for each factory indicated the costs of materials and labor expended for each product within each of its departments.

Only Barksdale objected to Pierre's reasoning.[7] When one unit within the company purchased from another unit, he preferred to have the purchasing unit pay charges based on current market prices rather than on costs. If the intracompany price was lower than the market price, well and good. But if the price was higher, the buying unit should not be penalized by having to purchase supplies at a greater expense. Moreover, the Executive Committee should know that the selling unit's costs were so high that its products could not meet the current market price. Since relatively few items were involved in intracompany transfers, the Executive Committee at this time supported Pierre's plan. However, when the company began to control a much larger portion of its own sources of supply, the question of interdepartmental billing did once again become pertinent. When it did, Coleman and one or two of the committee came to support Barksdale's view.[8]

Even then, Coleman, Barksdale, and the others could not convince Pierre or his assistants in the Treasurer's Office of the propriety of basing interdepartmental billing on a market rather than cost basis.[9] In addition to their earlier arguments, the former stressed that by using market prices performance of individual units and their managers could be properly determined. Only by such a method could the Executive Committee know which operations were returning a satisfactory return on investment, and which were not. Pierre and Dunham, however, remained adamant and in the end had their way.[10] They insisted that, first, charging within the company at anything but cost violated all canons of proper accounting procedures; and secondly, that the determination of market prices for many products purchased from one unit in the company by another would be exceedingly difficult to determine. The underlying reason for these differences was that Coleman and the operating executives wanted to use accounting data to appraise the performance of the company's departments, whereas Pierre and the Treasurer's Office saw the information only as useful in determining the profit and loss and the return on investment for the company as a whole. Many years later, when Pierre became responsible for the success of General Motors, he finally began to appreciate and then accept Barksdale's views on the matter of intracompany billing.

The most complex problem involved in the initial setting up of a uniform accounting system was the determination of how to allocate general overhead charges against the cost of manufacturing of each of the company's products. In the first place, practices continued to vary between departments. For example, in February 1905 Irénée, speaking for Pierre, who was on his way to Europe, reported to the Executive Committee that the High Explosives Department did not follow the normal practice of dividing general overhead among all the articles manufactured.[11] Overhead was charged solely to dynamite and not to acids, packing boxes, etc. But Barksdale's department would not change. Nor did the committee itself come to an agreement even on the general schedule for the distribution of overhead accounts until the end of the year 1905.[12] Then it accepted with minor modifications the schedule of charges Pierre had submitted in August on his return from his overseas trip. This list indicated how much was to be allocated to each of the different products for Works Accident Insurance, for bad debts (½ of 1% of gross sales monthly), for depreciation of plant (½ of 1% of plant value monthly), for depreciation of furniture and fixtures (1 ¼ % of value monthly), for marine insurance, depreciation of transportation facilities, for magazine insurance and other items. These schedules were reviewed and adjusted annually and new items added, but the basic charges remained about the same.[13]

Even so, the High Explosives Department continued to do some accounting in its own way. For example, it refused to place uniform interest charges on raw materials. Finally, in February of 1906 the Executive Committee supported the treasurer in insisting that "all records coming to the Executive Committee should have the same distribution of charges," while still permitting department heads to keep "special statements" for their own use only.[14] Apparently problems continued, for in the summer of 1908 the Executive Committee voted that "distribution of charges be placed entirely under the control of the Accounting Department."[15]

Well before this time, the Accounting Department had defined and the Executive Committee had approved of methods to determine and to allocate nonmanufacturing overhead charges. Except for Experimental Station's costs, there was little debate in the Executive Committee or the Treasurer's Office over such allocations. Sales expenses were relatively easily divided among the several products, as both the central and district offices were operated largely along product lines. The expenses of the Wilmington office and its bureaus were prorated according to the volume of sales. The expenses of Pierre's department, of Coleman's office, of the secretary's office, and of the Purchasing Department were prorated among the major products in much the same way as were selling expenses. For example, the Purchasing Department's expenses were divided among the three manufacturing units, with Black Powder taking 25%, High Explosives 56%, Smokeless Powder 17%, and Torpedo 2% (Torpedo was essentially a unit of the High Explosives Department, and made explosives used in the drilling of oil wells).[16] This method was used to allocate the expenses of the Development Department, except for the Experimental Station. These charges were added together and listed for each product as "administrative" costs. This item was subtracted from the net operating receipts to give the "net" return for each product on the monthly and annual income from sales reports.

The Legal Department's costs were handled in a different way. It charged the departments on a job basis. Moxham and Francis I. du Pont hoped that the Experimental Station would be able to pay its way in much the same manner as the Legal Department. Their original plan was to have all improvements developed by the laboratory considered its own property, and have the operating departments pay a fair royalty for inventions or new processes, or buy them outright. Such a proposal, however, did not make clear how to charge for those experiments that were not successful and how to allocate the other general expenses of the Experimental Station.[17]

Pierre turned his attention to the problem of accounting for Experimental Station's expenses shortly after returning from his long trip to Europe and South America in 1905. By the plan he finally proposed, the Executive Committee would review each January the sums expended that year for experiments, dividing the expenses among the three manufacturing departments. Against the fund would "be charged all general expenses of experimentation which cannot be properly brought against any one experiment" plus "the entire net cost of unsuccessful experiments."[18] The cost of successful experiments would be carried on the Patent, Goodwill, and Plant Account and, on the approval of the Executive Committee, this cost would either "be capitalized permanently" or "be gradually reduced by the payment of royalties by the Department benefited." Early in 1907 the Executive Committee agreed to account for the experimental expenditures at the Eastern Laboratory in the same way.[19] A little later, procedures to account for the costs of each individual experiment and to determine whether it had been successful or not were established. On the whole, however, the methods devised by Pierre remained relatively unchanged for many years.[20]

The determination of cost-accounting policy involved the treasurer largely with the manufacturing and auxiliary departments. Pierre's Auditing Office, however, had a closer relation with the Sales Department than did his accounting unit. The company's traveling auditors checked all the accounts for the sales in all the branch offices and the one hundred or so storage magazines and delivery points as well as those of the different explosives works.[21] Also most of the branch offices had their representatives of the Treasurer's Department who handled the collection of the overdue accounts and submitted to Wilmington daily reports of sales made.

One of Pierre's first tasks in setting up his department was to work out the procedures for billing and collecting as well as for making the daily audit of sales. By December of 1903 he and Haskell had agreed that the new branch offices of the Sales Department would do the billing and that duplicate bills were to be immediately forwarded to the Accounting Department in Wilmington. Employees of the Treasurer's Department in the branch offices were to have "direct supervision and control of all local billing."[22] Moreover, the Executive Committee added that "everything in the nature of dunning . . . should be done only through the branch offices of the Accounting Department." The salesmen should not have to be handicapped by being forced occasionally to become bill collectors. The initial procedure for dunning was, Pierre explained to the Executive Committee:

> to write a stereotype letter to each customer as soon as his account becomes due, calling his attention to the fact and adding that not hearing from him to the contrary, we will understand that it is satisfactory that you have us draw at sight on a certain day (naming a day ten days from the date of the letter).[23]

The plan was proving quite successful and 80% of these drafts were paid immediately.

The Sales Department, however, was far more concerned with pricing than costing and accounting policies. From its beginning the Executive Committee turned over the setting of specific policies to Haskell's department, but it did maintain its prerogative of deciding basic price policy.[24] Even here the initiative was left to Haskell. Yet Haskell and the rest of the committee were fully agreed on the basis for pricing policy. The company should make its profit on volume, not on markup, that is, make only a small profit on each of a large number of units sold. Such a policy had been one of the basic motives for the formation of the "Big Company." Economies resulting from the consolidation meant that the manufacturing departments could produce the various types of black powder, dynamite, and smokeless powder at lower costs than their competitors. So the Sales Department could undersell the competition. Pricing, therefore, was based on the setting of a margin high enough above costs to assure the company of an income to meet its financial obligations, to maintain, repair, and replace its physical assets, and to pay a dividend on its common stock as well as to provide funds for future expansion. At the same time the price needed to be low enough to discourage competition from growing, particularly by the entry of new firms into the industry. But it did not need to be so low as to drive efficient competitors out of the business. As Moxham had earlier stressed, the ideal position for the Du Pont Company would be to run its plants steadily at relatively full capacity and let the other smaller units adjust to short-term fluctuations in demand.

The factors involved in defining such a price policy were best indicated in a report submitted to the Executive Committee in May 1905 on the pricing of "B" blasting powder, the Black Powder Department's major product. (By that time the operating departments had developed fairly good cost data.) This report Pierre read with care and approval when he returned in June from his trip abroad. The vice-president in charge of sales began his statement by pointing out that consolidations both without and within the explosives industry had actually increased competition. Within the industry, consolidation had meant that a number of men—salesmen and managers—had found themselves without jobs. Since the new consolidated Powder Company had more effectively stabilized prices than the old Gunpowder Trade Association, several former employees as well as former owner-managers of smaller constituent companies had, after 1903, started new explosives firms largely to exploit local markets. Outside the industry there had been consolidation in industries that were major buyers of explosives, particularly mining. The coming of new large enterprises made "it difficult to get abnormal prices even if we thought it was wise to do so."[25] For the new big customers now had the funds to produce their own explosives, if they considered the Du Pont price too high.

Internal and external conditions thus reinforced the earlier plans to have a pricing policy based on high-volume output and small profit per unit. The Powder Company should set prices at a level that would discourage competition and satisfy the large customers. Haskell now specifically recommended that,

> if we frame our policy along such lines as will yield to us a small, very uniform profit when applied to a large production, and one that will leave the well managed competitors a close manufacturing margin while to a greater majority not so well managed it will mean no profit or a loss, we shall come more nearly conserving the best interests of our concern and yield in the longest run the greatest average of profit.

He estimated that if Du Pont set prices to make a profit of ten to fifteen cents a keg, the "well managed" competitors could make eight to ten cents, and the "average competitors" from nothing to five cents. However, "in order to do this we must have an average amount of business, run the mills we desire to run, and keep them going, as nearly as possible, all the time with the exception of the spring decrease in trade."

The Executive Committee, fully agreeing with Haskell's analysis, accepted his final recommendations for setting the price of "B" blasting powder, after "reduction for freight," at 90¢ a keg. The salesmen should try to get 95¢ if possible. A year later the Sales Department dropped the price to 85¢ at the mill.[26]

How much Haskell's department adjusted their prices to meet local competition or the demands of large competitors is not clear from the records of the committee or Pierre's or Coleman's papers. Pierre, Haskell, and the committee did discuss discounts given on standard prices. Pierre, for example, wanted to charge a standard 2% discount for the payment of bills within 10 days to the "Interest and Discount" account, but to charge any special discounts to the Sales Department as reductions in prices received.[27] Haskell and Barksdale preferred to have all discounts regarded as price reductions. "It seems very desirable," Haskell told the Executive Committee, "that we should know what we are averaging for our goods; under the present system [of accounting for discounts] we do not."[28]

The precise extent to which discounts were used is uncertain, but it was limited. During the expansion of business following the 1907 economic recession, the allocation of discounts "over the various branches of goods covered by remittances" had come to require the full time of a senior clerk.[29] Yet the total amount of price reductions appears to have been small. The regular and special discounts on blasting powder "B" totaled $151,121 in 1908 on over $7 million in gross sales. Moreover, there is little evidence presented in the antitrust suit the Justice Department later brought against the company in 1907 to suggest any widespread use of discounts as a competitive weapon after 1903.

## The Allocation of Financial Resources

In the formulation of financial policies the allocation of funds between the different and continuing demands for money had far greater long-run implications than costing and pricing. By 1905 the basic costing and pricing policies had been defined. Adjustments in the costing were left to Pierre's subordinates, and in pricing to Haskell's department. Thus the treasurer could focus his attention increasingly on the central activity of top management in a modern corporation. In working out the complex decisions required to meet the many different calls for working capital, for permanent plant and equipment, for investment in raw materials and properties, and for dividends, Pierre first faced the new challenges in the over-all management of a large business enterprise. It was his success in handling these challenges that proved his worth as a modern business executive.

The basic problem of allocating financial resources existed from the very beginning of the Powder Company. During most of 1903, however, Coleman, Pierre, and others were far too involved in planning and carrying out the consolidation and in building their own administrative offices to give such financial planning their serious attention. Money was needed on every side. The arrangements for the legal and financial consolidation required funds, as did the reorganization of the production and distribution facilities of a large part of the American explosives industry. Expanded volume necessitated, for the first time, large amounts of funds for bulk purchases and shipments of raw materials, such as nitrates, sulphur, and pyrites. The manufacturing departments could achieve economies of some scale by relocating plant facilities, but none of the three department heads believed that the objectives of the consolidation could be achieved without increasing investment in plant and equipment. Even the new centralized Sales Department needed more money to build and expand its branch offices and magazines.

Yet dividends had to be paid. If they were passed or slightly reduced, the outside stockholders in the firms coming into the consolidation who had not yet exchanged their stock for that of the Powder Company would be unlikely to do so, while those who already had would certainly protest. Without a regular flow of dividends through 1904, the consolidation might have been jeopardized. Nor would Du Pont & Company be able to meet the interest payments on its funded debt, payments that were to be paid from the Powder Company dividends.

During most of 1903 Pierre, concentrating as he was on consolidation and on department building, was only vaguely aware of the need to sort out these conflicting claims. In June, after reviewing the financial commitments of the Powder Company, he did suggest to Coleman that "we should be somewhat careful in our cash expenditures."[30] The only response to this from Coleman and Moxham was that young Pierre was being overcautious.[31] During the summer the new operating departments turned in their first estimates of expenditures for plant and planning equipment for the following year or so. These estimates did not trouble Pierre even though they totaled a good deal more than anticipated income.

In July 1903 Pierre conservatively predicted earnings for the next twelve months at $1.96 million. (This was for the existing Du Pont & Company and not for the new Powder Company which was just being formed.) He had available another $2.0 million of retained earnings of Du Pont, Laflin & Rand, and Eastern Dynamite in the form of negotiable securities.[32] Against a total available fund of $3.96 million, the treasurer expected to pay out $860,000 on interest and sinking fund accounts on outstanding loans. Moxham's Development Department had asked for $1.5 million for experimental laboratories and the purchase of nitrate lands in Chile. Barksdale had requested $1.24 million for high explosives, Alfred wanted less—but still a substantial $800,000 for black powder. In addition, the Smokeless Powder Department would probably need as much. These calls totaled over $5.2 million.

Possibly these figures did not worry Pierre just because they were so vague and imprecise. When he had more time, he and his department could ask for more realistic data. By December, however, when the treasurer began to study his books, he became a little worried. He warned the operating departments to pay more heed to their expenditures.[33] In response to this admonition Coleman appointed a committee of Haskell, Barksdale, and Alfred to report on items of capital expenditure that might be temporarily deferred.[34]

Then suddenly, early in January 1904, Pierre found himself without funds. The situation was clearly a temporary one, resulting from the fact that the consolidation was not yet legally completed. As Pierre was preparing to pay the Powder Company's January dividend on the preferred stock, he realized that he did not have full legal control over the several subsidiaries. This lack meant that he could not carry out his plans for pooling the cash balances of the constituent concerns.

Pierre was aghast when he realized the full implication of his position. The Powder Company had hardly any funds at all in its own name. Over $4.0 million had been authorized for capital expenditures, and its cash balances stood at $16,920.53. Pierre wanted to stop everything immediately and get the company's finances straightened out. On the morning of January 8 he dictated a memorandum to the Executive Committee outlining the situation and his fears about it. In it he drafted a resolution for the committee's approval which, as he stressed, "means its abandonment of all present plans of consolidation and of complete stopping for at least two months of the expenditures of appropriations until our affairs can be made to meet our requirements."[35]

The others on the committee felt less urgency and panic. Haskell, Barksdale, and Alfred told Pierre to calm down. The immediate difficulties could be easily met, and long-term plans need not be altered. The Executive Committee readily admitted that funds had to be found immediately to provide the $510,000 that Pierre required in working capital to meet the operating expenses for the next thirty days. The arrangements would have to be made to provide temporarily the funds for long-term capital expenses until the consolidation was completed and full legal and financial control of the subsidiaries obtained. The operating men agreed that Pierre had some legitimate concern about the long-term implications of the situation. Even if the accounts had been consolidated, expenditures for the whole enterprise were clearly greater than income. They argued, however, that these difficulties could be eased merely by postponing payment on current obligations and by reducing cash reserves.

Pierre quickly agreed with the others as to ways to meet the first of the temporary needs, although he was reluctant to call so soon on the family holding company for financial help. At a special meeting on January 28 the Executive Committee of the Powder Company arranged to get $225,000 from the E. I. du Pont de Nemours & Company, while Laflin & Rand was asked to pay $150,000 it still owed the Wilmington office.[36] The rest of the needed working capital, it was felt, could come from current income. Pierre also agreed that temporary arrangements could be made with the subsidiaries not yet consolidated to finance some of the existing capital expenditures. He protested vehemently, however, against the suggestion that the company's longer-term financial stringency could be met by enlarging and extending the floating debt and by reducing cash reserves. The specter of the Johnson Company clearly informed Pierre's attitudes. Cuts must come, he insisted, from the appropriations of capital expenditures, not from working capital.

During January Pierre continued to maintain that the operating departments must reduce their spending for plant and equipment as much as a million dollars.[37] At the meeting on January 28 Barksdale, Haskell, and Alfred, as the subcommittee appointed to review capital expenditures, made their position clear. They saw no pressure for major reductions. Indeed they "were positively of the opinion that the very important work provided for in these appropriations should go ahead."[38] The treasurer was being too cautious; the needed monies could come out of funds set aside for dividends, cash reserves, and working capital. Specifically they proposed that the estimates in the consolidated account for dividends be reduced by $200,-000, as much of the Powder Company stock was not yet exchanged; that cash reserves be reduced by $250,000; and that the payment of $130,000 for nitrate of soda be postponed. They further proposed that one-half, or $400,000, of the remaining $800,000 of bills outstanding also be postponed. These and other minor cuts would reduce claims on the financial estimates by $1,337,000. If Pierre would agree to these suggestions, the three operating chiefs could see their way to cuts in capital appropriations of $275,000.

At the meeting Pierre argued forcefully against endangering the brand new company's solvency by cutting into its cash reserves and by greatly increasing its floating debt. Solvency must be maintained, not by endangering working capital, but by reducing expenditures for fixed capital.[39] In the following week Pierre outlined his position in a report that he submitted to the Executive Committee for discussion on February 5. He began this memorandum by reminding his listeners of the precariousness of their situation. None of them had any experience managing a $50 million enterprise. "Our organization is admittedly incomplete in all departments, as much through a lack of knowledge of what is desired in the way of changes as to the lack of time in carrying out well established plans."[40] The present financial position of the company indicated these weaknesses. During the past year the Executive Committee had not only authorized expenditures of $3 million but had also "expended an additional amount equal to the present floating indebtedness, delayed accounts payable and reductions in cash balances to $1,430,000." In addition obligations incurred for the present year reached $1,788,000, thus making total authorized commitments of over $6,218,000. "We begin our second year with an estimated rate of expenditures of over $6,000,000 per annum, with decreased cash balances, with a floating debt of $800,000 (now $900,000) and with practically the entire income of the present year expended. In addition, $1,100,000 of invested surplus is pledged for development of the Nitrate business, while the balance is pledged as collateral for our floating debt."

The treasurer then repeated his strictures about using working or operating capital for long-term expenditures. "The impairment of working capital will be credit suicide and the shortest road to financial embarrassment." Because of the "present press of new work and reorganization difficulties, it seems absolutely impossible to count upon economy in the management of our working capital." Moreover, the volume of business had recently increased as much as 10%. If it remained as high, an additional $675,000 in working capital was required to meet current and continued needs. The proposed cut in amounts allocated for preferred stock dividends, Pierre contended, was certainly not practical. Some cuts elsewhere were more acceptable. Nevertheless, with the maximum paring of the Powder Company's financial commitments and obligations, they still totaled $4,078,-866.88. Even with the cuts in appropriations accepted by the special committee, the spending of all income and most of the existing surplus meant a deficit of $308,866. "Should we elect to continue our appropriations and to count on a floating debt of $300,000 it must be with the understanding that no expenditure whatsoever in addition to those already planned shall be made during the year 1904. Also that working capital for more than 5% increase in our business must be provided for by increasing our floating debt."

Pierre had defined the issue and made his arguments. The operating men were still unimpressed. They were willing to risk a continuing floating debt in order to have their long-term improvements. In this argument Coleman and Moxham finally decided that the treasurer was being too hesitant, and so supported Haskell, Barksdale, and Alfred. Once the committee had decided on a policy, the treasurer and his departmental colleagues stopped their arguing and immediately began to work out a way to finance temporarily the capital expenditures until the consolidation was fully completed.

At a meeting on February 15 the Executive Committee approved plans to have the still existing subsidiaries finance expenditures from their own treasuries.[41] So the cost of the new dynamite works near Ashland, Wisconsin, was temporarily transferred to the Lake Superior Powder Company, that of the proposed works in the Indian Territory to the Indiana Powder Company, and that in Colorado to the California Powder Works. This took a total load of $765,000 off the Powder Company's treasury, but that weight was still not lightened enough. The committee therefore agreed to further financial adjustments by authorizing the sale of the Ferndale Works to E. I. du Pont de Nemours of Pennsylvania for $225,000, by a reduction of $90,000 in a stock subscription to the Wilmington Trust Company, and by the sale of $275,000 worth of securities held as investments by Laflin & Rand. Finally Pierre agreed, despite his earlier vehement protests, to the postponement of half the current bills payable, which amounted to $400,000. This, in addition to the $275,000 cut in appropriations agreed to by the special committee, gave a reduction of current claims totaling $2,030,000.

Once Pierre accepted the risk of maintaining a sizable floating debt, the crisis proved relatively easy to solve by this reshuffling of internal accounts. Nevertheless, it had significant repercussions. In the first place, it helped convince everyone on the committee, and particularly Haskell, of the need to wind up the legal and financial aspects of the consolidation as quickly as possible. By summer enough of the legal and financial changes were completed to assure the consolidation of all the cash balances of the Du Pont interests under the Alexis I. du Pont account and so to remove the causes of the January cash shortage. At this time the consolidation of purchasing and sales accounts gave Pierre a still firmer control of the Powder Company's financial resources.

Secondly, everyone now agreed with Pierre on the need to develop more systematic procedures for approving and authorizing long-term capital expenditures. In the previous November the Executive Committee had stated that while appropriations for new construction not involved in routine operations and maintenance of over $5,000 required the committee's approval, those less than that needed only the president's signature.[42] Presidential approval was all that was required on orders for equipment. In 1903, too, the committee had asked the department heads to include in their monthly reports the "physical progress" on authorized expenditures, while the treasurer reviewed the same expenses from "a financial point of view."[43]

Then after the financial contretemps of January and February of 1904, the Executive Committee tightened up on ways of approving long-term, nonroutine appropriations. It agreed not to pass on any request "unless accompanied by engineering estimates and wherever necessary blueprints outlining the nature of the work to be done."[44] Three weeks later the committee added that no order of construction or equipment could be placed until the Accounting Department had given the request an appropriations number which was to be attached to all records pertaining to that appropriation.[45] Next the Executive Committee insisted that the selection of new plant sites had to have the approval of the Traffic and Sales Departments as well as the manufacturing departments involved. This condition was laid down so that the company could be more certain of getting the advantages of "connections and freight arrangements from the railroads."[46] At the same time, the committee permitted more flexibility in equipment purchases by allowing the department heads to approve those up to $5,000.[47] Then, in the summer of 1904, considerations of appropriations became a scheduled part of every regular monthly Executive Committee meeting. The committee also began to keep tabs, though not yet in a systematic manner, of overruns on appropriations as they appeared in the monthly reports. It did not yet check on the day-to-day use of the funds appropriated and the over-all rate of expenditures.

Nevertheless, these new appropriation procedures were significant, for the allocation of funds for capital expenditures became the Executive Committee's most important and time-consuming task. This fact in itself emphasizes a basic difference between the new Powder Company and the old Gunpowder Trade Association, between the old cartel and the new centrally administered operating company. As late as 1903 the Special Committee and the Advisory Commiteee of the Gunpowder Trade Association, working closely with the Eastern Dynamite Company (these committees were the nearest thing to a central office for the industry), concentrated their meetings wholly on the setting of prices. They never considered capital expenditures. Within a year, the Executive Committee of the Du Pont Company, the central office for 65% or more of the industry, rarely considered pricing and spent much of its time on appropriating funds for capital expenditures needed to maintain its current position and to assure its future growth. By early 1905 half the committee's regular meetings were specifically allotted to this task.

After the further systematizing of appropriations procedures, Pierre turned his attention to stabilizing the company's finances by obtaining more effective control of working capital, and particularly by paying off the unfunded debt incurred by the January decision. By that summer the demands on the treasury could now be more accurately anticipated and more easily met. The postponed bills for supplies had been paid, and growing income permitted a reduction of the floating debt. These short-term loans for supplies, and especially for nitrates, were made on such banks as the Guaranty Trust in New York and the American Exchange Bank and the First National Bank in Philadelphia.[48]

By October 1904 Pierre was already looking forward to paying all the unfunded debt, keeping cash balances at about $1.0 million and paying a small dividend of 2% (¼% quarterly) on common stock as well as the regular 5% on the preferred.[49] In fact, Moxham and one or two of the other members of the committee were already suggesting that common stock dividend be raised to 4%.[50] This was quite an improvement, for even in June Coleman was writing on the question of the common stock dividend: "The feeling is that we had better be a little conservative, at least for the present and let surplus earnings which are in the neighborhood of 12% on the common go into surplus or improvements."[51]

Once Pierre had achieved control of short-term expenditures, he began to discuss with Coleman the need to formulate a long-term policy of growth for the Powder Company. Such a policy would be a base line on which to tie all decisions involving the allocation of capital and other resources, the payment of dividends, and the size of cash reserves. Basic in this planning was a growing demand for explosives in the United States. Much less obvious to anyone, except Coleman, was the possibility of investment abroad.

In the second part of 1904 the demand for explosives began to recover from a slump that depressed the industry during the last of 1903 and the first part of 1904. In the first half of 1904 the dynamite business had dropped 9% below the same period for 1903. The situation in black powder was about the same. This decline meant that in 1904 Barksdale's department would manufacture 103.2 million pounds of dynamite as compared to 109.5 million produced the year before, and Alfred's department would produce 5.2 million kegs of "B" blasting powder as compared to 6.4 million kegs for the same period during the previous year.[52] Then Haskell, in his monthly report for September 1904, pointed to the large demand for supplies in the Midwest which was creating an "extreme shortage" of powder in that area.[53] In his next month's report, he noted "a very marked increase" in demand in nearly all parts of the country.[54] Therefore, at the regular October meeting Coleman and Alfred were appointed a subcommittee of the Executive Committee to study means of increasing capacity of black powder production, while Barksdale and Baldwin began to study the best ways to expand dynamite-making capacity.[55] At this same time, too, Coleman was beginning to develop ambitions of expanding Du Pont activities into Europe and Mexico, and earlier plans for purchasing nitrate lands in South America appeared to be coming into fruition.

After again conferring with Pierre, Coleman on November 4 asked the department heads (except for the treasurer) for estimates of their expenditures, "in the way of improvements and heavy repairs" for 1905, giving some attention to the needs of 1906.[56] On the same day he wrote the Executive Committee members describing a brief, basic financial policy for the company and asking each member for his criticism and comment.[57] Coleman began his statement of the proposed policy by pointing out that the experience of 1903 and 1904 indicated earnings at about $4.0 million per year, and certainly at least that amount could be assumed for 1905. (The net earnings were precisely $3,971,335 in 1903 and would be $4,061,469 in 1904.)[58] Of this sum, $1.25 million would go to dividends on preferred stock. If $1.0 million was set aside for capital improvement, $500,000 could be used for the common stock dividend and $250,000 could go either to the reserve fund or to other improvements. The president did not want the common stock dividends to exceed $500,000, or 2%, until the earnings were definitely over $4.0 million. If earnings rose, then the amounts allocated to dividends and to improvements could be increased. If earnings declined, then the dividends on common stock should be cut first, next the amount allocated to pay off debts or increased cash reserves, and only then should the amount available for improvements or capital investments be reduced.

The key figure in this memorandum was $1.0 million a year to be allocated for capital expenditures. It was based on the roughest of estimates made on the past experience of the explosives industry. Coleman hoped that that figure would be a guide to the committee in making its appropriations. If capital expenditures averaged over $83,000 a month (that is, $1.0 million divided by 12), then the committee would be warned to examine any further requests with a "very careful consultation or consideration."[59]

Pierre, who agreed with Coleman's proposal, now listened attentively to a growing debate between Barksdale and Moxham over ways to finance the Powder Company's growth. Each attacked Coleman's plan from an entirely different point of view. They represented alternative courses of action which Pierre, Coleman, and the Executive Committee would have to balance. Barksdale favored continuing conservative dividend policy. He was opposed to any increase in dividends until all debts were paid off and until the company had completed expenditures for plant and facilities "intended to strengthen our defensive position and cheapen our manufacturing costs."[60]

Moreover, new plant capacity would soon be required to meet the growing demand. Why raise the dividend now if later it would have to be cut back because of lower earnings or, what was more likely, the need for further capital expenditure? Such cutbacks could only cause the company embarrassment. Barksdale, while agreeing on the value of having a limit to expenditures, considered the $1.0 million a year set by Coleman too low for the next one or two years. He further reminded the president that he had made estimates only "for improvements and additions to our explosives factories, and not for lands and equipment to produce pyrites, sulphur, nitrate of soda and other interesting and most important matters that are in the hands of our Development Department."

Moxham, on the other hand, favored a liberal dividend policy. He argued that the dividends should have prior call on the company's resources even before capital improvement. He urged the declaration of a 4% dividend on common stock as soon as possible. He was certain that since the initial reorganization had been so successful in reducing costs, improved and more systematic organization could provide funds needed for both dividends and capital expenditures. He proposed a continuing analysis of long-term demands for powder and the best way to meet them in view of the company's over-all financial position. The more rational the company's procedures, Moxham always claimed, the more certain and the larger its earnings should be.

> As to the method of appropriation [he told Coleman] I hold that we are today erratic and not sufficiently careful about this. The concern is of sufficient magnitude to demand a broader gauged policy than that which has heretofore applied to this method. I see no reason why this point should not be handled as in the case of a Government budget;—to wit—A Committee should be selected whose duty it should be to criticize all requests for appropriations before the same were presented to the Executive Committee. They should personally not alone pass on the general idea and look into the engineer's estimates, etc. but should visit the ground and study in minute detail the proposed expenditures. An important duty of the committee would be to correlate improvements in one department with those which might be under construction in another, and so harmonize the work, and I do not see why it should not be possible for that committee to look a year ahead on some broad and comprehensive plan and so in a measure achieve what you suggest in your letter. The committee should be disinterested and should not consist of those who request the appropriations. It should be small.[61]

The two differing responses of Moxham and Barksdale led to further studies. Coleman appointed one subcommittee to look further into Moxham's proposal, and another to report, after more detailed investigation, on the specific needs of Barksdale's High Explosives Department in enlarging its capacity to meet the growing demand.

In the following April the Executive Committee acted on Moxham's proposal for a continuous review and coordination of appropriations. The committee, however, preferred to have a single man who would report monthly to the Executive Committee, giving in tabulated statements the details of the work done, amounts still to be expended, and the probable monthly rates of expenditures.[62] As Pierre was away, the selection of the man to fill this position was postponed until his return. In the summer of 1906 Irénée took the job. He not only carried out the tasks outlined by Moxham quite effectively; but, as time passed, he took on new ones given him by the treasurer and the Executive Committee.[63]

In the meantime the argument between Moxham and Barksdale over dividends versus capital expenditures led to an even broader discussion of the directions toward which the company should expand. At the first regular meeting the Executive Committee held in 1905, these issues were argued for two days. Barksdale and Haskell outlined the reasons for expanding domestic dynamite production by 20 million pounds above the current capacity of roughly 125 million pounds (this included the recently completed works at Ashland) and for the building of an additional acid plant. The cost of the total would be $1.8 million to be spent equally over two years.[64] Baldwin, who emphasized the growing demand for military powder, particularly by the navy, wanted $1.0 million for his branch. Alfred asked for much less, a mere quarter of a million. Moxham reported that he needed $400,000 for the Experimental Station and for the possible purchase of pyrites, sulphur, and nitrate properties. This figure, he warned, could come to much more if an exceptional bargain appeared, particularly in the purchasing of nitrate beds. And Pierre insisted that $300,000 be put aside for contingencies. These requests came to a total of $4.4 million, of which $3.0 million would be spent in 1905 and $1.4 million in 1906. These sums were indeed far more than Coleman had anticipated in his November letter to the committee.

At the same time the committee reviewed Coleman's new and still nebulous plans for expanding the Du Pont empire overseas.[65] Haskell and Barksdale vigorously opposed this idea, even though Coleman thought such expansion might be achieved with relatively little cash outlay. Possibly because no decision was made on overseas activities, Moxham was able to win his point about increasing dividends, even though the committee had supported plans for the expansion of domestic production. Moxham pointed out that the earnings were rising above the $4.0 million limit that Coleman had set before he would pay higher dividends. Coleman now estimated the earnings for 1905 at $5.0 million; even the conservative Pierre set them at $4.5 million.[66] (The exact figures turned out to be $5,193,294, with net earnings, after paying interest and other fixed charges, at $4,715,461.) But, if both Moxham and Barksdale had their way, a possible deficit of $750,000 faced the company. Finally, at the end of the two-day debate the committee accepted both positions. The minutes read "that after full discussion of this subject it was the consensus of the Committee that it would be advisable to increase the dividend on common stock to 4% and it will be safe to undertake the contemplated improvements thereafter."[67]

Pierre was deeply concerned about the outcome of the meeting of January 25–26. A compromise that gave the protagonists in an argument what each wanted might help to get a consensus needed for adjournment, but it was hardly a sensible way to run a business. Still he made no open protest, for he appreciated the complexities involved in making the decision. Barksdale, experienced and probably the most able of the company's professional managers in charge of the company's most productive operating department, should be accommodated if possible. Pierre had not pushed too hard earlier in his efforts to get uniform accounting. He preferred not to do so now on capital expenditures. Pierre was less sympathetic to Moxham's position, particularly as all through 1904 the Development Department's head had been alerting the Executive Committee to the possibility of increased expenditures for nitrate properties in South America. On the other hand, the treasurer had the highest respect for Moxham's business acumen. Moreover, Pierre was far more aware than the others of Coleman's ambitions to build a European empire.

While all these positions had legitimacy, clearly they could not all be adopted. Some order of priority had to be set. Major expansion, even if dividends were not increased, could not be paid for out of current income. Capital would have to be raised by the sale of securities. Yet the funds that could be realistically raised would hardly pay for all these projects. The members of the Executive Committee all realized that until they decided how much to spend abroad, they could hardly take a rational position on how much to spend at home. And until they had agreed on the amounts of money to be spent both at home and abroad, the committee could hardly talk intelligently about how much capital to raise and about the ways to carry out this financing. As the company's executives talked over these problems, they agreed that the first decision would have to be on whether or not to invest abroad. They further decided that Pierre should be the one to handle the critical negotiations involved in such possible overseas expansion. The need to define priorities for capital expenditures and so to reach a decision on the formulation of financial policy in this way took Pierre away from Wilmington to Europe and then to South America.

# Investment Overseas?

DURING THE EIGHT MONTHS following November 1904, Pierre du Pont traveled as far and as extensively as he had ever done or ever would. First came an emergency trip to California, then a transatlantic voyage to France, and finally a long sea and land journey to Chile. These travels gave the young treasurer a firsthand acquaintance with the explosives industry and an intimate view of the area that produced the Du Pont Company's primary raw material. On the trip Pierre proved himself a cautious, levelheaded negotiator. The knowledge of men and places gained from the journey critically affected his formulation of financial policy and, therefore, the final direction of growth that the Executive Committee accepted for the company. And since he, rather than Coleman, carried out these critical negotiations, they enhanced his ever-growing influence at the Du Pont Company.

Shortly before beginning his extended travels, Pierre had to carry out a shorter but tiring and quite disagreeable mission in California. In late November, just as the issues which would lead to Pierre's trip abroad were coming under discussion, the treasurer's Accounting Department reported irregularities in the accounts of Coleman's most trusted and respected West Coast manager, Edward G. Lukens.[1] The accountants produced convincing evidence that Lukens had deliberately cheated the Du Pont Company out of $47,000. Pierre took on the difficult task of confronting Lukens with this evidence. At first the Californian protested his innocence, but when Pierre showed him the tampered accounts, he confessed. Pierre then asked for his immediate resignation. Because public knowledge would not only ruin Lukens' reputation but also injure his son's promising political and business career, Pierre agreed not to make the embezzlement public knowledge if Lukens promised to reimburse the Powder Company by turning over to it $47,000 worth of stock in the California Investment Company and in the Coast Manufacturing & Supply Company.

By the time he had returned to Wilmington, the treasurer had become fully involved in the policy-making discussions that led the Executive Committee to send him abroad. The primary purpose of the trip was to carry out negotiations for the purchase of the major share in the French company that controlled the "Latin Group" of explosives makers. Once these negotiations were completed, Pierre was to join the company's Chilean agent, Elias Ahuja, who was then visiting his family in Europe, and to return to Chile with him. This way the treasurer might get to know the agent and evaluate for himself all aspects of the nitrate situation in Chile. He could then better determine how much and in what way the Du Pont Company should invest in or control the sources of one of its basic raw materials.

In handling the European negotiations, Pierre came to work with and understand Old World businessmen. In viewing the nitrate fields, he met with Europeans and Chileans who were bent on making their fortunes from the initial development of a colonial area's basic resources. The story of the first tells much about the workings of an international cartel at the turn of the century and suggests the nature of international negotiations between powerful national business groups. That of the second says something about the problems of doing business in a distant, speculative, frontierlike boom economy. An understanding of one calls for a brief review of the Du Pont Company's contacts abroad; the other, of the methods the company had used in obtaining its nitrate supplies.

### Negotiations with the French

In 1905 the world markets for most explosives makers in the United States and Europe had been explicitly defined by an agreement they had signed in 1897. That agreement, in turn, had its beginnings in one drawn up in 1888 between European and American manufacturers of that still relatively new product, dynamite. Patented by Alfred Nobel in 1864, its manufacture spread quickly in Europe and the United States during the 1870s and 1880s. By the middle of the latter decade production capacity was beginning to outrun demand, and competition became severe in the markets of Asia, Africa, and South America, as well as in the United States. Therefore in October 1886 several of the leading British firms joined to form the Nobel-Dynamite Trust Company, Ltd. In the following year the new British combination made a series of agreements with explosives manufacturers on the Continent, the most important of which were the firms which became the Köln-Rottweiler Pulverfabriken. All these arrangements culminated into two major agreements between what became the "Anglo-German Group"—the General Pooling Agreement of 1889 and the Mueller Agreement of 1890. Before these were signed, representatives of the British company came to New York and successfully completed negotiations with the dynamite companies—Repauno, Hercules, Giant, California, Atlantic Dynamite, and Hecla—who took the name the "American Group."[2] By this arrangement the British agreed to stay out of the United States and the Americans to keep out of Europe, Africa, Australia, and much of Asia. Both groups were to have equal rights in Canada, Mexico, Central America, South America, Korea, China, and Japan. In addition, the British were to "use their best efforts" to get Continental companies, besides their German allies, to agree to this general arrangement. During the next year or so, contracts were signed between the American group and individual European companies. Outside of these arrangements between the Americans and Europeans remained the *Société Générale pour la Fabrication de la Dynamite* and the *Société Continentale de Glycerine et de Dynamite*. These two foremost French firms became, in time, key units in the second largest European association, the "Latin Group," which operated under a single holding company, the *Société Centrale de Dynamite*.

The 1888 Agreement was to continue until 1893, when it was apparently allowed to lapse. Then in 1897, after the leaders of the Anglo-German Group started to build a plant in New Jersey, the Americans again met with the Europeans to sign a contract even broader than the earlier one.[3] This contract not only divided up the world market among the signers but also included the manufacturing and sales of black and the new smokeless powder as well as dynamite. The black and smokeless powder makers, like Du Pont, Laflin & Rand, and firms owned by the Fay and Lent interests, joined this agreement (which was to last until July 1907).

By the 1897 Agreement, the American companies basically promised to stay out of Europe and the Europeans out of the United States in the making and sale of propellants for gun and cannon ammunition whether manufactured with black or smokeless powder. On military smokeless powder, should one or more of the American companies receive a bid from a European government or should one or more of the Europeans have a bid from the American government, each group was to check with the other about the prices to be charged. As the Americans were using European processes, they had to pay a royalty to the Europeans on all military smokeless powder sold to the American government. If the United States purchased powder from Europe, then the American company would get the royalty.[4] The arrangements on high explosives, that is, "all explosives fired by means of Detonators" (primarily dynamite), were more detailed and more complex. The Americans were to have the exclusive market in the United States, Mexico, Central America (except British Honduras), Columbia, and

Venezuela. The rest of South America, British Honduras, and the Caribbean Islands not in Spanish possession were to be common or "syndicated" territory where neither Americans nor Europeans would build plants but where they would jointly market their products. This would be done by selling powder on a joint account, usually through the same agent with profits to be distributed equally and at prices to be decided by the chairmen of the two groups.[5] The remainder of the world was to be exclusively the territory of the Europeans except for Canada and the Spanish possessions in the Caribbean, which were "to be a free market unaffected by this Agreement." Communications between the two groups, particularly in regard to price determination in the syndicated territories, were to be handled by a chairman and a vice-chairman of each group.

The agreement covered patents but paid much less attention to them than to market prices. It merely read that "no legal proceedings are to be taken in respect to any alleged infringement until an attempt has been made to settle the matter amiably," through an "arbitral tribunal." Each side agreed not to purchase patents from local people, "except after having given the parties interested in manufacturing in the country in question the right of pre-emption on the same terms as the Patents offered them."

The revolution Coleman, Pierre, Alfred, and Moxham created in the American powder industry had little impact on the Agreement of 1897. Although, in transforming the old Association into the big consolidated company, the du Ponts had eliminated domestic agreements, they had made no changes in the European one. Apparently even Moxham did not urge the elimination or alteration of the overseas compact, although in 1905 Haskell was writing the Nobel Trust of the Powder Company's concerns about the agreement, which he and others feared violated the Sherman Antitrust Act. The only change resulting from the consolidation in the relations between the American and European manufacturers was the appointment of Coleman as chairman of the American Group.[6] The only new major interest in European markets to come out of the consolidation was the hope of the Du Pont subsidiary, Du Pont International Smokeless, to sell military explosives to European governments. When Colonel Buckner of International went to Europe to solicit orders, Coleman, Moxham, and Haskell agreed that he should keep the chairman of the European group informed of his activity.[7]

Coleman and Pierre realized that these international agreements were much easier to maintain than domestic ones, since they were much easier to enforce. Producing or marketing in a foreign country could be hidden only with difficulty. If a company openly broke the agreement, local representatives of the cartel could quickly harass the intruder with discriminatory taxes and tariffs and other political action. Moreover, the allocation of territories had followed the existing patterns of trade. Since nearly all of

Asia and Africa was under European dominance at the end of the nineteenth century, and since American trade had concentrated in the Western
Hemisphere, the American companies were quite satisfied with exclusive
rights in most of the Caribbean area and with an opportunity to trade on
equal terms in Canada and South America.

The challenge to these agreements came, not surprisingly, from the
European group that was not a partner to them. In 1901 the *Société Centrale
de Dynamite Nobel,* the holding company for the Latin Group, which had
not joined the 1897 Agreement, moved into Mexico. The *Société Centrale*
planned to oust the Americans from Mexico by political rather than economic means. It had formed, with a number of leading Mexicans, the
Mexican National Dynamite Company (Compania Nacional Mexicana de
Dynamita y Explosives). That firm then obtained from the government of
Dictator Porfirio Diaz a concession to build a dynamite plant in Mexico and
to have a monopoly of the powder business of that country, but only after
it had met certain conditions.[8] If the company was able to supply the
country with its dynamite needs and if it established at least fifty sales
agencies in all parts of that nation, it could charge the price agreed upon
at the signing of the concession contract. Other explosives firms were to be
kept out of the country by the levying of a high protective tariff.

The Americans, who after the 1897 Agreement had worked out their
own marketing arrangements for Mexico, protested.[9] However, since the
French had not signed that agreement, there was very little the European
chairman could do. Since the French had the strong support of Mexico's
Finance Minister, José Ives Limantour, political counteraction in Mexico
seemed futile. So the American Group and then Coleman and Pierre decided to wait to see if the French company could build the plant in the time
required and meet the other conditions of the concession. In the summer
and early fall of 1904 it seemed clear that it was meeting its deadlines. Its
factory was getting into production, and the new prohibitive tariff duties
were about to be imposed.[10]

It was hardly by chance then that in October 1904, Coleman met Siegfried Singer, the director and most active manager of the *Société Centrale,*
in St. Louis, where Singer was visiting the World's Fair on his way to
Mexico.[11] Singer and Coleman immediately took a liking to one another.
Coleman was impressed by the business ability and technical understanding
of this Austrian. Singer had been one of Alfred Nobel's earliest technical
advisers and had later become a research director for Nobel. In addition to
his scientific talents, Singer was, in the words of one correspondent, "a
gentleman of keen judgment, prompt of action, devoted to his work and of
great organizing and administrative ability." Coleman, and Pierre too,
agreed with this evaluation and marked him as a sharp, shrewd but basically
honest businessman.[12]

After Coleman and Singer had exchanged pleasantries, their conversation quickly moved to Mexico and soon to even larger matters. They reviewed the recent developments which gave the du Ponts dominance in the American market, and those in France which had given control of the Latin Group to Singer's *Société Centrale.* Should not these two now join forces? Combined, the Americans and the Latins would be able to bargain more effectively with the Anglo-German Group when the time came to renew the various agreements. Not only did such an alliance promise to enlarge markets but also to assure the most effective use of technological developments in many parts of the world. Coleman was particularly impressed by this point, one which Singer stressed. The Austrian described new developments in ordnance, chemicals, and artificial silk. He even boasted that dynamite was becoming a mere by-product of his company.[13]

As they parted, Coleman to return to Wilmington and Singer to go on to Mexico, both reaffirmed a strong interest in developing a close alliance. Coleman promised to discuss in detail with his younger cousin Pierre the possibility of arranging such a compact. As a first step he would try to get the Executive Committee to formalize an arrangement between their company and the *Société Centrale* to work together in the Mexican market.[14] On his return Coleman immediately reviewed with Pierre, and with Pierre alone, his conferences with Singer and discussed the possibility of an alliance with the Latin Group. Only after Pierre had left for California to investigate the Lukens affair did the president confer at length with Haskell and Barksdale about a possible agreement on the Mexican market. He then invited Singer to stop over in Delaware on his way back from Mexico to New York City. Singer, wife, maid and innumerable suitcases and trunks reached Wilmington on December 6.[15] While Elsie entertained Mrs. Singer, the Austrian talked with Coleman and Moxham about the larger plan and with Haskell and Barksdale about Mexico.

Before Singer and his entourage left Wilmington, two tentative arrangements had been signed.[16] The first outlined the terms by which Du Pont might obtain control of the *Société Centrale.* The second was an agreement by which Du Pont was to supply explosives to Singer's Mexican subsidiary after the Mexican government had laid down the new high tariffs. According to the first the Powder Company would purchase 10,000 of the 14,000 shares outstanding of the *Société Centrale.* Singer was to "arrange for carrying 75% of the money required." In return for control by Du Pont, Singer was to be assured of a larger share of the company's profits than he had been getting up to now. Both sides were to study this proposal and work out a course of action by March 1. By the second agreement Du Pont was to supply powder to the west coast of Mexico, where railroad transportation did not yet exist, until the time when the railroads were built or the French company was required to supply that area by the terms of the concession.

Profits resulting from this treaty were to be divided between the Powder Company and the *Société Centrale.* Coleman presented to the Executive Committee the second agreement but held back on revealing the first.

After extended debate at an Executive Committee meeting on December 20 (Pierre was still absent in California), its members quite unexpectedly turned down the agreement to supply Singer's Mexican company.[17] Recent news from Mexico strengthened Moxham's dislike of the proposal and caused Barksdale and Haskell to shift their views.[18] The three Du Pont Company agents in Mexico City all reported that the *Société Centrale's* Mexican subsidiary was in serious trouble. These informants did not see how the Mexican company could meet the terms of the concession and provide for the explosives needs of the country. Moreover the company had discovered its operating costs were higher than expected and so had asked for permission to charge higher prices than those set by the original contract. Such a raise would mean that the Mexicans would have to pay more than the existing price charged by American companies. Two of the agents urged Haskell to drop the price of American dynamite in Mexico immediately and to refuse to sell the Mexican company the dynamite it would need to meet its existing contracts.

Haskell, convinced of the validity of this course, urged war on the French. If by dropping prices and cutting back shipments they made it impossible for the French company to meet the terms of the concession, new tariffs would not be imposed and the Mexican market would remain open to the Americans. The others agreed.

Only Coleman held back. He began then, really for the first time, to describe the possibilities of a larger alliance to his colleagues informally at lunch and in their offices and more formally at the meetings of the Executive Committee.[19] Haskell, however, was too much impressed by the immediate opportunity in Mexico to trouble himself with long-term considerations. Barksdale fully backed Haskell's position. Moxham had asked Coleman a series of searching questions about Singer's capabilities, motives, and resources. Since Coleman had found it difficult to answer with any precision, the Development Department chief remained skeptical.[20] Baldwin, still a newcomer to the Executive Committee, took no position; and Alfred was away in Florida recuperating from the hunting accident that had seriously damaged his eye. Pierre, who had just returned from California, said little, although he was becoming increasingly troubled by the growing demands on the Powder Company's available funds.

During January, as the operating departments were drawing up proposals for capital expenditures, Haskell began to carry out the new sales policy in Mexico. Prices were cut, and requests for explosives for the French company in Mexico were turned down. On learning of these developments Singer cabled in anguish: "Cannot some arrangement be made? Surely peace is preferable to war."[21] Haskell replied in a series of letters which Pierre most certainly reviewed. In these notes he gave excuses for the change in position, but made very clear the basic reason for the new policy. He explained that the prices had to be cut in order to prevent other American companies from entering the Mexican market. Difficulties involved in obtaining necessary acid used in production prevented their West Coast factories from provisioning Singer's company. Then he warned that the Executive Committee had decided that a temporary share in the Mexican profits, once the concession was enforced, was hardly worth the abandoning of such a valuable market. "We do not desire war, but feel compelled to defend ourselves in the continued possession of a profitable business enjoyed during a long period of years and conceded to us as our exclusive property in return for other valuable considerations by our European friends."[22] While approving Haskell's letter, Coleman still demurred.

After the critical meeting of the Executive Committee on January 25 and 26 dealing with future capital expenditures in the United States, the question of the French alliance became central.[23] On the issue of whether to expand at home or abroad, Coleman continued to insist on the importance of the latter, while Barksdale and Haskell clearly preferred the former.[24] Pierre and Moxham were becoming more favorable to Coleman's ideas. Possibly at Pierre's urging, Moxham had arranged for L. M. Howland, a friend living in Paris, to make a detailed report on Singer, his *Société Centrale* and its widespread holdings.[25] Pierre clearly had come to the position that the European possibilities should be thoroughly investigated. If the proposed purchase could be arranged by the exchange of stock, the opportunity to move into foreign marketing and production might be seized with relatively little cash outlay. Both Pierre and Moxham became more enthusiastic after receiving a very favorable report from Howland.[26] The three were able to swing the committee to their view.

The resulting decision to send Pierre to Paris to open negotiations with Singer and then to return via Valparaiso to inspect and possibly to purchase nitrate lands pleased Coleman. "I trust," he wrote Singer, "we may be able to work out the scheme we talked over or one along the same lines which will accomplish the same results."[27] Coleman also told Alfred that if Pierre was successful in bringing these negotiations to a mutually satisfactory arrangement, he planned to join him "on a flying visit for a final discussion."[28] Pierre, who was also optimistic, made sure that Raskob could come along, as the financial aspects of the contract promised to be complicated. He wanted Alfred to join them. The trip might hasten his recovery from the recent hunting accident. In any case it would give Pierre a chance to regain contact with his cousin, who even before the accident had shown a declining interest in the company's affairs. Alfred, pleased by the invitation, regretted, saying that the condition of his eye still prevented him from making the trip.[29]

Pierre arrived in Paris with Raskob on February 28 and immediately began to survey the situation. That day they saw four men—L. M. Howland, Elias Ahuja, J. Wrampelmeier (the Du Pont Company's representative on the Continent), and Singer himself. With Ahuja, the company's agent in Chile, he made the necessary arrangements for the journey to South America. From Howland and Wrampelmeier he received more information about the French company and its holdings in Italy, Spain, Belgium, and South Africa. He was particularly interested in Howland's later reports even though they were based solely on published materials. These pointed out that the French company's control was not as tight over its subsidiaries as Singer had indicated. From Singer his first request was for more information.[30]

In his initial conversation with Singer, Pierre probed as to the various products manufactured by the companies controlled by the *Société Centrale*. The data Singer provided convinced the American that while the Latin Group produced nitric and sulphuric acid and other nitrate sulphates as well as glycerin and fertilizer, "all of these are manufactured in amounts as to lead me to believe that dynamite is the main product." On the following morning Singer turned over more vital information, the balance sheets of the several companies. These Pierre and Raskob broke down into meaningful tables, including assets, net earnings, and shares held by the *Société* in its subsidiary and allied companies. Then by comparing earnings to assets they computed the value of a share of the parent company stock to be $113 per share, which was a little below the current market value of between $118 and $120.

As he gathered information, Pierre became more certain of his negotiating strategy.[31] On the first day they met, Singer repeated his earlier proposal. Singer would turn over 10,000 of the 14,000 shares outstanding of the *Société Centrale* which would assure Du Pont control. However, of the 10,000 shares Singer and his family owned only 4,000. (It soon turned out that he owned only 3,000 and claimed to control 1,000 more.) He would have to buy the remaining 6,000 on the open market. A ten-year period would be needed to complete the purchase in order not to advance the price of the stock. This was, Pierre reminded Coleman, "much less atrractive than the first impression he gave, i.e., that he could immediately turn over shs. acquiring the balance on open market."[32]

On the afternoon of March 2, Pierre made a counterproposal. First, he presented basic objections to Singer's plan. It would be too expensive. "Locking up so much capital without adequate return" would take too long and was too risky, particularly as even large expenditures might not assure control. He then proposed financing the purchase through the exchange of

Du Pont Powder Company stock for that of the *Sociéte Centrale.* Singer reacted sharply. This was too novel an idea. The practice of exchanging stock had not been used extensively in Europe. "No one but Singer," he insisted, "would make the exchange."

The following discussion led to a suggestion by Singer which Pierre thought had merit.[33] By this plan the du Ponts would purchase 5,000 shares on the open market at $120 a share for a total of $600,000. These shares plus the 4,000 held by Singer would give the two groups control of the next general meeting of stockholders. At that meeting Singer and the du Ponts could authorize an issue of 12,000 new shares of stock. These could then be sold to the Powder Company at $118 or $120 a share. The issue plus the total of 9,000 shares which Singer and the du Ponts held between them would assure control of the *Société Centrale.* Then at its following meeting the French company would authorize a purchase of an amount of Powder Company stock equivalent to the amount of money used to purchase the French company shares. Thus the total cost of obtaining control would be the $600,000 necessary for the original 5,000 shares. Pierre informed Singer that the complex details of such a scheme could undoubtedly be worked out, but, as he wrote Coleman, he still was "not entirely satisfied in my mind that the acquisition is worth the sacrifice of six hundred thousand dollars in cash even though Singer has repeated that he can carry us for three-fourths of any amount that we can put up."

By March 4 the two negotiators had agreed on a general outline and Pierre cabled Moxham the proposal.[34] Moxham cabled back on March 7 that Coleman was out of town but should be back for the Executive Committee meeting the following day.[35] For that meeting he wanted more information. Would the purchase be made openly? How did the proposal affect the European Agreement? Could the financial data be confirmed by an examination of the books of the *Société Centrale?* Would the Powder Company have to pay cash before the exchange of stock is completed? What would be the maximum cash expenditure? Was control assured?

To these queries Pierre answered that buying was to be kept secret until 5,000 shares had been purchased.[36] The deal did not violate the agreement signed between the French and German Groups and, therefore, did not affect the American agreement of 1897. Confirmation of financial information was to be done by detailed examination of books and accounts. Cash would have to be paid before the exchange, but the maximum outlay would be $600,000 except for approximately $1.4 million that would be needed for the six weeks involved in carrying out the legal and financial transactions, that is, between the time of the Powder Company's purchase of the *Société Centrale*'s 12,000 shares and its repayment by purchase of the Powder Company stock.

The Executive Committee had Pierre's reply when it met on March 8. Coleman was still in the South, but Alfred had returned from Florida. No one on the committee was enthusiastic about the proposal. As Alfred wrote Pierre: "The very information which we should have had in order to act intelligently was missing, and, of course, it would have been the height of folly to have gone into an investment of this kind with the meagre information which we had at our command, despite the fact that our President seems to think otherwise."[37]

Moxham outlined the committee's position in more detail to Pierre.[38] The advantages of the purchase were distant and "abstract." The "strategic advantage" vis-à-vis the Anglo-German Group would not be a reality for more than two years. The only other gain was a technological one acquiring "knowledge of the evolution of powder abroad [which] may guide us in our future evolution here." Against this there was the disadvantage of tying up a large block of capital, "of undertaking the management of a complicated foreign business at the time when we are still lacking good men to round out our own management," and the real danger of "an ugly contest with the Anglo-Germans" which could be costly and for which the du Ponts were certainly unprepared. Haskell, with his eyes still focused on Mexico, continued to believe the whole deal was part of a plot to force the du Ponts out of their strong position in that area. But everyone agreed that the most serious problem of all was the lack of information. Therefore, the committee decided that if Pierre had the time, he was to supply further operational and financial data and to learn more about Singer's motives and about the effect of the change on the relations with the Anglo-German Group. If he did not have the time, he should postpone decisions on the arrangements until the information was acquired. "If this is impossible, it is our judgment that the proposition should be declined."[39]

However, even before Pierre received the Executive Committee's cable, he had on his own account rejected Singer's proposition. In a letter to Coleman written on March 4, Pierre reported that he had asked Singer why he wanted to make the move. Singer replied that he would gain from the increase of stock. Moreover, Pierre was sure that the Austrian planned to be the Du Pont representative in the new company. Also, he would be in a better position in Mexico and in the later negotiations with the Anglo-German Group.[40] Since he was quite sure Singer had much to gain, Pierre was surprised when he also objected to several clauses in the detailed contract that he and Raskob had drawn up. Singer was particularly unhappy about the one they had inserted to insure that the du Ponts had control of the *Société Centrale* before putting up the $1.4 million by requiring Singer to guarantee the sale of the projected new issue of stock to the Powder Company.[41] Singer would certainly call the tune, Pierre realized, if he was not fully and legally committed to the sale of the new issue before the plan began to be carried out. Singer also refused to open the company's accounts and books to Du Pont inspection before the 5,000 shares had been acquired. (The balance sheets that Pierre and Raskob had reviewed earlier merely showed results of operations and were useful primarily to determine the value of the shares of the *Société Centrale*.) Since the other members of the board of the French company were not involved in the transaction, Pierre realized that such an inspection would be embarrassing to Singer. He therefore agreed to this and some other points on which the Austrian had valid objections. But on the first point in which Singer was to guarantee the sale of the new stock to the Powder Company, Pierre wrote Coleman, "We entirely fell apart."

With the failure of this complicated plan Pierre returned to the idea of exchanging stock, which Singer now found more acceptable.[42] Then to his relief Pierre received Moxham's cable outlining the views of the Executive Committee. Even if the Executive Committee had given its approval, Pierre wrote Coleman, "I think I should not have put it through owing to the impossibility of providing for the details of the agreement," on which he would have insisted.[43] Moreover, in the course of negotiations he had become aware of other disadvantages involved in taking over the French firm. Tariffs made shipments from one country to another difficult, so control of the French company might not affect their bargaining position with the Germans and British as much as he and Coleman had anticipated. This was even more true since the *Société Centrale* did not have the major control in plants in Belgium, South Africa, and even in Mexico. Only in France, Italy, Switzerland, and Sardinia did it fully control its subsidiaries. Once Pierre and Singer had agreed to break off negotiations, Singer suggested that the du Ponts continue "fighting" in Mexico.[44] If they did later purchase the *Société Centrale*, they should then be able to obtain the Mexican company at a cheaper price. If they did not buy the parent company, then Singer would find it easier to get full control of the subsidiary, which now included a number of Mexican stockholders.

Coleman was, of course, disappointed by the turn of events. "Somehow I have a feeling," he wrote Pierre, "that we should have made an affiliation with Singer. On the other hand I feel there is something we do not quite know but we certainly know more since your visit than before."[45] Thus Pierre's rejection of these proposals did not fully shut off negotiations with Singer. For the next two years—indeed, until after the signing of the European Agreement in 1907—Coleman continued to scheme to buy control of the *Société Centrale*. In these same years the Mexican situation continued to involve the Executive Committee in discussion and decisions.

## The Nitrate of Chile

On the long trip from Cherbourg to Buenos Aires, Pierre and Raskob turned their attention from markets to raw materials, from the ways of doing business in the accepted framework of high finance and from the challenges of advanced technology to those of negotiating in a distant underdeveloped land then experiencing the boom that comes with the initial exploitation of natural resources. The voyage provided as complete a rest as Pierre had ever enjoyed. Ahuja proved to be a pleasant and amusing companion. In time he became one of Pierre's close personal friends. Pierre wrote Alfred how sorry he was he could not take part in such a long period of pure relaxation. "After the first few days," he told his cousin, "you realize there is no hope of news or any information that can cause worry or trouble so the voyage is bound to be one unadulterated loaf."[46] But leisure had its price. Pierre put on so much weight that upon arriving in Buenos Aires he had to buy a whole new wardrobe.

As his letters to Coleman reveal, however, business was not completely forgotten. For on the trip Pierre and Ahuja reviewed in detail the history of the Du Pont Company's interest in Chile; the procedures and policies it had followed in purchasing its raw materials; and the immediate objectives of Pierre's trip to Chile. Both men had been close to the evolution of the company's policies from their beginning. The initial interest in obtaining a closer connection with Chile, was, of course, a direct result of the consolidations of 1902 and 1903. Prior to that time the few plants operated by the du Ponts purchased their nitrates from commissioned agents (importers) in New York, and did so largely from a firm headed by Schuyler Parsons, whose family had long been connected with Laflin & Rand.[47] After the consolidation, purchases which formerly had come to the thousands of dollars began to run into hundreds of thousands of dollars. For after 1902 a single department of the new and then the "Big Company," first the Purchasing and later the Essential Materials Department, was purchasing nitrates and other supplies, not for one family firm, but for more than two-thirds of the entire industry. In fact, even before the completion of the consolidation, Moxham estimated that the new Powder Company was buying close to half of all the nitrates imported into the United States as well as taking close to half the glycerin manufactured in this country.[48]

As soon as the Development Department was organized, one of its major tasks became an investigation of supplies. Moxham, with Coleman and the rest of the Executive Committee, decided from the start that the company should control at least part of the sources of its raw materials. Although such investments would have to be made with care, they agreed they were necessary to assure the regular supply of essential material at reasonable prices. In the spring of 1903 Moxham put several of his subordinates to work on analyzing sources and suppliers of charcoal and wood, pyrites, sulphur, glycerin and, above all, nitrate. By the end of 1904 the company had a plant in Bay City, Michigan, for the production of charcoal and it was starting to buy its own timber tracts.[49] It had also opened its own pyrites mine in Labrador.[50] During that year the Development Department continued to search for a satisfactory source of sulphur and to work out the best method for obtaining its huge supplies of nitrate.[51]

Within a week or two after the formation of the Development Department, Moxham had sent a mining engineer, David Lawson, to the west coast of South America to make a study of existing and potential nitrate properties and the costs involved in buying and working them.[52] Moxham instructed Lawson to send back detailed descriptions of the working of nitrate beds, the processing of plants used, the machinery and other materials required to work the fields, equipment to run the plants and to transport raw and semifinished products. He was to check labor supply, relations with governments, prices, and particularly to make a study of the operation of the "so-called Syndicate" that apparently controlled most of the current nitrate production. Did each individual company maintain a separate and legal identity, Moxham asked, or did the syndicate "absolutely own the separate plants and run them as an Operating Department?"

Even before Lawson had completed his report, Moxham had opened negotiations in Peru "on supposition that large beds of nitrates exist, the truth of which is to be tested later."[53] The situation looked promising enough "to send a diplomatic representative properly accredited to the government of Peru." For this task Moxham had selected Elias Ahuja, who had been working in a New York firm that imported nitrates. Probably Parsons had recommended him. Ahuja's mission in Peru was unsuccessful. The fields had not been fully explored, and the government was still uncertain as to its policy on developing them. So Ahuja moved south to join forces with Lawson in Chile.

In the meantime Lawson completed his investigation and forwarded the results to Wilmington in November 1903.[54] Lawson's report only hinted at the complexities and hazards of doing business in Chile. The nitrate fields were located in arid, sparsely inhabited areas far from ports or shipping facilities. Their development would require the building of railroads, piers, housing and other facilities, as well as the importation of labor. Moreover, the titles to the fields were often vague and confused, with individuals, the members of the companies belonging to the cartel, and the Chilean government, all having claims on the properties. But Lawson played down these difficulties, stressing instead the opportunities for purchasing. Nitrate beds could be bought reasonably. Since the cartel was keeping up the price, the Du Pont Company should be able to produce nitrate from its own beds at

$14–$15 per ton below existing prices. When Ahuja joined him, Lawson began investigating possible purchases. He was so convinced of the value of buying that he sent one of Chile's most prominent engineers to Wilmington to work out the details of building processing plants.[55]

By spring of 1904 the purchase of large nitrate properties seemed imminent. In April Ahuja cabled that he had the opportunity to buy an extensive tract known as the Boquete property.[56] The shipping firm of W. R. Grace & Company, the most influential American business concern on the west coast of South America, had already offered the Powder Company a share in its subsidiary, the Chilean Nitrate Company, which it planned to have buy and operate the Boquete property. However, Ahuja learned that the owners were not committed to Grace but would willingly sell to the highest bidder. The field had an estimated production of 3 million tons and would require the construction of about 100 miles of railroad, pipe lines for water, port facilities, and a large processing plant. The cost in addition to the sum paid for the nitrate bed, Lawson estimated at £300,000, or $1.5 million.

The deal nearly went through. Moxham obtained the approval of the board of directors as well as of the Executive Committee to buy the Boquete property for £250,000 to be paid in four payments at ten-month intervals. Before signing, Moxham asked Ahuja to procure some kind of guarantee as to the output of the fields. On June 16 the Du Pont representative cabled back that the owners insisted on receiving payment in "a lump sum without any regard to quality."[57] At the same time he reported a rumor that the Chilean government was planning to repossess the property, claiming that it had been fraudulently obtained. That news ended the possibility of buying the Boquete lands.

During the summer Ahuja and Lawson continued their searches. Soon they opened negotiations for a large area in the Tatal region. Moxham then decided to bring Lawson back for consultation and send H. G. Smith, formerly vice-president of the Rutland Railroad, to assist Ahuja in carrying out that deal.[58] But in this case and in others the negotiators made little headway. In November Moxham recalled Ahuja to Wilmington to review the whole nitrate situation. The Spaniard reached Delaware in January before Lawson had returned.[59] He conferred at some length with Moxham and talked only briefly with Coleman, Pierre, and others. To all, the gist of his message was to reject the policy advocated by Lawson of buying properties in areas where the output of the beds was still untested. Ahuja then asked if he might visit his family in Spain before returning to Chile. So, when some days later the Executive Committee decided to send Pierre to France, Coleman and the others agreed that he should meet Ahuja in Paris and accompany him to Valparaiso.

The long talks with Ahuja on the slow boat to Buenos Aires gave Pierre a chance to size up the Spaniard's abilities. "Being thrown together constantly," he told Coleman, "I have had so many conversations with him on different subjects that I feel I am better able to judge as to how far we should entrust ourselves to his judgement in matters pertaining to S. America." Pierre had no concern about Ahuja's honesty and uprightness, only about his business judgment and ability. "While his views seem entirely sound, I do not think he is a man who could accomplish a result by any brilliant scheme or strategy, nor do I think he is in the class of born traders."

In their shipboard conversations Ahuja convinced Pierre that because of the dangers of purchasing property during the current speculative boom in nitrates, nitrate lands, and other Chilean natural resources, "it will be difficult," as Pierre wrote Coleman, "if not impossible, to bring any of the propositions into shape where we can accept them at a stated figure after examining the property. Of course it is useless to consider a purchase unless examination is permitted, so I am rather less enthusiastic on the whole question than I was on leaving New York."[60] A few days in Chile would make him still more skeptical.

Smith, the former railroad man whom Moxham had sent to Chile to work with Ahuja, met the boat in Buenos Aires. He reported the availability of excellent nitrate beds near Antofagasta. Pierre decided to have Smith and Ahuja go directly to Valparaiso to begin negotiations for the purchase of these properties. He and Raskob would spend a couple of days sight-seeing in the Argentine capital and then come to Chile to close the deal.[61] On his arrival Pierre found that Ahuja was quite right. He was unable to draw up a careful, businesslike contract that the sellers would accept. Before he had been in Chile a week, he had realized that for the time being, at least, land purchases were out of the question.

He then turned to the second of his objectives. For Pierre had come to Chile for more than just the buying of nitrate properties. The Executive Committee had instructed him to obtain an overview of the nitrate business including its operations, finance, labor, training methods, technology, existing port, rail and other transportation facilities, governmental relations including taxes, tariffs, licensing and titles, and so "to confirm in a general way, by personal observation, the data which had previously been in the 'It is said' class."[62] On the basis of these observations he was to recommend to the committee the policies it should adopt in the purchasing, financing, and shipping of their company's most important raw material. After a week or so in Valparaiso, Pierre, Raskob, and Ahuja traveled north through the desolate desert country to view the recently opened fields.

Pierre outlined the result of this trip in a long report which he submitted to the Executive Committee well after his return to Wilmington in June. This 45-page report, illustrated with photographs, reveals Pierre's observing eye and inquiring mind. In his descriptions he answered in detail the questions asked by the committee. His recommendations were, basically, two.

He advised strongly against the purchase of nitrate lands at this time, and he proposed the formation of an office in Valparaiso to be manned by salaried company personnel.

Purchasing of land, Pierre maintained, would continue to be risky until the Chilean economy returned to normal. Even though a financial panic had recently slowed the boom, "the check to speculation has not been sufficient to dampen the ardor of the promoters, who are still ready to go ahead if the opportunity occurs. Particularly is this true in Nitrates where the combination arrangements in maintaining prices seem to favor the promoter."

Nevertheless, Pierre believed these conditions were only temporary. The best statistics available indicated that nitrate productive capacity was already ahead of demand. Since 1897 the number of operating firms, *oficinas* as Chileans called them, had increased from 42 to 76. The existing combination of the British, German, and Chilean producers formed in April 1901 would certainly have trouble maintaining itself as output continued to increase. Moreover, if the prices remained high, demand itself might decrease, for the fertilizer industry, particularly in Europe, would begin to rely on the growing chemical industry to supply its needs at a more reasonable cost. If this happened, then there would be ample stocks of Chilean nitrate available for explosives manufacturers. "Under such circumstances it has seemed useless," Pierre concluded, "and in fact imprudent to attempt active negotiations. By this I do not advise dilatory methods in following up this important question. If good property is available and proper opportunity for investigation is afforded, prompt action is certainly advisable."

Pierre pointed to one other risk in buying nitrate lands. Their operation presented administrative difficulties. The great distance from the central office required the obtaining of the best possible managers. Yet it would be hard to find good men to stay in this forsaken area of the world for any length of time. The recruitment of an efficient labor force presented further problems.

The postponement of buying nitrate lands caused Pierre to urge immediate changes in the company's present methods of purchasing its raw material. The Powder Company was then buying through agents and brokers in New York including Parsons & Petit, W. R. Grace & Company, and Wessel, Duval & Company. Commissions paid to these firms on purchases of nearly $5.0 million a year averaged an annual charge of $380,000. The salaries of one or two representatives in Chile would be far less than that amount. As important as any money saved, these representatives could provide a steady flow of information into the Wilmington office—information that certainly could not be obtained from brokers.

Again the basic problem in setting up even a small nitrate-buying office was that the job "demands not only that the man have the capacity to trade advantageously, but requires a man of great integrity, the remote distance from the home office and the inaccessibility of the country making our interest more dependent on one representative" than any other office in the Western Hemisphere or in Europe. Ahuja certainly seemed to be the man for the job, although Pierre did point out that he was still inexperienced. The office, the treasurer recommended, should be set up in Valparaiso, with commission agents in the field who would trade through local brokers. Pierre further urged that the Executive Committee look into the methods of improving shipments north. It should not only investigate the chartering of ships but even make a study of coal and lumber as possible return cargoes.

Pierre and Raskob enjoyed another leisurely trip on their way home up the west coast and across the Panama Isthmus.[63] Shortly after his return to Wilmington in June, the Executive Committee began to carry out Pierre's recommendations. In August Ahuja became the Du Pont representative in Chile, with an office and a small staff in Valparaiso. That autumn he and Frank G. Tallman, the head of the Purchasing Department, worked out methods of buying.[64] They agreed that the timing of purchases was the critical matter. As long as the combination of nitrate producers remained united, both men thought the prices would continue to rise. But it seemed more likely that the producers would not stick together.[65] Then prices would surely fall. Tallman, in a perceptive report to the Executive Committee, repeated Pierre's analysis of overproduction in Chile. He further pointed out that the labor shortages and transportation difficulties, which had kept the *oficinas* below their assigned quotas, had now been solved and as a result there was great pressure to change the existing quota arrangements. Long-term commitments should therefore be avoided and flexibility permitted in the main purchases.

To buy rationally under these conditions, Ahuja asked that he might be sent as detailed an estimate of the company's nitrate requirements as the manufacturing and purchasing departments could devise. Secondly, he requested permission to follow the standard practice "of buying for an extended period, say one year," specifying delivery of "a certain average quantity per month and exchange or resell such quantities as may not be needed in certain months for excess quantities required in other months."[66] Finally Ahuja wanted "a rather free reign" in making individual purchases in order to take advantage of short-term fluctuations.

Even though this policy meant that Ahuja would be in fact speculating on fluctuations in the nitrate market, Tallman endorsed his proposal and Pierre and the Executive Committee approved it. All agreed under existing conditions that speculation could hardly be avoided. Ahuja's suggestions seemed to reduce the risks and permit him to carry out the Executive Committee's basic policy of "buying as cheaply as our competitors."[67] The committee also approved of Tallman's proposal to have the company handle its own shipments. The chartering of ships on its own account would assure the regular deliveries so essential in planning manufacturing runs. In addition, such a move would place Ahuja's buying less at the mercy of outside shipping companies, some of which were controlled by nitrate producers or other large purchasers. As a result, in December 1906 Tallman chartered the S.S. *Tauris* to carry nitrates back from Valparaiso.[68]

The nitrate purchasing policies, as proposed by Pierre and approved by the Executive Committee in the summer and fall of 1905, remained basically unchanged until the du Ponts finally bought nitrate properties in Chile in 1910. Ahuja continued to handle the purchasing, and Tallman took care of the shipping in Du Pont chartered bottoms. And for nearly two years the nitrate producers' combination in Chile continued to dominate the market and maintain prices.

Once the basic policy was settled, Pierre's primary concern with the raw material was the financing of the nitrate imports. This financial policy had to be worked out in relation to many others involving the control and allocation of financial resources, and its final definition had to wait until other critical decisions were made. Of these matters none was more important than the continuing question of whether to expand at home or abroad. For, although Pierre's trip to Chile had for the moment eliminated the need for funds to buy nitrate properties, Coleman's strong interest in expanding the Du Pont Company's activities in Europe meant a continuing possibility of heavy investment overseas.

## The Final Resolution of European Policy, 1905–1907

For the two years following Pierre's journey to France and then to Chile the formulation of the company's overseas policies remained of major interest to Pierre and to the Executive Committee as a whole. The results of Pierre's stay in Paris were far less clear than those of his trip to Chile. For this reason alone, European affairs took much more of his time and that of the committee than did those involved in nitrate purchases. For another, the formulation of European, and the related Mexican, policy involved far more complex activities—marketing, manufacturing, finance and over-all administration and possibly larger amounts of money—than did the purchasing and development of nitrate properties.

During the latter part of the year 1905 and the first half of 1906, the interrelated plans for Mexico, the *Société Centrale,* and the renewal of the European Agreement had blossomed under Coleman's watchful guidance into a broad and ambitious scheme of overseas expansion for the Du Pont Company. Coleman still hoped to use the Mexican situation as leverage to acquire, with Singer's help, the control of the Latin Group and then to use that control to wring concessions from the Anglo-German Group at the negotiations to renew the European Agreement in 1907. Coleman, indeed, even began to dream of uniting Du Pont, the *Société Centrale*, and the Anglo-German Group into a single, mammoth, worldwide explosives enterprise.

The minutes of the Executive Committee of August 6, 1906, a little more than a year after Pierre had returned from Chile, emphasize the progress Coleman was making in his imperial schemes.[69] The committee authorized the purchase of the French-oriented Mexican National Dynamite Company for $2.0 million. It "favorably considered" the formation of a holding company to be chartered in Switzerland and to be called the Du Pont–Nobel Company to permit the Powder Company to obtain control of the *Société Centrale* and with it the whole Latin Group. Its estimated cost was $4.4 million. Next the committee acknowledged the proposed new European Agreement, but since time was growing short did not review it. In addition, it accepted an offer to build a smokeless powder plant near Rio de Janeiro for the Brazilian government. Finally at this same meeting the committee authorized Pierre to develop plans for raising capital through the sale of $2.0 million of common stock to present stockholders.

In the spring and summer of 1906, however, just as Coleman was transforming his ambitions into well-defined projects, the demand of the domestic market for explosives, particularly dynamite, expanded sharply. By September 1906 the Executive Committee had to make the critical choice. Should it follow Coleman's plan to build a Du Pont empire overseas, or should it concentrate its financial resources on enlarging domestic production to meet the growing home market? In this decision the treasurer had the crucial say. The majority of the Executive Committee preferred the home markets, so only with Pierre's strong support would Coleman have his way.

An evaluation and understanding of these critical decisions require a brief review of three interrelated parts of Coleman's overseas plans—the Mexican purchase, the continuing negotiations with Singer for control of the Latin Group, and the agreement with the Anglo-German Group. The first of these, the authorization of the purchase of the Mexican National Dynamite Company on August 6, 1906, had its roots in Haskell's "war" on that company, which began shortly before Pierre sailed for Europe in February 1905. The strategy then outlined worked well. In mid-April an explosion at the recently opened Mexican factory made victory easier. This explosion, which only slowed production, was followed by an even more serious one in August, which meant that the plant would be out of production for six months.[70]

The resulting dynamite shortage created a critical situation for Mexico's essential mining and railroad construction industries. The Mexican company itself proposed to the Du Pont representatives that the Wilmington company buy it out. Should the du Ponts turn down this proposal, the

Mexican company asked it to supply Mexico with its dynamite needs for the next year or eighteen months.[71] The Executive Committee rejected the idea of purchase but did agree to supply explosives south of the border along the lines worked out in the Mexican Agreement drawn up by the American Group in 1898. By this arrangement, both the Giant and Aetna companies had a share in the trade.

In the following spring, however, the committee, and most particularly Coleman, began to look more favorably on the possibility of obtaining the Mexican company. Rumors reached Wilmington of the probability of its sale to another company.[72] At about the same time the Du Pont Company's president made up his mind to go abroad to confer with Singer and with the managers of the Anglo-German Group. Before leaving for London in early June 1906, Coleman decided that when he reached Europe he would sound out Singer and the officers of the company about selling the whole Mexican enterprise—factories, sales office, and the concession from the government —to the Powder Company. Then after conferring in Paris in July with Singer and P. Martinez del Rio, a prominent Mexican who with Finance Minister Limantour had long advocated and supported the concession, Coleman drew up terms for buying that company.[73] By this proposal the Powder Company would spend up to $2.0 million in improving and enlarging the existing factory and in building new works so that the company would be certain to meet Mexico's explosives needs. Until these improvements were completed, the company would be permitted to import without paying the high tariff. Both Coleman and Martinez del Rio signed this proposal, agreeing to submit it to their respective directors for approval.

The purchase of the Mexican company was only a minor objective of Coleman's European trip. His primary purpose was to complete negotiations with Singer for control of the Latin Group and then to work out a new general agreement with the Anglo-German Group. Coleman hoped to go even further and form a worldwide alliance or even a tighter combination of all three groups—American, Latin, and Anglo-German.

Coleman had refused to be discouraged by the failure of the March negotiations with Singer. In the discussions that followed (when Pierre was in South America), Moxham and Haskell continued to be skeptical of Coleman's ambitions.[74] They were, however, willing to have Singer as a personal ally and suggested he be made a confidential agent for the Powder Company in Europe. The Austrian turned down this proposal when Haskell offered it to him on a visit to Paris in June 1905.[75] Singer, however, did impress Haskell with his sincerity and ability and seems to have convinced the Sales vice-president of the advantages of an alliance. After this discussion Haskell also believed that the control of the Latin Group by Du Pont would not violate the existing agreements in Europe and that such control would not antagonize the Anglo-German Group. At that time Singer had urged Haskell, and early in 1906 again urged Coleman, to have the Powder Company consummate the alliance with the Latin Group before Coleman came to London in the following summer to draw up a new agreement with the Anglo-German Group.[76]

Moxham still held back. In February he was warning Coleman to use "extreme caution in how you deal with this gentleman," for a misstep in Paris could lead to "an extremely ugly complication" in the negotiations in London.[77] In any case he urged Coleman not to act until Dr. Carl Hagen, Du Pont's London representative, had made his detailed report on the whole European explosives industry. Since Coleman talked with, rather than wrote to, Pierre about his plans, the treasurer's views on the purchase of control of the Latin Group are not recorded in his papers. Yet his statements and actions during the spring and summer of 1906 indicated that Pierre was still favorable to European expansion if it could be financed at reasonable cost.

Coleman did have time to study Hagen's report before he left for Europe in mid-June. That report carefully described the complex commercial and financial relations between European companies, and particularly between the Anglo-German and the Latin Groups. It also pointed out that the Du Pont Company could place its dynamite and other explosives products on the European market at one cent or one and one-half cents less per pound than could the Europeans themselves. These lower costs appear to have resulted from Du Pont's high-volume manufacturing operations. The report also made clear that the Europeans would fight vigorously any challenge in these markets.[78]

Neither the report nor Moxham's Development Department proposed any course of action. Nor did the Executive Committee give Coleman any formal instruction when he departed for London and Paris. Left to his own devices Coleman moved fast. He had planned to spend a couple of weeks in Britain getting the lay of the land.[79] He had been in London only a day or so when he conferred with Singer who, on learning of Coleman's arrival, had crossed the Channel. The two quickly worked out a "trade" about which Coleman immediately wrote Pierre.[80] They would set up a company in Switzerland, which offered tax and legal advantages. By this time Singer was most willing to use the exchange of stock method for financing. For the proposed new Du Pont–Nobel Company, Singer agreed to put in 28,000 shares of the *Société Centrale*'s stock and receive in return 28,000 shares of the new company. The Powder Company would, in its turn, take $4.4 million worth of stock, some 32,000 shares, in return for comparable value of Powder Company preferred and common stock. In this way the Powder Company would control the *Société Centrale* and with it the Latin Group. When Coleman crossed the Channel in July to work out arrangements for the purchase of the Mexican company, he and Singer agreed on the final arrangements including details on the purchasing of stock and the provision that Singer would be the managing director of the proposed company. However, this agreement was far less carefully and rigorously defined than the one Pierre and Raskob had presented Singer sixteen months before.

Both Singer and Coleman hoped to use this proposal in the negotiations with the Anglo-German Group. When Coleman arrived in London, he had suggested to the senior executives of that group that they join with him and Singer (that is, with the Du Pont–Nobel Company) to form a single giant confederation. In financing this combination, he estimated that the Du Pont Company's share would come to $6.0 million. The British, however, appeared to show little interest at all in Coleman's scheme. "I do not think they know what I am talking about," Coleman wrote Pierre. "They admit a consolidation would be an advantage, but they evidently do not want to lose control of the European situation."[81]

Actually the audacity of Coleman's suggestion had stunned Henry de Mosenthal, the chief executive of the British Nobel Dynamite Trust. In a note to Thomas Johnston, the general manager of its largest subsidiary, he exclaimed about Coleman and his plans:

> His whole style was decidedly breezy. He stated that he thought that a closer union between him and us would be desirable, and then he developed the plan of amalgamation. . . . In short, it looks as if he had come over with the idea of buying up the Trust, the Powder Group, the Société Centrale and in addition all and any small fry that may have agreements with us. He asked me why smokeless powder was selling so cheap to the Government here. I said it was due to Kynochs, Mr. Arthur Chamberlain not wishing to join any convention. He asked me where the man lived, that he would like to have a look at him, and that when a man talked like that he wanted to be bought up.
>
> In short he absolutely staggered me, and I think I was right in telling him that in my opinion his proposal would stagger the Board. I hope you [Johnston] will be able to join me [in meeting him] on Monday evening, as I hardly feel strong enough by my wee self.

After outlining his plans for both the French and British mergers Coleman asked Pierre his opinion, by cable if possible. If Pierre replied by cable his answer cannot be found in either the Pierre or Coleman papers. On the other hand, Pierre at this time was very much involved in checking on the legality of these plans and may have postponed his answer to Coleman until he had received the lawyers' advice. In any case Pierre undoubtedly suspected that the British would hardly be enthusiastic about Coleman's plans. Why should they want to jeopardize their control over the European market in any way, particularly if they may have realized what Hagen had pointed out, that Du Pont could produce for the European market as efficiently and cheaply as most Europeans?

Coleman was not too distressed at the British refusal to merge with the proposed Du Pont–Nobel Dynamite Company. He and his colleagues on the Executive Committee had always looked on the arrangement with Singer as a means to win concessions from the Anglo-German Group. Here Coleman was successful. In outlining the new agreement, the British and Germans accepted having France, Italy, and Switzerland as "neutral" territory "not affected by this Agreement."[82] After obtaining this gain Coleman concentrated on enlarging more fully the exchange of patents and processes. As Singer kept stressing, the du Ponts still had much to learn from the Europeans on the chemistry and by-products of explosives.

Then suddenly the patent arrangements became the focal point of the whole European Agreement. In Wilmington the threat of an antitrust suit had raised questions about the legality of the existing agreement with the Anglo-German Group and about the one that Coleman was then negotiating.[83] Moxham, after conferring with Townsend, the senior partner of Du Pont's outside legal firm, was now certain that these agreements would be considered illegal. He quickly convinced Haskell and Pierre. Pierre then cabled Coleman that the present European Agreement should be immediately abrogated and the new one largely redrawn. Coleman accepted the advice. The old agreement was formally renounced by Coleman as chairman of the American Group, and by Sir Ralph Anstruther of the Anglo-German Group. Then for good measure it was burned in the presence of the chairmen and the representatives of the firms that had originally signed it.

Coleman waited until he received legal advice to redraw the new agreement. This advice came in a long letter written by Pierre on July 11 and another from Townsend, Avery and Button mailed the following day. Both resulted from a "lengthy interview" between Haskell, Pierre, and the lawyers. The lawyers stressed that "the law on this subject is in a very unsettled and formative condition." To be safe, however, the new agreement should be solely a patent and trade name agreement and should not involve pricing or the exclusive allocation of marketing territories. Pierre and Haskell felt that such a change from marketing to patenting agreements would not affect the underlying purpose of the arrangement "as the inability of the European countries (to use their patents and trade names) would form such a handicap that they would not undertake such an enterprise."[84]

The tentative agreement Coleman brought back to Wilmington early in August was then basically one for the exchange of methods, processes, and patents.[85] It was between the Du Pont Company (not the American companies as was the 1897 Agreement) and the Anglo-German Group, which identified itself in the contract as "the European Factories." It covered all types of explosives, but not industrial by-products of the manufacturing of explosives. The European Factories granted the Du Pont Company the sole right to use European methods or products made by such methods in the American territories and, except for military powders, to sell (but not to manufacture) such products "in neutral and syndicated territories." The Du Pont Company in turn granted sole rights to the European Factories to make and sell products with their processes, again with the exception of military powders, in the neutral and syndicated territories. The contract defined American territories as North America (except for Canada and British Honduras) and Columbia and Venezuela. Syndicated territory where the two marketed jointly was to be the rest of South America, while neutral territory was defined as Canada and, as Coleman had arranged, Italy, Switzerland, and France. The rest of the world was to be European territory.

The major part of the agreement dealt with the methods of interchanging information and patents and the payment for their use. The European Factories agreed to supply ample drawings and other information needed to permit the Du Pont Company to install European processes and to supply expert chemists and engineers and foremen if requested. They were to transfer all patents they currently possessed or developed in the future for use in the American territory. The European Factories were to impart their methods and secret processes to "chemists or other confidential person or persons," and were to "draw the attention" of the Du Pont Company to any new methods and processes they developed. The du Ponts were to do exactly the same thing for the Europeans. In payment the du Ponts were to credit to the European Factories one-half of the savings or additional earnings resulting from the use of European processes. If the improvement did not affect earnings and savings, but rather safety and quality, they were to pay a royalty of 10%. In any case the du Ponts were to guarantee a minimum payment of $100,000 a year to the Europeans. This figure was based on the average royalty payments the Americans had paid the Europeans annually under the 1897 Agreement on the manufacture of improved smokeless powder. On the other hand, Coleman had agreed that in any one year the Europeans would not have to pay an assured minimum of any size. Nor were they ever to be charged more than $300,000 in any one year for the use of American methods and processes. This concession to the Europeans troubled the Executive Committee. For unless the Du Pont Company could show equivalent value received in technical knowledge, Moxham, Townsend, and others thought that the courts would read it (and quite rightly) as an extension of the 1897 Agreement. It delayed the signing of the contract for several months. The new arrangement further defined the methods to be used in determining profits and savings resulting from the new processes and set up an arbitration procedure to settle disputes that might arise as to the amounts calculated. Finally, both sides agreed that in powder for military use "government prohibition shall be a valid plea . . . to decline to reveal a method which but for this prohibition would come within the operation of this Agreement."

Coleman must have been elated when he made his report to the Executive Committee immediately after his return to Wilmington in early August. Although he had not achieved his ultimate objective of a single worldwide unit, he surely had prepared the way for the Powder Company to enlarge its overseas operations. He reported to the Executive Committee at the first scheduled meeting on August 6 after his arrival back in Wilmington. The session had been called to discuss plans to build a Smokeless Powder plant for the Brazilian government near Rio de Janeiro. This was, incidentally, the one overseas project in which Coleman was not ultimately involved. As three of the committee's members were out of town, Haskell and Barksdale on business and Alfred in South Dakota, where he was obtaining a divorce, the initial critical discussion of Coleman's accomplishments involved only Moxham, Pierre, Baldwin, and Connable, the latter attending as Alfred's representative.

The meeting opened with a discussion and authorization of the Brazilian contract. The Du Pont Company was to build the factory and then run it for a year after its completion, all costs being covered by the Brazilians. After further correspondence, the company signed a contract with the Brazilian government on October 9, 1906.[86]

Next, in the order of business, Coleman presented the tentative contracts for the purchase of the Mexican company. Pierre and Moxham approved but voiced some reservations. Finally the members agreed "that it would be well to accept the proposition as outlined," provided that the Du Pont Company "finds that the assets are reasonably close to the estimated $2,000,000, say at least 10% thereof," and also if the three absent members of the committee specifically approve.[87]

The proposal to form the Du Pont–Nobel Company led to a more serious debate, with Moxham apparently still strongly opposing and Pierre supporting the purchase of the French or Latin Group. In the end the committee voted to record that the proposition was "favorably considered" but "that the details governing the same shall be put into proper form and be submitted to each member of the Executive Committee for study with a view to action early in September." Since there was no immediate pressure to ratify the new European Agreement, the committee decided to postpone action until the other members returned. Given the amount of appropriations approved during the afternoon, it is hardly surprising that the committee wound up the meeting by asking Pierre to "take up" with the proper experts the question of making an open market for our securities "in order to meet the clear need for more capital."

Before the crucial meeting set for September, Coleman worked hard to get support for his plan to obtain control of the Latin Group. He talked to the lawyers, getting their approval, and answered questions of different members of the Executive Committee. The more the committee members studied the plan, however, the less they liked it. Moxham again expressed his fears of the dangers involved in trying to move into the tightly controlled European market. Alfred had written Coleman from South Dakota that he would agree about the "strategic" advantages of the plan, but he could not see "how on earth you figure it will pay."[88]

More serious to Coleman was Pierre's growing concern about placing so large an amount of capital into purchasing control of the French company. For one thing, Pierre was far more skeptical about the accuracy and reliability of Singer's financial statements than Coleman had ever been. On August 13 he wrote Coleman asking him to get more detailed information from the Austrian.[89] By then, too, Pierre was thinking seriously of the alternative uses for this money, particularly in expanding dynamite production capacity at home. At the meeting held September 12, which even Alfred attended, Pierre supported the rest of the committee in refusing to approve Coleman's project until they had more accurate and detailed information. Despite the steady stream of his most persuasive arguments, the best Coleman could get from the committee was authorization to cable Singer that "generally speaking our people think well of plan," and that financing might involve an increase in preferred and a decrease in common stock. "Can you come on flying visit to explain details organization and manufacture to us perhaps bringing Mr. Falcouse [the French company's technical director]?"[90] Although Coleman continued to correspond with Singer, the purchase of the French company and the control of the Latin Group were never seriously considered after the September 12 meeting. Business commitments caused Singer and his technical director to postpone their trip. Even if they had come, it seems doubtful that their visit would have made a difference.[91]

For at this very moment, developments in the domestic market were forcing the Executive Committee to turn their attention to capital expenditures at home. During the spring and summer of 1906 the domestic demand for dynamite continued to grow. The heavy call for explosives that began in the autumn of 1904 had continued throughout the following year. General prosperity in the United States and throughout the world had kept mining, and railroad and building construction booming. By late spring of 1906 the demand for dynamite was becoming so great that a serious shortage loomed. Barksdale now believed that he needed to increase his department's productive capacity far beyond the 20 million-pound figure he had proposed to the Executive Committee in January 1905. Since the plant near Ashland, Wisconsin, was reaching completion that spring, his department had begun construction of a new plant in Colorado and to plan another in the state of Washington. At a meeting of July 25, 1906, held just before Coleman returned from Europe, the Executive Committee had agreed to a crash program to meet the expanding demands for dynamite by enlarging the capacity of three existing plants by a total of nearly a million pounds.

Then on September 22, only ten days after the meeting concerning expansion abroad, the committee had a long session to study a massive expansion program outlined by Hamilton Barksdale for his High Explosives Department.[92] While no clear-cut decision was made during September at any one meeting of the Executive Committee, the senior executives had definitely decided, before the month was out, to eliminate overseas expansion as a real alternative to growth at home. To Pierre, as well as the others, investment in the well-known domestic market seemed more attractive than a risky venture in the less-known, more distant European trade. At the end of the month, Pierre had completed a plan for financing the purchase of the French company (dated October 2). Yet only a week later he wrote William du Pont: "It now seems unlikely that there will be any necessity of investing funds in Europe, a fact of considerable relief to the Treasury, in view of the demands for funds in developing our own country."[93]

Although Pierre submitted a proposal for financing the foreign venture to the Executive Committee early in November, it was never discussed there. Unquestionably, Pierre never expected that it would be. For by early October he had decided that the Du Pont Company's existing resources and those he had planned to raise by the sale of stock would be allocated to domestic rather than foreign expansion. His decision set the company on a course that would not be altered for forty years. If Pierre had approved Singer's plan in Paris in 1905, or if he had strongly supported Coleman in August and early September in 1906, the Du Pont Executive Committee might have authorized the president's imperial overseas plans. But once he had decided to back domestic expansion, Coleman had almost no chance of getting his plan accepted.[94]

The decision to build at home rather than to buy abroad affected Coleman's other plans. It took the drive out of the scheme to buy the Mexican company and it favored the signing of the patent agreement with the Anglo-German Group. On August 6, only a week after he had presented the tentative agreement for the purchase of the Mexican dynamite company, Coleman received a telegram from Noetzlin, the Mexican company's local manager, who was then in Europe, approving the agreement.[95] On August 17 the Executive Committee agreed to accept the contract on condition that the Mexican company's assets were reasonably close to the two million Mexican dollars as claimed and that the Du Pont Company would have ten years to meet the terms of the concession. Until that time, it would have the right to import all the dynamite it was unable to manufacture to meet Mexican needs. In October Coleman traveled to Mexico to confer with Martinez del Rio, Limantour, the finance minister, and August Genin who, with Noetzlin, directly managed the company. At the resulting conference both sides seemed to be in agreement after Coleman said that he was willing to cut down the time needed to meet the terms of the concession.[96]

Nevertheless, neither side took positive action.[97] The du Ponts were slow in sending appraisers to Mexico. Limantour became involved in other political and governmental matters and failed to concentrate on adjusting the terms of the concession. Then, as the Mexican company again moved into full production after repairing the damages from the explosion, its manager and Singer and other officers of the French parent company became less interested in selling out. Any lingering hopes Coleman had about buying or building in Mexico came to an end with the international financial panic which suddenly began in September 1907.[98]

Of the three proposals Coleman brought back from Europe, only the agreement with the Anglo-German Group was finally signed. This agreement was in line with the policy of domestic expansion which Pierre and the Executive Committee had reached in September. It cut off the possibility of investment abroad, except in France, Italy, Switzerland, and Canada. At the same time, it encouraged technological advances that promised to make the home market even more profitable. Even here, where the Executive Committee was essentially in agreement, the papers were signed only after a good deal of discussion between the du Ponts and the representatives of the Anglo-German Group.

The first meeting of the Executive Committee devoted primarily to the agreement, held on September 8, brought out two major objections to the proposal.[99] Pierre and Moxham remained troubled by the legality of the agreement, particularly as to the operations in the syndicated South American territory. Secondly, Barksdale and Haskell disliked the provision that required the du Ponts to guarantee $100,000 in payments while the Europeans guaranteed nothing. After some exchange of correspondence as to where to meet to iron out these differences, both the Du Pont and the European–Nobel group agreed to alternate meetings until a compromise agreement was reached.[100] A session in New York in November was followed by a trip of Haskell and Moxham to Europe, and finally the Europeans returned to New York in May to sign the finished document.

By the time of the November conference, the Executive Committee had agreed to accept the guarantee if the Europeans could demonstrate the savings promised. They had assured Coleman that by their processes Du Pont could improve the safety of gelatine dynamite and increase the nitroglycerin yield. However, at the conference in November Moxham made it clear that Du Pont was in no way convinced about the real value of the $100,000 annual payment. At the February meetings with the Nobel representatives he and Haskell simply refused to discuss the proposal. So the Europeans dropped the demand.[101]

On the second objection, Pierre and Moxham recommended the formation of two jointly owned companies to be financed by the exchange of stock. One was to hold patents and the other to market in the syndicated territories.[102] Neither the American lawyers nor the European manufacturers appeared enthusiastic about these proposals. So when the new European Agreement was finally signed in June, its terms on this point were quite close to the one Coleman had originally brought back with him.

Once the managers of the Anglo-German Group had signed with the Americans, they took up negotiations with Singer for a comparable revision and extension of an agreement made in 1887 with the Latin Group.[103] In the midst of these discussions Singer was struck down with a fatal heart attack. After Singer's death, the directors of the French company became still more anxious to complete plans for an alliance that Coleman and Singer had advocated for so long a time. Even de Mosenthal temporarily urged Coleman to pick up the project again. But if Coleman still had hopes of expansion abroad he never voiced them. By the summer of 1907 Pierre's financial policies had definitely committed the Du Pont resources at home beyond the point of any return. In September, therefore, the Anglo-German Group began to negotiate with the Latin Group an arrangement that did not involve the Americans.

Both the Americans and Europeans were quick to reap the benefits of their new agreement. They started to exchange information by letter, and then all through 1908 senior executives, both Europeans and Americans from the Powder Company, began extended tours of each other's plants, offices, and laboratories and met for long periodic conferences.[104] Pierre himself enjoyed pleasant and instructive visits to the offices and plants of the Nobels on a trip he made to Europe in the late winter of 1910. There he met, for the first time, Harry McGowan, one of the ablest young executives in the Nobel Company, who would become a lifelong friend and business ally. The information and patents exchanged or offered during the first two years after the signing of the agreement included methods for improving detonators by using a dry process, new propellants for navy shells, electric safety fuses, experiments in obtaining nitrates from the air, and even such developments beyond explosives as the use of pyroxylin products for industrial purposes. The Du Pont Company certainly gained in technical and scientific knowledge by this exchange.

The Europeans, on the other hand, were primarily interested in the Americans' mechanical equipment and business methods. They asked for information concerning the determination of costs, the operation of pension funds and workmen's compensation, insurance and shipping arrangements. Besides exchanging information on patents and other rights, each side kept the other informed on new competition and legal and political developments, including the antitrust actions and decisions.

While some adjustments were made in the 1907 Agreement, it remained relatively unchanged until 1913. Then it was altered only because of the

United States government's successful antitrust suit against the Du Pont Company. During 1907 and 1908 the formula to determine profits for savings owing to interchange of patents and processes was worked out in detail. The two groups decided that straight royalty payments involved too many technical details and complex bookkeeping. So they agreed that a certain percentage of profits beyond those made in 1906 would be considered as a return from the use of new methods, equipment, and materials. If the Du Pont Company's profit exceeded $5.3 million (the 1906 profit), 36½% of the excess (after 6% interest was deducted) would be paid to the Anglo-German group for the "European Inventions." If the European profit, after allowances, exceeded $12.7 million, 63½% of that excess would go to the Americans for the use of their processes and methods. (Each of these percentages was that of the total assets of both groups held by each group.) While these payments were at least nominally paid for new information, they were basically used to keep both sides satisfied with the continuing division of the world markets.[105]

After the American and world economy had recovered from the panic of 1907, Pierre worked closely with de Mosenthal after the British proposed forming a jointly owned company, Canadian Explosives, Ltd., to manufacture and sell in Canada. That venture merged four Canadian companies, the largest of which, the Hamilton Powder Company, the du Ponts had had an interest in since the days of Eugene du Pont. The Du Pont Company took 45% and Nobel 55% of the stock in the new company and so began a partnership in Canada that lasted more than forty years.[106] On the other hand, the Executive Committee in 1911 dropped plans to develop a similar scheme for South America because of Pierre's insistence that such a program was contrary to the European Agreement and, of more importance, to American antitrust legislation.[107]

The rejection of Coleman's plans to move into Europe and Mexico and the acceptance of the new agreement with the Anglo-Germans thus fundamentally affected the growth of the Du Pont Company and the career of Pierre du Pont. Not only would the company concentrate in the future on the domestic market, but it would also be able to tap quickly and fully the scientific skills and resources of Europe's industrial laboratories. Its dominant position in North America seemed assured; the only threat to its power could come from the United States government itself.

For Pierre the decisions in the autumn of 1906 meant that he could finally begin to define the company's financial policy in terms of clearly defined goals rather than several quite different alternatives. Moreover, in making these plans, Pierre became increasingly independent of Coleman's attitudes and ideas. His decision against overseas expansion marked the first time he had broken with his cousin over basic policy for their company. The division between the president and the treasurer on overseas policy had subtly changed the relationship between the two cousins and between them and each of the individual members of the Executive Committee. Pierre found he could resist Coleman's persuasive arguments when on the basis of his own information and analysis he found them unsound. Moreover, because in the issue of overseas versus domestic expansion he came to advocate the views of the majority of the Executive Committee, he also came to be looked on more and more as the natural leader of that group.

# Maintaining Financial Control

W ITH THE DECISION in the fall of 1906 to grow at home rather than abroad, Pierre and the Executive Committee returned to the issues they had been debating before Coleman became intrigued by the opportunities abroad. Pierre now felt that his department had adequately shaped and tested the Powder Company's instruments for financial control. He was satisfied that, in most respects, cost, production, and other accounting data collected and compiled in the Treasurer's Office gave him and the Executive Committee an accurate picture of the company's widespread activities. He thought too that he had most of the information he needed for rational long-term planning.

They now had to decide on which of the products, and in which geographic areas, domestic production capacity would be increased; and they had to agree on how the funds were to be raised and from what sources. As before, the operating executives' ambitions exceeded the availability of funds. So Pierre took the lead in developing methods to evaluate the various alternatives so that the limited supply of money would be channeled into the most profitable areas.

In planning the financing of the expansion of plant capacity at home, Pierre kept two points constantly in mind. First, he wanted to raise the necessary funds without diluting the du Pont family's control of the Powder Company. This presented a challenge, for if retained earnings were not enough, then capital must come from the sale of stock and bonds. Such securities had to be made attractive to the family or sold to outsiders. The treasurer's second goal was to maintain a careful balance so that the allocation of funds for the expansion of plant and equipment would not adversely affect the continuing supply of working capital. Pierre's memories of the Johnson Company's difficulties and of his distress in January 1904 when he found the Du Pont Company temporarily without adequate working capital etched this objective sharply in his mind. He was determined not to let large capital expenditures threaten his cash reserves, nor lead to the creation of a large floating debt.

Nevertheless, the sums involved were so large that maintaining control of working capital was tricky business, even when large fixed capital expenditures were not being made. In his monthly report to the Executive Committee in June 1906 Pierre made this point to his colleagues. The events of a single month, including unusual expenditures coupled with a delay in the receipt of funds owed to the company by the United States government, had created a cash deficit of nearly $800,000. Pierre announced that the corporation would be able to borrow the money, but he took the occasion to consider the long-term significance of this event. "Our average deposits," he said, "are about $1,500,000 of which we require $500,000 . . . for current balances, leaving a possible $1,000,000 free for extraordinary requirements such as have appeared during the past thirty days."[1] Pierre added that the corporation's usual monthly cash outflow varied between $2.0 million and $2.5 million and that a cessation of collections for but half a month would exhaust the entire surplus. So large were the Powder Company's cash requirements that a moderate miscalculation, an increase in commitments that coincided with a fall in the demand, or payments for explosives, or a sharp business recession could within a matter of weeks bring the corporation to the brink of financial ruin.

Pierre could not, of course, foresee that in little over a year the onslaught of the nation's most severe financial panic between the gold crisis of 1895 and the stock market crash of 1929 would create precisely these conditions. In the summer of 1906 Pierre fully appreciated the problems of calculating demand, planning production, accumulating raw materials to meet the schedules, and providing cash to pay for payrolls and raw materials. In doing all these things he and the Executive Committee had to be sensitive to rapid changes in the economy which could quickly affect the level of demand or the availability of raw materials, credit, or cash. For Pierre, as for all managers of the new centrally administered industrial corporations, nearly all of which had been formed since the depression of the 1890s, the panic of 1907 was to be a critical test of their ability to maintain financial control of the new giant enterprises.

*Tightening Financial Control*

Even before Pierre began to work out his long-term financial plans for funding the anticipated plant expansion, he and the Executive Committee were aware of two major weaknesses in the recently developed financial and statistical controls. One lay in the purchasing of raw materials; the other, in the use of monies which had already been appropriated for new plants, offices, and equipment. The second problem resulted from the chance that the operating departments might simultaneously undertake major construction or maintenance projects which would result in large demands on the company's cash reserves. If the treasurer were unaware of how specific appropriation commitments were being spent until the bills were presented for payment, the Powder Company would risk serious financial distress.

At Pierre's urging, on January 4, 1906, the Executive Committee adopted a plan to insure that an appropriation would be programmed into the treasurer's planning prior to the expenditure of any money. In some ways the new procedures were more liberal than those first adopted in 1903. Pierre aimed to reduce red tape and simultaneously to increase the ability of top management to control—that is, to stop or alter—appropriations if deemed necessary. The major emphasis, therefore, was to improve the quality of information that the treasurer received about appropriations and to make these data available as rapidly as possible. As in the original appropriation procedure established in 1903, the expenditure of less than $5,000 required only the signature of one of the major department heads (Smokeless Powder, Black Powder, or High Explosives). In contrast, however, the rules for expenditures between $5,000 and $10,000 were liberalized to the extent that the Executive Committee no longer needed to approve. Such outlays could be rapidly initiated by a department head with the president's approval. The key refinement, however, proposed to make more use of the office in charge of the coordination and review of the appropriations procedures, an office first proposed by Moxham, late in 1904, and held by Irénée since the summer of 1905. The committee directed Irénée to pass upon, prior to any commitment to spend, "appropriations of every kind" and report the total immediately to the treasurer and to the Executive Committee as a regular part of its twice monthly meetings.[2] In theory, therefore, expenditures could not be made without the treasurer's knowledge, and the danger that a sudden flurry of bills from projects initiated by the various department heads could drain away cash reserves would be eliminated. Furthermore, the Treasurer's Office, if it found that appropriations would undermine the corporation's cash position, could alert the Executive Committee, which could rapidly suspend the grants until such time as the company's finances permitted them.

To initiate the rules was one thing; to achieve compliance was another.

Every month Irénée carefully evaluated each department's behavior. In October 1906 he reported that the "scheme for handling appropriations appears to be working rather more satisfactory than formerly," but he complained that "we still have expenditures coming before the corresponding appropriation has been granted."[3] Irénée, as Pierre's assistant, explained that this was unnecessary, since all irregular expenditures were concentrated at the black powder works, whereas neither the High Explosives nor the Smokeless Powder Departments violated established procedures. Irénée explained that from "a bookkeeping point of view violations were only a slight inconvenience." What concerned him was that management's control over the level of expenditure, a vital factor in time of crisis, was being undercut.

Irénée's report, however, pointed up the system's success rather than its failure. In September 1906, for example, violations amounted to only about $2,000 out of total appropriations of nearly $200,000. And Irénée was able to pinpoint incorrect procedures in such minor cases as $3 at the Mooar and $23 at the Rosendale black powder works.[4] Pierre's procedures had succeeded in giving top management a continuous accurate view of appropriations expenditures and a method to effect reductions instantly should that be necessary.

### Nitrate Purchases—Special Problems

No single phase of the big company's operations presented more challenge than purchasing. In 1906 its Purchasing Department spent over $19.25 million, and of this amount more than $8.5 million went for two essential materials, nitrate of soda and glycerin.[5] The Powder Company, which in mid-1906 had total net assets of slightly more than $37.0 million, could ill afford mistakes in acquisition of its raw materials.

Of these materials the item that tied up the largest amount of money and caused the most worry for the Treasurer's Office was nitrate of soda. The established procedures set up by Pierre and the Executive Committee on Pierre's return from Chile permitted Ahuja, operating from an office in Chile and assisted by Pierre's cousin Charles A. Belin, to purchase nitrates for the company on a very large scale, and to do so with a good deal of independence. This caused the working capital required for nitrates to rise from $1.6 million to $4.0 or $5.0 million annually.[6] Such large-scale speculation on the rise and fall of nitrate prices placed enormous responsibility on Ahuja, the senior South American representative. Pierre approved of the delegation of authority to Ahuja, but the Executive Committee felt that closer supervision was necessary.

Because of the size and cost of these shipments Pierre finally agreed with the rest of the Executive Committee in January 1907 to give Tallman, director of purchases, the power they had delegated to Ahuja.[7] Tallman, acting with the advice of a subcommittee consisting of Pierre and Hamilton Barksdale, was to decide the amount and the time at which nitrates were to be purchased. In addition, Tallman and his committee were to approve all nitrate resales and exchanges. Thenceforth, Wilmington, not Valparaiso, regulated the volume and timing of purchases and sales.[8]

The most difficult and immediate task, however, which faced the Powder Company in Chile was arranging to pay for the purchases. In the twentieth century's first decade Chile's economy was linked closely to that of Europe, especially England and Germany. English and German banks served most Chilean trading centers; in contrast, the influence and reputation of the United States financial institutions counted for little. In Chile, specie was scarce, and nitrate sales provided most of the foreign exchange. In fact, drafts issued in payment for nitrates often circulated a considerable time within the country as a money substitute.

Du Pont's problem was typical of those encountered by many American concerns that were expanding their activities into distant nations in the early part of the century. In short, the du Ponts found that their drafts would not be accepted as first-class notes, and since there were no American banks in Chile, they had to establish credit with a foreign institution. In February 1906 Pierre outlined a complex solution to the Executive Committee. Brown Brothers & Co. of Philadelphia, acting through their London agents, Brown and Shipley Co., had opened letters of credit in favor of Huth & Co., Valparaiso bankers. This arrangement granted Ahuja credit of between $3.0 million and $5.0 million at a Chilean bank. Ahuja, therefore, gave nitrate firms drafts drawn on Huth & Co. which in turn were guaranteed in London by Brown and Shipley. Huth & Co., however, sent the drafts, ideally with the nitrate shipping documents, directly to Philadelphia for payment. For this, Brown Brothers then transferred funds to London to complete the circle. Brown Brothers charged a commission of ¼ of 1% and Huth & Co. $\frac{3}{16}$ of 1%, making a total of $\frac{7}{16}$ of 1%, which amounted to $21,875 on transactions of $5.0 million. For the Powder Company the agreement was especially desirable, since it provided first-class banker's bills in Chile without loss of exchange and it also gave them short-term credit for as much as ninety days; that is, from the time when Ahuja paid the nitrate companies to the time when the drafts drawn on Huth & Co. were received by London for payment. For this accommodation interest was charged, but collateral was not required.[9]

Experience demonstrated that interest on the notes was significant. In July 1907 Pierre reported to the Executive Committee that the minimum charge covered a forty-five day period, that is, the time it took for steamers to carry the drafts from Chile to London for final payment and cancellation. But as the notes frequently circulated in Chile for weeks or even months, the interest charges became much higher. Wrote Pierre, "This is an item of great moment to us."[10]

Pierre proposed that the Powder Company aim toward the issuing of drafts in its own name payable directly on its London account. This would have eliminated the necessity of operating through Huth & Co. and with it the interest that accumulated from the time a draft on Huth & Co. was tendered a nitrate owner to the time that draft had been transported to England for final settlement. Pierre rejected using the services of the American Express Company on the grounds that it was so little known in Chile that drafts drawn on it would not be accepted as first class. Even in July 1907, one and a half years after the opening of its Chilean operation, Pierre still felt that the Du Pont Company needed more time before drafts in its own name on a London bank would be accepted at par.[11] In the midst of these negotiations, in the fall of 1907 a worldwide financial panic struck and forced a complete revamping of the arrangements for importing nitrates.

### The Increase of Capital and Domestic Expansion Plans

Besides building credit lines in Chile and improving methods of funneling information to the Executive Committee and of achieving more certain control of day-to-day expenses, Pierre also began in the first part of 1906 to obtain more precise and systematic information on long-term needs of the operating departments. Although the treasurer realized that few decisions could be made on how much to spend until the Executive Committee had agreed whether to move abroad or at home, he saw no need to wait on this decision before collecting essential information. Despite prodding from the Executive Committee, prior to 1906 no department had worked out a comprehensive long-term plan for increasing productive capacity. Each department had, as early as 1904, at the time of the formation of the big company, begun to develop plans for the rationalization of its production, that is, the closing of inefficient mills and the building of new ones strategically located with regard to sales. Despite promising starts toward long-term planning in high explosives and black powder, each department soon began to respond more to market demands of the moment than to pressure of top management for comprehensive programs.

Of the three departments, Black Powder, the Du Pont's oldest endeavor, had the least critical requirements, for it had ample plants to meet any foreseeable demand.[12] New markets in some regions, such as the recently opened Oklahoma coal fields, had created localized sales that necessitated shipping powder from distant works, thus increasing expenses and lowering profits. Still these exceptions were few. Even though black powder was gradually losing ground to dynamite and other high explosives, some pressure existed for modernization and relocation to keep pace with changing sales patterns.

Smokeless Powder also had little immediate need for capital funds, for its rifle and shotgun market was small in comparison to the demand of the one major customer, the United States government. And starting in 1906, Du Pont, or the "Powder Trust" as its opponents were beginning to refer to it, came under increasing attack. In Congress efforts to prohibit the government from purchasing its powder from any trust clouded the Smokeless Powder Department's future.

In contrast, growth in mining operations in Alaska and the Pacific Northwest as well as in Colorado and Michigan, continued large-scale railroad construction in Washington, Oregon, and California, together with the constantly growing urban centers which meant many major excavations for buildings, water mains, subways, and the like, put increasing demands on Du Pont's dynamite plants. Early in 1906 the High Explosives Department started making plans for a large new works in Washington State. That April, the Executive Committee appropriated $115,000 for the necessary real estate, even though detailed construction plans had not been formulated.[13] When the company found itself short of dynamite capacity by early summer of 1906, Barksdale presented an emergency plan, calling for an appropriation of $115,000 to increase the monthly production at three plants (Repauno, Sterling, and Joplin) to a combined total of 925,000 pounds. So great was the need for increased capacity that on July 25 the Executive Committee approved, even though Barksdale presented no detailed plans.[14]

The Executive Committee, and particularly Pierre du Pont, were not happy with the failure of the operating departments to produce systematic plans for long-term expansion. In April 1906 the committee asked the High Explosives Operating Department to make a study of the company's dynamite plant requirements for the forthcoming two years. Barksdale assigned W. B. Lewis, a man in his own department who was familiar with both selling and manufacturing of high explosives, to gather facts. On September 22, Barksdale presented the Executive Committee with a summary of Lewis's findings, together with some recommendations of his own.

This was the report that influenced Pierre to reject Coleman's overseas adventures and to decide to concentrate the company's resources on domestic expansion. The study embraced three years, 1907, 1908, and 1909, rather than the two for which the Executive Committee had originally asked. Barksdale, using past sales records as a guide, postulated an increase in dynamite consumption of 15% each year. The report divided the United States into six regions, each of which was "fixed by careful consideration of the relationship between the localities and the volume of consumption on the one hand, and the location and the capacity of Plants, both present and prospective, on the other."[15] Barksdale used actual sales for 1905 as a base and simply added 15% for 1906. He repeated the process to get statistics for 1907, 1908, and 1909. Then in one column he matched existing capacities in each region with estimated sales; a second column displayed existing capacities plus increase already authorized by the Executive Committee but not yet in operation. In this way the head of the Explosives Department was able to recommend a construction program that would match production in each region with prospective consumption through 1909. Barksdale admitted that "an annual increase of 15% may prove to be quite erroneous, and we also know that if the future demonstrates this assumed rate to be approximately correct it will not be uniformly so all over the country."[16] Nevertheless, he felt that his general conclusions were "plausible," and on the strength of them he recommended a vast increase in new construction.

His program was most ambitious. He proposed to finish the rationalization of production made possible by the consolidation. This meant the closing of several small, less well-located and less efficient works, including the Forcite, Enterprise, Mauch Chunk, and Hartford City plants. His main recommendation, however, was to erect four new large units: three with an annual capacity of 15 million pounds each, one in Pennsylvania's anthracite fields, a second unit at Joplin, Missouri, and the one already authorized in Washington State; and a 19 million-pound-per-annum plant in the Michigan copper country. Furthermore, Barksdale proposed additions to existing works that would raise annual production some 16 million pounds. All this was in addition to a new plant under construction but not paid for in Colorado. The magnitude of Barksdale's recommendations can be measured against the Washington plant which would cost at minimum $1.2 million. And only $100,000 of this outlay had been provided for as of September 1906. Barksdale's entire plan envisioned at least a total capital expenditure of $6.0 million, or $2.0 million per annum, in addition to the more than $2.5 million of work then programmed. The new capacity of 80 million pounds would expand the company's total output by 50%.

Barksdale's report was so comprehensive and impressive that it convinced the Executive Committee to persuade the Black Powder Department to make similar long-range projections. In 1907, faced with an urgent request to build new black powder plants at Middlesboro, Kentucky, and Springfield, Illinois, the committee asserted that "individual mills cannot be wisely located on local lines, but their location should be governed by broad trade considerations."[17] Therefore, it refused its authorization until Black Powder, in conjunction with the Sales and Traffic departments, had made a "general study covering the probable developments of the next three years (as was recently done in the High Explosives Department)."

Smokeless Powder, plagued as it was by antitrust attacks, made only a superficial survey of its further needs. In May 1907, H. F. Baldwin, the retiring head of the Smokeless Powder Department, commented in his final report that there "was no immediate probability of obtaining sufficient orders to warrant us in increasing our capacity."[18] On June 10, 1907, the committee referred the entire matter for restudy to J. A. Haskell who had temporarily taken charge of the department.[19]

The Barksdale plan for expanding high explosives production presented to the Executive Committee in September 1906 gave Pierre his first solid information on which to base long-term financial planning. Even so, Pierre was unable to give any kind of long-range financial considerations much realistic attention until that same summer, for the final settlement of the financing of the consolidation was not completed until that June. There were two reasons for this long delay. First, the bondholders of Delaware Securities and Delaware Investment—the holding companies used in the purchase of Laflin & Rand—continued to refuse to exchange these securities for preferred stock in the Powder Company. They had been perfectly willing to let the Powder Company use preferred stock as collateral for the bonds of the two holding companies. They were unwilling to make the next step and exchange those bonds for Powder Company securities and so permit the dissolution of the two holding companies, and with them Laflin & Rand. At the same time a few stockholders of those firms coming into the consolidation, particularly those in the California companies (the C.P.W., Vigorit, Judson, and California Investment), were disgruntled because, after they had made the exchange for the preferred stock of the Powder Company, its price on the open market had dropped to 89. Some holdouts continued to refuse to make the final exchange that would have permitted the winding up of these companies. In January 1906 Pierre and Moxham began to work out a plan to meet this situation. Then in February came a threat of an antitrust suit which increased the pressure for dissolving these remaining vestiges of preconsolidation companies.

The plan proposed by Pierre and Moxham called for the issuance of $16.0 million worth of 4½% gold bonds to be exchanged for the bonds of the investment companies and the preferred stock of the Powder Company. To assure the continuance of the 5% return as given on the preferred stock, a $100.00 worth of bonds was to be exchanged at $92.50. Pierre expected that this transformation would not only complete the financing of the consolidation but would also increase the du Pont family control of the company; for he hoped that many of the outside holders of preferred would be willing to give up the voting rights that went with the preferred stock for the extra security they assumed to be inherent in bonds. The Executive Committee approved these plans, and by July 1906, $6.6 million of this $16.0 million in issue had been used to obtain the bonds of the two holding companies, and $9.2 million more had been exchanged for the preferred stock of the Powder Company.[20]

As soon as this transaction was completed, Pierre began to plan for the financing of the company's future expansion, although he was not yet sure whether its growth would be concentrated at home or abroad. In this planning Pierre reviewed two sources of capital funds. The first was the direct reinvestment of the Powder Company's profits, or, in today's terminology, retained earnings. The second was the sale of its securities.[21]

Of these two sources Pierre thought first of earnings. On June 26, 1906, he forecast that the company's "net earnings" would equal 15% of its "net assets." Pierre noted that the Powder Company's net assets and its capital structure were not the same things, for as of January 1906 he calculated that the company's actual worth in tangible terms, that is, in real estate, working capital, investment surplus, etc., totaled $37.0 million, whereas against this had been issued $16.0 million of 4½ % gold bonds, $13.0 million of preferred stock, and $24.15 million of common stock. This totaled $53.15 million; the difference between that figure and the net assets of $37.0 million, some $16.15 million, was, following the accepted accounting practice of the day, euphemistically termed "good will." In the long run Pierre planned to squeeze out this water through retaining earnings.

Significantly Pierre regarded the new issue of $16.0 million of gold bonds as capital, rather than as a loan against the shareholders' property, that is, the $37.15 million of preferred and common stock. Furthermore, Pierre had no desire to use future earnings to reduce the bonded debt. But he did feel it unwise to calculate the earning power of "good will," so he used the more conservative "net assets" valuation of $37.0 million when he forecast that the company would earn 15%, or $5.6 million in 1906. (The actual earnings for that year turned out to be $5,332,802.00.)

Pierre presented his first long-term capital-raising program in June 1906 (that is, less than three months before Barksdale made his report and before the Executive Committee had turned away from Coleman's overseas plans). It covered a two-year period; in October of the same year, after plans for overseas expansion had been clearly abandoned, he extended it to seven years. He recommended that the Powder Company add approximately $3.5 million in new capital during the initial two years. Of this he proposed that nearly $2.5 million would come from earnings retained, and $1.0 million from the security sales. Pierre concluded that at the end of the first two years the Powder Company would have assets of $44,215,000. "If we subtract the par value of the preferred stock and bonds, namely $29,000,000 there remains a balance against the common stock of $15,215,000 or about 60 per cent of net asset [par] value. The value of our Good Will," he continued, "necessary to make common stock worth par would then be only $10,000,000 an amount that could be made good by laying up a surplus of $2,000,000 per annum for 5 years only."[22]

Pierre rested his expansion program directly upon his estimates of the

Powder Company's earnings. This, of course, is obvious in the case of the $2.5 million of profits which he hoped to retain annually, but he similarly linked the sale of the $1.0 million of securities to earnings.

The treasurer enumerated the three types of securities which might be sold. Bonds he rejected; there were but few of the 4½ % gold bonds left in the company's vaults and he did not relish a new issue. In 1906 the company's gold bonds had sold at a price which yielded 5% (92¼). He felt a new issue might not be sold on the same terms as the old, and a series with higher interest rates might have caused discontent among the existing bondholders and forced the refinancing of the entire debt. Preferred stock faced similar problems, for it paid a fixed, cumulative annual dividend of 5%; in July 1905 it sold at an average of 89, 11 points below par.[23] Pierre commented that the company was legally obligated to sell preferred stock at par and he was "doubtful if any extended market . . . [could] be made during the next two years."[24] That left only the common stock.

The Powder Company's main problem in the sale of any of its securities was finding buyers. In 1906 the public generally regarded the company as a family concern; its offerings were not listed on the New York, Philadelphia, or any other exchange where securities were regularly traded. As long as these conditions prevailed, it was difficult to open a broad market for new shares and those who wished to convert their holdings into liquid assets.

Pierre recognized that listing of his company's securities on the nation's main exchanges, especially the New York Stock Exchange, was essential to his long-term financial program and in the late fall of 1906 he investigated this possibility. After several conferences with William Lanman Bull of the New York Stock brokerage firm of Edward Sweet and Company, the treasurer reluctantly concluded that the chances were dim. Bull told Pierre that the Exchange disapproved of any company in which there was a "single holding of so large a portion of the stock as might make possible either a 'corner' or throw a large amount of the stock in the market suddenly."[25] Pierre's pessimism proved well founded. In November 1906 he asked the Guaranty Trust Co. of New York, which had acted as his agent since the Federal Steel Syndicate days of the late 1890s, "to ascertain whether the New York Stock Exchange would list our securities" in view of the fact that they were held by comparatively few individuals.[26] The Trust Company's query based on a hypothetical question which it submitted to the secretary of the Exchange convinced Pierre that "it would be practically hopeless to attempt listing at this time."[27]

Frank Connable, the acting head of Black Powder, disagreed. (Alfred I. was then in South Dakota getting a divorce.) Connable urged that the Powder Company's reputation and influence were such that listing was certain if an open and formal application were made. After all, he said, the "acknowledged fact that many of the most active stocks on [the ex]change today are dominated and controlled by one or a few individuals should lend encouragement to our effort."[28] Guided by Pierre's cautious conservatism, however, the Executive Committee did not care to risk the loss of prestige that a formal rejection might bring.

For a brief moment Pierre looked abroad for possible new sources of capital. Beginning in December 1906 he investigated placing Powder Company bonds with the French American Bank in Paris. As late as April 1907 the treasurer was still considering French capital markets, but nothing came of this effort. The decision to expand at home rather than abroad undoubtedly lessened his interest. Finally, the financial panic in the fall of 1907 made it almost impossible to place American securities abroad at favorable rates.[29]

Even though immediate listing upon the New York Stock Exchange was not possible, Pierre felt it imperative to create a market for Du Pont securities outside the family. He accomplished this in what was becoming the accepted way for new industrial firms to establish a demand for their securities on Wall Street. First he moved to have a New York investment house undertake the broad trading of all types of Powder Company securities. Thus, public quotations would appear in New York's unlisted securities departments. He was particularly anxious to insure that the owners of all the company's securities, bonds and stocks alike, would immediately receive a fair value for them should they want to sell. Hence he proposed to fix a price for Powder Company shares by placing standing orders of 92¼ (a yield of 5%) on the bonds, 89 for the preferred stock, and 100 to 102 for the common stock. He felt that bids would "not bring us any [common] stock, and will yet continue a satisfactory quotation. As to preferred stock and bonds," the treasurer continued, "we must be prepared to purchase small amounts" and he proposed that the company appropriate funds totaling $200,000 for that purpose.[30]

In October of 1906 Pierre worked out an agreement with New York's Edward Sweet and Company and placed a bid with them for stock so that they could enter it on the New York Curb. Pierre considered the curb list inferior to that of the New York Stock Exchange, but he felt the risk of having "our securities more or less discredited . . . [was] one of the disadvantages that we must be willing to accept. Listing on the Philadelphia Exchange," he concluded, "even if possible, will not bring us better company than we can obtain on the New York curb."[31]

Pierre recognized that his efforts to build a name and a reputation for Du Pont securities among the general public was a long-term project, and that no large amount of capital could be raised in this way short of offering securities so speculative in nature as to tempt the Wall Street gambling element. Consequently Pierre was forced back once again upon family resources. His problem was to attract capital from the family and at the same time to enhance the public image of the Powder Company's stock.

Pierre's strategy was simple; he advocated raising the already increased common stock dividend from 6% to 7%. This, he felt, would cause the shareholders to purchase new stock. "There can be no doubt," Pierre argued as early as June 1906, "of our ability to place any required amount of common stock at par should the dividend rate be raised to 7%."[32] In reality, Pierre's plan rested on the assumption that shareholders would simply plow the majority of their dividends back into the company. His plan called for the payment of $1,690,000 of dividends on the common stock. This was more than enough to enable the three cousins and the former partners or their heirs to pay for an issue of $1.0 million of new stock. Simultaneously the retention of the $2.5 million of earnings would give additional value to the old common shares.

The linkage of Pierre's capital-raising program to earnings meant that a downturn in business or any other factor that might reduce profits could have an immediate and disastrous effect on expansion plans. Nobody realized this better than Pierre himself, but, as he told the Executive Committee in October, he hoped that "if reasonable care is taken in making our plans of expenditure conform with my schedule," financial difficulties could be avoided.[33] The company had resources of at least $4.9 million including an invested surplus (in high-grade bonds and stocks) of $3.0 million; real estate to be sold worth $900,000; and a current borrowing power of at least $1.0 million. These assets should protect the company against a failure of income, "at least sufficiently long to enable us to curtail expenditures or provide other income." Phrased differently, Pierre's plan presupposed that any program for capital expenditures should be thoroughly controlled by the Executive Committee and arranged so that it could be immediately curtailed should circumstances warrant. It emphasized "pay as you go" as opposed to a program that could immediately tap a vast source of capital through large-scale loans or through widespread stock sales underwritten by investment banking houses. In contrast, many of America's most prestigious firms, such as Westinghouse Electric, were financing expansion with borrowed money.[34]

Pierre also suggested the approximate allocation of the capital that he proposed to raise. In the early (June 1906) discussion of long-range planning, before a positive decision had been made on overseas commitments and before Barksdale had submitted his reports on dynamite expansion at home, Pierre had proposed that the Powder Company spend in each of the first two years $500,000 for general appropriations, $500,000 for black powder expansion, and $1,150,000 for new dynamite capacity. Furthermore, he advocated that working capital be increased each year by 20%, or $1,400,000, the first year.[35]

These tentative recommendations were much too conservative. They neglected possible requirements for expansion by vertical integration, especially the purchase of nitrate properties and production facilities in Chile. More immediately, they misjudged Barksdale's needs which, as has been pointed out, included four large completely new works in addition to expanding existing facilities at a total cost of at least $6.0 million. During the late fall and winter of 1906–1907 Pierre continued to work out plans for financing the scheme even though no decision was reached on Barksdale's proposal. Then ominously the Powder Company's earnings began to drop.

In March of 1907 Pierre sounded a warning that prospects for the year looked "somewhat unfavorable." A combination of capital expenditures which totaled more than $3,760,000 including a little more than $2,500,000 for plants, real estate, and houses, together with a drop in the total volume of business, promised a deficit of more than $430,000. This, Pierre commented, was not serious enough "to warrant a change of policy or a wholesale reduction in expenditures," but it did mean a substantial reduction in the company's cash balances. To offset this, Pierre recommended "temporarily deferring part of our plant improvements."[36]

The Executive Committee responded by ordering that the Black Powder Department, whose trade was depressed, cease building additional capacity after the completion of its Indian Territory works.[37] This, however, was largely an empty gesture, since the High Explosives Department was consuming the majority of the new capital, and as yet the committee had taken no stand on Barksdale's demands.

On March 21, 1907, Barksdale presented the Executive Committee a request for an appropriation of $913,000 to finance construction of the new plant in Washington State as outlined in his September proposals. Barksdale's request brought on a sharp debate, for the High Explosives Department program required far more capital than Pierre at that time thought possible to raise. Although the Powder Company, thanks to its soon-to-be-completed Colorado works, had sufficient dynamite capacity to meet probable orders in 1907 and 1908, Barksdale estimated that continued growth would soon require still further capacity. Furthermore, a surge of demand in the Pacific Northwest and Alaska was crowding the company's Hercules facility in California. Should an accident occur, the company would be in a "very unfortunate position," Barksdale argued, and, equally important, he estimated that the company was losing $30,000 a month owing to the cost of overworking the Hercules plant.[38] Indeed, it was inefficiency as much as lack of capacity that disturbed Barksdale, and he soon presented the board with a long list of capital improvements that were desirable in that they reduced costs, yet were not immediately necessary.[39]

The argument was similar to the one Pierre had carried on with Barksdale, Alfred du Pont, and Haskell in the first weeks of 1904. The treasurer did not quarrel with most of Barksdale's basic objectives, yet he strongly opposed granting the appropriation for construction of the Washington plant at this time. He argued that building additional dynamite capacity violated his concepts of financing plant expansion as outlined in June 1906. "According to this plan we were to expend in new plants and construction during the twelve months from July 1, 1906, to July 1, 1907, $2,500,000."[40] This schedule, he pointed out, had already been met. Besides, the Colorado plant by going into full operation in 1908 would give the company adequate facilities until 1909. Pierre further felt that the needs of the entire company, not just a single department, should be taken into account when allocating capital. This being the case, he reminded the Executive Committee that he thought the most attractive area for investment was not additional production capacity, but essential raw materials, especially nitrate of soda. This area was so important, he maintained, that the Powder Company should not place itself in a position where it would lack the investment capital should an opportunity arise.

Pierre's most potent objection, however, centered upon the Powder Company's business prospects and its financial position and this, in turn, resulted from the data flowing into his office. He reported that as of March 21, 1907, the company was committed for $3,620,000 of capital expenditures but that it had provided only $2.5 million of capital, a figure that included $1.0 million of new stock. Lower sales had reduced earnings nearly $800,000 below estimates. Only the sale of $2.0 million of additional stock or the depletion of the vital cash reserves could make up the anticipated deficit and provide financing for the Washington plant. Pierre argued that sales trends made it unwise to reduce cash reserves; similarly he felt it unsafe to rely upon disposing of more than the planned $1.0 million of stock.[41]

At the Executive Committee's meeting on March 21, Pierre led the fight to stop further expenditures on the Washington plant for at least six months, or until the company's financial position became stronger. After long and heated discussion, Pierre's arguments convinced the Executive Committee to postpone a final decision on Barksdale's motion to grant a $913,951 appropriation for the new plant by agreeing to reconsider the question in thirty days.[42]

A month later, on April 22, 1907, Pierre went to the Executive Committee meeting even more convinced that the company should not commit itself to the Washington project. To clinch his point he submitted a revised forecast of expenditures and receipts for the year 1907, "showing a deficit of over $900,000 at the end of the year without making allowance for work on the Washington plant. This," he concluded, "is a summary of the Treasurer's argument against further construction expenditures at this time."[43] But the Executive Committee felt that Pierre was overcautious, and it passed, with Pierre alone voting in the negative, a motion to proceed with the Washington plant. The only restriction in the appropriation of more than $900,000 was a proviso that the High Explosives Department would "reduce the commitments during the next sixty days as much as possible without holding back the work."[44]

The decision effectively undermined Pierre's entire program for financial expansion. In the words of the Executive Committee, "the appropriation for the High Explosives Plant in Washington, and the situation generally . . . demonstrated . . . that the estimate of expenditure for the next four years which was prepared by the Treasurer some time since, will not meet the conditions facing us."[45] Consequently, the Executive Committee appointed a subcommittee consisting of Pierre du Pont, Coleman du Pont, and Arthur Moxham to develop a plan that would accomplish the goals of the committee's expansion program.

The financial plan that the three proposed differed surprisingly little from Pierre's original scheme, largely because it was based on the same data, that is, the information which came through the bureaucratic channels that the Treasurer's Department had established. Guided by Pierre's persuasive reasoning and statistics, the committee found that the average earnings of the Powder Company between 1895 and 1907 were 12.4% per annum and that the average annual increase in capital investment for these years had been 8.04%. The subcommittee concluded that "the experience of the past years" was the best guide to future growth; consequently, it recommended an average investment each year equal to 8% of the company's net assets. In dollar terms, this projected a gradually rising injection of new capital starting with $3,120,000 in 1907 and increasing to $4,245,000 in 1911. In general the amounts averaged $200,000 to $400,000 below Pierre's original plan, this due mainly to his less sanguine estimates for the powder business.

Coleman du Pont and Arthur Moxham agreed with Pierre that the main source of the additional capital would necessarily come from a mix of retained earnings and common stock sales. They desired to maintain a common stock dividend of 7% per annum, and simultaneously increase the common stock each year by 5%. The hope was, in effect, to make it possible for shareholders to subscribe for their full share of stock and still receive a cash dividend of 2%. Common stock sales were to provide $1.25 million of new capital in 1907 and approximately $1.5 million in 1911. The remaining capital, between 60% and 65% of the total, was to come from retained earnings.

The subcommittee made no effort, as Pierre had done earlier, to allocate specific amounts for improvements or additions to the various departments. To guard against fluctuations in income, it advocated that a $3.0 million reserve, invested in high-grade securities that could be immediately converted into cash, be maintained in the treasury at all times. This was to be in addition to the ordinary cash balance of approximately $1.0 million.

The guidelines for expenditure also echoed Pierre's thought. These specifically rejected the suggestion of "strictly maintaining our percentage of the total trade in each year" and gave the first consideration "to such improvements as will furnish cheaper raw material or cheaper production leaving as a second consideration the actual increase in the volume of business." Taken as a whole the subcommittee's revised financial plan kept the spirit of Pierre's original schemes, though some of the details were changed. It also officially de-emphasized Barksdale's desire to expand capacity and instead favored expenditures that would increase the efficiency of existing operations. In short, the policy of vertical integration and improvement of existing processes was given priority over the construction of new production facilities.[46]

On July 31, 1907, the full Executive Committee, over Hamilton Barksdale's vigorous objection, adopted the new financial plan. Barksdale accepted defeat gracefully, and in a separate motion the Executive Committee unanimously directed the various departments to submit at the September meeting "estimates as to the probable appropriations that will be required during the year 1908."[47]

All through the formulation of a capital expansion program Pierre's awareness of the close relationship between long-range financial planning and short-term working capital requirements grew. He was deeply mindful of the large cash outflow that was necessary to pay for the Powder Company's raw materials. Pierre recognized that the failure to keep business conditions under close observation could result in large purchases of raw materials during a period of falling sales—this in turn might dangerously deplete working capital. Pierre also knew that binding his long-term capital expansion program to retained earnings and stock sales stimulated by regular and high dividends made it doubly important to monitor business conditions carefully. His main goal became to control the exact level of expenditures for both short-term needs and capital expansion. He felt that, armed with information provided by the Sales, Purchasing, and Treasurer's departments, he could immediately detect overspending in raw materials, and so he could cause a rapid reduction of purchases. From the same data he would also be able to predict revenue and thus recommend to the Executive Committee when capital expenditures ought to be reduced. But for this to succeed he had to have knowledge of the exact state of capital expenditures. The treasurer hoped that the revised appropriations methods of January 4, 1906, especially the viewing by his brother Irénée of all appropriations before actual expenditures, would accomplish this, but as yet there had been no real test of this or his other financial concepts.

*Policy and Control in Time of Crisis*

The Powder Company's top management had finally agreed on how much to invest annually for expansion and how the new capital should be acquired. But in mid-1907 little of Pierre's program had been accomplished, nor had his system weathered the test of a major storm caused by forces originating outside the company.

Even before the Executive Committee's revised capital expansion program could take effect, the Powder Company encountered the most severe crisis it had faced since 1902, a crisis that gave Pierre a chance to demonstrate the value of his ideas about financial policy. The trouble did not come without warning. On June 14, 1907, a full six weeks prior to the Executive Committee's acceptance of the revised fiscal program, Pierre wrote that "our financial situation . . . has been so acute and extraordinary that it has been impossible to report progress."[48] The treasurer blamed higher raw material costs, "large expenditures in new plants, . . . decreased income from sales. . . ." as well as a sudden $600,000 purchase of nitrate. To surmount the trouble he sold virtually all the securities the company held as investments and contracted with banks and the New York financial house of Hathaway and Company for short-term loans amounting to $2,350,000.[49] This situation weighed heavily on Coleman du Pont, Pierre du Pont, and Arthur Moxham as they drew up the new financial program; and undoubtedly resulted in the reduced capital outlay requirements and assured the triumph of Pierre's conservative principles.

July did not see the Powder Company's financial position improve; the company ended the summer shorn of most of its invested surplus, with a reduced cash balance, and with a short-term debt in excess of $2.0 million. This was exactly the kind of predicament which Pierre had fought continuously to avoid and which he had particularly in mind when he opposed the appropriations for the new dynamite plant in Washington State.

At the moment the Powder Company's financial reserves were depleted, an international panic struck. During September, prices on the New York, London, and Continental stock markets dropped sharply. Credit became correspondingly strained. The panic itself began October 16, 1907, when the collapse of the Morse and Heinze copper corner caused a run on the New York banks. On October 23, the Knickerbocker Trust Company failed. Credit lines snapped and cash almost disappeared. Despite the deposit of $25.0 million of the federal government's funds in New York banks and J. P. Morgan's forceful measures to prevent further banking and Wall Street failure, the situation remained critical through November and December.[50] Fortunately for all concerned the effects of the panic were short-lived. By early 1908 further government action had restored confidence in American banks and the nation's over-all credit structure. By the summer of 1908 the economy was again prospering.

Pierre, of course, could not foresee this outcome as he and the Powder Company faced a critical situation in November 1907. Pierre's cash forecast submitted on the fifteenth of the month for three two-week periods (the remaining two weeks of November, the first half of December, and the last half of December) made alarming reading. The minimum goal was to provide a cash balance of $500,000 at the end of each period. On November 30 Pierre foresaw a balance of only $171,000; two weeks later a deficit of $445,000; and by the last day in December he predicted red ink amounting to more than $2,460,000. "You will also note," he added glumly, "that the deficit is of increasing proportions."[51] The treasurer expected to make up nearly $1.25 million of the amount by bank loans and another $750,000 by postponing acceptances from Brown Brothers, but even this left him $500,000 short. Pierre hoped to provide the $500,000 by selling the remaining invested securities and by holding up cash payments on bills.

The financial crisis, painful as it was, did not threaten to plunge the Powder Company into ruin, but it came close to destroying much of what the treasurer had labored two years to build. In two areas, consequences were especially serious. The first of these was in nitrate purchases. As late as October 1907 Pierre was still attempting to reduce the commission paid to the Chilean and British bankers who provided credits for the South American transactions by dealing directly with London and thereby eliminating the services of Huth & Company in Valparaiso.

In the midst of these negotiations, Brown Brothers, who had been handling the Powder Company's business without requiring the deposit of collateral, informed Pierre that they would "be unwilling to continue the business [any] longer on . . . [that] basis."[52] Reluctantly the Executive Committee voted to authorize that collateral by issuing of $1.25 million more of Du Pont 4½%, thirty-year gold bonds and by using an additional $1.0 million of bonds of other companies.[53] Before this arrangement could be consummated, Brown Brothers made still new demands. They insisted on a monopoly of all the Powder Company's nitrate of soda transactions for at least a year and they imposed more rigorous requirements for the deposit of collateral. Pierre found the new demands "obnoxious." Brown Brothers & Co., he wrote, "have assumed a very arbitrary attitude in these negotiations and on two weeks notice and in a severe financial crisis, have thrown over an arrangement which has been running for over two years."[54] Fortunately the Powder Company had more than a year's nitrate supply on hand and so was under no immediate pressure to come to terms. Therefore, upon the treasurer's recommendation the Executive Committee voted on November 9, 1907, to "discontinue negotiations with Brown Brothers," to suspend nitrate purchases in Chile, and to "sell all available surplus" of that material.[55]

In Pierre's mind the panic posed a second and more important threat: the destruction of his financial program, and with it the impairment of the company's prospects for future growth. As he contemplated the crisis a year later in December of 1908, the treasurer explained that "we were dangerously near a break in our dividend record, which to me would have been a catastrophe beyond future repair."[56] Indeed, the entire expansion program was especially vulnerable to business recessions because it hinged upon earnings, either those retained or those passed on in the form of dividends which in turn provided the whole stimulus for stock purchases. "It has been my intention," wrote Pierre,

> to place our common stock on such a secure basis as will make it possible to sell moderate amounts, say $1.0 million to $2.0 million without any question at any time. This . . . means that the stock must be made so attractive to the stockholders . . . that they cannot afford to let offers . . . go unsubscribed. If we can place our stockholders in a frame of mind to thoroughly believe in their securities, the public will undoubtedly follow.[57]

Even before the panic Pierre recognized that raising capital through stock sales was the weakest link in his program to raise new funds. In July of 1907, when the Executive Committee adopted the revised financial program which called for the sale of $1.25 million of common stock in 1907 and a total of more than $3.5 million of stock for the years 1907, 1908, and 1909, Pierre feared that many of the company's shareholders would fail to find the new issues irresistible even with the promised dividend of 7%. The worldwide financial pressures in the spring and summer of 1907 had affected the value of the Powder Company stock, along with that of many others. In June and July small quantities of Powder Company common had been offered below par.[58] This, combined with the acute fiscal strain within the Powder Company, made Pierre feel less optimistic about disposing of stock even to current holders. Thus he reacted in August by scaling down the proposed stock offerings for the three-year period to a total of $2.5 million to be issued in November of 1907 and 1909, but even so the treasurer feared that it would not be possible to sell the requisite amount of stock. To guard against failure he tried to commit family funds on a formal basis. He recommended that a syndicate composed of "E. I. du Pont de Nemours & Co. and such other parties as may wish to join" underwrite the entire $2.5 million stock issue.[59]

A syndicate was formed, just before the panic hit, consisting of the three cousins who had more than a 70% interest in the E. I. du Pont de Nemours & Company, other family members such as Colonel Henry du Pont, Alexis I. du Pont, the heirs of Francis G. du Pont, and others. The underwriting agreement, approved by the Powder Company on September 17, 1907, protected the interests of all the Powder Company's common shareholders, since it gave them the right to participate in the underwriting to the extent of 10% of their holdings, yet it committed the syndicate to acquire any shares not otherwise purchased. All underwriters received a 10% commission which, in effect, reduced the cost of the stock to 90% of par value. The first $1.0 million of stock was to be taken by November 1, 1907, and the remaining $1,500,000 by November 1, 1909.[60] The letters that Pierre had sent in July of 1907 to prospective syndicate members assured them that, although "the net result [for the Powder Company] this year has not been as favorable as last year," the final six months would "be better than the first" and that the company's finances were "in admirable shape."[61] The syndicate members acted with the faith that the Powder Company's dividends would continue and would provide the cash necessary to purchase the stock. If dividends had been suspended or reduced in 1907, many family members, whose cash resources were already severely strained, would have been forced to borrow money to pay for their Du Pont stock. Nothing could have been more disastrous for the Powder Company or Pierre's reputation within the family.

That fact remained constantly in the treasurer's mind during the crisis days in the fall and winter of 1907. From the beginning he saw that the real trouble lay not in the panic itself nor in the decline of the company's business that accompanied it, but in management's failure to bring expenditures in line with the ability of the firm to afford them. "The tendency of large corporations," wrote Pierre to Cousin William on July 9, 1907, "is to run into large expenditures on permanent investment without due thought to financing but I am trying to ward off this danger for our Company."[62] Nothing better illustrated Pierre's observation than Westinghouse Electric, which financed its expansion with more than $14.0 million of floating debt, a policy that led to insolvency and receivership at the first breath of financial panic in late October 1907.[63]

Because Pierre blamed most of the difficulties upon excessive appropriations for the enlargement of capacity, especially by the High Explosives Department, he tied salvation to large-scale reduction of expenditures and to the creation of a system that would automatically insure that outlays would be adjusted to revenues. Significantly the treasurer rejected the most obvious and time-honored method of reducing expenses, that of cutting wages and salaries. Of course he would have done so as a last resort and, in fact, on November 18, 1907, the Executive Committee passed a resolution calling for each department to devise a program of salary reductions and to be prepared to implement its recommendations not later than January 1, 1908.[64] Yet such plans were clearly a safety valve and on December 5, 1907, the Executive Committee voted to delay wage and salary reductions indefinitely pending the outcome of Pierre's other reforms.[65]

It was on the control of capital appropriations and of inventory, especially raw materials bought by the Purchasing Department, that Pierre focused his attention, for he was determined to make expenditures in these areas conform more exactly to the company's needs. Since he held excessive capital outlays most responsible for the trouble, it was only logical to cancel all outstanding appropriations other than those necessary for vital repair or maintenance. Here the system of reporting and controls which Pierre and Irénée had established in 1906 made it possible to gauge with great accuracy the amount of money appropriated for repairs and capital improvements, the rate of its expenditure, and how much of it remained in the treasury. In September, as conditions grew worse, Pierre asked each department to determine which of its appropriations could be canceled. On October 29 he reported to the Executive Committee that of outstanding appropriations totaling $1,112,000, $848,000 had been spent or irrevocably committed. This left a disappointingly small balance of $264,000, which the treasurer felt must be canceled. Accordingly the Executive Committee ordered the three operating departments to defer all construction work until further notice.[66]

Pierre early saw, however, that much as excessive capital expenditures might have been a basic cause of the Powder Company's ordeal, the major relief would have to come elsewhere. The treasurer found the answer after a careful search through the mass of data that flowed upward to his office. Inventory control proved to be the key. In August 1907 he noted that working capital, especially in the form of payments for materials and supplies, had increased almost $1.8 million during the period between February 28, 1907, and July 31, 1907. The treasurer immediately developed tables that plotted the ratio of materials and supplies to business done at different times in the company's experience since 1902. He concluded that "if we were to reduce this item [materials and supplies] to the same ratio as shown July 1, 1905, January 1, 1906 and 1907, a saving of approximately $900,000 would be effected."[67] He then launched a study to determine if and how such reductions could be accomplished.

Frank G. Tallman's October reports, which itemized the inventory of essential materials, provided just the information needed. They demonstrated what Pierre suspected. Although Tallman's department had done a superb job of buying essential materials at favorable prices, it had not coordinated buying with consumption trends. This was because Tallman seized upon price slumps to make large purchases, a policy that served the firm well in the long pull, but which absorbed large amounts of cash at a time when the Powder Company could least afford it. For example, Tallman had stockpiled a 7.8 months' nitrate supply at the planned consumption rate, or a 9 months' supply at the actual rate of use. Furthermore, despite the company's difficult financial position, he had instructed Ahuja to make still further purchases. Of crude glycerin there was a 13.5 months' supply, and Tallman was "seriously considering the advisability of immediately purchasing some more foreign crude." There was a seven months' stockpile of fusel oil and a six months' supply of sulphur. In addition, more than $800,-000 had been invested in miscellaneous materials and stores.[68]

Pierre felt that this information demonstrated that working capital had absorbed too much money. Lacking hard data about necessary stockpiles and guided by Pierre's advice, the Executive Committee on October 29, 1907, took drastic action: it ordered that "all stocks of essential materials and supplies on hand be limited to a maximum of two months' supply," and "in the matter of minor materials . . . the heads of the operating departments . . . [were] requested to keep these as much below two months' supply as . . . possible."[69] Furthermore, steps were taken to ensure that the miscellaneous materials available at each plant were inventoried, and the Purchasing Department was directed to shift stocks from one factory to another rather than to purchase additional items.

By far the most important step taken, however, was the order to the Purchasing Department to study ways to reduce raw material inventories and the effect this would have on the corporation's business. Tallman's report, submitted to the Executive Committee on January 24, 1908, was the first really comprehensive effort to determine minimum stock levels for eight key raw materials—nitrate of soda, refined glycerin, crude glycerin, pyrites, sulphur, crude saltpeter, muriate of potash, and fusel oil. Tallman argued that simply to maintain a two months' reserve of certain materials, notably nitrate of soda, pyrites, saltpeter, and glycerin, was impractical for in the case of these resources the nature of the market or the transportation time from the purchase point to the consuming factories required as much as a six or seven months' supply. Nevertheless, Tallman admitted that the company needed only a six or seven months' crude glycerin supply, not the thirteen months' reserve he had accumulated. And, in the case of sulphur, direct purchasing from the Union Sulphur Company had reduced the necessary stock of that material from a six months' supply to virtually none.[70]

The Executive Committee looked upon Tallman's report as merely the starting point for achieving better control of the raw material inventory. On February 7, 1908, it ordered the Operative Committee to make a further and more detailed study of the stock level requirements. The ideal goal remained the reduction of reserves to not more than a two months' supply. And the Executive Committee wanted to find techniques for canceling orders and reducing reserves during financial panics or business recessions.[71]

Because the international panic was so short-lived, Pierre's measures proved most effective. The financial adjustments he had outlined in December successfully met the company's immediate financial needs; while those taken on the financing and control of inventory had strengthened its long-term outlook. The Powder Company's business, which fell to 50% of normal during January and February of 1908, jumped back to 80% by midsummer. The company's position was even stronger than these statistics indicated, as it had been able to maintain its prices while those of raw materials had declined. Equally important in restoring the firm's financial health was the reduction of expenditures which came from the near cessation of capital outlays during the first seven months of 1908, and the liquidation of excess raw material. "We have been very successful," wrote Pierre to his cousin William on August 20, 1908. "Our total outstanding indebtedness in the shape of bills payable is now $705,000 represented by notes due in September, all of which we expect to pay at maturity; in fact, our financial situation is better today than it has ever been."[72]

On the whole, Pierre reflected in the same letter, "the lesson [of the panic] has been a good one for us, and we have gained information that will be valuable when the next call comes."[73] The major lesson, of course, for Pierre was the absolute necessity to coordinate appropriations, especially capital outlays, with a financial plan that was based upon the company's ability to raise revenues. Almost as important was the need to control inventories. On the first point Pierre emphasized that management had to have both the information and ability to reduce or defer such expenditures the instant that conditions demanded it. Addressing Coleman and Alfred in December of 1908, Pierre wrote: "You will remember that I prepared a plan under the date of June 1907 showing the financial prospect for several years. I have rewritten this plan to cover the financial record of the years 1907 and 1908, and have carried forward the estimate for a period of fifteen years, that is, up to January 1, 1924."[74]

Pierre's postpanic financial plan differed little from his prepanic ideas. Thus the treasurer proposed that his company increase its invested capital by about 8% each year, as he had previously recommended. This would amount to $3,480,000 in 1909 and $3,750,000 in 1910. Pierre kept his concept that new capital should be drawn from a mix of retained earnings and new stock sales. Thus, about two-thirds of the new capital would come from retained earnings and one-third from new common stock sales. As in his earlier plans, Pierre hoped that the old shareholders would plow back their dividends into new shares.[75] The end of the panic in early 1908 marked the real beginning of Pierre's iron rule in financial matters, an authority which, although it did not always determine the exact allocation of company resources, did at least ensure that appropriations would fall within established guidelines.

Further, the panic demonstrated the need for more planning and control in the purchase of essential materials; this was especially vital, since working capital represented such a significant portion of the Powder Company's entire resources. The centralization of buying under Frank Tallman's able direction in 1905 had not harmonized the complex operations of the Essential Materials Department with short-term fluctuating requirements. Indeed, at first glance, effective bulk purchasing seemed to demand cash outlays precisely when business recession and slack orders also lowered raw material costs. Finally, the panic made clear the conflict of interest between the various Powder Company departments. It was Tallman's attempt to capitalize on favorable prices for essential materials, not inefficiency or incompetence, which resulted in the large increase in working capital at the exact time consumption was dropping. The crisis of 1907 emphasized that Pierre, in his position as treasurer, had to act as arbitrator between conflicting interests. He was the one person who saw the firm's over-all financial picture. Pierre, therefore, rethought the Essential Materials Department's role and instituted the first comprehensive attempt to achieve simultaneously the advantages of large-scale, long-term buying, and minimum inventories. Only in this manner could Pierre be certain that spending on the part of Frank Tallman's office would not undermine the company's short-term financial requirements.[76]

Once Pierre had recognized the problem, the large inventories of essential materials such as nitrate of soda and glycerin proved a strength rather than a weakness, for they were readily turned into cash, and their sale greatly stimulated the Powder Company's rapid recovery in 1908. But the Executive Committee's attempt to establish permanent guidelines for raw material reserves only emphasized the necessity for further study. A two months' stock of certain reserves, though it might have sufficed in the crisis months of 1907 and 1908, was unrealistic. Nitrate, for example, averaged "50 days in transit from Chile to Atlantic Ports," and it took an additional week to unload a cargo into railroad cars and another three weeks to move it to the consuming mills. Furthermore, it was difficult to charter boats in Chile at the exact times they were needed.[77] Finally, there was a whole range of problems associated with purchasing nitrates from South America. Similar difficulties plagued crude glycerin, much of which was imported from Europe and required an average of two months for transit. Pyrites, too, had to be stockpiled for as much as six months, since the waterways at the source of the supply in Newfoundland froze during the winter. The problem of securing a raw material supply at the lowest cost and of coordinating that supply with the company's requirements defied an easy solution.

The studies initiated by the Executive Committee inevitably raised the issue of vertical integration. In fact, Pierre had already envisioned the ownership of nitrate fields in South America as the ultimate answer to the nitrate problem, even prior to his Chilean trip in 1905. Now that he had finally achieved control of capital expenditures, it was only logical that he should attempt to further enhance his financial planning by gaining a more precise control of the company's essential raw materials. It is no accident, therefore, that the policy of vertical integration, as one of the most promising means of bringing about this result, dominated much of the treasurer's thought in the years immediately following the panic of 1907.

# Toward Vertical Integration

T HE PANIC OF 1907 made clear Pierre du Pont's dominant position in the Powder Company. Prior to the crisis the treasurer played an important but secondary role to Coleman. While it is true Pierre's importance and value to the firm rose steadily during the prepanic era, still at the start of 1907 the treasurer found his advice overruled even on such matters as the amount of capital to be spent on expansion. Coleman, influenced by Barksdale and Moxham, regarded Pierre as overcautious. The panic proved Pierre right and the others wrong.

At the very time the financial crisis demonstrated the wisdom of Pierre's policies, Coleman became less important in company affairs. This was partly because Coleman, ever restless for new fields to conquer, was already beginning to take an interest in New York City real estate ventures. He turned also to politics. In 1906 he helped Colonel Henry become United States Senator from Delaware and two years later became his state's Republican National Committeeman. The Kentucky-bred Coleman, unlike Pierre, Alfred, and other kinsmen who had been born and raised on the Brandywine, never felt the satisfaction they did to remain in the relatively small family circle in Wilmington. Another important factor was a prolonged illness that lasted off and on from 1908 through 1915 and sapped Coleman's vitality. Starting in 1908 he was often absent from Wilmington's Du Pont Building, and Pierre substituted as chairman of the vital Executive Committee. Then on January 7, 1909, Pierre became acting president of the company. Although Coleman remained influential, Pierre, sitting in the chair at the Executive Committee meetings, became the natural leader.

Pierre's dominant role derived also from a different source. Before the panic the emphasis in the Du Pont firm had been on consolidating the explosives industry into the "Big Company." This involved negotiations to buy out or merge with other firms, which was the kind of activity at which Coleman excelled. There had also been the search for potential new areas for investment either in the domestic market or abroad. Coleman had taken the leadership in this too. The decision in 1906 to expand at home rather than overseas shifted the emphasis to planning, and to providing and allocating resources among various alternatives. Such work was Pierre's strength, as the financial program of June 1907 indicated.

After the crisis Pierre continued to refine his plans to raise capital and allocate it. But the panic taught him that mere control of appropriations and the ability to cut capital expenditures to harmonize with the firm's current financial position were not enough to assure the company full protection from disaster. Supply emerged as a central problem in planning. This meant obtaining reliable sources for raw materials at the least cost.

After 1907 Pierre and the Executive Committee devoted much of their energy to the problem of supply. This led first to a study of purchasing and secondly to an analysis of buying or controlling the sources of raw materials —what has come to be known as the policy of vertical integration. After 1907 Pierre not only had to help set policy in the allocation of funds between different production departments, but he had to help determine whether money might be better spent for such integration.

At the same time that supply problems were absorbing the energy of Pierre and his colleagues, the Powder Company became the target of an antitrust prosecution by the federal government. Although Pierre spent relatively little energy combating antitrust activity during the early years of the attack, the agitation caused a reduction of government orders for military smokeless powder, which left the company with surplus capacity. This forced Pierre to consider the question of alternative uses for the idled resources and led to the Powder Company's first major program of product diversification.

Before Pierre could give full attention to the areas of supply and vertical integration, however, he had to complete policies that had been put aside during the financial crisis of 1907. A first step was to tighten still further appropriations procedures. The second was to re-embark on domestic expansion. The primary difficulty with the appropriations procedures was that the Purchasing Department, in buying materials for construction, was still not informed as to the status of any appropriation and thus had no way to check whether or not a requisition had been authorized. The Executive Committee appointed a special committee consisting of Pierre, Coleman, and Moxham to study the problem. The three recommended increased centralization of planning. For this purpose they suggested, as had been done at the time of the formation of the big company, that all engineering be consolidated in a single independent Engineering Department. Furthermore, the special committee proposed the establishment of an appropriations clerk to be charged with processing all appropriations.[1]

The Executive Committee considered the special committee's report on March 19, 1908. Again Barksdale, backed by Alfred du Pont, successfully fought to retain departmental control over the engineering function. But the Executive Committee adopted other vital provisions of the report.[2] Of these the most important were the initiation of special appropriation requisition forms and the establishment of the appropriations clerk.[3] Under the new rules the clerk entered the appropriation in a central record and stamped the completed requisition form prior to the expenditure of any funds. Without the stamped form, neither Purchasing nor any other department could take action on a project. Only in case of emergency repairs made necessary by breakdowns or explosions could work begin prior to an approval of a formal appropriation request, but even here the department head had to provide a temporary appropriation form which estimated the cost, and the regular procedure had to be accomplished within sixty days. As under the old system, reports of appropriations granted were sent to the Treasurer's Office, which in turn furnished the Executive Committee with a statement of appropriations approved at its regular monthly meeting devoted to appropriations.[4] It was Pierre's hope that these new rules would make top management instantly aware of all expenditures. Thus the Executive Committee could stop or modify an appropriation before any funds were committed.

At the same time that he was reshaping the appropriation procedures Pierre was beginning to study expansion of domestic production. The anti-panic corrective measures he had adopted had halted Barksdale's ambitious program to expand dynamite capacity. The massive new plant at Du Pont, Washington, stood idle, three-quarters finished. Although Pierre had opposed much of Barksdale's program, his position rested upon the dictum that available financial revenues should strictly limit expansion. The treasurer's differences with the head of the High Explosives Operating Department were over short-run measures, not long-term goals. He now looked forward to starting work again on the capital improvement program which he, Coleman du Pont, and Arthur Moxham had formulated and which the Executive Committee had adopted in July 1907. Two weeks after the adoption of the revised appropriations procedure, the Executive Committee considered both a report from Pierre which indicated that limited funds were again available for capital improvements and an urgent request from Hamilton Barksdale to resume work on the new Washington dynamite plant. After a short discussion, with Black Powder's Frank Connable the lone dissenter, the Executive Committee voted to appropriate up to $500,-000 to complete the Washington plant.[5] By the end of April 1908 construction had again resumed. By June 1908 the Powder Company was well on its way toward fulfillment of the capital improvements envisioned under the revised financial plan adopted by the Executive Committee in July of 1907.

### Nitrate Supply

The resumption of steady progress toward expanding productive capacity proved much easier than achieving an inexpensive and reliable raw materials flow. And in this area early in 1908 rebuilding the vital but complex nitrate purchasing arrangements offered the most pressing challenge. Here Pierre's major concern was to reduce the very large sums of working capital absorbed in nitrates.

The panic-inspired program that the Executive Committee adopted to control essential material inventories attempted to limit the quantity of nitrate of soda on hand in the United States to a two months' supply. This alone in 1908 required a vast stockpile of 44 million pounds of soda worth in excess of $1,095,000.[6] But this was only the beginning for, in addition, the Powder Company had to assure itself of a further three or four months' supply, which was either in Chile awaiting shipment or afloat enroute to the United States. Thus, if the Powder Company paid cash for nitrates at the time of purchase in South America, this increased the working capital tied up in that material by $1.5 to $2.0 million.

Moreover, since the company's 90-day sight notes on Brown Brothers circulated in Chile in lieu of money for up to 120 days and since Brown Brothers required no collateral to secure the sight notes, the Powder Company was able to purchase as much as a four months' supply of nitrates without utilizing any precious capital. Thus Brown Brothers' demand at the height of the panic of 1907 for at least $2.0 million of collateral had the effect of requesting the company to supply $2.0 million additional working capital just at the time when Pierre was trying to contract the cash committed for raw materials.

The break with Brown Brothers gave only temporary relief, and Pierre informed the Executive Committee on December 4, 1907, that if the Powder Company were to continue direct nitrate purchase in Chile he would need an additional $2.0 million.[7] Since the panic dictated a retrenchment rather than an enlargement of the nitrate account, the only possible course seemed a return to purchasing nitrates from American brokers. So the Executive Committee ordered the Nitrate Committee to purchase only 25% of its requirements through Valparaiso and the balance from brokers in the United States. This would allow a reduction of capital allocated to nitrates from $3.0 million to about $1.0 million.[8]

The large quantity of nitrate of soda on hand at the end of 1907 made it possible to delay execution of the Executive Committee's new policy until it could be restudied.[9] At the beginning of 1908, F. G. Tallman presented the results of this inquiry to the Executive Committee. Buying from brokers, he argued, was attractive because the company could delay payment until thirty days after the nitrate had arrived in the United States. On the other hand, Tallman demonstrated that the Powder Company had always purchased in Chile at prices below those quoted by the brokers. In 1906 and 1907, for example, Du Pont's costs averaged 7⅔ cents per 100 pounds less than those charged by the leading importer, W. R. Grace & Company.[10]

Pierre considered the savings resulting from direct purchasing significant and noted that if the Powder Company relied solely upon importers their quotations might have been substantially higher. Certainly there was abundant evidence that Grace had done everything in its power to cut its prices to a minimum in order to regain the Du Pont business.[11] In January 1908 Pierre devised a temporary arrangement to finance continued nitrate purchases in Chile. The method was simple; it consisted of bank loans with title to the nitrate (in the form of shipping documents) serving as collateral. This procedure allowed the Du Pont Company to avoid tying up capital in nitrate until after it was received at an American port. But from Pierre's viewpoint there were still two difficulties: first, interest charges started from the day nitrate purchases were made in Chile and, secondly, financing for each shipment had to be separately negotiated, which made the credit line dangerously uncertain.

It was not until the fall of 1909 that Pierre finally solved this problem. Then he told the Executive Committee that the National City Bank of New York had granted the Powder Company a $2.0 million revolving credit to be made available at two key English banks, the London City & Midland Bank and the Union of London & Smith's Bank Ltd. Pierre explained that the Powder Company would issue 90-day drafts at Wilmington and forward them to Valparaiso, where they would be signed by R. R. M. Carpenter's younger brother Walter S. Carpenter, Jr., who had recently been sent to South America on his first assignment with the Du Pont Company. Either Carpenter or Ahuja would then endorse the drafts to the order of the nitrate sellers. Pierre stated that the Powder Company's growing reputation and the fact that the notes were payable in sterling at London banks would make them first-class paper which would circulate in Chile for as much as thirty days prior to being presented at a bank or other institution for payment. These Du Pont notes, unlike the previous Brown Brothers' notes, carried no interest until discounted, and thus had the same effect as granting the Powder Company an additional $500,000 interest-free loan.[12]

Pierre's favorable arrangement with the National City Bank of New York was a tribute to the high regard in which financial circles had come to hold the Powder Company. This was another bonus from Pierre's policies during the panic. By the terms of the contract, the Powder Company was to maintain at the National City Bank a minimum balance of $500,000 and, as in the earlier agreements, shipping documents served as collateral, and title for the nitrate remained with the bank until it arrived in the United States. In addition, the bank made a nominal interest charge. Reviewing the plan, the treasurer concluded that it was the "equivalent to our borrowing $2,000,000 year in and year out . . . at a cost of 1½ per cent per annum, which," he added, "is an exceptionally low rate of interest."[13]

The fall of 1909, therefore, marked the culmination of Pierre's long drive to finance direct nitrate purchases in Chile. From that date Du Pont notes circulated in Chile as first-class paper, and working capital required by nitrates was reduced to the approximately $1.25 million for American stockpiles (a two months' supply) and the $500,000 minimum balance that the company was committed to carry in New York's National City Bank. But even the new agreement did not completely eliminate the nitrate problem. For one thing, the National City Bank could cancel the agreement upon six months' notice, thus requiring a new search for credit—a prospect which might not be a pleasant one, as the panic of 1907 proved.[14] More important, Du Pont still remained at the mercy of the European-controlled nitrate firms and combinations in Chile. Pierre, therefore, felt that only when the Powder Company produced a substantial portion of its own nitrate would it be assured of a steady supply at the lowest prices.

Pierre was, in fact, already deeply involved in a drive to acquire an operating works in Chile. On June 3, 1908, the Executive Committee appointed a special committee of three consisting of Pierre du Pont, Hamilton Barksdale, and William B. Dwinnell, director of the Development Department, to analyze the possible purchase of South American nitrate production facilities.[15] The problem that faced the committee was not one of shortage. Indeed, by 1908 the nitrate oversupply that Pierre had anticipated in 1905 had materialized, bringing with it a disintegration of both the nitrate combination and the price structure. Prices which had risen steadily from 5/9d per hundredweight in 1899 to 9/4d in 1907 fell to 7/3d in 1908 and 6/5d in 1909.[16] In March 1909 the Executive Committee's regular Nitrate Committee, of which Pierre was a member, reported that there had "been a gradual accumulation of stock above ground during the past ten years, the amount being now so large as to constitute a serious menace to the selling price of Soda."[17] It had been this very prospect that had caused Pierre after his 1905 Chilean trip to recommend that the Powder Company delay the purchase of any South American nitrate lands.

If nitrate was both cheap and abundant, then why enter production? The reasons hinged upon the importance of nitrate as a resource for the du Ponts and the importance of the Du Pont Company as a nitrate consumer. In 1908 approximately 2 million tons of nitrate left the west coast of South America for world markets. Of this, Europe consumed nearly 1.4 million tons and the United States 300,000 tons. The du Ponts' purchase of more than 110,000 tons valued at $5.0 million represented 5% of the world's consumption and 30% of that in the United States.[18]

Clearly nitrate of soda was vital to the Powder Company. Yet at this time no outside pressure dictated a policy of vertical integration. In 1909 all other American explosives companies combined consumed only 60,000 tons, little more than half the quantity used by Du Pont. Furthermore, no competing firm had instituted its own direct purchasing in Chile, and all relied on the three major importers—W. R. Grace & Company, Wessel, Duval & Co., and Parsons & Petit—whose selling prices averaged consistently above Du Pont's costs. In fact, the major nitrate buyers in the United States (aside from the Du Pont Powder Company) were fertilizer concerns including such large enterprises as the Virginia-Carolina Chemical Company and the American Agricultural Chemical Company. In 1909 the fertilizer business absorbed almost the same amount of nitrates as did the entire explosives industry.[19]

Nor did the need to improve the coordination of the flow of raw material from the extractive process to the manufacturing stage provide a solid reason for the buying of properties in Chile. The Powder Company had already achieved this by direct purchasing and the chartering of steamships to move the nitrate of soda from Chile to American ports.

The major impetus for purchasing Chilean nitrate fields came not from without, but from within; it stemmed from the logical desire to lower still further over-all costs. Phrased differently, Pierre and his colleagues on the Executive Committee felt that money carefully invested in nitrate production for use by the company could mean an increased profit on its final product. They had always wanted a more certain control over the supplies of raw materials. They were unhappy with their dependence on the six-month contracts with the National City Bank in financing the flow of nitrates. And the possibility of an effective combination of nitrate producers remained a threat. But as long as their nitrate costs stayed consistently below those of their competitors, they saw no reason to take the final step in the policy of vertical integration, that is, actually investing large amounts of capital in the production of raw materials. Such purchases could wait until they could be had at bargain prices. In other words, they could wait until the Executive Committee was certain that the return on investment would be as high, or higher, from the purchase of these properties as it would if it were placed in explosives plants, sales activities, or other aspects of the business.

The Special Nitrate Committee's report of July 18, 1908, to the Executive Committee was cautious. It avoided any hint of an immediate purchase for the purpose of supplying all of Du Pont's nitrate requirements. Instead it recommended that the company send, as it had sent five years earlier, a "competent engineer to Chile" to investigate both undeveloped government lands and an operating *oficina* (nitrate mine and works).[20] On August 5, 1908, the Executive Committee approved the hiring of an engineer and directed that he study the acquisition of a "small property within a moderate expenditure, to be used as a means of education as to wise investment for the total ultimate supply that may be needed."[21] In other words, where in 1903 Du Pont representatives in Chile were investigating the possibility of purchasing undeveloped nitrate lands, they were now to investigate fully equipped operating plants.

Events did not begin to move rapidly until early in 1909. In March the Executive Committee discharged the Special Nitrate Committee and gave its full duties to the Development Department, which since 1908 had been managed by Pierre's brother Irénée du Pont.[22] On March 8, 1909, Irénée selected Edmund N. Carpenter (an uncle of Walter S. Carpenter) to make the investigation.

Carpenter left almost immediately for London, where he conferred with Elias Ahuja, and then on April 16 he took passage on the S.S. *Aragon* for Chile, arriving on May 12. He spent the next several months in North Chile's nitrate fields, where he made detailed inspections of the various properties and came to know the influential men.[23] Following the Executive Committee's instructions, Carpenter directed his main effort toward finding a suitable pilot works where Du Pont could gain much needed experience.

By September 1909, Carpenter decided that a property known as *Gloria* in the San Antonia District of the Tarapaca Pampa offered an attractive investment. The location was excellent; a 40-mile railroad connected it to a deepwater port at Iqueque; its machinery, barely two years old, was in good condition, although, because of the satiated market, it was not then in operation. But best of all it had a confirmed nitrate reserve of 180,000 tons and an annual production of 24,000 tons. In short, *Gloria* would be able to supply one-fifth of Du Pont's annual requirements; its reserves gave it a life of eight years. The property was large enough to provide vital experience; yet it did not require a long-term commitment. In Irénée's words, it was "a very desirable one on which to 'cut our teeth.' "[24]

For the Executive Committee and its acting chairman, the basic problem had been less in locating a suitable property and more in being sure of purchase of it at a suitable price. Carpenter, by limiting his attention to smaller properties that had been developed by small, ill-financed firms, obviously hoped to profit from the current depression in the nitrate fields. His main job, however, was to provide accurate data to be sent to the Development Department for analysis. He found estimates made by the owners of nitrate property to be totally unreliable and he employed experienced local engineers to make detailed surveys to determine as nearly as possible the exact quantities of nitrate reserves and the cost of working

Lammot du Pont (father of Pierre)       Mary (Belin) du Pont (mother of Pierre)

exis I. du Pont and Pierre S. du Pont (ca. 7)       Pierre S. du Pont and William H. Fenn at M.I.T. (1890)

Family picture—St. Amour (ca. 1896)

*Top row—left to right*

    Isabella Mathieu (du Pont) Sharp
    Pierre Samuel du Pont
    William Kemble du Pont
    Mary Alletta Belin (du Pont) Laird
    Lammot du Pont
    Margaretta Lammot (du Pont) Carpenter

*Bottom row—left to right*

    Irénée du Pont
    Mary (Belin) du Pont
    Henry Belin du Pont
    Louisa d'Andelot (du Pont) Copeland

Senior partners in 1900

Colonel Henry Algernon du Pont (1838-1926)

Francis Gurney du Pont (1850-1904)

Eugene du Pont (1840-1902)

Alexis Irénée du Pont (1843-1904)

The three cousins (ca. 1903), members of the Executive Committee
prior to the 1911 reorganization

T. Coleman du Pont

Pierre S. du Pont

Alfred I. du Pont

Other members of the first Executive Committee, 1900

Hamilton Barksdale

J. Amory Haskell (*Courtesy H. G. Haskell and E. L. Fleitas*)

Arthur J. Moxham (*Courtesy Arthur Moxham, grandson*)

Francis Irénée du Pont

# Close associates of Pierre S. du Pont

John J. Raskob

William du Pont

Henry Belin, Jr.

Tom L. Johnson

Senior executives at the Powder Company

Russell H. Dunham

Colonel E. G. Buckner

Major William Ramsay

Elias Ahuja (left); Walter S. Carpenter (right). *(Courtesy W. S. Carpenter, Jr.)*

Pierre S. du Pont and the War Executive Committee. (Top row–left to right) Lammot du Pont, William Coyne, R. R. M. Carpenter, H. Fletcher Brown, Merritt Fisher. (Bottom row–left to right) Frank Connable, J. J. Raskob, Pierre S. du Pont, Irénée du Pont, H. G. Haskell, F. G. Tallman.

The Family Fight—a cartoon from the Cleveland *Plain Dealer*. (*Copyright 1916 by the Cleveland Company. Reprinted by permission.*)

Pierre S. du Pont and Alice B. du Pont on their wedding trip.

# Brothers-in-law of Pierre S. du Pont

Charles Copeland *(Courtesy L. du Pont Copeland)*

H. Rodney Sharp *(Courtesy Mr. and Mrs. H. R. Sharp, Jr.)*

W. W. Laird *(Courtesy W. Winder Laird)*

R. R. M. Carpenter

The conservatory at Longwood,
November 1921 .

Senior executives at General Motors

W. C. Durant

Alfred P. Sloan, Jr.

Donaldson Brown *(Courtesy G. B. Layton and W. S. Carpenter, Jr.)*

Pierre and the copper-cooled engine. *(New York Globe, 1922)*

GENERAL MOTORS CORPORATION GUESTS
at the
MUNCIE CHAMBER OF COMMERCE ANNUAL SPRING DINNER.
Tuesday Night, May 15th, 1928, 6:30 o'clock, Masonic Temple

Top row—CHARLES F. KETTERING, Vice President; DONALDSON BROWN, Vice President; HENRY F. CRANE, Technical Adviser to Mr. Sloan; JOHN L. PRATT, Vice President; CHARLES S. MOTT, Vice President E. F. JOHNSON, Assistant Group Executive.

Bottom row—GEORGE WHITNEY, J. P. Morgan & Co.; JUNIUS S. MORGAN, Jr., J. P. Morgan & Co.; ALFRED P. SLOAN, Jr., President; C. E. WILSON, General Manager, Delco-Remy Division; W. S. KNUDSEN, President and General Manager, Chevrolet Motor Company; WALTER S. CARPENTER, Jr., Vice President, E. I. du Pont de Nemours Co.; R. SAMUEL McLAUGHLIN, President, General Motors of Canada.

General Motors Corporation guests at the Muncie Chamber of Commerce Annual Spring Dinner, May 15, 1928. *(Courtesy du Pont Public Relations Department)*

Pierre S. du Pont (left) and John J. Raskob (right) at Longwood (ca. 1950).

the property. *Gloria*'s owners, for example, claimed that nitrate in the ground totaled 360,000 tons, whereas a mining engineer whom Carpenter employed could find only 180,000 tons.[25]

Irénée's department took the raw data that Carpenter supplied and prepared reports for the Executive Committee. The basic goal was a 15% return upon investment. The Development Department based its calculations upon the quantity of nitrate in the ground, the cost of production and transportation to the coast, and a planned amortization of the capital. In its estimates the Development Department assumed that the price of nitrate would remain at its 1909 low, which they maintained was conservative, since they felt that the possibilities were excellent for a gradual, but long-term rise. For *Gloria*, Irénée recommended that the Powder Company offer "6 cents per 101 pounds of workable nitrate . . . plus $437,000 for maquina [machinery and production facilities], iodine and stores."[26] This came to a total of $667,000. On October 26 the Executive Committee, with Pierre presiding, approved Irénée's plan but *Gloria*'s owners refused the offer.[27] They still disputed Du Pont's estimate of nitrate reserve, claiming the figure of 180,000 tons was far too low.

Since *Gloria* could not be purchased at a satisfactory price, Carpenter turned his attention toward the *Carolina oficina*, which was located less than 80 rail miles from the deepwater port of Taltal.[28] *Carolina*'s owners claimed they had 15 million Spanish quintals of nitrate reserve and they demanded £205,000 sterling. *Carolina*'s potential yearly output was twice that of *Gloria* and thus it could fulfill 40% of Du Pont's annual nitrate requirements.[29]

In the bargaining for the *oficina* the du Ponts enjoyed an advantage which they lacked in their negotiations for *Gloria*. *Carolina*, unlike *Gloria*, which was an active producer, stood idle in need of major repairs to its machinery. Furthermore, since *Carolina*'s owners did not have adequate financial resources, they were anxious to sell. The campaign to purchase *Carolina* was a three-cornered affair. In Santiago, Chile, E. N. Carpenter bargained directly with the owners. Although Carpenter's role was primary, he worked within limits set by the Powder Company's top management. In Wilmington, Irénée du Pont and his Development Department analyzed Carpenter's data and reported the findings to the Executive Committee. At all times, Irénée collaborated with Pierre who, throughout the negotiations, served as acting president as well as treasurer.

The Executive Committee met on March 14 and on the basis of Irénée's detailed analysis it voted unanimously to empower the Development Department to offer £160,000 cash and the remaining £45,000 asked by *Carolina*'s owners "in bonds bearing not over 6% interest payable in fifteen years, with the provision that the bonds shall become immediately payable when 8,000,000 quintals of nitrate have been elaborated." The Powder

Company was to have the right to forfeit the property in lieu of payment of the bonds.[30] In effect, the Executive Committee voted to pay cash for the plant and confirmed nitrate reserves and to give additional £45,000 of bonds payable at the Powder Company's option only after the confirmed reserves of 8,000,000 quintals had been extracted.

E. N. Carpenter, however, had a free hand to negotiate as long as he did not exceed the Executive Committee's offer. Armed with this authority and detailed estimates of the nitrate reserves he came to terms with the owners. On September 22, six months after the decision to buy, Pierre informed the Executive Committee that "the Carolina property is ours." The sole price for all rights was only £160,000.[31] The Executive Committee then voted an appropriation of $975,000 to cover full payment for *Carolina*, to finance repairs, and to start production.[32]

Shortly afterward, on October 6, the Executive Committee authorized Carpenter to pay $7,000 for an option on a nearby *oficina*, *Negra de Taltal*.[33] The negotiations for the new property justified the extreme caution with which Du Pont had approached *Carolina*'s purchase, for although *Negra de Taltal*'s owners claimed 10 million Spanish quintals of reserves, the Development Department's engineers found only 3 million quintals.[34] When Carpenter attempted to recover part of the investigation expenses from *Negra de Taltal*'s owners as provided for in the option, he found them bankrupt and unable to pay.[35] As 1910 ended, the Powder Company temporarily stopped the acquisition of more nitrate fields and turned toward the problem of administering their new property.

Pierre and the Executive Committee initially placed the full responsibility for *Carolina*'s management in the Development Department.[36] And almost simultaneously the committee approved the change of *Carolina*'s name to *Oficina Delaware*. While Edmund Carpenter worked to bring the *oficina* into production, Pierre planned to provide it with a permanent management. He soon concluded that a separate corporation must be organized to handle the business. Pierre argued that this would limit the amount of property "which would be subject to attack on account of misdeeds and unwise actions on the part of our South American representatives." Secondly, he felt that it would simplify still further making payments in Chile, since the South American corporation would draw drafts against the home firm. These, bearing two signatures of the officers of the Chilean company, would finally meet the long-sought goal of Du Pont notes in Chile which had the safeguard of a double signature and which would circulate as first-class paper without the liability of requiring the backing of a bank. Like the other Du Pont paper this would go to London for redemption. Finally, Pierre thought that the financial success of the new nitrate company would make it possible within three years to issue bonds based solely on that property, thus expanding the Powder Company's ability to raise capital beyond what would be feasible if the nitrate operation were merged directly into the American company.[37] On December 8, the Executive Committee accepted Pierre's recommendations and directed that he take the necessary action.[38] In the following May of 1911, Pierre had the legal department organize the Du Pont Nitrate Company, of which he became president. The new corporation, chartered in Delaware, had a capital of $800,000 consisting of 7% cumulative nonvoting preferred stock and $800,000 of common stock.[39]

The energy and capital that the Powder Company executives expended on nitrate of soda inevitably caused the Executive Committee to consider the production and marketing of that commodity as an end in itself, separate from explosives business. Throughout 1910 and 1911 the Executive Committee discussed selling nitrate of soda to the large and growing fertilizer market in the United States. Irénée's Development Department carefully studied the feasibility of such diversification, a move that would bring Du Pont into direct competition with W. R. Grace & Company and other importers. Irénée reported that the 41 soda storehouses maintained by the Powder Company could form a distribution system superior to that of any other nitrate importer. But he warned that success in fertilizer might require the sale of a full line including potash and phosphates with which the company was unfamiliar.[40] After full consideration the Executive Committee decided against expanding into an unknown business where the return lacked the certainty of the explosives field. Furthermore, limited productive capacity of *Oficina Delaware* inhibited sales to outside consumers.

Even after the *oficina* was operating at full capacity, the Powder Company still had to purchase over 50% of its annual requirements.[41] The policy of not purchasing nitrate fields capable of supplying Du Pont's total needs was deliberate. The threat of moving still further into nitrate production encouraged the Powder Company's suppliers to quote the lowest possible prices in order to discourage further Du Pont entry into production. In addition, the company also benefited in depressed times because it could keep its own *oficinas* running at full capacity, reducing only outside orders.

With the formation of the Du Pont Nitrate Company in 1911 Pierre and his associates completed a major step in making their horizontal consolidation into a vertical one. From the very beginning of the Powder Company its Executive Committee and Development Department had concentrated much attention on assuring that the greatly increased productive capacity of the Du Pont enterprise—two-thirds of the industry—receive an uninterrupted flow of basic materials at the lowest possible cost. Yet Pierre, Moxham, and the others were extremely cautious in taking the final step of assuring control—that is, the actual purchase of nitrate properties. They wanted to be sure that the capital investment would bring a satisfactory return. The motive for such vertical integration was control in order to be sure of supplies; the timing for the execution of the strategy depended on the price of the properties.

## Glycerin

As the Powder Company moved toward vertical integration in nitrate of soda, it faced critically different problems with its other essential resources. Chief among these was glycerin. In the hectic aftermath of the panic of 1907, the Executive Committee at Pierre's urging directed the Purchasing Department to stop buying glycerin until further notice.[42] The committee issued this order on February 6, 1908; and it still stood at the end of July. The action stemmed from Pierre's concern that the Purchasing Department was routinely buying in advance as much as a twelve to fourteen months' supply of crude glycerin. Pierre hoped to reduce reserve stocks to as little as a two or three months' supply and to harmonize closely buying and consumption. This proved to be neither practical nor desirable.

Glycerin was absolutely vital. In 1908 every 100 pounds of high explosives required 14.28 pounds of glycerin, for which there was no substitute.[43] In mid-1908 Frank Tallman and Hamilton Barksdale both argued that a growing worldwide glycerin shortage made the goal of a two or three months' supply dangerous. In 1908, for example, the United States consumed approximately 30,000 tons of refined glycerin. This amounted to one-half the world's production. The Powder Company alone used 11,000 tons, one-third of America's requirements, and one-sixth of the world's production.[44]

The purchase of glycerin posed special problems. Unlike nitrate of soda, which existed in a natural state and could be mined directly in vast quantities, glycerin was a by-product. It occurred in animal and vegetable oils and was produced incidentally to the manufacture of laundry soaps and tallow candles. A sharp decline in candle manufacture during the last decades of the nineteenth century—caused by the use of kerosene, gas, and electricity for lighting—had left the entire glycerin supply tied ever more closely to soapmaking. From 1900 through the First World War, glycerin demand increased at a much faster rate than the supply, and the price reflected this. Tallman estimated that soapmakers could profitably recover glycerin if the price were 3½¢ per pound. In 1906 crude glycerin sold at 6¢ per pound; by 1907 the price had advanced to 14¢; it fell momentarily to 11¢ in early 1908, but by 1910 it was 17¢.[45] By February 1911 the price had leapt to 24¢ per pound and threatened to go to 35¢ or higher. Wrote Tallman: "I styled [in June 1910] glycerine our *second* most important raw material." Now in February 1911 he changed his mind; for glycerin had become "the *most* important raw material, not only on account of the dangers attending its purchase, but for the further reason that it [had] . . . so advanced in price as to elevate it, in the near future, to the head of the list of purchases, as far as the amount in money was concerned."[46] Tallman predicted to the Executive Committee that at the 1911 consumption rate (1,700 drums per month) the annual cost could reach more than $5,385,000.[47]

The glycerin problem that faced Pierre and his colleagues was, therefore, more than one of cost. It involved securing a supply at any price. There were still further complications. In 1908 the Powder Company purchased two kinds of glycerin: crude and refined. Only the refined product was used for explosives manufacture, and the du Ponts had provided Repauno with a refinery that manufactured from crude glycerin an amount equal to one-third of the company's refined glycerin consumption. Thus Tallman had to enter the crude market for Repauno and to purchase the remaining two-thirds of the refined glycerin from independent American refiners. The nature of the crude glycerin market added further problems. Although the United States consumed half of the world's production, it produced only a quarter of the world's supply. This forced the du Ponts and other refiners onto the world crude glycerin market.

The Executive Committee, therefore, had to answer several vital and related questions. Should the Powder Company build additional refining capacity, and if so how much? How could the company secure a more adequate supply of crude glycerin? And would this entail a program of vertical integration—by purchasing or expanding plants, equipment, and personnel—or simply better purchasing arrangements?

Almost immediately after the panic the Executive Committee decided to expand its refining. In November of 1908 Tallman argued that "with our present refining capacity at Repauno; i.e., one-third of our present consumption, we must purchase the remaining two-thirds [of our requirements] as refined from refiners in this country, or purchase the equivalent crude abroad and have it refined here for us."[48] Buying from American refiners was not practical because they, in turn, purchased their crude abroad, thus becoming direct competitors for the scarce resources with Du Pont and thus unnecessarily forcing up prices. But buying crude abroad and then sending it to American refiners for processing was also unsatisfactory, for, wrote Tallman, "we have never been able to contract with them at a difference between crude furnished and refined obtained, which has been less than 1½ cents per pound above our refining cost at Repauno."[49] Tallman recommended that the Powder Company build a new refinery at Repauno equal in output to the old. This would provide 660,000 pounds of capacity per month and promised annual savings of $118,000. The total necessary investment was approximately $100,000.[50] This more than met Pierre's requirement that capital invested show a return of 15% per annum.

Pierre, in the absence of Coleman, approved a preliminary appropriation for the new glycerin refinery during the first week of December 1908. Then on December 16 the Executive Committee authorized an additional $94,-000 to complete the improvements.[51] The new capacity, when added to the old, provided for two-thirds of the Powder Company's refined glycerin needs. Significantly, both Tallman and the Executive Committee rejected advice from Nobel that the Powder Company construct refineries capable of manufacturing all the required glycerin. Tallman argued that the new refinery, coupled with an underlying threat to build still more capacity, would enable the Du Pont Company to force better terms from the American refiners.[52] The policy of integrating backward to ensure the flow of a large part, but not all, of the company's raw material requirements became a standard Du Pont strategy. In most cases this forced suppliers to meet Du Pont's own prices. In effect, the company obtained the economy of complete vertical integration while not committing capital to capacity which might stand idle during times of slack production. In almost every case, however, the Powder Company stood ready to defend itself by an increase in its commitment to integration should the return upon investment warrant it.

Pierre and the Executive Committee examined the strategy of vertical integration as an answer to the crude, as well as the refined, glycerin problem. As Tallman put it, the Powder Company was "a large buyer in a limited market."[53] Every year after 1900 supplies became more scarce and the specter of a glycerin corner loomed. By 1910 the situation had become so acute that Tallman told the Executive Committee that it would require only a "limited amount of capital" for a speculator or promoter either in the United States or abroad to "buy up the little spot glycerine, contract ahead for that which remains uncovered this year and next, and to contract for 1912 and possibly later, and in this way control the situation and compel those of the consumers like ourselves who have no known substitute for glycerine to pay abnormally high prices."[54]

Pierre worked closely with Tallman to meet this threat. They both agreed that the manufacture of crude glycerin directly from animal or vegetable oils was not feasible. Though crude glycerin prices were high, their level reflected demand, not increased production costs. Because it was a by-product of soapmaking, its producers recovered glycerin at about 3½ ¢ per pound. Tallman did not know the exact cost of direct manufacture, but he estimated that if a plant were built to make only glycerin, costs of manufacturing would be in excess of 16¢ per pound. While it was true that glycerin might sell as high as 35¢ per pound, the Powder Company was such a high-volume buyer that its withdrawal from the market might cause prices to drop below 16¢. In short, if Du Pont went into the direct manufacture of glycerin, the price for everyone else might drop below the costs of making glycerin as a primary product directly from animal or vegetable oils. Therefore, nothing short of entering soapmaking, an unacceptable alternative, would allow the Powder Company to make crude glycerin at a price competitive with that on the market.

Pierre took an oblique approach. He encouraged a search for substitutes. On December 2, 1908, the Executive Committee, at his request, granted an appropriation of $1,500 for the Experimental Station to start the development of synthetic glycerin. Thus began a prolonged, but frustrating, drive for a glycerin substitute.[55] As the crisis deepened, the Executive Committee ordered the High Explosives Operating Department to find ways to reduce glycerin consumption.[56] By August 1910, Hamilton Barksdale could report that new techniques and the substitution of other ingredients for nitroglycerin had decreased the glycerin needed per 100 pounds of high explosives from 14.33 in 1907 to 12.43 in 1910.[57] But neither substitutes nor synthetics eliminated the need for crude glycerin and the Powder Company's consumption in terms of pounds for 1910 stood just about where it had in 1906 and 1907 and far above the figures for 1905.[58]

The impracticability of vertical integration (by investment in a direct operation or production facility for crude glycerin) and the inability to develop a synthetic kept the main responsibility for crude glycerin procurement in Tallman's department. "Our purchases," he wrote, "practically make the market. We *can* control the world situation in glycerine more easily than anyone else, on account of the relatively large amount required by us and our relations with other large users."[59] But achieving control meant abandonment of Pierre's program to reduce commitments to as little as two to four months' reserve stockpiles.

Pierre quickly reversed himself. Beginning in 1908 he supported Tallman in bold moves which systematically contracted for glycerin for at least a year and sometimes as much as two years in advance. Early that year the Powder Company took advantage of the recently renewed alliance to buy jointly with the English Nobels 15,200 tons of glycerin on the European market. Of this, Nobel took 8,000 tons, which was their entire requirement, and the Powder Company took 7,200 tons, which left about 4,000 tons for it to purchase in the United States.[60] In early 1910, when Pierre was in Europe, Nobel officials informed him that they desired to terminate the joint purchasing. They later changed their minds and renewed the agreement, but they rejected Pierre's suggestion that the two explosives giants buy jointly their entire glycerin requirements. Even so, a new purchasing agreement provided for a joint purchase of 22,000 tons: 10,000 for the Nobels and 12,000 for the Powder Company. As under the old arrangement, this was the European firm's whole requirement, but it left about 2,000 tons for Du Pont to acquire in America.[61]

Contracting for glycerin for a year in advance and cooperating with the Nobel firm protected the Powder Company against a corner. It also produced substantial savings. Tallman reported to the Executive Committee on November 22, 1910, that for the calendar year 1909 the Powder Company's costs had been but 14.008¢ per pound, while the market price had been 18¢. In 1910 the savings were even more substantial, Du Pont paying 14.6¢ per pound, while the market price was 20.5¢. This alone represented a saving of more than $1.3 million.[62]

But there was always the danger that a sudden price break would find the Powder Company with large contracts at figures substantially above the market price. In November 1910, for example, Tallman predicted a sharp price increase that would force crude glycerin to 30¢ per pound in 1911 and 35¢ per pound in 1912. Two months later the Purchasing Department, in its monthly report, indicated decreasing crude prices. Fearful that the company was accumulating stocks at inflated price levels, the Executive Committee demanded an explanation. Tallman's answer asserted that the price decrease was both slight and temporary and that the company was still buying below the market.

Tallman's concluding remarks summarized the problems that would continue to plague his department. At no time, said he, has the Purchasing Department ever "attempted to maintain that there would never be either a temporary or permanent recession [of crude glycerine prices] but have in fact called attention to the possibility under certain conditions of an extreme permanent decline, with its accompanying grave danger." Furthermore, he argued, "the study of the glycerine situation in all its various aspects is a continuous, steady and painstaking one from day to day, with the most energetic attempts to obtain all available information and with frequent consultations often more than once a week, at which times all information is gone over in detail."[63] But, concluded Tallman, there was no alternative, short of finding a glycerin substitute.

## Other Raw Materials

Crude glycerin was not the only raw material that caused the Purchasing Department anguish. Fusel oil, essential to the Smokeless Powder Department, like glycerin, was a by-product (in this case, of the manufacture of industrial alcohol) and was in limited supply. In fact, one-third of the fusel oil used in the United States was consumed by the Powder Company. Since Du Pont's requirements were twice America's fusel oil production, the company had to turn to a highly speculative European market for most of its supply.[64]

Pierre fully recognized that fusel oil could become a major problem. In 1908 the Executive Committee approved his request for an initial appropriation of $4,000 so that the Experimental Station could investigate the synthetic production of amyl acetate, a fusel oil substitute.[65]

In 1911 the fusel oil situation suddenly became critical. In January of that year the Purchasing Department's John B. Niles informed the Executive Committee that Honeywill & Company of London had cornered the market, forcing prices to abnormal levels.[66] Niles observed that the Experimental Station had developed a method to manufacture amyl acetate synthetically, and that a plant could be built to produce annually 500,000 to 800,000 pounds of amyl acetate. This would displace a like quantity of fusel oil. The problem, however, was exactly that of glycerin: amyl acetate could be manufactured at a lower price than the current market quotation for fusel oil, but should Du Pont withdraw from the fusel oil market, the result would be to break Honeywill's corner and to send fusel oil prices below the cost of making amyl acetate synthetically. Even so, Pierre and the Executive Committee voted unanimously to have the Development Department "prepare plans, and select a site, and submit a request for the necessary appropriation for the construction of a plant for the synthetical manufacture of amyl acetate, with the expectation that . . . we shall proceed as quickly as possible."[67] Simultaneously, however, the Executive Committee directed the Development Department to investigate fusel oil production and consumption patterns. Perhaps the committee hoped to impress Honeywill with the seriousness of its preparation for the manufacture of a fusel oil substitute and thus extract a better price. If so, the strategy proved a failure.

By spring 1911 the Development Department had finished its estimates. Pierre summarized the department's findings to the Executive Committee on April 11, stating that because of numerous mechanical and production problems in the synthetic amyl acetate process, a pilot plant should be constructed to gain experience prior to any large-scale manufacturing effort.[68] The Executive Committee seemed mildly favorable to a test plant. On May 9, 1911, however, when the Development Department presented hard cost data, the Executive Committee voted unanimously to drop the project. The data revealed that it would cost $134,000 for a pilot plant with a capacity of 165,000 pounds per annum, and more than $246,000 for a plant capable of producing 660,000 pounds per annum, which was about half of Du Pont's requirements. Concluded the Executive Committee, the investment was "so large in comparison with the value of the product" that it seemed unwise to proceed further.[69]

This action left the Purchasing Department at Honeywill's mercy and throughout the summer and fall it tried to come to an agreement with the head of the London firm. Honeywill was persuaded to come to Wilmington to discuss the matter in June 1911.[70] On September 12, however, Tallman told the Executive Committee that, despite further interviews with the London speculator, no satisfactory terms could be made. The Executive Committee had no choice, therefore, but to approve Tallman's policy of purchasing fusel oil in small amounts on a month-to-month basis at the market price. The Executive Committee, however, refused to abandon the search for a substitute and encouraged continuous research for one by the Development Department.[71]

Most of Du Pont's raw materials did not present the problems of nitrate of soda, crude glycerin, and fusel oil. Nevertheless, by 1912 the Powder Company had gained control of the sources of other materials. The reason was primarily defensive; that is, the du Ponts had been dissatisfied with the prices quoted by suppliers and had begun a limited production themselves in order to force commercial manufacturers to lower prices. Typical of this was the policy in regard to acid, both nitric and sulphuric. In 1905 the Purchasing Department became convinced that the large acid producers, especially the Grasselli Chemical Company and the General Chemical Company, were not giving the Powder Company "as low prices as the volume of our business and other considerations deserve."[72] Since no amount of selective buying seemed to change things, the Powder Company undertook direct manufacture of both acids. By 1909 Du Pont production, together with limited purchases from smaller acid concerns, enabled the Powder Company to demonstrate its total independence of the Grasselli Chemical and General Chemical companies. This gave the Purchasing Department a powerful bargaining lever.[73]

By 1912 the du Ponts had put to work a substantial amount of capital to produce the following raw materials or supplies: sulphuric acid, nitric acid, charcoal, wood pulp, alcohol, boxes, and pulp kegs. Their importance ranged from $1.58 million in sulphuric acid production and $1.22 million in nitric acid facilities to $143,000 for charcoal works. The company also had minor investments (less than $100,000) in the production of, or experimentation with, production of other materials such as sulphur and pyrites.

Pierre never regarded vertical integration as an end in itself. Although he appreciated the need for defensive actions, he always desired that capital so invested show profits at least equal to funds employed in explosives. His minimum goal remained a 15% return. In early 1912 he asked the Accounting Committee of the Executive Committee to prepare a statement "of our investment in acid plants and other plants for the manufacture of raw materials and preliminary products, together with the estimated profit thereon for the year 1910."[74] This quickly developed into a comprehensive analysis of vertical integration's profitableness—not only in 1910, but in 1911, and in previous years as well. A report presented to the Executive Committee on June 11, 1912, showed that of those plants studied only the glycerin refinery and the nitric acid facilities returned 15% or more on their invested capital. For glycerin the return was 95% per annum on an outlay of $204,000; for nitric acid it was 50% on $1.22 million. For sulphuric acid, however, the return was a bare .004 of 1% on $1.58 million; charcoal returned less than 5%, and wood pulp about 1%.[75] Boxes and pulp kegs showed actual losses. As a result, the Executive Committee ordered the general manager to study the possible abandonment of sulphuric acid manufacture, a move which by 1914 caused the liquidation of a substantial portion, but not all, of this activity.[76] Pierre's study also was one of the many factors that led to the end of pulp keg production.

More important, however, was the Executive Committee's decision to direct the Accounting Committee to make periodic reports that would analyze the financial success or failure of the various ventures involved in producing its own supplies and materials. Although the Accounting Committee's method, which compared the market price with Du Pont's own production costs, gave a somewhat deceptive picture (because the results did not take into account the influence that Du Pont's production exercised on the market price), it nevertheless gave a useful yardstick with which to measure the success of each capital outlay.

Concurrently with Pierre's evaluation of vertical integration, Moxham reopened the debate on the wisdom of the Purchasing Committee's nitrate of soda and crude glycerin policies. Moxham reverted to Pierre's original idea that it was dangerous to carry large raw material inventories. Not only did this tie up substantial quantities of needed capital but it risked what had actually happened to glycerin in 1911, when the company purchased "ahead on an *assumed* monthly consumption, to find consumption falling off rapidly and the stock on hand of high price material therefore accumulating rapidly on a falling market."[77] Though the glycerin reserves did not increase to the crisis point, the experience motivated Moxham to support a restoration of the measures instituted during the financial panic of 1907 to control raw material inventories—that is, that nitrate of soda and glycerin purchases be made for no more than two to three months in advance. Moxham would have liked to purchase no more than a week ahead had that been practical. In a lengthy analysis of both nitrate of soda and crude glycerin purchases he compared the prices that the Powder Company paid under its policy of buying "futures" (for as much as a year or more in advance) with the price that the Purchasing Committee would have paid had it bought its requirements three months ahead of consumption.

Moxham figured that in the case of nitrate of soda "we would have been better off purchasing on the market" rather than stockpiling during the years 1908, 1909, and 1910; but he agreed that there had been a saving during 1911. Nevertheless, he asserted that during the four years preceding 1912 had the Powder Company purchased three months in advance it would have saved approximately $144,000, or about 2% of the total cost of nitrate of soda. Moxham admitted that savings in glycerin had been substantial—over $1.0 million during the four years from 1908 through 1911—but even here he felt that the Purchasing Committee did not appreciate the risks. He postulated that buying "futures" worked only when raw material prices were advancing, but failed in a falling market. Nitrate of soda prices had declined three of the four years studied, he pointed out, a fact which explained why the Purchasing Committee's cost exceeded the market prices at the time of consumption during three of the four years. On the other hand, glycerin prices had risen steadily (except for the one brief reverse in 1911) and this accounted for the success in that field. But Moxham argued that crude glycerin prices could not be expected to rise indefinitely. Essentially he concluded that long-term purchases, whether of crude glycerin or nitrate of soda, were speculative and over the long pull the losses usually canceled out the gains. Therefore, he could see little justification for investing capital in large inventories or for the risks of guessing wrong on the state of the market a year hence.[78] The Executive Committee referred Moxham's analysis to the Purchasing Committee, of which Pierre was a member.[79]

Tallman's reply, on August 1, 1912, spoke for Pierre and the Purchasing Committee; it sharply defended long-term buying of both essential materials. Tallman attacked Moxham's nitrate data, asserting that his "market" price was in reality the quotations for spot sales, which were very limited and could not be used to gauge the nitrate price. As proof that the Du Pont nitrate purchasing policy had been effective during the years 1909 through 1911, Tallman offered a detailed statistical comparison of the nitrate purchases of the five largest buyers, two of which were European and three (including Du Pont) American. Although Du Pont did not receive as good a price as the two European concerns, each of which purchased three times as much nitrate as the Powder Company, the Purchasing Committee could point to a four-year average price of 7/2.55d, which very nearly equaled that of the W. R. Grace & Company (7/2.49d) and was substantially below that of Wessel, Duval & Co. (7/3.86d). For 1911 Du Pont boasted the lowest nitrate cost of all the five large buyers.[80] And Tallman argued that the crude glycerin record spoke for itself, for even Moxham admitted that it had been phenomenally successful with "right guessing" in all of the years studied.

Actually, Tallman insisted, Moxham had missed the point of the long-term buying. It had little to do with "speculation." While the director of Purchases agreed that advance buying carried risks, he asserted that the Powder Company had never bought beyond its intention to consume. True speculation, he declared, would be "more properly confined to purchases made beyond our necessities, purchases made for re-sale at a higher price than that of regular brokerage commissions, or failure to purchase until our stock was reduced dangerously low, waiting for an expected recession in the market," none of which had been done. The vital fact behind the decision to give the Purchasing Committee a relatively free hand to make long-term purchases was the importance of both nitrate of soda and crude glycerin to the Powder Company. No automatic method which involved buying at fixed times at whatever the market price happened to be would work, for, argued Tallman, "such a method would be quickly revealed to others who would take advantage of our necessities and force us to pay higher prices than would be necessary under a flexible—that is, nonmechanical—method of purchasing." This was especially true with glycerin, where buying had never been solely for "the purpose of making advantageous purchases, as far as the price is concerned, but" for defensive reasons, in order "to positively insure a supply of one of our most important raw materials, the production of which is limited by the production of other industries."[81]

Pierre supported the Executive Committee in its motion to endorse Tallman's recommendations that "no change be made in our present methods of purchasing [glycerin and nitrate of soda]." While the treasurer opposed unprofitable vertical integration for the minor raw materials—especially in cases where the market was competitive and not subject to the wiles of speculators—he recognized that the Powder Company could not leave to chance the acquisition of its two most essential material resources. Moxham, who had carried on his fight to change the Purchasing Committee's policies for almost a year, saw that his cause was lost, so in the interests of harmony he went along with his fellow members of the Executive Committee, thus making their decision in support of Tallman unanimous.[82]

For Pierre and the Executive Committee the underlying basis of their policy of vertical integration in relation to all their raw materials was to assure a steady and certain flow of supplies into their plants at the cheapest possible over-all costs. The precise way in which this policy was carried out depended on a wide variety of business and economic circumstances. Rarely, however, was Pierre willing to expand the business by buying properties producing raw materials unless the capital so expended would bring as high a rate of return as funds invested in plants, offices, and other facilities used in its basic activities—the making and selling of explosives.

## Diversification

Expansion through a policy of vertical integration was only one of the possible ways to allocate new capital. Diversification into fields allied to the powder business by common skills and resources was another. For the Powder Company the first major diversification experiment, which took place in 1910, was in the field of artificial leather. This came, however, not as a result of theory or planning, but as a response to problems thrust upon the Powder Company from outside. In this case, the cause was excess capacity in smokeless powder and a need to keep plants, resources, and workers fully employed.

Starting in 1906 the Du Pont Company came under increasingly heavy attack because of its dominant position in the powder industry. It became labeled the "Powder Trust," and the government initiated an antitrust suit in 1907 which, after several years of bitter litigation, led to a court-ordered dissolution of the Powder Company in 1912. The antitrust case, the subject of the following chapter, had important consequences for diversification because it threatened Du Pont's sale of smokeless powder to the army and navy. In 1908, Congress, in order not to have the armed services buy from a trust, authorized measures to double the capacity of the government's own powder-making facilities at Picatinny, New Jersey, and Indian Head, Maryland. Although the armed forces could not immediately dispense with Du Pont powder, starting in 1908 the Smokeless Powder Department experienced reduced orders.

The company fought to protect its military business. J. A. Haskell, since 1907 the head of the Smokeless Powder Department, and Colonel E. G. Buckner, who was responsible for Military Sales, rallied the company's congressional friends to its support and they were able to block in 1908 and 1909 amendments to the Military and Fortifications Bill and the Panama Canal Appropriations Bill, which were aimed at preventing government orders for powder from going to Du Pont. But they were powerless to stop an unfavorable amendment to the 1909 Naval Bill, which specified that "no part of any appropriation made in this act for the purchase of powder shall be paid to any trust, or combination in restraint of trade, nor to any combination having a monopoly of the manufacture and supply of gunpowder in the United States except in the event of an extraordinary emergency." Haskell's report to the Executive Committee on February 27, 1909, showed a substantial drop in powder made for the government in January 1909 as compared with the same month of the previous year. Production of Army and Navy Cannon Powder was just 200,000 pounds, 63,000 pounds less than in 1908. PYRO 30-Caliber production was less than 75% of the previous year and Dense Rifle less than a third of 1908. And Haskell had no illusions about the future, writing that "notwithstanding the fact that we know both Ordnance Departments' desire to be friendly and give us a sufficient share of their business to justify our continuing to keep large plants in existence for their use, the subservice of Congress to the opinions of a few radicals in their own body and whose votes they do not dare jeopardize, should, in my opinion, lead us to consider the Government as a competitive manufacturing organization. . . ."[83]

The growing threat of prolonged excess capacity in the Smokeless Powder Department led the Executive Committee on December 16, 1908, to appoint a committee consisting of J. A. Haskell, Pierre du Pont, and William B. Dwinnell to investigate alternative uses for the department's major product—guncotton.[84] The newly appointed committee worked closely with Irénée, who had just taken Moxham's place as the head of the Development

Department. Systematically they made investigations of all important products that consumed nitrocellulose (guncotton), including artificial leather, artificial silk, celluloid, and boat bottom paints.

Of all the new markets examined, artificial leather, a commodity that was enjoying a rapidly expanding use, seemed the most promising. Its use for seat covers in the booming new automobile industry seemed to assure a growing market. "The simplest solution," wrote Irénée, "would be to sell the guncotton to the makers of artificial leather," but he did not believe that this would work.[85] The Fabrikoid Company, located in Newburgh, New York, he reported, was the largest and most successful of the artificial leather concerns. It made its own nitrocellulose and had no interest in purchasing from Du Pont. Therefore, Irénée recommended that the Powder Company establish a small pilot plant that would give the corporation valuable experience and enable it to construct a factory large enough to compete on the artificial leather market. This way Irénée hoped it would be possible to convince Fabrikoid of the advantage of buying their guncotton from Du Pont or, better still, of merging with the Powder Company.[86]

By the summer of 1909 the Executive Committee had approved plans drawn up by the Development Department for an experimental artificial leather works at the closed-down smokeless powder plant at Oakland, New Jersey, and actual work was under way. The effort was on a small scale; only $2,500 was appropriated for it, which was 5% of the estimated cost of a small commercial factory.[87] Pierre quickly raised the question of how costs should be allocated for the new venture. The Executive Committee unanimously reaffirmed a decision made in February 1909: "That the Development Department shall have charge of the study of any new business or product which is not embodied in the company's regular process of manufacture, until the study is completed."[88] Under this arrangement all costs were to be borne by the Development Department until the transfer of the commercially perfected process to an operating department, which would then repay the Development Department for its work.

Experiments continued throughout 1909 and into 1910. The Development Department strove to perfect a new solvent recovery process that would enable the recapture of nearly 60% of the expensive amyl acetate solvents used in the manufacture of artificial leather. The Development Department thought that no potential competitor had a solvent recovery process and that the possession of one would give Du Pont an advantage so great as to ensure success in the new field. Quite by accident in February 1910, a fire in Fabrikoid's solvent recovery area disclosed to the Development Department that their potentially most important rival already had a recovery process. This discovery emphasized the desirability of diversification by acquiring Fabrikoid, and shortly thereafter efforts to this effect were begun.[89]

The senior executives in the Development Department undertook the negotiations and they moved with surprising speed. Irénée and Pierre, certain that artificial leather was a growing and profitable field, hoped to exploit the fact that Fabrikoid's owners lacked the capital to take advantage of their experience. On July 19, 1910, less than five months after the decision to approach Fabrikoid, Irénée du Pont brought a tentative contract to the Executive Committee. Although Irénée did not have "actual figures," he estimated that Fabrikoid's assets amounted to "about $780,000" and that its annual profits were "between $200,000 and $250,000." The proposed contract specified that the Powder Company pay Fabrikoid's owners an amount equal to five times the company's "net earnings for the year 1909, provided, however, that in no event shall . . . [the] purchase price exceed $1,300,000."[90] The contract further stipulated that an examination of the company's books and physical plant had to confirm the tentative estimates and that the tangible assets must amount to at least $780,000; otherwise the price was to be reduced accordingly. Irénée's contract made possible the expansion without the use of cash. Fabrikoid's owners were to receive 50% of their payment in Powder Company 5% cumulative preferred stock, 30% in Powder Company 4½% gold bonds, and the remaining 20% in Powder Company common stock. The securities newly issued for this purpose were to be taken at their par value.

At the Executive Committee meeting which made the decision, Coleman du Pont was absent, as were J. A. Haskell and C. L. Patterson, who, as head of the Sales Department, had come on the committee in 1907. After much discussion, Pierre, Arthur Moxham, and Hamilton Barksdale voted to accept the deal over the strong objection of Alfred I. du Pont, who preferred to confine the company to the powder business.[91]

The Development Department closed the agreement, paying Fabrikoid's owners a total of $1,195,000 in Powder Company securities.[92] The Executive Committee then decided to operate Fabrikoid as an administrative part of the Powder Company rather than as a separate corporation.[93] On September 1, 1910, the Executive Committee directed the Development Department to transfer the Fabrikoid plant to the Smokeless Powder Department.[94]

About six months after Fabrikoid had become an integral part of the Smokeless Powder Department, Pierre ordered an analysis of artificial leather's profitability. The results were not encouraging. Pierre reported to the Executive Committee that the Powder Company was receiving a return of 4.66% on the $1,195,000 worth of securities they had issued.[95] It soon became evident that the Development Department in its haste had erred by basing its purchase price on Fabrikoid's earning record for the single year 1909. Pierre remained optimistic that the long-term prospects for artificial leather were favorable, but he realized that it would take considerable time to attain his original hopes.

The Executive Committee continued to encourage the Development

Department to investigate alternative uses for nitrocellulose, such as boat bottom paints and artificial silk; but no commercial ventures in these areas were started, thus reflecting a more cautious attitude resulting from the Fabrikoid experience. It was only after the antitrust suit and a decline in the market for smokeless powder that the Executive Committee's interest in diversification revived. Nevertheless, Pierre and the Du Pont Executive Committee initiated the program of diversification to find uses for excess capacity in the smokeless powder plants and not as a new route to corporate growth. They searched for alternative uses only for nitrocellulose processed in the making of smokeless powder for the government market. They made no attempt to find other uses for resources involved in the production of black powder or dynamite. Even in seeking new nitrocellulose products, Pierre continued the same test of return on investment that he applied in determining the allocation of funds in new explosives capacity and in the production of raw materials.

## Continuing to Maintain Financial Control

Hand in hand with the attempt to analyze the profitability of new ventures, Pierre continued to increase his control over the administration of new capital expenditures. This remained crucial because the level of profits directly affected how much new capital could be infused into the company. With this in mind, he embarked on a program to improve his forecasts of future revenue so that he could better plan for over-all financial needs.

For forecasting purposes the treasurer wanted exact knowledge of the corporation's running expenses. He also needed to know earnings trends and the rate and direction of growth within the firm's various activities. To achieve these ends, he introduced a continuous review of the use of funds allocated by the formal appropriations procedures, the segment of expenditures most difficult to control.[96] On May 18, 1910, Pierre appointed Arthur Moxham, Alfred I. du Pont, and Hamilton Barksdale a committee to study further the appropriations procedure.[97] The subcommittee's report, made to the Executive Committee on December 9, 1910, and unanimously adopted, is worthy of detailed attention, for it exemplifies the kind of control Pierre wanted to achieve and the vital role that the treasurer played in shaping the company's development.

Under the revised system the old method of endorsing appropriations and reporting them to the Executive Committee, which was *pro forma*, statistical, and designed to give top management an exact picture of expenditures at any one moment, was continued as usual. The new refinements to the appropriations procedure attempted to review systematically all proposed capital expenditures, establish a priority for them, estimate available resources, and allocate the funds to the projects most needed by the various departments. Thus the president on the first of January of each year was to appoint an Appropriations Committee, of which he was the permanent chairman. The heads of the corporation's several departments were to submit to this committee on each first of January an estimate of projects for the coming year, listing them in order of their importance. At the same time the treasurer was to submit a forecast of the Powder Company's "earnings by months for the ensuing year, and the net total which he estimated would be available each month for duly approved and authorized appropriations." Furthermore, the treasurer was to send to the Appropriations Committee on the first of each month

> the estimated amount which would be available for expenditure during the current month, [the] actual amount shown by records as available for expenditures during the current month, [the] amount actually expended by the different departments to date as compared to their respective allotments, [and finally] a statement submitted once in six months or oftener showing the actual earnings on construction investment as compared with those forecasted by the departments at the time the appropriation was requested.

The Appropriations Committee's main work came early in January, and it consisted of comparing the expenditures advocated by the heads of the different departments with the treasurer's estimates of funds available and of making recommendations to the Executive Committee as to the allocation of the available resources. The final decision, of course, remained with the Executive Committee. Once it acted, the various departments were charged with immediately notifying the Executive Committee of any deviation from their allotments.[98]

During the period from 1908 through 1911 Pierre's most important duty. as the appropriations procedure suggests, was providing the funds and planning for the Powder Company's continuous expansion. Both the corporation and Pierre quickly recovered from the panic. On December 23, 1908, the treasurer wrote Coleman and Alfred that "the developments of the past year have shown the real strength of the company so fully that I feel the whole situation has improved . . . [as the result of] last year's panic. . . ."[99] But the rapid resurgence brought a need for much additional capital, not only to support the growing vertical integration ventures, but also to keep pace with the requirements for new capacity. By 1910, for example, the High Explosives Operating Department was pressing for the full realization of Barksdale's program for expanded dynamite output. That year the Executive Committee granted over $600,000 for a new 15 million-pound-per-year works at Joplin, Missouri; plans were far advanced for a new 15 million-pound plant on the East Coast to replace the obsolete Mauch Chunk and

Forcite works, which were to be abandoned; and preliminary studies were under way to provide 20 million pounds per annum additional capacity on the West Coast.[100]

Basically Pierre continued the financial strategy that he had initiated prior to the panic. The core of his program had combined the use of retained earnings with the sale of Powder Company common stock. The panic had left undisturbed the policy of using retained earnings, but had come near to dealing a mortal blow to the efforts to sell securities. Consequently, early in 1908 Pierre began with renewed vigor his efforts to make Powder Company stocks and bonds more attractive. First on the agenda was obtaining a listing on the New York Stock Exchange. In this effort Pierre worked closely with J. A. Haskell, who had close connections with the New York brokerage firm of Henry Brothers & Company, influential members of the Exchange. In March 1908, Pierre and Haskell had a meeting with the chairman of the Exchange's Committee on Listing Stocks and discovered that there would be "no trouble whatever in listing our bonds as far as their distribution is concerned." Further, they determined that preferred and common stocks could be listed as far as they were held by outsiders. Thus the listing could be accomplished through special arrangement made with the Exchange's registrar; this policy would prohibit the transfer on the Exchange of stock held by the Powder Company or E. I. du Pont de Nemours & Company (the family holding company). Pierre saw no objection to such an arrangement, since "E. I. du Pont de Nemours & Company has no intention of selling its holdings and if such intentions should develop there would be no objection to the listing on showing that the stock was to be distributed."[101] However, after further meetings with officers of the Exchange, Pierre decided to request listing for only the 4½% gold bonds and the 5% cumulative preferred stock. This proposal was finally accomplished in October of 1909.[102] Besides having the company's bonds and preferred stock on the New York Stock Exchange, Pierre listed the common stock on the New York Curb in January 1910, and all three varieties of securities on the San Francisco Stock Exchange.[103]

Pierre took other steps to facilitate the sale of Du Pont securities. He reported to the Executive Committee on December 10, 1908, that many brokers handling the stock exacted a higher than usual commission. The treasurer argued that such practices decreased the value of the securities. To remedy this he arranged with Henry Brothers & Company to buy and sell Du Pont stocks for 1/4% commission.[104]

But making it easier to buy and sell Powder Company securities was only a minor part of Pierre's program to raise capital through the sale of common stock. The keystone of this effort had been raising the common stock dividend to at least 7%, a rate of return he thought would make it an irresistible investment. But this had not guaranteed stock sales during the crisis, and only the underwriting agreement with the E. I. du Pont de Nemours & Company had saved the day. Pierre soon concluded that a 7% dividend was too low; hence in December of 1908 he recommended, and the Executive Committee agreed, that the common dividend be raised to 8%.[105] At the same time he resumed the efforts to support the market for Du Pont shares. During the year 1910, for example, he maintained with Henry Brothers & Company bids for preferred stock ranging from 85 to 87 and for common stock bids varying from 134½ to 138. The few shares the company obtained attested to the growing esteem in which they were held.[106]

The sale in December 1909 of the final common stock allotments under Pierre's revised financial plan of 1907 forced the treasurer to develop a new program. At the same time plans for additional dynamite capacity and $1.5 million required to float the nitrate venture in Chile intensified the needs for new capital. After eight months of consideration, Pierre proposed on June 27, 1910, that the company raise $2,396,000 by the sale of securities to be issued in 1911. His plan involved both common and preferred shares. He argued that the sale of relatively low dividend preferred stock added to the income of the common stockholder without forcing upon him the obligation to purchase new securities.[107] The problem, however, was that the 5% preferred shares sold at a discount at a price of about 85% of par. To alleviate this, Pierre decided to balance an issue of preferred with an issue of common, which was selling at a premium (about 14% of par with the dividend at 8%). To insure that common shares would rise in price Pierre proposed that the dividend be raised from 8% to 12% per annum.

The treasurer's program favored the stockholders. The common owners were to receive rights to purchase shares up to 3% of their holdings at a price of 140. Preferred shareholders were to be offered an allotment at a price of 80, equal to 10% of their holdings. And the price of both issues was designed to make the subscription rights of value.[108]

Pierre's plan was adopted by the Executive Committee on July 7, 1910. Although it made the Powder Company stock attractive to the general public, it still continued the tradition of drawing investment largely from the original stockholders. From the time he initiated his plans for financing expansion, Pierre always viewed high dividends as a method of retaining earnings, for how could shareholders fail to reinvest their money when doing so brought them such a high return? Pierre rested his program upon the assumption that the Powder Company could maintain high dividend rates indefinitely and he regarded the measures taken to improve the purchasing of raw materials, to develop selective vertical integration and so begin limited diversification as important steps toward his goal.

By 1911 the transformation of the Du Pont Company from a small family firm to a large modern corporation had been virtually completed. The first step had been the consolidation of the four major units in the industry —Du Pont, Hazard, Eastern Dynamite, and Laflin & Rand—into a single, centrally managed enterprise. After the briefest trials with the older ways of competition, Pierre, Moxham, and Coleman decided to extend this consolidation to over two-thirds of the powder industry. The years 1903 to 1906 were spent in completing the legal and financial arrangements of this consolidation, in building its administrative organization, and then in getting it functioning smoothly. By June 1906 the financing of the consolidation was completed; and in that September the Executive Committee finally decided to concentrate on expanding its activities at home rather than abroad.

In the years after 1906 the company's Executive Committee began a carefully planned program of expansion. The panic of 1907, which tested and proved the value of its financial and statistical controls, temporarily set back these plans. But in 1908 the Executive Committee started to carry out a long-range strategy of expansion to be financed largely by earnings, both those retained by the company and those returned in the form of stock purchases by the stockholders who invested their increased dividends. In the allocation of these funds the first priority went to enlarging production facilities—primarily in dynamite capacity and located in the West to meet the demands of the growing markets in the Mountain States and Pacific Coast areas. Capital was also placed in raw materials production to help assure adequate supplies. As time passed, however, Pierre tried to make certain that such investment offered as satisfactory a return as that allocated to facilities for production and sale of explosives. The needs and opportunities came often enough to transform this horizontal consolidation into a vertical one. At this time Pierre and his colleagues did not view diversification into new products for new markets as a profitable form of expansion. It was initiated only to use excess capacity in the small Smokeless Powder Department. By 1911 the Powder Company had become almost a prototype of the large vertically integrated enterprise producing a full line of products for one major market. It was an entirely different species of business corporation from the E. I. du Pont de Nemours & Company of a decade earlier.

As treasurer and then also as acting president, Pierre du Pont had played a critical role in creating this new corporation, in charting the direction of its growth, and then in carrying out its strategy of expansion. Pierre's influence had decided that the company would grow at home rather than abroad. Pierre had outlined the policy of financing this growth through profits; and he had the most to say about allocating those funds to be reinvested between investment in explosives plants, sales activities, and raw material production. He, more than Coleman or Alfred or any other member of the Executive Committee, was in this way the creator of the modern Du Pont Company.

# PART III

# THE NEW CHALLENGES

# The Powder Company Assailed

A T THE BEGINNING of 1911 Pierre could view the Du Pont Company with a feeling of deep satisfaction. Most of his duties had become routine. Long-range financial policies and methods of control had been established. The firm's direction of growth had been decided. Overseas expansion had been discarded in favor of concentration on the domestic market and on vertical integration. Consequently even Coleman's illness and Pierre's rise to the position of acting president in 1909 did not present new challenges, although it did put him more in the center of the decision-making process.

The first decade of the twentieth century had seen decisive family changes. His beloved brother Henry Belin lost a long struggle with tuberculosis in July of 1902, leaving a young wife and a 4-year-old son. Pierre immediately assumed the role of guardian and counselor to his sister-in-law Eleuthera and his nephew Henry Belin du Pont, Jr. Pierre's younger brother, William K., living in Wilmington with his wife and three young children, contracted typhoid fever in the summer of 1907. He literally died in Pierre's arms.

Sad family times were offset by happy ones as the clan periodically gathered for weddings: first, Irénée to Francis G.'s daughter Irene du Pont; then Lammot to Natalie Wilson; sister Louisa to Charles Copeland; Mary to William Winder Laird; Margaretta to Robert Ruliph Morgan Carpenter; and Isabella to Hugh Rodney Sharp. Pierre's relationship with his immediate family remained much as it had always been, enlarged to include the new in-laws. He retained his position as head of his father's clan, and his brothers and sisters still called him Dad and turned to him for guidance. Deeper changes would come with his mother's death in 1913 and his marriage to Cousin Alice Belin in 1915.

Even though at the start of 1911 things seemed to be going smoothly, new business challenges soon overtook Pierre. The first was the adverse outcome of the antitrust suit in May and the consequent difficulties involving the Powder Company's dissolution and reorganization. As soon as the antitrust question was settled, the problem of succession in the company's top management rose to the surface. By 1912 both Pierre and Coleman wished to step aside and give younger executives a chance. Relationships among the various branches of the du Pont family as well as those between non-du Pont members of the Executive Committee complicated the succession process. Coleman and Pierre's attempt to work out a plan to bring young men up the ladder into top management in 1914 brought on a sharp challenge from William and Alfred which culminated in a bitter fight for control of the firm. Before either the family dispute or the problems of succession could be solved, World War I brought a new challenge, that of expansion without jeopardizing financial solvency or family control.

Of all these challenges the decision of Judge Gray's court in May of 1911, which found the Powder Company in violation of the Sherman Antitrust Act and ordered it dissolved, seemed to Pierre the most ominous. The antitrust storm did not come without warning. Indeed it had been brewing since 1906, when a former Du Pont executive made a spectacular charge against the company. Consequently ever since 1906, while Pierre had been working out his methods of financial control, meeting the crisis of the panic of 1907, and solving the problems of vertical integration, the company had been fighting off the antitrust attack.

At first Pierre played only a minor role in the firm's defense. This was true even after he became acting president in 1909. The Executive Committee considered the attack to be supported by politicians who hoped to benefit by establishing reputations as trustbusters. Pierre knew little of politics. Not so Coleman, who became Delaware's Republican National Committeeman in 1908 and, once on the National Committee, assumed chairmanship of its Speakers Bureau.

Naturally the company's antitrust defense fell to Coleman. Despite Coleman's involvement in Republican politics and his excellent contacts within the administrations of Presidents Roosevelt and Taft, he had little understanding of the issues involved and his defense proved an utter failure. So out of touch with reality were Coleman and Pierre that the court's decision came as a mighty shock to both of them. This was true even though the Supreme Court had ruled against the Standard Oil Company of New Jersey and the American Tobacco Company in precedent-setting cases weeks prior to the decision of the Circuit Court for the District of Delaware in the Du Pont case. In fact Coleman refused to accept the verdict, and

Pierre was forced to take charge of the final stages of the antitrust fight.

The entire episode deeply scarred Pierre. He could not understand why people might rationally oppose the concentration of economic power in the hands of large corporations, as long as they were properly managed and charged reasonable prices. Because Pierre shared with his colleagues on the Executive Committee the view that the antitrust movement was simply a tactic by unscrupulous politicians to win votes, he was surprised when what he considered a basically conservative and responsible federal administration and court system insisted that his corporation be broken up. Pierre developed a deep mistrust of government officials—both elected and appointed. This was to hinder him later in his crucial dealings with the Wilson administration.

## The Attack

Beginning in February 1906 Robert S. Waddell, for twenty years an able and aggressive Du Pont Powder Company sales agent in Cincinnati and for a short time head of Coleman's newly centralized sales office in Wilmington but now the president of his own Buckeye Powder Company, launched a bitter attack against his former employers.[1] Waddell's charges, aired before the United States Senate Appropriations Committee, asserted that the "Du Pont Powder Trust" made "enormous profits" by virtue of its position "as an absolute and exclusive monopoly for the manufacture" of all government military powder. Further, Waddell asserted that the du Ponts "daily, continually, and openly defy and break the [antitrust and other] laws of the states and the United States." Knowing this, he asked rhetorically, "how much faith can be placed in [the du Ponts'] . . . loyalty and patriotism in time of emergency and national distress?"[2] Waddell urged that the government strike against the Du Pont monopoly in two ways: first, that it build its own plants to manufacture military powder and, second, that it bring a suit against the Powder Company under the Sherman Antitrust Act.

Waddell's attack made sensational reading and it received widespread newspaper coverage. "Nation in Grip of Powder Trust" headlined the Chicago *Tribune,* which continued in subcaptions, "Robert S. Waddell of Peoria Files Charges Against the Du Pont Company—Says Law Is Violated —United States Declared to be Mulcted of $2,520,000 a Year in Illegal Profits."[3] The attack came as no surprise to Elliott S. Rice, Du Pont's general sales agent in Chicago from 1882 through 1902, and who continued to manage Colonel Henry du Pont's extensive Chicago real estate holdings after retiring from the Powder Company. Rice had headed the Chicago agency during much of the time that Waddell was at Cincinnati, and the Chicagoan had come to hate his opposite number in Ohio. In 1902 Rice sent repeated letters to Coleman which protested Waddell's appointment as general sales agent and warned of possible trouble.

Waddell's initial broadside in early 1906 evoked in Rice a feeling of justification, and he happily clipped the story from the *Tribune* and sent it to Coleman. In the accompanying letter Rice wrote: "I haven't very much sympathy for you personally because of Waddell's present antics (for you were warned and urged to heed warnings very liberally in May, June, and July of 1902) yet in the face of these warnings you placed this miserable, sneaking Waddell in a position to gather together just the information that he is attempting to use against the house of Du Pont. . . ." Rice, however, maintained that he did not feel "at all vindicative [*sic*]" and offered his help in what he foresaw as a long fight ahead. The *Tribune*, he reminded Coleman, "is a conservative carefully-censored and responsible Chicago Daily. If the pettifogging R. S. Waddell has found it possible to reach the columns of such a paper we may expect 'red fire' and 'circus lemonade' in less particular publications."[4]

Coleman was absent from Wilmington on a short vacation when Rice's letter arrived, so Pierre answered it. The treasurer seemed more amused than alarmed by the whole affair. "I suppose," he wrote, "Waddell goes on the principal that all is fair in war, but I believe that he has overreached himself in this attempt to injure us and on that account I think that his article will miss fire."[5]

But Waddell's bombshell was not a dud, for it coincided with the widespread protest in America against the concentration of economic power in the hands of large corporations—a reaction which Moxham had predicted at the time of the big company's organization. Exposés of wrongdoing by leading businessmen were the order of the day. Indeed, in February 1906, almost simultaneously with Waddell's attack, William Randolph Hearst's *Cosmopolitan* magazine started a sensational series of nine articles by David Graham Phillips under the general title of "The Treason of the Senate." Phillips argued that the United States Senate was a rich man's club that daily sold out the rights of the common people to the trusts. Let there be no misunderstanding, wrote Phillips, "a man cannot serve two masters. The senators are not elected by the people; they are elected by the interests."[6]

For Waddell, therefore, Colonel Henry A. du Pont's campaign for and election to the United States Senate in 1906 provided an opportunity. "The Du Pont Company is going to send Col. du Pont to the Senate as a result of my disclosures in order that their interests will be protected," Waddell charged in the Peoria *Herald Transcript* of May 24, 1906. The Peoria newspaper headlined the story "Waddell Would Unseat Du Pont. Promises to Cause Indictment of Trust Magnate. Has Facts in Hand. If Du Pont Is Made Senator of Delaware, Violation of Anti-trust Laws Will Be Presented to Jury."[7] Waddell deliberately portrayed the colonel as the Du Pont Company's head.

Waddell's threats did not prove idle. During his long association with the du Ponts, he had accumulated a large file of letters, price agreements, and other documents that gave detailed information about the Gunpowder Trade Association's efforts to control prices and restrict competition. He could, through these documents, specifically link the three cousins to the association. In mid-July 1906 Waddell went to the attorney general's office in Washington and presented what amounted to a ready-made case against the Powder Company. The evidence seemed so strong that Attorney General William H. Moody, who had been in the center of President Roosevelt's antitrust prosecutions and who had personally argued the government's case against Swift and the other meatpackers before the Supreme Court, sent Special Agent Victor H. Roadstrum to Peoria for a detailed examination of Waddell's data.[8]

The du Ponts had no direct knowledge of the attorney general's decision until weeks afterward, but continued rumors caused the Powder Company's Executive Committee on August 7, 1906, to direct the Development Department to "investigate to the best of its ability the present situation at Washington."[9] The management of this inquiry fell to the director of the Development Department, then William B. Dwinnell, who asked influential Washington friends to contact appropriate officials in the Departments of Justice and Commerce and Labor. A letter sent on August 30, 1906, from Colonel E. J. Dimmick of Army Ordnance brought Dwinnell's first positive information. In response to Dwinnell's appeal, Dimmick had called on his friend Assistant Attorney General Charles H. Robb and learned that Special Agent Roadstrum of the Justice Department had been sent to Peoria to begin an official investigation of Waddell's charges. Colonel Dimmick reported that the assistant attorney general advised the Du Pont executives to ask that the Department of Justice make a formal and "searching inquiry" into the Powder Company affairs. Should such a request be made, Dimmick wrote, Robb would give it his personal attention and if the investigation showed that the Powder Company had "not violated the law he [would] . . . be only too glad to make a report that will be pleasing to the owners."[10]

Upon receipt of Dimmick's letter, Dwinnell optimistically informed the Executive Committee that although an investigation has been started " . . . the serious features . . . have in this [case] been emasculated. . . ."[11] On November 4, the Executive Committee held a lengthy conference with their New York attorneys who had been their constant advisers during the formation of the Powder Company, the senior partners of Townsend, Avery and Button. All present agreed that the company should cooperate with the government and make freely available any documents the attorney general's office wanted.[12] This was not the same as requesting an investigation, or as giving the attorney general's men unlimited access to all company files, but the Executive Committee had supreme confidence that their action would more than satisfy the government.

The plain fact was that neither Pierre nor Coleman, and indeed no one in Wilmington, took the inquiry seriously. On January ?, 1907, Pierre wrote William du Pont that "the government investigation seems to be dragging along slowly and judging from the reports of our friend, R. S. Waddell, there will be many terrible things to divulge when the time comes." Pierre concluded that "we are reserving our ammunition and have little doubt that most of the 'errors' can be routed with ease."[13]

The slow pace of the government's probe, however, indicated thoroughness rather than lack of determination. And much to the three cousins' surprise the Department of Justice on July 31, 1907, brought formal suit against the Powder Company, its officers, and the other firms which had comprised the Gunpowder Trade Association, charging violation of the Sherman Antitrust Act.[14] Newspapers across the country gave the government's action top billing. Headlined the San Francisco *Examiner:* "U.S. SUES POWDER TRUST,—SENATOR ITS CHIEF." The paper repeated as fact Waddell's assertion that Senator Henry du Pont, who was assumed to have ended his relations with the trust when he entered the Senate was now shown to be "the real power in the Trust." Similar headlines appeared in such widespread papers as the Detroit *Free Press,* the Wilmington, North Carolina, *Star,* and the Topeka *Daily Capital.*[15]

From the date of the government's suit the muckraking press, especially Hearst's papers, began an attack against the Powder Company and the two members of the du Pont family who were most prominent in politics— Republican Senator Henry A. du Pont and the senator's chief organizer and backer, T. Coleman du Pont. Pierre, who held no public office and whose activities inside the Powder Company had received little public attention, escaped the brunt of this notoriety. But the publicity damaged Coleman's position as a Republican leader. On September 25, 1908, Hearst's Los Angeles *Herald* announced under the banner "Traitor resigns," that "T. C. du Pont, the unsavory Powder King . . . [was] no longer Chairman of the Committee on Speakers of the Republican National Committee." The *Herald* gave itself much of the credit for "this victory for decency." In the same article, the *Herald* referred to the Du Pont Company as a "traitor Trust" and asserted that it "sold the Government bad powder."[16]

Despite the suit and the unfavorable press, both Coleman and Pierre remained optimistic that they would win, almost up to the date of the adverse court decree in July of 1911. In a confidential letter to Henry Belin on August 2, 1907, Coleman stressed the difficulty of separating the Powder Company into its original components. "I do not think you can unscramble an egg," he expressed it.[17] Most of Pierre's correspondence radiated confidence. In a letter to Coleman in September of 1910 Pierre took a cynical attitude toward the prosecution. It would be useless, he asserted, to appeal directly to either President Taft or former President Roosevelt for "it would be bad politics to admit that anyone accused was in reality innocent. It is much easier to assume all corporations guilty until through the courts they may prove themselves innocent. By the time this is accomplished," he felt, "the argument will have served its end politically." Thus Pierre felt "rather confident that we will come out alright" in the courts.[18] Even on March 25, 1911, immediately after the Supreme Court had ordered the dissolution of the Standard Oil Company, Pierre wrote to William that although "the decision in the Standard Oil case has not altogether cleared the air," the situation in respect to our suit "seems materially brighter. It is quite conceivable that . . . we shall receive a favorable decision."[19]

Both Pierre and Coleman had sound reasons for their optimism. They saw that Waddell's charges fell into two categories: first, that Du Pont enjoyed an unfair monopoly of the military business and, second, that the Powder Company had used the ruthless competitive tactics which had characterized the days of the Gunpowder Trade Association. Pierre and Coleman had unwavering confidence that once the case moved from the newspapers to the courts they could prove that their Powder Company bore little resemblance to the E. I. du Pont de Nemours & Co. of Eugene du Pont's day. Ingrained in Pierre's mind were the debates among the various Executive Committee members during the last six months of 1903 when the big company was being shaped. Pierre, it will be recalled, supported Moxham and the legal adviser, James Townsend, in the struggle to bring all Du Pont holdings into a single legal and administrative structure that would abandon the competitive tactics of the Gunpowder Trade Association. The treasurer could not believe that minor exceptions allowed at the insistence of Hamilton Barksdale and J. Amory Haskell were significant. Pierre was certain that the Powder Company had been transformed from an association created for the purpose of restricting entry and fixing prices into a centrally managed corporation that competed on the basis of economic efficiency.

Coleman du Pont's political activities also seemed an advantage. Coleman stood high with the professional politicians of the ruling Republican party. He was a liberal contributor to the party war chests. And as Delaware's representative on the Republican National Committee (beginning in 1909 and remaining until 1930), he came into frequent and friendly contact with powerful administration officials and members of Congress. By 1910 his close friends in the Senate included men of diverse political beliefs such as Wisconsin's conservative John Spooner and Idaho's progressive William Borah. The Republican high command might appease public pressure by removing Coleman from the political scene—as had happened in 1908 when they had forced his resignation as chairman of the Republican National

Committee's Speakers Committee—but the Wilmington powder maker had every right to think that key party officials would listen to and respect his opinion. In fact, almost to the day of the final court decree Coleman felt that he could solve the company's troubles by direct appeals to highly placed officials.

Without doubt both Pierre and Coleman and their able legal advisers correctly assessed the issues which formed the basis of the attack against them. James Scarlet, special assistant to the attorney general of the United States, confirmed the cousins' views of the government's case when he introduced Robert S. Waddell as a witness for the prosecution on October 21, 1908. "This witness is called," Scarlet asserted, "to show the history of . . . [the Du Pont] combination from the time of his [Waddell's] association with it, from 1882 to 1902, and its various forms; the overt acts committed in pursuance of it; the methods pursued, from time to time in monopolizing trade in interstate commerce. . . ." After Waddell had testified as to his part in Du Pont's illegal operations, Scarlet promised "evidence showing the existence of the conspiracy at the time of the filing of the bill [1907], and that the present form of combination of corporations is merely a device for the continuance of the conspiracy and for the purpose of evading the Federal Anti-Trust laws."[20]

Because Pierre, Coleman, and their close associates considered the onslaught against the Powder Company politically motivated, it is not surprising that they gave the outgoing, politically minded Coleman the major role in directing the counterattack. Coleman remained in the forefront even after 1908 when, because of illness and other interests, he turned over most of the presidential duties in the company to Pierre. Had Coleman's efforts met with success, the whole antitrust episode might have been but a footnote in Pierre's life. But Coleman's efforts failed, and in the end it was Pierre who guided the company through the final phases of court action, dissolution, and reorganization. Pierre's approach contrasted sharply with Coleman's, but everything Pierre did was shaped or influenced in some way by the campaign waged by his elder cousin.

### Coleman Leads the Defense—The Government Market

The nature of Waddell's attack gave Coleman a dual problem. Simultaneously he had to oversee the Powder Company's legal defense against the antitrust suit and he had to fight an attempt to deprive his firm of its total government sales. Du Pont's government business consisted largely of smokeless powder sales either to the navy for use in large guns or to the army for cannons and small arms. Even though the company sold explosives for use in the construction of the Panama Canal, these sales were relatively small and transitory. Panama sales, moreover, did not involve smokeless powder nor did Du Pont have a monopoly there, so, although the company's enemies tried to cut off all its government business, they concentrated their fire upon the military sales.

In absolute terms, both the investment in smokeless powder manufacturing facilities and the total amount sold to the government were substantial. J. Amory Haskell, testifying before a subcommittee of the House Appropriations Committee in January 1907, estimated that Du Pont capital absorbed in smokeless powder plants amounted to between $4.8 million and $7.5 million, depending upon the method of valuation used, and that sales to the armed forces were as much as $3.0 million a year.[21] Haskell further admitted that such sales were profitable; and that on a pound of powder in 1906 his company received 69¢ from the government and had expenses of 47¢, leaving a gross profit of 22¢ to go toward return on the investment. At this rate Du Pont's profit on their invested capital ran considerably above the minimum 15% that Pierre considered necessary in order to justify a capital outlay.[22] The smokeless powder sales did not bulk large when compared to the company's total business. In 1906, for example, sales of smokeless powder amounted to $3.0 million, slightly more than 10% of gross Powder Company sales of $29.0 million.[23] This business, however, in 1905 and 1906 produced nearly 20% of the company's total profits. The army and navy were clearly most important customers.

Waddell viewed Du Pont's government business as the most vulnerable part of the Powder Company's operations. His main aim was not so much to hurt the company financially as to dramatize Du Pont's monopoly position. Waddell hoped that Congress would prohibit the army and navy from making purchases from the Powder Company and that by so doing the "National Legislature would come out directly against the Powder Trust." Congressional pressure, Waddell felt, would substantially benefit the government in its antitrust suit. Therefore, from the very first, most of Waddell's public assaults concentrated on the government rather than the private portion of Du Pont business. The Justice Department seemed slow to grasp the effectiveness of this strategy, but by 1908 the prosecution joined Waddell in a concentrated barrage on the army and navy business.

Waddell's tactics were exceedingly effective. In May 1906 he retained Frank S. Monnett, who had prosecuted suits under Ohio law against Standard Oil and who was prominent in the National Antitrust League, to represent him. Monnett's first act was to file pleas with the War and Navy Departments charging that they "had been made partners [with the du Ponts] in a plan to practice extortion upon the government."[24] The Navy Department, it was claimed, commissioned two officers to develop a superior type of smokeless powder. The Peoria powder maker said that the officers patented the resulting discoveries and then sold them to the Du Pont Company. "The government pays . . . 70 cents a pound for . . .

smokeless, which cannot be purchased elsewhere on account of protecting patents."[25] The powder, however, Waddell contended, was worth only 35 cents per pound.

The next step in Waddell's campaign was to link Du Pont's monopoly of government business to its preponderance in the commercial sphere. Thus, he argued that profits from military sales enabled the Powder Company to "meet practically all the fixed charges" upon its plants and thereby permitted it "to sell common powder at an actual loss for the purpose of destroying . . . competitors."[26] Coupled with this was the charge that Du Pont had drastically reduced black powder prices in Waddell's own area of Illinois, Indiana, and Ohio and was selling below production costs.[27] Finally, Waddell introduced the European Agreement of 1897 into the argument.

Coleman du Pont, acting on the advice of several of his Washington friends and with Pierre's full concurrence, decided not to respond directly to Waddell's attacks. Public denials or pressure tactics designed to influence congressmen, Colemen agreed, would only give Waddell's charges more publicity. Besides, the Powder Company's president planned to rely on the friendship of key senators and representatives to protect the company's interests in Congress. He was sure the military officials would support the company. Coleman thoroughly acquiesced with Arthur Moxham, who wrote that "anything done by Monnett [Waddell's lawyer] . . . must take the nature of an application to the War and Navy Departments," where it will meet with men "who know the truth of the situation so thoroughly that it cannot hurt us." And Moxham concluded almost maliciously that the War and Navy Departments "cannot condemn us without also condemning themselves, and if the case is pushed it seems to me to open up the best possible opportunity for us to have the real truth . . . ventilated in the most favorable way to our side of the case."[28]

There was no question but that the military officials looked with favor upon the Du Pont Company. Of course they did not oppose expansion of government production facilities; in fact, the Navy Department had long fostered the development of a government smokeless powder works at Indian Head, Maryland. By 1907 this facility manufactured nearly one-third of the navy's requirements; but Indian Head's main purpose was to serve as a yardstick against which to measure desired quality and prices. Congressmen who passed appropriations for Indian Head did so with the clear understanding, backed by the views of the Chief of Army Ordnance Brigadier General William Crozier and the Chief of the Navy's Bureau of Ordnance Rear Admiral Newton E. Mason, that private smokeless powder facilities were necessary to provide a reserve in case of national emergency.[29]

But Coleman, Pierre, and Arthur Moxham badly misjudged Waddell's strategy. The Peoria powder maker had no intention of bringing the War and Navy Department officials to his support; the sole purpose of his pleas to them was to force a thorough congressional investigation of his charges. In this he was successful.

Starting in 1907 Waddell put into the hands of every senator and representative data which he claimed gave the facts about Du Pont's monopolistic agreements and gouging prices on government powder. He seized on the company's policy of silence, intimating that the du Ponts did not answer because they dared not. Although Congress continued to vote appropriations to purchase Du Pont powder in 1907 and in 1908, opposition grew.

By January 1909 Waddell's assault reached its peak, and he had convinced the Justice Department that it should extend its campaign against the Powder Company from the courts to the Congress. Just as Congress was considering the Naval Appropriations Bill with its provision for the purchase of powder, Waddell pulled from his file a copy of the 1897 European Agreement and gave it to Attorney General Bonaparte, who laid it before Theodore Roosevelt. The president considered sending the agreement to Congress, together with a special message proposing legislation to curb the Powder Company. Although the president dropped that idea, the attorney general called a news conference, where he made the full text of the European Agreement public with the statement that he believed the document still to be in full force. Within the Justice Department itself, there was talk of bringing criminal proceedings against the du Ponts.[30]

Almost simultaneously, the Powder Company came under attack in the House of Representatives. The House added three amendments to the Naval Appropriations Bill. These provided "that no part of this appropriation shall be paid to any trust or combination in restraint of trade nor to any corporation having a monopoly of the manufacture and supply of gunpowder in the United States, except in the event of an emergency." The second amendment added $250,000 to the budget "for the maintenance and enlargement of the [government] powder factory." And the final amendment specified that "no part of this appropriation shall be expended for powder other than small arms powder, at a price in excess of sixty-four cents a pound."[31] The effect of the three amendments would have been to make illegal any purchase of naval powder from the Du Pont companies and to reduce the price which the government could pay for powder from 1¢ to 5¢ per pound even if a way could be found to circumvent the prohibition against buying Du Pont powder. The increase in the size of the government powder-making capacity would still have left over 50% of the powder to be purchased from private sources. Since only Du Pont had the facilities to produce smokeless powder, just where the government would obtain this powder was not made clear.

Coleman had been confined to his house by his doctors at the time of the attorney general's announcement and the House of Representatives' unfavorable action, but he lost no time in launching a counterattack. He now recognized that the policy of silence had been a mistake. He moved to establish a Washington lobby consisting of Colonel Buckner, the head of the Powder Company's Military Sales Office, Brainard Avery from the law firm of Townsend, Avery and Button, and former Senator Spooner of Wisconsin, who had resigned his seat in mid-1907 to start practice as a Washington lawyer. Furthermore, Coleman aided his men with letters of introduction to key politicians such as Idaho's Senator William E. Borah.[32] Coleman also made lists of all members of Congress who might favor the Powder Company's case.[33] His efforts were too late to prevent the Senate's approval of the House amendment to the Naval Appropriations Bill of 1909.[34] But Coleman's political knowledge and friendships soon began to tell.

The Powder Company's lobby reached the chairmen of the House committees which were considering the Military Fortifications Bill (army) and the Sundry Civil Appropriations Bill (which included money for the powder to be used in the construction of the Panama Canal). The efforts of the House committee chairmen caused their respective committees to report bills that contained no restrictions upon the purchase of powder from any domestic manufacturer and set no price limitations. Subsequently both branches of Congress passed the bills as they emerged from the committees in the lower house. In a tone of relief, Brainard Avery wrote Coleman, "Had the attack succeeded in the House, we would have had considerable trouble in the Senate. . . ."[35]

Avery also worked quietly and effectively to block any chance of criminal prosecutions. The Justice Department felt that it could successfully bring such action, and both Avery and Coleman feared that "the expiring Administration would endeavor to obtain public approval by the institution of criminal proceedings."[36] To thwart this, Avery worked through Frank Hitchcock, Taft's campaign manager and a close friend of Coleman du Pont. "We used the argument, and with effect," Avery wrote Coleman, "that action on the criminal side, pending the event of the civil suit, should not be taken by the Roosevelt Administration and left to the Taft Administration to be disposed of."[37] Fortunately for the Du Pont Company, Roosevelt did not want to do anything that would hamper the actions of his successor.

Having blunted Waddell's attack, Coleman moved to make certain that in the congressional sessions of 1910 and thereafter the Powder Company's interests would be protected. Thus, Coleman maintained a small permanent lobby in Washington headed by Colonel Buckner. The former army officer was especially effective because of his contacts with key ordnance personnel, and his efforts paid big dividends.

The Congress passed the 1910 appropriations bills without attaching any of the anti-Du Pont amendments of the previous year. "I feel," Buckner wrote to the Executive Committee of the Powder Company in March 1911, "that our work completely reversed the sentiment that had been created in Congress against the Company and changed it from a spirit of malevolence to one of friendship."[38] Certainly if one could measure success in terms of retaining government orders for smokeless powder, Coleman and Buckner had indeed won a major victory.

### Coleman Leads the Defense—The Antitrust Case

The fight to protect the Powder Company's government business was only one aspect of the larger struggle against Waddell's anti-Du Pont crusade. The main battle, of course, centered upon preventing the Justice Department from dissolving the Powder Company. Both Coleman and Pierre insisted that their firm bore little resemblance to the company of Eugene du Pont's day, and in large measure this was true. Yet the old business practices that Moxham, Townsend, and Pierre had fought to end at the time of the formation of the big company had not been totally eliminated, and as Powder Company executives looked about them in 1906, they saw almost everywhere embarrassing vestigial remains. Thus, the first act in Coleman's counter antitrust strategy was to remove root and branch all remnants of unfair competitive practices and agreements in restraint of trade. Concurrently he launched an intensified drive to complete the merging of all properties and interests under the single roof of the Powder Company so as to verify further the argument that the du Ponts were operating one large corporation, not an association of separate firms. Connected with this step was the issuing of the 4½% bonds to complete final exchange of securities of the subsidiary companies for those of the Powder Company. The Powder Company's moves in 1906 to wind up the existing nonoperating subsidiaries provide an indication of the wisdom of the original arguments of Pierre and Moxham, and testimony as to how far these views had won out. By the same token, that action still had to be taken suggests the company's vulnerability to prosecution.

Despite a clear declaration by the Executive Committee on November 29, 1905, prior to Waddell's antitrust attack, which repeated the policy first enunciated by Moxham in 1903, "to the effect that anything in the nature of subterfuge or trade deceit would be done away with," tricky practices had not entirely ceased.[39] The Powder Company's relationship with Elmer Brode's Enterprise High Explosives Company was a case in point. It will be recalled that Brode had sold his firm to Eastern Dynamite in 1897 on the condition that he "would preserve the secrecy of ownership" and represent his Enterprise Explosives as an independent firm.[40] Largely through

J. A. Haskell's influence this arrangement continued even after the big company's formation.

In April 1906 Pierre's new accounting procedures brought the continuing deceit at Enterprise to his attention. In accord with new directives, Alexis du Pont, the assistant treasurer, asked Brode to deposit all his collections to the credit of the Powder Company and to make clear that he was a Du Pont subsidiary. Brode argued that since he had been forced to "continually act the lie, if now the truth be admitted," his reputation would suffer and he claimed his company would lose business. Irénée du Pont reported the problem to the Executive Committee. He sympathized with Brode's plight, but he felt that Brode should be told to "visit those whom he has been systematically deceiving" and tell them that his company now was controlled by Du Pont "and that he does not wish to secure their patronage by deception but can assure them that they will receive at least equally good treatment from the new owners." Irénée felt by being vague about the actual date of transfer, Brode could "escape from . . . [his] embarrassing position with a reasonable amount of grace and presumably will lose only such of his customers as are cranks."[41] On April 26, 1906, the Executive Committee, mindful that business tactics similar to Brode's had caused much of the criticism leveled against Standard Oil, voted to reaffirm their three-year-old ban against subterfuge and trade deceit; the committee formally approved Irénée's plan to make it clear that Enterprise had been purchased by Du Pont.[42]

The Powder Company's relationship with the King Powder Company posed a much more serious problem. In 1901, Gershon M. Peters, president of King Powder, which was hard pressed in the competitive wars, negotiated a 25-year contract to sell almost his firm's entire output to the E. I. du Pont de Nemours & Company and Laflin & Rand. The two then organized the King Mercantile Company, to which they gave the sole function of marketing the powder received from the King Powder Company. Despite the arguments in 1904, the Executive Committee failed to abrogate this arrangement after the organization of the big company.[43]

Nor did it take any action even after Robert S. Waddell wrote Virginia's Senator John W. Daniel a letter that accused the allegedly "independent" King Powder Company of being part of the Powder Trust and conspiring with the du Ponts to defraud the government. The senator promptly read Waddell's letter on the floor of Congress. Gershon Peters reponded by writing a frantic letter to Senator Daniel asserting that Waddell's charges were "a malicious falsehood" and arguing that "the King Powder Company [did] not belong, and never [had] . . . belonged to a 'Powder Trust.' " Furthermore, Peters concluded, he did "not believe that there is such a thing in existence as a 'powder trust,' " and he asked the senator to give "these corrections the same publicity that he had given to Mr. Waddell's statements."[44] Concurrently Peters wrote Coleman a letter enclosing a copy of his correspondence with Senator Daniel bemoaning the fact that "your company and ours have been put in a very false light."[45]

Coleman's initial reply to Peters indicated that the matter did not trouble him. "I am sincerely glad you wrote [to Senator Daniel]," the president of the Du Pont Company told Peters. "I agree with you fully that there is no such thing as the Powder Trust. In the old days there was an Association, but that is a thing of the past."[46] But Coleman's optimism faded after a consultation with his lawyers, who now insisted that the contract with King should be terminated. The Powder Company had two alternatives: it could purchase King Powder outright or it could break the contract. Peters again rejected any idea of purchase; and now demanded $150,000 damages, which was finally compromised to $100,000. Pierre paid the amount in October 1906, thus separating the two firms but, unfortunately for the du Ponts, the circumstances made it clear that the action resulted from Waddell's attack.[47] The King Powder Company contract became an important link in the chain of evidence the Department of Justice was forging to prove that the Du Pont Company had changed only its legal framework, not its business methods.

The European Agreement was even more damning. Waddell had a copy of this and used it with devastating effectiveness, as has already been evidenced in the attack on the du Ponts' military business. Here again the Powder Company made no effort to cancel the agreement until after the antitrust attack had started. Only then did the lawyers advise the Executive Committee that the agreement was illegal. Then, as has been pointed out, Pierre and Moxham cabled to Coleman, who was in Britain trying to culminate his imperial schemes. It was this cable that brought the end of the old type of agreement and led to the substitution of a patent agreement for one allocating marketing territories. The European Agreement, like the King Powder contract, became a vital part of the government's case.

Waddell's initial attack speeded the final reshaping of the company's legal structure. By early summer, even before Waddell had taken his case to the attorney general, Pierre and Moxham had completed the refinancing necessary to assure the final dissolution of those companies that had joined the Powder Company but still remained separate legal entities. James Townsend, working with Pierre, was able by January 1, 1907, to eliminate the California Powder Works, Vigorite, and Judson companies. Legal difficulties, however, prevented the final dissolution of the three holding companies used in earlier purchases—Delaware Securities, Delaware Investment, and California Investment.[48] Similar legal problems delayed action on the ending of the Hazard Powder Company and Eastern Dynamite;[49] while at Laflin & Rand the failure of holders of a small block of stock to make the final exchange forced a continuation of that company. Furthermore, it remained necessary to retain E. I. du Pont de Nemours & Co. of Pennsylvania, and International Smokeless. As Pierre testified, Pennsylvania law forbade a corporation chartered in another state to hold property in the Commonwealth, thus forcing the Powder Company to retain a subsidiary in that state.[50] At International Smokeless, which was held by the Powder Company through the Du Pont International Company, minority stockholder demands had prevented its merging into the Powder Company at the time the du Ponts acquired control. Since then the precarious position of the government business, which represented almost International's entire market, made impossible any amalgamation of International with the Powder Company on terms acceptable both to the minority stockholders and Du Pont.[51]

Although Coleman warmly endorsed the various attempts to put his company right with the law, he continued to believe that his standing in the Republican party would enable him to reach an accommodation with influential Washington leaders. When the Justice Department started its investigation in the fall of 1906, Coleman acted to cooperate with Assistant Attorney General Milton Dwight Purdy, who was in charge of the case. Coleman thought that Purdy, after analyzing information made available to the Justice Department by the Powder Company's lawyers, would quash the investigation. When this did not happen and the government announced on July 31, 1907, that it had formally begun antitrust proceedings, Coleman remained undaunted. He blamed Justice Department underlings for the decision and he felt that appeal to the attorney general or to the president would stop the suit. Coleman's friend in San Francisco, Captain John Bermingham, agreed. He wrote, on August 3, 1907, that some Powder Company stockholders have "questioned me about . . . the probable outcome of the case. . . . I tell them that you proceeded in consolidating the various Co.'s under advice or as good counsel as was procurable [and] that [you had] personally explained all your company's transactions to President Roosevelt. . . ." Bermingham blamed most of the sensational press dispatches on Waddell. "Will we have to 'Kow Tow' to Waddell? Guess not," he concluded.[52]

The government's suit encompassed not only the Du Pont Powder Company but all firms which had made up the Gunpowder Trade Association including those that had been merged into the big company and those such as Olin's Equitable Powder Manufacturing Company that had not. In addition the government action included Eastern Dynamite, Delaware Securities, Delaware Investment, and California Investment companies. In all, a grand total of twenty-eight corporate entities were defendants, together with seventeen individuals among which were the three cousins, Senator Henry A. du Pont, Irénée du Pont, Arthur Moxham, Hamilton Barksdale, Edmund Buckner, and Frank Connable.[53]

Coleman's strategy in 1907 was double edged. The first thrust was to defend his company in the courts. Then, if that should fail, Coleman was prepared to use his political influence to reach a compromise with officials of the Republican administration. Both Coleman and Pierre had strong faith in the courts. They took a cynical attitude toward Roosevelt's trust busting, a policy they felt he adopted largely to gain votes. The two cousins followed closely the government antitrust suits against Standard Oil and American Tobacco. They felt that the Supreme Court would vindicate the two corporations before the culmination of the Du Pont trial, thus stopping further action against the Powder Company. Coleman retained Townsend, Avery and Button to represent his company in the United States Circuit Court for the District of Delaware and he urged the other defendants to form a united front with Du Pont. Pierre, writing to Charles A. Belin in October of 1907, summarized his feelings as follows: "the country seems trust mad at present, though I believe most people base their faith on the future in the conservatism of our judges. Of course, the failure on their part might quickly result in a condition of affairs which should make the most insistent 'trust breakers' more than glad to reverse their policy."[54]

But even if the conservatism of the courts should fail, Coleman thought his second line of defense impregnable. Because Coleman was certain that the Republicans lacked sincerity about the antitrust cause, he felt he could work out a deal with the prosecution that would make it appear that the Justice Department had won a victory and would still leave the big company intact. The bone that he was prepared to throw to the government was for the Powder Company to declare a dividend of the stock of the Du Pont International Company. If this were done, Coleman explained to his Wilmington lawyer William Hilles, "the Big Co. would not own a single share of the Du Pont International."[55] But there would be no real change, since the Du Pont Company Executive Committee, through their direct ownership of International Smokeless stock, would still be able to set that firm's policies and receive the company's profits.

Coleman recognized that a "compromise" of the kind he had in mind might not be appropriate or possible immediately prior to the presidential election of 1908; consequently, he planned to wait until after a new president took office before trying to come to terms with the Justice Department. Even before the election, however, things appeared to brighten at the Justice Department as hostile Assistant Attorney General Purdy resigned to accept a judgeship in Minnesota.[56] But to Coleman, all depended on the election. Taft's nomination seemed to provide a sound opportunity to ensure that the Powder Company would be heard at the right time by the proper people, for Coleman's good friend and colleague Frank Hitchcock, the chairman of the Republican National Committee, assumed the management of the presidential national campaign. Taft's victory and Hitchcock's subsequent appointment to the postmaster generalship gave Coleman what he thought was an effective access to the new administration's inner circle.

By early 1910 the government's suit had sputtered on for more than two and a half years. In September of 1908, testimony had begun before Judge George Gray. Coleman, partly because of illness, but also possibly because he felt it unimportant, did not testify. Instead Pierre, aided by Alfred and a host of other company officials, served as the chief defense witness. Pierre emphasized in his prepared testimony of October 1909 the essential discontinuity between the old Gunpowder Trade Association and the new Powder Company.

By January of 1910, however, no decision was yet in sight; nor had the Supreme Court ruled on the Standard Oil and American Tobacco cases. With Purdy's departure, the Justice Department shifted the main burden of the prosecution to a Cincinnati Republican and former Ohio attorney general, Wade H. Ellis, who in 1908 had become assistant attorney general of the United States. His associate on the case was James Scarlet, a Pennsylvania lawyer and Roosevelt Republican who had become a special assistant to Attorney General George Wickersham.[57] As indicated earlier Scarlet was aided by Roadstrum, a special agent of the Justice Department, J. Harwood Graves, a special assistant to the attorney general, and John P. Nields, the United States district attorney for the District of Delaware.

Coleman soon became tired of waiting for a judicial solution and he decided to attempt to use his political influence to settle the case. He carried out most of the negotiations personally, bypassing Townsend, Avery and Button, the lawyers who had the main burden of defending the Powder Company. Aiding Coleman in his mission was William S. Hilles, who had also been retained to aid the New York lawyers. Coleman relied upon Postmaster General Frank Hitchcock to gain intelligence about attitudes and strategies within the Justice Department. This proved to be an error for, although friendly to the du Ponts, Hitchcock had little real influence with either Attorney General Wickersham or his subordinates.

Despite Hitchcock's assurance that the Justice Department's Wade Ellis would react sympathetically to Coleman's proposal to terminate the suit by having the Powder Company dissolve Delaware Securities, Delaware Investment, California Investment, Eastern Dynamite, and Hazard (these concessions were of no consequence, since the firms in question had long been in the process of dissolution) and declare a dividend of the stock of Du Pont International, nothing happened.[58] In fact, it soon became clear that Ellis opposed Coleman's suggestion for ending the suit.[59]

Even though Coleman made other attempts to stop the government's prosecution, the suit dragged on until June 21, 1911, when Judges George Gray, Joseph Buffington, and William M. Lanning of the United States Circuit Court for the District of Delaware found that Pierre, Coleman, and

Alfred du Pont, and the Powder Company (together with Irénée du Pont, Hamilton Barksdale, Edmund Buckner, Frank Connable, and others) had violated and were still violating the Sherman Antitrust Act. Essentially, the court accepted without reservation the government's argument that prior to 1904 the Du Pont interest had formed and maintained an illegal association to dominate trade in explosives, fix prices, and "regulate same not according to any law of supply and demand, but according to the will of the parties to said contract." The court ruled that Coleman, Pierre, and Alfred had "utilized" the combination until June 1904 in "suppressing competition and thereby building a monopoly." In other words the use of the combination in restraint of trade which violated Section I of the Sherman Act led directly to monopoly in violation of Section II. "The proofs satisfy us," the court added, "that the present form of combination is no less obnoxious to the law than was the combination under the trade association agreement, which was dissolved on June 30, 1904."[60] The judges' opinion took great pains to emphasize that although the defendants, by creating the Powder Company and dissolving the Gunpowder Trade Association, had changed the outward form of their business, they still continued to restrain trade and to monopolize in defiance of the law.

The judges based their opinion upon the Supreme Court's decision on the Standard Oil and American Tobacco cases, both of which had been decided in May 1911. In neither of the previous cases did the Supreme Court attempt to work out an actual scheme for dissolution. In both instances the Supreme Court left that task to the lower courts. The High Court allowed eight months for American Tobacco to be split into new competitive firms. The dissolution of Standard Oil was to be accomplished in six months. Obviously neither company was close to working out an acceptable dissolution plan at the time of the Du Pont decision.[61]

In the Du Pont case the court issued an interlocutory decree. The court recognized that "the dissolution of more than sixty corporations since the advent of the new management in 1902 and the consequent impossibility of restoring original conditions in the explosives trade" narrowed any final decree. This, however, said the court, "should not make the decree any the less effective." The court asked that there should be "recreated out of the elements now composing said combination [the big company] a new condition which shall be honestly in harmony with and not repugnant to the law." The court demanded that at the very least there be real and effective competition in explosives.[62]

The court asked the Powder Company to return before it in October with an outline of a plan that would help the court to draw a final decree.[63] If the du Ponts did not like the decision, which they most avowedly did not, they had two choices. They could ask for a rehearing before the courts; or they could appeal to the Supreme Court. The latter could be done only after the circuit court had issued a final decree.[64]

The court dismissed the charges against Senator Henry A. du Pont, and this was about the only good news. Colonel Henry's lawyer, David Marvel of Wilmington, argued that the senator had terminated his relationship with the management of the Powder Company in 1902 and that since then he had no interest in it "except . . . [as] a stockholder, but not a large one."[65] Marvel maintained that his client had no voice in running the Powder Company. Although the Justice Department refused to dismiss the action against Colonel Henry, the court accepted Marvel's argument.[66] The removal of Senator Henry from the antitrust litigation did relieve Coleman, Pierre, and the others, since it took much of the sting out of charges by Waddell and the more sensational press that the colonel was the Powder Company's real head and that he had used his senatorial position to benefit his holdings.

On the whole, however, Coleman's reaction to the court's decision was one of "great surprise," disbelief and anger.[67] "We are not a monopoly, cannot be a monopoly and are not in restraint of trade, nor can we be," he wrote Pierre.[68] If this were true, it logically followed that the lawyers had mishandled the case. To Moxham, Coleman wrote: "I am very much displeased at the showing made by our lawyers and don't think anything they said in the evidence or otherwise was taken in by the court. In fact, I feel sure that the true position of our company is even now not known to the court."[69] Coleman's anger at the lawyers increased when he thought of their bill. By October of 1907 the Powder Company had appropriated in excess of $200,000 for the litigation and was planning to spend an additional $100,000.[70] In December of 1907, the company agreed to pay Townsend, Avery and Button a maximum of $7,500 per month for their services, and this proved to be only a start, for costs soon exceeded $100,000 annually.[71] Coleman had always thought the legal fees to be high. Now that the lawyers had lost, he was furious: "We have already had three meetings of the attorneys [to find a solution to the court's decree] taking up a great deal of time and [they] have each I suppose made the usual unreasonable charge with the net result of no suggestion."[72]

Hatred and anger so obsessed Coleman that he began to lose touch with reality. On October 5, 1911, in a memorandum made for his own file entitled "The Powder Case Briefly Stated," Coleman summarized: "In 1905 or 6, an employee, R. S. Waddell, who had left the Powder Company after purloining certain old papers for blackmailing purposes [Coleman and Pierre felt that Waddell wanted Du Pont to buy his Peoria mill at a high price] and when unable to collect blackmail [he] went to the government with a lot of purloined records and a long story well put together (for the man had great ability, and was as slick as they make them, I never met his equal at deception . . . )." But T.C. did not confine his rage to any one person. He summarized that the suit had been "started by [a] blackmailer," was "brought for broken promises of [an] Attorney General" (Bonaparte), "argued for the broken promises of the President" (Taft), and that the Company had been "found guilty by Courts who know the wishes of the only power that can promote them."[73]

Hatred and the placing of blame, however, did not solve the Powder Company's most pressing problem, which was deciding upon a response to the interlocutory court decree. There were two initial paths. First, the defendants could attempt to reopen the case. Second, they could try to work out a dissolution plan which would satisfy the Justice Department and Judge Gray's court. Because Coleman blamed his New York law firm for the court's adverse decision, he turned increasingly to his Wilmington lawyer, William Hilles. In spite of everything that had happened, Coleman still believed that the government would accept a sham settlement. Consequently soon after the court's decision he asked Hilles to contact Special Assistant to the Attorney General William A. Glasgow who, with Scarlet's aid, had directed the prosecution after Wade Ellis had resigned from the Justice Department in February of 1910. Coleman told Hilles to propose approximately the same concession that had been offered to Ellis in January of 1910, that is, the dissolution of the old corporate shells—Eastern Dynamite, Hazard, Laflin & Rand, Delaware Investment, Delaware Securities, and California Investment. Glasgow proved to be unreceptive and informed Hilles that there would have to be a real breakup of the big company.[74]

Upon learning this, Coleman's first impulse was to ask for a rehearing. "In my judgment," he wrote Moxham, "I think we had better urge a reopening of the case so that I may be allowed to give evidence."[75] In line with this thinking, Pierre wrote Townsend on September 7, 1911, that it would be "wise to prepare for a request for a rehearing or a reopening of the case for the production of further evidence."[76] Pierre explained that Coleman's "chief value in the case would be to give his personal story of the transactions of 1902, in order to make stronger the dividing line between the old associations and the new corporation."[77] But privately the treasurer was not convinced that reopening the case was proper, and he added in his letter to Townsend, "You understand, of course, that we have made no decision . . . but we think it wise to make preparations. . . ."[78] Pierre's quiet concern about Coleman's strategy had already been expressed much more forcefully by Senator Henry du Pont through his attorney David Marvel, who had written Coleman: "The more I consider the proposition of reargument . . . the stronger I am confirmed in the opinion that it would be a mistake. . . . I am convinced . . . that the sooner this proposition is abandoned and all energies bent to presenting such a case before the court as might secure the most favorable decree the better it will be."[79]

Although Coleman did not altogether give up the idea of reopening the case before the court, he soon turned his energies toward another solution. The more he thought about it, the less he placed his confidence in lawyers. "I can see no use in taking . . . [ideas for settlement] up with our attorneys in New York as it would only enable them to increase the size of their already unreasonable bill," Coleman wrote Moxham in early September of 1911.[80] The Du Pont president could think only of using his political influence more effectively. The previous failures did not seem to daunt him. Coleman's strategy, therefore, was to gain a rehearing not before the courts, but before Attorney General Wickersham, whom he hoped to convince that the judges had erred when they found the big company in violation of the Sherman Act. As Coleman had done so often before, he contacted his two most trusted and influential political friends, William F. Stone, Sergeant at Arms of the Republican National Committee and Collector of the Port of Baltimore, and Postmaster General Hitchcock.[81]

Almost immediately after the court's decision, Postmaster General Hitchcock prepared the way for an interview between Coleman and Attorney General Wickersham. William Stone advised Coleman that the Powder Company's lawyers should make no attempt to arrange a settlement until after such a meeting.[82] Coleman met the attorney general on August 7, and he told Wickersham that he felt the court's decision was unfair and should be modified. The attorney general responded that although he sympathized with the Du Pont Company's problems, he could take up the case only on the basis of the decree rendered by the circuit court. Two days later Wickersham wrote Coleman that while "I have no disposition to evade any of the responsibilities put upon me, nor to withhold myself from any conference with you which may tend to the working-out of the requirements of the court, I do not think that any further conference merely for the purpose of advising me of your views of the controversy would be helpful. . . ."[83]

Blinded to even this flat rejection, Coleman was still convinced that he could win his point. In the last week of September, Wickersham agreed to meet Coleman in New York City at the federal district attorney's office. The plan that the Powder Company's president tried to persuade Wickersham to adopt was the measure proposed to Ellis in January of 1910 and then to Glasgow in June of 1911, one which left the big company almost untouched except for smokeless powder.[84] The attorney general, who was returning to Washington, D.C., from a few days' stay at the Mount Washington Hotel in Bretton Woods, New Hampshire, told Coleman that the proffered plan did not meet the court's decree and that nothing further could be decided until the government's attorneys had more detailed information on the Powder Company's black powder and dynamite sales. Coleman promised to provide the data. Wickersham indicated that if comprehensive and accurate statistics could be obtained, he saw no reason why the attorneys for the government and those for the Powder Company would be unable to reach a satisfactory settlement.[85]

Nothing that had happened convinced Coleman that the government was serious. On October 8 he wrote Wickersham asking for another meeting. Coleman began, "I don't want you to think me a nuisance or that I don't understand the English language," and he continued that he wanted to present a modified plan and that "you and I can do more toward doing what is fair and just in 3 hours than Glasgow and Hilles can in 3 weeks."[86] At the resulting meeting on October 12, the attorney general requested still more data and promised Coleman that when he received it he would personally evaluate it. The following day, Coleman met the attorney general at Washington's Metropolitan Club and gave him the desired information. About a week later Wickersham responded that he had examined the papers that had been passed to him at the Metropolitan Club. "So far as I can make out," he said, "they are all written for the purpose of demonstrating that the United States Circuit Court erred in rendering the decision it did. . . . As I have told you before," the attorney general emphasized, "I may not enter into a discussion of that proposition. I must accept the decision of the court as conclusive until reversed."[87] Wickersham asked that negotiations be continued between Hilles and Glasgow, and he added ominously that if a satisfactory plan were not worked out, the matter would be "submitted to the court for such proceedings as it may deem expedient."[88]

Incredibly, Coleman still did not think that Wickersham meant what he said. On October 26 the Du Pont president sent three letters: one to Frank Hitchcock, a second to Wickersham, and a third to President Taft's brother Charles, who in 1910 had joined Coleman in a syndicate to build New York's McAlpin Hotel. They all said approximately the same thing. To Hitchcock, Coleman wrote, "I have had a very, very careful analysis made of our business and want to show you some figures that will surprise you."[89] The burden of the argument was that the big company's black powder and dynamite business should not be broken apart. To Wickersham, Coleman wrote a letter which seemed oblivious of all that had transpired since the court's decree. "My thought was," Coleman concluded, "that if you knew the real facts in the case . . . you will know that there has been no restraint of trade nor any monopoly."[90] As a parting shot, the Du Pont president told Wickersham: "I am going to try to run down and lunch with you at the [Metropolitan] Club next Tuesday, not to bother you with a lot of details that you do not care to be bothered with . . . but simply to have the pleasure of dining with you and of suggesting one or two thoughts that have come to me. . . ."[91] How annoyed the attorney general must have been! In the letter to Charles Taft, Coleman asked for an interview with President Taft. Coleman promised to present the "actual facts and true conditions."[92]

As one can well imagine, none of these appeals bore fruit. Hitchcock was sympathetic but could do nothing. President Taft thought an interview would accomplish nothing and preferred to leave the matter to his attorney general. Wickersham had lunch with Coleman but stated that if any settlement were reached, it would have to be worked out at lower echelons.

Coleman seemed willing to do almost anything except face the reality that the Powder Company would have to be split into several competitive units. Therefore, despite his inability to change Wickersham's mind, Coleman attempted to influence the Justice Department officials directly in charge of the case. In late September 1911 he tried to reach William Glasgow but failed.[93] From November 1911 through mid-1912 Coleman tried to approach James Scarlet through a mutual friend, S. A. Yorks, who was vice-president and treasurer of the Central Coal and Iron Company of Central City, Kentucky (a company with which Coleman had begun his business career and of which he was still the president).[94] Nothing that Yorks did moved Scarlet. In fact the pressure seemed to backfire, for during the talks between the Justice Department and the company, Scarlet came out on the side of harsh treatment for the Du Pont interests.[95]

As time wore on and the negotiations went into the election year of 1912, the matter became of ever-increasing concern to the Taft administration. In March the president and Wickersham traveled to Philadelphia to a session of the circuit court convened to work out a settlement. The session was attended by Du Pont executives, court officials, and lawyers representing both the Powder Company and the government. At the meeting Wickersham, by accident, met Alfred I. du Pont during a recess and took him aside and told him, with President Taft looking on, that "it had been arranged with the court to appoint a receiver for our company and to continue the receiver in charge even though the case were appealed."[96] This would have automatically transferred the Powder Company's management from Pierre and Coleman to an outsider, who would take orders from the court. The receiver's duties would have been to dissolve the firm. It seemed clear to Pierre that any settlement made by a receiver might endanger the family control of the enterprise and would, in any case, be less favorable than an agreement worked out by the Du Pont management itself. Although Coleman still refused to face facts, Pierre had finally realized the previous October that he had to step in to reach some kind of settlement with the Justice Department and so end the litigation.

### Pierre Takes Control

Although Pierre held the position of acting president as well as treasurer during almost the entire antitrust litigation, he deferred to Coleman during the first phase of the suit. Throughout the affair, the two cousins held many beliefs in common. They agreed that Waddell had started the suit for blackmailing purposes, that the Roosevelt and Taft administrations had prosecuted it for political advantage, and that the Powder Company was absolutely legal. Pierre also shared Coleman's initial optimism as to the outcome of the suit.

But in early 1910, after the litigation had simmered along for almost three years with no end in sight, Pierre began to doubt the efficacy of Coleman's political approach. The more the treasurer pondered the situation the more he blamed both Coleman and Senator Henry's adventures in politics for the trouble. After much hesitation, on January 3, 1910, Pierre picked up his pen and prepared a letter to Senator du Pont: "At the time of the attack made on our company [to take away the smokeless powder business] in Congress last year . . . it was suggested . . . that the supposed entrance of our Company into the political field, through the instrumentality of yourself and Coleman had brought about this antagonistic feeling." Pierre continued that although Washington observers were thoroughly convinced of the truth of that statement, he had withheld judgment. Now, however, he wrote: "Our Executive Committee has finally come unanimously to the conclusion that your political connections, as well as those of Coleman's have worked injury to our company and will probably continue to do so."[97] Pierre had his letter typed, thought it over and then destroyed it, but he kept the handwritten original for his records. The treasurer, ever sensitive to other people's feelings, evidently felt that, although his letter rang true, it could do nothing but stir mistrust and recrimination. The document, however, is important, for it marks the beginning of Pierre's strong disapproval of Coleman's handling of the antitrust case.

Because Pierre remained confident that the lawyers would triumph in court, he withheld his criticism of Coleman. But Senator Henry's political career continued to grate on Pierre, and his worry turned to panic when in March 1911 Buckner reported that the senator might become chairman of the Senate Committee on Military Affairs. Pierre agreed with Buckner that if this happened it "would prove one continuous invitation of assault, misrepresentation and scandal."[98] Pierre counseled Coleman to tell Colonel Henry to decline the position if offered.[99] Reluctantly Coleman complied with Pierre's wishes. Fortunately the senator's committee assignments did not produce a crisis.[100]

Pierre had little more to do with the antitrust case until the court handed down its decision. The treasurer's initial reaction was much the same as Coleman's, one of shock and disbelief. The two cousins agreed that the court was politically motivated, but for Pierre the decree tended to confirm his growing distrust of Coleman's methods. With Coleman the failure was not his but the attorneys', and thus he came to believe even more in a political settlement. Although Pierre had no love for the lawyers, he thought that men of law, not politics, would finally settle the issue.

Still, Pierre made no immediate attempt to seize the initiative from Coleman. In fact Pierre was thrust almost by accident into assuming leadership in the settlement of the suit. Because Coleman had lost confidence in Townsend, Avery and Button, he sought the advice of other attorneys who he hoped might find a way to win. Through Colonel Henry he came into contact with David Watson of Pittsburgh, who had been associated with David Marvel in his successful attempt to remove the senator from the antitrust litigation. On October 10, 1911, Coleman retained Watson, who proposed a meeting in Philadelphia on Friday the thirteenth. Coleman actually had little expectation that the lawyer would help, and, since he had another engagement that day, he sent Pierre and Hilles in his place.[101] At that meeting Watson supported the advice that Townsend, Avery and Button had given since the interlocutory decree. Watson stressed that the court would demand that competition be created in the explosives business and that to do this at least some of the plants that were incorporated into the "Big Company" from Laflin & Rand and other powder companies would have to be turned over to new non-Du Pont firms. The main question, according to Watson, was not could the big company be left whole, but what parts of it would have to be assigned to new corporations. On this there was no easy answer, but Watson felt that if genuine concessions were offered, the court would not insist on too drastic a decree.[102]

Pierre returned to Wilmington from the Philadelphia meeting seething with anger at the handling of the case. Almost four months had elapsed since the decision of Judge Gray's court, and less than five weeks remained until the new deadline of November 21 when the Powder Company would have to return to the court to report on progress. The sole thing that had transpired during the four months was Coleman's informal negotiation with the attorney general. And this had resulted only in the knowledge that the government did not consider Coleman's ideas acceptable. As far as Pierre could see, there had been no progress at all, and the Powder Company's attorneys would appear before the court "without the least suggestion of a plan of action."[103] Pierre wrote Coleman that he was "very much disturbed at the present situation" and that he thought it "most important that . . . a plan should be agreed upon. . . ."[104]

Pierre recognized that a major problem was that no one knew what kind of plan would be acceptable either to the Department of Justice or to the court. Coleman's solution to this was to talk to the attorney general in the hopes of bringing him around to the Powder Company's point of view. Pierre saw that this was leading nowhere. The Powder Company's attorneys should draw up, he reasoned, a mild dissolution plan and present that directly to the court. If that should be rejected, Pierre proposed that the lawyers have a second scheme ready which yielded additional concessions. In the event that this second line of defense proved inadequate, he proposed a third one be presented, and so on, until finally a point of agreement could be reached. The treasurer felt so strongly about the need to present a definite proposal quickly that he told the Executive Committee that if his ideas did not meet their approval, he would insist upon being "relieved of all further responsibility in the handling of the Government suit" and of his duties as acting president.[105]

Thus, on October 18, 1911, Pierre, who turned back to the company's original law firm, ordered Townsend, Avery and Button to draft a plan that he felt was the smallest possible concession the court might approve: "the segregation of Du Pont International by declaration of a dividend of its stock; the final liquidation of Laflin & Rand, Hazard, Eastern Dynamite, and other inactive companies; dissolution and division of assets of E. I. du Pont de Nemours & Company plus segregation into another company of the four blasting powder factories of Laflin & Rand; i.e., Rosendale, Pleasant Prairie, Pennsylvania & Kansas, and Columbus."[106] Pierre, like Coleman, hoped to save the entire high explosives capacity.

During a conference between Pierre and James Townsend, the lawyer argued that the treasurer's plan for black powder was defensible, but the attempt to keep the dynamite capacity intact was not. Pierre reluctantly accepted Townsend's view and suggested the transfer to the proposed new company of dynamite plants equal to approximately 18% of the Powder Company's capacity (in addition to the four former Laflin & Rand black powder mills). Nothing better illustrates the divergent paths that Pierre and Coleman were taking than the sequence of events that followed this conference in October of 1911. On the eighteenth, Pierre ordered the lawyers to rush preparation of his trial plan. It was on the following day that Coleman wrote Hilles that there seemed to be no hurry in the negotiations with the government. He added that Wickersham was personally considering data which he, Coleman, had submitted.[107] It was on October 20 that the attorney general accused Coleman of submitting statistics prepared for the purpose of "demonstrating that the United States Circuit Court erred in rendering the decision it did."[108] The attorney general's letter made it clear that the Powder Company would have to split its dynamite capacity among two or more competitive companies. Coleman still had refused to take Wickersham seriously, and it was on October 26 that he wrote letters to the attorney general, the postmaster general, and Charles Taft which argued again that the court was wrong. By contrast, on the same date Pierre notified James Townsend that he agreed on modifying his plan so as to prepare splitting the four black powder mills plus 18% of the dynamite capacity from the big company.[109]

In all fairness to both Coleman and Pierre, it should be remembered that the dissolution of the Powder Company under the Sherman Act was without precedent. In the only comparable situation, neither Standard Oil nor American Tobacco had yet had time to finish working out a plan of dissolution in conformance with the Supreme Court's ruling in their cases. Besides, the situations were different enough so that no one pattern could fit all. In addition to the perplexing problem of what action was necessary to cease being in violation of the Sherman Act, there was the unanswered question of who would make the final decision as to what would be acceptable. Would it be the court or the Department of Justice? In October of 1911 Pierre thought the Powder Company could bypass the Department of Justice and present plans for reorganization directly to the circuit court. By November Pierre began to know differently. The court, he complained to the Executive Committee, had refused "to grant preliminary hearings, though we had been led to believe that such a course was open and recommended."[110] One judge told the Du Pont lawyers that the Justice Department and the Powder Company would have to get together and work out a solution which, if in harmony with the law and satisfactory to the government, would be ratified by the court. Consequently, when November 21, 1911, the date of the next hearing, came and the attorney general was not ready, the court postponed action.

In a sense Coleman had been right; the decision was not to be made by the courts but rested in the hands of the attorney general. Coleman's mistake was in misjudging the extent of his own influence and the commitment of President Taft and Attorney General Wickersham to the antitrust prosecutions. The administration had gone too far to back down in the Standard Oil, Tobacco, or Powder cases. The litigation which proved front page news much of the time had dragged on through almost all of Taft's term; the election of 1912 was approaching and the president wanted a decision. Coleman, as deeply involved in politics as he was, seemed unable to see this.

In making the settlement with the government Pierre had, since the court's decision, believed it could be done without inflicting a mortal wound upon the company. On July 20, 1911, he wrote his cousin William: "Our attorneys seem confident of two main points: (a) That the actual liquidation of E. I. du Pont de Nemours Powder Company will not be insisted upon if a sufficient segregation of assets into other companies can be accomplished. [And] (b) That the Government, under no condition, will endeavor to separate from the present company the factories constructed by it or by its predecessors, E. I. du Pont de Nemours & Co."[111] In other words, at this early stage Pierre felt that it would be possible to keep together all the plants operated by the Du Pont Company in 1901 and all those constructed by the Powder Company since that date. "If these essentials can be obtained," Pierre thought, "it does not seem that other dismemberment would be fatal to the company's interests."[112]

After his October conferences with the lawyers, Pierre began to get a clear picture of the situation. The government and the courts, he told the Executive Committee on November 10, 1911, "have determined to make a showing with our company." Pierre commented that he agreed with his friend, the former key man in the California Powder Works, E. S. Pillsbury of San Francisco, who had visited Wilmington in early November and had recommended that "we get under cover as things are liable to grow worse."[113]Thus, at the very time when Coleman was still trying to preserve the Powder Company as an indivisible entity, Pierre directed Townsend, Avery and Button and William Hilles to work with the government attorneys to formulate a definite plan that would separate from the Powder Company the following units: the Forcite, Emporium, and Hercules dynamite plants; the Rosendale, Pleasant Prairie, Pennsylvania & Kansas, and Columbus black powder mills; and International Smokeless Powder in its entirety.[114]

Pierre's actions to resolve the crisis did not mean that he had softened his views. The treasurer was every bit as bitter as Coleman, perhaps more so. To Richard M. Jones, head of the Penn Charter School in Philadelphia, Pierre's longtime friend and former teacher, he wrote on October 10, 1911:

> Under the Interlocutory decree of the Circuit Court . . . the company and its officials, including the writer, have been found guilty and the ensuing negotiations with the Government attorneys are far from reassuring as to their desire to see justice is meted out . . . I and my associates have a profound conviction that our intentions in the conduct of our business are free from adverse criticism. This is admitted by the Court in the rather remarkable statement "that the 28 defendants are associated in a combination, which, whether the individual defendants are aware of the fact or not has violated and still plans to violate both section one and section two of the Anti-Trust Act." To me this seemingly unwarranted accusation is sufficiently galling and it is the more so when the transactions of the company dating back to 1872 are brought into question and supposed criminal acts of my father, whom you knew personally, and other relatives of equal integrity are brought forward to show that the present generation should be punished. The whole business makes one ashamed of his American citizenship and casts doubt on the sincerity of our Government officials and their friends. . . .[115]

Pierre experienced nothing in the final negotiations with the government to cause him to change his mind.

The treasurer had hoped that his second line of defense, that is, the offer to split away three dynamite plants in addition to the four ex-Laflin & Rand black powder works, and International Smokeless Powder would satisfy the court. In this he was doomed to disappointment. In mid-December Hilles informed him that the Justice Department probably would not agree. Yet there was still no counterproposal, and the several government attorneys appeared to take diverging views.[116]

Despite Hilles' fears that the situation in Washington was deteriorating, Pierre remained determined to present his second line of defense directly to the court. After several postponements the court finally convened on

March 4, 1912, in Philadelphia to consider progress made toward a decree. By this time the government had decided upon a course of action. President Taft was there, accompanied by Attorney General Wickersham. At the formal court session, the Powder Company's lawyers presented a decree based upon Pierre's ideas for the judge's consideration. The government attorneys maintained that the concessions did not go far enough and then asked that the court appoint receivers for the Powder Company. At that point the court recessed and Pierre and his attorneys were invited to an informal session in the judge's chambers. There, Judge Gray told them that "the Court could not make a plan of dissolution" nor administer it and that unless the Justice Department and the Powder Company came to a voluntary settlement and signed a "consent" decree, the "only alternative was a receivership."[117] President Taft and Attorney General Wickersham arrived after the court's formal session, and it was then that they chanced upon Alfred I. du Pont and told him that the government would demand that receivers be appointed for the Powder Company. Alfred quickly relayed that message to Pierre.

The day's events angered the treasurer. "The whole judicial procedure has been a farce from beginning to end," he wrote to William. But he added, "however disagreeable all this may be, the practical effect is more important, as wounded feelings will work out their own cure in the proper time."[118]

It is quite clear in retrospect that neither Wickersham nor Taft had any desire to put the Powder Company into receivership, for at the informal session in the judge's chambers the government attorneys came forward with a counterproposal. Since Coleman was still saying that the Powder Company should not be broken apart, the attorney general wanted to make certain that the other important executives understood the government's determination; he would thereby create a favorable climate for acceptance of the Justice Department's plan. The threat to put the Du Pont interests in receivership, even though an appeal to the Supreme Court were undertaken—a condition which neither the Tobacco nor the Standard Oil trusts faced at the time they made their appeals to the Supreme Court—proved effective. After Alfred's "interview with the Attorney General," Pierre commented, "we decided to learn as rapidly as possible the plan that [Wickersham] . . . would insist upon, with the determination to accept that plan if it were within the range of possibility."[119]

The government's proposals, which were made by the Justice Department with President Taft's brother Charles serving as the president's personal representative, proved surprisingly conservative.[120] By authority of the decree that was finally accepted the du Ponts agreed to create two new companies and to turn over to those firms plants with the capacity to supply about 42% of the dynamite business and 50% of the black powder business.

The concept of splitting up an existing firm into three parts on the basis of share of output was, of course, a new one because the problem was new. The very first time an American corporation had divided into smaller parts had just been carried out with the final dissolution of Standard Oil and American Tobacco. At Standard Oil the task had been relatively easy because most of its subsidiaries were operating as well as legal units. So the decree could essentially make these subsidiaries into independent companies. American Tobacco also had a number of subsidiaries that became legally independent. But because the operations of a number of major companies coming into that consolidation had been fully integrated into a single centrally managed unit, the American Tobacco Company, the court decided to split that unit into three separate companies (American Tobacco, Liggett & Myers, and P. Lorillard) by allocating plants and brands to each of the three.[121] At Du Pont, of course, the existing subsidiaries—Laflin & Rand, Eastern Dynamite, Delaware Securities, etc.—were purely legal forms. They neither controlled nor operated any properties. So, in dissolving the Powder Company, the Justice Department used a criterion similar to the one developed in the Tobacco case. The two new companies to be created out of Du Pont would be allocated a specific share of the industry's operating capacity.

Fortunately for Pierre the government did not take into account asset value. The parts of the Powder Company to be split off met the requirements as to output and operating capacity, but the value of their assets was little more than $20.0 million compared to assets in excess of $60.0 million to be retained by the Powder Company.[122] The final decree specified that the new companies were to pay for their property by issuing $10.0 million of income bonds and $10.0 million of common stock. At least one-half of the income bonds were to be sold or distributed to the Powder Company's stockholders, and all of the common stock was to be distributed or sold.[123] Pierre summarized the effect of the attorney general's demands: in this way "the reduction of the assets of the parent company will be $10,000,000 [this represented the stock of the new firms. The $10.0 million of income bonds Pierre planned either to sell or to retain in the Powder Company treasury to serve as collateral] and will reduce our surplus of $17,000,000 to about $7,000,000, or in other words, E. I. du Pont de Nemours Powder Company will be reduced to approximately its condition in the year 1906." Writing ten weeks before the court ratified the plan, Pierre was worried. "I am fearful that the Government may try to cause further trouble when they find how little injury has been wrought by the plan so far agreed upon."[124]

The greatest irony of all was the attorney general's decision to allow the Du Pont Powder Company to retain the entire smokeless powder business. Admiral Austin M. Knight, president of the Special Board of Naval Ordnance, and General William Crozier, chief ordnance officer of the army, argued that Du Pont's smokeless production facilities were so closely interwoven with those of the military that segregation of them among separate companies would be unwise. Furthermore, the army and the navy preferred that a large well-financed company should retain the smokeless powder business, which required the maintenance of substantial reserve capacity, both in plants and personnel. Should war emerge the military officials felt that Du Pont experience would provide the means for rapidly expanding powder production. The court endorsed the position taken by the military officers. The judges in their opinion accompanying the final decree referred to the "highly beneficial" cooperation between the Du Pont Company and its subsidiary, International Smokeless Powder, and the government. The judges noted that the powder used by the army and navy was made entirely either by the government at its own plants or by Du Pont. "The decree leaves this situation unchanged," the court explained, "for the following reasons:

> First because the Government, through the ownership and operation of its own plants, is enabled to control the price it pays for such powder; and the whole matter will continue to be, as it now is, within the control of Congress and the executive departments.
> Second, because a division of that business among the several competing companies (there being only one customer) would tend to destroy the practical and scientific co-operation now pursued, between the Government and the defendant company just named, and to impair the certainty and efficiency of the results thus obtained. No benefit would accrue to the public by dividing this business (a business which cannot properly be designated as interstate commerce) between several competing concerns, while injury to the public interests of a grave character might and could probably result therefrom.[125]

Despite Pierre's fears, the attorney general did not press for drastic last-minute concessions, and on June 13, 1912, the court approved the final decree. The Powder Company had until December 15, 1912, to reorganize, with the option of applying for more time if it was found necessary.[126]

The final struggle with Waddell had a happy ending for Pierre and Coleman. In late August 1911, just a few weeks after the circuit court's interlocutory decree, Pierre received a letter from the New York legal firm of McFarland, Taylor & Costello informing him that Waddell, through his Buckeye Powder Company, had decided to sue for damages under the seventh section of the Sherman Act. Waddell asserted that Buckeye had sustained losses of more than $600,000 as a result of unfair competition by Du Pont, and his attorney reminded the Powder Company that under the provision of the Sherman Act which allowed the injured to collect triple damages, the total came to $1,919,691.[127] Pierre put the matter into the hands of the Powder Company's general counsel, John P. Laffey, who was aided by Townsend, Avery and Button.[128] Since the suit came before the United States Circuit Court in Trenton, New Jersey, the Powder Company also retained a Trenton lawyer, Frank S. Katzenbach.

At no time did anyone in the Powder Company show an interest in compromising with Waddell. Pierre felt that the Powder Company had a good chance, since Waddell had to prove that specific acts by the du Ponts had actually damaged Buckeye.[129] During the litigation, which lasted for well over two years, the Powder Company's lawyers sought to prove that Waddell had started the Buckeye Company for blackmailing reasons, that is, for the specific purpose of selling it to the du Ponts at an inflated price.[130]

The case finally went to the jury in February 1914, and the decision was a total victory for the du Ponts. Coleman's first reaction was to attempt to prosecute Waddell for perjury. The Powder Company's executives abandoned this idea, however, when further investigation disclosed that the Buckeye Powder Company was bankrupt and in the hands of a receiver and that Waddell himself was broke. As Moxham gleefully put it, "Waddell's credit for big lawsuits . . . [was] zero."[131] But this was small consolation for the loss of the antitrust case, the suit that Waddell did so much to institute.

## Dismemberment

The court order outlined the way toward dissolution. The actual task of implementing the decree fell almost entirely upon Pierre. In simple terms, the court demanded, first, that the du Ponts place their holdings in a single legal framework and, second, that they split off enough of their manufacturing capacity in high explosives and black powder to found two independent, competitive firms. For Pierre the significance of the first requirement was not the dissolution of the remaining subsidiaries. Their elimination had been his goal and Moxham's ever since the formation of the Powder Company. It was rather that it meant the end of the E. I. du Pont de Nemours & Company, the holding company by which the three cousins assured their control of the Powder Company. Pierre had hoped that he could carry out the second requirement without endangering the Powder Company's ability to continue as a successful profit-making institution. The first requirement he could do little but accept. The second provided a challenge that he met most effectively.

Immediately after the final decree Pierre placed most of the Du Pont holdings within a single corporation: the E. I. du Pont de Nemours Powder Company. By January 1913 he could report to the court that E. I. du Pont de Nemours & Company, Hazard Powder Company, Delaware Securities Company, Delaware Investment Company, Eastern Dynamite Company, California Investment Company, and the Laflin & Rand Powder Company had all been dissolved and that their assets, which consisted almost entirely of stock in the big company, had been distributed among their stockholders. This left intact only Du Pont of Pennsylvania and International Smokeless

Powder, which the du Ponts controlled through the Du Pont International Powder Company. The final decree specifically permitted the Powder Company to keep its control of International Smokeless Powder and maintain its corporate identity if it wished. Since there was no pressure to abolish these two corporations, the du Ponts maintained them until 1915, when they finally dissolved the firms and gave their stockholders securities of the Powder Company.[132] The decree also permitted the Powder Company to continue in operation provided it split away enough of its assets to set up two competing firms. Thus, in 1913 the du Ponts (with the exception of International Smokeless Powder, Du Pont of Pennsylvania, and the Du Pont Nitrate Company) achieved a single corporate structure with their holdings concentrated in a single firm, the E. I. du Pont de Nemours Powder Company (New Jersey).[133]

The heart of the circuit court's decree, however, was the order to "organize two corporations in addition to E. I. du Pont de Nemours Powder Company (1903 New Jersey Corporation)" and to transfer to them such manufacturing capacity as would make them substantial competitors. In sum, plants transferred to the new firms would give them capacity to supply 50% of the nation's black powder requirements and 42% of the dynamite market. The court order, which in reality represented Attorney General Wickersham's desires, modified in some degree because of Pierre's last-minute negotiations, was so explicit in certain parts that the acting president had little opportunity for maneuvering. The decree specified, for example, the manufacturing facilities to be turned over to each new corporation and those to be retained by Du Pont.[134]

The court decree provided specific guidelines on these provisions, but left a degree of latitude in carrying them out. The du Ponts were permitted to reactivate the Laflin & Rand and Eastern Dynamite corporate charters and to assign to them the assets to go to the two new firms; or the du Ponts could create two entirely new corporations as they chose. Furthermore, the old Powder Company was to "furnish [the two new] . . . corporations . . . with sufficient working capital . . . and cash," but the exact amount was not designated. Similarly the decree established a formula for the valuation of the transferred property which set the compensation to be received by the Powder Company on the inventory it held at the time of transfer plus a sum to equal "a fair valuation for the brands and good will." The new companies were to pay for their assets by turning over to the E. I. du Pont de Nemours Powder Company their securities, 50% of which were to be 6% bonds unsecured by mortgage and 50% stock; the Powder Company was obligated to accept the stock at par value and to "distribute the said stock and one half of the bonds or the proceeds of the sale of said bonds among [its common] stockholders." The new stock was to be of two classes—one-half with voting power, the rest without. Such shares were to be distributed "among the stockholders of E. I. du Pont de Nemours Powder Company." Those that went to any one of the twenty-seven defendants were to consist of one-half voting and one-half nonvoting stock. This provision, following in the American Tobacco precedent, kept control of the new firms in the hands of the original shareholders. Next, the court ordered that the Powder Company transfer to the new firms a fair proportion of its business and allow them to retain access to any desired information from the Du Pont Company's trade records for at least five years.[135] Finally the court directed the parent company to provide for its offsprings' facilities for the purchase of materials and research.

In the days following the final decree, Pierre's main concerns were two: first, the creation of two new viable explosives companies which would satisfy the circuit court's decree; second, the accomplishment of this in such a manner as to do the least damage to the old E. I. du Pont de Nemours Powder Company. To Pierre, the selection of the key personnel who would manage the new firms posed "the most important question." After much discussion the Executive Committee decided to place two able executives whom Pierre had supervised in the Powder Company: Russell H. Dunham (then its comptroller) in charge of the larger of the two new companies, and William J. Webster (head of the Powder Company's Sales Department in San Francsico) in the top executive position of the smaller of the new firms.[136] As for naming the new corporations, Pierre accepted the suggestion of his Sales Department that the larger of the new companies be called the Hercules Powder Company, and the lesser the Atlas Powder Company. Pierre explained to the Finance Committee that "we have two valuable brands of dynamite, Hercules and Atlas, the rights to which are not protected in any way."[137] The acting president urged that the Du Pont Powder Company could not utilize the old trade names, but if the new firms took them as the basis for their corporate titles, they would have a proprietary right in them. It was far better, he concluded, to name the new corporations after established powder brands than to resurrect the Eastern Dynamite and Laflin & Rand corporations.

Pierre's primary concern remained the safeguarding of the Du Pont Company's capital assets and ability to grow. In this the acting president succeeded better than he dared hope. During the final negotiations he had won an agreement from the attorney general's office and the court that the Powder Company should be allowed to retain those facilities which it had constructed since 1903. Thus the Du Pont Company entered the postsuit era with control of its best plants, such as the new dynamite works at Louviers, Colorado, and Du Pont, Washington, and the new black powder mill at Patterson, Oklahoma.

As important was Pierre's determination to see that the court-ordered breakup did not destroy or undermine the Powder Company's financial strength. In order to understand the problems he faced, it is necessary to return to May 1911, a few weeks before the circuit court handed down its decision on the antitrust case. At that time Pierre, together with Hamilton Barksdale, then general manager of the Powder Company, re-examined the entire problem of financing the company's future capital requirements. In a lengthy report the two proposed a bold new course. They began their statement by noting that the Powder Company's financial structure was built upon three kinds of securities: $16,548,000 of 4½% 30-year gold bonds; $15,893,000 of 5% cumulative preferred stock; and $29,426,000 of common stock.[138] The more the two examined the company's financial structure the more they began to see the various types of securities in new perspectives. Both agreed that there was less use for bonds, and a new role for preferred stock. "Originally," Pierre told the Executive Committee, corporate bond issues "were in such amounts and maturities as implied an intent to liquidate the debt." But as time went on, bond issues became so large that for most corporations, including Du Pont, they came to be regarded as capital not to be repaid "except by refunding."[139] Pierre felt now that because the refunding requirements might come at an unfavorable time, bonds were undesirable as a permanent part of the Powder Company's capital structure.

Preferred stock also began to take on new meaning. When it was created, Pierre observed, "our limited knowledge of preferred stocks and the state of uncertainty existing in the minds of most investors regarding the proper position which preferred stock should occupy in relation to the general security market" caused the Executive Committee to debate two points: the amount of the dividend and the voting privilege.[140] Pierre originally opted for a 5% cumulative dividend and the granting of full voting rights to the stock. Consequently, as of 1911 all Powder Company stock, preferred and common, carried a vote. This he maintained was in accord with the general procedure of the day. It also reflected the normal practice that preferred shares represented a firm's tangible assets, whereas common shares had as their basis good will and earning power.

As Pierre viewed the situation in 1911, he recognized that preferred stock had begun to acquire the characteristics of bonds rather than of stock. Two differences were of crucial significance. First, the senior stock represented an equity in the firm rather than a lien against its assets. And second, preferred shares carried a vote, whereas the bondholders had no voice in management except in case of default. But on the most important point the two kinds of securities were similar: both yielded a fixed rate of return which had prior claims on earnings to the common shares.

Pierre felt the financial reputation of the Powder Company in 1911 was such that few would question its ability to service its debt and maintain the preferred stock dividends. He thought that by raising the preferred dividend it would be possible to market substantial amounts of such stock. This would enable the retirement of the bonded debt, as well as provide the basis for expansion. The major obstacle was the vote attached to the preferred shares. As long as the senior shareholders retained a voice in the management of the Powder Company, Pierre felt that he and the family could not afford to offer the preferred stock in large quantities to the general public.

The new financial program that Pierre and Barksdale recommended in May 1911, shortly before the circuit court's adverse opinion, had as its main purpose the creation of a security that could be sold widely to small investors, both in the United States and abroad. They proposed a preferred stock that would be regarded as a "permanent" debt of the company, in contrast to ordinary bonded debt, which matured at fixed times. In order to ensure that the sale of preferred securities would not endanger the family's control, they specifically advocated that the Powder Company issue a new 6% cumulative preferred stock that had no voting privilege. These securities, they suggested, should be used to retire all 5% cumulative preferred stock on a share-for-share basis. The increased return should provide an immediate incentive to induce the old preferred stockholders to accept the new voteless shares.

Furthermore, Pierre and Barksdale proposed that preferred stock issues eventually replace the bonded debt; and that all future capital be raised through the sale of common and preferred shares at the ratio of 1½ to 1. This, Pierre explained, would maintain the current relationship between the amount of common shares and of debt (preferred stock plus bonds). Pierre argued that the 6% dividend rate would allow the shares to be sold at par both in New York and in France, and he urged that the new stock be placed on the Paris Bourse.

After refinancing the outstanding preferred stock and bonds, Pierre assumed that new stock (common and preferred at the ratio of 1½ to 1) issues would increase the capital employed by the Powder Company at approximately 5% per year. While the proposed growth rate was no larger than previous estimates, all earlier capital expansion rested either on retained earnings or upon the purchase of new issues by the old security holders, that is, mainly the du Pont family. The new program promised a way to allow the public to subscribe up to 40% of future capital requirements and still not endanger the old pattern of family control.

But, as in the case of Pierre's first comprehensive financial program of 1907, fate intervened to delay action on the proposals of 1911. The circuit court's interlocutory decree in the antitrust suit made any financial reorganization impossible. Nothing could be done until the court's decision had been made final, or until the antitrust case had been resolved in some other manner. On June 24, 1911, the Executive Committee held a special meeting and—over the objections of Pierre, who argued that the suit should not affect reform of the Powder Company's financial structure—officially post-poned action on his plan.[141]

Whether Pierre liked it or not, the government-ordained split would dominate all financial planning during the years between 1911 and 1913. Therefore, Pierre's main concern became the reconciliation of the ideas he and Barksdale had developed, and the problem of surrendering a substantial portion of the Powder Company's assets without reducing the original firm's financial power. Pierre recognized that the new corporations would require a substantial infusion of working capital in the form of cash as well as the turnover of factories and raw materials. If the Powder Company simply spun off to its own shareholders the securities it received from Atlas and Hercules, the parent corporation would lose from $5.0 million to $7.0 million in hard capital. Pierre developed a scheme to prevent this leakage; its success goes far to explain the very modest setback that characterized the firm's compliance with the court's decree.

The first part of Pierre's plan was to lessen the new companies' need for capital. This he accomplished by working out an agreement with the Justice Department that allowed Atlas and Hercules to use the Powder Company's Purchasing Department, plants producing raw materials, and research facilities for a "transitional" period of at least five years. By this maneuver Pierre eliminated an immediate need by the two new firms for several millions.

More important still were Pierre's plans for the capital structures of the new firms; he intended their capital to consist of 50% bonds and 50% stock. Pierre explained that bonds were to represent the solid assets transferred whereas the stock was to stand for intangibles such as earning power, patent rights, and good will.[142] Pierre planned to distribute the stock to the Powder Company's common shareholders and thus to satisfy the court's decree by removing from the Powder Company's control the management of the new companies. But Pierre was determined to keep the Atlas and Hercules bonds in the Powder Company's treasury, where they could be used as the basis for credit—perhaps as collateral for nitrate purchases. In short, through retaining the new firms' bonds, the acting president planned to keep the use of most of the tangible capital that he was forced to turn over to the new companies.

The court nearly accepted Pierre's recommendations without alteration. But at the last minute the Justice Department imposed two annoying changes. First, the attorney general specified that the bonds were to be "income bonds," that is, they could not be a lien against the property of the new firms. Nor was interest to be paid on them unless it was actually earned. Furthermore, the interest was not to be cumulative; hence, even if the bonds paid no return, the holders had no claim to future earnings. In effect, the bonds of the new companies were to have fewer rights than the preferred stock of the Powder Company. This naturally reduced the worth of the new securities as collateral. The second change required by Attorney General Wickersham forced the Powder Company "to distribute . . . one half the bonds . . . retaining the other half only."[143]

Although the Justice Department's action appeared to jeopardize his financial program, the acting president was determined not to let any precious capital escape if he could prevent it. In his report to the Powder Company's Finance Committee on May 25, 1912, Pierre explained how he had arrived at the proposed capital structures of the two new firms. The appraised value of the transferred plants plus the money in working capital would total $13,594,000. This would be divided as follows: bonds of the Hercules Powder Company, $5,750,000, and stock of the same firm $5,-885,000; bonds of the Atlas Powder Company, $2,750,000, and stock $2,-942,000.[144] The stock, of course, had to be distributed immediately to the Du Pont Powder Company's common shareholders as a dividend, but Pierre still hoped to retain the use of the full $8.5 million of capital as represented by the bonds of the two firms.

Pierre reverted to his financial plan of 1911, in which he had programmed for the Powder Company the abolition of the old preferred stock as a first step in the creation of a new nonvoting senior security. He therefore seized upon the 6% bonds of the new companies as a vehicle by which he could eliminate much of the old 5% preferred stock. "The bonds," he pointed out, "will be sufficient to retire approximately one-half of the outstanding preferred issue. If this exchange were consummated E. I. du Pont Powder Company could earn its outstanding preferred stock dividend more than ten times. This makes a very strong security and one which can be readily sold for future financing."[145] On further thought he decided to use the bonds to retire the Powder Company's bonds instead of preferred stock.

The final agreement that Pierre worked out with the officials of the Hercules and Atlas companies, and that the court accepted, inflated Pierre's proposed capital structure for the new firms slightly. In all, the Powder Company received $6.5 million in bonds from Hercules and $3.0 million in bonds from Atlas for a total of $9.5 million.[146] On October 5, 1912, he presented a proposal to exchange one-half of the Powder Company's holdings of bonds of the new companies (par value $4.5 million) for a like amount of the Powder Company's 4½% gold bonds. On October 8, 1912, the Executive Committee approved this plan, and to make it more attractive to the Du Pont Company's bondholders, the original company pledged itself to guarantee the interest on the Hercules and Atlas securities. This action opened the way for the retirement of more than one-fourth of the Powder Company's bonded debt.[147] The rest of the Hercules and Atlas bonds remained in the Du Pont Company treasury to be sold when additional capital was needed. This time came in late 1913, when the Executive Committee authorized the sale of the Hercules bonds to the Powder Company's share-holders at 85% of par value. As had been done before, Pierre, Alfred, and Coleman formed a syndicate to purchase the securities not taken up by the common stockholders under their rights.[148]

Then during the late months of 1913 the Powder Company finally adopted Pierre's financial program of 1911. On October 20, 1913, the Executive Committee approved an issue of 6% nonvoting preferred stock sufficient to retire both the old voting cumulative 5% preferred stock and the remaining half of the 4½% gold bonds.[149] This would have given the Du Pont Company a total capital of about $62.0 million, divided between $33.0 million of preferred stock and $29.0 million of common stock. But before all the changes could be made, World War I broke out, causing still greater changes in the company's financial structure.

The new Atlas and Hercules corporations began their active careers during the first three months of 1913. Although Pierre's main concern had been to protect the Du Pont Powder Company, he had every interest in the success of the new corporations. Only prosperous and profitable firms could pay the interest on their bonds and thus give solid value to the $9.0 million of their securities which the Du Pont Powder Company held and which Pierre was using to retire the Du Pont gold bonds and to raise additional capital for his company.

Furthermore, the Department of Justice and the court were watching carefully the relationship between the old Powder Company and the two new firms. The failure of either for whatever reason might have jeopardized the settlement, and hence the Du Pont Company itself. Coleman finally accepted the dissolution as a fact. In a confidential letter to Judge J. P. Laffey, the Powder Company's chief counsel, he wrote: "It is our desire to carry out not only the letter, but the spirit of the Decree to the utmost and rather than have our people do anything that could be considered in any way to [sic] stretching the Decree in a way that would favor us, they should be instructed to lean the other way and even give up trade or lose business rather than put themselves in a position where their smallest act would be open to criticism."[150]

Pierre backed Coleman's views, and took charge of putting into operation that part of the court's order that gave the new companies access to the Du Pont files (for the period prior to the breakup of 1913) and the full use of the purchasing and research facilities. Among the most complex of these arrangements was the determination of the charges to be assessed against the Hercules and Atlas corporations. In March 1913, Pierre, with the aid of the Manufacturing and Sales Committee and his staff, set price policies for the goods to be provided the new companies. Initially, for example, nitrate was to be sold at cost plus a 1¼% commission. In addition, Atlas and Hercules were to advance their share of funds needed to finance nitrate purchases. The new firms were given the choice of either paying cash at the time the Du Pont Company issued drafts for nitrate in Chile, or putting up collateral "as security for the drafts lodged in New York."[151] The Du Pont Powder Company agreed to sell crude glycerin for 1⅛% commission.[152] And supplies the Du Pont Powder Company produced in its own plants were to be sold at cost plus 15%.[153] For the access to the Du Pont Company's experimental facilities, Atlas and Hercules paid $60,000 out of a total research appropriation of $225,000 for the year 1913.[154] In following years the three firms came to new agreements that shared appropriations and the results of experimental work.

The year 1913 and the first three-quarters of 1914 was not a robust time for the powder business; during this period the three firms lost ground slightly to their competitors in the fields of black powder and dynamite. Statistics indicated that the two new firms lost relatively more of the proposed share of the market than did the Du Pont Powder Company, but in no cases were the declines enough to threaten the profitability of any of the three firms. The Executive Committee watched the relatively poor showing of the Atlas and Hercules companies, but out of fear of the antitrust laws voted on September 9, 1913, that "the question of loss of business to competitors on the part of the Hercules and Atlas Companies is not a proper subject for discussion."[155] Before permanent trends could be established, however, World War I changed all previous market patterns and provided a surplus of orders for all three firms.

The antitrust suit had several important consequences. It led to the formal abrogation of the European Agreement in 1913. Since Pierre recognized the value of maintaining connections with the Europeans, he agreed with the Executive Committee that a new compact that would not violate the Sherman Act should be drawn up. Pierre conducted some of these negotiations personally on a trip to Europe early in 1913. Then in August Pierre and his associates decided that the agreement should be dropped altogether, but that the Du Pont representatives should continue to consult regularly with the Anglo-German Group. In the following summer a new agreement was finally negotiated. Payments would now be paid specifically for royalties on patented and licensed processes and equipment and not on a percentage of an excess above a set profit figure. This conference in London was completed on July 2, shortly after the assassination of Archduke Franz Ferdinand at Serajavo. While the British considered the arrangement a lasting one, the du Ponts believed that the outbreak of the war put the new treaty in abeyance. After all, the British and the German members of the group were on opposite sides in a major war. When peace finally came the Du Pont Company was ready to start from scratch in drawing up a new alliance.[156]

A second consequence was that the outcome of the antitrust suit turned

the attention of the Executive Committee to examining with more seriousness the possibilities of diversification. The plans for capital expenditures for
1914 included a sizable amount to increase the capacity of the fabrikoid
plant and to renew the search for other products based on nitrocellulose
technology. Of more significance, of course, was the coming of a new
structure for the powder industry. In place of one dominant enterprise,
three strong companies began to compete for business. However, World
War I came before any definite new patterns of competition emerged. By
the end of the conflict all three companies had been transformed into
general chemical firms. Above all, Pierre had met the challenge of preserv-
ing the Powder Company as a powerful profit-making institution and one
that the du Pont family still completely controlled.

# The Problem of Succession

CHAPTER *11*

Uɴᴛɪʟ ᴛʜᴀᴛ ᴅᴀʏ in June 1911, when Judge Gray's court ruled the Du Pont Company was in violation of the Sherman Antitrust Act, neither Coleman nor Pierre considered the government suit their most important problem. Instead the two cousins in 1910 and early 1911 centered their major attention on one of the most difficult challenges facing any family business: the problem of succession. Perhaps it seems strange that two comparatively young men (in 1910 Coleman was forty-seven and Pierre was forty) should think of giving way to a still younger generation. But for different reasons each wanted to step aside. Even if in 1909 illness had not forced Coleman to relinquish the active duties of the company's presidency, he would not have been interested in continuing to run the Powder Company.

Coleman, by nature restless, saw little challenge left in Wilmington. New York seemed more attractive and, as the years after 1910 slipped by, Manhattan real estate development commanded ever more of his time and capital. In addition, Coleman's close association with Henry du Pont's successful bid for the U.S. Senate in 1906 made a deep impression. The gregarious Coleman enjoyed power and associating with those who ruled the nation. He viewed his selection as the Republican National Committeeman from Delaware in 1908 as a stepping-stone to bigger things, perhaps a senatorship or, in his more ebullient moments, to even the presidency itself. By comparison, the Powder Company seemed tame and, if Coleman were to continue as an officer, he would have preferred to be chairman of the board of directors, a position with no administrative responsibilities.

Pierre viewed his future differently. Between 1904 and 1910 he had taken the leading part in constructing for the company an administrative framework that almost automatically and impersonally fed forward precise, accurate, and meaningful information. This had taken most of Pierre's time at the expense of his private ambitions. Now that his company seemed on sure footing and he had become financially secure beyond his fondest hopes, Pierre wanted to take time to realize his childhood dream. Pierre had two related and intense interests: horticulture and water fountains. During his youth he vowed that if he ever had the money he would own large green-houses and develop gardens with elaborate fountains. He had these ambitions in mind in July 1906, when he purchased Peirce's Park, a 200-acre estate near Kennett Square, Pennsylvania, a few miles from the Delaware state line. The fact that Peirce's Park, which Pierre renamed Longwood, had traditionally been open to the public as a picnic and recreation ground probably attracted him, for he could remember as a child wistfully pressing his nose against the glass while looking into private greenhouses in Philadelphia. From the first, Pierre planned that the gardens and greenhouse he hoped to construct would not be restricted for his sole pleasure. Indeed, he continued without interruption the park's tradition by welcoming the public to his garden during the daylight hours, seven days a week. In addition, Pierre thought continually of his immediate family. He had unbounded confidence in his two surviving brothers, Irénée and Lammot. Pierre had brought both into the company and looked forward to the day when they would follow his footsteps into top executive positions.

Pierre and Coleman were not to find it easy to step aside. Although the two had dominated the company since 1902, others had to be considered. Besides Pierre and his brothers and Coleman, there were other du Pont family interests, notably those of Alfred and the two sons of General Henry, Senator Henry and William. Alfred's divorce and remarriage in 1907 had altered his relationship with both Pierre and Senator Henry. The hatred that Senator Henry and his brother William had for each other further complicated the problem of succession and family representation in company affairs. In addition, there were the non-du Pont members of the Executive Committee to be taken into account, particularly Arthur Moxham and Hamilton Barksdale, neither of whom wanted to give up active decision-making within the company.

In 1910 both Pierre and Coleman agreed that before any major change could be made, a new generation of top executives would have to be trained. Coleman was a strong believer in formal organization and he proposed that a new managerial structure be erected to give younger men the experience they would need to move to the top. Pierre, although not enthusiastic about Coleman's ideas, went along.

The resulting reorganization of February 1911 failed. Instead, it helped to start a conflict among the various du Pont family branches and also within the Executive Committee itself. The ensuing struggles stunned Pierre. He found himself the balance wheel as long as he remained in the company, but unable to move toward his goal of stepping aside in favor of his brothers. Blocked, Pierre turned to a sympathetic Coleman, hoping that his cousin's return to active participation in the management of the firm would clear the air.

The period between 1911 and 1914 marked Pierre's time of greatest uncertainty. Because he could not contain what seemed to him irrational personal conflicts within the Executive Committee and between family members, Pierre almost gave up and retired from the fray without achieving his goal. The period also was a crucial one for experimentation with means for achieving an orderly transference of power from one generation of executives to another. It made clear the special problems of a family corporation in perpetuating itself in the top management and demonstrated the difficulty of achieving unity as long as family ownership and control resided in several diverse branches.

## The 1911 Reorganization

The Power Company had prospered since the end of the panic of 1907. From a bottom of $28,027,000 in 1908, gross receipts increased to $30,805,000 in 1909 and to $33,240,000 in 1910. Profits kept pace. From a trough of $3,929,000 in 1907 they climbed to $4,929,000 in 1908, to $5,984,000 in 1909, and to $6,270,000 in 1910. In line with Pierre's program to increase dividends in order to make common stock a still more attractive investment, the dividend rate had been raised from 7% in 1908 to 7¾% in 1909, and 12% in 1910. This had been accomplished while still carrying forward substantial surplus earnings each year ($1,437,000 in 1908, $1,988,000 in 1909, and $1,339,000 in 1910) which were added to the firm's capital.[1]

The company's rising fortunes made early 1911 seem to both Pierre and Coleman an ideal time to launch their efforts to train a new generation of top management. The plan that emerged was clearly Coleman's; most of it was worked out while he was at his estate on Maryland's Eastern Shore. Pierre's main role, although he had consulted with Coleman at every step, was to put the plan into effect, a task that proved far more difficult than either had anticipated.

Coleman had examined the old administrative structure and concluded that it failed to train leaders because both the policy-making and day-to-day operational positions were combined in the same people. This prevented new talent from rising into key operational jobs where it could gain experience and be evaluated. Coleman reasoned that the old organization had the additional disadvantage of forcing top management to narrow its vision by being concerned with routine administration. Top management, he felt, should concentrate exclusively upon such broad problems as raising funds, planning future capital expenditures, and evaluating objectively existing operations. The central idea that guided Coleman in his reorganization was a more explicit separation of routine administration from the long-range policy-making activities.

The new structure, therefore, largely attempted to redefine the duties of the Executive Committee and to change the relationship of major decision-making agents in the Du Pont Company; it did not try to reorder administration within the firm's basic departments (that is, Black Powder, High Explosives, etc.), nor did it propose to change or abandon any of Pierre's channels that funneled information to top management. As in the old organization, Coleman's new structure kept the seven-man Executive Committee in the dominant position, and directly under it the chief administrative office was still the president. The basic change came at the next level. The three manufacturing units, Black Powder, High Explosives, and Smokeless Powder, together with the engineering function and the chemical research facilities (the latter two made into new departments), were placed under a single administrative jurisdiction and headed by a general manager. Specialized nonmanufacturing activities which, in most cases, served the entire company—Sales, Military Sales, Purchasing, Legal Matters, Real Estate, and Development—each retained its separate department and, as under the old system, continued to report directly to the president. (Compare Charts II and III.)

Coleman's ideal was to create in the Executive Committee an experienced group of long-range planners freed from any routine administrative tasks. The members of the Executive Committee would have the title of vice-president but, with the exception of the general manager, have no direct administrative link with any production, engineering, or research department. Coleman, however, was reluctant to cast the operating departments and other functions adrift without some contact with the pool of experience in the Executive Committee.

Therefore, eight new subordinate committees were established: Manufacturing and Sales, Purchasing, Appropriations, Development, Legal, Employees (under which functioned the Board of Pensions and the Board of Benefits and Awards), Reports, and Accounting. (See Chart IV.) The Finance Committee remained separate, although it continued to report to the Executive Committee. The idea behind the establishment of the subordinate committees was to relieve the Executive Committee of routine and detailed work, and yet put at its disposal organs that could undertake at its command sophisticated studies of complex and difficult problems. The subcommittees also were to be a meeting ground for the top policy-making and the top administrative management. Thus, while at least one member of the Executive Committee served on each subcommittee, usually as chairman, he was supported by the appropriate administrative head from one of the operating units.[2]

An analysis of the personnel who took over the major positions in the new structure demonstrates the attempt to separate policy-making decisions from operational problems. The Executive Committee, the long-range planning and policy-making group, remained the preserve of the old guard. It consisted of Coleman du Pont (president), Pierre du Pont (acting president and treasurer), Alfred I. du Pont, Hamilton Barksdale, Arthur Moxham, Charles L. Patterson (his title vice-president in charge of sales was eliminated), and J. Amory Haskell. All existing department heads except Pierre and Patterson were to give up their jobs as heads of departments. Only Barksdale, the new general manager, had administrative supervision of a routine executive type. And Barksdale's responsibilities were supposed to be of a more general nature, since his more routine duties were to fall on an assistant general manager. That position was to go to Pierre's brother Irénée, who both Coleman and Pierre hoped would soon become the company's leader. At the manufacturing level, two of the former departments had new heads: Harry G. Haskell in High Explosives and H. Fletcher Brown in Smokeless Powder. Frank Connable, at Alfred's insistence, carried on in Black Powder. William Ramsay headed the new Engineering Department; Charles L. Reese, a new Chemical Research group; and Colonel Edmund D. Buckner, a new Military Sales Department. Other department heads tended to remain the same as before: Sales, Charles L. Patterson; Purchasing, Frank G. Tallman; Legal, John P. Laffey; Development, R. R. M. ("Ruly") Carpenter; and Real Estate, Daniel Cauffiel.

The attempt to mix policy-making and operational personnel in the Executive Committee's subcommittees can be seen in the composition of those to which Pierre was assigned. The Purchasing Committee had three members: Frank G. Tallman, chairman, Pierre du Pont, and Hamilton Barksdale; the Appropriations Committee, four members: Pierre, who acted as chairman, J. Amory Haskell, Harry G. Haskell, and Irénée du Pont; Pierre also acted as chairman of the Development Committee, which included three additional men: Arthur Moxham, R. R. M. Carpenter, and Charles L. Reese.

Pierre's task of putting the new plan into effect was very difficult, and the results proved disappointing. One trouble stemmed from the timing. Coleman devised his plan at the height of an illness which made it difficult for him to be active in Wilmington and to circulate among the key men on the Executive Committee. Much of the plan was hammered out by Coleman at "The Moors," his place on the Eastern Shore near Hillspoint, Maryland,

and details were discussed with Pierre, Arthur Moxham, and Hamilton Barksdale either in person or by letter. Outside of Coleman's three collaborators, few knew of the reorganization more than a few weeks prior to its adoption.

But the plan's first setback resulted from Alfred I. du Pont's opposition. Ever since his divorce from Bessie G. du Pont in 1906 and his remarriage to Alicia Bradford in 1907, Alfred's actions had been the center of a controversy within the du Pont clan. Some of the family, like Colonel Henry, strongly disapproved, while others, such as William, defended Alfred. Coleman, sensitive to Colonel Henry's wishes, advised Alfred to retire from active participation in the company. Although Pierre remained friendly with Alfred, he felt that Bessie had been treated unfairly and he became her financial guardian. Alfred did not retire, nor did he break openly with his two cousins. The contretemps did, however, reduce his workload with the company. In 1906 he was absent for six months in South Dakota while he established residence there for a divorce, and during that year he surrendered his place on the Executive Committee to Frank Connable, who also assumed Alfred's duties in the Black Powder Department (although Alfred retained his title of vice-president). Not until March 1909 did Alfred replace Connable on the Powder Company's Executive Committee, a group over which Pierre then presided in place of the ill Coleman. From then on both Pierre's recollection and the minutes confirm that Alfred was a "very regular attendant at the meetings."[3]

Coleman's physical absence from Wilmington, the coolness between the two cousins, together with the general preoccupation with the antitrust suit, helped explain why Alfred was not consulted about the new organization. Furthermore, administrative details bored Alfred, and it was natural that Pierre would not seek Alfred's advice.

On January 18, 1911, Coleman made a special trip from the Eastern Shore to Wilmington, and for the first time presented the new plan of organization to the Executive Committee. Pierre chaired the meeting; Alfred was absent. By the plan previously mentioned, all officials were to resign from their administrative posts, and the president would appoint the general manager and the heads of the Sales, Purchasing, Legal, Development, and Real Estate departments. The general manager was to be left free to name the chiefs of the various units under his control. For Pierre, Coleman, Moxham, and Barksdale this was a formality, as they had already decided who would occupy the new positions.[4] The Executive Committee voted to put Coleman's plan into operation on February 1, 1911, and it appointed Pierre, Hamilton Barksdale, and Arthur Moxham a committee to make last-minute changes and adjustments as necessary.[5]

Under the new plan Alfred was still to be a vice-president and a member of the Executive Committee, but would give up his titular role as head of

CHART III

URE AFTER

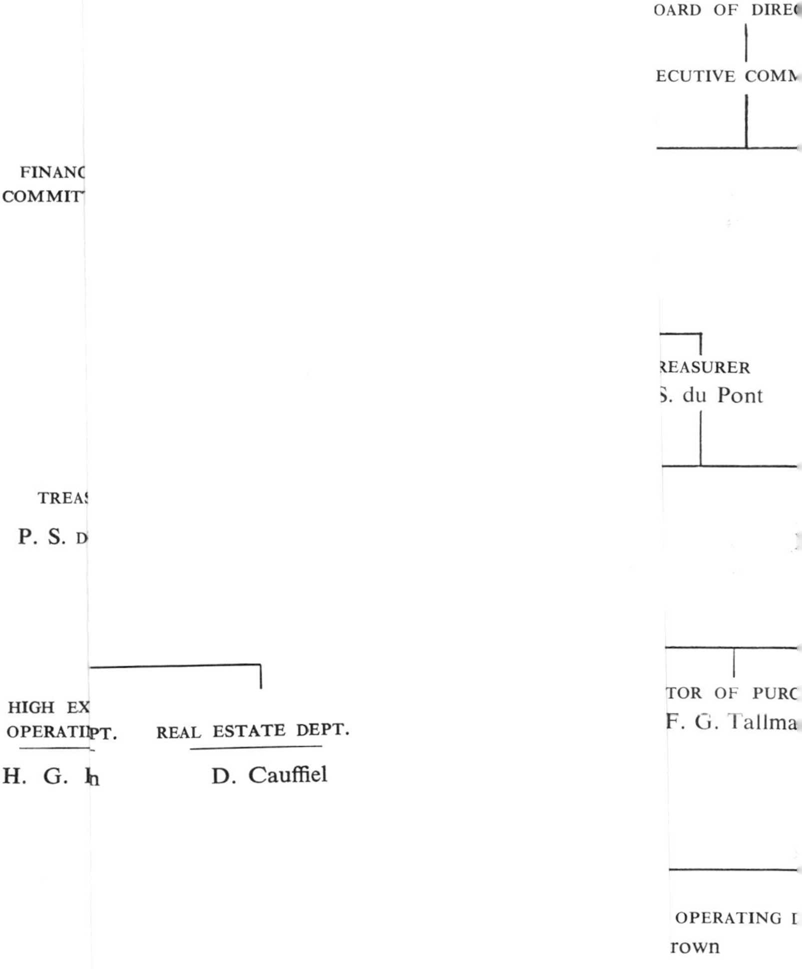

OARD OF DIRE(

ECUTIVE COMM

FINAN(
COMMIT"

REASURER

S. du Pont

TREAS

P. S. D

HIGH EX
OPERATI PT.          REAL ESTATE DEPT.

H. G. h               D. Cauffiel

TOR OF PUR(

F. G. Tallma

OPERATING [

rown

THE REORGANIZATION OF 1911

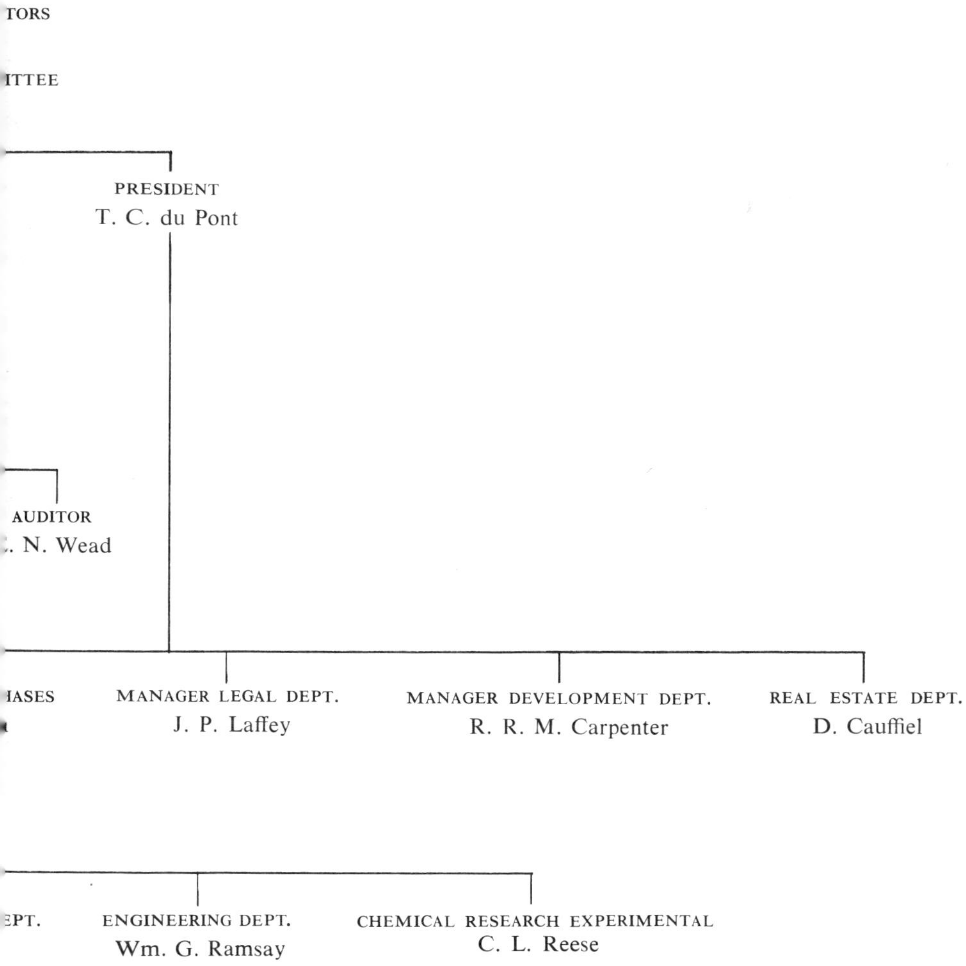

TORS

ITTEE

PRESIDENT
T. C. du Pont

AUDITOR
. N. Wead

IASES    MANAGER LEGAL DEPT.    MANAGER DEVELOPMENT DEPT.    REAL ESTATE DEPT.
J. P. Laffey     R. R. M. Carpenter     D. Cauffiel

EPT.    ENGINEERING DEPT.    CHEMICAL RESEARCH EXPERIMENTAL
Wm. G. Ramsay     C. L. Reese

Black Powder. He reacted with disbelief and anger when he learned of the change. It "was sprung on me so suddenly, and approved so soon afterwards, that I had little time or opportunity to express my views for and against it," he wrote Coleman on January 27, 1911.[6] It did not take Alfred long to formulate his ideas. On the same day he wrote the Executive Committee that he felt that the change had "not . . . been given the careful thought which it should have had before being finally adopted. . . ." Alfred went on to say that the company "during its existence, thrived under the old plan of organization to a remarkable extent; and that this success has been due largely to past methods, and not in spite of them."[7] Alfred asked that action on the new organization be delayed, that its provisions be put into effect "over a period of not less than six months, preferably longer." Alfred particularly urged that the present heads of the manufacturing departments "retain positions which will permit . . . the new Departmental Heads to consult them."[8] Alfred mistrusted Barksdale and wanted to keep him out of Black Powder. In short, Alfred wanted to continue his old role as an adviser and overseer of Black Powder manufacturing.

Coleman did not want to fight with Alfred, and he quickly wrote a conciliatory though formal and distant letter. "This is a matter," said Coleman, "that should have consideration by the [Executive] Committee and I have asked Mr. Pierre du Pont to bring it up at the next meeting . . . so that you can have a full opportunity of presenting your views to the members of the Committee."[9] Pierre, however, felt differently. He realized that the damage had been done and that further discussion would only deepen the wound. "The less said the sooner mended" was his motto.[10]

Alfred's rather bitter reply to Coleman's overture confirmed the wisdom of Pierre's attitude. Wrote Alfred to Coleman: "I beg to call your attention to the fact that my views are clearly expressed in my letter to the Executive Committee. . . . My one regret was that I had not opportunity to present the matter to the Executive Committee before the scheme was approved in detail . . . as I am confident that my logic is sound and it may have had the effect of making the Executive Committee's action somewhat more conservative. But," Alfred concluded, "to bring up the letter for discussion at a meeting . . . after the scheme of reorganization has been fully approved by every member save myself, it will only result in a waste of valuable time and nothing will be accomplished."[11]

Alfred's opposition proved to be an ill omen rather than an actual hindrance. Pierre was right; a short bit of time and avoiding the subject preserved Alfred's active cooperation. Alfred continued to serve on the Finance Committee. The Executive Committee records show that he attended the vast majority of the meetings from 1911 through 1914. And, as already mentioned, Alfred went with Pierre in March of 1912 to the crucial court session in Philadelphia, where the government—represented by President Taft and Attorney General Wickersham—put forward proposals for a final antitrust decree.

The real problem was, as Alfred suggested, that the new organization in practice did exactly the opposite of what it was supposed to do. Partly the reason lay in the choice of the general manager, Hamilton Barksdale. Probably better than anyone else Coleman du Pont knew Barksdale's limitations. The new general manager had performed well in his past job as head of the High Explosives Operative Department. He knew plant management and the special problems in the manufacture of dynamite, but he had been constitutionally unable to delegate authority. This was an unfortunate trait for a man who was to occupy a position created to give subordinates enough power and responsibility to prove themselves. Actually Coleman had wanted to make Barksdale a vice-president (like the rest of the Executive Committee) to serve in the capacity of general planner and adviser, much the same as Moxham. Coleman really desired that Irénée become general manager and start obtaining the experience he would need if he was to become president.

Barksdale, however, pushed hard for an opportunity to become general manager, and he had urged Coleman to give him a chance at the job. Barksdale had also received strong support from his old friend, J. Amory Haskell.[12] Pierre, who had grown to respect Barksdale deeply, was less aware of his limitations. Besides, Pierre disliked the idea of forcing his young brother ahead too rapidly, especially since this would cause Barksdale's resentment. Pierre also felt that Barksdale would train Irénée, who was to be assistant to the general manager. Pierre's active support for Barksdale had caused Coleman to consent reluctantly with "an absolute understanding that . . . [Barksdale] would find someone to take his place within two years."[13]

Thus, Barksdale received this crucial position. Coleman, seeking to make the best out of the new start, asked Pierre, prior to the initiation of the new organization, to send a circular letter to all plants and sales offices giving Barksdale a good send-off.[14] Pierre, harassed with the full responsibilities of the presidency, sent a routine announcement. "You will note," Pierre wrote Coleman, "that my circular letter failed to include a proper 'bouquet' for Barksdale but it . . . [is] too late to rectify that."[15] On this happy note the plan took effect.

It did not take long for Coleman to have misgivings about the new general manager. At the end of March Pierre wrote his cousin, who was still at his residence on Maryland's Eastern Shore: "The organization seems to be working well so far, but I cannot say that Mr. Barksdale has been in any measure relieved. I hope," Pierre concluded, "that after a few months he will be able to relieve himself of details." In disgust Coleman scribbled on the margin of the letter, "He never will—not built that way."[16] The next years gave no reason for Coleman to change his mind, and Pierre could do nothing but quietly agree. Barksdale could not understand the cousins' attitude.

Three years later, when Coleman and Pierre again reorganized the company, abolishing the position of general manager and finally pushing Barksdale up to a purely policy-making position, he protested strongly. Coleman in a conciliatory, but frank, letter told the erstwhile general manager that "I have felt the work you have been doing for the past three years has been both a loss to the Company in not giving you more important matters to attend to and unfair to you. . . . Frankly, Barkie," Coleman concluded, "I cannot understand your present attitude when P.S., Al. and I all tell you we believe you fitted for bigger, better, more important things, [and] believe the present grindstone, confining routine work is not fair to you. . . ."[17]

Barksdale's inability to give the younger men a chance to run their departments was not the only flaw in the new organization. The committee system posed even more of a problem. Right from the first, Coleman, whom Pierre kept informed on the progress of the reorganization, complained that the "members of the Executive Committee have not entirely grasped my idea of the re-organization. . . ."[18] In theory the subgroups were supposed to relieve the Executive Committee of work and to provide a meeting place for the routine administrators and top management. Pierre and Coleman both agreed that the committees should initiate little, if any, work, but should largely resolve questions either passed up to them from the various departments or down to them from the Executive Committee itself. But when Pierre came to writing up the duties of each new committee, he found it hard to put the ideal into words. The Manufacturing and Sales Committee, for example, had the responsibility for passing "upon questions of general policy in connection with the main manufacturing operations such as the character and distribution of manufacturing units including the location of new plants and the abandonment of old," or, in selling, such questions of general advance or reductions in prices.[19] The danger lurking in this description was that a zealous committee would insert itself into the running of the various departments. The mere presence of a member of the Executive Committee, who usually served as chairman, might overawe the operational men in the various departments, who would be reluctant to disagree with their superiors. How could Harry Haskell in High Explosives really stand up against a Manufacturing and Sales Committee that had on it such strong-minded old-guard members as his older brother, J. A. Haskell, Alfred I. du Pont, Hamilton Barksdale, C. L. Patterson, and F. L. Connable? Such important questions as the closing of the less efficient plants and probable locations for expansion would almost by default be decided by the committee. The system, instead of fostering new executive ability, encouraged government by committee.

In a little more than a year dissatisfaction with the plan became acute, and the Executive Committee appointed a special subcommittee consisting of Pierre, Arthur Moxham, and J. A. Haskell to study the committee system. Pierre and Moxham in their majority report of August 7, 1912, found the record "inconsistent and far from clear." "Nowhere," they said, was there a "clear-cut definition as to what particular [committee] duties are to be considered as 'Executive' and what as 'Advisory,' and the power embodied in the word 'Executive' is not defined." They further discovered committee meddling in the affairs of the operating departments. To stop this, they suggested that all committees become "unit" committees, that is, confined to the problems of a specific department and that the representative from that department become chairman of the committee, with increased power to make decisions.[20] This meant the separation of the Manufacturing and Sales Committee, a recommendation that J. A. Haskell opposed in a minority report asserting that the majority of matters handled by that organ were of joint interest to the manufacturing and sales departments.[21] All agreed, however, that there were too many committees and that the system had increased, rather than lessened, work for the members of the Executive Committee.

On September 10, 1912, the Executive Committee, sitting as a whole and with Coleman's approval, rejected both the majority and minority reports because neither attacked the central problem, the reduction in the number of committees. Pierre had argued that it was still too early to make a final judgment, and he had asked that the majority's recommendations be given a trial. Despite this, however, the Executive Committee voted, as of January 1, 1913, to abolish the Manufacturing and Sales, Legal, Employees, Appropriations, Reports, Accounting, and Development committees. This would have left only the Finance and Purchasing committees.[22] The Executive Committee did not stand by its decision, and one month later it voted to reconsider its stand; in December it revoked its action and called for still further study.[23]

The treasurer's sentiments undoubtedly swayed the Executive Committee to reverse itself. Pierre was not against change; he knew that the Powder Company's administrative structure required modification, but already in late 1912 he was beginning to be even more concerned about the difficult problem of who would lead the company in the years ahead.

The failure of the general managership and the other organizational reforms of 1911 must be understood against a background of personality clashes. It is true, as Pierre soon discovered, that the committee system did not lend itself to building strong independent executives in the various departments, but a squabble among the Du Pont top management dwarfed this problem.

Despite the Powder Company's large size and rapid growth, and its adoption of a modern and scientific system of management, Pierre and his two cousins continued to regard it as a family preserve. Coleman, in his more emotional moments, thought of the company as "My Baby."[24] Although he had said that the "President of the Company should be the man who had worked up to that position on merit," he concluded that the "position of President should always be filled by a du Pont."[25] Pierre admitted to the "same sentimental attachment" and "family pride" in the "old institution," and Pierre, even more than Coleman, felt that a du Pont should always lead the company.[26] These views complicated any program of reorganization that had as its aim the development of new talent and leadership.

But it was Coleman's personal ambitions that created the real crises. T.C., who turned fifty in 1913, was still a long way from retirement and there was no objective reason why he should have stepped down from the Du Pont Company presidency in 1914. Although illness had sapped his strength between 1909 and 1912, by 1913 he seemed to be on the mend; indeed by December of that year he felt so well that he declared himself completely recovered.[27] It was not sickness, therefore, that forced Coleman to retire, but his restless nature. Finding the Du Pont Company routine and Wilmington dull, Coleman had started to transfer his activities to New York City in 1910. Then he put $500,000 into a syndicate that constructed the McAlpin Hotel at 34th and Broadway. One of Coleman's partners was Charles P. Taft, brother of President Taft.[28] The glamour and prestige of this venture made Coleman hungry for more.

In January of 1912 the home office of New York's Equitable Life Assurance Society burned, and Coleman formed a corporation to erect an office building on the blackened site. The skyscraper, when completed, contained more usable space than any other business building in the world. By terms of the contract, signed in October of 1912, Coleman paid $13.5 million for the burned-out plot, and he agreed to complete his 36-story structure by May 1915. The building's estimated cost was $14.9 million, but before it was finished the project absorbed nearly twice that amount, or about $28.5 million. Equitable agreed to lease three floors of the giant edifice, and it financed a considerable portion of Coleman's venture by taking a long-term mortgage in lieu of cash for the purchase price of the land. For the building itself, Equitable loaned $20.5 million.[29]

Coleman's Equitable Building devoured ever more of his time and it was this, together with the lure of still further business opportunities in New York, which made him try to lessen his responsibilities to the Du Pont Company. Coleman was exasperated because the 1911 reorganization had not fostered young leadership.[30] He blamed Hamilton Barksdale for not advancing Irénée du Pont, the assistant general manager, into the general managership. By 1913 it had become clear that Barksdale wanted to remain general manager himself. "From what has recently developed," wrote Coleman in early 1914, "I do not think Barkie has had any idea of making him [Irénée] General Manager . . . and think perhaps he never did have the idea of recommending him for that position."[31]

For Coleman, therefore, the 1911 reorganization had proved a major disappointment. Barksdale had dominated the manufacturing division, inserting himself into the most trivial details. Furthermore, in both 1913 and 1914 the Powder Company felt the full effect of the antitrust breakup; this slack was magnified by a national business recession that reduced the total demand for explosives. The company's gross receipts dropped from a high of $36,524,000 in 1912 to $26,675,000 in 1913, and net earnings from $6,871,000 in 1912 to $5,347,000 in 1913. This forced a reduction in the rate of dividend from 12% to 8% (1913). Clearly the Powder Company needed a strong hand and close attention.

Pierre was the logical person to provide the needed leadership. At forty-four, he was a comparatively young man. But Pierre felt tired. Except, he wrote, "for business trips to California in 1904 and Chile in 1905 and to Europe in 1910 and 1913 [he] had not taken any prolonged vacation from home office duties since March of 1902."[32] And Pierre was more eager than ever to devote more time to Longwood, his country estate.

As years progressed, Pierre had improved Longwood, but the press of work that came with his assumption of the Du Pont Company's acting presidency in January 1909 had taken most of his time. He had begun to reconstruct the gardens and the house. With the settlement of the antitrust suit and the reorganization that followed, he began to look forward to retirement from business so that he could devote much of his time to the park. By 1912 his house there had been remodeled. The home was not large or lavish by the standards of those mansions built by tycoons such as William K. Vanderbilt, whose residence occupied a square block between Fifty-first and Fifty-second streets on Fifth Avenue in New York. Pierre's house, nevertheless, provided ample room to entertain and required a staff of servants.

In September 1912 Pierre started an instruction pamphlet that prescribed the duties of his employees. This book, which came to more than 140 pages, provided an excellent insight into the style of life at Longwood. Pierre often entertained at his country estate; his table rivaled that of any well-managed house of that period. Breakfast, served between 7:15 and 7:30 on weekdays and at 9:00 A.M. on Sundays, usually consisted of three courses: fruit, cereal; coffee with hot bread; meat or fish, eggs, potatoes, eggplant, or another vegetable. The 1:00 P.M. lunch was comparatively light and offered rolls, meat, fish or eggs, olives, pickles and other relishes such as garden-fresh celery or radishes. For dessert there was pie, pudding, or fruit. Dinner at 7:00 P.M. was the most elaborate meal. Served in six courses it started with hors d'oeuvres, such as caviar; soup; roast, poultry, or other meat; several vegetables, celery, olives, and other relishes; a salad; dessert, and finally coffee.

Pierre was fastidious. He looked after the wine cellar himself and he left detailed instructions for the care of his house. The silver, for example, was in charge of the caretaker. The tableware and nearly all other pieces were plated and hence of little real value; but the knives, forks, and spoons were sterling silver. Pierre directed that they be "guarded and counted frequently, so as to insure against loss." All tableware was to be polished at least once a week or more frequently if necessary. Pierre even concerned himself with the use of candles. "The metal candle sticks throughout the house," he instructed, "are to be placed in their various positions about the dwelling each morning and, at the same time, are to be replenished with fresh candles, excepting the single bed room candlesticks, where the partially burned candles may be allowed to remain." Pierre's directions for the care of every phase of his house and garden were equally detailed.[33]

In anticipation of spending more time at Longwood, Pierre had already taken steps to provide an able successor in the Treasurer's Department. Starting in 1909, the year he assumed the burden of acting president, Pierre began to transfer more and more of his chores as treasurer to his capable subordinate, John J. Raskob. On August 30, 1911, Raskob became the official assistant treasurer, but, in reality, even at that date he was performing all the duties of that office.[34] In January of 1914, Pierre had Raskob made the official treasurer.

Pierre never seriously considered that Alfred I. du Pont could lead the firm. In Pierre's words, "Alfred disliked 'office work' . . . looked down upon it," and of consequence "had no ambitions for a leadership that required him to be chained to a desk." Besides, an impairment of Alfred's hearing, which was noticeable as early as 1902, made it "difficult if not impossible for him to conduct even a small meeting, such as that of the Executive Committee."[35]

While Alfred could not take over, Pierre definitely wanted a young team to carry the burden of work in the Powder Company. Two of his brothers, Irénée and Lammot, were the brightest of the rising du Pont stars. Pierre hoped that they, his handpicked treasurer J. J. Raskob, his brother-in-law R. R. M. Carpenter, together with other talented younger men such as Major William Ramsay, Frank Connable, Harry Haskell, Walter Carpenter, William Coyne, Frank Tallman, and H. Fletcher Brown, would inherit the Powder Company's top leadership. For this to happen, however, there had to be a modification in the Powder Company's organization and its personnel. Pierre knew that Barksdale, Alfred I. du Pont, and Haskell (albeit for different reasons) wanted few changes in the old ways and they did not see any pressing need for new faces.

*Reorganization 1914*

The last months of 1913 were a difficult time for Pierre. He agreed with Coleman that the 1911 reorganization had failed to produce new leadership. He recognized, however, that it was the force of personality rather than a defect in organizational structure that thwarted the rise of new men. The problem, as Pierre saw it, was how to move the older generation of managers aside gracefully. Pierre, perhaps because he viewed his own family as the chief beneficiary of change, hesitated to take strong action himself. In his view only Coleman had enough prestige within the whole du Pont family and among the top executives to remold the company's structure and install new managers without a major row. Pierre urged Coleman not to retire, but again to become a full-time president. Thus Coleman, against his real wishes, returned to Wilmington in January of 1914, and for the first time since 1909 he gave his total commitment to the company he had done so much to build.

Pierre expected Coleman to concentrate his attention on reorganization and then to ease Irénée into the presidency. Coleman's actions during the first few weeks of 1914 pleased Pierre, for the two together worked out a plan of organization that the Executive Committee approved on February 9, 1914, and that took effect on March 1.[36] The new structure abolished the subcommittees of the Executive Committee and the position of general manager. The purpose of the plan was, oddly enough, almost identical with that of the 1911 reorganization. Coleman explained: "The present men who compose the Executive Committee should fit themselves for bigger things by frequent contact with the big things done elsewhere, and with the big men who guide or do these things. To have the necessary time for this they should give up that portion [of their duty] which is connected with the practical routine." The president observed that twelve years previously the "Executive Committee performed simultaneously, (1) those functions usually performed by Directors and important officers of the company and (2) those functions performed by the head of the practical side of the business."[37] In fine, Coleman still sought to separate policy-making activities from the operational routine. Thus, he tried once again to create a structure that removed the Executive Committee and its members as far from active administration as possible. In a preamble to the new plan, Coleman wrote: "The Board of Directors and their Executive Committee delegate to the President full responsibility for the management of the Company's affairs and the results obtained thereunder."[38] Although both the board and the Executive Committee were to retain "the right to interfere in the management," Coleman emphasized that this power ought to be used only in unusual circumstances. He emphasized that the president was normally to make "independent decisions" and that the chief executive would refer to the "Executive Committee such broad questions of policy or action as may be properly set before them."[39] The new structure created eight vice-presidents subordinate to the president. Hamilton Barksdale was to be vice-president in charge of the Manufacturing, Chemical, Engineering and Light, Heat and Power divisions; C. L. Patterson, Non-Government Sales; E. G. Buckner, Government Sales; Irénée du Pont, Purchasing, Nitrates and Development; and Pierre du Pont, Auditing, Treasury and Accounting. In addition, J. A. Haskell, Alfred I du Pont, and Arthur J. Moxham were made vice-presidents without specific duties. The make-up of the Executive Committee remained the same as before: Coleman du Pont, Pierre du Pont, Alfred du Pont, Hamilton Barksdale, Charles L. Patterson, J. Amory Haskell, and Arthur Moxham. Coleman made it clear that the vice-presidents were acting only in a "supervisory capacity" and that the heads of the various departments were to be given wide latitude and held "responsible not only for the results obtained but also for their judgment in exercising their authority."[40]

Pierre approved of the plan, but it was instituted only over the strong opposition of Hamilton Barksdale and J. Amory Haskell, both of whom voted against it when it came before the Executive Committee.[41] Barksdale's behavior annoyed Coleman greatly. Prior to the adoption of the new organization, the general manager had threatened to resign, and he won the support of Haskell, who pestered Coleman not to make the changes.[42] Coleman wrote bitterly that "in the matter of organization of the company, my own mind as to what is best for the company is as clear as a bell, is just what it was twelve years ago, and is opposed as it was and by the same people in the same way it was twelve years ago." He would gladly have relieved Barksale of even supervisory responsibility and made him, as Arthur Moxham had long been, a vice-president without specific administrative duties.[43]

Pierre, who felt that Barksdale's opposition had a legitimate, although distorted, basis, and that the general manager might be brought to see the right way, had persuaded Coleman to make Barksdale a vice-president in charge of actual departments. Even so, Coleman wrote Barksdale a long official letter explaining his new duties. "I," wrote the president, "should like you to . . . be responsible for the Department[s] indicated and in distributing the duties, I think . . . [that you should] take the same position in this case as was taken by me from 1905 to 1908, letting Mr. Harry Haskell take the place you then occupied as head of the High Explosives Operating Department, Mr. Connable take the place Mr. Alfred I. du Pont held then, and Mr. Brown the place Mr. J. A. Haskell held when he was head of the Smokeless Powder Operating Department . . . provided that this does not require more than one-quarter of your time. If it should require more than one-quarter of your time, please

EMPLOYEES
COMMITTEE
Alfred I. du Pont, Chairman
F. L. Connable
Wm. G. Ramsay

REPORTS
COMMITTEE
A. J. Moxham, Chairman
Alfred I. du Pont
R. H. Dunham

ACCOUNTING
COMMITTEE
R. H. Dunham, Chairman
Irénée du Pont
J. J. Raskob

BOARD OF PENSIONS
J. P. Laffey, Chairman
H. G. Haskell
H. F. Brown
Wm. Coyne
Geo. Patterson

BOARD OF BENEFITS & AWARDS
J. P. Laffey, Chairman
H. G. Haskell
H. F. Brown
Wm. Coyne
Geo. Patterson

brought up the question of William's directorship. Barksdale, who disliked William more than he did Moxham, "was in bitter opposition."[47] Pierre was even more hostile because he valued Cousin Henry's and Barksdale's feelings more than William's pride. Pierre later wrote, "To make William a director seemed unthinkable even if [he] . . . did deserve recognition."[48] Despite this, Coleman felt guilty about William's long exclusion and decided justice lay on his side.

This conflict provoked a crisis. Pierre's vehement opposition stunned Coleman, who had counted on his cousin's support. Time did not alter Coleman's feeling that Pierre had let him down. Toward the end of 1914 Coleman's illness returned and he had to remove himself from active leadership. In December he went to the Mayo Clinic for an operation that would save his life. From the Hotel Green in Pasadena, California, where he had gone to recuperate, Coleman sent an anguished, handwritten letter that tried to explain his views to Pierre. He wrote his cousin:

> from say April 1914 though I had taken up the active duties of president more at your request than for any 10 other reasons, you took several positions that from a business standpoint I could not understand I could not approve and *would* not go against you though my business judgment was not with yours. . . . It became evident [the president continued] that one of us had to take a back seat . . . neither being built that way this was impossible, so I then offered for the good of the Co. (and your family) to sell (or buy) at a figure that I thought so low you would jump at, and with your brothers to help and brothers in law with you, it was best for me to take a back seat, and you to take the lines, to my surprise you thought the price high and did not buy.[49]

Pierre, who wrote a memorandum upon receipt of Coleman's letter, explained that he had not accepted his cousin's offer because it was made after a heated argument "over the value of some of our men and over methods of solving the company's problems." In fact, Pierre felt that T.C. did not really desire to sell. With some emotion Pierre told Coleman at the time of the affair "that I did not care to break the partnership which we had established. . . . It was evident," he felt, "that our failure to agree was influencing T.C. to make a suggestion contrary to his own wishes."[50]

Coleman made his proposal to sell in early August 1914. Pierre's rejection of Coleman's offer contained an impassioned plea to continue as usual. This soothed matters for only a few days. In reality neither had changed his views. On August 26, Pierre again approached Coleman, arguing against William's appointment as a director and criticizing Moxham's behavior. Coleman, who had actually never recovered from his gallstone operation in 1909, was again feeling ill. Pierre's constant pressure proved too much for him. That afternoon Coleman took pencil in hand and on a sheet of graph paper wrote Pierre a confidential letter that set forth his views as forcefully as possible.

From what you told me this morning I realize for the first time that you are from a business standpoint very bitter against Moxham and that you think he has been the cause of all or nearly all our present troubles, this was a surprise to me because I think his criticisms have been of value to the Company and should be more valuable. My feeling is that Barkie's position is more directly responsible for our present situation than any other one thing, or ten things. From what you said this morning my feeling toward Barkie *in a business way* is a good deal like yours toward Moxham. On Sept. 1st I will have had 8 months of the hardest most disagreeable and unsatisfactory period of my life. . . .

1st. I took the Presidency Jany 1st/14 against my own personal interest and desires knowing it would mean a financial loss of about half a million dollars to me and it has and knowing I would have disagreeable work but because *you wanted me to,* expecting your support but don't feel I have had it. 2nd. I have offered to get out and give you my proxy for a term of years but this did not seem agreeable to you. 3rd. I offered to give a million dollars in stock rather than do what I conceive to be simple justice [appoint William a director]. 4th. I have offered to back any plan you want *because it is your plan* wheather [*sic*] I approve it or not.

5th. The Powder Co. I consider largely "My Baby" and as such dislike more than I am able to express to part with it and only two things make this possible. 1st my fondness for you and 2nd my fondness for it, and you will never know how hard it was for me to come to the conclusion that I ought to take a chance of parting with it from a sentimental stand point as well as from a practical stand point in the later [*sic*] case to agree to burden myself with additional obligations at this time and only my great love for "my baby" and absolute faith in its future causes me to do it. Should you buy my interest you would have my unqualified support and co-operation and visa verse [*sic*].

6th I will make one more offer; to leave to arbitration any differences between us by the three best men we can get not personally interested, paying them well for their work and agree that we will both be bound by their decision and on any point that we may differ carry out their decision.

7th I have always said and felt when a President cannot control his board of directors and have the support of his board it was time for him to quit and for the board to get a new President. I am now so close to the line that were it not for my beleif [*sic*] that it would make your task harder my resignation would go in to take effect Sept. 1st.

8th I feel I have done all mortal man can do and were it not that *I know you are sincere* in the position you take and don't realize that you are letting your heart govern your head and did I not know you are doing what you honestly think best and that you believe I am doing what I honestly think best I would have raised cane long ago as it is life is too short good freinds [*sic*] too scarce to continue longer as we are going so I sincerely hope you will do either No. 5 or No. 6.[51]

Pierre did not receive this letter until August 27. It was accompanied by a second handwritten note in which Coleman asked his cousin to take again the office of acting president on September 1, 1914. Coleman promised to "keep hands off on any future questions unless you want to talk to me."[52]

Coleman's letters moved Pierre deeply. "Your interest in the Powder Co. is justified by all that you have done for its organization and subsequent conduct," he wrote Coleman in reply. "There seems to be no reason for either [of us] withdrawing in favor of the other, but there is every reason for standing together as heretofore. Before giving further thought to parting, let us take another try at it on the old basis as you suggest. I will accept the Acting Presidency, or perhaps it will be better to assume your duties under the title of Vice President which I now have, and will endeavor to carry out a successful policy guided by the past and the information that has come up during the discussions of the past eight months."[53] Coleman agreed.

Thus, Pierre, with the title of vice-president, again moved into the Powder Company's top policy-making position. In a show of genuine compromise he supported William's election to the board of directors, and nomination to the Finance Committee as well. But Pierre's most immediate task was to institute further reorganization. Both he and Coleman realized that the administrative readjustment of March 1, 1914, had not provided the company with active new leadership. Coleman blamed Barksdale, who continued to meddle in the affairs of the divisions he supervised. Pierre saw Moxham as the villain. Actually there was some truth in both views. The main problem, however, was that although Coleman's rhetoric had deemphasized the role of the Executive Committee in practice the old guard continued to dominate that committee, and they kept supervisory control over the major company activities as well. The personalities of the older men—whether Hamilton Barksdale or Charles Patterson or Arthur Moxham—together with the traditions that had been established for years, were so strong that simply drawing an organization chart could not change the company's administration.

By August 1914 both Pierre and Coleman had recognized that the solution of their problem lay in a change of men rather than of organization. Since Pierre did not want to assume the presidency, Coleman approached Irénée, who refused outright. Irénée wrote to Coleman: "Pierre's desire not to be President should not be given consideration. It is his duty to take the position because it is to the Company's best interest that he do so. In weighing my opinion in this matter," continued Irénée, "please bear in mind that I have worked shoulder to shoulder with Pierre for twelve years, and I know him and myself better than any of you. If you have sufficient confidence in my judgment to risk me in the position of Chairman, you should surely take it in a matter in which I am so well posted."[54]

The agreement that Pierre piloted through the board of directors and that took effect on September 19, 1914 (see Chart V), reflected the combined wishes of its three major architects: Pierre, Coleman, and Irénée.

Although Coleman continued as president, and Pierre took the title of acting president, the real responsibilities for administering the company were transferred to a younger group of men. The change removed from the Executive Committee all the incumbents, including Coleman and even Pierre himself. Although Alfred I. du Pont, Hamilton Barksdale, J. Amory Haskell, Arthur Moxham, and Charles Patterson were retained as advisers with the title of vice-president, they were stripped of all their administrative and executive responsibilities. An entirely new Executive Committee emerged, with Irénée as chairman; Frank Connable, the new head of Purchasing; H. Fletcher Brown, director of Smokeless Powder; R. R. M. Carpenter, director of the Development Department; William Coyne, director of the Sales Department; Lammot du Pont, director of the Black Powder Department; Harry G. Haskell, director of the High Explosives Department; and John J. Raskob, treasurer.

The board of directors amended the Powder Company's by-laws to omit the requirement that the president be a member of the Executive and Finance committees. To provide the chief stockholders with an active check on the actions of the new Executive Committee, the Finance Committee was expanded from three to four members—Pierre, Alfred, William, and Coleman du Pont. The Finance Committee was no longer responsible to the Executive Committee but reported solely to the board of directors. Among that committee's important duties were the recommendation of the dividends to be paid, "the approval of the annual or semi-annual estimate of appropriations," the "approval of all detail estimates of appropriations committing the company to an expenditure of $300,000 or more at the time the Executive Committee recommends starting work," the authorization of "appropriations not in the annual or semi-annual estimate" which committed the company to any expenditure of $150,000 or more, and the approval of future capital expenditure plans.[55]

In reality, Pierre and Coleman hoped that the Finance Committee would approve, almost as a matter of routine, the recommendations made by the fresh young Executive Committee. Thus, the Powder Company's organization had swung a full cycle since 1911. The new Executive Committee had, "subject to the Board of Directors and Finance Committee . . . . full power in the control of the Company's affairs."[56] Although Pierre and his cousin hoped that the new committee would throw as much responsibility on to the heads of the individual departments as possible, they did not repeat the mistake of 1911: that is, they did not attempt to place in the departmental slots young men who were immediately supervised by a representative of the old guard with executive and administrative responsibility and authority over his subordinates. Pierre and Coleman recognized that organizational schemes alone could not create and install new leadership; it was the responsibility of each generation to train and appoint a new top management and then step aside and let the new executives take control. If this were done early enough, the old could lend encouragement and advice to the new.

The Executive Committee that Pierre and Coleman installed proved a happy choice, for it was to provide the talent needed to meet the challenge of World War I. Writing years later, in 1941, Pierre gave Coleman lavish credit. "Coming events," he said, "demanded youth, optimism, courage and cooperation. This Coleman gave to the Company in the new Executive Committee of 1914, probably his most important contribution to the Company's success and renown. No other person would have done this—no other person could have done it. Coleman's genius was fed by master strokes of foresight, once more he seized upon a difficult situation to place the Company in line for more successful development."[57] While Pierre may have overstated the case, there is no question that both he and his brother Irénée would not have appointed an almost entirely fresh Executive Committee. Both, for example, would have retained Hamilton Barksdale and probably J. A. Haskell.[58] Had Coleman been left to his own judgment, the change most likely would have come earlier, perhaps in 1911, and certainly in 1912, after he recognized the failure of the 1911 reorganization. As it was, Coleman shaped his ideas and planning to meet the strong objections of the older members of the Executive Committee, notably Haskell and Barksdale, to whom Pierre lent decisive support.

Pierre might have hoped that the strained events leading to the reorganization of September 1914 would usher in a time of stability in the company's top management—stability that was so essential if it was to meet unexpected demands created by the outbreak of war in Europe in August 1914. Acutally the reverse was true. The skirmishes of the fall of 1914 were just the prelude to events that would remove Coleman, Alfred, and William from power and leave Pierre undisputed master of the Du Pont Company.

# The Cousins Split

T HE EVENTS LEADING to the reorganization of 1914, which placed Pierre back in the role of acting president with a fresh Executive Committee, forced him to face the central problem involved in the transformation of a family firm into a modern corporation. He had to resolve the conflict between kinship and business. For all his strong sense of family identity, Pierre always saw the need for an impersonal administrative structure staffed by professional managers. He wanted all branches of the du Pont clan to continue to occupy key posts within the firm, yet he expected them to rise on the basis of ability and to make business decisions in terms of long-range return on investment.

The troubles at the top during the years between 1911 and 1914 brought home to Pierre the insecure grasp that he and his ideas still had upon the company. Everything depended upon at least three main branches of the du Pont clan working together: those headed by himself, Alfred, and Coleman. Despite minor friction the three had worked harmoniously since 1902. Then in 1914 Coleman, who with Pierre had created the Powder Company and who agreed with him wholly on the need for modern management and managers, began to reduce both his financial and personal involvement in the firm. Pierre felt that neither Alfred nor the other major stockholder, the long-excluded William, had a solid commitment to new business methods. Both made decisions, Pierre felt, on the basis of snap judgments and personal whims.

For Pierre, therefore, 1914 was a period of danger and uncertainty. Above all, he was determined to keep the company solidly on the track on which he and Coleman had set it. When Coleman, the largest shareholder, moved to sell a major block of his stock, the crisis for control that Pierre feared was at hand. The result was a bitter family fight.

"The schisms of the Church . . . created violent animosities frequently because of differences in regard to religious beliefs. Years tempered their violence and, without change in sentiment, the opposing sides have learned to forgive and forget. The schism in the du Pont family was born of no more important differences; let us hope that the lapse of almost thirty years has tempered if not completely cured its animosities."[1] So wrote Pierre du Pont in August of 1943, more than twenty-eight years after the day in February 1915 when he purchased Coleman's stock and thus simultaneously achieved personal control of the Du Pont Company and its presidency.

The family row that resulted permanently seared his mind, and for the remainder of his life he often relived the months of the purchase and the ensuing fight, trying to reconcile his own stand and the position taken by the other du Ponts. That the family schism remained during Pierre's lifetime and still lingers there can be no doubt. The publication of Marquis James's *Alfred I. du Pont, The Family Rebel,* in 1941, a book sympathetic to Alfred and critical of Pierre, caused Pierre to write during the next three years several different accounts of his role in the purchase of Coleman's stock. Said Pierre: "The chapter of the biography of Alfred I. du Pont by Marquis James entitled 'Coleman Sells Out' is inaccurate in omissions, part of which might have been avoided by more careful examination of the records—all could have been avoided by consultations with those available to him and who had played a part in the transaction."[2] Pierre asserted that he would gladly have discussed the matter with James, but, significantly, Alfred's biographer, even after the lapse of twenty years since the sale, did not feel free to show his manuscript to Pierre before publication.

Still the events reverberate. In 1964 John W. Donaldson, Coleman's son-in-law, published a perceptive pamphlet entitled *Caveat Venditor, A Profile of Coleman du Pont,* which devoted 23 of its 41 pages to recounting the sale. Hindsight, however, shaped much of Donaldson's thinking. He could not forget that "the common stock which Coleman sold for somewhat under thirteen million dollars has a market value today of well over a billion." Nothing less, he wrote, than "the control of a great industrial enterprise had been at stake" and "Pierre had beaten [everyone else] to the punch." Thus Alfred's attack on Pierre appeared to lack "moral principal as a motivating force" and smacked of "sour grapes."[3]

Knowledge of the Du Pont Company's pre-eminent position in American industry after 1920 and its fabulous profits during the First World War can distort any attempt to reconstruct the way participants in the events between 1914 and 1916 viewed their own times and to determine why they acted the way they did. It should be emphasized, therefore, that the Powder

Company, successful as it had been under the three cousins, was, prior to
the war, a modest venture compared to what it would become. Rapid
growth that would by 1965 make Du Pont the seventh largest industrial
concern in the United States, with its assets of $4.4 billion exceeding those
of the giant Pennsylvania Railroad and International Harvester combined,
could not have been predicted.[4] In 1909, although Du Pont ranked as the
twenty-seventh largest American industrial firm, its $60.0 million of capital
made it a pygmy when compared to the United States Steel Corporation
with a capital structure in excess of $1 billion, or the more than $560 million
that Standard Oil was worth prior to its dismemberment in 1911. Even after
its breakup, Jersey Standard was nearly five times as large as Du Pont.[5]

But size alone does not tell the whole story. Although the year 1913, the
Powder Company's first year of operation after accomplishing the court-
ordered dissolution, produced unspectacular, but adequate, profits, the next
year, 1914, in Pierre's words, dawned "very inauspiciously." His financial
forecasts indicated that "prospect of larger sales and satisfactory earnings
was discouraging."[6] Acting upon these estimates and the advice of the
Finance Committee, then composed of Alfred, Coleman, and Pierre, the
board of directors approved a continuation of the lower dividend on
the common stock, which in 1913 had been reduced from 12% to 8%. The
Executive Committee also ordered a 20% reduction in cash to be expended
for capital projects. For a few weeks Pierre feared that even the 8% dividend
rate could not be maintained. On May 1, 1914, revised estimates presented
a more hopeful picture, predicting that the revenue would enable the Powder Company to pay the interest on the bonded debt, the normal 5% return
on the preferred stock, and the 8% on the common shares, and still allow
20% of the earnings for reinvestment in budgeted projects. Even so, the
business recession had cut orders and the 1914 earnings forecast was for
only $4,900,000 as compared to actual earnings of $5,347,000 in 1913.[7] The
search for economies continued. At the same time Pierre and the Executive
Committee turned from investing funds in dynamite and black powder
capacity and gave priority to the purchasing of nitrate lands and expansion
of nonexplosives products, primarily fabrikoid. Of the 1914 capital expenditure program, more than half went for these two purposes.

The outbreak of the World War in August of 1914 did not immediately
change the picture. In fact, commercial business declined, and the Powder
Company executives, feeling that the European conflict would be of short
duration, were afraid to make any expenditures to accommodate potential
military orders. Hamilton Barksdale, writing two weeks after the war
started, approved "with no little reluctance" two projects amounting to less
than $16,000 requested by H. F. Brown to facilitate the manufacture of
smokeless military powder. Although the equipment might "be important,"
warned Barksdale, "its utilization may be temporary; therefore economy in

installation rather than reduced manufacturing cost should be considered."[8]

Not until two months after Germany declared war on Russia did the Du Pont Company receive substantial military orders. October of 1914 saw the first massive contract (in this case from France) for $14,659,000; followed in November by one for $15,161,000; in December, $18,292,000; in January, $36,763,000; and in February, a contract for $58,932,000.[9] The February orders alone were twice the Powder Company's gross receipts for the entire year of 1913!

Larger orders, however, did not mean immediate or even certain profits. Pierre explained that the contracts required the erection of new factories within a precise time schedule, the hiring and training of new workmen, the massive purchase of raw materials. Twelve million dollars for new plants had been spent prior to February 1915 and even more for raw materials. "Nobody knew," testified Pierre in 1916; "it was a mere guess as to whether the company could carry out these contracts. The Executive Committee ... were all comparatively new ... in their positions and were ... on trial." Pierre emphasized that if Du Pont fell down on strict times set for delivery, "the purchaser had the right to cancel the part of the contract yet undelivered. . . .Had the war terminated . . . or had the quality of our powder failed [because of the inexperience of new management and ill-trained workmen in untried plants], I am quite sure that such a cancellation would have been made."[10]

Between the beginning of 1914 and March of 1915 the Powder Company, therefore, underwent a revolution in fortune. Declining orders, reduced profits, and dull hopes marked the first nine months of 1914. For the six months between October 1914 and March of 1915 the commercial demand, which normally accounted for 90% of the company's sales, fell even more rapidly. Unprecedented military orders that required totally new factories and a vast new labor force gave promise of profit—a promise that could be realized only by extraordinary effort, planning, managerial skill, and luck. Success, even by mid-1915, was not self-evident, and more than one astute observer agreed with Edward Kraftmeier, a British Nobel Company representative who was sent by English interests in January 1915 to evaluate the du Ponts and who upon his return to London predicted that the Powder Company had "assumed obligations that would bankrupt it before the end of the year."[11] The Powder Company's common stock reflected the firm's shifting opportunities. In the last quarter of 1913 it ranged in price from between $124 and $130 a share. From a low of around $120 in early 1914, it gradually rose to $137 a share on November 11, to the $160s in December, and to $200 in February 1915.

Coleman du Pont's hopes and goals must be viewed in the perspective of 1914–1915, not that of later years. For the first eight months of 1914, he tried to bring unity to the Powder Company's top management and to transfer the key executive posts to younger talent. In this he failed, and, although he remained the Powder Company's titular head, real authority passed to Vice-President Pierre du Pont and his brother Irénée, who served as chairman of a brand new Executive Committee. Thus, after September 1914 Coleman could devote his full time to his other interests.

## Pierre Buys Coleman's Stock

Looking backward and with no knowledge of Coleman's activities, it seems almost impossible to explain why he decided to get out of the Powder Company just prior to the moment when it was to reap its largest profits. Coleman certainly did not plan to sever all of his connections with the company that bore his family name. His original idea was to retire to an honorific position such as chairman of the board of directors. His decision to sell all of his holdings came suddenly and surprised nobody more than Pierre. "I still wonder, Coleman, why you did it," wrote Pierre on March 8, 1915, a few weeks after the sale.[12]

Although Coleman made up his mind to sell in a split second, the events that led to his action extended back over many months and even years. Time had not lessened Coleman's ambitions. He continued to expand his political career. Ever since his management of Senator Henry du Pont's campaign, he had been the acknowledged Republican political boss of his adopted state. In 1911 he further set out to enhance his reputation by starting construction on a highway to run from Wilmington southward a hundred miles to the Maryland line. He planned to finance the road himself and to donate it to the people. He suspended construction on his highway a year after he started because he felt downstate farmers acted like Jesse James when it came to selling land for a right of way, but Coleman later continued, a bit at a time, to make his dream a reality. In 1916 he resumed construction—a coincidence that some cynically regarded as perfectly timed with a self-initiated boomlet to boost Coleman into no less an office than the presidency of the United States.[13]

More important were Coleman's real estate ventures in New York. The Equitable Building alone took at least $8.0 million of his fortune, much of which had to be raised during the crucial months between October 1914 and February 1915. On June 11, 1915, Coleman surprised the country by purchasing from J. P. Morgan and Company for $4,394,540.10 the controlling interest of the Equitable itself, the world's largest life insurance company. Coleman's purchase of the Equitable yielded one substantial benefit: it allowed him to redraw the agreements under which he had financed the Equitable building and so to meet immediate financial obligations acquired in constructing the edifice. Coleman completed these transactions when he mutualized the company in 1917.[14]

All of Coleman's activities took money. It would be a mistake to picture him as a man with unlimited funds. The Equitable Building, by today's standards, or even those of the Powder Company in 1917, may not seem like a vast undertaking. But the more than $41.0 million invested in the tower and the land on which it stood loomed large beside the $60.0 million prewar capitalization of the Powder Company. And the Equitable investment bulked even larger when compared to his own financial resources. In 1914 almost all of Coleman's wealth was tied up in his Powder Company holdings. The $13,831,865 that he received for all of his interest in that company, while small in comparison to what the stock was later worth, was substantially more than he would have received for it at any previous time. Coleman was a wealthy man, even though his riches were dwarfed by those of John D. Rockefeller, Carnegie, or the Vanderbilts.

In 1914 Coleman pictured himself as moving from the small-time and provincial town of Wilmington to the financial capital of the United States, where he would, through investments in hotels, office buildings, and insurance, parlay his money into a fortune that would rival that of the steel, oil, and railroad magnates. Such success, he felt, could only enhance his political aspirations.

A crisis came for both Coleman du Pont and the Powder Company in December of 1914. Although Coleman had already put up 10,500 shares of Powder Company common stock as collateral to Equitable, he still needed at least $3.0 million more. At first he made tentative arrangements to borrow the money from New York banks. Then he began to reflect that he could meet his financial requirements in other ways.

It will be remembered that neither the Powder Company's bonus program nor its scheme to sell stock to employees had been designed for top management. In fact, both specifically excluded the Executive Committee from participation. And as long as the old guard, who were also the major stockholders, dominated the Executive Committee, this made sense. But the new committee appointed on September 19, 1914, contained no large shareholders. Both Pierre and Coleman thought it essential that those who ran the company should have a major financial stake in it. Thus, Coleman reasoned that his and the company's needs were the same, and that both could benefit if the corporation financed the purchase of a large block of his stock and resold it on easy terms to the new key administrators.

Before Coleman could advance very far with his idea, he was again stricken with a severe internal illness. On December 14, he left Wilmington for the Mayo Clinic at Rochester, Minnesota, where shortly after Christmas the doctors operated upon him for adhesions resulting from his original gallstone surgery in 1909. Coleman's illness was serious; for a few days he hovered near death, and, although he eventually recovered his usual vigor, he did not return to the East Coast until after March 1, 1915.

All of Coleman's negotiations to sell stock to the company were carried out through Pierre, at first in person and, after Coleman left for Minnesota, either by letter or through an intermediary, Coleman's private secretary, Lewis L. Dunham. It is not surprising that Coleman turned to Pierre. Despite the stormy first nine months of 1914, Pierre and his cousin had always been close; seldom had either taken a major step without consulting the other. Coleman's relationship with the Powder Company's other two major stockholders, who were, of course, the two other men most concerned in any substantial shift in Du Pont Company stock ownership, was not easy. Although Coleman had used his influence to elect William du Pont to the Powder Company's board of directors in 1914, the two had always been distant. As has been pointed out, Alfred's divorce and remarriage in 1907 had intensified the feeling of mutual mistrust and lack of confidence that had long existed between Coleman and Alfred. By 1915 suspicion had ripened into deep enmity. "I of course know Alfred has some ulterior motive in mind, as he has tried to do what he could agin [*sic*] me at every opportunity, but this we both know and I always take it into consideration," Coleman complained to Pierre on January 6, 1915.[15]

Early in December 1914, prior to his departure for Rochester, Coleman approached Pierre with an offer to sell to the Powder Company 20,000 shares of his common stock for resale to key employees. In the following days, Coleman wrote to Pierre the details of the plan they had worked out. The proposal advocated that each member of the new Executive Committee be allotted 1,500 shares and that any other employee whose salary was $500 a month or over be allowed to subscribe for three times the amount of his annual earnings.[16] Coleman set a price of $160 per share for his stock (which would bring him about $3.2 million) and he asked that Pierre take the matter up "with Alfred I. to see whether he approved of such a procedure."[17]

Alfred responded favorably to Pierre's casual verbal inquiries, but both agreed that the company's Finance Committee would have to consider Coleman's offer. Thus began innocently enough the series of events which led Coleman to sell his entire holdings to Pierre. All the participants, though greatly divided on their views of the outcome, agreed upon almost all of the essential facts. The dispute arose almost entirely over a difference of interpretation of the facts.

Coleman left Wilmington on December 14, 1914, thinking that he had arranged for the sale of about $3.2 million of his stock. Actually Alfred was having second thoughts. On the day Coleman departed, Alfred sent Pierre a letter which maintained that $160 per share was too much. A second letter on December 21 amplified Alfred's views. He argued that in order to attract employee investment it was imperative to offer them a return of at least 6½%. Since the dividend rate on the common stock for 1914 would be 8%, he reasoned that the company should not pay more than $125 per share for Coleman's stock.[18]

Alfred's thoughts ignored the possibility that the large war orders, if they were fulfilled, would drastically improve the company's profit position and make possible a substantial increase in the dividend. Alfred, of course, had full information about the war business. He had attended the Finance Committee meetings in October, November, and December, at which he had listened to H. F. Brown (head of Smokeless Powder), John Raskob (the treasurer), and other Executive Committee members detail earning forecasts, new orders, and appropriations that the Finance Committee had to approve. Alfred, along with William and Pierre, had voted the appropriations.

Alfred's evaluation, therefore, did not stem from ignorance of the company's prospects. It arose partly from his pessimistic analysis of the firm's situation. Even Pierre, writing years later, admitted that there were a "number of occurrences that might have seriously hampered or even prevented the realization of the Treasurer's [Raskob's] optimistic forecast. Though enormous orders had been booked, the plants required to fill them had not yet been completed."[19] Furthermore, most observers thought the war would not last beyond the year 1915. There was also a threat that Congress might prohibit the shipment of munitions to belligerent countries. And, concluded Pierre, "granting that these external interferences were overcome, could the personnel of the company carry out a program that required 100 per cent performance for a year without serious delay or mistake?"[20]

Alfred had other reasons for his caution. Coleman did not propose to give his stock away. Indeed, his price was near the highest mark it had reached prior to the time he broached the matter with Pierre. For most of the year common had been quoted below $120 a share. During October it ranged from 117–118 to 127–128; in November the stock rose steadily, but it reached 162–163 only on the last day of the month. Coleman, bullishly viewing the war business, felt his price was low. "I have, as you know, always thought well of the common stock and put a higher figure on it than you have," he wrote Pierre on December 7. "I think it is well worth 185 today and think it will get to 190 to 200 before the year 1915 is many months old."[21] Events made Coleman's predictions seem timid, but Alfred, reacting partly out of a growing distrust of his cousin and partly out of past experience that had often failed to support Coleman's buoyant optimism, refused to accept Coleman's valuation.

Alfred hoped that the Finance Committee would review Coleman's offer at its regular meeting on December 30, but the press of war business forced the committee to convene earlier. On December 22, 1914, Alfred and William held an informal meeting of the committee at which Irénée du Pont and Colonel E. G. Buckner of Military Sales discussed the war problems.

Pierre could not attend, hence no binding action could be taken, but the following day Pierre joined Alfred and William, and the three, as the full committee (with only Coleman absent), acted on a variety of questions. The main topic concerned military orders.[22] Pierre noted that all the smokeless powder that could be manufactured by existing plants before November 1, 1915, had been sold, but explained that excess guncotton made it possible with new facilities to increase production by 400,000 pounds per month. The committee agreed unanimously to approve plant expansion.[23]

Coleman's offer was the final order of business. Pierre argued that it was a "very good one." Alfred, who had determined his stand prior to the meeting, agreed that it was desirable for the company to purchase stock to resell to key employees, but he opposed paying Coleman's price of $160 per share. Alfred was backed by William who, however, did not, as Pierre later recalled, "express himself quite as freely."[24] The Finance Committee concluded by voting 2 to 1 (Pierre voting No) to instruct Pierre "to advise Mr. L. L. Dunham, attorney for Mr. T. C. du Pont, that we do not feel justified in paying more than $125 per share for this stock."[25]

The minutes were typed and duly signed by the three Finance Committee members present: Pierre, Alfred, and William. The accuracy of the minutes later became one of the few factual points to be disputed. About eighteen months later, in July 1916, Alfred and William maintained that the minutes should have read "we do not feel justified in paying more than $125 per share for this stock 'now' or 'at this time.' "[26]

Such a wording would have implied continued negotiations. Pierre testified that the minutes were correct, a position consistent with his later contention that the Finance Committee had firmly rejected Coleman's offer.[27] Neither William nor Alfred, however, thought the point important enough to correct the minutes, which they signed shortly after the meeting.

The Finance Committee's action disappointed Pierre, who knew that it left unsolved two crucial problems: Coleman's need for money, and the question of how to make stock available to the new Executive Committee. Pierre began to think about ways to circumvent the Finance Committee's decision. Of course there was the possibility that rising profits and quotations for the shares might cause Alfred and William to reappraise the value of the stock. And there was the further possibility that Pierre could arrange to have Coleman sell the shares directly to the men concerned without going through the company. But, then, few of these men were wealthy enough to pay for such large blocks of stock.

Nothing could be done until after Coleman's operation. That ruled out any reconsideration by the Finance Committee at its meeting of December 30, 1914. Shortly after New Year's Day Pierre received word from Lewis Dunham that Coleman had survived his surgery, had even been out of bed for a few minutes, and was slowly gaining strength. Pierre's letter of January 4, 1915, to Coleman was apologetic. "I have been intending to write you about the reception of your proposition by the Finance Committee. Unfortunately, Alfred, who had approved the plan before you went away, got somewhat crosswise in the meeting and I think it wise to let the matter rest for the moment, preferably until I can see you, before taking any other step. I am sorry and provoked that the proposition did not go through," Pierre continued, " . . . but like many other things the final result cannot be obtained quickly."[28] Coleman replied that the refusal would cause him to reopen negotiations with New York bankers for additional money. He seemed especially bitter toward Alfred and suggested that Pierre should consider withdrawing the proposition.[29] Pierre answered, on January 9, that he understood Coleman's disappointment. "Possibly," wrote Pierre, "I could have put it through by insisting, but at great risk of having the other side pitted against me; that might have complicated the whole plan for good and all. As it remains now, I feel that the proposition is open for reconsideration at your option, of course." William had left Wilmington on the first of January and was not to return for about three weeks. When William returned, Pierre promised to "take up the work again, unless I have word from you to the contrary," and he added, "My judgment is that the deal will go through this time."[30]

Coleman, however, began to sour. Pierre's letters to him, crowded as they were with details about war orders and progress, filled Coleman with optimism. He was already beginning to feel that he should receive a higher price than $160 per share. On January 15, he wrote Pierre to withdraw the offer.[31] On January 18, Pierre replied that he thought "there will be some disappointment, as I believe that the members of the Executive Committee were anxious to take the stock."[32] Coleman's reply indicated that he was not in a hurry to sell his shares and that he had abandoned hope of getting his plan accepted by the company. He agreed with Pierre that it might be possible for him to sell stock directly to the employees, but added that "if this is left until I get home we can work it out better."[33]

Up to this point, the evidence is clear that Pierre's main concern was to obtain stock for the key employees. But in the third week of January, Pierre began to fear that events were in the making which might endanger family control of the Powder Company. A turning point was what Pierre came to call the "Kraftmeier Incident." Edward Kraftmeier, as was mentioned earlier, was affiliated with the British Nobel Company, and his sympathies were so pro-English that he later changed his name to Kay. It all began innocently enough. Kraftmeier cabled from London stating that he and his wife would arrive in New York on the *Lusitania* on Saturday, January 23, 1915. He asked Pierre and Irénée to meet him.[34] Pierre assumed that Kraftmeier desired to talk about still more Allied purchases of military powder, and so he asked Colonel Buckner to accompany him. As Pierre wrote Coleman two days later, he had been "much surprised to find that Mr. Kraftmeier made no mention of orders. Finally," Pierre continued, "after he succeeded in drawing me aside, he told me that they had had a report that Kuhn, Loeb & Company of New York (who are pro-German) had gained control of our company through the embarrassment of one of our largest stockholders and that they on that account had fears concerning the orders placed with us."[35] Pierre immediately assured Kraftmeier that the report had no basis in fact.

Kraftmeier's doubts worried Pierre, because the key to protecting Du Pont interests had been his company's ability to receive sufficient advance payments from the Allies to eliminate much of the risk from constructing new facilities to manufacture war orders. British and French confidence was vital. Thus, Pierre brought up Kraftmeier's rumor at the January 27 meeting of the Finance Committee, whose four members (of whom only Coleman was absent) owned enough stock to control the company. Pierre described the meeting in a letter to Coleman. "It was suggested that we four large stockholders place our stock together for a period of time covering this extraordinary war condition with an agreement that the certificates would not be sold or used as collateral unless by common consent." Alfred further proposed that any outstanding loans on such stock "be taken up by the Company" and then proceeded to make a survey of those present, which confirmed that none had used their stock for collateral.[36] This made it very clear that it was T.C., with his deep commitment to real estate ventures in New York, who was the object of the rumors. William and Alfred then asked Pierre to communicate with Coleman to see if he would agree to the stock-pooling plan. Pierre left no doubt about his own position. "Personally," he urged Coleman, "I think it is a good idea, as our ability to state positively that control of the stock was absolutely safe would put our foreign orders in much better position."[37]

Coleman, however, faced with a still undetermined need for further capital to finance his New York ventures, did not relish any restrictions that might tie up his Du Pont stock. Furthermore, the critical nature of Coleman's illness made him dubious about any plan to encumber his stock. He therefore refused to pool his stock or to accept loans from the company. Upon learning this, Pierre reacted with disappointment. "I think you somewhat misunderstand the situation," he wrote. "Kraftmeier made no such request. . . . The purpose of depositing a majority of the stock was to [give] definite assurances . . . that . . . [it] was in a safe position for a period of time necessary to complete war orders. From the company's standpoint this would have the advantage of bringing to us a greater share of the business than might be obtained if the matter were left uncertain. If uncertain the Allies can easily get others in this country interested in the powder business."[38]

Events moved to a rapid climax. On February 15 Pierre received a letter from Coleman, who was still at Rochester, which told of a sudden relapse on February 7, and a recovery that took about five or six days. Then Coleman dropped his bombshell. He was certain that the Powder Company common would rise in value from its current quotations to about $300 a share. He argued that the men "now at the helm and actually doing things should make the profit. . . . So clear I am that this is the right time to get them interested that I am willing to let go . . . 20,000, 30,000 or even 40,000 shares at today's market, which I assume is about 200." Coleman added that as to the "details of working this out I am entirely willing to leave this to you and Lew [Dunham]."[39]

Pierre was surprised, but he still did not know Coleman's full intentions. On February 17 he met Dunham and "asked him to find out if T.C. would pool his remaining stock." Dunham replied that he thought Coleman would "or perhaps sell all."[40] For the first time Pierre realized that the sale of all Coleman's stock was "possible or probable."[41] Pierre wanted the full story as quickly as possible, so he had Dunham send Coleman the following telegram: "Wire me if you would be willing to sell forty thousand shares and pool balance for voting purpose. Another proposition would you be willing to sell entire holdings. Both cash."[42]

After his conference with Dunham, Pierre made a quick estimate of the money needed to purchase all of Coleman's stock, and that afternoon conferred with Raskob. The next day, February 18, Pierre, together with his brothers Irénée and Lammot, his brother-in-law R. R. M. Carpenter, and Raskob, met to discuss the situation. In the midst of the conference Dunham came in to say that "T.C. would sell all of his stock, but would not go into a voting pool unless he knew of the terms."[43] At that moment Pierre and his associates decided to make an offer for all of Coleman's stock, a proposition they felt would require about $14.0 million.

Cash was the immediate problem, for none of the prospective purchasers had the amount necessary. In fact, as Pierre later testified, all together had assets of only about $11.0 million.[44] Therefore, they sent Raskob to New York the next day to ask J. P. Morgan and Company for a loan based upon Du Pont stock as collateral. To Pierre this procedure was both natural and desirable, for the New York banking house had become the purchasing agents for the Allies in the United States, and it was through Morgan that Du Pont received most of its orders. In the light of the rumors of the instability in the Powder Company ownership and the feeling of some that it was overextended, what better way could the managers of the Powder

Company display faith in their corporation than to risk a large portion of their personal fortunes in the purchase of stock in their own company? Furthermore, it would demonstrate explicitly that there was no danger of outside control.

Raskob boarded a train for New York soon after the conference. The next morning, February 19, he conferred with William H. Porter, a Morgan partner. Raskob left New York on the 3:30 train for Philadelphia, where he met Pierre at the Bellevue Hotel. Raskob's news was good; Porter was almost certain that "at least ten millions of the necessary fourteen millions could be placed, and gave hope that the whole of the fourteen millions" could be found.[45] The following day, Pierre and his two brothers met with R. R. M. Carpenter and John Raskob in Wilmington where, by telephone, they learned from Porter that he could secure at least $10.8 million. At this point Pierre decided to ask Coleman if he would take part payment in cash and the rest in a note. Pierre's telegram to Coleman explained the proposition. Pierre offered to buy all the common shares (63,214 shares) at 200, and all the preferred (13,989 shares) at 80, paying $8.0 million in cash and $5,762,000 in seven-year 5% notes.[46] Coleman telegraphed back that he "would rather keep the preferred than sell at 80" and that he wanted 6% instead of 5% on the deferred payment.[47] By return wire, Pierre agreed to the 6% interest on the deferred payments and offered 85 for the preferred stock.[48] In a telephone conversation later the same day, Coleman and Pierre talked out the final details of the sale. To summarize the agreement, Pierre sent Coleman a further telegram: "I understand I have purchased from you 63,214 shares of the common stock of the E. I. du Pont de Nemours Powder Company at 200 dollars per share and 13,989 shares of the preferred stock . . . at 85 per share. Also you are to be paid $8,000,000 in cash and $5,831,865 in 6 per cent 7 year notes . . . the collateral on the notes being 36,450 shares of the common stock."[49] Coleman confirmed Pierre's memorandum, and the deal was set.

Pierre, however, did not make the purchase alone. He took into partnership with him five trusted associates. Besides the four who had worked out the agreement, they included A. Felix du Pont, a son of Francis G. du Pont, who had proved his ability as a professional manager while superintendent at Carney's Point and who was at this time playing a critical part in the expansion of the smokeless powder plants to meet the war demand. Under Pierre's leadership the six became a syndicate that formed the Du Pont Securities Company, incorporated under the laws of Delaware with a capital issue of 75,000 shares. Into the Du Pont Securities Company was placed all the stock, preferred and common, purchased from Coleman, plus an additional 610 shares of preferred and 28,277 shares of common most of which belonged to Pierre. He sold them to Du Pont Securities so that he would have absolute control of that holding company. Pierre agreed to provide the collateral to underwrite the purchase of half of Coleman's shares, and the other five agreed to supply the rest. The stock of the holding company Pierre received in exchange for his half of Coleman's purchase and these additional securities came to 60% of Du Pont Securities stock outstanding.

It was the Du Pont Securities Company which formally purchased Coleman's stock and which gave to the Bankers Trust Company of New York (acting for Morgan) a 6% note for $8.5 million, secured by 54,591 shares of Du Pont Powder Company common stock and 14,599 preferred shares of the Powder Company. But the syndicate members gave an additional pledge. In the event that the Securities Company defaulted, they guaranteed "severally but not jointly" to pay to the Bankers Trust Company the following sums: Pierre du Pont, $4.25 million; Irénée du Pont, $1.36 million; Lammot du Pont, $1.36 million; John Raskob, $340,000; A. Felix du Pont, $680,000; and R. R. M. Carpenter, $510,000. Similarly, Coleman received $8.0 million in cash and a 6% seven-year note for $5.9 million from the Du Pont Securities Company backed by 36,900 shares of Powder Company common as collateral. Beyond that Coleman neither demanded nor received a further guarantee for his loan.[50]

Pierre had formed the Du Pont Securities Company to enable him, since he alone held approximately 60% of the Securities Company's stock, to control for voting purposes all of Coleman's shares, even though he did not own all of them. By forming the Securities Company and distributing its shares rather than Coleman's stock, Pierre made it possible for others to participate in the profits, but he did not risk control. From the first, Pierre planned to, and soon did, make the new Executive Committee members partners in his venture. Had he, however, given them Coleman's stock directly and had the other members of the syndicate owned their shares separately, Coleman's block of stock would have been split among so many owners that control of the company might again be in danger. Even more important, the combined holdings of Alfred and William would permit them to have much more powerful say in the affairs of the company. Consequently, the new Executive Committee members, like Pierre's five associates, became shareholders in the Du Pont Securities Company. Thus, Pierre, controlling the Du Pont Securities Company, which in 1918 became Christiana Securities Company, and the Powder Company shares that he owned outright, could vote 105,000 shares out of a total of approximately 606,000 voting shares. In short, Pierre emerged from the whole affair master of the Powder Company's destiny.[51]

Pierre and his five associates conducted their negotiations with Coleman and their final purchase of his stock with great speed and in absolute secrecy. Alfred and William du Pont did not know, nor did the members of the Executive Committee who were not among Pierre's five associates. Pierre, himself, was anxious that no word of the affair get out prior to its conclusion. "Important this be kept confidential for present" were the last words of Pierre's first telegram to Coleman on February 20, 1915.[52]

### The Family Reaction

Such a large and important transaction could not long be hidden. Pierre and Coleman reached agreement on February 20, although it took twelve days before all the papers were finally processed. On February 26, Seward Prosser of the Bankers Trust Company called Raskob to say word of the deal had leaked out on Wall Street and he suggested that some statement ought to be made. Pierre agreed and notified the Wilmington *Star*, which published a brief account in its Sunday edition of February 28.[53] Even so, Pierre gave as little information as possible. He talked to reporters at Longwood, his country place, and verified that a syndicate headed by himself had purchased Coleman's entire holdings. When asked the price, Pierre "replied that he did not care to give this information. . . . When queried on the personnel of the syndicate, he said he was not at liberty to give the names of the others. 'I can only speak for myself,' he replied." He did say that "only those now active in the du Pont company are included."[54] This led the Philadelphia *Public Ledger* to speculate that Alfred and William were part of the syndicate.[55]

But Alfred and William were as much in the dark as the Philadelphia papers. Both were stunned. On Monday, March 1, 1915, the morning after the first newspaper account, Alfred demanded an interview with Pierre. The meeting took place in Alfred's office. As Pierre testified the following year, Alfred "asked me whether the report was true that I had purchased T. C. du Pont's stock. I told him it was. He said, 'I suppose that was for the company?' I said, 'No, not at all; a personal transaction.' He said, 'I think you ought to turn that over to the company.' I inquired of him why he thought that; told him I differed from him in that opinion, and he said that I could not have purchased that stock without using my position or the credit of the company and therefore the company should have the right to take the stock." Pierre ended the interview by stating that he "could not consider turning the stock over to the company."[56] The following day, Pierre received from William du Pont, who was vacationing in Brunswick, Georgia, a telegram that warned: "Paper states you have purchased Coleman's stock, I presume for the company. Any other action I should consider a breach of faith."[57] Thus began the fight that was to destroy forever Pierre's friendship with his cousins Alfred and William.

Pierre's enemies made much over the secrecy of his negotiations. John Johnson, attorney for Pierre's opponents at the resulting trial, accused him of resorting to secrecy because of a fear "that the news would get out and something would be done in the interest of the company to block it,"[58] and much later Alfred's sympathetic biographer Marquis James castigated Pierre and his five fellow syndicate members as the "secret six."[59]

What motivated Pierre? Certainly he must have known that both Alfred

and William would react unfavorably. Newspapers looking at the transaction even a few months later seized upon the enormous rise in value of
Powder Company stock which followed from the war profits and concluded
that Pierre and his associates saw the chance to make a lot of money and
grabbed it. They also agreed that those who opposed him did so in order
to get a larger slice of the pie. In fact, from the first, the papers exaggerated
the financial side of the affair. The Philadelphia *Public Ledger* reported that
the purchase involved "$20,000,000."[60] By 1916, the press was having a
field day. A Sunday feature in a February 1916 issue of the Cleveland *Plain
Dealer* was typical. "How War Profits Split the du Ponts" emblazoned the
article which was subcaptioned "Squabble over $60,000,000 or $70,000,000
profits brings breach that even time may not heal."[61]

But Pierre, who had to act in February 1915, viewed the entire problem
differently. The cardinal fact to him was not war profits, for the first of these
was yet in the future, but that his company had assumed the largest obligations for the manufacture of powder in its history and that success rested
largely upon the confidence of those placing the orders. Pierre knew that
Coleman's illness, his construction ventures in New York, and his attempts
to borrow money on Wall Street had resulted in unsettling rumors about his
financial status. These were undermining confidence in the Powder Company just at the time when it needed the trust of the banking community
and its customers most. Coleman's offer faced Pierre with a crisis. He felt
he had no other choice but to act. Had he not just assured Kraftmeier that
the control of the Powder Company would remain in family hands? Pierre
felt he could not explain the sale of stock to outsiders. In fact, had Coleman,
the president and largest owner of Du Pont securities, sold his holdings to
outside speculators at a historically high price, it would have looked suspi-
ciously as though the man who knew most about the company was deserting
a sinking ship. This would have lent strong support to the unfavorable report
that Kraftmeier was about to make about the Powder Company on his
return to London. In this way Pierre could convince himself that the family
concern's very survival seemed at stake.[62]

Yet clearly the reason Pierre moved so fast and secretly when the offer
from Coleman came was that he wanted to obtain control of the family
company. He preferred to face Alfred and William with a *fait accompli.*
Those two cousins, even if the events of the previous months had not
occurred, would not have permitted a transaction to go through that gave
Pierre voting control of the company any more than Pierre would have
quietly accepted a similar move by Alfred and William. Given the present
events, Pierre had come to feel that he could not work with Alfred and
William. He had tried earlier to leave the company partly because he had
tired of keeping the different personalities working together. Coleman now
was getting out. If Pierre was to stay in, if he was to be responsible for the

future of the Powder Company, he wanted the necessary authority to carry out this responsibility.

Another reason for Pierre's quick action was that he hoped to give key Powder Company executives a substantial claim on the profits of their firm. Pierre and Coleman had for some time agreed on the value of such a move, but it had been blocked by the Finance Committee's rejection of Coleman's initial offer. Pierre felt that the only way he could make a management incentive plan based on Coleman's stock a reality was through his purchase of that stock. Alfred, though in sympathy with his cousin's desire to make stock available to the new Executive Committee, had consistently refused to support the purchase of any of Coleman's shares at a price above $125. As late as February 16, 1915, on the eve of Pierre's purchase (when Du Pont common had sold on the market as high as 200), Alfred had written Coleman defending the Finance Committee's offer to purchase stock at $125 per share.[63] Alfred's intransigence and his distrust of Coleman intensified Pierre's fear that any consultation with Alfred could erupt in a fight that might be fatal not only to the management incentive plan but even for the company's war obligations. As for talking to William, Pierre's opposition to William's directorship in 1914 had created strained feelings, which made cooperation at the initial stages of the Coleman purchase risky. Besides, William had supported Alfred in his evaluation of Powder Company common at $125.

Pierre had no thought of keeping the profits of the purchase to himself. On March 19, 1915, he moved to distribute a bonus to the key men directing the Powder Company's war expansion. On the sole condition that the recipients stay with the firm for a full year, Pierre distributed 1,250 shares of Du Pont Securities stock to each of ten men: Irénée du Pont, Lammot du Pont, R. R. M. Carpenter, A. Felix du Pont, William Coyne, Harry G. Haskell, Harry F. Brown, John J. Raskob, William G. Ramsay, and Frank G. Tallman. J. P. Laffey also received 500 shares.[64] Taking the value of Coleman's stock at the $200 per share that Pierre paid for it, the gift amounted to around $250,000 for each executive except Laffey, whose bonus was $100,000. Of course, the rapid rise in the value of the stock made each of the bonuses worth several times as much by the war's end.

Nor did Pierre try to freeze out members of the family who had not played a major part in the management of the company. On April 16, 1915, he sent letters to Alexis I. du Pont, Eugene du Pont, Eugene E. du Pont, Francis I. du Pont, Ernest du Pont, E. Paul du Pont, Archibald M. L. du Pont, Philip F. du Pont, Henry F. du Pont, Charles Copeland, W. W. Laird, and H. Rodney Sharp inviting them to enter the Du Pont Securities Company on the same terms as the original six syndicate members who, Pierre wrote, "now hold stock in the Du Pont Securities Company in the proportion of 500 shares of the latter for each 222.75 shares of the common stock of the E. I. du Pont de Nemours Powder Company acquired from the syndicate members by the . . . Securities Company. . . . If you will transfer to me 223 shares of [Powder Company] common stock . . . I will transfer to you 500 shares of Du Pont Securities Company and $50 in cash, representing the quarter share of . . . Powder common at the original price of $200 per share."[65] Considering the rapid rise in the value of the Powder Company's securities, this was an attractive offer. It did not, however, affect Pierre's control of the Du Pont Securities Company. Indeed, it was the sale of his own Powder Company stock to the holding company that made it possible for him to make this offer and still maintain control of the new holding company.

But weeks prior to Pierre's formal offer to other key Powder Company owners to join in the Du Pont Securities Company, the battle lines had been formed. The cynical and Pierre's enemies alleged that his generous offers to the Executive Committee and other du Ponts were merely bribes.[66] Much water had flowed down the Brandywine in the weeks between Pierre's offer to the du Ponts and his purchase of Coleman's shares. The meeting between Pierre and Alfred in the latter's office on March 1, the day after the papers announced the sale, had not placated Alfred. In fact, he remained more determined than ever to block Pierre's plans.

Alfred searched for support; he immediately contacted William and advised his cousin to speak out. This led Pierre to suspect that William's telegram charging Pierre with bad faith had really originated in Alfred's mind. On March 3, 1915, Alfred arranged a meeting in his office in the Du Pont Building of all those du Ponts who were not involved in the purchase of Coleman's stock. Pierre was not invited, but when he learned of the conference through Alexis du Pont, Pierre became determined to go and force a showdown.

Alfred scheduled the meeting for 8:00 on the morning of March 4. Pierre, accompanied by his brother Irénée, arrived early. Alfred was already there, as was William, who had hurried back from Georgia. So were Eugene du Pont, Philip du Pont, and Alexis du Pont. A little later Francis I. du Pont and Henry F. du Pont came in. For a while everyone evaded the reason for the meeting and talked aimlessly of other things. Finally, after a full hour, Pierre himself broke the ice. He said "the transaction had been completed" and that William du Pont had in a telegram accused him of bad faith. Pierre asked William to explain his charge. William replied that Pierre could not have made the purchase if he had not used his official position with the Powder Company and the firm's credit as well. William argued, therefore, that Pierre was obligated to offer the stock to the Powder Company. Alfred agreed. Pierre listened to William's statement and then took the floor and denied using "the company's credit in any way." Pierre reiterated that the purchase had "been purely a personal transaction," and concluded that he "resented very much their finding fault and their accusation against" him. Pierre then withdrew "after having inquired whether they had any more charges to bring against . . . [him or his] associates." As none was made, Pierre later testified that he told Alfred and William to "make no more charges to those present as they had refused to make them before me." Alfred in a direct challenge to Pierre then asked him if he refused to sell the stock to the company. Pierre answered forcefully that he "did refuse to sell it."[67]

Pierre left the meeting aware that there was to be a fight. He quickly decided that his statement to Alfred had been a tactical error. Pierre, certain that his actions were not selfish, but were taken to save the Powder Company, was also confident that the majority of the firm's directors and shareholders would support him. Consequently, he met Alfred's challenge head on; the day after Pierre's bold refusal to sell he wrote the company's directors that "I withdraw a statement made on . . . March 4th that I will not sell the stock. I am now open to consider a proposition. I have not formed a final opinion, nor have I and my associates discussed the acceptance of a proposition. The question is absolutely open as far as we are concerned."[68] Pierre, however, did not expect his offer to be accepted. His letter made that clear. Pierre attached a copy of Alfred's note of February 16 to Coleman which argued that Powder Company stock still had a value of $125 per share. And immediately before making the offer to give the company a chance to buy Coleman's stock, Pierre declared that "neither I nor any of my associates have used or attempted to use the company's name in this transaction. I have been greatly surprised that Messrs. Alfred and William du Pont consider that the Company has in any sense the right to take this stock, and still more surprised that some others of our directors have at least entertained such a feeling, if they do not now possess it."[69]

The special meeting of the board of directors that followed on March 6 was momentous. For one thing, it marked the formal end of T.C.'s reign. Pierre read Coleman's letter of resignation from the presidency of the Powder Company, its board of directors, and the Finance Committee. The board unanimously elected Pierre president and made him chairman of the Finance Committee. Irénée became the new Finance Committee member by a vote of 12 to 4; thus, the committee consisted of Pierre, Irénée, Alfred, and William. The board of directors also took up the question of filling vacant directorships caused by T.C.'s resignation and the departure of Arthur Moxham, who had organized with two of Pierre's cousins, Charles A. and Ferdinand L. Belin, the Aetna Explosives Company—a consolidation of several small companies. The board unanimously chose A. Felix du Pont a director, but neither of the other two candidates, William G. Ramsay and J. P. Laffey, received a majority vote, and the matter went over to a future meeting.[70]

The consideration of the purchase of Coleman's stock was the main business of the meeting. Two days after the event Pierre explained his actions in a letter to Coleman, who was then residing at the Hotel Green in Pasadena, California, as a part of his recuperation. "We had in mind," wrote Pierre, "to invite some of the other du Ponts in when the whole plan was upset by A.I. and Wm. starting a terrible 'hell-raising' because I had not taken the stock for the Powder Co. . . . I insisted on taking the whole question before the Board where we had the hottest meeting ever, ending in A.I. getting mad and leaving. I then had a motion made offering to buy the stock from us at cost and had Laffey come in and explain at length that it would be illegal for the company to invest more than its surplus, $7,500,000 on which the law is very emphatic. After this," he continued, "the question was referred to the Finance Committee for recommendation. As I cannot vote on this, it means that A.I. and Wm. must either advocate an illegal act, or acknowledge that they are all wrong in their whole plan. They will do the former and I think that the Board will give them a very decided 'turn down' on Wednesday."[71]

And that was precisely what happened. The board at its meeting on Wednesday, March 10, voted 14 to 3 against the purchase of Coleman's stock. Only Francis I. du Pont sided with Alfred and William, and Frank Connable abstained. Before adjournment the board elected J. P. Laffey a director.[72]

Pierre hoped that the directors' decisive action would end the fight. As in the past his philosophy remained "the less said the sooner mended." The board's action left him free to make his offer to the other du Ponts to exchange 222.75 shares of their Powder Company stock for 500 shares of Du Pont Securities. The response, however, certainly indicated that hard feelings had not died. It also emphasized that the family split along specific lines. Those who accepted included Henry F. du Pont (Colonel Henry's son) and Eugene E. du Pont (of the Alexis I. branch), both of whom were directors of the Powder Company, Charles Copeland, a brother-in-law, who had worked in the treasurer's office since 1903, and two other of Pierre's brothers-in-law, William Winder Laird and Hugh Rodney Sharp.[73]

Those who rejected the offer tended to be those who had little active connection with the Powder Company. Of these only two were on its board and none in its active management. Of the two directors, Francis I. (a son of Francis G. du Pont) had left the company's Development Department when he had been forced to choose between outside interests and full-time work as head of the Experimental Station. Francis I. said he appreciated Pierre's offer, but because of " 'friendship and sympathy' for Alfred" he thought it best not to take it.[74] The other director, Alexis I., may have been acting in deference to the feelings of his brother Eugene, for, although he refused the offer, he did come out strongly for Pierre as the battle continued.

His brother Eugene (both were sons of Eugene du Pont, the president of the company in 1902) had never held responsible executive positions in the company. Neither had Philip du Pont (Eugene E.'s brother), who admitted that he considered it "a generous offer and a good business opportunity."[75] Neither had the others who rejected the offer, including Archibald, Ernest, and E. Paul du Pont.[76]

For a while, war problems crowded the issue from Pierre's mind, but time and the rush of business failed to heal the family split. In September he began to hear rumors that a complaint had been lodged with the Department of Justice charging that the Du Pont Securities Company was a violation of the antitrust laws. He could not trace the accuracy of the story, but he knew that Alfred still bristled with resentment. Furthermore, after one disastrous brush with the Justice Department's antitrust division, Pierre feared another. He determined to go directly to Washington to trace the rumor. On September 14, 1915, he met John Davis, solicitor general of the Department of Justice. From Davis and George Carroll Todd, assistant to the attorney general in charge of antitrust litigation, Pierre learned that a charge had indeed been made. He found Todd familiar with the whole Powder Case, but no amount of digging could unearth the source. A direct inquiry as to whether Alfred du Pont was the complainant brought the terse reply that it was the "policy of the department not to give out such information."[77] Pierre took care to explain his conception of the formation of the Du Pont Securities Company. He tried to minimize the idea that his purpose had been to control the Powder Company and asserted that the main reasons "were to provide the means of purchasing the holdings of T. C. du Pont, and incidentally, to interest financially some of the more important men of our company." Pierre obtained an agreement that the attorney general would make no move against the Du Pont Securities Company without due notice and without giving the persons concerned a chance to reply to criticism and to rectify improper acts. He was relieved to find Todd friendly and of no "firm opinion on the subject."[78]

Nevertheless, Pierre returned to Wilmington uneasy. He wrote a further letter to the Department of Justice in which he attempted to show his willingness to cooperate.[79] Pierre approached Alfred directly and asked him if he had made the complaint. Alfred refused to say Yes or No, and this action convinced Pierre that his cousin was the troublemaker.[80]

## The Suit

Pierre had good reason to worry. Although little came of the antitrust agitation, Alfred was planning a legal challenge. The blow fell on December 9, 1915. On that date Pierre was served papers bringing suit against him and others in the United States Court for the District of Delaware. The com-

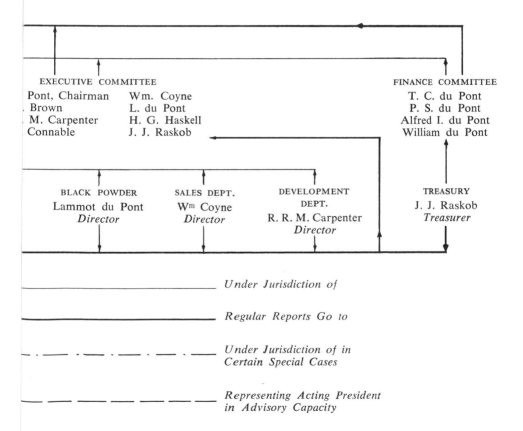

EXECUTIVE COMMITTEE
Pont, Chairman    Wm. Coyne
. Brown           L. du Pont
. M. Carpenter    H. G. Haskell
Connable          J. J. Raskob

FINANCE COMMITTEE
T. C. du Pont
P. S. du Pont
Alfred I. du Pont
William du Pont

BLACK POWDER
Lammot du Pont
*Director*

SALES DEPT.
Wᵐ Coyne
*Director*

DEVELOPMENT DEPT.
R. R. M. Carpenter
*Director*

TREASURY
J. J. Raskob
*Treasurer*

*Under Jurisdiction of*

*Regular Reports Go to*

*Under Jurisdiction of in Certain Special Cases*

*Representing Acting President in Advisory Capacity*

plaint alleged that the Powder Company had the right to Coleman's stock and asked that it be turned over to the firm. Alfred's attack, however, was oblique. His strategy was to pose as the protector of the small stockholders, and he had the suit brought by Philip F. du Pont of Merion, Pennsylvania, a son of the deceased Alexis I. du Pont. Philip named his brother Eugene E. du Pont as a defendant in the case, along with Pierre, Irénée, Lammot, Henry F., A. Felix, John J. Raskob, and others.[81] Although Philip brought the suit, few, except possibly for the first few weeks, thought he was acting alone. The day after the papers were served, the Philadelphia *Public Ledger* explained: "The generally accepted story is that Alfred I. du Pont and his friends were endeavoring to secure control of the powder company; that it was believed that they had it, but that Pierre S. and his syndicate secured control. Alfred I. and William took no action, but Philip F. did not like to see the stock passing into the hands of a syndicate instead of coming to the company itself, and therefore brought the suit."[82]

It did not take long for Alfred to show his colors. On January 10, 1916, he joined the suit,[83] and by the fifteenth of that month much of the du Pont family had taken sides. The split pitted brother against brother, mother against son, daughter against daughter, cousin against cousin, and longtime friend against longtime friend. Yet the pattern held—those who joined Alfred were family members who had not held responsible positions in the Powder Company's management.

Four of the late Francis G. du Pont's sons—Francis I., E. Paul, Archibald M. L., and Ernest—joined the suit on Alfred's side. One son, A. Felix, long an active company executive, was a defendant with Pierre. One of Francis G.'s daughters, Eleanor Perot, filed a petition in support of Philip and Alfred. Another daughter, Irene, was the wife of defendant Irénée du Pont. Cousin William, although never formally a party to the litigation, later testified on Alfred's side. One of the most poignant letters came to Pierre from Philip's mother, Bessie, who wrote: "I am much distressed that Philip who has always expressed the greatest admiration for you—and still does —should have brought this suit. He never told me, and I knew nothing of it until the day the papers came out with it. Had I known of it, I could have tried to persuade him not to bring it. I realize how you have borne the burden of this business for 7 years while Coleman was ill and other big stockholders absent and what we all owe to you and can only say again how sorry I am that my son should have anything to do with such a suit."[84]

For Pierre certain aspects of the affair were especially galling. Among these was the choice of counsel by Alfred's side. In charge of the case was Philadelphia's John G. Johnson, a 74-year-old corporation lawyer who had a distinguished record in the antitrust field. He had argued the company side of the Northern Securities, Standard Oil, and American Tobacco cases. Johnson, "who had spent a lifetime defending the majority interests of corporations," told Alfred "he would take the case in the hope of establishing a precedent for better protection of the interests of minority stockholders."[85] He had a big reputation for skillful cross-examination and courtroom pyrotechnics. William A. Glasgow, Jr., also of Philadelphia, assisted Johnson. Pierre knew Glasgow as a hard-bargaining and successful prosecutor for the Justice Department in its fight against the Powder Trust. Pierre had decidedly unpleasant memories of the erstwhile government lawyer; furthermore, the fact that both advocates had taken active roles in antitrust cases seemed ominous. News releases, obviously inspired by Alfred's camp, worried Pierre as they had after his interview with Justice Department officials in September. An article in the Philadelphia *Evening Ledger* for December 30, 1915, reported that the Department of Justice had several complaints, presumably originating with one of the warring factions, that the Du Pont Company still controlled one of the powder firms established after the dissolution.[86] Another story, headlined "Morgan's part in Du Pont deal may be probed," promised close government scrutiny of the Du Pont Securities Company.[87]

Pierre grew angry. In December 1915, immediately after receiving notice of the suit, he called upon Alfred to discuss the matter. This Alfred refused to do. Nor did he attend a Powder Company board of directors meeting, despite the fact that he had been the first consulted as to a time and place and had agreed to come. When questioned about his absence, Alfred declined to give an explanation. Alfred further aroused Pierre's ire by "signing a notice to the President and Treasurer of the Company to the effect that the dividends recently declared . . . should not be paid" to the holders of Coleman's stock.[88]

Although Alfred had not yet admitted his support of Philip's litigation, Pierre had decided on January 8, 1916, that it was "quite impossible that this suit should have been brought without the connivance and co-operation of Mr. Alfred I. du Pont, and it is equally evident that he has given aid in the bringing of his suit, and has refused aid to the Company and its officers."[89] Pierre had only one response. The directors must affirm confidence in their president by removing Alfred from his positions as a vice-president of the company and member of the Finance Committee. This the directors did on January 10, 1916, and, immediately following their action, Alfred announced his intention to join Philip.[90]

Pierre did not stop. He would not be content until all who opposed him were removed from the Powder Company's board of directors. His plan was to drop Alfred, William, and Francis from the board at the company's annual meeting in March and replace them with Hamilton Barksdale, William Ramsay, and Frank G. Tallman. Thus, with the avowed intent of electing his hand-picked slate of directors and of winning approval for the board of directors' refusal in 1915 to buy Coleman's stock, Pierre appealed for proxies. His letter to the stockholders of January 18, 1916, enclosed copies of both Philip's Bill of Complaint and Pierre's answer. Pierre concluded his plea asserting that he either owned in person or controlled through proxy 55% of the total voting stock. This, of course, included the disputed shares that the syndicate purchased from Coleman du Pont.[91]

It is not surprising, therefore, that Pierre had his own way. "With the smoothness of a well-oiled machine," reported the Philadelphia *Public Ledger*, "the annual meeting of the E. I. du Pont de Nemours & Co., the big powder company, was held at noon today [March 13, 1916] and at the close of the meeting Alfred I. du Pont, who has been connected with the powder manufacturing business in this country as an active official all of his life; William du Pont, also interested actively in the powder business for many years; and Francis I. du Pont, chemist of note and inventor of a number of smokeless powder processes, had ceased to be directors of the biggest powder company in the world."[92] The vote was decisive. Pierre's slate got 411,053 out of a total voting issue of 593,224 shares. Alfred's side voted only a token 3,621 of the 181,191 shares they controlled. By a similar lopsided majority the shareholders affirmed Pierre's purchase of Coleman's stock.

From this it can be seen that Alfred began his fight against Pierre at a great disadvantage. The minimal vote received by Alfred's side was deliberate. He asked his supporters to withhold their endorsement of any action until the court had ruled upon Philip's suit.[93] Even so, the vote made it clear that Pierre commanded a decisive majority of the Du Pont stock.

The general support that Pierre could claim from the company's shareholders forced Alfred into a complex strategy. He could not hope to win any direct contest in a stockholders' meeting. He knew that before he started. Alfred's fight, therefore, had two distinct parts, each vital to victory. The first was court action. Through this he hoped to win a ruling that Pierre had acted illegally in purchasing Coleman's stock and that he should have bought the shares and offered them to the company. Yet Alfred knew that this was only half the battle, for no court could force the stockholders to take advantage of an offer that Pierre might make to sell. What a legal victory could do was to cause a fresh stockholders' meeting, one in which Pierre would be prevented from voting Coleman's shares, thus reducing his strength. But even this would fall short of giving Alfred his way. He would win only by changing the minds of many of the du Pont family, employees, and other stockholders. Therefore, the second part of Alfred's attack, which he waged both in and out of the courtroom, was to attack Pierre's integrity. The stockholders had to be convinced that Pierre had betrayed his trust and had acted for personal gain at the expense of his company and the outside stockholders. This second part of Alfred's strategy was essential to his ultimate victory and helps explain the lasting bitterness that resulted from the struggle.

The year 1916 for Pierre was not a happy one. He found himself the center of unwanted, but seemingly all-pervasive, attention from the press. The family fight would have drawn much comment in any case, but the Du Pont Company's spectacularly profitable role in supplying the Allies with munitions assured that the affair would be front page news in every newspaper in the nation. To Pierre many of the stories were just repulsive. In this category was a full-page feature run early in 1916 by the Cleveland *Plain Dealer*. The story prominently displayed pictures of Pierre, Coleman, and Alfred and his wife, Alicia; the photographs were set off against a large cartoon depicting two armies of du Ponts dressed as Chinese warlords fighting each other over fat sacks of money. This account took no sides but raked over all of the most recent family scandals such as Alfred's divorce and remarriage. It took the attitude "a plague on both your houses." Pierre's response was remarkably detached. "Thanks for your enclosing a copy of 'Plain Dealer'," he wrote to W. A. Donaldson. "Such articles are very unsatisfactory, but I see no way of preventing them as long as people want to read."[94]

Pierre was by now, however, aware of his opponent's strategy, and he kept sharp watch for attacks on him that might be fostered by his enemies in the guise of "news releases." A series of five articles entitled "The Great Powder Romance: A True Story of Strong Men and Their Millions" written by Henry B. Loos of the Philadelphia *Evening Ledger*, which began on January 25, 1916, worried Pierre. The *Ledger*, one of Philadelphia's leading and most respected papers, had a wide audience among Du Pont shareholders, and misinformation sown by it might reap dissension among his supporters. Loos's articles were especially dangerous, for, though they were flamboyant, they lacked the harsh muckraking quality that characterized the feature in the Cleveland *Plain Dealer*. More irksome to Pierre, though the articles appeared to be impartial, they contained statements damaging to his cause. "Should the suit be successful," said Loos in the first piece, "the stock in question will go into the treasury of the powder company and every outstanding share of common stock will be enhanced in value by about $200."[95] To Pierre this seemed calculated to rouse the small shareholders against him.

Therefore, while Pierre ignored much of what he considered obnoxious newspaper publicity, he responded quickly to Loos's articles. To Cyrus Curtis, the *Evening Ledger*'s "accredited owner," Pierre wrote, complaining: "I do not ask you to waste time in reading . . . [Loos's articles] for they are ill written, serve no proper purpose and, though based largely on allegation, they are filled with misstatements. To the intelligent reader it is possible that no wrong impression is conveyed, but to the mass of shallow thinkers the effect cannot be other than a false and damaging viewpoint as to the character and activities of the writer and his associates." Pierre argued that if the *Ledger* investigated and uncovered "the originator of the articles," it would discover that it had "been much imposed upon." He concluded by asking that "in the future the *Evening Ledger* make careful inquiry as to the truth of the data in regard to the du Pont family and the E. I. du Pont de Nemours & Company before publication," and he suggested that Charles B. Landis, who was in charge of the company's Publicity Department, could answer any question.[96] Owner Curtis passed Pierre's letter over to his executive editor who made a correct, but cold and formal, reply.[97] It was apparent that no attempt could stop Alfred from gaining wide publicity for his side among Du Pont shareholders, for since December 1911 he had owned the Wilmington *Morning News,* which poured forth a steady stream of anti-Pierre propaganda.

The much-awaited trial began on June 28, 1916, in Wilmington before Judge J. Whitaker Thompson of Philadelphia. Judge Edward Bradford of Wilmington, before whom the case was originally brought, had asked to be relieved because he was related to both sides.[98] The case that Alfred's lawyers constructed contained the following assertions: that the Powder Company had never officially terminated its negotiations with Coleman du Pont to purchase stock for the benefit of key company employees; that Pierre had never been released by the Powder Company from his task of consummating a deal for the stock with Coleman and was, therefore, not free to act for himself; that Pierre needed and used his position as a Powder Company officer to obtain the loan which the Du Pont Securities Company received through J. P. Morgan; that the decision of the directors on March 10, 1915, not to purchase Coleman's shares from Pierre was invalid because Pierre had stacked the deck by corrupting a majority of the directors by bringing or offering to bring them into the Du Pont Securities Company; that, further, Pierre had misled the uncorrupted directors, first, by having the company's counsel John P. Laffey—who was later bribed by a gift of 500 shares of the Du Pont Securities Company—give a legally incorrect opinion that the company could not invest more than its surplus of less than $8.0 million in Coleman's shares, and, second, by withholding information on the enormous profits that would result from the war contracts.

Alfred's counsel made much of the spectacular rise of daily cash balances at those banks, especially J. P. Morgan, that had participated in the loan to Pierre. Alfred's side asserted that such banks received large Du Pont Company deposits as payoffs. The daily Du Pont Company balance records at all such banks became a major exhibit of the complainants.[99]

Woven into the legal case ran a message to the Du Pont shareholders that Pierre and a few insiders had privileged knowledge. "These men," Alfred's counsel Johnson said, "played with marked cards. They were blinded by the gigantic fortunes before them. When Raskob went to New

York to begin negotiations with the Morgans for the $8,500,000 ... he knew that he could not have obtained any such loan if it had not been for his connections with the Du Pont Company and the Morgans' knowledge of his knowledge of the vast profits that were in sight for the company."[100]

Pierre emerged as a selfish and untrustworthy man who surrounded himself with sycophants such as John J. Raskob, "a $12-a-week clerk who was advanced to Treasurer when Pierre got control of the Powder Company."[101] In the complainant's version, Alfred became a staunch independent. William A. Glasgow, in his final four-hour argument to the court, quoted a letter to the Du Pont directors in which Pierre said it became his "painful duty to recommend the removal of Alfred I." "Can you imagine," Glasgow sneered, "the tears in the eyes of Raskob, his weeping, such weeping as has not occurred since the time Rachel was weeping for her children and would not be comforted. But they ousted him . . . because he was an independent director. Pierre wanted men on that board he could control. . . . "[102] But even more stinging was Glasgow's charge against Pierre's integrity. "He double-crossed the Powder Company and he double-crossed Coleman who was selling the stock." Glasgow argued that the Powder Company "had on hand ... $38,000,000. . . . There was no question about the ability of the Company to buy it . . . [but] Pierre had never made a legitimate offer to sell the stock which he had purchased [and he knew] J. P. Laffey, the counsel for the Powder Company, was ready with an opinion that the company could not legally make the purchase. This, your Honor," remarked the lawyer, "is what you would call a lead pipe cinch."[103]

One of the major problems facing the defense was the rapid change in the Powder Company's fortune from December 1914 to July of 1916. What had been hope in December of '14 and promise in February of '15 had become reality in January of '16 and history by the time of the trial. Johnson took great delight in pretending to drag from Pierre during the cross-examination the information that in the fifteen months since the purchase of Coleman's shares Du Pont common had received dividends of $273 a share more than their cost.[104]

For Pierre the trial must have had an uncomfortable similarity to the antitrust litigation. Many of the faces were the same. Glasgow was opposing Pierre's legal experts—William Hilles, J. P. Laffey, George S. Graham, and William H. Button—all of whom had been involved in the antitrust defense. Then, too, there was Pierre's feeling that right was on his side and his confidence that he would be upheld. He wrote Barksdale during the trial: "I can not see that they [Alfred I., Philip, Francis I., and William] have made any steps toward proving any of their contentions." The Du Pont president concluded: "They have brought out nothing new although they have tried to by reading a lot of their elementary material. I hardly believe this will fool the court."[105]

Pierre felt that his opponents had no case. For him the Finance Committee's decision of December 23, 1914 (which he had opposed)—"that we do not feel justified in paying more than $125 per share"—virtually ended any company negotiations. "Alfred and William du Pont have testified that the words 'at this time' were omitted in the minutes, but," commented Pierre wryly, "as Alfred had signed the minutes, he took refuge in the statement that he was in the habit of signing papers without looking at them."[106]

Pierre's attorneys built their defense upon an attempt to re-create the problems that faced Pierre at the time he purchased Coleman's stock. Thus Pierre testified at length of the risks involved in the war contracts, of Coleman's need for money, of the Kraftmeier incident, and of the need to reward key employees. Pierre explained that his continued attempts in January 1915 to arrange a purchase of some of Coleman's shares was necessitated by his desire to make stock available to the new Executive Committee. And Pierre pointed to Alfred's continued belief in mid-February 1915 that Powder Company common was still worth only $125.

Pierre felt that the argument that he used his position with the Powder Company to obtain a loan from J. P. Morgan had no merit. Pierre pointed out that he gave collateral in the form of Du Pont stock which exceeded the value of the loan. The deal was strictly a personal business transaction, and he regarded the rapid rise of Powder Company deposits at J. P. Morgan and other banks that participated in the loan as inevitable under the circumstances. The Powder Company established its Morgan account on December 9, 1914, only because the New York house was the Allied purchasing agent. Since Morgan acted as paymaster for Great Britain and France, it was hardly surprising that Du Pont's cash balance with Morgan rose sharply as war contracts increased and moved toward fulfillment. The company had carried substantial accounts with thirteen major New York banks and the Philadelphia National Bank long before the war. Morgan's role in the Du Pont Securities loan was one of broker. That is, it acted as the intermediary between the du Ponts, who received the money, and the institutions that actually furnished the cash. Morgan placed the loan with fourteen major New York banks and one Philadelphia firm, all of which (except the Coal and Iron National Bank of New York) were Du Pont depositories.

Pierre testified that he did not even know until March 1915 which banks had taken part in the loan, and he found that out only incidentally. He argued that, although it might seem as though deliberate policy had caused cash deposits to rise at participating banks, the coincidence could be easily explained. Morgan dealt primarily with the major New York banks, and the du Ponts traditionally had deposits with only the strong Manhattan institutions. This being the case, coupled with the extraordinary cash flow into the company, it was inevitable that Powder Company balances would rise with participating banks. One thing is clear. Though Manhattan's Coal and Iron

National Bank took part in the loan, it never became a Du Pont depository during the time in question.[107]

The charge that Pierre had bribed the board of directors seemed the most unkind cut of all. Pierre maintained that he purchased Coleman's stock for only two reasons—to ensure the continued management of the company by the team that Coleman had placed in charge in September 1914, and to provide a way to reward the men who were carrying on the war burden. Pierre's personal correspondence makes it clear that he planned to give the stock to the new Executive Committee and other leading managers long before Alfred's opposition became a serious matter. And, in fact, Alfred's behavior only delayed Pierre's offer to other family members.[108]

## Defeat and Victory

The court's decision handed down on April 12, 1917, by Judge Whitaker Thompson proved even more shocking to Pierre than had the ruling in the antitrust suit. Thompson's forceful opinion followed Alfred's interpretation of most of the facts. The judge seized upon Pierre's statement to Coleman's representative, L. L. Dunham, which said that the Finance Committee had on December 23, 1914, rejected Coleman's offer to sell shares at $160 but had omitted that it would pay $125. The judge agreed with Alfred that this conveyed the false impression that the committee's turndown had been absolute. The court further castigated Pierre for keeping secret the letters that flowed between him and Coleman after the Finance Committee's turndown. According to Judge Thompson, if Pierre "had with fidelity carried out his trust, had correctly reported to Coleman the substance of his instructions from the Finance Committee and had fully and freely disclosed to the Finance Committee what had transpired between him and Coleman, and the Finance Committee or the Company had determined to proceed no further, or had determined not to purchase Coleman's stock, his position of agency and trust for the Company would have been at an end and he would have been free to act for his own interests and those of his associates."[109]

"The Finance Committee," asserted the judge, "was in favor of purchasing the stock, but that fact and the reasons for not buying it at $160 had not been stated to Coleman, although it was rapidly rising in value and Coleman knowing this was kept by Pierre in ignorance of the facts which Pierre should have disclosed to him. He, in whom confidence was reposed of faithfully representing the Company in the transaction, cannot, after betraying his trust through suppression of the facts and through abandonment of his principal by suggestion of a sale through an outside financing, now take advantage of his own wrong and successfully claim that the resulting withdrawal of the offer, thus brought about and concealed from his principal until the trial of the cause, relieves him of any further responsibility and puts him in a position to thereafter deal for himself."[110] Thompson ruled that Pierre's machinations invalidated the actions taken by the board of directors in 1915 and the stockholders in 1916, which had refused to purchase Coleman's stock from the Du Pont Securities Company. Reasoned the judge: "The only course remaining, therefore, is to put the question [of the company's purchase of Coleman's stock] before the stockholders of the E. I. du Pont de Nemours & Company for their decision at a meeting called for that purpose, to be conducted under the supervision of a Special Master. . . ."[111]

Thompson's decision appeared to give Alfred nearly everything he wanted. There would be a stockholders' meeting to decide the issue, one in which Pierre would be prevented from voting any of the shares he had acquired from Coleman. But, of more importance, the judge had cast grave doubt on Pierre's integrity. Alfred took full advantage of this. The day following the decision his Wilmington *Morning News* headlined: "DUPONT COMPANY WAS DEFRAUDED IN $58,000,000 STOCK DEAL BY DEFENDANT DIRECTORS, COURT RULES." The lead article began with a special box outlined in black entitled "Defendant Directors Who Betrayed the Powder Company." The list, headed by Pierre, included his brothers Irénée and Lammot, John J. Raskob, A. Felix du Pont, R. R. M. Carpenter, Henry F. du Pont, Eugene E. du Pont, William Coyne, Harry Haskell, John P. Laffey, and H. Fletcher Brown. Alfred's paper printed Judge Thompson's entire ruling, but those portions most obnoxious to Pierre were excerpted and placed so that even the casual reader could not avoid them.[112] For weeks thereafter the columns of the *Morning News* maintained a running attack on Pierre's character. These became so blatant that on April 17 George Carter, the editor of the Wilmington *Evening Journal,* a paper which Pierre's supporter Colonel Henry du Pont owned and which had been silent for most of the trial, disobeyed Pierre's wishes and printed an editorial defending him. Carter's act received Pierre's gratitude. He wrote the editor: "I thoroughly appreciate your honest intention to benefit me . . . and I must admit with equal candor that your act has been a benefit, much as I regret that it has been necessary to disregard my expressed wishes."[113] By this time Pierre felt he had good need of newspaper support, for Alfred sent copies of the *Morning News* to most of the independent Du Pont shareholders, especially those who lived far from Wilmington.[114]

Just prior to Judge Thompson's ruling, Alfred's side launched still another attack, a suit that challenged the whole bonus system. This litigation, had it been pressed to a successful conclusion, would have deprived most of the employees of their bonuses. But Irénée thought that the real reason for it was to lay the groundwork for disallowing the votes of bonus stock in the coming showdown over Coleman's shares.[115] Whatever Alfred's reason, his new tactic threw a scare into many bonus holders.

Pierre's anger at the court's decision was deep. His brother Irénée expressed their joint attitude when he wrote A. Felix du Pont, who was in Charleston, South Carolina, that "Judge Thompson handed down an opinion which might have been written by the late Mr. Johnson [Alfred's attorney], so far as its one-sidedness is concerned." Thompson "even goes to the ridiculous extent of claiming that Pierre wilfully prepared a fraud just as Johnson claimed. . . . You doubtless read," Irénée added bitterly, "that Mr. Johnson dropped dead at breakfast the day after the opinion came out. You also probably heard before you left that Pizeck, Alfred's publicity man, who engineered the *Morning News* attack last summer, had a stroke of paralysis. It looks as tho providence were taking a hand in the matter."[116]

But anger did nothing to solve Pierre's problems. If he could not immediately defeat the attack on the bonus system, he could at least calm the minds of those executives who had guided the company during the war crisis. Thus, he wrote on April 4, 1917, to Irénée, Lammot, J. J. Raskob, R. R. M. Carpenter, F. G. Tallman, J. P. Laffey, William Coyne, H. G. Haskell, H. F. Brown, and Mrs. Caroline Ramsay that it was "pitiful that a Court of Justice . . . [might take] from you the well earned fruits of your endeavors and that a handful of evil doers who have bourne [*sic*] no part of the burden but who have shared liberally in the rewards, should seek to deprive you of the payments which their own agreements gave you under the Bonus Plan . . . . Through flaunting the name of du Pont, they have brought it to shame and dishonor. . . ." Pierre continued that "in February and March 1915 . . . you were offered . . . shares of the Du Pont Securities Company whose appreciation under your guidance was to form part of your reward. Now that the security of the possession of this stock is threatened, I shall immediately set aside a number of shares of the common stock of E. I. du Pont de Nemours & Company equivalent to your Du Pont Securities Company investment, which shares will accrue to your benefit in the event of a final adverse decision of the Du Pont Securities Case."[117]

Thus, with one stroke Pierre protected the key employees. "One of the bright spots of this trying episode," said the Du Pont Company's president, "is the opportunity afforded to show you the sincere affection and admiration that I hold for you and to recognize the wonderful support that you have accorded to me in all the trials and perplexities of the years that we have been associated together."[118] No one received Pierre's letter with more gratitude than did Mrs. Caroline J. Ramsay, wife of the Du Pont Company's Chief Engineer William G. Ramsay, whose 1,250 shares of Securities Company stock worth in excess of $736,000 formed the bulk of her estate. The fact that Pierre had no legal obligation to protect her interests made his message especially welcome. "I had one of my happiest moments since my husband's death, last night, when I read your letter to me," she wrote. "The feeling of your high appreciation of the work into which he threw his whole soul, the knowledge of your thoughtful care that all you considered his due should be secured to us, touched the depths of my heart."[119]

Pierre saw a clear duty to aid his trusted associates and he acted quickly. But not so obvious was the kind of response he should make to Judge Thompson's decision. Ought he to appeal, or could he trust to the outcome of a stockholders' meeting? Pierre considered both alternatives seriously. If he were to appeal, Pierre determined that he needed the counsel of an attorney whose reputation was at least equal to the late John Johnson, so he consulted Charles Evans Hughes, who advised that the chances for a higher court's overturn of Judge Thompson's ruling were good.[120]

But the more Pierre sounded opinion in Wilmington, the more it became evident that he had an excellent chance of winning a decisive victory at a stockholders' meeting. Therefore, he decided that he would submit to a formal court decree which would fix such a meeting. The date set was October 10, 1917. Should the vote go the way he hoped, he felt the case would be terminated.

Pierre then set about to ensure that Alfred's campaign to influence stockholders would fail. Since Pierre could not with propriety solicit proxies, he asked Hamilton Barksdale, J. A. Haskell, and C. L. Patterson to undertake that task. Pierre told Barksdale to warn the stockholders of the consequences of supporting Alfred. Such a vote would have upheld "charges of fraud and misconduct." Pierre wrote: "It is difficult to believe that the stockholders would wish to retain me if they so believed. However that question need not be reached as I should not be willing to continue with them. I believe that the other defendants in this case who have likewise been found guilty will concur in my views and will be unwilling to serve the stockholders further in event of a vote favorable to purchase of the stock and the affirmation of the Lower Court's decision by the Appellate Court."[121]

Pierre also asked Barksdale to stress the "moral question involved . . . namely: the present holders of a large part of the stock in question are those [that is, the key employees] who were to be benefitted by T. C. du Pont's original offer. . . . Their attention," Pierre emphasized, "was not called to the question of ownership of the stock until long after they had made good in their performance and had added enormous sums to the assets and earnings of the stockholders."[122] Finally, Pierre desired that a letter which Coleman had written to the Du Pont Company directors should receive maximum publicity. In this, T.C., who had stood by Pierre during the entire fight, tried to refute the charges that Pierre had withheld information from him. Said Coleman, "Mr. Pierre S. du Pont, then Vice-President of the Company, wrote me fully of the affairs of the company during my . . . [illness], and, on again reading his letters, I find that he left unreported no material fact in regard to the proposition made by me nor to its non-acceptance by the Finance Committee." He concluded by asserting that the "stockholders should know directly from me that I believe that they have no right or interest whatever in the stock which I formerly owned, and that, if for any reason the sale to Mr. Pierre S. du Pont was not effective, then title to stock is properly mine."[123]

By early September Pierre had a majority of the proxies and it was clear that he would win. Even the opposition realized this and began to explore ways of forcing Pierre to turn Coleman's stock over to the company without holding a stockholders' meeting. However Judge Thompson would not follow this course.[124] But even the prospect of victory held scant cheer for Pierre. The court's opinion and Alfred's attack had struck at Pierre's most precious possessions, his honor and his integrity. Ever since his father's untimely death he had been the leader of his large family and the guardian of their many interests. Pierre's brothers and sisters continued to refer to him affectionately as Dad and, as his responsibilities grew, Pierre became the guardian of the affairs of many men and women both in and out of the du Pont family. It was no accident that Bessie G. du Pont, Alfred's first wife, had turned to Pierre to serve as her financial trustee. His action in offering to make good any loss suffered by the key employees or their heirs as a result of the bonus suit was a typical case of the way he kept his word. Pierre had promised the bonuses, and he had arranged for them at his own expense. The recipients had made good on their obligations, and Pierre would see that their bonuses were made good as long as he had the money to do it.

Pierre had prided himself upon having the trust of the entire family, and this was certainly true prior to his purchase of Coleman's stock. He had been on good terms with both William and his brother Colonel Henry du Pont. He had mediated between Alfred and Coleman, and between Alfred and his first wife Bessie. Pierre had strong opinions about some relationships; he sympathized with Colonel Henry and Barksdale in their dispute with William du Pont, but for more than ten years he had managed to avoid taking sides openly in that dispute and had been friendly with all. Although in a family as large and as polarized as the du Ponts nobody could be a strong leader and keep the good will of everybody all the time, Pierre did not realize this until the fight over Coleman's stock. And even then Pierre kept wishing that something would happen to restore the old relationships. The family was still as important to him as the firm.

Nothing better illustrates Pierre's anguish than his correspondence with May Saulsbury. May had been William du Pont's wife prior to a divorce and remarriage to Willard Saulsbury. May's marital status had become as controversial in Wilmington society as had Alfred du Pont's. Mrs. Saulsbury, who had a fiery temper and a suspicious mind, created additional turmoil in 1905 by causing her husband to file a memorandum in the New Castle

Court of Chancery against the E. I. du Pont de Nemours & Company because she felt her rights as a holder of $150,000 of company purchase notes had been compromised.[125] Although this had been settled amicably, May's husband Willard had been anything but neutral toward the du Pont family. In 1912 the Democrats sent him to the United States Senate. Previously he had unsuccessfully tried to unseat Senator Henry du Pont for "alleged wholesale corruption," and claimed that were he, Saulsbury, sent to the Senate, Colonel Henry "would go out by the back door."[126] Colonel Henry was still a senator when Saulsbury was elected, and hatred between the two had grown so intense that Delaware's senior senator ignored long-time tradition and refused to present his new colleague to the Senate. Through all this Pierre and May remained good friends.

May did not get around to considering sending in a proxy until well after Pierre had received more than enough to win a stunning victory. Then May wrote Pierre, enclosing a letter from her husband urging that she vote to support Alfred's side.[127] May asked for more information and advice. Pierre replied that he was "disappointed that your proxy did not come without hesitation, as the failure shows a doubt in your mind which I hoped to have been spared." But, he continued, as "your letter indicates that your mind is still open . . . I believe that I can place before you further information of interest if you will spare me a few minutes to talk it over."[128] When May delayed an answer, Pierre wrote an impassioned plea. "If one thing is certain about this case," said Pierre, "it is that I personally know that I either *did* or *did not* intentionally and deliberately perpetrate a fraud upon our stockholders. Whether I am telling the truth when I say—as I have said under oath—that *I did not do this thing* is a statement to be believed or not as the hearer may elect. . . . My friends must choose between two courses. First: to believe that I wilfully committed a fraudulent act and have perjured myself in its denial, in which event they should oust me from my position in the company; or Second: That the court with most meager evidence, none of which consists of testimony or direct statements of witnesses, has erred. There seems no middle ground."[129]

May's reply, equally troubled but sympathetic, explained that she had avoided a meeting because of an "excitable disposition." Said she, "I have always liked you." She felt that Pierre's "desire to have the safe control of the company had confused the question" in his mind, but she added, "I do think that in this matter you have made a mistake and I have never had a doubt that the stockholders should have been consulted."[130] She held to her belief that Pierre should have turned the profits over to the company. She stressed that she looked at the whole matter as a legal one and that she still had the "kindest feelings" toward Pierre. Her letter left no doubt that she would vote to uphold Alfred's cause. Pierre still did not give up. He argued that the question was not a business or a legal one and that the personal side

was paramount. "I am," he wrote, "disappointed that it does not appeal to
. . . you more strongly. Perhaps I am oversensitive on the subject. For my
part I do not distinguish between business and personal integrity. You may
have an indefinite idea of things gone wrong, but at heart you cannot believe
that I am involved in any fraudulent transactions such as those pictured by
the Court. If so, it seems incredible that you should endeavor to justify your
intuitions by subscribing to gross charges of misconduct which must be the
reason for a vote to acquire the stock in question."[131]

Despite May Saulsbury's painful defection, Pierre's victory at the stockholders' meeting held on October 10, 1917, left no doubt that the vast
majority of the du Pont family and the other stockholders found no fault
with his action. As Pierre analyzed the returns, he noted that every officer
and director of the company, together with 60 of 65 members of the du Pont
family (excluding the plaintiffs), voted with him. Of the noninterested
shares (owned neither by a plaintiff, defendant, nor a du Pont), 203,937, or
71.3 %, were voted against Alfred. "Of the eight hundred Wilmington
stockholders, 763, or 95%, voted with the Defendants. Of 171 shareholders
holding more than 200 shares, 158, or 92% sided with the Defendants."
Pierre must have been pleased to note that although "Mr. Alfred I. du Pont
has been heralded as the champion of the small stockholder, the Defendants
voted the proxies of 1258 individuals out of a total of 1414 stockholders
owning less than 20 shares."[132] Pierre's margin of victory was more than 2
shares to 1.[133]

Alfred still did not want to admit defeat. His paper charged that Pierre
had influenced the stockholders' meeting by "wrongful methods" and he
urged the court to compel Pierre to give up the disputed stock despite the
vote. [134] But Judge Thompson did not take Alfred's advice and the court,
taking note of the stockholders' decision, dismissed the original bill of
complaint. Commented the *Wall Street Journal:* "This practically ends the
long-fought litigation instituted by Alfred I. du Pont . . . unless he and his
co-plaintiffs take an appeal to the United States Circuit Court of Appeals
which is said to be impossible."[135]

Alfred did appeal. The case dragged on after the war had ended in 1919.
Finally, the United States Circuit Court of Appeals filed its ruling on March
6, 1919. The opinion, written by Judge Buffington, who had previously ruled
against the Powder Company in the antitrust case, quashed all of Alfred's
hopes; it reinterpreted much of the massive testimony of the original trial
in a manner very favorable to Pierre. Buffington emphasized that the long
delay in filing the original suit had hurt Alfred's case. The stock "was
acquired by the Syndicate in February [1915], the directors declined to take
. . . [it] for the Company in March, and this Bill was not filed until December. In the meantime the stock had increased to an extraordinary value. It
was known in March that the Company by its directors had declined to take

it. If the directors took this step in violation of their duty, the wrong was done then and the basis for legal redress then existed." But nothing was done until nine months afterwards and in the meantime "uncertainties had become certainties, and the business had proved so successful, such large profits were so certain that the stock increased rapidly in value." This made the whole question different from the "uncertain speculative question it was in March preceding, and this Bill, filed in December, stands in a very different light before a court of equity from what would have been the case had it been promptly filed. If the Company had been unsuccessful [in its war contracts], if the fears of Alfred I. du Pont and those who thought with him, [that Powder Company stock was worth only $125 a share] had proved well founded and the Syndicate had not been able to take the stock and there had been an effort to compel the Company to take it, there can be little doubt, indeed, the proof by one of the stockholders is, that legal steps would have been taken to prevent the Company taking it if such attempt had been made."[136]

The circuit court's ruling stopped Alfred's attack and he soon made conciliatory moves. The day following the decision he and William came to see Pierre to discuss the Du Pont Company's annual report. It was a chilly meeting. Nobody mentioned the decision, but William did bring up the bonus suit, which still lingered on. He offered to mediate that issue between Pierre and Alfred. Pierre spurned the offer. He remarked "that there was . . . no need for [a] mediator . . . in the bonus suit, the question was between Alfred and the beneficiaries of the bonus plan and not between him and me."[137] Pierre later wrote his attorney George S. Graham that he hoped the interview indicated that Alfred was ready to drop the suit. Although Alfred finally terminated that action, the once friendly relationship between Alfred and Pierre had been permanently smashed. Oddly enough, Francis I. du Pont, who also came into the Du Pont Building the day after the court decision, avoided Pierre.[138] In his case, however, time effected a reconciliation. Thus ended the tragic and bitter events that left Pierre in full control of the Du Pont Company.

The most critical period in the history of any modern large impersonal corporation comes when the founder or his family have to make terms with the requirements of large-scale enterprise. If the company is to continue long as a force in its industry, the needs of the enterprise must come before those of the family. Above all, managers of the company must be chosen for their technical and administrative competence and ability. The direction of the firm can no longer be left to untrained, unskilled men just because they are members of the family.

For the Du Pont Company the case of du Pont versus du Pont symbolized the culmination of this transition. Pierre had done much more than any other du Pont of his generation to ease this critical readjustment. But in the end he had to decide between the family and the enterprise. Those who were not part of the new corporation, or who, like Alfred and Francis I., found it hard to meet its demanding requirements, were unable to fully accept the change. They still felt that they should have a say in the family "birthright" and were disturbed that outsiders should have a larger role in and receive larger rewards from the activities of the Du Pont Company. Pierre was able to keep these discontents muted until Coleman's ambitions and his plans to sell out forced the issue of control. Pierre then felt he had to choose between the needs of the enterprise and the continuance of family solidarity. Searing as the experience was, Pierre du Pont never doubted that he had made the right choice. Surely the E. I. du Pont de Nemours Powder Company would have had great difficulty in meeting the greatest challenge of its history—that raised by the coming of the first world war in a hundred years—without the services of the most competent and best-trained managers in the industry.

# Supplying the Allies

T HE YEAR 1914 marked the first of five of the busiest and most demanding years of Pierre's life. During this period he faced simultaneously the problem of succession and the resulting bitter family fight, the unprecedented demands brought on by World War I, and the unexpected problems posed by a major personal investment in the new and dynamic automobile industry. The challenge created by the outbreak of World War I came on the Powder Company just at the moment that Pierre and Coleman had resolved the related issues of succession and the restructuring of the company's administrative organization by making Pierre again acting president and by installing a new Executive Committee chaired by his brother Irénée.

Meeting the demands of a major modern international war would during the twentieth century become part of the experience of most large American corporations. But in 1914 the challenges were totally new. The Civil War had been over for almost half a century, and it never called for the expansion of output that World War I did. The Spanish-American War was only a momentary affair, although it was one that did provide the Du Pont Company with some guidelines in 1914.

The First World War was one of the most significant events in the history of the Du Pont Company because it demanded such sudden and enormous expansion. Prior to the American entry into the war in 1917, the Du Pont Company had amassed enormous profits. From any point of view the war business was truly staggering. In 1912, the Powder Company's best prewar year, its gross receipts amounted to $35,524,000 and the net earnings were $6,871,000. The court-ordered dissolution reduced the gross to

$26,675,000 and the net to $5,347,000 in 1913. The economic recession of 1914 caused both the net and gross to shrink still further.[1] In 1915, however, even though commercial business fell sharply, gross receipts soared to $131,142,000, and net earnings, after providing for amortization, came to $57,399,000. The next year, 1916, gross receipts increased almost two and one-half times, to $318,845,000, and net earnings to $82,107,000.[2] In short, in the single year 1916, the company's gross receipts and net earnings both exceeded the combined totals for all the prewar years since the three cousins had taken control! Pierre himself never tried to minimize the huge sums made by his company. Testifying before the Senate Committee chaired by Senator Gerald P. Nye of North Dakota, which investigated the munitions industry in 1934, Pierre tried to insert into the record the correct statistics. But, he commented, "I am not trying to fight the figures, because no matter what the figures are, the profit was very large."[3]

Viewed from hindsight, it has seemed almost inevitable that the du Ponts would get rich out of the war. They were in the munitions business at a time when a prolonged armed conflict engulfed most of the civilized world. For more than two years they were in the fortunate position of selling their wares to foreign nations. This made it possible for them to garner high profits on such sales without vulnerability to charges of unpatriotic profiteering. H. C. Englebrecht and F. C. Hanighen, in their book *Merchants of Death, A Study of the International Armament Industry*, emphasized that almost any munitions maker was bound to prosper. "Du Pont did very well during the war," they said and then they asserted that "Winchester Repeating Arms Company, manufacturers of rifles, bayonets, and ammunition, could hardly complain of bad business." There followed a summary of Winchester's war production record, which was indeed impressive.[4]

## The Problems of War Business

Nothing was further from the truth, however, than the axiom that war business brought automatic profits. The cases of Winchester and the Remington Arms Company give eloquent testimony to the pitfalls of war business. No other American corporations manufactured goods more directly relevant to warfare, and both companies won large Allied contracts. In October 1914 Remington received orders from the British for a minimum of 1 million Enfield rifles. This necessitated raising production at the Ilion, New York, plant from 500 guns a day to 2,000 a day. In 1915 Russia ordered 1 million rifles and 100 million rounds of ammunition to be manufactured at Remington's Bridgeport, Connecticut, plant.[5] Winchester also obtained large Allied orders. By December of 1914 the company had contracts worth over $16.0 million on its books; by the end of 1915 total Allied orders stood at approximately $47.5 million.[6]

Despite the extraordinary business, both companies came near disaster. In order to meet its commitments, Remington embarked on a large-scale expansion. By 1916 the company encountered delays, and as a result expenses continued to mount, and creditors became concerned. In order to restore confidence, Samuel Pryor stepped down from Remington's presidency. A creditors' committee was formed, and Harry S. Kimball became president to act for the committee. Then, just as things seemed to be going well, the Russian Revolution occurred, and the new Kerensky government repudiated the contract for the 1 million rifles. This left the Remington Company with 750,000 completed guns and an apparent loss of $10.0 million. Only America's entry into the war and the United States government's subsequent purchase of 600,000 of the Russian rifles saved the company from bankruptcy.[7]

Winchester had no better luck with Allied business. Russian and English rifle needs forced the company into a large expansion. Although the Russian orders were finished almost on schedule, Winchester ran into trouble in the production of two British orders totaling 400,000 Enfield rifles. The contracts had been signed in November of 1914 and March of 1915, and it was expected that the last guns would be finished by mid-1916. But the company failed to meet its delivery timetable, and in September 1916, after only about 235,000 of the 400,000 rifles had been accepted, the British canceled the contract. In 1916, therefore, when the Du Pont Company enjoyed an enormous profit, Winchester faced a financial crisis. In the words of Harold Williamson, Winchester's historian, "The war contracts with the Allies, which had been expected to total $47.5 million and yield a manufacturing profit of $15.5 million, actually totaled $30.7 million and returned a manufacturing profit of $5.47 million."[8] If, Williamson continued, Winchester's Allied business had been charged with its share of the overhead, the net profit "would be reduced to nothing."[9] And these figures did not allow a penny for the amortization of more than $24,706,000 that had been invested in new plants to produce the war goods, of which more than $16.0 million had been borrowed from the Boston investment banking house of Kidder, Peabody & Company.[10]

It is not surprising, therefore, that in April 1916 Winchester's management, through Kidder, Peabody, made a persistent effort to unload the company onto the du Ponts, who, they felt, had both the capital and the skill to rescue Winchester from its financial troubles. After an initial interest the Du Pont Company's Executive Committee, with Pierre's concurrence, concluded that there was little chance that the Allied orders would produce a profit. Thus the Du Pont offer to Winchester wrote off the war business as "highly speculative" and valued the company's stock on the basis of its prewar earning record. Winchester's management, still hoping to complete the British orders, felt that in the end they could turn a profit, and did not accept the Du Pont valuation of their stock.[11] Shortly thereafter the British cancellation of the Enfield contract confirmed Du Pont's estimates and left the Winchester management with no profit on the war business and a large debt incurred to pay for the required new facilities. Only the fortuitous entrance of the United States into the war provided orders to utilize Winchester's new capacity and to make possible an over-all profit on the World War I military business.[12]

The problems that faced Remington and Winchester were similar: each company came near disaster for identical reasons. In both cases, the war produced orders far in excess of each concern's facilities, thus forcing construction of extensive new plants. Further, the orders were not for regular merchandise, but were for special guns and other matériel designed to meet Russian or English military specifications. This caused many problems in tooling up for production. Indeed, both companies encountered severe difficulties in manufacturing products that would meet the rigid standards of Russian and British inspectors. Williamson blames inspection troubles for much of the delay on Winchester's Enfield contract. In fact, such problems were almost inevitable, since the Enfield rifle was in the process of being redesigned at the time the British let their war contracts, and the American manufacturers had only a model from which to hastily develop production capacity. It would be easy to blame technical difficulties and bureaucratic tangles for the troubles of the gun manufacturers, but the real problem lay elsewhere.

The root difficulty for both Winchester and Remington was their managements' faulty conception of the problems of war business. Allied orders required the construction of new facilities and other capital investments for which there would be little if any use after the war's end. Further, the very nature of war itself presented major difficulties. No one knew how long it would last or what its effect would be on world price levels. The vital fact of war business was a high degree of uncertainty, particularly in relation to the volume of orders and deliveries. Among the immediate questions that should have been asked by management were: What will happen if the war ends, or if prices of supplies rise? The record indicated that neither Winchester nor Remington considered these questions.

Both managements seemed to regard the war as an opportunity rather than a risk. Indeed, in September 1914 Winchester contacted British sources soliciting contracts.[13] Neither Winchester nor Remington took measures to differentiate war business from their normal civilian work, which they continued at a usual pace until the American entry in the war. Management's attitude led both companies to make contracts that placed the burden for financing the required capital expansion on themselves. The data given here are for Winchester, but Remington followed the same pattern. Although Winchester received approximately an $8.6 million advance from the Allies, this provided only one-third of the new money necessary for the war business.[14] In order to raise the rest, Winchester had to divert profits from its civilian earnings and to borrow. This, in effect, caused Winchester to assume most of the risk of wartime expansion, and made it easy for England or Russia to cancel or modify a contract without bringing upon themselves much financial loss. Indeed, the Enfield contracts had vague cancellation clauses which were later interpreted to mean that the contracts could be terminated "on 90 days' notice."[15] Add to this the comparatively long-term nature of the production schedule. In the case of the Enfield rifles there was a lapse of almost two years from the time the first contract was signed in 1914 and the last gun was to be delivered in 1916. Despite this, Winchester fixed prices on the guns in 1914 and figured its paper profits margins in terms of costs as of that date. No provision was made for a rise in the cost of labor or raw materials. This item alone cost Winchester a reduction of $7.93 million in its expected profit of $15.5 million.[16] It is no wonder, therefore, that the Du Pont Executive Committee, in April 1916, wrote off Winchester's war contracts as of no value. The committee analyzed all of the rifle maker's problems: the fact that the Allies could cancel their orders and leave Winchester with a loss; the rise in the cost of raw materials and labor over previous estimates; and the very unfavorable ratio between the capital invested in the war business and the profits expected from it. For Du Pont, Winchester had a good potential in its normal civilian business, but its war contracts were almost a guide for those who wanted to bankrupt themselves.[17]

## Drawing the Allied Contracts

The Du Pont Company faced most of the problems that plagued the gun manufacturers. Black powder and high explosives (dynamite), the two divisions that in prewar years normally accounted for about 85% of the company's business, languished between 1915 and 1917 as plants produced well below their capacities.[18] Military explosives, the kind purchased by the Allies and later by the United States government, were largely limited to three types. First and most important was smokeless powder, followed by trinitrotoluol (TNT) and picric acid. None of these three enjoyed any widespread commercial sales during the prewar period; nor was there much prospect that civilian demand for these products could be developed after the war. All required special manufacturing facilities that were not readily adaptable to other purposes. In 1914 Du Pont production capabilities for these products were small, or, in the case of picric acid, nonexistent. Despite the company's near monopoly of the nongovernment production of smokeless powder, Du Pont capacity was rated at only about 700,000 pounds per month, almost nothing compared to the actual output of nearly 38 million pounds reached in March of 1918.[19] In the prewar years, however, Du Pont's rated smokeless capacity of 700,000 pounds had seldom been operated for any sustained period of time. In fact, by mid-1914 attacks against the Du Pont "Powder Trust" had so restricted government orders that the business had shrunk to about 8% of the company's total, and in May the Finance Committee was giving serious consideration to concentrating smokeless production in a single factory and to abandoning two of Du Pont's three smokeless powder plants.[20] Du Pont was even less established in the manufacture of TNT, which it had begun to produce in 1912. Commercial hopes for this explosive had led to an investment of $360,000 and a monthly capacity of 300,000 pounds on the eve of the war. Yet only 10% of the capacity had ever been sold. By 1918, however, TNT sales amounted to 3,318,000 pounds per month, requiring that the prewar capacity be increased tenfold.[21] Picric acid, used as a filling for armor-piercing shells, did have a commercial use in the dye industry. Prior to 1914, however, this had been realized only in Europe, especially in Germany, which, at the time World War I started, had been supplying most of the chemical dyes used in the United States. Du Pont as yet had not moved into dyes, which required a technical competence and an investment far beyond the mere ability to manufacture picric acid.

The Allied orders, therefore, for Du Pont as well as for Winchester and Remington, demanded the immediate erection of new production units, for which there would be little or no use in a postwar market economy. Like the gun manufacturers, Du Pont had to raise vast amounts of capital. It was no accident but, rather, good foresight and extremely competent management that enabled Du Pont to succeed where the others had failed.

It was, of course, by chance that the war started just as Pierre had assumed the full direction of the company. It was in late August, the first month of the war, when Coleman, under pressure from both his outside interests and health, stepped aside. Irénée, who both Pierre and Coleman had hoped would lead the company, was under the circumstances reluctant to take over, so Pierre remained the senior executive officer, and Irénée assumed charge of operations as the chairman of the new Executive Committee. By December Coleman's worsening health took him out of even an advisory capacity, and the sale of his stock in February 1915 removed him completely. Alfred, obviously, left the center of power by his decision in December 1914 to oppose Coleman's efforts to sell his stock. The subsequent fight with Pierre removed Alfred from the company's inner councils entirely by the end of 1915. Of the principal executives who had from the first helped the three cousins transform the Du Pont interests from a family enterprise to a modern corporation, few survived the reorganization of the fall of 1914. Moxham resigned, and by early 1915 was trying to get in on the new war business by helping to form the Aetna Explosives Company consisting of a merger of three small explosives companies. J. A. Haskell retired; Charles L. Patterson and Pierre's trusted friend Hamilton Barksdale remained active in the company's affairs, but they served not in an administrative capacity but as vice-presidents, advisers, and troubleshooters, with few specific duties.

Nearly all the day-to-day operations of the company would be handled by the new Executive Committee, which included, besides its chairman Irénée, another of Pierre's brothers, Lammot, as head of Black Powder; a brother-in-law, R. R. M. Carpenter, in charge of the Development Department; H. Fletcher Brown, as director of Smokeless Powder; Harry G. Haskell, as director of High Explosives; William Coyne, as director of Sales; and John J. Raskob, as treasurer. Frank Connable remained on the committee, with nominal charge of purchasing. After March 1916, when Frank Tallman came on the committee as vice-president in charge of purchasing, Connable became more an elder statesman like Patterson and Barksdale.[22]

Pierre, therefore, concentrated his attention on broad policies, particularly on fixing the terms that would define the relationship between the Allies and the company. His decisions, more than any other person's, ensured that Du Pont would emerge from the war with a profit. And in making these decisions he continued to rely on the advice of Hamilton Barksdale.

Unlike the gun manufacturers, Pierre refused to regard the outbreak of the war as an opportunity. In fact, his initial reaction was just the opposite, since he felt that normal civilian business would suffer. Consequently, shortly after the start of the war, on August 24, 1914, he joined with the other members of the Executive Committee in urging that capital expenditures and major repairs for all departments, commercial and smokeless powder, be curtailed.[23] Every instinct bolstered by past experience told Pierre that war brought with it more danger than opportunity for his company. Pierre's first experience with the explosives industry under Eugene du Pont had culminated during the Spanish-American War. Then Pierre had seen the company turn its full energies toward the manufacture of powder for the United States Army and Navy. This had included a rapid enlargement of facilities to make brown prismatic military cannon powder of no commercial value. Spain's unexpectedly quick defeat left the company with expanded facilities, large quantities of prismatic powder on hand, and canceled contracts. Since brown prismatic powder had become outmoded by the smokeless variety, Du Pont was left with a product that had become almost valueless. Immediately after the war, the navy canceled a contract for 1 million pounds of brown prismatic and asked the du Ponts to substitute a similar quantity of smokeless powder at a price that would compensate for the cost of increasing the brown prismatic powder facilities. Eugene du Pont stated that his company would prefer to take the loss rather than go into more military business.[24]

The Spanish-American War left an indelible impression on Pierre's mind. It taught him that wars, because of their unpredictable nature, presented an enormous risk to commercial enterprises and that any plans for war production were subject to immediate cancellation. One of the main reasons that Pierre and Coleman desired to bring International Smokeless under Du Pont control in 1903 was that they feared that company, which depended entirely upon military orders, would inevitably encounter periods of large orders followed by canceled contracts or slack demand. This, they felt, would tempt International's management to expand their activities into the more stable commercial business. Thus, it was the desire to keep a potentially strong competitor from arising in the nonmilitary sphere that brought International Smokeless into the Du Pont orbit.[25]

The big company's experience with smokeless powder did not bring happy results. Ever since Waddell's attack (in 1906) launched the antitrust fight, the company had been under a hail of criticism for its role in supplying military and naval powder. Hostility in Congress had restricted military orders and had lowered prices for those that were allowed. By February 1914 smokeless prospects looked so bleak that Pierre joined with the other members of the Powder Company's Finance Committee to vote that "no expenditures be made for the purpose of maintaining or increasing . . . [the smokeless powder] plants until the policy of the Government as to purchasing explosives has been more clearly defined."[26]

It is ironic, but it is nonetheless true, that it was a mistrust of war business created by years of frustration in the production of military powder that guided Pierre in his management of the company during World War I. Even more paradoxical, this mistrust was, in large measure, responsible for much of his success. At the beginning, Pierre, in common with most observers both in Europe and America, expected the war to be of short duration. They felt that the war would resemble the most recent European conflict, the Franco-Prussian War. Pierre's brother Irénée regarded the conflict as an annoyance. On August 10, 1914, he wrote to H. J. Mitchell of England's Nobel Dynamite Trust Company that "I do hope this unfortunate war will soon be over and appreciate that it must be more of an inconvenience to you than to us." Consequently, two weeks after the start, Pierre agreed with Barksdale that caution should be exercised before even as much as $15,000 was spent on improvements in the smokeless powder plants. Both felt that although new equipment might be beneficial, its use would probably be temporary. Thus, on August 20, 1914, when the Finance Committee considered two appropriations totaling less than $16,000 recommended by H. F. Brown for the Carney's Point factory, Pierre and his colleagues approved them "with the understanding that they . . . [would be] made only upon the receipt by us of large additional orders for Smokeless Powder either from Foreign Governments or our own government."[27]

Pierre's attitude was that no expenditures, however minor, should be made without definite orders in hand. This cautious policy was but the corollary of Pierre's assumption that the war could end tomorrow. Throughout the conflict Pierre never changed that assumption. Every plan was made with provisions to protect the company from a sudden end to hostilities and the consequent cancellation of orders.

In October of 1914, after the war had been raging a little over two months, it became evident that Du Pont would be offered large Allied contracts. The French alone talked of placing a single order for 8 million pounds of cannon powder. This was equal to an entire year's capacity of the existing Du Pont smokeless plants. Russia and England also expressed interest in buying Du Pont powder. Thus, within a few weeks after the outbreak of war, it became clear that the Powder Company would have to build new capacity if Allied orders should materialize.

For Pierre, therefore, the problem was the terms on which the company should take war orders. Du Pont had supplied smokeless cannon powder to the United States government at the congressionally fixed price of 53¢ per pound. This figure had produced a profit, although Pierre felt that the government orders were too small relative to the size of the fixed capital investment the company had to maintain to fulfill them and consequently there was not adequate compensation for the resources invested. In short, had the government ordered enough powder to keep plants running at near full capacity, instead of 30% to 40%, the company would have made substantial return on its investment.

In dealing with the Allies, Pierre never let nonbusiness considerations sway his judgment. Return on investment was his goal, and although he later became strongly pro-Allied, in the early months, in the true spirit of a neutral, he would have dealt with either side. On February 5, 1915, he wrote Coleman that if the Germans "came forward with orders in quantity similar to the orders of the Allied nations we would be willing to sell."[28] Thus business, not sentiment, controlled Pierre's thinking. Since orders from the Central Powers could hardly have been expected to materialize, these considerations remained purely academic.

Pierre realized that he was negotiating with the Allies from a position of strength. As he later phrased it: "We went into this war business at the solicitation of the Allies, not at our solicitation. They wanted powder, and the reason they wanted it was they could not manufacture it themselves. It required anywhere from 4 to 9 pounds of raw materials to be taken across the water to produce a pound of powder on the other side. We know what the shortage of vessels was at that time. The Allies did not want to take four times as much material over there to make the powder in the plants that they were obliged to build at a greater cost than we could build them on this side."[29]

Because the raw materials for cannon powder (cotton and nitrate of soda) came from the Western Hemisphere, Pierre was better able to insist that the Allies, not the Powder Company, should take the risk of building any new capacity. Since Pierre felt that the war would soon end, he determined that the price per pound of powder should be high enough so that an initial order would at one swoop amortize the construction of all needed facilities, and also provide a profit. The figure that Pierre set in consultation with H. Fletcher Brown, Irénée, and Colonel Buckner was $1 per pound. This was nearly twice what the United States government paid for smokeless powder. Pierre felt that 50¢ per pound would, on large orders, provide enough to cover the cost of manufacture, allow a cushion for rising costs, and give a substantial profit. The remaining 50¢ would finance the cost of building new factories. The French, who were the first to negotiate with the company, agreed to pay $1 per pound. The French government suggested that it insure the Du Pont Company by depositing 25% of the face value of the contract in a bank of the government's choice.[30]

Pierre rejected this idea. The contract, which was finally signed on October 12, 1914, provided for the Du Pont Company to manufacture 8 million pounds of cannon powder at $1 per pound and 1.25 million pounds of guncotton at 75¢ per pound. The French were to supply cash equal to 50% of the face value of the contract prior to October 23, 1914; another 30% came due when the powder was placed in the dry house, and the remainder when the powder was ready for shipment. (Terms for the guncotton, which did not need drying, were 50% in advance and 50% upon delivery at the dock in New York.) This contract ensured that the French would supply the capital for constructing all new munitions plants and that the du Ponts would receive the money before being committed to any expenditures. The risks that the Powder Company took in the first phase of the French contract owing to capital investments were thus almost eliminated.

There was, however, a risk in the second part. Because of France's need for maximum speed, the Powder Company committed itself to a tight delivery schedule. In the case of the cannon powder, 300,000 pounds were to be delivered before November 1914; 450,000 pounds in December 1914; 625,000 pounds monthly January to April 1915; 750,000 pounds May to October 1915; and 250,000 pounds in November 1915.[31] If this timetable was not met, the French had the right to cancel at any time. The du Ponts risked the working capital that they had to advance to purchase raw materials and the cost of manufacture against their ability to meet their delivery schedule. Yet, even here, the risks might be reduced. Unprocessed raw materials such as cotton might be sold or, in the case of the nitrates, diverted to peacetime explosives such as dynamite. In any case, the Du Pont Company's risks were small compared to those taken by Winchester and Remington, who financed their capital expansion by borrowing money against payments they would receive only after they had delivered the goods.

The most unusual part of the original Du Pont contract with the French was that government's willingness to advance 50% of the price of the powder with no security. This feature became a standard part of all the Du Pont–Allied contracts that required capital expenditures. Had Du Pont failed to construct the munitions works, the Allies would have taken the loss. Speaking in June of 1918, Pierre attributed the Allies' willingness to take such a risk to the company's financial standing. The foundation of this strength, he argued, stemmed from the consolidation of the explosives industry initiated by Pierre and Coleman after purchasing the Du Pont interests in 1902.[32] Consolidation also gave the company a new technological strength that grew in the following decade. Had the industry remained fragmented, no such contracts could ever have been made. Left unsaid by Pierre, but equally as important, had been the reputation for fiscal strength he had established during his reign as treasurer. Pierre's successful efforts to build an international credit rating, the ease with which the company had ridden out the panic of 1907, and the strong fiscal posture maintained through the dissolution crisis had been noted in the financial community, and paid big dividends in the fall of 1914. And in 1915 Pierre regarded his purchase of Coleman's stock as an important part of retaining the confidence of the financial community and the Allies.

In the building of the new units Pierre continued his conservative policy. Soon after arranging the French contract he chaired a Finance Committee meeting that voted "as soon as the first payment of $4,000,000 is received from the French Government on its order for 8,000,000 pounds of powder [that] $1,500,000 of this amount be set aside for the purpose of further increasing our smokeless powder capacity approximately 5,000,000 [per annum] by building another plant at such a point as may be recommended by the Executive Committee."[33] This was but the beginning of a long string of actions which turned advance payments into new munitions plants. The following month the Finance Committee explicitly defined an amortization policy. All expenditures that it authorized in connection with increasing smokeless output were to be amortized immediately "out of the profits on our export business."[34] This meant that before any dividends were declared, the company paid for the new plants, and for accounting purposes wrote off their value. In actual fact, of course, as long as the plants were operated, the capital invested in them would produce profits. It was, therefore, the confirmation of Pierre's hard bargain with the Allies, together with the unexpectedly long continuation of the war, that was the key to big profits for the Du Pont Company. Since capital costs were amortized on the first order, new orders meant high profits. The continued rush of demand at the end of 1914 and during the early months of 1915 kept the Powder Company building new facilities at such a rate that it was not until the end of 1915 that the size of the profit margin became clear. For cannon powder, for example, the Du Pont Company received orders for over 15 million pounds by the end of December 1914; and in January and February of 1915 additional orders for over 34 million pounds were placed. It is no wonder that Pierre, writing to Coleman at the end of January 1915, found it "difficult to judge of the effect of earnings by the extraordinary business." He guessed that it would be "in the neighborhood of 100 per cent."[35] But with the general picture changing so rapidly, Pierre wanted to be on the cautious side. He looked forward to raising the dividend from 8% to 12%, but he was reluctant to make public much data. He preferred to confine information to company officials—that is, administrators and directors. Consequently he considered not publishing the usual quarterly reports. The increase of the dividend, together with the rumors of large orders, would, he felt, keep stockholders from selling. But at the same time the lack of hard data would cool overheated expectations, thus giving management more room to maneuver in case the war ended suddenly or events reduced profit margins.[36] But reality exceeded the most hopeful thoughts. Gross receipts for 1915 totaled over $131.0 million and soared to more than $318.8 million in 1916. And, as has been pointed out, net earnings after providing for amortization were over $57.4 million in 1915 and $82.1 million in 1916.[37]

Indeed, by the middle of 1916 the du Ponts found themselves with a large manufacturing capacity that had been completely amortized. This forced them to review their prices. Through May of 1916 the Du Pont Company had made a standard charge to the Allies of $1 per pound of smokeless powder. Sales to Bethlehem Steel, a company that had large munitions orders for shells and bought powder from Du Pont to load them, had been at 80¢ per pound. Pierre justified this price on the ground that "Bethlehem Steel were old customers of ours. We felt they were entitled to a [lower] price on powder furnished by our original plant, on which there was a heavy amortization."[38] Pierre's reasoning led the Allies to request a reduction in price on orders placed in 1916. This caused the unusual spectacle of a falling price for powder throughout the war, a development that was the exact opposite of almost all other price trends. By May of 1916 Bethlehem Steel's price had dropped to 60¢ per pound. In June of the same year France paid 80¢ per pound, but by the following month prices to the Allies were reduced to 60¢ per pound. They fell to 55¢ in October and to 51.3¢ for Italy's huge order of 20,460,000 pounds in May 1917. Thus, by America's entry into the war the price of smokeless powder had dropped below prewar levels.[39]

Pierre and his brothers later took pride in the price decline. By 1918 not only were the Allies purchasing powder at a price below that set by Congress at the height of the powder trust agitation, but the United States Army had made contracts for over 194 million pounds at prices ranging from a

high of about 46¢ per pound to a low of approximately 43¢ per pound.[40]
During the Nye Investigation, Irénée insisted that the committee place
charts of powder prices alongside those it had developed to depict the price
rises in other fields. Such data put Du Pont in a most favorable light. For
example, cotton, one of the main ingredients of smokeless powder, sold in
January 1918 at prices 2½ times those of 1914. On the first of January 1918
corn sold for twice the price it brought in 1914, and the average of all
commodities stood 75% higher than in 1914.[41]

There were good reasons for the decline in powder prices. The first was
the total amortization of all Du Pont's smokeless powder plants. This eliminated capital costs. The second was volume. Pierre had considered prewar
prices to the United States government too low because orders were in such
small quantities that they failed to produce an adequate return on the capital
invested. But the quantity orders during World War I changed this, and thus
largely offset rising labor and other costs. Beyond this, despite the increase
in cotton prices after 1916, factors were in operation that mitigated many
of the rising costs of raw materials. These will be discussed later in this
chapter.

### Financing Allied Purchases

The nature of the war business confronted Pierre with some unprecedented financial problems. The most important of these concerned the large
quantity of foreign securities that came into the company's possession. On
the first contracts the French and British paid strictly in cash. Had those
two governments desired to pay for part of their orders with bonds, Pierre
undoubtedly would have agreed. But the first such discussion arose with the
Russians. Early in January Colonel Buckner and Pierre met with the Russian financial representatives in New York and discussed a possible order
for 30 million pounds of smokeless powder. The Russians proposed that
payment be made one-half in cash and the rest in bonds. The tsar's representatives, who were used to financial dealings in Europe and were complete
strangers in the United States, frankly told Pierre that they were anxious
to establish their credit in America and that placing a large quantity of
bonds with the Powder Company would be desirable. Pierre advanced an
alternative proposition that he hoped would guarantee the use of the
new powder facilities then under construction for the British and French
after their contracts had been filled. Under this arrangement 500 million
pounds would be supplied, with delivery running three months in 1917.
Payment would be half in bonds and half in cash with the company making
an additional public purchase of $5.0 million of Russian bonds at the time
the contract was signed. This again was designed to boost the Russian credit
rating.

Pierre was enthusiastic. "Of course," he wrote Coleman, "the final result will be equivalent to accepting 40% in cash and 60% in bonds. As the cash payment will let us out with some profit, it seems unlikely that the net result will be anything but very satisfactory."[42] Besides, Pierre did some very naive calculations which determined the ratio of debt to population comparing Russia with France, Germany, England, and the United States, and he concluded that "considering the vast and enormous resources of the Russian Empire, it would seem their bonds are the safest of all the warring nations."[43] So impressed was Pierre by Russian financial strength that he would even have considered taking all payment in bonds.[44] That such a proposition failed was not Pierre's fault, but was due instead to a hesitation on the part of tsarist officials in St. Petersburg to issue bonds.[45] Russia's reluctance was certainly Pierre's luck. In 1916 the Du Pont Company, under pressure from the Allies to shore up Russia's faltering credit, purchased $1,550,000 of Imperial Russian Government external loan bonds. The Russian Revolution a year later taught Pierre how risky foreign bonds could be. By 1919 the tsarist bonds were hopelessly in default, and, of course, they became totally worthless.[46]

Fortunately the Du Pont Company had better luck with British and French securities. After initial cash purchases, both of these countries had to rely upon mass borrowings to raise money to pay for American goods. It was only logical that the Powder Company, as one of the major suppliers of the Allies and a company that stood to profit largely from such business, would become deeply involved in floating British and French paper. At first Du Pont participated in underwriting Anglo-French borrowings. The first appeal came to Pierre in September 1915 from J. P. Morgan, the financial house that the Allies had placed in charge of coordinating their American purchases. Morgan asked the Powder Company to underwrite the bonds "to the extent of $35,000,000" which the Finance Committee agreed to do.[47] This was but the beginning. By 1916 Du Pont had to accept British and French notes in partial payment for some of the powder deliveries. By 1918 the company had supported British and French borrowing to the extent of over $54.0 million and had accepted almost $55.0 million more in the form of notes in payment for goods delivered.[48] The importance of Allied paper to the company can be gauged against the following. During the entire war years, 1915 through 1918, the total net earnings after providing for amortization approximated $235.6 million while the British and French securities totaled about $110.0 million, or nearly half the total.

The problem for Pierre was, therefore, to find a way to turn the British and French securities into cash. Such a conversion had pitfalls. The company had such amounts of these securities that a mass sale would have depressed their price below par. Such an action would not only have been costly to the Du Pont Company, but might have fatally undermined confidence in the securities themselves. Indeed, as the war dragged on, exchange ran so heavily against the Allies that toward the end of 1917 they requested the major holders of short-term notes to renew them. In fact, November of 1917 found Edward R. Stettinius, Jr., of J. P. Morgan, who was acting in behalf of Great Britain, pleading with the Du Pont Company to renew part or all of some $12,986,600.75 of British notes due to mature on December 15, 1917.[49]

For Pierre, the Allied securities represented a dilemma. His company's cash requirements did not allow him to lock up over $100.0 million, yet a way had to be found to dispose of them which would not depress the market or otherwise embarrass the Allies. At first Pierre, as chairman of the Finance Committee, approved of the sale of some Allied paper in small lots. In February 1916 the committee authorized the sale of slightly more than $100,000 of the French Franc Loan 3¾% bonds at a price which yielded a profit of $706.52 in addition to interest accumulated during the time the securities were held.[50] As turning bonds into cash in small lots was a slow process, Pierre sought other methods. In mid-May of 1916 he decided to accept a recommendation from the treasurer, Raskob, that the Anglo-French bonds be paid to the company's stockholders in the form of a dividend. Raskob's was an almost ideal solution. It made possible large dividends, preserved the company's cash to use in its investment program, and transferred the Anglo-French bonds to individual holders, some of whom would hold them for a while, whereas others would dispose of them in small lots. In accord with this, the Finance Committee on May 31, 1916, voted to declare a 25% dividend on June 15, 1916, 5.8% of which would be in cash and 19.2% in Anglo-French bonds.[51] This move enabled the company to get rid of $11,770,840 of the bonds.[52] By the end of the war Du Pont had used as common stock dividends $34,992,800 worth of Allied bonds.[53]

Using foreign securities for dividend purposes succeeded in transferring, however, only about one-third of the Allied securities which the Du Pont Company received. Indeed, at the time of America's entry in the war in April 1917, the company still held over $40.0 million of Allied paper in its treasury. Pierre recognized that Du Pont would be expected to invest heavily in securities the United States would issue to finance the war. In fact, by the war's end Du Pont had purchased in excess of $115.0 million of such offerings.[54] But obligations of the United States government were quite different from those of Britain or France. American securities were easily negotiable, and, in point of fact, the Du Pont Company seldom held them for more than a few weeks. It used them for tax payments and dividend payments, or it sold or discounted them. In short, Pierre regarded holdings of United States securities almost the same as he did cash. His policy was, therefore, to purchase such paper freely, treating it in the same manner as the company traditionally had treated high-grade corporate bonds or government securities in peacetime—that is, as a convenient way to invest a temporary surplus so that it would earn interest, but at the same time be readily convertible into cash.

To Pierre, therefore, the United States entrance into the war in April 1917 seemed to provide an opportunity to dispose of the foreign bonds. President Wilson and Secretary of the Treasury William G. McAdoo immediately launched large-scale drives to sell bonds. Pierre and Raskob felt that the government's effort provided the Du Pont Company a method of accomplishing two very important objectives: first, the company could support the war loan drive by taking a large subscription; and, second, it would pay for the securities by tendering the British and French paper. If this could be done, the company would at one blow transform its Allied holdings into securities instantly convertible into cash. Thus, on May 21, 1917, the Finance Committee authorized Pierre and Raskob to discuss with the secretary of the treasury the purchase of $30.0 million of 3½% United States bonds paying for them with the British and French notes in the company's treasury maturing after December 1, 1917.[55] On June 1, 1917, Pierre and Raskob went to Washington and made their offer to Secretary of the Treasury McAdoo. They promised that the company would subscribe for $30.0 million in the initial Liberty Bond drive, provided they could pay with the Allied securities. Pierre hoped that since sales had yet to match the hoped-for goal McAdoo would react favorably to the idea. But the secretary was cool. He was confident that the first Liberty Loan would be oversubscribed, perhaps as much as two to three times. Furthermore, McAdoo stressed that he had no authority to purchase foreign notes.[56] Pierre recognized that it was futile to press the matter further. In consequence Du Pont made a straight bid for $7,525,000 of the Liberty Loan. The issue was so oversubscribed that the company was allotted only $2,590,000. Even so, Du Pont disposed of the bonds immediately. Of the total, $552,250 worth were held to sell to employees who had agreed to purchase them; the remainder, slightly over $2,037,000 worth, were sold largely to J. P. Morgan & Company and Laird & Company.[57] This turned out to be the first in a series of subscriptions to Liberty Loan drives.

Pierre's failure to convert Allied securities into U.S. bonds left the company with the problem of negotiating the paper itself. This became important, since the program of diversification into the chemical industry needed an infusion of cash. Therefore, those British and French notes not used for dividend purposes were discounted at banks. Even when J. P. Morgan pleaded with Du Pont to extend the due date on the $12,986,600.75 of British notes maturing December 15, 1917, Pierre was not enthusiastic. Acting on the president's advice, the Finance Committee on November 21, 1917, agreed to renew only half of the notes, and only then with the understanding that retained British paper would be endorsed and discounted at a bank.[58] Such maneuvers removed all Allied paper, with the exception of the Imperial Russian bonds, from the company's treasury by December 1918.[59] Pierre and Raskob's careful management of British and French paper ensured that it was converted into cash at little loss to the company and with slight loss in the Allied credit position.

### Monitoring Physical Expansion and the Control of Working Capital

One of the most impressive facts of the Du Pont Company's wartime history was the vast increase in its physical volume of business. This necessitated the massive construction of new plants and large-scale purchasing of raw materials. Du Pont's accomplishment is further magnified when it is realized that, unlike the arms manufacturers who slipped behind their production schedules and who failed to estimate price behavior correctly, the Powder Company met, and in some cases surpassed, contract times for the delivery of powder, and forecast with surprising accuracy production costs and profit margins. Du Pont's success in these spheres was due to a combination of good management and luck.

For Pierre, all his experience with the big company from its founding until the outbreak of hostilities in Europe must have seemed like a dress rehearsal for his role in the war. Although Pierre concentrated on vital policy decisions and although he delegated both the authority and responsibility for tasks of expanding capacity, purchasing raw materials, and meeting production capacity, he, neverthless, kept a keen interest in and watch over these matters. Although not a member, Pierre often attended the Executive Committee's meetings, especially when its members were considering basic issues of expansion and control. As president he carefully reviewed all its activities. As chairman of the Finance Committee he passed on every appropriation that was made for the construction of new plants.

In meeting the challenge of expansion, luck played its part in several ways. For example, the war's outbreak deepened the commercial recession, which had begun to idle much of the company's high explosives capacity in 1914. This temporarily left idle the superb engineering team that had constructed the new dynamite plants. Furthermore, this team had never worked to capacity; lack of capital had curbed expansion. The slack commercial business and the absence of any current plans for commercial development made it possible to put the trained engineering staff immediately to work building smokeless powder capacity. Such work was similar enough to the high explosives factories that had been built to pose no unusual technical problems.

Pierre's team for smokeless powder had grown up with the big company. Harry Fletcher Brown, who headed the Smokeless Powder Department during World War I, was a Harvard-educated chemist who started his career at the navy's Newport, Rhode Island, Torpedo Station. After becoming chief chemist there, he resigned to go to the newly formed International Smokeless Powder and Chemical Company in 1900. When the three cousins bought International, they brought Brown to Wilmington to be the second in command of the then relatively unimportant Du Pont Smokeless Powder Division.[60] Then in 1911 he became its head. The key engineering personnel came from the high explosives side. William G. Ramsay, the Du Pont Company's chief engineer until his untimely death in 1916, was a University of Virginia-educated civil engineer, who in 1892 joined the Repauno Company and, after the consolidation, moved into the engineering division of the High Explosives Operating Department. His assistant, Harry M. Pierce, who became chief engineer upon Ramsay's death, had begun at Repauno in 1893.[61] Together the two had directed the large-scale building of dynamite plants which occurred after 1906.

The minutes of the Executive and Finance committees give ample evidence that the appropriation and control procedures established by Pierre during the period of capital expansion between 1904 and 1911 continued to be used during World War I. After binding contracts for military powder had been signed, H. Fletcher Brown submitted to the Executive Committee detailed appropriations for new construction, whether for the enlargement of the works at Carney's Point or the building of entirely new facilities such as those at Hopewell, Virginia. All during the war, when contracts were signed requiring expanded capacity, the Executive Committee immediately held special meetings to consider the necessary appropriations. When the Executive Committee acted, it sent its decision on to the Finance Committee for final approval at one of its bimonthly meetings. In cases of extreme urgency, Pierre, in consultation with his brother Irénée, who was chairman of the Executive Committee, gave tentative approval to appropriations. Pierre later submitted them for final ratification to a regular meeting of the Finance Committee.[62] During the rush of orders beginning in 1915, H. F. Brown sometimes made preliminary appropriations estimates which both the Executive Committee and Finance Committee acted upon in that form. These were always followed by detailed appropriations data. In all cases, both the Executive Committee and the Finance Committee, and Pierre, had extensive knowledge of the orders that the company had received, the money appropriated for new capacity *prior* to its expenditure, and a continuing flow of data that indicated the rate at which appropriated money was being spent. Because the top engineering staff and H. Fletcher Brown had used this system prior to the war, it was easy for Pierre to keep a tight rein on expenditures during a time of massive expansion.

In the purchasing of supplies, which Frank Tallman continued to handle, fortune favored the Powder Company during the end of 1914 and throughout most of 1915. For example, glycerin, which was in short supply and essential to dynamite, was not a component in smokeless powder. Moreover, the most important raw materials declined or remained stable in price. The outbreak of the war broke the market for the two key smokeless powder ingredients: nitrate of soda and cotton. Nitrate came almost exclusively from Chile. There, despite the vertical integration moves by Du Pont, the main production had remained under the control of British and German interests. The British blockade kept South American nitrate shipments from reaching the Central Powers, thus demoralizing the German companies and depriving Chile of both the German market for nitrate used in explosives and the even larger one for fertilizer. Only Germany's development of large factories that could extract nitrates from the air kept its explosives factories producing. The loss of Continental markets, of course, kept the price of nitrates down.

The British blockade also cut off much of the Central Powers' supply of American cotton. Indeed, cotton prices plummeted at the war's outbreak; by November of 1914 they were almost 50% below the level of 1913. In fact, by 1915 Britain moved to purchase large quantities of American cotton to help raise price levels, thus hoping to end hostility of southern congressmen to its German blockade. Even so, cotton prices remained below 1913 levels all during 1915, and only in July 1916 did they finally soar above those of the last full prewar year.[63]

For the Du Pont Company the immediate problem was one of procuring the necessary raw materials to fulfill its contracts; next, there was the question of whether the company ought to go further and secure supplies beyond those actually needed in order to be prepared for still further expansion of the war business. The risk, of course, was clear; it meant locking up several millions of dollars in materials for which the company would have no use if the war ended suddenly and the contracts were canceled.

Tallman recognized that the drop in cotton prices that accompanied the war's outbreak was an opportunity that should be seized. Consequently he approached the Finance Committee on October 28, 1914, the very time when the first Allied contracts were about to be signed, and asked for permission to purchase 48 million pounds of raw cotton linters worth approximately $720,000. Pierre backed Tallman's suggestion, undoubtedly feeling that cotton prices were so depressed that there was very little risk in case the company had to dispose of the linters on the open market. Consequently, the Finance Committee voted Tallman's purchase of the $720,000 worth of cotton and further set a general policy in regard to that material. It authorized the Purchasing Department to buy linters "to cover our normal supply as may be required to cover special orders on hand and 10 to 15% in excess of such orders."[64] This allowed the acquisition of large amounts of cotton at depressed prices, and when prices finally rose in mid-1916 the company already had a large supply on hand.

The nitrate problem was a bit more complex. The removal of the Central Powers from the market depressed nitrate so that it sold "at approximately the average cost of production."[65] Thus the German nitrate firms were squeezed, and it appeared that there might be opportunities to pick up good properties at bargain prices.[66] By January 1915 the magnitude of the Allied orders became clear, and advance payments began to roll in. That month the company had about $12.0 million excess working capital. Consequently the Executive Committee directed the Purchasing Department to make a special investigation as to the advisability of stocking nitrate of soda.[67] This led to the purchase by March of 1915 of 193,000 tons of nitrate of soda worth approximately $7.7 million, of which 108,000 tons were stored in Chile until needed.[68] As in the case of cotton, advance nitrate purchases worked well, since, as the war dragged on, prices rose substantially, finally soaring above prewar levels.

Although Pierre approved of large advance purchases of nitrate of soda, he and the Executive Committee had doubts about buying more nitrate properties. All felt that if a real bargain could be found it should be investigated, but Pierre knew the risk was great. War conditions were temporary, and new nitrate sources such as Germany's process for extracting it from the air might undermine the value of all Chilean *oficinas*. Indeed, with Pierre's backing the Du Pont Company, in May 1915, moved to form the American Nitrogen Company, which had as its purpose the acquisition of the North American rights of the Norwegian Nitrate Company's process for the manufacture of atmospheric nitrogen.[69] Unfortunately, the Norwegian process required electric power in quantities unavailable in North America in 1915. Pierre hoped that such power could be produced by the harnessing of waterpower at a site either in Canada or in the United States. But to develop sites such as Niagara Falls or the Columbia River the company needed the support of the federal government. And Wilson's administration refused to back the sale or lease of valuable waterpower resources to the du Ponts.[70] Red tape snarled acquisition of Canadian waterpower, and so the scheme to make atmospheric nitrogen languished. Consequently the company remained interested in Chilean properties.[71]

The Purchasing Department, with the backing of Pierre and the Executive Committee, also authorized buying other raw materials besides nitrate of soda in advance of needs. In some cases, however, if supplies of vital materials, such as sulphuric acid and toluol, were short, the company followed the policy it had developed in the prewar period. It matched the prices it would have to pay on the outside market against the cost of manufacturing the product itself. Sulphuric acid was an important example. In July 1915 it became clear that the company would need 105,000 additional tons in 1916. The High Explosives Department estimated that twelve units capable of making 120,000 tons of acid per annum could be built at a cost of $1,930,000 and that 120,000 tons of acid could be produced at a cost of approximately $2,700,000. This included the amortization of 75% of the capital required for the plants and all production expenses. The Executive and Finance Committees balanced this information against the price of a similar amount of sulphuric acid on the open market, which the Purchasing Department estimated would be approximately $4,560,000. The two committees authorized unanimously the construction of new acid capacity.[72] Similar statistical studies resulted in the construction of plants to make toluol as well.[73] Here again, by following practices already well established, Pierre and the Finance and Executive committees were able to determine quickly whether raw materials should be purchased on the open market or manufactured by the company itself.

Always cautious, Pierre took definite steps to protect his company against inventory losses if the war should suddenly end. For this purpose, Pierre and, of course, the Executive Committee used the Purchasing Department's fortnightly reports. These had been perfected by Tallman and Pierre in order to control working capital after the raw material inventory difficulties experienced during the panic of 1907. But as the European conflict dragged on, Tallman tailored his fortnightly reports to give the exact information that he felt was needed in the new war situation. The reports indicated the length of time for which the company was covered on the various materials it purchased, the average costs, and the status of the raw material markets. In addition, the monthly reports summarized the fortnightly reports and compared the current consumption with that of past years. [74]

For each of the four major substances consumed, that is, nitrate of soda, cotton, sulphur, and alcohol, the Executive Committee set special guidelines for the Purchasing Department. For other materials it established the general rule that supplies would be bought in quantities only in order "to take care of war orders in hand, plus the usual margin of safety on the basis of normal [that is, peacetime] consumption."[75] Both Pierre and the Executive Committee took special care to examine the Purchasing Department's reports to see that it followed instructions.

Nitrate and cotton linters received the most attention. For example, on March 29, 1916, the Executive Committee directed the Purchasing Department to buy enough cotton linters to run the smokeless powder plants at full capacity until November 1, 1916. Yet on May 8, 1916, a report indicated that cotton on hand would operate plants at full capacity through all of 1916 and one-third of a month into 1917.[76] The Executive Committee demanded an immediate explanation, and the following week it ordered a report to determine how much cotton could be sold month by month from the surplus stocks.[77] The Executive Committee minutes show that throughout 1916 and 1917 it reviewed the vital cotton situation, usually on a weekly basis, but sometimes more frequently.[78]

As the war continued on into 1916, the outcome became even more uncertain. Massive summer offensives on both sides made it possible that the French might break through on the Somme or that the Germans might shatter Allied defenses at Verdun. Rumania's war effort against the Central Powers seemed to give a brief flicker of hope for the Allied cause in the Balkans. Through the summer, therefore, it seemed possible that a decisive victory by one side or the other might end the war. By the fall the situation had changed. The certain defeat of Rumania ended Allied hopes in the Balkans; and the failure of offensives by both sides in France continued the stalemate there. In November Wilson's re-election to the presidency on a campaign that stressed the avoidance of active American participation in the war and the seeming inability of either side to win caused rumors of peace negotiations to fill the air.[79]

Pierre remained constantly alert to war developments, and his company prepared itself for a sudden end of the conflict, whether it came from the victory of one side or the other or through mediation. In mid-summer of 1916, Pierre, Irénée, Frank Tallman, and John Raskob discussed the formation of a general policy for the Purchasing Department to follow to protect the company should the war stop suddenly. This resulted, on July 8, 1916, in an Executive Committee order that the company dispose of all materials and supplies in excess of the amounts necessary to manufacture 100 million pounds of powder in addition to war orders now in hand. Further, the Purchasing Department was requested to make arrangements so that starting August 1, they could "quickly dispose of all our materials and supplies in excess of the amounts necessary to manufacture 40 million pounds of powder should no additional orders be received by the end of July."[80] Furthermore, Treasurer Raskob, in August 1916, set up an amortization fund charged against the cost of the war business of $3.0 million "to cover possible losses due to our having an abnormal supply of raw materials on hand at excessive prices after" the war contracts ceased.[81] Significantly the increased interest in curbing excessive investments in raw material occurred precisely at the time when prices for most ingredients for military explosives began to rise sharply above normal peacetime levels. Although details of the plans to cope with the dangers of excessive investments in raw materials varied to meet the specific conditions of the moment, the Du Pont Company's top management continued to devote much time and effort to this problem. The system of reports which Pierre and Tallman had perfected helped to ensure that the key decision-makers would have exact knowledge of such conditions as the size and number of the contracts for war explosives, the materials necessary to fulfill these obligations, the materials on hand, and the cost of any materials needed, whether they were purchased at market cost or manufactured by building facilities to produce them. Also available to Pierre were thorough studies that attempted to forecast price and demand trends and matched wartime prices with those of the prewar years. These kinds of data enabled the Du Pont Company to make decisions that would maximize its wartime profits and minimize the risk of any sudden transition from war to peace.

## The War and Diversification

Pierre's keen realization that the war was a temporary condition had another extremely important consequence. It turned the company to exploring peacetime uses for its war-created facilities and skills. Such exploration would transform the Du Pont Company from the nation's largest explosives manufacturer into its largest chemical producer. The resources available for this transformation were impressive. During the war years, 1914 through 1918, the gross capital employed by the company increased from $83,432,000 to $308,846,000.[82] But these figures do not tell the whole story. Gross income during the war amounted to $1,049,000,000, of which $200,000,000 went for constructing smokeless powder, TNT, or other plants producing military explosives.[83] The company paid dividends to the stockholders amounting to $140,983,000. In addition, the company retained earnings totaling slightly more than $89,287,000.[84] The war, therefore, provided vast new physical facilities and a surge of new cash. In addition, it produced an important intangible: new human capital. The Engineering Department alone, for example, increased from a nucleus of about 800 men to a force numbering at times 45,000. By 1916 the company had an expanded force of managers and technicians trained in the ways of nitrocellulose technology whose skills might be applied to the production of a wide variety of peacetime products. Between 1914 and 1918 the number of such executives (men receiving salaries of $4,200 or more) employed had risen from 94 to 259.[85]

Pierre knew that the war's end would render worthless much, if not most, of the new physical plants. Consequently he amortized—that is, wrote off as of no value—any new construction required. But such a policy did not preclude the company from attempting to salvage something out of the wartime plants. Besides, the new capital—both human and monetary— demanded profitable employment. Therefore, as the Du Pont Company embarked upon its massive wartime expansion, Pierre made certain that its officials began to investigate both peacetime uses for the new plants and virgin areas for the investment of any new capital that might be acquired.

The main job of planning diversification fell to the Development Department, run by Pierre's brother-in-law Robert Ruliph ("Ruly") Morgan Carpenter, who was greatly assisted by his younger brother, Walter S.

Carpenter. During 1915 the Carpenters spent most of their time investigating the problem of using the new smokeless powder capacity then under construction. As the war lengthened and the magnitude of the retained earnings became clear, they widened their investigation to include any appropriate field for Du Pont investment. Their task was to determine products that would fit best into the company's capabilities and to decide whether to have the company develop such products itself or to find firms that could be brought into the Du Pont orbit.

Even prior to the massive war contracts, the Development Department had been investigating the manufacture of celluloid, which, like smokeless powder and artificial leather, could be made from nitrated cotton. In November of 1914 the Executive Committee appropriated $26,000 for the Experimental Station to conduct developmental work in celluloid. As a result of the Development Department's investigation conducted by Walter Carpenter, the Executive Committee in December approved moving into the production of celluloid and, in this case, fabrikoid, by purchasing a "going concern" in the field.[86] But war orders caused this to be put aside until September 1915. Then Du Pont bought the Arlington Company, a manufacturer of pyralin-based celluloid, for more than $5.0 million.[87] Not only did Arlington offer a use for nitrated cotton, but it could also absorb some of the solvents the Powder Company made for the explosives business and support possible development in the film and lacquer fields.[88] The Executive Committee moved rapidly to integrate Arlington's management with Du Pont's. To assure communication the committee voted that one of its members take Arlington's presidency. After consulting with Pierre, Irénée gave the job to Lammot du Pont.[89]

During 1915 (the first full war year), no one could tell for certain how much capital would be available for expansion. Consequently the Development Department could do little more than explore in a general way potential opportunitites for peacetime business. Toward the end of 1915, however, it became certain that there would be at minimum $20.0 to $30.0 million surplus capital to invest, and possibly more; in addition, at the war's end massive facilities would become surplus at Deepwater, Carney's Point, Haskell and Parlin in New Jersey, and at the huge new guncotton facilities constructed at Hopewell, Virginia.

Consequently Pierre and the Executive Committee began to press the Development Department for a comprehensive investigation into possible new uses for the future excess capacity. On January 17, 1916, the Executive Committee instructed the Development Department to make a report within a week on what had been accomplished toward finding new uses for Hopewell.[90] The Executive Committee at its next meeting listened to the report with interest and then ordered the investigation expanded to review possible uses for all major war plants including Parlin, Haskell, Deepwater, and Carney's Point. It also recommended the hiring of an industrial chemist to evaluate opportunities in the chemical field at large. Further, the Executive Committee urged that prior to any decision to alter the military powder plants, the federal government ought to be consulted as to whether it wanted to retain the new factories for possible use by the army or the navy.[91]

From 1916 onward, Walter Carpenter made systematic, and even more sophisticated, studies to find peacetime uses for Du Pont's wartime capacities. The Development Department made its work known to both Pierre and the Executive Committee in formal reports it produced every two weeks, or more often if the situation required. Walter Carpenter had at first concentrated on finding uses for Hopewell and other physical facilities that Du Pont was accumulating. Seven months of intensive investigation, however, changed this attitude, for it seemed clear that the company's vastly expanding human and organizational capital, together with the rapidly increasing cash surplus, was the real challenge. In August of 1916 the Executive Committee recognized this and unanimously resolved that efforts to find "uses for our excess plant capacity after the completion of our present foreign orders need not be confined to studies of industries which are allied to the business of our company." The committee did ask, however, that "preference should at all times be given to studies of allied industries."[92] In February 1917 the Executive Committee drew up a priority list of areas upon which it felt that R. R. M. Carpenter and his department should concentrate their efforts. The fields were, in order of desirability: first, dyestuff and allied organic chemicals; second, the vegetable oil industry; third, paint and varnish; fourth, water soluble chemicals; and fifth, industries related to cellulose and cotton purification.[93] This listing emphasized the utilization of the technical and managerial experience that the company was achieving through the manufacture of TNT and other more sophisticated munitions; the priorities downgraded the quantitatively large, but more routine, capacity that had been engaged in cellulose and cotton purification at Hopewell and other plants.

In its investigations of 1916 the Development Department's work consisted of two related activities: First, the initiation and evaluation of studies that were made in the company's growing experimental laboratories; these centered on using company output and skill to make new products such as motion picture film. Secondly, once a decision had been made that a field showed promise, the Development Department studied how best to enter it. Sometimes, as in the case of dyes, it built its own plants. At other times, as in the case of paints and varnishes, it purchased a going company. The latter step required a careful evaluation of possible candidates for merger. In general, no investment was considered unless it was indicated that capital so employed could earn at least 12½%. Finally there was the delicate, prolonged and often unsuccessful purchase negotiation.[94] Thus, investment in new industries went slowly. By May 1917 there was a surplus of more than $60.0 million in prospect, yet only about $18.0 million had been invested. A month later Ruly Carpenter reported that he believed the company had embarked on projects that would eventually require $66.0 million of capital, but so far only about $21.0 million had been appropriated.[95]

Though diversification occurred gradually, the years 1916, 1917, and 1918 saw the foundations laid for the transformation of the Du Pont Company from an explosives manufacturing concern to a chemical company. A large effort went into carving out a foothold in dyes. Prior to the war this industry had been almost a German monopoly, although some English firms also had developed a base in the field. As Pierre later explained, the chemical composition of several explosives, particularly picric acid, was similar to that of dyes. The company hoped that part of the apparatus used to make picric acid could be diverted at the end of the war to dyemaking.[96] But, more important, the company needed to acquire technical knowledge. Therefore, the Development Department entered into negotiations with Levinstein, Ltd., Manchester, England, dyemakers. The agreement worked out at the end of 1916 gave the Du Pont Company access to all the technological data in possession of Levinstein upon the payment of a royalty of $125,000 per year for a period of ten years.[97] The following March the Executive Committee voted to construct a $600,000 indigo plant near the company's picric acid facilities at Deepwater, New Jersey.[98] This was only the beginning. By June 18, 1917, the company was planning an investment in dyes of approximately $7.0 million.[99] Two months later, in August, the total stood slightly in excess of $8,736,000. By 1930 the dye investment equaled $50.0 million.[100]

From the start Pierre strongly supported the move into dyes. His enthusiasm was bolstered by pressure from the textile industry and the State Department, both of which wanted an alternative to the German dye industry. Young Walter Carpenter and the other men opposed a large investment in dyes, fearing that the company could not compete with the Germans after the return of peace. In this they were right. Of all Du Pont diversification efforts, dyes were slowest to return a profit.

Closely allied to dyes was the manufacture of paints, varnishes, and colors. Like dyes, paints and varnishes shared a common base with explosives, the link here being chemicals such as alcohol, benzol, solvent naptha, dead oil, pitch, ether, and pyroxylin solutions, already manufactured at company facilities.[101] The Development Department also emphasized that the paint and varnish business was a large, growing, and profitable one, and that Parlin, with its close proximity to the rich New York market and its excellent transportation facilities, provided a good base to expand into the industry.

The plan agreed upon for the move into paints and varnishes was to purchase old-line companies with substantial and profitable factories; Du Pont would operate them during the war at their old locations and then when the war was over convert the facilities at Parlin and other smokeless powder plants into the production of their peacetime manufacture. The largest and most important of the purchased firms was Harrison Brothers & Company, a Philadelphia paint and varnish manufacturer, which Pierre described as a "concern well-known and of long standing for a period even longer than the life of the Du Pont interests."[102] Negotiations for Harrison started in early December of 1916; on January 15, 1917, Ruly Carpenter reported that the firm had been purchased for $5.7 million.[103]

Other paint and varnish concerns purchased included Cawley, Clark & Company and its subsidiary, the Beckton Chemical Company of Newark, New Jersey, both of which were absorbed in June of 1917 for a total cost in cash of $1.95 million.[104] A few months later Du Pont bought the Bridgeport (Connecticut) Wood Finishing Company for $300,000.[105] In 1918, after the investment in General Motors, two more companies were acquired. In April Du Pont took control of the Flint (Michigan) Varnish & Color Company at a cost of $325,000, and in September the Executive Committee appropriated $650,000 for the New England Oil Paint & Varnish Company of Everett, Massachusetts.[106]

In 1917 Dr. Fin Sparre, director of the Development Department, undertook one of the most exhaustive of Du Pont's diversification studies— an investigation of the vegetable oil industry. For this the Executive Committee made an appropriation of $105,000. In June Dr. Sparre reported that his team had worked out preliminary plans for an investment of approximately $14.0 million, half of which would be working capital. Impressed, the committee ordered further studies. These were not completed until well into 1918. By this time, however, major commitments had been made in pyralin, dyes, paints and, for different reasons, automobiles. In September 1918, when Ruly Carpenter pressed for a decision on the plans for vegetable oil, the Executive Committee, although favorable to further investigation, refused to authorize any negotiations for purchase of firms in this field. The absorption of funds to help finance the massive postwar expansion in General Motors had undoubtedly ended, temporarily at least, diversification into vegetable oil during the final period of the war.[107]

The Development Department also paid close attention to Du Pont's original venture outside explosives, that is, artificial leather. Expansion occurred in Canada where Fabrikoid invested $231,000 to relocate its Toronto plant and increase its capacity.[108] The Canadian venture proved a major success, but results from the United States plants were disappointing. Rising costs and sales at long-term contracts with fixed prices cut profits.

In June of 1917 the Toronto plant, with but 12% of the artificial leather business of the company, contributed 40% of Fabrikoid's earnings.[109] Artificial leather's relatively poor record tended to discourage large-scale investment during the war. Indeed, during August 1916 the Executive Committee approved H. F. Brown's recommendation that "no further additions be made to our [United States] Fabrikoid Capacity at this time."[110] Thus, artificial leather took only minor amounts of the new capital generated by the war.

As the Du Pont Company expanded into so many new and diverse fields, Pierre worried about the organization problems that were being created. In the case of the Arlington Company, although Pierre had Irénée appoint their brother Lammot as president, and although Arlington reported its doings to the Executive Committee, which had ultimate control over it, the subsidiary's operations remained quite separate. Arlington officials drew up expansion plans, purchased many of their materials, and controlled sales. The Executive Committee had the power to shape Arlington's decisions, but rarely did. In January 1917, when Harrison Brothers was purchased, Pierre recommended that as a temporary measure the Arlington precedent should be followed. The Executive Committee took Pierre's advice and placed Lammot in charge of the new firm.[111]

As soon as Pierre had settled Harrison's short-term managerial problem, he set into motion machinery that he hoped would solve the novel questions arising from the changing composition of Du Pont's activities. In a special report to the Executive Committee on May 5, 1917, Pierre suggested that a specific person on the Executive Committee should be designated to look after the new industries and "that a new Department should be formed to carry these acquisitions either permanently or until a better resting place can be found." The president recommended that Lammot, already in charge of Arlington and Harrison, be assigned this job and that the dye industry be put in his care as soon as the Development Department could arrange it. Pierre urged that Lammot be given time to manage the new firms by relieving him of his duties as head of Black Powder. In turn, H. G. Haskell's High Explosives Department would be enlarged to include all black powder and other explosives, with the exception of smokeless powder.[112] The Executive Committee approved Pierre's report without change. His actions evaded the more difficult problems of constructing a permanent organizational structure to accommodate the new endeavors. He wisely recognized that acquisitions yet to be made might pose still further problems. Lammot du Pont's Miscellaneous Manufacturing Department provided a way to manage new fields until the final outline of the new Du Pont Company could be seen more clearly. This put off the major problems of reorganization until after the war.

## *Financial Reorganization and the Formation of E. I. du Pont de Nemours & Company*

Although administrative reorganization had to await peacetime, the war gave Pierre an opportunity to achieve his long-delayed plans for financial reorganization. In 1911, it will be recalled, Pierre, then acting as treasurer, had worked out, with Hamilton Barksdale's help, a comprehensive financial program that had as its goal the elimination of the Powder Company's bonded debt and the creation of a new voteless preferred stock. Pierre desired to use the preferred stock to replace the 4½ % and 5% gold bonds, and then to raise new capital at the rate of about 5% per year through the sale of common and preferred shares at the ratio of 1½ to 1. Besides eliminating the Powder Company's debt, the voteless preferred stock would have allowed Du Pont to attract substantial outside money without sacrificing family control. Before Pierre's plan could be adopted, the government's victory in the antitrust case made any change in the company's financial structure inappropriate, and the Executive Committee postponed action. The problems of rearranging the explosives industry in the wake of the antitrust verdict and then the commercial recession of 1914 kept Pierre from resubmitting his financial plan.[113]

The huge inflow of new capital into the Powder Company's treasury that accompanied Allied war orders in 1915 caused Pierre to think again of his 1911 financial proposals. Consequently in mid-1915 he asked the treasurer, John Raskob, to formulate a plan to restructure the company's finances. After lengthy discussions with Pierre, Raskob drew up a plan, which the Powder Company's board of directors and stockholders approved almost without alteration. The 1911 goals remained unchanged. In accord with this plan a new company called the E. I. du Pont de Nemours & Company and incorporated in Delaware was created. This new firm which, as Pierre emphasized, had "a corporate name . . . [identical] to that adopted by the founder of the business in 1802,"[114] was approved by the board of directors of the E. I. du Pont de Nemours Powder Company on August 19, 1915. The Powder Company stockholders ratified it on September 8, 1915, and it came into being officially on October 1, 1915.[115] The new organization, referred to by Pierre and Raskob as the "Delaware Corporation" in contrast to the Powder Company (which was incorporated in New Jersey), had authority to issue securities worth at par value a total of $240.0 million, of which $160.0 million were to be nonvoting 6% cumulative debenture stock and $80.0 million of common stock. At the time of its formation the company issued only part of the authorized stock.

In accord with Raskob's plan the new Delaware Corporation purchased all the assets of the old Powder Company. It paid for them the sum of

$120,000,000. The payment consisted of $1,484,000 in cash, $59,661,700 in debenture stock at par value, and $58,854,200 in common stock at par value. The New Jersey company which received the above payment used the cash and securities to liquidate itself. The Powder Company purchased from its bondholders its outstanding $14,166,000 of 4½% bonds, with a like amount of new Delaware Company debenture stock. Thus the owner of $10,000 worth of Powder Company bonds paying 4½% interest received $10,000 worth of Delaware Company debenture stock paying 6%. The Powder Company exercised its right to call the $1,230,000 of 5% bonds at 105 and paid cash. The owners of the $16,068,600 of Powder Company 5% cumulative preferred stock were offered a like amount of the 6% cumulative debenture stock. Raskob counted on the attractive features of his proposal to cause the holders of Powder Company securities to make the exchange. He observed that the preferred owners received what amounted to a 20% increase in their income and a safer security too, since in the new company there would be no bonds that would stand ahead of debenture stock claims. The old bondholders received an even larger rate of increase by making the exchange. Finally, the Powder Company issued a dividend to the holders of its common shares of 200% "payable in Delaware Corporation common stock at par." In effect, the New Jersey Company transferred Delaware Company common shares worth $58,854,200 at par value to its stockholders, giving the New Jersey's common stock owners two shares of the new company for one share of the old. In practical terms, this amounted to a 2 for 1 stock split, since no money changed hands and the par value of $100 per share was arbitrary and had no relationship to the market value of the stock (which was as much as 4 times higher than the par value of the Delaware shares). When these exchanges were completed, the Powder Company had no assets left, and it was simply dissolved.[116]

The legal and financial reorganization of 1915, that is, the creation of the E. I. du Pont de Nemours & Company of Delaware, accomplished all of Pierre's goals of 1911. It eliminated the bonded debt from his firm's capital structure. In the new debenture stock the Delaware Corporation had a senior security which enabled it to "obtain new capital at all times by paying the minimum rate therefor and one which will admit of the company's credit expansion keeping pace with its trade expansion." Raskob, who had the job of putting Pierre's ideas into written form, explained that he had recommended that the new securities be called "debenture stock" because while they were not a mortgage against the company, as would be the case with bonds, they offered better security than that found in the average preferred stock.[117]

Following Raskob's thinking, the Delaware Corporation's new debenture stock had voting privileges only in case the firm's earnings in any calendar year were equal to less than one and one-half times the accrued interest on the debenture stock issued and outstanding. Further, the debenture stock had the sole voting privileges, to the exclusion of the common stock, in the unlikely case that the company failed to pay any quarterly dividend on the debenture stock and remained in default for six months. Raskob argued that this limited voting privilege strengthened the security in that it gave holders of the senior stock "the opportunity to come into the management of the property in a case of trouble before the assets are so dissipated as to make rehabilitation of the company practically impossible, or such as to require an exorbitant amount of new capital." Raskob concluded that although such a security could not be called a bond, he was "not warranted in justice to ourselves and successors to class it with American preferred stock, that English Debenture stocks are exactly in line with the nature of security contemplated and command a high position in the category of investment securities and we are, therefore, justified in selecting 'Debenture Stock' as the name of our senior security."[118]

In this way the new Delaware Corporation through the creation of debenture stock had been able to retire both the old bonded debt and the old voting preferred shares. The new shares effectively assured that the company's control would stay with the common shareholders. As the new corporation entered the middle of the war years, it had in reserve approximately $100.0 million worth of debenture stock at par value which could be issued as bonuses, used to purchase new companies in the diversification program, or sold to the public. Also approximately $20.0 million worth of common shares remained to be issued. This provided the company enormous flexibility in obtaining capital and made it possible to tap sources not before available without a lessening of du Pont family control.

The period between 1914 and 1917 demonstrated the value of professional management as well as the mastery of Pierre's control of the Du Pont Company. The company was able to undertake huge contracts during most uncertain times and protect itself against potential loss. Equally important, Pierre's native caution and previous experience prevented a false optimism, which enabled the Du Pont Company to earn large profits while other major war contractors, such as Winchester and Remington, fell on hard times. Simultaneously, by reshaping its financial structure and by beginning its transformation into a chemical enterprise, Pierre had placed the company in an excellent position to rapidly liquidate the war business and move into large peacetime markets. But before the company could seriously develop the potentialities of its diversification program, its Executive Committee, and particularly Pierre, had to meet a challenge even more complex than the supplying of the Allies. In 1917 and 1918 Pierre's most time-consuming task was to work out the terms by which the Du Pont Company would supply the American military forces.

# The American War Effort:
# Negotiations Begun

A MERICA'S ENTRY into the war against Germany posed a whole range of challenges for Pierre du Pont and his company. The central issue was the nature of the relationship between a large firm manufacturing munitions and the government. World War I differed vastly from all previous conflicts involving the United States in that it was the first time that the nation had fought since it had developed a highly industrialized economy. Furthermore, this was the first time the American government had attempted large-scale mobilization of both manpower and economic resources. The government's problem was to devise a war plan and then allocate the national resources to meet the desired goals. For Pierre and the other leaders of major corporations the problem was different. They had to work out the terms on which they would take government work. They had to learn how to operate within a controlled economy in which their efforts were part of a larger plan. Since neither Pierre nor the government officials with whom he dealt had had any comparable experience nor any precedents to guide them, it is hardly surprising that things did not always go smoothly.

## Marriage

In the summer of 1915 the pace of Pierre's life slowed a bit. The problem of succession seemed to have been solved at last. Coleman had sold his stock, Alfred had removed himself from management, and Pierre and his brother Irénée had a firm grasp on the reins. Philip du Pont would not bring his suit until the very end of the year. The crucial decisions about the terms of the war contracts had been made, and policies had been developed to guide expansion. Supplying munitions to the Allies was beginning to become routine. For a short period Pierre had time to think about his personal affairs.

For Pierre the death of his mother in June of 1913 brought changes in his way of life. St. Amour, his mother's large stone house located in Wilmington on the northeast corner of Pennsylvania Avenue and Rising Sun Lane, had always been a welcome haven from the rush of business. It now became lonely and empty. Consequently Pierre decided to take up residence in a suite of rooms in the Hotel Du Pont. He turned St. Amour over to his brother Lammot. This freed Pierre to spend most of his leisure time at Longwood.

Pierre saw even more of his close-knit group of friends. He entertained frequently at Longwood, but on busy days he often stopped for dinner with Lammot at St. Amour or with his sister Isabella and her husband Rodney Sharp, who lived a short walk from St. Amour in a house called Gibraltar. At Gibraltar Pierre saw much of the Sharps' frequent house guest, Alice Belin of Scranton.

Alice was Pierre's first cousin. Her father, Henry Belin, Jr., was a brother of Pierre's mother. Pierre had known Alice since childhood; he had many times visited Scranton, where the Belin family was one of the town's richest and most influential. Henry Belin, Jr., was president of Scranton's Traders' National Bank and, more important, president of the Du Pont Company of Pennsylvania which manufactured black powder for the anthracite coal district. He had helped Pierre and Coleman approach the owners of Laflin & Rand at the time of the formation of the big company. Alice's family was strict and formal. After graduating from Bryn Mawr College in 1892, she returned home to help her mother manage the household servants and to participate in the family's active social life.

Because Alice liked to travel, Pierre had included her in two European excursions. In February 1910 the Rodney Sharps, the Lammot du Ponts, and Alice accompanied Pierre on a trip to England. After spending time in London, where Pierre transacted business with the Nobel representatives, the group went to France. There Pierre met his cousin Roger de Trégomain, who introduced the visitors to many du Ponts who had not migrated to America.[1] Three years later, in January 1913, when Pierre made another voyage to England, Alice was in the party of six, which included Ruly and Peggy Carpenter and Charles and Louisa Copeland. After Pierre finished conferring with the Nobel group, the six crossed the English Channel to Paris, where they renewed their friendship with the French du Ponts. Then came a motor trip from Paris to Naples by way of Nice, Florence, and Rome.[2]

As 1915 wore on, Pierre looked forward to Alice's visits. Some days they met in Philadelphia, where they enjoyed dining out and then attending a play or concert. Pierre found Alice wonderful company. Both had similar interests. They liked music and shopping; architecture and gardens fascinated them. On other days Pierre would drive out from his office, and the two would walk in the Sharps' rose garden. It was there, on June 17, that Pierre asked Alice to marry him.

Pierre's courtship of Alice Belin had been so prolonged and so casual that the announcement of their wedding plans came as quite a surprise to many, even in the du Pont family. In fact, Alice commented in her diary that Pierre's proposal came as an awful (but pleasant) shock. Her parents, probably because the two were first cousins, may have doubted the wisdom of the marriage, but most others regarded the match as a good one. Immediately after the announcement Coleman, who was aboard his yacht *Tech* off Boston, sent Alice his "hearty congratulations" and then added, "You know my theory is that any girl who gets married is a goose, but if all men were like Pierre I would change my theory."[3]

Pierre, who hated to appear in public, desired a quiet, intimate ceremony that could be enjoyed by his and Alice's close friends. Because Pennsylvania's laws prohibited the marriage of first cousins, the couple decided to be wed in New York City at the Park Avenue home of Alice's brother Ferdinand Lammot Belin. The wedding, which took place at 5:30 P.M. on October 6, 1915, was simple, but beautiful. About 200 guests, largely members of the family, attended. The Reverend Dr. Joseph Odell of the First Presbyterian Church of Troy, New York, but formerly pastor of Scranton's Second Presbyterian Church, presided at the ceremony. Alice's father gave her in marriage; her attendants were her young nephew, Wells Belin, and Wilhelmina du Pont. Rodney Sharp was Pierre's best man.[4] Alice confided to her diary that it was "the best day of [her] life."

Following the ceremony the guests attended a dinner and reception; then Pierre and Alice left by train for Philadelphia, where they stopped at the Ritz. The war business made it impossible for Pierre to take a prolonged honeymoon, so they limited their trip to the mid-Atlantic states. From Philadelphia they continued southward to Washington, stopping at the Willard. The highlight of their two-week honeymoon was an automobile journey from Washington through back country Virginia, West Virginia, and southern Pennsylvania, where autumn was turning the forests crimson, orange, and gold. They spent several days at Hot Springs, Virginia, and White Sulphur Springs, West Virginia, returning to Longwood through Chambersburg and Gettysburg.[5] After Pierre had returned to Wilmington, he was quickly engaged in the powder business, although until the following spring he spent as much time on his new venture into the automobile industry as he did on the Du Pont Company's war trade.

*Pierre Views American Entry into the War*

Like most civilized people at the start of the twentieth century, Pierre was stunned by the outbreak of the European war. Although proud of his family's distant French heritage, he never considered himself anything but an American. He enjoyed his visits with his relatives in France, and he cherished the business friendships he had developed with the English Nobel interest, particularly those with Dr. Carl Hagen and Harry McGowan. But Pierre also worked well with the German Nobel group.

For the first few months, Pierre, in common with most Americans, thought the war would end quickly. As for American involvement, that seemed so remote that he did not consider it at all. But as weeks wore into months, and months into a year, Pierre began to develop a strong attachment to the Allies. Of course, by the end of 1915, not only did his company stand to profit from British and French orders, but it was also holding millions in Allied paper that depended for its value upon the success of Allied armies.

More than business considerations influenced Pierre. Toward the end of 1915 he received vivid descriptions of French suffering and urgent appeals for money from two cousins, Madeleine de Trégomain and Marguerite Bidermann, whom he and Alice had visited in Paris during the trips of 1910 and 1913. Both relatives had become deeply involved in large-scale aid to war victims. Marguerite Bidermann founded a hospital to care for wounded soldiers, while Madeleine de Trégomain set up a fund to help disabled soldiers and their families, the dependents of those killed in battle, and civilians displaced by the fighting.

Pierre responded immediately to his cousins' appeals. To each in January 1916 he sent $1,000. He wrote to his cousin Mrs. Lentilhon Foster: "It is always a pleasure to assist our relatives because I feel that in sending to them the aid goes directly where it is needed."[6] A few days later he sent $1,000 to the *Comité d'Assistance en Alsace-Lorraine* largely for the purpose of evacuating children from the war zone.[7] These were but the first of an ever-increasing flow of donations to French relief. The grateful recipients of his money soon began to send back graphic descriptions of war suffering. He received detailed information about Marguerite Bidermann's hospital and Madeleine de Trégomain's activities.[8]

French organizations recognized Pierre's contributions. In October 1916 the *Comité Central de la Colonie Française de Philadelphie* elected him an honorary member. Pierre, in his acceptance of the honor, gave evidence of his increasing admiration for the Allied cause. Said he, "It is a great pleasure to be useful in a small way to France during this time of great trial. The wonderful devotion of the French People to their country and their efficiency at this time of necessity is one of the greatest features of the European war."[9]

Pierre's letters indicate that by the start of 1916 he had lost any hint of neutrality and was committed in sympathy as well as economic interests to an Allied victory. But what of his attitude toward United States involvement? First, it should be made clear that nothing in Pierre's correspondence indicates that he ever believed that the Allies required American military intervention to win the war. Even German submarine warfare, which to some openly challenged America's freedom to ply the seas, to Pierre posed little threat to the vast commerce flowing between North America and England. As late as February 1917, after the Germans had declared their unrestricted submarine warfare, Irénée wrote Pierre: "The submarine activity certainly is not as serious as the Germans wish us to believe."[10] Principle might force America to defend its right against what the du Ponts, in common with many other Americans, thought were barbaric attacks on the high seas, but it is doubtful that Pierre considered the military needs of the Allies.

For Pierre the question of American involvement revolved about two points: first, the relationship of his company to the preparedness movement; secondly, a concern for the role that his firm, the world's greatest manufacturer of military powder, would play in supplying the nation's armed forces should war erupt. The preparedness controversy proved most vexing. Almost as soon as the European war started, some of the nation's distinguished Republican leaders, such as Theodore Roosevelt and Representative Augustus P. Gardner, began agitation to increase the size and training of the armed forces. They were quickly supported by the military lobbies, especially the army and navy leagues. In May 1916, after German torpedoes sank the *Lusitania*, the preparedness movement became a crusade.[11]

Pierre tried to keep away from involvement with the preparedness movement. During the antitrust fight he had learned his lesson well; the company's near monopoly of the private smokeless powder manufacture made it vulnerable to attack. As he explained to Mrs. Lindon Bates, chairman of the Women's Section of the Movement for National Preparedness, "Our company has found it necessary to take the position of neutrality in the effort for preparedness. We are large manufacturers of powder for military purposes, and, therefore think it unwise to take part in a movement which should be settled without bias by the country at large."[12] This became Pierre's standard reply to anyone seeking Du Pont's support for building America's military might.

But such a position did not prevent attacks on the company. Its fabulous war profits from the Allied business made it too attractive a target. During the political campaign of 1916, important Democratic leaders and insurgent Republicans charged that big business, especially arms makers who hoped to receive large government orders, motivated the preparedness drive. On August 28, for example, the Milwaukee *Journal* quoted Senator Robert M. La Follette as saying, "You have seen the Battle Cry of Peace, paid for by the Maxims and the du Ponts, a picture that shows invaders uniformed as Germans, firing upon and destroying buildings." The St. Louis *Republic* quoted Senator William J. Stone, Democratic Senate leader, as making a similar statement.

Pierre regarded such speeches as irresponsible, and he labored hard to counteract them. He respected Senator La Follette's open-mindedness and honesty; consequently the Du Pont president wrote the senator that "while it is a faraway assumption that a newspaper report is necessarily correct, I must trouble you to learn exact facts, as the Du Pont Company has not contributed a dollar toward the 'Battle Cry of Peace' or to any organization that has had for its object the advocacy of Preparedness."[13] In fact, he continued, "at the beginning of the agitation I, as President of the Du Pont Company, issued a circular requesting that the officers and employees of the company refrain from contributions to and active interest in such organizations."[14] Pierre hoped that La Follette would retract or modify his views, but despite two additional letters La Follette did not even bother to reply.[15]

With Senator Stone's statements, Pierre reacted differently, for he regarded the senator and the Democratic party as hopelessly hostile. Under Pierre's direction the company's publicity agent placed before the St. Louis *Republic* the "facts" which the paper used as the basis for an article on December 17, 1916, that answered the senator.[16] This too had frustrating results. Nothing that Pierre could do seemed able to stop critics of the company from accusing it of fomenting preparedness agitation.

Never far from Pierre's mind was the problem of his company's role in supplying powder for the United States armed forces. Two questions troubled him. First, almost from the start of the conflict Allied orders had booked Du Pont's entire military capacity for months ahead. Pierre would have liked to work out a plan with the government that would define his company's responsibility for providing powder for the American military should the United States go to war. To Pierre it was clear that even Du Pont's capacity would not be enough to supply both Allied and American needs without new plants. Second, there was the problem of what to do with the enormous new military power plants the du Ponts had constructed for the Allied business once orders fell off and capacity lay idle. The Allied contracts with the Powder Company provided for the total amortization of the new factories upon the completion of the initial orders, but Pierre hoped that something could be salvaged from the plants through diversification. However, before converting the new facilities to new products, he felt obligated to offer them to the government. Pierre had no definite program in mind, yet he considered that it might be to the government's advantage if the Du Pont Company maintained the plants under contract for future military use or sold them to the armed forces outright at a nominal price. In June 1916 Pierre reported to the secretaries of the army and navy the current Du Pont capacities, and he asked for a meeting to discuss the future use of the plants.[17]

This overture was unsuccessful. Much as Pierre desired to cooperate with government officials, events thwarted him. In fact, by the end of 1916 he had become almost totally alienated from President Wilson and his appointees in the War and Navy departments. At the root of the trouble was the feeling within the administration and among highly placed Democrats in Congress that the Powder Company was making too much money out of the war. In the summer of 1916 Congress translated hostility to the du Ponts into what Pierre regarded as a punitive measure against his company. A bill, popularly known as the "Munitions Tax," placed a special surcharge of 12½% on the profits from sales of "gunpowder and other explosives." While the measure was being considered, Pierre complained to Representative Claude Kitchen, chairman of the House Ways and Means Committee, that "the Bill discriminates against the manufacturers of explosives, singling out their industry for drastic treatment amounting to penalization, while others engaged in the manufacture of munitions of war and making equal or greater profits are permitted to go free." Then he listed a sample of exports for military sales to Europe that included trucks and passenger automobiles valued at $142.0 million, aircraft worth $7.8 million, and woolen goods of $70.0 million. Also unaffected, said Pierre, were profits made from the sale of guns, tanks, submarine parts, and cases of food.[18] The law finally passed by Congress contained a clause making the tax retroactive so as to include profits during the whole of 1916. This particularly enraged Pierre. He regarded taxes as a cost of doing business, and he argued that any such measure should apply to future transactions, thus giving the corporations affected an opportunity to adjust prices to reflect the tax.

Efforts by the Du Pont Company to stop the bill in Congress had only minimal effects. The firm did succeed in changing the base on which the tax was levied from 8% on the gross income from munitions sales to a flat 12½% of net profits.[19] But the discrimination remained. Irénée later estimated that his company alone paid about 90% of all the money that the government collected under the tax, and that Hercules and Atlas, in which he, Pierre, and other du Ponts had large blocks of stock, paid most of the rest.[20] Pierre personally flayed the tax in the Du Pont Company's Annual Report for 1916: "It is regrettable that the United States Government has made our stockholders the victims of excessive taxation. Under the Corporation and Ammunition tax laws, the tax levied against our company *for the year 1916* alone will result in our paying to the United States Government an amount equal to the entire profit made on sales of military [smokeless] powders to the United States Government by this company and its predecessors since the inception of the industry about twenty years ago. To state it in another way, the tax levied against our company for 1916 under these laws will aggregate an amount equal to 170 per cent of our entire net earnings for the year 1912 in which . . . we had the largest earnings in the history of the company prior to the war."[21] In practice the tax was more a symbol of Congress's disapproval of the Du Pont profits than an attempt to confiscate them. The company, in 1916, earned in excess of $82.0 million, and of this paid out more than $62.0 million in dividends on the common shares, which amounted to a return of exactly 100%.[22]

In 1934 the Nye Committee senators seized upon Pierre's statement (in the 1916 annual report) arguing that the tax allowed "a very good showing." Even in 1934 both Pierre and Irénée, however, still resented that their company "had been singled out . . . to be taxed retroactively . . . ," but Pierre admitted to the Senate Committee that "the stockholders naturally were not very much concerned about it, [since] they made extremely good profits." Irénée added that "I do not think we would have put . . . [the comment] in the report, if we were writing it today [1934]."[23] In 1916, however, the tax stung sharply.

A second clash with the Wilson administration came over the issue of extracting nitrogen from the air. Despite the abundance of nitrates in Chile, Pierre worried that German sabotage at the *oficinas*, a shortage of shipping, or highly successful submarine warfare might restrict the importation of that vital raw material. The obvious answer to this was to develop the patents the du Ponts had obtained for the recovery of atmospheric nitrogen. But this required vast waterpower resources, which government conservation measures had withdrawn from commercial development. Pierre took the problem to Washington, urging Congress to allow Du Pont development of a waterpower site such as the famed Muscle Shoals on the Tennessee River. Early in 1916 he wrote newly appointed Secretary of War Newton Baker, asking for support. Neither Congress nor the secretary of war responded favorably. In the legislative halls Senator Oscar Underwood, Democrat from Alabama, referred to the bill as a "grab" and accused the du Ponts of "lobbying."[24] Instead, Congress passed a measure to empower the government to construct, own, and operate a plant to fix nitrogen from the air.

Simultaneously, Secretary of the Navy Josephus Daniels openly attacked private military powder manufacture and advocated more government-built and -operated plants. Ruly Carpenter took note of one of Daniels' blasts in March of 1916. "The private manufacturers," asserted the secretary of the navy, "first demanded $1 a pound [for smokeless powder]. This was reduced to 80 cents when the Government began to manufacture. Now . . . enough is manufactured by the navy for its needs in time of peace at a cost of 24 cents a pound—34 cents with the overhead charges, interest and such items—and the price in the open market is 53. 'The difference between 53 and 34 cents in a programme of preparedness,' " he said, " 'is well worth saving.' " The combination of Daniels' and the other attacks on the Du Pont military powder business so annoyed Carpenter that he recommended that "we write off this year every pound of military powder capacity we have and consider that we will secure no more of this business."[25] Pierre probably agreed.

Against this background it is not surprising that no conclusive talks were held between government officials and the company either about its role in case of an emergency or about the new Du Pont smokeless plants. Indeed, Pierre widened the gap between himself and the government by his statements during the election campaign in 1916. On October 18, the New York *World* published a report that the Du Pont Company had issued an order prohibiting its employees from wearing Wilson buttons. Said Pierre in a letter to the *World*, "No such order has been given to any of our men in any of our plants. Every individual in the employ of this company is free to vote as he pleases and to work for whatever candidate, national, state or local he pleases." But the president of the Du Pont Company added that "there is a growing realization that many acts of the present administration have been inimical to the interests of the company and therefore inimical to the individuals who, as employees or stockholders, depend on it for their daily bread. Men of both national parties, who have studied these acts in an impartial, non-partisan light have reached the conclusion that they and their families will benefit by a change at Washington. They have expressed their views openly both within the plants and without; and neither they nor those who think otherwise have been interfered with in the slightest degree. . . ."[26] Among the Wilson administration's inimical acts Pierre included "the discriminatory tax on munitions profits," the "cavalier dismissal of the Du Pont Company's offer to build a plant for the fixation of atmospheric nitrogen," and the construction of additional government powder plants, combined with the failure to take full advantage of the existing private powder plants.

With his company unable to work out any plans with the United States government, and with the Allied business becoming routine, Pierre, in early 1917, decided to take a well-earned rest and to give his wife a real honeymoon. On January 28, at 8:00 P.M., Pierre and Alice, together with her sister and brother-in-law Mary and Nathaniel Robertson, two friends, Percy and Mary Nields, and Pierre's sister Louisa Copeland and her husband Charles, boarded the private railroad car "Commonwealth" at Philadelphia's Broad Street Station and headed west for a twenty-eight day trip that took them to San Francisco, Del Monte, Santa Barbara, and Pasadena in California, and the Grand Canyon of Arizona.[27]

Almost as soon as Pierre left, America and Germany began to drift toward war. By the end of January, Wilson's dramatic attempt to mediate between the Central Powers and the Allies had failed. On February 1, while Pierre and Alice were staying at San Francisco's Fairmount Hotel, Germany announced that it would begin unrestricted submarine attacks. War seemed near. As Pierre left San Francisco on February 3 for Del Monte, Wilson announced that he had broken relations with the Imperial German Government.[28] When Pierre and Alice left the train at Santa Cruz for a side trip to view the big trees, he could think of little else except the responsibilities that he felt war would thrust upon his company. Early the following day, Pierre telegraphed Irénée from the Hotel Del Monte that he would come to Wilmington immediately if his services were needed. Irénée's return telegram encouraged Pierre to continue his trip. That evening Pierre met and talked at length with Rear Admiral William Mayhew Folger, retired former commander of the American Asiatic Fleet and an expert on naval ordnance. Late that night Pierre wrote Irénée, reporting that the admiral had suggested that the company ought to tender its services to the government in the event of a declaration of war. "The suggestion appeals to me," wrote Pierre, "and if you all think well of it pass such a motion taking care that the wording is such as will not be open to unfair criticism or misunderstanding." Again Pierre emphasized that he wished "to return if anything turns up either to demand my presence or to make it even remotely advisable that I be in Wil." He added that if war were declared, "it would seem right that I return immediately and I shall probably do so though I shall wire you first if I have time."[29]

But war did not erupt immediately. For several weeks following the diplomatic break, German submarines sank no American ships, and Wilson and the nation lived in hope that the crisis might be resolved without armed conflict.[30] Pierre, therefore, had ample time to finish his trip; and while Pierre traveled, Irénée kept him informed. Irénée's letter of February 10 addressed to Pierre, in care of the Hotel El Tovar at Grand Canyon, reported a perplexing situation. "You naturally would think," Irénée reasoned, "that if this country goes to war, the Du Pont Company first of all would be the one to get active immediately. I believe on the contrary that should war be declared we will not be called on to do anything actively for a considerable period." Although the government knows that the war "is imminent," the War Department is not active. "It will take, I think, some months before they really get under way." Most likely, Irénée concluded, "in the course of two or three months, at the shortest, this country will awaken to the fact that we can be of some assistance in terminating the war . . . providing we get to work and when that time comes, we may . . . be called upon to expand still more."[31] Pierre read his brother's letter, but he discounted the government's lack of interest in the expansion of the Du

Pont Company's production capacity. Pierre probably felt that Wilson's hope of negotiating with Germany on the submarine issue made the president reluctant to commit the nation to any large munitions expenditures.

### The Initial Government Contract

When Pierre arrived back at Wilmington on February 20, 1917, the formal declaration of war with Germany was still almost six weeks away. Despite what his brother Irénée had written him, Pierre continued to believe that war would bring an immediate call from the government for Du Pont's services. There was some evidence for this. In early March he received a letter from Bernard Baruch of the Advisory Commission of the Council of National Defense inquiring about the status of all raw resources needed for explosives. Pierre replied that all materials used in military propellant powders were "obtainable in sufficient quantity . . . without going outside of the limits of the States excepting Nitrate of Soda," which came entirely from Chile. Because of the large European contracts, he continued, "our company is now carrying and will continue to carry until well into the summer a stock of nitrate of soda which any day will be available for the manufacture of some seventy or eighty million pounds of military explosives on the above mentioned contracts, exclusive of the explosives already manufactured and on hand at that time."

Also the company would have enough nitrate of soda to produce a three months' supply of commercial explosives necessary for mining and other operations during a period of active war. Beyond that the nation would have to depend upon Chilean imports. Pierre warned against reliance upon the fixation of nitrogen from the air. Such production might be possible "within a year or eighteen months, but the risk of failure [was] too great to permit this source of supply being reckoned as available." Pierre commented that the Du Pont Company was attempting to make a beginning on extracting nitrate from the air, but "unfortunately," he said, "the method of manufacture by the arc process, which we would proceed with immediately if power were available, is blocked by the present prohibition on use of undeveloped water powers in the United States." Consequently Pierre recommended that the government purchase a two-year reserve of Chilean nitrate immediately and that it be stockpiled in the United States to guard against the possibility that German submarines could interrupt the supply.[32]

On March 22, fifteen days before the declaration of war, Pierre sent unsolicited letters packed with data about his company's military powder capacity to both Newton D. Baker, the secretary of war, and Josephus Daniels, the secretary of the navy. "Our orders with the Entente Allies," Pierre wrote, "are sufficient to run our factories to their full rated capacity of 27,500,000 pounds per month until September 15, 1917."[33] Beyond that the Du Pont Company could supply only small amounts to the United States. There would be 2.3 million pounds per month capacity added by June when extensions to existing plants had been finished, and "under favorable conditions" Pierre felt that his company could make an immediate 3.0 million pounds per month above its rated capacity for current delivery. Pierre also included comprehensive data on the raw resources available at the various company plants. The message of the letter, although unstated, was clear: if the United States expected to consume powder in quantities comparable to those used by England and France, there had better be immediate planning for increased new military powder capacity.

It is certain that Pierre misjudged the initial impact the war was to have upon American industry. He thought that hostilities would bring immediate large-scale mobilization, with simultaneous plans to build vast munitions plants. Most Americans thought otherwise. After Congress finally declared war on April 3, 1917, the impression persisted, even in the highest levels of the government, that America's part "would be largely one of moral support, with expanding preparation in the background as insurance against any unforeseen disasters."[34] Although the United States sent a division to France in the late spring of 1917, it served merely as a gesture of solidarity. The action did not indicate that the nation now realized it would take a massive infusion of American troops to stop the Germans. Not until Colonel Edward House's mission to Europe in late autumn of 1917 did the full magnitude of the need for American participation become clear. Then the Supreme War Council and the Interallied Conference worked out a program to put 1 million U.S. troops in France by June 1918 (there were only 129,000 there on December 1, 1917), and by 1919 there were to be over 2 million in the field, all equipped with American supplies.[35]

Not until the late fall was the American government interested in large-scale munitions orders. Meantime, the powder demands of the armed services were modest. The record emphasizes this forcefully. On April 7, 1917, the day following the declaration of war, Pierre received a communication from Brigadier General William Crozier, chief of Army Ordnance, advising that "the present and anticipated needs . . . for smokeless powder . . . during the next twelve months" amounted to approximately 78 million pounds.[36] Pierre, Irénée, and Colonel Buckner of Military Sales compared the army's requirements with their own rated capacity, which was 330 million pounds per year. In addition, they estimated that with extraordinary effort the factories could annually produce 36 million pounds over and above the rated capacity. Furthermore, in June new facilities would be completed that would yield approximately 23 million more pounds that could be sold to the army during the year ahead. Production in excess of rated capacity and new facilities would allow the du Ponts to fill most of the requirements, and unsold capacity to become available after September 1917 would make it possible to supply the rest.

Before Pierre could convey this information to General Crozier, he received a telegram from F. A. Scott, chairman of the General Munitions Board. Scott asked, "Can you meet me, Colonel [William W.] Dunn and possibly General Crozier at Hotel Willard" on Sunday April 15, 1917?[37] Pierre replied that Irénée du Pont and H. F. Brown would go to Washington as his representatives. At the meeting it appeared that Aetna Explosives Company, which Arthur Moxham and Pierre's brothers-in-law Ferdinand Lammot Belin and Charles A. Belin had organized, was on the verge of receivership. Colonel Dunn of Ordnance feared that this would endanger a substantial source of smokeless powder and he suggested that Du Pont take over Aetna's operations. Irénée argued that Du Pont had been approached several times by Aetna, but had always rejected any takeover because the firm had "undesirable contracts," had purchased raw materials at exorbitant prices, and furthermore had inefficient plants. Irénée told Dunn that the government should not go to any expense to keep Aetna in operation; then he added that the Du Pont Company "had carefully considered the Government's forecast of their requirements and were prepared to meet them without interfering with our contracts with the Allies, and further that we could probably furnish 2,000,000 pounds of guncotton per month for the French Government if they wished it to replace a million pounds a month order which they have with Aetna."[38]

Five days later, on April 20 at a meeting of the General Munitions Board in Washington, Colonel Buckner, H. F. Brown, and three other Du Pont executives made the company's formal proposal to sell powder. It included an offer to furnish the entire needs of both the army and navy, selling .30 caliber powder at 60¢ per pound and cannon powder at 47½¢ to 50¢ per pound. Of the four companies submitting bids, only Du Pont had the capacity to fulfill the requirements in anything approaching the required time, and its prices were the lowest as well. Colonel Jay E. Hoffer of the Ordnance Department commented that it was not the government's present policy "to urge an increase of capacity where existing free capacity is in excess of estimated requirements," and that Du Pont's prices for cannon powder were "lower than the present cost of manufacturing this powder at the Army powder factory."[39] Thus it was recommended that Du Pont receive contracts from both the army and navy. By July 30, 1917, such contracts aggregated some 67 million pounds for the army and 56 million pounds for the navy. At that point, the entire Du Pont capacity had been booked up to and including the month of May 1918. As of July 1918, however, Du Pont had almost its entire capacity still unsold.[40]

There were several notable characteristics of these initial government powder orders. First, even though the negotiations were done in the name of the General Munitions Board, the key arrangements were made by representatives on that board from General Crozier's Ordnance Department, that is, Colonels Hoffer and Dunn. These men, like General Crozier, had done business with the Du Pont Company for years. Both sides trusted one another. This was clearly indicated in Irénée's report to Pierre on the Aetna affair. Irénée gave Colonel Dunn an appraisal of Aetna, and then followed it with the statement that Harry Fletcher Brown would testify later. Colonel Dunn "said he had the highest regard for Brown's opinion and would follow whatever Brown recommended."[41] In short, so great was the confidence of the army men in Brown that resuscitating Aetna was never seriously considered again.

A second important point was that the negotiations required the construction of no new capacity, but were merely for powder made from plants in being. Thus the question revolved solely about price. Du Pont quotations were almost precisely the same as the government powder cost in its own plants. These prices, because of Du Pont's larger, more efficient, and totally amortized factories, which operated at a high volume and hence had low unit costs, provided an ample profit for the company. Thus the negotiations went smoothly for both sides.

Conditions changed radically, however, in the fall of 1917. In late September the Wilson administration began to recognize that massive American armies would be needed in Europe, and that existing munitions plants were insufficient to supply projected requirements. Indeed, Army Ordnance estimated that by the end of 1918 smokeless powder production in the United States would need to be twice that of the Du Pont capacity in October 1917. This meant the construction of units equal to almost the entire existing Du Pont works, that is, plants with a proposed capacity of one million pounds per day to cost approximately $90.0 million. The problem confronting the American government in the fall of 1917 was not unlike that which faced the British and French at the start of the European war. Since the requirements could not be purchased from industries in being, large factories had to be created that would become useless the day the hostilities ceased. In short, the commercial attractions of such plants were almost nil. Pierre saw the analogy immediately; in his negotiations with the government he constantly referred to his company's experience in building a vast smokeless powder capacity for the Allies.[42]

For the government, the war supply problems of 1917 were unprecedented in its history. Always before, such supplies had been purchased largely from the civilian economy, from factories in being. In the less complex Civil War days munitions meant food, horses, uniforms that could be made in existing factories, and explosives manufactured in commercial mills. While the Civil War did utilize some government arsenals and did require the expansion of some private factories, few, if any, large contracts to build plants had to be made. But neither the long-past Civil War nor the short-lived Spanish-American War provided the government with any useful guidelines.

The World War was both new and different. Not only was it large-scale, but it broke out at a time when the nature of war reflected the increasing complexity of technology and industry in the twentieth century. Not only did armies require the traditional food, rifles, horses, and uniforms, but they needed vast quantities of highly sophisticated machines such as tanks, railway artillery, and aircraft—all of which could be manufactured only in specialized plants. Of all the requirements, smokeless powder turned out to be the largest in terms of cost. Indeed, the government contract that eventually went to Du Pont for the construction of the Old Hickory smokeless powder factory turned out to be the biggest of the war.[43]

For the government, therefore, acquiring munitions was not simply going to the economy and buying the necessary supplies; it was rather the task of creating the industrial capacity to meet highly specialized requirements, a task new to all concerned. There were many unanswered questions in September of 1917. Who was to build these new industrial ventures? Private industry? If so, on what terms? And who in the government was to negotiate the contracts? Or would the government itself build the required factories? If so, where would it get the manpower, organization, and managerial and technical talent? All these were real questions, and there was no consensus either in or out of government as to how they should be answered. Adding to the confusion was the shortness of time. The war demanded rapid solutions. There was little opportunity to sit back and formulate an over-all plan.

The obvious responsibility for creating munitions capacity lay with the executive branch, that is, with Wilson and his appointees in the War and Navy departments. But the many problems that descended on the president and the secretaries of the War and Navy departments made it impossible at the start for them to give close personal attention to the problem of procurement. Much of the real responsibility, therefore, fell on the lower levels, especially on General Crozier, chief of Army Ordnance, and his staff. But Woodrow Wilson, in response to the advice of his secretary of war, Newton D. Baker, had recognized even before the war that ordinary means would not suffice, and had supported the establishment of the Council of National Defense, and late in October of 1916 an Advisory Commission of the Council of National Defense. These were organizations made up of key administrators in the government, including the secretaries of war and the navy, important men in business and labor, such as Daniel Willard, president of the Baltimore and Ohio Railroad, Bernard Baruch of Wall Street, and Samuel Gompers, president of the A. F. of L.. Out of the Advisory Commission of the Council of National Defense grew, almost informally at first after the declaration of war in April 1917, the War Industries Board chaired by Daniel Willard and composed of ordnance experts from the armed services and top businessmen who, like Willard, had been recruited for the duration of the emergency. Since the nature of the Council of National Defense, including its Advisory Commission and the War Industries Board, was advisory rather than executive, the exact role which they were to play in the creation of new defense industries was unclear at the time the Du Pont contracts were negotiated.

Pierre du Pont watched the formation of the government groups with some misgiving. He had definite ideas about how the nation's munitions requirements should be provided. He believed that the government should turn to its private businessmen as the source of the best-trained managerial and technical skills. More than that, Pierre had a hearty distrust of government, which years of antitrust litigation and the attacks upon the company for the Allied business had only heightened. He resented especially the assaults on the company's profits. While some politicians and administrators might regard money made from Allied contracts as ruthless exploitation, Pierre saw such profits as the incentive for doing a job quickly and well. As he was to express it to Newton Baker: "There is no doubt we have made large profits, but their making has enabled us to complete work that has not been duplicated elsewhere. It has also placed us in a position to name prices for powder to the United States Government below those in force before the war without any amortization charge whatever to cover the use of factories which will shortly be permanently dismantled."[44] Others might rely on a surge of patriotic zeal for motivation, but for the president of the Du Pont Company the one way to ensure success was to pay for it. To him it was the emphasis upon rewarding men for a job well done which made private ventures succeed while government, with its employees having no financial stake in the outcome, often failed.

Pierre's beliefs convinced him that his firm could effectively carry out government war work only under certain specific conditions. These beliefs became explicit when the contract he devised was challenged by government officials. First, Pierre insisted, if new capacity were to be built by the Du Pont Company, he wanted complete control, from the construction of factories to their operation. Pierre later phrased it this way to Daniel Willard: "We shall not be responsible for mistakes of others, that is, we will not operate a factory built by others, nor will we build a factory to be operated by others; and on any one factory site the entire work shall be done by us." In short, Pierre wanted "the responsibility . . . for ultimate success of the undertaking without interference." Next he wanted to "receive a rate of compensation that is fair, even though the total amount of money so received may seem large if the magnitude of the work involved is not considered."[45] Pierre did not feel he could afford to give away the company's services. Part of this may have been the worry that, should he do so, Alfred du Pont might use this as a rallying point in his continuing attack against the company's management. Pierre expressed this idea in a letter to Colonel Buckner: "There is another point on which we have touched lightly, but whose importance I wish to impress upon you, namely, that we have among our stockholders a very aggressive and wealthy minority who are spending much time in trying to harass the present administration of the company. We cannot undertake any work of the magnitude contemplated in these Government factories without including in our charges the profit that one might reasonably expect from the use of our stockholders' money. If we should fail to do this, the unfriendly minority would have a case of some merit to promote against those in charge of the company's affairs."

More important to Pierre was his belief that profits provided the best incentive for success. After all, Pierre had always planned to use part of Coleman's stock as a way to reward the key executives for their work. Pierre had also moved swiftly to guarantee the bonus payments when they had been challenged by Alfred. Said Pierre to Colonel Buckner: "I do not think . . . [the building of the plants for the Allies] could have been done without the stimulus of our bonus plan. We cannot divert our principal men in this new work without similar payments to them, not only because we would be unwilling to undertake the work without making such provision of payment of those employed, but because we could not hold the men in our service unless such outlay be made, either in salary, or as we prefer to do, in bonus."[46] Therefore, Pierre insisted that any agreement with the government make it possible to pay substantial bonuses to key men.

Beyond this, Pierre desired to write into any agreement both a minimum compensation and an incentive for the company to raise its profit if it could better the minimum expectations. He felt that this tactic was most appropriate for the manufacture of powder after the plants had been constructed. He had in mind setting a base price for powder that would allow a minimum profit, with the provision that should his company be able to lower costs of production beyond a certain point, both the government and the firm would share equally in the savings. Therefore, throughout Pierre's thinking ran the general principle that he should have total control over any project his company might undertake, and that profits were a tool to obtain the best possible results for the company and the customer.

The first negotiations between the Du Pont Company and the government to have the firm build new smokeless powder facilities came early in October 1917. By then the government fully realized that munitions plants then in being would not be adequate for the demands of the army which it was planning to put in Europe by late 1918. Army Ordnance estimated that projected needs for smokeless powder would require the construction of new factories with a total capacity of one million pounds of finished powder per day. In addition to a total projected cost for the new construction of approximately $90.0 million, the government planned initial orders for 450 million pounds of powder that would cost about $155.0 million. The combined total of the plant construction and possible munitions orders of $250.0 million dwarfed proposed single contracts to any other firm during the World War.[47]

At no time did the Army Ordnance Department consider anything but government ownership of the new facilities. The proposal was that the Du Pont firm act as agent for the government. No other course would have been practical, since the plants had no peacetime value. But neither the army nor any other branch of the government had the available manpower or talent to allow rapid construction of the proposed factories. It was only logical that the army should turn to the Du Pont Company, which had so recently constructed plants similar in size.

The negotiations between the army and the company were carried out by General Crozier and his staff, particularly Colonel Hoffer, who had arranged previous government purchases of Du Pont powder, and Captain E. A. Hamilton. Du Pont's head of Military Sales, Colonel Buckner, represented the company in the early stages, but he always acted in close consultation with Pierre and Irénée. The army and the company reached quick agreement on the basic outline of a contract. The terms of remuneration (which were later to cause so much trouble) were initially drawn without argument. For constructing the plants, the government was "to pay directly or . . . reimburse . . . for all cost of the construction of the plants, and in addition . . . [pay] at the time of making payments on account of such construction, whether directly . . . or . . . in reimbursement—(a) A sum equal to seven (7) per cent thereof to cover preparation of plans, the procurement of sites, engineering supervision other than local supervision, and services in connection with purchasing and forwarding deliveries of material necessary for the construction of the plants, and, (b) A sum equal to eight (8) percent to cover administration other than local administration, pro rata share of overhead expense other than local expense, and to cover profit."

The company was also to undertake the manufacture of the powder. For this the government was to pay "all the cost of operation of the plants and in addition . . . the sum of five (5) cents per pound for all smokeless powder delivered and accepted." Furthermore, "at the end of the first full month of operation of any unit or fraction of a unit, the cost of the water-dried powder, exclusive of the cost of boxes and amortization and depreciation of the plant, but including the cost of components and the conversion thereof, repairs, power, transportation, general works expense, works accidents, and plant superintendence, and all other proper items of cost shall be determined, and in the event that such cost shall be found to have been less than forty-four and one-half (44½) cents per pound the Government

. . . [would] pay . . . in addition to the five (5) cents per pound as above, fifty (50) per cent of the difference between the amount by which the actual cost is less than the base cost of forty-four and one-half (44½) cents per pound." Pierre insisted on the last provision which gave incentive to the company to lower the production costs and of course increase profits by sharing in the savings.[48]

The clause that caused the most extended discussion in the negotiation was also specifically demanded by Pierre. This provision called for the Du Pont Company to create an entirely new corporation called the Du Pont Engineering Company. To this subsidiary would be transferred all men who would work on the government plant, and it would be this company, not the E. I. du Pont de Nemours & Company proper, which would undertake the work. Captain E. A. Hamilton of the Ordnance Department, writing on October 21, summarized Pierre's major reason for dealing through a subsidiary company; mainly Pierre had "a desire to limit liability which 'lies in the possibility of its being hereafter held that the Ordnance Department exceeded its lawful powers in making this contract, in which event the agent might be held liable on its implied warranty of authority on all contracts signed by it as agent of the Government. The Du Pont Company desires to assume no risk of financial loss to itself.' " The captain emphasized that it was not so much fear of the validity of the contract, as "the magnitude of the undertaking which gives rise to the apprehension."[49] Pierre recognized that if his company accepted the contract and started to build the plants, speed would be vital, and that his firm would immediately have to undertake large financial commitments for construction materials, machinery, and other goods. Either the courts or some arbitrary government official might then deny the validity of the commitments and refuse to pay—leaving the company liable.

The contract that Pierre and General Crozier signed in Washington on October 25, 1917, contained all of the clauses mentioned above and seemed to clear the way for Du Pont construction and operation of the giant new powder venture. Indeed the company moved quickly to start work. Since the Du Pont engineering staff, with the encouragement of General Crozier, had as early as April 21 started looking for suitable sites for new smokeless powder factories, the company had a detailed list of available properties, the most promising of which were at Charleston, West Virginia, and Nashville, Tennessee.[50] Immediately after the signing of the contract in October, the company took options on the Nashville and Charleston sites; it also purchased for $700,000 the Betts Machine Company in Wilmington for the express purpose of manufacturing much of the machinery for the new factories and, in addition, placed orders for other machinery amounting to $2,373,912. Within a week after the contract had been signed, the company had spent or committed a total in excess of $3,073,000.[51]

Pierre was pleased as he surveyed the position of the firm on October 30, 1917. The negotiations with the military officers had gone smoothly, as they had in the past. The company, with its large contract for new government smokeless powder plants, was already making major steps toward its fulfillment. But the next day, on October 31, 1917, just six days after the contract was signed, Pierre learned the surprising news that the largest government contract in American history had been canceled. Pierre was stunned. This momentarily left the Du Pont Company with large resources —financial, technical, and managerial—that would be idle. The company remained without a government contract into January of 1918. It was in December, when it looked as though Du Pont might not play any part in building or managing the government's new smokeless powder facilities, that Pierre decided to commit a significant portion of his firm's resources to a new venture in General Motors.

# The American War Effort: Negotiations Completed

PIERRE HAD NO ADVANCE WARNING that senior officials within the War Department were disturbed with the contract he had signed with the Army Ordnance Department to build a smokeless powder plant with a million-pound-per-day capacity. His first knowledge came from a telegram from Newton D. Baker:

> I have just had presented to me the details of the proposed contract with regard to increased capacity for powder production. This matter is large intricate and important. Do nothing about it until you hear further from me. Stay all action under the order until I can acquaint myself thoroughly with all features of the matter.[1]

## Negotiating the Old Hickory Contract

Unknown to Pierre, a disagreement had developed between Army Ordnance on one side and the War Industries Board and Secretary of War Baker on the other.[2] The trouble came because the chief of Ordnance, General Crozier, acting on his own initiative, had negotiated the contracts. He did not inform the Explosives Committee of the War Industries Board of his actions until all the important parts of the Du Pont contract had been formulated. Even then Crozier only informally telephoned the chairman of the board's Committee on Explosives who, thereupon, reported to the committee that the chief of Ordnance "had decided to recommend that . . . [Du Pont] be permitted to expend . . . $90,000,000 to double their smokeless powder capacity." He added that this would be done "without bringing the matter before the War Industries Board."³ Several members of the War Industries Board's subcommittee seemed uneasy at the news, especially since General Crozier provided no details of the proposed agreement. In consequence, one critic of the contract commented that "since the government was so vitally interested in this matter that such additional facilities should be the property of the Government and not of a private interest."⁴

If General Crozier knew of the doubts that existed on the War Industries Board, he paid them little heed. On October 31, 1917, he presented the Du Pont contract to Secretary of War Newton D. Baker for what he expected to be a routine ratification. The secretary, who at first seemed favorable, began to have second thoughts. For one thing, Baker, former Democratic mayor of Cleveland, who ironically enough had started his career as city solicitor under the late mayor and Pierre's earliest mentor Tom Johnson, had become critical of the profits that Du Pont had made on Allied contracts. Baker's opinion was shared by most of the other Wilson appointees to major executive posts. Baker's attitude to the du Ponts had already been manifested in his opposition toward the firm's efforts to gain waterpower rights for a factory to extract nitrogen from the air. Baker now decided, in the tradition of Tom Johnson's attitude toward public service corporations, that if Du Pont did any work for the government, there should be no large profits. Thus, rather than signing the contract Crozier offered, he telegraphed Pierre to halt work; and he called in Bernard Baruch and Robert Brookings of the War Industries Board to investigate the agreement.⁵

Had it not been for Baker's decision, the War Industries Board would probably not have become involved in the matter, but his request brought to the surface latent hostility to the du Ponts. Foremost among the opponents of the company was Leland L. Summers, a consulting engineer who interrupted his practice to become a technical adviser on Allied munitions purchases for J. P. Morgan and who then became a member of the War Industries Board in 1917. Robert Brookings, an idealistic 67-year-old St. Louis philanthropist who had made his fortune with the Cupples Company, a manufacturer of wooden articles, equally mistrusted the du Ponts. Later he was to take a leading part in founding Washington's Brookings Institution. Brookings' attitude became openly known during the ensuing negotiations, when Irénée recalled that Brookings had remarked that "he would rather pay a dollar a pound for powder for the United States in a state of war if there was no profit in it rather than pay the Du Pont Company 50 cents a pound for powder if they had 10 cents profit in it." Irénée contemptuously put down Mr. Brookings "as a woodenware manufacturer in St. Louis or somewhere. He evidently did not appreciate that we might have a war on the east coast of the United States. I was fearful of war," Irénée added. "Apparently he thought that he was far enough inland so that it did not matter much."⁶

Brookings, who was certain that Army Ordnance had erred in its proposed contract with the Du Pont Company, set out to prove the case. He motored with Admiral Ralph Earle, chief of the navy's Bureau of Ordnance, to the Indian Head smokeless powder factory, where he collected information. In a letter to Newton Baker, Brookings stated his case forcefully. Based upon data the superintendent of Indian Head provided, Brookings estimated that the cost of a pound of powder at the proposed new Du Pont plant would not exceed 35¢ per pound, "so that under the Du Pont contract they would make during the first year of operation a profit of about 10¢ per lb., or approximately $30,000,000 in addition to the $13,500,000 construction commission provided for." And he added, "I would place very little value upon the super-expert knowledge of the Du Ponts, or patents or other privileges attached to their service, for the government already has the experience and talent necessary."[7]

While Brookings was building his case, General Crozier attempted to find justifications for the original contract. The general asked that Pierre du Pont put in writing the reasons that his company required a commission of 15% to build the proposed factory. On November 1 Pierre wrote the general a lengthy letter. The commission of 15%, "which may amount in maximum to $13,500,000 . . . covers not only profit, but many indirect expenses which are so involved in the daily conduct of our business as to prevent segregation except by an estimated division of thousands of expense items incurred in the period of construction." In addition, Pierre argued that out of the commission the company would pay a bonus to the key men such as had been the practice on the construction of Hopewell plants. Of the 15% Pierre estimated that there would be a minimum six categories of direct costs which included preparation of plans, supervision of construction, bonuses to key employees, the expediting of materials to be purchased, administrative expense at Wilmington, and the depreciation of the Betts Machine shop. In addition, he found two indirect costs: interference with the company's newly expanding dye industries by the transfer of the engineering staff and other employees to government work; and loss in economies in the current operations owing to diversion of the engineering department. At minimum, Pierre estimated, these factors would amount to 8.19% of the total of the government contract, leaving the maximum profit to the company 6.81%. And it was possible that the costs might approach 14.97%, leaving a bare .03 of 1% profit. In short, Pierre felt that the company would make little, if any, money from the construction. Profit, if any, would ride largely upon long-term operation of the plants after completion. "You appreciate," he wrote Crozier, "that the task imposed upon our company is enormous and fully justified the alternative offer made last night when Mr. Buckner offered to furnish the Government our existing plans from which to build these plants without charge, if in return you can arrange to have the work done by other engineers and builders, thus relieving us entirely of the burden. I believe," Pierre added, "that this counter offer should not be accepted. These factories can be constructed more cheaply and efficiently and with greater certainty of immediate maximum output if the work is conducted by E. I. du Pont de Nemours & Company than if handed over to contractors who cannot place themselves in immediate contact with similar plants in actual operations."[8]

Armed with this information, General Crozier invited the members of the War Industries Board to a conference on November 14, 1917. Colonel Hoffer and a civilian expert joined General Crozier to represent the Ordnance Department, while Judge Robert Scott Lovett, Bernard Baruch, and Brookings attended for the War Industries Board. Pierre's brother Irénée spoke for the Du Pont Company. At the meeting, Crozier unveiled a compromise contract that reduced the company's proposed commission to 8% and made some reductions in the profit the firm would make from the operation of the plants.[9] During the meeting, Colonel Hoffer criticized the cost data that Brookings provided from Indian Head.

Brookings left the meeting unconvinced. He wrote Newton Baker that "while our protest has produced changes in the contract which will probably save the government $5,000,000 or $6,000,000, . . . it still remains in shape where those who expressed themselves, Judge Lovett, Mr. Baruch, and myself declined to approve it. . . ." Brookings emphasized "the conviction which I think we all have in the War Industries Board that when a large sum of money like this is to be expended, unless we participate in the first stages of the conference and are able to mold it along lines which we feel to be fair and equitable, it is almost impossible to do anything with it." No amount of argument made any impression upon the Ordnance Department, complained Brookings, for they still maintained that the original contract "was not only a reasonable one, but one which evidenced the greatest generosity upon the part of the du Ponts. . . . I have the feeling," Brookings continued, "that if we had participated in this negotiation from the beginning we could have just about reduced it one-half, i.e. 7½% on construction and probably 2½¢ per lb. for operation. Even this would have given them an absolutely secured profit of 7½ million dollars per year for nothing on earth but directing the policy of the company from their main office, as, of course, everything else was chargeable to the cost of powder and the Government furnished absolutely all the capital, and, by the terms of the contract, assumed risk of every kind and character."[10] From this it was clear that Brookings did not value the Du Pont Company's experience very highly, nor did he feel that the diversion of its key engineering and managerial staff from its other duties deserved compensation. He felt the company assumed absolutely no risk, a view that Pierre clearly did not share.

Thus General Crozier's meeting failed to produce an agreement. On leaving the conference, the general said "he felt that, regardless of price the Government must have immediate action on this, and . . . [this] could only be had through the du Ponts."[11] As the members of the War Industries Board refused to modify their strong stand, the contract had to go to Newton Baker for a final decision.

The secretary did two things: he urged the War Industries Board to prepare a proposal of its own; then he discussed the matter with President Wilson, who agreed that an attempt ought to be made to find an alternative to relying on the du Ponts. In the emergency, Baker invited bids on the project from Louis J. Horowitz of Thompson-Starrett, one of the nation's biggest construction companies. (This was, incidentally, the firm that had built the Equitable Building for Coleman du Pont.) Baker's request took Horowitz by surprise. Thompson-Starrett had had no experience with building explosives plants, and Horowitz suggested that the War Department turn to Pierre du Pont. Horowitz recalled that "Baker became solemn and fixed his eyes on me as he said, 'I have just come from the White House. I may tell you that we have made up our minds that we are going to win this war without Du Pont.' " Baker then charged that the du Ponts wanted too much money.[12] Reluctantly, therefore, Horowitz agreed to submit a bid.

While Secretary Baker attempted to find an alternative to the use of the Du Pont talent, Pierre grew more and more irritated at the delay in reaching an agreement. He felt that his company had acted generously and in good faith from the beginning. The original October 25 contract had been negotiated with the ordnance officers quickly and almost without argument, and Pierre felt that the War Department had approved the percentage charges by his company. He had moved rapidly to put the contract into effect, taking options on property, purchasing a $700,000 machine shop in Wilmington, and placing orders for over $2,370,000 of equipment. In addition, the company had received quotations for approximately $15,600,000 of other necessary items. In the weeks that followed, Pierre's frustration and sense of anger increased. For one thing, he had talked to Secretary Baker almost immediately after the cancellation order and had come away deeply hurt. In Pierre's words: "We had a different point of view in regard to the amount of profit on the 15 per cent. The Secretary said to me, in substance, these words: 'I think it is time for the American people to show they can do things for themselves.' " Pierre continued, "I thought up to that time I was an American citizen, but he seemed to indicate that he considered we were a species of outlaws, and I . . . resented the remark."[13]

Nevertheless, Pierre had hopes that Irénée could work out some agreement at the meeting that Crozier called on November 14. In fact, Pierre, looked with favor upon the Ordnance Department's compromise contract.

Although the agreement committed the company to build the plant almost without profits, it did provide that the firm could operate the completed factories for a period long enough to allow "reasonable compensation for our services." But days went on and still no decision had been made. On November 23, 1917, Pierre wrote the War Department to force a decision. "With the assurance of our earnest desires and entire willingness as always, to aid the government in any way in our power," he wrote Baker, "we feel that this matter has now been delayed so long and has become so complicated that we should express to you in writing our willingness to withdraw or proceed under the modification of the order suggested by the Ordnance Department on Saturday, November 17. May we ask for a prompt decision as to which of these courses is to be pursued."[14]

Newton Baker had delayed because the War Department was divided. The secretary himself favored turning the whole project over to Thompson-Starrett. The War Industries Board, however, hesitated. Influenced by the arguments of the Ordnance Department, Daniel Willard, speaking for the board, wrote that there was "much technical expert service to be rendered in the construction and equipment of this plant not fully covered in the Graham-Sterritt [*sic*] proposition." He concluded that the "du Pont people are in every way the best fitted" for the task. "Inasmuch, however, as we have so far been unable to agree with the du Ponts as to what would be fair compensation for the erection and operation of the plant," the War Industries Board recommended that Baker invite the responsible heads of the company to meet him at his office and that the secretary say to them "that the emergency nature of the Government needs is such that . . . [he] must insist upon . . . [the du Ponts] taking hold of the project without further delay." The board recommended that the War Department pay the Du Pont Company a sum of $1.0 million on account for the net profit and that after the plant had gone into operation there be negotiation as to what further payments should be made, if any, to the du Ponts for profit. If no agreement were possible, the case should be submitted to binding arbitration.[15] Daniel Willard sent his letter to Newton Baker on November 26. The following morning Pierre received a telegram from General Crozier asking the Du Pont Company president to attend a meeting that afternoon at 4:30 in the secretary of war's office. Pierre replied that he would be there.[16]

The meeting between Pierre and Newton Baker only heightened the tension between the two. The secretary of war started the conference by stating that he favored relieving the du Ponts of any responsibility of building new smokeless powder capacity and giving the work to other companies such as Thompson-Starrett, but that General Crozier argued against such a policy as had Daniel Willard, representing the War Industries Board. Consequently Baker told Pierre that the Du Pont Company would be asked to undertake the work on the terms recommended by the War Industries

Board on the previous day. Pierre objected to the proposed compensation of only $1.0 million, whereupon Baker said that under the original contract drawn by the Ordnance Department on October 25 the Du Pont profit "might be anywhere from $13,000,000 to $30,000,000 [and] that his mind could not conceive of services of anyone being worth such a price."

Baker's comments angered Pierre. "It appears to me that Washington does not value our services highly," he wrote the following day. Then Pierre proceeded to defend the profit figures for the original contract. "Assume the cost of powder at 35¢ per pound and the amount manufactured at 450,000,000, the total transaction including the cost of plant at $90,000,000 will amount to about $250,000,000. The profit named by the Secretary will amount to from 5 to 12%. The $1,000,000 proposed by the War Industries Board is ¼ of 1 per cent. . . . " Pierre's inclination was to refuse the proposition on the spot, but he told Newton Baker that he "would not assume the responsibility of a decision," but would put the matter before a meeting of the company directors with the recommendation that it be refused.[17]

Pierre returned to Wilmington, and the following day, November 28, met with his board. Pierre related to them the secretary's hostile attitude. He also emphasized a more practical concern. The proposed $1.0 million profit was so small that it would not even compensate for the risk the company was being asked to take. Although Baker might argue that the government would assume the entire burden of risk by offering to pay promptly for all bills the du Ponts would incur, Pierre insisted that the company could not evade all risks. "In the first place," as he had told Baker, "the validity of our agency cannot be established outside the courts, and no matter what precautions may be taken through the organization of the subsidiary engineering company we may become liable in some way. Furthermore, if the work is to be accomplished we must proceed with it without stoppage or delay of any kind. If the Government should suddenly command us as their agent to cease work as they have already done twice, we would be obligated to assume great financial responsibilities in order to avoid a complete collapse of the project. This," said Pierre, "the Secretary could not deny."[18] For Pierre the logic was clear. Under the terms proposed at Washington, the company could earn no profit from the venture, but it would assume substantial risk. Finally, Pierre did not feel much remorse at refusal, since the secretary of war had said he preferred that others should act.

However much the terms proposed by Secretary Baker angered Pierre, neither he nor his board felt comfortable about a total rejection of the government's work. The nation was at war, and no one more than Pierre wanted rapid victory. While it is true that he constantly argued that his company should make a 15% profit on the business, this was not the main issue. The real problem was the mistrust that had been developing between the du Ponts and the Wilson administration ever since the company had begun earning large profits on the Allied business. "We have not the implicit confidence of the Government which will be necessary if we are to do this work successful [*sic*]. [And] in the opinion of the Secretary, who is the responsible head of the War Department, we are not necessary to the project and our services are being forced upon him against his recommendation," wrote Pierre.[19]

Consequently, the board refused to agree to build and operate the new plants for the sum of $1.0 million, as the War Industries Board had proposed. The members stated that they would be willing to undertake the project if they were given a contract that would allow them to earn approximately (but not more than) 10% on the construction and 15% of the operating cost.[20] Pierre communicated the board's decision to Daniel Willard of the War Industries Board on December 1, with the almost certain knowledge that the counteroffer would be rejected.[21]

The War Industries Board, with the secretary of war present, held a special meeting on December 3 to consider what should be done. They reached no decision. Secretary Baker and the civilian members of the board were strong for going ahead without the help of the du Ponts. But General Crozier and Army Ordnance felt that the Wilmington powder firm's participation in the project was essential. Newton Baker failed to decide the question, and this gave Crozier a chance to get in touch with Pierre to see if the firm would modify its stand. The general emphasized to Pierre that without the Du Pont Company's aid the war effort might falter. Pierre had already begun to worry about the consequence of his company's stand. He and Colonel Buckner had decided to ask General Crozier, on his visit to Wilmington of December 9, "whether there is general agreement at Washington that our company's services are necessary to the Government and whether we are right in supposing that the question of compensation is alone responsible for the delay." Out of this meeting came a new offer from Pierre, a proposal that the matter of compensation be submitted to arbitration.[22] Pierre made his new bid on December 10, but by this time Secretary Baker had made up his mind not to deal with Du Pont. This should have ended the entire negotiation, and it is certain that Newton Baker intended that it would.[23]

At this point it must be said that the documents suggest that Baker and his civilian advisers had but a scant idea of who they thought would build the powder plants if the du Ponts did not. The secretary kept talking of direct government construction of the smokeless powder capacity. Baker, in his letter of December 12 to Pierre, phrased it this way: "After the receipt of the letter from your company definitely declining to accept a proposition from the Government as formulated in the suggestion of the War Industries

Board and presented by me to your company, the War Department proceeded to work out a plan for the direct creation of this capacity by the Government itself."[24] Pierre kept remembering that Baker had told him that the " 'Government should undertake this work itself' and that 'it is an opportunity for the American people to show that they can do things for themselves.' " The big problem was, of course, that the government had no organization in existence that could build the required plants. Nor could one have been put together rapidly enough to meet the projected military powder demands. This meant that the War Department would have to hire some already organized engineering firm. General Crozier knew this, and his every effort had been directed to bringing the secretary of war to accept that the du Ponts were necessary; such acceptance would enable the War Department to concentrate upon working out an agreement that would fix a price for their services.

The second problem was the development by the government of criteria for war contracts—for example, just how much profit would be allowed? It is clear that few, if any, either outside or inside the government had done much thinking on this question. It is probable that Pierre, because of his experience with drawing wartime contracts with the Allies, had pondered the matter more than anyone else. Certainly Pierre phrased his concepts clearly and concisely. If the Du Pont Company president had had his way, he would have attempted to award work to those who could meet the government requirements most rapidly and cheaply in terms of absolute costs to the government. Pierre felt that his firm was the best qualified. "It is probable—approaching to certainty—" he wrote, "that E. I. du Pont de Nemours & Company can complete the construction work and bring the factories into operation more quickly and more cheaply than any other organization even though others should be willing to work without compensation and E. I. du Pont de Nemours & Company should charge a maximum of 10% on cost of construction and 15% on base cost of operation. . . ."[25] If this were true, Pierre could not understand why his company should not be allowed the aforementioned profit. Failing in that, Pierre preferred a contract that would return a certain fixed profit unit—preferably one that was common to all contractors undertaking similar work. Pierre rejected one contract from the War Department because his company had been offered less compensation than another firm to do comparable work.[26]

Secretary Baker approached the war contracts with the feeling that since the United States faced a war emergency, private companies should be willing to accept nominal profits. Nothing better illustrates this than Baker's conversation with Louis Horowitz about the fee that Thompson-Starrett was to be offered. Baker suggested $1.0 million for doing $100.0 million of work.[27] What is equally clear is that Baker considered the du Ponts to have made excessive profits out of the Allied business. Throughout the negotiations ran the feeling, stated blatantly by Robert Brookings, that the War Department and the civilian group would rather pay a higher price for some other contractor to do the work with no profit than have Du Pont undertake the project at a lower figure and make a substantial profit.

In mid-December 1917, when Newton Baker decided to have the government "create directly" its own powder capacity, he called upon Daniel Cowan Jackling, a western mining executive who had headed one of the nation's largest corporations, American Smelting and Refining, producers of copper, to undertake the task. Jackling agreed, but quickly recognized that he could succeed in building the plants only if he employed the services of others. His first efforts were to continue the government's negotiations with Thompson-Starrett. That firm refused to build the entire 1-million-pound-a-day capacity needed by the army, but agreed to construct plants that would manufacture only half that amount, or 500,000 pounds per day. More important, Thompson-Starrett made it clear that they did not have the necessary experience to design, plan, and erect even a 500,000-pound-a-day complex in the time required, without the aid of the du Ponts. Consequently on December 17, 1917, Jackling went to Wilmington to see Pierre. In Pierre's words: "Mr. Jackling announced that he wished to learn the nature of the assistance that the officers of E. I. du Pont de Nemours & Company were willing to give him and to obtain the preliminary 'lay out' of the proposed plant which this company was asked to build under General William Crozier's order of October 25, 1917."[28]

Pierre told Jackling that Du Pont would give limited help to Thompson-Starrett by having its Engineering Department furnish the details of plans, including maps of the Charleston site, numerous blueprints of powder plants, and an analysis of the Charleston water supply.[29] Pierre emphasized to Jackling, however, that the company would not divert its manpower to any detailed supervision of Thompson-Starrett's work.[30]

Jackling's agreement with Thompson-Starrett provided only one-half of the War Department's estimated needs, and there was some uncertainty whether it could do so in the time required. Consequently Jackling decided, after two weeks, that the Du Pont Company must be given the contract to provide the other half of the requirements. Newton D. Baker then authorized him to reopen negotiations with Pierre du Pont.

Early in January, therefore, Pierre realized that his company would have to come to terms with the government to build a great new powder works. Pierre felt anger and frustration, but he was also beginning to feel fear as well because he knew that, should a powder shortage develop, the public would place much of the blame upon himself and his company. Somehow, he thought, a way had to be found to break the impasse and to make certain that those who he felt were responsible for the state of powder production would be exposed to public view. Pierre naively thought that the best course was to bring the whole controversy out in the open, in the hope that public outrage would force the administration to change its ways. Preparedness critics of Wilson's administration in both the Republican and Democratic parties seemed to offer Pierre an excellent opportunity. Among the most influential critics were former President Theodore Roosevelt and Oregon's Democratic Senator George Earle Chamberlain, who was chairman of the Senate Committee on Military Affairs. Chamberlain had little use for Baker, and suggested in a public speech before the National Security League in January 1918 that the supply of munitions be removed from the jurisdiction of the secretary of war and lodged in a new cabinet level department headed by a minister of munitions. Roosevelt, who heard the speech, applauded warmly.[31] Pierre, aware of Chamberlain's views, caused many of the details of the Powder Company's negotiations with Baker to be leaked to the senator, who used the information in an attempt to embarrass Baker before a public hearing of his Senate Committee on Military Affairs.

Just what Pierre's inner thoughts were on the eve of Chamberlain's hearings is not recorded, but any hope that Newton Baker could be damaged quickly evaporated. Senator Chamberlain began his examination of the secretary of war on January 11, with the statement that "there is quite a general feeling amongst those with whom I have come in contact that the outlook for the production of powder is not good. . . . [That] there will . . . not be a sufficient amount of powder to meet the requirements of ourselves, and possibly, the demands of the allies upon America." Baker easily thwarted a public discussion by implying that security demanded that questions of the quantity of powder and the provisions for its manufacture be discussed in a private or executive session of the committee. In response to some pressure, however, Baker did admit that no contractor had been found to build the projected powder plant at Nashville, and he gave a brief account of the payments that the du Ponts had demanded to undertake the work.[32]

Baker's testimony was just enough to throw a bad light upon the Du Pont Company. *The New York Times* gave this account: "Senator Chamberlain referred to the Du Pont offer to build and operate a plant at cost, but Secretary Baker explained the offer was to build a plant for a commission of 15 per cent and operate it for eighteen months. On the basis of a $90,000,000 investment, he explained, the du Ponts would have made a gross profit of $20,000,000 to $40,000,000. 'They never at any time offered to erect a plant without compensation,' he said."

*The New York Times* account alarmed Pierre, who clipped it from his paper and enclosed it in a letter to Newton Baker with the following comment: "Erroneous conclusions may be drawn. . . . The profit of from Twenty to Forty Million was not obtainable from the Ninety Million Dollar investment in factories, but from the construction and operation contract amounting to Three Hundred and Twenty-five Millions, of which the larger sum of Forty Million Dollars represented 12.5%, the smaller 6.15% only." After some other comments, Pierre added: "However, our company is not disposed to enter into any argument or public discussion and we do not ask correction of the statement above mentioned."[33]

The *New York Times* article increased Pierre's apprehension about the failure of the government to find a contractor to build the proposed Nashville powder plant. Therefore, a friendly reply from Baker, and Jackling's continued interest in a possible Du Pont contract, caused Pierre again to consider offering his company's services. This time Pierre was determined that he would enter into no negotiations unless they had the explicit approval of Secretary Baker.[34] The secretary of war, who had also come to the realization that Du Pont was necessary, was more than glad to start such discussions. In a formal letter to Pierre on January 19, Baker stated that Jackling had "full authority to discuss and negotiate with you with regard to any work in connection with the proposed military powder factories of the Government."[35]

Upon receipt of Baker's assurance, Pierre arranged to meet Jackling in Wilmington on January 24. On that day the Du Pont president, aided by Colonel Buckner, hammered out an understanding with Jackling; this was turned into a specific contract on January 29, 1918.[36]

The so-called Jackling Contract represented a compromise, but Pierre yielded most. Under its terms the specially created Du Pont Engineering Company agreed to construct near Nashville a smokeless powder plant to be called Old Hickory capable of producing 500,000 pounds of cannon powder per day. This was one-half the amount specified in the original contract. The Engineering Company was to act as an agent for the government, to supply no capital, and for its services receive $500,000 to be paid in four equal installments as the work progressed. This part of the contract clearly represented a victory for the views of Daniel Willard and the War Industries Board, since they had proposed a payment of $1.0 million for building twice as much capacity. The Du Pont Engineering Company was to operate the Nashville plant after its completion, and the terms for this complied more with the original agreement that Pierre and General Crozier had signed. Under the rejected contract of October 25, the government was to pay all costs of operation plus a commission to the du Ponts of 5 cents per pound of powder accepted. And should production cost fall below 44½ cents per pound, the company would receive an incentive payment of half of the saving. The Jackling contract reduced the Du Pont commission to 3½ cents per pound, but retained the incentive payment provision of the original agreement almost word for word. To protect the company and the government against figures distorted by inflation, the contract specified a formula that would adjust for changes in the price of raw materials.[37]

Pierre signed the Jackling contract because he dared not do otherwise. A failure to agree meant risking America's military effectiveness in the war with Germany. But Pierre still worried that the War Department would prove uncooperative, and he seethed with anger at the treatment he had received at the hands of Newton Baker and the War Industries Board. Pierre still innocently felt that the American public ought to know the story. With this in mind, in early February Pierre consulted his friend Joseph H. Odell, the Presbyterian minister who had performed his marriage in 1916. Odell, besides his ministerial duties, was active in progressive Republican politics. He had been an editorial writer for the Philadelphia *Public Ledger and Evening Ledger,* and in 1913–1914 editor-in-chief of the Scranton *Tribune Republican* and *Scranton Truth.* In 1918 Odell joined the staff of the progressive national magazine *Outlook,* managed by Theodore Roosevelt's friends Lyman and Lawrence Abbott, and for whom Odell was to serve as a war correspondent on the western front.[38]

Pierre told Odell the entire story of his dealings with the War Department. The minister asked for exact data so that the editors of *Outlook* could review the facts as the basis for a story of the Wilson administration's bungling. Consequently, on February 4, 1918, Pierre gathered together most of the important documents of the dispute and sent them to Odell.

Fortunately for Pierre, *Outlook's* Lawrence F. Abbott did not act rashly. He had Pierre's documents read by the magazine's lawyer and then by Elihu Root. Roosevelt's former secretary of war saw the issues clearly and he advised against any publication of the affair, for reasons that Pierre should have known himself. Root pointed out that the Du Pont Company was "engaged in important Government work which is of great value to the country and to the winning of the war and that any public discussion of past controversies might cause friction and interrupt this work." But equally as important, he maintained that "the attitude of a very large element of our people is still such toward the great corporations that there is some possibility of stirring up a feeling that the War Department was championing the cause of the plain people as against 'Big Business' and thus diverting . . . attention from the one thing that . . . ought [to be kept] . . . in mind, that is, how to win the war."[39]

Root's arguments made such good sense that Pierre immediately dropped all plans to publicize his company's fight with Newton Baker and the Wilson administration.[40] The whole episode, however, reveals much about Pierre. The Du Pont Company president, despite his losing brush with antitrust and the bad press that resulted from his fight with Alfred, still could not think of himself as a great capitalist or the big businessman. Pierre had started life as a well-off member of America's upper-middle class. From the first, he had freely associated with such business radicals as Tom Johnson and Arthur Moxham. Furthermore, of all political leaders, Pierre most admired Theodore Roosevelt. To Pierre, Big Business was Standard Oil or the House of Morgan, not Du Pont. And even when Du Pont became a giant, Pierre continued to view all controversy in the light of the narrow issues at hand; he could not comprehend that he and his company had become to many the very embodiment of the overmighty corporation.

## Building Old Hickory

Despite Pierre's reservations about the Wilson administration, he and his company plunged with vigor into building Old Hickory. He sincerely believed that Du Pont could provide the nation with new powder capacity at the least cost and in the fastest time, and he regarded the contract that Jackling had made with Thompson-Starrett to build a factory of similar output and design, called Nitro, at Charleston, West Virginia, as a challenge. When, in January, it seemed certain that Du Pont would find it necessary to build the Nashville plant, Pierre held a meeting with Colonel Buckner and the Du Pont Company's chief engineer, H. M. Pierce, at which it was decided that when the company signed an agreement with Jackling no effort would be spared to finish Old Hickory ahead of Nitro. In that spirit, Buckner, who negotiated the Jackling document in its final form on January 29, sent Pierre a telegram which read: "Contract signed by all concerned. . . . Turn loose the wolves."[41]

Building Old Hickory was not quite like Du Pont's experience in erecting the giant Hopewell complex to supply Britain and France. The big difference was control. Du Pont had nearly total freedom in its work for the Allies. It selected the sites, built the plants according to its own design, bought raw materials from whom it pleased—and it did everything in a peacetime economy. In building Old Hickory, Du Pont acted as agent. The difference was crucial. Whereas with Hopewell the British and French supplied large cash advances and let Du Pont build plants for its own account, the Jackling contract specified that Du Pont would merely construct plants to be owned by the government. Thus the company found itself building to specifications not of its own making. All had to be accomplished in an atmosphere of crisis and shortage, and efforts had to fit into an overall plan dictated by the war as a whole.

Pierre did not enter into the Old Hickory construction unaware of the problems. His biggest fear was that red tape or Jackling's subordinates might delay government approval of plans, or interfere in the supply of raw materials. The chief engineer, Harry Pierce, reinforced Pierre's own thoughts. Pierce argued that he had to have freedom to do things his own way, "unhampered. If this cannot be arranged," said Pierce, *"we will fail."* Furthermore, Pierce emphasized that Du Pont must do its own purchasing. To the chief engineer this meant that Jackling's agents would do no more than routinely approve decisions made by the Du Pont staff.[42] In addition to Pierce's concerns, Pierre had another: finance. By the nature of what they were doing, the Du Pont Company had to move quickly, and this meant contracting obligations rapidly. The Du Pont president had still not put aside his fears that the government might not honor the obligations entered into by the du Ponts, thus leaving the company liable to large losses.

As the work began, many of Pierre's worst fears started to materialize. In mid-February Jackling's representative in Wilmington insisted that "everyone connected with the Du Pont Engineering Company and engaged on work in connection with the Nashville plant [had become] . . . employees of the government . . . and subject to all rules and regulations relating to government employees." Pierre recognized that if this were not fought, his authority would be seriously undermined. Consequently he sent William S. Gregg of the company's legal department to Washington to confer with the controller of the treasury and men from Jackling's office. In the capital, Gregg worked out an uneasy agreement which concluded that the "Du Pont Engineering Company should retain its identity as Agent" and that "it would be left to the . . . Engineering Company to determine as to the employees who should be considered Government employees and those who should not be regarded as such."[43]

This still did not end the friction, and government officials continued to intrude into such areas as plant design. On March 5, for example, Pierce wrote Pierre that while "Mr. Jackling's personal attitude towards us and towards all phases of the design and construction work . . . has been at all times of the broadest character. . .[that] the work as a whole suffers to the extent . . . it is necessary to reach all important decisions through a third party." A case in point was the purchase of rails for the plant railway. Here the director of military railways attempted to set up specifications that would apply to lines in France as well as those in military plants. "We consider this question of rails a typical example of 'too many cooks.' There are a number of other cases like this and we are scarcely started," complained Pierce to Pierre.[44]

Fortunately for the Du Pont Company, War Department officials in February 1918 began to re-examine their estimates for powder requirements, and they came to the conclusion that even with the added capacity of Nitro and Old Hickory more would be needed. Consequently, during March the government began negotiations to have Du Pont build additional smokeless powder plants. By this time the animosity between Pierre du Pont and Newton Baker was starting to dissipate in the common effort to win the war. Du Pont vigor on the Old Hickory job impressed Baker. Further, Jackling was strained to supervise the relatively inexperienced Thompson-Starrett team and recognized that he was of little use in aiding the du Ponts. Consequently Newton Baker allowed the negotiations for new factories to shift back to the Ordnance Department, where they were handled by Colonel Samuel McRoberts.

The War Department at first asked Du Pont to build a plant the size of Nashville (500,000 lbs. per day) on a site at Louisville, Kentucky, but Pierce suggested that it would be quicker and less costly to double the size of Old Hickory instead. A rapid study confirmed that Pierce's suggestion would save $15.0 million. These new negotiations gave Pierre a chance to rethink the entire position of his company. He knew that the Jackling contract, with its $500,000 payment for building Old Hickory, represented a surrender of his original demand for adequate compensation for his company's services. The government might consider the payment significant, but compared to Du Pont's profits either on its war business or even on its peacetime output, the half million dollars was a small amount. High wartime taxes made the sum even less attractive. But if the reward under the Jackling contract was small, Pierre still felt the dangers to his company were great, since it might bog down in a mass of red tape or incur large obligations the government would not honor.

Pierre let it be known that if the old contract were canceled, his company would agree to build at Nashville a plant with a capacity of 900,000 pounds per day of 24 hours (400,000 pounds more than under the Jackling contract) for the sum of one dollar. In return for this, the government must give the Du Pont Engineering Company absolute control over construction and relieve it from substantially all financial risk. Pierre suggested that the government make an advance payment of $18.75 million that the company could draw on. This payment would serve as a revolving fund to be replenished as bills were verified and checked by government agents.

The growing trust between Pierre and Newton Baker, which had fortunately not been destroyed by Pierre's rash move to vindicate his company in the pages of *Outlook*, made it possible for the War Department to accept Pierre's ideas almost unchanged. The new contract negotiated by E. G. Buckner and Colonel Samuel McRoberts on March 23 embodied all of Pierre's suggestions. The du Ponts were to run Nashville after its completion and receive the same fees called for under the Jackling contract.[45]

The new document freed Du Pont from interference and, in the words of Chief Engineer Pierce, "things began to 'hum.' " Despite a later start, Old Hickory soon overtook the Thompson-Starrett venture at Nitro. On June 22 Pierre reported the progress to his friend E. N. Carpenter. Old Hickory's sulphuric and nitric acid factories started running on June 11, and on June 22 the first of nine smokeless powder units, each able to produce 100,000 pounds daily, was about to be completed. "By comparison," Pierre wrote, "the construction at Charleston, being undertaken by other contractors . . ., shows an average condition about equal to that of our Nashville construction at the end of last April. It is true," he continued, "they have started one unit of sulphuric acid, but as their guncotton and powder apparatus is not nearly ready for use the acid must be shipped elsewhere or operations discontinued at the Charleston plant until their operations 'catch up'. . . ." Pierre did not blame Thompson-Starrett. "The whole fault," he argued, "had been one of bad judgment in arranging for the entire work. It is quite impossible for contractors who have never had experience in an entirely technical line to compete with those who have recently done exactly similar work. In fact," he concluded, "those engaged at Charleston deserve a good deal of credit for tackling a difficult job which should never have been forced upon them."[46]

From July through November 3, 1918, the Du Pont Engineering Company brought the first six of nine units into full operation, and on November 11, Armistice Day, unit number seven was 90% finished, and the remaining two units approximately 55% complete. Of course, the war's end stopped construction; thus, Old Hickory, although ahead of schedule, never operated at its total capacity.[47]

Pierre took justifiable pride in his company's performance. Measured by any standards, except profits, the war work undertaken for the United States was enormous. The money expended by the Du Pont Engineering Company for the construction of Old Hickory alone came to more than $83,820,000, and Du Pont produced $24,320,000 worth of powder at the plant while the war was in progress. Altogether, including Old Hickory and four other government factories built by Du Pont Engineering, the company expended a total of $129,535,000. For this, Du Pont received a total gross profit of $2,670,000. The profit included $2.0 million for construction fees at Old Hickory and another small works at Penniman; the rest came from operation. But net profits were much less. Federal income and excess profits taxes took $2,030,000, which made the net profit approximately $632,000, a figure that was further reduced by a total of $193,000 in stock bonus awards to employees, payments which were entirely borne by the E. I. du Pont de Nemours & Company. Thus, Du Pont's total compensation for handling approximately $129,500,000 of work stood at $439,000, or far less than ½ of 1%.[48]

Years later, in 1934, when the Nye Committee investigated the company's wartime activities, Alger Hiss, then an attorney for the committee, angered Pierre by charging that the Du Pont Engineering Company made the fantastic profit of $1,961,000 (for the operation of Old Hickory) on an investment of $5,000. This, said Hiss, was a profit of 39,321%! Pierre explained that the Engineering Company's nominal capital of $5,000 had little significance, for the firm had been devised as part of a legal arrangement to protect the E. I. du Pont de Nemours & Company itself from excessive risk. Pierre pointed out that despite all efforts in drawing the agreements, there was considerable risk even in the final contract. For example, $300,000 expended on Old Hickory was disallowed by the government. Pierre argued that this could have amounted to much more and could have substantially reduced profit or caused a major loss. "Expenses were so arbitrarily thrown out [by the government accounting officers]. They were just thrown out. There was no question about the $300,000 having been expended on the plant." Pierre continued that even recourse to the courts could have failed. "There might have been some quirk of a legal phrase that we did not know anything about that might have disbarred us."[49] But even if there had been absolutely no risk, Pierre agreed with Michigan's Senator Arthur Vandenburg that it was not right to measure the profits against any money invested by the company. The du Ponts were not primarily risking their capital; they were selling their knowledge and experience much as does a physician.

One thing Pierre knew and felt that the government and the American public ought to appreciate was that the plants built by his company cost less per unit of production than those of the rival Thompson-Starrett firm. Both Pierre and H. M. Pierce were avidly interested in comparing the difference in cost between Nitro and Old Hickory. After the war, Pierce secured a copy of Jackling's data and came to the following conclusions: the unit cost of powder at Nitro was $109.32 compared to $90 for the Du Pont plant. Using this data, had Jackling constructed Old Hickory, it would have cost $109,320,000 instead of $90,000,000. This meant that the public saved approximately $19,300,000.[50] Pierce also concluded that had Du Pont built Nitro the cost would have approximated $63,000,000 instead of the $76,525,000 it did cost, thus saving the taxpayers a further $13,525,000. In addition, the du Ponts were speedier than their rivals. Old Hickory manufactured more than 35 million pounds of acceptable cannon powder up to the date of the Armistice. Nitro, on the other hand, was just getting into production on the day the war ended, and it is doubtful if powder acceptable to Army Ordnance had yet been finished.[51] Pierre took special notice of Pierce's conclusions and planned to include them in his own account of Old Hickory when he wrote it, which he never did.

### Pierre Steps Down

The Armistice ended an era for Pierre du Pont and his company. Since 1914 Pierre had desired to leave active business and to turn his attention to Longwood and his other interests. The conflict within the company's top management prevented his retirement in 1914; then came war, and the fight with Alfred. As long as the war lasted, Pierre felt he could not relinquish his post.

The period between 1914 and 1919 saw many changes, not the least of which were large-scale diversification and the rise of a new generation of managers. Pierre had assumed the leadership in 1914 because no other man could command the respect of the company's owners and key executives. The war years changed this. One by one, the old guard was replaced. Moxham left the company, Coleman sold his stock, Pierre defeated Alfred in the bitter family fight, and Barksdale, who stayed at Pierre's side throughout the contest with Alfred, died in 1918 after a long illness. Chief Engineer Ramsay died in 1916. J. Amory Haskell and John Raskob became involved in General Motors. Of the old group, only Frank Connable continued on the Executive Committee, and he had not taken an active role after Tallman joined the committee in 1916 as the executive primarily in charge of purchasing.

In 1914 Pierre had wanted to hand the reins to his brother Irénée, who had pleaded lack of experience. By 1918 that was no longer true. The new group that had manned the Executive Committee since 1914 had become a skillful team and, in turn, had developed a strong second rank of young executives beneath them. Irénée had served as first vice-president and chairman of the Executive Committee and had been at Pierre's side when nearly all the major wartime decisions had been made. Another of Pierre's brothers, Lammot, also served on the Executive Committee and gained administrative skills as vice-president in charge of black powder production and then, even more, as head of the new Miscellaneous Manufacturing Department, which managed the new ventures in paint, dyes, fabrikoid, celluloid, and chemicals. Furthermore, men like H. Fletcher Brown in Smokeless Powder and Harry G. Haskell in High Explosives had proved themselves. Below the Executive Committee, but still vitally important, Harry M. Pierce had demonstrated himself a worthy replacement for Major Ramsay. In short, the Du Pont Company entered 1919 with a young, highly experienced and dedicated top management group.

Du Pont also entered the postwar period with a host of unsolved problems. The company bore only slight resemblance to its prewar self. Its assets had increased from $83.4 million in 1914 to $308.0 million in 1918.[52] But sheer size alone did not tell the story, for the company had changed from a narrowly based explosives firm to an organization with interests in new fields such as paints, chemicals, and dyes, each almost equal to the original powder investment. The firm also had a surplus of more than $68.0 million to allocate for new ventures. Despite growth and diversification during the war, Pierre brushed aside all questions of organizational changes. For one thing, despite the new investments, nearly all effort remained concentrated on the war production, which accounted for most of the profits. For this, the highly centralized control developed prior to the war worked perfectly. Pierre considered the new products as ones for the postwar markets to make use of capital and talents accumulated during the conflict. Consequently he postponed a review of the company's organization until the war was over.

Pierre stayed long enough to oversee the immediate deactivation of wartime plants, an event for which he had prepared. But he was determined to turn active management of the company over to a younger team as quickly as possible. Therefore, as the war business closed down, Pierre prepared to pass the presidency to Irénée. Pierre explained that he would always stand ready to offer advice from his position as chairman of the board of directors. He would continue to serve as president of the Du Pont Securities Company (which in June 1919 was renamed the Christiana Securities Company), through which he and his immediate family controlled the Du Pont Company. However, Pierre insisted that initiative for reorganization or new investment would, of necessity, originate with the new team. He expected it to enjoy a freedom similar to that exercised by the three cousins when they took command in 1902.

Late in 1918 and early in 1919, even before Pierre stepped down from the presidency, Irénée and his key advisers started to examine the question of organization. To do this, the Executive Committee appointed a subcommittee headed by Harry Haskell. Flushed by wartime success the Haskell committee opted for a refinement of the highly centralized managerial system already in use. The revised organization that went into effect in the summer of 1919 made no provision for semiautonomous divisions for the newly important nonexplosives enterprises. Thus the centralized sales and production departments, for example, served explosives, paints and dyes, and all other units as well. Within two short years problems forced massive rethinking of the entire concept of an organization for a diversified company, but by that time Pierre had shifted his full-time attention to General Motors.[53]

For Pierre, men, not organizations, were the primary consideration, and when he formally relinquished the presidency to his brother Irénée on May 1, 1919, he looked with confidence on a new team that included another brother, Lammot du Pont, as first vice-president and chairman of the Executive Committee. Equally important to the three brothers had been the selection of the new postwar Executive Committee. The three, but especially Pierre, felt it vital to encourage new talent much as Pierre and Coleman had tried to do in 1914. Pierre phrased it this way in explaining the change to the board of directors in April 1919: "I am firmly of the opinion that we have now reached another turning point in the conduct of the affairs of E. I. du Pont de Nemours & Company; therefore it would seem wise to place responsibility for future development and management of the business on the next line of men."[54] Thus, such valued old hands as Harry Haskell, William Coyne, Frank Tallman, and Frank Connable were retired from line administration and the Executive Committee. In their places were F. D. Brown as treasurer, who had already taken Raskob's place in October 1918; F. W. Pickard, Sales; W. C. Spruance, Production; C. A. Patterson, Explosives Manufacturing Department; W. S. Carpenter, Jr., Development Department; J. B. D. Edge, Purchasing Department; and C. A. Meade, Miscellaneous Manufacturing Department.[55]

Pierre, at his departure, could look back upon the most significant years in the Du Pont Company's long history. Since 1914, assets had almost quadrupled to a total of $308.0 million, and profits had reached undreamed-of levels. Net earnings peaked at $82.0 million in 1916 and, despite greater volume, shrunk to $49.0 million in 1917 and $47.0 million in 1918. The drop came with the reduction in powder prices to the Allies as plants became totally amortized and, also, with the shift to low-profit contracts with the United States government. Even so, net earnings stood more than seven times higher than they had been in the highest prewar year, 1912.

In the period between 1911 and 1919 Pierre left a permanent mark upon the Du Pont Company. First, he met the crisis of the antitrust suit by guiding the company through the complex dissolution procedures, to emerge stronger than ever. Next, he led the firm during the dangerous problems of wartime expansion. During this time his primary goal was always the preparation of his company for the postwar world. Thus, diversification started under his tenure laid the basis for Du Pont's rise as the leading broad-based chemical firm in the United States. Pierre accomplished all this while he took decisive steps to ensure that the company would remain under family control. At the same time Pierre carried the company through the most critical period in the transformation of a small family firm into a large, modern corporation. Even if family-owned, he insisted that it must be professionally managed. The executives were to be chosen and promoted on the basis of administrative and technical skills, not on family connection.

After 1919 Pierre never again gave the Du Pont Company his undivided attention. He placed his entire reliance upon the new men. Despite Pierre's desire to retire, however, his career as a corporation builder was not over. Within a year and a half he was to be devoting all his time to reorganizing and rejuvenating the General Motors Corporation which, within a little more than a decade, had already become the fifth largest industrial company in the nation.[56]

PART IV

THE GENERAL MOTORS STORY

# Initial Involvement, 1915–1917

DURING THE SAME YEARS that Pierre du Pont was supervising his company's huge wartime expansion and setting its postwar directions, he was also chairman of the board of General Motors Corporation. He became the automobile company's chairman when it was only seven years old. By then it was already second, although a very distant second, to the Ford Motor Company in size of assets and in volume of production. By the end of 1920, when Pierre became its president as well as chairman, it was one of the largest corporations in the world. By 1928 it had replaced Ford as the leading American automobile company, a position it still holds today. In that year the General Motors Corporation reported the highest net profits ever made by an American corporation up to that time.

During his first years as chairman, however, General Motors was not Pierre's primary concern. He was responsible for having the Du Pont Company make a large investment in the automobile company in 1917. He then helped to determine its financial policies and sought with little success to have it adopt Du Pont administrative and financial methods. The sharp postwar recession, which dramatized the need for financial and administrative reform, forced Pierre to take the presidency of the corporation in December 1920. For the next three years he spent nearly all his time in restoring the company's health and vigor. Once its business procedures had been rationalized, Pierre turned the presidency over to capable Alfred P. Sloan, Jr. After 1924 Pierre devoted less time to the affairs of General Motors. As chairman, the position he held until 1928, his major task was to keep a watchful eye on the huge Du Pont investment in the automobile company.

Pierre du Pont's career at General Motors, therefore, falls into four quite different phases: initial involvement, the crisis of 1920–1921, the rebuilding of the giant corporation from 1921 to 1924, and the following years, through 1928, of success and fulfillment. The story can be viewed from three vantage points. From each of these viewpoints Pierre's experiences were quite different from those he had had at Du Pont.

At General Motors Pierre was no longer working in a familiar situation with brothers, cousins, and lifelong associates. The only person he knew intimately in the automobile company was John J. Raskob. This relationship is, then, one key to understanding and evaluating Pierre's contribution in the automobile industry. For Pierre, the General Motors venture was always a partnership with John Raskob. During part of the time Raskob was actually the senior partner. The other two men Pierre worked closely with in New York and Detroit were William C. Durant and Alfred P. Sloan, Jr. The first Pierre found stimulating and charming, but he never fully trusted Durant. In the second, Pierre discovered a man of less charm, but one with a more powerful mind and a far stronger will. Pierre came to have a greater respect for Sloan than for any other businessman he had ever known, and because of this, Sloan was one of the very few men who could take issue with Pierre on basic business problems and have his way.

Pierre's fundamental concern at General Motors was to see that the investment of the Du Pont Company and the du Pont family in that corporation remained profitable. The investment was one of the largest ever made by an American company and family in an outside firm. A study of Pierre's role at General Motors, therefore, provides a useful look at the nature and process of financial control. Clearly the most important lesson Pierre and his associates learned was that financial control exercised with inadequate administrative and statistical techniques was hardly any control at all.

In making General Motors into a profitable investment, Pierre had to devote his energies to a new set of business, as well as industrial, problems; these were quite different from those he had learned to handle at Du Pont. The automobile industry was young and swiftly growing, whereas the explosives industry had been long established. At Du Pont, Pierre's initial task had been to transform an old-line cartel into a modern integrated operating company and then to learn to meet the needs and requirements of this new type of industrial organization. The company's massive expansion during World War I was based on a firm administrative and managerial framework which Pierre had played a large part in creating. Except for the disastrous recession of 1920–1921, the story at General Motors was one of continuous, if fluctuating, growth. There were no cartels in the industry. From the first, the integrated enterprise had been the industrial form used. The financing and management of a corporation of great size in the nation's swiftest-growing industry—and one in which short-term demand fluctuated widely

—was, then, Pierre's basic task at General Motors. An analysis of how he handled such fundamental industrial problems provides a third theme for the following chapters. It reveals as much about personnel, product policy, technology, administration, and finance in American big business as did the story of Pierre's experience at Du Pont.

## Becoming Chairman of the General Motors Board

Few decisions had a greater impact on Pierre or the du Pont family than his decision to become chairman of the board of the General Motors Corporation. Yet the opportunity came almost by accident, and even that chance would not have occurred except for John J. Raskob, who first interested Pierre in General Motors. Furthermore, Raskob was responsible for getting Pierre to cause the Du Pont Company to invest a large block of wartime profits in the motor company. During General Motors' great period of expansion, Raskob took the initiative in setting its financial policies. Only after the Du Pont ties to General Motors became more than financial did Pierre come to play a positive and creative role in the automobile company.

Raskob had seen the promise of General Motors as early as 1914, before the outbreak of the war in Europe and before the final rupture between Pierre, Coleman, and Alfred. In February 1914 he purchased 500 shares of General Motors common and convinced Pierre to buy 2,000. He argued that a low price of $70 a share reflected "only the fact that they were not paying dividends."[1] The company's excellent earnings and competent management, Raskob believed, should double the value of the shares in a year's time. This prediction turned out to be right. The boom set off by the demands of the European war intensified the already strong interest of Americans in automobiles. By the summer of 1915 General Motors stock was selling at over 200. By September it had reached 350.[2] By December the stock he had bought at 82 reached 558. At this time over half the value of Pierre's investment portfolio (outside of his Du Pont and other powder industry holdings) was in General Motors.

This last rise, however, resulted more from an internal fight for control than from external demand. In 1910 the company's founder, William C. Durant, had been forced to borrow $15.0 million from a group of Boston and New York bankers headed by the venerable banking house of Lee, Higginson and Company of Boston. As a condition of the loan, Durant was to retire from active management, and the bankers were to have full control for five years through a voting trust. The loan, and with it the trust, were to terminate on October 1, 1915. As the time neared, Durant and his friends began buying up trust certificates. No one was more active in helping Durant than Lewis G. Kaufman, president of the Chatham & Phoenix Bank of New York City.[3] Because the Du Pont Company had used the bank to handle its New York transactions, Kaufman had earlier asked Pierre to be one of the bank's directors. Then, just before the General Motors Board met to determine policies needed on the expiration of the voting trust, Kaufman invited Pierre to come on the automobile company's board.[4] He assured Pierre that the company would pay off its loan in full. The voting trust, he reported, would be dissolved, and Durant, having acquired the controlling shares, would take over the company's management. The change would occur at the board meeting scheduled for September 16. Pierre accepted the invitation and agreed to attend the meeting even though he had to be in Washington on September 14 about an antitrust complaint that he feared Alfred might have instigated. He carefully arranged to have Raskob come with him to New York.

At the September 16 meeting, Pierre found that Kaufman's description of the situation was not at all true.[5] Durant did not have a controlling interest of the stock. He and his supporters formed one faction. The bankers who formed the voting trust were the other. Both factions could agree on dividend policy. The excellent earnings that Raskob had earlier noted permitted the company to pay off the $15.0 million loan and, in addition, to declare a dividend of $50 a share on common stock, the first dividend to be paid since the company's formation in 1908. But neither group would agree to the makeup of the slate of directors to be presented to the stockholders at the November annual meeting. Pierre was astonished at the " 'absolute' deadlock" between "the old and the new factions." After six hours of tiring debate, twelve of the fifteen directors had been agreed on, with each side nominating six men. Pierre's name had been approved as one of the Durant-Kaufman nominees.

After a brief consultation among themselves, the spokesman for the bankers, James J. Storrow, a senior partner of Lee, Higginson and Company and chairman of the General Motors Finance Committee, proposed a way to break the deadlock. He suggested that Pierre nominate three "neutral" directors. When the Durant group agreed, Pierre recommended the names of Raskob, J. Amory Haskell, and Pierre's cousin and brother-in-law Lammot Belin, who was in New York working for the Aetna Explosives Company. The meeting ended harmoniously with the formation of a proxy committee including two from each side—Durant and Kaufman, Storrow and Charles W. Nash, the president of the company, and Pierre—although not yet officially a director—as chairman. It would present the agreed-upon fifteen directors to the stockholders. After the meeting, Pierre and Raskob had long discussions with both groups about the present and future of General Motors.

Both sides were pleased to have Pierre take the role of peacemaker. His quiet way, his searching questions, and his desire to achieve solutions won the confidence of all. Storrow wrote: "May I congratulate you and Mr.

Raskob upon the success of your day's work in New York? Certainly it was an irksome job for all concerned; but it seems pretty clear that the stock-holders are much better off than otherwise would have been the case."⁶ The conservative Boston banker urged that either Pierre or Raskob become chairman of the Finance Committee, a position he himself had long held and through which he had strongly influenced the affairs of the company. Pierre thanked Storrow "for the very candid way that you have discussed affairs with Mr. Raskob and me. As outsiders, unacquainted with the opera-tion of the Company, we feel much complimented in being trusted with confidential information and hope that we shall be of sufficient service to merit your confidence."⁷ But he declined the offer to chair the Finance Committee. Both he and Raskob were far too busy with the Du Pont Company. The position eventually went to Kaufman, in whom Pierre had expressed confidence.

Durant, too, was pleased by Pierre's actions. Writing him on September 25, he congratulated Pierre on a draft of the letter prepared for proxies. "I think you have handled the matter splendidly and will hold myself in readiness to attend the meeting [of the Proxy Committee] any time next week at your convenience."⁸

The plans accepted at the September 16 meeting were carried out with little difficulty. Haskell and Belin and, of course, Raskob agreed to come on the board. Pierre, however, was a little embarrassed and a little annoyed because Durant had leaked the news to the press about the arrangement even before he had time to write Haskell or Belin.⁹ When informed at the November 16 meeting, the stockholders approved of the slate and, as a part of the larger agreement as of September 16, Pierre became chairman of the board of General Motors Company, a position he would continue to hold for the next thirteen years.¹⁰

This unexpected chance to take part in the management of General Motors came at an opportune moment for Pierre. Du Pont Company affairs were going well. The purchase of Coleman's stock and the creation of the Du Pont Securities Company had been successfully carried out. As yet, there had been no overt reaction from Alfred, although Pierre was still worried that there might be. The new Executive Committee, beneficiaries of the stock purchase, were doing an excellent job. The building of the first war plants under Major Ramsay's guidance was almost completed. That summer, too, Pierre had made his decision to wed. In fact, he and Alice were married only three weeks after the directors' meeting that made Pierre the board's chairman. The fall of 1915 was indeed a time for new ventures.

Pierre was clearly interested in his new position. He wrote Haskell that he had "no intention of being a 'dummy' director."¹¹ He planned to get a clear picture of the motor company's operations and then to see if the methods of over-all control that had worked so well at Du Pont might not

438 ]    THE GENERAL MOTORS STORY

be applied to General Motors. On returning from his two-week wedding trip through the Virginia mountains, Pierre turned his attention to General Motors, not to Du Pont. After conferring with Raskob, he decided the two should visit Detroit and Flint, taking Alice and Helena Raskob with them.

The trip was most informative.[12] The two men inspected General Motors' plants and offices and talked at length with senior executives and local financiers. They met Charles W. Nash, who managed Durant's carriage company and headed Durant's first automobile venture, the Buick Motor Company, before Storrow and the other bankers had offered him the presidency of General Motors. They talked with Walter P. Chrysler, the very competent young executive whom Storrow had brought from American Locomotive to take Nash's place at Buick, and Henry M. Leland, the elderly, still brilliant machine-maker who, as president of Cadillac, had already given that automobile a reputation for high-quality performance. Pierre was particularly impressed with Emory W. Clark, the president of the First and Old National Bank of Detroit. Because he had initially helped finance Durant's company and then remained close to the Storrow regime, Clark had been on the board of directors from the earliest days of the company.

In talking with Clark and Nash in Detroit and with Kaufman and Durant in New York, Pierre and Raskob repeatedly urged that the automobile company pattern its Finance and Executive committees on those of Du Pont.[13] The Executive Committee should be made up of the heads of the major car-making units, and the Finance Committee should be representative of the major financial interests. Pierre wanted the Finance Committee to approve annual budgets (a financial device that did not then exist at General Motors), as well as large appropriations for capital expenditures. Pierre, however, found much more interest in his suggestions in Detroit than he did in New York.

At Detroit Pierre and Raskob had learned a great deal about William Crapo Durant. When Pierre had met the founder of General Motors at the September 16 meeting, he could hardly have suspected the critical part Durant would play in his and Raskob's lives during the next five years. Everyone agreed that Durant's imagination and drive had created General Motors. Both Clark and Leland, however, emphasized what Storrow had already suggested. Durant, an able and experienced industrial organizer, was becoming more and more a promoter and financial manipulator. His return to full control of General Motors, warned Clark, would bring, at the very least, administrative confusion and difficulties; at worst, it could threaten financial disaster. Durant's brilliance and charm were too dangerously combined with an oversanguine optimism and enormous self-confidence. With these traits came a fatal weakness—he wanted to manage everything himself. As one of Storrow's associates later stated:

Durant is a genius, and therefore not to be dealt with on the same basis as ordinary business men. In many respects he is a child in emotions, in temperament, and in mental balance, yet possessed of wonderful energy and ability along certain other well-defined lines. He is sensitive and proud; and successful leadership, I think, really counts more with him than financial success.[14]

Yet Durant's formation of General Motors was the culmination of a brilliant business career.[15] Before getting into motors he had made a fortune as one of the largest producers of carriages in the country and had done so by creating a corporation based on high-volume production and marketing. In his hometown of Flint, Michigan, he had set up factories producing wheels, bodies, axles, springs, and even whip sockets, and then built large specialized plants to assemble these parts into 200 carriages a day. Further, he organized a country-wide network of dealers and distributors to sell his product. To assure himself of essential supplies, Durant integrated backwards by financing the growth of paint and varnish works in Flint, and even by purchasing stands of hardwood and hickory.

By 1900 Durant, who was still under forty, was ready for a new venture. The automobile provided a threat to his existing carriage business and a challenge to his entrepreneurial talent. In December of 1904 he purchased the tiny Buick Motor Company and immediately adapted his empire-building methods to automobile production. He encouraged parts and accessory makers to come to Flint: Charles S. Mott, maker of axles and wheels, moved from Utica; Alfred Champion, producer of spark plugs, came to Flint from Boston. Durant built large assembly plants in or close to Flint and created a nationwide distributing network for the marketing of cars. The results, indeed, were impressive. In 1903 the Buick Motor Company built and sold 16 cars. In 1904 the output expanded to 31. By 1906 Durant raised production to 2,295 vehicles, and by 1908, 8,487. In four years Buick Motor Company had become the largest producer of automobiles in the United States. In 1908 Ford was running second, with a production of 6,181 vehicles, and Cadillac was trailing third, with 2,380.

In 1908, the year in which Ford manufactured the first Model T and started on his huge expansion, Durant decided to form the General Motors Company around the nucleus of Buick and his other Flint operations. Like Ford, Durant saw the potentialities of a high-volume market for the inexpensive automobile. Both men realized that volume production could reduce unit costs and, by lowering prices, expand the market. Because he was a salesman and a financier, rather than a mechanic like Ford, Durant decided that the quickest and surest way to provide the capacity necessary to produce the essential volume was through combining existing plants and distributing outlets into one giant enterprise. So in 1908 he organized the new company to include Buick and three other firms that both manufactured and distributed (the Olds Motor Works, the Oakland Motor Car

Company, and Henry Leland's Cadillac Motor Car Company); one distributing firm, the McLaughlin Motor Car Company, Ltd., of Canada; five minor motorcar companies (which provided little more than small factories or patents); three truck-making companies; and ten parts and accessories firms. In financing these purchases Durant used very little cash. He relied, as the du Ponts had done earlier, on merely exchanging the stock of the new holding company for that of the purchased operating company.

In carrying out his strategy of expansion through combination and vertical integration, Durant rarely troubled himself about temporary declines in the demand for cars. So he was caught totally unprepared for a slight business recession in the summer of 1910. Even though General Motors' income from sales had almost doubled between 1908 and 1910—going from $29.0 million to $49.4 million (and most of this coming from Buick)—when sales dropped off, the promoter found himself without cash enough to pay his workers or suppliers.[16] It was this need that brought him to Lee, Higginson and Company and that led to the $15.0 million loan and the five-year voting trust.

After Storrow took over the management of General Motors, Durant, in a sense, started all over again. In 1911 he formed, with Louis Chevrolet, the Chevrolet Motor Company, and within the next four years had created another nationwide organization of assembly plants, wholesale offices, and retail agencies. Soon this organization was making money. For the two years ending August 14, 1915, Chevrolet's net sales totaled close to $11.8 million, and profits were just over $1.3 million.

In the meantime, Storrow and Nash had tried to bring some order into the sprawling General Motors empire. They consolidated several of the operating units, changed the top personnel and, in an effort to help control and coordinate the company's widespread activities, they even tried to form a central organization for purchasing, accounting, engineering, and research. Yet when Pierre visited Detroit in the fall of 1915, General Motors was still a loose combination—of producing and distributing firms of automobiles, trucks, parts, and accessories—with little control from any central office. It was a very differently organized and administered corporation from the Du Pont Company.

This is why Pierre urged Clark, Nash, Durant, and the others to pattern the General Motors top management after Du Pont. He proposed studying these changes at a meeting of the Finance Committee on November 12, four days before the stockholders' annual meeting that approved of the new board.[17] At the same time he urged the committee to adopt a set of proposals Raskob had drawn up for a systematic dividend policy based on estimates of the company's long-term earnings which he and the Du Pont treasurer were quite certain would assure an annual dividend of 4½% on common stock.

Nothing came of these proposals. In fact, Pierre reported to Clark, the Detroit banker, that at the November 12 meeting "developments were quite discouraging."[18] Durant had appeared at the meeting, Pierre explained, and "stated, among other things, that the developments of the past two or three weeks (whatever that may mean) had led him to determine to take an active interest in the management of the General Motors Company. This statement is quite the opposite of that he made to me and Mr. Raskob at the time of our first and only previous meeting (excepting that of the Proxy Committee)." Pierre quickly learned what Durant meant.

December 1915 was a month of surprises. On the ninth Pierre was served the papers of the Philip du Pont suit. On December 21 he discovered by the morning press that William C. Durant had reacquired control of the General Motors Company.[19] He headed a syndicate, the papers reported, that now proposed to offer the controlling share of that company to the Chevrolet Motor Company, of which he, Durant, was president and which he fully controlled. Durant had begun to prepare for this move right after the critical meeting of September 16. On September 23 he reorganized his Chevrolet interests by forming the Chevrolet Motor Company (Delaware) capitalized at $20.0 million, and then he exchanged $13.2 million of this stock for the shares of the companies that built and sold Chevrolet. He offered the remaining $6.8 million worth of shares to the public. Because of Chevrolet's good profit record, the public stock apparently sold well. The books on its sale were closed on November 1. Clearly Durant then used the funds acquired from the sale of Chevrolet stock to purchase more General Motors shares. Then on December 21 he made his announcement that he had purchased enough General Motors stock to control it and planned to offer to exchange Chevrolet stock for that of General Motors at the very favorable rate of 5 Chevrolet shares for 1 of General Motors. (To make possible the exchange Durant, at a special stockholders' meeting of December 23, increased Chevrolet's capital stock from $20.0 million to $80.0 million.)

All this was unknown to Pierre when he picked up his newspapers on the morning of December 21. He was amazed to read of Durant's claim that he had the backing of the powerful Du Pont and Remington Arms interests and that with these allies he controlled 60% or 70% of General Motors stock. Other directors were surely just as surprised. Clark, and probably others, immediately got in touch with Pierre. Pierre replied to Clark by letter (and probably to others by phone) that he knew nothing more than what was in the papers.[20] He thought the press statements could only refer to common, and not preferred, stock and added that "it is hardly fair to say that Mr. Durant has been 'backed in his fight' by the du Pont interests." He and the other neutral directors were, he insisted, concerned with the best interests of the stockholders, and "in this particular business I cannot see how a Director of General Motors could turn in his stock to Chevrolet without arranging that a similar offer be made to all other stockholders."[21] No offer had been made yet to him, "but I do not see how my decision could be other than to stay out unless a general offer was made. As to the general offer I should have to know what it meant before I could reach a decision or recommendation."

Pierre was cautious. He thought it unlikely that Durant actually had control. If the exchange offer was bona fide, and enough stockholders did accept the offer to turn their General Motors over to Chevrolet at the rate of 5 to 1, and if Durant kept control of the majority of Chevrolet shares, he would certainly have control of the combined holdings. But just as certainly the bankers would not go along even if there was a general offer to exchange. Durant's proposition, Pierre was certain, was directed at him and his associates, for the exchange of their stock would probably be enough to tip the scale in Durant's favor.

In any case, Pierre was determined that he and the other three "neutral" directors should, in fact, remain neutral in the coming second round of the battle between Durant and the Storrow forces. He, Raskob, Haskell, and Belin refused Durant's offer to make the exchange, and they did so more than once.[22] At the same time Pierre did not support the efforts of Storrow and the others to block Durant's scheme and then to remove him once again from office. Despite strong pressure from the majority of the General Motors board (for two Durant men—Charles S. Mott and Samuel S. Pryor, president of Remington Arms—whose support Durant had claimed, had joined with the bankers on this issue), Pierre refused to sign a statement protesting any attempt by Chevrolet to control or change the present General Motors management.[23] Nor would he back the bankers' plan to set up at the next stockholders' meeting in November a three-year voting trust that they would dominate. As one can imagine, both sides continued to woo Pierre and his associates during the early months of 1916.

By April it became apparent that Durant had, without Du Pont assistance, acquired at least 50% of the General Motors common stock. The bankers, who had sent out appeals in February and again in March urging the formation of a voting trust, found the replies disappointing.[24] The first indication Pierre had of Durant's victory was in mid-April when he had a visit from president Nash. Shortly afterward, Nash sent the chairman his resignation to take effect August 1.[25] (He would actually leave his office in June.) In May and early June, Storrow, Clark, and Pryor followed suit. Soon the last of the bankers, Albert H. Wiggin, president of the Chase National Bank, also resigned and Leland then left General Motors rather than work for Durant.[26] Storrow and Clark immediately turned to a new venture, forming the Nash Motor Company, which was headed by the former president of General Motors.[27] At the same time Leland began the Lincoln

Motor Company, which some years later Henry Ford purchased.

By May Pierre and Raskob agreed that there was no longer any reason to remain neutral. Durant had won, and the Storrow group was about to retire from the field. Pierre and his associates therefore decided to accept the latest of Durant's several offers to exchange Chevrolet stock for General Motors at the 5 to 1 rate. "Developments of recent months," Pierre wrote Durant on May 9, "have considerably altered my opinion relative to the propriety of making this exchange; principally because of the fact that the control of General Motors is now definitely fixed beyond anybody's question."[28] He had hesitated in accepting the offer only because of his previous refusals, but, if Durant was still agreeable, he would exchange the 2,350 shares he controlled. Moreover, since the ownership had changed, Pierre told Durant that he would willingly give up his place on the board. "Should your plans make it advisable to make the change I will not be aggrieved in any way."

Even though Durant had won control without any active help from Pierre du Pont, he was obviously not willing to lose an ally of Pierre's stature and financial resources. He urged the Wilmingtonian and his associates to remain on the board; he asked Pierre to continue as chairman when he, Durant, took over the presidency in June on Nash's retirement. Durant replaced the bankers who were retiring from the board with the general managers of the major operating units—Buick, Cadillac, Oakland, Olds, and the General Motors Truck Company.[29] The two directors who had remained steadfastly loyal to Durant (Arthur G. Bishop, a Flint banker, and J. H. McClement, a New York broker) remained on the board. This, then, was the General Motors board of directors over which Pierre du Pont presided after he ceased to be a "neutral" director mediating between the two factions that had fought so long and hard for the control of the General Motors Company.

## The Durant Regime

Durant, the victor of that battle, however, had no intention of working closely with his board. He considered it merely a paper organization that he had to have to meet legal requirements and accepted business practices. The founder, who had regained his company, was going to run it by himself. For many weeks after he took over the presidency in June, Durant neither phoned nor wrote Wilmington. Finally, on August 25 Pierre wrote Durant: "Am I wrong in waiting for advice from you relative to G.M. matters? It is my understanding that you wish to talk to me on the subject. As I have not heard from you I fear that through misunderstanding I have failed to communicate with you as to a convenient date of meeting."[30]

There was no misunderstanding. Durant wanted Pierre's support, not his advice. He distrusted industrialists from Wilmington almost as much he did bankers from State Street and Wall Street. In planning the legal reorganization of his company that September, Durant directed lawyers to set up a new General Motors Corporation with only a five-man board, a three-man Executive Committee, and no Finance Committee at all.[31] To such an organization, however, Pierre, Raskob, and other members of the board would not agree. After some debate they had their way. The new board remained a large one, with Finance and Executive committees. Nevertheless, these committees met most infrequently. Even the meetings of the board itself were called only on the shortest notice and then at the initiation of the president, not the chairman.[32]

Nor did Durant see the need for extensive executive assistance in managing his company. Although General Motors' activities were concentrated in Michigan, he preferred to stay in New York. The members of his small administrative staff, which included the treasurer, Herbert H. Rice (who also served as the company's advertising and purchasing adviser), Meyer L. Prensky, the comptroller, and John T. Smith, the legal counsel, had to divide their time between New York and Detroit. As late as 1920 the central administrative organization at General Motors consisted of only seven executives and their secretaries.

Durant not only expected to run his own show but to do so with very little help. He saw little need for the type of systematic group management that Pierre had done so much to create at the Du Pont Company. In the youthful automobile industry of that day, however, Durant's views were not unique. The other founding fathers of the industry—Olds, the Dodge brothers, Leland and, above all, Henry Ford—were individualistic, strong-minded men who ran their companies almost single-handedly. And, as was to be the case with Durant, none was ever able to meet the administrative needs required to manage a large enterprise. None transformed successfully the companies they had founded into efficient modern corporations.

Once back in power Durant began to carry out long-held plans for the expansion of General Motors. By the early fall of 1916 he had completed a legal and financial reorganization that set up a new company, the General Motors Corporation, which acquired the assets of the existing General Motors Company and its subsidiaries.[33] This move not only resulted in a new capital structure consisting of just under 200,000 shares of 6% preferred and just over 825,000 shares of common stock (par value $100) but also transformed the old subsidiaries into divisions. In other words, the new corporation legally controlled and operated all the major units by itself rather than through legal subsidiaries. The change, it should be stressed, was only legal. The many operating divisions continued to be managed as independent units held together only by Durant himself.

Even before this legal reorganization was completed, Durant embarked on a program to greatly enlarge the corporation's automobile-producing capacity. From July 31, 1916, until December 31, 1917, investment in plant and equipment at General Motors almost doubled to reach a figure of just over $40.1 million.[34] High profits permitted Durant to finance much of this expansion out of retained earnings. During the same period $27.8 million of earnings was plowed back into the corporation, and over $11.0 million was distributed as dividends. Chevrolet, which Durant had not brought into General Motors, enjoyed a similar type of expansion. New factories for transmissions, motors, and axles were built in Toledo and Flint, and assembly plants in Oakland and Fort Worth.

Durant always believed that the expansion of automobile-producing capacity required a comparable growth in parts and accessories plants. In May 1916, as soon as he was certain of his control over General Motors, Durant, with Kaufman, formed the United Motors Corporation—a holding company whose stock Durant planned to use to purchase a number of firms making parts.[35] For this purchase 1.2 million shares (no par value) were authorized, of which only 5,000 shares had voting rights. The only legal connection between United Motors and General Motors was that Durant was the major and probably controlling stockholder in each. Largely through exchange of stock, United Motors quickly obtained two roller-bearing companies (Hyatt and New Departure), two electrical system manufacturers (Dayton Engineering Laboratories and Remy Electric), and the Perlman Rim Corporation.

Durant placed the president of one of these firms, Alfred P. Sloan, Jr., in charge of the new holding company. As a young graduate of the Massachusetts Institute of Technology, Sloan had founded the Hyatt Roller Bearing Company with a capital of $5,000 in 1898. He had built an eminently successful company, which eighteen years later he was able to sell out to Durant for $13.5 million. In 1917 Durant and Sloan had United Motors buy into the Harrison Radiator Company, purchase the Klaxon Company (producers of horns), and form the United Motors Service, Inc., to provide repair and maintenance service to the United Motors' several lines of accessories.

In carrying out the program of expansion during the summer and fall of 1916, Durant continued to ignore his board of directors. Pierre was disturbed, but he was too involved with the Du Pont Company's war activities and postwar planning and with the suit of *du Pont vs. du Pont* to force any changes. He decided instead that Raskob should be his deputy and spokesman at General Motors. He knew that John would not take any action without consulting him. Raskob had always had a stronger interest in General Motors than Pierre and was even more optimistic about the automobile's future. Raskob, too, admired Durant's financial skills and expansive ambitions. The two had much in common. Moreover, the Du Pont Company's treasurer was less involved than Pierre and other executives in the wartime expansion that called for administrative and technical rather than financial skills.

Pierre and Raskob agreed that they would increase their influence at General Motors by strengthening the Finance Committee which, besides the two, included only Durant, Kaufman, and McClement. The two further agreed that their first objective must be the legal and financial amalgamation of Chevrolet and United Motors into General Motors. Only after such a merger of Durant's major properties was completed could an over-all rational administrative structure for this industrial empire be instituted.

On December 1, 1916, Raskob wrote Kaufman, chairman of the Finance Committee, stressing that the committee must have essential information such as monthly balance sheets and comparative earning statements if it was to act responsibly.[36] The same day he asked for clarification on the existing relationships between Chevrolet and General Motors.[37] Kaufman and Durant gave this information reluctantly. When Raskob finally received it, he urged that Chevrolet be combined with General Motors "in order to receive a better and more concentrated organization, and incidentally avoid excessive costs in the way of duplicate income taxes which are now becoming quite heavy, and to clarify the atmosphere generally."[38] Such a plan would also add, Raskob pointed out, "a perfectly splendid low price car" which would "round out" the General Motors line.

Durant and Kaufman held back, for it was by maintaining the separate legal identities of the three companies that they controlled their automobile empire. Chevrolet held 450,000 of the 825,000 shares of General Motors common stock outstanding. In 1916 Durant and his immediate family held by far the largest block of stock in Chevrolet—at least 30%, and probably 40%, of the stock issued. He and his close financial associates, Kaufman and McClement, could unquestionably vote over 50% of the shares. They also appear to have held over half of the 5,000 voting shares of stock in United Motors.

After much discussion Raskob and Pierre persuaded Durant to place Hamilton Barksdale on the Chevrolet board as the representative of the du Pont interests. Then Durant reviewed an arrangement proposed by Raskob to merge the two companies by having General Motors purchase Chevrolet's assets and so transform Chevrolet into a holding company whose only function was to hold General Motors stock. General Motors would pay for the Chevrolet assets by a further stock issue. The amount issued would be such that the ratio of assets to capital outstanding at General Motors would be the same after the purchase as it was before the purchase.[39] Durant accepted this first step, for, by increasing the General Motors stock held by Chevrolet, his control over General Motors was strengthened. He was for the same reasons less enthusiastic about the second step of Raskob's plan, which was to eliminate Chevrolet as a separate corporation by exchanging its stock for that of General Motors at a rate of 1¼ shares of General Motors and $5.90 in cash for each share of Chevrolet.

These proposals were discussed in detail at a meeting of the Finance Committee late in March 1917.[40] Not only did Pierre join Raskob at the meeting, but Pierre also made certain that Barksdale was there. Raskob opened the discussion by stressing the conservative nature of his proposal. He pointed out that General Motors could issue the stock needed to purchase Chevrolet and a 12% stock dividend still be paid. The debate over the value of Chevrolet's assets was settled when Durant agreed to let the leading New York accounting firm of Haskins & Sells appraise the assets of both General Motors and Chevrolet in order to have the basis for the amount of stock to be issued. The decision on the final exchange and the elimination of Chevrolet was postponed. At the same meeting the committee considered, but took no action on, the Du Pont men's suggestion of purchasing United Motors in a similar manner.

The Chevrolet merger moved slowly. During May and June the auditors from Haskins & Sells conferred with the comptrollers of the two companies, checked the books, and viewed the plants and offices in New York, Detroit, Flint, and elsewhere.[41] They found their task more complicated than they had anticipated because of Durant's haphazard methods of accounting; particularly difficult was "the treatment of several hundreds of thousands of dollars in Intra-Company accounts."[42] Legal technicalities over the dissolution of the old General Motors Company also caused delays. As Smith explained, the dissolution had to be complete before the stock issue of the new General Motors Corporation could be increased.[43]

The entrance of the United States into the war with Germany raised new difficulties. The possibility of a critical reduction in automobile production because of the rationing of steel and other materials, and the introduction of large excess profits taxes, all affected the assumptions about sales and earnings on which Pierre, Raskob, and Durant had based their plans for merger.[44] In addition, Pierre urged (somewhat to Durant's distress) that General Motors follow the example of the Du Pont Company and contribute to the current Red Cross drive to raise $100.0 million for war victims.[45] He was anxious to back the plan proposed by Judge Elbert Gary of the United States Steel Corporation and Theodore Vail of the American Telephone and Telegraph Company to have the major American corporations declare a special dividend of 1% or 2% as their contribution to the Red Cross.

The most serious problem of all was that uncertainty created by war caused the price of automobile stocks to drop precipitously—and General Motors more than most. Stock buyers, like the automobile company's executives, were worried that war would curtail the automobile company's sales and profits. Raskob's proposed financing of the Chevrolet merger and further expansion assumed that earnings would increase but that the price of General Motors stock would remain at about $200 a share. By the end of June the price had dropped to $115 and it continued to fall throughout July.[46] Durant and Raskob now apparently agreed to put off the merger and the issuing of the new common stock until the market for that stock had revived.

Anxious to keep the price from dropping further, Durant formed in July 1917 a syndicate to buy General Motors stock.[47] He found a ready partner in John Raskob. Possibly—although the evidence is not clear—Raskob, like Durant, was using General Motors stock as collateral for speculative and other loans. While Pierre did not participate in the syndicate, he was fully informed of its activities by its major managers, Durant and Raskob. In mid-August, just as the syndicate was getting under way, General Motors' prices again broke. Durant blamed "viciously untrue and scurrilous" articles which, among other things, claimed that the company had failed to negotiate a $12.0 million loan at a 12% interest rate.[48] He first urged Pierre and Raskob to join him in purchasing stock independently of the syndicate. Raskob resisted the suggestion and may not have even told Pierre about it.[49] Instead he told Durant that it was as important to maintain a 12% dividend on the stock as to try to support its price by purchasing in the open market. The syndicate, however, continued to buy through Nathan Hofheimer of the brokerage house of C. I. Hudson and Company. Despite this buying, the value of General Motors stock continued to drop. By mid-September it had reached 86. Both the coming of steel-rationing and the imposition of large excess profits taxes were influencing the market, and Durant again pressed Raskob to purchase stock "for individual accounts."[50]

When Raskob reviewed the situation with Durant at the end of October, he realized that the buying syndicate had expended its resources without achieving its ends. He also saw that the corporation's president, whose purchases on his own account had been with funds loaned on the basis of General Motors stock as collateral, had reached the limit of his funds. Yet when the syndicate stopped buying, the price of General Motors common quickly fell to 75. A further drop would force Durant, and possibly the syndicate, to provide more funds or more collateral. Durant's position had become critical.

He and Raskob then began a desperate search for money. Their first thought was to have Durant ask General Motors for a loan. At a Finance Committee meeting of November 8, attended by all the members except Durant, Raskob proposed that the corporation make a loan "to Mr. Durant for the benefit of himself and certain associates in the company." The collateral for the loan was to be General Motors common stock valued at $50 a share.[51] Raskob argued that Durant had been heavily involved in the market because he considered it "his duty to protect the market of General Motors and its availability as collateral for the benefit of stockholders." As a result the "financing of such operations was absorbing his time and atten- tion to the detriment of the company's interests."

In the discussion that followed, McClement, who knew the least about Durant and his syndicate, agreed with the rest of the committee's members (including Pierre) to recommend such a loan. He tied three conditions to the agreement: the holders of 700,000 shares must assent to the loan (the total outstanding was still only 825,590); the holders of these shares must agree not to sell or loan any during the duration of Durant's loan; finally, the 450,000 shares of General Motors which gave Chevrolet control of the corporation "should not be marketed or loaned during the continuation of the loan."

The next day, however, McClement changed his mind and decided to oppose the proposed loan in the committee and on the board. The arrange- ment, he had come to feel, could lead to "severe future criticism and perhaps individual liability of assenting Directors." This opposition con- vinced Pierre to vote against the loan and, as a result, Raskob and Kaufman decided not to pursue the proposal further. Instead they suggested that Durant be helped by authorizing him a salary of $500,000 a year with immediate payment for two years. Apparently Durant's need was so great that McClement and Pierre decided to risk criticism of paying what was for that time a huge salary. On November 15 Pierre, acting for the Finance Committee, approved the payment of $1.0 million in salary to the corpora- tion's president.[52]

While this amount helped Durant meet immediate calls for funds, it was not a long-range solution. The bearish market continued to drive prices down. Durant and Raskob then turned to another obvious source, Pierre du Pont himself. Sometime between November 15 and 20 the two, working with Pierre, drew up a tentative proposal. It was written in the form of an agreement between Durant and associates and P. S. du Pont and associates. As might be expected, the arrangement was an extremely complex one. Essentially there would be a holding company, the Motors Security Com- pany, to hold 212,000 shares of Chevrolet and 120,000 shares of General Motors. Pierre would put $12.5 million into it in such a way that he and Durant would have equal holdings and so have equal control of Chevrolet and the General Motors Corporation.[53]

In return for Pierre's $12.5 million investment, the proposed agreement read, "Du Pont will assume responsibility for financial management of Chevrolet-General Motors affairs thus making it possible for Durant to give his entire time and attention to the operating end." And, as Pierre had always wanted, the procedures of appropriating funds for plants and facili- ties and the organization of the Finance and Executive committees (upon which both Du Pont and Durant would be represented) would be patterned explicitly on those of the Du Pont Company.

The proposal was not accepted. Who rejected it, the existing evidence fails to indicate. It would have been somewhat difficult for Pierre, even with his wartime dividends, to raise $12.5 million in a relatively short time. For Durant the arrangement had a greater disadvantage, for it eliminated his control over General Motors through Chevrolet and explicitly divided his control with Pierre du Pont. In any case, Durant and Raskob had to begin once more their search for funds.

### The Du Pont Company's Investment in General Motors

One reason that Pierre may have been unsympathetic to the proposal to become Durant's partner at General Motors was that he was so completely engrossed in the affairs of the Du Pont Company. During the fall of 1917 the War Department, it will be recalled, had decided, after months of little action, to increase vastly the nation's powder-making facilities.[54] In September and October Pierre and his associates had worked out the contract with the War Department for building one of the largest smokeless powder plants in the world—a contract that General Crozier signed on October 25. Then came Newton D. Baker's refusal to accept it. On December 14 the Du Pont Executive Committee accepted Baker's rejection of the October 25 contract. During these weeks Pierre had little time to keep an eye on Durant's activities or to work out clearly in his own mind what should be done about Durant's difficulties. In the circumstances, he could hardly have thought much about his long-range relationship to the automobile company.

Having been unsuccessful with Pierre, Durant and Raskob decided to approach the Du Pont Company itself. No one knew better than John Raskob of the vast wartime surpluses, $50.0 million of which were still not allocated to the postwar diversification program. Moreover, if the Du Pont Company could be persuaded to use a portion of this sum to purchase General Motors stock in the open market instead of buying it directly from Durant as the earlier proposal had called for, Durant would retain his large block of Chevrolet stock and therefore control of General Motors. At the same time such large purchases on the open market by the Du Pont Company would do what Durant and the syndicate could not do and maintain the price of General Motors stock. Pressure on Durant to find more money or collateral would be ended.

After considering this new approach, Durant and Raskob checked with Hofheimer, the broker who did the buying for Durant and the syndicate.[55] Then during late November and early December they worked out an arrangement that they presented first to Pierre and then to the Du Pont

Company itself. By this plan the Du Pont Company and its stockholders were to invest in $25.0 million worth of General Motors common stock. Of this amount, $3.0 million was to be taken from Durant and Hofheimer and the rest was to be purchased on the open market. To carry out this scheme Raskob proposed the formation of a holding company, this time to be called the Du Pont Motor Company. It would issue two types of stock, Class "A" 12% cumulative nonvoting common stock, and Class "B", which would have the sole voting power. Raskob suggested that the Du Pont Company immediately buy through an exchange of stock $7.0 million of the Class "B" stock and so insure its control of the holding company. He then proposed that the holders of Du Pont common be allowed to buy up to the value of 30% of their holdings, for a total purchase of $18.0 million worth of Class "A." These purchases would be made easier if the Du Pont Company would agree to pay an extra dividend of 32% which should be paid quarterly during 1918. With the $25.0 million received from the sale of its stock, the new holding company would purchase Chevrolet at not over $115 per share and General Motors at a price of not over $95 per share. This was well above the price at which General Motors was selling at the end of November.[56]

Raskob showed this plan to Pierre just at the moment that the Du Pont Company's directors voted to acknowledge the War Department's rejection of the contract for the new powder works. Pierre now saw the General Motors proposal in a different light. It provided a specific alternative to the great smokeless powder plant as a means of using funds and managerial and technical talents. Some of the $1.0 million already put into the government project might be used for the construction of facilities for General Motors. Once the war was over, Pierre fully agreed with Durant and Raskob, there would be a great opportunity for the Du Pont engineering staff in the construction and operation of factories at General Motors, for the rapid growth of the automobile industry seemed as certain as anything could be in business.

The arrangement proposed was much more advantageous to Durant than the earlier one. Since he did not have to share explicitly his control with the Du Pont Company, and since the very large purchases of General Motors common in the open market would certainly maintain General Motors stock at the price desired, Pierre insisted on two points. First, he wanted the same type of administrative control he had asked Raskob to spell out in the earlier proposal. The Finance and Executive committees at General Motors and the appropriations procedures must be patterned after those at Du Pont. Durant would be represented on both committees. Even more specifically than before, Durant would have to agree to let the Du Pont Company run the finances of General Motors through the Finance Committee, while he, working through the Executive Committee, would have full authority and responsibility for its operations. The second point Pierre required was that Durant must complete the merger of Chevrolet and United Motors into General Motors and the elimination of both subsidiary companies. Durant quite willingly accepted these terms.

By the week ending December 16, Raskob and Durant had worked out, and Pierre had approved, the plan for the $25.0 million purchase of General Motors stock. Raskob then immediately moved to present it to the Du Pont Company.[57] He knew perfectly well that the proposal would come, in his words, "as quite a shock" to most of the Du Pont executives.[58] Up to this time neither he nor Pierre had discussed it with anyone except possibly Irénée and Donaldson Brown. The latter was Raskob's senior assistant in the Treasurer's Office. Raskob may have hoped by surprise to forestall the development of arguments against it. On Monday the sixteenth, he tried to set up a meeting of the Du Pont Finance Committee for the following day and a joint meeting with the Executive Committee on Wednesday.[59] As too many members were out of town, the meetings were set for the end of the week. On Thursday, December 19, Raskob completed a report that outlined his proposal and presented the reasons that the investment would benefit the Du Pont Company.

On Friday, December 20, the Du Pont Finance Committee (Pierre, Irénée, Raskob, and Henry F. du Pont) would meet and then confer with the Executive Committee. On Saturday the full board would convene. Only three weeks before, the board had made a decision on the largest contract ever negotiated by a private firm with the United States government. Now it had to approve of one of the largest investments ever made by one industrial company in another operating in a very different field. The Finance Committee quickly informed Henry F. du Pont of the details of the plans. He was the only member not yet fully acquainted with them. The committee then promptly approved the proposal.[60] After the members of the Executive Committee joined the discussion at 10:30, the argument became more serious, the questions more searching, and the opposition more obvious. Ruly Carpenter, as head of the Development, was particularly skeptical. Surely there were still many excellent opportunities for investment in the chemical industry, where the Du Pont men had the technical knowledge and experience in production, marketing, and research. A. Felix du Pont, senior executive in the Smokeless Powder Department, and possibly Lammot du Pont, expressed doubts. At one o'clock the meeting adjourned, with no vote taken.

The next morning the debate began again.[61] When the remaining directors were called in at 11:30 in order to have a full meeting of the board, Pierre was forced to announce that no agreement had yet been reached on the proposal to invest in General Motors. Again Raskob repeated his arguments. Again the others asked if there were not better uses for the money. This time Colonel Buckner expressed his opposition. He undoubtedly argued, as Felix could have the previous day, that the government contract was still a very real possibility. The secretary of war would have to come back to Du Pont as the only company with the necessary technological and managerial skills to carry out the government's work. Buckner was disturbed at the thought of investing in a totally new business until the company was absolutely certain that the money and men might still not have to be used on the vast smokeless powder project. Raskob probably replied that even the signing of the contract with the government would not affect this transaction, as any such contract would provide for cash advances before major construction. In fact, Raskob used as a basis for his report a cash forecast made before the cancellation of the contract. In any case, after a break for a late lunch, the Finance and Executive committees met as a single unit and unanimously accepted Raskob's recommendation to invest $25.0 million in General Motors and Chevrolet. At three o'clock the board met again and, after some further discussion, approved the recommended purchases of stock—with only Colonel Buckner, Felix, and Eugene E. du Pont voting in the negative.[62]

Throughout the two days Raskob carried the brunt of the argument for the investment, and he appears to have stuck pretty closely to the points made in his report of December 19 to the Finance Committee.[63] The main thread of his argument was that General Motors provided an unexcelled opportunity for the investment of surplus funds. The treasurer estimated that the company had $90.0 million available for investment. So far only $40.0 million had been put into new chemical industries under the program agreed to in the previous February. Of the $50.0 million "still seeking employment" certainly one-half could be placed as ' an attractive investment in one of the most promising businesses in the United States." For the past year or two the automobile industry had been enjoying "phenomenal" profits which—at the price proposed for the stock—would yield 40% on the investment. Since Durant had returned to the control of General Motors, earnings had jumped from $13,409,000 in 1915 to $27,740,000 in 1916 and, even with war taxes, would again be over $27.0 million in 1917. The profits promised to be still higher in 1918. Chevrolet had enjoyed a similar profit record.

In addition to the profitability of the investment, Raskob drummed on two points. First, he pointed out that the purchase gave the Du Pont Company, with Durant and a few individual du Ponts and close associates, full control of General Motors and Chevrolet. Pierre would remain chairman of the board and Durant president and "the directorates of the motor companies will be chosen by du Pont and Durant." Moreover, the Du Pont interests were "immediately to assume charge and be responsible for the financial operation of the Company," and "the Finance Committee will be ours." On these points, Raskob was, in his report at least, less than candid

454 ]   THE GENERAL MOTORS STORY

with the Du Pont executives. He did not mention the events leading up to the proposal. While he did point out that Chevrolet had a controlling interest in General Motors, he did not indicate that Durant came close to, if not actually, controlling Chevrolet. Clearly, however, Raskob and Pierre counted on Durant's promise to complete the Chevrolet merger, including the final exchange of stock, and to give the du Ponts full control of General Motors' finances. After all, Durant could hardly renege on promises made to these powerful and much needed allies.

Raskob aimed his second theme at the Carpenters, Lammot du Pont, and others working on the diversification program. He stressed that "our interest in General Motors will undoubtedly secure for us the entire Fabrikoid, Pyralin, paint and varnish business of these companies, which is a substantial factor." Finally, he emphasized that some of the Du Pont executives might well find more use for their talents in the motor than in the chemical industry in postwar years. The purchase, he was certain, would "afford many opportunities to keep our important men occupied with big things after the war."

In supporting Raskob's arguments, Pierre appears to have used a somewhat different emphasis.[64] He suggested, as he had done so often to Kaufman and Durant, how General Motors might benefit from Du Pont experience in management and, for the moment, particularly financial management. Equally important, the automobile company could use the services of the Du Pont Engineering Department and other staff units. The Engineering Department had been greatly expanded to build the plants that produced the powder for the Allies. These plants were now completed, and Pierre was at that moment much less sanguine than was Buckner about the possibility that the Engineering Department would soon build a plant for the War Department. In fact, Pierre, burned by the experiences of the fall, was not sure that the company should ever take on a sizable amount of government business. In any case, he was certain that in the postwar period the construction of automobile plants would be a profitable way to make use of the Engineering Department's talents and experience.

Pierre further emphasized, though in a different way from Raskob, the value of the investment to the diversification program. Large dividends from General Motors would be of special value during the period when new ventures such as paints, dyes, and artificial silk were still in their development stage and so not yet returning a profit. This argument, Pierre later remembered, was "the most attractive feature of all." It may have done more than the others to convince those executives who were most involved in the Du Pont Company's diversification program.

Pierre's strong support was convincing enough for most of the Du Pont directors. The high respect they held for him unquestionably affected their vote as much as did his arguments and those of Raskob. If he had opposed the proposal, the Du Pont Company would never have made its long and profitable alliance with General Motors. On the other hand, it is just as certain that the Du Pont Company would not have made this initial investment in automobiles if Durant, assisted by Raskob, had not tried unsuccessfully to hold up the price of General Motors stock in the fall of 1917. It seems likely, too, that if the War Department had not questioned the contract of October 25, and if the Du Pont Company by December had been devoting its full energies to building the new explosives work, the investment in General Motors would have been much less attractive.

Once the Du Pont board had approved, Raskob's plans were carried out without a hitch. The holding company, initially called General Industries, Inc. (it soon became Du Pont American Industries), was approved by the Finance and Executive committees on January 21 and by the board on January 30, 1918.[65] Moreover, by the end of January the War Department had signed the Jackling contract for constructing the plant at Old Hickory.[66] Under that contract the War and Navy departments agreed to make a 25% down payment, and so its signing made it possible to use the company's surplus to take up the $18.0 million worth of Class "A" stock that Raskob was planning to offer the Du Pont stockholders, as well as the $7.0 million Class "B" stock. The Finance Committee had, however, already approved Raskob's proposal to declare a 32% year-end dividend in order to encourage the purchase of the Class "A" stock by the Du Pont Company stockholders. With funds paid in by the Du Pont Company, the new holding company purchased 97,875 shares of General Motors and 133,690 shares of Chevrolet for a total of $25,183,758.84. This gave it a total of 23.83% of the combined General Motors-Chevrolet stock outstanding.[67] Of these shares it bought $1.2 million directly from Durant, $1.8 million from Hofheimer, his broker, and the remainder on the open market. For this the company used $7.2 million from the 32% year-end dividend; the rest of the $18.0 million came from Du Pont Company surplus funds. Of the $7.2 million, $1.3 million came from dividends on Du Pont stock that the new holding company had in its treasury from sale of Class "B" stock to the Du Pont Company. The other $5.9 million came from a temporary arrangement with the Du Pont Securities Company. These very large purchases on the open market, of course, effectively maintained the price of General Motors in the 90s. Through the Du Pont Company, Durant and Raskob were able to do what they never could have done by themselves, individually. As Raskob later reported, the first $20.0 million worth of shares were bought at an average of $93.75. Because of the boost this gave to the market, the remainder came somewhat higher.

Next came the required changes in the Finance Committee and the board. Kaufman agreed to resign from both whenever Pierre thought it advisable.[68] Pierre asked him to leave the Finance Committee but to stay on the board. In March McClement resigned from the board and, therefore, from the Finance Committee. Irénée and Henry F. du Pont then came on the board and the committee. As a result, the new Finance Committee included Raskob as chairman, Pierre, Irénée, Henry F. du Pont, Haskell, and Durant.[69] Only Haskell was added to the revived Executive Committee, which was made up of the heads of the leading operating divisions—with Durant as chairman.

At Raskob's suggestion Pierre du Pont announced publicly his company's investment in General Motors and the resulting changes in top management. Pierre made the announcement on February 21 at an elaborate dinner at the Metropolitan Club in New York attended by fifteen leading bankers from New York and Philadelphia.[70] After Pierre described the Du Pont Company's move into automobiles, Durant gave a glowingly optimistic account of the present situation and future growth of the industry. The newspapers and financial reporters enthusiastically described the affair. "There's not a doubt," Raskob reported, "that the dinner resulted in the General Motors Corporation becoming definitely established in the minds of the important bankers of the country."[71]

Shortly after the dinner, the final provisions of the purchase were completed. The board approved the carefully defined duties of the Finance Committee as written by Pierre and Raskob. The committee would meet monthly. As at Du Pont it would approve twice a year the estimate for capital expenditures and "a general financial plan" necessary to finance these appropriations.[72] No further approval would be necessary on expenditures unless an item ran over $300,000 or for a new appropriation not in the general budget costing more than $150,000 or for the sale of any real estate property valued at over $100,000. Plans to finance these capital costs were to be based on adjusted monthly financial forecasts.

The board did less to define the role of the Executive Committee.[73] This may have been because of Pierre's agreement to let Durant run the operations if Du Pont handled the finances. As its chairman, Durant continued to operate the company in the same fast-moving, free-wheeling manner as he had done in the past. Pierre, Raskob, and the others assumed that financial control, carefully and rationally defined, would assure a systematic businesslike development of the lucrative automobile trade. In less than three years they learned they were wrong. Financial control did not bring effective administrative control.

# Du Pont "Control"
# at General Motors 1918–1920

AFTER MARCH 1918 the du Ponts dominated the General Motors Finance Committee. Through the committee, they and others believed they "controlled" the corporation. Their influence was as strong in General Motors as that of J. P. Morgan; Lee, Higginson; Kuhn, Loeb and Co.; and other investment bankers in the large railroad or industrial corporations they had helped to finance. Like the bankers the du Ponts did affect the corporation's policies; but their control over General Motors operations and the men who managed them was all too limited.

The members of the Finance Committee, and particularly its chairman, John J. Raskob, were influential in determining important financial policy. The committee pushed through the administrative and legal mergers with Chevrolet (but not the final exchange of stock) and with United Motors. The committee, always working closely with Durant, determined how to provide capital essential for the rapidly growing business. The committee and Durant agreed fully that they should avoid obtaining funds from investment bankers and should instead finance the massive expansion by plowing back profits made at General Motors and Du Pont.

In the end, however, the Finance Committee failed to finance growth from within, and indeed brought the corporation to the edge of financial disaster. It failed because it was unable to keep an effective oversight and control over either the short-term operating or the long-term capital expenditures of the company. The ineffectiveness of the Finance Committee illustrates limits of outside financial control in a large, modern corporation. Moreover, an understanding of how and why this control was insufficient to prevent a crisis is essential to understanding the basic challenges facing Pierre when he became president of General Motors in December 1920.

The fundamental reason the Finance Committee was unable to carry out its function was that control remained personal rather than institutional. Pierre and Raskob did not develop the type of statistics and reports they had created in the Du Pont Company. Pierre failed to do so simply because he did not have the same commitment to General Motors that he had to Du Pont. Until the end of 1920 he continued to let Raskob take the initiative in the affairs of the motor company. Raskob's genius, however, had always been for financial manipulation rather than management. He had devised brilliant schemes for raising capital at very little cost and for thus making the most effective use possible of existing credit—credit based on the output and the profit record of General Motors and Du Pont. Raskob was far less interested in the mundane task of building and running the apparatus needed to secure control of operating activities.

The difficulty with the personal control of the du Ponts and General Motors was that the persons involved had so many other concerns and interests. Irénée, as general manager, and then, after Pierre's retirement in April 1919, as president of the Du Pont Company, was completely immersed in Du Pont business in Wilmington. Harry F. du Pont, the senator's oldest son, had more time but had neither the inclination nor the training to understand fully the financial needs, problems, and issues of the giant automobile corporation. Pierre and Raskob had counted on the superb training and experience of two retired Du Pont executives, J. Amory Haskell and Hamilton M. Barksdale. But both were old and had lost their earlier energy. Barksdale, already a sick man, died in October 1918. Haskell, now well in his sixties, remained active at General Motors, but, like the rest of the committee, had little experience in or understanding of the details of making and selling automobiles.

After his retirement from the Du Pont Company's presidency, Pierre too turned with eagerness to the more leisurely country life at Longwood. He at last could spend his time developing his extensive horticultural plans. In 1919 he began the construction of the great greenhouses.[1] Completed in 1921 they soon housed one of the most famous botanical collections in the world.

Pierre, too, began to meet his broader obligations to the community. Shortly before the end of the war he had formed, endowed with $90,000, and become president of the Service Citizens of Delaware. Its purpose was "to work for the improvement of social conditions in the State."[2] Its methods were characteristic of Pierre and of many business and political leaders of the prewar progressive period. Through the use of experts and careful studies whose findings were to be widely published, the Service Citizens expected the voters and state legislature to reform existing institutions and conditions. Pierre's organization began by having the New York Bureau of Municipal Research survey Delaware's state and local governments. On the basis of the bureau's report, the Service Citizens prepared a plan for a thoroughgoing reorganization and centralization of the state's 117 administrative offices. A similar survey was made on public health programs and another on the Americanization of recent immigrants.

After Pierre's retirement from the Du Pont Company, he and the Service Citizens concentrated on the state's educational system. Even before the war Pierre had given large sums to the Massachusetts Institute of Technology and Delaware College. His gifts of over $1.5 million to the latter marked the beginning of its transformation into the modern University of Delaware. Then after the war Pierre's attention turned to the state's schools. The reports made by the Service Citizens and by the federal government and the General Education Board of the Rockefeller Foundation defined and deplored the "utter inadequacy" of the Delaware school system. As a result the legislature formed a Delaware State Board of Education, and the governor immediately appointed Pierre a member. As the most active member of the commission, Pierre first arranged for a survey of all school buildings in the state. He then engaged three Columbia University professors to set standards and to plan model schoolhouses. He visited schools regularly throughout the state. By setting up five separate trust funds managed through the Delaware School Auxiliary, a subsidiary of the Service Citizens, he gave $3.8 million of his own funds to be used largely for new school buildings. As a result of these new activities, he had relatively little time to do more than attend meetings of both the Du Pont and General Motors Finance committees. He did not give close attention to the affairs of General Motors.

For Raskob, on the other hand, retirement from day-to-day activities at Du Pont meant more time for General Motors. The last thing he wanted to do was to settle down to a quiet country life and to take over local responsibilities. Even before April 1919, he came to spend more and more of his time in New York. He relished trips to Detroit, Flint, and other auto-making towns. So he soon came to know Durant, Chrysler, Sloan, Mott, and John T. Smith far better than Pierre did. He enlarged his acquaintances in the New York banking community. He became involved with broader business issues and problems, reading widely on taxes, on labor organizations, and on the new field of public relations. He delighted in arranging dinners for eminent men at the Metropolitan Club to discuss these issues and to develop the business community's proposals or positions on these matters.

Nevertheless, Raskob rarely, if ever, made an important move or decision at General Motors without consulting Pierre and being certain of his support. Despite his dislike of going to New York, Pierre missed very few meetings of the General Motors Finance Committee. He played a personal role in important financial negotiations of the corporation. Moreover, he found the time to encourage significant administrative reforms, an area in which Raskob had little interest. Although Pierre played a relatively passive role in General Motors before 1920, he remained, next to Raskob and Durant, the most influential man in the corporation.

## The Merging of Chevrolet and United Motors

When Pierre, Raskob, and their associates took over the General Motors Finance Committee early in 1918, the corporation's greatest challenge was still the adjustment to the uncertainties of wartime conditions.[3] By summer, 18 of the 23 operating units were working on government contracts turning out automobiles, ambulances, and officers' cars. Buick and Cadillac were starting on an order for 10,000 Liberty airplane engines, and Cadillac was producing the power plant for a 2½ ton "artillery tractor," while another division was concentrating on the production of trench mortar shells.

Pierre and the others on the Finance Committee were always aware of the temporary nature of this new business.[4] Yet war production was essential to the corporation, for early that summer the expected restrictions on the use of steel and other materials in nonessential products, including pleasure cars, had been imposed. To meet this cut in car production Durant proposed taking the corporation into the tractor business. To develop a large-scale production of tractors, he first asked the Finance Committee to approve the purchase of a major interest in the Sampson Sieve-Grip Tractor Company, and then in July 1918 to buy the Janesville Machine Company in Wisconsin to provide the necessary plant and equipment.[5] At the same time Durant began to search for a product his dealers might sell during the temporary famine in cars. This investigation brought General Motors in the marketing and then production of refrigerators, still a new and little-tried household appliance.

The new Finance Committee supported Durant's plans to meet the changing wartime markets. It approved the expensive Janesville purchase without question. When the government curtailment of steel seemed certain, and with it a reduction of the output of steel users, Pierre and Raskob agreed, as Pierre wrote Barksdale, "that the opportunity of acquisition of shops manufacturing parts and accessories will be made broader through the slackening off of business."[6] So the Finance Committee fully backed the proposal of Durant and Sloan to purchase the Lancaster Steel Company, makers of cold drawn steel, to buy the remaining stock in Harrison Radiator Company, and to take over the Scripps-Booth Company for its plant and equipment.

The primary concern of both Pierre and Raskob at General Motors was not, however, financing of expansion but simplification of General Motors' financial and corporate structure. The first order of business was to complete plans for the amalgamation of Chevrolet and United Motors into General Motors. This had been part of the December deal with Durant. When Pierre announced publicly the Du Pont entry into General Motors, he made the point clear. There he stressed both the intention to merge Chevrolet with General Motors and also to increase the capitalization of the corporation by expanding the par value of the common stock from $82.6 million to $150.0 million, and 6% preferred from $20.0 million to $50.0 million.

The sale of Chevrolet assets to General Motors went off without a hitch even though the price paid of 282,684 shares was lower than Raskob had earlier estimated.[7] The price probably reflected both the Haskins & Sells audit and the improved bargaining position of the Du Pont group. By May 1918 Chevrolet had become an operating division of General Motors and that company's remaining function was to hold the controlling block of General Motors stock. At this time the Du Pont Company increased its holdings in Chevrolet by purchasing 25,425 shares.

In October the Chevrolet board agreed to the last step of the merger, the final exchange of stock, and the elimination of the company. No deadlines were set on the exchange. Hofheimer, Kaufman, and some others did begin to trade Chevrolet stock for General Motors, but Durant did not. The du Ponts did not either, for their total of 159,115 shares was still much smaller than Durant's block of at least 250,000. As late as November 1920, after a sizable amount of the stock had been exchanged, Durant and his immediate family were still holding 30% of the Chevrolet stock outstanding.[8] Durant was reluctant to let go of this leverage on the du Ponts, for Chevrolet still had the majority of General Motors stock. The evidence is not clear why Pierre and Raskob did not insist on the culmination of the merger. Probably they assumed that the increase in share capital of General Motors stock from 826,000 to 1,500,000 authorized for the purchase of Chevrolet stock would make that company's block of 450,000 shares less vital for control.

Kaufman and Durant also initially resisted the merger of United Motors into General Motors.[9] But at a meeting of the General Motors Finance Committee in the spring of 1918 they agreed to sell to General Motors by a stock exchange whereby $30 worth of General Motors preferred and $10 worth of common would be traded for each share of United Motors, for a total of just over $33.0 million worth of preferred and $11.0 million of common.

To provide the securities needed for the purchase of United Motors, and capital for other projects, the Finance Committee decided to expand still further the corporation's capitalization. It proposed, and the board and stockholders approved, having a total capitalization of $100.0 million worth of preferred and $200.0 million of common.[10] Because the New York Stock Exchange's listing committee thought the new preferred might adversely affect the old, Pierre and Raskob decided to issue, instead of the new preferred, $150.0 million worth of 6% cumulative debentures (no par value but redeemable at $115), with voting rights and other privileges similar to the Du Pont debenture issue of 1915.[11] After this change was approved by the General Motors stockholders in December 1918, those of United Motors agreed to take their payment in $30.0 million in debentures and $16.0 million in common.

With this last exchange, the first major part of the program Pierre and Raskob had outlined for General Motors was completed. All parts of Durant's empire were now under a single corporate roof and within one operating company. The only unfinished business was completing the final exchange with Chevrolet and dissolving that company. But if legal centralization had been achieved, central administrative control had hardly begun.

### The Postwar Expansion Program

The mergers with Chevrolet and United Motors and the increase in capitalization were completed just in time. The sudden end of war in November 1918 permitted Durant, with the enthusiastic backing of Raskob, to turn at once to plan for massive peacetime production to meet what both men considered to be a huge and ever-increasing demand for automobiles, trucks and other commercial vehicles.

For Raskob and even Pierre expansion would have priority over administrative changes. Less than three weeks after the Armistice, Durant and Raskob, after a brief consultation with Haskell, drew up a prospectus of the initial financial needs required to begin a program of postwar growth. The plan they presented to the Finance Committee on December 12, 1918, called for raising $52.8 million, of which $36.15 million "should be arranged for immediately."[12] Raskob admitted that these estimates were only very rough guesses. Certainly he prepared no careful analysis such as the Du Pont Company had long used in planning its capital appropriations. But the market was there, the potential profits high. So the enthusiasm of Raskob and Durant was hard to resist.

Part of the funds the two men requested was needed to complete the arrangements resulting from the merger of Chevrolet and United Motors and the purchase of Scripps-Booth and of the Canadian properties. The Finance Committee had approved this last purchase as part of its program to obtain full control of its subsidiaries. By far the greatest amount, however, was for machinery and equipment to increase the output of the old and the building of new automobile, truck, and tractor factories, branch assembly plants, foundries and forges, and works making axles and frames. Raskob, more than Durant, saw the need for enlarging marketing facilities as well as production units. He wanted $4.0 million to form credit and insurance companies to help dealers finance their customers' purchases. He asked for another $4.0 million to build a great new central office building to house the staff and administrative offices of the new company—a project that Durant, significantly, never favored.

Of the $52.8 million asked for, Raskob recommended that $24.7 million be provided out of earnings and $21.6 million be raised through the sale of $18.0 million with a par value of $100 of common (not debenture) stock at 120. He proposed that the stock be "offered to a Syndicate at $120.00 per share in which Syndicate all the common stockholders of the Company shall have the opportunity of participating pro rata." The remaining $6.5 million he wanted to issue separately to complete payment for the Canadian properties. To all this, Pierre and the Finance Committee agreed.

Raskob expected the Du Pont Company to provide much of the capital for the initial postwar expansion at General Motors which could not come from retained earnings. On returning to Wilmington and talking again with Pierre and Irénée, Raskob drew up a proposal for the approval of the Du Pont Finance Committee.[13] It had two parts. The less important section referred to the purchase of the Canadian companies. Since Samuel McLaughlin, their president, wanted cash rather than stock, Raskob suggested that the Du Pont Company take the General Motors common stock at $130 per share and pay McLaughlin in cash. He further urged the Du Pont Company to act as the syndicate to underwrite the entire offering of 180,000 shares at 120. Raskob pointed out that the company then had in its treasury enough money to take the whole issue at that price, to continue as planned on its diversification program, and still to pay 18% annual dividend on its common stock.

Pierre asked the Du Pont Finance Committee to meet with him at Longwood on the evening of December 17.[14] All members attended, as did Donaldson Brown, who had taken Raskob's place as the Du Pont Company's treasurer only a few weeks before. Raskob and Pierre undoubtedly argued that the automobile industry promised a larger and quicker return on investment than further ventures in the chemical industry. They may also have pointed out that such purchases would strengthen the Du Pont control at General Motors by balancing the block of Chevrolet that Durant might still be able to control if he refused to make the exchange for General Motors stock. The rest of the committee appeared quite amicable, noting that the Du Pont Company had a large amount of "liquid capital" available for investment.[15] Further, it agreed to have the company act as a syndicate to sell all the stock, first to General Motors stockholders and then to take up what they did not buy. By early 1919 the Du Pont Company had acquired from the McLaughlin interests and from the underwriting of the new issue 108,597 shares of General Motors common, thereby almost doubling its holdings in the automobile company. At that time it held a total of 206,454 shares of General Motors and 159,155 shares of Chevrolet.[16]

When it was clear that the Du Pont Company had absorbed all it could and the General Motors stockholders would buy no more, Pierre and Raskob tried to persuade their European allies, particularly Sir Harry McGowan of the Nobel Company and the executives who managed the joint Nobel–Du Pont subsidiary in Canada, to purchase a large block of stock. In April 1919 the two arranged a dinner at the Metropolitan Club for McGowan to meet Durant "and talk over the motor situation."[17] But at the moment, McGowan was not interested. So Raskob, Pierre, and Durant decided to modify their basic policy and to reach a broader source of capital by selling to the general public through leading stockbrokers. In May the Finance Committee authorized a sale of $50.0 million worth of the new nonvoting debenture stock through four houses (Dominick and Dominick of New York, Hayden, Stone and Company of Boston, Montgomery and Company of Philadelphia, and Laird and Company of Wilmington).[18] This move only confirmed the committee's biases against outside financing; for the sale went badly, even though the underwriters received a commission of 15.25% as an incentive to move the stock. As a result the Finance Committee decided to withdraw the issue after $30.0 million worth had been sold. The sale, because of commissions, netted the corporation only $25,425,000.

Yet the demand for capital continued to grow. Expanded production schedules in all the operating divisions led to incessant calls for funds to enlarge plant and equipment and to obtain more cash to meet payrolls and to pay for supplies. At nearly every meeting the Executive and Finance committees authorized new expenditures.[19]

Rapidly expanding production also increased the need for assured sources of parts and accessories, semifinished and raw materials.[20] In the early months of 1919 Durant began to review possible shortages. He had studies made of existing sources of aluminum, leather, plate glass, tires, and gasoline. He asked for reports on the availability of wheels, storage batteries, magnetos, gears, machine tools, machines, and even housing for workers. As a result of these investigations Durant signed a contract with the Aluminum Company of America to assure a continuing supply of that raw material. He and Raskob recommended, and the Finance Committee approved, a $500,000 investment in the Goodyear Tire and Rubber Company, and even larger ones in the General Leather Company, the Doehler Die Casting Company, and the Brown-Lipe-Chapin Company. Large investments, too, were made in Ball Brothers Manufacturing Company and the Dunlop Rubber Company. As a result of the last investment, Pierre became a member of that tire company's board. Durant also proposed the formation and financing of housing construction companies in order to provide the necessary homes for workmen in Flint, Detroit, and elsewhere.

Pierre accepted the need for this program of vertical integration and took a personal part in negotiating for the two most significant purchases General Motors made. One involved buying control of the Fisher Body Corporation. That company had owned and managed one of Michigan's largest carriage businesses before it turned in 1908 to making automobile bodies.[21] This business the elder Fisher turned over to his several sons, Fred J. (the oldest), Lawrence P., Charles L., William A., Edward F., and Alfred J. From 1908 on, General Motors had been, quite naturally, one of their leading customers, particularly as Ford had moved so quickly into making his own bodies for the Model T. But the Fishers had many other customers. So Durant made an arrangement with them as early as November 1917 to purchase substantially all their output at cost plus 17.6%. The postwar expansion plans convinced Durant and the Finance Committee of the absolute necessity of having an assured control over General Motors' largest and most critical supplier. They simply could not afford to have the Fishers fail to renew their contract on acceptable terms. Any doubts Pierre might have had as to the need for this control were quickly resolved when he learned that automobile manufacturers in Cleveland (undoubtedly Willys-Overland) had opened negotiations to form a partnership with the Fishers in which they (the Fishers) would control.

After a series of conferences in the summer of 1919 between Pierre, Durant, and Raskob on the one hand and the Fisher Brothers and their largest financial backers, Louis and Aaron Mendelssohns, on the other, Pierre made the following offer.[22] General Motors would purchase 60% of the Fisher stock paying approximately $5.8 million in cash and $21,851,000 in five-year serial notes. To accomplish this move Fisher Body Corporation would increase its capitalization from 200,000 to 500,000 shares, the new issue of 300,000 shares going to General Motors at $92 a share. A majority of the stock was to be held in a voting trust, consisting of Pierre and Durant from General Motors and two men chosen by Fisher Body; the board of directors would have seven members from General Motors and seven from Fisher. Pierre agreed that the voting trust would pay a dividend of $10 a share for the next five years if a profit were made. He also suggested continuing the current contract at 15% rather than at 17.6% above cost. Finally, Pierre recommended that the Fishers set up an over-all committee structure similar to the ones he had developed at Du Pont and General Motors, with a Finance Committee concentrating only on finances and an Executive Committee "in complete charge of the operations of the company except for finances." The Fishers and the Mendelssohns accepted these terms, except that the contract was to be carried on at the old rate and was to last for five years, that is, until October 1924. They then dropped their negotiations with the Cleveland group.

The second purchase in which Pierre took a personal hand was equally significant. This was the buying of Charles F. Kettering's companies in Dayton, Ohio, including the Delco Light Company (formerly the Dayton Engineering Company), makers of farm lighting and power plants, and the Dayton Wright Airplane Company.[23] In this instance Pierre's aim, one strongly supported by Sloan but less so by Durant, was to get the ingenious inventor of the self-starter and one of the best-known engineers in the industry to devote his full time to the testing and improving of General Motors products.

During 1919 the Finance Committee reviewed and authorized the expansion of distributing facilities as well as those for producing automobiles and the supplies needed in that production. Raskob took the initiative in forming the General Motors Acceptance Corporation to assist dealers and customers to finance their purchases.[24] The idea was not a new one. Makers of durable goods for a mass market, like sewing machines, typewriters, and agricultural implements, had many years before worked out ways to finance dealers and consumers so that purchases could be made on time or installment plans. The General Motors Acceptance Corporation was, however, the first such company-managed consumer financing organization in the automobile industry.

Raskob, supported by Durant, sought to develop overseas sales. The General Motors Export Company was set up, with offices in New York, to handle distribution abroad except for that in Great Britain and Ireland, which was placed under General Motors, Ltd., of London. Other export companies handled the overseas marketing of parts and accessories. In the fall of 1919 Durant and the Finance Committee decided to investigate the possibility of securing a production base in Europe through the purchase of a European manufacturer.[25] A committee of Haskell, Sloan, Kettering, Champion, and Mott went to France to see about purchasing the Citroën company. After much discussion the committee decided against buying Citroën, but the reasons were technical and administrative rather than financial. Sloan felt that the Citroën plant was antiquated, and that with the postwar expansion program at home General Motors had absolutely no experienced managerial personnel it could spare to handle overseas production.[26]

The corporation's annual report for 1919 suggests the size and costliness of the postwar program for expanding production and for vertical integration. In that year alone General Motors had increased its investments in unconsolidated companies by over $50.5 million, spent $47.7 million for real estate, plant, and equipment, and acquired, through consolidation, property valued at $12.7 million.[27] During that first postwar year its permanent investment rose from $76.6 million to $153.8 million; expenditures for inventories and labor rolls increased proportionately. For example, its labor force rose from 49,118 to 85,980.

This huge expansion was planned and carried out in a haphazard way. Over-all production and investment goals were very vague. Individual requests for funds by the divisions were broad and general. Normally everyone received what he asked for. Thus, when Sloan, Raskob, and Durant quarreled over the allocation of funds, each for a favorite project (Durant for the tractor division, Sloan for the New Departure roller-bearing division, and Raskob for the new giant administration building in Detroit), the Finance Committee solved the controversy by authorizing all the funds desired for each project.[28] Such examples of laxity and generosity in granting appropriations apparently did not trouble Pierre as they had in the early years of the Du Pont Company. But they did intensify the need for money. The public sale of debentures had been most disappointing. Only a little over $25.0 million of the $50.0 million hoped for had been raised. In August 1919 Raskob quite naturally turned once again to the Du Pont Company. Members of the Du Pont Finance Committee who were not closely associated with General Motors agreed to the purchase of 22,000 shares at a total cost of close to $4.8 million. They insisted, however, that this was the last investment the Du Pont Company could make in General Motors.[29] The Du Pont Company simply could not put more of its surplus into outside investment. The diversification program required all that it had. The company had already invested over $47.0 million in the motors business and now held over 228,000 shares of General Motors as well as 159,115 shares of Chevrolet. Unfortunately, no record has been left of the debate on this purchase. It would have been useful to know where Pierre stood on the issue of using the family firm to continue to finance his new interest in automobiles clearly at the expense of further growth in the new chemical ventures.

Having received all they could from the Du Pont Company, the General Motors Finance Committee decided to turn again to its own stockholders. To tap this source Raskob came up with an ingenious plan that quickly won the backing of the Finance Committee.[30] He proposed that the 6% preferred and the 6% debentures be replaced by 7% cumulative nonvoting debentures. He recommended that the Finance Committee authorize an issue of $500.0 million of these 7% debentures redeemable at 120. Each holder of the present 6% preferred and debenture would be issued warrants entitling him to subscribe for two shares of the new debentures at par and to pay one-half the cost of these shares in cash and the other half by turning in either old preferred or debenture stock. From this exchange among the stockholders, the Finance Committee expected to raise $85.0 million. This amount, added to the corporation's surplus in cash, sight drafts, and Liberty bonds would provide the $175.0 million that Raskob estimated was still needed to pay the costs of the postwar expansion program. The board approved this plan on November 26 and at the same time authorized the amount of common stock to be raised from 5.0 million shares with par value of $100 (as approved by the stockholders in June) to 50.0 million shares of stock with no par value. They were to be exchanged for the existing shares of common at a rate of 10 to 1. These changes were ratified at a stockholders' meeting on January 6, 1920.

Durant and the Finance Committee were sorely disappointed by the outcome of this plan, which the stockholders formally approved in January.[31] By February, when, in the terms of the original announcement the right to subscribe was to be closed, only $11.0 million worth of the new debentures had been taken by exchange and sale. By May 1920 the total "fresh capital" the corporation received from the issue was only $12.5 million out of an anticipated $85.0 million. The failure of the sale and exchange of the new debentures was a clear sign of the financial problems facing the corporation in 1920. It was not until the late spring, however, that Pierre and Raskob began to appreciate the seriousness of its financial outlook. Only then did they finally agree that they must look to outsiders for funds. Even so, they still hoped to obtain capital from groups that could work with them as partners.

*Proposals for Internal Reform*

Although he had agreed that the Finance Committee would leave operations to Durant while he and Raskob took control of finances, Pierre remained constantly troubled by the lack of system in the management of General Motors. He was willing to wait to have Raskob institute financial and statistical controls for the corporation as a whole until the merger with Chevrolet and United Motors was completed. But from the summer of 1918 on, he, more than Raskob, tried to get Durant to adopt the administrative methods used at Du Pont. Pierre's initiative affected two areas—the formation of a central or general staff organization, and the development of a more adequate flow of information into the central office.[32] As a first step he asked Harry Pierce, in the summer of 1918, to have one of his men survey the General Motors plants and offices, with particular attention as to where and how the Du Pont Engineering Department could best assist the automobile company. Eric L. Bergland, one of Pierce's ablest assistants, completed his report in mid-September 1918. Pierce immediately forwarded a copy to Pierre.[33]

Every paragraph of Bergland's report stressed the lack of method and system at General Motors. It pointed out the total absence of a central engineering department, in fact, of any sort of permanent, well-organized central staff. Bergland did find "a very general admiration and appreciation of what the Du Pont Company had done and the value of their organization." Any assistance the Du Pont Company could give, he was sure, would be welcomed by individuals and departments at General Motors. They would certainly give "their heartiest cooperation."

The fundamental lack of system resulted, Bergland stressed, from the fact that General Motors continued to be essentially a one-man show. "Mr. Durant apparently has complete charge of all the planning and dictates largely the policies to be followed. His opinion is consulted for final decisions in a great many cases as there seems no one else in the organization who is the final arbitrator for the various plants or for the new developments." Durant personally made decisions on the small matters in a way that was "unnecessary with a properly equipped organization." He had "even heard of a case where details of designs for electric wiring were referred to him for decision, as controversy had risen and no one seemed able or of sufficient authority to decide." Because Durant maintained his offices in New York and came to Michigan only on visits, the need for approval often postponed action on critically important matters for weeks on end.

The procedures for authorizing construction, repair, and maintenance of General Motors facilities were most haphazard. The suggestions for changing or adding to an existing factory came either from the works manager, from Durant himself, or from Henry L. Barton, Durant's assistant on production matters (with the unofficial title of "the Efficiency Engineer"). After a general discussion by these three, requests for modifications or additions would go to the Executive Committee for approval. The request included only the most general specifications and usually called for little or no bidding on the contracts. The plant manager was normally so involved in supervising the production of the plant that he had little time to check on the contractor doing the work. Inevitably, the work progressed slowly, with "extravagant costs." With the construction of new plants the story was the same. As a result, valuable experience and techniques developing in one plant were not transmitted to other factories. Barton's office, consisting of little more than a man and a secretary, was far too small to act as such a transmitter of technical knowledge.

Moreover, Durant was always calling this assistant or another to check on some new suggestion, proposal, project, or idea:

> There is no system similar to our work order system for making suggestions [Bergland continued] or no central engineering organization for carrying out or developing these suggestions, and, therefore, it seems possible that only the more obvious and necessary things are done, and these only after considerable delay, as each case of new construction at plants puts a considerable burden on the plant managers. There is, I think, also a certain lack of cooperative spirit between the different plants. These plants are practically independent as regards the purchasing, accounting, and other organizations, and as they were independent operating organizations before the General Motors was formed, and have been more or less functioning ever since as independent organizations, it is very

easy to understand a feeling of this kind as there is no central organization directing them, except in the most general way.

Bergland then pointed to the high costs involved in not having central purchasing and to the dangers as well as cost of not having coordinated control over inventory buying. General Motors could obviously learn much from Du Pont Purchasing and other staff departments as well from the engineering staff.

Bergland's report verified Pierre's impression of General Motors' management. He talked to Durant about bringing in more system. Durant was very willing to make use of the Du Pont staff organization, but he never developed a commitment to building up General Motors' own central office and staff. After the Armistice, the Du Pont engineering department immediately began to work for General Motors.[34] It had little difficulty in shifting its extensive facilities from building munitions factories to constructing new or enlarging old automobile plants. By October 1919 Pierce's office had completed $17.0 million worth of engineering construction and design work as well as detailed studies and surveys for the many General Motors operating divisions.[35] The charge on this work, as Alfred Sloan wrote to the head of one of his operating divisions, was under 5% of the total cost, far less than outside architects and contractors would have charged.

Durant quickly began to make use of other Du Pont departments. He conferred with Dr. John H. Squires, the head of the Du Pont Personnel Office. Squires proposed a system to centralize control of personnel activities and suggested methods to standardize reports and to collect and index all information on all classes of employees. He further proposed keeping "an active waiting list" of all job applicants.[36] He also pointed out the advantage of having qualified men on tap to be available to move when technical difficulties appeared in production or construction work. Squires even talked with Sloan and others about the organizational structure of the General Motors factories, departments, and over-all corporation.[37]

At the same time, the Du Pont Development Department formed a Motor Development Section headed by John Lee Pratt. Pratt, a young executive, had come to work for the Du Pont Engineering Department in 1905, shortly after he graduated from the Engineering School at the University of Virginia.[38] It was Pratt who carried out most of Durant's investigations about the availability of supplies and materials and helped plan his strategy of expansion. At the same time, the Chemical Department began research in improved gasoline and other matters.[39] The Du Pont Legal Department even added its bit.[40]

Both Du Pont and Durant looked on these arrangements as temporary.[41] The du Ponts believed they were to provide an impetus for General Motors to build its own staff offices. Durant was, in fact, so pleased by the promising performance of the Du Pont departments that he asked both Squires and Pratt to come to work for him in his New York office.[42] After receiving this request, Ruly Carpenter wrote Pierre that Durant failed to realize that these men performed so effectively only because they were backed by a strong staff organization. "For example, aside from being a good man, Mr. Pratt had access to all the information in the Engineering Department and knew exactly where to go to get this information quickly, and could also consult with such men as Pierce, Foster, etc. . . . Indeed," he continued, "a very analogous case might be that of a man who heard an extremely good orchestra and immediately sent for the leader of this orchestra to come to his house and play for him individually, believing that he was going to get the same music." Carpenter urged Pierre to stress these facts to Durant.

Pierre pressed the point. Durant agreed but, for all his enthusiasm, he did very little. The only lasting move in the creation of a central staff was to obtain Kettering's services for research and development in automobile engines, machinery parts, and accessories. Pierre and Sloan had much more to do in bringing Kettering to General Motors than did Durant. Durant's lack of interest certainly was one reason that Pierre decided in December 1919 to urge Pratt to move permanently to General Motors. Even so, Pratt's primary task quickly came to be one of bringing system into financial procedures, rather than developing a larger and more systematic central staff.[43]

Pierre, undoubtedly, hesitated to push Durant harder because of their initial agreement to give Durant a free hand in operations. Pierre indicated this hesitancy in a letter to Durant written on January 2, 1920: "If we seem overzealous in recommending methods that have been successful in our organization, you and your practical men should not hesitate in combatting our views. We shall concede to you the benefit of the doubts in all cases and whatever policy is adopted will be the policy of all."[44] The significance, then, of Pierre's efforts to give General Motors a central staff organization was that he pointed out to the division managers and other executives in the automobile company the value of such central staff units. His infrequent and relatively mild suggestions also helped make him more aware of the deficiencies of the central offices and departments, an understanding that proved valuable when the crisis of General Motors affairs forced him to take its presidency.

In developing financial policies and system, Pierre and Raskob were not constrained by the agreement with Durant. However, both apparently thought they should wait for the completion of the merger with Chevrolet and United Motors before setting up financial controls for the corporation as a whole. And these legal changes were not fully completed until early 1919. Also, in the early months of 1919 Pierre was fully involved in turning over the Du Pont Company to Irénée and the younger executives. Nevertheless, the two men did send competent executives including Frank Turner, E.W. Proctor, and John F. Porter from the Du Pont Accounting Department to Michigan to help Buick, Champion Spark Plug, and other divisions to develop more systematic methods.[45]

On one financial policy Pierre did not wait. Early in the summer of 1918 he outlined a bonus plan for executives, similar to the one that Coleman had introduced at Du Pont in 1903. Pierre proposed that a bonus fund be set up amounting to 10% of net earnings "after deducting 5% on the capital employed in the business of the Corporation."[46] The money in this fund was then to be used to buy stock that would be allocated to salaried employees who had performed particularly well. In addition, Pierre proposed a "Royalty Bonus" for "inventions, suggestions, ideas or improvements of special value to the Corporation." General Motors executives were enthusiastic about these proposals. "Frankly," Sloan wrote Haskell, "there is nothing we need more than something of this kind."[47] The Finance Committee, the board, and the stockholders quickly approved.

The board also supported another, though somewhat different, recommendation from the Finance Committee for setting up an Employees' Savings and Investment Plan. Under that plan the financial office created a savings fund in which the employees could deposit 10% of their wages or salaries up to $300 a year; the corporation would then "duplicate 'dollar for dollar' the total amount of the Employees' savings."[48] Pierre and the Finance Committee apparently saw this plan as removing the need for a formal pension program.[49] In any case, a pension plan like that which had so long been established at Du Pont was not introduced at General Motors until the 1930s.

Finally, in June and July of 1919 Raskob, after consulting with Pierre and Durant, reorganized the central financial offices at General Motors. He promoted Meyer L. Prensky, Durant's comptroller, to treasurer, replacing Rice, who later became a vice-president and general manager of Cadillac. He then appointed as comptroller Frank Turner, who had served the Du Pont Company for thirty-two years before Pierre had sent him to Detroit.[50] "In making these appointments," Raskob told the senior executives at General Motors, "it is hoped to strengthen our financial and accounting organization and to bring about a uniform standard system of accounting and eventually effect a centrally controlled financial and accounting organization." He and the Finance Committee gave Turner full responsibility for organizing the Accounting Department, for "the installation of proper systems of accounting for the main office and all divisions and branches of this Corporation and its subsidiaries," and, finally, for devising an effective system of reports for the central and divisional offices as well as for the Finance Committee. Raskob further challenged the complete financial autonomy of the divisions by emphasizing that the financial officers of the divisions and subsidiaries "while directly responsible to the general manager of their particular division or company, will render their fullest support and cooperation to the Treasurer and Comptroller of General Motors respectively." Moreover, all future appointments of financial and accounting offices in the divisions and in the subsidiaries would require the approval of the treasurer and the comptroller.

As Turner and Prensky began to work on standardizing accounting and other internal financial procedures, they found much of the groundwork had already been surveyed by Alfred Sloan. As head of the organization supplying parts and accessories to the major manufacturing divisions, Sloan had a broader view of the corporation and a closer business relationship with the different divisional chiefs than did any other senior executive, except possibly Durant. He had long favored a stronger central organization. Before Kettering's arrival, for example, he had pushed for a central research unit.[51] A few months later he was urging the creation of an effective central engineering organization. Well before the setting up of the central accounting office, Sloan had a talk with Raskob and Durant about major and closely interrelated financial procedures.[52] In the summer of 1919, after Turner's appointment, he reviewed with the new comptroller his activities and ideas about handling billings and appropriations and his plans to develop uniform accounting procedures.

Ever since United Motors had become part of General Motors, Sloan had worked hard, and with little success, to improve managerial methods and statistical controls in the larger company. He wrote three penetrating reports on the weaknesses of the internal management at General Motors —analyzing problems and providing solutions. One, completed late in 1919, was on interdivisional billing. Here Sloan urged that the corporation replace its present chaotic system where "each deal seems to be worked out as an individually bargained arrangement with no relation to any general plan."[53] He proposed that the prices one division charged another be based on predetermined rate of return on invested capital and that if the price were too high for the buying division, it could purchase outside the company. The second report he drafted as chairman of a committee on appropriations procedures consisting of himself, Prensky, and Pratt, appointed late in 1919. This report, finished in the spring of 1920, outlined a set of rules for appropriating funds for capital expenditures in a rational and systematic way.[54] His review and proposals had many similarities to the work Pierre had done in developing appropriations procedures at the Powder Company after its formation in 1903. The third dealt with a fundamental reorganization of the corporation's operating structure.[55]

Because Sloan's reports concerned internal operations rather than external financing, they were considered by Durant and the Executive Committee, and not by the Finance Committee. Durant praised them highly but did so little to carry them out that Sloan seriously considered leaving General Motors to become an industrial analyist for Lee, Higginson and Company.[56] Pierre undoubtedly knew that the Executive Committee was reviewing methods of interdivisional billing and appropriations procedures, but he did not get a chance to read Sloan's reports on these matters. In September 1920, just as General Motors' administrative weaknesses were becoming painfully obvious, Sloan decided to bypass the president and talk these matters over, particularly that of organization, with the chairman.[57] The talk and a review of the report on organization impressed Pierre with Sloan's broad knowledge of the business and his clear, analytical mind. The fact that this was the first time Pierre and Sloan had had a serious discussion about General Motors affairs suggests how out of touch Pierre was with the day-to-day administration of the corporation.

Because of the agreement with Durant by which he became responsible for operations and the du Ponts for finance, Pierre did not fully realize how badly the automobile company was being managed. He appreciated the need for better financial and administrative controls, but was unaware of how little had actually been done to institute them. He knew that Durant was not a satisfactory administrator, but apparently failed to appreciate fully the weakness resulting from the lack of an over-all administrative structure. He was troubled when the corporation's most able executive, Walter Chrysler, whom Durant had made general manager in charge of all operations, resigned. Chrysler left in anger because he found it impossible to work with Durant.[58] Disturbed as he was, Pierre did not make Chrysler's departure a reason to study and improve the corporation's top management.

The emphasis on external expansion and financing and the disregard of internal efficiency and administration in the years immediately following World War I brought General Motors to a most serious crisis. By the end of 1920 the corporation was paying a price for the failure of its senior executives to bring order into its operations. The task of carrying General Motors through this crisis and restoring its vitality fell squarely on the shoulders of Pierre S. du Pont. During the crisis and the rebuilding that followed, Pierre du Pont and Alfred Sloan replaced John J. Raskob and William C. Durant as the most influential decision-makers at General Motors.

# The Crisis, 1920

DURING THE CHRISTMAS SEASON of 1919 Pierre fully enjoyed the holiday festivities. At the coming out parties, the family visits, and the decorating of the great Christmas tree at Longwood, he conversed with brothers, sisters, and close friends about the goings and comings of the younger du Ponts—their college plans, engagements, and weddings. He talked, too, about the long-anticipated trip he and Alice were going to take at the end of January to the West Coast and Honolulu. With his brothers and brothers-in-law he occasionally discussed business. He expressed his concern about operating weaknesses at General Motors as revealed by Chrysler's sudden departure. He and his brothers were uncertain, too, about the realism of John Raskob's plans for raising, through the sale of the new debentures, the large sums of capital that General Motors still needed. Yet these business uncertainties were not important enough to call off or postpone his trip to Hawaii.

He and Alice went to New York in the middle of January—she, to shop and he, to see an organ he wanted to put in the orangery at Longwood as well as to attend to General Motors business.[1] But he did find an occasion to talk to his good friend Seward Prosser, chairman of the board of the Bankers Trust Company; Prosser had been expressing serious doubts about General Motors' ability to finance its huge investment program, particularly in the face of mounting inflation.[2] Pierre, uncertain whether he had reassured Prosser, asked Raskob to confer with the banker and possibly one or two other leading financiers. Raskob made the right impression. Using the information he had presented to the Finance Committee when he first proposed the 7% debentures in November, he pointed out that by 1928 General Motors would have capital assets worth $1.5 *billion.* Of the funds used to acquire these assets, he predicted, 40% would be raised by the sale of senior securities. Raskob answered Prosser's questions so persuasively that the latter wrote Pierre he was completely satisfied by the "long heart to heart talk" he had had with John.[3]

The du Ponts thoroughly enjoyed their trip to Honolulu. The Harry Haskells accompanied Pierre and Alice most of the way, and the Charles Pattersons met them at Chicago and went with them to San Francisco and then met them again in Hawaii. In the Islands and on the West Coast (including a trip to Los Angeles) Pierre visited nurseries and botanical collections. He and Alice dined with, and were entertained by, old friends, including Elias Ahuja.[4]

The du Ponts returned to Longwood on February 28. Pierre immediately talked with Raskob and then went with him to a meeting of the General Motors Finance Committee. The news was depressing. The plan to have the corporation's stockholders provide an infusion of $85.0 million by the exchange of the new debentures for old had been going badly, having brought in at this time only about $7.0 million in new money. Moreover, expenditures were increasing at an unprecedented rate. At that meeting the Finance Committee was asked to approve of huge "over-runs" on appropriations already authorized. The division managers were finding that the rising costs, and sometimes the unexpected ones, made impossible the completion of major projects within the sums authorized. When Pierre read the minutes of the Finance and Executive committee meetings that had occurred since he was away, he became even more uneasy. At one meeting alone the Executive Committee had approved of "over-runs" amounting to $10.3 million made by Buick, Chevrolet, and the tractor company.[5] At the same time, the rising value of inventories indicated a rapidly growing need for working as well as investment capital.

Two basic matters demanded attention. The Finance Committee must develop plans to raise almost immediately millions on millions of dollars, or else the corporation's financial soundness would be jeopardized. It must also begin to get firm control over the massive expenditures of funds the division managers were making with almost no supervision from the Detroit or the New York offices. The first priority, Pierre agreed, was to obtain the capital.

*Finding New Partners*

As soon as Raskob realized that the debenture exchange was a failure, he began to look for other sources of capital. Even before Pierre returned from the West Coast, John had persuaded Sir Harry McGowan to make a visit to New York to consider whether the Nobel company and the joint Du Pont–Nobel subsidiary, the Canadian Explosives, Ltd., should invest in General Motors. They undoubtedly had discussed General Motors financing a few months before, when McGowan was in the country to sign a new agreement between the Nobel and Du Pont enterprises. In any case, Sir Harry was now quite receptive to the arguments of Raskob and Pierre. Within a day or two the Englishman was ready to put up some $30.0 million.

McGowan returned to Wilmington with Pierre and Raskob on March 19 and, while Pierre entertained him at Longwood, Raskob prepared a proposal under which the Du Pont Finance Committee would invite the Nobel enterprises to become partners in General Motors. Raskob stressed that the corporation needed $60.0 million to complete the current "development program."[6] Existing "investment conditions" made impossible the raising of capital from outside sources by selling debentures. Since the funds were needed for fixed, not working, capital, the corporation should not attempt to finance with short-term notes. Since neither of the two present sets of partners (the du Ponts and Durant) had the funds, and since "there is every reason to believe that there will be ample opportunity offered for expansion during the next few years," Raskob believed that the situation "affords splendid opportunity to interest new partners without the present partners sacrificing anything." As McGowan and his associates were interested, Raskob proposed that 360,000 new shares, which totaled 20% of the common stock then outstanding, be offered for sale to the existing stockholders at $200 a share (or $20 a share after the 10 to 1 exchange from old to the new common stock which had already been authorized by the stockholders' meeting in January). Since the du Ponts and Durant held the right to approximately 60% of the offering (that is, 216,000 of the new shares), they could safely turn over their right to $30.0 million worth of this block to the Nobel Explosives Trades, Ltd. After further negotiations McGowan's associates in Canadian Explosives, Ltd., agreed to subscribe $6.0 million, thus assuring the raising of $36.0 million from England and Canada through the sale of 180,000 shares of new stock (totaling 1,800,000 shares after the 10 to 1 exchange). The Finance Committee, as usual, supported the Pierre-sponsored Raskob recommendation without any recorded debate.

Raskob, however, did not mention who was to provide the remaining desperately needed $24.0 million. After the March meeting he suggested the possibility of bringing in the Hercules Powder Company as a partner.[7] Hercules, however, like Du Pont, needed its surpluses for a postwar diversification program. Finally, in April, Pierre, Raskob, and Durant agreed that they must go beyond their close associates and try to tap outside sources of capital. Since they were seeking partners who would invest in the business and who would be more than mere agents to market securities, they agreed to turn to the most eminent house of all, J. P. Morgan and Company.

Pierre had worked with that house off and on since 1914 and had full confidence in its competence to obtain funds. Durant grudgingly approved the move, though later he claimed to have opposed it.[8] For a brief time, early in 1920, he (like Raskob) clearly hoped to raise enough funds from the stockholders of General Motors and Du Pont to pay for the completion of the expansion program.[9] Indeed, he and Raskob had started a syndicate in March for the sale of that part of the new no par issue whose rights had not been turned over to the Nobels. But the falling stock market and the leveling off of demand for automobiles during the spring completely dampened Durant's hopes—as well as Raskob's and Pierre's—of raising funds from familiar sources. In any case, in mid-April, as the negotiations with Nobel were coming to a close, Durant, Pierre, and Raskob held their first meetings with members of the firm of J. P. Morgan and Company.[10]

The Morgan partners were no more enthusiastic about the proposed partnership than Durant had originally been. They had never made an investment in the automobile industry and they were wary of Durant's reputation as a speculator. As they later made clear, they had come only because Pierre had assured them of his own belief in the value of General Motors as a long-term investment and because he had stressed that he, Raskob, and Durant would work with them as partners. "I need not tell you," Edward Stettinius, the Morgan partner in charge, wrote Pierre after their negotiations, "that however attractive General Motors may have been, it would not have received the support we have given it, if it had not been for your active connection with and interest in the company."[11]

Durant announced the results of both the Morgan and Nobel negotiations early in June.[12] The Nobels agreed to pay 10% of their allotment of $30.0 million on June 1 and the rest in weekly installments until December 1. The Morgan Company would underwrite the $28.0 million. It would form a syndicate to distribute just over 1.4 million shares of the new no par value equal to 140,000 shares of old stock to be sold at $20 a share. Their commission would be $600,000, to be paid by taking 60,000 shares at $10 rather than $20 a share (that is, the firm would purchase $1.2 million worth of the issue for $0.6 million). In addition, each of the firms involved in the syndicate formed by Morgan to take up and distribute stock received a commission in stock of 5%, totaling in shares $1.34 million. So the total commission in shares, and not cash, was just under $2.0 million for a net return of just over $26.0 million. Both Pierre and Irénée thought this a reasonable commission under the circumstances of the rapidly declining stock market.[13] In addition, the house of Morgan was to appoint one member to the General Motors board of directors, and the companies in the Morgan-organized syndicate were to select five new board members. The Morgan representative became Stettinius; the five others included Prosser, George F. Baker of New York's First National Bank, Owen D. Young of General Electric, William H. Woodin of American Car and Foundry, and

Clarence M. Wooley of the American Radiator Company. Also to come on the board as representatives of the Nobel interests were Sir Harry McGowan, Arthur Chamberlain (another Britisher), and William McMaster (a Canadian).

The Morgan firm carried out the underwriting very successfully. It completed the distribution of the 1.4 million shares through the syndicate by July 15, the date agreed upon. Then the new directors came on the board and Prosser, Baker, and Stettinius became members of an enlarged Finance Committee. Next, to assist further sales by the group that had taken the stock, the Morgan company formed a syndicate of itself, the Du Pont Company, Chevrolet, and General Motors. Capitalized at $10.0 million it was to stabilize the price of General Motors stock during the final disposal.[14]

The Nobels were far less effective. As early as June 4, McGowan was writing: "Frankly the difficulty of finding our proportion—around about $30,000,000—between now and the end of the year is going to be extraordinarily great."[15] He then asked if he and the Canadian company could pay their installments over a period of a year rather than six months. After consulting with the Morgan men, Raskob replied that legally the payment could not be postponed. Then McGowan proposed an international syndicate to include Kuhn, Loeb and Company to assist in marketing his block. Again Raskob demurred. It would be as hard to raise money in New York as in London. Certainly the Morgans would not be interested in working so closely with their major competitor, Kuhn, Loeb. Next McGowan asked if Morgan would take $5.0 million of the $30.0 million block of stock.

Sir Harry arrived in New York early in August to try to work out some satisfactory plan. He brought with him Sir Josiah Stamp, economist and civil servant, who had joined the Nobel company in 1919 as its secretary. They quickly discovered that the Morgan firm would put in no more money. Neither would the National City Bank; nor would the Guaranty Trust, except under the harshest of terms. After much discussion with McGowan and Stamp, Pierre and Raskob worked out a plan to take up the $30.0 million.[16] The Nobels agreed that they could raise half of their allotment. Canadian Explosives would temporarily acquire $8.0 million (in addition to the $6.0 million it had already agreed to purchase) if Pierre assured that company that the du Ponts would take the block off its hands as soon as possible. Finally, Pierre, Raskob, and Durant decided to make use of the capital still held by Chevrolet. By taking the dividends received on its General Motors stock and by borrowing on short-term notes with that stock as collateral, they could raise the remaining $7.0 million. General Motors thus received "fresh capital" of about $60.0 million.[17] However, the $15.0 million that came from Chevrolet as well as Canadian Explosives was raised essentially on a short-term basis, as Pierre had committed the Du Pont Company to cover this amount.

In retrospect, it is apparent that the financing of General Motors' initial growth came largely from General Motors and the Du Pont Company. Up to the close of World War I, the corporation's expansion was paid mostly out of profits of the two companies. By the end of 1920, the corporation's fixed assets (real estate, plants, and equipment), which were listed in July 1916 at $24.4 million, had risen to $345.0 million. Of the capital raised to pay for this growth, $67.0 million had come from Du Pont, a little less than $20.0 million from the Nobels, and $51.0 million from outside, about half of which had been raised by J. P. Morgan and Company. The rest was paid for out of General Motors profits.

## The Inventory Crisis

The new capital came just in time. Without it (and, as Stettinius had made clear, only Pierre du Pont could have obtained it), the corporation would have had the greatest difficulty remaining solvent in the trying days to come. The actual crisis, however, resulted less from the demands for capital for fixed assets and more from the strident calls for working capital. Essentially it developed directly from the failure of the Finance Committee to obtain satisfactory control over expenditures of either working or fixed capital.

One basic reason that expenditures grew so rapidly in the first months of 1920 was that pent-up, postwar demands and the reconversion of the economy to peacetime activities pushed prices upward.[18] The managers of the operating divisions were unwilling to cut back their original expansion program. Instead, they willingly paid for construction in inflated prices. They also stocked inventory to assure themselves of supplies before shortages and inflation forced prices still higher.

At the end of 1919 the Executive Committee had created an Appropriations Committee chaired by John Lee Pratt. It, however, had little success in bringing order into the allocation of funds to the divisions for capital plant and equipment. For neither Pratt nor anyone else in the central office had the authority to check carefully on the validity of requests or to obtain additional information about costs, bidding procedures, and so forth. This is why the Executive Committee, consisting as it did largely of division managers, approved at meeting after meeting of large additional "overruns" on appropriations already made. The Finance Committee seemed to have little choice but to protest and to ratify. It could hardly argue that the work should be left uncompleted.

The Finance Committee had less to say about the expenditures for supplies, materials, and labor than it did about those for capital plant and equipment. Nevertheless, in March, well after Pierre returned from the West Coast, he might have tried to restrain Durant. The Finance Committee accepted Durant's production schedule of 876,000 cars, trucks, and tractors for the year beginning August 1920.[19] This sanguine forecast led to further buying of parts and materials. By May, however, with the negotiations with the Morgans moving along well and those with the Nobels almost completed, Pierre and Raskob finally turned their full attention to bringing operating expenses under some kind of central control. The negotiations themselves emphasized the need to conserve funds. The declining stock market had already suggested the possibility of a business recession abroad as well as at home.

On May 13 Pierre called—what was still unprecedented at General Motors—a joint meeting of both the Executive and Finance committees.[20] At this meeting he and Raskob stressed the dangers of continuing extensive buying for inventories. Both insisted that the division managers must curtail spending. Raskob pointed out that by the end of April the value of the inventories held by the divisions had risen to just under $186.0 million. At his suggestion, an Inventory Allotment Committee was appointed consisting of Durant, Haskell, Prensky, and Sloan. It was to allocate to each division its share of the $150.0 million of working capital that Pierre and Raskob estimated was available during the rest of the calendar year. At the same meeting the General Motors top executives reduced materially the production schedule Durant had outlined in March.

Still, even with lower production goals, the division managers made little effort to stay inside the limits set by the new Inventory Allotment Committee. The cautions, warnings, and even orders of the central office, went unheeded precisely because the division managers fully controlled their own funds for day-to-day production. They placed their own orders for equipment and material and paid for them out of division funds. They could even borrow on their own account if the money in the division treasury did not suffice. Given the prevailing postwar temper of expansion and inflation, these executives preferred to buy now and pay later from the proceeds of the sales of their completed cars.

But, while the division managers continued to stock supplies, demand for their products began to decline, first slowly and then precipitously. In August the Finance and Executive committees again warned the division managers to stay within the limits of expenditures set earlier. In October Pierre made Pratt chairman of a new Inventory Committee that was to spend its full time in bringing inventories under control. By then, however, the damage was done.

In September, as the general postwar business recession shook the economy, the demand for automobiles nearly disappeared. To meet the crisis Ford slashed his prices by 20% to 30%. Durant, supported by his division managers, attempted to maintain General Motors prices, but with little success. Before long, General Motors prices had to be cut if any sales were to be made at all. With the sharp drop in sales, production fell off and inventories of supplies and materials on hand soared. In late October the value of this inventory had reached $210.0 million, "exceeding by $60,000,000 the allotments of the Executive and Finance Committees," a later report noted. "This excess accounted for about 70% of the borrowing at that time."[21]

By the end of October working capital was disappearing. The return from the sale of new cars covered only a small part of running expenses. It was difficult to shift funds allocated for the completion of new construction and for the payment of equipment already ordered to pay wages and suppliers' bills. So many divisions fell back on short-term loans from local banks, usually at a high rate of interest.

In November, conditions worsened. The company sold only 13,000 vehicles, one-fourth of what sales had been in early summer. By January, production had reached a record low of 6,150 vehicles. Vast amounts of supplies already ordered or on hand could not be used in volume and, given the rapidly falling prices, they were soon greatly overvalued. Indeed, by the time the dust had settled, Pierre and his associates wrote off $84.9 million worth of inventory as a dead loss.

## Durant's Disaster

The postwar recession had as disastrous an impact on Durant's personal finances as it did on those of General Motors. For Durant attempted to do exactly what he had done three years earlier. In the summer and fall of 1920 he tried to maintain the price of General Motors by purchasing it on his own account. This time the over-all economic situation was far more serious than it had been in 1917. So, too, became Durant's difficulties.

During the summer of 1920 he formed, without informing Pierre or the Morgan company, a syndicate to deal in General Motors stock. Later, in telling his story of the events of 1920 to a journalist, Durant emphasized that he formed the group to maintain the price of General Motors stock. This is how the reporter recorded Durant's recollections:

> One day—it was July 27, 1920—one hundred thousand shares of General Motors stock were suddenly dumped into the market. The market was demoralized. General Motors stock broke to 20½. Durant—caring not one whit for money, and caring everything for the thousands who believed in him—bought that stock. More came into the market at a lower price. He bought that, too. Then [in the following months] more and more and more—always at decreasing prices, which made all his previously acquired holdings worth just so much less. Alone, unsupported, single-handed, and smiling, he fought the battle, purchasing the stock down to $12 a share, endeavoring to save General Motors for those who had made it possible more than ten years previous.[22]

But in the summer of 1920 there was another syndicate in which Durant, the president of General Motors and Chevrolet, was very much involved. It was the one the Morgan firm had formed for exactly the same purpose: that of maintaining the price of General Motors stock. In fact Durant, as president of the two firms, had signed an agreement with the other members —the Du Pont Company and J. P. Morgan—that none of the four companies would buy, sell, or borrow General Motors stock on their own account. For, as Pierre pointed out in November, two parties acting independently of one another could not effectively carry out their tasks of buying to stabilize prices.[23]

Possibly Durant thought the Morgan-managed syndicate was not being aggressive enough. Possibly he had already borrowed heavily and needed to keep the price of General Motors stock up in order to avoid further calls for collateral. Possibly he thought that through the heavy purchasing of General Motors stock he might once again be able to regain control of the company he now shared with the du Ponts, or at least to strengthen his influence in "his" company. The evidence is unclear.

What is clear is that, as he told the reporter, he was buying heavily. By late September he was urging Raskob to get the formal stabilizing syndicate to move in strongly to maintain the price of the stock. Raskob talked to Dwight W. Morrow and George P. Whitney, partners in J. P. Morgan, about Durant's proposal. Such an attempt to maintain prices under the existing conditions, they told Raskob, was hopeless and foolhardy. The only objective of the syndicate was to prevent the price from becoming demoralized as the general market dropped. When Raskob reported these comments to Pierre, the latter agreed that the Morgan approach was "the only proper and indeed only feasible way."

Nevertheless, Pierre did nothing to stop Durant from continuing to buy on his own. Indeed, he even, as he had in 1917, agreed to give him additional temporary assistance. A few weeks later Pierre admitted that while his "judgment was against this independent action [of Durant]," he had not made an issue of it. He was, he recalled, "not sure that the subject has been discussed in a way that indicated to Mr. Durant any clear cut ideas on my part; in fact, I have pictured his purchases to sustain the market as being limited to a number of shares well within his supposed purchasing power and that of his immediate friends who might be helping him in placing the stock."[24] Pierre also knew of the formation of the Durant Corporation that was created early in October specifically for the purpose of trading in General Motors shares. [25] In late October he was willing to approve Durant's request (forwarded by Raskob) for a loan from the Du Pont Company of the 1,307,479 shares of General Motors common. While this loan was redeemable on ten days' notice, and was well secured by 95,000 shares of Chevrolet stock, Pierre's approval of such a loan could only have encouraged Durant to continue his independent market operations.[26]

Pierre, however, was taken aback when, shortly after the approval of the loan, he began to read advertisements in the daily and financial press announcing that the Durant Corporation was offering blocks of General Motors stock to investors. The Morgan partners were even more alarmed. Pierre agreed with Morrow and the Morgan partners, who immediately got in touch with him, that such an announcement made clear to everyone Durant was operating heavily in the market on his own account.[27]

For the first time Pierre became seriously troubled by Durant's financial operations. He realized he was now, as he had been in the fall of 1917, quite in the dark about the General Motors president's over-all financial situation. He realized that Raskob knew little more. Given the general decline of the stock market, and with it the price of General Motors stock, the corporation's credit could be threatened if Durant was using its stock as collateral for large borrowings. A continued decline might force him to dump his stock. At Pierre's suggestion Raskob talked with Morrow and arranged for a conference between the Morgan and Du Pont representatives and Durant to review the latter's financial situation and especially the activities of the Durant Corporation.

Pierre opened this meeting, held on Wednesday, November 10, in New York, by stressing that it was essential that "the partners in ownership of General Motors stock should know each other's position." Morrow and Whitney then reviewed in detail the operations of the stabilizing syndicate, pointing out to Durant that the decline of General Motors stock was hardly out of line with that of most other stocks. Pierre, supported by Raskob, next emphasized that the Du Pont interests were not buying or selling General Motors stock in any significant amount, nor were they borrowing on it. Morrow then came to the point by saying he saw nothing to threaten the value of General Motors stock unless Durant or his friends were using it as collateral at the banks or the brokerage houses in order to obtain funds to be used in stock market operations.

Durant's reply was indirect. He explained the activities of the Durant Corporation, whose purpose he insisted was only to permit employers, dealers, and others vitally interested in General Motors to purchase stock at the current low prices. He reviewed in general terms how much the Durant Corporation had bought and sold. Then Morrow asked him directly if he knew of any weak accounts in the market. His answer was a strong No. When Pierre and Raskob and the two Morgan partners left the meeting that afternoon, they were certain that Durant's holdings were as clear as their own and that Durant was not borrowing on his General Motors stock. The Morgan partners were still troubled by the scope of Durant's activities. On departing, Whitney told Durant that he would be back within the next couple of days to review the Durant Corporation's accounts in more detail.

The next morning Durant called Pierre and Raskob, asking them to lunch with him. When they sat down at table, both men were surprised to find Durant distraught and agitated. "The bankers," he told Pierre, demanded his resignation as president. He would have to "play the game," Pierre recalled him saying, "for the reason that the Company as well as he personally 'was in the hands of the bankers' and must act accordingly." Pierre took sharp exception. What was Durant talking about? Despite the large number of recent short-term loans to meet the unexpected demands for working capital, the funds raised by the Morgans and the Nobels meant that the corporation could make good its obligations. Pierre was certain, he told Durant, that "our banking partners concur in this opinion and saw no difficulties in carrying out our loans, until liquidation through the operations of the business could be accomplished." Durant quieted down. But as the men left the luncheon table, he muttered something about being worried over his personal accounts. After lunch, Pierre, now thoroughly alarmed, insisted that Raskob get some idea of Durant's personal indebtedness before they returned to Wilmington the next morning. Did these debts amount to $6.0 million or $26.0 million? Raskob saw Durant briefly before Whitney arrived to go over the business of the Durant Corporation. In reply to Pierre's question, Durant merely told Raskob that "he would have to look the matter up."

Pierre and Raskob returned to New York on Thursday the eighteenth, determined to get a precise picture of Durant's financial situation. Before going to Durant's office Raskob called on Morrow. The Morgan partner reported that Whitney and another partner, Thomas Cochran, had spent Monday reviewing the affairs of the Durant Corporation; they had decided that although Durant "had behaved foolishly in handling the advertising, he was in no way involved in stock market operations."

Raskob returned to the General Motors Building to give Pierre this encouraging news. But as the day went on both became increasingly alarmed. As Pierre wrote Irénée: "Mr. Durant was very busy that day, seeing people, rushing to the telephone, and in and out of his room, so that although we waited patiently for several hours, interrupted only by lunch time, it was not until four o'clock that afternoon that Mr. Durant began to give us figures indicating his situation." Then rough penciled notes showed an indebtedness of $20.0 million, "all presumably on brokers' accounts" and "supported by 1,300,000 shares of stock owned by others and an unknown amount of collateral belonging to Durant." The 1.3 million shares were unquestionably the block the Du Pont Company had loaned Durant three weeks earlier. In addition, he owed $14,190,000 personally, against which he had 3 million shares of General Motors as collateral. But all these estimates were rough indeed. Durant had no personal books or accounts, and no summary of brokers' accounts outstanding. Even while Pierre and

Raskob were going over these notes, Durant received and met a call from one of his brokers for $150,000. "The whole situation, besides being very involved, seemed very serious. Mr. Durant promised to ask his brokers for accounts in order to make a more positive statement." On leaving the office, Pierre phoned Irénée to come to New York the next morning, while Raskob canceled his plans to attend Saturday's Harvard-Yale game in New Haven.[28]

On Wednesday, while Durant was trying to obtain more accurate data from his brokers, Raskob, Pierre, and Irénée first reviewed Durant's situation with Sir Harry McGowan, who had come to New York to check on the marketing of the securities he had taken. Then the Du Pont group began to work out a plan to prevent Durant from being forced to dump his stock on the market in order to meet calls from his brokers. By now the brokers' reports indicated debts aggregating $38.0 million! All were temporarily secured by General Motors stock, and the margins were narrow. A further decline in the price of General Motors common, which fell to $13½ that day, would, Irénée thought, surely result in a crash.[29] First, Raskob proposed to purchase 3 million shares from Durant at $11.0 million to be paid in cash and an additional $25.0 million in deferred payment. Durant protested that "he would be practically ruined" if he accepted this proposal. Raskob then suggested the formation of a company to hold Durant's stock. It would issue $20.0 million in notes to be used as collateral in place of the present stock, and $7.0 to $10.0 million in stock which the du Ponts would pay for in cash; the cash could then be used to pay off Durant's most immediate and pressing debts.

On Thursday, November 18, Durant's affairs came to a climax. During the day Russell E. Briggs, who had long been Durant's personal secretary, brought together a fairly complete tabulation of Durant's brokers' accounts. He handed the data to Pierre early in the afternoon. Pierre then made a rough summary in pencil which he had ready for the typist about four o'clock. This summary set Durant's indebtedness a little lower than the previous day's estimate, but also underlined the fact that a good deal more collateral or cash was needed. During the day Durant received several calls from brokers asking for additional margin. Pierre's summary made it clear to all that Durant had come to the end of his resources.

For the first time, Durant fully appreciated his precarious position. He frantically phoned Whitney at 23 Broadway without telling Pierre he was doing so. He urged the Morgan partner to use the stabilizing syndicate to buy 1,100,000 shares of General Motors from him at 13, the afternoon's closing price. Durant explained to Whitney on the phone that the continuing price drop of General Motors was "proving very embarrassing to some of his friends."[30] Whitney called in Morrow, who phoned Durant back to say that the function of the syndicate was not to buy from the participants in it, but only from the open market. Was Durant in trouble? Well, no, replied Durant, only his friends were. Did he have "any interest in the profits or losses of these margined accounts of his friends?" Morrow continued. "Well, under certain conditions, yes," Durant answered. Morrow asked him to come to 23 Broadway to talk over the situation. Durant, in turn, urged Morrow to come to his 57th Street Office on his way home, where he could then have a full review of Durant's accounts. Morrow agreed, saying he would bring Whitney and Cochran with him.

Durant then called Raskob and Pierre into his office, telling them of the expected visit from the Morgan partners and asking them to stay for the meeting. Pierre, angered by Durant's earlier duplicity, refused. "We told him that his position differed so entirely from that represented to us and to Morgan & Co. that it was impossible for us to sit in a meeting with him and the Morgan partners, unless he agreed to make a complete statement to them." Durant would not agree. So the two went back to Raskob's office, where they continued to work with Irénée and Briggs on Durant's accounts. At about seven o'clock Pierre, Irénée, and Raskob left the building for dinner. As they walked out one elevator, they met the bankers coming out of another.

Whitney, noticing Pierre, called him aside. They had just seen Durant, he reported, and were returning at his request at nine o'clock. Could they talk to the Du Pont group before then? Right now, Pierre suggested. All six returned to Raskob's office. There, Pierre asked the Morgan men if Durant had made a complete statement. They showed him a typed copy of the summary of the brokers' accounts that Pierre had drawn up earlier. Indeed, Durant had been even more precise with them. He had made it clear that unless he had $940,000 in cash before the opening of the stock exchange, he would be unable to meet his creditors' demands. The du Ponts and the Morgan partners agreed that the situation was serious. Durant's financial collapse might easily bring on failure of brokers carrying his loans. This, in turn, could precipitate a financial panic. There was a striking parallel between these events and the crisis in the affairs of the brokerage house of Moore and Schley during the panic of 1907. At that time, the Morgan firm sought to prevent a collapse by purchasing holdings of Moore and Schley of Tennessee Coal and Iron Company. Now the house of Morgan faced the same sort of problem with Durant and General Motors.

After a short snack the six returned to the General Motors office building. At nine o'clock the three Du Pont men and the three Morgan men were in Durant's office. With them were John Thomas Smith, the General Motors lawyer, a Dr. Campbell, who turned out to be Durant's son-in-law, as well as Durant and Briggs. In the outer office waited a partner of one of the largest brokerage houses in New York, who had come to ask Durant for more collateral to cover loans. For several hours the Du Pont and Morgan men reviewed Durant's complicated set of accounts. In many cases the accounts could only be explained orally by Durant or Campbell. When the figures were checked, the bankers and the du Ponts went to Raskob's office to work out a plan to raise the $30.0 million needed to meet Durant's major debts. Pierre then outlined Raskob's plan to form a company to buy and hold Durant's stock. Morrow was skeptical. Given the condition of the market, brokers could hardly be expected to take the securities of a brand new company as collateral. Moreover, Raskob's proposal did not take into account the need to raise almost a million dollars before 9:30 the next morning in order to prevent the dumping of 300,000 shares of General Motors stock on the market.

The only sure way to eliminate these debts was to pay them off in cash. The group finally decided that $27.0 million would cover Durant's most pressing needs and that the price paid represented a price per share of about 9½.[31] When the bankers said they would raise $20.0 million, and agreed to do so without cost, Pierre announced his willingness to raise the remaining $7.0 million without directly involving any banks. The Morgan men were pleased. "There are only two firms in this country who are real sports," Cochran laughed, "viz. Du Pont and Morgan." Having decided on a company to hold Durant's stock—which was to be paid for in cash—the discussion then turned to what Durant's equity should be in the holding company. Morrow thought that a fourth interest in the new company would be fair enough.

The group then returned to Durant's office, where Morrow outlined the proposal. Durant argued that a fourth share was too "harsh." He suggested that he be given 40% and Du Pont 60%. Finally, they agreed that one-third of the holding company's stock should go to Durant, and two-thirds to Du Pont. Next, they decided how to raise the cash that Durant needed immediately and worked out the relationship of Durant's debts and those of his friends in their buying syndicate. In Pierre's words: "checking of accounts and discussion continued without interruption until 5:30 o'clock Friday morning, about that time Mr. Durant and I signed a memorandum, agreeing to the general proposition of a $20,000,000 note issue and issue of stock to support $7,000,000 furnished by the Du Pont interests; also, the loan of additional collateral, estimated at 1,300,000 shares."[32] This 1.3 million shares and the 2.7 million which the new holding company would purchase from Durant would provide the collateral for the $20.0 million cash loan which the Morgan firm promised to raise from the New York banks. In addition, the Morgan partners agreed to furnish Durant $640,000 before 9:30 the following morning. Durant said he could hold off on the rest if Pierre could obtain for him a loan of $530,000 sometime during the next day.

After breakfast and a short nap, all were back at work.[33] The Morgans got the $640,000 to Durant in time for him to meet all calls before the exchange opened. Before the day was out, the Du Pont Finance Committee, whose members had come to New York on the morning train, made Durant a loan of $530,000. The members of the committee also gave their full approval to the agreed-on plan. By evening the house of Morgan had arranged for the $20.0 million loan. In order to complete these arrangements they found it necessary to give a commission to the banks making the loan. All agreed that it was best to pay this commission in the stock of the proposed new holding company. After some discussion with Durant, Pierre agreed to lower Du Pont's share and raise Durant's. They decided to call the holding company the Du Pont Securities Company, the same name as the holding company that had purchased Coleman's stock and that now had the title of Christiana Securities. Of its common stock, 40% (40,000 shares) would go to Durant, 40% (40,000 shares) to Du Pont, and 20% (20,000 shares) to cover the commissions.

The completion of all the arrangements had to wait until after the weekend. On Monday the new holding company, the Du Pont Securities Company, was formed with Pierre as president and Raskob as treasurer. Durant signed an agreement to sell 2,546,548 and 23/100 shares to be delivered on December 10.[34] In return he received 40,000 shares of common stock in the new company. The Morgan partners signed the agreement to raise the $20.0 million on the basis of the holding company's notes. A third agreement signed that day, between the new Du Pont Securities Company and the old Du Pont American Industries and Chevrolet, provided for the more than 1,300,000 shares of General Motors that were needed to complete the collateral necessary for the Morgan loan.[35]

In addition the du Ponts raised the $7.0 million they had promised. This was done by having Du Pont American Industries (the holding company the Du Pont Company used to hold its General Motors stock) purchase $4.2 million of Du Pont Securities preferred. Funds for this purchase came from $1.4 million in the former's treasury from dividends on its holdings and $2.8 million that was borrowed from Christiana Securities Company. The remaining $2.8 million came by having Chevrolet purchase $2.8 million worth of Du Pont Securities preferred. For this purchase Chevrolet undoubtedly borrowed some funds from banks on short-term notes.[36]

Pierre and Raskob had, therefore, used the large block of General Motors stock held by Chevrolet to provide the collateral for the $27.0 million cash needed to bail out Durant. They could make use of it, where Durant could not, because their arrangements were between corporations—holding companies—not persons, and also because they were only exchanging stock between companies and not, like Durant, seeking collateral for brokers' loans to purchase on the open market. Since Durant still owned by far the largest block of Chevrolet stock, his full approval to these arrangements was obviously essential.

Once the agreements were completed, one more critical decision remained. Durant, upon accepting the terms of the Du Pont and Morgan partners, agreed to resign. Morrow and the others considered him totally incompetent to manage the corporation. By now Pierre could only concur. Even Raskob favored the change. On Monday, November 22, the Du Pont Finance Committee, whose members were still in New York, urged Pierre to take the presidency of General Motors.[37] So too did Seward Prosser, Pierre's closest friend among the financiers who were aiding General Motors. Prosser's views were quickly supported by the other New York bankers. Alfred Sloan and his fellow operating executives at General Motors saw no other man in the corporation "who had the prestige and respect that would give confidence to the organization, to the public, and to the banks, and whose presence could arrest the demoralization that was taking place."[38]

Pierre hestitated. Since the war he had insisted that he could no longer participate actively in business. Longwood and Delaware were to have first call on his time. The task of carrying General Motors through the current crisis and of restoring it to administrative health would be difficult and time consuming. Moreover, Pierre realized that he had no real experience in the automobile industry. It seemed presumptuous for him to take the place of a man who had been with the industry from its beginning.

Yet he was at least partly responsible for the situation in which the corporation now found itself. If he had paid closer attention to its affairs in the past, if he had not left so much to John Raskob, if he had kept a closer watch on Durant and checked more carefully on his requests and those of John's for funds, neither the affairs of Durant nor those of General Motors would have been in such a crisis. He had a responsibility to the family and to the Du Pont Company which, through his intercession, had become involved with the automobile corporation.

Moreover, who else could do it? Clearly Raskob could not be left to manage General Motors without a guiding hand. Events had shown decisively that Raskob, the brilliant financier, was not a brilliant administrator. Haskell could not run the corporation by himself. He was over sixty years of age and in poor health, and besides, he knew relatively little about the intricacies of General Motors financing. Sloan was a possibility, but Pierre hardly knew him. He might be an able administrator, but he had no awareness of the corporation's over-all financial problems. Pratt was too young and inexperienced. None of the division managers had an over-all understanding of the corporation's affairs. They were little known outside their own divisions, and they had little financial experience. In fact, nearly all were having difficulty in handling the finances of production. Pierre considered these alternatives and talked them over with Raskob in New York and as they returned to Wilmington on the Wednesday afternoon train. Driving from the station to Longwood, he told Alice that he had decided to accept the presidency of General Motors.[39]

Years later he recalled that Raskob's arguments finally convinced him and "set his mind at rest."[40] Here was, John had pointed out, still a grand opportunity. General Motors was already a giant enterprise in the most promising industry in the nation. It had talented and experienced executives as well as great plants, research laboratories, and an international distributing network. All that was lacking was "a leader with the common sense to permit them to operate this great organization with the least interference." Above all, Raskob stressed, confidence in General Motors had to be restored. "All was ready for a reorganization and advance toward better days."

Pierre said nothing about his decision at the Bachelors' Ball in Wilmington Wednesday night. Nor did he mention it the next day at a large family Thanksgiving dinner at Longwood. On Friday, November 26, he returned to work. First, he completed an agreement for Durant's signature on minor matters such as bringing the Durant Corporation to an end and transferring salaries that Durant had paid from his own personal account to that of the corporation itself. Pierre then wrote Sir Harry McGowan, who had left New York before the final consummation of the arrangements resulting from Durant's difficulties. Next, he recited the story of the recent events in great detail in a letter to Irénée that was to serve as a record of the story.[41] Only then, at the afternoon meeting of the Du Pont Finance Committee, did he formally inform his associates that he would accept the presidency of General Motors. He was ready to take over on the following Wednesday, December 1, the day Durant officially retired.

# Reorganization
# and Regeneration, 1921

CHAPTER *19*

H is decision made, Pierre acted swiftly and decisively. On Monday, back in New York, he began to review accounts and reports, had a final talk with Durant, and telegraphed the division managers and senior executives to meet with him in New York on Wednesday. After lengthy conferences with top personnel he returned to Wilmington for the weekend. Monday saw him back in his 57th Street office in New York and on Tuesday, December 7, he was off to Dayton to consult with Kettering, accompanied by Haskell, Sloan, Raskob, and other executives.

So began a pattern of work that would continue uninterruptedly until Pierre resigned from the presidency in the spring of 1923. During the week he worked at the General Motors offices in New York, living at the nearby Carlton House, where he and Raskob had a large apartment.[1] Their wives, Alice and Helena, often spent the week in New York with their husbands; they enjoyed shopping, the theater, opera, and often helped with business entertaining. Every other week Pierre would take the night train to Detroit, Dayton, and other cities where General Motors plants and offices were located. Usually Sloan and Raskob and one or two other business associates would be on the train with him so that during and after dinner they could go over the next day's work and problems. Even on the weekends in Wilmington he was busy with business. Saturday was the only day that he could catch up on Du Pont Company and du Pont family affairs; Sunday he devoted to Longwood. While he tried to give some attention to the Delaware public schools, he found that he simply did not have the time, so in the fall of 1921 he resigned from the State Board of Education.

During his first two weeks as president, Pierre considered all the critical matters involved in meeting the company's crisis and in beginning its reorganization and regeneration. At the very first meeting of December 1 with the division managers and senior staff and financial officers, Pierre reviewed the ways of assuring effective control of inventory purchasing and of writing down and even writing off the existing surplus of supplies and materials.[2] On the trip to Dayton the following week he conferred at great length with Sloan about how best to reshape the corporation's administrative structures and procedures so as to regain and maintain control of its vast widespread activities. The primary purpose of that trip, however, was to discuss with Kettering ways to improve General Motors' products and to rationalize its conglomerate product line. On returning to Wilmington on the following weekend, he talked to Irénée about bringing Donaldson Brown, the Du Pont Company's treasurer, to General Motors to install essential financial and statistical procedures. The following week, in New York, he conferred with Raskob about putting on a permanent basis the financing of the Durant stock that had been purchased so hurriedly in the early hours of November 19.

## Structural Reorganization

Of the four critical areas requiring swift action—inventory control, organizational structure, product policy, and financial reform—Pierre acted most quickly upon organization. From the end of 1920 until 1924 administration and operation, rather than finance, became Pierre's central concern. With this shift Raskob, the financial expert, became definitely the junior partner. Pierre fully realized that until the lines of authority and responsibility were clearly and explicitly defined, the other reforms would be difficult, if not impossible, to achieve. In the area of administrative reform Pierre relied from the start almost completely on Alfred P. Sloan, Jr.

Pierre came to know Sloan really for the first time on the trip of December 7 and 8 to Dayton.[3] He had read over Sloan's organization study after the conversation in September; but he had not yet reviewed Sloan's reports on appropriations procedures and interdivisional billing. On the trip Pierre checked these reports and talked the longest about the second.

In their discussion on interdivisional billing, Pierre argued, as he had done many years before with Coleman, that in the billing and settling of accounts between the different divisions the company should be considered as an enlarged factory. The producing division, therefore, should bill the receiving one at cost. Sloan, on the other hand, favored, as Coleman had done earlier, using interdivisional billing as a method of evaluating divisional performance. He told Pierre of his proposal to have the selling division set its intercompany prices on a more sophisticated return on investment formula and at the same time to protect the buying divisions from paying over the market price for purchases made within the corporation. Before the train reached Dayton, Pierre had decided to appoint a committee of Pratt, Turner, and Barton, Durant's production expert, to study Sloan's earlier report on interdivisional billing and to make recommendations to the new Executive Committee.

On his return to New York, Pierre himself reviewed Sloan's reports on organizational structure and appropriations procedures. Just before and right after Christmas Pierre and Sloan worked out the final adjustments of a structure based on Sloan's study. The most important change Pierre asked for was the creation of a small temporary Executive Committee to guide the corporation through the crisis. After conferring with Raskob he also made some adjustments in the financial staff offices. The basic outlines of Sloan's plan, however, remained unchanged. At the first meeting of the board after Pierre became president, held on December 30, he proposed the plan and the board unanimously adopted it. On January 3 it went into operation as the corporation's fundamental constitution.[4] Its principles still govern General Motors today, half a century later.

Pierre had moved quickly because he saw in Sloan's plan the means to build the central, or general, executive and staff offices so essential to provide an effective over-all control of the autonomous operating divisions. He realized that the organizational problems were very different at General Motors from the ones that were concurrently challenging the Du Pont Company. At that time the Du Pont Executive Committee was beginning to study the administrative difficulties raised by the diversification program.[5] Its basic problem was to decentralize authority and responsibility so that the general office would not be overwhelmed with operating details. At General Motors the case was exactly the opposite. Overdecentralization had led to anarchy. Here an enlarged central, or general, office was essential to assure even a modicum of over-all control. Yet Sloan was keenly aware of the tradition of divisional independence that was so strong at General Motors. He believed, probably more than did Pierre, that such independence encouraged initiative and independence.

Pierre certainly approved of the opening sentence of Sloan's study: "The object of this study is to suggest an organization for General Motors Corporation which will definitely place the line of authority throughout its extensive operations as well as to co-ordinate each branch of its service, at the same time destroying none of the effectiveness with which its work has heretofore been conducted." The structure would then be based on "two principles":

1. The responsibility attached to the chief executive of each operation shall in no way be limited. Each such organization headed by its chief executive shall

be complete in every necessary function and enable[d] to exercise its full initiative and logical development.

2. Certain central organization functions are absolutely essential to the logical development and proper control of the Corporation's activities.[6]

Sloan proposed to achieve these aims by replacing personal controls with institutional ones. He did this first by explicitly defining "the functions of the various divisions constituting the corporation's activities, not only in relation with one another, but in relation to the central organization," so that "it will perform its necessary and logical place." He then assigned each of the many divisions into one of four "groups"—Car, Accessories, Parts, Miscellaneous. The first included the divisions that manufactured and sold "complete motor cars—purchasing part of their component parts from outside sources, part from the divisions of the Corporation, and manufacturing part with their own facilities."

In setting up the next two groups of divisions—the Accessories Group and the Parts Group—Sloan made a major change in the old Durant organization. Before 1921 a number of these divisions had been operated by Buick, Chevrolet, and other car-making units. Now those divisions that sold over 60% of their production *outside* the corporation were to form the Accessories Group. (In February 1921, Hyatt still sold 40% of its output of roller bearings to Ford and only 18.1% to General Motors divisions.) The Parts Group consisted, then, of those that sold 60% or more of their products *within* the corporation. The former had, Sloan noted, "common problems, such as sales and advertising policies, competitive conditions, proper placing of the Corporation's capital to effect the best results to the Corporation as a whole and many other questions which do not enter into the operations within the Corporation." The final group was a catch-all including the tractor, the refrigerator, overseas trade division, and General Motors Acceptance Corporation. In making adjustments to Sloan's plan Pierre decided that a Miscellaneous Group did not make much administrative sense, so he placed General Motors Acceptance Corporation directly under Raskob and gave Frigidaire to the Accessories Group. Tractor and overseas trade divisions were not placed in any group. On the first of these, Pierre preferred to wait until a decision was made on whether General Motors would remain in the tractor business. The second—overseas trade—became in time a separate group.

Each group of divisions was supervised by a "Group Executive" who would be a "General" executive but without line authority. Sloan defined the role of the group executives by specifically describing, as an example, the duties for the one in charge of the Accessories Group. This general officer was to have no specific day-to-day duties, nor was he to have actual line authority over the division managers. He could advise, but not order.

He was to keep a close eye on the performance of the divisions under his supervision and to be the channel of communication between them and the Executive and Finance committees.

The divisions in their groups formed the Operations Staff. To assist the operating units, the corporation was to have two other staffs—the Financial Staff and the Advisory Staff. (See Chart VI.) Pierre decided to leave most of the organizing of and recruitment for the Financial Staff to Raskob and Donaldson Brown; the latter began work at General Motors early in January. Pierre paid closer attention to the Advisory Staff, for he had, since 1916, urged Durant to create such an organization. In addition to its existing Research and Engineering offices, headed by Charles F. Kettering, and the Plant Lay-Out section headed by Barton, and the Patent and Legal offices, Sloan proposed that the corporation have its own Plant Engineering, Personnel, Real Estate, Purchasing, and Sales sections. (Of these the first became the Power and Construction and the second the Industrial Relations sections.) The function of all staff sections, Sloan repeatedly stressed, was only advisory. Staff executives could never give an order to a general or divisional executive. "The purpose of the staff is to advise the chief executives of the operations staff concerning problems of technical and commercial nature which are themselves so broad and require so much study as to be outside the scope of a single operation and which will be, when developed, of importance to the guidance of all operations."

In Sloan's plan the two senior committees—the Executive and the Finance—continued their duties as originally outlined by Pierre after the Du Pont Company purchase of General Motors stock, with the Executive Committee retaining "its entire supervision over the operations side of the Corporation's activities" while the Finance Committee continued to have "general control of the Corporation's finances and its financial staff." The latter was "to approve major appropriations, set dividends, decide salaries for the top officials and determine long-range financial goals."

For the moment, however, Pierre wanted a small, all-powerful Executive Committee to steer the corporation through the crisis. It would include, besides himself, only Raskob, Haskell, and Sloan. A small group of men could move more quickly than a larger committee. Besides, Pierre was not certain that the operating men on the existing Executive Committee were competent to handle high-level policy-making. If he put none of the division managers on the committee, he would then avoid appearing to "play favorites."[7] Each of the four members on the new Executive Committee had a specific job. He, as president, would be chairman. Raskob would continue as chairman of the Finance Committee and have only a very general supervision of the corporation's finances and the new Financial Staff. Sloan would become head of the Advisory Staff, and Haskell the vice-president in charge of the Operations Staff. The general managers of the cars, tractor, and truck divisions and representatives of the parts and accessories divisions formed a new Operations Committee which Pierre expected to handle the more routine operating matters. This committee would, in fact, have many of the same functions and much the same makeup as the old Executive Committee. In making his statement on December 29 announcing the new organizational structure to the General Motors personnel, Pierre emphasized that "it is my belief that 90% of all questions will be settled without reference to the Executive Committee and that the time of the Executive Committee members may be fully employed for the Corporation leaving the burden of management and the carrying out of instructions to the Line, Staff, and Financial Divisions."[8]

In the first months of 1921 the biggest task facing Pierre and the three other members on the Executive Committee was to transform Sloan's elaborate plan into a living and working system. Pierre was fully aware that in a company as large as General Motors the structure would have to be modified and adjusted. Even more important, Pierre noted, "the success of any scheme of organization adopted by our company will depend on the enthusiasm and sincerity manifested by the respective heads of the departments in carrying out the plan." As critical as defining the new organization was the finding of competent executives to man it.

The most difficult part was creating an effective Advisory Staff. This may be why Pierre initially put Sloan in charge of that staff. The Advisory Staff required more senior executives than did the Financial Staff or the operating divisions. Sloan also had to work hard in defining staff activities, many of them brand new, and in making the divisional executives aware of these services. Although Pierre conferred with John H. Squires of the Du Pont Personnel Department about men qualified for jobs at General Motors, he left the final selection up to Sloan and the executives in charge of each operation.[9] By June, Sloan had filled the more important offices. His greatest find was Norval H. Hawkins, Henry Ford's brilliant sales manager; Hawkins, who had only recently left Ford, now became head of General Motors' new Sales Analysis and Development Section.[10] Once the Advisory Staff had become a going concern, Pierre switched Haskell and Sloan around, making Sloan vice-president in charge of Operations and Haskell the head of the Advisory Staff.

Pierre wanted Donaldson Brown, the Du Pont Company's treasurer, to head the Financial Staff, because he realized that Raskob's strength lay in external financing rather than in development of internal financial procedures.[11] Brown had excelled in this field ever since he had devised in 1912 the basic return on investment formula used at Du Pont. During the past couple of years he had been developing uniform accounting and other statistical procedures for the new activities that the Du Pont Company had acquired through its diversification program.[12]

Brown's task was less difficult than Sloan's, because Raskob had already begun to reorganize the financial offices in the summer of 1919 when Prensky became treasurer and Turner comptroller.[13] Brown immediately set to work to enlarge his Financial Staff. Among his two successful appointments were Earl Clarke, who had worked with him in Wilmington and now came to Detroit to head the new statistical department, and young Albert Bradley, who became assistant treasurer. He also made a place for Russell E. Briggs, one of Durant's oldest and most confidential associates, as head of the Employees Bonus Department.

In the selection of top personnel Pierre's most critical task came in the appointment of the executives in the general office and of the division managers. Here he, rather than Sloan or Brown, had the final say. Pierre put Pratt in charge of the Accessory Group after his Inventories Committee had completed its work. He made Pratt's close friend, E. F. Johnson, a former Du Pont Company executive who had headed the Development Department in Wilmington, the group executive for the Parts Division. In late spring of 1921 he asked Charles S. Mott, a large stockholder and director who had been an executive at General Motors since the early Durant days, to take charge of the Car, Truck, and Tractor Group. A few weeks later, after Pierre had made Haskell the vice-president in charge of the Advisory Staff, he asked Mott also to act as the director of the Advisory Staff under Haskell. Haskell's health made it increasingly difficult for him to travel to Detroit. Moreover, Pierre wanted the responsible head of that staff to reside in Detroit, not New York. He soon asked Haskell to concentrate his energies on overseas sales.[14]

Even more difficult than selecting the group executives was the job of choosing the general managers of divisions. No appointments were more critical to the revival and future prosperity of General Motors. The corporation's salary scale fully recognized this fact. The division manager's salary of $100,000 a year was the same as Pierre's as president and chairman of the board and twice that of the general executives like Sloan, Haskell, and Mott.[15]

Pierre wanted to keep tested and able managers who would, nevertheless, accept the new general office procedures and controls. In the four important divisions—Buick, Chevrolet, Truck, and Canadian—he proposed relatively minor changes. At Buick, Henry H. Bassett had taken Chrysler's place as general manager in 1918 and had kept his division the most efficient and profitable at General Motors. At Chevrolet, Pierre removed A. B. C. Hardy, the division's senior executive, putting him temporarily in charge of the Advisory Staff's new purchasing section. He then made Carl W. Zimmerschied, a competent Hungarian-born engineer who had headed its production division, Chevrolet's general manager.[16] Although uncertain about the future of the Truck Division, Pierre decided to leave its experienced manager, William L. Day, in charge while Samuel McLaughlin continued to head the Canadian operations.

In Oldsmobile, Oakland, and Cadillac, Pierre did make major changes. In all three cases, managers had been drawing funds from the corporation for their own personal accounts.[17] Since Durant had permitted such practices, these men were not intentionally dishonest; nevertheless, such slipshod financial procedures had to be stopped. Fred W. Warner at Oakland and Richard H. Collins at Cadillac had a contract from Durant by which they were paid not a fixed salary but a percentage of profits which was to be determined after the audit. As they had determined and had drawn their pay without authorization and before the audit was made, Pierre insisted that they replace the funds. Both did, Collins with good grace and Warner under protest. Edward Ver Linden of Oldsmobile, deciding that the compensation Pierre had computed for him in 1920 was too low, decided to draw out the monies he felt were coming to him without further authorization. Pierre insisted that he return these funds.

By May all three men had left General Motors. Pierre was not concerned about the loss of Warner and Ver Linden, for their divisions were badly managed, but he may have been sorry to lose Collins, who was an able executive. After consulting with Sloan, Pierre appointed three close associates of Durant who had long experience with the corporation. He put A. B. C. Hardy in charge of Oldsmobile. George Hannum (for many years the general manager of the Jackson-Church-Wilcox Division, makers of rims, wheels, and stampings) took command of the Oakland Division. H. H. Rice, whose experience was more on the financial than the production side, became Cadillac's head.[18] These men proved to be competent, though not exceptional, divisional managers. Yet they quickly came to have as much confidence in Pierre as they had once had in Durant. Their attitudes, in turn, helped to persuade the divisional personnel to support the new management wholeheartedly. In the smaller Parts and Accessory divisions Pierre made relatively few changes. There his major problem was more which ones to drop or to merge.

Pierre's care and diplomacy in making changes in division managers helped him to win the confidence of the operating men, most of whom looked with great skepticism and often distrust on the representatives of eastern financial interests. His visits to the many plants and his quiet and persuasive talks about the future of General Motors and the automobile industry further reassured the divisional executives.[19] In these talks he also stressed the importance of carrying on the work in a businesslike, ethical way. He had already insisted that the general managers should not have their own personal accounts, nor would he permit general or sales managers to own stock in dealerships or suppliers. Such sound business practices had worked well at Du Pont, he emphasized. They should do so at General

Motors. His tactful but straightforward approach to the critical matter of selecting top-level personnel was one of Pierre's major contributions to the regeneration of General Motors.

## Statistical and Financial Controls

Absolutely essential to the new scheme of organization were executives who were in sympathy with its purposes. Necessary too was the development of impersonal statistical and financial controls. Only a constant flow of information on divisional activities and performance in terms of sales, output and, above all, rate of return on investment could permit the division managers to operate without constant personal supervision. The lack of such data and of automatic checks on spending for both permanent and working capital had been the underlying cause of the crisis at General Motors. In developing such new procedures and controls during the first half of 1921, Pierre followed the recommendations in Sloan's earlier reports on interdivisional billing and appropriations and those set forth by Pratt in his committee on methods of inventory control.

Sloan had pretty well convinced Pierre that methods used for interdivisional billing were more than mere accounting devices, but could become indispensable tools for evaluating operational performance. The committee that Pierre appointed on the trip to Dayton (Pratt, Turner, and Prensky) made its report to the new president on January 6. The three fully supported Sloan's earlier recommendations, agreeing that the divisions should charge a price for the products that would bring a specific return, say, of 15% on investment capital.[20] If the buying division found that the prices charged by the selling division were out of line with prices paid on the open market, its manager was to notify the Executive Committee. The committee would then have the price differential investigated. If the selling division was unable to bring its prices down, and if its production was not needed for assuring an adequate supply of critical items, then the division could be sold or put to other uses.

Uniform procedures of interdivisional billing were essential to the development of statistics that would indicate precisely the net return on invested capital produced by each operating division. Under the old methods that Pierre had favored at Du Pont, the statistics would not show clearly how much a car-making division, such as Buick, or how much an accessory one, such as Harrison Radiator, contributed toward the final profit on the product. This new information would be a guide to management in allocating capital and would improve the morale of the operating divisions by indicating the share each had in making the final profit. In addition, such procedures ended the constant bargaining between divisions.

In the discussion of its report the committee opposed one part of Sloan's proposal. It did not want the head of the new purchasing section to be the "arbitrator" to decide, in case of disagreement, whether the price charged by the selling division was in actual fact out of line with market prices. The committee also added to Sloan's report careful definitions of the terms cost, profit, and capital employed. It made these definitions partly to assist Turner in the work he had already started on developing a uniform accounting system for all the divisions within the corporation. During the following weeks Turner was able to standardize the classifications of accounts so that they would be the same throughout the corporation for the calendar year of 1921.[21] Although a number of refinements were still to be made, by the summer of 1921 the Executive Committee and the Finance Committee at last had the basic information-gathering schemes needed to determine costs in relation to output. They could now begin to compute realistically the rate of return on investment for each of the many General Motors activities.

Because Sloan's earlier report on appropriations procedures followed closely the Du Pont Company's pattern, Pierre saw no reason to appoint a committee to review it. He felt quite competent to evaluate by himself. On December 21 he sent Sloan his comments.[22] On the whole he expressed only enthusiasm with the recommendations. But he did have some major suggestions. He could not agree that "over-runs" on appropriations must necessarily continue or that the proposals and programs of "each separate division or subsidiary must necessarily be considered separately." To avoid "over-runs" Pierre proposed the setting up of a contingency fund when making the initial appropriation. On the second point he insisted that the basic purpose of making an appropriations program was precisely to consider requests as a whole and not separately. He further favored including in an appropriations request any special tools and equipment needed to put a factory project into operation; it should also list the initial working capital required. Both these items should be considered as "invested capital necessary for the development of profit."

Sloan readily agreed to these modifications.[23] He knew that special tools, dies, and jigs in a new assembly plant could cost over a million dollars. He told the treasurer, Prensky, of Pierre's interest in, and "very constructive" suggestions for, improving the appropriations procedures.[24] From one of Prensky's assistants Sloan had learned that the work on the Appropriations Manual was progressing well. He therefore suggested that he and Prensky meet with Pratt, the third member of the committee on appropriations, set up late in 1919, to consider Pierre's modifications and the "general aspects of the matter" before the directors' meeting scheduled for December 30.

At the evening session the three accepted Pierre's proposals, made some minor additional changes, and turned the work of completing the manual over to A. C. Anderson, whom Donaldson Brown had just appointed as the head of the new Appropriations Accounting Department of the Financial Staff. Anderson's manual, after a lengthy review by Brown and then by the general managers, was approved by Pierre and the Executive Committee and then by the Finance Committee in April of 1922. Its major procedures for "an independent impartial review and checking all phases of proposed projects outside the Division or Subsidiary itself" were already in use by the summer of 1921.[25]

Information compiled and checked by Anderson's office was then reviewed by the Executive Committee and, if over a certain sum, by the Finance Committee. In both these committees (and Pierre's voice carried the greatest weight in each) the members checked each project, not only on its own merit but in relation to the corporation's over-all development. Once the appropriation was approved, Anderson's office was to keep watch to see the funds so allocated were spent as planned. By April 1921 Pierre was assured that the procedures for the allocation of funds for long-term, permanent investment were as precise and as effective as those he had developed for the Du Pont Company more than a decade and a half earlier.

By late spring, too, the general office had achieved controls for the allocation of short-term working capital, as well as long-term capital investment. The failure to control such short-term expenditures for supplies, material, and labor had been at the heart of the General Motors financial crisis. On October 8, while Durant was still president, the Finance Committee had temporarily taken control of buying supplies away from the division managers and placed it in the hands of the new Inventories Committee headed by John L. Pratt.[26] All purchasing authorizations had to be approved by the committee. Then on the day he became president, Pierre, at the meeting with the senior executives, enlarged Pratt's committee and gave it the task of revaluing stocks on hand as well as controlling continued purchasing. At the same first meeting Pierre asked the division managers to give the Executive Committee "each month a revised estimate of sales for the succeeding four months."[27] On the basis of these estimates he asked for a revised estimate of funds needed to pay for necessary supplies, materials, and labor to meet the expected demand.

Talking with Pratt in early December, the new president was impressed with how much had already been accomplished. The first step, Pratt later reported, "was to send out, under the signature of the President of the General Motors Corporation, a letter instructing all General Managers to buy nothing; to stop shipment of all purchases released until the Inventories Committee could review the situation with each individual General Manager and decide on what material would be received and what would not be received. . . ."[28] This meant "sitting down with the General Managers in their own offices and going over their inventory situation with them in detail." It also meant talking to the suppliers individually. Pratt told the suppliers that they could "break" General Motors by insisting on payment.[29] If they held off, they could count on having a good customer in the future. Only one large steel company did insist on payment, and by February not a single lawsuit had resulted from the renegotiation or readjustments of the many contracts. Through persuasion, Pratt, in fact, passed on some of the financing of inventory stocks to the suppliers. By early February he reported to Pierre that a normal inventory on hand, in relation to expected sales, had been achieved at Buick and Cadillac. Olds' inventory was beginning to approach normal. Inventories were still badly unbalanced, however, at Chevrolet (where production was down 60%), at Oakland, the Truck Division, and particularly at the Samson Tractor Division.[30]

After control began to be restored, Pratt (following Pierre's suggestion in the meeting of December 1) asked each general manager to submit a monthly schedule forecasting estimated sales for the next four months and the amount and costs of materials and payrolls needed to meet these sales. Pratt and his committee "scanned" the estimates and discussed them with the general managers. "When an agreement had been reached, material for one month's production at a time was released by the Inventories Committee."[31] In reaching these decisions Pratt considered other matters besides demand and supply. One aim was to keep plants working even if their products could not be sold immediately, in order to maintain a nucleus of a trained working force.[32] By these controls Pratt had reduced the value of General Motors inventories by over $32.2 million by December 31, 1920, and by $6.0 million more during the first three months of 1921.[33]

As Pratt was achieving control over inventories, Prensky, as the committee's vice-chairman, began the "writing down" of existing supplies. In a detailed report to Pierre and the Finance Committee dated February 18, Prensky recommended a total write-off of $25.7 million. The report makes clear the nature of this accounting reappraisal. Of the total amount written off, $13.3 million resulted from "repricing in order to bring values down to market or cost whichever is lower." Excessive production of parts that had become obsolete by the discontinuance of the product or model added an extra $3.1 million to the write-off. The differences between the overhead manufacturing expense charged to inflated values and that of current inventory values added another $7.4 million. Discrepancies in cost accounting methods used in different plants and divisions came to $1.2 million more, and other adjustments to another $2.0 million. Finally there was $3.7 million which, Prensky reported, resulted from an astonishing overstatement of physical inventory in the Oakland Division in 1919. It was this revelation that first made Pierre suspicious of the ability of Oakland's general manager, Fred Warner.

Pierre accepted the need to write down the amount proposed by Prensky as an essential though painful piece of financial surgery. Neither Pierre nor

Prensky was fully aware of the fact that this estimate was only a beginning. The liquidation of some of the weaker divisions made further write-offs necessary as did the depressed market for automobiles for 1921. Before the final reading, which Pierre recorded in his Annual Report of 1922, the corporation was forced to write off $84.9 million in inventory adjustment and liquidation losses.[34] While the listing of such losses naturally brought protests from some stockholders, others praised the write-down. Pierre's old mentor, Arthur J. Moxham, wrote congratulating him on his courage in taking this step and in his "splendid handling of what I know was a difficult problem."[35]

By April 1921 Pierre agreed with Donaldson Brown that Pratt and Prensky had brought the inventories under control and that the committee should be disbanded. From the start all four had always considered Pratt's committee as a temporary measure. Continued direct control of purchases and allotments by the general office through the Inventories Committee, Brown emphasized, was "unwholesome and objectionable."[36] Under the decentralized scheme of management these decisions should be left to the divisions. Now they could be, Brown reported, because he and Pratt had worked out a set of procedures based on the experience of the Inventories Committee to provide a constant check on the divisional employment of working capital.

The basis for the new and more permanent procedures was a continuing use of the monthly forecast that Pierre had suggested on the first day of his presidency. Each division, Pratt proposed, would continue to make forecasts for the following four months (and even longer where they might be of value). These more detailed reports included forecasted demand and production schedules and the resulting supplies and working force needed to meet the estimated production. The approval of the Operating vice-president (Sloan, after May 1921) would be the authorization for the division managers to purchase the following month's supplies and materials. While improved and refined, these procedures which tied production schedules and purchases of supplies to monthly forecasts have remained ever since 1921 the basic tool for controlling both inventory and working capital at General Motors.

Once these procedures were installed, Pierre and Raskob asked the Financial Staff to remedy another weakness that the crisis of 1920 had revealed. This was the lack of means for controlling and pooling of the corporation's cash.[37] Much of the short-term borrowing had occurred in late 1920, because the divisions could carry out financial transactions on their own accounts, and because they could not draw on one another for funds. After 1920 the financial autonomy of the division managers was curtailed. All incoming receipts were placed in the corporation's account, in one or more of a hundred banks throughout the country, where General Motors had placed depository accounts. All disbursements from these accounts had to be authorized by the general Financial Staff.

Under the new system funds could easily be transferred from one part of the country to another. If deposits in one bank exceeded the fixed maximum set by the Financial Staff, the surplus was sent by telegraph to one of a number of reserve banks. Whenever a division needed funds, a general officer, after approving the request, would transfer the funds from the reserve bank to the one holding that division's account. Besides assuring a large pool of cash, these provisions also facilitated interdivisional payments. Intracorporation certificates based on these deposits were exchanged instead of cash. By establishing good working relations with so many banks in all parts of the country, General Motors also developed extensive lines of credit. Further savings were assured because this pooling of resources allowed for a reduction of total bank balances and so permitted the excess cash to be invested in income-producing, short-term government securities.

Even before the completion of the new cash control system, the crisis that had brought Pierre to the presidency had been surmounted. A basic new organizational structure had been created for the corporation, and its offices manned. Confidence had been restored. Procedures to ensure rational allocations of the corporation's capital had been started. Others had been formulated to control and reduce the working capital needed to finance the production of goods in the many divisions from supplier to customer.

### The Permanent Financing of the Durant Purchase

The one remaining task was the permanent financing of the Durant purchase. As might be expected, this was done by John Raskob. This time, however, Pierre and the Morgan partners kept a closer watch on his work than they had on his earlier financial schemes. These plans involved several different situations. One was the final settlement with Durant. The second was placing on a permanent basis the financial arrangements that Pierre, Raskob, and the Morgan partners had worked out so hurriedly on that long and hectic night of November 18. The third was to relieve Canadian Explosives and Chevrolet of the temporary purchases of General Motors stock that they had made.

In this refinancing Durant made the first move. Although he had received just under $26.0 million in cash from the Du Pont Securities Company as well as 40,000 shares (40% of its stock), Durant still had obligations.[38] Always optimistic, he was already beginning to think about new ventures. He needed cash. Also he still had an outstanding loan from the Du Pont Company of 1,307,499 shares of General Motors stock secured by collateral of 95,000 shares of Chevrolet. Much of that block of General

Motors stock he was continuing to use as collateral for brokers and other loans. So he approached Raskob to work out an arrangement that might give him more flexibility.

Before the end of 1920 the two had reached a mutually satisfactory agreement by which Durant sold his 40% block of stock in the Du Pont Securities Company to the Du Pont Company (i.e., the Du Pont American Industries) for 235,000 shares of General Motors stock. (The value of Durant's original block of Du Pont Securities shares was, in terms of the end-of-the-year market price, something over $3.0 million.)[39] Durant was to deliver 95,000 of the General Motors shares he received from Du Pont to "certain interests which he owes." The Du Pont Company would retain the balance of 235,000 General Motors shares it had sold to Durant as collateral for a loan of $500,000 cash. As part of the same agreement the Du Pont Company was to sell Durant the 1,307,499 shares he had borrowed from it in October. Durant would pay a price equal to $10 a share. The payment would be the 95,000 shares of Chevrolet which Durant had put up as collateral in October, and which then had an estimated value of about $13.0 million. This left Durant with half a million dollars in cash and a block of General Motors stock which, at the arranged price, was worth $13.1 million and had a market value at the time of the exchange of $17.0 million.

It was this agreement that Durant initiated, and not the November arrangement, that gave the Du Pont Company absolute control of Chevrolet and of the Du Pont Securities Company and, therefore, of General Motors itself.[40] For the very first time the Du Pont Company replaced Durant as the largest stockholder in General Motors. The control of Chevrolet meant voting control of 4.5 million shares of General Motors and that of Du Pont Securities some 2.5 million more (which had been purchased from Durant in November). The agreement was quickly carried out after the Du Pont Finance Committee approved it on January 17.[41]

Durant appeared to be more than satisfied. At a dinner for "his boys," men whose fortunes he had helped to make, he praised the du Ponts for bailing him out. If they had not raised overnight the many millions of dollars he needed, he reported, "General Motors would have been broke."[42] Clearly Durant was not too shattered by the course of events. Even before the final settlement had been approved by the Du Pont Company, he was planning to form a new automobile company. At the end of December 1920 the press was reporting that Wall Street was giving Durant three years to make a full comeback and, in fact, to recapture control of General Motors.[43] In the middle of January, six weeks after he left the presidency of General Motors, his successor received a telegram from the Chamber of Commerce of Flint, Michigan. The Chamber was anxious, the telegram read, to have Durant locate his new enterprise in Flint. But it also realized "the great obligation and debt of gratitude the city owed General Motors."[44] Pierre

immediately replied that although Durant would certainly be an active
competitor, "there was no objection or ill-feeling among those who remained in the old Corporation. I hope Mr. Durant will have your confidence
and assistance."

Durant did settle in Flint. He became an aggressive competitor, producing the low-priced Star, the Flint, the Durant, and other models.[45] But the
time of great opportunity for new firms was almost over in the automobile
industry. By the mid-twenties the market was leveling off. The advantage
now favored the existing companies. Durant kept going during the prosperous years of the twenties, but, like other smaller firms, his went under in the
depression of the 1930s. Yet, possibly, if Pierre had not effectively and
quickly resuscitated and regenerated Durant's original creation, Durant still
might have been able to make a lasting comeback.

With Durant off to a new start and the close association of five years
ended, Raskob turned his attention to putting the *ad hoc* financing of the
previous year on a permanent basis. Such a step was necessary if only
because the $20.0 million worth of notes issued by Du Pont Securities
would come due within a year. In addition, Raskob and Pierre still had to
carry out their promise to relieve the Canadian Explosives Industries, Ltd.,
of the $8.0 million worth of stock it had temporarily taken during the
previous summer.[46] At the same time they had to pay back the funds taken
from Chevrolet to pay for part of that issue, some of which had been covered
at Chevrolet by short-term loans using General Motors stock as collateral.
After that, Pierre and Raskob expected to carry out their long-planned
elimination of the Chevrolet Motor Company.

The first step in the refinancing was to liquidate Du Pont Securities and
turn its 2.5 million shares of General Motors over to the Du Pont Company
(i.e., to the Du Pont American Industries, Inc.). The December arrangements with Durant meant that the du Ponts came to hold his 40,000 shares
of Du Pont Securities as well as the 40,000 of their own (16,000 of which
they had turned over to Chevrolet and 24,000 of which to Du Pont American Industries to obtain the General Motors stock needed for the collateral
for the $20.0 million worth of notes). Liquidation required first obtaining
the remaining 20,000 shares promised the bankers for commissions, next
paying off the $20.0 million in notes, and then getting back from Chevrolet
the 16,000 shares of Du Pont Securities common and the 28,000 of its
preferred used to obtain General Motors stock for collateral. And Christiana Securities also had to be repaid the funds borrowed and used to raise
the $7.0 million cash as Du Pont's part of the November 18 bargain.

By the end of March 1921 Raskob had worked out a plan for this
refinancing.[47] Pierre, Irénée, and others on the Du Pont Finance Committee
modified it somewhat before it was approved in May. To provide the funds
to liquidate Du Pont Securities and to repay Canadian Explosives, Raskob

proposed that the Du Pont Company itself issue $35.0 million worth of 7½% gold bonds. J. P. Morgan and Company agreed to market the issue at 95. The discount of 5% as a commission was, in Raskob's opinion, hardly excessive, given the state of the market. Not only were securities selling at all-time lows, but the bond market had recently been saturated by a $200.0 million bond issue of the Chicago, Burlington and Quincy Railroad. The collateral for these Du Pont Company bonds was to be 7.0 million shares of General Motors common.

The transaction was quickly and efficiently carried out.[48] Of the somewhat over $33.0 million received, $20.2 million went to redeem the notes held by the banks and other firms, and to repurchase the 20,000 shares of Du Pont Securities those firms were to receive as commissions. The sum of $6,388,000 went to Chevrolet to buy back the remaining 16,000 shares of Du Pont Securities common stock, the 28,000 shares of preferred, and the $2.8 million acquired to raise part of the Du Pont $7.0 million share of the November 18 transaction. In addition $2.8 million was used to pay back the loan made by the Du Pont Company from the Christiana Securities in purchasing the Du Pont Securities preferred. After these transactions were completed, the Du Pont Securities Company was dissolved and its holdings of General Motors were turned over to Du Pont American Industries.[49]

After a discussion with Sir Harry McGowan and the Canadian company, all agreed that the du Ponts would take that block of 400,000 shares of General Motors stock at $20 a share, the price paid for it, and thus carry out the promise to relieve the Canadians of the purchase they had made the previous summer. Du Pont further agreed to use funds from the $35.0 million bond issue to purchase half the block. The rest would be paid in a year. Early in 1922, with the help of a $4.0 million loan from J. P. Morgan and Company, the Du Pont Company bought the remaining 200,000 shares at 20.[50]

The final step in the refinancing of the Durant purchase was the wind-up of Chevrolet. Its debts were paid off with cash received from the Morgan loan, and then in June the outstanding Chevrolet stock was exchanged for that of General Motors at a rate of 14.425 shares of General Motors for one of Chevrolet.[51] By this exchange the Du Pont Company received 3,177,428 shares of General Motors for its block (230,196 shares) of Chevrolet stock. When the refinancing was completed, the Du Pont Company held a total of 7,362,540 shares of General Motors (35.8% of the shares outstanding), for which it had paid $75,581,259. Nearly all these shares were needed to provide the 7.0 million shares of collateral called for by the $35.0 million loan marketed by J. P. Morgan.

Pierre was particularly pleased by how smoothly the refinancing had gone. He was grateful to the Morgan firm for arranging the marketing of the

$35.0 million loan, and especially for the redemption of Du Pont Securities common from the bankers at the low rate of $10 a share. When expressing his thanks to J. P. Morgan the younger and Stettinius, Pierre took the opportunity to review the work done at General Motors during the past six months:

> I must confess [he told Morgan] that last mid-winter was a most disquieting period, not only because of the collapse of Mr. Durant and the motor industry, but because of my very inadequate knowledge of the motor business.[52]

But now Pierre was certain that General Motors would be a productive investment:

> I am convinced that errors in expenditures are not as great as we had feared; in fact, I would not be surprised to find all the permanent investment usable in a profitable way. However, I do believe the organization as arranged by Mr. Durant was wrongly planned for carrying on business in the substantial manner you would recommend.
>
> The losses in personnel that have occurred are, I believe, due entirely to changes that are being made for the betterment of the organization. I have no regrets whatever at the loss of the men that are leaving us.

Morgan replied that he and all his partners had "complete confidence that under your guidance, or that of the men you may eventually select to take some of the work off your hands, the company will come through this present period of depression in excellent condition."[53] Stettinius added that he realized "the difficulty of the problems you have had to face and I admire your courage and wisdom."[54] Although he had no doubt at all about the ultimate outcome for General Motors, he did fear still "some rough weather before us, but under your leadership, the company will weather the storm and some of these days will come into smoother seas."

Certainly much remained to be done. Most important of all, General Motors products needed to be improved so that they could continue to compete in the current market. The product line itself still had to be put on a rational basis. Nevertheless, Pierre had accomplished a great deal in his first six months at General Motors. The general office had regained control of its vast complex business activities through a new organizational structure, through uniform cost accounting, and through procedures to systematize the use of short-term working capital and long-term investments. Moreover, as Pierre suggested to Morgan, the basic plant and facilities were completed. The postwar expansion had been finished and paid for. When the market for automobiles recovered, further expansion could undoubtedly be financed out of profits.

Yet the institution of new procedures, critically important as they were, was only part of Pierre's contribution to the recovery and regeneration of General Motors. Equally significant was his personal leadership. In a quiet,

undramatic but clear-headed way, he restored the confidence of all concerned with the future of General Motors and its new management. This
was easy enough with the bankers and stockholders, for they were impressed by Pierre's name and reputation. It was, however, much more
difficult to win the confidence of the managers and men, who looked on
Durant with respect and real affection, and who looked on the du Ponts and
Morgan as dangerous, exploitative outsiders. Pierre came to be respected
for himself. His visits to plants and the towns in which they were located
helped convince the executives of Pierre's concern and desire to learn about
the automobile industry. He persuaded them that his would be in fact less
of an absentee management than had been Durant's. Useful, too, were his
conferences with local businessmen and civic leaders in the midwestern
cities and towns where General Motors offices and plants were concentrated.[55] He assured these men that General Motors would not pull out, but
planned to stay and grow. These talks also helped to reassure General
Motors suppliers. Their growing belief that the great corporation would
remain solvent and become prosperous did much to make easier Pratt's task
of adjusting and renegotiating contracts for materials and equipment.

By the summer of 1921 the crisis had passed and the regeneration of
General Motors had begun. Recovery seemed quite certain. A beginning
had been made. The next few months would test the value of the new
procedures, the competence of the new senior executives, and the validity
of the new air of confidence.

# Product Policy and Technological Innovation, 1921–1923

A S STETTINIUS PREDICTED, rough weather still lay ahead. The new organizational structure and statistical and financial controls were still more theoretical than operational. The new senior executives had to learn how to handle their authority and meet their responsibilities. Finances, however, were no longer a problem. With plants operating at 40% and less capacity, no funds were needed for expansion. All the Finance Committee, including the three representatives of the bankers, agreed that dividends should be as low as possible and still retain the confidence of stockholders and investors. Income should be used to meet short-term debts and to build up a surplus account.

The fundamental test of the new men and procedures came, then, not in finance or even organization, but in meeting the most basic problem of any manufacturing business—the development and sale of a profitable line of products. At General Motors in the spring of 1921 this problem had two parts. First, the quality of existing cars, trucks, and other vehicles and of the parts and accessories used in them had to be improved. Second, decisions had to be made about the number and variety of vehicles and models. In other words, both a product policy and a market strategy had to be determined.

To Pierre du Pont, more than to most of his associates, the key to product improvement and market strategy was technological experimentation and innovation. He personally urged the development of coatings or paints so that the automobile would not need to be protected from the weather. In 1921 such a "garageless" car was a significant innovation. He encouraged cooperation between the Du Pont and General Motors laboratories to find ways of improving the driving power of gasoline, particularly by eliminating "engine knock." But for Pierre the most exciting technological innovation at General Motors was a radically different air-cooled engine. Since 1919 he had watched with growing interest the work being done in Kettering's laboratories on an engine that would have many advantages over the conventional water-cooled model.

While the air-cooled engine was not in itself new, Kettering's design to make its volume production practical was an innovation. By using copper fins on the cast iron block to draw off heat, he expected to produce engines in much larger numbers and at much lower cost than did the makers of the Franklin, the only other satisfactory air-cooled car then on the market. Both Kettering and Pierre came to see in the air-cooled engine the most certain way to revive the fortunes of the unprofitable car divisions and to permit General Motors to compete effectively against Ford and the other major automobile manufacturers.

## Defining the Product Line

Even before product improvements could be seriously considered, Pierre and the senior executives at General Motors had to decide on what to make for existing markets. Durant had paid almost as little attention to developing a rational product line as he had to fashioning systematic management procedures and controls. His basic strategy, it will be recalled, was to concentrate on output. Neither he nor his Executive Committee ever discussed how far the corporation should go into the production of its own supplies and materials. Nor had they considered how far they should move into nonautomobile products like tractors and refrigerators. They had not even decided whether the automobiles produced by one division should compete with those of another, and if so how and in what way.

As long as the market continued to grow, Durant and his division managers looked on such questions as academic. The recession of 1920, however, had made them painfully real. In the first place the drastic drop in demand in the fall of 1920 and the winter of 1921 shattered Durant's basic assumption—that of the ever-expanding market. At that time, only Buick and Cadillac enjoyed sales enough to show a profit, and Cadillac only barely so. By early 1921 the other five car and truck divisions were reporting serious losses. Some of the Parts and Accessories divisions were doing well enough. For others the record was dismal. Of the latter, the Central Gear, Central Foundry, and Canadian Products divisions reported the highest losses. Worse still was the record of the nonautomotive divisions. Although Delco Light, maker of home lighting plants for farmers, continued to stay in the black, Frigidaire's losses had by February 1921 reached $1.52 million, with a total estimated loss expected at $2.5 million, while Samson Tractor was losing $100,000 a month.[1]

Of all the statistics Pierre studied in the spring of 1921, the most discouraging were those of sales. Where General Motors had sold 344,334 vehicles in 1919 (20.8% of the domestic market), in 1921 it sold only 193,275 (12.8%).[2] In the meantime Ford, with 1,518,000 vehicles sold, had moved up from 40.1% to 55.7% of the home market. Buick, which of all the General Motors divisions suffered the least, dropped from 115,401 in 1920 to 80,122 in 1921.[3] The high-priced Cadillac was harder hit, declining from 19,790 to 11,130.

Nearly all the car-making divisions—Chevrolet, Oakland, Oldsmobile, Sheridan, and Scripps-Booth—competed with one another and with Buick in much the same middle-level market. None was producing volume enough to make a profit in 1921. The lowest-priced General Motors car, the Chevrolet "490," sold from $795 to $1,375, or for $300 more than Ford's Model T, while the "FB" model priced between $1,350 and $2,075 competed with all the other General Motors models except the Cadillac. Both models suffered from weak axles and an unreliable clutch. Chevrolet sales had dropped from 129,525 in 1920 to 68,000 in 1921 (4.0% of the market). In order to use up its inventory and still sell its cars, Chevrolet had to set its prices at a level that caused it to lose about $50 on each car sold. Neither the Sheridan nor the Scripps-Booth division produced enough vehicles to achieve any significant economies of scale. Both relied on other divisions for their motors. Sheridan used the Chevrolet "FB," and Scripps-Booth the Oakland 6-cylinder. Neither of these engines was of good quality. A new engine had been designed for the Oakland line, but the business recession had brought a halt to the construction of the factory to produce it. Partly because of the existing engine's poor performance, Oakland sales fell from 34,839 to 11,812 between 1920 and 1921. Oldsmobile continued to dissipate its energies by producing not only a 4- and 6-, but also an 8-cylinder model, none of which was of the quality of the Buick. Since its output fell from 41,127 in 1920 to 18,978 in 1921, Olds no longer had the volume necessary to produce a profit on any of the three models.

As Pierre turned his attention to product line, he was bombarded by advice from all sides. His division managers, staff men, executives, and even the bankers (through management consultants) expressed different opinions about what should be done. As the man who had to make the final decision, Pierre felt particularly handicapped by his lack of experience in the industry. His work at Du Pont had served him well in evaluating the proposed organizational and accounting procedures, but the production and the marketing of explosives had little in common with the making and selling of automobiles. Pierre listened to all points of view, often writing to Kettering and others for information. Normally he relied on the reports of small *ad hoc* committees of senior executives which he appointed to study specific problems. It was not until September, however, a full nine months after he had taken office, that he had clearly decided in his own mind what should constitute General Motors basic product lines.

Before then, however, he, Sloan, Raskob, and Haskell had made a number of important decisions about what General Motors should produce. On one of the first of these there was little debate. The Executive Committee and the division managers quickly voted against a policy of backwards integration beyond parts and accessories to the control of basic supplies— a policy which Durant had favored and in which Henry Ford was at that moment actively engaged. The decision was most clearly expressed in the Annual Report for 1920, which Pierre completed and signed on March 26, 1921.

> Thus: a comparatively small portion of the total tires produced are consumed by the automobile manufacturer, the larger percentage being sold directly to users of cars for replacement purposes; the greater part of the production of sheets and other forms of steel is consumed by trades other than the automotive industry; therefore investment in these fields has not been made. By pursuit of this policy, General Motors Corporation has become firmly entrenched in lines that relate directly to the construction of the car, truck and tractor, but has not invested in general industries of which a comparatively small part of the products is consumed in the manufacture of cars.[4]

As a result of this decision General Motors would not build a great plant with fully integrated operations such as Henry Ford was then constructing on the banks of the River Rouge.

By the same decision, however, General Motors would retain nearly all the Parts and Accessories divisions that Durant had collected. Although several executives had urged selling some of these divisions, Pierre strongly favored having an assured supply of all items essential in assembling an automobile. Day and Zimmermann, the management consulting firm hired by Seward Prosser and by J. P. Morgan and Company to evaluate General Motors prospects, was lukewarm about retaining them. While the consultants finally decided that most of these divisions would in the long run be advantageous to the corporation, their report recommended that they be "wholly divorced from the General Motors Corporation in as far as operations are concerned."[5] Pierre and his Executive Committee, however, argued that the new organizational structure and financial controls would make such a separation unnecessary, and the bankers quickly agreed.

There was, on the other hand, much more debate over retaining the nonautomotive divisions, particularly Frigidaire and Samson Tractor. Sloan, Haskell, and McLaughlin, head of Canadian operations, argued strongly for selling the refrigerator division.[6] Pratt, however, urged that

Frigidaire be handed over to Delco Light which, under the competent management of Richard H. Grant, had started to move into the production and sale of washing machines and other household appliances.[7] The Day and Zimmermann report backed Pratt's proposal. So in April Pierre and Sloan asked Grant and J. P. D. Fiske, the current manager of Frigidaire, to review the product's prospects, particularly the development of new models, including one with an air-cooled refrigeration compressor.[8] They were to recommend whether that division should be turned over to Delco, or liquidated. Since Delco had some excess manufacturing capacity and an extensive sales organization, the two men recommended, and the Executive Committee approved, that Frigidaire be managed by Delco.[9] In a short time the new refrigerators were bringing General Motors a satisfactory profit.

The decision on the tractor was slower in coming. In March Pierre asked Haskell to analyze the tractor situation for the Executive Committee.[10] Dissatisfied with Haskell's report completed in early May, which focused largely on prices, Pierre asked Sloan to continue the investigation. In July he requested William Coyne, still a Du Pont vice-president, to inspect the plants and to talk to the executives at Janesville, Wisconsin, and at the West Coast factory.[11] Sloan, using Coyne's data, made a detailed report in September in which he recommended that the tractor business should be dropped unless Kettering's staff could develop within a year a small, tough, inexpensive "utility" tractor.[12] Even if such a tractor could be produced, Sloan warned, its marketing would be costly. To compete with International Harvester, John Deere, and other farm implement firms would undoubtedly require the development of an expensive supplementary line of agricultural implements.

Continuing losses in a depressed agricultural economy finally convinced Pierre in 1922 to liquidate the tractor division.[13] He did, however, encourage Kettering to continue research work on the tractor and maintain a skeleton organization at the former Samson plant at Janesville.[14] He agreed with Kettering that such work was of great value in improving the automobile. He believed Kettering was quite right in pointing out to Sloan, when the latter suggested stopping the development program, that information acquired from it about carburetion alone covered the cost of the work. Pierre was also interested in developing the tractor as a hedge against a depression. If the demand for passenger cars declined, and Pierre warned Sloan that at some time this would certainly occur, the corporation could use some surplus capacity to make tractors.

Pierre found the least agreement of all on the most important of product policies—the types of passenger cars that General Motors should produce. From the first, the great point of contention was Kettering's air-cooled engine. On his trip to Dayton during the first few days of his presidency Pierre had become convinced that the innovation would revive the weak divisions. In January Pierre conferred at length with Sloan and Zimmer-schied, the general manager of Chevrolet, about the possibility of immedi-ately replacing the Chevrolet "490" with an air-cooled motor.[15] Sloan and Zimmerschied, supported by McLaughlin and other operating men, argued that such a car could not be ready for the model year, which began the following August. Moreover, Chevrolet had huge stocks of materials and supplies for existing models, inventories that should be used up. A month later the General Motors president discussed the possibility of replacing the Oldsmobile's obsolete engine with an air-cooled 6-cylinder.[16] Sloan was even more skeptical about this proposal than he was about the one for Chevrolet.

With these different points of view in mind, Pierre brought Kettering, Mott, Zimmerschied, and Bassett of Buick into an Executive Committee meeting on February 23, 1921.[17] The committee first approved Bassett's proposal to develop a water-cooled 4-cylinder engine for a less expensive Buick. Kettering then outlined an ambitious plan for putting a 4-cylinder air-cooled car into production at Chevrolet beginning the following August. He anticipated an output of 300 cars a day by January 1, 1922. Zimmer-schied again wanted to wait for the next model year. He not only had inventory to use up but also his engineers were removing the "mechanical defects" and were designing a new body for the existing "490." Pierre, who was becoming convinced by the inventory argument, asked the Chevrolet manager to give him a detailed report of these plans for the Chevrolet "490" during the next model year and directed Kettering to "proceed with the design and construction of the 6-cylinder air-cooled car."[18]

At this same time, Pierre, the Executive Committee, and the division managers were discussing the merits of continuing or dropping car lines in the three other unprofitable divisions. In March the discussion centered around the Sheridan and the Scripps-Booth. Sloan was certain that both divisions should be scrapped.[19] McLaughlin felt that both were producing well-designed cars with a good potential market.

The Executive Committee wavered back and forth. On March 16 it decided to discontinue the Sheridan; ten days later, after a convincing presentation by the division's manager, the committee rescinded its earlier decision. On April 6 it decided that the Sheridan should build a 4- and a 6-cylinder car and discontinue the 8, even though the division managers in the Operations Committee had agreed that only the 8 would sell.

To Pierre this decision was the last straw. He had become completely exasperated with this kind of *ad hoc* decision-making. The general princi-ples needed to be outlined and agreed upon, as they had been on organiza-tional and financial matters. Once the senior executives had decided on the general product policy, then the divisional products could be fitted in an orderly way into the larger program. So Pierre, at that very meeting, appointed a special committee consisting of Mott, Sloan, Bassett, Zimmerschied, Kettering, and Hawkins (of the Sales Staff) to study and report on "the future manufacturing lines of General Motors."[20]

This committee made its preliminary report to the Executive Committee on May 4. After a great deal of discussion, Pierre and the committee approved the final report on June 9.[21] It was one of the most important in the corporation's history. "The recommendations outlined, the basic product policy of the corporation, a market strategy, and some first principles," Sloan later wrote, "all together they expressed the concept of the business."[22] One such principle was that the primary object of the corporation was not just to make cars but to make money, and that the return on the investment was to be the criterion for decisions about individual products and the product line as a whole. A second principle was that the corporation's earnings and its future as a profit-making institution depended on increasing the value and utility of its vehicles to its customers and on decreasing the cost of producing and selling them.

To achieve these broad objectives the number of models offered needed to be reduced, and each model must be placed in its own distinct price range. The ideal line would have a car in each price level, ranging from a low-price, high-volume car able to draw customers away from Henry Ford's Model T to the high-price, high-quality, low-volume range in which Cadillac then sold. If possible, the divisions should not overlap or duplicate their offerings within a single price range. Without such duplication or models one division would be able to handle all General Motors volume in each price market. Economies of scale could be further increased by cooperation between the divisions so that they all could use many of the same parts, accessories, supplies, and materials, and so that new ideas, procedures, and technological innovations could be very quickly spread from one to another.

The report proposed that General Motors offer cars in six different price ranges: (I) $450–600, (II) $600–900, (III) $900–1200, (IV) $1200–1700, (V) $1700–2500, (VI) $2500–3500. At that time the seven car-making divisions produced nine different lines, since the two Chevrolet models, the "490" and the "FB," and two of the Olds models, the 6- and the 8-cylinder, were basically different price markets. Moreover, no General Motors car sold for less than $600. The report, therefore, called for a new car to fill in the lowest price range where General Motors products had not yet penetrated. It further proposed the elimination of four existing automobile lines in the middle range. The line that the committee recommended for each of the six price ranges, going from lowest to highest, was Chevrolet, Oakland, a new Buick 4, a Buick 6, Oldsmobile, then Cadillac.

The report then outlined a market strategy based on this basic product policy of bracketing the market. The corporation must use quality as its primary competitive weapon. With improved quality the cars could be priced at the top of their respective ranges. Better quality would then attract customers who were shopping in that price market, and, at the same time, its price could draw those who usually purchased in the next higher range. In competing with Ford the strategy had special significance. In the lowest-price class, Ford had a complete monopoly. His power was suggested by the fact that Ford had made more than 55% of all the cars sold in the United States in 1921, while Chevrolet produced only 4%. General Motors' greatest competitive hope lay, then, in making a quality car that could sell for about $500 or about $100 more than the average Model T.

Pierre du Pont wholeheartedly supported this report. One immediate result of its quick approval by the Executive Committee was the liquidation of the Sheridan and Scripps-Booth divisions.[23] Another was to approve Bassett's production plans for his 4-cylinder Buick. Because the report made quality the key to General Motors' marketing strategy, another significant result was to give even stronger reason for the rapid development of the air-cooled engine.

## Improving the Product

The air-cooled car, which Kettering believed was then ready for mass production, certainly promised, as nothing else did, excellent performance and low production costs.[24] It was 200 pounds lighter than any of its competitors. It required much less fuel, and could not freeze in the winter or overheat in the summer. For a given horsepower, the air-cooled engine provided more speed, more comfort and safety than a comparable water-cooled engine, and it had 25% fewer replacement parts. Kettering was certain that because of its lightness, fewer parts, lack of radiator and plumbing system, this car and its engine could be mass produced more cheaply than that of any other competitor, including Ford's Model T.

Given the obvious importance of the air-cooled engine to the new marketing strategy, Sloan had authorized Kettering to set up a small pilot plant in Dayton to manufacture 25 engines a day of both 4- and 6-cylinder types.[25] The major decision on how best to introduce the air-cooled engine into the General Motors line had to wait, however, until July when Sloan and Raskob returned from a long-planned business trip to Europe. On July 26 Pierre, Sloan, Raskob, and Haskell (this was one of the last trips Haskell was to make as the fourth member of the Executive Committee) took the train to Dayton, where they met Mott and Kettering. The latter exuded enthusiasm and optimism. "It is the greatest thing ever produced in the automobile world," he happily told Pierre.[26]

Again the debate centered on when to begin production of the new air-cooled models at Chevrolet and at Oakland. Kettering and Pierre wanted it to be as quickly as possible. As to Chevrolet, Mott and Sloan again emphasized the inventory problem, while Kettering recalled Zimmerschied's reluctance to move quickly. At Oakland, the picture was more promising. Kettering reported that the new general manager, George Hannum, had shown great interest in the engine and would be more than willing to have Kettering develop at Dayton the air-cooled 6 during the coming model year. The group then traveled to Detroit to confer with Hannum. There the Executive Committee agreed to go ahead on the 6 and hold back on the 4.[27] Once Oakland had moved into production, the Chevrolet executives could only profit from Hannum's experience.

Pierre, however, remained troubled by the decision to hold back on the 4-cylinder. After all, Chevrolet had the critical position in the new product lineup. Early in September, therefore, Pierre did what he had not done before at General Motors, and rarely did at Du Pont: he drew up a major report entirely on his own. He completed the report on September 8 and presented it to Sloan and Raskob on September 13.[28] In the report Pierre outlined emphatically and explicitly his views on product policy, particularly the changes still needed in its product lines. He began by emphasizing the need for improving the quality of the corporation's cars and for lowering their production costs. He underlined, as he had done in his first meeting as president, the importance of having all new designs carefully tested at the Dayton laboratories. He wanted standardized reports sent to the Executive Committee, and also to the division managers involved, on all special tests as well as on the regular 25,000-mile one. Once a design had been accepted, changes that might "raise the car to a higher [price] class" must not be permitted.[29]

His suggestions for the different divisions were quite precise. For Buick he proposed only that work be begun to find ways of obtaining more economic fuel consumption and of improving the parts so as to reduce its high replacement rate. For Cadillac his suggestion was broader. He presented detailed statistics to show that the existing volume in the price range of $3,000 and above was too small a one on which to build a profitable volume operation. Second, he wanted to modify the earlier proposal of the special committee on product policy that Oldsmobile fill the price gap between Cadillac and Buick. Since Cadillac's organization was far more efficient than that at Olds, Pierre proposed that the Cadillac Division increase its volume by developing a model to sell at between $2,000 and $2,500. For this purpose the Oldsmobile plant at Lansing should be turned over to Cadillac, and the Oldsmobile Division then be liquidated.

The other two weak divisions, Pierre insisted, must move into the production of the air-cooled car even more quickly than had been planned. He reaffirmed the decision made with Hannum at Detroit to have the 6-cylinder manufactured "in a small way" at Dayton, starting in November. He now wanted the new car to be exhibited at the annual automobile show in New

York in January and then go into production at the Oakland plant in February. At Chevrolet the "490" should "not be continued in production beyond the time necessary to reduce inventory and commitments." Therefore, he wanted an immediate decision on when production of the new model would begin. As current information indicated that inventories should be completely used up by July 1922, he proposed that the manufacture of the air-cooled car at Chevrolet's Flint plant, with its capacity of 25,000 cars a year, should begin on May 1, 1922, at the latest.

To achieve this goal Pierre carefully outlined a development program to be carried on jointly by Dayton and Flint. It included the 25,000-mile and other road tests to be made by both organizations. For all his commitment to the new car, Pierre heeded Sloan's words of caution. As "it seems wise to have another alternative open to Chevrolet in case of unforeseen complications or delay in the permanent use of air cooling," he recommended the development at Dayton of a 4-cylinder engine using a new Muir type of water-cooling system which Zimmerschied's engineers were adapting to the needs of the "490." But, he added, "this alternative should not be permitted to interfere in any way with the program of work on the air cooled car."

As long as Pierre included the alternative of developing a water-cooled engine, Sloan was quite willing to accept the president's proposal for Chevrolet and Oakland. On the other hand, he felt strongly that the Oldsmobile should continue in the General Motors line. It had a well-known name. Its national sales organization was a valuable asset. After much debate, Pierre reluctantly agreed. By September 20 the president had reviewed the contents of his report with all the division managers concerned, except Hardy of Olds.[30] Zimmerschied and Hannum agreed to the suggestions for getting the air-cooled car into production. On October 20 the Executive Committee formally approved Pierre's program for both the 4- and the 6-cylinder air-cooled engine.[31] At the same time Pierre agreed with Sloan that the committee "instruct" the Oldsmobile Division to develop a car with a 6-cylinder water-cooled engine to sell for between $1,900 and $2,300.

By the decision of this meeting of October 11, Oakland was to stop production of the water-cooled engine by December 1, less than six weeks away. In February the division would begin the production of the air-cooled 6 at its Pontiac plant at the rate of 100 cars a day, increasing its output during the following months. Pierre eagerly awaited the first reports. "Now that we are at the point of production of the new cars," he wrote Kettering, "I am beginning to feel like a small boy when the long expected circus posters begin to appear on the fences, and to wonder how each part of the circus is to appear and what act I will like best."[32]

On November 8 came the disappointing news. There would be no circus. Hannum wrote Pierre that the model sent from Dayton to Pontiac had failed to pass its road test.[33] The changes needed to make the car satisfactory would take at least six months. To bridge the time lag between the shutdown of production of the old model on December 1 and the new target date of the air-cooled, Oakland's general manager had decided to bring out a complete new line of water-cooled engines that would go into production in January. Both Sloan and Pierre were taken aback that Hannum had made the decision without consulting them, but, since it was done, they felt that they could do little but ratify it.

At the meeting Pierre called to decide what to do next, Sloan argued, and Bassett agreed, that it had been a mistake to start the air-cooled production with the more complex 6-cylinder engine.[34] The group then decided to send engineers and cost accountants from the Advisory Staff to determine whether a 4-cylinder could be built for the price Kettering had estimated and whether a 4-cylinder might be substituted for the 6 in the Oakland. At the end of the meeting Pierre, Sloan, and Mott wrote a note of confidence to Kettering. For that engineer was even more shaken by the first failure of his innovation than was Pierre. They had no doubts, they told him, of his ability "to whip all the problems in connection with the development of our proposed air-cooled car."[35]

Two weeks later, on December 15, the Executive Committee made its final decision on the car lines for 1922.[36] Pierre, Sloan, and Raskob approved of price reductions proposed by Buick, Chevrolet, and Oldsmobile. Then they turned to the question of the air-cooled car. Pierre reminded the other two of the desperate need for the new car. Chevrolet was losing from $1.0 million to $1.5 million a month on its old model, and Oakland was not much better off. Together the two divisions should be making $1.5 million. The corporation was, therefore, losing approximately $3.0 million a month waiting for the development of the air-cooled engine.

The president then suggested that the committee accept Hannum's proposal to bring out a water-cooled line at Oakland and turn the air-cooled car over to Chevrolet. He proposed that Bassett and Zimmerschied go with the chief engineers of Chevrolet, Oakland, and Buick to Dayton to review in detail the major problems involved with the air-cooled engine. The divisional engineers would stay in Dayton until the 25,000-mile road tests were successfully completed on the 4-cylinder job. Daily progress checks and all reports of tests would be sent to New York and Detroit as well as to the general managers of Chevrolet and Oakland. At the same time the three engineers would be making plans for mass-producing the air-cooled engine at Chevrolet by September 1922. If the 4-cylinder engine performed well for this division, they could then plan to use it in the Oakland. The Executive Committee approved of Pierre's suggestions and agreed to discontinue the Chevrolet "FB" without developing the Muir water-cooled engine as Pierre had earlier proposed. By the end of 1921 the production of the air-cooled car was still almost a year away. Chevrolet would be the great testing ground. Pierre had not lost faith in what he still considered to be the most important technological development at General Motors.

During 1921 Pierre encouraged other innovations besides the air-cooled engine.[37] He supported Kettering's work on improving performance of trucks and taxicabs.[38] More significant was his continuing interest in the development of all-weather automboile finishes and high octane, "no knock," gasoline.[39] Both innovations were greatly needed in the automobile industry. In 1921 cars were finished with paints or varnishes that normally peeled off if the vehicle were not kept under cover in a garage, barn, or shed. Moreover, the drying of paints and varnishes was the slowest part in the mass production of the automobile, often taking from two to four weeks; this intensified the manufacturer's inventory problems. At this time, large volume producers—Ford, Dodge, and General Motors—used only black enamel on their cars because of the drying problem. A fast-drying, all-weather finish would be of great value to both the producer and consumer, particularly if it could be had in different colors. A major defect in the gasoline of the time was its "knock," which reduced compression and put a severe strain on the engine. It resulted from the gasoline-air mixture's burning too fast in the cylinder. One result was that engines had to be designed with low-compression ratios. In collaboration with the Du Pont research men, Kettering had been working since 1919 on ways to eliminate the "knock," which, besides producing a better gasoline, would permit engines to be designed with higher compressions. Pierre du Pont did much to encourage development of a higher-compression engine, and was a key instigator of work on developing "no knock" gasoline.

Pierre's search for an improved finish came directly out of his interest in the air-cooled car. In August 1921 he wrote Irénée:

> On thinking over General Motors affairs, especially the air cooled car, it has occurred to me that the major cost of an automobile investment lies in the provision of a garage or storage place, and for the person who drives himself much trouble and time is consumed in taking the car to and from the garage.
>     Why not a garageless car?
>     A closed car covered with weather proof material, and air cooled, could be left at the door at any time, thus proving much more useful to the average owner of a small car than the apparatus which must be carefully housed against the weather. The above suggests improved fabrikoid for the purpose, either in shape of curtains for an open car or covering the outside of a closed car.[40]

In reply to a similar letter that Pierre had sent the same day to General Motors research laboratories, Kettering pointed out that Fabrikoid deteriorated rapidly in the sun and so would have to be painted. A baked enamel was still probably a better answer. "Any work which can be done on the paint subject, and enamel, would surely be of great value," he added.[41] After further discussion with Irénée and Kettering, Pierre dropped the idea of Fabrikoid, and the attention of both General Motors and Du Pont turned to fast-drying enamels and varnishes.[42] In April 1922 he sent Kettering another idea on the same subject. This time he suggested an "oxidized metal car" with a body made of steel so processed that its natural finish would be enough to withstand the weather.[43]

The solution was already under way in the Du Pont laboratories. In July 1920, largely by chance, there occurred in one of the laboratories a chemical reaction which created a lacquer with the qualities desired for automobile finishes. By fall of 1922 the development of this fast-drying, tough finish had progressed so far and its prospects seemed so promising that Pierre tried to get the Du Pont Company to give General Motors an exclusive contract for its use.[44] This proposal Irénée emphatically turned down. In 1923 the first cars using the new lacquer, given the trade name of Duco, came off the production line. This was the 1924 Oakland "True Blue" model. In 1924 Cadillac was beginning to use Duco on a large scale while Chevrolet and Buick were still experimenting with its use. By 1925 Duco was being used by all the major automobile producers.

Pierre had a less direct role in the development of the improved "no knock" gasoline.[45] Nevertheless, the new gasoline was a direct result of the partnership between Du Pont and General Motors which Pierre had promoted. By 1921 the project, which Pierre had studiously encouraged since 1917, was gaining momentum under the direction of Thomas Midgely. When Midgely decided that iodine was the best ingredient for eliminating the knock, Pierre had the Du Pont Purchasing Department give him a report on the availability of that product.[46] Since these reports showed that existing sources were inadequate, Midgely turned to bromide from salt. Finally, by the end of 1922 he had succeeded in developing a tetraethyl lead solution that did the trick. General Motors and Standard Oil of New Jersey formed the Ethyl Corporation, each owning 50% of its stock, to market the new product. The Du Pont Company then received the contract to produce the ethyl solution. Pierre approved, supported, and kept a watchful eye on this three-company venture in its formative stages.[47]

By December 1921, the completion of Pierre's first year as president, the General Motors product line seemed to be shaping up well. The executives had agreed on a clear-cut market strategy and product policy. To have cars that would sell on the expensive side of each price range, the corporation's senior executives and its divisional and general engineering and research staffs were concentrating their energies on finding more durable and attractive finishes, on developing a better gasoline, on improving mechanical performance, and, above all, on getting a less costly, more efficient air-cooled engine into mass production.

*Organizational Adjustment*

In reviewing the experience of the preceding year, Alfred Sloan decided that the shaping of the new product line, and particularly the development of the air-cooled engine, had revealed weaknesses in General Motors' organizational structure. The corporation was still too decentralized, he told Pierre and Raskob. The divisions still had too much autonomy and the general office still had too little authority to permit General Motors to get the maximum results from its combined resources. The situation reflected itself in two ways. First, the Executive Committee (and for practical purposes, now consisting of only Pierre, Raskob, and Sloan, as Haskell's health prevented him from attending all but a very few meetings after the fall of 1921)[48] was too much involved in operating details. As a result, the collective role of the three men—as differentiated from their individual functions as president, chairman of the Finance Committee, and vice-president in charge of Operations—was becoming confused and cloudy. In the second place, cooperation between the general Advisory Staff and the operating divisions was still sadly lacking.

On December 24, 1921, ten days after he and Sloan had made the final decision on the air-cooled program, Pierre received a long memorandum from the vice-president in charge of operations, analyzing the corporation's most significant current problems and proposing remedies. "The moment has been reached," Sloan began, "when we should have a general discussion on the general subject of Organization. I think that this is the most important thing before us at the moment."[49] First, he proposed to enlarge the small committee set up to meet the crisis by adding executives with operating experience. In addition, Sloan wanted to appoint an operative head "with the authority to act" (i.e., to give orders directly to the operating divisions), and to strengthen the power of the general executives. On the matter of staff and line coordination he hoped to develop procedures that would encourage direct contact between the staff and operating executives carrying out the same functions; that is, to bring together divisional sales, engineering, and research executives with those involved with comparable functions on the staff. At the moment the staff men rarely saw operating men other than the general managers and their immediate subordinates. "The policy of doing business exclusively with the General Manager is not only unsafe, in my judgment," Sloan told Pierre, "but absolutely dangerous and should not be further tolerated." This was true not only in research and development, where the air-cooled engine's problems made clear a lack of cooperation between Kettering's staff and the divisions; it was also the case in sales, where the division managers were not making use of Norval Hawkins' excellent ideas and plans, and in the area of plant engineering and construction.[50]

In a long memorandum attached to the letter of December 24 to Pierre, Sloan went into detail on each of his two main points. On the first, he stressed that the Executive Committee should confine itself to "principles . . . properly developed and thoughtfully carried out rather than to constitute itself as it now is as group management. . . ."[51] During the previous few months, Pierre could only agree that he, Sloan, and Raskob had been involved in setting production schedules and deciding on prices and other operating details. For this task, Pierre did not have to be reminded, neither he nor Raskob had much useful background. So Sloan recommended that Mott, McLaughlin, and, in time, Bassett be added to the committee and that the committee avoid operating details and concentrate on the formation of policy. He further urged that whoever had charge of operations "should be designated with real authority to be used in case of emergency." Such an operating head should be the president. If Pierre did not consider this plan "feasible," Sloan wanted an executive vice-president appointed with such power. Here Sloan specifically had in mind Hannum's abrupt cancellation of the air-cooled 6 and the Executive Committee's inability to react quickly to this decision.[52]

As to the assignment of the other senior executives, he urged that Mott should not continue to be saddled with the job of being the director in Detroit of the Advisory Staff as well as the general executive for the Car and Truck Group. He also protested against Pierre's habit of bringing Bassett to Detroit to assist the Executive Committee in making decisions about the air-cooled car and other matters. Bassett was responsible for General Motors' largest money-maker and must stay on the job. "It is far better that the rest of General Motors be scrapped than any chances be taken with Buick's earning power."

On analyzing the line and staff relations, Sloan began by reviewing what he called "the Dayton situation." The great error made in the development of the air-cooled car, Sloan maintained, was in the failure to define and specify the role of Dayton and the role of the divisions in this critical work. The engine, he was certain, would have been much further along if Kettering had completed its development, next had had it tested by outside experts, and only then turned it over to the divisions to produce. "Advanced engineering always, like advanced everything else, brings down upon it the discredit of ridicule of minds who cannot see so far." For this reason, Sloan continued, "such engineering must be demonstrated in such a way that facts must be accepted rather than theory." However, since the damage was done, and the divisional engineers now had a deep distrust of the research man at Dayton, the need to assure better line and staff contact was more essential than ever before.

The same was true for sales. Hawkins, drawing on his highly successful years at Ford, had worked out a series of programs on advertising, trade-in policy, sales methods, car maintenance and repair, and dealer organizations.[53] But the divisions had paid little or no attention to these suggestions. Three months earlier Pierre had given a talk at a joint meeting of the divisional sales managers and the Executive Committee to impress upon the sales force the need for cooperation among the several different divisions and between the divisions and the Advisory Staff. He had emphasized, too, that the divisions must carry on comparable sales policies.[54] Yet little had resulted.

As a first step in "defining the relations" between the divisions and the staff, Sloan turned to a suggestion that Raskob had made a few days earlier.[55] Raskob had compared the functions of the Advisory Staff with those of the Financial Staff. Each could be considered to have valuable auditing duties. Competent executives welcomed the financial auditing. Why then, Sloan argued, should division executives not approve and appreciate one that checked "the quality of its product, the efficiency of its Sales and Engineering Departments"? Such an audit, in Sloan's opinion, would make it "not only a privilege but a duty of the staff sections of Dayton and Detroit to familiarize themselves with the respective engineering, sales, construction and purchasing sections of each division." The staff men would report to the responsible divisional executives irregularities or areas for improvement. The Advisory Staff would remain, like the auditors' office, only advisory. The general executives in Detroit and New York as well as the divisional general managers would have "greater assurance as to the efficiency and effectiveness of the different functions of every different operation."

In reading over this report Pierre was impressed, as always, by the clarity of Sloan's analysis and the logic of his suggestions. He did not take offense at the tactful but clear criticism of the way Pierre had handled some of his presidential duties. He quite agreed. After all, he had been through similar discussions with Coleman and his Du Pont associates on the importance of keeping the Executive Committee out of operational detail. In fact, the massive internal reorganization that had just been completed at the Du Pont Company had been sparked by a similar need to avoid day-to-day group management by the senior committee.

Nevertheless, Pierre moved cautiously in making changes at the top, possibly because he may have been thinking of retiring as soon as the product line was settled. If Sloan took his place, he, not Pierre, should make the selection of the top committee. Until then, until he was sure the corporation had recovered, he wanted to keep firm control of top-level decisions. In any case, Pierre did not put Mott and Fred Fisher on the Executive Committee until the following autumn.[56] Even then, Fisher went on the committee primarily in order to assure better communications with the Fisher Body Company. Nor did Pierre relieve Mott of his duties as the Detroit head of the Advisory Staff, although this was probably because Sloan was unable to recommend a good replacement. Nor did he give Sloan the title of executive vice-president, which Sloan so clearly wanted.

Pierre did follow some of Sloan's suggestions. He stopped bringing Bassett to Detroit and allowed him to concentrate his attention on Buick. He also gave Sloan informally the authority he wanted over the division managers. It was to be used, however, only in case of emergency. And he did his best to keep the Executive Committee out of operating detail. Sloan, for example, was given, as vice-president in charge of operations, the authority to approve prices.[57] Pierre further wholeheartedly approved of giving the Staff Sections auditing functions and of establishing direct contact between executives on the staff and in the divisions concerned with the same activity—sales, research, and the like. Finally, he agreed with one of Sloan's earlier suggestions—which was to send to General Motors officers, particularly the "minor executives," who were less aware of organizational needs and concepts, a detailed explanation of the principles and precepts behind the new organization plan.

In January 1922 Sloan drew up such a document which, after modifications by Pierre and Raskob, was sent to General Motors executives over Pierre's signature. It was an impressive piece of work. Certainly one of the first treatises ever written on the administration of the modern decentralized enterprise, it fully expressed Pierre's views as well as Sloan's.[58] Sloan began on a historical note. A small firm producing a single line of products had really only one form of organization available to it, that is, functional departments, coordinated by a central office. But when a company expanded in size, especially through purchases and mergers, and diversified its product line, its organizational needs became exceedingly complex. It then had two choices available: it could remain "centralized" by having a single large central office administer functional departments that managed one function throughout the whole giant enterprise; or it could take the path that General Motors had chosen and be "decentralized," with autonomous divisions whose functional departments were not directly under executives in the general office—instead, the divisional managers ran their own functional units within policies and guidelines for the operating divisions set by a general office.

Sloan then rephrased the two basic principles under which General Motors was managed: "1. The chief executive of each operation controls the administration of all functions within that particular operation. . . . 2. Certain central co-ordinating and controlling functions are provided to insure a logical development of the Corporation's activities as a whole and for the better protection of its employed capital." He then made a distinction between administration and policy-making. "An organization based on the above two principles represents, therefore, decentralized control as to the administration of policies *with* centralized control as to their establishment, all made possible through proper co-ordination of the individual operations with a general or central administration."[59] The board and its committees would determine policy and the division managers would administer it. The top committees, for example, would not set specific prices but would work out price ranges in which the divisions could sell. They should set such standards of performance wanted in a car and the ways to test these, but they should not try to pass on the technical designs of individual models.

In defining the role of the executive in the general office, Sloan gave the executive vice-president (Pierre changed this title back to the existing one of vice-president in charge of operations) "complete authority and responsibility for the administration of operations." The vice-president in charge of operations, working with the group executive and the division managers involved, would then carry out the policies set by the board and its senior committees. The division manager was still to have the final say. Only in cases of emergency could the vice-president in charge of operations order a division manager to act. Clearly, however, Sloan had decided, after a year's experience in the general office, that the purely advisory status of senior executive officers was no longer valid and that at least one officer in the general office should have line authority. In defining the advisory and new auditing functions of the general staff, Sloan, however, continued to stress that "the Advisory Staff had no authority whatsoever over any function of any operation, its sole duties being of an advisory and auditing character."

Actual experience thus brought modification to the original structure. Properly enough, the creator of the structure was the first to suggest the changes. Nevertheless, even though the vice-president in charge of operations had seen the need for the changes and the president had approved of all of them, except for enlarging the Executive Committee, basic difficulties continued. The president and the Executive Committee fell back into making operational decisions and the line and the staff officers failed to settle their differences. The reason was again the air-cooled engine and the growing problem of getting it into production. A final decision on that engine would not come for a year and a half. Only after that decision was made would the final adjustments in the organizational structure of General Motors be fully worked out.

One organizational change did, however, come almost immediately. Early in 1922 Karl Zimmerschied had a complete physical and psychological breakdown.[60] The task of trying to meet Chevrolet's current engineering and production problems while introducing a radical new car at the same time proved too much for him. Pierre was fortunate to be able to get just at this moment the services of William S. Knudsen, who for many years had been performing so expertly as Henry Ford's production manager. In the years after World War I, Knudsen, like so many of Ford's most able executives, had become increasingly distressed by his chief's high-handed procedures. Not long after he left that company, Mott and Sloan convinced him in February 1922 to join General Motors' Advisory Staff as a production expert. In this capacity his first job with General Motors was to make a report for Mott on the problems involving the production of the air-cooled engine. Fully appreciating its value as General Motors' secret weapon against Ford, he urged that production begin immediately.

Pierre, delighted by this report, decided to give Knudsen Zimmerschied's job. Since Knudsen knew little or nothing about Chevrolet's overall management, Pierre gave him the title of vice-president in charge of operations at Chevrolet, becoming himself general manager as well as president of the division.[61] This move certainly came as a result of Zimmerschied's breakdown and Knudsen's availability. But it also meant that Pierre as well as Sloan was going to remain involved with operating decisions, at least until the air-cooled car was fully in production.

### The Continuing Issue of the Air-Cooled Car

Pierre considered the new arrangement at Chevrolet only temporary. If the air-cooled car was as successful as Pierre, Kettering, and Knudsen were sure it would be, then Knudsen would in a very short time be general manager at Chevrolet. But success was slow in coming. Even this most accomplished automobile production man began to have increasing difficulties in getting the new car to the market. Until the summer of 1923 the air-cooled car overshadowed all other matters of executive concern at General Motors.

Pierre's first request of Knudsen was that he formulate a long-term production program for Chevrolet on the basis of recent Executive Committee decisions. Late in February 1922, just before Knudsen made his report, Sloan, supported by the Car Division managers, had again cautioned Pierre that there was "nothing before the Corporation or the Chevrolet Division . . . to justify the positive conclusion that the air-cooled car should be put into production on the date specified," that is, September 1922.[62] Sloan had further proposed "a second line of defense," that of improving Chevrolet's existing water-cooled engine, a proposal which Pierre himself had suggested in October, but which had been dropped in the December 15 decision. Becaused Kettering's staff was so completely tied up in the development of the air-cooled engine, Sloan authorized the hiring of outside engineering consultants to carry out the new work on the water-cooled engine.

On the basis of these modifications of the December 15 decision, Knudsen outlined for Pierre's approval a program of "tooling up" for the manufacture of the 4-cylinder air-cooled to begin production at the rate of

10 cars a day on September 15, 1922, and to reach a rate of 50 a day by the end of the year.[63] Pierre, Raskob, and Sloan, and then the Finance Committee approved of Knudsen's request for $500,000 to begin work even before the road tests on the air-cooled engine were completed. At the same meeting of the Executive Committee on April 7, Pierre convinced his colleagues to call the new engine a "copper cooled" one because of the distinctive copper fins used to draw off the engine's heat; this, he felt, would clearly differentiate it from other air-cooled engines. In May the Executive Committee committed itself still further on the new car by directing McLaughlin to begin work on its production and sale in Canada and abroad.[64]

Since he had so emphatically urged these commitments, Pierre was delighted at the end of May to receive Kettering's glowing report of the car's 20,000-mile road test. "The valves and all the bearings were in perfect condition," the research chief wrote. "There was no carbon deposit in the motor and the oil mileage had been in the neighborhood of a thousand to twelve hundred miles per gallon. In all road tests here, we never have seen anything like this. . . ."[65] The divisional executives, Kettering crowed, simply did not appreciate what an impressive technological innovation the new engine in the car represented. They were "looking upon this as being a slight advance over the present thing instead of being a tremendous asset." On the basis of this performance, he advocated "a more extensive building of cars" than was planned and urged Pierre to come to Dayton to see the achievement for himself. Pierre did, and was more certain than ever that the car was General Motors' best hope.[66]

June brought more good news. The automobile market was beginning to boom. With the revival of the economy after months of depression, Americans were again enthusiastically buying cars. Buick was doing particularly well, Cadillac reported heavy sales, while Chevrolet's sales were rising above all expectations.[67] Colin Campbell, Chevrolet's sales manager, predicted a demand of 500,000 cars for that division.[68] So in July Pierre and Knudsen began planning a large increase in production of both water- and air-cooled models. They agreed to expanding facilities so that the division would acquire an over-all capacity of 500 air-cooled and 2,500 water-cooled cars per day by March 1923.[69] By October 1923 Chevrolet output would reach 50,000 a month. Total production scheduled for 1923 would be 425,000. This was indeed a far cry from the sales of the year just passed, when Chevrolet sold only 77,000 vehicles and the corporation as a whole just under 215,000.

To meet this schedule Pierre and Knudsen proposed building two new assembly plants—one at Buffalo and the other at Cincinnati—expanding others, and turning tractor plants in Wisconsin and California over to the Chevrolet division.[70] Pierre then talked to Harry Pierce and William Coyne of the Du Pont Company about ways and means of carrying out this construction.[71] The General Motors president worked closely with Fred Fisher to devise the best ways to raise the $5.0 million needed to enlarge the Fisher Body plants and to build a new glass plant needed for the expanded production program of Chevrolet and the other car divisions.[72]

At the same time Pierre asked the other division managers to outline what they would need in the way of funds to meet the new demand. Their requests were impressive indeed. For working capital alone, an increase of $130.0 million was required. In reporting these needs to the Finance Committee, Pierre anticipated surprise but hoped for support. "Our meeting is tomorrow," he wrote Raskob, who was in Europe, "and I expect to need a doctor to revive certain members from the shock of reading the report."[73] The members were shaken. The memories of the last expansion program were much too clear. They remained even more cautious than Pierre had anticipated. As Pierre wrote to one absentee, Sir Harry McGowan:

> We are in a curiously mixed position in General Motors Corporation. Our debts are paid, earnings good, volume of business fine and prospects encouraging. On the other hand, every endeavor to size up the situation as a whole for future guidance results in a pessimistic attitude on the part of our Finance Committee members, not warranted by our own current actions. I fear that they fail to absorb the "atmosphere" of the day.[74]

Sir Harry's response, however, was similar to that of his colleagues on the committee. On the one hand, he was "simply amazed at the programme for daily output of cars" and astonished at the idea of doing business on this "gigantic scale," but "on the other I think it is all to the good that the Finance company [obviously, Committee] are chary of encouraging fresh capital outlay at the present time."[75] So the committee appropriated funds for only a moderate expansion, providing $3.7 million for Chevrolet assembly plants and additional sums for the Fisher expansion.[76] In all, the authorization made possible an increase to output of 2,000 rather than 3,000 cars a day by the following September.

By the summer of 1922 Pierre was becoming almost as optimistic about the future of the automobile industry as Durant and Raskob had been in 1919. The difference was that his program would be based on much more solid information, would be much more carefully supervised from the general offices in New York and Detroit, and would be paid for out of General Motors earnings.

Pleasing and exciting as was this new demand for automobiles, it intensified the underlying differences within General Motors over the copper-cooled engine. If demand was growing so fast and if it was being met effectively with existing water-cooled models, why, the divisional executives asked, should the corporation risk the high cost of developing and producing a new car? Why let Ford with his obsolete Model T keep the market when, with just a few improvements in comfort and performance, customers were willing to pay a good bit more for the standard Chevrolet? On the other hand, Pierre, encouraged by the success of the tests at Dayton and by Knudsen's faith in the new car, was still certain that its development was necessary to give General Motors a lead in the fast-growing market. So strong was his conviction that he was undisturbed by the difficulties that forced Knudsen to delay the target date for starting production from September to November; he was also undismayed by the concurrent problem of making the dealers sell old models while everyone waited for the new.[77] Moreover, by November Pierre insisted to Sloan and other senior executives that Olds and Oakland must begin their plans to change over from the water-cooled to the air-cooled engine. Because Olds was doing least well in meeting the revival of demand, he particularly wanted it to move quickly into air-cooled production.

Knudsen's delays in getting the Chevrolet copper-cooled engine into production stiffened the opposition of the division managers. The delays also troubled Sloan, who had begun to act as their spokesman. At a meeting at Detroit, on November 8, 1922, that included Pierre, Sloan, Kettering, Bassett, and Mott the issue was joined.[78] Before the meeting, Pierre talked alone to Kettering who, suspecting that the operating men were out to scuttle his innovation, was "very much disturbed by the lack of interest of Hardy and Hannum." In the larger meeting Sloan took the lead in stressing the dangers of committing three divisions to a still unproved innovation. Pierre, determined to move forward, emphatically countered Sloan's argument. He insisted that the Executive Committee had already made the decision to have all three divisions produce air-cooled cars. Like Kettering, he was annoyed at the divisional executives' insistence that they continue work on the water-cooled engine. The only question before the meeting was, in Pierre's mind, the time of the changeover to the air-cooled. "I pointed out," he noted in a memorandum he dictated immediately following the meeting, "this [the change to the air-cooled car] had been decided some months ago by the Executive Committee and that the only decision left was a change of front, or the abandonment absolutely of all experiments with water-cooled and steam-cooled cars." The copper-cooled engine was not untried, Pierre argued. It had been thoroughly tested and proved and "therefore there is great deal more risk in committing ourselves to water cooled than copper cooled, especially as all troubles developed in four and six cylinder copper cooled relate to the chassis or parts of the engine that are common to both water and copper cooled jobs." Kettering then added that it was logical to have Olds and Oakland moved into the copper-cooled engines because they had not improved their water-cooled engines as effectively as Chevrolet. Because of existing plans for the production of both water-cooled and air-cooled engines at Chevrolet, Pierre was willing to put off until May 1 the decision on the timing of the complete shift over to air-cooled. But he wanted Olds and Oakland to stop work on water-cooled engines and to begin at once on working out plans for the production of the copper-cooled engine and car.

After a lengthy discussion, Pierre and Sloan reached a compromise. The Executive Committee agreed that after August 1, 1923, Oldsmobile would produce only a copper-cooled 6. In addition, "all experiments and developments of water cooled motors" were to be discontinued immediately.[79] On the other hand, Oakland was "under no circumstances" to produce a copper-cooled car of "any kind or description" until the other two divisions had fully tested, technologically and commercially, the value of innovation. Chevrolet was to "proceed with the development of its copper-cooled model cautiously, with a view to determining all factors involved . . . always recognized as being present in the development of any new product, in such a way that the hazard to the Corporation is at all times kept at a minimum."

As 1922 drew to its close, Pierre still had few doubts about the future of the copper-cooled car. In December Knudsen produced 250 of the new models.[80] In January they were unveiled at the annual automobile show in New York, where they created a sensation, even though they were priced at $200 more than the standard Chevrolet. In January, too, Knudsen optimistically promised his chief a total of 1,000 air-cooled cars by the end of February and a production schedule after that of 500 a month. After June he believed he could increase the output up to 1,500 a month if production on the water-cooled was stopped on July 1.

But by early March Pierre began for the first time to have serious doubts about the copper-cooled program. Knudsen clearly was not going to meet the schedule he had promised. Already the division was receiving complaints about the few copper-cooled cars that had been sold. He and his brothers and a few close friends, including Seward Prosser and Philip Cook, the Episcopal Bishop of Delaware, had received their cars and tried them.[81] Their performance was disappointing. Nearly all were plagued by mechanical troubles.

At the same time the demand for automobiles continued to grow even faster than previous estimates. Pierre now returned to his earlier plans, which would provide the funds to speed up Chevrolet's production from the 2,000 previously authorized to 3,000 a day.[82] This time he was sure the Finance Committee would go along. After conferring with Knudsen he worked out a detailed program that called for $11.9 million in working capital and an additional $6.4 million in permanent investment.

While Pierre was planning this program, several of the directors again cautioned him against committing Chevrolet completely to the air-cooled car.[83] He talked with Sloan about the possibilities of continuing on a basis of using both types of cars—air-cooled and water-cooled. The vice-president in charge of operations adamantly opposed any further compromise. The time had come to fish or cut bait. It would be exceedingly difficult for the production men, and even harder for the salesmen, to have to continue over a period of time to handle two very different models. If the air-cooled car proved itself, then adopt it; if not, then drop it. "To sum up," Sloan wrote, "the only real and best way of handling this proposition is to first be sure you are right and then go ahead, which, to me, means getting the job right before we try to push big production on it and then when we know the time has arrived, make our final plans." Sloan was sure Pierre would agree.

This time Pierre did. He realized he had pushed for the mass production and sale of the new car before it was fully tested and before it had proved itself (as Sloan insisted the year before that it should) in the eyes of the divisional men who would have to produce it. He was about to ask the Finance Committee for $28.0 million to meet the growing demand for Chevrolet alone. He could hardly ask them to risk this amount on a car whose performance was so questionable. Yet he refused to have the whole air-cooled engine scuttled merely because the development had been slow and the market had taken a turn for the better. On the other hand, prolonged indecisiveness between the two models would continue to cost the corporation millions of dollars in losses. A clear-cut decision would soon have to be made. It should be made by those who were directly and intimately involved in the manufacture and sales of cars. Sloan had been right: the president had become too much involved in operating details. So by the middle of April Pierre decided to resign as president. Sloan could take over the position and be responsible for the critical decisions; Pierre, as chairman of the board, would retain an overview of the corporation's activities.

Pierre had positive as well as negative reasons for deciding in April 1923 to retire from the presidency of General Motors. He had taken the post only to bring General Motors through a serious crisis. He had never considered it a permanent job. Only the need to solve the final major problem—the creation of an effective product line—had kept him in New York and Detroit this long. During 1922 he was beginning to think that others should make decisions on product policy. Then early in 1923 he made a review of his work at General Motors and this, too, must have emphasized to him that he had completed, and done so effectively, the task he had set out to do.

The occasion for the review came when, in February 1923, he began collecting data to write up the corporation's annual report.[84] He decided then to outline and discuss the causes and consequences of the crisis at General Motors and in the automobile industry as a whole during the postwar economic depression. His theme would be that the corporation's massive expansion between 1919 and 1920 had been essentially sound. The cause of the crisis had not been overexpansion of productive facilities, but rather the loss of administrative control, since this permitted the divisions to overextend working capital, largely through purchasing too much inventory.

Pierre opened the report by pointing out two long-term lessons of the 1920–1921 recession. One, the automobile was no longer a luxury, a mere "pleasure car."[85] It had become a basic form of transportation. Although new car purchases had dropped off drastically during the recession, the demand for gasoline had remained steady. The recession, then, did not cause a decline in automobile use. It only delayed purchases of new cars. The second result was that "the manufacture and sale of the automobile as a commercial necessity must follow the same careful economic and resourceful methods as found necessary in other standardized industries." This had certainly been the case at General Motors.

The strong revival of demand after the summer of 1922 had proven the validity of the expansion program of 1919 and 1920. During 1922, production had climbed to more than 70% of capacity over the year as a whole; in some months it was up to 80%. In that year General Motors had sold 456,763 vehicles (442,981 of them were passenger cars) as compared to 391,798 in 1919 and only 214,799 in 1921.

The expansion program of 1919 and 1920, with an estimated cost of $281.6 million, had not in itself put the crucial strain on the corporation's finances. The difficulty had arisen from excessive payments for materials and supplies purchased at inflated prices. It was these purchases that led to much of the borrowing of $82.8 million. Pierre then described in detail the failure of the Inventory and Allotment Committee to control such expenditures. Even so, he pointed out, the losses were concentrated in ten of the thirty-four divisions. The ten accounted for the operating losses of $15.3 million in 1921 as well as by far the largest share of liquidation losses, which had totaled $84.9 million. The other divisions broke even or turned in a profit. The divisions with heavy losses—including Olds, Oakland, Chevrolet, Sheridan, Scripps-Booth and, above all, Samson Tractor—had been either discontinued or reorganized.

"Three considerations," Pierre assured the stockholders, "make the recurrence of the 1920–1921 disaster seem unlikely if not impossible." A repetition of extreme inflation, engendered by the war and the resulting deflation, was hardly likely to occur again. Of more significance was the "complete system of inventory and purchase control" established by the corporation in 1921 and the system of cash control completed in the following year. In addition to the development of "system in management and control," the "regeneration" of General Motors had been aided by improving facilities, lowering costs, and bettering the corporation's products.

The company had profited from the lesson of 1920–1921 and the return of demand in 1922. At the end of that calendar year it had no indebtedness in the form of notes or bank loans. It had assets (cash, sight drafts, notes, and accounts receivable, materials, etc.) of $180.3 million. The only fixed indebtedness was money notes and mortgages totaling $2.3 million. Total permanent investment stood at $291.3 million. Net earnings for 1922 were $66.8 million as compared with $13.2 million for 1921. The dividend on preferred and debenture stock had been paid all through the recession. But, after paying a dollar a share (in quarterly payments of 25¢ each) during 1921 on common, the Finance Committee decided to pass the dividend in January 1922. As confidence had by that time been restored, and would probably not be weakened by the passing of the dividend, Pierre felt it prudent to use the funds to build up the surplus and contingency accounts.[86] In November 1922 the committee declared a 50¢ dividend, and after the payment of the dividend the surplus account stood at $89.9 million. Regular payments of common stock dividends now seemed assured.

The achievement of his goals as president, as well as his failure to build a new product line around a revolutionary car, led to Pierre's decision to hand over the presidency to Alfred Sloan. But the preparations for the annual stockholders' meeting on April 18 were completed before Pierre finally made his decision.[87] Pratt and DeWitt Page, head of the New Departure Roller Bearing Division, were to come on the board. Bankers and other New York directors were to have a trip to Detroit to view several plants. Pierre thought it best to wait to announce his decision until after the stockholders' meeting, at which he was duly re-elected president. Then he conferred, first with his brothers Irénée and Lammot.[88] With their approval he then discussed his decision more formally with the Du Pont Finance Committee. On April 25, the day he presented the $28.0 million program for the Chevrolet expansion, he wrote to Seward Prosser and other close associates of his intentions to resign. The same day a more stereotyped letter went to the members of the General Motors board. To all he pointed out that the corporation had gained "stability" and that during the past year Alfred Sloan had "assumed many of the most important duties entrusted to a President." He was, therefore, recommending this man for the presidency. He thought "it important that definite understanding be reached before calling a formal meeting. In meantime nothing has been said to Mr. Sloan." He also agreed that he would remain as chairman of the board and as a member of both the Finance Committee and Executive Committee. For a short time, he would continue on as the nominal head of Chevrolet.[89] After hearing from the members of the Finance Committee and the board, Pierre talked to Sloan on May 8. Two days later he officially submitted his resignation as president of General Motors.

# General Motors Rebuilt, 1923–1924

WHEN PIERRE RETIRED from the presidency in May 1923, he optimistically planned to remove himself from active participation in the affairs of General Motors. He expected to drop his influential role in policy-making and to remain largely an adviser. He would keep watch over the major, primarily financial, matters. He planned to give up his suite in the Carlton House in New York City and to end his regular trips to Flint, Detroit, Dayton and other General Motors centers. To be certain that he would not be drawn back into the daily affairs of the corporation, he started at once to work out a plan to assure the continuance of the able and expert management team that he had brought together at General Motors. He began to turn his attention again to improving Delaware's roads and schools, a task which, as was pointed out, he had put aside when he took over the General Motors presidency.

The change of pace was not, however, as easy to achieve as Pierre had hoped. Besides the formulation of a plan to tie the managers more closely to the corporation, three other matters continued to require his close attention: one was the fate of the copper-cooled car, and with it the completion of the General Motors product line; a second was a final adjustment of the organizational structure of the corporation resulting from the experience of developing the copper-cooled engine; a final concern was the completion of the major refinements in the corporation's statistical and financial controls.

## The Management Securities Company

On April 6, 1923, as Pierre was making up his mind to resign from the presidency, he asked his secretary to bring him all the information available on bonus, savings, and pension plans at General Motors and Du Pont. He and Raskob then began to discuss plans for a stock purchasing or partnership program for General Motors similar to that which led to the formation at Du Pont of the first Du Pont Securities (which became in 1918 the Christiana Securities Company).[1] Pierre had long been convinced that the Du Pont Company's impressive performance during the war years could be attributed in good part to the working out of the Christiana Securities plan. As he had written to one stockholder in March 1918: "We had in our organization at the beginning of the war a nucleus of men representing the best talent in their line. Not one of them has deserted the company, though flattering offers of salary and participation in profits were open to all of them."[2] These men had not been substantial stockholders in the company. Pierre could not have expected them to stay at a financial sacrifice, which could have been the case if they had not been able to participate in the Christiana Securities Company.

A similar situation now existed in the automobile industry. At the moment General Motors had, Pierre believed, the best set of managers in the business, but the competition for these men was strong. In 1922 General Motors produced only 15% of the cars manufactured in the United States. Ford, Dodge, Chrysler, Nash, Packard, Studebaker, Pierce-Arrow, and others were large and wealthy companies who needed, above all else, experienced managers to meet the demands of the rapidly growing market. They could make extremely attractive offers for talents that were probably the rarest of all the essential ingredients in this young industry.

Moreover, Pierre had looked on Christiana Securities as more than just a means of keeping competent senior executives. From the beginning of their own partnership in the Du Pont Company, both Pierre and Coleman had searched for ways to give professional managers financial incentives similar to those of a family firm. This was the reason for the development of bonus and stock purchase plans almost immediately after they set up the new company in 1902. This, too, was the purpose both had in mind for Coleman's stock in 1914. Such a large block of stock made it possible, for the first time, to provide the senior executives in the company with a far larger stake in its financial performance than could the existing stock and bonus purchase plans.

The beneficiaries of Christiana Securities had been the members of the Du Pont Company's War Executive Committee. After his retirement as president of the Du Pont Company in April 1919, Pierre wanted to make a similar arrangement for members of the new Executive Committee. Because the Du Pont Company was then so involved in its massive reconversion and diversification program, Pierre decided not to use company funds directly but to work out the arrangements personally. He offered to sell each member of the committee a block of 1,000 shares of Du Pont common at $320 a share. The purchase price would be financed by a loan of $320,000 from the Du Pont Company for which the stock would be collateral. The dividends from the stock could then be used to pay off the loan. Pierre's purpose was, he wrote the recipients:

> (1) To recognize the good work done by you for the Company;
> (2) To encourage you in further effort to benefit yourself and other stockholders by placing you in a position to share in the profits of the Company;
> (3) To continue the plan of insuring good management of the Company's affairs by enlisting permanently the services of able men through securing for them a personal interest in the Company's success apart from salary compensation.[3]

When the recession of 1920–1921 drove down the value of all stocks, Pierre, in April 1921, turned over to each of the recipients 400 shares of Christiana Securities, then valued at $400 a share, to be held as additional security on the loans. As he wrote to all of them, he did this so that each "would be free of worry over the unexpected outcome of your purchase and that your future efforts should result in substantial reward even though the values of a year ago are restored and no more." Pierre kept his right to redeem the 400 shares when the original loans had been repaid. Before that time he informed all the men involved that he surrendered this option and that the shares were theirs.[4] So by 1927 these seven executives, with no cash outlay of their own, had received 1,000 shares of Du Pont and 400 shares of Christiana Securities, then having a total value of nearly $800,000.

As Pierre contemplated retirement from the presidency of General Motors in the spring of 1923, he quite naturally thought of developing a similar "partnership" plan for the members of the top executive team at the automobile company. It was natural, too, that he considered using for this purpose part of the large block of stock that the Du Pont Company had so unexpectedly purchased from William C. Durant. The Du Pont Company was, however, still servicing the $35.0 million bond issue sold through J. P. Morgan to pay for this stock. This debt would have to be refinanced before the stock could be used in a manager incentive plan. Finally, in carrying out such a proposal, Pierre wanted to be sure that the Du Pont Company's control of General Motors was in no way jeopardized.

Raskob, who listened to Pierre's ideas with great interest, was particularly concerned about the last two points. He had been even more troubled than Pierre by the costs of the interest and amortization of the Du Pont Company's $35.0 million bond issue. Only two of the ten payments had been made, and the interest requirements were still substantial. In fact, the Du Pont Company was contemplating the possiblity of selling some General Motors stock to meet the payments. Only a month before, in March 1923, Raskob had formed a syndicate to maintain the price of General Motors stock if such a sale had to be made.[5]

Raskob, like Pierre, still considered Durant a threat to Du Pont control at General Motors. Both men remembered well Durant's brilliant comeback in December 1916. In 1923 Wall Street journalists and analysts were still predicting Durant's return as the owner-manager of General Motors. This concern was another reason for the syndicate that Raskob formed in March. As late as October 1925 Pierre was writing Raskob and Winder Laird, his brother-in-law, in Wilmington, about the possibility of Durant's obtaining control of a large enough block of General Motors stock to permit him to outvote the Du Pont interest.[6]

In mid-June 1923 Pierre asked Raskob and Donaldson Brown to draw up a plan that would carry out three objectives: (1) to create an opportunity for General Motors executives to acquire a larger interest in their own company at no out-of-pocket costs to themselves; (2) to insure payment of the Du Pont bond issue; and (3) to accomplish both without losing voting control of the 38% of General Motors common it then controlled. In addition Pierre wanted to sell a block of General Motors under the new arrangement to that company's executives.[7] This gesture, he believed, would convince many at the Du Pont Company of his own commitment to the scheme.

Raskob and Brown, working undisturbed in the tranquiliity of the late spring at Lake Placid, completed their plans on June 20. Copies of their proposal went to Pierre, the Finance Committee at Du Pont, and to Laffey, Du Pont's general counsel. Like most of Raskob's creations, the plan was complicated. It involved the use of two holding companies—the Du Pont American Industries (whose name would be changed to General Motors Securities Corporation) controlled by the Du Pont Company, and the Management Securities Company controlled by General Motors.[8] The first, which held the Du Pont Company's 7.5 million shares of General Motors stock, would sell a third of *its* stock (*not* the General Motors stock held by Du Pont) to the second for $37.4 million ($4.7 million in cash and $32.7 million in notes maturing in 1931). The Du Pont Company would use the funds from the matured notes to pay off the Morgan loan. (At the same time the first, Du Pont American Industries—and, therefore, the Du Pont Company—would retain control of all its shares of General Motors stock.) In addition, General Motors would turn over to the Management Securities Company annually for seven years an amount of stock equivalent to 6% (later 5%) of its earnings (after deducting 7% on capital invested). General Motors would then allocate $5.5 million of the stock of the second holding company (i.e., the Management Securities Company) to "its important men," retaining $1.1 million for future distribution. The recipients would give a small down payment for the stock and pay the balance in seven annual installments from the dividends received from that stock which, in turn, would reflect the earnings turned over to the holding company by General Motors. General Motors would have an irrevocable option to repurchase the stock from the recipient "should he resign, or should his position or performance in the corporation change."[9] By means of such complex arrangements, the plan met all three of Pierre's objectives.

Pierre found the Raskob-Brown plan much to his liking. But the senior executives at the Du Pont Company did not. Both Walter Carpenter, the treasurer, and Irénée du Pont, the president, had strong objections.[10] Their protests, however, were technical ones over the details of the plan and not over its general principles. Irénée was quite taken by the thought of using a General Motors management stock purchase program to help the Du Pont Company pay off its bonded indebtedness. He had been troubled, like Raskob, by the possibility of curtailing Du Pont dividends in order to do so. He disliked the alternative of selling General Motors stock to acquire the needed funds, for, as he wrote Pierre, "the fear of Du Pont selling might be a serious market depressant on General Motors common stock prices." Nevertheless, he thought that the plan, as outlined by Raskob, failed to provide properly for the amortization of the Du Pont Company's bond issue. Carpenter objected to a lack of flexibility in making later allocations of the stock. He also complained that the tax implications had not been thought out carefully enough. In the end he favored a more direct plan of allocating the Du Pont-held General Motors stock than this one, which involved going through two holding companies. If a direct sale was impractical, then one holding company, not two, should be enough.

During the summer of 1923 both the Du Pont Company and General Motors Finance Committees held meetings to review Raskob's plan. Occasionally the debate became quite heated.[11] After one meeting, on August 11, Pierre began to believe that Carpenter and Irénée had turned against the whole idea of "obtaining owner management in General Motors Corporation." Irénée wrote immediately to impress on him that this was not the case. "I am more than in accord with the principle, in fact, believe it is almost invaluable, so much so that I think the advantages outweigh the disadvantages of the rather unusual intricate route of interesting them through a Managers' Company."[12] The present arrangement he still considered to be "an improvident sale" for the Du Pont Company. Pierre, reassured, did his best to satisfy his brother. After the objections of Irénée and Carpenter were met by modifying certain details, the plan easily passed the finance committees and the boards of directors at Du Pont and General Motors. The final plan authorized the formation of the two holding companies and called for two types of stock to meet the concerns of Walter Carpenter and Irénée du Pont as to tax and amortization requirements.[13]

Sloan then broached the proposal to his executives. As he explained to Pierre and Raskob on the telephone, he did not want "in any way, shape or manner" to influence the potential participants.[14] "I believe they should be told frankly that here is an opportunity to go in business; they take the profit and they take the risk." For unless he did so, and the plan did not work out for the participants, Sloan emphasized that his position as chief executive would be an intolerable one. Pierre quite agreed. The risk was, of course, that if General Motors failed to make a profit, or made only a relatively small one, the recipients would not get the income to cover for the annual installment on the purchase price of their stock. They would then have to pay out of their own pockets for stock whose value would certainly drop below the price at which they had purchased it. Nevertheless, neither Sloan nor Pierre could have been surprised by the fact that every executive Sloan consulted was exceedingly enthusiastic about taking part in the Management Securities Company.

The final step was the initial allocation of Management Securities stock. The General Motors Finance Committee gave the task to a small subcommittee consisting of Seward Prosser, Arthur G. Bishop, and Pierre as chairman.[15] The committee agreed that this was a neutral board, as neither Prosser nor Bishop had any managerial connections with General Motors, and Pierre was planning to remove himself from day-to-day activities. Actually, the decisions as to the allocation of the stock were left almost entirely to Pierre and Sloan, with Brown probably giving the most additional advice. In November Pierre made the initial selection from names submitted to him by Sloan and probably Brown.[16] He preferred a list that included a large number of allotments. Sloan countered by giving bigger sums to fewer men. Pierre's initial allocation was to just over 150 executives, while Sloan divided the same amount of stock among close to 80 men. Pierre did not argue the point but accepted, as he tended to do, the judgment of the corporation's chief operating executive.

In any case the recipients were pleased and soon would be even more so. For the great increase in the value of the stock during the 1920s meant, as Sloan later pointed out, that a man who paid a down payment of $1,000 on his allotment in late 1923 would have paid $10,800 more in seven additional annual payments. By 1930, when all transactions involved in this plan were completed (a year ahead of time), the value of the $10,800 worth of shares had reached $61,128.[17] Nearly all the 80 participants received over $10,000, and the average initial allotment was $50,000 worth of stock. Therefore, the average value of these allotments was in 1930 over $3.0 million apiece. Several were allocated over $100,000, three got $300,000 and one, Sloan, $350,000. By the late 1920s Pierre's plan had created many new millionaries. The profits proved well worth the risks. The top professional managers at General Motors benefited personally by the performance of their company, and exceedingly few executives could be enticed to leave it.

### Still the Copper-Cooled Engine

During the first few months after his retirement from the presidency, Pierre was faced with a far more pressing and difficult problem than that of devising an incentive compensation plan. This was the continuing issue of the copper-cooled engine and car. The change in the top command at General Motors had been influenced by the misfortunes of the new car, and the change itself helped to speed a decision. Although he was no longer president, Pierre could hardly remove himself from this complex problem.

Sloan acted with characteristic speed and decisiveness on the copper-cooled engine. At the very first session of the Executive Committee (May 18) after he became president, Sloan opened the meeting by raising the question of the copper-cooled 6-cylinder model. He argued that it was extremely hazardous to completely commit Oldsmobile's production to the copper-cooled 6, as the committee had agreed back in November. "The continuing delay in producing the Chevrolet copper-cooled car is a constant reminder of the uncertainties and the difficulties in engineering and manufacturing which would certainly delay the program and might lead to serious embarrassment to the Olds Motor Works organization at the factory and throughout the world."[18] Pierre had gone to Detroit for the meeting, which was attended by Kettering and Knudsen as well as the new members— Fisher and Mott. After a good deal of discussion the group agreed to have three senior engineers (A. L. Cash, general manager of the Northway Division; Ormand E. Hunt, chief engineer of Chevrolet; and E. A. DeWalters, chief engineer of Buick) report whether the copper-cooled 6 was fully ready for production.

Neither Pierre nor Raskob was at the meeting of the Executive Committee, held ten days later in Detroit, when the engineers made their report. "The engine ignites badly after driving at moderate speeds in air temperatures from sixty to seventy degrees," they summarized. "It shows a serious loss of compression and power when hot, though the power is satisfactory when the engine is warming up from a cold condition."[19] In addition there were several minor difficulties. The committee then unanimously agreed to cancel the copper-cooled program at Olds, instructing that division to develop immediately a water-cooled engine that could use a chassis built for the copper-cooled engine. The long-range development of the copper-cooled 6 was turned over to A. L. Cash's Northway Division, a parts and engine-making division that concentrated on equipment for trucks.

Shortly after Sloan and the others had decided to kill the copper-cooled 6, a similar decision occurred on the copper-cooled 4 at Chevrolet. This move came, however, more from Knudsen than from the Executive Committee. By the end of June 1923 Chevrolet had produced a total of only 759 copper-cooled cars. Of these about 500 passed factory inspection. Of the 500, 150 were used by factory representatives and other corporation officials and about 300 were being used by dealers. So only a small number had been actually sold to customers. Because of continuing complaints from dealers and customers, Collins and Knudsen decided to recall all copper-cooled cars from the field late in June.[20] This move marked the abrupt end of the ambitious Chevrolet program, agreed to in April 1922, and reaffirmed in November of that same year and again in January 1923.

Kettering's response to these two moves was one of shock and disbelief. He, of course, knew that production was going badly. In fact, just before he learned of the recall of the copper-cooled car from the field, he had suggested to Sloan that if the car was not "commercialized" within the corporation, he would like to discuss ways and means of having it produced outside.[21] But the reality of the program's failure was a harsh and bitter blow. On June 30 Kettering wrote Sloan, sending a copy of the letter to Pierre: "I have definitely made up my mind to leave the Corporation unless some method can be arranged to prevent the fundamental work done here from being thrown out and discredited through no fault of the apparatus. . . ."[22] The fault, he was certain, was "an organized resistance within the Corporation. . . . My only regret, in severing my connection with the Corporation, would be the wonderful association I have had with yourself, Mr. du Pont, Mr. Mott and others." Sloan replied by reviewing the long, tedious history of the air-cooled car and particularly of the clash of opinions between Kettering's staff organization and the operating divisions. But he "could not agree [with Kettering] that the situation is in any sense hopeless."[23] In any case, neither he nor Pierre du Pont would consider accepting Kettering's resignation.

Sloan, Fisher, and Mott then met Kettering to talk over the best means of developing the car so that it still might be mass produced to the specifications desired by the Executive Committee. The four men agreed that the basic difficulty lay "with the divided responsibility between the Chief Engineer [at Chevrolet] and Mr. Kettering."[24] Little could be done "unless the responsibility is positively assured in the hands of one or the other party." So they reported to Pierre that they had decided, subject to his approval, to set up a new division in Dayton. Kettering would have complete charge of designing the car and engine. "The new operation will take over the four cylinder copper cooled engine and probably the six cylinder Olds and will market these two copper cooled jobs under their own names, starting with five or ten a day and building up as demand increases."

Although Pierre had retired from the presidency, he was still chairman of the board, a member of the Executive Committee, and nominally head of Chevrolet. He was annoyed by Sloan's abrupt moves and troubled by Kettering's response. Although it had Kettering's approval, this proposal, as he read it, would essentially mean abandoning the innovation. He wrote a sharp letter urging Sloan "not to put this plan in force until we have a conference. The fundamental defect in the plan is that it will encourage opposition instead of doing away with it."[25] The Chevrolet and Oldsmobile people would have to condemn the copper-cooled car as a failure "in order to explain their retirement from this field. Their opposition will be strengthened by everybody who is now doubtful or opposed to the copper cooled car and perhaps make converts of those who are still open minded."

On the other hand, if the copper-cooled was sold through Chevrolet and satisfied their dealers, the other divisions would take it up more quickly than if it were sold through a small special organization. Pierre had "no reason to think that the copper cooled is opposed by the Chevrolet Sales Organization at present." He approved of calling back the cars already sold, as the mass production of the copper-cooled engine and chassis had still not been properly worked out. He would be willing to have its manufacture moved from Chevrolet's Michigan plant to Kettering's in Dayton. Admittedly too, the engineering design still needed attention. If Hunt, Chevrolet's chief engineer, was unable to solve the problem, then another engineer should be hired. The engine's only major setback was the loss of compression, and Kettering had explained that this was caused by a design that permitted the drawing of hot air from around the exhaust pipe into the carburetor. Engineering as well as manufacturing could go to Dayton. But the copper-cooled must be sold through Chevrolet.

Pierre's angry response launched a series of conferences in New York and Detroit. At these, Sloan stressed how much the copper-cooled was hampering Chevrolet and delaying the expansion program essential to meet the new market.[26] By the summer of 1923 Collins' estimates of Chevrolet's market had reached 730,000 cars a year. Sloan and the division executives wanted to get into full production with an improved water-cooled car as soon as possible. At the meeting of July 18 the Executive Committee unanimously approved the expansion of facilities to assure the production of 3,000 water-cooled cars a day.[27] After continuing discussion of the future of the copper-cooled engine, the committee finally agreed to postpone decisions until Knudsen, who was away on an inspection trip, returned to Detroit.

The final decision on the copper-cooled car came on August 16, 1923.[28] The Executive Committee, including Pierre, voted unanimously to give the 4-cylinder to Chevrolet and the 6-cylinder to Dayton. Knudsen would remain responsible for the development of the 4-cylinder car, for its engineering and production as well as sales. H. D. Church, an experienced automotive engineer who had worked long for Packard, would be placed in charge of redesigning the engine and chassis. Kettering and a similar unit at Dayton would be responsible for redesigning the 6 for the existing Oldsmobile chassis. If this unit was successful, the corporation would then form a new division to produce and sell a limited number of 6-cylinder copper-cooled cars to get the reaction of dealers and customers in different parts of the country before going into high-volume production.

Pierre was pleased by the "new start." His confidence in the car's ultimate success remained unshaken.[29] Indeed, during the debate leading up to the August 16 decision, he told Kettering that once the chassis was modified, he expected 60,000 copper-cooled 4-cylinder cars to be sold by May 1924.[30] Kettering's encouraging reports kept up Pierre's hopes. "Your good letter of December 18 in regard to progress on the copper cooled cars made a fine Christmas present," Pierre wrote Kettering.[31]

## Completing the Corporation's Organizational Structure

The decision in August 1923 on the copper-cooled car brought significant adjustments in General Motors' organizational structure as well as in its production line. By that summer everyone on the Executive Committee was deeply disturbed by the wrenching controversy between the divisional executives and those of the staff over the new engine. Kettering remained convinced that the principal reason the copper-cooled car was not in full production was the refusal of the divisional executives and engineers to appreciate and to understand the innovation. Hannum, Hardy, and, in time, even Knudsen, and their subordinates felt that "idea men" in Dayton were too cavalier and too unconcerned about the basic engineering problems that had to be solved if the car was to be mass produced. In addition, Sloan continued to be troubled by the failure of divisional salesmen and plant managers to benefit from the work done by the experts on the staff.

On August 20, 1923, immediately after the Executive Committee decision on the future of the copper-cooled car development, Pierre wrote Knudsen two long letters.[32] In one he called for a detailed report of mechanical weaknesses in the present copper-cooled car. In the second he asked for a review of the history of the development of the car in order to pinpoint just what went wrong and what basically caused the "utter collapse of the program." He had, Pierre stressed, "no thought of trying to fix responsibility for the purpose of eliminating a culprit," but rather he wanted to know "the situation in order that a recurrence of the trouble may be avoided." Pierre pointed out that he himself was as much at fault as anyone. In a follow-up letter he added, "If there is anything to be criticised in our actions, it is the failure to record definitely the nature and causes of trouble promptly. I confess that I am ashamed of this record, particularly of the part that I have played in it, for I feel that I did not sufficiently insist upon making of records that would have saved us a lot of trouble."[33]

Knudsen's reply underlined the role of line and staff differences in causing the failure. "Unhappily, the engine troubles when reported caused a wide range of differences of opinion between the creators and producers, both as to their causes and their remedies."[34] Pierre's correspondence with Kettering, during the fall of 1923, served as a constant reminder of the continuing antagonism between the divisions and Dayton.[35]

The correspondence with Kettering and Knudsen also convinced Pierre of the value of an organizational response that Sloan had just developed to bring together the corporation's engineering and research executives. Sloan proposed the formation of a committee of divisional and staff engineers with its own permanent secretary, office staff, and budget. He had first used this type of permanent committee to coordinate the functional activities of the different divisions with the work done by the Advisory Staff in the field of purchasing.[36] In the spring of 1922 he proposed to give the corporation the advantages of volume purchasing, but still to keep buying decisions in the hands of the division managers by forming a General Purchasing Committee. Such a unit, Sloan was certain, could save the corporation between $5.0 million and $10.0 million a year as well as assist in the standardization of supplies and materials, in the control of inventory, and in the improvement of buying procedures.

A few months later Sloan proposed a similar permanent committee to supervise institutional advertising; that is, the advertising of the General Motors name and the line of products, rather than that of any one division. Pierre had been particularly impressed by the value of the meetings of this committee in encouraging a spirit of cooperation and a corporation point of view. He told Sloan that even if the advertising results were negligible, the cost of having such a committee was justified by "the development of the General Motors atmosphere and the working together spirit of all members of the committee representing the various phases of the Corporations' activities."[37]

In the summer of 1923 Sloan, like Pierre, was beginning to look on a comparable committee as the way to reduce the damaging staff and line tensions over product development. In September Sloan, after talking over his plans with the chairman of the board, formally proposed the formation of a General Technical Committee. That group would, he suggested to the Executive Committee, "deal in problems which would be of interest to all Divisions and would in dealing with such matters largely formulate the general engineering policies of the Corporation." It could also take over the functions of the present small Patents Committee and, most important of all, create "a more intimate contact" between the operating divisions and the research laboratories at Dayton. This would make it possible for the corporation "to capitalize" on the potential of the laboratories in a way they had not been able to do so far because of the lack of a "proper system of administration." Not only would the proposed committee be providing "better coordination with the Research Corporation but better coordination also among the Operation Divisions themselves."

Besides encouraging coordination and developing a better *esprit de corps,* the proposed committee could, Pierre agreed with Sloan, provide a running record of development on all projects, a record that he felt had been so lacking in the copper-cooled program. The Executive Committee quickly approved, and the General Technical Committee held its first meeting on September 14, 1923. It included chief engineers of as well as others from car-making divisions, Kettering, and representatives from Dayton, and was chaired by Sloan himself. (See Chart VII.) The committee went right to work. Although it handled all patent matters and supervised the vast new proving grounds then being built at Milford, Michigan, it was more an educational than an administrative organ.[38] Its meetings were largely seminars in engineering matters ranging from developing the design and production of new models to more specific developments like improved brakes, fuel consumption, steering mechanism, "balloon tires," and transmissions.

For a time Kettering, who remained upset by the initial failure of the copper-cooled engine, only grudgingly cooperated with the new committee. Pierre, who was much closer to him than Sloan and the operating executives, urged him gently to be more cooperative and involved with the General Technical Committee's activities. In his correspondence with Kettering on the new copper-cooled developments, Pierre reminded the research chief that, despite setbacks, 1923 "has been a most encouraging year in General Motors" and that a "cause for encouragement lies in the fact that there seems to be a continuing growth of cooperation and development of General Motors as a whole, instead of separate units."[39] By December Kettering was willing to say to Pierre: "The Technical Committee meetings are a fine thing and, certainly, the Division Engineers are beginning to see that some of the things we are doing have not been without foundation. . . . I am sure we are going to do much toward developing the spirit of cooperation in each of the divisions."[40] When the time came to test the newest modifications in the copper-cooled engine, Kettering was only too glad to turn to the General Technical Committee rather than have to work through one of the divisions. While conflict inevitably appeared now and then between the line and staff men, the senior executives at General Motors were so pleased with the success of this interdivisional committee for engineering and product development that during 1924 they set up similar General Sales, Works Managers, and Power and Maintenance committees. By the formation of the permanent interdivisional committee with its own staff and funds, Sloan, encouraged by Pierre, had found a way to strengthen the corporation as a whole without seriously impairing the autonomy of the division managers. Through the committees the corporation could benefit from economies of scale that it otherwise could not exploit. These economies came as much in the use of ideas about product design and improvement, marketing, and plant engineering as from the advantages of volume purchasing and the use of standardized parts, accessories, supplies, and materials.

Sloan also instituted other organizational adjustments shortly after he became president. They were quite similar to the measures he had proposed to Pierre late in 1921. As president, Sloan now had the authority he had asked for earlier and which Pierre had unofficially granted him as vice-president in charge of operations. In fact, Pierre began to fear that Sloan was taking on too much. "My only fear in the whole situation," he wrote Sloan at the end of 1923, "is that you carry too much of a load on your shoulders; but I hope that you will gradually remedy that trouble by shifting part of the burden to your lieutenants. I am sure they are willing to help you if you will permit them."[41] The chairman of the board was understandably relieved when in December 1924 Sloan increased the size of the Executive Committee so that it included more men with operating experience—men such as Bassett, Pratt, Brown, and two more of the Fisher brothers.

*Completing the Corporation's Statistical Controls*

As 1924 opened, Pierre could hardly have been more pleased by the state of affairs at General Motors. As he reminded Sloan, Kettering, and others, the year 1923 had been the best the industry had ever known. While Ford still dominated the low price market, General Motors, by selling 774,617 passenger cars (up from 442,981 the previous year), had increased its share to 21% of the market, made a net income of $72,009,955, and declared a dividend of $1.20 (30¢ a quarter) a share on its common stock.[42] Pierre still had high hopes for the copper-cooled engine as the innovation that would put General Motors ahead of Ford. With General Motors' finances in excellent shape and with Sloan's firm—perhaps a little too firm —grasp on the company, Pierre began to carry out his plans for retiring still more completely from active business affairs. Now, at long last, he felt he could concentrate on improving his state's educational system and building his botanical collection and displays at Longwood.

As he was finishing his plans to "sell out" his interest in Du Pont and General Motors to his immediate family, Pierre was startled to find General Motors business taking a sharp turn for the worse. In the late spring of 1924 the corporation was struck by an inventory crisis that had frightening similarities to that of 1920. The end result of this less critical emergency was beneficial. Just as the controversy over the copper-cooled engine in the summer of 1923 led to a rounding out of the General Motors organizational structure, so the inventory problem of 1924 resulted in putting the capstone on the basic set of statistical controls which Sloan, Brown, and Pratt had fashioned for General Motors. For the moment, however, the new crisis temporarily delayed Pierre's withdrawal from General Motors operating affairs.

The causes of the inventory troubles of 1924 were twofold. The first was statistical. The company still lacked accurate long-term forecasting techniques as well as ways to adjust continually the forecast to actual market demand. As in nearly all of American industry, the evaluation of the market rested on past experience. The second was a plan for producing and storing cars during the slack winter months, a policy that Pierre and the Executive Committee had approved in December 1923. In that month, as in the previous December, Donaldson Brown had asked each division to prepare a forecast of its next year's activities. A division was, in Brown's words, "required to present an outline of its view of probable operations for the succeeding year, embodying estimates of sales, earnings and capital requirements." He called for three sets of estimates: " 'pessimistic,' representing a minimum expectation, 'conservative,' representing what is considered a likely condition, and 'optimistic,' representing what the name implies with production and sales capacity as limitations."[43]

Because 1923 had been such a good year for the industry, the division managers tended to be optimistic even in their "conservative" estimates. Moreover, they remembered how they had been caught short of cars the previous spring by an unexpected, unprecedented demand. To avoid this situation the managers, late in 1923, urged the Executive Committee to adopt a storage plan. The committee approved. It agreed, for example, that Chevrolet should produce and store 15,000 cars a month until March 1. Such a storage plan, the committee thought, would help flatten out the seasonal peaks in the company's business and so lower costs and stabilize employment. Even if the spring demand did not materialize, the committee had reasoned that "the shut down or slackening of manufacture in the spring would cost no more than if it occurred as usual in the winter."[44]

Pierre had agreed with both the optimistic forecast and the specific plan to store cars. He, too, had been much impressed with the booming automobile market. Early in the fall he had strongly supported Sloan's request for an immediate $1.0 million appropriation to expand production at Chevrolet. In a letter to Sloan on this appropriation he laid down a very concise summary of his views on the way in which resources should be allocated to meet an expanding market.[45] It indicates that Pierre had somewhat different criteria for the allocation of funds for capital investment in the rapidly expanding automobile industry of the 1920s than he had for the more stable powder trade during the first decade of the century. Priority, he wrote Sloan, should be given to the car-making divisions, where as high as 25% return on investment could be expected. Nevertheless, funds must concomitantly be spent to increase the capacity of the parts and accessories divisions, even though the return on investment would probably be less there. Such a move was necessary "in order to insure our supply, to give information as to costs, and to control quality." This "insurance" should provide enough capacity to produce at least 1/3 of the parts and accessories required for the expanded automobile-making capacity. But Pierre stressed that the expansion of parts and accessories capacity was only "insurance." Even if some venture into this field could bring a higher return on investment than the corporation's main line of business, Pierre still urged that no further funds be deflected from the building of new car-making facilities. On this point Sloan wholeheartedly agreed.

By carrying out the plans of late 1923, the divisions manufactured more cars than in any previous winter. In the following March, when the anticipated high spring demand was expected to appear, Sloan and the Executive Committee carefully studied the divisions' inventories.[46] This review revealed disquieting figures. Sales had been lower than in previous months. As sales fell off, the Chevrolet Division, for example, had reduced its production for the first three months of 1924 from a planned 215,000 units to 181,300. Even so, in mid-March the division's dealers had 119,000 cars on hand, and the division itself had stored 32,000 vehicles. If production was to continue, even at a somewhat reduced rate of 30,000 units a month, the division would have to sell 225,000 cars during the next three-month period of April, May, and June in order to get inventories down to normal levels. Yet in the boom season of 1923, only 138,000 cars were sold during the same quarter. So, if the output continued at the 30,000 monthly rate, the dealers would have to sell 87,000, or 63%, more cars than they did in the previous year. Unless production of 30,000 a month was maintained, existing inventories of stocks and materials would not be cleaned up by the end of the period.

On the basis of these figures Sloan, after consulting Pierre and the Executive Committee, first urged Knudsen at Chevrolet to cut current production immediately to 30,000 cars a month; he also asked Oakland to make a comparable reduction.[47] Sloan then called on all the divisions to revise their March 25 monthly schedules. Because he did not want to discourage dealers and salesmen, he gave as his reason the excess production during the past months, rather than a drop in anticipated demand.[48] He further warned all division managers to keep an extremely careful watch over inventory and urged those who had not done so to set up a "daily index" of the movement of supplies and material (in terms of value), similar to the one he had set up in the general office.

Pierre, who talked to Raskob and other members of the Finance Committee about the inventory situation, considered Sloan's warning necessary. He also thought it quite adequate. During April, however, he became increasingly troubled by reports that sales were not up to expectations. So he thoroughly approved the Executive Committee's proposal to send Sloan and Brown on an extended trip to the West Coast and back to check personally on sales and the whole distributing and dealer network. Pierre asked Sloan to telegraph him immediately if sales were going badly. If they were, Pierre wanted to know why.

Sloan's first telegram came from Denver on May 15. It reported that conferences with dealers, distributors, and bankers in Kansas City and Omaha revealed serious weaknesses in the dealer organization.[49] Moreover, faulty transmissions, bad paint jobs, and other technical defects were hurting sales of Chevrolet and one or two other models of other divisions. Three days later Pierre received another telegram giving similar reports about Denver and the Mountain State towns. Still Sloan had said nothing about Pierre's basic concern about actual sales to customers and the resulting inventory situation.

Sloan's telegram in reply to Pierre's wire for such information read: "I am fully aware that sales to consumers are disappointing to say the least ... am in touch with all divisions and am insisting that schedules be further curtailed to reduce stock in field by July first to normal proportions." Sloan later recalled that his demand for a drastic curtailment of production was one of the very few direct orders that he ever gave as the chief executive of General Motors.[50] In the same telegram Sloan emphasized that the divisions had weakened the corporation's over-all distributing and sales network by overloading the dealers. Then, possibly thinking that the complaints about Chevrolet's quality might bring Pierre and Kettering to push more strongly for the copper-cooled car, he warned against inflicting "further burdens" on the dealers "on account of obsoleting stock on hand through new models or modifications of present models."

A few days after Sloan and Brown returned from their trip west, the Finance Committee had its first meeting since the seriousness of the inventory crisis became known outside the inner circle of top management.[51] Pierre's role in this discussion is not recorded. He undoubtedly explained, though probably did not condone, Sloan's delay in curtailing production. Others on the committee, particularly the bankers, were most upset by this evidence of managerial weakness in the divisions as well as in the general office. After "a very lengthy discussion" the committee passed a strong resolution, asking Sloan why the crisis had been permitted to arise and what was being done to prevent its repetition. "Why were steps not taken earlier by the Operating Divisions to drastically curtail their production more in line with the unsold stocks of cars in the field and the consumer demand?"

And then: "What steps will be taken to assure effective control of production schedules in the future to guard against over-production?" The committee also discussed the decline in the quality of the Chevrolet. A second resolution asked for a report indicating the causes of this deterioration in quality. What remedies were being taken? What would be the cost of correcting the trouble? How had the defects affected sales?

Sloan's response to the first of these resolutions was to work out with Brown the statistical procedures that brought together and integrated the techniques the two men, along with Pratt, had been developing since the beginning of 1921. The basic cause for the 1924 difficulties had been the lack of accurate data in the divisions and the general office on actual sales of cars by dealers to consumers. Sloan, therefore, asked the dealers to send through the general office, every ten days, reports listing sales of new cars and trucks to consumers and the number of new and used cars each dealer had on hand.[52] The information on used cars was particularly important, he pointed out, because a backlog on used cars had such a direct effect on the sale of new cars. In addition, Sloan asked R. L. Polk Company, a firm providing commercial business information, to expand data they were already giving monthly on new car registrations. These data supplied General Motors with a clear picture of the share of the market each of its products enjoyed and how that share was changing. The ten-day reports and the Polk registration figures made possible the swift adjustment of existing forecasts on the basis of actual demand. They also provided valuable data for drawing up future long-term forecasts.

On the eve of their departure for the West in mid-May, Sloan and Brown had asked the division managers to begin more accurate long-range forecasting on the basis of estimates that Brown's office had drawn up for the second half of 1924.[53] From this time on, the division estimates of demand and production, or Divisional Indices as they were called, were based on those worked up in the general office for the corporation as a whole. The details of these forecasting techniques need not be told here, since Pierre did little more than approve and praise them.[54] It is sufficient to say that by 1925 all short-term activities at General Motors—production schedules, purchases of supplies and materials, employment, and even prices (since costs and prices were so closely related to anticipated volume)—were based on the annual Divisional Indices; these were, in turn set within a statistical framework provided by the general office. Through this central set of statistics the executives could guide the divisions without encroaching directly on the authority and responsibility of the division managers.

These data, so essential in supervising divisional activities and in maintaining the flow of goods through the many facilities, also became exceedingly useful to Pierre and to other members of the Finance Committee in evaluating divisional performance. They found them invaluable, too, in determining the allocation of funds and other resources among the corporation's many divisions. Actual output, sales, and profit could be continually checked against the earlier estimates. The division managers could then analyze and explain the differences to the Executive and Finance committees. The members of these committees were in a better position than before to decide whether general business and marketing conditions or managerial ability accounted for these differences. On the basis of such information they could allocate capital funds and executive talent more rationally. As one financial executive outlined these procedures:

> The forecasting program should serve two separate and quite distinct general purposes. In its broadest aspects, the forecast affords means of gauging an operating program in terms of the fundamental policy of the Corporation regarding the rate of return on capital investment, as related to the pricing of the product, and the condition under which additional capital will be provided for expansion. The second and more frequent use of the forecast is as a tool for control of current operations.[55]

Pierre was immensely pleased and impressed with the report that Sloan wrote in September 1924 in answer to the June resolution of the Finance Committee.[56] So, too, were the bankers—Baker, Prosser, Stettinius, and George Whitney—and the other du Ponts on the committee. Pierre was at last fully confident, really for the first time since the Du Pont Company made its initial investment in General Motors, that he and his associates could maintain an effective oversight of their massive investment by doing little more than a careful reading of the statistical reports and regularly attending the meetings of the Finance Committee.

## The Rebuilding Completed

Sloan's response to the 1924 inventory difficulties reassured Pierre that he need not delay his plans for semiretirement. He was now certain that General Motors could move forward with efficiency that was still rare in the automobile industry. The end of 1924 indicated that the patterns of administration, finance, and product line were all fully defined. The years immediately following were to reveal just how successful had been the rebuilding of the nation's and, in fact, of the world's second largest automobile company.

By 1924 General Motors certainly had the best set of managers in the business. This was true at the top level, where General Motors had such automotive veterans as Sloan, Bassett, the Fisher brothers, Knudsen, Kettering, Mott, and DeWitt Page, as well as those trained in the Du Pont school—men like Pratt, Brown, Turner, Bergland, E. A. Johnson, and others. But, as Pierre realized when he began to work out the allocations for shares in the Management Securities Company, the second and third lines of management were also filled with highly competent men. Ford, Dodge, Chrysler, Nash, Studebaker, and Packard had, at best, some exceedingly capable senior executives but far fewer talented men down the line. Ford, in particular, had been losing many of his key executives during the very years Pierre and Sloan had been building up their management team. Pierre's plan to encourage the team to stay together by the formation of the Management Securities Company worked well. Very few of the eighty who took a part in the plan left the corporation before reaching retirement age.

By the end of 1924 Pierre believed that General Motors was organized to assure the most efficient use of the managerial talent. The decentralized structure gave the divisional managers a wide scope of action within the broad policies set by the senior committees. The steps taken since 1921 to increase the oversight of the general office and to assure more certain coordination of activities, all had Pierre's strongest support. He heartily approved the increase of the chief executive's power and the formation of the interdivisional committees to bring together the different divisional and staff executives working on the same kind of functional activity. He finally felt certain that the statistical and financial procedures at General Motors were refined and sophisticated enough to permit a constant oversight of the corporation's activities by the senior committees of the board.

Pierre's major contribution in the development of the organization and administrative techniques at General Motors was to accept their importance and to support those who were instituting them. Such support was of genuine importance in industry in which systematic methods of over-all management had not yet been employed and were little understood. In fact, the best-known producer, Henry Ford, was at this time openly ridiculing them. Nor did Chrysler, Dodge, Nash, and the other companies appear to have taken a real interest in organizational matters before General Motors' success led to imitation.

By the close of 1924 the corporation's financial structure was as sound as its administration. Raskob and Brown continued to be as constructive in finance as Sloan was in operations; they, like Sloan, never moved without full and careful consultation with Pierre. In 1924 the financial executives decided to consolidate the corporation's four different types of preferred and debenture stocks into a single issue of 7% cumulative preferred stock with no voting rights (except that if the corporation failed to pay 7% dividends, its holders could elect one-quarter of the board of directors). They further agreed to reduce the 20,646,379 shares of common stock outstanding with a capitalization of $10 for a no par value stock capitalized at $50. For four shares of old, each stockholder received one of the new. When the exchanges were completed, the preferred stock outstanding would have a book value of $110.0 million and the 5,161,600 shares of common, a book value of $258.1 million[57]

By 1925 the corporation's securities were a very sound investment. In 1924, even with the sharp drop in demand during the spring, General Motors' net income stood at $51,623,490, and the dividend remained at the same rate as during the more profitable year of 1923.[58] After that year, profits, dividends, and the value of the stock rose sharply. In 1925 income more than doubled to $116,016,000, and the dividends rose to $12 a year (as compared to $4.85 for the same value of stock the previous year). This was only the beginning. In the next few years General Motors turned in one of the most satisfactory profit records of any large corporation in this country.

By the fall of 1924 the only business involved in the rebuilding of the corporation still unfinished was the final definition of its basic product line. In this work Sloan concentrated first on improving Chevrolet and then on filling critical gaps in the product line. On the second, preliminary decisions had already been made. The president's response to the sharp criticism of the Finance Committee in June of 1924 about Chevrolet's quality was to make minor changes in the existing models. He urged Chevrolet to put its best engineering talent into having a first-rate car ready for the model year that began in the summer of 1925. These new models had a longer body, increased leg room, a Duco finish, a one-piece windshield with automatic wipers, an improved clutch, and a sound rear-axle housing. They met Sloan's expectations, as well as those of Pierre and of the Finance Committee.[59] With this model General Motors began, for the first time, to make serious inroads on Ford's low-priced market.

Until Pierre, Sloan, Kettering, Knudsen, and others had agreed in the summer of 1923 not to consider the copper-cooled motor as an immediate prospect, they had had little chance to consider how to fill the two most obvious gaps in that product line—gaps that Pierre had pointed out in his report of December 1921. Of these the most critical one to be filled was the low-priced, high-volume range between Chevrolet and Oakland in which Pierre had originally hoped to place the air-cooled Oakland. The other was the gap between Cadillac and Buick which Pierre had suggested the Cadillac Division could fill by building a car to sell for about $2,000.

In the fall of 1923 Sloan and Pierre agreed that the designing of a car to fill the first need would be an excellent task for the newly formed General Technical Committee. They both hoped that in carrying out this task the committee could draw on the development work already done on the copper-cooled car. Specifically, Sloan proposed that a water-cooled 6-cylinder engine be developed to be used in the chassis that Oldsmobile already had built for an air-cooled car.[60] From this suggestion came the Pontiac. Having learned the high cost of haste, the general executives were determined to move deliberately in the development of this car. When the designs were completed in the fall of 1924, George H. Hannum asked whether his Oakland Division might not take over production and marketing of the new car. This request led the Executive Committee to debate the wisdom of selling an automobile that would take away customers from both Chevrolet and Oldsmobile. But its skeptical members—and Pierre was not one of them— were convinced by Sloan that "it will be better that we take business from our own Divisions than have competitors do so."[61]

The Executive Committee agreed that the new car's design must be approved by the General Technical Committee before production could begin at Oakland. After being road-tested by Chevrolet, it would be returned to Oakland to be produced and sold. The development went off on schedule so that the new Pontiac was ready for volume production in the fall of 1925. It proved to be such a success that Oakland soon dropped its other, more expensive, model and concentrated all its efforts on the Pontiac. Soon it changed the name of its division to that of its new product.

In July 1924 Pierre took part in the discussions on the one last step in rounding out the General Motors product line. The Executive Committee, however, did not implement the resulting decision to develop what was to be the La Salle until the Pontiac had proved itself. Then, when the Oakland line was discontinued, Oldsmobile moved down into a price range between Buick and the new Pontiac. Cadillac was authorized, as Pierre had proposed in September of 1921, to build a $2,000 car. Although the Executive Committee did not give that division the go ahead until March of 1926, the La Salle was, nevertheless, ready for mass production by the fall of 1927.[62]

By the end of 1924 all of Pierre's plans were successfully completed— except the copper-cooled engine. And during that fall Pierre had finally begun to lose interest in the experiment. In spite of Kettering's continued reassurances, the copper-cooled engine's new start proved to be a slow one. In the late spring of 1924 Kettering had asked the General Technical Committee to run road tests on the 6-cylinder model he was developing at Dayton. He refused to let the divisions take part in the tests "for fear of the prejudice" against the copper-cooled. In August Knudsen had the redesigned air-cooled 4-cylinder Chevrolet tested. Both tests were disappointing; neither warranted a move to volume production.[63]

But Pierre and the majority of the Executive Committee simply could not bring themselves to drop the copper-cooled engine. At a meeting of the committee in September 1924 (the discussion was put off until a time when Pierre could attend), Sloan proposed to sell the patents to an automotive engineer who had spent many years with the Franklin Company, the only other major producer of an air-cooled engine.[64] Sloan's opponents no longer argued about the potential profitability of the car but rather stressed how much the corporation had already invested in the experiment. They recalled that Sloan had estimated in February 1924 the direct costs of the copper-cooled experiment to be $3.5 million.[65] Indirect costs resulting from delaying at least two years the completion of the General Motors product line were far, far greater. With so much money put into the innovation, they still hoped they might get something out of it.

In the following spring General Motors at last buried the copper-cooled scheme. In April 1925 Sloan sent the Executive Committee a memorandum saying the 6-cylinder was still not ready for production and enclosed Church's long report on the 4-cylinder car and engine.[66] In this report Church said that while there were still some minor problems to overcome, the major ones had been solved and that the car was finally ready for production and sale. By then, however, the Chevrolet water-cooled was becoming one of the fastest-selling cars in the country and was challenging Ford's Model T in the low-price class. Sloan was certain that "no member of the Executive Committee wants at this time to advance any argument that we should do anything in connection with Chevrolet considering its present position, earning power, etc." No one did, not even Pierre. Nor did Kettering or anyone else argue that the time had come to set up a new division to make and market the 6-cylinder. The Executive Committee did not even bother to discuss Church's recommendations or Sloan's letter analyzing them.

Pierre's experience with the air-cooled engine was certainly not a happy one. The project failed partly because development was too hurried and partly because the market was changing so rapidly. In order to revive the money-losing divisions Pierre pushed on them a product before it was ready for full-scale production and distribution. The intensified controversy that resulted between the line or staff executives at General Motors unquestionably lowered the chances of producing a successful car. More important, however, was the shifting demand for automobiles. The rapidly growing market made an entirely new product far less necessary as a competitive weapon than when the market was as depressed as it was from 1920 to 1922. High demand meant that the managers at Chevrolet and other General Motors divisions were certain that they could capture even more than their share of the market with the conventional water-cooled engine. Understandably, Pierre's only major setback at General Motors came in the field in which he had the least experience.

Yet, Pierre's very lack of experience in the industry may have pushed him into doing a more effective job at General Motors than he would have done otherwise. His broad administrative and financial experience stood him in good stead when he moved from managing a giant explosives and chemical company to managing a corporation in still another industry. Moreover, even though his knowledge of the engineering and design of this second corporation's product was extremely limited, he did make an important contribution in defining the basic product line and market strategy. In so doing he saw the genuine need for technological development and placed great faith in Kettering and his technically trained associates to innovate.

In any case, Pierre's insistence on using a radically different engine to improve the product line kept him involved with the affairs of General Motors after the corporation was administratively and financially back on its feet. The efforts to get the copper-cooled engine into mass production helped Pierre see the problems at General Motors far more quickly than if he had not been so involved. They made clear the importance of organizational adjustment, particularly the formation of the interdivisional committees; they gave him a clear picture of the abilities of the leading executives. It was to produce the copper-cooled engine that Pierre put Knudsen in charge of Chevrolet. Pierre, as much as anyone else, was responsible for bringing Kettering into the corporation in 1919 in order to develop such an engine. Certainly it was Pierre who kept Kettering from resigning over the first failure of the experiment. Even though Sloan was on the other side, his handling of the issues involved only increased Pierre's respect for him. He fully realized that Sloan had a better understanding of the problems involved in getting the copper-cooled engine into production and had, in spite of Pierre's protests, taken the necessary steps to avoid the full consequences of the failure of the experiment.

Pierre du Pont's achievements at General Motors essentially resulted from his critical appreciation of the problems the corporation faced, from an understanding of what talents were needed to meet these challenges, and from an ability to bring together into a working team extremely able and strong-minded men. To play this role Pierre had become himself intimately involved in the affairs of the corporation. He had not been involved during the time when Durant and Raskob ran General Motors. He became so only when he was forced, in 1921, to bring the corporation back from near disaster. He remained so committed until 1924, largely because of the copper-cooled experiment. After 1924, when the corporation had clearly reached a peak of administrative and financial excellence and when the copper-cooled car was clearly no longer feasible, Pierre was more than happy to give General Motors even less attention than he had in the years before 1921.

# Last Years at General Motors and Du Pont

CHAPTER 22

In the spring of 1924, before the growing inventories became a serious problem, Pierre was determined, come what may, that he would leave General Motors' affairs largely to others and turn his full attention to Longwood and the needs of his native state. In April he had enjoyed the festivities at the formal opening of the Kennett Pike, a modern highway running from Wilmington to Kennett Square, Pennsylvania, which he had personally helped finance.[1] A little later that spring, he, Raskob, and the Reverend James H. Odell met to revive plans made in 1920 to improve Delaware's public school system.[2]

At Longwood Pierre wanted to carry out long-held plans for water gardens and fountains. He had earlier built several ponds and lakes and in 1919 he had installed a large pumping station.[3] Before settling on a definite design Pierre wished to visit Europe to study famous fountains and gardens. But the affairs of General Motors had forced a constant postponement of the trip.

Such were the renewed projects and interests that decided Pierre in the summer of 1924 to "sell out" his major holdings to his brothers and sisters. Yet even after he had successfully carried out the transaction, he did not completely put aside business matters. For the next four years he continued as chairman of the board of both General Motors and Du Pont and also of Christiana Securities—the instrument through which his immediate family controlled the other two. From this vantage point he kept a watchful eye on the huge industrial empire he had done so much to create.

*Selling Out*

For some time before May 1924 Pierre had been troubled by the high cost of transferring his properties. Inheritance taxes promised to be so large as to force a sale of part of his securities, thus impairing the value of his estate and, of much more importance in Pierre's mind, of weakening his immediate family's control of the Du Pont Company and, through it, of General Motors. Moreover, any forced sale would drive down the price of the securities sold. As long ago as 1915, after the reorganization of the company which followed Coleman's sale of his stock, Pierre had taken out $6.0 million worth of life insurance, an amount he considered adequate to pay state and federal taxes coming due on his death. In this way he hoped to avoid a sale of securities.[4] By the early 1920s this sum had become inadequate. Nevertheless, Pierre resisted increasing his insurance because he disliked to tie up so much income. In addition, in the spring of 1924 a revenue bill was being debated in Congress which levied the highest inheritance taxes ever imposed by the federal government, reaching 40% on estates over $10.0 million.[5] That bill had passed Congress in May and was signed by President Calvin Coolidge on June 2.

By 1924 Pierre had given some thought to the transfer of his estate. He had followed Coleman's example by turning over 7,000 shares of Du Pont and 2,800 shares of Christiana Securities in 1919 and 1921 to members of the Du Pont Executive Committee. In the spring of 1923 he proposed doing the same with over $6.0 million worth of General Motors stock, which he planned to sell to the Management Securities Company. In September 1923 he proposed to Irénée to sell 20,000 shares of Du Pont common "with [the] similar object of interesting men prominent in the Du Pont Company."[6] But by the time the Management Securities Company arrangement had been completed and other General Motors business tidied up, Pierre (and his brothers and brothers-in-law) had turned to the idea of "selling out" to his immediate family rather than to the company and turning over nearly all his "powder holdings" rather than just the 20,000-share block. Such a move would insure a safe and inexpensive transfer of the basic family property. It would also make explicit his desire to remove himself from the active affairs of both Du Pont and General Motors. He probably would have waited until the inventory problems and the copper-cooled engine had been worked out. But he acted in May in order to have his estate settled before the passage of the new law on inheritance taxes.

Pierre's holdings included 12,500 shares of Du Pont preferred, 24,000 shares of Du Pont common, 51,000 shares of Christiana Securities preferred, and 56,000 shares of Christiana Securities common. Together these Christiana Securities totaled an equity of 107,000 shares of Du Pont and were now close to one-third the total stock outstanding in the family holding company.[7] Pierre held 12,000 shares of Hercules and 11,000 shares of Atlas that he had received when the Du Pont Company was split in 1912 after the antitrust suit. Besides these securities, Pierre looked on Longwood —its grounds, gardens, and greenhouses—as part of a larger family estate. Indeed, unless the family could arrange to care for it, Longwood could only be sold at a great loss. But these losses would be small compared to those that might result if part of Pierre's Christiana Securities or of Du Pont holdings had to be suddenly sold.

Winder Laird, Pierre's stockbroker brother-in-law, strongly supported by Irénée and another brother-in-law, Ruly Carpenter, favored making the transfer by setting up an annuity.[8] They proposed forming a holding company, to be called the Delaware Realty and Investment Company, to buy these holdings from Pierre and, in turn, pay him an annuity computed on the current return from the securities. The annuity, they were certain, was not taxable until the payment to the recipient exceeded the price of the annuity. They opposed, however, buying an annuity from an insurance company because they were certain that its very high cost would force, in the same manner as inheritance taxes, the sale of some of Pierre's holdings. By making the transaction within the family, that cost would be avoided. After reviewing these proposals, Pierre checked with the Equitable Life Assurance Society to see if all this information was correct.[9] Satisfied, he and Alice signed on May 31, 1924, the agreement setting up the holding company and defining the annuity.

By the terms of this agreement, Pierre turned over to the newly formed holding company all his Du Pont, Atlas, and Hercules shares and nearly all of his Christiana Securities stock (44,000 out of his 51,000 shares of preferred and 49,000 out of his 56,000 shares of common).[10] He also transferred to it 400 shares of Longwood, Incorporated, which included securities and insurance as well as title to the grounds and greenhouses. His residence and fifty acres of adjoining land were omitted from the agreement. On these properties was placed a book value of $13.5 million, apparently based on the par value of the stock. The current income from them was estimated at a little under $1.0 million a year. So the annuity was to pay Pierre and Alice $900,000 a year until their deaths.

In this way, then, Pierre and his immediate family were able to transfer the major part of Pierre's estate without losing any substantial income, or in any way threatening the control of the family holdings. Pierre's brothers and brothers-in-law then divided the shares of Delaware Realty into eight parts: one part went to each member of the immediate family, that is, to Irénée du Pont, Lammot du Pont, Louisa Copeland, Mary Laird, Isabella Sharp, and Margaretta Carpenter; a share went to Henry B. du Pont (Henry Belin du Pont's son); and one was divided among William K. du Pont's three children, Paulina, Wilhelmina, and Hallock. Several of these members, in turn, divided their allotment among their children. Thus, through Delaware Realty and their holdings in Christiana Securities, Pierre's immediate family continued to maintain the controlling interest of Du Pont and, through Du Pont, of General Motors.

Once the transaction was completed, Pierre informed the Du Pont Company and members of the larger family of the arrangement and the reasons for it. Most revealing was a letter to Alice's brother Paul.[11] In it Pierre dealt with the problems involved in a large inheritance and his desire to remove himself from an active business life. "A law that requires the holding of one-fourth of a large estate or devotion of about one half of the gross income to pay life insurance premiums seems to me to be the height of financial stupidity."[12] On the other hand, he eagerly looked forward to a change of pace and new kinds of work. "I often wonder why so many people hang on to their fortune and property instead of having the fun of watching the distribution processes themselves." Since the tax laws gave no incentive to accumulate, "why not then enjoy the dissociation processes. I have had much more satisfaction in planning for roads, schools and hospitals, etc. than in continuing the piling up process, and am sure that I shall enjoy much more the further development of the Du Pont interests as an outsider and adviser than as an owner and responsible head." Not that he would drop out entirely. As he said in a second letter, his "usefulness as an adviser will be problably as great without owning this block of stock."[13] Pierre concluded his first letter:

> It is curious how history repeats itself. In 1902 the sudden death of Eugene du Pont brought about the sale of the Du Pont business interests to T.C., Alfred and me, price paid $12,000,000 in bonds and one quarter stock in the new company. In 1915, T.C. sold out to Irénée, Lammot, John, Ruly, Felix and me, price paid $13,900,000. Now Irénée, Lammot and Winder offer to buy me out, price offered $13,500,000. It seems logical to let go does it not?

Paul Belin, who agreed, must have seen one significant fact in the progression in the change of ownership. Where, before, succession had begun within the clan, now it ended by being wholly within Pierre's immediate family. Moreover, Delaware Realty controlled properties and investments vastly larger than those that Pierre and his two cousins had purchased in 1902, or those that Pierre and his associates had acquired in 1915.

This transfer of his property turned Pierre further away from the affairs of General Motors and Du Pont, and more toward enjoying what he called the dissociation process. He was not yet old, just over fifty-four, and still active and vigorous. By September 1924 Pierre was engrossed in working out a plan that would require the approval of the state legislature for financing the expansion of the Delaware public school system.[14] His studies of the financing of the schools had led him to analyze and suggest reforms in the state's tax structure. These suggestions led in turn to his appointment in the fall of 1925 as State School Tax Commissioner.[15] In that same year Pierre and Alice made their long-postponed trip to Europe. In Italy he found the model for his water garden at the Villa Gamberaia near Florence. Pierre thoroughly enjoyed applying his technical training to aesthetic purposes. The pools of the garden at Longwood, as in the original in Italy, were precisely located to allow for optical illusion. From the viewing terrace they appear equidistant. Once these carefully planned pools, fountains, and planting were completed, Pierre began building a set of electrically operated and lighted fountains in front of the greenhouses. The fountains were fed by an intricate system of underground pipes, with the water falling back into recirculating basins; they were set in the formally designed garden of box-wood shrubs and trees. The lighting was so arranged that when the jets of water rose to heights of almost a hundred feet and fell again, the colors changed in harmonious sequence through the entire spectrum. Playing their ever-changing shapes and colors, from the subdued to the dramatic, the electrical fountains brought continual pleasure to the designer and also to the general public, who were welcomed to the vast gardens.

In the mid-1920s Pierre also began to sharpen his political views. Not only was he disturbed by what, even then, seemed to him punitive income and inheritance taxes, but he was also most unhappy about the outcome of that noble experiment, prohibition. In his letters to Paul Belin telling of the transfer of his holdings, Pierre inveighed against the Eighteenth Amendment.[16] It encouraged "an utter disregard of law," bringing graft and black-mail. Nor did it discourage drinking. In fact, he saw far more inebriates now than he ever had seen before prohibition. Since the Republicans then in office supported and endorsed what to him were unhealthy, indeed immoral, tax and antidrinking laws, Pierre began to question again his allegiance to the Republican party. His irritation at prohibition would soon carry him into taking a leading part in the repeal of the Eighteenth Amendment.

### The Christiana Securities Company

Although Pierre spent much more time on such nonbusiness interests after the summer of 1924, he continued for the next four years to maintain a careful oversight of his family's business interests. Even though he was no longer an owner, but in his words "an outsider and adviser," he remained one of the most influential men at Du Pont and General Motors. Besides being chairman of the board of both companies, he stayed on the Finance Committee of each. He also continued to serve at General Motors on committees that reviewed bonuses and salaries. But it was as chairman of the Christiana Securities Company that his power was most explicitly defined. His immediate family held over 60% of Christiana common stock, and Christiana in turn held over 30% of the Du Pont common stock outstanding (through Delaware Realty and personal holdings the share held by Pierre's family in Du Pont was even higher). Since the Du Pont Company still owned close to 35% of the voting stock of General Motors, the family had practical control of that corporation.

Pierre's desire to maintain this control over Du Pont and General Motors was essentially a negative one. He did not want that control in order to manage. After 1919 at Du Pont and after 1924 at General Motors he insisted explicitly that he did not want to be involved in setting policies, even the broadest ones on markets, strategies of expansion, and organizational structure. What he wanted was to be sure that the men who did make these decisions were competent professional managers. His experiences with nonprofessional "partners" at Du Pont and General Motors had seared him. At both companies some of his most difficult moments had been caused by other large stockholders—by Coleman, Alfred, and William at Du Pont, and by Durant at General Motors. Control for Pierre meant the assurance that a rational professional management was committed to the use of its energies to produce earnings for the stockholders. From such a management all branches of the du Pont family would benefit. Durant, Alfred, William, and even Coleman, Pierre felt, had not always put the firm and its stockholders before their own personal interests.

During the 1920s Pierre and his brothers were obsessively concerned about assuring control of their two companies. At least until 1925 they continued to fear a raid by outside speculators—such as Durant—or disgruntled family members—such as Alfred and William. This concern was shown in their extreme caution in refinancing the Christiana Securities bond issue. In 1924 they asked J. P. Morgan and Company to handle the refunding of $5.0 million worth of 7½% bonds of which part could be paid off in cash. (The issue originally resulted from the arrangements to pay for Coleman's block of stock.) When one of the Morgan partners, Edward Stettinius, suggested that this be done by the purchase of $4.0 million in call loans, Irénée replied:

> I have little doubt that carrying the $4,000,000 in call loans would be reasonably safe if the loss in case of serious trouble would not be out of all proportion to the cost of avoiding the risk. This unfortunately is the case, for the Christiana Securities Co. is in substantial control of the Du Pont Co. and that in turn in working control of the General Motors Corp., so that it is important not to in any wise jeopardize the collateral behind the loan, and though there is not one chance in a hundred of any real danger, we must avoid that chance.[17]

Irénée then proposed, and Stettinius agreed to, an issue of $3.0 million worth of 5½% bonds coming due serially between July 1, 1925, and July 1, 1931, and backed by 100,000 shares of Du Pont common.[18] The funds from this sale would then be used to retire $3.0 million of the existing $5.0 million worth of Christiana Securities 7% bonds. The remainder, Irénée and Pierre planned to pay off from the holding company's dividends. This refinancing reduced the interest payments on collateral required for the Christiana Securities bonds. At the same time the market value of the collateral made the notes "gilt edge" and assured a quick sale of the new issue.

Because of the caution of its owners the balance sheets of Christiana Securities during the 1920s showed little change in the nature of the assets listed. Pierre and his brothers never considered these assets with a book value of over $40.0 million as a pool of capital for investment. In periods of falling prices they occasionally used holding company funds to support Du Pont or General Motors stock and also to increase their holdings of both at bargain rates.[19] Only once during the 1920s and 1930s did Christiana Securities hold any other industrial stock. Then for a very brief period late in 1929 and in 1930 it owned small amounts of Kennecott Copper and Anaconda Copper.[20] The holding company's balance sheet looked very much the same in 1918, 1928, and 1938.

Pierre and his brothers did, however, use the capital for investments or financial moves that might affect the control of their interests. From the start Christiana Securities held a sizable block of stock in the Wilmington Trust Company, the bank Pierre had helped to found in the early years of the Powder Company. Pierre also used holding company funds for a short time at the end of 1920 to help finance the Du Pont Company's purchase of Durant's General Motors stock.[21] Earlier that year the holding company purchased Wilmington's two leading papers— the *Evening Journal* and the *Morning News.*[22] The first had been owned for years by Colonel Henry, and the second by Alfred I. du Pont, who had used it to attack Pierre and his brothers during the long and bitter legal suit of *du Pont vs. du Pont.* In 1920 Alfred had run into serious financial trouble.[23] The federal government was demanding over $1.8 million in cash in taxes on Alfred's 1915 income. He was being sued, too, by the officers and employees of a recent unsuccessful venture, the Nemours Trading Company, which had gone into bankruptcy. He was, therefore, forced to sell his paper, and Pierre, of course, was delighted to buy it. He and his brothers then arranged to have Christiana Securities purchase Colonel Henry's paper and to merge the town's leading morning and evening newspapers.

Alfred's troubles also forced him to consider selling his large block of 78,000 shares of Du Pont common. In December 1921 he approached Irénée to see if he and his brothers would be interested in buying.[24] As his asking price was $280 a share and as the market price was then just under a $100 a share, Irénée turned him down. In January 1922 Alfred asked Thomas Cochran of J. P. Morgan and Company to find a buyer for 75,000 shares of Du Pont common. "My feeling is," Alfred told Cochran, "that were this block of stock in the hands of some outsider, so to speak, it would be the means of bringing a new influence to the Board of Directors, of which, as I have frankly stated to you, they are in great need."[25] Alfred, however, continued to be most unrealistic about the price. When Cochran suggested that $280 was a little steep for a stock selling at about $75, Alfred indicated that he would let it go at $140. The Morgan firm was not interested at that price. Cochran pointed out to Alfred that he had only two alternatives available: he must either organize a group of outsiders to buy the stock, or turn to Pierre and his brothers. Alfred reluctantly agreed to the latter course and Cochran called in Irénée. After checking with Pierre and the other directors of Christiana Securities, Irénée proposed buying 30,000 of Alfred's shares at 83⅓ and the balance by deferred payments over a period of time at a somewhat higher price.[26] Alfred, however, insisted on $150 a share. Although Cochran thought that Alfred might come down to $125, he considered further negotiations "fruitless."[27] In the end Alfred made a satisfactory settlement with the government. By holding on to his stock he remained until his death the largest stockholder in the Du Pont Company except for Christiana Securities itself.[28] The whole episode could only remind Pierre of the importance of control and the value of Christiana Securities in maintaining it.

Nevertheless, later in the same year, 1922, Pierre permitted the one exception to his general rule and allowed Christiana Securities funds to be used in a way that was not directly concerned with the maintenance of family control. He agreed to the purchase of a block of stock of the Atlas Powder Company (one of the two firms formed by the dissolution of the old Powder Company in 1912). One reason that Pierre agreed to this move was his friendship with Sir Harry McGowan and his interest in maintaining the Du Pont alliance with the Nobel Industries. He may also have been worried that Coleman du Pont was beginning to take a new interest in the powder industry. For, although Coleman had been a United States Senator from Delaware since 1921, he retained his interest in business affairs; and, although he had sold his Du Pont stock, he still held the many shares he had received in Atlas at the time of its formation.

In March 1922 Pierre learned from William Coyne that Atlas officials were trying to have an import duty placed on explosives in order "to forestall a CXL [Canadian Explosives, Ltd.] invasion of the United States with its dynamite."[29] This move indicated that Atlas's president, William J. Webster, was "not in a conciliatory mood." Coyne added: "I will hazard a guess that he is either being coached or advised in this matter by T.C." CXL, it will be remembered, was the large Canadian company that the Du Pont Company and Nobel Industries had jointly owned since 1910. At about this same time Pierre learned that Atlas had enlarged its Canadian business by purchasing control of Northern Explosives, Ltd. Atlas itself had become a major force in the explosives industry when, in 1915, it purchased the largest independent, the Giant Powder Company of California and its several subsidiaries, including the Giant Powder Company of Canada.

Before taking any action Pierre decided to check with Atlas's president. Webster insisted that in protecting the interests of their stockholders neither Atlas nor the Giant Powder Company of Canada was "doing anything that is unfair." He did not want to remain in the shadow of the larger company. Their Canadian business should not "remain in a position where its success or failure is determined by Canadian Explosives, Ltd."[30] Despite this strong statement, Atlas and its Canadian subsidary, as well as the Du Pont Company, the Nobel Industries, and its subsidiary had, by summer, worked out a complicated but mutually satisfactory arrangement. Atlas would merge its Canadian companies (Northern Explosives and Giant of Canada) into a new firm, the Northern-Giant Explosives, Ltd. It would then sell stock in the new company to the Du Pont Company and Nobel Industries and in exchange would receive stock in Canadian Explosives, Ltd. While these negotiations were under way, someone, probably Sir Harry McGowan, proposed that they cement the alliance still further by having the du Ponts increase their holdings in Atlas. This could be done most easily through Christiana Securities Company.

Irénée at first strongly opposed the purchase of a block of Atlas stock by Christiana Securities. He disliked the proposal, he wrote Pierre, even though the head of the Du Pont legal staff had advised that Christiana Securities could purchase Atlas stock without transgressing the antitrust laws as long as its holdings and those of Pierre and his immediate family did not amount to 50% of the voting stock.[31] If it was important to have the majority shares of Atlas stock in "friendly hands," Irénée preferred to have Christiana Securities loan to individuals like Harry Haskell and Ruly Carpenter the funds necessary to make the purchase. However, at a meeting four days later, which Pierre and Raskob attended, the holding company's board agreed to bid on a new issue of stock that Atlas was floating to help finance the proposed merger.[32] By November, when the merger was completed, Christiana had purchased 16,500 shares out of 32,000 newly issued for just over $2.0 million.[33] In the following year, when Atlas split its stock 3 to 1, Christiana's holdings of Atlas rose to 49,500 shares out of a total of 261,438 shares outstanding.[34]

This purchase of a little over half of a new issue did not give the du Ponts formal control of Atlas, particularly as most of the 11,000 shares (33,000 after the split) held by Pierre and smaller amounts by his immediate family were still nonvoting stock. Nevertheless, this transaction gave Pierre and his brothers a powerful voice over the management of Atlas and one that might at least counter Coleman's. Then in April 1927 the Christiana Securities board agreed to buy from Coleman a block of 21,071 shares of Atlas at $60 apiece, thereby increasing Christiana's total holdings in Atlas to 70,000 shares.[35] Coleman, who was ill with cancer with only three more years to live, had finally taken himself out of the powder business.

By 1928, however, the relations between Christiana, Atlas, CXL, the Du Pont Company, and the Nobels were becoming so complicated that Pierre and his brothers decided to sever Christiana's connection. During the preceding years Atlas had been expanding its holdings in Canadian Explosives, much to the distress of Arthur B. Purvis, the president of CXL. In the summer of 1928 Purvis was insisting that Sir Harry McGowan and the du Ponts make Atlas sell much of its CXL stock back to the Canadian company. But at a meeting in Wilmington in September Sir Harry and Lammot du Pont (now the president of Christiana Securities as well as Du Pont) decided against such a change.[36] Purvis, who attended the meeting, was most annoyed. After all, he wrote McGowan, were not Nobel and Du Pont allied in CXL and did not the du Ponts through Christiana Securities control 52% of Atlas? Purvis admitted that he "did not feel it proper so to state at the meeting (in so far as the information came to me very confidentially)." The percentage of Du Pont control that Purvis did not mention openly was, even after the purchase of Coleman's stock, exaggerated.

The pressure from Purvis and possibly other rumors of control (talk that probably raised the specter of antitrust action) decided Pierre and his brothers to have Christiana dispose of its Atlas stock. In November 1928 they agreed to sell part of it back directly to Atlas and the rest to the brokerage house of Laird, Bissell and Meeds. Atlas, in turn, sold its shares of Canadian Explosives to Du Pont and Nobel Industries.[37] The sale ended any possible threat that the du Ponts might be accused of controlling Atlas through Christiana; kept the relationship of the Du Pont and the Nobel holdings in Canadian Explosives the same; and permitted Atlas managers through direct purchase and through Laird, Bissell and Meeds to increase their holdings in the stock of their company.

Pierre had watched the Atlas transaction with more than usual interest, because Sir Harry had become one of his close personal friends and because he had always favored the alliance with Nobel Industries. He felt that the du Ponts had greatly benefited from the patent and process agreement of 1907. Since his first visit in 1910 to the Nobel offices and factories, Pierre had kept in close touch with Harry McGowan. Then after the Armistice, Pierre had strongly supported, although he had taken almost no part in the negotiations, the formal arrangements between the Nobel Explosives Trades, Ltd., (which became Nobel Industries in November 1920) and the Du Pont Company that became known as the General Explosives Agreement of 1920.[38] Signed late in 1919, it was practically the same agreement that had been drawn up in 1914 and that the du Ponts considered to have been put in abeyance with the war in Europe. The only difference was, of course, that the German firms were not included in this new patent and process agreement. Later, in 1920, Pierre had worked closely with Sir Harry to persuade the Nobel firm to help finance General Motors expansion. During the 1920s, when Sir Harry came on regular trips to this country to check on both his automobile and chemical interests, he and his wife and daughter often stayed with Alice and Pierre at Longwood. When the du Ponts visited Britain, they enjoyed visiting the McGowans.[39]

Pierre had another opportunity to strengthen the Du Pont Company ties with Nobel in 1923. That summer Sir Harry and his associates began to protest vigorously against the Du Pont Company's sales of munitions in Europe, an area they considered to be their market. Pierre tried, in this case unsuccessfully, to soften the controversy.[40] Harry Haskell and Felix du Pont, who were then responsible for overseas sales of smokeless powder, argued that these sales did not violate the agreement with the British because that was a patent agreement, and the smokeless powder sold in Europe was no longer protected by patents. They further pointed out that the War and Navy departments, and even General John J. Pershing, had been urging the Du Pont Company to make these sales as the only way to assure continuing development and production of military powders. For in these years Congress had cut to almost nothing appropriations for the military services to buy or make powder.

Pierre agreed on the logic of the first point but was probably less than sympathetic to the second. He contended, however, that it was not prudent to antagonize the Nobels for such a small amount of business. He had always cherished the "free and frank exchange of ideas" for which Sir Harry continued to speak. The Du Pont Company's move into chemicals, Pierre pointed out, still further enhanced the value of the old alliance. Yet at this time the views of Haskell and Felix prevailed. Pierre made no effort to push his ideas after the Executive Committee had rejected them. The Du Pont Company, therefore, continued to sell military powders to Poland, Czechoslovakia, Spain, and other European countries.[41]

Although Pierre had not been able to alter the views of the Executive Committee, he undoubtedly helped to keep the alliance firm by assuring Sir Harry that the Britisher's views were getting a fair hearing in Wilmington. By the mid-twenties the connection between the two giant chemical firms was proving useful even beyond the exchange of technological information. In 1925 the Du Pont Executive Committee arranged with Nobel Industries for the licensing of production and marketing of its new "Duco" automobile finishes in Britain and on the Continent.[42] In the same year the Du Pont Company worked out with Nobel Industries, Ltd., and the German Badische Anilin the formation of a firm to produce and sell tetraethyl gasoline developed by the Ethyl Gasoline Corporation (jointly owned by General Motors, and Standard Oil Company of New Jersey). At this same time, too, the Du Pont and Nobel companies decided to join together to help finance the modernization and expansion of the two large German companies that before World War I had been part of the Nobel alliance, the Dynamit-Aktien-Gesellschaft vorm. Alfred Nobel and Company [DAG] and the Köln-Rottweil Pulverfabriken AG.[43] The Du Pont Company did not favor the idea of a loan but preferred to invest in the common stock of the companies. As the German companies wanted funds to embark on the production of new chemical products—celluloid, artificial silk, vulcanized fiber, and viscose products—the investment promised to be valuable in the exchange of technological information and in the development of new markets. At the same time Irénée hoped that the investment might soften the German companies' competitive aggressiveness in South America. Irénée therefore suggested that Du Pont and Nobel Industries each purchase 5 million shares (14% of the stock) in the two German companies. The plan was carried out without a hitch. The relationships between Du Pont and Nobel and the German firms remained relatively unchanged throughout the 1920s, even after the great mergers of 1926 that resulted in the formation of Imperial Chemical Industries (with Nobel Industries a major founder) in England, and I. G. Farbenindustries AG (which the German companies joined) in Germany.[44]

The growing success of both the Nobel and Du Pont companies in chemicals caused Sir Harry to propose in 1927 "a closer community of interests between Imperial Chemical Industries and the du Ponts."[45] His suggestion for tightening the alliance was to have his company sell its 100,000 General Motors shares and purchase with the money received 45,000 shares of Du Pont. Pierre approved of the exchange, but he was not at all sympathetic to a suggestion from Raskob that the Nobels be made even more explicit partners by offering them an equivalent amount of Christiana Securities stock.[46] With the money received from this sale Raskob proposed to buy into United States Steel, whose stock Irénée and other du Ponts were purchasing on their own account, or better yet to purchase more General Motors stock. Pierre undoubtedly approved of Lammot's reply to Raskob, for it expressed so precisely his own feelings about the family holding company. "Christiana Securities is almost entirely owned by a small group that are intimately connected and whose interests are much the same. If we get another substantial stockholder, such as I.C.I., the chances are that its interest would not be wholly with the other stockholders, and this would leave the way open to difficulties and misunderstandings."[47]

Pierre preferred not to use the holding company even to help finance a major venture proposed by the members of his own immediate family. When, in these same years, 1927 and 1928, his brother Irénée, his nephew Henry B. du Pont, and other family members and close friends decided to invest in the United States Rubber Company, Pierre approved.[48] He contributed to the initial investment, but took no part in the negotiations with Charles B. Seger which resulted in that group's purchase of 30% of the rubber company's stock, and with it practical control. Nor did Pierre make any suggestions for the resulting administrative and financial reorganization of the rubber firm after Francis B. Davis, an able Du Pont executive, became its president and after he installed the Du Pont form of decentralized operating structure and the Du Pont types of centralized financial and statistical controls.[49] Ownership of the rubber company's stock through Christiana Securities would have been the easiest way to maintain family control of this new large investment. Instead it was secured by setting up a voting trust consisting first of Irénée, young Henry B. du Pont, and Holliday Meeds.[50] Later Lammot and Felix du Pont became trustees. That this alternative was used emphasizes Pierre's determination to have Christiana Securities used for nothing except to assure him and his family control of the E. I. du Pont de Nemours & Company and its own massive investment in the General Motors Corporation. It was not to be a vehicle to increase the family's influence and income in other parts of American industry.

## Watching Over General Motors

At both Du Pont and General Motors Pierre viewed his job as chairman of the board as involving two tasks: one was to review and give a final approval as to dividends, capital appropriations, and other financial policies, the other was to make sure that the professional executives managing both companies were of the highest caliber. In carrying out these tasks Pierre concentrated much more on General Motors than on Du Pont. After the 1920 crisis at General Motors, he and his brothers had made an implicit agreement by which he would supervise the affairs of the automobile company and they would look after Du Pont. As the decade of the 1920s passed, Pierre became even more confident about the executive abilities of Irénée, who remained president of the Du Pont Company until 1925, and Lammot, who carried on that position until 1940.[51] Since Pierre had developed a far greater knowledge of General Motors than any one else in the du Pont family or the company, the division of labor between the brothers continued after Pierre had retired from the General Motors presidency and had sold his holdings to his brothers and sisters.

Pierre took his position as chairman of the board of General Motors seriously. He was, for example, quite shocked when Sloan suggested in 1927 that a quorum of the board might be less than a majority. Pierre summarized his indignant reply by saying: "First that this is an extraordinary arrangement, not consistent with the principle of majority rule; and, second, that it tends to belittle the value of the directors' meetings."[52]

The chairman left the details of financial policy at General Motors to

Raskob and Brown, just as he left operational policy and administration almost wholly to Sloan. His own wishes about financial policies were, however, very clear. He wanted expansion to be financed from within, dividends to be regularly maintained, with extra dividends being declared only when the surplus account was ample. Finally, he expected the financial structure of the company to become and remain relatively simple. With these policies, the rest of the Finance Committee, headed by John Raskob, were in full agreement. Besides reviewing budgets, Pierre took part in the Finance Committee's critical decisions on important capital investments.

After 1924 the precise formulation of financial policy at General Motors was an exceedingly pleasant, uncomplicated task. Earnings rose rapidly.[53] These were indeed years of fulfillment and reward for the work of reorganization and rejuvenation carried out between 1921 and 1924. Earnings, which stood at $116.0 million in 1925, rose to $186.2 in the next year and in 1927 almost doubled, reaching a figure of $235.1 million. (See Appendix, Table 6.) Then came the record earnings of 1928 of $276.5 million, the largest annual profit to be recorded by an industrial company anywhere in the world until after World War II. This impressive performance was a magnificent testimony to Pierre's achievements in the rebuilding of General Motors.

With such earnings, Pierre and the Finance Committee had little difficulty in maintaining a steady rate of dividends, in retaining earnings for expansion and replacements, and in finding enough money for sizable extra dividends. In 1925 the Finance Committee voted a regular dividend of $6 a share and extra dividends totaling $12 a share. In 1926 the regular dividend stood at $7 a share and then an additional $8 extra dividend was declared in July, and a 50¢ stock dividend in September. In the next year the total dividends per share on the no par value common stock rose to $17.50. In 1928 they totaled $19 for the same amount of stock. This was a far cry from the dividend of $4 in 1921 and $2 in 1922 for similar amounts of stock. In the same years, reinvested earnings went from $46.4 million in 1925 to $74.7 million in 1926 to $91.2 in 1927 and to $101.8 in that magnificent year of 1928. For 1929 dividends and surplus were down only a relatively small amount from 1928.

The upward climb of the market value of General Motors securities was one reason for changes in the corporation's capitalization.[54] Pierre and the Finance Committee agreed in 1924 that it was wise to have stock priced at about $50 a share, in order to interest the average investor, instead of the then low-priced shares which attracted the speculators. In 1924, therefore, the stock was reduced by the 4 to 1 exchange. When the value rose rapidly, the Finance Committee reversed the procedure, approving a 2 for 1 split on common stock in September 1927 and a second split in 1929, after Pierre had left the chairmanship of the board, of 2½ for 1.

The stock dividend and splits were responsible for the major increase in the amount of common stock outstanding. The 1926 stock dividend raised the total to about 7.6 million shares. The final purchase of the Fisher Corporation and the small amount of stock issued to the Management Securities Company and through the regular bonus plan increased the total stock outstanding to 8.7 million. With the 1929 split, the total stock outstanding stood at 17.4 million shares. Thus, during Pierre's tenure as chairman of the board, no common stock was sold to finance expansion or to maintain or even repair plant facilities. And only one relatively small issue of 664,000 shares—about 11% of the stock outstanding in 1926—was issued to purchase the remaining 40% of the Fisher Body Corporation, which General Motors still did not control.

During this same period of high dividends, the corporation experienced an expansion of plants, equipment, and facilities that even exceeded the massive Durant-Raskob program after World War I. The great increase in car production in all divisions, but particularly at Chevrolet, the plans to produce the Pontiac and then the La Salle, the parallel growth in parts and accessories units—all these developments called for heavy capital investment. The rapid shift from the open to the closed car created an extra pressure for new machines and plants. In these years, too, the foreign, particularly the European, markets added still further inviting opportunities for investment. As a result, a gross investment in real estate, plant, and equipment rose from $288.9 million in 1924 to $412.9 million in 1925 to $543.0 million in 1928, when Pierre left the chairmanship.[55] Investment in affiliated subsidiaries and miscellaneous units almost doubled, while total assets climbed from $384.4 million in 1924 to $1,242.9 million in 1928. Nearly all this impressive growth was financed from internal earnings. Unlike the railroad companies and those in the electrical and the iron and steel industries, General Motors was able to avoid going to the money markets to obtain funds for capital investment and was still able to pay exceedingly handsome dividends.

Such were the profits of the new technologies which permitted the economies of mass production and mass distribution on a scale hitherto unrealized. Yet no other large automobile or chemical company was as profitable as the two that Pierre had played such a critical part in organizing and managing. The comparison of the financial record of Ford and that of General Motors emphasizes dramatically the value of Pierre's style of systematic marketing and administration. For 1927 Ford had a net loss of $30.4 million, and in 1928 of $70.6 million. Even in his most lucrative year, 1929, when Ford showed a $91.5 million profit, his return was still far below that of General Motors for the same year. And that year's income hardly made up for the disastrous losses of the previous years and those that were yet to come.[56]

In February 1927, Pierre made the only exception to his general rule against external financing. He and the Finance Committee authorized the sale of an issue of $25.0 million worth of preferred stock with a par value of $100, which J. P. Morgan and Company agreed to market at $120.[57] Because of the corporation's large cash reserves and its surplus and high dividends, stockholders, brokers, and business analyzers criticized this issue. One former executive, William Day, wrote Pierre of his surprise; he knew of Pierre's aversion to outside financing. In his reply Pierre stressed that the issue was necessary "to keep the cash account large, making it possible to take advantage of opportunities for investment and insure the maintenance of common stock dividends without question."[58] Pierre added words of assurance in the long-term value of General Motors stock and ones of praise for Day's old boss, Alfred Sloan. "I do not think that the outlook for General Motors could be better than it is, not only in a financial and business way, but with respect to management and organization, which had been brought to a point of great perfection under Alfred Sloan's able management. It was a happy day when we secured him for his present position."

In the preceding months Pierre and the Finance Committee had had opportunities which were attractive and valuable enough to justify making this one exception to their general policy. These opportunities included the final purchase of Fisher Body, the possibility of buying Dodge Brothers, and the acquisition of European automobile companies. Of these the most important was the purchase of 40% of the Fisher Body stock still outstanding. In the negotiations for these securities Pierre played a major role. The independent-minded Fisher brothers, veterans in the carriage and automobile body-making business, resisted the absorption of the family firm, even though from General Motors' point of view logic appeared to demand it. Pierre was particularly anxious to make the purchase, partly to bring these able automobile executives fully into the General Motors management and partly to assure closer coordination between the body-making and the car-producing units. His tact, persuasiveness, and prestige were all needed in order to carry out these negotiations successfully.

Pierre had taken, it will be recalled, an important part in the original negotiations of 1919 which had given General Motors control of 60% of the body-making company and had led to the signing of a contract by which General Motors agreed to purchase substantially all of Fisher's output at cost plus 17.6%. By 1924, when the contract expired, Pierre, as well as the Fishers, realized how much conditions had changed.[59] General Motors was getting tooled up for another massive expansion. But now the closed car, and Fisher's major product was the closed body, was taking over the market. In 1921 Roy Chapin of the Hudson Motor Company produced a closed car that sold for only $300 more than the same model touring car. The enthusiastic response for this product was immediate. To meet the competition the General Motors divisions had to work more closely and precisely with Fisher Body. In 1923, while Pierre was still active with Chevrolet, he found that he and Knudsen were having difficulty in getting Fisher to meet Chevrolet's schedules.[60] As General Motors increased its closed car output, the need for coordination became still greater. During 1924 the corporation raised its production of closed cars from 40% to 75% of output and in the next year it stood at 80%

Moreover, Pierre and Sloan still needed experienced general executives to plan and carry out at the very top level the expanding production program. The Fishers, who had proved themselves exceedingly able, naturally tended to concentrate their efforts on Fisher Body rather than on General Motors. One reason that Pierre had placed Fred Fisher, head of the family and president of the company, on the General Motors Executive Committee in 1922 was to get him further involved in making the broad decisions about production, design, output, and pricing of General Motors products that inevitably affected the work of his own organization.[61] Then in the summer of 1924 Pierre began to talk privately with Fred Fisher about the possibilities of having him and one or two of his brothers devote all their energies to General Motors affairs. He proposed that they make this change at the time when the old contract between the two companies expired.[62]

Pierre appears to have suggested a complete merger of Fisher into General Motors. Fred Fisher favored a closer relationship, but he and his brothers balked at complete integration. Their profits had been generous. Besides, they hated to see the family business completely disappear. In this they were emphatically supported by their strong-willed mother. Pierre was sympathetic. He fully appreciated the commitment to the family firm. However, as he wrote to Fred Fisher late in July, "so far I have had some difficulty in picturing a situation whereby the Fisher brothers may stick together as a unit in the General Motors Corporation."

By the time the old contract had expired, Pierre, Raskob, and Sloan had worked out an arrangement they thought the Fishers might accept.[63] First, they would place Lawrence Fisher on the Executive Committee. He and Fred would devote all their attention to the larger affairs of General Motors. The Fisher Body Corporation would remain an autonomous legal as well as operating unit, with William as its president and the other three brothers as operating executives. Instead of a cost plus contract, its profits would be computed in the same manner as those of the operating divisions. In addition, Pierre proposed that each of the several brothers receive a share of the still unallocated allotment of the Management Securities Company stock. The Fishers apparently accepted this arrangement with little argument, for it was put into effect by the end of October 1924.[64]

Pierre and the Finance Committee waited almost a year before bringing up again the question of merger. The Executive Committee was still somewhat concerned that 40% of the stock in one of their most important units (about half of which was held by the Fishers themselves and a quarter by the Mendelssohns) might well be sold or transferred even before the death of the holders. The committee also agreed with Pierre about the value of having more of the Fishers devote more of their time to General Motors management. Given the greatly increased market value of the corporation's stock, this moment appeared to be a good one to purchase the rest of the Fisher Body stock through an exchange of shares.[65]

The committee made an offer to complete the merger by such an exchange of stock, but William Fisher and his brothers continued to hold out. They may still have been concerned about maintaining the family firm as a unit, or they may have sincerely felt that they could get a better price from General Motors. After Fred Fisher, who had been away when the negotiations opened, returned to New York, he and Pierre finally worked out a satisfactory arrangement. In so doing, Pierre pretty well accepted Fisher's argument about the large hidden values not fully indicated in the general accounts of inventory and overhead and the ability of the Fisher Body to expand its current plant capacity.[66]

By the terms of the agreement signed in May 1926, the holders of just under 40% of the stock were to turn over their securities to General Motors at a ratio of 1½ shares of General Motors for 1 of Fisher.[67] The book value of General Motors stock issued was $57.0 million for the $36.8 million book value of Fisher Body. At that time Fisher's assets were listed at $92.3 million (including $3.4 million for intangible assets). At market value, however, the General Motors stock issued was worth $136.0 million. So the Fishers clearly received an excellent price for these securities. On the other hand, given the corporation's high profits, the increase of capitalization by some 11.46% had little effect on the market value of General Motors common or on the dividend rate.

Pierre and Sloan now quickly moved the experienced Fisher executives into key posts.[68] Charles T. came on the Executive Committee and served as well on the Works Managers Committee. Lawrence P. remained on the Executive Committee and served on the Sales Committee. He soon became the general manager of Cadillac and one of the most competent division managers the corporation ever had. In fact, the Executive Committee in the latter part of the twenties was made up essentially of the three men Pierre had put in after the crisis—Sloan, Brown, and Pratt—and the three Fishers; for after 1924 Pierre and Raskob played little part in that group's deliberations. Fred Fisher served on the Finance Committee as well as the Executive Committee and was the only man, besides Pierre and Sloan, to do so. He was also on the Operations Committee and was the only executive, besides Sloan and Brown, to be on both that committee and the Executive Committee. In addition, William F. became group executive of the newly formed Body Group that included the Fisher plants plus recently acquired accessory divisions. Alfred J. Fisher represented that group on the General Technical Committee. Of the six brothers, only Edward F. did not become a senior General Motors executive.

Pierre was far less involved in other major negotiations during the mid-1920s. He had neither as strong an interest in nor as detailed an understanding of their background. He took very little part in the brief, but unsuccessful, bid General Motors made to buy Dodge.[69] The possibility of purchasing Dodge was important, however, insofar as it reminded Pierre and the Finance Committee of the value of having a strong cash position should a similar opportunity appear. Yet, realistically, this particular purchase had only a limited appeal. General Motors was already a well-balanced integrated firm with carefully laid plans to meet existing and potential demands. Pierre succinctly summarized his skepticism of the purchase in a letter to Thomas Cochran, who had handled the negotiations for the Morgan firm and General Motors:

> Now that the smoke of battle has blown away, I think we should all congratulate ourselves in not having been led to bid more for the Dodge properties. I am convinced that we "went the limit" in our bid. I figure—and John Raskob agrees with me—that the re-incorporation of Dodge will have to earn $2. to every dollar earned by our divisions in order to compete. That is quite a handicap, and I am glad it was not assumed by us.[70]

Better opportunities for further investment in the automobile industry existed abroad rather than at home. The European markets were growing rapidly and, as yet, no European automobile company had a large enough volume to benefit from many of the economies of scale. So despite transportation costs, American producers could easily compete in the European market. To meet this demand, General Motors had followed Ford's lead by setting up assembly plants in England and on the Continent.[71] Yet such plant expansion, as well as the formation of a worldwide distributing organization, did not fully meet the changing needs of that market. European governments were placing increasingly higher tariffs on American automobiles, and they were basing their licensing and insurance charges—as well as local taxes—on the registered horsepower of car engines. This factor plus the high price of gasoline put a premium on redesigning engines with a much lower horsepower than the cars built for domestic use. Such considerations encouraged the Finance and Executive committees at General Motors to do what Ford and other competitors had not yet done—purchase European automobile companies.

In 1925 the corporation gave its first attention to a European purchase since 1919. Pierre spent that summer in France touring the gardens in the Rhône and the chateau country, carefully studying those at Versailles, as well as viewing the du Pont ancestral homes and talking to distant relatives. He had been there, however, only a short time when he wrote Sloan a glowing account of the potential market in France, where he saw "a prospective repetition of the experience of the United States."[72] The French farmer had "already shown his ability to buy the bicycle, why not the motor car?" He added that the largest European company, the French firm of Citroën, was not at this time a much better buy than it was when Sloan, Haskell, Kettering, and the others had investigated the possibilities of its purchase in 1919. By the same token, it would not be a dangerous competitor. Pierre also saw the opportunity to mass-produce taxis, something General Motors had already done in the United States. He hoped that Sloan would bring these comments to the attention of the committee that was about to leave New York to investigate the possibility of overseas investment.

As Pierre knew well enough, the Executive Committee's interest was in England, not France. During the spring James D. Mooney, head of General Motors overseas operations, had made detailed reports to the Executive and Finance committees recommending Great Britain as the place to begin purchasing foreign properties.[73] In that highly industrial area the market was larger, and the tariff fees and gasoline even more costly than on the Continent. Mooney was particularly hopeful about purchasing the large and apparently well-managed Austin Company. After the Finance Committee approved, an *ad hoc* committee of Brown, Pratt, Fred Fisher, and Mooney had been formed to complete the negotiations with Austin. They could count on, the Finance Committee had told them, the support of Morgan's London house, Morgan, Grennell and Company.

Pierre was on his way home from Europe when the committee cabled its first favorable reports. The members reported that they had unanimously recommended that General Motors purchase all of Austin's common stock for just under $5.5 million. On this investment they expected a 20% return. Sloan approved. Then a few days later, Mooney unexpectedly notified Sloan and Pierre that the deal was off.[74] The Austin directors, Mooney reported, had refused to present the General Motors offer to their stockholders in a frank and truthful way, or to give the shareholders an honest picture of the value of Austin's assets and current financial position. Since the continuing good will of the stockholders would be important, the Mooney committee unanimously decided to withdraw the offer.

The committee may have then reviewed Pierre's suggestions for exploring possibilities in France. But, like Pierre, its members were skeptical of the Citroën, and, apparently, no other French firm looked much better. Instead, the committee proposed the purchase of Vauxhall Motors, Ltd., a British company much smaller than either Austin or Citroën. Its purchase would not be a substitute for Austin, but would be a pilot operation permitting General Motors to get a better understanding of the problems of managing an overseas corporation. Pierre and the Finance Committee quickly approved this purchase.

Sloan, Pierre, and the Finance Committee continued to keep a watch on the European market and other opportunities for investment. The demand continued to grow and the Vauxhall experiment was providing useful information. Pierre was undoubtedly pleased to learn that in 1927, despite tariffs and discriminatory fees, General Motors sold more cars in Europe than any other automobile company, European or American. In fact, only five companies of any nationality in the world did a larger business in Europe than General Motors.[75] In the spring of 1928 the corporation's top committees again began to study proposals to expand Vauxhall's production and to acquire a controlling interest in the Adam Opel AG, the largest automobile company in Germany. Before any decision was made, however, Pierre had resigned as chairman of the board. He was not involved in the negotiations that led to the purchase of Opel in the spring of 1929,[76] for after his resignation he no longer took a major part in shaping financial policy at General Motors.

As chairman of the board at both General Motors and Du Pont, Pierre always considered his second task—the reviewing of the performance of top management—as important as approving of financial policies and major capital investments. He tried to get to know the senior executives in both companies.[77] He often chatted informally with those in Wilmington at the Du Pont Building or at lunch at the Wilmington Club across the street. He met those at General Motors when he went to New York and occasionally to Detroit for a board or Finance Committee meeting. He made it a point to confer with the Fishers, whom he had done so much to get into the automobile company's top management. He remained close to Sloan, whom he continued to consider as General Motors' greatest single asset.[78]

As a member of the Finance Committee at Du Pont and the Bonus and Salary Committee (and also of the board of the Management Securities Company) at General Motors, Pierre reviewed in a regular and formal fashion the performance of all important executives. In deciding on salaries and bonus at General Motors he usually took his cue from Sloan; at Du Pont, from Irénée and then Lammot du Pont. Occasionally he would suggest changes on his own initiative. In 1925, for example, he proposed that Sloan's allotment of the Management Securities stock be increased from 350,000 shares to 450,000 shares; while Mott's be reduced from 300,000 to 200,000. This change, Pierre argued, was only fair, since Mott was taking a less active part in top management.[79] Pierre agreed to explain personally to Mott the reasons for this move.

The chairman of the board was also anxious to increase the commitments of senior executives to their companies through stock purchase plans.

As he wrote in 1925 to a long-time acquaintance, the Harvard economist William Z. Ripley, he and his brother believed that the completion of such plans to provide an incentive for managers in large-scale enterprise was "the best contribution that we can make to our industry before quitting time."[80] Pierre continued: "Manager ownership is not covered by the voting control of the company through ownership of a few shares of voting stock. The principle of manager ownership is that of financial interest."

At General Motors Pierre helped to bring some minor modifications in the Management Securities Company so that more of its shares could be allocated to executives who had taken no part in the initial allotment. Pierre and Sloan had specifically in mind the team that had so successfully developed the Pontiac. The key man of that team was then being courted by Studebaker with most attractive offers.[81] Pierre also began to take steps to set up a similar plan in 1931 when transactions involving the Management Securities Company would be completed. For this purpose he had General Motors start buying its stock in the open market.[82]

At Du Pont, more needed to be done than at General Motors, for there no formal plan permitting the purchase of large blocks of stock had been devised since Christiana Securities was used to reward wartime managers. Comparable arrangements with the postwar Executive Committee had been personal ones between Pierre and members of that group. In 1925 the chairman of the board, therefore, encouraged the adoption of a proposal to allocate stock to executives who had recently moved into highly responsible positions, particularly those "with moderate means," so as "to make them more nearly partners."[83] After much discussion the Du Pont Finance Committee decided to set up a plan using trust funds rather than a holding company.[84] Under its terms the recipients paid for their allotment of stock by giving the Du Pont Company notes to be redeemed in seven to ten years. The company then set up a trust fund to hold the stock of each recipient. The monies to pay off these notes came from the dividends of the stock itself, from any regular bonuses the recipients were awarded, and from a new fund set up by the company to which it turned over earnings after the company had made 6% return on investment. As in the case of General Motors these large blocks of stock could thus be acquired by those receiving allotments with little or no out-of-pocket costs to themselves. To make the allocations and administer the arrangement Pierre appointed a committee consisting of his two brothers, Irénée and Lammot, and a brother-in-law, R. R. M. Carpenter.[85]

Throughout the 1920s Pierre considered his review of top management and checking of financial policies as basic business tasks necessary to keep both these investments profitable. He always looked on each company as a distinct and separate enterprise. He fully agreed with a statement made by Raskob in 1922 that once the reorganization was completed, General

Motors "must stand on its own feet and never again have to look to the Du Pont Co. or anyone else for support."[86] For this reason he rejected a proposal by Irénée to move the General Motors offices from New York to Wilmington in order to make use of available space in the Du Pont-owned Wilmington Trust Building.[87]

Nevertheless, Pierre thought it was perfectly proper for General Motors to buy from Du Pont. All things being equal, Du Pont should have the General Motors business, but certainly not in any way that raised costs and so lowered profits of the latter. This relationship of buyer and supplier became the basis for the successful suit brought by the federal government against General Motors and Du Pont in 1949 to dissolve the formal connections between the two companies. A review of the vast amount of evidence presented by the government and the defendants as well as the records in the Pierre S. du Pont collection emphasizes two facts. First, Pierre rarely considered at all the question of General Motors purchasing from Du Pont. Fewer than a dozen letters of the hundreds he wrote on General Motors matters during his fourteen years as chairman of the board touched on General Motors purchases. Second, there is no evidence that Pierre ever ordered a manager at General Motors to buy supplies from Du Pont if he could get the product elsewhere for a lower price or better quality. At General Motors the divisions were permitted to buy parts and accessories that its own divisions produced from someone else if they could get a better price or quality. They had to make a report to the Executive Committee on why they preferred outside to inside sources.[88] But no one expected a division manager to make such a report if he chose not to buy from Du Pont.

Of course, the General Motors divisions did get many of their supplies from Du Pont. In 1921, when the sharp depression of that year was drying up the Du Pont markets, Pierre urged Irénée and R. R. M. Carpenter to go after General Motors business.[89] Then as general economic conditions improved and automobile sales expanded, the General Motors Purchasing Committee proposed, and the Executive Committee approved, that the corporation should always have at least two major sources of supplies.[90] When Knudsen enforced his policy at Chevrolet by not permitting the Du Pont Company to bid on further business in which it was already the major supplier, William Coyne sent Pierre a letter of protest.[91] Although Pierre replied to Coyne that he did "not think it advisable to interfere" unless the Executive Committee specifically agreed on such a policy, he did question Knudsen. "One good source, properly maintained, is more reliable than two sources," he suggested to the Chevrolet manager. Moreover he disliked shifting temporarily from one source to another.[92] As a result of this letter, the Du Pont Company salesmen were permitted to bid for the Chevrolet business and soon had its orders for coated fabrics. In the early 1920s the Du Pont Company remained the predominant, though not the sole, supplier to General Motors of products that it produced for the automobile market.

Pierre did not give General Motors purchasing any further attention until 1927 when, at a meeting of the Du Pont Finance Committee, he stated that he was "somewhat surprised at the statment that General Motors was not buying anywhere near all their requirements of products which Du Pont makes from Du Pont."[93] At Lammot du Pont's request, William P. Allen of the Paint, Lacquer and Chemical Department reported that of the total of $12.0 million worth of products which General Motors could purchase from Du Pont during the year ending June 30, 1926, General Motors had placed $8.0 million with Du Pont and $4.0 million with its competitors.[94]

Pierre learned that two types of arrangements encouraged the obtaining of this business. One was through reciprocity arrangements which George Kerr, a Du Pont staff executive, had proposed to Pierre in 1924. Following a plan then used by Bethlehem Steel and other large American corporations, Du Pont signed agreements with General Motors and other buyers and suppliers by which each would purchase products they needed from the other at somewhat lower prices.[95] The other was the "super discount" by which General Motors received goods from Du Pont at a lower price than Ford or other automotive companies.[96] Such arrangements, of course, made it attractive for General Motors divisions to buy from Du Pont, although the profits for Du Pont on the items were less than those on sales to other companies.

Pierre had the power to force General Motors executives to buy from Du Pont. As the Supreme Court pointed out in its decision on the antitrust case, the potential for developing a captive market certainly existed. The evidence suggests, however, that Pierre gave little attention to exploiting this potential. If Pierre had used the power, he would hardly have been a prudent guardian of the large Du Pont investment in General Motors. His basic concern was to make General Motors a profitable investment, and not a market for Du Pont. In 1926 the dividends the Du Pont Company received from General Motors were about $44.0 million, while the profits it made from its sales to General Motors could hardly have been more than $2.0 million.[97] For Pierre to have concentrated his attention on the latter at the expense of the former would have been an act of irrationality that would violate all the business and profit-making expertise Pierre had developed throughout his business career.

### Resignation as Chairman of the Board

Pierre clearly enjoyed his not too arduous role of keeping an eye on the Du Pont investment in General Motors. It was important, but not time-consuming, work. It did not interfere with his interest in expanding and improving the grounds, gardens, and botanical collections at Longwood, or his efforts to improve the Delaware public school system, or his work in revising the state tax laws. Nor did it keep him from taking an increasingly active part in the campaign against prohibition by becoming involved in the management of the Association Against the Prohibition Amendment.

Then unexpectedly, in the summer of 1928, Pierre resigned from the chairmanship of the board of directors of General Motors, a post he had held for thirteen of the twenty years of the corporation's existence. Pierre's resignation resulted directly from John Raskob's move into politics and Alfred Sloan's insistence that such activities required Raskob to retire from the chairmanship of the Finance Committee. This controversy between Sloan, Raskob, and Pierre was significant in that it ended Pierre's as well as Raskob's direct participation in the affairs of General Motors. It also shows much about the relationship of Pierre to his two closest business associates at General Motors.

Raskob's move into politics arose, interestingly enough, from Pierre's growing involvement in the fight against prohibition. In 1926 and 1927 Pierre became increasingly impressed by the work of the Association Against the Prohibition Amendment, founded in 1919 by a former naval captain, William H. Stayton. Also, during his visits to New York Pierre met and talked with friends at the Metropolitan Club and elsewhere who whole-heartedly agreed with him about the Eighteenth Amendment. It expanded the police power of the federal government in a futile attempt to prevent drinking, and it also helped to increase taxes by depriving the state and federal governments of a large source of revenue.

Late in 1927 Pierre and three well-known New Yorkers met with Stayton in Washington to re-form his association so that it could greatly enlarge its membership, its funds, and its pressure on the nation's legislatures.[98] These five men were, besides Pierre and Stayton, Charles Sabin, chairman of the board of the New York Guaranty Company, whom Pierre had known from the early General Motors days, Edward S. Harkness, eminent philanthropist, and the aristocratic New York Republican James Wadsworth, who had just retired from the United States Senate. The five formed an Organization Committee. They then agreed to set up a large board of managers of distinguished people whose tasks were to be largely honorific, an Executive Committee to set policies, a full-time director to carry them out, and subcommittees to operate in every state. For the director, the Organization Committee chose Major Henry H. Curran, an experienced and knowledgeable New York Democratic politician and an associate of Alfred E. Smith, then governor of the state of New York. In March Pierre became the chairman of the association's new Executive Committee and Irénée one of its members.

Pierre was soon spending much more time on enlarging and reorganizing the association than he was on the affairs of General Motors and Du Pont.

Quite naturally he had soon persuaded Raskob to join him.[99] By the late spring of 1928 Raskob, because of his wide set of acquaintances in New York and because he enjoyed making public appearances, had become one of the association's best-known spokesmen.

As an articulate "wet," Raskob attracted the attention of leading Democrats in New York; meanwhile his new interest had drawn Raskob, a lifelong Republican, into the Democratic party. In 1927 he had met Governor Smith through a mutual friend, William F. Kenny, a highly successful contractor.[100] Smith and Raskob immediately took a liking to each other. Both were devout Roman Catholics as well as "wets." Each considered the other a man of humble origin who had "made good" in his field. Moreover, Raskob's wealth and his business reputation (the press enjoyed extolling him as one of the financial wizards of the age)[101] made him especially welcome as a recruit to an organization that was devising plans to challenge the party of business and prosperity.

Immediately after Smith had won on June 28, 1928, the Democratic nomination for the presidency, he asked Raskob to be his campaign manager and to take the position of chairman of the Democratic National Committee. Raskob told Pierre, who enthusiastically encouraged him. But he did not mention this invitation to anyone else at General Motors or Du Pont. The day he came to New York to tell Sloan and the others at General Motors' 57th Street headquarters that he was accepting Smith's call, he learned that his son William had been killed in an auto accident on his way home from Yale.[102] The news immediately took him back to Wilmington before he met with any of his fellow executives. He returned to New York, still shaken by the tragic death of his son, just in time to attend a luncheon on July 11 announcing publicly his election as Democratic National Chairman.

The first inkling that Sloan or others at General Motors or Du Pont had of Raskob's political involvement came from the headlines.[103] The announcement was quickly followed by discussion in news and editorial columns, mostly in a critical vein, of the implications of having the chairman of the Finance Committee of one of the nation's largest and most powerful business corporations as the chairman of the Democratic party. Sloan, supported by the Fishers, insisted that Raskob resign as chairman of the Finance Committee. Raskob asserted vigorously that a leave of absence was enough. General Motors, he argued, should encourage, not discourage, such political activity. He made the point strongly to Coleman du Pont, who because of cancer had just resigned from the Senate. Even though the corporation should not in any way attempt to influence its employees politically, it should say that "if its employees will take an active interest in government, it will extend leave of absences to those employees during the period of campaigns, in order to enable them to run for Councilman, State

Senator, United States Senator or even President and hold their jobs open for them if they care to return after the election."[104]

At the Executive Committee meeting to discuss the Raskob situation, Pierre supported this position. Sloan, however, insisted that a leave of absence would only look like a "make-shift" arrangement and demanded resignation. Pierre emphatically replied that if Raskob had to resign, then he, Pierre, also should have to resign. If Raskob was being censured for being politically active while holding an important position at General Motors, so too should he, Pierre, for his work for the Association Against the Prohibition Amendment.

The possibility of Pierre's resignation disturbed the directors and senior executives at General Motors and Du Pont far more than the certainty of Raskob's leaving. Before taking further action, Sloan felt that he should poll the board of directors for their opinion about Raskob's resignation. While the majority approved, several expressed their concern about Pierre's threat. Irénée, for example, wrote that, while not agreeing with Sloan, he certainly accepted the majority vote of the board as indicated by the poll. But, he added: "It is of the utmost importance that the other resignation be not accepted, but on the contrary withdrawn."[105] Pierre was doing this, his brother was certain, "because of loyalty to a friend rather than the necessity of the case."

Before the board acted officially on these two resignations, Raskob, Pierre, and Sloan had another tiff. Raskob wanted to have the announcement made merely by having the newspapers print his letter of resignation written to Sloan, and Sloan's reply. Again Sloan disagreed. As he wrote Pierre: "The large amount of publicity extending over the whole United States in the most prominent position in practically all newspapers for a period of two weeks, is not going to be offset, even to a small degree, by the simple announcement of Wednesday."[106] Again Sloan had his way. At a major address that he made in Flint on August 1, he stressed the theme that "General Motors is not in politics. It will not permit its prestige, its organization, or its property to be used for political purposes."[107] While the corporation recognized "the right of each and every member of the organization to express his opinion as an individual on any public questions," it must be made absolutely clear that the individual speaks for himself and not for General Motors. The address received the publicity Sloan desired, for he saw to it that it was printed and sent to stockholders, dealers, suppliers, and newspaper editors.

At its next meeting the board accepted Raskob's resignation as chairman of the Finance Committee, with hopes that he would return to his job. It would not accept Pierre's resignation, but gave him a leave of absence. In his letters to Sir Harry McGowan and DeWitt Page explaining his actions, Pierre emphasized that the majority decision of the board and the Executive

Committee was agreed to "with the utmost grace and entire satisfaction of every one of us."[108] Yet he explicitly pointed out that Raskob "feels the whole thing more deeply than most of us imagine" and unquestionably would not return to General Motors. Implicitly Pierre indicated that he was as strongly affected.

Neither man did return to his position. Both remained on the General Motors board, although Pierre insisted on making his resignation from the chairmanship final, and turned it over to Lammot.[109] He did stay on the Finance Committee and, after the presidential campaign, Raskob once again joined that committee. But the two men rarely attended its meetings. Never again did they pay serious attention to the affairs of the giant corporation that they had done so much to create. Pierre turned the oversight of the Du Pont investment in General Motors entirely over to Lammot and to Walter Carpenter.

The nature of this departure reveals much about the men involved. Raskob raised the issue by his interest in the larger world and a liking for the public limelight, a taste Pierre never cultivated. Pierre left only because Raskob did so, and because Sloan forced Raskob out. For Pierre the venture at General Motors had always been a partnership with John Raskob. After the fiasco of 1921 Raskob had quickly regained Pierre's confidence. Pierre would not, even as a most inactive chairman, go it alone. Sloan deeply regretted having to take the strong stand on Raskob's resignation. Years later, he recalled it as the only real conflict he had ever had with Pierre or the du Pont family. As he insisted to Pierre in meetings and in letters, he had taken this position basically "to protect the Corporation's interests as I see it."[110] Sloan was the only member of the Executive Committee, or even of the board, except possibly Fred Fisher, who could stand up to Pierre. In fact, he was the only person in Pierre's long business career who opposed him on major issues and won. Significantly, on the two most important differences—over the copper-cooled car and Raskob's resignation—Pierre's response to such successful opposition was to withdraw: first from the presidency and then from the chairmanship of the board of directors of the General Motors Corporation

## Retirement

Pierre du Pont's resignation as chairman of the board of General Motors marked the end of his active business career. After 1928 he continued for some years to take part in business and governmental work. He served on boards of directors of several corporations and held positions in Delaware state and in federal government organizations. But far more of his energies were devoted to Longwood, building his collection of flowers, trees, and shrubs and enlarging the grounds and facilities. He devoted more hours than he had in the past to listening to music at home, in New York, Philadelphia, and Europe. For the first time he and Alice could indulge their taste for travel by spending nearly every summer in Europe and taking winter trips to Florida and Cuba. Abroad, Pierre particularly enjoyed their stays in France, where he began collecting seriously mementos of the du Pont family before it moved to America and works of eighteenth-century French literature and history.

These forays into the past turned Pierre to concerning himself with the papers of the American side of the family and the records of the Du Pont Company. He urged his cousins to have family letters properly preserved and checked carefully on the record-keeping methods of the Du Pont Company. He encouraged Alfred's first wife, Bessie, to write a brief history of the company during the nineteenth century based on these records.[111] At the same time, he supported a much larger project of editing in many volumes the papers of the first Pierre Samuel du Pont. This interest, in turn, started Pierre to bring together books on economics and economic history in his library at Longwood. These large and varied collections became the nucleus of the present Eleutherian Mills Historical Library in Greenville, Delaware, which now houses an excellent library in economic history and French studies.

The business and activities that he carried on until the mid-1930s were for the most part those he had started before 1928. His concern for elementary public education in Delaware continued. By 1935 he had personally contributed over $6.0 million, or 30%, of the monies used in the construction of new school buildings during the period from 1920 to 1935. He used a large portion of this money specifically to build schools for Negroes becaused the state legislature spent so little on them.[112] He continued on as State School Tax Commissioner (in 1929 the title was changed to Delaware Tax Commissioner) until 1937, long after he had reformed the tax structure so as to assure a steady flow of funds to the public schools.[113] He accepted the position again in 1944, holding it until 1949. Pierre prided himself on his success in installing and maintaining a simplified graduated income tax that he considered more equitable and productive than a sales or nongraduated income tax.

In the early 1930s Pierre carried on his work with the Association Against the Prohibition Amendment—efforts that brought him into some national prominence.[114] He remained on its Executive Committee until its demise in 1933, and thoroughly enjoyed being host in December of that year at a banquet in New York to celebrate the repeal of the Eighteenth Amendment.[115] Because of his interest in repeal, he actively supported Franklin D. Roosevelt in the 1932 campaign, even though Roosevelt had defeated Smith at the Democratic National Convention which, of course, ended Raskob's tenure as chairman of the Democratic National Committee.[116] Before the campaign Pierre had served on Herbert Hoover's Presidential Committee for Relief as well as on the Delaware Unemployment Relief Commission. In 1933 Roosevelt appointed him to the Industrial Advisory Board of the National Recovery Administration and then placed him on the NRA's National Labor Board.

By 1934 Roosevelt's failure to balance the budget and his increasing interest in welfare legislation turned Pierre back to his long-held Republican affiliation. He was even more irritated by the charges brought against him and the Du Pont Company in the spring of 1934 by Senator Gerald P. Nye and his congressional committee to investigate the munitions trade in World War I.[117] The charges that he and others had conspired to bring the United States into the war in order to protect their investment seemed so patently absurd to Pierre that he found it hard to believe that such allegations might be taken seriously. But he remembered that he had had the same attitude about the antitrust suit between 1910 and 1912. In any case Pierre found it easy to join many of his former colleagues in the Association Against the Prohibition Amendment to form the American Liberty League. He took a much less active role in the new organization, which became so hostile to Roosevelt's New Deal, than he had in the earlier association. He let his brothers, particularly Irénée, speak and act for him.[118]

The business activities he carried on after retiring from the General Motors chairmanship undoubtedly took less time than his civic or governmental duties. He continued to serve until 1934 on the boards of financial institutions that he had joined when he left the Du Pont presidency in 1919, including the Philadelphia National Bank and the Bankers Trust (of New York). He also stayed on the boards of the General Motors Acceptance Corporation, its associate, the General Exchange Insurance Company, and General Motors of Canada until 1934, and on the board of the parent company until 1944. After 1934, however, his most active directorship outside of Du Pont, Christiana Securities, and the Wilmington Trust Company was the Pennsylvania Railroad.[119] He joined the railroad's board in 1930 and remained on it until 1953, less than a year before his death. He also became in 1932 a member of its Finance Committee. During the depression years he took an advisory rather than an initiating role in developing plans for retrenching and refinancing the railroad's capital structure.

Other business activities took as little time as board meetings. In 1929 he did let Raskob venture fairly large sums of surplus capital on the New York money markets.[120] His old confidant talked him into participating in constructing in New York City the tallest building in the world. Although Pierre did become a director of the Empire State [Building] Inc., he took no part in its business direction, which Raskob and his new political associates handled.[121] That venture, like so many of Raskob's speculations and investments in the 1930s, turned out badly. After 1930 Pierre asked Raskob's advice on the money market much less often and rarely made changes in his investment portfolio. In the 1930s the two lifelong business partners began to drift apart. Raskob spent most of his time in New York while Pierre rarely left Wilmington except for his extended trips abroad and in winter to the South. So the two saw less of each other than they had since they joined forces in 1899.

For both Pierre and Raskob the 1930s were years of frustration. They were unable to grasp the meaning of the swift and deep economic and political changes going on about them. It was a strange and disturbing new world. While Raskob continued to meet it with his old energy and old ways, Pierre's response was to withdraw. If this study were a full-scale biography, a detailed analysis of Pierre's story after he left the chairmanship of General Motors would be essential for an understanding of the man's personality and his changing attitudes and continuing basic values. For the student of Pierre du Pont's business career, these last years are far less significant. His contributions to his family and its fortunes, and his achievements as a builder of modern corporations, all came before 1929.

# The Family and the Enterprise

Pierre's role at both Du Pont and General Motors after he retired from the presidency of each makes clear the major achievement of his business career. He created two of the most successful modern large American business corporations, and he did so without losing legal and financial control of these enterprises. The most critical period in the history of any modern corporation is when the founder or his family must come to terms with the needs of large-scale business enterprise. Few American business-men have handled this almost inevitable crisis in the growth of the modern corporation more effectively than Pierre S. du Pont.

In evaluating Pierre's achievement, two points need to be stressed. The first is that the needs and values of a family and those of a large impersonal enterprise are and have for centuries been in conflict. A family puts a premium on what sociologists term particularistic values; while large-scale enterprise demands universalistic ones. The family's first loyalty is to its individual members and the larger kinship group. In making decisions in a family economic or political unit, the needs of the family come first. The purpose of the family firm is to meet financial needs and help the family maintain its position in the larger society. When at all possible, sons and sons-in-law are recruited to head the firm. Managerial selection is thus based as much on family relationship as on ability, intelligence, or business performance. The Du Pont Company from 1802 to 1902 might well be considered a model or an almost ideal type of a family firm.

The large modern corporation, like large governmental offices or military commands, is little concerned with the family needs and loyalties. Its continuing successful operation requires managers with a specific type of training, experience, and abilities. In the modern industrial corporation, decisions are based on impersonal criteria, usually long-term return on investment, and managerial selection is based on business training and performance rather than on family connections. Performance, in turn, is judged by objective criteria such as production, marketing, and cost records, as well as return on investment. This process of selection encourages managers to develop a rational, objective, calculated approach to business problems and challenges.

The impersonalization of modern business enterprise is essentially a function of the large volume of goods it handles, and of the wide variety of activities with which it has become involved. Size, volume, and variety came when a small firm added new factories; when it expanded into new functions such as marketing, purchasing, transportation, and control of semifinished or raw materials through a policy of vertical integration; and when it moved into new markets and technologies through a strategy of diversification. No family firm could possibly provide the personnel to manage such an enlarged enterprise, and only rarely could a family find the funds to finance such growth.

Size, too, brought new problems of its own. It demanded, as the small family firm never did, attention to organizational structure, regularizing of selection and promotion of personnel, and the development of statistical and financial controls to make possible the evaluation and coordination of, and the long-term planning for, its varied activities. The answers to these needs had to be defined in impersonal, universalistic terms rather than in personal or particularistic ones. By the 1920s the Du Pont Company and General Motors were already models, ideal types, of the modern industrial corporation.

The second point that needs emphasizing is that the metamorphosis of the family firm into a modern impersonal corporation has occurred only recently and has come with surprising swiftness. The transformation from family to impersonal organization in the political life in the West began centuries ago and was centuries in coming; but the change in economic life began only in the nineteenth century. In Europe and in Latin America, too, family roots are deeper, and family traditions stronger. There the transformation is still going on. In the United States, however, the rise of the modern corporation in most major industries can be pinpointed in time to the period between the 1890s and the 1930s. During that generation, the coming of the modern corporation was one of the most important developments in the American economy. And of that generation few men were more involved than Pierre du Pont in shaping the formation of this powerful economic institution.

Before 1890 there were in the United States, except for the railroads, very few business enterprises of the modern type. Only a handful were capitalized at over $5.0 million and only a few employed salaried executives.[1] The railroads were the exception precisely because of their size and the complexity of their operations.[2] They were too large to be financed by a single man or family and too complex to be operated without a team of carefully trained men who administered through a precisely defined bureaucratic structure. Only one family—the Vanderbilt—was wealthy enough to finance and competent enough to have a say in the management of a railroad system. Even Vanderbilt control lasted for little more than a generation. The old Commodore did not enter the railroad business until 1863 when he was seventy-two years old. While his son William took an important part in building and managing the New York Central system, neither of William Vanderbilt's sons played as active a role in the affairs of their railroad as Pierre's nephews were to do in the affairs of the Du Pont Company.

In the great transformation from the small family firm to the impersonal enterprise that began in American industry during the 1890s, the family connections with the new large corporations tended to disappear. The majority of the new large enterprises were created, as was the Powder Company, through combination and then consolidation. This route to size tended to discourage the continuation of family connections with the firm, for rarely did one family among the several involved in the combination have the funds or entrepreneurial talent to dominate the new corporation. In many cases, outside financial investment bankers became responsible for financing the consolidation. As a result, the bankers' representatives on the boards of directors and the finance committees of the new corporations usually had more to say about their operations than did the spokesmen of individual firms that had gone into the consolidation. In any case, it was not long before the managers trained within the new corporation began, because of their experience and specialized know-how, to make nearly all the important decisions involved in the management and growth of the corporation.[3] There were some important exceptions to this general rule. The McCormicks at International Harvester and the Guggenheims at American Smelting and Refining are examples. Still, it seems safe to say that in none of the very largest American corporations was family control more clear and influence more powerful after the combination and consolidation than it was in the Du Pont Company.

In those firms that grew to great size through internal expansion rather than through combination with other firms, the founder or his family often failed to make terms with the requirements of the enterprise. Some of the nation's best-known industrialists, including Henry Ford, George Westinghouse, and the Armours, brought their companies close to financial disaster because they attempted to run their new giant enterprises as small family firms. Finally, when an individual and his partners were able to create a modern corporation, their family rarely carried on in top management. Very few Rockefellers, Chryslers, Eastmans, Schwabs, Clarks, Sinclairs, or Litchfields followed their fathers or uncles into senior executive positions in the great corporations the latter created.

Nevertheless, it was in this type of firm—one that grew by internal expansion rather than through combination—that family influence remained the longest. The Swifts in meat-packing, the Deeres in farm implements, the Reynoldses and Toms in cigarettes, the Firestones in rubber, the Dows in chemicals, the Houghtons in glass, and the Watsons in business machines—all continued to hold sizable blocks of stock and to take part in the management of their enterprises after those had reached great size. Their experiences were the closest to those of the du Ponts. They, too, successfully made the transition from family firm to modern, large-scale enterprise. Some have succeeded quite well. In fact, a recent study suggests that companies with even a small amount of family or personal control have a better performance record than those where such influences have disappeared or never existed.[4]

Family and personal interests have, however, not remained long, even in this type of enterprise. Such families as the Swifts and the Deeres no longer have a significant say in the management of the companies that carry their name. As another recent study has pointed out: in 1929, 56% of the 200 largest nonfinancial companies (which controlled 42% of the total assets held by these 200 firms) had at least 10% of their stock held by individuals, families, or a small number of associates.[5] By 1963, on the other hand, comparable holdings by individuals, families, and a small number of associates occurred in only 15.5% of the total number of companies owning 15.0% of the total assets held by the top 200. Clearly the family-controlled modern corporation is in itself a transitional form between the old family partnership and the new impersonal, professionally manned enterprise. It rarely lasts more than two generations.

Yet the way in which this transition from family firm to giant enterprise has been carried out affects the shape, style, and continuing success of that enterprise. An understanding of how precisely these transitions were accomplished is of great significance in the understanding of the development of the American business system. Here, then, lies the importance of reviewing Pierre du Pont's experience. Few, if any, American businessmen were more deeply involved, and on such a large scale, in the carrying out of this basic institutional change.

What, then, were precisely Pierre's contributions to the transformation of the Du Pont Company and General Motors into their modern form? What made him such a successful corporation builder? At Du Pont, Pierre's initial contribution was financial; that is, his fiscal inventiveness permitted him and his two cousins to use the capital and credit of the family and firm to finance the consolidations of 1902 and 1903 and the growth of the new enterprise in the years immediately following. Because of Pierre's financial ingenuity and Coleman's diplomacy, the du Ponts did not have to go to Wall Street investment houses or any other outsiders for funds. The success in financing the transformation of the firm was one central reason that Pierre and his family were able to retain control of the new corporations for so long a time.

Pierre's financial skills were essential, in another way, to the building of a modern corporation. He quickly developed and learned how to use the statistical and financial techniques necessary to its management. He used these new methods to guide the company through what were still to corporate managers uncharted waters. Early in the twentieth century few industrialists had yet devised ways to maintain financial control of a $50.0 to a $100.0 million corporation in an economy where demand, supply, and availability of short-term credit all fluctuated, often quite violently. Pierre met the test of the financial panic of 1907 which brought down such new giants as Allis-Chalmers and Westinghouse. He used these new methods also in making the decision to go against Coleman's overseas adventures and instead to concentrate on home markets. They helped him, too, in financing the growth of the company through a strategy of vertical integration and continued expansion of productive capacity.

At the Du Pont Company Pierre's contribution was also administrative. With Coleman he selected the men to run the new company; and, second only to Moxham, he paid close attention to devising detailed operating structures and systems that would permit the senior managers to make the most of their time and talents. In these administrative tasks Pierre was not a major innovator. He and his colleagues on the Executive Committee drew on the experience of two of the most technologically advanced industries of the day—steel and electrical machinery—and from the most managerially advanced enterprises—the railroads. Yet more than the heads of most family firms and more than any other du Pont except Coleman, Pierre appreciated the necessity to bring in managerial and entrepreneurial talent from outside the family. And more than most professional executives who came to head so many of the new industrial corporations, he and Coleman appreciated the importance of giving managers some of the same incentives that came with family ownership.

Pierre's special contribution to administration was, however, more than the introduction of men and systems. He was the catalyst who kept the company's senior executives working together and who, at the same time, kept the family interested and involved in the enterprise. Because of his clear analytical mind, his calm and somewhat cautious outlook, his sensitivity to the feelings and positions of others, and his ability to concentrate on the task at hand, Pierre quickly came to have the respect of both the family and professional managers. Thus, he soon came to have the most to say about the management of the Powder Company.

Because of the position he had achieved through the quiet force of his personality, Pierre became the executive who had to meet and solve the new challenges that began to face the company once its day-to-day activities became relatively routinized. He took over the preparation of the company's response to the government's antitrust action after Coleman's strategy was obviously failing to stave off an unfavorable verdict and dissolution. It was he, not Coleman, who devised the plan that met the government's requirements and still kept the Du Pont Company viable as a large-scale enterprise.

This challenge tired him. So did the continuing one of keeping top managers working together and at the same time assuring a flow of competent younger men to senior positions. In the fall of 1913, therefore, Pierre decided to lighten his load. He turned the company back to Coleman, expecting him in time to hand the reins to Irénée. Yet, in a very short time, it was clear that Coleman had neither the health nor the talent to keep top management working together. Pierre then had to return to his old job as the head of the company.

Coleman's decision to leave the presidency and to sell out precipitated one of the most difficult tests in Pierre's career. It provided an opportunity, if Coleman sold his stock to the company, to carry out plans both he and his cousin had agreed were necessary to tie the able professional managers to the family enterprise. It posed a threat of the possibility of interference with family control if Coleman sold to outsiders. Of more importance, Coleman's departure meant that Pierre would have to share control of the company with William and Alfred. These two, Pierre felt, were not aware, as Coleman always had been, of the requirements of managing a modern enterprise. Pierre then decided to buy Coleman's stock himself to assure that the company would continue to be managed as he and Coleman had run it in the past and, at the same time, to provide incentives for the professional managers to stay with the firm. This decision quickly led to a bitter family battle.

The legal fight dramatized the tensions caused by a shift from the personal values of the family to the impersonal ones of the enterprise. Except for Francis I., no member of the family who had long held a responsible executive position in the company joined Alfred in the suit against Pierre. Alfred, who arranged the suit, had been bypassed by Pierre and Coleman as not competent enough for top management. He had been joined by William, who until 1914 had been kept out of company affairs for twenty years and who had hurt feelings about this rejection. And Francis I., too, had been asked to devote all his time to the company or leave it. To all those who joined battle against Pierre, the family firm was as much a heritage as it was to him, Coleman, or Francis's brother Felix. They quite naturally blamed their failure to take part in it on those members of the family who managed the company. They had little difficulty in ascribing sinister motives to management that did not include them in its activities. The fight was a victory for Pierre and for the enterprise, yet it split the family wide apart. It convinced Pierre never to share control of the company again with anyone except his own brothers and brothers-in-law.

Pierre's final challenge at Du Pont came with the unexpected outbreak of World War I, which brought a sudden, unprecedented, astonishing demand for military powder. The temporary nature of this demand raised the question of how to finance enormous expansion without endangering the financial solvency of the company. This test Pierre met by his carefully defined contracts that would cover expenses if the war should end before the construction costs were met. Then, as the expansion was being completed and paid for, he encouraged development of postwar plans as sophisticated and far-reaching as those of any American corporation. He and his associates decided to use the company's enlarged resources, particularly the administrative and technological skills of its greatly enlarged managerial staff, to move into the production and marketing of several types of chemical products. By 1919 Pierre had met all his challenges successfully. The company was ready to compete with new products for the postwar market; a new and able young Executive Committee had taken over from the men who had managed the company throughout the war; and Pierre and his immediate family remained in full control of the E. I. du Pont de Nemours & Company.

At General Motors Pierre's contribution was more administrative than financial. This was true even though the Du Pont Company did provide a significant share of funds for the automobile enterprise's huge postwar growth and so obtained financial control of the company. At General Motors Pierre achieved what William C. Durant, its founder, could not. Durant believed, like Henry Ford and other founders of the first successful automobile companies, that he could manage the new giant as if it were a relatively small company. Despite warnings from his own executives and from Pierre himself, Durant failed to put General Motors' finances on a sound basis, to develop systematic statistical and financial information and controls, or to keep and to continue to recruit able professional managers. Nor was Pierre's closest friend, John J. Raskob, who had originally brought Pierre to General Motors, able to remedy the situation. While adept at financial manipulation, Raskob did not have the interest or probably the capability to introduce essential reforms. Only after Pierre became its president in December 1920 did the transformation of General Motors into a modern corporation really begin.

Before the crisis of 1920 Pierre concentrated on other matters. The Du

Pont Company required nearly all his attention through April 1919. On retiring from its presidency, he turned to enlarging Longwood and improving the Delaware school system. The disappearance of demand for automobiles that accompanied the postwar recession created a crisis that taught Pierre a critical lesson. Financial control did not necessarily mean administrative control. He now realized that although he and his associates controlled General Motors financially and legally, his suggestions, recommendations, and even orders, were not necessarily carried out. With the coming of the crisis Pierre put all other matters aside and turned his efforts to shaping Durant's sprawling industrial speculation into a well-managed modern enterprise.

At General Motors Pierre's basic contribution came in providing new men and methods. Of the two, men were more important than methods. The managers he placed in the senior executive positions were far more responsible than he himself was for introducing the new ways. While none of the new executives were members of the du Pont family, a number had had their training at the Du Pont Company. These not only included men at the top, like Donaldson Brown and John Lee Pratt, but also middle-level executives like E. F. Johnson, Eric Bergland, Alfred R. Glancy, and Frank Turner. Moreover, Pierre appreciated the value of Alfred Sloan in a way that Durant never had. His first act was to adopt Sloan's plan of organization, and within six months he had put Sloan in charge of operations.

Pierre's most significant role at General Motors, however, was, as it had been at Du Pont, to act as a catalytic agent. He was able, again by his reason and quiet sensible ways, to fashion a strong management team from disparate elements: men from Du Pont who knew the ways of modern management but little about the making and selling of automobiles; divisional and staff executives who understood their industry well but were skeptical about outside control and outside advice; and, finally, representatives of the bankers and J. P. Morgan and Company who had always been less than enthusiastic about their investment in the automobile business. At the very top he kept the strong, sharp-minded Sloan, the sanguine and inventive Raskob, the imaginative but sensitive Kettering, and the bluff and practical Pratt all working together harmoniously.

Because Pierre never had the same commitment to General Motors that he had to Du Pont, he always looked on his stay there as temporary. Once the company had been set back on its feet, he was ready to return to Wilmington. One activity, however, did continue to hold his interest, and this was Kettering's work in developing a new type of engine. When this technological innovation began to be costly and when it brought him into conflict with the senior executives whose views he respected, and so threatened his effectiveness, Pierre found it easy to step down and turn the presidency over to Sloan. Because of the knowledge he had gained at

General Motors, he remained the Du Pont Company's watchdog over its huge investment in the automobile concern. Yet again, when an essentially personal matter brought him into conflict with Sloan, Pierre willingly resigned as chairman, turning the job of supervising General Motors over to Lammot and Walter Carpenter.

This brief review of Pierre's experience suggests why he did so well at Du Pont and General Motors. In the first place, he understood the demands of a new and changing situation. At the same time, he wanted to retain old values. He fully accepted the needs of large-scale enterprise—that is, the use of experienced managers, the adoption of new technologies, and the bringing in of new financial and administrative techniques. At the same time he wanted to keep the loyalties, commitments, and incentives that existed in a small family partnership.

In the second place, Pierre's business knowledge was general rather than specialized. Equally important, he had the ability of getting specialists to work together. He had a good knowledge of the technical aspects of the powder industry (but not of the automobile business); he had at an early age a broad understanding of finance, and developed an excellent one of administration. Above all, he was willing to listen to and to work with other executives.

Such entrepreneurial talents became valuable only with the rise of the modern corporation. Before the coming of the large enterprise with its national and, indeed, international markets, with its factories and laboratories in all parts of the country, and with its own sources of supply at home and abroad, most American industrialists could manage their business by themselves or with, at the most, a handful of partners. They needed to have some understanding of new machinery, some ability at raising and handling capital, and some talent in recruiting and training a labor force. They carried on a single type of business activity and produced one type of product. They were functional specialists. But when the firm became multifunctional—when it began to do its own marketing, supplying its own raw and semifinished materials, as well as carrying on its own manufacturing—then a more general knowledge of the several activities became more essential than expertness in one. Then, too, the ability to make a number of functional specialists work together as a single management team became the most essential of business skills.

Training, lineage, and personality—all contributed to Pierre's success as a builder of modern corporations. Lineage, that is, being a du Pont, gave him a commitment to making a career in the family firm. As important, it provided him access to a pool of capital and assured him of a high credit rating that made it possible to secure funds essential for the formation and management of a large modern enterprise. Yet comparable amounts of capital were available, though probably at somewhat higher cost, to a good many entrepreneurs and corporation builders in these same years. Indeed, one of the most important developments of this period was the ability of the growing money markets on Wall Street to provide such funds. For Pierre the real significance of the availability of family capital was that the transformation of family firm could be financed without resorting to Wall Street, thus avoiding the sharing of control with outsiders.

Training, too, was invaluable. An education at M.I.T. and an exposure to the methods of the steel and electrical industries gave Pierre a useful introduction to modern technology. Even more important, they provided him with a rational and analytical approach to management and finance and showed him how such an approach had been successfully applied. Moreover, because of the early death of his father and then of his uncle, Pierre had had to learn the realities and responsibilities of handling large sums of money at a relatively young age. His management of the finances of the Johnson Company and the funding of the streetcar ventures furthered his financial education. While other du Ponts had the same access to the same pool of capital, and other du Ponts had comparable engineering training, of all the clan only Coleman was as well versed in finance as Pierre. Training alone, however, cannot account for Pierre's later achievements.

It was his personality that made the real difference. Because of his personality Pierre was able to use his family resources and his training more effectively than did other du Ponts or, indeed, other professional managers with whom he worked. Pierre's abilities seem to have rested on three traits: his sensitivity to the feelings and positions of others, his willingness to accept their views if they were presented and argued in rational business terms, and his facility for concentration.

Far more than Coleman or Alfred, or even William Durant, Pierre refused to let himself be distracted by personal or other business affairs. By the same token, when he resigned from an active position at Du Pont or later at General Motors, he concentrated on other matters and paid little direct attention to their problems. Again, more than Coleman or Alfred or any of his cousins, he had the patience and interest to read and comprehend the flow of statistical and financial data so essential to the management of the modern corporation.

At the Executive Committee meetings at Du Pont and then at General Motors, Pierre was probably the best listener of the group. More than Coleman, Alfred, Barksdale, Haskell, Moxham, Sloan, or Durant, Pierre was willing to examine dispassionately views that differed from his own. He rarely became psychologically involved in arguing and defending a position. He expected to win or lose his arguments on the basis of the accuracy and amount of data presented and the logical analysis of these data. This sense of psychological security may have added to his awareness of the strengths and weaknesses of the men with whom he worked. It also may have made it easier for him to encourage them to make the most of their talents. Such understanding of others quickly made him a natural leader among his able and strong-willed associates.

To explain how Pierre's personality developed is beyond the scope of this study. Yet two points can be briefly suggested. His lack of physical coordination and the resulting lack of athletic ability may have turned him inward, strengthened his interest in his studies, and intensified that shyness that made it so difficult for him to speak in public. Such attitudes may have encouraged habits of disciplined thought and the ability to listen carefully.

His place in his immediate family may have been important, too. After his father's death, when he was only fourteen, Pierre increasingly took over the responsibility as head of the household. He quickly won his mother's confidence as a family as well as a financial adviser. As his letters attest, he also remained very close to his brothers and sisters. Except when he was at the Institute or in Lorain, he lived with the family at St. Amour until his mother's death, and when he was away he wrote regularly. Pierre thus understood well the tensions, crises, and collective joys of a large family, yet more as a parent than as a sibling. For most of his life he was called Dad openly and with affection by his brothers and sisters. His place in the family and in the larger kinship group strengthened his psychological security. He was always fairly sure of where he was going and why, and from an early age became accustomed to making important decisions involving others.

Pierre, of course, had to pay a price for the very traits that so assisted him in becoming a creator of modern corporations. For one thing his devotion to family and firm and his ability to concentrate on the business at hand narrowed his outlook and horizons. He rarely reached beyond his family, firm, and close circle of friends to meet his needs. He never had the urgings of a Coleman du Pont or a John Raskob to try his talents on the larger national scene. New York failed to have the attraction for him that it had for the two men whose business skills he most admired.

The difficulty came when the family he had helped to raise had grown up, moved away, and begun to raise their own children. The death of his mother sharpened the break. It was at this very same time that Pierre was trying to maintain the integrity of the company from the attack by the government and was attempting to bring in a new and younger set of managers. This was probably the most difficult period in Pierre's life. He sold St. Amour to Lammot and planned to bring Coleman back as the active head of the company. Longwood was to take the place of the family and the firm. When this plan failed and Pierre realized that he could not escape the demands of the larger family and the enterprise, he again turned his energies to business. Because of these continuing commitments, Pierre rarely enjoyed at Longwood, even after his marriage to his first cousin, Alice Belin, the satisfactions of family life as fully as he had at St. Amour.

Throughout his career Pierre was guided by the hope that he could keep family and enterprise together. He appreciated the problems involved. One threat, he realized, came from the federal government, for he was aware that concentrated economic power had long been suspect in America. Nevertheless, he could not understand why actions in which he took great pride should be condemned by the government. That his efforts in building up the Du Pont Company, in working with Nobel Industries, and in revitalizing General Motors should be grounds for legal suits by the government surprised and disturbed him. He was proud of the record of his two companies and quite willing to open his records to government attorneys and, later, to historians. He therefore never could really believe that the government would bring to an end the enterprises he had done so much to create. Nor did he feel that governmental action could force a separation of family and enterprise.

Another threat troubled Pierre more. He appreciated, far more than most, the conflict between the needs of the enterprise and the demands of the family. Nevertheless, he had always expected that enough du Ponts, recruited from all branches of the family, would become trained, experienced managers. He hoped still that the members of the family would continue to play a critical part in governing their company. He wanted them to be on the Executive Committee and even become its president. The new threat to these hopes grew directly out of the company's ability to adjust to the needs of a modern industrial economy. Success had brought great wealth. And wealth, Pierre feared, would soften the old commitments to serving the family enterprise. It would undermine the willingness of the younger members of the family to accept the rigorous demands made upon the manager of a modern corporation.

These views Pierre expressed most clearly in a letter written in 1922 to one of his nephews for whom he had long acted as guardian. In presenting a final account of the guardianship, Pierre reviewed the background of the growth of "the family fortunes."[6] He described the work of the young man's great-great-grandfather in founding the company and the efforts of his great-grandfather and his great-great uncle and then his cousin Eugene to carry it on. After reviewing the course of events since 1902, Pierre made his point. With one or two exceptions, the members of his and the three preceding generations of the du Ponts had started life without great fortune. "It is not an exaggeration to say that nearly all were in a position 'requiring work for a living.' This condition had its problems, its advantages and disadvantages. The sum total of the effort has been successful financially and at the same time with due regard for the duties owed society in general. The du Pont family is entitled to a just pride in their name."

While "the past and passing generations" have had their challenges, "the generation of which you are a member and those that will follow will have a new line of difficulties. There are, and will be, many of these du Ponts born to a position of wealth that may not require the hard work and continued application which was the lot of our forebears." The new way of life would perhaps be more difficult and "require greater moral stamina to combat the temptations of wealth and luxury and to carry forward, in a manner becoming the family traditions. While there are many to represent the coming generation, there are comparatively few to set the pace in this new position of affairs." This small number had a great responsibility. They would determine "the name and position of the du Pont family in the world of affairs for a quarter of a century. If you fail in your example those immediately following you may do likewise, or be powerless to negative [*sic*] your error." New opportunities lie ahead, Pierre concluded, different perhaps from those of the past, but ones that call "for sober thought and the exercise of all the powers for good that lie within you. I have no doubt that you will win success and such is my earnest hope."

Pierre's hope was not completely in vain. Several of the coming generation did play a major part in the affairs of the Du Pont Company and did maintain a careful oversight of the General Motors investment. But the number was smaller than Pierre had anticipated. Through the years the separation of family and enterprise increased. Indeed, as the number of members of the clan eligible for posts in the Du Pont Company grew, those who reached the upper echelons of management progressively decreased. By mid-century the family had ceased to be not only a source of managerial talent but also a source of capital. Retained earnings and the impersonal money markets supplied the necessary funds for expansion.

Pierre's premonitions were at least partially correct. Time and wealth probably eroded the close relations between the family and its enterprises more than did government action. A federal antitrust suit in the early 1950s terminated Du Pont control over General Motors, but it did not affect the control of Christiana Securities in the Du Pont Company. Although Christiana Securities still owns 29% of Du Pont common, the holding company's stock is held in recent years by many more persons than Pierre's immediate family. Thus, General Motors has become similar to most large American corporations where the managers do not own and the owners do not manage. The Du Pont Company is moving in the same direction, for, as its shares and those of Christiana Securities become more widely held, fewer of the members of a much larger family are entering its management. The professional managers at General Motors are no longer responsible to a readily identifiable group of owners; and those at Du Pont are becoming much less so.

Given the technological, administrative, and financial requirements of a large, industrial corporation in the second part of the twentieth century, the separation of family from the enterprise appears unavoidable. Pierre himself would probably have understood and agreed. In business matters he never favored maintaining the *status quo*. His achievements resulted from an accommodation, not a resistance, to change. More than any other member of his family he appreciated the demands and requirements of a new form of industrial organization. Committed as he was to the values of the family, he still refused to let them get in the way of the needs of the enterprise. Because he understood and accepted the technological and managerial imperatives of an industrial economy, he created two of the most successful of the nation's modern corporations. Because of this achievement, the du Pont clan acquired and kept its reputation as the nation's foremost industrial family.

# APPENDIX

Table 1. ASSETS AND CAPITAL, E. I. DU PONT DE NEMOURS POWDER COMPANY AND SUCCESSORS 1904–1919
(in millions and rounded, so that totals may not add exactly)
Data as of December 31 year indicated unless otherwise noted.

| | 1904* | 1905* | 1906 | 1907 | 1908 | 1909 | 1910 | 1911 | 1912 | 1913 | 1914 | 1915 | 1916 | 1917 | 1918 | 1919 |
|---|---|---|---|---|---|---|---|---|---|---|---|---|---|---|---|---|
| *ASSETS* | | | | | | | | | | | | | | | | |
| Working Capital | 13.5 | 13.9 | 15.5 | 18.3 | 17.6 | 20.0 | 22.9 | 21.4 | 21.7 | 17.5 | 26.4 | 64.9 | 82.3 | 145.0 | 222.6 | 86.1 |
| Investments, including short-term investments and after 1915 permanent investments | 4.3 | 5.7 | 5.8 | 4.8 | 6.4 | 3.4 | 4.2 | 4.8 | 7.0 | 12.8 | 11.4 | 70.6 | 83.7 | 47.6 | 20.5 | 87.7† |
| Realty not including Plant Real Estate | 0.9 | 0.7 | 0.9 | 0.9 | 0.9 | 0.9 | 0.8 | 0.9 | 0.9 | 0.6 | 0.5 | 0.5 | 0.5 | 0.5 | 0.5 | 1.0 |
| Permanent Investment in Manufacture | 38.4 | 39.7 | 44.5 | 46.9 | 49.2 | 50.4 | 50.1 | 56.2 | 56.5 | 43.8 | 45.1 | 122.2 | 51.3 | 70.3 | 65.1 | 65.7 |
| Total | 57.2 | 60.0 | 66.6 | 70.9 | 74.1 | 74.8 | 81.1 | 83.2 | 86.0 | 74.8 | 83.4 | 258.3 | 217.9 | 263.4 | 308.8 | 241.0 |
| *CAPITAL* | | | | | | | | | | | | | | | | |
| Funded Debt | 5.1 | 5.0 | 14.3 | 14.4 | 16.9 | 16.4 | 16.5 | 16.7 | 16.8 | 16.9 | 17.0 | — | — | — | — | — |
| Preferred Stock Issued | 17.0 | 22.5 | 14.9 | 14.7 | 15.6 | 13.5 | 15.8 | 15.8 | 15.8 | 16.1 | 16.1 | 60.8‡ | 60.8‡ | 60.8‡ | 60.8‡ | — |
| Preferred Stock Held in Reserve | 7.2 | 1.8 | 0.1 | 0.1 | 0.1 | 0.1 | 0.1 | 0.1 | 0.05 | 0.05 | 0.05 | 0.05‡ | 0.05‡ | 0.05‡ | | |
| Common Stock Issued | 13.9 | 22.5 | 25.0 | 25.8 | 27.9 | 28.0 | 29.4 | 29.4 | 29.4 | 29.4 | 29.4 | 58.9 | 58.9 | 58.9 | 58.9 | — |
| Common Stock Held in Reserve | 9.9 | 1.4 | 0.1 | 0.1 | 0.05 | 0.05 | 0.05 | 0.05 | 0.03 | 0.03 | 0.03 | 0.03 | 0.03 | 0.03 | — | — |
| Total | 53.2 | 53.1 | 54.3 | 55.0 | 60.4 | 58.0 | 61.9 | 62.0 | 62.1 | 62.5 | 62.6 | 119.7 | 119.7 | 119.7 | 119.7 | — |

SOURCE: Annual Reports of the Du Pont Powder Co. and its successors.

* Data for this year as of January 1.
† Includes 22.7 million advances to controlled companies.
‡ Debenture stock.

Table 2  DU PONT POWDER COMPANY AND E. I. DU PONT DE NEMOURS & CO. ANNUAL COMMON STOCK DIVIDENDS 1904–1919

(Expressed as a percentage of par value)

| | 1904 | 1905 | 1906 | 1907 | 1908 | 1909 | 1910 | 1911 | 1912 | 1913 | 1914 | 1915 | 1916 | 1917 | 1918 |
|---|---|---|---|---|---|---|---|---|---|---|---|---|---|---|---|
| E. I. du Pont de Nemours Powder Company | ½ | 3½ | 6½ | 7 | 7 | 7¾ | 12 | 12 | 12 | 8* | 8 | 22† | 6 | 6 | 6‡ |
| E. I. du Pont de Nemours & Co. | | | | | | | | | | | | 30 | 100 | 51§ | 26** |

SOURCE: Annual Reports of the Du Pont Powder Co. and its successors.

* Does not include 48.474% paid in securities of Atlas Powder Co. and Hercules Powder Co.
† Does not include distribution of two shares of common stock of E. I. du Pont de Nemours & Co. for each share of common stock of E. I. du Pont de Nemours Powder Co.
‡ Based on par value of $10.
§ Includes 1% Red Cross dividend.
** Includes Red Cross 2% dividend, 1% United War Work dividend, 5% dividend in preferred stock of Du Pont Chemical Co. $5 par value.

Table 3  E. I. DU PONT DE NEMOURS POWDER CO. (and its successors) 1904–1919
Income Accounts as of Year Ended December 31 (in millions and rounded)

| | 1904 | 1905 | 1906 | 1907 | 1908 | 1909 | 1910 | 1911 | 1912 | 1913* | 1914 | 1915 | 1916 | 1917 | 1918 | 1919† |
|---|---|---|---|---|---|---|---|---|---|---|---|---|---|---|---|---|
| Gross Receipts | 26.1 | 27.7 | 30.8 | 31.7 | 28.0 | 30.8 | 33.2 | 33.4 | 36.5 | 26.7 | 25.2 | 131.1 | 318.8 | 269.8 | 329.1 | 105.4 |
| Net Earnings | 4.4 | 5.1 | 5.3 | 3.9 | 4.9 | 6.0 | 6.3 | 6.5 | 6.9 | 5.3 | 5.6 | 57.8 | 82.1 | 49.3 | 43.1 | 17.7‡ |
| Interest on Outstanding Bonds | 0.3 | 0.3 | 0.5 | 0.7 | 0.7 | 0.9 | 0.7 | 0.8 | 0.8 | 0.8 | 0.8 | 0.6 | — | — | — | — |
| Preferred Stock Dividends | 1.0 | 1.1 | 1.0 | 0.7 | 0.8 | 0.7 | 0.7 | 0.8 | 0.8 | 0.8 | 0.8 | 1.7§ | 3.6§ | 3.6§ | 3.6§ | 3.6§ |
| Common Stock Dividends | 0.1 | 0.8 | 1.5 | 1.7 | 1.8 | 2.2 | 3.4 | 3.5 | 3.5 | 2.4 | 2.4 | 24.1 | 58.9 | 30.0 | 15.3 | 10.6 |
| Surplus Carried Forward | 2.9 | 2.9 | 2.0 | 0.5 | 1.4 | 2.0 | 1.3 | 1.5 | 2.0 | 1.4 | 1.8 | 1.4 | 19.6 | 15.6 | 24.1 | 3.4 |
| Accumulated Surplus | 5.1 | 8.0 | 9.9 | 10.4 | 11.8 | 13.8 | 15.2 | 16.7 | 18.6 | 5.7 | 7.5 | 9.0 | 28.6 | 44.2 | 68.3 | 71.7 |

SOURCE: Compiled from Annual Reports of the Du Pont Powder Company and its successors.

* Marks year of split by the antitrust decree.
† Data for Du Pont Company and subsidiary companies (but not Du Pont American Industries).
‡ Includes adjustments due to termination of extraordinary war business.
§ Debenture stock dividends.

Table 4  DU PONT COMPANY OUTPUT OF SELECTED PRODUCTS 1904–1917

| | 1904 | 1905 | 1906 | 1907 | 1908 | 1909 | 1910 | 1911 | 1912 | 1913 | 1914 | 1915 | 1916 | 1917 |
|---|---|---|---|---|---|---|---|---|---|---|---|---|---|---|
| Black Powder ("B" Blasting) (millions of kegs) | 5.9 | 5.8 | 6.7 | 7.3 | 5.6 | 5.9 | 6.2 | 5.8 | 5.7 | 3.7 | 3.2 | 3.5 | 3.2 | 4.4 |
| Sporting Powder (millions of kegs) | 0.3 | 0.3 | 0.4 | 0.4 | 0.3 | 0.3 | 0.3 | 0.3 | 0.3 | 0.2 | 0.1 | 0.3 | 0.4 | 0.3 |
| Dynamite (millions of lbs.) | 103.2 | 114.5 | 153.2 | 161.8 | 131.8 | 158.8 | 172.0 | 164.8 | 182.4 | 116.5 | 102.7 | 110.8 | 125.9 | 128.0 |
| Smokeless Powder (millions of lbs.) | 4.8 | 6.1 | 3.9 | 3.8 | 4.5 | 4.3 | 4.2 | 5.9 | 5.5 | 5.5 | 5.5 | 208.2 | 583.3 | 776.9 |

SOURCE: Compiled from Treasurer's Annual Reports to the Executive Committee of the Du Pont Powder Company and its successors.

Table 5  DU PONT COMPANY PROFITS ON SALES OF SELECTED PRODUCTS 1904–1917
(in millions of dollars)

| | 1904 | 1905 | 1906 | 1907 | 1908 | 1909 | 1910 | 1911 | 1912 | 1913 | 1914 | 1915 | 1916 | 1917 |
|---|---|---|---|---|---|---|---|---|---|---|---|---|---|---|
| "B" Blasting | 1.06 | 0.73 | 0.39 | 0.15 | 0.46 | 0.83 | 0.98 | 0.89 | 0.75 | 0.54 | 0.59 | 0.71 | 0.73 | 2.10 |
| Black Sporting | 0.45 | 0.45 | 0.43 | 0.41 | 0.31 | 0.31 | 0.20 | 0.15 | 0.14 | 0.04 | 0.07 | 0.15 | 0.19 | 0.09 |
| Smokeless Sporting | 0.28 | 0.42 | 0.30 | 0.36 | 0.54 | 0.56 | 0.44 | 0.63 | 0.79 | 0.49 | 0.61 | 2.01 | 3.31 | 2.49 |
| X Rifle Smokeless | — | — | — | — | — | — | — | — | — | — | — | 7.52 | 14.57 | 4.99 |
| Army & Navy Smokeless | 0.38 | 1.07 | 1.06 | 0.43 | 0.59 | 0.44 | 0.38 | 0.82 | 0.74 | 0.91 | 0.69 | 0.73 | 0.31 | 2.08 |
| X Cannon Smokeless | — | — | — | — | — | — | — | — | — | — | — | 44.38 | 117.24 | 54.49 |
| Dynamite | 1.56 | 1.91 | 2.52 | 2.16 | 2.25 | 2.71 | 3.12 | 2.92 | 3.13 | 1.79 | 1.76 | 2.25 | 2.96 | 5.53 |
| Fabrikoid | — | — | — | — | — | — | 0.01 | — | 0.05 | 0.09 | — | — | — | — |
| Total Operating Profits from Sales of *All* Manufactured Products | 4.26 | 4.88 | 5.09 | 3.83 | 4.70 | 5.46 | 5.80 | 6.04 | 6.24 | 4.50 | 5.43 | 73.43 | 169.43 | 82.60 |
| Special Amortization of Wartime Plants | — | — | — | — | — | — | — | — | — | — | — | 14.46 | 76.06 | 9.40 |
| Total Net Earnings | 4.44 | 5.06 | 5.33 | 3.93 | 4.93 | 5.98 | 6.27 | 6.54 | 6.87 | 5.35 | 5.60 | 57.40 | 82.01 | 49.11 |

SOURCE: Compiled from Treasurer's Annual Report to the Executive Committee of the Du Pont Powder Company and its successors.

Table 6   GENERAL MOTORS CORPORATION

| Year | Net Income ($000) | Preferred Stock Dividends ($000) | Earnings on Common Stock — Amount ($000) | Common Stock Dividends — Amount ($000) | Reinvested Earnings — Amount ($000) |
|---|---|---|---|---|---|
| 1920 | 37,750 | 5,620 | 32,130 | 17,893 | 14,237 |
| 1921 | (38,681) | 6,310 | (44,991) | 20,468 | (65,459) |
| 1922 | 54,474 | 6,429 | 48,045 | 10,177 | 37,868 |
| 1923 | 72,009 | 6,887 | 65,122 | 24,772 | 40,350 |
| 1924 | 51,624 | 7,273 | 44,351 | 25,031 | 19,320 |
| 1925 | 116,016 | 7,640 | 108,376 | 61,935 | 46,441 |
| 1926 | 186,231 | 7,645 | 178,586 | 103,931 | 74,655 |
| 1927 | 235,105 | 9,109 | 225,996 | 134,836 | 91,160 |
| 1928 | 276,468 | 9,405 | 267,063 | 165,300 | 101,763 |
| 1929 | 248,282 | 9,479 | 238,803 | 156,600 | 82,203 |
| Avg. 1920–29 | 123,928 | 7,580 | 116,348 | 72,094 | 44,254 |

| Year | Net Sales ($000) | Value Added ($000) | Capital Expenditures (Excl. Tools) ($000) | Provision for Depreciation ($000) |
|---|---|---|---|---|
| 1920 | 567,321 | 188,427 | 79,162 | 10,388 |
| 1921 | 304,487 | 59,346 | 11,687 | 6,751 |
| 1922 | 463,707 | 172,530 | 13,847 | 13,585 |
| 1923 | 698,039 | 230,864 | 29,760 | 15,056 |
| 1924 | 568,007 | 182,190 | 16,143 | 16,079 |
| 1925 | 734,593 | 284,472 | 12,554 | 17,237 |
| 1926 | 1,058,153 | 464,350 | 66,108 | 20,398 |
| 1927 | 1,269,520 | 630,608 | 55,060 | 27,364 |
| 1928 | 1,459,763 | 711,200 | 79,806 | 31,177 |
| 1929 | 1,504,404 | 708,214 | 75,627 | 35,948 |
| Avg. 1920–29 | 862,799 | 363,220 | 43,975 | 19,398 |

Table 6  GENERAL MOTORS CORPORATION (*Continued*)

| At End of Year | Cash in Excess of Tax Liability ($000) | Inventories ($000) | Net Working Capital ($000) | Net Plant ($000) | Capital Stock and Surplus ($000) | Capital Stock, Surplus, and Long-term Debt ($000) |
|---|---|---|---|---|---|---|
| 1920 | 42,742† | 164,685 | 137,062† | 220,805 | 430,822 | 430,822 |
| 1921 | 38,176 | 108,763 | 92,723 | 213,397 | 366,194 | 366,194 |
| 1922 | 26,255 | 117,418 | 125,118 | 206,873 | 404,681 | 404,681 |
| 1923 | 38,807 | 138,678 | 139,163 | 219,975 | 437,079 | 437,079 |
| 1924 | 82,193 | 97,202 | 159,227 | 217,215 | 450,107 | 450,107 |
| 1925 | 131,230 | 112,092 | 179,968 | 199,508 | 487,016 | 487,016 |
| 1926 | 105,074 | 156,204 | 188,946 | 315,201 | 634,257 | 634,257 |
| 1927 | 172,952 | 172,648 | 269,324 | 348,527 | 757,735 | 757,735 |
| 1928 | 182,679 | 196,692 | 292,205 | 396,141 | 855,375 | 855,375 |
| 1929 | 98,651 | 188,473 | 247,575 | 429,967 | 954,476 | 954,476 |
| Avg. 1920–29 | 91,876 | 145,286 | 183,131 | 276,861 | 577,774 | 577,774 |

† After deducting $4,942,000 reserve for federal taxes and extraordinary expenses.

| Year | Average Number of Employees | Total Payrolls (000) |
|---|---|---|
| 1920 | 80,612 | 112,800† |
| 1921 | 45,965 | 66,020 |
| 1922 | 65,345 | 95,128 |
| 1923 | 91,265 | 138,291 |
| 1924 | 73,642 | 110,478 |
| 1925 | 83,278 | 136,747 |
| 1926 | 129,538 | 220,919 |
| 1927 | 175,666 | 302,905 |
| 1928 | 208,981 | 365,352 |
| 1929 | 233,286 | 389,518 |
| Avg. 1920–29 | 118,758 | 193,816 |

† Indicates red figure.

Table 7  COMPARISON OF NUMBER AND PROPORTION OF PASSENGER MOTOR VEHICLES SOLD BY THE PRINCIPAL MANUFACTURERS DURING ALTERNATE YEARS FROM 1911 TO 1929

[from Federal Trade Commission, *Report on the Motor Vehicle Industry* (Washington: Government Printing Office, 1939), p. 29]

| Year | Total Number Passenger Motor Vehicles Sold By All Manufacturers | Chrysler Corporation Sales | Ford Motor Co. Sales | General Motors Corporation Sales | Subtotal, Chrysler Corporation, Ford Motor Co., General Motors Corporation Passenger-Car Sales | Subtotal, Hudson, Nash, Packard, Studebaker Passenger-Car Sales | Total Passenger-Car Sales, 7 Companies Covered in Commission's Inquiry | All Other Manufacturers' Passenger-Car Sales, Except 7 Covered in Commission's Inquiry |
|---|---|---|---|---|---|---|---|---|
| | *Units* | *Units* | *Units* | *Units* | *Units* | *Units* | *Units* | *Units* |
| 1911 | 199,000 | — | 39,640 | 35,459 | 75,099 | 30,524 | 105,623 | 93,377 |
| 1913 | 462,000 | — | 182,311 | 56,118 | 238,429 | 44,004 | 282,433 | 179,567 |
| 1915 | 806,000 | — | 342,115 | 97,937 | 440,052 | 57,998 | 498,050 | 397,950 |
| 1917 | 1,746,000 | — | 740,770 | 195,945 | 936,715 | 75,348 | 1,012,063 | 733,937 |
| 1919 | 1,658,000 | — | 664,482 | 344,334 | 1,008,816 | 107,187 | 1,116,003 | 541,997 |
| 1921 | 1,518,000 | — | 845,000 | 193,275 | 1,038,275 | 120,459 | 1,158,734 | 359,266 |
| 1923 | 3,624,717 | — | 1,669,298 | 732,984 | 2,402,282 | 308,491 | 2,710,773 | 913,944 |
| 1925 | 3,735,171 | 134,474 | 1,494,911 | 745,905 | 2,375,290 | 515,066 | 2,890,356 | 844,815 |
| 1927 | 2,936,533 | 182,627 | 273,741 | 1,277,198 | 1,733,566 | 551,945 | 2,285,511 | 651,022 |
| 1929 | 4,587,400 | 375,381 | 1,435,886 | 1,482,004 | 3,293,271 | 563,405 | 3,856,676 | 730,724 |
| | *Per cent* | *Per cent* | *Per cent* | *Per cent* | *Per cent* | *Per cent* | *Per cent* | *Per cent* |
| 1911 | 100.00 | — | 19.92 | 17.82 | 37.74 | 15.34 | 53.08 | 46.92 |
| 1913 | 100.00 | — | 39.46 | 12.15 | 51.61 | 9.52 | 61.13 | 38.87 |
| 1915 | 100.00 | — | 38.18 | 10.93 | 49.11 | 6.48 | 55.59 | 44.41 |
| 1917 | 100.00 | — | 42.43 | 11.22 | 53.65 | 4.32 | 57.97 | 42.03 |
| 1919 | 100.00 | — | 40.08 | 20.77 | 60.85 | 6.46 | 67.31 | 32.69 |
| 1921 | 100.00 | — | 55.67 | 12.73 | 68.40 | 7.93 | 76.33 | 23.67 |
| 1923 | 100.00 | — | 46.05 | 20.23 | 66.28 | 8.51 | 74.79 | 25.21 |
| 1925 | 100.00 | 3.60 | 40.02 | 19.97 | 63.59 | 13.79 | 77.38 | 22.62 |
| 1927 | 100.00 | 6.22 | 9.32 | 43.49 | 59.03 | 18.80 | 77.83 | 22.17 |
| 1929 | 100.00 | 8.18 | 31.30 | 32.31 | 71.79 | 12.28 | 84.07 | 15.93 |

SOURCE: U. S. Department of Commerce, Bureau of the Census, *Statistical Abstract of the United States 1936*, p. 363 for years 1911–19 and Census of Manufacturers 1921–29. Figures for 1911–21 represent production and 1923–29 represent sales.

# SOURCES OF INFORMATION

The basic source of information for this study has been the Papers of Pierre S. du Pont. This collection of over one million documents is housed in the Eleutherian Mills Historical Library, Greenville, Delaware. There the entire collection is designated as The Longwood Manuscripts, Group 10, Papers of Pierre S. du Pont (1870–1954). The business and personal papers that make up the major part of the collection are known as Series A. In addition there are many personal writings by Pierre S. du Pont on subjects in which he was interested which are known as Series B. In this study we have cited all the papers from this collection as PSduP plus the citation number of the file in which the document resides. When we cite Pierre S. du Pont's own writings, we use the prefix B before the file number.

In telling the story of the Du Pont Company the papers of Thomas Coleman du Pont and the records of the E. I. du Pont de Nemours Powder Company, and its predecessors and successors, were absolutely essential. The first of these collections is also housed at the Eleutherian Mills Historical Library and includes business correspondence and other documents relating to the years during which T. Coleman du Pont served as president of the Du Pont Company. Those for 1902–1907 are known as Accession 1075. Those for 1908–1915 are listed under Accession 472, Records of EIDPDNCo. In this study they are referred to as 1075 plus the file number or 472 plus the file number.

The Executive Committee Minutes, the reports presented to the Executive Committee, and a number of other records of the E. I. du Pont de Nemours Powder Company and its predecessors and successors are located at the headquarters of the E. I. du Pont de Nemours & Company in Wilmington, Delaware, under the supervision of the Secretaries to the Committees Division.

One other source that proved useful was the letters of Colonel Henry du Pont, which are housed at the Eleutherian Mills Historical Library, where they are known as The Papers of Henry Algernon du Pont (1838–1926) in the Henry Francis du Pont Collection of Winterthur Manuscripts, Group 8.

The papers of John J. Raskob are also maintained at the Eleutherian Mills Historical Library as its Accession 473. These are extremely valuable for understanding both the Du Pont and General Motors stories. Besides his business papers relating to these two companies, this collection includes files of Mr. Raskob's personal finances, his property transactions, and his political career.

Other essential sources in the Du Pont section of the book came from the Wilmington and Philadelphia newspapers and the records of several legal transcripts including (1) In the Circuit Court of the United States, for the District of Delaware, No. 280. In Equity, *The United States of America, Petitioner, v. E. I. du Pont de Nemours and Company, E. I. du Pont de Nemours Powder Company (of New Jersey), Du Pont International Powder Company, Delaware Securities Company, California Investment Company, Delaware Investment Company, The Hazard Powder Company, Laflin & Rand Powder Company, Eastern Dynamite Company, E. I. du Pont de Nemours Powder Company (of Delaware) et al., (1909–1912)*; (2) In the District Court of the United States, for the District of Delaware, In Equity 340, *Philip F. du Pont, Original Complainant and Eleanor du Pont Perot, Eleuthère Paul du Pont, Archibald M. L. du Pont, Ernest du Pont, Alfred I. du Pont, Francis I. du Pont, Louis Albert deCazenova, Jr., Henry S. Morris, and Charles Ellis Gooden, Intervenors, v. Pierre S. du Pont, Irénée du Pont, Lammot du Pont, Alexis Felix du Pont, John J. Raskob, Robert Ruliph Morgan Carpenter, Henry F. du Pont, Eugene E. du Pont, William Coyne, Harry G. Haskell, Harry F. Brown, John P. Laffey, E. I. du Pont de Nemours & Company, Du Pont Securities Company, and E. I. du Pont de Nemours Powder Company, Defendants, (1916)*; (3) the Appeal, No. 2382, In the United States Circuit Court of Appeals for the Third Circuit, *Philip du Pont and others, Plaintiffs below, Plaintiffs in Error, vs. Pierre S. du Pont, and others, Defendants below, Defendants in Error,* before Buffington and McPherson, Circuit Judges and Haight, District Judge, Opinion of Court by Buffington, J. (Filed March 6, 1919). In addition we made use of *Munitions Industry Hearings before the Special Committee Investigating the Munitions Industry,* United States Senate, Seventy Third (Seventy Fourth) Congress Pursuant to S. Res. 206. A Resolution to Certain Investigations Concerning the Manufacture and Sale of Arms and other War Munitions (Washington: Government Printing Office, 1934–1937). Also in writing the chapters on General Motors the Pierre S. du Pont and the John J. Raskob documents were supplemented by the Trial Exhibits and Depositions of both the prosecution and the defense in the antitrust case, In the United States District Court, For the Northern Division of Illinois, Eastern Division, Civil Action No. 49 C–1071, *United States of America vs. E. I. du Pont de Nemours and Company, General Motors Corporation, United States Rubber Company, Christiana Securities, Delaware Realty & Investment, Pierre S. du Pont, Lammot du Pont, Irénée du Pont, Defendants.* (June, 1956)

In addition one of the authors had detailed notes based on interviews and documents which he used when he was a consultant to Alfred P. Sloan, Jr., in the publication of Sloan's *My Years with General Motors.* Also interviews with Walter S. Carpenter, Jr., John Lee Pratt, Mrs. R. R. M. Carpenter, James Eliason, Eugene E. du Pont, Jasper E. Crane, and Frederick A. Wardenburg provided useful material.

# NOTES

CHAPTER 1. The Family and the Firm

1. Pierre S. du Pont, "My Father," written February 28, 1943; rewritten June 29, 1948, the Eleutherian Mills Historical Library, Greenville, Delaware. Longwood Manuscripts, Group 10. Papers of Pierre S. du Pont (1870–1954), personal and business. Series A consists of correspondence and related publications such as reports and clippings. Series B consists of ninety-four memoirs on various subjects of personal interest. Hereafter the references to Pierre S. du Pont's collection, Series A, will be PSduP plus the file number; the references to his own writings, Series B, will be PSduP B plus the file number. The above quotation is PSduP B–7.
2. Henry Algernon du Pont was appointed Adjutant General of Delaware in 1846; in 1861 he was appointed major general, commanding the Delaware Volunteers.
3. All data about the Brandywine Mills at the time of Lammot du Pont, Pierre S. du Pont, "My Father," PSduP B–7.
4. Pierre S. du Pont, "Written at Chateau d'Andelot near Saint Amour, Jura, France," July 1935, PSduP B–5.
5. *Ibid.*
6. Mrs. Alfred V. du Pont to Bidermann du Pont, July 3, 1865, Du Pont, Belin, Lammot, d' Andelot Papers, Eleutherian Mills Historical Library, Accession 761, Box 2.
7. Sophie Madeleine du Pont to Amelia E. du Pont, October 1–3, 1865. Eleutherian Mills Historical Library, Winterthur Collection, Group 9, #23758.
8. Pierre S. du Pont, "My Induction to Explosives Manufacture," April 10, 1945. PSduP B–5.
9. Pierre S. du Pont, "Written at Chateau d'Andelot," PSduP B–5.
10. Marquis James, *Alfred I. du Pont, The Family Rebel* (Indianapolis: Bobbs-Merrill, 1941), pp. 19–20.
11. Pierre S. du Pont, Memoirs, 1945, PSduP B–5.
12. *Ibid.*
13. All quotations, Pierre S. du Pont, "Written at Chateau d'Andelot," PSduP B–5.
14. Pierre S. du Pont, Memoirs, 1945, PSduP B–5.

15. Pierre S. du Pont, "Written at Chateau d'Andelot," PSduP B–5.
16. *Ibid.*
17. *Ibid.* All quotations.
18. Pierre S. du Pont, "My Father," PSduP B–7.
19. Pierre S. du Pont, "Written at Chateau d'Andelot," PSduP B–5.
20. Arthur Pine Van Gelder and Hugo Schlatter, *History of the Explosives Industry in America* (New York: Columbia University Press, 1927), pp. 403–407.
21. *Ibid.*, p. 402.
22. B. G. du Pont, *E. I. du Pont de Nemours and Company, A History 1802–1902* (Boston: Houghton Mifflin, The Riverside Press, 1920), p. 140.
23. The Hazard Powder Company (fully owned by Du Pont) had one-third of the Repauno stock until the sale of Lammot's partnership was completed. P. S. du Pont to S. Hallock du Pont, December 28, 1922, PSduP 909.
24. Pierre S. du Pont, Memoirs, 1946, PSduP B–5.
25. *Ibid.*
26. Pierre S. du Pont, "My Father," PSduP B–7.
27. Pierre S. du Pont, Memoirs, 1946, PSduP B–5.
28. Pierre S. du Pont, "My Father," PSduP B–7.
29. Pierre S. du Pont, "Written at Chateau d'Andelot," PSduP B–5.
30. James, *Alfred I. du Pont*, pp. 50–51.
31. Pierre S. du Pont to Louisa du Pont, December 5, 1886, PSduP 388. Pierre du Pont and his sister Louisa wrote to each other every Sunday night for the four years that he was away from home attending Massachusetts Institute of Technology.
32. *Ibid.*, December 11, 1886.
33. *Ibid.*, January 9, 1887. Pierre du Pont's fraternity friends were Charles K. Lennig and Albert H. Smith.
34. *Ibid.*, February 13, 1887.
35. *Ibid.*, May 22, 1887.
36. *Ibid.*, December 4, 1887.
37. *Ibid.*, October 30, 1887.
38. *Ibid.*, April 20, 1890.
39. *Ibid.*, May 4, 1890.
40. *Ibid.*, May 4, 1890.
41. James, *Alfred I. du Pont*, p. 86.
42. Charles Irénée du Pont was one of the few members of Victor Marie du Pont's branch who joined the company. He was the great-grandson of Victor, the brother of Eleuthère Irénée du Pont who had started the Du Pont Company and was the father of Henry, Alfred Victor (Pierre's grandfather), and Alexis I. du Pont.
43. P. S. du Pont to L. du Pont, May 18, 1890, PSduP 388.

CHAPTER 2. The Apprenticeship

1. Pierre S. du Pont, "My Induction to Explosives Manufacture," written October 10, 1945. Papers of Pierre S. du Pont, the Eleutherian Mills Historical Library, Longwood Manuscripts, Group 10, Series B, File 5, hereafter cited PSduP plus the identifying file number.
2. *Ibid.*
3. Of Repauno stock Laflin & Rand owned one-third, Hazard one-third, and Lammot du Pont one-third. Upon Lammot du Pont's death, the company purchased two-thirds of his shares and his widow kept the remaining third. P. S. du Pont to E. Paul du Pont, January 31, 1949, PSduP 918.
4. The Cincinnati *Enquirer*, May 19, 20, 22, 1893.

5. Pierre S. du Pont, "Written at Chateau d'Andelot, near Saint Amour, Jura, France." July 1935, PSduP B–5.

6. Data on electric railroads, Harold C. Passer, *The Electrical Manufacturers 1875–1900, A Study in Competition, Entrepreneurship, Technical Change and Economic Growth* (Cambridge, Mass: Harvard University Press, 1953), p. 341.

7. The data on the Johnson Company and Arthur Moxham from Tom L. Johnson, *My Story* (New York: B. W. Heubsch, 1911), pp. 9–16, 31, and Michael Massouh, who is currently completing a biography of Tom Johnson. According to Massouh, sales offices were set up in Boston, New York, St. Louis, New Orleans, Chicago, Atlanta, and San Francisco.

8. Pierre S. du Pont, "Chateau d'Andelot," PSduP B-5.

9. P. S. du Pont to E. Paul du Pont, January 31, 1949, PSduP 918.

10. P. S. du Pont to T. C. du Pont, January 9, 1895, PSduP 26.

11. P. S. du Pont to T. C. du Pont, January 16, 1895; T. C. du Pont to P. S. du Pont, January 12, 1895, PSduP 26.

12. P. S. du Pont to H. B. du Pont, January 27, 1899, PSduP 19.

13. T. Johnson to P. S. du Pont, August 3, 1893, PSduP 26.

14. A. Moxham to P. S. du Pont, September 4, 1893, PSduP 26.

15. P. S. du Pont to E. Paul du Pont, January 31, 1949, PSduP 918.

16. Prospectus, The Johnson Company. P. S. du Pont received this undated document with a form letter, April 13, 1894, PSduP 26.

17. A. Moxham to P. S. du Pont, April 13, 1894, PSduP 26.

18. Prospectus, The Johnson Company; P. S. du Pont to A. Moxham, February 5, 1894; Statement of Financial Plan; A. Moxham to P. S. du Pont, June 26, 1894, all PSduP 26.

19. Bonds worth $4,400 at par.

20. Stock worth $17,300 at par.

21. P. S. du Pont to Johnson Company, April 12, 1895; A. Moxham to P. S. du Pont, May 9, 1894, PSduP 26.

22. P. S. du Pont to T. Johnson, April 12, 1895, PSduP 26.

23. T. C. du Pont to P. S. du Pont, January 31, 1896, PSduP 26.

24. A. Moxham to P. S. du Pont, July 18, 1896, PSduP 26.

25. A. Moxham to R. G. Dun & Co., September 29, 1896, PSduP 26.

26. A. Moxham to P. S. du Pont, October 7, 1896, PSduP 26.

27. In addition to the above citations, data on the Wilmington loans come from P. S. du Pont to T. C. du Pont, January 24; A. Moxham to P. S. du Pont, February 26; P. S. du Pont to T. C. du Pont, January 25; T. C. du Pont to P. S. du Pont January 27; T. C. du Pont to P. S. du Pont, January 31; P. S. du Pont to A. Moxham, September 26; A. Moxham to P. S. du Pont, September 29; P. S. du Pont to A. Moxham, October 4; T. C. du Pont to P. S. du Pont, December 10; all 1896, all in PSduP 26. Data on Taylor by Michael Massouh from his forthcoming study of Tom Johnson.

28. Johnson Co. to P. S. du Pont, August 3, 1893, PSduP 26; also Pierre S. du Pont, "Chateau d'Andelot," PSduP B-5. Data on U.S. Steel formation from Abraham Bergland, *The United States Steel Corporation, A Study of the Growth and Influence of Combination in the Iron and Steel Industry* (New York: Columbia University Press, 1907), pp. 55–56.

29. Arthur Pine Van Gelder and Hugo Schlatter, *History of the Explosives Industry in America* (New York: Columbia University Press, 1927), p. 795.

30. Pierre S. du Pont, Memoirs, January 19, 1949, PSduP B-5.

31. *Ibid.*

32. P. S. du Pont to E. Paul du Pont, January 31, 1949, PSduP 918.

33. P. S. du Pont to H. B. du Pont, April 13, 1895, PSduP 19.

34. H. B. du Pont to P. S. du Pont, March 19, 1899, PSduP 19.

35. P. S. du Pont to H. B. du Pont, February 12, 1899, PSduP 19.

36. P. S. du Pont to E. I. du Pont de Nemours & Co., January 20, and the answer to the above, January 23, 1899, PSduP 19.
37. P. S. du Pont to H. B. du Pont, January 22, 1899, PSduP 19.
38. H. B. du Pont to P. S. du Pont, January 23, 1899, PSduP 19.
39. P. S. du Pont to H. B. du Pont, January 27, 1899, PSduP 19.
40. *Ibid.*
41. *Ibid.*
42. H. B. du Pont to P. S. du Pont, June 29, 1988, PSduP 19.
43. P. S. du Pont to H. B. du Pont, October 24, 1899, PSduP 19.
44. P. S. du Pont to A. Moxham, June 25, 1900, PSduP 250.
45. P. S. du Pont to A. Moxham, July 22, 1900, PSduP 26; P. S. du Pont to A. Moxham, August 8, 1900, PSduP 250.
46. P. S. du Pont to A. Moxham, September 4, 1900, PSduP 250.
47. P. S. du Pont to the Directors of the Johnson Co., December 9, 1901, PSduP 26.
48. P. S. du Pont to Chas. H. Simonds, January 20, 1905, PSduP 26; Pierre S. du Pont, "Chateau d'Andelot," PSduP B-5.
49. P. S du Pont to T. C. du Pont, March 9, 1901, PSduP 431.
50. P. S. du Pont to Members of Federal Steel Syndicate, June 15, 1901; also minutes of the stockholders' meeting of the Dallas Consolidated Electric Street Railway, June 11, 1901, PSduP 431.
51. P. S. du Pont to H. B. du Pont, May 15, 1901, PSduP 431.
52. P. S. du Pont to George P. Bissell, July 19, 1901, PSduP 431.
53. P. S. du Pont to T. C. du Pont, July 2, 1901, PSduP 431.
54. G. P. Bissell to P. S. du Pont, July 15, 1901, PSduP 431.
55. P. S. du Pont to A. Beveridge, November 15, 22, 1901; A. Beveridge to P. S. du Pont, November 15, 1901, PSduP 431.
56. P. S. du Pont to W. Washington, September 18, 1901, PSduP 431.
57. E. T. Moore to P. S. du Pont, January 2, 1902; C. H. Alexander to P. S. du Pont, February 5, 1902; C. H. Alexander to E. T. Moore, March 22, 26, 1902; E. T. Moore to P. S. du Pont, March 19, 25, 1902; C. H. Alexander to P. S. du Pont, March 17, 1902. All PSduP 431.
58. E. Moore to W. K. du Pont, July 7, 1902; E. Moore to W. K. du Pont, July 7, 1902; P. S. du Pont to Messrs. Findley, Etheridge and Knight, January 13, 1902; P. S. du Pont to E. Moore, June 4, 1902; all PSduP 431.
59. P. S. du Pont to E. Moore, June 4, 1902, PSduP 431.
60. P. S. du Pont to W. K. du Pont, July 29, 1902, PSduP 431.
61. P. S. du Pont to Alexis I. du Pont, September 1, 1902, PSduP 431.

CHAPTER 3. The New Company

1. Mary du Pont to P. S. du Pont, January 14, 1902, The Eleutherian Mills Historical Library, Papers of Pierre S. du Pont, Longwood Manuscripts, Group 10, File 48. Hereafter cited by PSduP plus the identifying file number. Louisa du Pont to P. S. du Pont, January 14, 1902, PSduP 388.
2. Louisa du Pont to P. S. du Pont, January 27, 1902, PSduP 388; J. Raskob to P. S. du Pont, January 28, 29, 1902, PSduP 303; Mary du Pont to P. S. du Pont (telegram), January 28, 1902, PSduP 48.
3. Historical sketch written by P. S. du Pont, dictated 1948, "Reorganization of 1902," PSduP B-44.
4. T. C. du Pont to P. S. du Pont (telegram), February 6, 1902, PSduP 15.
5. T. C. du Pont to P. S. du Pont (telegram), February 11, 1902, PSduP 15.

6. The review of events given here is taken from recollections of several participants. While none have the same emphasis, all are remarkably consistent about the facts of the case. Alfred's version was first told on the witness stand of the antitrust suit against Du Pont and later expanded and embellished in Marquis James, *Alfred I. du Pont, The Family Rebel* (Indianapolis: Bobbs-Merrill, 1941). Colonel Henry A. du Pont gave his version in a long letter to Eugene E. du Pont, February 25, 1921, PSduP 418–4, a copy of which he sent to Pierre the following day. He was moved to write the letter because of comments about the 1902 change of command in the just published history of the company by Alfred's first wife, Bessie G. du Pont, *E. I. du Pont de Nemours and Company: A History 1802–1902* (Boston: Houghton Mifflin, 1920). In the antitrust suit Hamilton M. Barksdale, Francis I. du Pont, and Pierre S. du Pont all gave versions of these events. Pierre summarized his views in the rough historical sketch of 1948, PSduP B–44.

7. H. A. du Pont to E. E. du Pont, February 25, 1921, PSduP 418–4.

8. Testimony of Francis I. du Pont, *U. S. Circuit Court of Delaware, No. 280 in Equity, United States of America, Petitioner v. E. I. du Pont de Nemours and Company et al., Defendants* (hereafter cited *U.S. v. Du Pont*) *Defendants' Record Testimony*, II, 963–967.

9. This and the two following quotations are from H. A. du Pont to E. E. du Pont, February 25, 1921, PSduP 418–4.

10. For J. A. Haskell's and H. M. Barksdale's work at Repauno see William S. Dutton, *Du Pont: One Hundred and Forty Years* (New York: Scribner, 1942), pp. 146–147. Testimony H. Barksdale, *U.S. v. Du Pont* (1909), *Defendants' Record Testimony*, II, 625. The only significant discrepancy in the different versions of the story is in Barksdale's testimony. He testified that "about ten days" after Eugene's death he was asked to take the presidency in order to sell the company, and if not salable to run it. He further stated at the same time Alexis reported that Alfred "desired an opportunity to present a proposition, which the doctor told me had, of course, been granted." The other versions indicate that at least a week elapsed between the invitation to Barksdale and the final meeting in which the decision to sell was approved and was then followed by Alfred's request to buy the company. In any case the decision to sell the company and have Barksdale act as its agent was formally decided on February 14 (at least this seems the most likely date). This was seventeen days after Eugene's death. James's attempt to combine these versions leads to confusion, *Alfred I. du Pont*, pp. 143–147. The timing of the initial invitation to Barksdale does coincide closely in time to Coleman's brief visit to New York where he met Pierre.

11. H. A. du Pont to E. E. du Pont, February 25, 1921, PSduP 418–4. James mentions that Alfred about this same time "acted quietly slipping away to New York to see bankers about a loan for refinancing the company in case cash were needed to block the proposed sale to Laflin & Rand," James, *Alfred I. du Pont*, p. 143. James's source is an interview with Jessie Ball du Pont, Alfred's third wife.

12. The date is still not clear. Pierre, in his 1948 historical sketch, gives Friday, February 14. Colonel Henry remembers in his letter to Eugene two meetings on consecutive days. Coleman's wire to Pierre refers to a meeting on Wednesday evening. Possibly this may have been put off to Thursday morning, or Coleman may have been referring to a previous meeting with Alfred. The E. I. du Pont de Nemours & Co. have no records from late January until February 26.

13. H. A. du Pont to E. E. du Pont, February 25, 1921, PSduP 418–4.

14. James, *Alfred I. du Pont*, pp. 144–145. James states that this meeting was the first stockholders' meeting that Alfred had ever attended.

15. This and the following quotation, *U.S. v. Du Pont (1909) Defendants' Record Testimony*, I, 446–447.

16. This and the two following quotations, H. A. du Pont to E. E. du Pont, February 25, 1921, PSduP 418–4.

17. *Ibid.*

18. James, *Alfred I. du Pont,* pp. 147–150. James's story differs from the one told here in that he brings Coleman in for the first time after and not before the meeting of February 14. James had not seen Colonel Henry's letter to Eugene E. (at least there is no reference to it in his excellent citations). Colonel Henry's version does have an authenticity both in the timing of the events and in the personalities of the men involved.

19. P. S. du Pont to W. K. du Pont, February 20, 1902, *U.S. v. Du Pont (1909) Defendants' Record Exhibits,* 1, 39. There is no letter in the PSduP collection to Tom Johnson. In any case Johnson could have hardly answered before Pierre wrote his brother on the 20th that "Mr. Johnson knows the circumstances and thinks it is all right to act as I have." PSduP 19.

20. James, *Alfred I. du Pont,* pp. 149–150. Accounts of the blizzard fill the columns of the February 17 issue of the Wilmington *Every Evening.*

21. Historical sketch, "Reorganization of 1902," PSduP B–44. H. A. du Pont to E. E. du Pont, February 25, 1902, PSduP 918.

22. H. A. du Pont to E. E. du Pont, February 25, 1921, PSduP 418–4. The sellers were most fortunate to make this arrangement. The bonus was to be a bonanza. Each of the full partners received $2.4 million in bonds and just under 6,000 shares of stock. By 1925, Pierre estimated, the value of that block of stock was over $16.5 million. P. S. du Pont to I. du Pont, L. du Pont, W. W. Laird, September 28, 1925, PSduP 418.

23. H. A. du Pont to E. E. du Pont, February 25, 1921, PSduP 918. P. S. du Pont to W. K. du Pont, February 20, 1902, also to I. du Pont, *U.S. v. Du Pont (1909) Defendants' Record Exhibits,* 1, 38–39; to William Fenn, February 20, 1902, PSduP 257. The next day Pierre notified his uncle Henry Belin, PSduP 9. The following quotations are from the letters to W.K. and Irénée. The replies of his mother and uncle are interesting (PSduP 48 and 9). Raskob, in taking Pierre's dictation, had not yet learned the proper form for Brandywine.

24. Historical sketch, PSduP B–44. *U.S. v. Du Pont (1909) Defendants' Record Testimony,* I, 511–541. Minutes of the Board of Directors meeting, February 26, 1902, "Agreement made this first day of March A. D. nineteen hundred and two, by and between, Henry A. du Pont, Alexis I. du Pont, Francis I. du Pont, Charles I. du Pont, Alfred I. du Pont, Alexis I. du Pont and Eugene du Pont, executors of the last will and testament of Eugene du Pont, deceased, parties of the first part and E. I. du Pont de Nemours & Company, a corporation existing under the laws of the State of Delaware, party of the second part . . . .", PSduP 418; list of holdings in old and new company, PSduP 418; James, *Alfred I. du Pont,* pp. 157–158. The E. I. du Pont de Nemours Company was formed on February 26, and received its charter in Dover, Delaware, on the 27th. It changed its name to E. I. du Pont de Nemours & Co. on May 8, 1902. It took over the liabilities and received the assets of the E. I. du Pont de Nemours & Company. On November 1 another agreement was signed, PSduP 418. The old 1899 corporation was dissolved and the new E. I. du Pont de Nemours Company which had become & Company took over all the properties from the 1899 corporation. The March 1, 1902, agreement was declared null and void; J. H. Cassidy to the Secretary of State, Dover, January 28, 1947; William J. Story to J. H. Cassidy, January 29, 1947, in the present-day Du Pont Company files; Copy of Certificate of Incorporation for E. I. du Pont de Nemours & Co., PSduP 418.

25. Pierre du Pont, historical sketch, 1948 PSduP B–44. *U.S. v. Du Pont (1909) Defendants' Record Testimony,* I, 479–480: James, *Alfred I. du Pont,* p. 153.

26. James, *Alfred I. du Pont,* p. 158.

27. This allocation of duties was defined by the cousins in their first meeting. P. S. du Pont

to H. Belin, February 21, 1902: "Coleman will be President, Alfred Vice President, and I will be Treasurer though it may be some days before election is held." PSduP 9.

28. These plants were valued in Pierre's inventory, PSduP 418.

|  | *As of July 2, 1902* | *As of March 1, 1902* |
|---|---|---|
| Brandywine Mills | 457,791.31 | 400,000 |
| Iowa Mills | 365,923.70 | 275,000 |
| Sycamore Mills & | | |
| Other Assets | 112,531.32 | 123,866.22 |
| Wapwallopen | 326,163.47 | 275,000 |

The information on the Sycamore Mills, Arthur P. Van Gelder and Hugo Schlatter, *History of Explosives in America* (New York: Columbia University Press, 1927), pp. 134–135. The works were dismantled in 1903.

29. This table is a precise copy of "Data concerning inventories, E. I. du Pont de Nemours & Company." Prepared by Pierre and Raskob and filed in PSduP 418. Later detailed inventories for each category as well as totals are filed in PSduP 418. In listing the value of the stock held in other companies, Pierre includes only $160,163.50 for investment stocks, $4,533,339.99 for Powder Company stocks, and $937,509.75 for investment bonds. (See Table 3–1.) Pierre later recalled that the only issue over the evaluation of the property came in three pieces of property on the Hudson, Niagara, and Delaware rivers, which had been purchased for storage magazines. It was finally agreed that these would not be included in the property purchased. PSduP 632.

30. Dutton, *Du Pont*, pp. 176–177, says the purchase gave them joint control over 15 out of 22 important companies including both Hazard and Eastern. Pierre in his 1948 memoirs says that by purchase of Laflin & Rand the Du Pont Company gained majority holdings in 23 and substantial minority in 4 more, and without Laflin & Rand, Du Pont held large blocks of stock in only 5. James, *Alfred I. du Pont*, p. 170, says that the Du Pont Co. held 34.8% of Laflin & Rand, but all the evidence in the P. S. du Pont and T. C. du Pont papers shows that the Du Pont Company held little or no stock in Laflin & Rand.

31. P. S. du Pont to H. Belin, March 8, 1902. Pierre answered a letter to H. Belin, March 6, referring to "our conversation of the other evening" on both "the new deal" and "the purchase of L&R." PSduP 9.

32. The best coverage of the founding and growth of the Association and its agreements with the California companies is given in Van Gelder and Schlatter, *Explosives Industry*, pp. 128–158. Also useful is Lucius F. Ellsworth, "Strategy and Structure: The Du Pont Company's Sales Organization, 1870–1903," in *Papers Presented at the Annual Business History Conference*, ed. J. van Fenstermaker (Kent, Ohio, 1965), pp. 108–109. The general story of the Du Pont Company and the industry during the second half of the nineteenth century can be found in William S. Dutton, *Du Pont*, pp. 107–168; Bessie G. du Pont, *E. I. du Pont de Nemours and Company: A History*, chs. 9–11.

33. Van Gelder and Schlatter, *Explosives Industry*, pp. 139–141. The five new companies were Great Western, Lake Superior, Sycamore, Ohio, and Marcellus.

34. This control is indicated by the printed *Gun Powder Trade Association of the United States-Compendium of Rules, June 1st, 1881*, and later modification of the rules filed in the E. I. du Pont de Nemours & Co. records at the Eleutherian Mills Historical Library, Acc. 500–514. See also earlier "Resolutions passed by Gunpowder Trade Association, and to be observed by all agents, New York, April 13, 1876," Acc. 500–514; "Compendium of Rules, June 1st, 1881," Acc. 500–519.

35. *Census of Manufacturers for 1907* (Washington, 1907), pp. 8, 511.

36. For Henry du Pont's purchases, see Dutton, *Du Pont*, pp. 121–123. Particularly useful

for Laflin & Rand is a typewritten autobiographical sketch written by Solomon Turck for his grandsons La Motte T. Cohu and William Cohu, January 29, 1901. La Motte Cohu gave a copy of this letter to Alfred D. Chandler, Sr. See also Van Gelder and Schlatter, *Explosives Industry,* pp. 235–236, 251–252.

37. Solomon Turck, "Autobiography," and Van Gelder and Schlatter, *Explosives Industry,* pp. 132–137, 237. The only purchase in the anthracite region by Du Pont, alone, after 1875, was that of the Consumer's Powder Company bought in 1885, of which Henry Belin became president, *ibid.,* p. 218. Also, as indicated earlier, the Du Pont Company and Laflin & Rand sponsored the Hamilton Powder Company in Canada, which bought Windsor Powder Mills shortly thereafter. The Oriental Company later moved to Cincinnati; R. T. Coleman headed that firm until 1900 when his brother John B. Coleman became its president. Coleman's son John W. was treasurer and his son-in-law F. W. Pickard was its secretary. The same men held comparable offices in the King Mercantile Company, *ibid.,* p. 264.

38. Van Gelder and Schlatter, *Explosives Industry,* pp. 137–138.

39. *Ibid.,* pp. 140–148.

40. *Ibid.,* pp. 148–157.

41. Dutton, *Du Pont,* pp. 136–139; and Van Gelder and Schlatter, *Explosives Industry,* pp. 594–595. After the Cleveland plant was moved to Missouri, the Hercules Powder Company became only a selling organization, and Repauno operated the plant at the new location.

42. Van Gelder and Schlatter, *Explosives Industry,* pp. 426–427.

43. *Ibid.,* pp. 426, 596, 694–695. Also monthly report of High Explosives Department, Hamilton M. Barksdale to Executive Committee, Du Pont Company, Du Pont Co. records.

44. Dutton, *Du Pont,* pp. 146–152. Ernest Dale and Charles Meloy, "Hamilton MacFarland Barksdale and the du Pont Contribution to Systematic Management," *Business History Review,* Vol. 36 (Summer 1962), pp. 127–152.

45. James, *Alfred I. du Pont,* pp. 169–171.

46. H. Belin to P. S. du Pont, March 6, May 14, 1902; P. S. du Pont to H. Belin, March 8, 1902, PSduP 9; P. S. du Pont historical sketch written 1948, PSduP B–44.

47. Activities of H. Boies, J. A. Haskell, S. Parsons, and J. Riker in Van Gelder and Schlatter, *Explosives Industry,* pp. 219–220, 234, 239, 242–244. Also Solomon Turck letter, January 29, 1901, cited in note 36 above.

48. Van Gelder and Schlatter, *Explosives Industry,* pp. 213–214, 247.

49. H. Belin to P. S. du Pont, May 14, 1902, PSduP 9.

50. S. Parsons to H. Belin, July 22, 1902, PSduP 176.

51. S. Turck to grandsons, January 29, 1901. After the sale Pierre and Parsons purchased a block of Laflin & Rand stock at $370 per share, P. S. du Pont to S. Parsons, November 6, 10, 26, 1902, and S. Parsons to P. S. du Pont, November 25, 1902, PSduP 433. Pierre had hoped to get it at $350 per share.

52. Historical sketch, 1948, PSduP B–44.

53. Plan #1, August 8, initialed by P. S. du Pont and J. Raskob. PSduP 176. They named the holding company United States Explosives Company.

54. T. C. du Pont to P. S. du Pont, August 12, 1902, PSduP 176.

55. Plan #2, August 14, initialed by P. S. du Pont and J. Raskob, PSduP 176.

56. Notations indicating figures of Delaware Investment and Delaware Securities penciled on back of Earlington Hotel stationery, PSduP 176.

57. "Propositions to be made to Laflin & Rand stock-holders and to the owners of eleven hundred shares of Moosic Company," typed with blue carbon and a copy of an agreement with blank spaces filled in with Pierre du Pont's handwriting. By this plan the sellers of

Laflin & Rand would get $2.16 million worth of Delaware Securities bonds (i.e., 5,400 × $400) and a bonus of stock equivalent in par value to 20% of the bonds taken. In addition to this bonus of $432,000 worth of stock which would be divided among the four sellers, Haskell was to get an additional bonus of $200,000 worth of stock. The Du Pont Company would retain the remaining stock of that company. The second holding company, Delaware Investment, would be capitalized at $5.0 million with $2.5 million in 5% bonds and $2.5 million in stock. $2.39 million would go to the four sellers to cover the 5,400 shares at $300, plus the 1,100 shares of Moosic at $700 (i.e., 5,400 × 300/1100 × 700). In addition, a bonus in Delaware Investment stock, equivalent in par value to 25% of the bonds taken, would go to the four sellers and the remainder would be held by the Du Pont Company. In this way the sellers would get the asking price of $4.52 million in 5% twenty-year bonds ($2.16 million in Delaware securities bonds and $2.39 million in Delaware Investment) and the bonus of a little more than $1.0 million in stock.

58. This and the following quotations are from the revised "Proposition" to the shareholders of Laflin & Rand and to the owners of the eleven hundred shares of Moosic, PSduP 176. The information in the following paragraph is from the same source.
59. These can be seen by comparing the original and revised versions of the "Proposition" and the "Agreement," PSduP 176. One small modification was not carried out. Both sides agreed that, when the transaction was completed, the two holding companies would combine. However, the sellers decided to retain the two companies. T. C. du Pont to A. Moxham, January 3, and to J. A. Haskell, J. Riker, S. Parsons, and H. Boies, January 7, 1903, 1075–2.
60. Parsons to P. S. du Pont, August 21, 1902, PSduP 176.
61. Historical sketch, 1948, PSduP B–44. Pierre wrote Coleman about Parsons' note on August 22, and probably went to New York later that morning. PSdup 176.
62. This table is taken directly from "Laflin & Rand Treasurer's Statement—June 30th 1902" in PSduP 176 as is Pierre's re-evaluation of these accounts.
63. Historical sketch, 1948, PSduP B–44.
64. T. C. du Pont to J. A. Haskell, August 24, 1902; T. C. du Pont to S. Parsons, August 24, 1902; H. Boies to T. C. du Pont, August 26, 1902; all in 1075–2. Up to this time all calculations had been made on the assumption of the sale of the 5,400 shares of Laflin & Rand and the 1,100 of Moosic. The sellers had immediately available 5,524 shares of Laflin & Rand and 950 shares of Moosic. The holders of Laflin & Rand were to get $2,209,600 worth of Delaware Securities bonds (5,524 at $400) and $1,657,200 of Delaware Investment (5,524 at $300), and the Moosic holders, $665,000 (950 at $700) in Delaware Investment bonds. In addition they were to get a stock bonus of 20% on shares turned in to Delaware Securities, and 25% on those exchanged for Delaware Investment holdings. The stock bonus was then computed thus:

The 20% bonus of Delaware Securities; i.e.    $2,209,600 = $441,920 for L&R
The 25% bonus of Delaware Investment; i.e.    $1,657,200 = $414,300 for L&R
The 25% bonus of Delaware Investment; i.e.    $665,000 = $166,250 for Moosic

Of this total bonus of $1,022,470 on 6,474 shares, or $157.934 a share, the Moosic holders would receive a total $150,037.30 (i.e., 950 shares at $157.934) and the Laflin & Rand holders would get a total $872,432.70 (i.e., 5,524 at $157.934). Of the last, $441,920 would be in Delaware Securities, so the remaining $430,512.70 would have to be in Delaware Investment. The exchange rate for each share was to be these sums divided by the total Laflin & Rand shares (5,524) and would be $77.935 a share. So the bonus for each share of Laflin & Rand was $60 in Delaware Securities and $77.935 in Delaware Investment.

65. Benjamin Strong, Secretary, Metropolitan Trust Company, to T. C. du Pont, January 22, 1904, 1075–2. The trust company had changed its name from Atlantic to Metropolitan after the agreement had been made. Parsons too was to have an agreement. Coleman mentions that he and Pierre had been working something out, but the results are not clear from the existing letters, T. C. du Pont to S. Parsons, October 10, 1902, 1075–2; also H. Boies to T. C. du Pont, August 26, 1902, 1075–2; and T. C. du Pont to H. Boies, August 20, 1902, 1075–2.

66. *U.S. v. Du Pont (1909) Pleadings*, 347–348, answer of Alfred I. du Pont.

67. T. C. du Pont to J. A. Haskell, September 3, 14, 1902, 1075–2. Among other things Coleman was vice-president of the Du Pont Improvement Company, General Contractors, Owensboro, Kentucky, according to a letterhead on a letter dated May 17, 1902, 1075–1.

68. List "E. I. du Pont de Nemours & Co. stock put up as collateral on bonds of the Delaware Securities and Delaware Investment Companies," 1075–2. Also undated handwritten list. T. C. du Pont to Alexis I. du Pont, October 6, 1902, 1075–2. Benjamin Strong to T. C. du Pont, January 22, 1904, PSduP 433. Coleman with 36% of the stock provided 11,000 shares; Alfred with 20.5%, 6,150 shares; Pierre with 18%, 5,400 shares; and so on down the line. Some Eastern Dynamite came from Du Pont, but most of it was still carried in the name of Hazard, while the Du Pont Company provided all 9,000 shares of Hazard. "Memorandum of Eastern Dynamite Company stock taken to New York to Hypothicate as collateral of the Delaware Securities Company for the Delaware Investment Company," undated. 1075–2. B. Strong to T. C. du Pont, January 22, 1904. PSduP 443.

69. J. A. Haskell to T. C. du Pont, October 15, 1902. J. A. Haskell to C. Stebbins, October 15, 1902, 1075–2.

70. P. S. du Pont to S. Parsons, November 6, 10, 18, 19, 1902; S. Parsons to P. S. du Pont, November 14, 18, 19, 25, 26, 28, 1902, and December 3, 4, 1902; P. S. du Pont to Pauline du Pont, Irénée du Pont, Louisa d'A. du Pont, Henry Belin, December 1, 1902. Metropolitan Trust Company to P. S. du Pont, February 7, 1903, PSduP 433. Also at this time Coleman purchased the 61 shares of Laflin & Rand (Parsons selling 16, Boies 15, Riker, 30), as decided by the purchase agreement for $300. This was converted to Delaware Securities and Delaware Investment stock and bonds and turned over to the Du Pont Co. T. C. du Pont to S. Parsons, October 10, 1902, to H. Boies, October 12, 20, 1902, to P. S. du Pont, October 11, 20, 27, 1902, 1075–2.

71. Van Gelder and Schlatter, *Explosives Industry*, pp. 253–263; Dutton, *Du Pont*, pp. 121–122; historical sketch, PSduP B–44. Also E. S. Rice to T. C. du Pont, October 4, 1902; Rice wrote: "Some three years since, I was permitted by Prest. Covin of the Hazard Powder Co. to place upon my staff of Hazard employees, Mr. H. C. Hirschy, at that time residing at St. Paul," 1075–8.

72. Important letters on the transfer are T. C. du Pont to George Weightman, July 28 (2 letters), August 5, 8, 14, November 11, 1902. G. Weightman to T. C. du Pont, July 27, August 4, 7, 15, November 1, 1902. 1075–3. W. S. Colvin to T.C. du Pont, August 15, 26, 29, September 9, 25, October 1, 1902; T. C. du Pont to W. S. Colvin, August 18, 27, September 1, October 3, 1902, 1075–4.

73. T. C. du Pont to P. S. du Pont, August 14, 1902, 1075–3A. Colvin retired at $4,000 a year and Weightman at $2,500. Both were to be available for consultation at Du Pont. For instance Colvin agreed to be on hand "until Hazard business and its many branches shall have become sufficiently familiar to your several Wilmington departments to prevent annoyance and cost of time." W. S. Colvin to T. C. du Pont, September 2, 1902, 1075–4. The Hazard office in New York included a clerical staff of seven—two bookkeepers, two shipping clerks, a general clerk, a mailing clerk, and a stenographer. W. S. Colvin to T. C. du Pont, August 29, 1902, 1075–4.

74. Van Gelder and Schlatter, *Explosives Industry*, p. 262; and letters cited in note 72, above.

When Colvin retired he resigned as "Director, President, Treasurer, Secretary, Executive Committee member, for one or more, in thirteen separate concerns, twenty-one resignations in all." These separate companies included Eastern Dynamite Company (secretary), Lake Superior Powder Company, Phoenix Powder Company, Anthracite Powder Company. He was also a member of the Advisory Committee of the Gunpowder Trade Association, W. S. Colvin to T. C. du Pont, September 25, 1902. Weightman was treasurer and director of Hazard, and secretary and director of the Hecla Powder Company, Weightman to T. C. du Pont, August 15, 1902, 1075–4.

75. A. J. Moxham to T. C. du Pont, December 1, 5, 1902; T. C. du Pont to A. J. Moxham, December 20, 1902; E. S. Lentilhon to T. C. du Pont, January 9, 1902; T. C. du Pont to E. S. Lentilhon, January 19, 1902; T. C. du Pont to H. A. du Pont, January 20, 1903; 1075–3D. John L. Lequin was apparently dissatisfied, as he brought suit against the Hazard Powder Company—a suit that was dropped at the end of 1904, A. J. Moxham to T. C. du Pont, P. S. du Pont, H. M. Barksdale, and J. A. Haskell, December 14, 1904, 1075–3D.

76. E. Lentilhon to T. C. du Pont, May 1, 1902, and enclosed report of interview held between Captain Money and Lentilhon, April 30, 1902, 1075–32G. These reports show that Hazard tried to purchase the same company in June 1901.

77. Van Gelder and Schlatter, *Explosives Industry,* pp. 786–801.

78. A. W. Money to E. Lentilhon, July 11, 1902; P. S. du Pont to T. C. du Pont, July 18, 1902; P. S. du Pont to E. Lentilhon, July 18, 1902; T. C. du Pont to P. S. du Pont, August 14, 1904, 1075–32G.

79. "Production & costs . . . mos. July-December 1901" for Laflin & Rand initialed by P. S. du Pont and J. J. Raskob, October 20, 1902; data on output of Laflin & Rand plants for five years, 1897–1902, PSduP 433; also in Laflin & Rand Annual Report, Eleutherian Mills Historical Library, Acc. 500–533, EIDPDNCo. Papers.

80. T. C. du Pont apparently first planned to move to headquarters in New York City. James, *Alfred I. du Pont,* pp. 167–168.

81. *Ibid.* John J. Raskob, a typewritten sketch of the life of Pierre S. du Pont, 1944, p. 5, PSduP 384–2. Also W. Fenn to T. C. du Pont, contracts and leases, May 2, 1902, 1075–1.

82. Information concerning Russell Dunham comes from Mrs. Elizabeth Erickson, Public Relations, Hercules, Inc. Dunham became the first president of that company after its creation in 1912 following the dissolution of the Du Pont Company after the antitrust suit.

83. The formation of the Sales Department with Waddell as its head and the resulting problems can be followed in the correspondence between Coleman and E. S. Rice. T. C. du Pont to E. S. Rice, May 23, June 13, 18, 1902; E. S. Rice to T. C. du Pont, May 21, 27, June 24, 1902, 1075–8A, 8B.

84. The Du Pont Company's conservatism can be seen by examining the lists of the sales offices or agents for the members of the Gunpowder Trade Association, E. I. du P. de N. Co. records. The agents' role is well described in the detailed correspondence of E. S. Rice, the Chicago agent during the 1880s and 1890s, in these records at the Eleutherian Mills Historical Library.

85. E. S. Rice to T. C. du Pont, May 21, 22, 27, 31, 1902, 1075–8A, 8B.

86. This and the following quotations are from E. S. Rice to T. C. du Pont, May 27, 1902, 1075–8B.

87. T. C. du Pont to E. S. Rice, May 24, 30, June 2, 1902, 1075–8A, 8B.

88. E. S. Rice to T. C. du Pont, June 18, 19, 21, 1902; E. S. Rice to Treasurer's Office, E. I. du Pont de Nemours & Co., June 26, 1902, 1075–8A. In the last letter Rice writes: "While I regret that it has been considered necessary to submit the expense accounts of this office to one who can't possibly know but little of the conditions under which we obtain and maintain trade, I presume it was considered best by you."

89. A. J. Moxham to T. C. du Pont, October 14, 1902, 1075–26.

90. More accurate accounting figures showed that Rice had higher unit costs than other major selling offices, and so helped to bring about his retirement; E. S. Rice to T. C. du Pont, January 26, February 24, March 14, 1902; T. C. du Pont to E. S. Rice, February 26, March 11, 1902; T. C. du Pont to H. A. du Pont, January 29, February 16, 1902, 1075–8.

91. T. C. du Pont to J. A. Haskell, September 15, 1902, 1075–18.

92. A. J. Moxham to T. C. du Pont, October 14, 1902, 1075–26.

93. This and the following quotation are from T. C. du Pont to F. I. du Pont, J. A. Haskell, P. S. du Pont, Alfred I. du Pont, H. M. Barksdale, and A. J. Moxham, February 4, 1903, 1075–18.

94. *Ibid.*

95. A. J. Moxham to T. C. du Pont, February 7, 1903, 1075–18.

96. T. C. du Pont to A. J. Moxham, February 9, 1903, 1075–18.


CHAPTER 4. The Big Company

1. This and the following quotation are from minutes of the Executive Committee of E. I. du Pont de Nemours & Company (hereafter cited as Ex. Cte. Min. plus the meeting number), March 16, 1903, #3. The quotation in the first paragraph of the chapter is from P. S. du Pont to the Board of Directors, E. I. du Pont de Nemours Powder Company, April 19, 1904 (see note 13 below).

2. Holdings of the E. I. du Pont de Nemours & Company and subsidiaries as listed in several places, the most complete and probably the most accurate being the monthly report of the Treasurer's Department to the Executive Committee, December 7, 1903. Many reports, minutes and related correspondence filed by the Secretaries to the Committees Division at the E. I. du Pont de Nemours & Company were made available to the authors and hereafter are cited, Du Pont Co. Records.

3. The negotiations between the du Ponts and Lent are indicated in Du Pont & Co. to T. C. du Pont, December 5, 1902 (a telegram); Blandin, Rice, and Ginn to A. Lent, December 11, 1902; T. C. du Pont to A. Lent, December 20, 1902 (two letters), January 2, 3, 7, 20, 26, 29, 31, February 4, 1903; A. Lent to T. C. du Pont, December 29, 1902, January 5, 26, 1903; T. C. du Pont to W. S. Hilles, January 26, 1903; P. S. du Pont to T. C. du Pont, January 24, 1903; T. C. du Pont to P. S. du Pont, January 26, 1903. All these letters are from the Eleutherian Mills Historical Library, T. Coleman du Pont Presidential Papers, Accession 1075, File 23, hereafter cited 1075 plus identifying file number.

4. Bermingham refers to Coleman's sickness, but does not say what the disease is in J. Bermingham to T. C. du Pont, February 24, 28, 1903, 1075–23.

5. A. Lent to P. S. du Pont, February 14, 1903, 1075–32.

6. The negotiations with Olin are indicated in T. C. du Pont to F. W. Olin, December 27, 1902, January 7, 10, 1903; F. W. Olin to T. C. du Pont, January 3, 1903, all in 1075–32B.

7. T. C. du Pont to A. J. Moxham, June 5, 1902, 1075–23.

8. Belin's trip and his findings are described in detail in H. Belin, Jr., to E. I. du Pont de Nemours & Co., September 16, 17, 20, 26, 1902; also T. C. du Pont to P. S. du Pont, October 14, 1902, all in 1075–24; also P. S. du Pont to H. Belin, Jr., October 17, 1902, Papers of Pierre S. du Pont, Longwood Manuscripts, Group 10, hereafter cited PSduP plus the identifying file, in this case, PSduP 176.

9. Besides Belin's original reports, see T. C. du Pont to P. S. du Pont, April 25, 1903, and E. S. Pillsbury to T. C. du Pont, November 22, December 6, 16, 26, 1902; T. C. du Pont to E. S. Pillsbury, December 12, 22, 1902, January 3, 1903; J. Bermingham to T. C. du

Pont, November 10, 25, December 13, 15, 1902, January 9, 1903; J. Bermingham to Executive Committee of California Powder Works, monthly report, December 12, 1902, all in 1075-23.

10. At the moment Pillsbury was trying to alter the charter in such a way as to dilute du Pont control, H. Belin Jr. to E. S. Pillsbury, October 11, 1902; T. C. du Pont to E. S. Pillsbury, October 11, 1902; H. Belin Jr. to T. C. du Pont, November 1, 1902; E. S. Pillsbury to T. C. du Pont, October 22, 1902; T. C. du Pont to J. Bermingham, November 25, 29, 1902; J. Bermingham to T. C. du Pont, December 30, 1902, January 21, 1903, February 24, 28, 1903, all in 1075-23.

11. J. Bermingham to T. C. du Pont, February 6, 11, 1903, and also October 28, 29, 1902; T. C. du Pont to E. S. Pillsbury, December 22, 1902; E. Lukens to T. C. du Pont, November 27, December 19, 1902; T. C. du Pont to E. G. Lukens, December 9, 1902, all in 1075-23.

12. Ex. Cte. Min., April 6, 1903, #4.

13. P. S. du Pont to Board of Directors, E. I. du Pont de Nemours Powder Company, April 19, 1904, later corrected and revised in August 1904. The original is in the F. G. du Pont Papers, Eleutherian Mills Historical Library, Acc. 504-16. This was revised in August 1904. "This historical sketch was written in August 1904 and recopied at that time as shown. No changes have been made up to this date, Sept. 1, 1905, at which time the document was bound for preservation, P. S. du Pont." The five following quotations are from this document, PSduP B-44.

14. Minutes of the Advisory Committee of the Gunpowder Trade Association, 1902, records and correspondence for that committee for the same year, Eleutherian Mills Historical Library, Early Papers of E. I. du Pont de Nemours Co., Accession 500-Box 51, hereafter cited by accession number and identifying file.

15. *Ibid.* The role of the Special Committee in typewritten "Compendium of Rules," in amended form, amended October 2, 1902, and minutes of the meeting of the Advisory Committee.

16. Shell and cartridge companies also received discounts.

17. Minutes of the general meeting of the Gunpowder Trade Association, October 2, 1902, Acc. 472.

18. Typewritten "Procedure in the matter of employment of Auditor" and A. J. Moxham to J. A. Haskell, December 23, 1902, enclosing a suggested letter to be sent to the Associated Companies, Du Pont Co. Records. The cost of the investigation was to be paid by the defendant if found guilty. If not, then the Complainant would pay one half and the Association the other. See also E. Greene to M. Ballou, February 16, 1904; also letter drafted by Moxham, "To all the Associated Companies," forwarded to J. A. Haskell on December 23, 1902, all items in 500-518.

19. Letters from all the member companies are *ibid.*, as are all the letters of the next three notes. W. A. Beecher of Ohio was skeptical as to the plan's value, W. A. Beecher to E. Greene, January 1, 1903. The Fay companies' response is from M. Ballou, secretary of American Powder Mills to E. Greene, January 9, 1903 (the two quotes are from this letter). A. D. Fay's personal secretary sent a similar letter to E. Greene on January 12, 1903, *ibid.*

20. *Ibid.*, F. W. Olin to E. Greene, January 9, 20, 1903.

21. *Ibid.*, "Charges and findings," Oscar E. Morton, C.P.A., "Auditors' findings in matters of charges against American Powder Company by E. I. du Pont de Nemours & Co. and Hazard Powder Co."

22. P. S. du Pont to T. C. du Pont, July 15, 28, 1903, September 1, 1903, and P. S. du Pont's "Report on Negotiations with Austin Powder Co.," undated, all 1075-32A. The quotation is from the September 1 letter.

23. Arthur Pine Van Gelder and Hugo Schlatter, *History of the Explosives Industry in America* (New York: Columbia University Press, 1927), pp. 688–689; also J. A. Haskell to T. C. du Pont and H. M. Barksdale, November 17, 1902, and T. C. du Pont to J. A. Haskell, January 7, 1902, 1075–40; A. J. Moxham to T. C. du Pont, May 9, 1903, 1075–23. At the same time the Du Pont Company purchased a small fuse plant owned by the Macbeth family for $175,000 plus $39,000 for supplies on hand, P. S. du Pont to T. C. du Pont, April 21, 1903, 1075–32; also Ex. Cte. Min., April 14, 1903, #5.

24. These negotiations were carried out in a series of letters between Coleman and J. A. McGhee starting August 18, 1902; also J. K. Love to G. R. McAbee, October 2, 1902; memorandum of conversation with J. A. McGhee, undated; and T. C. du Pont to J. A. Haskell, November 4, 1902; J. A. McGhee to T. C. du Pont, November 8, 1902, all 1075–32.

25. A. I. du Pont to E. I. du Pont de Nemours & Co., November 8, 1902 and T. C. du Pont to J. A. McGhee, November 10, 1902, 1075–32.

26. H. Davis to T. C. du Pont, August 1, 1903. T. C.'s request for information was dated July 3; also T. C. du Pont to H. Davis, August 5, 1902. All letters cited in this and the following notes relating to the Jellico Company are in 1075–16B.

27. T. C. du Pont to J. A. Haskell, August 5, 1902, and for the second notification, T. C. du Pont to J. A. Haskell, November 13, 1902; also H. Davis to T. C. du Pont, November 5, 25, 1902, 1075–16B.

28. T. C. du Pont to H. Davis, April 7, 1903; also W. S. Dwinnell to A. J. Moxham, May 7, 1903; T. C. du Pont to A. J. Moxham, May 14, 1903; A. J. Moxham to T. C. du Pont, May 18, 1903, 1075–16B.

29. A. J. Moxham to T. C. du Pont, March 20, 1903; 1075–32. The letter forwarding the *McClure* article is A. J. Moxham to the Executive Committee, February 17, 1903. Coleman replied on March 1 to Moxham: "It looks pretty bad in some cases but I think it is exaggerated." 1075–18.

30. A. J. Moxham to T. C. du Pont, June 2, 1903, 1075–32.

31. T. C. du Pont to A. J. Moxham, June 8, 1903, 1075–32.

32. This and the following four quotations in this paragraph are from Report of P. S. du Pont to Board of Directors April 19, 1904 (revised August 9, 1904). Quotations are from the August report, PSduP 418–4.

33. The initial proposals are described in detail in the Ex. Cte. Min., April 6, 1903, #4. After obtaining Laflin & Rand, some of the small companies had been dissolved or combined with others.

34. These two quotations are from Report of P. S. du Pont to Board of Directors, April 19 (revised August 9, 1904), PSduP 418–4 as are the remaining quotations in this paragraph except for the last two which are from the Ex. Cte. Min., April 6, 1903, #4. These two items were the primary sources for the facts on the initial proposals for the consolidation and the arguments for it.

35. P. S. du Pont to T. C. du Pont, May 2, 1903, 1075–23.

36. These bonds were to be issued at $105. Why the difference between $12,000,000 worth of notes or purchase notes and $10,000,000 worth of funded bonds at $105 is not clear. Probably a million and a half had been repaid in the past year. Also, as Pierre wrote Coleman, May 2, 1903, so much preferred stock was needed as collateral that they would have to take a third of their commission in common stock rather than in preferred stock, 1075–23.

37. Du Pont & Co. would be responsible for these payments. The Powder Company would pay the interest in sinking fund payments, charging Du Pont & Co. for this together with a 4% interest charge. Also, other small bonded issues which had been made largely to

purchase small companies were to be treated as "current liabilities" of the new Powder Company.

38. Ex. Cte. Min., April 6, 1903, #4; Van Gelder and Schlatter, *Explosives Industry*, pp. 213-214.

39. The quotations in this and the following sentence are from the Report of P. S. du Pont to Board of Directors, April 19, 1904 (revised August 9, 1904). Quotations are from the August 9 version, PSduP 418-4.

40. This and the following quotation are from P. S. du Pont to T. C. du Pont, April 21, 1903, 1075-32.

41. P. S. du Pont to T. C. du Pont, May 2, 15, 1903; T. C. du Pont to P. S. du Pont, June 25, 1903, 1075-23.

42. P. S. du Pont to T. C. du Pont, June 19, 1903, 1075-23; also printed notices to the constituent companies filed in 1075-32, and Agreement of Consolidation dated June 18, 1903, in the same file.

43. P. S. du Pont to T. C. du Pont, July 14, 1903, 1075-32.

44. P. S. du Pont to T. C. du Pont, July 14, 1903; P. S. du Pont to George S. Cappelle, July 9, 1903, 1075-32; also mentioned at a special meeting Board of Directors of E. I. du Pont de Nemours & Co., July 1, 1903, 1075-32.

45. This and the two following quotations are from A. J. Moxham to T. C. du Pont, May 2, 1902, 1075-32. The only important explosives manufacturers that Moxham did not mention were George L. Rood and his son Norman. After selling a black powder firm in Indiana and a dynamite firm, in 1902, they had organized a dynamite plant in Missouri and a black powder plant in Indiana two years later.

46. T. C. du Pont to A. J. Moxham, April 13, 1903, 1075-32, May 5, 1903, 1075-23; A. J. Moxham to T. C. du Pont, April 18, 1903, 1075-32.

47. A. J. Moxham to T. C. du Pont, May 15, 1903; Coleman fully agreed, T. C. du Pont to A. J. Moxham, May 20, 1903, 1075-32.

48. P. S. du Pont to the Ex. Cte., June 6, 1903 filed, with Ex. Cte. Min., June 9, 1903, #8. P. S. du Pont to T. C. du Pont, September 1, 1903, summarizes the negotiations, 1075-32B; also A. J. Moxham to T. C. du Pont, July 17, 1903, and F. W. Olin to P. S. du Pont, September 3, 1903, 1075-32.

49. P. S. du Pont to T. C. du Pont, July 14, 1903, 1075-32; P. S. du Pont to Ex. Cte., July 21, 1903, "Report on the Consolidation" filed with Ex. Cte. Min., July 21, 1903, #9.

50. H. A. Beecher to T. C. du Pont, July 13, 1903; P. S. du Pont to T. C. du Pont, July 14, 1903; T. C. du Pont to P. S. du Pont, July 21, 1903, 1075-32; and P. S. du Pont to Ex. Cte. "Report on Consolidation" in Ex. Cte. Min., July 21, 1903, #9.

51. T. C. du Pont to P. S. du Pont, July 14, 1903, 1075-32.

52. Ex. Cte. Min., April 14, 1903, #5.

53. The course of the negotiations is indicated in A. J. Moxham to T. C. du Pont, August 3, 1903; Ex. Cte. Min., August 4, 1903, #11, including a letter W. S. Smith to J. A. Haskell, July 25, 1903, and "memorandum of understanding in reference to matters of securing E. C. & Schultz Co."; also Powder Company Ex. Cte. Min., November 18, 1903, #9. See also Van Gelder and Schlatter, *Explosives Industry*, pp. 799-802.

54. As Moxham pointed out, the rental "could be covered by laying aside preferred stock of the amount we would have been willing to give them had they joined our holding co.," A. J. Moxham to T. C. du Pont, August 3, 1903, 1075-32.

55. This and the following quotation are from A. J. Moxham to T. C. du Pont, June 15, 1903, 1075-23.

56. P. S. du Pont to T. C. du Pont, July 10, 1903, "Memorandum of Conference prepared between P. S. du Pont and W. W. Gibbs for a proposed combination of the Government Large Calibre Smokeless Powder Plants, consisting of the plants of the International

Smokeless Powder and Chemical, the du Pont, Laflin & Rand, and the California Powder Works," undated, both in 1075–32H. P. S. du Pont to Ex. Cte., July 20, 1903, "Report . . . on the International Smokeless Powder Company" in Ex. Cte. Min., July 21, 1903, #9. Pierre was uncertain whether the government work could be separated from commercial production at Carney's Point, but Francis I. was confident that this could be done.

57. This and the following quotation are from T. C. du Pont to P. S. du Pont, July 16, 1903, 1075–32H; also Ex. Cte. Min., July 21, 1903, #9.

58. P. S. du Pont to Ex. Cte., July 20, 1903, "Report on Consolidation" filed with the Ex. Cte. Min., July 21, 1903; also P. S. du Pont to T. C. du Pont, June 19, 1903, 1075–23.

59. This and the following quotation are from A. J. Moxham to T. C. du Pont, June 18, 1903, 1075–23.

60. T. C. du Pont to P. S. du Pont, April 20, 1903, 1075–32.

61. T. C. du Pont to P. S. du Pont, April 25, 1903, 1075–23.

62. T. C. du Pont to A. J. Moxham, May 2, 1903, 1075–32.

63. T. C. du Pont to P. S. du Pont, April 25, 1903, 1075–23.

64. T. C. du Pont to A. J. Moxham, May 8, 1903, 1075–32. Moxham later asked: "What makes so many things crooked in California? I often have wondered whether Colonel Sellers was innocent or a villain. I think the result of your trip indicates the latter," A. J. Moxham to T. C. du Pont, May 19, 1903, 1075–23.

65. T. C. du Pont to Officers and Board of Directors, California Powder Works, May 29, 1903, 1075–23.

66. T. C. du Pont to A. J. Moxham, May 25, 1903; also J. Bermingham to T. C. du Pont, July 3, 1903, 1075–23.

67. Van Gelder and Schlatter, *Explosives Industry*, pp. 283–291, 497–502; William S. Dutton, *Du Pont: One Hundred and Forty Years* (New York: Scribner, 1942), pp. 122, 127, 128. J. Bermingham to T. C. du Pont, May 27, 1903, 1075–32J, indicated when and how the du Ponts obtained 6,500 shares.

68. Van Gelder and Schlatter, *Explosives Industry*, pp. 431–450.

69. A. J. Moxham to T. C. du Pont, May 25, 1903, 1075–23.

70. Van Gelder and Schlatter, *Explosives Industry*, pp. 640–646, 681–686.

71. *Ibid.*, pp. 449, 684, 729–730.

72. Van Gelder and Schlatter, *Explosives Industry*, pp. 644–646. Christian de Guigné of Stauffer and Vigorite told E. S. Pillsbury of C.P.W. "that he had only gone into the dynamite business—the Vigorite Company—because Capt. Bermingham had persisted against his protest, in breaking the price of acid, and he was compelled to find a market for his product through that channel." E. S. Pillsbury to T. C. du Pont, December 6, 1902, 1075–23. After the Du Pont interests took over the Vigorite management the spelling on that company's letterhead drops the "e" and in correspondence it is referred to as Vigorit.

73. The Metropolitan company was being financially aided by de Guigné and the Stauffer Chemical Company. When Coleman asked the Metropolitan people to join the Powder Company, they replied that they were afraid to give up their powder plant because they had been unable to purchase fuse powder. This is because the C.P.W. discriminated against them in favor of the fuse company which it had helped to finance, T. C. du Pont to P. S. du Pont, June 5, 1903, 1075–23.

74. This and the following quotations in this paragraph are from T. C. du Pont to A. J. Moxham, May 19, 1903; also important is T. C. du Pont to E. G. Lukens, May 8, 1903, and T. C. du Pont to C. C. Bemis, May 8, 1903, all in 1075–23. Also T. C. du Pont to E. G. Lukens, May 18, 1903; T. C. du Pont to W. S. Hilles, May 27, 1903, 1075–32D. Agreement between T. C. du Pont and California Investment Company, May 21, 1903, PSduP 418.

75. T. C. du Pont to A. J. Moxham, May 25, 1903, 1075–23.
76. At this late date Haskell and Barksdale began to express doubts about the purchase of Vigorite. Pierre and Moxham on the other hand supported Coleman fully on the purchase of Vigorite and the other companies, A. J. Moxham to T. C. du Pont (telegrams), May 29, 30, 1903; T. C. du Pont to H. M. Barksdale, June 1, 5, 1903, 1075–23; A. J. Moxham to T. C. du Pont (telegram), June 1, 1903; H. M. Barksdale to T. C. du Pont (telegram), May 28; H. M. Barskdale to T. C. du Pont, May 27, 28, 1903; A. J. Moxham to T. C. du Pont (telegram), May 28, 1903, 1075–32E.
77. T. C. du Pont to A. J. Moxham, May 25, June 1, 1903, 1075–23.
78. This and the following quotation are from A. J. Moxham to T. C. du Pont, June 2, 1903, 1075–23; A. J. Moxham to T. C. du Pont, June 2, 3, 1903, 1075–32J–II. Although Coleman agreed with Pierre that in a showdown the du Ponts "could probably control," he pointed out that "this means a fight which would be undesirable," T. C. du Pont to A. J. Moxham, June 8, 1903, 1075–23.
79. Pierre reported the results of the meeting in two handwritten letters. "I wish the club would provide typewriters for illiterate members," he commented. The first letter was undated and the second was dated June 8; both quotations are from the first letter; also P. S. du Pont to T. C. du Pont (telegram), June 7, June 9, 1903, 1075–32J.
80. T. C. du Pont to A. J. Moxham, June 1, 5, 1903, 1075–23. On June 1 Coleman was flat on his back. He was up again on June 5, but a relapse sent him to the hospital almost immediately. As early as May 9, he had written to Pierre that "Elsie and I go to Monterrey for a day or two as I have had a slight attack of my Johnstown trouble but hope it is only temporary," 1075–23. This illness may have been an attack of gallstones, for which Coleman was operated on some years later.
81. T. C. du Pont to P. S. du Pont, July 13, 1903, 1075–32.
82. T. C. du Pont to P. S. du Pont, June 11, 1903, 1075–23; T. C. du Pont to P. S. du Pont, July 13, 18, 25, 29, 1903; P. S. du Pont to T. C. du Pont, July 20, 24, 1903; T. C. du Pont to W. S. Hilles, July 14, 1903; T. C. du Pont to H. G. Scott, July 15, 1903; T. C. du Pont to Stockholders E. I. du Pont de Nemours & Co., September 5, 1903, all in 1075–32D.
83. T. C. du Pont to P. S. du Pont, June 11, 1903, 1075–32; T. C. du Pont to C. de Guigné, July 10, 25, 30 (2 letters), 31, August 1, 7, 1903; A. J. Moxham to T. C. du Pont, June 1, 1903 (telegram); T. C. du Pont to P. S. du Pont, August 17, 1903; T. C. du Pont to H. M. Barksdale, June 19, August 13, 17, 1903, all in 1075–32E.
84. T. C. du Pont to E. S. Pillsbury, July 30, 1903. The course of negotiations is indicated in J. Bermingham to T. C. du Pont, July 7, 8, 10, 1903; T. C. du Pont to M. A. de Laveigo, July 9, 23, 24, 30, 1903; T. C. du Pont to E. S. Pillsbury, July 11, 23, 1903; T. C. du Pont to P. S. du Pont, July 24, 1903, all in 1075–32J–II.
85. T. C. du Pont to C. C. Bemis, T. T. Bishop, L. Monteagle, July 25, August 1, 1903; C. C. Bemis to T. C. du Pont, July 29, August 1, 1903. Coleman made a second offer in May 1904 which Giant's president turned down. T. C. du Pont to C. C. Bemis, May 12, 30, June 24, 1904; C. C. Bemis to T. C. du Pont, June 13, 1904; E. G. Lukens to T. C. du Pont, June 7, 1904; T. C. du Pont to E. G. Lukens, June 15, 1904, all in 1075–32C.
86. T. C. du Pont to A. J. Moxham, June 1, 1903, 1075–23; T. C. du Pont to C. F. Legge, June 17, July 27, August 7, 1903; also to L. Schwabacker, August 1, 1903; T. C. du Pont to J. Bermingham, July 29, 1903; T. C. du Pont to W. C. Peyton, July 31, August 11, 1903; W. C. Peyton to T. C. du Pont, August 5, 1903; T. C. du Pont to A. I. du Pont, July 20, 1903, all in 1075–32F.
87. A. H. Merritt, Ensign, Bickford and Co., June 17, 18, 1903, unsigned, to S. J. Eva, June 13, 1903; T. C. du Pont to S. J. Eva, August 1, 13, 1903; T. C. du Pont to R. S. Ensign, March 24, August 1, 8, 25, September 4, 1903, 1075–10. The West Coast fuse makers

hoped that Coleman would be able to make an arrangement with the National Fuse Company of Denver, the remaining large fuse concern in the West.

88. Van Gelder and Schlatter, *Explosives Industry*, pp. 730–731.

89. T. C. du Pont to P. S. du Pont, June 11, 1903, 1075–23; T. C. du Pont to C. de Guigné, July 30, 1903; T. C. du Pont to P. S. du Pont, August 17, 1903, both in 1075–32E. E. S. Pillsbury to T. C. du Pont, May 7, 1903; T. C. du Pont to E. S. Pillsbury, May 7, 1903; T. C. du Pont to Pres. of Board of Directors of C.P.W., May 29, 1903; J. Bermingham to T. C. du Pont, June 1, 1903; T. C. du Pont to P. S. du Pont, June 2, 28, 1903. The resulting transaction with the Peyton Chemical Company involved a lawsuit which delayed the sale of Du Pont holdings in that company.

90. These negotiations are indicated in T. C. du Pont to J. A. Haskell, June 8, 1903; A. C. Rulosfon to T. C. du Pont, May 5, July 14, 1903; A. S. Ralston to T. C. du Pont, June 10, 1903; T. C. du Pont to A. C. Rulosfon, July 13, 17, 1903; T. C. du Pont to J. Bermingham, June 15, 17, July 15, 1903; H. M. Barksdale to T. C. du Pont, July 24, 1903; J. Bermingham to T. C. du Pont, June 18, July 17, 1903; E. S. Pillsbury to T. C. du Pont, September 12, 1903; statement by C.P.W., June 11, 1903, on prices of shotgun cartridges and attached comments, all in 1075–32.

91. T. C. du Pont to H. M. Barksdale, July 29, 1903, 1075–23.

92. A. J. Ralston to T. C. du Pont, June 27, 1903, 1075–23.

93. C. F. Leege to T. C. du Pont, November 4, 1903, 1075–32F.

94. P. S. du Pont to T. C. du Pont, September 1, 1903, 1075–32H.

95. For policies and procedures of the appraising process see H. M. Barksdale to T. C. du Pont, July 10, 1903, 1075–23; P. S. du Pont to Ex. Cte., July 20, 1903, "Progress of the Consolidation," filed with Ex. Cte. Min., July 21, 1903, #9; T. C. du Pont to J. Bermingham, August 17, October 3, 30, 1903, and J. Bermingham to T. C. du Pont, September 24, October 8, 1903, 1075–32J; T. C. du Pont to R. H. Dunham, October 3, 1903; T. C. du Pont to J. Bermingham, September 30, 1903, 1075–32J–II. Above letters deal only with the appraisal of the C.P.W. Similar letters for the process in other companies can be found in their folders in the T.C. Papers. Especially useful are T. C. du Pont to E. G. Lukens, September 5, 1903, 1075–32D; T. C. du Pont to C. de Guigné, November 16, 1903, 1075–32E; E. G. Lukens to T. C. du Pont, September 9, 1903, 1075–32. Biographical data on Jackson and Ramsay are given in Van Gelder and Schlatter, *Explosives Industry*, pp. 571–573, 593, 611–612.

96. T. C. du Pont to E. S. Pillsbury, September 4, 1903, 1075–32J–II.

97. R. H. Dunham to T. C. du Pont, October 20, 1903; T. C. du Pont to C. de Guigné, October 27, 1903, 1075–32J–II. California had shown concern for the need for modern accounting methods in late 1902 when Pillsbury encouraged Coleman to send a competent auditor.

98. E. G. Lukens to T. C. du Pont, September 21, 1903 (telegram), 1075–32D.

99. Treasurer's Department report, October 12, November 10, 1903, January 6, 1904, filed with Ex. Cte. Min., October 21, 1903, #7, January 20, 1904, #13.

100. For some reason Coleman considered this step unnecessary, but was willing to have the form letter sent when Pierre was fully supported by the Executive Committee. P. S. du Pont to T. C. du Pont, December 29, 1903, enclosing the form letter; T. C. du Pont to P. S. du Pont, November 30, 1903; January 1, 1904; also Townsend and Avery to J. J. Raskob, November 23, 1903, all three in 1075–32. A good example of such a circular letter as was sent out to the stockholders is J. Bermingham to the stockholders of C.P.W., March 11, 1904, 1075–32J–I.

101. Ex. Cte. Min., August 13, 1903, #12.

102. P. S. du Pont to J. Bermingham, January 8, 1904; T. C. du Pont to J. Bermingham, January 16, 1904, 1075–32J–II.

103. On the whole de Guigné was highly pleased with the general outcome of this appraisal; see de Guigné to T. C. du Pont, November 20, 1903. Disagreement over real estate values, T. C. du Pont to C. de Guigné, November 30, 1903; E. G. Lukens to T. C. du Pont, December 3, 7 (telegram), 11, 13 (telegram), 18, 23 (telegram), 28, 1903; January 20, 1904; T. C. du Pont to E. G. Lukens, December 12 (telegram), 14 (telegram), January 26, 1904, all in 1075–32E.

104. P. S. du Pont to T. C. du Pont, September 1, 1903; also A. Lent to T. C. du Pont, September 8, 1903; T. C. du Pont to A. Lent, September 4, 9, 1903, 1075–32A. The continuing Olin negotiations are given in P. S. du Pont to T. C. du Pont, September 1, 1903; F. W. Olin to P. S. du Pont, September 3, 1903; P. S. du Pont to F. W. Olin, September 9, 1903; F. W. Olin to T. C. du Pont, September 11, December 8, 1903; A. J. Moxham to F. W. Olin, September 26, December 18, 1903, 1075–32.

105. Van Gelder and Schlatter, *Explosives Industry,* pp. 155, 275–281; *U.S. Circuit Court of Delaware, No. 280 in Equity, United States of America, Petitioner v. E. I. du Pont de Nemours and Company et al., Defendants* (hereafter cited as *U.S. v. du Pont*) *Defendants' Record Testimony,* II, 708–710.

106. Pp. 272–273 of the present book.

107. Ex. Cte. Min., September 3, 1903, #2.

108. This and the following three quotations are from P. S. du Pont to T. C. du Pont, September 4, 1903, 1075–32H.

109. Ex. Cte. Min., September 3, 1903, #2.

110. The following information on International comes from Van Gelder and Schlatter, *Explosives Industry,* pp. 867–873.

111. P. S. du Pont to T. C. du Pont, September 4, 1903, 1075–32H.

112. T. C. du Pont to W. W. Gibbs, September 14, 17, 24, 29, October 5, 17, 23, 1903; W. W. Gibbs to T. C. du Pont, September 23, 26, 29, October 6, November 2, 1903, 1075–32H.

113. Undated memorandum on Proposal "To organize a new company to be known as the Du Pont International Powder Company," 1075–32H; also Ex. Cte. Min., November 5, 1903, #8.

114. W. W. Gibbs to T. C. du Pont, November 13, 23, 1903; T. C. du Pont to W. W. Gibbs, November 14, 19, 1903; T. C. du Pont to E. G. Buckner, November 16 (telegram), December 14, 19, 1903; E. G. Buckner to T. C. du Pont, November 16 (telegram), December 9 (telegram), 1903; G. S. Graham to T. C. du Pont, December 4, 12, 19, 1903; T. C. du Pont to Trust Company of North America, December 14, 19, 1903; T. C. du Pont to W. S. Hilles, December 23, 1903; T. C. du Pont to P. S. du Pont, May 24, 1904, 1075–32H; T. C. du Pont to M. A. de Laveago, February 12, 1904, 1075–32J-I.

115. P. S. du Pont to T. C. du Pont, February 23, 1904. The outside stockholders were not too happy about the later developments, either. Gibbs and others were upset because Coleman refused to list the stock of the new company on any stock exchange, thus preventing them from using it as collateral for loans; while Buckner thought that the dividend should have been higher. See particularly W. W. Gibbs to T. C. du Pont, February 24, March 23, April 2, 1904; T. C. du Pont to W. W. Gibbs, March 25, 1904; E. G. Buckner to T. C. du Pont, March 23, April 8, 11, 1904; T. C. du Pont to E. G. Buckner and H. F. Baldwin, April 7, 1904. The stock of the Powder Company and its subsidiaries remained unlisted; in fact, the only explosives companies that were listed on any stock exchange were California and Giant, both on the San Francisco Exchange. T. C. du Pont to E. G. Buckner, March 25, 1904, 1075–32H. Coleman gave Buckner the primary reason for not listing was his preference to keep the fiction of separate companies for government bidding. T. C. du Pont to E. G. Buckner, H. F. Baldwin, April 7, 1904, 1075–32H. Since the chartered holding company was called the Du Pont International

Smokeless, Coleman could hardly have kept this arrangement secret, but apparently felt that there was little to gain in widely broadcasting the new connection.

116. P. S. du Pont to T. C. du Pont, June 3, 1904; T. C. du Pont to P. S. du Pont, May 28, June 7, 1904, 1075–32H. Coleman's estimate was based on 12½% of earnings of $208,333.33, while Pierre's was on $159,275.52.

117. *U.S. v. du Pont, Opinion of the Court and Interlocutory Decree,* 30.

118. A. J. Moxham to T. C. du Pont, May 2, 1903, 1075–32. Pierre and Moxham's earliest plan called for a single selling company to take over all interstate business and possibly the entire selling end of the business, Ex. Cte. Min., April 6, 1903, #4.

119. A. J. Moxham to T. C. du Pont, June 18, 1903, 1075–23.

120. A. J. Moxham to T. C. du Pont, August 3, 1903, 1075–32.

121. For example, T. C. du Pont to A. J. Moxham, June 24, 1903, 1075–23.

122. That these issues were discussed is clear from A. J. Moxham to T. C. du Pont, June 2, 1903, 1075–32; A. J. Moxham to T. C. du Pont, June 18, 1903, 1075–23.

123. Report of J. A. Haskell to Executive Committee, September 3, 1903, filed with Ex. Cte. Min., September 8, 1903, #3.

124. Moxham's policy statement continued:

We will not bribe men to get information. We will not employ detectives, nor will we sell under false pretences in meeting the outside world whether our competitors are or not. Our duty is to get the fullest information that it is possible for us to get about every move made by our competitors whether building or in operations so long as that information probably belongs to the world at large and if we succeed in doing that to the full we will be in a position to do all that can legitimately be done to reduce the effect of competition. Beyond this I have decided that we will not go.

A. J. Moxham to W. B. Dwinnell, August 25, 1903, 1075–18. Dwinnell reported on the business value of the new policy in his annual report to Moxham, January 12, 1904, filed with Ex. Cte. Min., January 20, 1904, #13.

125. This and the following quotation are from A. J. Moxham to T. C. du Pont, June 18, 1903; also A. J. Moxham to T. C. du Pont, June 2, 1903, both in 1075–23.

126. The information for the following paragraph comes from "Preliminary Report of James M. Townsend to E. I. du Pont de Nemours Powder Co., New York Dec. 1, 1903"; "Report of Edwin Walker of Winston, Payne, Strown, Chicago, Dec. 4, 1903 to James M. Townsend"; "Supplementary Report of James M. Townsend to A. J. Moxham Chairman of Committee on Reorganization, Dec. 19, 1903"; A. J. Moxham, "Minority Report to the Executive Committee Jan. 2, 1904"; "Report from the Committee to Consider the Question of Reorganization as Agreed to at Meetings Held Dec. 23, 24, 30," all filed with Ex. Cte. Min., January 13, 1904, #12. Also important are Ex. Cte. Min. for the meeting held January 21, 1904, #14.

127. This and the following quotations are from the Report of J. M. Townsend, December 1, 1903, Ex. Cte. Min., January 13, 1904, #12.

128. *Ibid.* This and the following quotation are from the report of E. Walker, December 4, 1903.

129. *Ibid.* This and the following quotation are from the Report of J. M. Townsend, December 1, 1903.

130. *Ibid.* Supplementary Report of J. M. Townsend, December 19, 1903.

131. *Ibid.* This and the following two quotations are from Report of J. M. Townsend, December 1, 1903.

132. A. J. Moxham to T. C. du Pont, June 2, 1904, 1075–23.

133. Report of J. M. Townsend, December 1, 1903, Ex. Cte. Min., January 13, 1904, #12.

134. *Ibid.* This and the following nine quotations are from Moxham's "Minority Report," January 2, 1904.
135. The validity of this point is indicated in W. W. Dwinnell to A. J. Moxham, January 12, 1904. Part of the annual report of the Development Department filed with the Ex. Cte. Min., January 20, 1904, #13.
136. Treasurer's Report, October 12, 1903, filed with Ex. Cte. Min., October 21, 1903, #7.
137. Report of the Committee to Consider the Question of Reorganization, undated, filed with Ex. Cte. Min., January 13, 1904, #12. The two quotations in this paragraph are in this report.
138. Ex. Cte. Min., January 13, 1904, #12.
139. Ex. Cte. Min., January 21, 1904, #14. Only the number of votes, not who voted, are recorded in the minutes. But it seems likely that if Coleman had joined Pierre and Moxham, the others' debate would not have continued so strongly.
140. P. S. du Pont to Board of Directors, E. I. du Pont de Nemours Powder Company, April 19, 1904 (later revised in August 1904), Acc. 504; T. C. du Pont to P. S. du Pont, April 21, 1904, 1075–32. There is a mass of routine, and some not so routine, correspondence involving the final bringing in of the many companies into the consolidation in the folders for these individual companies in the T. C. du Pont Presidential Papers.
141. P. S. du Pont to T. C. du Pont, December 31, 1903; T. C. du Pont to P. S. du Pont, January 1, April 20, 1904; T. C. du Pont to J. Bermingham, January 16, February 6, 1904; T. C. du Pont to E. S. Pillsbury, January 22, March 1, 1904; T. C. du Pont to R. S. Penniman, February 3, 4, 13, 1904; E. S. Pillsbury to T. C. du Pont, January 23, February 12, 18, 24, March 7, 1904; R. S. Penniman to T. C. du Pont, January 28, February 12, 13, 24, 1904; T. C. du Pont to H. M. Barksdale, March 11, 1904; H. M. Barksdale to P. S. du Pont, March 8, 1904; J. Bermingham to T. C. du Pont, March 17, 18, 30, April 3, 28, May 4, 1904, 1075–32J–I, II.
142. T. C. du Pont to R. S. Penniman, January 30, 1905; R. S. Penniman to T. C. du Pont, February 13, 1905, 1075–32E. For delays with the California Investment Company, see E. G. Lukens to T. C. du Pont, December 18, 1904, 1075–32E. Treasurer's Report, May 16, 1904, filed with Ex. Cte. Min., May 25, 1904, #29, and Treasurer's Report, July 20, 1904, filed with Ex. Cte. Min., July 22, 1904, #37 show that the Powder Company controls 99.25% of the California Investment Company stock, but in the Treasurer's Report, May 1905 (no date) filed with Ex. Cte. Min., June 28, 1905, #63, 285 shares of California Investment Company's total 4,000 shares are still outstanding.
143. Ex. Cte. Min, July 29, August 4, 1903, #10, #11; Ex. Cte. (Powder Company) Min., November 18, December 17, 1903, #9, #10; J. A. Haskell to A. J. Moxham, April 25, 1904; A. J. Moxham to T. C. du Pont, April 26, 1904; T. C. du Pont to J. A. Haskell, April 28, 1904; J. A. Haskell to T. C. du Pont, P. S. du Pont, H. M. Barksdale (as directors of the Laflin & Rand Company), December 23, 1904; P. S. du Pont to J. A. Haskell, December 23, 1904, 1075–32, and pp. 273–274 of the present book.
144. Pierre's Treasurer's Report, July 21, 1904, filed with Ex. Cte. Min., July 27, 1904, #37, indicated that in two companies large blocks of stock were still held by outsiders— Chattanooga (45.39%) and Fairmount (40%). In six more, outsiders held 15% to 22%; these included Delaware Investment, Delaware Securities, Globe (a small selling company), King Mercantile, Schaghticoke, American Storage and Delivery, E. I. du Pont de Nemours of Pennsylvania, and the California Powder Works. By May 1905 the only companies with any outside stockholders at all were the California Powder, Vigorit, California Investment, Delaware Investment, Delaware Securities and E. I. du Pont de Nemours of Pennsylvania, Treasurer's Report, May 1905, presented to Ex. Cte. meeting of June 28, 1905, #63. The best place to follow the proceedings are the monthly reports of the Committee on Reorganization to the Executive Committee, Du Pont Company Records.

145. J. A. Haskell to E. Greene, March 30, 1904, 1075–23.

146. Ex. Cte. Min., March 30, 1904, #22.

147. Ex. Cte. Min., February 9, 1904, #17.

148. I. du Pont to Ex. Cte., April 21, 1906, #85, and pp. 271–272 of the present book.

149. Moxham explained the Powder Company's position in the industry to Lent of Austin when the latter decided not to join the big company:

> In our consolidation we have started out with the belief, first that our position is one of such strength that if we manage, as we ought to manage, we need not fear small competition; second, whether we fear it or not we are going to have it, and in the long run we believe that it is essential to our well being that it should exist. If we consistently adhere to these lines I do not see why there should be any special question of differences between ourselves and the Austin Powder Company. We have plenty of competition in addition to your good selves. 1075–32A.

### CHAPTER 5. The Treasurer

1. A. J. Moxham to T. C. du Pont, August 3, 1903, the Eleutherian Mills Historical Library, T. Coleman du Pont Presidential Papers, Accession 1075, File 23, hereafter cited 1075 plus the identifying file number.

2. A. J. Moxham to T. C. du Pont, April 23, 1903, 1075–23.

3. A. J. Moxham to T. C. du Pont, May 2, 1903, 1075–23.

4. This and the following three quotations are from A. J. Moxham to T. C. du Pont, June 18, 1903, 1075–23.

5. *Ibid.* Moxham added that Francis "is not unwilling to assume responsibility if he understands it belongs to him and he is going to turn out to be one of the able men of the crowd in time."

6. A. J. Moxham to T. C. du Pont, August 3, 1903; A. J. Moxham to T. C. du Pont, June 18, 1903. In the August 3 letter Moxham also wrote that "Alfred is acquiescing in the general development with good grace." 1075–23.

7. The Board of Directors Minutes, March 4, 1904.

8. The Board of Directors Minutes, July 8, 1904.

9. Connable replaced L. R. Beardslee, essentially a dummy director, in 1906. Another dummy director, Edmund B. Coy, was replaced by H. F. Baldwin when he took charge of the Smokeless Powder Department.

10. Pierre also made certain that the several branches of the family were represented on the small board of the family holding company, the E. I. du Pont de Nemours & Company. In 1905 that board included Colonel Henry and the three cousins who founded the new company (each of the four represented a different branch of family). In addition, Lex was there representing the Eugene branch; Philip the Alexis I.; and Francis I. the Francis G. interests.

11. Memorandum of P. S. du Pont on sale of Coleman's stock in the Eleutherian Mills Historical Library, Papers of Pierre S. du Pont, Longwood Manuscripts, Group 10, File B–49, hereafter cited as PSduP plus the identifying file number.

12. T. C. du Pont to H. F. Baldwin, January 9, 1904; H. F. Baldwin to T. C. du Pont, December 24, 26, 1903, January 9, 1904, 1075–18. Baldwin had married Coleman's sister Pauline. Coleman and Pierre would not let Francis I. resign from the Powder Company Board when he left the Executive Committee.

13. An interview with P. S. du Pont by A. Rae duBell on February 1, 1954, a copy of which duBell forwarded to P. S. du Pont in a letter dated March 4, 1954, PSduP 303.

14. Barksdale's interests and achievements are enthusiastically outlined in Ernest Dale and Charles Meloy, "Hamilton MacFarland Barksdale and the Du Pont Contributions to

Systematic Management," *Business History Review,* Vol. 36 (Summer 1962), pp. 127–152.

15. Executive Committee Minutes (hereafter cited as Ex. Cte. Min.), June 7, 1903, February 15, 1904, #6, #18; also H. M. Barksdale to Executive Committee, December 5, 1903, 1075-18.

16. Ex. Cte. Min., March 20, 1904, #22.

17. Ex. Cte. Min., February 15, August 31, 1904, #18, #39.

18. Ex. Cte. Min., June 5, 27, 1906, #88, #89. The quotations in this paragraph are all from the minutes of the June 27 meeting. Also see Ex. Cte. Min., July 26, 1906, #91.

19. Ex. Cte. Min., July 11, 1906, June 27, 1905, #91, #63.

20. Particularly useful on the problems involved in defining interdepartmental boundaries are A. J. Moxham to T. C. du Pont, October 11, 1903, and T. C. du Pont to A. J. Moxham, October 13, 1903, all in 1075-33.

21. Ex. Cte. Min., July 12, October 14, 1904, #35, #43.

22. The limit had been initially set at $100, Ex. Cte. Min., December 31, 1903, #11, and raised to $150 on March 30, 1904, Ex. Cte. Min., #22, and lowered again to $100 in 1906, Ex. Cte. Min., April 21, 1906, #85.

23. T. C. du Pont to W. S. Hilles, December 9, 1902, 1075-31. Coleman informed Haskell and Barksdale, who were then in California, of the plan after Moxham and Pierre and the others had reviewed it, T. C. du Pont to J. A. Haskell and H. M. Barksdale, December 31, 1902, 1075-31. It seems unlikely that the inspiration for the plan came from Haskell's informal bonus schemes developed earlier at Repauno, mentioned in William S. Dutton, *Du Pont: One Hundred and Forty Years* (New York: Scribner, 1942), p. 151. Possibly Haskell and Coleman had talked over the plans, but it is hard to say just what nature "Haskell's Bonuses" at Repauno actually were.

24. Standard Oil had a pension plan adopted also in 1903 but no bonus plan, Ralph W. Hidy and Muriel E. Hidy, *Pioneering in Big Business, 1882–1911* (New York: Harper & Brothers, 1955), p. 602. According to one source five employee stock purchase plans existed before 1901. National Industrial Conference Board, *Employees Stock Purchase Plans in the United States* (New York, 1928); but these were not necessarily bonus plans.

25. T. C. du Pont to W. S. Hilles, December 9, 1902. Among the first of the beneficiaries of the new stock purchase plan were E. S. Rice, William McBlair, long the Hazard agent at St. Louis, and J. A. McGhee, who had long been active in the company's business in the anthracite area. T. C. du Pont to E. S. Rice, January 10, 1903; E. S. Rice to T. C. du Pont, January 13, 1903; P. S. du Pont to T. C. du Pont, July 3, 1903; T. C. du Pont to P. S. du Pont, July 9, 1903, all 1075-31.

26. This and the following quotation are from Ex. Cte. Min., December 31, 1903, #11.

27. Ex. Cte. Min., May 27, 1904, #31.

28. This and the following quotation are from Ex. Cte. Min., December 28, 1904, #51.

29. Ex. Cte. Min., April 28, September 27, November 10, 1905, #59, #69, #72; February 19, June 4, 1906, #82, #87.

30. Ex. Cte. Min., May 24, November 30, 1904, #28, #40; June 1, 1905, #61. The pensions were charged against the departments and offices in which the employee had worked. Ex. Cte. Min., November 10, 1905, #72. For most employees the pension formula gave "for each year of service one per centum of average regular monthly pay for the ten years preceeding retirement." Ex. Cte. Min., May 27, 1904, #31.

31. Ex. Cte. Min., October 10, 1907, #141; July 1, October 21, 1908, #167, #175.

32. These figures are from "Treasurer's Annual Report to the Executive Committee for 1905," passed by the Executive Committee, April 25, 1906, #85. Unless otherwise indicated, the departmental reports to the Executive Committee are under the jurisdic-

tion of the Secretaries to the Committees Division of the E. I. du Pont de Nemours & Co. Hereafter cited Du Pont Co. Records.

33. A. I. du Pont to F. L. Connable, February 19, 1904; T. C. du Pont to A. I. du Pont, February 25, 1903, 1075–18; F. L. Connable to T. C. du Pont, July 13, August 3, 5, 22, September 9, 28, 1904, 1075–18, 1075–16; T. C. du Pont to F. L. Connable, July 16, August 4, 22, 1904, 1075–16D.

34. Arthur P. Van Gelder and Hugo Schlatter, *History of Explosives Industry in America* (New York: Columbia University Press, 1927), p. 207.

35. Ex. Cte. Min., May 25, 1904, #30; also Ex. Cte. Min., October 21, 1903, #7; and A. I. du Pont to Executive Committee, November 9, 1903, #9. The five plants to be shut down were Lake Superior, Sycamore, Birmingham, Conemaugh, and Farmingdale. Those whose permanency was questionable were Dorner, Shenandoah, and Oliver (the last included smokeless as well as black powder works). The two new mills were Gardner and Nemours. A third one, planned for Arkansas, was postponed because of lack of funds early in 1904. By the end of 1904, five in the first category, plus Dorner and one other, had been permanently shut down, while Weldey was added to the questionable list. "Annual Report for Black Powder Operating Department for 1904," passed by Executive Committee, April 26, 1905, #59. By the end of 1905, 25 mills were producing B blasting powder. Three small mills at larger units—Brandywine, Wayne, and Schagticoke—were making sporting powder, "Annual Report of Black Powder Operating Department for 1905," passed by Executive Committee, April 5, 1906, #84.

36. Ex. Cte. Min., October 5, 1904, #43. Annual Reports of High Explosives Department for 1904 and 1905 passed by Executive Committee, January 25, 1905, and January 31, 1906, #53, #88, respectively. The Judson works at San Francisco were shut down in early 1906, "Annual Report of High Explosives Department for 1906," passed by Executive Committee, January 30, 1907, #114. Also, Dale and Meloy, "Barksdale," *Business History Review*, (Summer 1962), pp. 127–152; Van Gelder and Schlatter, *Explosives Industry*, pp. 597–598. Lucius Ellsworth, "Strategy and Structure: The Du Pont Company's Sales Organization, 1870–1903," J. van Fenstermaker, ed., *Papers Presented at the Annual Business History Conference* (Kent, Ohio), pp. 108–109, provides an excellent summary of the background of the Du Pont sales organization, particularly the work of Haskell at Repauno.

37. The department also operated a small charcoal plant. The department's Annual Reports to the Executive Committee made clear the nature of the centralized control. Also, Barksdale made a report on appraising current operations and future changes in the Smokeless Powder Department, dated March 31, 1904, Ex. Cte. Min., #23. See also Ex. Cte. Min., March 30, 1904, #22. The legal and financial relationship between the Du Pont Company, the International Company, and the Powder Company are made clear in H. F. Baldwin to T. C. du Pont, December 30, 1904, February 15, 1905; T. C. du Pont to A. C. Watts, April 7, 1904, February 8, 1905; E. C. Buckner to T. C. du Pont, January 5, 11, 1905; T. C. du Pont to E. C. Buckner, January 10, 11, 13, 1905; T. C. du Pont to H. Philler, February 7, 1905; W. W. Gibbs to T. C. du Pont, February 9, 1905, all in 1075–32H.

38. T. C. du Pont to A. J. Moxham, October 13, 1905, 1075–13.

39. Sales Department's Monthly Report to Executive Committee, March 23, 1904, #22. A little earlier Haskell reported that the salesmen and the branch offices had been reorganized into three classes, to be known as "A," "B," and "Local." The "A" salesmen "will be used to handle important trade in the territory of the office to which they may be attached. 'B' to be used for visiting blocks sufficient to contain one month's work. 'Local' salesmen are those used as city salesmen or located where important trade exists," Sales Department's Monthly Report, January 12, 1904, #13. In this plan Haskell was following marketing patterns earlier developed by Cyrus H. McCormick in the reaper business and John H. Patterson in cash registers. In taking on the storing and delivering of

explosives to storage magazines and then to the customers, the branch offices took over a function which the American Storage and Delivery Company, sponsored by the Gunpowder Trade Association and formed in 1901, was just beginning to handle in 1902 for the association's members. For example, W. Olin to E. Greene, January 12, 1903, Eleutherian Mills Historical Library, 544–51, and Sales Department Monthly Reports in 1904. For continuing change in consolidation of branch sales offices, see Sales Department Report, November 2, 1904, #47.

40. The formation of the temporary West Coast management unit is covered in correspondence between T. C. du Pont and Bermingham, Pillsbury, Lukens, and Penniman, 1075–32J and 32J–II.

41. T. C. du Pont to J. A. Haskell, July 17, 1903; E. C. Ferriday to T. C. du Pont, July 22, 1903; T. C. du Pont to A. Hyndaman, May 18, 1904, 1075–18; P. S. du Pont to T. C. du Pont, December 19, 1903, 1075–16E.

42. These difficulties are described in the Sales Department Monthly Report, March 23, 1904, #22, and other reports of that year.

43. T. C. du Pont to J. A. Haskell, February 12, 1904. Other letters on the Frederick Waddell situation are T. C. du Pont to J. A. Haskell, February 25, March 9, 25, April 1, 4, 1904; J. A. Haskell to T. C. du Pont, March 2, 4, April 2, 1904; T. C. du Pont to F. J. Waddell, February 21, 1904; F. J. Waddell to T. C. du Pont, September 16, January 24, 1905; C. L. Patterson to A. J. Moxham, June 28, 1905; A. J. Moxham to C. L. Patterson, June 28, 1905, all in 1075–18. Those covering Rice's failure to adjust are E. S. Rice to T. C. du Pont, January 26, February 29, March 14, 1904; T. C. du Pont to E. S. Rice, February 26, March 11, 1904; T. C. du Pont, to H. A. du Pont, January 29, 1904, all in 1075–18. P. S. du Pont to J. A. Haskell, July 12, 1906, with enclosures, 1075–18.

44. For an amusing reference to one of these conventions, T. C. du Pont to P. S. du Pont, March 22, 1905, 1075–32H. The minutes were printed with photographs and bound and sent to all participants.

45. F. G. Tallman, employed April 11, 1905, at age 45 after twenty years' experience in the steel and machinery industry, including assistant foreman in Corliss Steam Engine Shops; plant superintendent in Carnegie—Phipps; sales manager, Yale & Towne; and sales engineer, Brown Hoisting. Ex. Cte. Min., November 5, 1903, #8; J. A. Haskell to P. S. du Pont, January 4, 1904; T. C. du Pont to J. A. Haskell, January 5, 1904; F. G. Tallman to T. C. du Pont, March 28, 1905, April 24, 1906; A. I. du Pont to T. C. du Pont, April 27, 1906; T. C. du Pont to F. G. Tallman, March 28, 1905, May 16, 1906, 1075–18.

46. F. G. Tallman to Executive Committee, November 20, 1905, #76; F. G. Tallman to T. C. du Pont, May 17, 1906, 1075–18; Ex. Cte. Min., March 4, 1908, #159.

47. Ex. Cte. Min., November 5, 1903, March 31, 1904, #8, #22. In case of emergency purchasing such as would be needed after an explosion, the departments could make direct equipment orders up to $1,500, the chairman of the Executive Committee up to $5,000, and the Executive Committee over $5,000.

48. A. I. du Pont to Manufacturers Contracting Company, September 25, 1903, PSduP 418; T. C. du Pont to A. J. Moxham, October 13, 1903; Ex. Cte. Min., November 5, 1903, #8. Continuing efforts to combine the two departmental engineering staffs are indicated in A. J. Moxham to T. C. du Pont, May 20, 1904, 1075–13; Ex. Cte. Min., December 1, 1904, #47; October 31, 1907, #145; March 9, #160; April 2, 1908, #161.

49. A. J. Moxham to P. S. du Pont, February 25, 1904; T. C. du Pont to A. J. Moxham, June 1, 1904, both in 1075–13. In the latter, Coleman says Laffey's unit is to handle all legal matters that are not referred to Townsend or Hilles.

50. This and the following quotation are from J. P. Laffey to A. J. Moxham, October 10, 1905, 1075–13.

51. T. C. du Pont to A. J. Moxham, February 7, 1903, and, particularly, June 13, 1904, 1075–18.

52. T. C. du Pont to A. J. Moxham, October 13, 1903, 1075–18.

53. Development Department Monthly Report, December 17, 1903, #10.
54. Francis I.'s monthly report submitted with the Development Department Monthly Report provided the best brief summary on the numerous and various products handled by the Experimental Station; a particularly good one is that of October 14, 1904, #42, and February 22, 1905, #57.
55. However, when Haskell requested the formation of a Technical Bureau in the Sales Department, the Executive Committee did vote to keep such work at the Experimental Station, Ex. Cte. Min., September 27, 1905, #68. The annual reports of the Development Department and those of the High Explosives Department indicate the nature of the work carried on at both the Experimental Station and the Eastern Laboratory at Repauno.
56. Treasurer's Monthly Report, September 1903, #3. The delay in moving the Laflin & Rand accounting is mentioned in P. S. du Pont to T. C. du Pont, June 6, 1906, 1075–32J.
57. This and the following quotation are from the Treasurer's Monthly Report, September 1903, #3. The report lists offices and their heads.
58. Handwritten memorandum gives a list of salaried employees in the department and how much each was paid, PSduP 418. A similar memorandum from P. S. du Pont to the Executive Committee, June 4, 1904, #34, indicates the great expansion of the department by that date.
59. The activities of Dunham's department, including the function of the traveling auditor, are indicated in his regular reports to the Treasurer, Du Pont Co. Records.
60. P. S. du Pont to the Executive Committee, June 22, 1904, #33.
61. T. C. du Pont to Victor du Pont, July 15, 1904; A. D. Hasbrook to the Executive Committee, January 20, 1904, 1075–13. Coleman had placed Hasbrook in charge of a small, new Real Estate Department before the formation of the big company.
62. A letter from P. S. du Pont to J. J. Raskob, March 14, 1910, best illustrates this relationship. Also, P. S. du Pont to President's Committee on Awards, November 29, 1909. Both letters are in the Eleutherian Mills Historical Library, John J. Raskob Papers, Accession 473, hereafter cited as Raskob Papers.
63. Treasurer's Monthly Report, October 12, 1903, #7.
64. P. S. du Pont to Executive Committee, January 8, 1904, #13.
65. Chapter 6, pp. 159–162.
66. P. S. du Pont to Executive Committee, September 28, 1903, #7.
67. P. S. du Pont to Executive Committee, May 24, 1904, #30. This scheme is most succinctly described in P. S. du Pont to William du Pont, May 17, 1904, PSduP 616; also, Treasurer's Monthly Report, October 8, 1904, #43.
68. Treasurer's Monthly Report, July 21, 1904, #37.
69. Treasurer's Monthly Report, November 16, 1904, #47. Under the new system, Pierre wrote, the old books of the still existing subsidiaries were "continued separately, though the consolidated accounts will be left without reference to the subsidiary corporations," Treasurer's Monthly Report, October 18, 1904, #43. P. S. du Pont to J. A. Haskell, November 28, 1904; T. C. du Pont to P. S. du Pont, December 29, 1904, #51; Ex. Cte. Min., May 25, 1905, #61.
70. This can be found in the Treasurer's Monthly Reports, for example, July 21, 1904, #37.
71. "Treasurer's Annual Report to the Executive Committee of E. I. du Pont de Nemours Powder Co. for 1905" is the first full report, although the report for 1904 is quite detailed.
72. A. J. Moxham to T. C. du Pont, June 10, 1904, and T. C. du Pont to A. J. Moxham, June 13, 1904, both in 1075–13. Coleman phrased Moxham's point in the following way:

I agree with the statement in your letter which is as follows:—That it should be understood that no department heads should in any way interfere with the subordinates of another department but that the cooperation of one department with another department should be finally arranged by the heads of the separate departments and the heads of both departments then give their respective subordinates such instruction as will enable the company as a whole to derive those benefits which come from united effort.

73. P. S. du Pont to William du Pont, January 3, 1906, PSduP 616.
74. Ex. Cte. Min., September 27, 1905, #68. The Du Pont subsidiary, the Manufacturing Contracting Company, put up the building, Ex. Cte. Min., January 4, 1906, #78.
75. Much of the detailed work is described in the correspondence in 1075–16.
76. This and the following quotation are from A. I. du Pont to T. C. du Pont, January 12, 1907, 1075–16.
77. This and the following quotation are from P. S. du Pont to A. I. and T. C. du Pont, January 17, 1907, 1075–16.
78. T. C. du Pont to P. S. du Pont, January 18, 1907, 1075–16. To this Alfred insisted it was not a question of "the length of the name or how it sounds or how it looks, but rather the naming of the building 'The du Pont de Nemours' was 'palpably our duty,'" A. I. du Pont to T. C. du Pont, January 21, 1907, 1075–16.

CHAPTER 6. Formulating Financial Policy

1. The development of comparable cost sheets can be seen by comparing those used by the three operative departments as they were summarized in their annual reports to the Executive Committee for the years immediately following the consolidation. Hereafter reports, letters, and minutes of the Executive Committee are cited Ex. Cte. Min. plus the date and the meeting number.
2. Ex. Cte. Min., March 30, 1904, #22.
3. Ex. Cte. Min., October 26, 1904, #43.
4. For example: Ex. Cte. Min., December 8, 1905, #74; Ex. Cte. Min., February 1, 1906, #80; P. S. du Pont to Ex. Cte., February 28, 1906, #83; I. du Pont to R. H. Dunham, April 30, 1906. The achievement of uniformity required careful definition and classification of each item the company made. Final agreement on standard classification did not come until 1908. Whereas the breakdown had been for 16 products in 1905, it included 28 in 1908. P. S. du Pont to Ex. Cte., May 1, 1908, #163; J. H. Haskell to L. R. Beardslee, June 8, 1908, #167.
5. This and the following quotation are from P. S. du Pont to J. A. Haskell, October 8, 1903, Ex. Cte. #4; Also Ex. Cte. Min., September 3, October 13, 1903, #3, #6; from the start Barksdale did not agree with Pierre's position.
6. Ex. Cte. Min., September 3, December 18, 1903, #3, #10.
7. Ex. Cte. Min., September 26, 1906, #100.
8. See Chapter 9, pp. 242ff.
9. Memorandum to H. M. Barksdale, P. S. du Pont, J. A. Haskell from T. C. du Pont. This memorandum is undated but 7–21–08 is penciled on the margin. The following quotations are from this memo. The specific issue which raised the matter at this time was whether the products of the Metallic Cap Company should be charged to the receiving plant at cost or market value; Ex. Cte. Min., June 3, 1908, #165.
10. Monthly Report of Operating Committee, July 1, 1908, #167.
11. I. du Pont to Ex. Cte., February 9, 1905, #56.
12. Ex. Cte. Min., August 30, November 29, 1905, #66, #73. For adjustments after Pierre's initial proposals in August see Treasurer's Monthly Report, October 18, 1905, #70; also report to Ex. Cte., Oct 25, #70; Ex. Cte. Min., January 25, March 30, 1905, #53, #58. The company in 1905 decided to carry its own marine insurance agency "with a view to saving commissions made by insurance brokers," Ex. Cte. Min., December 20, 1904, #51; also Ex. Cte. Min., September 27, 1906, #100.

13. An example of an additional significant new item was the inclusion of interest charges of plant investment. Ex. Cte. Min., December 26, 1906, #110, January 3, 1908, #153, May 20, 1908, #164.

14. Ex. Cte. Min., February 1, 1906, #80; also L. R. Beardslee to F. L. Connable, October 15, 1906, #103.

15. Ex. Cte. Min., July 1, 1908, #167.

16. Ex. Cte. Min., October 31, 1907, #145; Department Monthly Reports, December 17, 1903, #10, December 8, 1905, #68.

17. For example, Ex. Cte. Min., March 17, 1904, #21.

18. These and the two following quotations are from Ex. Cte. Min., December 27, 1905, #76,; see also Ex. Cte. Min., December 8, 1905, #74.

19. Ex. Cte. Min., February 13, 1907, #115.

20. With relatively solid agreement over allocation for general overhead charges about the many mills and departments, the one remaining problem for the Accounting Department to work out was a comparable allocation of special charges. Such charges had usually been determined when a special case first appeared. So, in December 1908, Pierre, at the request of the Executive Committee, submitted a report outlining all these special charges and the amounts to be paid for them by the different departments and occasionally by different mills. These special charges included costs of litigation, such as the recently opened antitrust suit, the bonding of employees who handled large sums of money under a blanket premium, the cost of the London and Valparaiso offices, certain types of advertising, special depreciation on manufacturing government smokeless powder, and variance in costing involved in the production of by-products. At the same time Pierre and the committee made a review of the distribution of general overhead charges. In nearly every case the committee followed the treasurer's recommendation, P. S. du Pont to Ex. Cte., December 31, 1908, #181; Ex. Cte. Min., January 9, 1909, #182; Ex. Cte. Min., April 2, 1908, #161; Ex. Cte. Min., March 17, 1909, #186.

21. E. N. Wead to P. S. du Pont, February 4, 1909, Annual Report of "the work of the Auditing Department," provides the best summary of the work of this unit. Ex. Cte. Min., February 6, 1909, #184.

22. This and the following quotation are from Ex. Cte. Min., December 17, 1903, #10; Ex. Cte. Min., November 18, 1903, #9.

23. P. S. du Pont to Ex. Cte., January 8, 1904, #13. In the following April Pierre wrote the Executive Committee about the double checking on powder sold both by the Sales and the Accounting departments; Pierre recommended ending this duplication of work and having only the Accounting Department do it. The committee took no action. P. S. du Pont to Ex. Cte., April 18, 1904, #26.

24. For example, Ex. Cte. Min., April 28, 1904, #26. Haskell did confer with the treasurer's office on the handling of discounts, I. du Pont to Ex. Cte., January 31, 1905, #55.

25. This and the following quotations are from J. A. Haskell to Ex. Cte., May 2, 1905, #60.

26. Ex. Cte. Min., April 6, 1906, #84, approving recommendations dated March 28, 1906. Pierre had written William du Pont earlier in the year: "prices for 'B' Blasting Powder have been very materially reduced during the last year so that at present this product is selling at a lower price than it has ever sold in the history of the powder business, if allowance is made for the difference in price of nitrate of soda compared with past years," P. S. du Pont to William du Pont, January 3, 1906, PSduP 616.

27. Treasurer's Monthly Report to Ex. Cte., December 28, 1904, #51; I. du Pont to J. A. Haskell, December 12, 1904, #51; the Treasurer's Report was not signed but Pierre was in California at that time and Irénée was acting for the treasurer; Also Irénée comments on Haskell's letter cited below, note 28.

28. J. A. Haskell to Ex. Cte., November 22, 1904, #47.

29. This and the following quotations are from P. S. du Pont to Ex. Cte., December 31, 1908, meeting January 7, 1909, #181.
30. P. S. du Pont to T. C. du Pont, June 9, 1903, the Eleutherian Mills Historical Library, T. Coleman du Pont Presidential Papers, Accession 1075, File 23, hereafter cited 1075 plus the identifying file number.
31. A. J. Moxham to T. C. du Pont, June 18, 1903, 1075-23.
32. Ex. Cte. Min., July 29, 1903, #10; H. M. Barksdale to Ex. Cte., July 10, 1903, #10; A. I. du Pont and J. A. Haskell to Ex. Cte. for the same meeting.
33. Treasurer's Monthly Reports, November 10, December 7, 1903, for meetings #9 and #10.
34. Ex. Cte. Min., December 17, 1903, #10. The committee favored the investigation because of "the prospects of a possible reduction in trade," and not because of a shortage of funds.
35. These and the following quotations are from P. S. du Pont to Ex. Cte., January 8, 1904, #13. The event that undoubtedly triggered the cash shortage was the refusal of Riker and Parsons to permit Laflin & Rand cash balances to be consolidated in the "Alexis I. du Pont Scheme," J. L. Riker to Metropolitan Trust Co, Trustee, Papers of Pierre S. du Pont, at the Eleutherian Mills Historical Library, File 418-4, hereafter cited PSduP plus the file number.
36. Ex. Cte. Min., January 28, 1904, #14; also Ex. Cte. Min., February 4, 15, 1904, #16, #18. $200,000 of this was a short-term loan, the collateral of which was 2,000 shares of Eastern Dynamite stock, valued at $200 per share, which had not yet been exchanged for Powder Company stock. The Du Pont & Co. also purchased $25,000 worth of Eastern Dynamite stock.
37. P. S. du Pont to Ex. Cte., January 19, 1904, #13, and A. I. du Pont, J. A. Haskell, and H. M. Barksdale report to the same meeting.
38. A. I. du Pont to J. A. Haskell and H. M. Barksdale report to the Ex. Cte., January 28, 1904, #15. They also proposed small reductions allotted by the International Smokeless purchase and for the stock of the Wilmington Trust Fund. The reduction of $1,337,000 meant a cut of total commitments from $4,635,306 to $3,298,306.
39. Ex. Cte. Min., January 28, 1904, #15.
40. This and the five following quotations are from P. S. du Pont to Ex. Cte., February 1, 1904, #18. Pierre also reported how these obligations fell upon the three major Du Pont companies; Du Pont, Laflin & Rand, and Eastern Dynamite. The deficit for the first came to $685,502.59; for the second, $601,899.63; and for the third, $363,426.04—a total of $1,650,828.26. He made this analysis to the committee because "the obligations would necessarily fall upon the three companies above named as we have no means of committing the other companies to expenditures. At present we cannot receive funds from other companies except by the declaration of dividends," and it would be "very unwise" to credit such dividends beyond those needed to pay on preferred stock. For if such dividends were paid the stockholders in the subsidiaries would have little incentive for exchanging stock for that of the Powder Company. P. S. du Pont to Ex. Cte., February 10, 1904, #18.
41. Ex. Cte. Min., February 15, 1904, #18. The committee also agreed at the next meeting that a possible reduction in business would permit the equipment to be transferred from the eastern mills to the western ones, where the demand was much higher. Ex. Cte. Min., March 10, 1904, #20. A little later it was decided, much against Alfred's wishes, to ask Olin to build a mill in Arkansas which the Black Powder Department was planning to undertake. Ex. Cte. Min., March 30, 31, 1904, #22, and May 25, 1904, #30.
42. Ex. Cte. Min., November 18, 1903, #9.
43. Ex. Cte. Min., September 30, 1903, #5.

44. Ex. Cte. Min., March 10, 1904, #20.
45. Ex. Cte. Min., March 31, 1904, #22.
46. Ex. Cte. Min., April 27, 1904, #26.
47. Ex. Cte. Min., March 31, and May 25, #22, #30; also requisition orders were not needed on construction orders under $100, and equipment orders under $500.
48. As indicated in Treasurer's Monthly Reports to Ex. Cte., 1904.
49. Treasurer's Monthly Report, October 18, 1904, #43. Because of the somewhat unexpected demands and the continued lack of long-range financing, Pierre did not succeed in completely eliminating the floating debt until 1906. Treasurer's Monthly Report, February 21, 1906, #83.
50. To Ex. Cte., November 2, 1904, #47. A. J. Moxham to T. C. du Pont.
51. T. C. du Pont to Frank L. Connable, January 11, 1904, 1075-68.
52. Operative Department Report for year 1904, January 25, 1905, 2. Black Powder Department Reports for 1904, 1905, first page.
53. Sales Department Monthly Report, October 18, 1904, #43; November 22, 1904, #47. Haskell also noted that there was a slight decline in demand for blasting powder and dynamite in the East, and a continuing normal demand in the South.
54. Sales Department Monthly Report, November 22, 1904, #47.
55. Ex. Cte. Min., October 18, 1904, #43.
56. T. C. du Pont to A. I. du Pont, H. M. Barksdale, H. F. Baldwin, November 1, 1904, #47.
57. T. C. du Pont to Ex. Cte., November 4, 1904, #47.
58. Treasurer's Annual Report to Ex. Cte., 1905, #85. Dated April 25, 1906, it gives a breakdown of profit and loss for the years 1903, 1904, 1905.
59. T. C. du Pont to Ex. Cte., November 4, 1904, #47.
60. This and the following quotations are from H. M. Barksdale to T. C. du Pont, November 8, 1904, copies to Ex. Cte, #47.
61. A. J. Moxham to T. C. du Pont, November 2, 1904, copies to Ex. Cte. #47.
62. Ex. Cte. Min., April 28, 1905, #59.
63. See Chapter 8.
64. These estimates are summarized in Ex. Cte. Min., January 26, 1905, #54. Also Haskell's monthly report, January 18, #53, gives an excellent detailed analysis of the growing demand and the ability of Du Pont and competing companies to meet it.
65. See Chapter 7, pp. 174-176 of the present book.
66. Coleman's estimate of $5.0 million of earnings in a penciled note in PSduP 418. The estimate accepted by the committee: $4.5 million.
67. Ex. Cte. Min., January 26, 1905, #54.

CHAPTER 7. Investment Overseas?

1. The most important letters on Lukens' falsifications of records are P. S. du Pont to T. C. du Pont, November 29, December 3, 5, 7 (two letters), and 10 (two letters), 1904; T. C. du Pont to P. S. du Pont, December 8, 12, 18, 1904. The Eleutherian Mills Historical Library, T. Coleman du Pont Presidential Papers, Accession 1075, File 32D, hereafter cited 1075 plus the identifying file number. Pierre S. du Pont also kept a separate file concerning Lukens' embezzlement and all correspondence relating to it, Eleutherian Mills Historical Library, Papers of Pierre S. du Pont, Longwood Manuscripts, Group 10, File 181, hereafter cited PSduP plus the identifying file number. Because the Judson-California Investment merger with the Powder Company had not yet been completed, Lukens legally took the money from Judson rather than from Du Pont. It was therefore legally possible for them to accept payment in full from Lukens and not prosecute.
2. There are copies of both the 1886 Agreement between the European firms and the 1888

Agreement between the Anglo-German Groups at The Eleutherian Mills Historical Library, E. I. du Pont de Nemours & Co. Records, Accession 472, hereafter cited by the Accession number; also, William J. Reader, *Imperial Chemical Industries—A History*, Vol. I, *The Forerunners, 1870–1926* (Oxford: Oxford University Press, 1970), pp. 125–137, 156–159.

3. A copy of the 1897 Agreement is in 472. It is also printed in the Government Exhibits in *U.S. Circuit Court District of Delaware, No. 280 in Equity, United States of America, Petitioner v. E. I. du Pont de Nemours and Company et al., Defendants* (hereafter cited as *U. S. v. du Pont*), *Petitioner's Record Exhibit*, II, 1123–1132. Also Arthur Pine Van Gelder and Hugo Schlatter, *History of Explosives Industry in America* (New York: Columbia University Press, 1927), pp. 426–428. All quotations in following paragraph from copy in Antitrust suit Exhibits.

4. The working out of these terms can be ascertained by reviewing the correspondence between T. C. du Pont and the European chairman, 472; also, Reader, *Imperial Chemical Industries*, I, 159–160.

5. The method of operation is indicated in J. A. Haskell to Ex. Cte., February 12, 1907, #115. The Americans took only a small part of the market. In 1904 the Europeans sold $1,218,873 worth of goods on the joint account, the Americans only $275,550. The agreement of the "Common Syndicate Fund" was to be set up by payment of a fixed amount on each case sold, "For the purpose of protecting the common interest against outside competition."

6. Reader, *Imperial Chemical Industries*, I, 168. We have been unable to locate the formal appointment of T. Coleman du Pont as chairman. But in all correspondence after 1902, Coleman du Pont speaks for the American Group, 472.

7. The relations of the purchase of International Smokeless to the European Agreement are given in T. C. du Pont to J. A. Haskell, March 4, 1904; J. A. Haskell to T. C. du Pont, April 6, 9, 1904; A. J. Moxham to T. C. du Pont, April 20, May 10, 30, 1904; T. C. du Pont to A. J. Moxham, April 14, May 9, 20 (telegram), 21, 1904; T. C. du Pont to E. G. Buckner, June 8, 1904; all in 1075–32H.

8. While Van Gelder and Schlatter, *Explosives Industry*, pp. 714–715, mentions briefly the story of the Mexican Company, the details are found in the correspondence between the du Ponts and the French cited in notes below.

9. *Ibid.*, 428. The Mexican Agreement was signed October 1, 1898.

10. Moxham Report on the Mexican Situation to the Executive Committee, June 30, 1904, #34. On October 1, 1904, the Development Department submitted a report on the *Société Centrale*. There is also another detailed report on Mexico, October 22, 1904, 1075–32K.

11. S. Singer to T. C. du Pont, written from the fair asking T. C. du Pont to lunch, October 19, 1904, 1075–32K.

12. Quotation from report of L. M. Howland to A. J. Moxham, February 19, 1905, 1075–32K.

13. Coleman du Pont seemed to have some vague thoughts about developing the foreign markets before talking to Singer. Writing Moxham, October 13, 1904, a week before he met Singer concerning the duties of the Development Department, Coleman du Pont commented that "should we determine to invade the foreign field; for example in South Africa, or in Europe, my judgement is that negotiations concerning all questions of policy up to the time of deciding same should rest with your department," 1075–32K. On the other hand, after receiving a report from T. J. Wrampelmeier listing companies controlled by the Nobel Dynamite Trust Co., sent to Coleman du Pont, September 29, 1904, Coleman du Pont asked Moxham, "Any reason I should know about this?"

14. T. C. du Pont to S. Singer, October 31; S. Singer to T. C. du Pont, November 14; S. Singer

to T. C. du Pont (telegram) November 25; J. A. Haskell to T. C. du Pont, November 29, December 8, 1904, 1075–32K.

15. T. C. du Pont to S. Singer, November 2, 1904; S. Singer to T. C. du Pont (telegram) November 25, 1904, 1075–32K.

16. Both memoranda, 1075–32K; also J. A. Haskell to S. Singer, December 14, 1904.

17. Ex. Cte. Min., December 20, 1904, #51. J. A. Haskell to S. Singer, December 22, 1904 (cable), 1075–32K.

18. The three agents were C. B. Lewis, who was closely connected with the National Metal Company; J. P. Nolan, who represented the California Powder Works in Mexico; and Arthur Moxham's brother Egbert, who was checking the Mexican situation for the Development Department, J. P. Nolan to W. A. Sullivan, November 9, 1904; C. B. Lewis to W. A. Sullivan, January 10, 1905; especially C. B. Lewis to J. A. Haskell, January 18, 1905, all 1075–32K.

19. Ex. Cte. Min., January 26, 1905, #54.

20. Answers to Moxham's queries labeled Letter A and Letter B, no date, 1075–32K.

21. S. Singer to J. A. Haskell, January 13 (cable); letter also January 9, 16 (cable), 17 (cable); J. A. Haskell to S. Singer, January 10 (cable), 14 (cable), 20, 23, 1905; T. C. du Pont to J. A. Haskell, January 3, 6, 1905; T. C. du Pont to S. Singer, January 19 (cable), 1905, 1075–32K.

22. J. A. Haskell to S. Singer, January 14, 1905, 1075–32K.

23. Ex. Cte. Min., January 26, 1905, #54.

24. J. A. Haskell to T. C. du Pont, January 24, 1905, 1075–32K.

25. L. M. Howland to A. J. Moxham, January 19, 1905; the report did not arrive in time for the January 26 meeting.

26. Howland followed up his first report of January 19 with a second one, February 19, after completing a ten-day trip to Switzerland and Italy, getting information at all cities where the *Société Centrale* controlled plants, 1075–32K.

27. T. C. du Pont to S. Singer, February 10, 1905, 1075–32K.

28. T. C. du Pont to A. I. du Pont, February 17, 1905, 1075–32K.

29. A. I. du Pont to P. S. du Pont, February 15 (telegram), 1075–32K.

30. P. S. du Pont to T. C. du Pont, March 2, 1905, 1075–32K. There are four letters on this date numbered 401–404. The quotation in the following paragraph is from 404.

31. P. S. du Pont to T. C. du Pont, March 2, 1905, 1075–32K.

32. P. S. du Pont to T. C. du Pont, March 1, 1905. The two following quotations are from P. S. du Pont to T. C. du Pont, March 2, 1905, 1075–32K.

33. P. S. du Pont to T. C. du Pont, March 2, 1905, 1075–32K.

34. P. S. du Pont to A. J. Moxham, March 4, 1905 (cable). P. S. du Pont to T. C. du Pont, March 4, 1905, 1075–32K.

35. A. J. Moxham to P. S. du Pont, March 7, 1905, 1075–32K.

36. P. S. du Pont to A. J. Moxham, March 8, 1905 (cable), 1075–32K.

37. A. I. du Pont to P. S. du Pont, March 21, 1905, PSduP 407.

38. A. J. Moxham to T. C. du Pont, March 8, 1905, 1075–32K.

39. Ex. Cte. Min., March 8, 1905, #57.

40. P. S. du Pont to T. C. du Pont, March 4, 1905, 1075–32K.

41. P. S. du Pont to T. C. du Pont, March 9, 1905, 1075–32K. "In the first place Singer refused to deliver our right to subscribe to shares mentioned in subparagraph 'b' prior to our payment for five thousand shares, six hundred thousand dollars, purchased in open market." Singer further "refused to deliver to us the right to subscribe to more than five thousand shares of new stock if we bought but five thousand shares in open market," if the Powder Company bought six thousand shares then Singer was willing for Du Pont to take six thousand additional shares.

42. P. S. du Pont to T. C. du Pont, March 9, 1905, 1075–32K.
43. *Ibid.*
44. *Ibid.* Pierre du Pont suggested that Singer may have proposed this scheme in order to sound him out on the Du Pont Company's plans in Mexico.
45. T. C. du Pont to P. S. du Pont, March 22, 1905, 1075–32K.
46. P. S. du Pont to A. I. du Pont, March 24, 1905, PSduP 407.
47. In fact, Parsons protested because the Du Pont Company began to centralize nitrate buying, Ex. Cte. Min., September 19, 1905, #67.
48. Development Department Report to Ex. Cte., October 13, 1903, #7.
49. A. J. Moxham to T. C. du Pont, March 25, 1903, 1075–32. Development Department Report to Ex. Cte., January 8, 1904, #8. Ex. Cte. Min., July 15, 1905, #64.
50. Development Department Report to Ex. Cte., December 9, 1903, #10. April 10, 1904, #24, April 25, 1904, #26.
51. For sulphur exploration, Development Department Report to Ex. Cte., January 15, 1905, #53, March 31, 1904, #22, September 8, 1904, #40, October 13, 1904, #42.
52. A. J. Moxham to D. Lawson, February 11, 1903, 1075–38. The two following quotations are from these instructions.
53. This and the following quotations are from the Development Department Report to the Ex. Cte., December 11, 1903, #10. For Peruvian negotiations see reports in Ex. Com. Min., February 13, 1904, #18, March 21, 1904, #23, April 25, 1904, #26, October 13, 1904, #42.
54. Development Department Report, Ex. Cte., November 12, 1903, #9.
55. Development Department Report, Ex. Cte., April 25, 1905, #59.
56. The Boquete negotiations may be followed in the correspondence between A. J. Moxham and W. R. Grace & Company, Ahuja and Lawson, filed with the minutes of Ex. Cte., May 25, #33, June 30, 1904, #34. Also Board of Directors' minutes, May 18, July 6, 1904.
57. E. Ahuja to A. J. Moxham, June 16, 1904, #34.
58. Ex. Cte. Min., August 23, 1904, #38.
59. Development Department Report to Ex. Cte., November 23, 1904, #47, and January 17, 1905, #53.
60. P. S. du Pont to T. C. du Pont, March 24, 1905, 1075–18. This and the quotation in the paragraph above were written at sea.
61. *Ibid.*
62. This and the three following quotations are from P. S. du Pont to Ex. Cte., July 17, 1905, #88, filed with report on Chile, November 1905, pp. 1, 5, 11, and 4.
63. J. J. Raskob to E. Ahuja, June 13, 1905, Raskob Papers at the Eleutherian Mills Historical Library, Accession 472. Hereafter, cited Raskob Papers.
64. The operations and combinations are well described in the report of F. G. Tallman to Ex. Cte., November 20, 1905, #74; Tallman's report also gives names of nitrate brokers in New York.
65. *Ibid.*, 3. "It seems incredible," wrote Tallman, "that the large and favored producers would . . . submit to operating their plants at one-third capacity only."
66. *Ibid.*, 8–9. The next quotation is from page 9.
67. *Ibid.*, 11. Ex. Cte. Min., December 8, 1905, #74. P. S. du Pont to William du Pont, January 3, 1906; PSduP 355. Ahuja's role in the spring of 1906 is well covered in Ahuja to A. J. Moxham, April 4, 1906, attached to the Development Department Report to the Ex. Cte. June 6, 1906, #88. Copies of the letter were sent to P. S. du Pont and F. Tallman.
68. Ex. Cte. Min., November 28, 1905, #75.
69. Ex. Cte. Min., August 6, 1906, #92.
70. C. L. Patterson to T. C. du Pont, April 25, 1905; forwarding letter of E. L. Wettig,

describing explosion damage, 1075–32. Also J. A. Haskell to Ex. Cte., April 27, 1905, #59.

71. Ex. Cte. Min., August 24, 1905 (Special), #67, and accompanying letter W. S. Simpson to J. A. Haskell, November 15, 1904. Also Ex. Cte. Min., August 23, 1905, #66. Also E. L. Wettig to C. L. Patterson, December 30, 1905, filed with Ex. Cte. Min., January 4, 1906, #78.

72. T. C. du Pont to S. Singer (cable), April 18, 1906, S. Singer to T. C. du Pont, April 21, 1906, 1075–32K. Shortly before this time the question of building a dynamite plant in Mexico was again raised and in May the Ex. Cte. Min. record that it was "the concensus of opinion that the present situation does not call for any positive action on the part of the Committee." May 29, 1906, #86.

73. Ex. Cte. Min., August 6, 1906, #92. The Paris meeting and later developments are indicated in S. Singer to T. C. du Pont, July 2, 21, 1906, 1075–32K.

74. S. Singer to T. C. du Pont, April 4, 1905, and another undated (but refers to Pierre's recent negotiations), June 22, 26, 1905; T. C. du Pont to S. Singer, May 4, 1905; March 23, 1905, all 1075–32K.

75. J. A. Haskell to T. C. du Pont, June 13, 1905; S. Singer to T. C. du Pont, January 9, 1906, 1075–32K.

76. T. C. du Pont to S. Singer, January 23, 1906, 1075–32K.

77. A. J. Moxham to T. C. du Pont, January 22, 1906, 1075–32K.

78. Hagen's report was dated May 22, 1906, filed with Ex. Cte. Min., May 28, 1906, #88.

79. Coleman du Pont had written his old friend Tom Johnson June 4, 1906: "Not knowing the ground as well as some of the older ones [who had negotiated the 1897 Agreement] I am going to 'rubber' for a couple of weeks. Then if I am pushed in a corner I will cable for Arthur, Pierre, Barksdale or anyone else who could be of service. Elsie and all the children are going to see their French cousins and use the French language."

80. T. C. du Pont to P. S. du Pont, June 26, 1906; for Singer's trip to London, Edna Smith to T. C. du Pont, June 19, 1906; S. Singer to T. C. du Pont, June 21, July 2, 13, (two letters) 1906; T. C. du Pont to S. Singer, June 22, July 19, 1906, 1075–32K. L. Dunham to S. Singer, June 26, 1906. (Just as Raskob always accompanied Pierre du Pont, so Lew Dunham, Coleman du Pont's secretary and right-hand man, always went with him on his business trips.) The official name of the company was to be *Société Centrale de Dynamite du Pont–Nobel.* S. Singer to T. C. du Pont, July 21, 1906, 1075–32K.

81. T. C. du Pont to P. S. du Pont, July 21, 1906, 1075–32K. The next quotation, de Mosenthal's note about Coleman, June 22, 1906, is from Reader, *Imperial Chemical Industries,* I, 198–199.

82. The version of the European Agreement which Coleman du Pont brought with him is filed with Ex. Cte. Min., September 12, 1906, #98. Singer wrote T. C. du Pont on July 21, asking whether the Anglo-German Group had been told yet whether "you are free for France," 1075–32J.

83. The story of the problem of the legality of the European Agreement is told in detail in J. M. Townsend to T. C. du Pont, July 12, 1906, filed with Ex. Cte. Min., September 20, 1906, #99. Resolutions of the European-American chairman to renounce the 1897 Agreement are filed in 1075–32–II. Coleman du Pont tells of the burning of the agreement in a letter to R. S. Penniman August 31, 1906, 472.

84. And this was the opinion of the federal courts forty-three years later. *United States District Court, Southern District of New York, Civil No 24–13, United States of America against Imperial Chemical Industries, Ltd., E. I. du Pont de Nemours et al.* (April 1949). *Opinions and Final Judgements,* 23–26. Pierre's comments are in J. M. Townsend to T. C. du Pont, July 12, 1906, #99. William H. Button had recently become a senior partner in Townsend and Avery.

85. All the following quotations are from this copy of the European Agreement, filed with Ex. Cte. Min., September 12, 1906, #98.

86. Ex. Cte. Min., October 9, 1906, #102; also Ex. Cte. Min., August 27, September 20, 27, 1906, #95, #99, #100.

87. This and the following quotations are from the Ex. Cte. Min., August 6, 1906, #92; T. C. du Pont to S. Singer, August 8, 10, 1906; T. C. du Pont to Ex. Cte., August 8, 1906, 1075–32K.

88. A. I. du Pont to T. C. du Pont, August 29, 1906; T. C. du Pont to A. I. du Pont, September 6, 1906, 1075–32K.

89. P. S. du Pont to T. C. du Pont, August 13, 1906. Coleman du Pont forwarded this letter to Singer, August 14, 1906. T. C. du Pont even authorized Singer to begin stock purchases. T. C. du Pont to S. Singer, August 17, 1906 (cable), T. C. du Pont to P. S. du Pont, August 18, 1906, R. de Tregomain to Cousin (probably Pierre), September 19, 1906, 1075–32K.

90. T. C. du Pont to S. Singer, September 13, 1906 (cable); also a letter on the same date. In his letter Coleman du Pont told Singer, "there were so many detail points about manufacturing and physical conditions that I could not answer, our Executive Committee felt we should like to have a talk with you and with this end in view I wired. . . .," 1075–32K.

91. S. Singer to T. C. du Pont, September 15 (cable), November 23, 1906, 1075–32K.

92. Ex. Cte. Min., July 25, 1906, #91; Ex. Cte. Min., September 22, 1906, #99 (see Chapter 8 of the present book).

93. P. S. du Pont to William du Pont, October 10, 1906, PSduP 355. The plan to finance the du Pont-Nobel Co., dated October 2, 1906, is filed with the Ex. Cte. Min., November 2, 1906, #103.

94. Ex. Cte. Min., September 16, 1906, #98.

95. Ex. Cte. Min., August 17, September 26, 1906, #94, 100.

96. Ex. Cte. Min., November 2, 1906, #103; S. Singer to T. C. du Pont, April 29, 1907, 1075–32K.

97. These developments are covered in S. Singer to T. C. du Pont, April 29, May 10, June 20, 1907; T. C. du Pont to S. Singer, May 18, June 1, 1907, all 1075–32K.

98. A. J. Moxham to H. Mosenthal, November 22, 1907, H. Mosenthal to A. J. Moxham, November 27, 1907, 472, Ex. Cte. Min., October 8, #101.

99. Ex. Cte. Min., September 8, 1906, #98.

100. Ex. Cte. Min., September 26, 1906, #100.

101. Ex. Cte. Min., November 10, 14, 1906, #104, #105; also, Reader, *Imperial Chemical Industries*, I, 200–202.

102. A. J. Moxham to J. A. Haskell, February 27, 1907, filed with Ex. Cte. Min., #115; Ex. Cte. Min., April 21, 1907, #122.

103. Data from this paragraph come from S. Singer to T. C. du Pont, May 10, June 20, 26, 1907; S. Singer to H. de Mosenthal, May 19, 1907, H. de Mosenthal to S. Singer, June 25, 1907, all 1075–32K.

104. The examples of these important exchanges are T. Johnson to Du Pont Powder Co., August 9, 1907; T. C. du Pont to H. de Mosenthal, November 2, 1907; A. J. Moxham to H. de Mosenthal, December 19, 1907; T. Johnston to J. A. Haskell, January 14, 1908; T. C. du Pont to Nobel-Dynamite Trust Co., Ltd., January 3, 1908; H. de Mosenthal to T. C. du Pont, February 4, 1908; H. J. Shand to C. L. Patterson, March 30, 1908; W. S. Simpson to H. de Mosenthal, April 13, 1909; H. de Mosenthal to P. S. du Pont, December 13, 1909; C. L. Patterson to H. de Mosenthal, April 26, 1909, all in 472. The examples of visits and conferences are T. C. du Pont to H. de Mosenthal, February 5, 1908; T. Johnson to Du Pont Powder Co., February 7, 1908; H. de Mosenthal to T. C.

du Pont, April 10, 1908; memorandum of discussion in C. L. Patterson's room in Du Pont Building, May 29, 1909, all 472.

105. T. C. du Pont to H. de Mosenthal, July 11, 1908, American Agreement Accounts 1907, 472; Ex. Cte. Min., August 7, October 9, 14, 1907, #136, 141, 142; other minor modifications are in P. S. du Pont to Ex. Cte., September 2, 1908, #172; Reader, *Imperial Chemical Industries*, I, 203–204.

106. The Canadian venture is covered in H. de Mosenthal to P. S. du Pont, April 28, 1911. This letter illustrates that type of information being exchanged in later periods of the agreement. Reader has a detailed analysis of developments in Canada in *Imperial Chemical Industries*, I, 203–211.

107. Pierre's rejection of the South American proposal is covered in P. S. du Pont to Ex. Cte., April 4, 27, 1910; C. L. Patterson to Ex. Cte., April 28, 1910; P. S. du Pont to H. de Mosenthal, September 29, 1910, #219, 220, 224, 231. See also Van Gelder and Schlatter, *Explosives Industry*, pp. 703–711; and *U.S. v. Imperial Chemical Industries, Ltd. et al.*, plans for ending joint interests of I.C.I. and Du Pont. *Opinions and Final Judgements*.

## CHAPTER 8. Maintaining Financial Control

1. Treasurer's Report to the Executive Committee, June 20, 1906, #89. The filing of the minutes, reports and letters to the Executive Committee is under the supervision of the Secretaries to the Committees Division of the Du Pont Company. Hereafter all documents in this category are cited Ex. Cte. plus the date and the meeting number.

2. Ex. Cte. Min., January 4, 1906, #78.

3. This and following quotations in paragraph from Irénée du Pont to the Ex. Cte, October 9, 1906, #102.

4. *Ibid.*

5. F. G. Tallman to the Ex. Cte., July 9, 1907, #135.

6. *Ibid.*, and Tallman to the Ex. Cte., November 20, 1905, #73.

7. Tallman had replaced Coyne as head of Purchasing when the latter was appointed as Director of Sales and Charles L. Patterson became vice-president in charge of sales.

8. Minutes of the Ex. Cte., January 31, 1907, #114.

9. P. S. du Pont to the Ex. Cte., February 27, 1906, #84. We have been unable to get the precise rate of this accommodation interest.

10. P. S. du Pont to the Ex. Cte., July 24, 1907, #135.

11. *Ibid.*

12. After 1904 Alfred I. du Pont was assisted in managing the Black Powder Department by Frank Connable, who came to Du Pont from the Chattanooga Powder Company. Connable became a director of Du Pont in 1906, and during that year assumed much direct responsibility for Black Powder because of Alfred's frequent absences. In 1911 Connable became director of the Black Powder Operating Department. See Arthur P. Van Gelder and Hugo Schlatter, *History of Explosives Industry in America* (New York; Columbia University Press, 1927), p. 144.

13. Ex. Cte. Min., April 5, 1906, #84.

14. Ex. Cte. Min., July 25, 1906, #91.

15. Hamilton Barksdale to the Ex. Cte., September 22, 1906, #100.

16. *Ibid.*

17. This and the following quotation, Ex. Cte. Min., January 30, 1907, #114.

18. H. F. Baldwin to the Ex. Cte., May 8, 1907, #127.

19. Ex. Cte. Min., June 10, 1907, #130.

20. A. J. Moxham to William Dwinnell, January 18, 1906, Eleutherian Mills Historical Library, T. Coleman du Pont Papers, Accession 1075, File 13 (hereafter cited 1075 plus

the file number). A. J. Moxham to T. C. du Pont, March 19, 1906, 1075–18; also Treasurer's Report to the Ex. Cte., January 18, 1906, #80. For reasons not clear from existing evidence the wholly owned Hazard Powder Company had not been dissolved. This may have been because of state laws like those of Pennsylvania, which penalized out-of-state corporations.

21. Pierre and Irénée du Pont to the Ex. Cte., June 26, 1906, #88. Statistics for this and the following two paragraphs are drawn from this document.

22. *Ibid.*

23. For quotations of prices, see P. S. du Pont to the Ex. Cte., July 23, 1906, #93.

24. P. S. and Irénée du Pont to the Ex. Cte., June 26, 1906, #93.

25. P. S. du Pont to the Ex. Cte., October 26, 1906, #104.

26. P. S. du Pont to the Ex. Cte., November 20, 1906, #107.

27. *Ibid.*

28. F. Connable to the Ex. Cte., November 24, 1906, #107.

29. P. S. du Pont to the Ex. Cte., December 13, 1906, #110; T. C. du Pont to Pierre du Pont, April 3, 1907, #123; Pierre du Pont to the Ex. Cte., April 9, 1907, #123; Pierre du Pont to the Ex. Cte., April 16, 1907, #123.

30. P. S. du Pont to the Ex. Cte., July 23, 1906, #93.

31. P. S. du Pont to the Ex. Cte., October 26, 1906, #104.

32. P. S. and I. du Pont to the Ex. Cte., June 26, 1906, #88.

33. This and the following quotation from P. S. du Pont to the Ex. Cte., October 2, 1906, #103.

34. See Theodore J. Grayson, *Leaders and Periods of American Finance* (New York: Wiley, 1932), pp. 369–374.

35. P. S. and I. du Pont to the Ex. Cte., June 26, 1906, #88.

36. P. S. du Pont to the Ex. Cte., March 6, 1907, #117.

37. Ex. Cte. Min., March 6, 1907, #117.

38. Ex. Cte. Min., March 21, 1907, #119.

39. H. M. Barksdale to the Ex. Cte., July 27, 1907, #135.

40. P. S. du Pont to the Ex. Cte., March 21, 1907, #119.

41. *Ibid.*

42. Ex. Cte. Min., March 21, 1907, #119.

43. P. S. du Pont to the Ex. Cte., April 20, 1907, #123.

44. Ex. Cte. Min., April 22, 1907, #123.

45. *Ibid.*

46. Detail in above paragraphs comes from the financial plan submitted by P. S. du Pont, T. C. du Pont, and A. J. Moxham to the Ex. Cte., June 14, 1907, #132.

47. Ex. Cte. Min., July 31, 1907, #135.

48. P. S. du Pont to the Ex. Cte., June 14, 1907, #132.

49. *Ibid.*

50. O. M. W. Sprague, *History of Crisis Under the National Banking System* (Washington, D.C.: Government Printing Office, 1910), pp. 246-280.

51. P. S. du Pont to the Ex. Cte., November 15, 1907, #150.

52. P. S. du Pont to the Ex. Cte., November 8, 1907, #150.

53. Ex. Cte. Min., October 31, 1907, #145.

54. P. S. du Pont to the Ex. Cte., December 3, 1907, #150.

55. Ex. Cte. Min., November 9, 1907, #146.

56. P. S. du Pont to T. C. du Pont and A. I. du Pont, December 23, 1908. EMHL; EIDPD-NCo, Accession 472–24. Old records of the E. I. du Pont de Nemours & Company at the Eleutherian Mills Historical Library are hereafter cited by Accession number.

57. *Ibid.*

58. P. S. du Pont to William du Pont, July 9, 1907, PSduP 616.
59. P. S. du Pont to the Ex. Cte., August 24, 1907, #138.
60. *Ibid.*, and Ex. Cte. Min., September 17, 1907, #139.
61. P. S. du Pont to William du Pont, July 9, 1907, PSduP 616.
62. *Ibid.*
63. Grayson, *Leaders and Periods of American Finance*, pp. 370–371.
64. Ex. Cte. Min., November 18, 1907, #148.
65. Ex. Cte. Min., December 5, 1907, #150.
66. See Ex. Cte. Min., October 29, 1907, #144.
67. P. S. du Pont to the Ex. Cte., August 24, 1907, #138.
68. Reports of F. G. Tallman to the Ex. Cte.; Nitrate of Soda, dated October 26, 1907; Glycerine, dated October 28, 1907; Fusel Oil, dated 28 October 1907; and Sulphur, dated October 28, 1907, all Ex. Cte., #145. Also, October 29, 1907, #144.
69. Ex. Cte. Min., October 29, 1907, #144.
70. F. G. Tallman to the Ex. Cte., January 24, 1908, #156.
71. Ex. Cte. Min., February 7, 1908, #156.
72. P. S. du Pont to William du Pont, August 20, 1908, PSduP 616.
73. *Ibid.*
74. P. S. du Pont to T. C. du Pont and A. I. du Pont, December 23, 1908, 472–24.
75. P. S. du Pont to A. I. du Pont and T. C. du Pont, December 23, 1908, 472–24. See also P. S. du Pont to the Ex. Cte., December 21, 1908, #180; and J. J. Raskob to P. S. du Pont, December 24, 1908 (two letters), 472–24.
76. P. S. du Pont to A. I. du Pont and T. C. du Pont, December 23, 1908, 472–24.
77. F. G. Tallman to the Ex. Cte., January 24, 1908, #156.

CHAPTER 9. Toward Vertical Integration

1. P. S. du Pont, A. J. Moxham and T. C. du Pont to the Executive Committee, February 29, 1908, Executive Committee Meeting #160. The filing of the minutes, letters, and reports to the Executive Committee is under the supervision of the Secretaries to the Committees Division of the Du Pont Company. Hereafter all documents in this category are cited to Ex. Cte., plus the date and the meeting number.
2. Ex. Cte. Min., March 19, 1908, #160.
3. The details of the new appropriations procedures were as follows: A formal request for appropriations was required for any capital project whose cost exceeded $100. A $500 expenditure was allowed without appropriation if it were charged to the repair account. Under the new system, as under the old, a department head or his deputy could authorize an expenditure of less than $5,000; the president, or in his absence, a member of the Executive or Finance committees other than the head of the requesting department could approve those between $5,000 and $10,000; and only the whole Executive Committee could allow those for $10,000 or more.
4. I. du Pont, Report on Appropriations, to Ex. Cte., April 11, 1908, #162.
5. P. S. du Pont to Ex. Cte., March 27, 1908, #161, and Ex. Cte. Min., April 2, 1908, #161.
6. P. S. du Pont to Ex. Cte., May 12, 1909, #191.
7. Ex. Cte. Min., December 4, 1907, #150.
8. *Ibid.*
9. F. G. Tallman, Nitrate Committee Report to Ex. Cte., February 5, 1908, #156.
10. F. G. Tallman to Ex. Cte., February 5, 1908, #156.
11. F. G. Tallman to Ex. Cte., November 20, 1905, #76.
12. J. J. Raskob for P. S. du Pont to Ex. Cte., October 25, 1909, #201; P. S. du Pont to Ex.

Cte., November 16, 1909, #206; P. S. du Pont to Ex. Cte., November 29, 1909, #207; P. S. du Pont to Ex. Cte., December 10, 1909, #207.

13. P. S. du Pont to Ex. Cte., November 16, 1909, #206.
14. The full agreement between the Powder Company and the National City Bank is appended to Pierre's report, Ex. Cte., November 29, 1909, #207.
15. Ex. Cte., Min., June 3, 1908, #165.
16. I. du Pont, Special Report on Nitrate Property Carolina de Taltal, to Ex. Cte., February 19, 1910, #212.
17. F. G. Tallman for the Nitrate Committee to Ex. Cte., March 17, 1909, #186.
18. *Ibid.*
19. I. du Pont, Special Report on Sale of Nitrate to Farmers, to Ex. Cte., October 31, 1910, #234.
20. H. M. Barksdale, P. S. du Pont and W. B. Dwinnell to Ex. Cte., August 5, 1908, #169.
21. *Ibid.*
22. Ex. Cte. Min., March 3, 1909, #185.
23. Monthly Reports, Development Department to Ex. Cte., February 1909, pp. 4–5; March 1909, p. 6; July 22, 1909, pp. 5–6; August 26, 1909, p. 6, #184, #185, #195, #197.
24. I. du Pont to Ex. Cte., September 20, 1909, #200.
25. *Ibid.*
26. *Ibid.*
27. Ex. Cte. Min., October 5, 1909, #202, Ex. Cte. Min., October 26, 1909, #203.
28. Ex. Cte. Min., January 13, 1910, #208.
29. I. du Pont to Ex. Cte., March 12, 1910, #215.
30. Ex. Cte. Min., March 14, 1910, #215.
31. P. S. du Pont to Ex. Cte., September 16, 1910, #230.
32. Ex. Cte. Min., September 22, 1910, #230.
33. Ex. Cte. Min., October 6, 1910, #232.
34. Development Dept. Monthly Report to Ex. Cte., November 1910, pp. 4–6, #237.
35. Development Dept. Monthly Report to Ex. Cte., December 1910, pp. 3–4.
36. Ex. Cte. Min., September 22, 1910, #230.
37. P. S. du Pont to Ex. Cte., December 2, 1910, #236.
38. Ex. Cte. Min., December 8, 1910, #236.
39. Pierre explained to the Executive Committee that the par value of the preferred stock was equal to two-thirds of the Powder Company's investment in *Oficina Delaware* and that he had arrived at the figure of $800,000 of common stock by deducting the 7% to be paid on the preferred stock ($56,000) from the $175,000 which the Development Department estimated would be earned by the Nitrate Company. This left $119,000. Pierre assumed that common stock should earn 15%, which would be achieved if it totaled $800,000. It should be emphasized, however, that Pierre created the new securities not to distribute, but to serve as collateral for loans or bonded debt. The ownership of the stock and control of the company remained with the Powder Company. Nothing indicated the relationship of the Powder Company to the Nitrate Company better than the list of its officers. Its directors were Hamilton Barksdale, Pierre du Pont, Frank Tallman, R. R. M. Carpenter, Elias Ahuja, C. A. Belin, and E. N. Carpenter. Besides Pierre as president, the Nitrate Company had C. A. Belin, E. Ahuja, and Ralph Derr (manager of the *oficina*) as vice-presidents, H. T. Baird as secretary, and Walter Carpenter as treasurer. P. S. du Pont to Ex. Cte., April 7, 1911, #248; Ex. Cte. Min., May 9, 1911, #248.
40. I. du Pont's Special Report to Ex. Cte., Sale of Nitrate to Farmers, Ex. Cte., October 31, 1910, #234.
41. Ex. Cte. Min., November 10, 1910, #234; Ex. Cte. Min., January 6, 1911, #238; Ex.

Cte. Min., January 25, 1911, #240; Ex. Cte. Min., February 10, 1911, #243.

42. F. G. Tallman to Ex. Cte., July 29, 1908, #169.

43. H. M. Barksdale and Charles Patterson to Ex. Cte., August 24, 1910, #229.

44. H. M. Barksdale and F. G. Tallman to Ex. Cte., November 4, 1908, #177.

45. F. G. Tallman to Ex. Cte., July 29, 1908, #169; F. G. Tallman to Ex. Cte., November 22, 1910, #236.

46. F. G. Tallman to Ex. Cte., February 9, 1911, #245.

47. *Ibid.*

48. F. G. Tallman and H. M. Barksdale to Ex. Cte., November 4, 1908, #177.

49. *Ibid.*

50. *Ibid.*

51. Ex. Cte. Min., December 16, 1908, #179.

52. F. G. Tallman and H. M. Barksdale to Ex. Cte., November 1908, #177.

53. F. G. Tallman to Ex. Cte., July 29, 1908, #169.

54. F. G. Tallman to Ex. Cte., June 2, 1910, #222.

55. Ex. Cte. Min., September 2, 1908, #172.

56. Ex. Cte. Min., June 2, 1910, #222.

57. H. M. Barksdale and C. L. Patterson to Ex. Cte., August 24, 1910, #229.

58. *Ibid.*

59. F. G. Tallman to Ex. Cte., June 2, 1910, #222.

60. F. G. Tallman to Ex. Cte., November 22, 1910, #236.

61. *Ibid.*

62. *Ibid.*, p. 18.

63. F. G. Tallman to Ex. Cte., March 28, 1911, #246.

64. R. R. M. Carpenter to Ex. Cte., March 20, 1911, #246.

65. Ex. Cte. Min., September 16, 1908, #173.

66. Ex. Cte. Min., January 18, 1911, #239.

67. *Ibid.*

68. Ex. Cte. Min., April 11, 1911, #246.

69. Ex. Cte. Min., May 9, 1911, #248.

70. Ex. Cte. Min., July 11, 1911, #256.

71. Ex. Cte. Min., September 12, 1911, #255.

72. F. G. Tallman to P. S. du Pont, April 8, 1910, old records of E. I. du Pont de Nemours & Co., Eleutherian Mills Historical Library, Accession 472, hereafter cited 472.

73. *Ibid.*

74. Ex. Cte. Min., March 20, 1912, #269.

75. Accounting Committee Report, L. R. Beardslee to Ex. Cte., May 31, 1912, #272.

76. Ex. Cte. Min., June 11, 1912, #272.

77. A. J. Moxham to Ex. Cte., May 6, 1912, #271.

78. *Ibid.* Quotations and reasoning.

79. Ex. Cte. Min., May 15, 1912, #271.

80. Charles Petze to F. G. Tallman, August 2, 1912, exhibit "B" Report to Ex. Cte., September 11, 1912, #276.

81. F. G. Tallman to Ex. Cte., August 1, 1912, #276.

82. Ex. Cte. Min., September 11, 1912, #276.

83. J. A. Haskell to Ex. Cte., February 27, 1909, #186.

84. Ex. Cte. Min., December 16, 1908, #179.

85. Development Department Report, January 1909, p. 1, #182.

86. Development Department Report to Ex. Cte., February 1909, pp. 1-2, #184.

87. Development Department Report to Ex. Cte., August 1909, #197.

88. Ex. Cte. Min., March 16, 1910, #216; H. M. Barksdale, A. J. Moxhan, J. A. Haskell

and I. du Pont to Ex. Cte., February 10, 1909, #185.

89. I. du Pont and R. R. M. Carpenter, Final Report on Artificial Leather to Ex. Cte., September 29, 1910, #233.

90. Ex. Cte. Min., July 19, 1910, #225.

91. *Ibid.*

92. Ex. Cte. Min., March 14, 1911, #245.

93. Ex. Cte. Min., August 4, 1910, #227.

94. Ex. Cte. Min., September 1, 1910, #229.

95. Ex. Cte. Min., March 14, 1911, #245.

96. Ex. Cte. Min., March 19, 1908, #160; Ex. Cte. Min., March 16, 1910, #212; Ex. Cte. Min., June 2, 1910, #216.

97. Ex. Cte. Min., May 18, 1910, #221.

98. Information given above, and all quotations from Ex. Cte. Min., December 9, 1911, #236.

99. P. S. du Pont to T. C. du Pont and A. I. du Pont, December 23, 1908, 472–24.

100. Ex. Cte. Min., May 18, 1910, #221; June 9, 1910, #223; July 7, 1910, #224; October 6, 1910, #232.

101. P. S. du Pont to Ex. Cte., March 13, 1908, #160; Ex. Cte. Min., March 5, 1908, #159.

102. Application of the E. I. du Pont de Nemours Powder Co. to list the 4½% thirty-year bonds and the 5% cumulative preferred stock on the New York Stock Exchange, September 30, 1909, 472–13.

103. P. S. du Pont to Ex. Cte., December 30, 1909, #208; Ex. Cte. Min., January 19, 1910, #209.

104. P. S. du Pont to Ex. Cte., February 22, 1909, #185; P. S. du Pont to Ex. Cte., December 10, 1908 and Ex. Cte. Min., December 16, 1908, #179.

105. P. S. du Pont to T. C. du Pont and A. I. du Pont, December 23, 1908, 472–24.

106. P. S. du Pont to Ex. Cte., June 29, 1910, #224.

107. P. S. du Pont to Ex. Cte., June 27, 1910, #224.

108. *Ibid.*

CHAPTER 10. The Powder Company Assailed

1. *U.S. Circuit Court District of Delaware, No. 280 in Equity, United States of America, Petitioner v. E. I. du Pont de Nemours and Company et al., Defendants,* Petitioner's Record Testimony, Vol. I, pp. 244–251; hereafter cited *U.S. v. E. I. du Pont, antitrust case of 1911.*

2. Chicago *Tribune,* February 24, 1906. Clipping in letter, E. S. Rice to T. C. du Pont, February 24, 1906. The Eleutherian Mills Historical Library, T. Coleman du Pont Presidential Papers, Accession 1075, File 41, hereafter cited 1075 plus the identifying file number.

3. *Ibid.*

4. *Ibid.*

5. P. S. du Pont to E. S. Rice, March 1, 1906, 1075–41.

6. David Graham Phillips, *The Treason of the Senate* (introduction by George E. Mowry and Judson A. Grenier) (Chicago: Quadrangle Books, 1964), p. 59.

7. Peoria *Herald Transcript,* May 24, 1906, clipping in letter to Charles L. Patterson, May 31, 1906, 1075–41.

8. E. J. Dimmick to W. B. Dwinnell, August 30, 1906, 1075–41.

9. Executive Committee Minutes, August 7, 1906, Meeting #93 (hereafter cited as Ex. Cte. Min. plus the meeting number).

10. E. J. Dimmick to W. B. Dwinnell, August 30, 1906, 1075–41.

11. W. B. Dwinnell to Ex. Cte., August 31, 1906, 1075–41.

12. Ex. Cte. Min., September 4, 1906, #97.

13. P. S. du Pont to William du Pont, January 2, 1907, PSduP 616, Papers of Pierre S. du Pont, Eleutherian Mills Historical Library. Hereafter cited PSduP plus the file number.

14. T. C. du Pont to Townsend, Avery and Button, July 31, 1907, 1075–57.

15. San Francisco *Examiner*, July 31, 1907; Detroit *Free Press*, August 3, 1907; Wilmington North Carolina *Star*, July 31, 1907, and Topeka *Daily Capital*, August 4, 1907. All clippings sent to T. C. du Pont by E. G. Buckner, March 2, 1911. Part of a large collection of clippings used for the company's defense against the government suit in the E. I. du Pont de Nemours Company papers at the Eleutherian Mills Historical Library, Presidential Papers, Accession 472. Hereafter cited 472.

16. *Ibid.*, Los Angeles *Herald*, September 12, 1908.

17. T. C. du Pont to H. Belin, Jr., August 2, 1907, 1075–15.

18. P. S. du Pont to T. C. du Pont, September 16, 1910, 1075–151.

19. P. S. du Pont to William du Pont, May 25, 1911, PSduP 616.

20. Quotations from *U.S. v. E. I. du Pont, antitrust case of 1911, Petitioner's Record Testimony*, I, 93.

21. *Additional Supplement of Hearings Before the Subcommittee of the Committee on Appropriations House of Representatives, Consisting of Messrs. Walter I. Smith (Chairman), J. W. Keifer, J. V. Graff, J. J. Fitzgerald, and Stephen Brundidge, Jr., in Charge of the Fortification Appropriation Bill, Smokeless Powder* (Washington: Government Printing Office, 1907), pp. 26–27. Hereafter *Additional Supplement, Fortification Bill, 1907.*

22. *Ibid.*, 29.

23. *Ibid.*, 26.

24. Development Department Supplementary Report to Ex. Cte. by A. J. Moxham, June 4, 1906, #88. Data on Monnett from *Who's Who in America, 1906–1907* (Chicago: Marquis & Co., 1906), p. 1249.

25. Development Department Supplementary Report to Ex. Cte., A. J. Moxham, June 4, 1906.

26. *Additional Supplement, Fortification Bill, 1907*, 20.

27. *Ibid.*

28. Development Department Supplementary Report to the Ex. Cte., A. J. Moxham, June 4, 1906, #88: also P. S. du Pont to C. A. Belin, January 4, 1907, PSduP 438.

29. *Congressional Record*, April 13, 1908. Cover letter J. A. Haskell to the Ex. Cte., April 24, 1908, #163; E. G. Buckner to Ex. Cte., March 1, 1911, #245.

30. Brainard Avery to J. A. Haskell, March 26, 1909. Report on the Powder Company's smokeless powder lobby with cover letter, J. A. Haskell to Ex. Cte. April 7, 1909, #187.

31. W. B. Dwinnell to T. C. du Pont, P. S. du Pont et al. Ex. Cte. January 23, 1909, #185.

32. T. C. du Pont to W. Borah, January 22, 1909, 472.

33. T. C. du Pont to J. A. Haskell, January 27, 1909. Wrote Coleman: "I know well enough to talk entirely frankly to the two Senators and the Representative from Delaware, Senator Borah from Idaho, Senator Dixon, Senator Penrose, Senator William Alden Smith, Senator Elkins, Senator Scott, Senator Crane, Senator Burrows . . ." There follows a lengthy list of other Congressmen whom Coleman thought could be influenced, 472.

34. Brainard Avery to J. A. Haskell, March 26, 1909. Report on the Powder Company's smokeless powder lobby, with cover letter to the Ex. Cte., April 7, 1909, #187.

35. *Ibid.*

36. *Ibid.*

37. *Ibid.*

38. E. G. Buckner to the Ex. Cte., March 1, 1911, #245.

39. Ex. Cte. Min., November 29, 1905, #73.

40. Irénée du Pont to Ex. Cte., April 21, 1906, #85; Arthur Pine Van Gelder and Hugo

Schlatter, *History of the Explosives Industry in America* (New York: Columbia University Press, 1927), p. 694.

41. This and the above quotations from Irénée du Pont to the Ex. Cte., April 21, 1906, #85.

42. Ex. Cte. Min., April 26, 1906, #85.

43. *U.S. v. E. I. du Pont, antitrust case of 1911, Defendants' Record Testimony*, II, 708–710.

44. G. M. Peters to Senator Daniel, March 26, 1906, 1075–41.

45. G. M. Peters to T. C. du Pont, March 26, 1906, 1075–41.

46. T. C. du Pont to G. M. Peters, April 7, 1906, 1075–41.

47. *U.S. v. E. I. du Pont, antitrust case of 1911, Defendants' Record, Testimony*, I, 506–507.

48. Townsend, Avery & Button to J. A. Haskell, May 6, 1908, memo regarding letter to wind up Laflin & Rand and Delaware Securities, 472. *U.S. v. E. I. du Pont, antitrust case of 1911, Defendants' Record Testimony*, I, 501. Also Government Exhibits, 392, Vol. V, 2746–2747.

49. *Ibid.*, I, 542.

50. *Ibid.*, I, 503.

51. *Ibid.*, I, 553.

52. J. Bermingham to T. C. du Pont, August 3, 1907, 1075–57.

53. Full list of defendants included: E. I. du Pont de Nemours & Company; E. I. du Pont de Nemours Powder Company (New Jersey); Du Pont International Powder Company; Delaware Securities Company; Delaware Investment Company; California Investment Company; Hazard Powder Company; Laflin & Rand Powder Company; Eastern Dynamite Company; E. I. du Pont de Nemours Powder Company (Delaware); E. I. du Pont de Nemours & Co. of Penna.; the King Powder Company; Austin Powder Company of Cleveland; California Powder Works; Conemaugh Powder Company; Fairmont Powder Company; International Smokeless Powder and Chemical Company; Judson Dynamite and Powder Company; Metropolitan Powder Company; Peyton Chemical Company; the Aetna Powder Company; the American E. C. & Schultze Gunpowder Co. Ltd.; the American Powder Mills; the Equitable Powder Manufacturing Co.; the Miami Powder Co.; Alexis I. du Pont, Alfred I. du Pont, Eugene du Pont, Eugene E. du Pont, Henry A. du Pont, Henry F. du Pont, Irénée du Pont, Francis I. du Pont, Pierre S. du Pont, Thomas Coleman du Pont, Victor du Pont, Jr., Jonathan A. Haskell, Arthur J. Moxham, Hamilton M. Barksdale, Henry F. Baldwin, Edmund G. Buckner, and Frank L. Connable.

54. P. S. du Pont to C. A. Belin, October 8, 1907, PSduP 438.

55. T. C. du Pont to W. Hilles, January 14, 1910, 472.

56. J. A. Haskell to the Ex. Cte., March 27, 1908, #161.

57. Brainard Avery to T. C. du Pont, February 17, 1909, 472.

58. T. C. du Pont to W. Hilles, January 14, 1910, 472; W. Hilles to T. C. du Pont, January 19, 1910, 472; W. Hilles to T. C. du Pont, January 19, 1910, 472.

59. W. Hilles to T. C. du Pont, June 25, 1910, 472; T. C. du Pont to F. H. Hitchcock, June 27, 1910, 472.

60. *U.S. v. E. I. du Pont, antitrust case of 1911, Opinion of Court and Interlocutory Decree*, June 21, 1911.

61. Ralph W. Hidy and Muriel E. Hidy, *Pioneering in Big Business 1882–1911* (New York: Harper & Brothers, 1955), pp. 709–711; and Richard B. Tenant, *The American Cigarette Industry* (New Haven, Conn.: Yale University Press, 1950), pp. 59–60.

62. The above quotation and interpretation, G. W. Wickersham to T. C. du Pont, October 20, 1911, 472. Also *U.S. v. E. I. du Pont, antitrust case of 1911, Interlocutory Decree*, p. 44.

63. This deadline was further extended to November 21 and then still further as the participants in the suit worked out a solution compatible with the final decree.

64. P. S. du Pont to William du Pont, July 20, 1911, PSduP 616.

65. D. Marvel to J. Scarlet and W. Glasgow, January 18, 1911; Henry Francis du Pont Collection of Winterthur Manuscripts, Group 8, Box 39.

66. *Ibid.*, D. Marvel to H. A. du Pont, January 30, 1911.

67. T. C. du Pont to G. Sladovich, September 29, 1911, 472.

68. T. C. du Pont to P. S. du Pont, October 27, 1911, PSduP 418.

69. T. C. du Pont to A. J. Moxham, July 21, 1911, 472.

70. T. C. du Pont to Ex. Cte., October 4, 1907, 1075-57.

71. T. C. du Pont to J. Townsend, December 16, 1907, 1075-57.

72. T. C. du Pont to A. J. Moxham, September 2, 1911, 472.

73. Memorandum, T. C. du Pont, October 5, 1911, "The Powder Case Briefly Stated," 472.

74. W. Hilles to T. C. du Pont, June 29, 1911, 472.

75. T. C. du Pont to A. J. Moxham, Sept. 2, 1911, 472.

76. P. S. du Pont to J. M. Townsend, September 7, 1911, 472.

77. P. S. du Pont to A. J. Moxham, September 8, 1911, 472.

78. P. S. du Pont to J. M. Townsend, September 7, 1911, 472.

79. D. Marvel to T. C. du Pont, July 20, 1911, 472.

80. T. C. du Pont to A. J. Moxham, September 2, 1911, 472.

81. W. F. Stone to T. C. du Pont, July 27, 1911; T. C. du Pont to W. F. Stone, July 31, 1911, 472.

82. W. F. Stone to T. C. du Pont, July 27, 1911, 472.

83. G. W. Wickersham to T. C. du Pont, August 9, 1911; T. C. du Pont to H. P. Scott, August 5, 1911, 472.

84. Telegrams from T. C. du Pont to G. W. Wickersham, September 21, 1911; G. W. Wickersham to T. C. du Pont, September 21, 1911; and T. C. du Pont to G. W. Wickersham, September 22, 1911, 472.

85. G. W. Wickersham to T. C. du Pont, October 20, 1911, 472.

86. Draft of letter, T. C. du Pont to G. W. Wickersham, October 8, 1911, 472.

87. G. W. Wickersham to T. C. du Pont, October 20, 1911, 472.

88. *Ibid.*

89. T. C. du Pont to F. Hitchcock, October 26, 1911, 472.

90. T. C. du Pont to G. W. Wickersham, October 26, 1911, 472.

91. *Ibid.*

92. T. C. du Pont to C. P. Taft, October 26, 1911, 472. For Taft's business relationship with Coleman du Pont see Lewis J. Horowitz and Boydon Sparks, *The Towers of New York* (New York: Simon and Schuster, 1937), pp. 102-103, 133.

93. T. C. du Pont to A. H. Martin, September 28, 1911, 472; T. C. du Pont to S. A. Yorks, November 10, 1911, 472.

94. S. A. Yorks to T. C. du Pont, November 17, 1911; T. C. du Pont to S. A. Yorks, December 30, 1911, 472; T. C. du Pont to J. Scarlet, March 10, 1912, 472.

95. T. C. du Pont to S. A. Yorks, March 18, 1912, 472.

96. Pierre to the Ex. Cte., March 18, 1912, #269; also P. S. du Pont to William du Pont, April 3, 1912, PSduP 616. Attention is called to the fanciful account of Alfred I. du Pont's role in the antitrust litigation found in Marquis James, *Alfred I. du Pont, The Family Rebel* (Indianapolis: Bobbs-Merrill, 1941), pp. 243-246. According to this account Alfred opposed an appeal, which was true, and then through former Senator J. F. Allee of Delaware arranged a meeting in March 1912, between Taft, Wickersham, Coleman du Pont, and William Glasgow at the White House. It is clear from Pierre's letter that this meeting never took place. Marquis James's footnote reveals the cause of the error, a letter from J. F. Allee to A. I. du Pont, July 13, 1921, and a hearsay account given by Jessie Ball du Pont (Mrs. Alfred I.) and her brother Edward Ball. It should be noted that Allee and Coleman du Pont were on bad terms before the government suit started in 1906.

Allee quoted Taft as "denouncing Coleman du Pont as 'slippery as an eel and crooked as a ram's horn.' " Allee had helped Waddell prepare his attack against the Du Pont Company and therefore it is highly unlikely that Coleman or Pierre would have had any dealings with Allee at all. It is more probable that Allee and Alfred became friends after Pierre and Alfred I. split when Coleman sold his shares in the Du Pont Company. The rest of James's source was from an oral account of the White House conference given as Mr. Alfred I. told it to his wife, Jessie Ball du Pont, and Edward Ball some ten years later. The trouble here is that James is relying on a hearsay account repeated ten years after the fact. Alfred did meet Taft, but it was in Philadelphia on March 4, not in Washington. Pierre's description written shortly after the event makes this very clear.

97. P. S. du Pont to H. A. du Pont (not sent), January 3, 1910, PSduP 418.
98. E. G. Buckner to T. C. du Pont, March 10, 1911, 472.
99. H. M. Barksdale to T. C. du Pont, March 13, 1911, 472.
100. T. C. du Pont to H. M. Barksdale, March 16, 1911; T. C. du Pont to H. A. du Pont, March 16, 1911, 472.
101. T. C. du Pont to D. Watson, October 10, 1911, 472.
102. D. Watson to T. C. du Pont, October 9, 1911; D. Watson to H. Hilles, November 1, 1911, 472.
103. P. S. du Pont to Ex. Cte., October 8, 1911, #257.
104. P. S. du Pont to T. C. du Pont, October 18, 1911, 472.
105. P. S. du Pont to Ex. Cte., October 18, 1911, #260.
106. *Ibid.*
107. T. C. du Pont to W. Hilles, October 19, 1911, 472.
108. G. W. Wickersham to T. C. du Pont, October 20, 1911, 472.
109. P. S. du Pont to J. Townsend, October 26, 1911, 472.
110. P. S. du Pont to Ex. Cte., November 10, 1911, #261.
111. P. S. du Pont to William du Pont, July 20, 1911, PSduP 616.
112. *Ibid.*
113. Both quotations from P. S. du Pont to Ex. Cte., November 10, 1911, #261.
114. *Ibid.*
115. P. S. du Pont to R. M. Jones, October 10, 1911, PSduP 564.
116. W. Hilles to office of the president of E. I. du Pont de Nemours Powder Co., December 18, 1911, 472.
117. P. S. du Pont to William du Pont, April 3, 1912, PsduP 616.
118. *Ibid.*
119. *Ibid.*
120. W. H. Button to C. P. Taft, April 22, 1911, 472.
121. George Sweet Gibb and Evelyn H. Knowlton, *The Resurgent Years* (New York: Harper & Brothers, 1956), pp. 1–14; Richard B. Tennant, *The American Cigarette Industry,* pp. 60–66.
122. P. S. du Pont to Ex. Cte. March 18, 1912, #269.
123. P. S. du Pont to William du Pont, April 3, May 8, 1912, PSduP 616.
124. *Ibid.,* April 3, 1912.
125. *Final Decree, June 13, 1912,* 4, 5, 6, of *U.S. v. E. I. du Pont.*
126. P. S. du Pont to William du Pont, June 13, 1912, PSduP 616.
127. MacFarland, Taylor, and Costello (signed L. G. Abbot) to E. I. du Pont de Nemours Powder Co., August 26, 1911, 472.
128. P. S. du Pont to J. P. Laffey, September 26, 1911, 472.
129. P. S. du Pont to Townsend, Avery and Button, August 28, 1911, 472.
130. T. C. du Pont to J. P. Laffey, October 30, 1913; J. P. Laffey to T. C. du Pont, January 2, 1914, 472.

131. A. J. Moxham to T. C. du Pont, April 7, 1914, 472.
132. Van Gelder and Schlatter, *Explosives Industry,* p. 874.
133. *In the District Court of the United States, for the District of Delaware. In Equity, No. 280. The United States of America vs. E. I. du Pont de Nemours & Company and others, Defendants' Report in Compliance with Final Decree of June 13, 1912. Filed January 15, 1913.* 2, 3. Hereafter, cited *Defendants' Compliance with Final Decree, June 13, 1912.*
134. *In the District Court of the United States for the District of Delaware, in Equity, No. 280. The United States of America, Petitioner, v. E. I. du Pont de Nemours & Company and others, Defendants. Opinion of Court and Final Decree. June 13, 1912.* Opinion, p. 4. Hereafter cited *Final Decree, June 13, 1912.* The du Ponts were to transfer to the first of the new corporations dynamite plants at Kenvil, New Jersey; Marquette, Michigan; Pinole, California. For the manufacture of black blasting powder: Rosendale, New York; Ringtown, Pennsylvania (two plants); Youngstown, Ohio; Pleasant Prairie, Wisconsin; Turck, Kansas; Santa Cruz, California. For the manufacture of black sporting powder, Hazardville, Connecticut; Schaghticoke, New York. To the second of said corporations transfer the following plants: for the manufacture of dynamite: Hopatcong, New Jersey; Senter, Michigan; Atlas, Missouri; Vigorit, California. For the manufacture of black blasting powder: Riker, Pennsylvania; Shenendoah, Pennsylvania; Ooltewah, Tennessee; Belleville, Illinois; Pittsburg, Kansas. Transfer or furnish the first of the two corporations with a plant for the manufacture of smokeless sporting powder at Kenvil, New Jersey, or some other suitable eastern point and it was to be of a capacity of 950,000 pounds per annum. The du Ponts were to retain for the manufacture of Dynamite: Ashburn, Missouri; Barksdale, Wisconsin; Du Pont, Washington; Emporium, Pennsylvania; Hartford City, Indiana; Louviers, Colorado; Gibbstown, New Jersey; Lewisburg, Alabama. For the manufacture of Black Blasting Powder: Augusta, Colorado; Connable, Alabama; Oliphant Furnace, Pennsylvania; Mooar, Iowa; Nemours, West Virginia; Patterson, Oklahoma; Wilpen, Minnesota. For the manufacture of Black Sporting Powder: Brandywine, Delaware; Wayne, New Jersey: For the manufacture of Smokeless Sporting Powder: Carney's Point, New Jersey; Haskell, New Jersey; for the manufacture of Government Smokeless Powder: Carney's Point, New Jersey; Haskell, New Jersey. *Ibid.,* pp. 4–6.
135. This and the two quotations above are from the *Final Decree, June 13, 1912,* 7–8.
136. P. S. du Pont to William du Pont, July 26, 1912, PSduP 616.
137. P. S. du Pont to Finance Committee, May 25, 1912, 472.
138. *Ibid.,* for par value of outstanding securities only.
139. P. S. du Pont and H. M. Barksdale to the Ex. Cte., April 24, 1911, #248.
140. *Ibid.*
141. Ex. Cte. Min., June 24, 1911, #250.
142. Note: In the big company, bonds and preferred stock stood for solid assets, while the common stock stood for intangible values such as controlling power.
143. P. S. du Pont to William du Pont, May 8, 1912, PSduP 616.
144. P.S. du Pont to Finance Committee, May 25, 1912, PSduP 616.
145. *Ibid.*
146. Defendants' Compliance with *Final Decree, January 15, 1913,* 8, 12.
147. L. R. Beardslee, Secretary of Ex. Cte., October 5, 1912; also Ex. Cte. Min., October 8, 1912, #278.
148. Ex. Cte. Min., December 9, 1913, #299.
149. Ex. Cte. Min., October 20, 1913, #297.
150. T. C. du Pont to J. P. Laffey, February 13, 1913, Ex. Cte. meeting, #286.
151. Accounting Committee to Ex. Cte., March 29, 1913, #288.
152. *Ibid.*
153. Manufacturing and Sales Committee to Ex. Cte., March 28, 1913, #288.

154. Ex. Cte. Min., May 14, 1913, #290.
155. Ex. Cte. Min., September 9, 1913, #296.
156. Data here courtesy of W. J. Reader of London, England, who is currently writing a history of ICI. From *Imperial Chemical Industries—A History,* Vol. I, *The Forerunners, 1870–1926* (Oxford: Oxford University Press, 1970), pp. 212–215.

CHAPTER 11. The Problem of Succession

1. Annual Report, E. I. du Pont de Nemours Powder Company 1911, p. 9.
2. For T. Coleman du Pont's ideas, see T. C. du Pont to P. S. du Pont, February 4, 1911. Records of E. I. du Pont de Nemours Company at the Eleutherian Mills Historical Library, Accession 472, hereafter cited as 472. Also, Executive Committee Minutes, January 18, 1911, Meeting 289, hereafter cited as Ex. Cte. Min. plus date and meeting number (#).
3. Marquis James, *Alfred I. du Pont, The Family Rebel* (Indianapolis: Bobbs-Merrill, 1941), chs. XII and XIII, especially pp. 194–195, 204–205. Also P. S. du Pont "Coleman Sells Out," written in 1941, file 54 in the collection of the personal writings of Pierre S. du Pont at the Eleutherian Mills Historical Library, hereafter cited as PSduP Series B plus the file number.
4. See chart.
5. Ex. Cte. Min., January 18, 1911, #239.
6. A. I. du Pont to T. C. du Pont, January 27, 1911, 472.
7. A. I. du Pont to Ex. Cte., January 27, 1911, 472.
8. *Ibid.*
9. T. C. du Pont to A. I. du Pont, February 3, 1911, 472.
10. P. S. du Pont to T. C. du Pont, February 1, 1911, 472.
11. A. I. du Pont to T. C. du Pont, February 7, 1911, 472.
12. T. C. du Pont to J. A. Haskell, January 13, 1914, 472.
13. *Ibid.*
14. T. C. du Pont to P. S. du Pont, January 25, 1911, 472.
15. P. S. du Pont to T. C. du Pont, January 30, 1911, 472.
16. P. S. du Pont to T. C. du Pont, March 31, 1911, PSduP 418.
17. T. C. du Pont to H. M. Barksdale, February 12, 1914, 472.
18. T. C. du Pont to P. S. du Pont, February 4, 1911, 472.
19. P. S. du Pont to Ex. Cte., January 31, 1911, 472.
20. Data and quotations, above, P. S. du Pont and A. J. Moxham to Ex. Cte., August 7, 1912, #274.
21. J. A. Haskell to Ex. Cte., August 19, 1912, #276.
22. Ex. Cte., Min., September 10, 1912, #276.
23. Ex. Cte. Min., November 12, 1912, #279; Ex. Cte. Min., December 11, 1912, #282.
24. T. C. du Pont to P. S. du Pont, August 24, 1914, PSduP 15.
25. Undated draft written in 1914 on Organization, by T. C. du Pont, 472.
26. P. S. du Pont to T. C. du Pont, August 28, 1914, PSduP 418.
27. T. C. du Pont to Directors of E. I. du Pont de Nemours Powder Company, December 2, 1913, 472.
28. Lewis J. Horowitz and Boyden Sparks, *The Towers of New York, The Memoirs of a Master Builder* (New York: Simon and Schuster, 1937), pp. 102–103, 133.
29. Roscoe Carlyle Buley, *The Equitable Life Assurance Society of the United States: One Hundredth Anniversary History: 1859–1959* (New York: Appleton-Century-Crofts, 1959), p. 185.

30. T. C. du Pont to Directors, E. I. du Pont de Nemours Powder Company, December 2, 1913, 472.
31. Undated draft written in 1914 on Organization, 472.
32. P. S. du Pont, "Coleman Sells Out," written in 1941, PSduP B–54.
33. At the time Pierre du Pont bought Peirce's Park, it consisted of 202 acres. He renamed his property "Longwood" and added surrounding land to the estate until at the time of his death it totaled more than 1,000 acres. The data on the Longwood story are found in PSduP 516–2, and the housekeeping details are in P. S. du Pont's book of instructions for the Longwood staff in the same file.
34. Ex. Cte. Min., March 20, 1911, #269.
35. P. S. du Pont, "Coleman Sells Out," PSduP B–54.
36. Ex. Cte. Min., February 9, 1914, #303.
37. T. C. du Pont to Ex. Cte., February 7, 1914, notation VOID written on this document, as this is not the final organization plan which was also written on the same day, 472.
38. T. C. du Pont to Ex. Cte., February 7, 1914, 472.
39. *Ibid.*
40. *Ibid.*
41. Ex. Cte. Min., February 9, 1914, #303.
42. P. S. du Pont, "Coleman Sells Out," PSduP B–54.
43. Undated draft written in 1914 on Organization by T. C. du Pont, 472.
44. T. C. du Pont to H. M. Barksdale, February 12, 1914, 472.
45. P. S. du Pont, "Coleman Sells Out," PSduP B–54.
46. P. S. du Pont's "The Schism of 1914–1915," written 1943, PSduP B–53, and "Coleman Sells Out," PSduP B–54.
47. P. S. du Pont, "Coleman Sells Out," PSduP B–54.
48. *Ibid.*
49. T. C. du Pont to P. S. du Pont, March 17, 1915, PSduP 15.
50. P. S. du Pont, "Coleman Sells Out," PSduP B–54.
51. Handwritten letter, T. C. du Pont to P. S. du Pont, August 24, 1914 (Pierre notes on the bottom of this letter that he thinks it was written on the 26th), PSduP 15.
52. T. C. du Pont to P. S. du Pont, August 27, 1914, handwritten but unsigned, PSduP 15.
53. P. S. du Pont to T. C. du Pont, August 28, 1914, Defendants' Exhibit No. 15. *In the United States District Court for the Northern District of Illinois, Eastern Division, United States of America, Plaintiff vs. E. I. du Pont de Nemours and Company, General Motors Corporation, United States Rubber, Christiana Securities Company, Delaware Realty & Investment Corporation, Pierre du Pont, Irénée du Pont, Defendants.* Civil Action, No. 49C–1071.
54. I. du Pont to T. C. du Pont, August 11, 1914, Du Pont Co. Records.
55. P. S. du Pont to the Board of Directors, E. I. du Pont de Nemours Powder Company, September 11, 1914, 472.
56. *Ibid.*
57. P. S. du Pont, "Coleman Sells Out," 1941, PSduP B–54.
58. I. du Pont to T. C. du Pont, August 11, 1914, Du Pont Co. Records.

CHAPTER 12. The Cousins Split

1. "The Schism of 1914–1915," 1943. Eleutherian Mills Historical Library, Pierre S. du Pont Manuscripts, Series B (memoirs written by P. S. du Pont), File 53. Hereafter, PSduP B– plus the file number.
2. *Ibid.*

3. Quotations from John W. Donaldson, *Caveat Venditor, A Profile of Coleman du Pont* (privately printed, 1964), p. 38.

4. "1965 Profitability Rankings," *Forbes*, Vol. 97, No. 1 (January 1, 1966), pp. 10–11, 147–150.

5. Abraham D. H. Kaplan, *Big Enterprise in a Competitive System* (Washington, D. C.: Brookings Institution, 1954), p. 144. George S. Gibb and Evelyn H. Knowlton, *The Resurgent Years, 1911–1927* (New York: Harper & Brothers, 1956), p. 7.

6. "The Schism of 1914–1915," 1943, PSduP B–53.

7. Pierre S. du Pont, Memoirs, 1941, PSduP B–54.

8. *Ibid.*

9. *Philip F. du Pont et al. v. Pierre S. du Pont et al., Record of Final Hearings, U.S. District Court, District of Delaware, No. 340, in Equity.* Hereafter Philip du Pont Suit, Final Hearing, Complainants' Exhibit No. 29, Vol. IV, 237.

10. Philip du Pont Suit. Final Hearing, Testimony of Pierre S. du Pont, Vol. III, 926–927.

11. Pierre S. du Pont, Memoirs, 1941, PSduP B–54.

12. P. S. du Pont to T. C. du Pont, March 8, 1915, PSduP 15.

13. Marquis James, *Alfred I. du Pont, The Family Rebel* (Indianapolis: Bobbs-Merrill, 1941), pp. 281–283.

14. R. Carlyle Buley, *The Equitable Life Assurance Society of the United States, 1859–1964* (New York: Appleton-Century-Crofts, 1967), Vol. II, pp. 817–823.

15. T. C. du Pont to P. S. du Pont, January 6, 1915, Philip du Pont Suit, Final Hearing, Vol. II, 626.

16. Philip du Pont Suit, Final Hearing, Testimony of Pierre S. du Pont, Vol. II, 616–617: T. C. du Pont to P. S. du Pont, December 7, 1914, Vol. II, 475–476; T. C. du Pont to P. S. du Pont, December 14, 1914, Vol. II, 476.

17. Philip du Pont Suit, Final Hearing, Testimony of Pierre S. du Pont, Vol. II, 617.

18. This equaled a rate of 6.4%, A. I. du Pont to P. S. du Pont, December 14, 1914; A. I. du Pont to P. S. du Pont, December 21, 1914, Philip du Pont Suit, Final Hearing. Vol. I, 165–166.

19. Pierre S. du Pont, Memoirs, 1941, PSduP B–54.

20. *Ibid.*

21. T. C. du Pont to P. S. du Pont, December 7, 1914, Philip du Pont Suit, Final Hearing, Vol. IV, 291.

22. "The Schism of 1914–1915," 1943, PSduP B–53.

23. *Ibid.* Finance Committee Minutes, Meeting number 56, December 23, 1914; hereafter, Fin. Cte. Min. plus date and number.

24. Philip du Pont Suit, Final Hearing, Pierre S. du Pont Testimony, July 10, 1916, Vol. II, 621.

25. Fin. Cte. Min., Special Meeting, December 23, 1914, #56.

26. Philip du Pont Suit, Final Hearing. Testimony of Alfred I. du Pont, June 28, 1916, Vol. I, 175–178.

27. Philip du Pont Suit, Final Hearing, Testimony of Pierre S. du Pont, July 10, 1916, Vol. II, 620.

28. P. S. du Pont to T. C. du Pont, January 4, 1915, Philip du Pont Suit, Final Hearing, Vol. IV, 295.

29. Philip du Pont Suit, Final Hearing, T. C. du Pont to P. S. du Pont, January 6, 1915, Vol. II, 296–297.

30. Both quotations: Philip du Pont Suit, Final Hearing, P. S. du Pont to T. C. du Pont, January 9, 1915, Vol. IV, 298.

31. Philip du Pont Suit, Final Hearing, T. C. du Pont to P. S. du Pont, January 15, 1915, Vol. IV, 305 (telegram); T. C. du Pont to P. S. du Pont, January 17, 1915, Vol. IV, 310;

T. C. du Pont to P. S. du Pont, January 19, 1915, Vol. IV, 311.

32. Philip du Pont Suit, Final Hearing, P. S. du Pont to T. C. du Pont, January 18, 1915, Vol. IV, 310–311.

33. Philip du Pont Suit, Final Hearing, T. C. du Pont to P. S. du Pont, January 19, 1915, Vol. IV, 311.

34. Pierre S. du Pont, Memoirs, 1941, PSduP B–54.

35. Philip du Pont Suit, Final Hearing, P. S. du Pont to T. C. du Pont, January 25, 1915, Vol. IV, 315.

36. P. S. du Pont to T. C. du Pont, January 28, 1915, cited *in the United States District Court for the Northern District of Illinois, Eastern Division, United States of America, Plaintiff vs. E. I. du Pont de Nemours and Company, General Motors Corporation, United States Rubber, Christiana Securities Company, Delaware Realty & Investment Corporation, Pierre S. du Pont, Lammot du Pont, Irénée du Pont, Defendants, Civil Action No. 49C–1071.* Hereafter cited as *U.S. v. Du Pont, GM et al. Defendants' Exhibit, 28.* Also PSduP 15.

37. *Ibid.*

38. P. S. du Pont to T. C. du Pont, February 5, 1915, PSduP 15.

39. T. C. du Pont to P. S. du Pont, February 13, 1915, PSduP 15.

40. Memorandum in pencil by P. S. du Pont, undated but written at the time of the Philip du Pont Suit, PSduP 15.

41. *Ibid.*

42. Telegram, L. L. Dunham to T. C. du Pont, February 17, 1915, Defendants' Exhibit, 33, *U.S. v. Du Pont, GM et al.*

43. Memorandum in pencil by P. S. du Pont, undated but written at the time of the Philip du Pont Suit. PSduP 15. Note: A voting pool would have been an arrangement whereby Coleman, Pierre, and Alfred I. would have agreed to vote their stock as a bloc. As in the electoral college, a majority of shares could determine the vote of the entire unit.

44. Philip du Pont Suit, Final Hearing, Testimony of Pierre S. du Pont, July 12, 1916. Vol. II, 763.

45. *Ibid.*, July 10, 1916, 660–661.

46. Telegram, P. S. du Pont to T. C. du Pont, February 20, 1915, PSduP 15.

47. Telegram, T. C. du Pont to P. S. du Pont, February 20, 1915, PSduP 15.

48. Telegram, P. S. du Pont to T. C. du Pont, February 20, 1915, PSduP 15.

49. Telegram, P. S. du Pont to T. C. du Pont, February 20, 1915, PSduP 15. This was the third telegram to go from P.S. to T.C. on this date.

50. Note that last-minute adjustments cause final figures to differ slightly from those in Pierre du Pont's telegram of confirmation. All data in the above paragraphs are in the correspondence of Pierre S. du Pont and were used as exhibits and testimony in the Philip du Pont Suit.

51. Data of the Philip du Pont Suit, Testimony, and Exhibits.

52. Telegram, P. S. du Pont to T. C. du Pont, February 20, 1915, PSduP 15.

53. Memorandum in pencil, undated, but written at the time of the Philip du Pont Suit, PSduP 15.

54. Philadelphia *Public Ledger*, February 28, 1915.

55. Philadelphia *Public Ledger*, March 1, 1915.

56. Philip du Pont Suit, Final Hearing, Testimony of Pierre S. du Pont, July 11, 1916, Vol. II, 696–697.

57. Telegram, William du Pont to P. S. du Pont, March 2, 1915. PSduP 15.

58. Philip du Pont Suit, Final Hearing, Cross Examination of Pierre S. du Pont by J. Johnson, July 12, 1916, Vol. II, 838.

59. James, *Alfred I. du Pont*, p. 277.

60. Philadelphia *Public Ledger*, February 28, 1915.
61. Clipping, Cleveland *Plain Dealer* (date torn off), enclosed with letter, W. A. Donaldson to P. S. du Pont, early February 1916, PSduP 639–1.
62. Pierre recorded his thoughts along these lines in his memoirs in 1941, PSduP B–54.
63. A. I. du Pont to T. C. du Pont, February 16, 1915, PSduP 15.
64. Agreement, March 19, 1915, between Du Pont Securities Company and Irénée du Pont et al., Defendants' Exhibit No. 45, *U.S. v. Du Pont, GM et al.*
65. Copies of the letters sent by P. S. du Pont to H. F. du Pont and others, April 16, 1915, PSduP 15.
66. For James's interpretation, *Alfred I. du Pont*, pp. 275–276.
67. All quotations from Philip du Pont Suit, Final Hearing, Testimony of Pierre S. du Pont, Vol. II, 698–699. Additional data from memorandum written in pencil by P. S. du Pont, undated but written at the time of the trial, PSduP 15.
68. P. S. du Pont to Board of Directors of E. I. du Pont de Nemours Powder Company, March 5, 1915, PSduP 15.
69. *Ibid.*
70. Memorandum of Discussion at Special Meeting of Board of Directors of the Powder Company, March 6, 1915, PSduP 15, reprinted in Philip du Pont Suit, Final Hearing, Vol. IV, 492–509, especially 508. The four individuals who voted against Irénée are not listed, but they were Alfred I., William, Francis I., and Frank Connable.
71. P. S. du Pont to T. C. du Pont, March 8, 1915, PSduP 15.
72. Adjourned meeting E. I. du Pont de Nemours Powder Company, March 10, 1915. Reprinted in Philip du Pont Suit, Final Hearing, Vol. IV, 510–520.
73. Eugene E. du Pont to P. S. du Pont, May 20, 1915; H. F. du Pont to P. S. du Pont, April 29, 1915, both PSduP 15.
74. Copy of memorandum in pencil by P. S. du Pont after "call from Francis I. du Pont 5/10/15," PSduP 15.
75. Philip F. du Pont to P. S. du Pont, May 5, 1915, PSduP 15.
76. Eugene du Pont to P. S. du Pont, May 20, 1915; Archibald M. L. du Pont to P. S. du Pont, May 17, 1915; E. Paul du Pont to P. S. du Pont, May 10, 1915; Alexis I. du Pont to P. S. du Pont, May 6, 1915; Ernest du Pont to P. S. du Pont, May 12, 1915; all in PSduP 15.
77. P. S. du Pont to W. Hilles, September 17, 1915, PSduP 15.
78. *Ibid.* Both quotations.
79. P. S. du Pont to G. C. Todd, September 18, 1915, PSduP 15.
80. Philip du Pont Suit, Final Hearing, Testimony of Pierre S. du Pont, July 12, 1916, Vol. II, 783–784.
81. The others were Coyne, R. R. M. Carpenter, Haskell, H. F. Brown, J. P. Laffey, the Powder Company, the E. I. du Pont de Nemours & Co., and the Du Pont Securities Company.
82. Philadelphia *Public Ledger*, December 10, 1915.
83. *Ibid.*, January 11, 1916.
84. Mrs. Alexis I. du Pont to P. S. du Pont, December 21, 1915, PSduP 639.
85. James, *Alfred I. du Pont*, p. 279.
86. Philadelphia *Evening Ledger*, December 30, 1915, clipping in PSduP 639–1.
87. Philadelphia *Evening Ledger*, December 29, 1915, clipping in PSduP 639–1.
88. P. S. du Pont to Board of Directors E. I. du Pont de Nemours & Company, and to the Board of Directors of the Powder Company, January 8, 1916, PSduP 639.
89. *Ibid.*
90. Minutes of the Board of Directors, January 10, 1916, indicate that the decision to remove Alfred I. du Pont "upon being put to a vote . . . was carried; all the directors voted in

the affirmative except Francis I. du Pont who voted in the negative and Mr. Alexis I. du Pont who desired to be recorded as not voting, giving as his reason for this action that he felt that not sufficient notice had been given to the directors for the full consideration of this subject." Alfred I. du Pont's decision to join Philip du Pont announced in Philadelphia *Public Ledger,* January 12, 1916.

91. P. S. du Pont et al. to Stockholders, E. I. du Pont de Nemours & Company, and E. I. du Pont de Nemours Powder Company, January 18, 1916, PSduP 639.
92. Philadelphia *Public Ledger,* March 14, 1916.
93. *Ibid.,* January 20, 1916.
94. Clipping (date missing, but in February 1916), PSduP 639-1; also, P. S. du Pont to W. A. Donaldson, February 11, 1916, PSduP 639.
95. Philadelphia *Evening Ledger,* January 25, 1916, clipping PSduP 639-1.
96. Quotations from P. S. du Pont to Cyrus H. K. Curtis, February 4, 1916, PSduP 639.
97. P. H. Whaley to P. S. du Pont, February 10, 1916, PSduP 639.
98. Philadelphia *Public Ledger,* June 28, 1916.
99. Philip du Pont Suit, Final Hearing, Complainants' Exhibit, 27, Vol. IV, 199–209. "Daily balances on deposit with banking institutions."
100. Philadelphia *Public Ledger,* July 21, 1916.
101. *Ibid.,* January 20, 1916.
102. *Ibid.,* July 27, 1916.
103. *Ibid.*
104. Philip du Pont Suit, Final Hearing, Cross Examination by J. Johnson of Pierre S. du Pont. Vol. II, 770–772.
105. P. S. du Pont to H. M. Barksdale, July 10, 1916, PSduP 639.
106. *Ibid.*
107. Philip du Pont Suit, Final Hearing, Testimony of Pierre S. du Pont, July 11, 1916, Vol. II, 741–750. Also Complainants' Exhibit, 27, Vol. IV, 199–210.
108. P. S. du Pont to T. C. du Pont, March 8, 1915, PSduP 15.
109. Philip du Pont Suit, Opinion of Court, by Hon. J. Whitaker Thompson, U.S. District Judge, April 12, 1917, p. 70.
110. *Ibid.,* pp. 73–74.
111. *Ibid.,* p. 75.
112. Wilmington *Morning News,* April 13, 1917.
113. P. S. du Pont to G. Carter, April 18, 1917, PSduP 639.
114. P. S. du Pont to J. R. Ensign, May 1, 1917; J. R. Ensign to P. S. du Pont, May 2, 1917, PSduP 639.
115. I. du Pont to A. F. du Pont, April 20, 1917, PSduP 639.
116. *Ibid.*
117. P. S. du Pont to H. G. Haskell, H. F. Brown, Caroline Ramsay (the widow of Major W. G. Ramsay), F. G. Tallman, J. P. Laffey, William Coyne, Irénée du Pont, Lammot du Pont, J. J. Raskob, R. R. M. Carpenter, April 4, 1917, PSduP 15.
118. *Ibid.*
119. Caroline J. Ramsay to P. S. du Pont, April 15, 1917, PSduP 639.
120. P. S. du Pont to E. S. Pillsbury, August 14, 1917; also B. Nields to P. S. du Pont, April 14, 1917, PSduP 639.
121. P. S. du Pont to H. M. Barksdale, August 21, 1917; P. S. du Pont to H. McGowan Esq., July 3, 1917, PSduP 639.
122. P.S. du Pont to H. M. Barksdale, August 21, 1917, PSduP 639.
123. Printed copy of T. C. du Pont to Directors of the E. I. du Pont de Nemours & Co., May 11, 1917, PSdup 639.
124. P. S. du Pont to B. Clark, September 14, 1917, PSduP 639.

125. *W. Saulsbury v. E. I. du Pont de Nemours & Co. et al.*, 1075–50.
126. John K. Winkler, *The Du Pont Dynasty* (New York: Reynal & Hitchcock, 1935), p. 295.
127. W. Saulsbury to May Saulsbury (Mrs. Willard Saulsbury), September 19, 1917, PSduP 639.
128. P. S. du Pont to May Saulsbury, September 25, 1917, PSduP 639.
129. P. S. du Pont to May Saulsbury, September 28, 1917, PSduP 639.
130. May Saulsbury to P. S. du Pont, October 1, 1917, PSduP 639.
131. P. S. du Pont to May Saulsbury, October 3, 1917, PSduP 639.
132. Analysis of vote, October 10, 1917, PSduP 639.
133. 312,587 shares against Alfred I. du Pont to 140,574 shares for him, Appendix to Report of Special Master, Philip du Pont Suit, Record After Final Hearing, Vol. VI, 1967–2029.
134. Wilmington *Morning News,* November 15, 1917.
135. Evening Edition, *Wall Street Journal,* March 20, 1918.
136. *No. 2382. In the United States Circuit Court of Appeals for the Third Circuit, Philip du Pont, and others, Plaintiffs Below, Plaintiffs in Error, vs. Pierre S. du Pont, and others, Defendants Below, Defendants in Error, before Buffington and McPherson, Circuit Judges, and Haight, District Judge, Opinion of Court by Buffington, J., Filed March 6, 1919,* 78–79.
137. P. S. du Pont to G. S. Graham, March 7, 1919, PSduP 639.
138. P. S. du Pont to I. du Pont, March 7, 1919, PSduP 639.

CHAPTER 13. Supplying the Allies

1. E. I. du Pont de Nemours Powder Co. Annual Report, 1914, p. 7.
2. E. I. du Pont de Nemours & Co., Annual Report, 1918, p. 30.
3. Hearings Before the Special Committee Investigating the Munitions Industry, United States Senate, Seventy-third Congress Pursuant to S. Res. 106, Part 5, Sept. 1934, p. 1031. (Hereafter Nye Committee Investigation.)
4. H. C. Engelbrecht and F. C. Hanighen, *Merchants of Death, A Study of the International Armament Industry* (New York: Dodd, Mead, 1934), pp. 180–181.
5. Alden Hatch, *Remington Arms in American History* (New York: Rinehart, 1956), pp. 214, 217.
6. Harold F. Williamson, *Winchester, the Gun That Won the West* (Washington, D.C.: Combat Forces Press, 1952), p. 220.
7. Hatch, *Remington Arms,* pp. 222–224.
8. Williamson, *Winchester,* p. 233.
9. *Ibid.,* p. 234.
10. *Ibid.,* pp. 234–235.
11. EIDPDN&CO., Ex. Cte. Min., April 27, 1916, #54; April 28, #55; May 1, #56; May 8, #58; June 5, #65. The Du Pont Company was legally reorganized in 1915. On October 1, 1915, the E. I. Du Pont de Nemours & Co. (referred to in notes as EIDPDN & Co.) was created to replace the E. I. Du Pont de Nemours Powder Co. (EIDPDN Powder Co.).
12. Winchester Arms data, unless otherwise noted, Williamson, *Winchester,* 217–249.
13. Williamson, *Winchester,* p. 218.
14. *Ibid.,* pp. 232, 234.
15. *Ibid.,* p. 226.
16. *Ibid.,* p. 232.
17. EIDPDN & Co., Ex. Cte. Min., April 27, 1916, #54; April 28, #55; May 1, #56.
18. C. L. Fry, *Prices of Explosives,* War Industries Board Price Bulletin No. 56 (Washington: Government Printing Office, 1919), pp. 7–8.

19. EIDPDN & Co., *Annual Report for 1918*, p. 9.
20. Finance Committee and H. M. Barksdale to EIDPDN Powder Co. Executive Committee, May 2 and 5, 1914, Du Pont Co. Records.
21. Nye Committee Investigation, Part 5, Testimony of Pierre S. du Pont, pp. 1030–1031.
22. P. S. du Pont to J. A. Haskell, March 4, 1916, Du Pont Co. Records. In 1916 Connable became a vice-president with advisory capacities similar to Haskell and Patterson. Because Tallman continued to be the real head of Purchasing, even after Connable moved over from Black Powder, it was he rather than Connable who received the Du Pont Securities bonus.
23. EIDPDN Powder Co., Ex. Cte. Min., August 24, 1914, #317.
24. Marquis James, *Alfred I. du Pont, The Family Rebel*, (Indianapolis: Bobbs-Merrill, 1941), pp. 129–130. Also William Dutton, *Du Pont: One Hundred and Forty Years* (New York: Scribner, 1951), pp. 161–163.
25. P. S. du Pont to T. C. du Pont, September 4, 1903, Eleutherian Mills Historical Library, T. Coleman du Pont Papers, Accession 1075, Box 32H. Hereafter 1075 plus the box number.
26. EIDPDN Powder Co., Fin. Cte. Min., February 4 and 5, 1914, #6.
27. Pierre S. du Pont, "Coleman Sells Out," Eleutherian Mills Historical Library, Papers of Pierre S. du Pont, Personal Memoirs Series B, File 54. Hereafter PSduP B– plus the file number. Also EIDPDN Powder Co. Fin. Cte. Min., August 20, 1914, #42. Irénée du Pont to H. J. Mitchell, August 10, 1914, courtesy of W. J. Reader.
28. P. S. du Pont to T. C. du Pont, February 5, 1915, cited *in the United States District Court for the Northern District of Illinois, Eastern Division, United States of America, Plaintiff, vs. E. I. du Pont de Nemours and Company, General Motors, United States Rubber, Delaware Realty and Investment Corporation, Pierre S. du Pont, Lammot du Pont, Irénée du Pont, Defendants. Pierre S. du Pont Deposition,* Exhibit #30. Hereafter *U.S. v. E. I. du Pont, General Motors et al.*
29. Nye Committee Investigations, Part 5, p. 1054.
30. Address of Colonel E. G. Buckner, Vice-President in Charge of Military Sales, E. I. du Pont de Nemours & Co. On the Relations of the Du Pont American Industries to the War, Du Pont American Industries Sales Convention, Atlantic City, N.J., June 19, 1918, p. 7, Du Pont Co. Records.
31. Above contract data from *Philip F. du Pont et al. vs. Pierre S. du Pont et al.*, Record of Final Hearing, U.S. District Court, District of Delaware, No. 340, in Equity (hereafter Philip du Pont Suit, Final Hearing), Vol. IV, 211–235.
32. Pierre S. du Pont to General Sales Convention, Atlantic City, June 18, 1918. Du Pont Co. Records.
33. EIDPDN Powder Co., Fin. Cte. Min., October 14, 1914, #49.
34. EIDPDN Powder Co., Fin. Cte. Min., November 11, 1914, #52. For taxation purposes the Du Pont Co. could not amortize until after the war.
35. P. S. du Pont to T. C. du Pont, January 25, 1915, Philip du Pont Suit, Final Hearing, Vol. IV, 316.
36. *Ibid.*
37. EIDPDN & Co., *Annual Report, 1918*, p. 30.
38. Nye Committee Investigation, December 13, 1934, Part 13, p. 2324.
39. *Ibid.*, pp. 2990–3005.
40. *Ibid.*, pp. 2928, 2929, 3003.
41. *Ibid.*, pp. 2928–2929, and Part 15, December 17, 18, 1934, p. 3856.
42. P. S. du Pont to T. C. du Pont, January 9, 1915, Philip du Pont Suit, Final Hearing, Vol. IV, 300.

43. *Ibid.*

44. P. S. du Pont to T. C. du Pont, January 14, 1915, Philip du Pont Suit, Final Hearing, Vol. IV., 307.

45. *Ibid.*, P. S. du Pont to T. C. du Pont, January 25, 1915, Vol. IV, 314.

46. Report, Treasurer to Fin. Cte., July 17, 1919, Du Pont Co. Records.

47. EIDPDN Powder Co., Fin. Cte. Min., September 29, 1915, #89.

48. Summary of Treasurer to Fin. Cte., December 27, 1918, Du Pont Co. Records.

49. EIDPDN & Co., Fin. Cte. Min., November 21, 1917, #80.

50. EIDPDN & Co., Fin. Cte. Min., February 9, 1916, #18.

51. EIDPDN & Co., Fin. Cte. Min., May 31, 1916, #29.

52. EIDPDN & Co., Fin. Cte. Min., June 2, 1916, #30.

53. Treasurer to Fin. Cte., December 27, 1918, Du Pont Co. Records.

54. *Ibid.*

55. EIDPDN & Co., Fin. Cte. Min., May 21, 1917, #59.

56. EIDPDN & Co., Fin. Cte. Min., June 2, 1917, #66.

57. EIDPDN & Co., Fin. Cte. Min., July 11, 1917, #69.

58. EIDPDN & Co., Fin. Cte. Min., November 21, 1917.

59. Treasurer to Finance Cte., December 27, 1918, Du Pont Co. Records.

60. Arthur Pine Van Gelder and Hugo Schlatter, *History of the Explosives Industry in America* (New York: Columbia University Press, 1927), pp. 810, 811.

61. *Ibid.*, pp. 592, 593.

62. For example, on February 5, 1915, Pierre du Pont approved an appropriation exceeding $4,180,000, which the Executive Committee did not formally approve until February 10, 1915, EIDPDN Powder Co., Fin. Cte. Min., #59.

63. Nye Committee Investigation, Part 15, December 17 and 18, 1934, p. 3856; also, Ernest R. May, *The World War and American Isolation 1914–1917* (Chicago: Quadrangle Paperbacks edition, 1966), pp. 343–344.

64. EIDPDN Powder Co., Fin. Cte. Min., October 28, 1914, #50.

65. EIDPDN Powder Co., Ex. Cte. Min., January 11, 1915, #342.

66. EIDPDN Powder Co., January 24, 1915, #348.

67. EIDPDN Powder Co., Ex. Cte. Min., January 11, 1915, #342.

68. EIDPDN Powder Co., Ex. Cte. Min., March 22, 1915, #360.

69. EIDPDN Powder Co., Ex. Cte. Min., March 8, 1915, #358, May 3, 1915, #371.

70. P. S. du Pont to Editor, New York *World*, October 20, 1916, Du Pont Co. Records.

71. EIDPDN & Co., Ex. Cte. Min., February 12, 1917, #118; April 9, 1917, #129; April 18, 1917, #131.

72. EIDPDN Powder Co., Ex. Cte. Min., July 28, 1915, #391; EIDPDN Powder Co., Fin. Cte. Min., July 28, 1915, #81.

73. EIDPDN Powder Co., Ex. Cte. Min., July 6, 1915, #385.

74. EIDPDN & Co., Ex. Cte. Min., May 15, 1916, #59.

75. EIDPDN & Co., Ex. Cte. Min., June 5, 1916, #65.

76. EIDPDN & Co., Ex. Cte. Min., May 8, 1916, #58.

77. EIDPDN & Co., Ex. Cte. Min., May 15, 1916, #59.

78. EIDPDN & Co., Ex. Cte. Min., November 20, 1916, #73.

79. May, *The World War and American Isolation*, pp. 362–363.

80. EIDPDN & Co., Ex. Cte. Min., July 8, 1916, #73.

81. EIDPDN & Co., Ex. Cte. Min, August 14, 1916, #81.

82. EIDPDN & Co., *Annual Report, 1918*, p. 4.

83. *Ibid.*

84. EIDPDN & Co., *Annual Report, 1919*, p. 16.

85. EIDPDN & Co., *Annual Report*, 1918, p. 4, and Alfred D. Chandler, Jr., *Strategy and*

*Structure: Chapters in the History of the Industrial Enterprise* (Cambridge: M.I.T. Press, 1962), pp. 83–91.

86. EIDPDN Powder Co., Ex. Cte. Min., November 23, 1914, #333; December 21, 1914, #339.

87. EIDPDN & Co., Ex. Cte. Min., September 29, 1915, #408.

88. Excerpt from Report of the Executive Committee to the Board of Directors, September 22, 1915, Du Pont Co. Records.

89. EIDPDN & Co., Ex. Cte. Min., November 15, 1915, #15.

90. EIDPDN & Co., Ex. Cte. Min., January 17, 1916, #26.

91. EIDPDN & Co., Ex. Cte. Min., January 24, 1916, #27.

92. EIDPDN, Ex. Cte. Min., August 14, 1916, #81.

93. EIDPDN & Co., Ex. Cte. Min., February 5, 1917, #117.

94. Unsuccessful negotiations to purchase Fels Naptha in Ex. Cte. Min., December 11, 1916, #102; January 22, 1917, #115; February 5, 1917, #117; unsuccessful negotiations to purchase O'Bannon Co. (artificial leather) February 21, 1916, #14; March 2, 1916, #37; March 13, 1916, #39; March 14, 1916, #40; March 20, 1916, #41; March 23, 1916, #43; April 19, 1916, #50.

95. EIDPDN & Co., Ex. Cte. Min., May 14, 1917, #136; July 2, 1917, #145.

96. EIDPDN & Co., *Annual Report, 1918*, p. 22.

97. EIDPDN & Co., Ex. Cte. Min., December 12, 1916, #103.

98. EIDPDN & Co., Ex. Cte. Min., March 5, 1917, #123.

99. EIDPDN & Co., Ex. Cte. Min., June 18, 1917, #143.

100. EIDPDN & Co., Ex. Cte. Min., August 17, 1917, #153; Nye Committee Investigation, September 1934, Part 5, p. 1080.

101. Development Department to Ex. Cte., "The Manufacture of Paints and Varnishes at Parlin," August 11, 1916, Du Pont Co. Records.

102. EIDPDN & Co., *Annual Report, 1918*, p. 22.

103. EIDPDN & Co., Ex. Cte. Min., December 11, 1916, #102; January 15, 1917, #114.

104. EIDPDN & Co., Ex. Cte. Min., June 11, 1917, #142.

105. EIDPDN & Co., Ex. Cte. Min., November 30, 1917, #175.

106. Development Committee Report, April 17, 1918, Du Pont Co. Records. Also Ex. Cte. Min., April 19, 1918, #203; September 3, 1918, #234.

107. EIDPDN & Co., Ex. Cte. Min., June 4, 1917, #141; September 30, 1918, #242.

108. EIDPDN & Co., Ex. Cte. Min., September 18, 1916, #87.

109. EIDPDN & Co., Ex. Cte. Min., March 26, 1917, #126; July 2, 1917, #145.

110. EIDPDN & Co., Ex. Cte. Min., August 21, 1916, #82.

111. EIDPDN & Co., Ex. Cte. Min., January 22, 1917, #115.

112. EIDPDN & Co., Ex. Cte. Min., May 5, 1917, #123.

113. For Pierre's earlier financial program see Chapter 10, pp. 294–296, of the present book.

114. EIDPDN & Co., *Annual Report, 1915*, p. 1.

115. *Ibid.*, 2.

116. Although formal dissolution of the Powder Company did not take place until May 22, 1926, by January 1916 the Powder Company had distributed most of its assets and had ceased to be a factor.

117. Raskob gave his reasons in the following words:

American industrial corporations usually have large bond issues ranking ahead of their preferred stocks and after the payment of bond interest the margin of earnings to secure the preferred stock dividend is generally comparatively small. These preferred stocks have no preference except as against common stock, and it is usual to give the preferred shares a vote in order that they may have a voice in the maintenance of their slender margin of safety. . . . England has apparently recognized the necessity for corporations to be in position to issue securities with some degree of elasticity and under Act of Parliament passed in 1863, with various amendments since that time, corporations have been granted the right to issue 'Debenture Stocks.' A few of these Debenture stocks are secured by mortgage, but as a rule the security is a floating charge on the entire properties and earnings. . . . J. J. Raskob to Finance Committee of Du Pont Powder Company, July 24, 1915, Du Pont Co. Records.

118. All quotations from this section come from John J. Raskob to Finance Committee of the Du Pont Powder Co., July 24, 1915, Du Pont Co. Records.

## CHAPTER 14. The American War Effort: Negotiations Begun

1. Bowring & Co. to J. B. D. Edge, January 24, 1910; Pierre to R. de Trégomain, February 2, 1910; P.S. du Pont to Bowring & Co. (dictated by P. S. du Pont's secretary H. Rodney Sharp), January 26, 1910; all PSduP 668. Also diary of Alice B. du Pont, PSduP 628–12.
2. P. S. du Pont to C. Hagen, January 6, 1913; P. S. du Pont to Cunard Steamship Co., January 6 and 14, 1913; Cunard Steamship Co. to P. S. du Pont, January 10, 1913, PSduP 668.
3. T. C. du Pont to Alice Belin, June 26, 1915, PSduP 628–3.
4. See announcement and newspaper clippings in PSduP 628–3.
5. Alice du Pont Diary, PSduP 628–12.
6. P. S. du Pont to Mrs. A. Lentilhon Foster, January 18, 1916; P. S. du Pont to Marguerite Bidermann, January 18, 1916, PsduP 346.
7. *Comité d'Assistance en Alsace-Lorraine* to P. S. du Pont, February 16, 1916, PSduP 346.
8. Dr. E. Lambert, Chief Physician of the 268th Territorial Infantry, to P. S. du Pont, May 6, 1916 (translation); M. Berthias to P. S. du Pont, June 9, 1916, PSduP 346.
9. P. S. du Pont to the *Comité Central de la Colonie Française,* November 6, 1916, PSduP 346.
10. I. du Pont to P. S. du Pont, February 10, 1917, PSduP 18.
11. Arthur S. Link, *Woodrow Wilson and the Progressive Era, 1910–1917* (New York: Harper & Brothers, 1954), pp. 174–190. Augustus P. Gardner was Senator Henry Cabot Lodge's son-in-law.
12. P. S. du Pont to Mrs. Lindon Bates, January 31, 1916, Du Pont Co. Records.
13. P. S. du Pont to R. M. La Follette, September 7, 1916, Du Pont Co. Records.
14. *Ibid.*
15. P. S. du Pont to R. M. La Follette, November, 2, 1916, March 23, 1917, Du Pont Co. Records.
16. P. S. du Pont to R. M. La Follette, March 23, 1917, Du Pont Co. Records.
17. P. S. du Pont to E. I. du P. de N. & Co., Ex. Cte., June 23, 1916, #66.
18. P. S. du Pont to C. Kitchen, July 8, 1916, Eleutherian Mills Historical Library, Irénée du Pont Papers, Accession 228, File 392, hereafter 228 plus the file number.
19. W. Saulsbury to P. S. du Pont, April 27, 1918, Du Pont Co. Records.
20. *Hearings Before Special Committee Investigating the Munitions Industry, United States Senate, Seventy-third Congress, Pursuant to S. Res. 206 (Nye Committee),* Part 5, September 1934, p. 1045. Hereafter cited Nye Committee Investigation.
21. E. I. du Pont de Nemours & Co., *Annual Report, 1916,* pp. 5–6. Note: Pierre himself dictated these pages.
22. E. I. du Pont de Nemours & Co., *Annual Report, 1919,* pp. 14–17.
23. Nye Committee Investigation, Part 5, September, 1934, pp. 1045–1049.
24. R. R. M. Carpenter to E. I. du Pont de Nemours & Co., Ex. Cte., March 31, 1916, #48.
25. *Ibid.*

26. P. S. du Pont to the Editor, New York *World,* October 20, 1916, Du Pont Co. Records, for this and quotations immediately below.
27. J. D. Anderson to F. B. Barnitz, January 19, 1917, PSduP 668.
28. Link, *Wilson and the Progressive Era,* p. 268.
29. P. S. du Pont to I. du Pont, February 4, 1917, PSduP 18.
30. Link, *Wilson and the Progressive Era,* pp. 266–282.
31. I. du Pont to P. S. du Pont, February 10, 1917, PSduP 18.
32. P. S. du Pont to B. M. Baruch, March 21, 1917, Du Pont Co. Records, for above data and quotations.
33. P. S. du Pont to N. D. Baker, March 22, 1917, quotation and data following it, Du Pont Co. Records.
34. Benedict Crowell and Robert Forrest Wilson, *How America Went to War—The Armies of Industry,* Vol. 1 (New Haven: Yale University Press, 1921), p. xvi.
35. *Ibid.,* pp. xvi–xviii.
36. W. Crozier to E. I. du Pont de Nemours & Co., April 6, 1917, Du Pont Co. Records.
37. F. A. Scott to P. S. du Pont (telegram), April 14, 1917, Du Pont Co. Records.
38. Memorandum of I. du Pont on his trip to Washington, April 15, 1917., Du Pont Co. Records.
39. J. E. Hoffer to F. A. Scott, April 21, 1917, Nye Committee Investigation, Part 13, December 13, 1934, pp. 3130–3132.
40. E. G. Buckner to F. A. Scott, July 30, 1917, Nye Committee Investigation, Part 13, December 13, 1934, pp. 3133–3134.
41. Memorandum of I. du Pont on his trip to Washington, April 15, 1917, Du Pont Co. Records.
42. P. S. du Pont to N. D. Baker, November 23, 1917, Du Pont Co. Records.
43. Nye Committee Investigation, Part 14, December 14, 1934, p. 3209.
44. P. S. du Pont to N. D. Baker, November 23, 1917, Du Pont Co. Records.
45. P. S. du Pont to D. Willard, December 1, 1917, Du Pont Co. Records.
46. P. S. du Pont to E. G. Buckner, November 1, 1917, Nye Committee Investigation, Part 13, December 13, 1934, pp. 3144–3145.
47. E. G. Buckner to Chief of Ordnance, October 8, 1917, Nye Committee Investigation, Part 13, December 13, 1934, pp. 3137–3137; P. S. du Pont to Board of Directors, E. I. du Pont de Nemours & Co., November 26, 1917, Du Pont Co. Records.
48. Note the base on air-dried powder was to be 47 cents per pound. These data and the two paragraphs, above, from the contract signed by Pierre S. du Pont for his company and William Crozier, Chief of Ordnance, October 25, 1917, Nye Committee Investigation, Part 13, December 13, 1934, pp. 3141–3143.
49. E. A. Hamilton to War Department, Gun Division, Office of Chief of Ordnance, October 21, 1917, Nye Committee Investigation, Part 13, December 13, 1934, pp. 3140–3141.
50. H. M. Pierce, Memorandum, Investigation and securing sites for smokeless powder plants by E. I. du Pont de Nemours & Co. in the interests of the United States Government, December 13, 1917, Du Pont Co. Records.
51. Memorandum, P. S. du Pont to H. M. Pierce, undated but probably November 1, 1917, Du Pont Co. Records.

CHAPTER 15. The American War Effort: Negotiations Completed

1. N. D. Baker to P. S. du Pont (telegram), October 31, 1917, from the files under the jurisdiction of the Secretaries to the Committees Division of the E. I. du Pont de Nemours & Co. Hereafter, Du Pont Co. Records.

2. *Hearings Before the Special Committee Investigating the Munitions Industry, United States Senate, Seventy-third Congress, Pursuant to S. Res. 206 (Nye Committee), Part 14, December 14, 1934, p. 3188.* Hereafter cited Nye Committee Investigation.
3. Minutes of the War Industries Board, October 11, 1917, Nye Committee Investigation, Part 13, December 13, 1934, pp. 3139–3140.
4. *Ibid.,* October 16, 1917, Part 13, December 13, 1934, p. 3140.
5. *Ibid.,* October 31, 1917, Part 13, December 13, 1934, p. 3144.
6. Nye Committee Investigation, Part 14, December 14, 1934, p. 3177.
7. R. S. Brookings to N. D. Baker, November 7, 1917, Nye Committee Investigation, Part 14, December 14, 1934, p. 3264.
8. P. S. du Pont to W. Crozier, November 2, 1917, Nye Committee Investigation, Part 13, December 13, 1934, pp. 3147–3150, for the data and quotations given above.
9. See revised unofficial contract between War Department and the Du Pont Company, W. Crozier to E. I. du Pont de Nemours & Co., November 19, 1917, Du Pont Co. Records.
10. R. S. Brookings to N. D. Baker, November 14, 1917, Nye Committee Investigation, Part 14, December 14, 1934, pp. 3269–3270.
11. *Ibid.*
12. Louis J. Horowitz and Boyden Sparks, *The Towers of New York* (New York: Simon and Schuster, 1937), p. 177.
13. Nye Committee Investigation, Part 14, December 14, 1934, p. 3188.
14. P. S. du Pont to N. D. Baker, November 23, 1917, Du Pont Co. Records.
15. Data and quotations given above, from D. Willard to N. D. Baker, November 26, 1917, Nye Committee Investigation, Part 14, December 14, 1934, p. 3274.
16. W. Crozier to P. S. du Pont (telegram), November 27, 1917. Also P. S. du Pont to W. Crozier, November 27, 1917, Du Pont Co. Records.
17. P. S. du Pont to the Board of Directors of the E. I. du Pont de Nemours & Co., November 28, 1917, PSduP 639.
18. *Ibid.*
19. *Ibid.*
20. Extracts from the minutes of the Meeting of the Board of Directors of E. I. du Pont de Nemours & Co., November 28, 1917, Nye Committee Investigation, Part 14, December 14, 1934, p. 3276.
21. P. S. du Pont to D. Willard, December 1, 1917, Nye Committee Investigation, Part 14, December 14, 1934, pp. 3277–3280.
22. P. S. du Pont to N. D. Baker, December 10, 1917, Nye Committee Investigation, Part 14, December 14, 1934, pp. 3281–3282.
23. N. D. Baker to E. I. du Pont de Nemours Powder [sic] Co. Attention Pierre S. du Pont, December 12, 1917, Nye Committee Investigation, Part 14, December 14, 1934, p. 3286.
24. *Ibid.*
25. P. S. du Pont to Board of Directors, E. I. du Pont de Nemours & Co., January 10, 1918, PSduP 418.
26. P. S. du Pont to E. G. Buckner, January 9, 1918, PSduP 418.
27. Horowitz and Sparkes, *Towers of New York,* pp. 177–178.
28. P. S. du Pont to E. G. Buckner, January 9, 1918, PSduP 418.
29. H. M. Pierce's memorandum to P. S. du Pont, January 14, 1918, PSduP 418.
30. P. S. du Pont to E. G. Buckner, January 9, 1918, PSduP 418.
31. C. H. Cramer, *Newton D. Baker, A Biography* (Cleveland: World Publishing, 1961), p. 145.
32. The public testimony before Chamberlain's committee, copied with appropriate comments by Du Pont officials, can be found in PSduP 418.
33. P. S. du Pont to N. D. Baker, January 11, 1918, and the *Times* clipping in PSduP 418.

34. P. S. du Pont to N. D. Baker, January 16, 1918, Nye Committee Investigation, Part 14, December 14, 1934, p. 3288.
35. N. D. Baker to P. S. du Pont, January 19, 1918, PSduP 418.
36. See memorandum of understanding between Jackling et al. for the government and Pierre du Pont et al. for the Du Pont Co., January 24, 1918, Ex. Cte. report, for meeting #190.
37. "Construction of Explosives Plant near Nashville, Tenn." (Jackling Contract), Nye Committee Investigation, Part 14, December 14, 1934, pp. 3289–3296.
38. *Who's Who in America,* Vol. XI, 1920–1921 (Chicago: A. N. Marquis, 1920), p. 2130.
39. L. F. Abbott to J. Odell, March 4, 1918, PSduP 418.
40. P. S. du Pont to J. Odell, March 13, 1918, PSduP 418.
41. H. M. Pierce to P. S. du Pont, January 22, 1940, PSduP B–46.
42. H. M. Pierce to P. S. du Pont, February 8, 1918, PSduP 418.
43. W. S. Gregg to P. S. du Pont and J. J. Raskob, February 26, 1918, PSduP 418.
44. H. M. Pierce to P. S. du Pont, March 5, 1918, PSduP 418.
45. Contract between the Du Pont Engineering Co. and Chief of Ordnance, March 23, 1918, Nye Committee Investigation, Part 14, December 14, 1934, pp. 3297–3305.
46. P. S. du Pont to E. N. Carpenter, June 22, 1918, PSduP 418.
47. H. M. Pierce to P. S. du Pont, January 22, 1940, PSduP B–46.
48. Exhibits #1169 and #1170 of the Du Pont Co. for the Nye Committee Investigation, Part 14, December 14, 1934, pp. 3310–3312.
49. Nye Committee Investigation, Part 14, December 14, 1934, pp. 3222–3224.
50. Actual savings were slightly lower, since the last three units of Old Hickory's nine were abandoned prior to their completion.
51. Data from H. M. Pierce to P. S. du Pont, June 22, 1940, PSduP B–46.
52. Du Pont Powder Co., *Annual Report, 1914,* p. 6; E. I. du Pont de Nemours & Co., *Annual Report, 1918,* p. 29.
53. See informal, nonnumbered meeting, E. I. du Pont de Nemours & Co., Minutes of Ex. Cte., April 29, 1919; Alfred D. Chandler Jr., *Strategy and Structure* (Cambridge: M.I.T. Press, 1962), pp. 67–68.
54. Informal, nonnumbered meeting, E. I. du Pont de Nemours & Co., Ex. Cte. Min., April 29, 1918.
55. Report of Pierre S. du Pont to Board of Directors, April 7, 1919; Chandler, *Strategy and Structure,* p. 67.
56. By assets, A. D. H. Kaplan, *Big Enterprise in a Competitive System* (Washington D.C.: Brookings Institution, 1954), p. 148.

CHAPTER 16. Initial Involvement, 1915–1917

1. J. J. Raskob to H. P. Scott, February 12, 1914, DTX DP 37; and J. J. Raskob to W. A. Brady, February 28, 1914, DTX DP 38. All citations using GTX (Government Trial Exhibits), DTX DP (Defense Trial Exhibits, Du Pont) and DTX GM (Defense Trial Exhibits, General Motors) are from the exhibits of the Du Pont-General Motors Antitrust Suit, which was instituted in 1949. *In the United States District Court for the Northern District of Illinois, Eastern Division, Civil Action No. 49C–107, United States of America, Plaintiff, vs. E. I. du Pont de Nemours and Company, General Motors Corporation United States Rubber, Christiana Securities, Delaware Realty & Investment Corporation, Pierre S. du Pont, Irénée du Pont, et al., Defendants.* Hereafter cited as Du Pont–GM Antitrust Suit, except that Government Trial Exhibits will be cited only as GTX, and Defense Trial Exhibits as DTX plus indication of the defendant(s)—DTX DP for Du Pont and DTX GM for General Motors. Often these same documents are in the Pierre S. du Pont or the John J. Raskob collections at the Eleutherian Mills Historical Library. Where they are

in both or one of these collections, and also in the antitrust suit records, the notes here cite to the antitrust suit because of the availability of these printed exhibits in major libraries. On October 21, 1915, Pierre held just under 2,300 shares of General Motors, 2,205 in his own name, and the rest in the accounts of younger du Ponts whose accounts he handled as trustee, Central Trust Company to P. S. du Pont, October 2, 1915, the Eleutherian Mills Historical Library, Papers of Pierre S. du Pont, Longwood Manuscripts, Group 10, File 624. Hereafter cited by PSduP plus the identifying file number. Nearly all these shares had been purchased in 1914, P. S. du Pont, "Net Purchases of Common Stock of General Motors Company, Chevrolet Motor Company and General Motors Corporation, 1914-1917," GTX 114.

2. Lawrence H. Seltzer, *A Financial History of the American Automobile Industry* (Boston: Houghton Mifflin, 1928), pp. 173-174.

3. *Ibid.*

4. *Deposition of Pierre S. du Pont* in the Du Pont-GM Antitrust Suit, May 21, 1951, p. 121.

5. The story of the meeting is covered in *Deposition of Pierre S. du Pont*, pp. 123-127; P. S. du Pont to J. A. Haskell, September 17, 1915, GTX 116. The quotations in this paragraph are from this letter; see also *Automotive Topics*, September 25, 1915, pp. 447-448.

6. J. J. Storrow to P. S. du Pont, September 20, 24, 28, October 5, 1915, PSduP 624. The quotation is from the September 20 letter. See also Henry G. Pearson, *Son of New England—James Jackson Storrow* (Boston: Thomas Todd Co., 1932), p. 140.

7. P. S. du Pont to J. J. Storrow, September 22, October 5, 1915. The quotation is from the first letter. In the second, Pierre suggested that Alfred Wiggin, president of the Chase National Bank and a new director, become Chairman of the Finance Committee, PSduP 624.

8. W. C. Durant to P. S. du Pont, September 25, 1915, PSduP 624.

9. P. S. du Pont to J. A. Haskell, September 17, 1915, GTX 116.

10. A clipping from *Automotive Topics*, November 1915, PSduP 624.

11. P. S. du Pont to J. A. Haskell, September 17, 1915, PSduP 624.

12. The details of the trip are indicated in P. S. du Pont to J. J. Storrow, October 25, 1915, DTX DP 39; P. S. du Pont to C. W. Nash, November 9, 1915; P. S. du Pont to E. W. Clark, November 10, 1915, both in PSduP 624; and diary of Alice du Pont, November 2-5, PSduP 628-12.

13. Discussed in letters to Nash and Clark, cited in note 12 above; also P. S. du Pont to L. G. Kaufman, L. Belin, J. A. Haskell, all on November 6, 1915; also in a copy, undated, "Proposed Duties of the Executive Committee—General Motors Corporation" and "Proposed Duties of the Finance Committee—General Motors Corporation," all in PSduP 624.

14. Pearson, *Storrow*, p. 139. The warnings of Clark and Leland are indicated in E. W. Clark to P. S. du Pont, December 29, 1915, PSduP 624.

15. The story of the founding and early growth of General Motors is summarized in more detail in Seltzer, *Financial History*, pp. 145-172; Pearson, *Storrow*, pp. 123-140; Alfred P. Sloan, Jr., edited by John McDonald with Catharine P. Stevens, *My Years with General Motors* (Garden City, N.Y.: Doubleday, 1964), pp. 3-11; Alfred D. Chandler, Jr., *Strategy and Structure—Chapters in the History of Industrial Enterprise* (Cambridge: M.I.T. Press, 1962), pp. 115-122; Arthur Pound, *The Turning Wheel—The Story of General Motors Through Twenty-Five Years, 1908-1933* (Garden City, N.Y.: Doubleday, 1934); ch. 10 is a discursive account of the corporation's early years.

16. The figures on sales and those in the next paragraph on Chevrolet sales come from Seltzer, *Financial History*, pp. 151, 173-174, respectively.

17. P.S. du Pont to E. W. Clark, November 13, 1915; P. S. du Pont to L. G. Kaufman, November 19, 1915; P. S. du Pont to C. W. Nash, November 18, 1915; P. S. du Pont to A. H. Wiggin, November 22, 1915; L. G. Kaufman to P. S. du Pont, December 1, 1915, all in PSduP 624.

18. This and the following quotations are from P. S. du Pont to E. W. Clark, November 13, 1915, PSduP 624.

19. Clipping in Detroit *Free Press,* December 21, 1915, sent to Pierre by E. W. Clark and from *Newsletter* of C. W. Harris & Company, New York stockbrokers, and clipping, New York *Daily Journal,* December 24, 1914, all in PSduP 624 accompanied by a handwritten, unsigned note—"This kind of thing naturally perhaps troubles Mr. Nash and disturbs many others in the organization." See also Seltzer, *Financial History,* pp. 173–174.

20. E. W. Clark to P. S. du Pont, December 22, 1915, PSduP 624.

21. This and the following quotation are from P. S. du Pont to E. W. Clark, December 27, 1915; Clark in reply to P. S. du Pont, December 29, 1915, PSduP 624.

22. Memorandum "handed P. S. du Pont by L. G. Kaufman on Friday, March 17, 1916 in New York," P. S. du Pont to L. G. Kaufman, March 21, 1916, DTX DP 40, J. J. Raskob to W. C. Durant, April 10, 1916, GTX 120; W. C. Durant to J. J. Raskob, April 12, 1916; J. J. Raskob to W. C. Durant, April 13, 1916; J. J. Raskob to E. G. Buckner, April 13, 1916; J. J. Raskob to Chatham & Phoenix Bank, April 18, 1916, all in the Eleutherian Mills Historical Library, Papers of John J. Raskob, Accession 473. Hereafter cited as Raskob Papers.

23. "Statement received over phone from New York, December 27, 1915." The revised printed version of the statement, December 31, 1915, and received by Pierre, January 3, 1916, both in PSduP 624. Important, too, is E. W. Clark to P. S. du Pont, December 29, 1915; J. J. Raskob to C. S. Sabin, A. H. Wiggin, and S. Prosser, December 30, 1915. On the same day Raskob wired an officer of Lee, Higginson in Boston saying, "Regret we cannot sign at this time I will see you Tuesday." (The officer's name was F. W. Allen.) These two telegrams are in the Raskob Papers.

24. Seltzer, *Financial History,* pp. 176–177.

25. C. W. Nash to P. S. du Pont, April 18, 1916; P. S. du Pont to Board of Directors, General Motors, April 28, 1916, PSduP 624.

26. The letters of resignation of all these men are in PSduP 624. Of the original bankers' slate, only Charles H. Sabin remained.

27. Pearson, *Storrow,* pp. 142–144.

28. This and the following quotation are from P. S. du Pont to W. C. Durant, May 9, 1916, GTX 122; J. J. Raskob to Lammot Belin, May 6, 1916, GTX 119; J. J. Raskob to W. C. Durant, May 3, 9, 25, June 3, 1916, Raskob Papers. Raskob held 1,215 shares.

29. The information on Durant's activities comes from *Annual Report of General Motors Company, July 31, 1916* (dated September 30, 1916). Chandler, *Strategy and Structure,* p. 123; and the report of E. L. Bergland and H. M. Pierce, September 12, 1918, PSduP 624; *Automotive Industries* (August 30, 1917), 37:390.

30. P. S. du Pont to W. C. Durant, August 25, 1916, PSduP 624.

31. "Draft of By-Laws of General Motors Corporation," prepared by Standish Bachus, and attached letter, S. Bachus to W. C. Durant, October 11, 1916, from author's notes made while doing research for Alfred P. Sloan, Jr., *My Years with General Motors.* Citations whose source is not otherwise indicated are from these notes.

32. Notices of these meetings are in the P. S. du Pont and Raskob Papers and show that members, including Chairman of the Board, were usually notified only a day or two before the date of the meeting.

33. Seltzer, *Financial History,* pp. 178–179. The shares in the new corporation were to be exchanged for old at the rate of 1 share of 6% preferred in the new for 1.3 shares of 7%

of preferred in the old, and 5 shares of the new for 1 share of the old common stock (both old and new common having the same par value of $100). A total of 199,803 of the preferred and 825,590 common were taken by the exchange.

34. Seltzer, *Financial History*, pp. 179–180. This figure is before deducting $1.5 million for depreciation. In the same period, value of inventories rose from $25.1 million to $46.6 million, and assets from $22.7 million to $55.9 million. The annual reports for the year give more details on this performance.

35. Seltzer, *Financial History*, pp. 183–188; Sloan, *My Years with General Motors*, pp. 23–24. For their part in organizing the company, Durant and Kaufman received a bonus of 9,000 shares.

36. J. J. Raskob to L. G. Kaufman, December 1, 1916, January 30, 1917, Raskob Papers. Also in DTX DP 43.

37. J. J. Raskob to W. C. Durant, December 1, 1916, in Raskob Papers. Durant's reply of December 12, 1916, is GTX 118, and Raskob's follow-up letter of December 20, 1916, is in Raskob Papers.

38. These and the two following quotations are from J. J. Raskob to W. C. Durant, January 30, 1917, DTX DP 43; also, J. J. Raskob to W. C. Durant, January 24, 1917, DTX DP 42; J. J. Raskob to L. G. Kaufman, February 1, 1917, Raskob Papers.

39. Raskob made this point by saying that "the same relationship to a share of General Motors stock paid therefore as to assets of the General Motors Corporation to its common stock now outstanding." "Suggested plan for Amalgamation of Chevrolet Motor Company and General Motors Corporation," typewritten, undated, in PSduP 624.

40. J. J. Raskob to W. C. Durant, March 6, 10, 1917; W. C. Durant to J. J. Raskob, March 10, 1917; R. I. Eads to J. J. Raskob, March 13, 1917, all in Raskob Papers. W. C. Durant to P. S. du Pont, undated telegram, March 1917; P. S. du Pont to J. T. Smith, March 26, 1917, all in PSduP 624.

41. J. J. Raskob to J. T. Smith, May 21, 1917, Raskob Papers; Haskins & Sells to J. J. Raskob, May 25, 1917, PSduP 624.

42. Haskins & Sells to J. J. Raskob, June 29, 1917; also June 25, July 5, 1917, all in Raskob Papers.

43. J. T. Smith to J. J. Raskob, June 2, 1917, Raskob Papers; W. C. Durant to P. S. du Pont, April 17, 1917; P. S. du Pont to M. J. Martin, June 29, 30, 1917, PSduP 624.

44. These issues are mentioned in W. C. Durant to P. S. du Pont, May 7, 1917; P. S. du Pont to W. Saulsbury, May 8, 9, 1917; P. S. du Pont to A. F. Polk, May 8, 1917; and reply of both to Pierre, May 9, 1917, in PSduP 624. Also, J. J. Raskob to W. C. Durant, July 30, 1917, DE 78. (Defense Exhibits, not Defense Trial Exhibits—the former were used in the District Court trial and not in the final Supreme Court trial.)

45. P. S. du Pont to W. C. Durant, June 6, 1917; P. S. du Pont to L. G. Kaufman, June 6, 1917, both in PSduP 624; W. C. Durant to J. J. Raskob, July 27, 1917; W. C. Durant to J. W. Fordney; W. C. Durant to J. J. Raskob, September 26, 1917, all three in Raskob Papers.

46. General Motors Corporation Stockmarket Prices, June 30, 1917–December 31, 1917, DTX 127.

47. J. J. Raskob to W. C. Durant, July 24, 30, 1917, DE 76, 78; W. C. Durant to J. J. Raskob, July 28, 1917, DE 77; *Deposition of Pierre S. du Pont*, May 21, 1951, pp. 142–143; J. J. Raskob to J. T. Smith, September 27, 1917, Raskob Papers. While direct evidence is hard to find, it seems clear that at this time and then again in the summer and fall of 1920 Durant was using his General Motors stock as collateral for speculative securities. An old friend of Durant, Howard F. Hansell, Jr., told one of the authors on September 20, 1969, that he recalled that Durant had bought heavily in Industrial Fibre Corporation of America, Wilcox Oil & Gas, and other nonautomotive concerns.

48. W. C. Durant to J. J. Raskob, telegram, August 12 (1917), and letter, September 12, 1917, GTX 149 and DE 80.
49. J. J. Raskob to W. C. Durant, July 30, 1917, Raskob Papers.
50. J. J. Raskob to W. C. Durant, October 24, 1917, DE 81.
51. This and the following three quotations are from J. H. McClement to members of Finance Committee, General Motors Corporation (L. G. Kaufman, Chairman, J. J. Raskob, P. S. du Pont, W. C. Durant), November 9, 1917, DE 82; also, J. J. Raskob to W. C. Durant, November 6, 1917, Raskob Papers.
52. P. S. du Pont to L. G. Kaufman, November 15, 1917, PSduP 624. Pierre refers to the majority of the Finance Committee approving this proposal, so, apparently, McClement too voted against this move.
53. Agreement between W. C. Durant and P. S. du Pont, undated, DTX DP 45. The quotation in the next paragraph is from this agreement. The Motors Security Company was to purchase 162,000 shares of Chevrolet at 120 and 120,000 shares of General Motors at 100 from Durant and 100,000 shares of Chevrolet from Pierre at 120. It would then issue an equivalent amount of 7% nonvoting preferred and common stock. Pierre was to obtain his block of 100,000 shares of Chevrolet or the equivalent in General Motors by buying 52,800 shares of Chevrolet from Durant for $5,115,000, of which a small part would be paid in notes. Of the remaining 47,200 Pierre had about 20,000 and would purchase the remainder in the open market; that is, he would buy about 27,000 shares for about $3.0 million. Durant would then sell 4,170,000 shares of Motors Security for $4,500,000 cash to Pierre in order that Durant and Pierre would have equal ownership in the common stock of the new Motors Security Company and which, in turn, would control Chevrolet and which, in turn, would control General Motors.
54. See pp. 407–423 of the present book.
55. Durant's movements during this period can be traced in J. J. Raskob to W. C. Durant, November 26, 30, 1917; W. C. Durant to J. J. Raskob, November 28, 1917; and N. Hofheimer to J. J. Raskob, November 30, and Raskob's reply, December 1, all in Raskob Papers.
56. Outlined in Treasurer to Finance Committee (Du Pont Company), December 19, 1917, GTX 124.
57. On December 7, 1917, Raskob wired Durant, "Please call me twelve o'clock tomorrow. Sending Special Delivery to you tonight." On December 17, Raskob wired Durant again that meetings on the plan were to be held during the coming week. Both telegrams are in Raskob Papers.
58. J. J. Raskob to W. C. Durant, December 17, 1917, Raskob Papers.
59. Minutes of Finance Committee (Du Pont Company), December 20, 1917 (#84). Minutes, reports, and other records of the I. E. du Pont de Nemours & Company are located at the company's headquarters in Wilmington, Delaware, under the supervision of the Secretaries to the Committee Division. Hereafter cited as Du Pont Co. Records.
60. Minutes of Special Joint Meeting, Executive and Finance Committees, December 20, 1917 (#178, Executive Committee), Du Pont Co. Records. In addition to members of both committees, A. Felix du Pont attended. The minutes did not record the arguments, merely listing who voted negatively. In an interview in November 1957, Donaldson Brown told the author that Raskob's report of December 19 was directed at the Carpenters of the Development Department who were expected to be the most opposed to the proposal. P. S. du Pont, in his *Deposition* of May 21, 1951, p. 155, gives the arguments offered by men like Felix du Pont and Col. Buckner. Lammot du Pont as head of the Miscellaneous Manufacturing Department had, like the Carpenters, his eye on usages for funds closer to the company's basic lines. For example, he strongly favored the purchase of the Winchester Repeating Arms Company, Minutes of Executive Committee, Febru-

ary 1, 1918 (#192), also Minutes of Joint Meeting of Executive (#217) and Finance Committee (#110), June 25, 1918, Du Pont Co. Records.

61. Minutes of Adjourned Special Joint Meeting of Executive and Finance Committees, December 21, 1917, GTX 124.

62. Minutes of Special Meeting of Board of Directors of E. I. du Pont de Nemours & Company, December 21, 1917, DTX DP 47.

63. Treasurer to Finance Committee (Du Pont Company), December 19, 1917. The following eight quotations are from this report, GTX 124.

64. These are best expressed in *Deposition of Pierre S. du Pont*, May 21, 1951, pp. 155–156. The quotation at the end of the paragraph is from this testimony.

65. Minutes of Joint Meeting of Finance and Executive Committees, January 21, 1918 (#91 Finance Committee, #188 Executive Committee); Treasurer to Finance Committee, January 17, 1918 (#9981), DTX DP 48. The Army Ordnance and the Navy Department's Bureau of Ordnance agreed to make a 25% advance payment in cash on the signing of a contract, and so such contracts released reserve funds for the purchase.

66. Pierre made this point in his *Deposition* of May 21, 1951, p. 161.

67. This and the following figures are from the report of Treasurer to Finance Committee, March 8, 1918 (#10267), GTX 128; minutes of Finance Committee, March 13, 1918 (#98) and including report (#10267). Also important are minutes of Finance Committee, February 9, 1918 (#88), and February 27, 1918 (#96), Du Pont Co. Records.

68. L. G. Kaufman to J. J. Raskob, January 15, 1918, PSduP 624; P. S. du Pont to L. G. Kaufman, January 22, 1918; J. J. Raskob to W. C. Durant, January 23, 1914, GTX 129.

69. Treasurer to Finance Committee (Du Pont Company), March 8, 1918, GTX 128; minutes of meeting of General Motors Board of Directors, February 21, 1918, GTX 130. Barksdale, who was on the Chevrolet board, was to take his place on the General Motors board as soon as the former was "wound up." GTX 129.

70. J. J. Raskob to W. C. Durant, January 23, 1918, GTX 129. These letters of invitation are all in PSduP 624.

71. Raskob described the dinner in Treasurer to Finance Committee (Du Pont Company), March 8, 1918, GTX 128.

72. Minutes of meeting of Board of Directors, General Motors Corporation, February 21, March 21, 1918, GTX 130, 131.

73. On March 26 Raskob did send Durant "suggested rules of procedures for the Executive Committee." He also enclosed a "copy of our Appropriation Rules which contain much food for thought," Raskob Papers.

CHAPTER 17. Du Pont "Control" at General Motors, 1918–1920

1. "Chronological Growth of Longwood," prepared by Construction Division, January 1948, pp. 7–8, PSduP 516.

2. The charter of the Service Citizens is quoted in a letter from J. H. Odell to Mrs. P. S. du Pont, April 12, 1924, which provides an excellent summary of Pierre du Pont's educational enterprises, PSduP 628.

3. The information in this paragraph on war production comes from *Annual Report of General Motors Corporation for 1918*, pp. 1–12. Also, documents cited in notes 44 and 45 of Chapter 16.

4. P. S. du Pont to H. M. Barksdale, July 29, 1918, GTX 133.

5. Tractors and refrigerators are considered in Arthur Pound, *The Turning Wheel: The Story of General Motors Through Twenty–five Years, 1908–1933* (Garden City, N.Y.: Doubleday, 1934), ch. 12; Alfred P. Sloan, Jr., *My Years with General Motors*, (Garden City, N.Y.: Doubleday, 1964), p. 15; J. L. Pratt, *Direct Testimony*, p. 1403.

6. P. S. du Pont to H. M. Barksdale, July 29, 1918, GTX 133. Purchases indicated in this paragraph are mentioned in Lawrence H. Seltzer, *A Financial History of the American Automobile Industry* (Boston: Houghton Mifflin, 1928), pp. 184, 187–189; Pound, *The Turning Wheel*, ch. 12; and *Annual Report of General Motors Corporation for 1918*, pp. 12–13.

7. Seltzer, *Financial History*, pp. 180–182, outlines the Chevrolet-General Motors merger; also printed notice to stockholders, Chevrolet Motors Company, October 11, 1918, Raskob Papers; Treasurer to Finance Committee (Du Pont Company, December 19, 1917), GTX 124; also "History of the Du Pont Company's Investment in General Motors Corporation," August 17, 1921, GTX 166.

8. Statement to Chevrolet Motor Company stockholders, December 1, 1920, forwarded in letter from I. du Pont to F. D. Brown, December 27, 1920, Du Pont Co. Records.

9. United Motors purchase is outlined in Seltzer, *Financial History*, pp. 183–188; also, printed notice to stockholders of the United Motors Corporation, October 3, 1918, and January 18, 1919, PSduP 624. P. S. du Pont to H. M. Barksdale, June 29, 1918, describes Kaufman's protest that the exchange was unfair even though he made at least $4.0 million on the stock he received as a promoter's bonus, GTX 133.

10. These developments are indicated in Seltzer, *Financial History*, pp. 184–185; printed notice to stockholders of General Motors Corporation, August 15, 1918, November 25, 1918, Raskob Papers; P. S. du Pont to J. T. Smith, November 14, 1918, PSduP 624. There were two notices dated November 25. One was signed by Durant and the other by T. S. Merrill, Sec. The data in the paragraph are from the November 25 notice signed by Durant.

11. Seltzer, *Financial History*, pp. 185–187; P. S. du Pont to J. T. Smith, November 14, 1918; and printed notice to stockholders, November 25, 1918, signed by W. C. Durant, PSduP 624.

12. This and the following quotations are from J. J. Raskob, chairman, General Motors Finance Committee, December 12, 1918, GTX 134.

13. J. J. Raskob to Finance Committee, December 14, 1918, GTX 135; also, *Deposition of Pierre S. du Pont*, May 21, 1951, p. 186. Raskob proposed that the stock be issued at $120 a share and rights at $10 a share. The company would buy all the rights and then sell stock to stockholders or take up the shares itself.

14. Minutes of the Du Pont Company Finance Committee, December 17, 1918, #127; printed notice to common stockholders of General Motors Corporation, January 6, 17, 1919, PSduP 624. Notice to stockholders, Chevrolet Motor Company, January 18, 1919, Raskob Papers.

15. Raskob suggested specifically that the funds be taken from "the obsolescence fund that had been set aside during the war years."

16. The Du Pont Company acquired (through its Du Pont American Industries Inc.) 43,000 shares of General Motors common from the McLaughlin interests at $130 per share, for a total cost of $5.59 million. In addition, it retained from underwriting the larger issue, 65,597 shares at a total cost of $8,407,833 at the average price of $128.21 per share. J. J. Raskob to R. S. McLaughlin (telegram), February 3, 1919, Raskob Papers; Minutes of the Du Pont Finance Committee, February 26, 1919; "History of the Du Pont Company Investment in the General Motors Corporation," August 17, 1921, pp. 2–3, GTX 166.

17. J. J. Raskob to P. S. du Pont, J. Haskell, and others, April 7, 1919, Raskob Papers. This conversation did, however, encourage McGowan to have the Nobel company invest in the British-based automobile industry, William J. Reader, *Imperial Chemical Industries —A History*, Vol. I, *The Forerunners, 1870–1926* (Oxford: Oxford University Press, 1970), 383–384.

18. J. J. Raskob to F. W. Warner, April 7, 1919. The terms and the process of carrying out the sale are indicated in Seltzer, *Financial History*, pp. 192–193. Also, printed notice to stockholders, General Motors Corporation, May 20, 1919, Raskob Papers; P. S. du Pont to B. S. Dominick, July 8, 1919, PSduP 624.

19. The scope of the expansion of plant and facilities is outlined in an article describing a $37.4 million program in *Motor Age* (April 10, 1919).

20. This expansion program is summarized in Pound, *The Turning Wheel*, chapter 13; *Annual Report of General Motors Corporation for 1919*, p. 10; J. L. Pratt, *Direct Testimony*, in Du Pont–GM Antitrust Suit, pp. 1392–1396. Printed letter to stockholders of Chevrolet Motor Company, April 23, 1921, signed by P. S. du Pont, mentions Ball Brothers Glass Manufacturing Company holding 150,000 shares of General Motors, which were apparently given as part payment for the General Motors investment in that company, PSduP 624. The Dunlop Rubber Company was a British-based firm, and the purchase of its stock was made after consultation with Sir Harry McGowan. Possibly for this reason Pierre agreed to go on its board. See pp. 575–576, Chapter 22 of the present book; also Reader, *Imperial Chemical Industries*, I, 384.

21. Pound, *The Turning Wheel*, p. 288.

22. P. S. du Pont to F. J. Fisher, September 11, 1919, GTX 425; Seltzer, *Financial History*, pp. 217–218; a letter from the Fisher brothers and Louis and Aaron Mendelssohns to the General Motors Corporation, September 25, 1919; and P. S. du Pont to F. J. and C. T. Fisher, September 25, 1919, GTX 426 and 427.

23. T. A. Boyd, *Professional Amateur—The Biography of Charles Franklin Kettering* (New York: Dutton, 1957), pp. 117–119; *Automotive Industries* (April 22, 1920), 42:980; A. P. Sloan to J. J. Raskob, July 25, 1919, Raskob Papers; and J. J. Raskob to General Motors Finance Committee, August 22, 1919, PSduP 624.

24. *Deposition of Pierre S. du Pont*, May 21, 1951, p. 194; Sloan, *My Years with General Motors*, pp. 303–304; printed pamphlet "GMAC—Retail Financing Plan," which Raskob received in July 1919, describes well and briefly the activities of the Acceptance Corporation and lists its officers, Raskob Papers; also C. C. Cooper to P. S. du Pont, March 12, 17, 29, 1919; I. W. Seeley to P. S. du Pont, October 18, 1920. Haskell became the president of the General Motors Acceptance Corporation and other members of the General Motors Finance Committee including Pierre its directors. Two New Yorkers, Paul Fitzpatrick and Curtice C. Cooper, became its operating head and legal counsel respectively.

25. *Annual Report of General Motors Corporation for 1919*, pp. 7, 13; *Annual Report of General Motors Corporation for 1921*, p. 24; Sloan, *My Years with General Motors*, pp. 315–318; P. S. Steenstrup to P. S. du Pont, March 6, 1919, PSduP 624.

26. Sloan, *My Years with General Motors*, p. 317.

27. *Annual Report of General Motors Corporation for 1919*, pp. 9–11, 16; Seltzer, *Financial History*, p. 192.

28. Sloan, *My Years with General Motors*, pp. 27–28.

29. "History of the Du Pont Company's Investment in the General Motors Corporation," August 17, 1921, GTX 166; Minutes of Du Pont Company Finance Committee, August 4, 15, 1919, #147, #149, Du Pont Co. Records.

30. Seltzer, *Financial History*, pp. 194–195; "Printed Notice to Stockholders in the General Motors Corporation," November 20, 1919, January 10, 1920. This first is in PSduP 624, the second in PSduP 624–11.

31. Minutes of the Regular Quarterly Meeting of the Board of Directors of Du Pont American Industries, May 26, 1920, GTX 141.

32. Pierre makes his point strongly in the *Annual Report of E. I. du Pont de Nemours & Company for 1918*, p. 24.

33. E. L. Bergland to H. M. Pierce, September 12, 1918. The quotations in the next four paragraphs are from the Bergland report, PSduP 624.

34. J. A. Haskell to H. M. Pierce, December 26, 1918, and letters to Pierre, Irénée, and J. A. Haskell from H. M. Pierce, December 27, 1918, in which he outlined how his organization might carry out the General Motors' engineering work, Du Pont Co. Records.

35. A. P. Sloan to H. C. Harrison, January 12, 1920. In another letter to Harrison, December 30, 1919, on the value of the Du Pont engineering staff, Sloan praised "the wonderful capacity of the organization."

36. Memorandum from J. H. Squires, Wilmington, at request of W. C. Durant, December 1918; K. W. Zimmerschied to H. L. Barton, January 14, 1919.

37. J. H. Squires to A. P. Sloan, October 30, 1919; A. P. Sloan to J. H. Squires, November 10, 1919.

38. J. L. Pratt, *Direct Testimony*, pp. 1391–1395.

39. The Chemical Department's assistants became significant only after Kettering joined General Motors. The Du Pont researchers began to work with Kettering's assistants to develop a more effective antiknock gasoline, for example, C. M. Stine to C. F. Kettering, February 2, 1920, DTX DP 94; C. M. Stine to L. du Pont, May 1, 1920, DTX DP 95.

40. For example, in August 1918, the Du Pont Legal Department advised against the proposed purchase of Reo and of Scripps-Booth by General Motors, as they might be construed as a violation of Section 7 of the Clayton Act, P. S. du Pont to W. C. Durant, August 15, 1918.

41. R. R. M. Carpenter to Executive Committee (Du Pont Company), March 19, 1919, GTX 557.

42. J. L. Pratt, *Direct Testimony*, p. 1396; R. R. M. Carpenter to P. S. du Pont, February 18, 1919, DE GM 195. The two quotations are from the letter, above.

43. J. L. Pratt, *Direct Testimony*, p. 1401. Pratt remembers that Durant had three assistants at the end of 1919. Besides himself and K. W. Zimmerchied, there was a man named Wagner.

44. P. S. du Pont to W. C. Durant, January 2, 1920, PSduP 624.

45. P. S. du Pont to W. P. Chrysler, November 8, 1918; P. S. du Pont to Frank Turner, June 2, 1919; F. Turner to P. S. du Pont, May 13, 25, 1919; J. F. Porter to J. J. Raskob, May 3, 10, 1919, all in Raskob Papers. Raskob closed the May 10 letter which acknowledged a long one from Porter dealing with the weaknesses in the accounting and the administrative methods at Champion by saying, "Mr. du Pont and I are very interested . . . in the progress all you boys are making and sincerely hope that work continues to be as interesting as it has worked out to be."

46. This and the following quotations in this paragraph are from a printed circular, "General Motors Corporation—Bonus Plan," which was enclosed with a printed "Supplementary Notice of Special Meeting of Stockholders, August 20, 1918," Raskob Papers. At the same time the Finance Committee worked out a systematic plan of paying directors bonuses as well as compensations by establishing "a contractual relationship which is not subject to criticism in the same way as if the bonuses were awarded under the general scheme directly or indirectly by the Directors to themselves." J. A. Haskell to P. S. du Pont, September 4, 1918; P. S. du Pont to J. A. Haskell, September 19, 1918. PSduP 624.

47. A. P. Sloan to J. A. Haskell, July 16, 1918, DTX GM 27; also, J. A. Haskell to A. P. Sloan, July 16, 1918, DTX GM 26.

48. Undated printed circular, "General Motors Corporation—Employees' Savings and Investment Plan," 1919, PSduP 624.

49. P. S. du Pont to N. F. Doughterty, January 24, 1928, PSduP 624.

50. J. J. Raskob, Chairman of Finance Committee, to all officers of General Motors Corpora-

tion and subsidiary companies, July 11, 1919. The following quotations in this paragraph are from this letter, Raskob Papers.

51. A. P. Sloan to W. P. Chrysler, April 11, 1919; A. P. Sloan to C. F. Kettering, June 26, 1919.

52. Sloan, *My Years with General Motors*, pp. 49–50; also A. P. Sloan to W. C. Durant, March 5, 1918.

53. "Report of the Committee Appointed for the Purpose of Studying Inter-Divisional Business," undated. The report is discussed in Sloan, *My Years with General Motors*, p. 50.

54. Sloan, *My Years with General Motors*, pp. 119–121. A. P. Sloan to M. L. Prensky, August 30, 1920; "Advice of action on method of handling appropriations," October 2, 1920; and A. P. Sloan to P. S. du Pont, December 27 (dictated December 24), 1920.

55. Sloan, *My Years with General Motors*, pp. 45–55.

56. Sloan, *My Years with General Motors*, p. 31.

57. P. S. du Pont to A. P. Sloan, September 15, 1920, PSduP 624. This letter and Sloan's initial letter are presented in full in Sloan, *My Years with General Motors*, pp. 51–52.

58. Sloan, *My Years with General Motors*, p. 27; Chandler, *Strategy and Structure*, p. 126.

## CHAPTER 18. The Crisis, 1920

1. Alice B. du Pont Diary, January 13, 1920, PSduP 628-12.

2. S. Prosser to P. S. du Pont, January 10, 1920, PSduP 624.

3. S. Prosser to P. S. du Pont, January 20, 1920; J. J. Raskob to P. S. du Pont, January 23, 1920. For example, Prosser asked Raskob to recast the data to show what would happen if financing was done out of earnings and no more debentures were sold after the present offering. Raskob sent Pierre, as well as Prosser, a copy of his reply. J. J. Raskob to P. S. du Pont, January 23, 1920, PSduP 624.

4. Alice B. du Pont Diary, entries for January 23 to February 28, 1920, PSduP 628-12.

5. Alfred P. Sloan, *My Years with General Motors* (Garden City, N.Y.: Doubleday, 1964), p. 29.

6. This and the following three quotations are from J. J. Raskob to Finance Committee of the Du Pont Company, March 19, 1920, GTX 140; also Minutes of Quarterly Meeting of Board of Directors of Du Pont American Industries, May 26, 1920, GTX 141; and Alice B. du Pont Diary, March 20, 1920, PSduP 628-12. In these discussions with McGowan, Pierre and Raskob appeared to have stressed the value of the Nobel connection in helping General Motors to penetrate the British and other foreign markets, William V. Reader, *Imperial Chemical Industries, —A History*, Vol. I: *The Forerunners* (Oxford: Oxford University Press, 1970), 368.

7. Memorandum of M. D. Fisher to I. du Pont, June 4, 1920, Du Pont Co. Records.

8. W. A. P. John, "That Man Durant," *Motor* (January 1920), pp. 250–253; reprinted in Alfred D. Chandler, Jr., *Giant Enterprise: Ford, General Motors and the Automobile Industry* (New York: Harcourt, Brace & World, 1964), pp. 77–81.

9. An unsigned syndicate agreement, March 10, 1920, PSduP 624.

10. J. J. Raskob to W. C. Durant, April 16, 1920, Raskob Papers; D. Morrow to P. S. du Pont, January 17, 1920 (draft with corrections by George Whitney), PSduP 624.

11. E. R. Stettinius to P. S. du Pont, July 20, 1920, GTX 145. This was a reply to a letter Pierre wrote to Stettinius, as he did to all the other new board members, welcoming them to General Motors and thanking them for their assistance, PSduP 624.

12. Minutes of Quarterly Meeting of Board of Directors of Du Pont American Industries, May 26, 1920, GTX 141; W. C. Durant to J. P. Morgan & Company, June 2, 1920, GTX 142; H. McGowan to J. J. Raskob, June 25, 1920, Raskob Papers; printed letter, W. C.

Durant to holders of common stock, June 2, 1920, Raskob Papers.

13. I. du Pont to J. J. Raskob, May 21, 1920, GTX 143; also, I. du Pont to P. S. du Pont, May 1920, PSduP 624.

14. J. T. Smith to I. du Pont, July 1, 1920. The Du Pont Company's share of the syndicate was $1.0 million and then raised to $1.5 million, "History of Du Pont Company's Investment in General Motors Corporation, August 17, 1921," GTX 166.

15. H. McGowan to J. J. Raskob, June 4, 1920. Information for this paragraph comes from this letter and H. McGowan to J. J. Raskob, June 25, 29, July 6, 14, 27, 28, 1920; and J. J. Raskob to H. McGowan, June 30, July 6, 13, 16, all in Raskob Papers; and P. S. du Pont to J. J. Raskob, August 24, 1920, PSduP 418.

16. J. J. Raskob to P. S. du Pont, August 31, 1920, enclosing a letter of J. J. Raskob to L. Lankford (First Vice-President of Canadian Explosives, Ltd.), August 27, 1920; P. S. du Pont to H. McGowan, September 1, 1920, Raskob Papers; Finance Committee to Executive Committee, Du Pont American Industries, October 18, 1920; printed statement from P. S. du Pont to the stockholders of Chevrolet Motor Company, April 23, 1920, PSduP 624; "History of Du Pont Company's Investment in General Motors Corporation, August 17, 1921," GTX 166. When this financing was fully completed, the Nobel company held 609,428 shares of General Motors plus a block of 200,000 it took from CXL (while CXL still held somewhat more than 250,000 shares). H. McGowan to J. J. Raskob, January 12, 1926, Raskob Papers; and W. Carpenter to Finance Committee at Du Pont Company, October 15, 1925, GTX 170. Even the smaller block of stock taken by the British firm became, and remained throughout the twenties, the largest investment the Nobel company ever made in an outside undertaking. In fact, the shares of only one of its constituent firms had a higher value. Reader, *Imperial Chemical Industries*, I, 385–386, 421.

17. Of the total $64.0 million raised, $2.0 million went to the New York bankers as commissions and probably the same amount to the Nobel group, although the evidence is not clear on this point. Also, about 250,000 shares were not fully paid for by the end of 1920, Lawrence H. Seltzer, *Financial History of American Automobile Industry* (Boston: Houghton Mifflin, 1928), p. 197.

18. The story of the failure to control expenses for capital equipment and inventory is reviewed in Sloan, *My Years with General Motors*, pp. 29–31; and Alfred D. Chandler, Jr., *Strategy and Structure: Chapters in the History of the Industrial Enterprise* (Cambridge: M.I.T. Press, 1962), pp. 128–129.

19. *Annual Report of the General Motors Corporation for 1922*, p. 9.

20. *Ibid.*, pp. 9–10. The information for this paragraph comes from this report and the sections in the Sloan and Chandler studies cited in note 18 above. Nevertheless, in mid-October Durant was still assuring Raskob, and through him Pierre, that the inventories were under control and that all would be well by the end of the year, W. C. Durant to J. J. Raskob, October 13, 1920, PSduP 624.

21. Chandler, *Strategy and Structure*, pp. 128–129.

22. "That Man Durant," cited in Chandler, *Giant Enterprise*, p. 81.

23. This and the following quotations are from a letter Pierre wrote Irénée for the record dated November 26, 1920, DTX DP 50, reprinted in Chandler, *Giant Enterprise*, pp. 81–86. This letter and a draft of a letter to Pierre from Dwight Morrow of J. P. Morgan & Company with corrections by G. Whitney, January 17, 1921, PSduP 624, are the two basic sources for this account of the story of the events leading to Durant's departure. These long, separately, and independently written reports agree on all points but, of course, have quite different emphases. Also useful is the *Depositon of Pierre S. du Pont*, May 21, 1951, pp. 205–220. Unless otherwise indicated all quotations in the rest of this chapter are taken from the letter of Pierre to Irénée of November 26, 1920. The incident

is briefly referred to in Harold Nicolson, *Dwight Morrow* (New York: Harcourt, Brace & World, 1935), pp. 156–157.

24. D. W. Morrow to P. S. du Pont, January 17, 1921, PSduP 624.

25. On October 15, Pierre wrote young Walter J. Laird at the Durant Corporation, PSduP 418.

26. It was equivalent to 130,748 shares of old stock and for which Durant gave 95,000 shares of Chevrolet as collateral. The loan was specifically from the Du Pont American Industries Corporation, the holding company the Du Pont Company had set up to hold its General Motors stock, W. C. Durant and Du Pont American Industries, October 26, 1920, GTX 147.

27. Besides Morrow's comment on this point there is a letter from Pierre to Durant on November 8 in which Pierre protests strongly against the rumor that Durant was having the Durant Corporation solicit Delaware school teachers in the sale of its stock. Yet even here he protested because of the fact that Durant had placed him in "a very unfortunate position" as a member of the state school board.

28. J. J. Raskob to Thomas Hildt, November 11, 1920, Raskob Papers; Memorandum, Irénée du Pont, "written for the purpose of the record" November 18, 1920, PSduP 624; Alice B. du Pont Diary entries for November 3, 17, and 18, PSduP 628–12.

29. Irénée du Pont Memorandum, "written for the purpose of the record," November 18, 1920, PSduP 624.

30. This and the following two quotations, D. W. Morrow to P. S. du Pont, January 17, 1921, PSduP 624. Harold Nicolson in his *Dwight Morrow,* pp. 156–157, summarized the phone call and subsequent events.

31. D. W. Morrow to P. S. du Pont, January 17, 1921, PSduP 624.

32. A copy of the agreement dated November 19, 1920, GTX DP 52, is initialed by P. S. du Pont and is also in PSduP 624. Minutes of the Finance Committee (Du Pont), November 19, 1920, #196, held in New York at General Motors Building, 24 West 57th Street, GTX 149; also Minutes of Finance Committee, November 26, #128, held in Wilmington.

33. P. S. du Pont to I. du Pont, November 26, 1920, DTX DP 50. This information for the following two paragraphs comes from Agreement between Du Pont Securities Company and W. C. Durant, Du Pont American Industries, and Chevrolet Motor Company, part of GTX 154 (the original and somewhat differently worded draft is in PSduP 624); Agreement between Du Pont American Industries and the Chevrolet Motor Company and Delaware Securities Company, November 22, 1920, GTX 153; George H. Gardner, Vice-President, Du Pont Securities Company to Du Pont American Industries, Inc., and Chevrolet Motor Company, November 22, 1920, GTX 154; Minutes of meeting of Board of Directors of Du Pont Securities Company, November 22, 1920, GTX 155; J. P. Morgan & Company to Du Pont American Industries, Inc., and Chevrolet Motor Company, November 21, 1920, PSduP 624.

34. The final figure came from a further review of accounts and after making an adjustment for the Friday transactions in which some of Durant's holdings were put up for collateral for loans made that day.

35. This was done by turning over 24,000 shares of Du Pont Securities common to Du Pont American Industries in return for 824,178 shares of General Motors common, and the other 16,000 shares of the Du Pont allotment of common to Chevrolet for 549,435 shares of General Motors.

36. For in April 1921 Chevrolet bank loans outstanding were $5.25 million, only part of which was used to raise money to pay for the $7.0 million block of General Motors stock which Chevrolet took in September.

37. Fin. Cte. Min., Du Pont Company, November 22, 1920, #198; *Deposition of Pierre S.*

*du Pont,* p. 215; and Pierre's handwritten comments on "The Reorganization of General Motors" written in March 1951, PSduP B–63.

38. Sloan, *My Years with General Motors,* p. 43.
39. Alice B. du Pont's Diary entry for November 24, PSduP 628–12.
40. This and the following quotations are from "The Reorganization of General Motors," March 1951, written by P. S. du Pont, PSduP B–63.
41. The letters to Durant, McGowan, and Irénée of that date are all in PSduP 624.

CHAPTER 19. Reorganization and Regeneration, 1921

1. Pierre describes this pattern of life in *Deposition of Pierre S. du Pont,* p. 222, and Alice's Diary fully verifies these statements, PSduP 628–12; also as did John L. Pratt in an interview, October 2, 1962.
2. Minutes of Meeting between President and Plant Managers, December 1, 1920, DTX GM 196. Other events mentioned in this paragraph will be discussed in detail in the following pages.
3. Memorandum—Discussion en route to and from Dayton, December 7, 8, 1920. This trip is described and the memorandum quoted in Alfred P. Sloan, Jr., *My Years with General Motors* (Garden City, N.Y.: Doubleday, 1964), pp. 73–74. It is also mentioned in a newspaper clipping in PSduP 624.
4. A. P. Sloan to P. S. du Pont, December 27, 1920 (dictated December 24), PSduP 624; Memorandum P. S. du Pont to Officers, Directors, and Heads of Departments, December 29, 1920, DE 303; General Motors Organization Chart, January 23, 1921, DTX GM 171; reprinted in Sloan, *My Years with General Motors,* p. 57. The modifications made by Pierre can be seen by comparing this chart to the one at the end of Sloan's Organization Study, DTX GM 1, which is reprinted in Alfred D. Chandler, Jr., *Strategy and Structure* (Cambridge, Mass.: M.I.T. Press, 1962), pp. 136–137.
5. Chandler, *Strategy and Structure,* pp. 91–96.
6. This and the following seven quotations are from General Motors Corporation—Organization Study, DTX GM 1.
7. *Deposition of Pierre S. du Pont,* p. 226.
8. This and the following quotation are from the Memorandum of P. S. du Pont to Officers, Directors, and Heads of Departments, December 29, 1920; Sloan, *My Years with General Motors,* pp. 44–45, 56, tells of the new committee as does *Automotive Topics,* January 8, 1921.
9. P. S. du Pont to J. H. Squires, December 6, 1920, PSduP 624.
10. Sloan's appointments are indicated on the General Motors Organization Chart, May 31, 1921 (see Chart VI, p. 501). Norval Hawkins' career is described in Allan Nevins and Frank E. Hill, *Ford: Expansion and Challenge, 1915–1938* (New York: Scribner, 1954), pp. 340–345. Besides Hawkins, Kettering, and H. L. Barton as head of the Factory Section, Sloan appointed Eric L. Bergland head of Power and Construction, J. H. Main as head of Purchasing, H. A. Austin as head of General Motors Building Section, Charles McNamee head of Real Estate, and Lloyd Blackmore remained the chief in the Patent Section. Harry Bassett headed Housing in addition to his duties as Buick's division manager, for most of the housing was at Flint for Buick employees, and a little later S. P. Bunker became the manager of Industrial Relations. Soon chiefs of Traffic, Advertising, and Publicity and Service sections were appointed. The role of the Traffic Department, for example, in a decentralized structure is well described in William Coyne to A. P. Sloan, December 22, 1924, PSduP 624.
11. I. du Pont to Finance Committee (Du Pont Company), December 21, 1921, GTX 180; J. J. Raskob to I. du Pont, January 8, 1921, GTX 181.

12. Irénée and others in Wilmington fully agreed that Brown was the man to bring the Du Pont financial system to General Motors. The problem became Brown's replacement at Du Pont. Irénée wanted Walter Carpenter, while Raskob very strongly urged the appointment of one of Brown's assistants, Angus Echols. That Carpenter became the new Du Pont treasurer against Raskob's strongest opposition suggests that the crisis at General Motors had somewhat diminished his influence with Pierre and his brothers. I. du Pont to Finance Committee (Du Pont Company), December 31, 1920, and to Board of Directors (Du Pont Company), January 4, 1921; J. J. Raskob to I. du Pont, January 8, 1921, Minutes of Finance Committee (Du Pont Company), December 27, 31, 1920, Du Pont Co. Records.

13. The manning of the Financial Staff is indicated in General Motors Corporation Organization Chart, May 31, 1921, and F. Turner to A. P. Sloan, January 10, 1921; A. P. Sloan to F. Turner, January 17, 1921. Sloan stressed in this letter to Turner the obvious need for adjustment and modification of the original organization structure. "It was so very vitally necessary that we should get something started in order to shape things around, that the time did not permit the working out in detail of all the various departments that we have in Detroit." The appointments of Pratt, Johnson, and Mott are indicated in Organization Charts, January 3 and May 31, 1921, and also in Minutes of the General Motors Executive Committee. Unless otherwise indicated, references to the Executive Committee and Finance Committee will be to those at General Motors.

14. Organization Chart, May 31, 1921, shows Haskell headed the General Motors Export Company, assisted by P. S. Steenstrup.

15. Salaries are given in Executive Committee Minutes.

16. *Automotive Topics*, January 1, 1921.

17. *Testimony of J. L. Pratt*, pp. 1387-1502; Pratt went into more detail on these changes in an interview on October 2, 1962. P. S. du Pont to R. H. Collins, March 18, 1921, DTX DP 63; and P. S. du Pont to the Finance Committee, May 11, 1921, DTX DP 64; P. S. du Pont to R. H. Collins, July 7, 12, 1921, Du Pont Co. Records, stresses that Collins left the company satisfied with the arrangements. The Executive Committee on May 25 received a resolution from the Finance Committee saying:

> That it should not be possible for anyone in the Corporation to draw a check payable to himself when signed by himself or for a Division Manager to cause a check to be drawn on the Division's bank balance to his order or for his account, except with the approval of the Treasurer of the General Motors Corporation.

> On June 7 Raskob asked the Executive Committee what steps had been taken to see that the Finance Committee's resolution was being effectively carried out, Executive Committee Minutes, May 25, June 7, 1921.

18. The careers of these men are given in Arthur Pound, *The Turning Wheel* (Garden City, N.Y.: Doubleday, 1934), pp. 96-97, 165, 224. Mott's appointment is mentioned in the Minutes of the Executive Committee, March 31, 1921.

19. Pratt described these talks in his interview, October 2, 1962.

20. Memorandum to P. S. du Pont, President, from Committee on Inter Divisional Pricing, January 6, 1921. The committee enclosed a copy of the earlier "The Report of the Committee Appointed for the Purpose of Studying Inter Divisional Business" which Sloan wrote and is described on pp. 477-478 of the present book, and in *My Years with General Motors*, pp. 49-50. Sloan's report and that of the committee's went to Brown for comment and, with few modifications, was fully incorporated into the General Motors accounting procedures by the following fall.

21. Sloan, *My Years with General Motors*, p. 143.

22. P. S. du Pont to A. P. Sloan, December 21, 1920, enclosing Pierre's "Memorandum on

Report: Appropriation and Organization Study." The two following quotations are from this memorandum.

23. A. P. Sloan to P. S. du Pont, December 27, 1920 (dictated December 24), PSduP 624.

24. This and the following quotation are from A. P. Sloan to M. L. Prensky, December 24, 1921.

25. The quotation is from Sloan's earlier Appropriation Organization Study, Sloan, *My Years with General Motors*, p. 120.

26. Sloan, *My Years with General Motors*, p. 124.

27. Minutes of meeting of President and Plant Managers, December 21, 1920. The inventory crisis was also discussed on the trip to Dayton, mentioned above, and also P. S. du Pont to A. P. Sloan, December 14, 1920.

28. This and the following quotation are from Memorandum, J. L. Pratt to J. J. Raskob, April 14, 1921, cited in Sloan, *My Years with General Motors*, pp. 124–125.

29. Interview with J. L. Pratt, October 2, 1962.

30. Minutes of conference held in Sloan's office, February 10, 1921. (The minutes of this meeting are cited in another connection in Sloan, *My Years with General Motors*, pp. 60–61.) Pratt's reference to not having a single suit resulting from the renegotiation or postponement of payment is given in this memorandum.

31. J. L. Pratt to J. J. Raskob, April 14, 1921.

32. J. L. Pratt to J. J. Raskob, April 14, 1921.

33. Report from Treasurer to Executive Committee, February 18, 1921. The following quotation is from this report.

34. *Annual Report of the General Motors Corporation for 1922*, p. 9.

35. A. J. Moxham to P. S. du Pont, March 21, 1923, PSduP 624.

36. D. Brown to Finance Committee, April 21, 1921, quoted in Sloan, *My Years with General Motors*, p. 126.

37. Sloan succinctly described the development of cash controls in *My Years with General Motors*, pp. 121–124.

38. In the final settlement Durant received $25,954,157 in cash for 2,626,368 shares of General Motors. *Annual Report of E. I. du Pont de Nemours and Company for 1922*. The best summary of refinancing is in this report.

39. Agreement between Du Pont American Industries, Inc., Du Pont Securities Company, and W. C. Durant, December 31, 1921, GTX 157; J. J. Raskob to Finance Committee (Du Pont Company), January 17, 1921, GTX 156.

40. In November 1920 Durant personally held 109,769 shares of Chevrolet and Du Pont American Industries, 37,350 shares. By the exchange the Du Pont's block went up to 132,000 and Durant's down to 14,769. Chevrolet Motor Company's List of Stockholders, December 1, 1920, Du Pont Co. Records.

41. Advice of Action taken by Finance Committee (Du Pont Company), January 17, 1921, GTX 156; Minutes of Finance Committee (Du Pont Company), January 10, 24, 1921, #205.

42. J. L. Pratt, *Direct Testimony*, p. 1412. Pratt was and still is a strong admirer of Durant. His biases come out not so much in an anti-Du Pont view but rather in an anti-Sloan position.

43. Clipping from *Evening Mail*, December 30, 1920, PSduP 624.

44. This and the following quotation are from a clipping from the *Flint Daily Journal* which gives in full the telegram from the Flint Chamber of Commerce, January 16, 1921, and Pierre's reply, PSduP 624.

45. By June 1921 Durant had a large factory getting into production at Lansing, Michigan. He had started another at Flint and was planning a third at Oakland, California, P.S. du Pont to J. J. Raskob, July 1, 1921. Pierre also reported to Raskob that Stettinius had told

him that Durant "had applied for a loan on General Motors stock, presumably on the shares that he obtained by exchange for Durant Motors," Raskob Papers.

46. E. R. Stettinius to J. J. Raskob, March 7, 1921, Raskob Papers.
47. The best summary of the plan is in "History of Du Pont Company's Investment in General Motors Corporation, August 17, 1921," GTX 166; also, J. J. Raskob to Finance Committee (Du Pont Company), April 2, 1921, GTX 161, and Advice of Action (Du Pont Company), May 10, 1921, GTX 165.
48. "History of Du Pont Company's Investment in General Motors Corporation, August 17, 1921," GTX 166. Du Pont American Industries, Inc., Board of Directors, offer of Chevrolet Motor Company to sell and deliver to E. I. du Pont de Nemours and Company its entire interest in the Du Pont Securities Company and assignment of said offer to this company, May 31, 1921, *New York Times,* May 13, 1921, *Annual Report for E. I. du Pont de Nemours and Company for 1922,* GTX 158.
49. The Morgan commission plus costs came to $1,885,000. Also $1,020,400 became available with the final liquidation of the Du Pont Securities Company.
50. Minutes of meeting of Finance Committee (Du Pont Company), December 30, 1921, GTX 169.
51. A printed statement to stockholders of Chevrolet Motor Company from P. S. du Pont, dated April 23, 1921. With Durant's departure, Pierre became president of Chevrolet Motor Company. By January 1922, all the stock had been exchanged except 600 shares held by Arthur G. Bishop and 400 by Katharine B. Minor, J. J. Raskob to Finance Committee (Du Pont Company), January 30, 1922; J. J. Raskob to A. G. Bishop. April 28, 1922, and W. S. Carpenter to Finance Committee (Du Pont Company), February 6, 1922, GTX 168.
52. This and the following quotation are from P. S. du Pont to J. P. Morgan, June 3, 1921, GTX 159; Pierre also wrote Stettinius on June 3, 1921, GTX 160; all this correspondence is in PSduP 624.
53. J. P. Morgan to P. S. du Pont, June 6, 1921, GTX 159.
54. This and the following quotation are from E. R. Stettinius to P. S. du Pont, June 8, 1921, GTX 160.
55. Pound, *The Turning Wheel,* p.196, makes the point about P. S. du Pont restoring confidence to General Motors, while Pratt in his interview of October 2, 1962, stressed the importance of giving the suppliers confidence in General Motors' future.

CHAPTER 20. Product Policy and Technological Innovation, 1921-1923

1. The situation of all divisions was summarized by Pratt in Sloan's Detroit office, February 9 and 10, 1921. The meeting is covered in Alfred P. Sloan, Jr., *My Years with General Motors* (Garden City, N.Y.: Doubleday, 1964), pp. 60-61, 356.
2. The figures for domestic sales are from Federal Trade Commission, *Report of the Motor Vehicle Industry* (Washington, D.C.: Government Printing Office, 1939), p. 29. (See Appendix, Table 7.) The figures for total sales are from *Annual Report of the General Motors Corporation for 1922,* p. 20. Total General Motors Sales at home and abroad were 391,798 in 1919, 393,075 in 1920, and 80,122 in 1921.
3. These figures on divisional production are from the corporation's records and given in Sloan, *My Years with General Motors,* pp. 60–61. The Chevrolet figures not listed in Sloan's are given in General Motors Corporation, "Comparison of number and proportion of motor vehicles (Passenger and Truck) sold by Ford, General Motors and other manufacturers, 1921," DTX GM 35.
4. *Annual Report of General Motors Corporation for 1920,* p. 8.
5. Preliminary Report No. 1691–1 on General Motors Corporation to J. P. Morgan and

Company, March 30, 1921, by Day & Zimmermann, Inc., Engineers. Pierre mentions this investigation which he says was for the Bankers Trust Company as well as for J. P. Morgan and Company in a letter to Harry Pierce, February 26, 1921, PSduP 624.

6. R. S. McLaughlin to J. A. Haskell, January 18, 1921. The letter, plus another written February 21, 1921, reviews the situation in all the divisions and is therefore a useful supplement to Pratt's comments in Sloan's office, February 9 and 10. Also, Minutes of the Executive Committee Meeting, February 2, 23, 1921. Unless otherwise indicated, the committees refer to those of General Motors.

7. Minutes of meeting in Sloan's office, February 9, 1921, and Day & Zimmermann Report, March 31, 1921. J. L. Pratt, *Direct Testimony*, p. 1403. His comments were elaborated in an interview in October 1962.

8. Minutes of Meeting of Executive Committee, April 13, 1921.

9. Sloan, *My Years with General Motors*, pp. 356–357.

10. Minutes of Executive Committee, April 7, May 11, 1921.

11. Telegram, P. S. du Pont to H. H. Rice, K. W. Zimmerschied, W. A. Day, H. H. Bassett, J. H. Craig, July 9, 1921; P. S. du Pont to G. H. Hannum, July 11, 1921, PSduP 624; also P. S. du Pont to J. J. Raskob, July 1, 1921, Raskob Papers.

12. Minutes of Executive Committee, September 21, 1921; the report was dated September 12, 1921.

13. *Annual Report of the General Motors Corporation for 1922*, pp. 10–11.

14. P. S. du Pont to A. P. Sloan, December 4, 1923, and copy of letter C. F. Kettering to A. P. Sloan, August 23, 1923, both in PSduP 624.

15. Minutes of Executive Committee, January 19, 1921, cited in Sloan, *My Years with General Motors*, p. 74. Also R. S. McLaughlin to J. A. Haskell, January 18, 1921.

16. Minutes of Executive Committee, February 16, 1921, cited in Sloan, *My Years with General Motors*, p. 74.

17. Cited in Sloan, *My Years with General Motors*, p. 75.

18. This and the previous quotation are from the Minutes of the Executive Committee, February 23, 1921.

19. Minutes of Executive Committee, March 2, 9, 16, 29, April 6, 1921.

20. Minutes of Executive Committee, April 6, 1921.

21. Minutes of Executive Committee, May 4, June 9, 1921.

22. Sloan, *My Years with General Motors*, p. 63. The report is described in detail on pp. 62–70.

23. The decisions are indicated in report, P. S. du Pont to the Executive Committee, September 8, 1921. Sloan mentions this report in *My Years with General Motors*, p. 77. P. S. du Pont to J. J. Raskob, July 1, 1921, tells of plans to increase Buick's production by using the Scripps-Booth factory, Raskob Papers.

24. The best brief description of the advantages of the air-cooled car is in the report of P. S. du Pont to Executive Committee, September 8, 1921.

25. Minutes of Executive Committee, June 7, 1921.

26. The meeting of July 26, 1921, is quoted in Sloan, *My Years with General Motors*, p. 76.

27. The meeting of August 3, 1921, and decision is mentioned in P. S. du Pont to Executive Committee, September 8, 1921.

28. Minutes of Executive Committee, September 13, 1921.

29. This and the following are from P. S. du Pont to Executive Committee, September 8, 1921. His strong and continuing commitment to testing new designs at Dayton is indicated in Minutes of Executive Committee and Plant Manager, December 1, 1920 (DTX GM 1962) and Minutes of Executive Committee, March 13, 1921.

30. Minutes of Executive Committee, September 20, 1921.

31. Minutes of Executive Committee, October 20, 1921, cited in Sloan, *My Years with General Motors*, p. 77.
32. Quoted in Sloan, *My Years with General Motors*, p. 77.
33. P. S. du Pont to G. W. Hannum, November 8, 1921, quoted in Sloan, *My Years with General Motors*, p. 78.
34. Minutes of Executive Committee, November 30, 1921, quoted in Sloan, *My Years with General Motors*, p. 78.
35. Quoted in Sloan, *My Years with General Motors*, p. 79. Pierre wrote Kettering a week before asking for information to "get me straight on a number of points," P. S. du Pont to C. F. Kettering, November 23, 1921, PSduP 624.
36. Minutes of Executive Committee, December 15, 1922, cited in Sloan, *My Years with General Motors*, p. 79.
37. Pierre's interest in a variety of technological innovations is indicated by his active interest in and financial support of talking motion pictures. In 1920 he became a vice-president and director of the Webb Talking Picture Company.
38. P. S. du Pont to C. F. Kettering, October 8, 1923, for taxicabs; Minutes of Executive Committee, September 21, for trucks.
39. Sloan briefly reviews the development of automobile finishes in *My Years with General Motors*, pp. 235–237, and "no knock" gasoline, pp. 221–226. As General Motors and the Du Pont Company worked closely together on both these products, there is a vast amount of material on each in the form of exhibits and testimony in the Du Pont–GM Antitrust Suit.
40. P. S. du Pont to I. du Pont, August 11, 1921, Du Pont Co. Records.
41. C. F. Kettering to P. S. du Pont, August 16, 1921, Du Pont Co. Records.
42. I. Du Pont to P. S. du Pont, August 24, 1921; P. S. du Pont to I. du Pont, August 25, 1921; C. L. Petz to P. S. du Pont, November 30, 1921, PSduP 624; *Deposition of Pierre S. du Pont*, August 11, 1921, pp. 236–238; F. O. Clements to A. P. Sloan, November 8, 1921.
43. P. S. du Pont to C. F. Kettering, April 12, 1922, mentioned in *Deposition of Pierre S. du Pont*, p. 238.
44. P. S. du Pont to I. du Pont, October 19, 1922, mentioned in *Deposition of Pierre S. du Pont*, p. 240; I. du Pont to P. S. du Pont, November 6, 1922, PSduP 624; F. O. Clements to A. P. Sloan, June 20, 1923 (copy sent to P. S. du Pont), an excellent summary of the progress of General Motors in the use of Duco.
45. Work had begun on this development before Pierre became president, *Deposition of Pierre S. du Pont*, pp. 261–265. In addition to documents cited earlier and the many exhibits in the Du Pont–General Motors Antitrust Suit, useful letters are F. O. Clements to C. M. Stine, January 29, 1920, Du Pont Co. Records. Pierre's strong continuing interest is indicated in memorandum re "Doping of Fuel" March 3, 1922, April 4, August 30, October 9, November 20, 1922; "Memorandum of a visit to Dayton with Mr. Irénée du Pont," July 6, 1922—all in PSduP 624. Also, Pierre du Pont to J. J. Raskob, July 18, 1922, Raskob Papers. In addition, correspondence on an agreement between General Motors and the Du Pont Company on the allocation of costs of research done at the Du Pont Company for General Motors, I. du Pont to P. S. du Pont, November 8, 1921, Du Pont Co. Records; P. S. du Pont to L. du Pont, November 7, 10, 1921; L. du Pont to P. S. du Pont, October 31, November 8, 19, 1921, all in PSduP 624.
46. P. S. du Pont to C. F. Kettering, May 13, June 26, 1922, PSduP 624.
47. For example, in P. S. du Pont to A. P. Sloan, July 28, 1924, PSduP 624, Pierre opposed a reduction in the amount of tetraethyl lead in gasoline because of shortage of supplies, as such a move "would be equivalent to reducing the quality" of the product. Standard Oil's part in developing the improved gasoline is described in George S. Gibb and Evelyn

Knowlton, *The Resurgent Years* (New York: Harper & Brothers, 1956), pp. 532–547.

48. Also, because of Haskell's poor health and because of a trip Sloan and Raskob had made to Europe in the summer of 1921, the Executive Committee had authorized a major overhaul of the overseas marketing division, placing James D. Mooney in charge, Minutes of Executive Committee, September 9, 1921.

49. This and the following three quotations are from A. P. Sloan to P. S. du Pont, December 24, 1921. Sloan quotes from this letter in *My Years with General Motors*, pp. 100–102. Sloan asked that the next Tuesday's meeting of the Executive Committee be set aside for this purpose.

50. The Minutes of the Executive Committee discussing the proposal of Eric Bergland and Willis Johnson to improve and check on the planning and carrying out of new construction suggest the lack of line and staff coordination in this area.

51. This and the following four quotations are from a "Memorandum of Items to discuss at the earliest possible moment with Mr. P. S. du Pont regarding the general subject of Organization," attached to letter of A. P. Sloan to P. S. du Pont, December 24, 1921.

52. A. P. Sloan to J. J. Raskob, February 13, 1922 (dictated February 10).

53. Besides Sloan's memorandum, other evidence of Hawkins' ideas are indicated in C. S. Mott to A. P. Sloan, August 19, 1921; *Printer's Ink* (September 29, 1921), 116:3, and Minutes of Executive Committee, September 20, 1921.

54. Minutes of Executive Committee, September 20, 1921.

55. This and the following four quotations are from Sloan's "Memorandum of Items to discuss with Mr. P. S. du Pont regarding the general subject of Organization," cited in note 51, above.

56. Minutes of Executive Committee, December 6, 1922, show that this was the first meeting attended by Mott and Fisher.

57. Minutes of Executive Committee, January 3, 1922.

58. Sloan forwarded the plan to Pierre and Raskob and Mott for comment with a covering letter, February 8, 1922. A. P. Sloan to J. J. Raskob, February 13 (dictated February 10), 1922, indicates Raskob's response and has a valuable discussion of the problem of distinguishing policy from the administration. The following six quotations are from Sloan's memorandum to be signed by Pierre entitled "Plan of Organization." There is a long unsigned memorandum elaborating and spelling out in detail the role and functions of the board and the Finance and Executive committees which was probably written by Sloan, but just might have been done by Pierre. Sloan quotes from this edition in *My Years with General Motors*, p. 101. The final version was sent out in May, Secretary to A. P. Sloan to C. S. Mott, May 6, 1922.

59. Raskob proposed that the sentence read: "An organization based upon the above two principles represents, therefor, decentralized control as to *operation and administration* with centralized control as *to determining and adopting policies to govern* the operation and administration of our various units and their functions, all made possible through proper coordination of the individual operations with a general or central administration."

60. P. S. du Pont to Mrs. C. W. Zimmerschied, June 28, 1923; P. S. du Pont to A. P. Sloan, June 28, 1923; P. S. du Pont to C. W. Zimmerschied, July 28, 1924, all in PSduP 624. Interview with J. L. Pratt, October 2, 1926; Norman Beasley, *Knudsen: A Biography.* (New York: McGraw-Hill, 1947), pp. 115–123. Knudsen's biographer tells of his experiences at Ford. Allan Nevins and Frank E. Hill, *Ford: Expansion and Challenge, 1915–1933* (New York: Scribner, 1957), pp. 15–16, 70–73, 168–169, 356–360, emphasize his valuable contributions at Ford.

61. Minutes of Executive Committee, March 22, 1922.

62. This and the following quotation are from the minutes of a meeting between Sloan, Mott,

Bassett, and Zimmerschied, cited in Sloan, *My Years with General Motors*, p. 81.

63. Minutes of Executive Committee, April 7, 13, 1922; also, P. S. du Pont to W. S. Knudsen, August 20, 1923, PSduP 624.
64. Minutes of Executive Committee, May 11, 1923.
65. This and the following two quotations are from C. F. Kettering to P. S. du Pont, May 24, 1922, PSduP 624.
66. Telegram, J. T. Ardis to I. du Pont, L. du Pont, and J. J. Raskob, May 31, 1922, PSduP 624.
67. P. S. du Pont to J. J. Raskob, July 18, 1922, Raskob Papers; also, P. S. du Pont to H. McGowan, July 21, August 16, 1922, PSduP 624.
68. P. S. du Pont to H. McGowan, July 21, 1922, Du Pont Co. Records.
69. Memorandum on Chevrolet Schedule, Detroit, July 11, 1922, PSduP 624.
70. P. S. du Pont to J. J. Raskob, July 18, 1922; and Minutes of Executive Committee, August 31, 1921, Raskob Papers.
71. H. M. Pierce to P. S. du Pont, August 30, October 4, 1922; also, copy of H. M. Pierce to I. du Pont, August 19, 22, 1922; and W. Coyne to I. du Pont, September 6, 1922; P. S. du Pont to W. S. Knudsen, September 25, 1922, all in PSduP 624.
72. Memorandum: "Fisher's Finances in connection with Chevrolet assembly program, Detroit, July 12, 1921—meeting with Mott, Kettering, Fisher and du Pont;" also P. S. du Pont to W. S. Knudsen, June 10, 1922 (telegram); P. S. du Pont to F. Fisher, July 17, 1921, all in PSduP 624.
73. P. S. du Pont to J. J. Raskob, July 18, 1922, Raskob Papers.
74. P. S. du Pont to H. McGowan, July 21, 1922. Pierre mentions in this letter his request to division managers for estimates of financial requirements for expansion, Du Pont Co. Records.
75. H. McGowan to P. S. du Pont, August 14, 1922, PSduP 624.
76. P. S. du Pont to H. McGowan, August 26, 1922, PSduP 624; Minutes of Finance Committee, July 19, August 2, 31, 1922; Appropriation for Chevrolet was $3,743,000; also, P. S. du Pont to Finance Committee, April 25, 1923, PSduP 624.
77. Chevrolet schedule was readjusted October 24, 1922, memorandum of that date; also, P. S. du Pont to A. P. Sloan, November 8, 1922; P. S. du Pont to C. Campbell, October 19, 1922, all in PSduP 624.
78. Memorandum on 6 Cylinder Copper Cooled Car—Meeting with Mr. Kettering, November 8, 1922. The following three quotations are from this memorandum, which is quoted in Sloan, *My Years with General Motors*, pp. 84–85.
79. This and the three following quotations are in the Minutes of Executive Committee, November 16, 1922, and are given in Sloan, *My Years with General Motors*, p. 85.
80. Sloan, *My Years with General Motors* covers developments in December and January. The January schedule is given in memorandum of meeting with Knudsen, January 24, 1923, PSduP 624.
81. P. S. du Pont to W. S. Knudsen, November 18, 1922; P. S. du Pont to C. Campbell, February 23, 1923; P. S. du Pont to W. de Kraft, March 30, 1923; P. S. du Pont to W. S. Knudsen, March 30, April 9, May 12, 1923; J. P. Tyler to P. S. du Pont, April 6, 1923, all in PSduP 624. Tyler, the service manager of the Wilmington Auto Company, told Pierre that the clutch on his and Irénée's copper-cooled cars stopped revolving too quickly, and so made shifting of gears impossible. Also the number one and two pistons were pumping oil.
82. P. S. du Pont to C. Campbell, February 23, 1923; W. S. Knudsen to P. S. du Pont, April 21, 1923; P. S. du Pont to Finance Committee, April 25, 1923, all in PSduP 624. The program is given in this last letter. The exact figure was $6,426,000 for permanent investment and $11,918,000 for working capital.

83. A. P. Sloan to P. S. du Pont, April 16, 1922. The quotation at the end of the paragraph is from this memorandum.

84. Pierre drafted the report in late February; talked it over with the bankers on the board; and then had its figures and wording checked in early March. He signed it as of March 19, 1922. P. S. du Pont to J. T. Ardis, February 28, 1922; P. S. du Pont to R. P. Lindaberry, February 28, 1922, PSduP 624.

85. This and the following six quotations are from *Annual Report of General Motors Corporation for 1922*, March 18, 1923, as are the figures and statistical data. These figures differ from those in Table 7 in the Appendix of the present book which are just for passenger vehicles produced for the U.S. market.

86. Printed statement of P. S. du Pont, President, to the Stockholders, January 24, 1922, PSduP 624; P. S. du Pont to J. J. Raskob, July 1, 1922, Raskob Papers; P. S. du Pont to H. McGowan, January 5, 7, 1922; H. McGowan to P. S. du Pont, January 7, 1922, all cables, PSduP 624.

87. P. S. du Pont to J. L. Pratt and DeWitt Page, April 13, 1923; P. S. du Pont to D. Morrow, G. F. Baker, S. Prosser, March 30, 1923, all in PSduP 624.

88. P. S. du Pont to Col. H. A. du Pont, May 8, 1923, outlines the steps involved in announcing his resignation. P. S. du Pont to S. Prosser, April 25, 1923; P. S. du Pont to Directors of General Motors, April 25, 1923. The three quotations in this paragraph are from the letter to the directors. Useful too is "Suggested Announcement" of resignation, all in PSduP 624. Also, Minutes of Finance Committee (Du Pont Company), April 24, 1923, GTX 182. The letter to the directors is GTX 183. Sloan was elected a director in the Du Pont Company, a move Raskob strongly opposed. J. J. Raskob to P. S. du Pont, May 15, 1923; Minutes of Board of Directors (Du Pont Company), GTX 185, 186.

89. Pierre wrote Knudsen about his resignation from the presidency, saying that no definite arrangement had yet been made about Chevrolet, "As I have been more or less of a figure head the division will not suffer greatly if it seems best for me to retire from my ornamental position." He praised Knudsen and his methods, his lack of prejudice, and his willingness to cooperate. "Your patience in straightening out Chevrolet troubles has been wonderful. You have won the gratitude of the whole management as well as the writer." P. S. du Pont to W. S. Knudsen, May 12, 1923, PSduP 624.


CHAPTER 21. General Motors Rebuilt, 1923–1924

1. T. Geesey to J. Ardis, April 6, 1923, PSduP 624. In making his statement in the General Motors–Du Pont Antitrust Suit, Pierre recalled that Raskob brought the matter up, but that Raskob claimed that it was Pierre's idea. *Deposition of Pierre S. du Pont*, May 28, 1951, pp. 272–273.

2. P. S. du Pont to H. E. Ellsworth, March 8, 1918, DTX DP 60.

3. This and the following quotation are from P. S. du Pont to A. F. du Pont, April 1, 1921. Pierre summarizes the arrangements made in December 1919 and makes his offer to turn over 400 shares of Christiana Securities in this letter. Similar letters went to F. W. Pickard, J. B. D. Edge, C. A. Meade, W. C. Spruance, F. D. Brown, L. du Pont, and W. S. Carpenter. Also relevant is P. S. du Pont to H. B. Robertson, December 21. 1922. All are in PSduP 632.

4. P. S. du Pont to seven executives listed in previous note, September 26, 1925, all in PSduP 632. In a letter of thanks of September 29, 1925, W. S. Carpenter wrote:

You will probably disclaim that you were prompted by any conscious motive other than good business. Without granting or questioning this I hope, nevertheless, to be able to justify it. I cannot, however, have this pass without letting you know that I appreciate and admire your part in this matter more than I will be able to express.

5. J. J. Raskob to Finance Committee (Du Pont Company), March 31, 1923; also D. Brown to J. J. Raskob, May 23, 1923. Both in Raskob Papers.

6. P. S. du Pont to W. W. Laird, October 23, 1925, PSduP 624. The letter includes a list of stockholders friendly to Du Pont and the amount of their holdings. By this time Pierre felt that it would be impossible for Durant to seize control. P. S. du Pont to J. J. Raskob, July 1, 1921, Raskob Papers, suggests their earlier concern.

7. P. S. du Pont to I. du Pont, September 4, 1923, PSduP 624.

8. The plan was carried out in the following fashion. The first step was to place all of the 7.5 million shares of General Motors stock held by the Du Pont Company (at the current price of $15 per share, their total value would be $112.5 million) into the account of the Du Pont American Industries (the Du Pont-controlled holding company that had been formed to purchase the stock from Durant) and then change the name of that company to General Motors Securities Corporation. That holding company would next issue 600,000 shares of common stock at a par value of $100. Then General Motors would form another holding company to be known as the Management Securities Company which would issue $5.5 million worth of shares of common stock, all to be held by General Motors. As a third step the new Management Securities Company would then purchase 200,000 shares, or one-third interest, in the General Motors Securities Corporation, paying for the stock $37.4 million (that is, one-third of the value of the total holdings of $112.5 million). It would pay for them with $4.7 million in cash and $32.7 million in 8% notes maturing in 1931, the same date that the du Ponts' present bonds used to pay for the Durant purchase would come due. The Du Pont Company would get $4.7 million in cash plus having General Motors responsible for amortizing the remaining $28 million worth of Du Pont debt. That is, at each time that the du Ponts' 7% notes became due at J. P. Morgan, the General Motors Securities would provide the same amount on its 8% notes due at Du Pont. Cash paid would be used to pay off part of the debt. As a fourth step, Pierre would sell a block of 433,334 shares of General Motors to the Management Securities Company at $15 per share and receive a payment of $800,000 in cash and $5.5 million in bonds. Finally, General Motors would sell the $5.5 million worth of stock (466,666 ⅔ shares at $15 a share) it received from Management Securities Company to its most effective executives, reserving $1.0 million of this amount for future allotments. J. J. Raskob to Finance Committee, E. I. du Pont de Nemours & Company, June 20, 1923, GTX 235.

9. Alfred P. Sloan, Jr., *My Years with General Motors* (Garden City, N.Y.: Doubleday, 1964), p. 412.

10. I. du Pont to P. S. du Pont, June 29, 1923, PSduP 418 and August 14, 1923, GTX 237. The quotation is from the first letter. W. S. Carpenter to F. D. Brown, July 19, 24, 1923, GTX 236, 238; and F. D. Brown to W. S. Carpenter, July 20, 1923, GTX 237.

11. The issues are suggested in J. J. Raskob to Finance Committee, General Motors Corporation and E. I. du Pont de Nemours and Company, July 20, 1923, GTX 240; and extract from Minutes of Board of Directors, General Motors Corporation, August 9, 1923, GTX 241.

12. I. du Pont to P. S. du Pont, August 14, 1923, GTX 242.

13. The final arrangement differed from the original one only in detail. Besides meeting the Du Pont Company's objections, adjustments had to be made for the rapid rise in the price of General Motors stock during the summer and fall of 1923. In July General Motors common had been selling below 15; it was up to 60 in October. The two holding companies were retained. To meet tax and amortization needs, the Management Securities Company was to issue two types of stock: (A) with dividends paid from General Motors earnings contributed to Management Securities and (B) with dividends paid from the stock received from the Du Pont Company (i.e., the Du Pont American Industries). Towards the first, General Motors was to pay 5% rather than 6% of its net earnings. To satisfy Irénée, the Du Pont Company would sell 30% rather than 33 ⅓ % of its General

Motors holdings. In return Management Securities paid the same amount of cash ($4.7 million) and $28.8 million in convertible 7% preferred stock rather than $32.8 million in 8% bonds. The cash would be used to pay the next installment on the retirement of the bond issue. With this much paid off and the clear recovery of General Motors, the Morgan firm was willing to take the remaining Management Securities 7% preferred as security for the remainder of the bond issue still outstanding. Pierre apparently also was paid by Management Securities in preferred stock rather than bonds for his block of General Motors stock, although the details on this point are not clear. The plan was to work by having Management Securities' income allocated in two different ways. The *annual payments* from General Motors' earnings (and it was agreed that if these should fall below $2.0 million because of low earnings, General Motors would make up the difference in an unsecured loan at 6% interest) were to be credited to the Class "A" stock account and used to pay dividends of the Class "A" stock. The *dividends* from the block of General Motors stock held by the Securities Corporation through Du Pont American Industries were to be credited to the Class "B" stock account. Part of this income would be used to pay the small dividends on the Class "B" stock and also on the 7% on the preferred issue, and the rest would be used to retire the preferred stock. In this way Irénée was sure of having a regular fund to amortize the Du Pont Company bonds used to purchase the Durant stock. So by 1931 when the preferred issue was retired (and the Du Pont Company bonds paid off), the holders of Management Securities would own outright the holding company that held equivalent to 30% of the Du Pont investment in General Motors. The final plan is most succinctly outlined in Sloan, *My Years with General Motors,* pp. 410–414. Good also is the draft of the letter by Raskob to General Motors stockholders attached to a letter of Pierre du Pont to J. J. Raskob, July 1, 1926, PSduP 624. See also Minutes of Special Meeting of Board of Directors, E. I. du Pont de Nemours and Company, August 23, 1923, GTX 243; J. J. Raskob to Finance Committee (Du Pont Company), October 10, 1923, GTX 244; J. J. Raskob to Finance Committee (General Motors Corporation), October 2, 1923, GTX 244; Board of Directors to Finance Committee (Du Pont Company), October 15, 1923, GTX 244; Excerpts from Minutes of Finance Committee (Meeting #285), October 15, 1923, GTX 245; J. J. Raskob to Board of Directors (Du Pont Company), October 27, 1923, GTX 247; and particularly J. J. Raskob to W. S. Carpenter, Jr., November 6, 1923, GTX 249. Also J. J. Raskob to P. S. du Pont, July 26, 31, 1923; and P. S. du Pont to I. du Pont, September 4, 1923, both in PSduP 624.

14. This and the following quotation are from A. P. Sloan to J. J. Raskob, October 8, 1923, DTX GM 29.

15. Extracts from Minutes of Board of Directors (unless otherwise indicated committees and boards will be those of General Motors), November 8, 1923, GTX 250.

16. *Deposition of Pierre S. du Pont,* May 28, 1951, pp. 273–274; P. S. du Pont to S. Prosser and H. G. Bishop, November 22, 1923, GTX GM 30. This letter includes Pierre's original list and Sloan's modifications. The three who received $300,000 allotments were Bassett, Mott, and Raskob. Their allotments, like that of Sloan, were determined by Pierre and the Finance Committee.

17. Sloan, *My Years with General Motors,* p. 414.

18. Minutes of Executive Committee, May 18, 1923, quoted in Sloan, *My Years with General Motors,* pp. 86–87; Kettering, Hunt, and Knudsen also attended the meeting.

19. Minutes of Executive Committee, May 28, 1923, quoted in Sloan, *My Years with General Motors,* p, 87.

20. Sloan, *My Years with General Motors,* p. 87.

21. C. F. Kettering to A. P. Sloan, June 26, 1923, quoted in Sloan, *My Years with General Motors,* pp. 87–88.

22. This and the following quotation are from C. F. Kettering to A. P. Sloan, June 30, 1923, Sloan, *My Years with General Motors,* p. 89. Kettering's biographer noted that "the

discontinuance of the copper-cooled Chevrolet in the summer of 1923 was a staggering blow to him [Kettering]. It was then that his spirits reached the low point in his research career." T. S. Boyd, *Professional Amateur—The Biography of Charles Francis Kettering* (New York: Dutton, 1957), p. 123.

23. A. P. Sloan to C. F. Kettering, July 2, 1923, quoted in Sloan, *My Years with General Motors*, pp. 89–91.

24. This and the following two quotations are from A. P. Sloan to P. S. du Pont, July 6, 1923, Sloan, *My Years with General Motors*, pp. 91–92.

25. This and the following two quotations are from P. S. du Pont to A. P. Sloan, July 7, 1923, PSduP 624.

26. Series of telegrams between P. S. du Pont and C. F. Kettering, July 9–12, 1923. Sloan's views are particularly well stressed in A. P. Sloan to P. S. du Pont, J. J. Raskob, C. Mott, and F. Fisher, July 25, 1923, quoted in Sloan, *My Years with General Motors*, p. 93.

27. Minutes of Executive Committee, July 18, 1923. Collins' estimate of 730,000 cars a year was given at this meeting. Minutes of Executive Committee also show that on August 23, 1923, it approved of the construction of additional West Coast plants at Los Angeles and Seattle for Chevrolet, with Buick taking over the plant at Oakland, California. Because of continuing demand, Sloan on October 15 asked for an appropriation, in addition, of $1,000,000 to increase capacity 25%. P. S. du Pont to A. P. Sloan, October 18, 1923, PSduP 624. On October 24, the Executive Committee approved of the construction of a Chevrolet plant in London, England, and the construction of a small Buick 6-cylinder car, Minutes of Executive Committee, October 24, 1923, PSduP 624.

28. Minutes of Executive Committee, August 16, 1923.

29. P. S. du Pont to W. S. Knudsen, August 20, 1923. Pierre protested against Campbell's letter to copper-cooled car owners which relieved the company of all responsibility. The Division should stand by its products, he wrote. "If we take this attitude of evading responsibility, how can we expect to sell copper-cooled cars in the future?" P. S. du Pont to C. Campbell, August 18, 1923, PSduP 624.

30. P. S. du Pont to C. F. Kettering, July 12, 1923 (telegram), PSduP 624.

31. P. S. du Pont to C. F. Kettering, December 21, 1923, PSduP 624.

32. Both in PSduP 624. Earlier, when Pierre had told Knudsen of his resignation, he had written: "The only point on which we have crossed swords is on the question of cooperation with other divisions." P.S. du Pont to W. S. Knudsen, May 12, 1923.

33. P. S. du Pont to W. S. Knudsen, September 4, 1923, PSduP 624.

34. W. S. Knudsen to P. S. du Pont, September 1, 1923, PSduP 624.

35. C. F. Kettering to P. S. du Pont, September 28, October 4, December 12, 21, 1923; P.S. du Pont to C. F. Kettering, September 24, October 1, 8, December 18, 1923, PSduP 624.

36. Sloan describes the development of the Inter-divisional Committee in *My Years with General Motors*, pp. 102–114.

37. This and the following five quotations are from A. P. Sloan to the Executive Committee, September, 1923, cited in Sloan, *My Years with General Motors*, pp. 105–108.

38. As described in Sloan, *My Years with General Motors*, p. 109.

39. P. S. du Pont to C. F. Kettering, December 21, 1923; also, P. S. du Pont to C. F. Kettering, September 24, November 1, 1923, PSduP 624.

40. C. F. Kettering to P. S. du Pont, December 28, 1923, PSduP 624.

41. P. S. du Pont to A. P. Sloan, December 21, 1923, PSduP 624.

42. *Annual Report of General Motors Corporation for 1923*, pp. 5, 19, 21.

43. Donaldson Brown, "Pricing Policy in Relation to Financial Control," *Management and Administration* (February, March, 1924), 7:196, 285; also, Sloan, *My Years with General Motors*, pp. 128–130.

44. Production Plan, Chevrolet Division, March 26, 1924, PSduP 624.

45. P. S. du Pont to A. P. Sloan, October 18, 1923, PSduP 624. The quotation in the paragraph is from this letter.
46. Production Plan, Chevrolet Division, March 26, 1924, PSduP 624; also, A. P. Sloan, Report to the Finance and Executive committees, March 14, 1924, cited in Sloan, *My Years with General Motors*, p. 130.
47. Production Plan, Chevrolet Division, March 26, 1924, PSduP 624.
48. A. P. Sloan, General Letter Nos. 141, 142, March 24, 25, 1923, mentioned in Sloan, *My Years with General Motors*, p. 130.
49. This and two other telegrams from A. P. Sloan to P. S. du Pont, May 15, 18, 27, 1924, PSduP 624. The quotations in the following paragraph are from the third telegram, PSduP 624.
50. Sloan, *My Years with General Motors*, p. 131.
51. Minutes of Finance Committee, June 13, 1924, cited in Sloan, *My Years with General Motors*, pp. 131–132. The quotations in this paragraph are from these minutes which are given more fully in Sloan's book.
52. Sloan, *My Years with General Motors*, pp. 136–137.
53. A. P. Sloan, General Letter No. 145, May 12, 1924, cited in Sloan, *My Years with General Motors*, pp. 134–135.
54. These techniques are described most succinctly in Sloan, *My Years with General Motors*, pp. 134–139, and Albert Bradley, "Setting up a Forecasting Program," American Management Association, *Annual Convention Series*, No. 41 (March 1926), pp. 3–18, reprinted in Alfred D. Chandler, Jr., *Giant Enterprise: General Motors, Ford and the Automobile Industry* (New York: Harcourt, Brace & World, 1964), pp. 127–141. See also Alfred D. Chandler, Jr., *Strategy and Structure: Chapters in the History of the Industrial Enterprise* (Cambridge: M.I.T. press, 1962), pp. 150–152.
55. Bradley, "Setting up a Forecasting Program," p. 3.
56. Sloan made his formal reply to the Finance Committee on September 29. It is quoted quite fully in Sloan, *My Years with General Motors*, pp. 132–133.
57. These changes are summarized in *Annual Report of General Motors Corporation for 1924*, p. 6, and printed leaflet "Preferred and Common Stock of General Motors," August 1, 1924. For further details of the proposal see an undated printed circular to the stockholders signed by J. J. Raskob. F. M. McHugh acknowledges receiving it on May 15, and on May 20, A. C. Ketcham wrote to P. S. du Pont saying that the Wilmington Trust Company would send Pierre's proxies unless they heard to the contrary. All three items are in PSduP 624.
58. These and the following figures on income and dividends come from the *Annual Report of General Motors Corporation for 1924*, pp. 5, 21, and for 1925, p. 5. The dividend rate in 1924 was 30¢ a quarter for the first three quarters and $1.25 on the new stock based on 4 to 1 exchange. So the total was 5¢ more than 1923.
59. Sloan, *My Years with General Motors*, pp. 153–154.
60. The story of the development of the Pontiac is well told in Sloan, *My Years with General Motors*, pp. 155–158.
61. A. P. Sloan to the Executive Committee, November 12, 1924, report on the "Status of the Pontiac Car So-Called," quoted in Sloan, *My Years with General Motors*, p. 157.
62. Minutes of Executive Committee, July 23, 1924, March 30, 1926, January 25, 1927, L. P. Fisher to P. S. du Pont, February 4, 1927, and P. S. du Pont to L. P. Fisher, February 12, 1927, suggest Pierre's continuing interest in the La Salle, PSduP 624.
63. Minutes of Executive Committee, September 18, 1924. Here the copper-cooled development was fully reviewed.
64. At the meeting of September 3, 1924, Raskob asked the Executive Committee to postpone discussion until the 18th so that Pierre could be there.

65. Sloan made this estimate in a report to the Executive Committee, Minutes of Executive Committee, February 27, 1924.

66. A. P. Sloan to Executive Committee, April 27, 1925, and H. D. Church's report of April 9, 1925. The quotation is from Sloan's letter.

CHAPTER 22. Last Years at General Motors and Du Pont

1. This is best described in a long letter from J. H. Odell to Mrs. P. S. du Pont, April 12, 1924, which tells of Pierre's nonbusiness activities in some detail, PSduP 628.

2. J. J. Raskob to P. S. du Pont, September 5, 8, 1924; J. J. Raskob to J. H. Odell, September 8, 1924; and memorandum entitled "To Citizens and Taxpayers of Wilmington"; also, P. S. du Pont to O. F. Odell (J.H's. brother), November 30, 1923; all in Raskob Papers.

3. "Chronological Growth of Longwood," prepared by its Construction Division, January 1948, PSduP 516–2.

4. *Deposition of Pierre S. du Pont*, p. 278.

5. Sidney Ratner, *Taxation and Democracy in America* (New York: Wiley, 1967), pp. 418–421. The maximum rate on inheritance tax had in earlier acts been only 25%. The reason for high estate and gift taxes in 1924 was the cuts made in the same bill on income taxes.

6. P. S. du Pont to I. du Pont, September 4, 1923, PSduP 624. For the transfer of shares to members of the Du Pont Executive Committee in 1919 and 1921, see pp. 543–544 of the present book.

7. Pierre gave this list in a letter to P. B. Belin, June 4, 1924, GTX 90, *U.S. A. Plaintiff vs. EIduPdeN, G.M. et al. Defendants;* hereafter exhibits cited by identifying initial and number.

8. In the letter to Belin cited above, Pierre mentioned that Irénée and W. Winder Laird made the proposal. Later, on the witness stand, Pierre recalled that it came from Laird and R. R. M. Carpenter. "I know Laird was the first one that spoke of it." *Deposition of Pierre S. du Pont*, p. 288.

9. William H. Graham, second vice-president of the Equitable Life Assurance Society, to F. A. McHugh, May 2, 1924, DE DP 32.

10. "Indenture Granting Annuity from Delaware Reality and Investment Company to Pierre S. du Pont and Alice Belin du Pont," May 31, 1924, GTX 94.

11. P. S. du Pont to P. B. Belin, June 4, 12, 1924, GTX 90, 91; I. du Pont to Sophie, Margaretta, and Constance du Pont, July 15, 1924, GTX 97.

12. This and the two following quotations are from P. S. du Pont to P. B. Belin, June 4, 12, 1924, GTX 90, 91.

13. P. S. du Pont to P. B. Belin, June 12, 1924, GTX 91. The following quotation is from the June 4 letter cited in note 12, above.

14. See letters cited in note 12.

15. Pierre was appointed Tax Commissioner in early November 1925, PSduP 1057.

16. The two letters cited in note 12. The quotation is from the June 4 letter.

17. I. du Pont to E. R. Stettinius, June 19, 1924 (copy to P. S. du Pont), PSduP 632. Background for this refinancing is covered in I. du Pont to J. J. Raskob, August 21, 1923, GTX 65; J. J. Raskob to I. du Pont, September 13, 1923, GTX 66; I. du Pont to J. J. Raskob, December 17, 1923, and I. du Pont to J. J. Raskob, April 11, 1924; J. J. Raskob to I. du Pont, May 9, 1924, all in PSduP 632. Copies of all these letters went to P. S. du Pont.

18. The plan is most succinctly described by Paul Willard Garrett in the financial section of the New York *Post* of July 16, 1924, and is spelled out in I. du Pont to E. R. Stettinius, June 19, 1924, PSduP 632.

19. For example, I. du Pont to P. S. du Pont, June 23, 1921; I. du Pont to Board of Christiana Securities, December 22, 1921, and January 5, 1922; I. du Pont to P. S. du Pont, October 29, 30, 1929; L. du Pont to Board of Christiana Securities, November 5, 1929, and November 10, 1930, all in PSduP 632.

20. As indicated in the Balance Sheets of Christiana Securities for these years, PSduP 632. At most the copper stock held never amounted to more than 1% of the value of the holdings.

21. Also the holding company paid in 1919, $850,488 for the cost of the Philip F. du Pont, that is, the suit that threatened its legal validity.

22. Memorandum from R. R. M. Carpenter to directors of Christiana Securities Company, August 16, 1920, PSduP 632.

23. Marquis James, *Alfred I. du Pont, The Family Rebel* (Indianapolis: Bobbs-Merrill, 1941), pp. 331-334.

24. I. du Pont to board of Christiana Securities, December 12, 1921; I. du Pont to P. S. du Pont, December 30, 1921, PSduP 632.

25. Quoted in James, *Alfred I. du Pont*, p. 347.

26. I. du Pont to Board of Christiana Securities, March 22, 1922, PSduP 632.

27. T. Cochran to I. du Pont, April 11, 1922 (enclosing a letter from A. I. du Pont to T. Cochran, April 8, 1922), all in PSduP 632.

28. James says that by 1926 Alfred was the second largest stockholder, holding more than 580,000 shares, but he cites no source. (The Du Pont shares had split since 1921.) According to James, Alfred had been buying Du Pont stock. However, in 1928, when Christiana held just over 800,000, Alfred held just under 180,000 shares; other holdings may have been held in other accounts, Stockholders List, August 31, 1928; and James, p. 922.

29. This and the two following quotations are from W. Coyne to P. S. du Pont, March 28, 31, 1922, PSduP 418.

30. W. J. Webster to P. S. du Pont, March 31, 1922, PSduP 591-2. The resulting agreement is covered in A. B. Purvis to H. G. Haskell, May 26, 1922, Government Exhibit, 22; W. S. Carpenter, Jr., to L. du Pont, H. G. Haskell, and William Coyne, November 18, 1922, and the attached memorandum, Government Exhibit, 23. *United States vs. Imperial Chemical Industries, Ltd. et al., District Court of the United States for the Southern District of New York, Civil No. 24-13.* Hereafter cites to this case will be indicated by (ICI) to distinguish exhibits and other documents from the citations to the Du Pont–GM Antitrust Suit. Also citations to government exhibits will be GE and to defendants' exhibits DE.

31. I. du Pont to P. S. du Pont, June 20, 1922, GTX 54; J. B. Laffey to I. du Pont, June 19, 1922, PSduP 632. The quotation is from Irénée's letter.

32. Extracts from Board of Directors Meeting, Christiana Securities Company, June 26, 1922, GTX 55.

33. I. du Pont to Board of Directors, Christiana Securities Company, August 17, 1922, GTX 56; and extracts from minutes of Christiana Securities meeting, June 26, 1922, GTX 55. W. S. Carpenter, Jr., to L. du Pont, H. G. Haskell, and W. Coyne, November 18, 1922 GE 23 (ICI). As a chart of the Du Pont Company's holdings in 1923 indicates, the Du Pont shares of Northern Giant Explosives, Ltd., were held by Associated Securities of Canada, a holding company that also held the Du Pont shares of Canadian Explosives, Ltd., PSduP 418.

34. As indicated in Balance Sheet, Christiana Securities, 1923, PSduP 632.

35. Minutes of Special Meeting of the Board of Directors of Christiana Securities Company, April 8, 1927, GTX 58. The total cost was $1,264,260.

36. This situation is indicated in A. B. Purvis to H. McGowan, October 15, 1928, GTX 59. The two following quotations in this paragraph are from this letter.

37. The board of Christiana Securities agreed to sell 30,000 shares of Atlas stock back to the Atlas company at 66⅔ per share. 15,000 shares of stock were to be used in that company's stock subscription plan, and 15,000 were to be paid for by Atlas executives. The remaining 40,571 shares were to be sold to the brokerage house of Laird, Bissell and Meeds at the same price. With these funds Christiana then bought from Atlas the 52,494 shares which it held in CXL and sold these to the Du Pont Company and the Nobel Industries (now Imperial Chemical Industries) in a way so that the holdings of each in the Canadian company remained the same proportion. R. R. M. Carpenter to Board of Directors of Christiana Securities Company, November 5, 1928, GTX 61; and Minutes of above, November 6, 1928, GTX 62.

38. A copy of the Agreement is printed as GE 1 (ICI). The relations between the Nobel Explosives Trades, Ltd. and Du Pont as they were worked out in 1920 is well described in William J. Reader, *Imperial Chemical Industries—A History,* Vol. I: *The Forerunners* (Oxford: Oxford University Press, 1970), pp. 394–398, and in *Pleadings, Opinion and Final Judgment* of the ICI case.

39. P. S. du Pont's letter to McGowan and Sir Harry's reply, 1937, suggest the strength of this friendship. It deals with Pierre congratulating Sir Harry upon his elevation to the peerage, PSduP 637.

40. R. R. M. Carpenter to P. S. du Pont (undated), PSduP 418; and a similar letter to Irénée on these matters, dated June 29, 1923, which is GE 35 (ICI). The memorandum of Harry Haskell of July 27, 1923, and H. G. Haskell to P. S. du Pont, July 21, 1923, PSduP 418; see also, I. du Pont to H. G. Haskell, July 18, 1923, GE 38 (ICI); unsigned note from Nobel to W. S. Carpenter, undated, in PSduP 418. The quotation in the following paragraph is from this note.

41. The Du Pont Company continued to sell in these countries even after Irénée, Haskell, and Felix du Pont had conferred with Sir Harry in London in the spring of 1924. A year and a half later when, at the close of 1925, modifications were made in the 1920 agreement, a compromise was reached. Then the du Ponts were to continue to concentrate selling nitrocellulose powders in Europe, while the Nobels were to have "the priority on TNT and nitroglycerin powders." H. G. Haskell to A. Felix du Pont, Du Pont Executive Committee, March 21, 1924, GE 45 (ICI); notes of conference at Nobel House, May 2, 1924, GE 50 (ICI); and W. T. Taylor to Major Casey, May 27, 1926, GE 51 (ICI).

42. The arrangement for the marketing of Duco and antiknock gasoline is mentioned in J. E. Crane to I. du Pont, February 4, 1925 (a cable with a copy to P. S. du Pont); J. E. Crane to H. G. Haskell, September 18, 1925, PSduP 418.

43. I. du Pont to P. S. du Pont, August 24, 1925; notes from a meeting in Hamburg, Germany, September 7, 1925; J. E. Crane to H. G. Haskell, September 14, 1925, PSduP 418; an extract from minutes of Finance Committee (Du Pont Co.), October 5, 1925, GE 88 (ICI). In Reader, *Imperial Chemical Industries,* I, 408–410 indicate the relationship of the German competition in South America.

44. The Du Pont Company sold all its stock interest in DAG September 1940. Shortly after the stock purchase, representatives of Du Pont and DAG drew up a patents and process agreement similar to the one the Du Pont Company had with the Nobel Industries. When unable to agree on the terms of the agreement, "an informal understanding was arrived at between them which was not binding on either of them, under which each indicated a willingness to offer the other such rights to patents, processes and technical developments." These were to be negotiated on an individual basis, and reciprocal plant visits were encouraged. No information or visits were exchanged after 1937. *Pleadings,* in the ICI case, pp. 23–25; the quotation is from page 24. Several different negotiations led to

another agreement in 1929, which involved the Germans as well as the British. *Pleadings, Opinion and Final Judgment* (ICI), 51; also Reader, *Imperial Chemical Industries,* I, 411–413.

45. H. McGowan to J. J. Raskob, March 28, 1927, PSduP 624.

46. J. J. Raskob to P. S., I. and L. du Pont, June 16, 1927, GTX 67. More than seven years earlier, in December 1919, McGowan had proposed a somewhat similar exchange of stock, but the matter was not taken up. Reader, *Imperial Chemical Industries,* I, 396. The year before, McGowan had unexpectedly sold 22,500 shares of General Motors largely because of changes in the international exchange rate, J. J. Raskob to H. McGowan, December 23, 1925, and H. McGowan to J. J. Raskob, January 12, 1926, Raskob Papers. Some months later the Du Pont Company purchased 40,000 shares of General Motors from CXL, L. du Pont to H. McGowan, August 23, 1926, GTX 172.

47. L. du Pont to J. J. Raskob, June 17, 1927, GTX 68.

48. H. B. du Pont to P. S. du Pont, December 30, 1927; P. S. du Pont to H. B. du Pont, January 3, 1928; I. du Pont to Syndicate purchasing U. S. Rubber Company stock, September 6, October 20, November 7, 1928, PSduP 229–40.

49. There is a brief summary of Du Pont's role in reorganizing United States Rubber in Alfred D. Chandler, Jr., *Strategy and Structure: Chapters in the History of the Industrial Enterprise* (Cambridge, Mass.: M.I.T. Press, 1962), pp. 350–351.

50. H. B. du Pont to P. S. du Pont, January 25, 1928, and Trust Agreement, December 28, 1928; I. du Pont, H. B. du Pont, H. S. Meeds, Jr., to P. S. du Pont, December 28, 1928, PSduP 229–40.

51. After Pierre went to General Motors in 1920, he immediately turned any questions, requests, or proposals concerning the company over to this brother Irénée and after 1925 his brother Lammot, telling the correspondent that since 1919 he had almost nothing to do with the business of the Du Pont Company. There are many examples of such letters in PSduP 418.

52. A. P. Sloan to J. T. Smith, March 21, 1927 (copy sent to P. S. du Pont), and P. S. du Pont to A. P. Sloan, March 24, 1927, PSduP 624.

53. These figures on earnings and those in the next paragraph on dividends come from the Corporation's Annual Reports for these years. Earnings are listed as somewhat higher in the Federal Trade Commission *Report on the Motor Vehicle Industry* (Washington, D.C., 1939), pp. 525–526. For example, for 1927 the Federal Trade Commission Report listed net profit for General Motors at $262.3 million, for 1928 at $296.3 million.

54. The figures in changes of stock issued come from the Corporation's annual reports. Also stock changes are described in a letter to stockholders by A. P. Sloan, January 7, 1926, and by M. L. Prentiss, September 14, 1927, both in Raskob Papers.

55. Gross investment rose to $609.9 million in 1929. The investment in affiliated subsidiaries and miscellaneous units went from $61.5 million in 1924 to $117.7 million in 1928 and to $203.3 million in 1929. Total assets reached $1,324 million in 1929. These figures are all in the Corporation's Annual Reports for these years.

56. Figures on Ford's financial performance come from Federal Trade Commission, *Report on the Motor Vehicle Industry,* p. 649. Ford's total assets were more than half of General Motors'. In 1929 they were listed at $761.0 million as compared to General Motors' assets of $1,324.9 million. A. D. H. Kaplan, *Big Enterprise in a Competitive System* (Washington, D.C.: Brookings Institution, 1954), p. 149. At that date, 1929, General Motors was the third largest company in the United States by assets, and Ford the sixth. Also, Alan Nevins and Frank E. Hill, *Ford: Expansion and Challenge, 1915–1933* (New York: Scribner, 1957), chs. 15–16, 22.

57. Lawrence H. Seltzer, *A Financial History of the American Automobile Industry* (Boston: Houghton Mifflin, 1928), p. 219.

58. This and the following quotation are from P. S. du Pont to W. L. Day, March 9, 1927, PSduP 624.
59. Alfred P. Sloan, Jr., *My Years with General Motors* (Garden City, N.Y.: Doubleday, 1964), pp. 160–161.
60. P. S. du Pont to C. Campbell, February 23, 1923, PSduP 624.
61. P. S. du Pont to L. du Pont, October 31, 1922, GTX 435. This reason was probably more important to Pierre than was Sloan's plea to add more operating men to the top committee.
62. P. S. du Pont to F. J. Fisher, July 28, 1924, PSduP 624. The next quotation is from this letter.
63. P. S. du Pont to A. Bishop, October 14, 1924, PSduP 624.
64. H. McGowan to P. S. du Pont, November 7, 1924, PSduP 624. McGowan was delighted that the Fishers agreed to become full-time executives, as he felt Sloan was "overburdened. . . . In addition it cements the relationship for all time with the Fisher Corporation, to which we all attach great importance." Also, P. S. du Pont to General Motors Finance Committee, January 26, 1925, PSduP 624.
65. Seltzer, *Financial History*, pp. 218–219; F. D. Brown to J. J. Raskob, March 13, 1926, DE GM 34; A. P. Sloan to J. J. Raskob, February 13, March 13, 1926, Raskob Papers.
66. F. J. Fisher to P. S. du Pont, January 19, 1927, PSduP 624.
67. W. A. Fisher to Stockholders of Fisher Body Corporation, June 30, 1926, GTX 507.
68. These changes are indicated in the Corporation's Annual Reports and its organization charts for these years. Particularly revealing is the chart dated April 1927, which is DE GM 3. In a letter to W. S. Fisher, February 15, 1927, Pierre stressed to the Fisher brothers their involvement in the "broader responsibilities of the enlarged company," PSduP 624.
69. Seltzer, *Financial History*, pp. 241–243, has the best brief account of this sale.
70. P. S. du Pont to T. Cochran, April 7, 1925, PSduP 418.
71. Nevins and Hill, *Ford: Expansion and Challenge*, ch. 14; Sloan, *My Years with General Motors*, pp. 315–318. Durant had set up Bedford Buicks, Ltd. of London before World War I to assemble cars on Buick's chassis. The first really large overseas assembling operations began in 1924 when Chevrolet set up a plant near London and another near Copenhagen.
72. This and the following quotation are from P. S. du Pont to A. P. Sloan, July 17, 1924, PSduP 624.
73. The following account of the Austin negotiations is from Sloan, *My Years with General Motors*, pp. 318–319.
74. J. D. Mooney to A. P. Sloan, undated cable on the bottom of which is written "Copy to Kennett Square," PSduP 624.
75. J. D. Mooney to J. J. Raskob, January 8, 1928 (forwarded to Pierre), PSduP 624. The largest company was the German Vereinigte Steel Works; then came the British, Egyptian-based Peel & Company, producers of raw cotton; Anderson & Clayton, American cotton sellers; Copper Export Company, also an American firm; and the German General Electric Company. Pierre had little interest in the Far Eastern market.
76. Sloan, *My Years with General Motors*, p. 326. By the final agreement General Motors received 80% interest in Opel for $25,967,000 and with an option to buy the remaining 20% for $7,395,000. This final purchase came in 1931.
77. As chairman, Pierre, of course, had a major say in the selecting of new and dropping of old members from the board. For example, when American Car and Foundry became involved in the manufacturing of trucks, it was Pierre who arranged with the Morgan firm for the resignation of William Woodin, the Morgan-sponsored director who was president of American Car and Foundry, to resign from the board. P. S. du Pont to J. P. Morgan, June 6, 1927; J. P. Morgan to P. S. du Pont, June 8, 1927; P. S. du Pont to

W. S. Woodin, June 20, 1927. Also, P. S. du Pont to G. W. Pepper, October 22, 1926, P. S. du Pont to J. P. Morgan, September 23, 1925; C. C. Cooper to P. S. du Pont, August 15, 1927, all in PSduP 624.

78. For example, when Raskob and Brown became worried about Sloan's health, they went to Pierre to have him urge Sloan to extend a Palm Beach vacation for another week. "No one else can convince him," Raskob wrote; "Alfred will pay no attention to anyone except you, and perhaps not even you." J. J. Raskob to P. S. du Pont, March 3, 1925; P. S. du Pont to A. P. Sloan, March 5, 1925, PSduP 624. Pierre also kept in touch with retired managers of General Motors. There is correspondence in PSduP 624 to K. Zimmerschied, W. Day, H. H. Bassett, and H. H. Rice.

79. J. J. Raskob to P. S. du Pont, April 30, 1925; P. S. du Pont to J. J. Raskob, May 8, 1925; P. S. du Pont to C. S. Mott, May 8, 1925, PSduP 624. Management Securities apparently purchased 100,000 shares of Mott's allotment and sold them to Sloan.

80. P. S. du Pont to W. Z. Ripley, November 17, 1925, PSduP 1075.

81. That man was Alfred R. Glancy. A. P. Sloan to P. S. du Pont, Chairman; S. Prosser and A. G. Bishop, July 7, 1926, PSduP 624. Also, A. R. Glancy to P. S. du Pont, September 17, 1923, and September 25, 1925, PSduP 624. After the initial allocation of Management Securities stock in November 1923 and January 1924, there were further allotments in November 1924 (and early 1925) when the Fishers received their shares and again in April–May 1925 and July 1926. See list of the Allocation of Management Securities stock in GTX 260.

82. J. J. Raskob to P. S. du Pont, June 29, 1926; P. S. du Pont to J. J. Raskob, July 1, 1926, and attached "Suggested Alternative Wording," J. J. Raskob to P. S. du Pont, February 16, 1927; P. S. du Pont to J. J. Raskob, February 21, 1927, PSduP 624.

83. I. du Pont to P. S. du Pont, July 24, 1922. This letter has three important enclosures, PSduP 418.

84. The provisions of the plan are outlined in the *Annual Report of the E. I. du Pont de Nemours & Company for 1926*, pp. 9–10.

85. M. D. Fisher, Sec. Executive Committee, to P. S. du Pont, October 22, 1926; L. du Pont to P. S. du Pont, January 24, 1929, both in PSduP 418.

86. J. J. Raskob to P. S. du Pont, January 30, 1922.

87. Irénée's proposal to move the General Motors offices from New York to Wilmington was first proposed by Daniel Cauffiel, head of the Du Pont Real Estate Department. Irénée argued that the move would strengthen the partnership between the two companies and mean that Pierre would not have to spend so much time in New York. Moreover, it would help to fill up some of the unused office space. D. Cauffiel to P. S. du Pont, July 19, 1921; I. du Pont to P. S. du Pont, April 19, 1922, both in PSduP 624.

88. Chandler, *Strategy and Structure*, p. 144.

89. F. W. Pickard to P. S. du Pont, July 9, 1921, Du Pont Co. Records; L. du Pont to P. S. du Pont, August 10, September 2, 1921, GTX 420, 422; P. S. du Pont to L. du Pont, August 23, 1923, GTX 421.

90. "Closing Argument on Behalf of the Government," in the Du Pont–General Motors antitrust case, December 8, 1953, p. 7250; W. Allen to Executive Committee, Du Pont Company, February 1923, GTX 406.

91. W. Coyne to P. S. du Pont, July 18, 23, 1923, PSduP 418.

92. P. S. du Pont to W. Coyne, July 19, 1912, PSduP 418; P. S. du Pont to W. S. Knudsen, July 27, 1923, PSduP 624.

93. L. du Pont to P. S. du Pont and J. J. Raskob, January 27, 1927, GTX 460.

94. W. P. Allen to P. S. du Pont, June 25, 1927, GTX 460.

95. G. W. Kerr to P. S. du Pont, June 25, 1924, with enclosure; also, August 26, 1924, PSduP 624.

96. "Closing Argument" . . . in the Du Pont–GM antitrust Suit, December 8, 1953, p. 7266.

97. *Annual Report of E. I. du Pont de Nemours & Company for 1926*, pp. 14–15.

98. "Resolution to be Presented at a Meeting to be held at the Residence of Senator James W. Wadsworth, Washington, D.C., January 6, 1928;" W. H. Stayton to P. S. du Pont, February 6, 1928; Minutes of Special Meeting of the Directors of the Association Against the Prohibition Amendment held at the home of Charles Sabin, New York City, at 7 P.M. the 15th day of March 1928, all in PSduP 1023. See also W. H. Stayton to Organization Committee (P. S. du Pont, E. S. Harkness, and Charles H. Sabin), January 9, 1928. (The membership of the Organization Committee was enlarged at that meeting.); also in PSduP 1023.

99. Pierre proposed Raskob as one of the fifty directors in the reorganized Association, W. H. Stayton to P. S. du Pont, February 6, 1928, PSduP 1023.

100. Oscar Handlin, *Al Smith and His America* (Boston: Little, Brown, 1958), pp. 87, 127–128. The correspondence between Raskob and Smith in the Raskob Papers begins February 18, 1928.

101. Clippings in the Raskob Papers.

102. Pierre describes these events succintly to Sir Harry McGowan in a letter of August 27, 1928, PSduP 624. *New York Times* of July 11 gave the announcement.

103. P. S. du Pont to H. McGowan, August 27, 1928, PSduP 624; P. S. du Pont to D. Page, August 11, 1928, PSduP 624; A. P. Sloan, Jr., to I. du Pont, July 25, 1928, DE GM 17, review the issues raised in the Executive Committee. Clippings in the Raskob Papers indicated some of the press response, as does Sloan's letter just cited.

104. J. J. Raskob to T. C. du Pont, August 17, 1928, DE GM 20.

105. This and the following quotation are from I. du Pont to A. P. Sloan, July 27, 1928, DTX GM 18. Irénée's letter mentions the poll of directors.

106. A. P. Sloan to P. S. du Pont, July 27, 1928, PSduP 624.

107. This and the following quotation are from a printed pamphlet "General Motors Is Not in Politics—Extracts from a speech by Alfred P. Sloan, Jr. . . . Aug. 1, 1928 . . ." The covering statement by Sloan, August 3, 1928, PSduP 624.

108. This and the following quotation are from P. S. du Pont to H. McGowan, August 27, 1928; also, P. S. du Pont to D. Page, August 11, 1928. Also significant is P. S. du Pont to M. S. Rukeyser, August 14, 1928, all in PSduP 624.

109. P. S. du Pont to F. D. Brown, January 25, 1929. Pierre sent similar letters to other members of the board. All are in PSduP 624–3.

110. A. P. Sloan to P. S. du Pont, July 27, 1927, PSduP 624. In a conversation with Sloan in the fall of 1962, while making a final review of *My Years with General Motors*, I [Chandler] told him I was planning to write a biography of P. S. du Pont and had been in Wilmington. Sloan's first question was, did anyone mention Raskob's and Pierre's retirement? It was, he said, the only real difference of opinion he had with Pierre and the Du Pont group. Only after he had reviewed many of the records of the postwar crisis did Sloan fully recall the copper-cooled controversy.

111. B. G. du Pont, *E. I. du Pont de Nemours and Company, A History, 1802–1902* (Boston: Houghton Mifflin, 1920), and PSduP 533.

112. Important files on Pierre S. du Pont's efforts for Delaware schools are PSduP 712. Also, Harold C. Livesay, "Delaware Negroes, 1865–1915," *Delaware History* (October 1968), 13:11. During this period all Delaware public schools were segregated. See also Henry C. Reed, *Delaware: History of the First State* (New York: Lewis Historical Publishing Co., 1947), pp. 72–74.

113. Pierre du Pont's activities as tax commissioner are indicated in PSduP 1057.

114. Pierre du Pont's continuing activities in the Association Against the Prohibition Amendment are indicated, PSduP 1023.

115. P. S. du Pont and S. W. Lambert, December 12, 1933; Seating Arrangement and Table Diagram, "Victory Dinner of the Board of Directors of the Association Against The Prohibition Amendment," The Waldorf Astoria, December 5, 1933, all PSduP 1023.
116. Raskob's tenure as Democratic National Chairman and Smith's defeat and his are described in Arthur M. Schlesinger, Jr., *The Crisis of the Old Order*, Vol. 1: *The Age of Roosevelt* (Boston: Houghton Mifflin, 1957), chs. 27–28. Also, Handlin, *Al Smith and His America*, ch. 7.
117. There are copies of the hearings, newspaper clippings and other papers pertinent to the Nye investigation in PSduP 418–9.
118. The file concerning the Liberty League is PSduP 771. The fullest published account is George Wolfskill, *The Revolt of the Conservative: A History of the Liberty League* (Boston: Houghton Mifflin, 1962); chs. 3, 5 indicate the part played by Pierre and his brothers.
119. Before joining the Pennsylvania Railroad, Pierre had been a director of the Philadelphia, Baltimore and Washington Railroad—a subsidiary of the Pennsylvania Railroad—from 1915 to 1918. Pierre also served as a director of the General Reduction Corporation of Detroit, 1927–1936; the American International Corporation of New York, 1916–1933; and the Regents Corporation of Dover, Delaware, 1930–1937, as well as the Wyoming Shovel Works, Wyoming, Pennsylvania, 1914–1930, and director of the Wilmington Trust Company from its founding in 1903 until his death, PSduP 229.
120. Investment Accounts, 1928, 1929, 1930, PSduP 229.
121. There is little besides routine printed material in the file on the Empire State, Inc., PSduP 229–15.

## CHAPTER 23. The Family and the Enterprise

1. Thomas R. Navin and Marion V. Sears, "The Rise of a Market for Industrial Securities, 1887–1902, *Business History Review* (June 1955), 29:109–112.
2. Alfred D. Chandler, Jr., *The Railroads, The Nation's First Big Business* (New York, 1968), pp. 43–70 and 97–125.
3. Thomas C. Cochran describes and analyzes in detail this transformation in the railroads in his *Railroad Leaders, 1845–1890: The Business Mind in Action* (Cambridge, Mass.: Harvard University Press, 1953), chs. 5 and 6.
4. R. Joseph Monsen, John S. Chiu and David E. Cooley, "The Effect of Ownership and Control on the Performance of the Large Firm," *The Quarterly Journal of Economics* (August 1968), 82:435–451.
5. Robert J. Larner, "Ownership and Control in the 200 Largest Non-Financial Corporations, 1929 and 1963," *American Economic Review* (September 1966), 56:779–780.
6. P. S. du Pont to S. H. du Pont, December 28, 1922, PSduP 1909.

# Index

*While the various reorganizational names of the du Pont parent company have been indexed, all subentries have been, for the reason of clarity, listed under the general name of the "Du Pont Company."*

Abbott, Lyman and Lawrence, 422
Adam Opel AG, 580
Addyston Pipe and Steel case (1899), 112
Aetna Powder Company, 189, 340, 364, 402, 403
Ahuja, Elias, 170, 177, 181, 182, 183–84, 186–87, 204–05, 222, 231, 234, 476
Alexander, C. H., 45
*Alfred I. du Pont, The Family Rebel* (James), 323
Allen, William P., 583
Aluminum Company of America, 464
American Agricultural Chemical Company, 233
American Exchange Bank, Philadelphia, 164
American Express Company, 206
American Group, 171, 172, 189, 192
American Liberty League, 589
American Nitrogen Company, 378
American Powder Company, 58, 60, 83
American Smelting & Refining Company, 593
American Sugar Company, 112
American Tobacco Company, 260, 275, 276, 277, 285, 286, 288, 289, 293
Andelot, Henry Victor d', 7
Anderson, A. C., 501–02

Anglo-German Group, 171, 179, 187, 188, 189, 192, 196, 197, 198, 199, 299
Anstruther, Sir Ralph, 192
Anthony Powder Company, 117
Antitrust suits, 208, 228, 248, 260–91, 299-300
*Aragon,* S.S., 234
Arlington Company, 382, 386
Army Ordinance Department, U. S., 406–407, 410, 413, 416
Artificial leather, production of, 249–50, 385–86, 454, 522–23
Ashland (Wisc.) Works, 59, 139, 162, 195
Asheville, North Carolina, 36
Association Against the Prohibition Amendment, 584–85, 586, 588, 589
Atlantic Giant Company, 61, 171
Atlas Powder Company, 293, 296–99, 396, 567–69
Austin Company, 579
Austin Powder Works, 58, 59, 60, 79–80, 90, 99, 101
Automobile industry, 343, 444, 451, 463, 478, 507, 531, 534, 538, 578
Avery, Brainard, 270

Badische Anilin, 570
Baker, George F., 478, 479, 554

Baker, Newton D., 397, 400, 404, 405, 410, 411, 413, 414, 415–16, 417–19, 420–21, 422, 424, 425, 450
Baldwin, Henry F., 128, 129, 131, 139, 167, 175, 208–09
Baldwin, Matthias W., 10
Ball Brothers Manufacturing Company, 464
Bankers Trust Company, New York, 335, 589
Bank of Delaware, Wilmington, 31, 32
Barksdale, Hamilton M., 49–50, 61, 62, 74, 80, 90, 91, 94, 97, 110, 111, 112, 115–16, 117, 118, 124, 216, 218, 219, 130, 131, 133, 138–39, 140, 141, 143, 147, 152, 157, 159, 160, 162, 166, 167, 168, 174, 175, 176, 195, 196, 197, 205, 207–08, 214, 217, 227, 229, 232, 238, 241, 250, 251, 265, 274, 277, 294, 295, 296, 302, 305, 306, 307, 308–09, 311–312, 313, 315–16, 317, 318, 319, 320, 321, 324–25, 344, 353, 365, 366, 428, 446, 447, 458
Barton, Henry L., 469, 494
Baruch, Bernard, 400, 404, 411, 413
Bassett, Henry H., 498, 516, 517, 518, 521, 525, 527, 532, 549
Bates, Mrs. Lindon, 394
Bay City, Michigan, 182
Beckton Chemical Company, 385
Beecher, Walter A., 90
Beecher, William, 82
Belin, Charles Augustus, 6, 204, 275, 340, 402
Belin, Ferdinand Lammot, 340, 392, 402
Belin, Henry, 44, 57, 62, 68, 80, 94, 264, 391
Belin, Lammot, 436, 437, 442
Belin, Paul, 563, 564
Belin, Wells, 392
Bergland, Eric L., 468–70, 554, 598
Bermingham, John, 80, 96, 97, 274
Bethlehem Steel Company, 71, 370, 583
Betts Machine Company, 408
Beveridge, Alven, 43
Bickford Company, 98
Bidermann, Marguerite, 393
Birmingham Powder Company, 60, 90
Bishop, Arthur G., 443, 542
Bishop, George T., 41
Bissell, George P., 43
Boies, Henry M., 62, 63, 64, 68, 90
Bonaparte, Charles Joseph, 269, 279
Bonta, A. K., 44, 45
Boquete property, Chile, 183
Borah, William E., 265, 270
Boston, Massachusetts, 17, 18, 43
Bradford, Edward, 347
Bradley, Albert, 498

Brandywine Creek, 5
Brandywine Mills, 4–14, 54, 130, 139
Brazil, 194
Bridgeport (Ct.) Wood Finishing Company, 385
Briggs, Russell E., 486, 487, 498
British government, 372–73
British Nobel Dynamite Trust, 191
Brode, 118, 271, 272
Brookings, Robert, 411–12, 413–14, 419
Brooks, Philip, 19
Brown, Donaldson, 452, 463, 496, 497–498, 501, 504, 540, 549, 550, 552, 553, 554, 555, 573, 577, 579, 598
Brown, Edmund L., 90, 91
Brown, F. D., 429
Brown, Henry Fletcher, 103, 131, 139, 305, 313, 315, 320, 324, 329, 338, 351, 352, 365, 366, 368, 375–76, 386, 402, 403, 428
Brown & Shipley Company, 205
Brown Brothers & Company, 205, 219, 230
Brown-Lipe-Chapin Company, 464
Buckeye Powder Company, 73, 111, 261, 290, 291
Buckner, Edmund G., 102, 172, 270, 271, 274, 277, 283, 305, 315, 329, 332, 368, 371, 401, 406, 407, 417, 421, 423, 425, 452–53
Buenos Aires, Argentina, 181, 184
Buffington, Joseph, 276, 356–57
Buick Motor Company, 438, 439, 443, 476, 498, 500, 503, 512, 518, 519, 525, 530
Bull, William Lanman, 211
Button, William H., 348

Cadillac Motor Car Company, 439, 440, 443, 499, 503, 512, 519, 530, 557
California Investment Company, 97, 103, 170, 209, 273, 274, 276, 279, 291
California Powder Works, 58, 59, 78, 79, 80, 90, 93, 94–95, 96, 97, 98, 99, 100, 102, 116, 140, 162, 171, 209, 273
Cambria Powder Mill, 84
Campbell, Colin, 530
Campbell, Dr., 487, 488
Canadian Explosives, Ltd., 199, 477, 479, 505, 507, 567, 568, 569
Carnegie, Andrew, xxi, 135, 327
Carney's Point, New Jersey, 34, 35, 37, 54, 70, 74, 126, 139, 152, 366, 376, 382, 383
*Carolina oficina,* 235–26
Carpenter, Edmund N., 234–35, 236, 425
Carpenter, Peggy, 391

Carpenter, R. R. M. ("Ruly"), 259, 305, 313, 320, 333, 334, 335, 338, 351, 352, 365, 381, 383, 384, 385, 391, 397, 398, 452, 471, 562, 568, 581, 582
Carpenter, Walter S., 313, 381–82, 383, 384, 541, 542, 587, 599
Carpenter, Walter S., Jr., 231, 430
Carter, George, 351
Cash, A. L., 543
Cauffiel, Daniel, 305
Caveat Venditor, A Profile of Coleman du Pont (Donaldson), 323
Cawley, Clark & Company, 385
Celluloid, production of, 382, 383
Census Bureau, U. S., 59
Central Coal & Iron Company, 26–27
Chamberlain, Arthur, 191
Chamberlain, George Earle, 420
Champion, Alfred, 439, 466
Chapin, Roy, 575
Charleston, West Virginia, 408
Chattanooga Powder Company, 60, 90, 152
Chester, Pennsylvania, 14
Chevrolet, Louis, 440
Chevrolet Motor Company, 440, 441, 445, 446, 447, 449, 452, 453, 460–62, 476, 479, 498, 505, 507, 508, 513, 518, 519, 529, 544, 545, 551, 556, 558, 574, 582
Chicago, Burlington & Quincy Railroad, 508
Chicago Tribune, 261, 262
Chile, nitrate supply from, 151, 181–87, 205–06, 214, 222, 230–38, 245, 254, 377, 378, 397, 400
Chilean Nitrate Company, 183
Christiana Securities Company, 335, 429, 489, 538, 539, 561, 563, 564–72, 581, 603
Chrysler, Walter P., 438, 459, 474, 475, 498
Chrysler Motor Company, 538, 555
Church, H. D., 546, 558
Cincinnati Enquirer, 24
Citroën Company, 466, 579
Civil War, 20, 359, 403–04
Clark, Emory W., 438, 440, 441
Clarke, Earl, 498
Cleveland, Ohio, 26
Cleveland Plain Dealer, 337, 346
Climax Powder Company, 62, 84
Coast Manufacturing & Supply Com-pany, 170
Cochran, Thomas, 485, 487, 488, 566–67, 578
Coleman, John B., 82, 90, 91
Collins, Richard H., 499, 544, 545
Columbia Investment Company, 79

Colvin, William S., 69
Comité Central de la Colonie Francaise de Philadelphie, 393
Comité d'Assistance en Alsace-Lorraine, 393
Commerce Department, U. S., 263
Connable, Frank L., 90, 91, 100, 127, 138, 139, 211–12, 229, 274, 277, 305, 306, 309, 313, 320, 341, 365, 428, 429
Consumer Powder Company, 89
Cook, Philip, 533
Coolidge, Calvin, 561
Copeland, Charles, 144, 149, 259, 338, 341, 391, 397
Cosmopolitan magazine, 262
Cotton supply, 377–78, 379–80
Council of National Defense, 404–05
Coyne, William, 131, 313, 320, 338, 351, 352, 365, 429, 515, 530, 567, 582
Crimean War, 6
Crozier, William, 268, 289, 401, 402, 403, 404, 407, 408, 410, 411, 412–13, 414, 415, 417, 418, 419, 450
Curran, Henry H., 584
Curtis, Cyrus, 346–47

Dallas, Texas, 41, 43, 44, 47
Dallas Consolidated Electric Street Rail-way, 41, 43, 44–46
Dallas Electric and Standard Light and Power Company, 44–45, 46
Daniel, John W., 272, 273
Daniels, Josephus, 397–98, 400
Davis, Francis B., 572
Davis, Hywel, 84
Davis, John, 342
Day, William L., 499, 514, 515, 575
Dayton, Ohio, 518
Dayton Engineering Laboratories, 445
Dayton Wright Airplane Company, 466
Deepwater, New Jersey, 382, 384
Deere, John, 515
Delaware College, 459
Delaware Investment Company, 88, 89, 90, 117, 209, 273, 274, 276, 279, 291
Delaware public school system, 458, 537, 549, 557, 560, 563–64, 584, 588, 598
Delaware Realty & Investment Company, 562, 563
Delaware School Auxiliary, 459
Delaware Securities Company, 65, 68, 88, 89, 90, 117, 209, 273, 274, 276, 279, 289, 291
Delaware Unemployment Relief Com-mission, 589
Delco Light Company, 466, 512, 515
Detroit Free Press, 264
DeWalters, E. A., 543
Dimmick, E. J., 263

Dodge Brothers Motor Company, 444, 527, 538, 555, 575, 578
Doehler Die Casting Company, 464
Dominick & Dominick, 464
Dominion Iron & Steel Company, 39
Donaldson, John W., 323
Donaldson, William A., 51, 53, 346
Duco finish, 523, 570
Dunham, Lewis L., 328, 330, 333, 350
Dunham, Russell H., 71, 72, 73, 74, 100, 124, 143, 144, 146, 149, 152, 153, 293
Dunlop Rubber Company, 464
Dunn, William W., 402, 403
Dun's Reports, 32
Du Pont, A. Felix, 334, 335, 338, 340, 343, 351, 352, 452, 453, 570, 572, 597
Du Pont, Alexis I., 35, 44, 46, 49, 50, 51, 52, 53, 90, 127, 162, 220, 272, 338, 339, 341
Du Pont, Alexis (Lex) Irénée, II (son of Cousin Eugene), 8, 17, 18, 20, 127
Du Pont, Alfred I., 3, 16, 17, 22, 26, 27, 31, 35, 44, 48, 49, 50–52, 54, 56, 62, 68, 73, 74, 84, 89, 90, 91, 119, 124, 125, 126, 127, 128, 130, 135, 138, 139, 147, 148, 159, 160, 162, 165, 175, 176–177, 179, 181, 195, 211, 214, 224, 229, 250, 251, 260, 276, 277, 282, 288, 302, 305, 306–08, 309, 313, 320, 321, 322, 323, 324, 328–29, 330, 331, 332, 335, 336, 337, 338, 339, 340, 341, 342–43, 344, 345–46, 347, 348, 349, 351, 353, 354, 356, 357, 358, 364, 390, 406, 436, 437, 563, 565, 566–67, 596
Du Pont, Alfred Irénée (Pierre's cousin), 9, 11, 20–21, 22, 24, 36, 37
Du Pont, Alfred Victor (Pierre's grand-father), 4
Du Pont, Alfred Victor (Pierre's Uncle Fred), 7, 8, 16, 17, 20, 21, 24, 25, 26–27
Du Pont, Mrs. Alfred Victor, 7
Du Pont, Alice Belin (Pierre's wife), 260, 391–92, 398, 437, 438, 475, 476, 490, 492, 562, 564, 601
Du Pont, Alicia Bradford (Mrs. Alfred I.), 306, 346
Du Pont, Annie Rogers Zinn, 128
Du Pont, Antoine Bidermann, Jr., 31
Du Pont, Archibald M. L., 338, 342, 343
Du Pont, Bessie G. (Mrs. Alfred I.), 306, 343, 354, 588
Du Pont, Bidermann (Pierre's uncle), 6, 8, 17, 20, 24, 25
Du Pont, Charles Augustus (Pierre's uncle), 6
Du Pont, Charles I., 21, 23, 33, 35, 37, 48, 49, 50, 52
Du Pont, Charlotte, 16

Du Pont, E. Paul, 338, 342, 343
Du Pont, Eleuthera (Henry Belin's wife), 259
Du Pont, Eleuthère Irénée, 4
Du Pont, Eleuthère Irénée (Pierre's uncle), 9, 16
Du Pont, Elsie (Mrs. T. Coleman), 51, 174
Du Pont, Emma Paulina, 41
Du Pont, Ernest, 338, 342, 343
Du Pont, Eugene (Pierre's cousin), 8, 9, 19, 20, 21, 22, 24, 34, 35, 36, 37, 44, 47, 49, 53, 61, 84, 102, 199, 338, 339, 342, 365
Du Pont, Eugene (son of Cousin Eugene), 8, 52, 127, 563
Du Pont, Eugene E., (son of Alexis I.), 127, 338, 341, 343, 351, 453
Du Pont, Francis G., 20, 22, 34, 35, 37, 38, 48, 49, 50, 51, 52, 53, 54, 89, 90, 127
Du Pont, Francis I., 22, 34, 74, 90, 126, 128, 142, 154, 338, 339, 341, 343, 344, 345, 357, 358, 596
Du Pont, Hallock, 562
Du Pont, Colonel Henry A., 20, 21, 35, 41, 44, 49, 50, 51, 52, 53, 63–64, 66, 68, 82, 89, 90, 127, 128, 220, 227, 262, 264, 274, 278, 279, 283, 284, 301, 302, 316, 351, 354, 355, 526, 565, 567
Du Pont, Henry Belin (Pierre's brother), 7, 13, 17, 35, 36–37, 38, 39, 41, 42, 48, 259, 562, 571
Du Pont, Henry Belin, Jr., 259
Du Pont, Henry F. (son of Henry A.), 127, 338, 339, 341, 343, 351, 452, 456, 458
Du Pont, Henry H. (Pierre's uncle), 4, 5, 6, 9, 13–14, 19, 24, 59
Du Pont, Irene (Irénée's wife), 259, 343
Du Pont, Irénée (Pierre's brother), 7, 17, 25, 39, 41, 43, 71, 100, 127, 134, 138, 149, 153, 167, 203, 204, 234, 235, 248, 249, 250, 259, 272, 274, 277, 302, 305, 308, 311–12, 313, 314, 319, 320, 321, 326, 329, 333, 335, 338, 340, 343, 351, 352, 359, 364, 365, 366, 368, 371, 376, 380, 382, 386, 394, 397, 398, 400, 401, 402, 403, 411, 413, 428, 429, 452, 456, 458, 463, 471, 478, 487, 491, 493, 507, 523, 536, 541, 542, 561, 563, 565, 566, 567, 568, 571, 572, 580, 581, 582
Du Pont, Isabella (Sharp) (Pierre's sister), 8, 259, 391, 562
Du Pont, Lammot (Pierre's brother), 8, 138, 259, 302, 333, 335, 338, 343, 351, 352, 365, 382, 386, 391, 428, 429, 452, 536, 562, 563, 571, 572, 580, 581, 583, 587, 599

Du Pont, Lammot (Pierre's father), 4–7, 8, 9, 12–14, 15, 16–17, 25, 59–60, 61

Du Pont, Louis Cazenove (Pierre's cousin), 9

Du Pont, Louisa (Copeland) (Pierre's sister), 7, 11, 13, 16, 19, 24, 41, 47, 259, 391, 397, 562

Du Pont, Margaretta Lammot (Pierre's grandmother), 26, 27

Du Pont, Margaretta Lammot (Carpenter) (Pierre's sister), 16, 259, 562

Du Pont, Mary (Laird) (Pierre's sister), 8, 259, 562

Du Pont, Mary Belin (Pierre's mother), 6–7, 11, 14, 16, 19, 38, 260, 391

Du Pont, Mary V., 11

Du Pont, Maurice (Pierre's cousin), 9, 17, 18, 19

Du Pont, May, 128

Du Pont, Natalie Wilson (Lammot's wife), 259

Du Pont, Paulina, 25, 562

Du Pont, Philip F., 338, 343, 390

Du Pont, Pierre Samuel, xix–xxii; achievements of, evaluation of, 591–601; acting president of du Pont Company, 77, 227, 255, 259, 305, 318, 319, 320, 322, 359; American entry into war viewed by, 393–400; antitrust suit and, 282–91; apprenticeship of, 23–46; birth of, 4, 7; boyhood of, 7–14; chairman of du Pont Company board, 560, 564; chairman of General Motors board, 433, 435–43, 437–38, 534, 536, 537–559, 560, 564, 572–83, 583–87; Coleman's stock bought by, 326–35; consolidation organized by, 85–93; courtship of, 391–92; Delaware State School Tax Commissioner, 564, 588; dismemberment of the Powder Company, 291–300; du Pont Company purchased by, 48–54; education of, 15–22; executive ability of, 3–4; family background of, 4–6; family loyalties and traditions, 125, 259–60, 322, 601–04; family suit against, 342–53, 356–58; financial control, maintaining, 201–26; financial policy, formulating, 149–68; financial responsibilities of, 24–28; French and Chilean negotiations, 149, 151, 176–86, 187–200; initial involvement in General Motors (1915–1917), 433–56; interests, personal, 302, 427, 458–59, 537, 549, 560, 563–64, 583–84, 587–589, 598; Johnson Company financing by, 28–33; last years at General Motors and du Pont, 560–90; Longwood estate of, 302, 312–13, 336, 391, 427, 458, 463, 475, 476, 477, 490, 491, 492, 549,

Du Pont, Pierre Samuel (*continued*) 560, 562, 564, 570, 583, 588, 598, 601; marriage of, 6–7, 392, 437; organization of the Big Company by, 77–120; overseas investment and, 169–200; panic of 1907 and, 218–26; preparation years of, 47–120; president of du Pont Company, 323, 340, 375; president of General Motors Corporation, 490–536; president of the Johnson Company, 36–40; religious views of, 16; reorganization of 1911, 303–13; reorganization of 1914, 314–21; resignation as president of du Pont Company, 427–30; resignation as president of General Motors, 534, 536; retirement of, 587–90; schism in the du Pont family and, 336–42; selling out, 561–64; shyness of, 11–12, 15 17, 21; siblings of, 7–8, 16; smokeless powder invention of, 34–35; stockholders' meeting of 1917, vindication by, 353–56; street railway ventures of, 40–46; succession at du Pont, problem of, 301–321; transformation of General Motors Corporation, contribution to, 597–99; transformation of the du Pont Company, contribution to, 594–97; treasurer of the du Pont Company, 54–70, 77, 115, 123–48, 149–68, 169, 201–26, 227, 255, 305; vertical integration, toward, 227–55; vice-president of the du Pont Company, 319, 326; World War I and, 359–89, 393–409, 410–27

Du Pont, Sophie (Pierre's sister), 7, 13, 24

Du Pont, Thomas Coleman, xxi, 4, 8, 9, 11, 17, 21, 22, 24, 26, 27, 28, 30, 31–32, 33, 36, 38, 40, 41, 42, 44, 48, 50, 51–52, 53, 54, 55, 56, 57, 62, 63, 64, 65, 66, 68, 69, 70, 72, 73–74, 75, 76, 77, 78, 79, 80, 82, 83, 84, 85, 90, 92, 93–99, 100, 101, 102, 103, 104, 110, 111, 116, 118, 119, 120, 124, 125, 216–227, 128, 129–30, 133, 134, 135, 136, 140, 141, 142, 147, 148, 151, 152, 153, 158, 159, 162, 164, 165, 172, 173–74, 175, 176, 178, 180, 181, 187, 188, 189–193, 194, 195, 196–97, 198, 199–200, 216, 218, 224, 227, 228, 229, 250, 255, 260, 262, 264, 265–82, 283, 284, 285, 288, 291, 298, 301–02, 303, 304, 306, 307, 308–09, 311–12, 314, 315, 316, 317–19, 320, 321, 322, 323, 325–31, 332, 333, 334, 335, 336, 337, 338, 340, 353–54, 358, 364, 366, 390, 392, 428, 472, 561, 563, 569, 585, 595, 596, 600

Du Pont, Victor, 127

Du Pont, Washington, 293

Du Pont, Wilhelmina, 392, 562

Du Pont, William (Pierre's cousin), 221, 224, 260, 264, 286, 302, 306, 316–17, 319, 320, 321, 322, 328, 329, 330, 331, 332, 335, 336, 337, 339, 340, 341, 343, 344, 349, 354, 357, 565

Du Pont, William (son of Henry H.), 20, 21, 22, 61, 128

Du Pont, William K. (Pierre's brother), 7, 13, 14, 28, 41, 43, 44, 45, 48, 53, 259

Du Pont American Industries, Inc., 507, 540

Du Pont Building, Wilmington, 147–48

Du Pont Company, Accounting Department, 143, 144, 145–46, 151, 154, 155, 163, 169, 472; administrative structure, new, 70–76; Advertising Bureau, 140; Allied contracts, drawing, 362–71; Allied purchases, financing, 371–75; Allies supplied by, 359–89; artificial leather, production of, 249–50, 385–86, 454, 522–23; antitrust suits against, 118–19, 157, 192, 199, 208, 228, 248, 260–91, 299–300; Black Powder Department, 138, 156, 206–07, 208, 214, 304; bonus system, 136–37, 338, 351; branch offices, 140–41, 155; capital, increase of, 206–16; celluloids, production of, 382, 383; Chile, nitrate negotiations in, 151, 181–87, 205–06, 214, 222, 230–38, 245, 254, 377, 378, 397, 400; Coleman du Pont in California, 93–99; competing companies, buying of, 59–70, 78–85; consolidation of subsidiary companies, 78–120; costing and pricing policies, 151–57; cotton supply, 377–78, 379–80; department building, 137–47; Development Department, 142, 166, 181, 182, 190, 234, 235, 237, 238, 242, 243, 249, 250, 381–386, 470; dismemberment of, 291–300; diversification, 247–51, 300, 381–86, 427, 467; dividends of, 164, 253–54, 294–95, 344, 370, 373; domestic expansion plans, 206–16; dyes, production of, 383, 384; Eastern Laboratory, 143, 155; Engineering Department, 229, 381, 419, 454, 468, 470; European policy, final resolution of (1905–1907), 187–200; Essential Materials Department, 142, 181, 224–25; Executive Committee, 125–37, 304–05, 314–315, 322, 359, 365, 376, 383, 429, 450, 452–53, 494, 561, 570; Experimental Station, 142–43, 154–55, 241; family schism, 336–42; family suit, 342–53, 356–58; final form of, 104–20; Finance Committee, 477, 507, 536, 541, 581,

Du Pont Company (continued) 583; financial control, maintaining, 201–26; financial policy, formulating, 149–68; financial reorganization, 387–389; financial resources, allocation of, 158–68; formation of E. I. du Pont de Nemours & Company, 387–89; France, negotiations in, 151, 176–80, 187–200; fusel oil supply, 242–44; General Motors "control" by (1918–1920), 457–74; glycerin supply, 238–42, 245, 377; government contract, initial, 400–409; High Explosives Department, 138–139, 141, 151, 153–54, 166, 195–96, 204, 207, 214, 216, 221, 241, 252, 304, 376, 386; holding companies, 61, 65, 68, 78, 79, 81, 85, 86, 88, 91, 113, 209, 334, 339; Information Bureau, 140–41; international agreements, 102, 116, 118, 171–73, 180, 187–200, 268, 269, 273, 299; investment in General Motors, 433, 434, 450–56, 467, 506; Jackling Contract, 421–22, 423, 425; Laflin & Rand purchased by, 62–69, 82, Legal Department, 142, 154, 470; Mexico, negotiations in, 173, 174, 179, 187, 188–89, 199; military orders, 325; Miscellaneous Manufacturing Department, 386, 428; motion picture film, production of, 383; new leadership, search for, 301–13; new strategy, 54–70; Nitrate Committee, 230, 232, 233, 234; nitrate supply, 161, 168, 181–87, 204–206, 222, 230–38, 245, 254, 377, 378, 379, 397, 400; nitric acid supply, 244–245; Old Hickory plant, building, 421, 423–27; organizing, 85–104; overseas expansion plans, 188–95, 197–200, 570; overseas investment, 166, 167, 168, 169–200; paints, varnishes, and colors, production of, 383, 384–85; panic of 1907, 218–26; pension plan, 137; physical expansion, monitoring, 375–81; purchase of E. I. du Pont de Nemours & Company, 48–54; Purchasing Department, 141, 142, 154, 181, 204, 221, 223, 228, 243, 244, 296, 378, 379, 380; reorganization of 1911, 303–13; reorganization of 1914, 314–21; Salary Department, 144; sales agents, 71–73; Sales Department, 140–41, 155–56, 157, 158, 163, 208; Smokeless Powder Department, 138, 139–40, 159, 204, 207, 208–09, 248, 376; staff departments, 141; stock and securities of, 211, 212, 253–54, 294–95, 325, 326–335, 338–39, 346, 387–89, 561–62; stock sales to employees, 135–36; subsidiaries of, 6, 14, 56–57, 111–13, 152,

Du Pont Company (*continued*)
162, 172, 408; succession, problem of, 260, 301–21; sulphuric acid supply, 244–45, 378–79; Traffic Department, 141, 163, 208; transformation of, contributions of Pierre S. du Pont to, 594–597; Treasurer's Department, 74, 138, 143–47, 151, 153, 155, 201, 203, 204, 216, 313; vertical integration, toward, 227–55; war business, problems of, 360–63; working capital, control of, 375–81; World War I production, 359–389, 393–409, 410–30

Du Pont Company of Pennsylvania, 6, 88, 162, 274, 291, 292, 391

Du Pont de Nemours, Pierre Samuel, 4, 588

Du Pont de Nemours & Company, E. I. ("Delaware Corporation"), 387–89

Du Pont de Nemours Powder Company (New Jersey), *see* Du Pont Company

Du Pont Engineering Company, 408, 421, 425, 426

Du Pont International Powder Company, 103–04, 172, 275, 276, 292

Du Pont Motor Company, 451

Du Pont Nitrate Company, 237, 292

Du Pont-Nobel Dynamite Company, 188, 190, 191, 192, 194

Du Pont Securities Company, 334–35, 338, 339, 342, 344, 347, 429, 437, 455, 489, 506, 508, 538

Durant, William C., 434, 435, 436, 437, 438–40, 441–42, 443–50, 453, 454, 455, 456, 457, 459, 460, 461, 462, 463, 464, 465, 467, 468, 469, 470–71, 473–74, 477, 478, 479, 480, 481, 482–90, 491, 492, 496, 499, 502, 505–07, 510, 512, 514, 439, 540, 565, 597

Durant Corporation, 483, 484, 485, 491

Dwinnell, William B., 232, 248, 263

Dyes, production of, 383, 384

Dynamit-Aktien-Gesellschaft vorm, 571

Earle, Ralph, 412

Eastern Dynamite Company, 56–57, 61–62, 66, 70, 71, 73, 74, 86, 100, 117, 118, 163, 255, 271, 273, 274, 276, 279, 285, 289, 291, 292

Edge, J. B. D., 430

Eighteenth Amendment, 564, 584, 588

Electric street railroad industry, 30–31, 40–46

Eleutherian Mills, 5

Eleutherian Mills Historical Library, 588

Ellis, Wade H., 276, 279, 280

Empire State Building, Inc., 589

Englebrecht, H. C., 360

Ensign Company, 98

Enterprise High Explosives Company, 61, 88, 117, 208, 271, 272

Equitable Life Assurance Society, 311, 326, 327, 414, 562

Equitable Powder Company, 60, 79, 90, 99, 274

European agreements on foreign markets, 102, 116, 118, 171–73, 180, 187–200, 268, 269, 273, 299

Explosives industry, 57–62, 76, 81, 88, 118, 142, 169

Explosives Supply Company, 117

Fabrikoid Company, 249–50, 385, 386, 454, 522–23

Fairmont Powder Company, 60, 84

Faithorne, L., 141

Falcouse, Mr., 195

Fay, Addison G., 82

Fay family, 58, 83, 87, 90, 93, 104, 127

Federal Steel Company, 33, 36, 38, 40, 71

Federal Steel Syndicate, 40, 41

Fenn, William H., 18, 28, 39, 43, 52, 71, 100

Ferndale Mill, 84, 85

First National Bank, Philadelphia, 164

Fisher, Alfred J., 578

Fisher, Charles L., 465

Fisher, Charles T., 577

Fisher, Edward F., 465, 578

Fisher, Fred J., 465, 526, 531, 543, 544, 576, 577, 579, 587

Fisher, Lawrence P., 465, 576, 577

Fisher, William A., 465

Fisher, William F., 577

Fisher Body Corporation, 465, 526, 531, 574, 575-78

Fiske, J. P. D., 515

Flint, Michigan, 439, 506–07

Flint Varnish & Color Company, 385

Folger, William Mayhew, 399

Forcite Powder Company, 61, 152, 208, 287

Ford, Henry, xxi, 439, 443, 444, 517, 555, 593, 597

Ford Motor Company, 433, 439, 465, 481, 495, 518, 522, 538, 549, 555, 574, 578

Fort Worth, Texas, 41

Foster, Mrs. Lentilhon, 393

France, negotiations in, 151, 176–80, 187–200

Franco-Prussian War, 366

Franz Ferdinand, Archduke, 299

French American Bank, Paris, 212

French government, 368–69, 370, 372–373, 402

Frigidaire, 495, 512, 514–15

Fusel oil supply, 242–44

Galey, Samuel Maxwell, 4
Gardner, Augustus P., 394
Gary, Elbert, 447
General Chemical Company, 244
General Education Board, 459
General Electric Company, 26, 44, 45, 46
General Exchange Insurance Company, 589
General Explosives Agreement (1920), 569
General Industries, Inc., 455
General Leather Company, 464
General Motors, Ltd., 466
General Motors Acceptance Corporation, 466, 495, 589
General Motors Corporation xx, xxi, 123, 144, 385, 409, 428, 429, 430; Accounting Department, 472–73; Advisory Staff, 497–98, 524, 525, 526, 527, 528, 547; air-cooled engine, 512, 515–16, 518, 519, 520, 521, 529–36, 558; Appropriations Committee, 480; bonus plan, 472; Buick Division, 439, 443, 476, 498, 500, 503, 512, 518, 519, 525, 530; Cadillac Division, 439, 440, 443, 499, 503, 512, 519, 530, 557; Chevrolet and United Motors merged with, 460–62; Chevrolet Division, 440, 441, 445, 446, 447, 449, 452, 453, 460–62, 476, 479, 498, 505, 507, 508, 513, 518, 519, 529, 544, 545, 551, 556, 558, 574, 582; copper-cooled engine, 532–33, 537, 543–46, 548, 552, 557, 558, 559, 561; crisis of 1920, 475–91; Delco Light Company, 466, 512, 515; dividend payments of, 440, 445, 479, 573, 574; du Pont "control" (1918–1920), 457–74; du Pont investment in, 433, 434, 450–56, 467, 506; Durant purchase, financing, 505–10; Durant's disaster, 482–91; Durant regime, 443–50; Employees' Savings and Investment Plan, 470; Ethyl Corporation, 523, 570; Executive Committee, 476, 480, 481, 482, 501, 516, 518, 519, 520, 527, 528, 533, 543, 545, 546, 549, 550, 551, 557, 558, 579; Finance Committee, 457–58, 460, 461, 462, 463, 464, 465, 466, 467, 468, 475–76, 479, 480–81, 482, 490, 501, 502, 511, 530, 533, 541, 542, 552, 553, 554, 556, 573, 575, 578, 579, 580, 586, 587; Fisher Body Company, 465, 526, 531, 574, 575–78; General Purchasing Committee, 547; General Technical Committee, 547–48, 556, 557; initial involvement of Pierre S. du Pont (1915–1917), 433–56; in-

General Motors Corporation (continued)
ternal reform, proposals for, 468–74; Inventory Allotment Committee, 481; inventory crisis, 480–82; Management Securities Company, 538–43, 555, 561, 574, 576, 580, 581; New Departure Roller Bearing Division, 445, 536; new partners, finding, 476–80; "no-knock" gasoline, 522, 523; Oakland Division, 499, 503, 513, 518, 519, 532, 533, 556, 557; Oldsmobile Division, 499, 503, 513, 519, 520, 532, 533, 543; organizational adjustment, 524–529; organizational structure, completing, 446–49; overseas trade, 466, 495, 578–80; Pontiac Division, 557, 574; postwar expansion program, 462–68; product policy (1921–1923), 511–36; rebuilt (1923–1924), 537–59; refrigerator production, 460, 495, 512, 514–15; reorganization and regeneration (1921), 492–510; statistical and financial controls, 500–05, 549–54; stock and securities of, 435, 441, 442, 447, 451, 455, 462, 463, 464, 467–68, 477, 482, 483, 486, 505, 506, 507–08, 540, 542, 555–56, 561, 573–74, 577, 580; storage plan, 550; structural reorganization, 493–503; technological innovations (1921–1923), 511–36; transformation of, contributions of Pierre S. du Pont to, 597–99; Tractor Division, 460, 503, 513, 514, 515; Truck Division, 498, 503; watercooled engine, 520, 521, 529, 532, 534, 556, 558
General Motors Export Company, 466
General Motors Securities Corporation, 540
General Motors Truck Company, 443
General Pooling Agreement (1889), 171
Genin, August, 196
George, Henry, 26, 316
Giant Powder Company, 13, 94, 96, 97, 98, 189, 568
Gibbs, W. W., 93, 102, 103, 117
Glancy, Alfred R., 598
Glasgow, William A., 279, 280, 281, 282
Glasgow, William A., Jr., 344, 348
Gloria oficina, 234–35
Glycerin supply, 238–42, 245, 377
Gompers, Samuel, 404
Goodyear Tire & Rubber Company, 464
Grace & Company, W. R., 183, 185, 231, 233, 237, 246
Graff, Elizabeth (Pierre's Aunt Betty), 9, 10–11, 15
Graff, Fred (Pierre's Uncle Fred), 10, 15
Graham, George S., 348, 357

Grant, Richard H., 515
Grasselli Chemical Company, 244
Graves, J., Harwood, 276
Gray, George, 260, 276, 279, 284, 288
Great Western Powder Company, 60
Greene, Edward, 82, 117
Gregg, William S., 424
Guaranty Trust Company, New York, 164, 211, 479
Guigné, Christian de, 96, 98
Gunpowder Trade Association, 14, 20, 24, 58–61, 69, 72, 78, 82–83, 86, 94, 99, 117, 156, 163, 263, 264, 265, 274, 276, 277

Hagen, Carl, 190, 393
Hamilton, E. A., 407, 408
Hanighen, F. C., 360
Hannum, George H., 499, 519, 520, 521, 532, 546, 557
Hardy, A. B. C., 498, 499, 520, 532, 546
Harris & Company, 43, 44
Harrison Brothers & Company, 385, 386
Harrison Radiator Company, 445, 460, 500
Harvard University, 18, 19
Haskell, Harry G., 62, 138–39, 305, 309, 315, 320, 338, 351, 352, 365, 386, 428, 429, 476, 568, 570, 579
Haskell, J. Armory, 49, 61, 62, 63, 64, 65, 66, 68, 74, 82, 84, 90, 91, 97, 110–11, 112, 115–16, 117, 118, 124, 126, 128, 129, 130–31, 135, 140, 141, 147, 155, 156, 157, 158, 159, 160, 162, 164, 172, 174, 175, 176, 179, 188, 189, 190, 192, 197, 209, 214, 248, 250, 251, 253, 265, 267, 272, 305, 308, 309, 310, 313, 320, 321, 353, 365, 428, 436, 437, 442, 456, 458, 462, 466, 472, 481, 490, 492, 496, 497, 498, 514, 515, 518, 524
Haskell, New Jersey, 139, 382
Haskins & Sells, 447, 461
Hathaway & Company, 218
Hawkins, Norval H., 497, 517, 524, 525–526
Hayden, Stone & Company, 464
Hazard Powder Company, 56, 58, 59, 69, 70, 78, 86, 255, 273, 276, 279, 285, 291
Hearst, William Randolph, 262
Henry Brothers & Company, 253, 254
Hercules Powder Company, 61, 171, 214, 287, 293, 296–99, 396, 477
Hilles, William S., 79, 135, 136, 275, 276, 279, 281, 284, 285, 287, 348
Hiss, Alger, 426
Hitchcock, Frank, 270, 275–76, 280, 281

Hoffer, Jay E., 402, 403, 407
Hofheimer, Nathan, 448, 450, 451, 455, 461
Homberg, Moses, 7
Honeywill & Company, 243
Hoover, Herbert C., 589
Hopewell, Virginia, 376, 382, 383
Horowitz, Louis J., 414, 418
House, Edward M., 401
Howland, L. M., 176, 177
Hudson & Company, C. I., 448
Hudson Motor Company, 575
Hughes, Charles Evans, 353
Hunt, Ormund E., 543, 545
Huth & Company, 205, 206, 219
Hyatt Roller Bearing Company, 445, 495

I. G. Farbenindustries AG, 571
Illinois Steel Company, 33
Imperial Chemical Industries, 571
Indiana Powder Company, 60, 162
Indian Head, Maryland, 248, 268
Ingersoll, Robert G., 16
Inheritance taxes, 561, 564
International Harvester Company, 324, 515, 593
International Smokeless Powder and Chemical Company, 91, 92, 100, 102, 103, 117, 140, 274, 287, 291–92, 366, 376
Iron National Bank, New York, 349–50

Jackling, Daniel Cowan, 419, 421, 423, 424, 427
Jackson, Oscar R., 100
James, Marquis, 323, 336
Janesville Machine Company, 460
Jellico Coal Company, 27, 84, 111
Johnson, E. A., 554
Johnson, E. F., 498, 598
Johnson, John G., 336, 343–44, 347–48, 353
Johnson, Tom, 25–28, 29, 30, 31, 32, 33, 36, 38, 40, 41, 51, 53, 73, 316, 411, 422
Johnson Company, 25, 27, 28–33, 36, 38–39, 40, 43, 47, 51, 160, 202, 316, 600
Johnston, Thomas, 191
Johnstown, Pennsylvania, 26, 27, 29, 30
Jones, Richard M., 15–16, 17, 287
Joplin, Missouri, 207, 208, 252
Judson Company, 94, 96, 97, 98, 99, 209, 273
Judson, Egbert, 94
Justice Department, U. S., 118, 157, 263, 264, 267, 269, 270, 271, 273, 274, 275, 276, 278, 279, 282, 284, 286, 288, 289, 296, 297, 298, 342

Kanny, William F., 585
Katzenbach, Frank S., 291
Kaufman, Lewis G., 435–36, 445, 446, 449, 454, 455, 461
Kenvil, New Jersey, 58
Kerr, George, 583
Kettering, Charles F., 466, 471, 492, 493, 496, 512, 513, 515, 516, 517, 518, 519, 521, 522, 523, 525, 529, 530, 532, 543, 544–45, 546, 547, 548, 552, 554, 556, 557, 558, 559, 579
Kidder, Peabody & Company, 361
Kimball, Harry S., 361
King family, 101–02
King Mercantile Company, 101, 272
King Powder Company, 101–02, 104, 272–73
Kingsbury, E. P., 63
Kirk & Sons, Arthur, 84
Kitchen, Claude, 396
Klaxon Company, 445
Knickerbocker Trust Company, New York, 218
Knight, Austin M., 289
Knight case (1895), E. C., 112
Knudsen, William S., 528–30, 532, 533, 543, 544, 545, 546–47, 551, 554, 556, 557, 559, 576, 582
Köln-Rottweiler Pubverfabriken, 170, 571
Kraftmeier, Edward, 325, 313–33, 337
Kuhn, Loeb & Company, 119, 332, 457, 479

Labor Department, U. S., 263
Labor unions, 112, 115
Labrador, 182
Laffey, John P., 142, 290, 298, 305, 338, 340, 341, 347, 348, 351, 540
Laflin & Rand Powder Company, 14, 49, 50, 56–57, 58, 59, 60, 61, 62–69, 70, 73, 74, 77, 78, 82, 86, 93, 116–17, 118, 130, 139, 152, 160, 162, 209, 255, 273, 279, 285, 289, 291, 292, 391
Laflin Powder Manufacturing Company, 63, 88
La Follette, Robert M., 395
Laird, William Winder, 259, 338, 341, 540, 562
Laird, Bissell & Meeds, 569
Laird & Company, 374, 464
Lake Superior Powder Company, 60, 78, 90, 162
Lancaster Steel Company, 460
Landis, Charles B., 347
Lanning, William M., 276
Latin Group, 171, 173, 174, 177, 187, 189, 194–95, 198
Lawson, David, 182–83

Lee, Higginson & Company, 435, 440, 457, 474
Leland, Henry M., 438, 440, 442–43, 444
Lennig, Charles, 18
Lent, Mr., 82, 83, 90, 91, 93, 101, 104
Lentilhon, Mr., 69
Lequin, Mr., 69
Levinstein, Ltd., 384
Lewis, W. B., 207
Liberty Bond drives, 374
Limantour, Finance Minister, 189, 196, 197
Lincoln Motor Company, 442–43
Linden, Edward Ver, 499
London City & Midland Bank, 231
Longwood estate, 302, 312–13, 336, 391, 427, 458, 463, 475, 476, 477, 490, 491, 492, 549, 560, 562, 564, 570, 583, 588, 598, 601
Loos, Henry B., 346
Lorain, Ohio, 30, 31, 33, 36, 38, 47, 53
Lorain Steel Company, 39, 71
Lorain Street Railway, 38, 40
Los Angeles *Herald*, 264
Louisville, Kentucky, 25
Louviers, Colorado, 293
Lovett, Robert Scott, 413
Lukens, Edward G., 96, 169–70
*Lusitania* disaster, 394

Management Securities Company, 538–543, 555, 561, 574, 576, 580, 581
Marcellus Powder Company, 60
Marsden Company, 102–03
Martinez del Rio, P., 189, 196
Marvel, David, 279, 284
Mason, Newton E., 268
Massachusetts Institute of Technology, 17, 18, 19, 21, 22, 27, 35, 129, 459, 600
Mauch Chunk plant, 208
McAdoo, William Gibbs, 374
McClement, J. H., 443, 446, 449, 456
*McClure's* magazine, 85
McFarland, Taylor & Costello, 290
McGowen, Sir Harry, 198, 393, 464, 476–77, 479, 486, 491, 508, 531, 567, 568, 569, 570, 571, 586
McLaughlin, Samuel, 463, 499, 514, 516, 525, 530
McLaughlin Motor Car Company, Ltd., 440
McMannis, William J., 143
McMurray, C. F., 91
McRoberts, Samuel, 425
Meade, C. A., 430
Mendelssohn, Louis and Aaron, 465, 577
*Merchants of Death* (Englebrecht and Hanighen), 360

Metropolitan Match & Fuse Company, 94, 97, 98
Mexican Agreement, 189
Mexican government, 117
Mexican National Dynamite Company, 173, 188–89, 194, 196
Mexico, negotiations in, 173, 174, 179, 187, 188–89, 196–97, 199
Miami Powder Company, 58, 60, 83
Middleborough, Kentucky, 208
Midgely, Thomas, 523
Milford, Michigan, 548
Military and Fortifications Bill, 248, 270
Miller, John G., 141
Milwaukee *Journal,* 395
Mitchell, H. J., 366
Money, Albert W., 70
Monnett, Frank S., 267, 268
Montgomery & Company, 464
Mooar (Iowa) Mill, 54, 139, 204
Moody, William H., 263
Mooney, James D., 579
Moore, Edward T., 43, 45
Moore & Schley, 487
Moosic Powder Company, 62, 63, 64, 65, 66, 88
Morgan, Grennell & Company, 579
Morgan, J. P., 33, 119, 218
Morgan, J. P. (the younger), 509
Morgan & Company, J. P., 326, 333, 347, 349, 372, 374, 411, 457, 477–79, 480, 483, 484, 485, 486, 487, 489, 505, 508, 514, 539, 565, 566–67, 575, 578, 598
Morrow, Dwight W., 483, 484, 486–87, 488, 490
Morton, Oscar E., 55, 83
Mosenthal, Henry de, 191, 198, 199
Motors Security Company, 449
Mott, Charles S., 439, 442, 459, 466, 498, 516, 517, 518, 525, 526–27, 529, 532, 543, 544, 554, 580
Moxham, Arthur J., 25, 26, 28, 29–30, 31, 32, 33, 36, 38, 39, 73–75, 77, 80, 81, 82, 83, 85, 86, 89, 90–91, 92–93, 94, 97, 99, 101, 104, 110, 111, 112, 114–15, 116, 117, 118, 119, 120, 126, 128, 129, 130, 133, 134, 142, 143, 147, 151, 154, 159, 162, 164, 165, 166, 167, 168, 172, 175, 179, 181, 182, 183, 189, 190, 192, 193, 194, 195, 203, 209, 216, 218, 227, 228, 229, 237, 245–46, 255, 263, 265, 268, 271, 273, 274, 278, 291, 302, 305, 306, 308, 310, 316, 317, 318, 319, 320, 340, 364, 402, 422, 428, 504, 595
Mueller Agreement (1890), 171
Munitions Tax Bill, 396–97
Munroe, Charles E., 34

Nash, Charles W., 436, 438, 440, 442
Nash Motor Company, 442, 538, 555
Nashville, Tennessee, 408
National Antitrust League, 267
National City Bank, New York, 231–32, 233, 479
National Recovery Administration, 589
National Security League, 420
Naval Appropriations Bill (1909), 248, 269, 270
Navy Department, U. S., 267, 268, 269
*Negra de Taltal oficina,* 236
Nemours Trading Company, 566
New Departure Roller Bearing Company, 445, 536
New England Oil Paint & Varnish Company, 385
Newport, Rhode Island, 34
New York automobile show, 519–20, 533
New York curb market, 212, 253
New York Powder Company, 61
New York Stock Exchange, 211, 212, 253, 462
*New York Times, The,* 420, 421
New York *World,* 398
Nields, Percy and Mary, 397
Niles, John Barton, 71, 141, 243
Nitrate supply, 161, 168, 181–87, 204–206, 214, 222, 230–38, 245, 254, 377, 378, 379, 397, 400
Nitric acid supply, 244–45
Nitro plant, Charleston, West Virginia, 423, 424, 425, 427
Nobel, Alfred, 13, 170, 173
Nobel and Company (DAG), Alfred, 571
Nobel-Dynamite Trust Company, 170, 198, 241, 366
Nobel Explosives Trades, Ltd., 477, 478, 479, 481, 485, 569
Nobel Industries, Ltd., 567, 568, 569, 570
Noetzlin, Mr., 196
North Dallas Circuit Railway Company, 41
Northern Explosives, Ltd., 567
Northern Securities case, 113
Northwestern Powder Company, 60
Norwegian Nitrate Company, 378
Nye, Gerald P., 360
Nye Committee investigation, 360, 371, 397, 426, 589

Oakland, New Jersey, 70, 91
Oakland Motor Car Company, 439–40, 443, 499, 503, 513, 518, 519, 532, 533, 556, 557
Odell, James H., 560

Odell, Joseph H., 422
*Oficina Delaware,* 236, 237
Ohio Powder Company, 60, 90
Old Hickory smokeless powder plant, 421, 423–27
Olds, R. E., 444
Oldsmobile Motor Company, 499, 503, 513, 519, 520, 532, 533, 543
Olds Motor Works, 439, 443
Olin, Franklin W., 60, 79–80, 82, 83, 90, 91, 93, 101, 104
Oliver Dynamite Company, 62, 89, 139
Oriental Powder Mills, 58, 60, 90, 91
*Outlook* magazine, 422

Packard Motor Company, 538, 555
Page, Dewitt, 536, 554, 586
Paints, varnishes, and colors, production of, 383, 384–85
Panama, 186
Panama Canal, 266, 270
Panama Canal Appropriations Bill, 248
Panic of 1907, 151, 199, 218–26, 227, 230, 255, 595
Parlin, New Jersey, 103, 140, 382, 384
Parsons, Schuyler, 62, 63, 64, 66, 90, 181
Parsons, William Barkley, 60, 62
Parsons & Petit, 185, 233
Patterson, C. A., 429
Patterson, Charles J., 62
Patterson, Charles L., 74, 131, 140, 141, 250, 305, 309, 315, 319, 320, 353, 365, 476
Patterson, George, 100
Penn Charter School, William, 15–16, 17
Penniman, Russell S., 140
Pennsylvania Railroad, 324, 589
Pennsylvania Steel Company, 29
Peoria *Herald Transcript,* 262
Perlman Rim Corporation, 445
Perot, Eleanor, 343
Pershing, John J., 570
Peru, 182
Peters, Gershon M., 101, 117, 272–73
Peters Cartridge Company, 101
Peyton Chemical Company, 99
Phi Kappa Sigma fraternity, 19
Philadelphia, Pennsylvania, 9, 12, 13, 15
Philadelphia Centennial Exposition (1876), 9
Philadelphia National Bank, 349, 589
Philadelphia *Public Ledger,* 336, 337, 343, 345, 346, 347
Phillips, David Graham, 262
Phillips Andover Academy, 17
Phoenix, Arizona, 39
Phoenix Powder Company, 60
Picatinny, New Jersey, 248

Pickard, F. W., 429
Pierce, Harry M., 62, 376, 423–24, 425, 427, 428, 468, 530
Pierce-Arrow Motor Company, 538
Pillsbury, E. S., 80, 96, 97–98, 116, 287
Pizeck, Mr., 352
Polk Company, R. L., 553
Pompton Lakes, New Jersey, 70, 74
Pontiac Motor Company, 556–57, 574
Porter, John F., 472
Porter, William H., 334
Pratt, John Lee, 470, 473, 480, 481, 494, 498, 500, 502–03, 504, 510, 514–15, 536, 549, 550, 553, 577, 579, 598
Prensky, Meyer L., 444, 472, 473, 481, 498, 500, 501, 504–05
Proctor, E. W., 472
Prosser, Seward, 336, 475–76, 478, 479, 490, 514, 533, 536, 542, 554
Pryor, Samuel, 361, 442
Purdy, Milton Dwight, 274, 275
Purvis, Arthur B., 569

Ramsay, Caroline J., 352
Ramsay, William G., 62, 305, 313, 338, 340, 344, 352–53, 376, 428, 437
Raskob, Helena, 438, 492
Raskob, John J., 39, 41, 43, 47, 51, 53, 55, 63, 64, 66, 71, 74, 124, 144–45, 146, 147, 149, 176, 179, 180, 184, 186, 313, 320, 329, 333, 334, 338, 343, 348, 351, 352, 365, 373, 374, 375, 380, 388, 389, 428, 429, 434, 435, 436, 437, 438, 440, 441, 442, 443, 444, 445–446, 447, 448–49, 450–51, 453–54, 455, 456, 457, 458, 459–60, 461, 462–463, 464, 465, 466, 467, 468, 471–73, 475, 476–77, 478, 479, 481, 483, 484, 485, 486, 487, 488. 489, 490, 491, 492, 493, 495, 496, 497, 504, 505, 506, 507–08, 514, 518, 519, 521, 524, 525, 526, 527, 530, 531, 538, 539–40, 541, 543, 552, 555, 560, 568, 571, 573, 576, 577, 578, 581, 584, 585–87, 588, 589–90
Raskob, William, 585
Remington Arms Company, 360–361, 362–363, 364, 368, 389, 441
Remy Electric Company, 445
Repauno Chemical Company, 14, 17, 20, 24, 49, 56, 61, 62, 72, 125, 171, 239, 376
Rice, Elliott S., 72–73, 141, 261, 262
Rice, Herbert H., 444, 472, 499
Riker, John L., 62, 64, 68
Rio de Janeiro, Brazil, 188, 194
Ripley, William Z., 581
Roadstrum, Victor H., 263, 276

Robb, Charles H., 263
Robertson, Nathaniel and Mary, 397
Rockefeller, John D., 327
Rockefeller Foundation, 459
Rood, George L., 91, 104
Rood, Norman P., 91, 104
Roosevelt, Franklin D., 588, 589
Roosevelt, Theodore, 260, 263, 265, 269, 270, 394, 420, 423
Rosendale black powder works, 204
Russian government, 371–72
Russian Revolution (1917), 361, 372

Sabin, Charles, 584
St. Louis *Republican,* 395
Samson Tractor Company, 460, 503, 513, 514, 515
San Francisco *Examiner,* 264
San Francisco Stock Exchange, 253
Saulsbury, May, 354–56
Saulsbury, Willard, 25, 28, 354–55
Scarlet, James, 266, 276, 279, 282
Schaghticoke Company, 59
Schism in the du Pont family, 336–42
Schultze Company, E. C., 70, 91–92, 140
Scott, F. A., 402
Scripps-Booth Company, 460, 513, 516, 518
Seger, Charles B., 572
Service Citizens of Delaware, 458–59
Sharp, Hugh Rodney, 259, 338, 341, 391, 392
Sheffield Land Company, 38, 39
Shenandoah Powder Mill, 84
Sheridan Company, 513, 516, 518
Sherman Antitrust Act (1890), 57, 60, 112, 113, 172, 260, 261, 264, 277, 280, 285, 290, 299
Singer, Siegfried, 173–74, 175–76, 177–178, 179–80, 188, 189–91, 192, 195, 196
Sloan, Alfred P., Jr., 433, 434, 445, 459, 466, 467, 470, 471, 473–74, 481, 490, 492, 493–97, 499, 500, 501, 504, 514, 515, 516, 517, 518, 519, 520, 521, 524–26, 527–28, 529, 530, 532, 533–534, 536, 542, 543, 544, 545, 547–48, 549, 550, 551, 552, 553, 554, 555, 556, 558, 559, 572, 575, 576, 577, 579, 580, 581, 584, 585, 586, 587, 598, 599
Smith, Ab, 18
Smith, Alfred E., 584, 585, 588
Smith, H. G., 183, 184
Smith, John Thomas, 444, 459, 487
Smokeless Powder Mill, Carney's Point, New Jersey, 34, 35, 37, 54, 70, 74, 126, 139, 152, 366, 376, 382, 383

Société Centrale de Dynamite, 171, 173, 174, 175, 176, 177, 178, 179, 180, 187, 188, 190
Société Continental de Glycerine et de Dynamite, 171
Société Generale pour la Fabrication de la Dynamite, 171
Society of Friends (Quakers), 15, 16
*Some Mistakes of Moses* (Ingersoll), 16
Southern Powder Company, 60
Spanish-American War, 36, 359, 365, 366, 404
Sparre, Fin, 385
Spooner, John, 265, 270
Spruance, W. C., 429
Squires, John H., 470, 471, 497
Standard Oil Company, 324
Standard Oil Company of New Jersey, 260, 265, 267, 272, 275, 276, 277, 285, 286, 288, 289, 523, 570
State Department, U. S., 384
Stauffer Chemical Company, 94, 96, 98
Stayton, William H., 584
Steel Motors Company, 26
Stettinius, Edward R., 478, 479, 480, 509, 511, 554, 565
Stettinius, Edward R., Jr., 373
Stone, William F., 280
Stone, William J., 395
Stone & Webster, 43, 46
Storrow, James J., 436–37, 438, 440, 442, 443
Studebaker Company, 538, 555, 581
Subsidiary companies, consolidation of, 78–120; trade agreements and legal status of, 111–13
Sullivan, John L., 17
Sulphuric acid supply, 244–45, 378–79
Summers, Leland L., 411
Sundry Civil Appropriations Bill, 270
Supreme Court, U. S., 112–13, 260, 265, 275, 276, 277, 285, 286, 288, 583
Sweet & Company, Edward, 211, 212
Switzerland, 190
Sycamore Mill, 54, 59

Taft, Charles, 281, 285, 288, 311
Taft, William Howard, 260, 265, 275, 279, 281, 282, 286, 288, 308
Tallman, Frank G., 141, 142, 186–87, 204–05, 222, 223, 224, 225, 231, 238–239, 240, 241, 242, 243, 246, 305, 313, 338, 344, 352, 365, 376, 379, 380, 429
*Tauris,* S.S., 187
Taylor, Frederick W., xxi, 32
Tennessee Coal & Iron Company, 487
Textile industry, 384

Thompson, J. Whitaker, 347, 350–51, 352, 353, 354, 356
Thompson-Starrett Company, 414, 415, 418, 419, 423, 424, 425–26
Tiers, William T., 43
Todd, George Carroll, 342
Topeka *Daily Capital,* 264
Townsend, Avery & Button, 192, 263, 275, 276, 278, 284, 285, 287, 290
Townsend, James A., 89
Townsend, James M., 110, 11–12, 113–114, 192, 193, 265, 273, 279, 285
Townsend & Avery, 89
Trégomain, Madeleine, 393
Trégomain, Roger de, 391
Turck, Solomon, 14, 59, 60, 61, 62
Turner, Frank, 472, 473, 494, 498, 500, 501, 554, 598

Underwood, Oscar, 397
Union Bank, Wilmington, 31, 32
Union of London & Smith's Bank, Ltd., 231
Union Sulphur Company, 223
United Motors Corporation, 445, 446, 447, 452, 457, 460–62, 473
United Motors Service, Inc., 445
United States government, 102, 202, 207, 248, 363, 368, 371, 373–74, 396–99, 401, 404, 405, 406–09, 416–18, 423, 424, 425, 459, 561, 566
United States Rubber Company, 571–72
United States Steel Corporation, 47, 87, 324, 571
University of Delaware, 459

Vail, Theodore, 447
Valparaiso, Chile, 184, 185, 186, 187
Vandenburg, Arthur, 427
Vanderbilt, Cornelius, 593
Vanderbilt, William K., 312, 593
Vauxhall Motors, Ltd., 579–80
Vegetable oil industry, 385
Vigorite Powder Company, 90, 94, 97, 98, 101, 116, 209, 273
Virginia-Carolina Chemical Company, 233
Von Lengerke & Detmold Company, 70

Waddell, Frederick W., 141
Waddell, Robert S., 71, 72, 73, 74, 111, 118, 141, 261–63, 264, 265, 266, 267, 268, 269, 272, 273, 274, 278, 282, 290, 291, 366
Wadsworth, James, 584
Walker, Edward, 111, 112–13, 114

*Wall Street Journal,* 356
Wapwallopen Mill, 6, 54, 88
War Department, U. S., 399, 410, 414, 415, 417, 418, 422, 424, 450, 451, 454, 455
War Industries Board, 405, 410–11, 413, 414, 415, 416, 417, 421
Warner, Fred W., 499, 503
Washington, William D'H., 46
Watson, David, 284
Wead, Edward N., 143–44, 146, 149
Webster, William J., 293, 567, 568
Weightman, Mr., 69
Weldy, Henry A., 91
Weldy Powder Company, H. A., 90
Wessel, Duval & Company, 185, 233, 246
West Court Manufacturing Company, 98
Western Cartridge Company, 91
Westinghouse, George, 593
Westinghouse Electric Company, 26, 213, 221
Whitney, George P., 483, 484, 485, 486, 487, 554
Wickersham, George, 276, 280–82, 285, 286, 288, 290, 292, 308
Wiggin, Albert H., 442
Willard, Daniel, 404, 405, 415, 417, 421
Williamson, Harold, 361, 362
Wilmington, Delaware, 5, 74
Wilmington Classical Institute, 4
Wilmington *Evening Journal,* 351, 566
Wilmington *Morning News,* 347, 351, 566
Wilmington *Star,* 336
Wilmington (N.C.) *Star,* 264
Wilmington Trust Company, 162, 566
Wilson, Woodrow, 374, 380, 396, 398, 400, 404
Winchester Repeating Arms Company, 360–63, 364, 368, 389
Winston, Payne & Brown, 111
Woodin, William H., 478
Wooley, Clarence M., 479
Works Accident Insurance, 153
World War I, xxi, 12, 260, 298, 300, 321, 323, 324, 359, 364–89, 390–409, 434, 447, 597
Wrampelmeier, J., 177

Yorks, S. A., 282
Young, Owen D., 478

Zimmermann, 514, 515, 516, 517
Zimmerschied, Carl W., 498, 519, 520, 521, 528, 529

71 72 73 10 9 8 7 6 5 4 3 2 1